CERTIFICATION CIRCLE™

MOUS

Microsoft Office XP

Bunin, Clemens, Friedrichsen, Hunt, Pinard

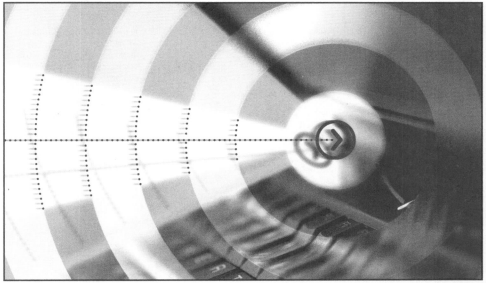

MASTER

APPROVED COURSEWARE

COURSE TECHNOLOGY™

Australia • Canada • Mexico • Singapore • Spain • United Kingdom • United States

MOUS Microsoft Office^XP

CERTIFICATION CIRCLE™ MASTER

Bunin, Clemens, Friedrichsen, Hunt, Pinard

Managing Editor:
Nicole Jones Pinard

Product Managers:
Debbie Masi
Julia Healy

Editorial Assistant:
Elizabeth Harris

Production Editor:
Debbie Masi

Contributing Author:
Carol Cram

Developmental Editors:
Holly Lancaster, Kim Crowley
Laurie Brown, Helen Clayton

Composition House:
GEX Publishing Services

QA Manuscript Reviewers:
Nicole Ashton, John Freitas, Harris Bierhoff
Jeff Schwartz, Alex White

Book Designers:
Joseph Lee, black fish design

Thank You, Advisory Board!

This book is a result of the hard work and dedication by authors, editors, and more than 30 instructors focused on Microsoft Office and MOUS certification. These instructors formed our Certification Circle Advisory Board. We looked to them to flesh out our original vision and turn it into a sound pedagogical method of instruction. In short, we asked them to partner with us to create *the* book for preparing for a MOUS Exam. And, now we wish to thank them for their contributions and expertise.

ADVISORY BOARD MEMBERS:

Linda Amergo	Old Westbury
Shellie Besharse	Mississippi County Community College
Margaret Britt	Copiah Lincoln Community College
Becky Burt	Copiah Lincoln Community College
Judy Cameron	Spokane Community College
Elizabeth T. De Arazoza	Miami-Dade Community College
Susan Dozier	Tidewater Community College
Dawna Dewire	Babson College
Pat Evans	J. Sargent Reynolds
Susan Fry	Boise State University
Joyce Gordon	Babson College
Steve Gordon	Babson College
Pat Harley	Howard Community College
Rosanna Hartley	Western Piedmont Community College
Eva Hefner	St. Petersburg Junior College
Becky Jones	Richland College
Mali Jones	Johnson and Wales University
Angie McCutcheon	Washington State Community College
Barbara Miller	Indiana University
Carol Milliken	Kellogg Community College
Maureen Paparella	Monmouth University
Mike Puopolo	Bunker Hill Community College
Kathy Proietti	Northern Essex Community College
Pamela M. Randall	Unicity Network
Theresa Savarese	San Diego City College
Barbara Sherman	Buffalo State
Kathryn Surles	Salem Community College
Beth Thomas	Hagerstown Community College
Barbara Webber	Northern Essex Community College
Jean Welsh	Lansing Community College
Lynn Wermers	North Shore Community College
Sherry Young	Kingwood College

Preface

Welcome to the
*CERTIFICATION CIRCLE
SERIES*. Each book in this
series is designed with one
thing in mind: preparing you to
pass a Microsoft Office User
Specialist (MOUS) exam. This
strict focus allows you to target
the skills you need to be successful. You will not need to
study anything extra—it's like
getting a peek at the exam
before you take it! Read on to
learn more about how the book
is organized and how you will
get the most out of it.

Skill Overview
Each skill starts with a paragraph
explaining the concept and how
you would use it. These are
clearly written and concise.

File Open Icon
We provide a realistic
project file for every
skill. And, it's in the
form you need it in
order to work through
the steps; there's no
wasted time building
the file before you can
work with it.

Skill Steps
The Steps required
to perform the skill
appear on the left
page with what you
type in green text.

Tips
We provide tips
specific to the skill
or how the skill is
tested on the exam.

Table of Contents
This book is organized around
the MOUS exam objectives.
Each Skill on the exam is
taught on two facing pages
with text on the left and figures on the right. This also
makes for a terrific reference;
if you want to brush up on a
few skills, it's easy to find the
ones you're looking for.

Getting Started Chapter
Each book begins with a
Getting Started Chapter.
This Chapter contains skills
that are *not* covered on the
exam but the authors felt
were vital to understanding
the software. The content
in this chapter varies from
application to application.

Skill Set 8
Integrating with Other Applications

Import Data to Access
Import Data from an Excel Workbook

You can import data into an Access database from several file formats, including an Excel workbook or another Access, FoxPro, dBase, or Paradox database.
It is not uncommon for a user to enter a list of data into Excel and later decide
to convert that data into an Access database, because the user wants to use
Access's extensive form or report capabilities or wants multiple people to be able
to use the data at the same time. (An Access database is inherently **multi-user**;
many people can enter and update data at the same time.) Since the data in an
Excel workbook is structured similarly to data in an Access table datasheet, you
can easily import data from an Excel workbook into an Access database by
using the **Import Spreadsheet Wizard**.

Activity Steps
📁 Classes01.mdb

1. Click **File** on the menu bar, point to **Get External Data**, then
   click **Import**
2. Navigate to the drive and folder where your Project Files are
   stored, click the **Files of type list arrow**, click **Microsoft Excel**,
   click **Instructors**, then click **Import** to start the Import
   Spreadsheet Wizard
   See Figure 8-1.
3. Select the **First Row Contains Column Headings check box**,
   then click **Next**
4. Click **Next** to indicate that you want to create a new table, then
   click **Next** to not specify field changes
5. Click the **Choose my own primary key option button** to set
   InstructorID as the primary key field, then click **Next**
6. Type **Instructors** in the Import to Table box, click **Finish**, then
   click **OK**
7. Double-click **Instructors** to open it in Datasheet View
   See Figure 8-2. Imported data works the same way as any other table
   of data in a database.
8. Close the Instructors table

tip

Step 4
You can also
import Excel
workbook data
into an existing
table if the field
names used in the
Excel workbook
match the field
names in the
Access table.

98   Certification Circle

Additional Projects

For those who want more practice applying the skills they've learned, there is a project for each skill set located at the back of each book. The projects ask you to combine the skills you've learned to create a meaningful document – just what you do in real life.

Project for Skill Set 1
Working with Cells and Cell Data

Sales Projection for Alaska Adventures

You work for Alaska Adventures, a small company based in Juneau, Alaska, that offers sea kayaking, mountain biking, and hiking tours. You've received a workbook containing a sales projection for the sea kayaking tours that the company hopes to sell in the busy summer months of June, July, and August. In this project, you will complete and format this worksheet. The workbook also contains a second worksheet that includes a list of the guests who purchased sea kayaking tours on a single day during the previous summer. You'll use the AutoFilter features on this list to determine the number of customers who came from countries other then the United States and Canada.

Activity Steps

open EC_Project1.xls

1. Clear the contents and formats of cell A3, drag cell A4 up to cell A3, then delete cell D14 and shift the cells left

2. Merge cell A3 across cells A3 to E3, then check the spelling in the worksheet and correct any errors

3. Enter Total in cell E5, use the Go To command to navigate to cell C13, then change the value in cell C13 to 1200

4. Use the SUM function in cell E12 to add the values in cells B12 through D12, then copy the formula to cells E13 through E15

5. Select cells B12 through B16, then use the AutoSum button to calculate the totals required for cells B16 through E16

6. In cell B18, enter the formula required to subtract the value in cell B16 from the value in cell B9, then copy the formula to cells C18 through E18

7. Use Find and Replace to locate all instances of 1500 and replace them with 500

Step 8
To save time, press and hold the [CTRL] key, select each group of cells, and then click the Currency Style button.

8. Format cells B7 through E7, B9 through E9, B12 through E12, B16 through E16, and B18 through E18 with the Currency style, format cells B8 through E8 and cells B13 through E15 with the Comma style, then compare the completed worksheet to Figure EP 1-1

9. Switch to the Customers worksheet, then use AutoFilter to show only the International customers in the Category column. The filtered list appears as shown in Figure EP 1-2

close EC_Project1.xls

Skill 1
Import Data to Access

Figure 8-1: Import Spreadsheet Wizard dialog box

Figure 8-2: Imported Instructors table in Datasheet View

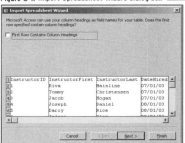

Seven records were imported

extra!

Using delimited text files
You can import data from a **delimited text file**, a file of unformatted data where each field value is delimited (separated) by a common character, such as a comma or a tab. Each record is further delimited by a common character, such as a paragraph mark. A delimited text file usually has a **txt** (for text) file extension. You can use delimited text files to convert data from a proprietary software system (such as an accounting, inventory, or scheduling software system) into a format that other programs can import. For example, most accounting software programs won't export data directly into an Access database, but they can export data to a delimited text file, which can then be imported by Access.

Figures

There are at least two figures per skill which serve as a reference as you are working through the steps. Callouts focus your attention to what's important.

Extra Boxes

This will *not* be on the exam—it's extra—hence the name. But, there are some very cool things you can do with Office xp so we had to put this stuff somewhere!

Target Your Skills

At the end of each unit, there are two Target Your Skills exercises. These require you to create a document from scratch, based on the figure, using the skills you've learned in the chapter. And, the solution is provided—there's no wasted time trying to figure out if you've done it right.

Additional Resources

There are many resources available with this book—both free and for a nominal fee. Please see your sales representative for more information. The resources available with this book are:

INSTRUCTOR'S MANUAL

Available as an electronic file, the Instructor's Manual is quality-assurance tested and includes unit overviews, lecture topics, solutions to all lessons and projects, and extra Target Your Skills. The Instructor's Manual is available on the Instructor's Resource Kit CD-ROM, or you can download if from www.course.com.

FACULTY ONLINE COMPANION

You can browse this textbook's password protected site to obtain the Instructor's Manual, Solution Files, Project Files, and any updates to the text. Contact your Customer Service Representative for the site address and password.

PROJECT FILES

Project Files contain all of the data that students will use to complete the lessons and projects. A Readme file includes instructions for using the files. Adopters of this text are granted the right to install the Project Files on any stand-alone computer or network. The Project Files are available on the Instructor's Resource Kit CD-ROM, the Review Pack, and can also be downloaded from www.course.com.

SOLUTION FILES

Solution Files contain every file students are asked to create or modify in the lessons and projects. A Help file on the Instructor's Resource Kit includes information for using the Solution Files.

FIGURE FILES

Figure Files contain all the figures from the book in bitmap format. Use the figure files to create transparency masters or in a PowerPoint presentation.

SAM, SKILLS ASSESSMENT MANAGER FOR MICROSOFT OFFICE XP SAM^xp

SAM is the most powerful Office XP assessment and reporting tool that will help you gain a true understanding of your students' proficiency in Microsoft Word, Excel, Access, and PowerPoint 2002.

TOM, TRAINING ONLINE MANAGER FOR MICROSOFT OFFICE XP TOM

TOM is Course Technology's MOUS-approved training tool for Microsoft Office XP. Available via the World Wide Web and CD-ROM, TOM allows students to actively learn Office XP concepts and skills by delivering realistic practice through both guided and self-directed simulated instruction.

Certification Circle Series, SAM, and TOM: the true training and assessment solution for Office XP.

Preparing for the MOUS Exam

Studying for and passing the Microsoft Office User Specialist (MOUS) exams requires very specific test preparation materials. As a student and reviewer of MOUS exam materials, I am proud to be a part of a team of creators that produced a new series specifically designed with the MOUS exam test taker in mind.

The Certification Circle Series ™ provides a fully integrated test preparation solution for MOUS Office^{XP} with the powerful combination of its Core and Expert textbooks, testing software with Skills Assessment Manager (SAM^{XP}) and Training Online Manager (TOM^{XP}). This combination coupled with the Exam Reference Pocket Guide for quick test taking tips and Office^{XP} materials will provide the skills and confidence a student will need to pass the MOUS exams.

How does the Certification Circle Series provide the best test preparation materials? Here's how:

▶ Core and Expert texts are based entirely on MOUS exam objectives.

▶ Table of Contents in each book maps directly to MOUS exam objectives in a one to one correlation.

▶ "Target Your Skills" exercises in the end of unit material presents problem solving questions in similar fashion to the MOUS 2002 exams.

▶ Skills Assessment Manager (SAM^{XP}) provides a simulated testing environment in which students can target their strengths and weakness before taking the MOUS exams.

If you are an experienced Access user, you'll probably want to go directly to the Target Your Skills exercise at the end of the Skill Set and Test your mastery of the objectives in that Skill Set. If you are unsure about how to accomplish any part of the exercise, you can always go back to the individual lessons that you need to review, and practice the steps required for each MOUS objective.

If you are relatively new to Access, you'll probably want to complete the lessons in the book in a sequential manner, using Target Your Skills exercise at the end of each Skill Set to confirm that you've learned the skills necessary to pass each objective on the MOUS test.

The Target Your Skills exercises simulate the same types of activities that you will be requested to perform on the test. Therefore, your ability to complete them in a timely fashion will be a direct indicator of your preparedness for the MOUS exam.

Judy Cameron, Spokane Community College
and the Certification Circle Series Team

SAM, Skills Assessment Manager for Microsoft Office XP

SAM XP–the pioneer of IT assessment.

How can you gauge your students' knowledge of Office XP? SAM XP makes teaching and testing Office XP skills easier. SAM XP is a unique Microsoft Office XP assessment and reporting tool that helps you gain a true understanding of your students' ability to use Microsoft Word, Excel, Access, and PowerPoint 2002, and coming soon Outlook 2002, Windows 2000 and Windows XP.

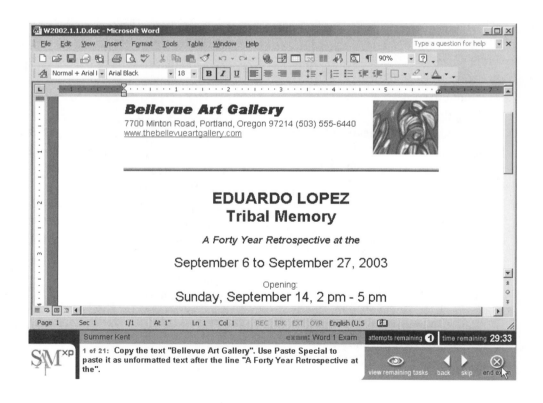

TOM, Training Online Manager for Microsoft Office XP

TOM—efficient, individualized learning when, where, and how you need it.

TOM is Course Technology's MOUS-approved training tool for Microsoft Office XP that works in conjunction with SAM XP assessment and your Illustrated Office XP book. Available via the World Wide Web or a stand-along CD-ROM, TOM allows students to actively learn Office XP concepts and skills by delivering realistic practice through both guided and self-directed simulated instruction.

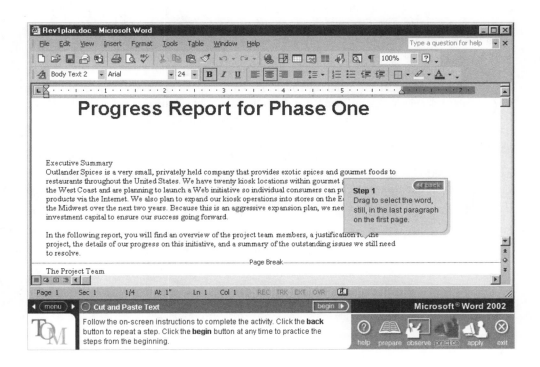

Certification Circle: Exam Reference Pocket Guide

The Microsoft Office ^{XP} Exam Reference Pocket Guide is a reference tool designed to prepare you for the Microsoft Office User Specialist (MOUS) exams. The book assumes that you are already familiar with the concepts that are the basis for the skills covered in this book. The book can therefore be used as a study companion to brush up on skills before taking the exam or as a desk reference when using Microsoft Office programs.

There are six chapters in this book. The first chapter in the book, *Exam Tips*, provides some background information on the MOUS Certification program, the general process for taking an exam, and some helpful hints in preparing and successfully passing the exams.

The remaining five chapters each cover a different Office program: Word, Excel, Access, PowerPoint, and Outlook. Each program-specific chapter begins by covering program basics in a brief *Getting Started* section. This section covers the basic skills that are not specifically covered in the MOUS exams, but that are essential to being able to work in the program. The *Getting Started* section is followed by the complete set of skills tested by the Microsoft MOUS Certification exams, starting with the Core or Comprehensive exam, and then followed by the Expert exam where applicable. These sections are labeled and ordered to exactly match the Skill Sets and Skill Activities tested in the MOUS Certification Exam. Clear, bulleted steps are provided for each skill.

Because there are often different ways to complete a task, the book provides multiple methods where appropriate for each skill or activity, including Menu, Button, Keyboard, Mouse, and Task Pane methods. The MOUS exams allow you to perform the skills using any one of these methods, so you can choose the method with which you are most comfortable to complete the task. It is the perfect companion to any of the Certification Circle Series textbooks or as a stand-alone reference book.

Contents

MOUS Microsoft Office^{XP}

CERTIFICATION CIRCLE™ *MASTER*

MOUS Microsoft Office^XP

CERTIFICATION CIRCLE™ MASTER

MOUS Microsoft Office^{XP}

CERTIFICATION CIRCLE™ MASTER

MOUS Microsoft Office^{XP}

CERTIFICATION CIRCLE™ *MASTER*

MOUS Microsoft Office^{XP}

CERTIFICATION CIRCLE™ *MASTER*

MOUS Microsoft Office^{XP}

CERTIFICATION CIRCLE™ *MASTER*

MOUS Microsoft Office^{XP}

CERTIFICATION CIRCLE™ *MASTER*

MOUS Microsoft Office^XP

CERTIFICATION CIRCLE™ MASTER

MOUS Microsoft Office^{XP}

CERTIFICATION CIRCLE™ *MASTER*

MOUS Microsoft Office^{XP}

CERTIFICATION CIRCLE™ *MASTER*

MOUS Microsoft Office^{XP}

CERTIFICATION CIRCLE™ *MASTER*

MOUS Microsoft Office^XP

CERTIFICATION CIRCLE™ *MASTER*

MOUS Microsoft Office^{XP}

CERTIFICATION CIRCLE™ *MASTER*

Skill List

1. Start and exit Word
2. Understand toolbars
3. Understand task panes
4. Open and close documents
5. Work with more than one open document
6. Navigate in the document window
7. Understand views
8. Save the files you create
9. Use smart tags
10. Get help

Microsoft Word is a **word-processing program**, a program that makes it easy to enter and manipulate text in documents. A **document** is any file that you create using Word.

Before you can start creating your own documents, you need to learn a few fundamentals about working with Word, including how to start and exit the program, open and close documents, navigate in a document, open and close task panes, change views, save files, use smart tags, and use Help.

Getting Started

Getting Started with Word 2002

Start and Exit Word

Before you can create documents, you need to start Word. In this lesson, you will learn how to start and exit the Word program. When you start Word, you open the Word program window and a blank document window.

Activity Steps

Step 5
You can also click Exit on the File menu to exit Word.

1. Click the **Start button** 📲Start on the Windows taskbar

2. Point to **Programs**
   See Figure GS-1.

3. Click **Microsoft Word**

4. If necessary, click the **Maximize button** ☐ in the Word program window title bar
   See Figure GS-2.

5. Click the **Close button** ☒ in the program window title bar

---

extra!

Understanding filename extensions

Each Windows program uses a different **filename extension,** the three letters that follow a period after the filename itself. The unique extensions identify each document's file type. Word creates document files with the **.doc** file extension. Word also uses the extension **.dot** to identify template files, documents that have built-in formatting that you use as a starting point for creating a new document. Word can also create and open files with the extension **.htm,** which identifies Hyper Text Markup Language (HTML) files, the file type that Web pages use.

Figure GS-1: Starting Word

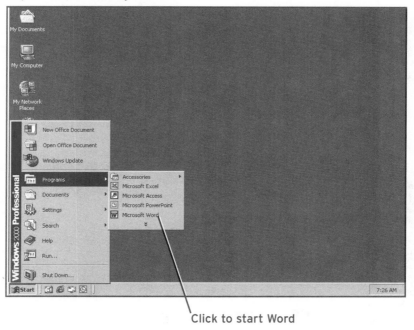

Click to start Word

Figure GS-2: Word program window

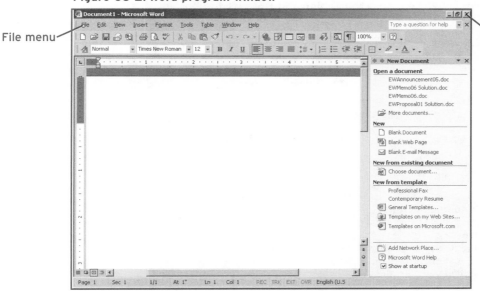

File menu

Program window Close button

Understand Toolbars

Toolbars contain buttons that provide one-click access to frequently used commands. When you start Word, usually only the Standard and Formatting toolbars are visible. Word provides 30 toolbars that contain buttons grouped by specific tasks. For example, the Tables and Borders toolbar contains buttons that you click when you are working with a table in a document. Toolbars are either **docked** along a screen edge, or they are **floating** in the middle of the screen.

If you keep the Standard and Formatting toolbars on one line, the button you want may not be visible, so click the Toolbar Options button on either toolbar, then click the button you need.

Activity Steps

1. Start Word

2. If the Standard and Formatting toolbars are on one line, as shown in Figure GS-3, click either **Toolbar Options button**, then click **Show Buttons on Two Rows**
   The figures in this book show the Standard and Formatting toolbars on two lines.

3. Click **Tools** on the menu bar, click **Customize** to open the Customize dialog box, then click the **Options tab**, if necessary

4. Make sure that the **Show Standard and Formatting toolbars on two rows** check box is selected, then click the **Always show full menus check box** to select it, if necessary

5. Click **Close** in the Customize dialog box

6. Right-click any toolbar, then click **Tables and Borders** to open the Tables and Borders toolbar
   See Figure GS-4.

7. If the Tables and Borders toolbar is not floating as shown in Figure GS-4, position the pointer over a blank area on the toolbar (not over a button), press and hold the mouse button so that the pointer changes to $+$, then drag the toolbar down into a blank area of the window and release the mouse button

8. Click the **Close button** ✕ in the Tables and Borders toolbar title bar, then exit Word

---

extra!

Using toggle buttons
Toggle means to turn something on or off. Toggle buttons are buttons that are either active (selected) or inactive (deselected). For example, the Drawing button on the Standard toolbar is a toggle button. Clicking it causes the Drawing toolbar to open (usually at the bottom of the window). A blue, square outline appears around an active button, and the button background changes from gray to a light blue. When you click the Drawing button again, the toolbar closes and the button is no longer selected.

Figure GS-3: Word program window with Standard and Formatting toolbars on one line

Toolbars on one line

Toolbar Options buttons

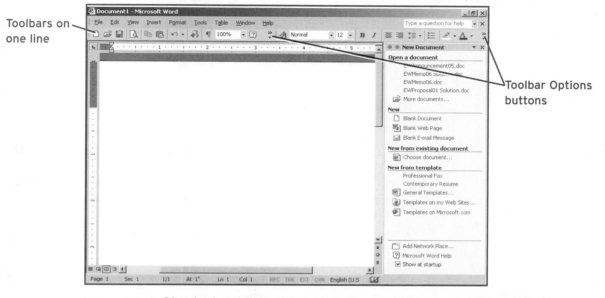

Figure GS-4: Standard and Formatting toolbars on two lines and a floating toolbar

Toolbars on two lines

Tables and Borders toolbar

Toolbar Close button

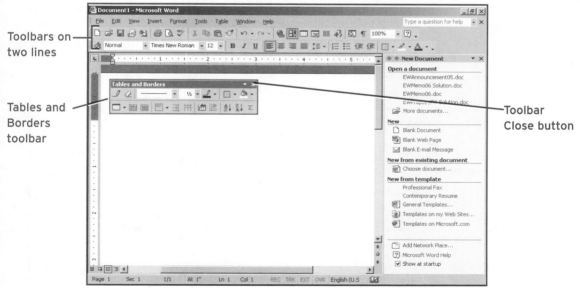

Getting Started

Getting Started with Word 2002

Understand Task Panes

Task panes provide lists of hyperlinks (links) to commonly used commands. They usually appear on the right side of the document window. When you move the pointer over a hyperlink in a taskpane, the pointer changes to 🖑 and the link becomes underlined (similar to links in your browser window). Clicking a link has the same effect as executing a command using the menus or toolbars. Word provides eight task panes (see Table GS-1).

Activity Steps

1. Start Word

2. If a task pane is not open, click **View** on the menu bar, then click **Task Pane**

3. Click the **Other Task Panes list arrow** ▼ in the task pane title bar, then click **Reveal Formatting** to open the Reveal Formatting task pane

4. Move the pointer over the **Font link** to see the pointer change to 🖑
   See Figure GS-5.

5. Move the pointer over the **Sample Text box** at the top of the task pane to see the list arrow appear

6. Click the **Back button** ◀ in the task pane title bar to return to the previously displayed task pane

7. Click the **Close button** ✕ in the task pane title bar to close the task pane
   See Figure GS-6.

8. Exit Word

tip

Right-click any toolbar, then click Task Pane to open or close task panes.

TABLE GS-1: Task panes in Word

task pane	description
New Document	Contains commands for opening new and existing documents
Clipboard	Opens the Office Clipboard, a special area for holding text and objects that you want to paste into the document
Search	Contains commands and options for searching for files that meet specific criteria
Insert Clip Art	Contains commands for searching for clip art (saved images) that meet specific criteria
Styles and Formatting	Contains lists of Word styles (pre-defined formats for text)
Reveal Formatting	Displays a description of the formatting in the selected text
Mail Merge	A set of six panes that helps you merge names and addresses with a form letter
Translate	Contains commands for translating selected text or the entire document to and from French or Spanish

Figure GS-5: Reveal Formatting task pane open

k button

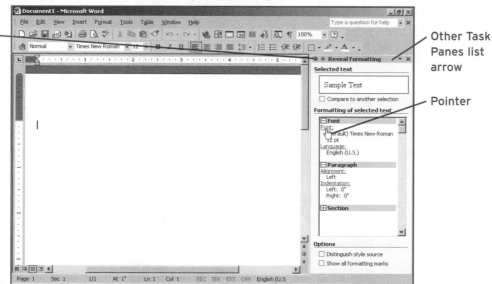

Other Task Panes list arrow

Pointer

Figure GS-6: Document window with no task pane open

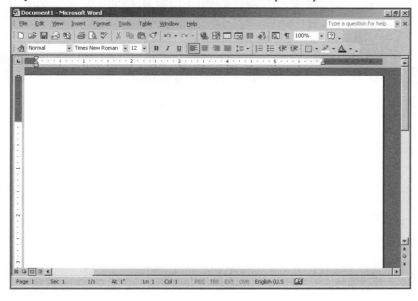

Open and Close Documents

In Word, you can create new, blank documents and you can open existing documents to edit them. When you open documents, you can click the list arrow next to the Open command in the Open dialog box to choose one of a variety of ways to open the document (see Table GS-2). When you have finished working on a document, you should close it. It's a good idea to close all open documents before exiting Word.

Activity Steps

Click the New Blank Document button to open a new, blank document; click the More documents link in the New Document task pane to open the Open dialog box.

1. Start Word, make sure the New Document task pane is open, then click the **Blank Document link** under **New** in the task pane as shown in Figure GS-7 to open another new, blank document

2. Click the **Close Window button** ☒ in the menu bar to close the document

3. Click the **Open button** 🖆 to open the Open dialog box

4. Click the **Look in list arrow**, then select the drive or folder where your project files are stored

5. If your project files are stored within another folder, double-click that folder in the list to display its contents

6. Click the **CCAnnouncement01** file to select it
See Figure GS-8.

7. Click **Open** to open the selected file

8. Click **File** on the menu bar, then click **Close** to close the document

Note: In the rest of the book, we assume that you will have Word running or that you will start Word before completing the steps, and that you will exit Word when you have finished.

When you need to open a file to complete a set of steps, the complete filename will appear next to 📄 before Step 1. 📄 will appear again at the end of the steps to remind you to close the file or files you worked on in the skill.

Figure GS-7: Closing a document

New Blank Document button

Open button

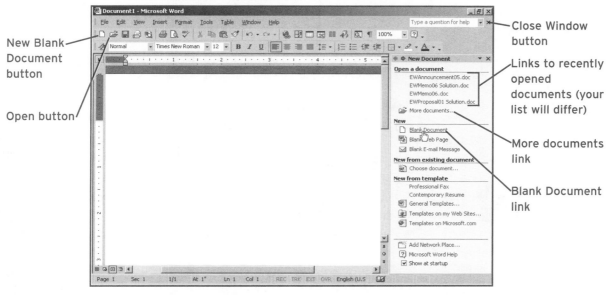

Close Window button

Links to recently opened documents (your list will differ)

More documents link

Blank Document link

Figure GS-8: Open dialog box

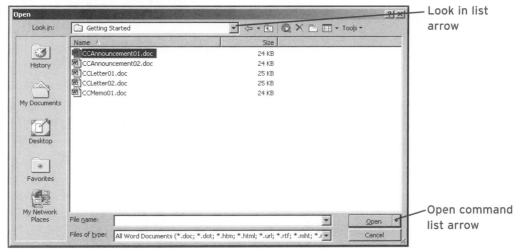

Look in list arrow

Open command list arrow

Getting Started

Getting Started with Word 2002

Work with More Than One Open Document

You can open more than one document at a time in Word. The **active document** is the document that you are currently working on. The other documents are **inactive**. You can switch between open documents by clicking the document button on the Windows task bar; by clicking Window on the menu bar, then clicking the document name; or by displaying all of the open document windows on the screen at once and clicking in the one you want to make active.

Activity Steps

 open CCAnnouncement01.doc

1. Make sure that Word is running, then make sure you opened the **CCAnnouncement01** file as indicated above

2. Click the **Open button** [icon], navigate to the drive and folder where your project files are stored, click the **CCMemo01** file, then click **Open** to open a second document

3. Click **Window** on the menu bar, then click **CCAnnouncement01**, as shown in Figure GS-9, to make it the active document

4. Click **Window** on the menu bar, then click **Arrange All** to display both documents at the same time
   See Figure GS-10.

5. Click in the **CCMemo01 document window** to make it the active document

6. Press and hold **[Shift]**, click **File** on the menu bar in the CCMemo01 document window, then click **Close All**

7. Click the **Maximize button** [icon] in the Word program window

Step 3
You can also click the document button on the taskbar to switch to another document.

Figure GS-9: Switching between documents using the Windows menu

Checkmark appears next to active document

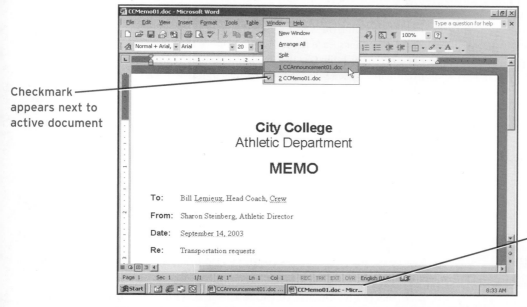

Document button for active document appears indented

Figure GS-10: Two open documents displayed on screen at the same time

Title bar of active document is blue

Title bar of inactive document is gray

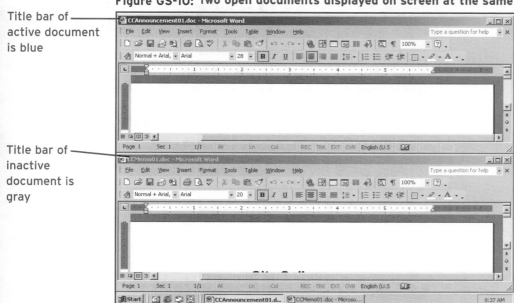

Getting Started

Getting Started with Word 2002

Navigate in the Document Window

One of the benefits of working with Word is how easy it is to move around and edit different parts of the document. You can click anywhere in the document to position the **insertion point**, the blinking vertical line that indicates where the text you type will appear. You can also use the keyboard to move the insertion point around in the document (see Table GS-3). Some keys need to be used together to move the insertion point. When you see two keys listed next to each other, such as [Ctrl][Home], you must press and hold the first key, in this case, the [Ctrl] key, then press the second key, in this case, the [Home] key, and then release both keys.

Activity Steps

 open CCLetter01.doc

1. Make sure that you opened the **CCLetter01** file as indicated above, then click immediately before **crew** in the first line of the body of the letter to position the blinking insertion point there *See Figure GS-11.*

2. Press [➡] five times to move the insertion point to the word **program** in the next line

3. Press **[Page Down]** to move the insertion point down a screen

4. Drag the scroll box in the vertical scroll bar down to the bottom of the scroll bar to see the end of the document without moving the insertion point

5. Click above the scroll box in the vertical scroll bar to jump up a screen

6. Click the down scroll arrow in the vertical scroll bar to scroll down one line

7. Press **[Ctrl][Home]** to move the insertion point to the beginning of the document

8. Make sure you close the **CCLetter01** document as indicated below

 close CCLetter01.doc

The horizontal scroll bar works the same way as the vertical scroll bar except the document moves sideways in the window.

Figure GS-11: Insertion point in document

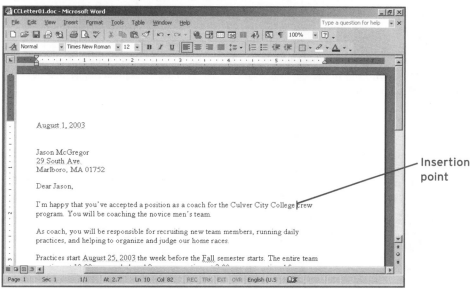

TABLE GS-2: Shortcut keys for moving the insertion point

key	effect
[→], [←]	Moves the insertion point to the right or left one character at a time
[Ctrl][→], [Ctrl][←]	Moves the insertion point to the right or left one word at a time
[↓], [↑]	Moves the insertion point down or up one line
[Page Down], [Page Up]	Moves the insertion point down or up one screen at a time
[Ctrl][Home]	Moves the insertion point to the beginning of the document
[Ctrl][End]	Moves the insertion point to the end of the document
[Home]	Moves the insertion point to the beginning of the current line
[End]	Moves the insertion point to the end of the current line

Getting Started

Getting Started with Word 2002

Understand Views

Word allows you to look at your document in different ways called **views** (see Table GS-3). The default view is Print Layout view. To change the view, you click one of the view buttons located to the left of the horizontal scroll bar. You can also change the **zoom**, the magnification of the document on screen, by clicking the Zoom button list arrow , then selecting another zoom setting from the list, or by clicking in the Zoom box, then typing a new magnification. Changing the view or zoom does not affect how the document will look when printed.

Activity Steps

file open CCAnnouncement02.doc

1. Make sure that you open the **CCAnnouncement02** file as indicated above, then click the **Normal View button** 📄 *See Figure GS-12.*

2. Click the **Web Layout View button** 📄

3. Click the **Outline View button** 📄

4. Click the **Print Layout View button** 📄

5. Click the **Zoom button list arrow** [100% ▾], then click **Whole Page** *See Figure GS-13.*

6. Click in the **Zoom box**, type **60**, then press **[Enter]**

7. Click the **Zoom button list arrow** [60% ▾], then click **100%**

8. Make sure that you close the **CCAnnouncement02** document as indicated below

file close CCAnnouncement02.doc

tip

You can also change views by selecting a view on the View menu.

TABLE GS-3: Document views	
view	**what you see**
Print Layout view	All of the text, any graphical elements, and headers and footers as they appear on the printed page
Normal view	Formatted text, but not some graphical elements or headers and footers; does not show the document as it will look when printed
Web Layout view	Document as it would look if you published it to a Web page
Outline view	Headings indented to show the structure of the document

Figure GS-12: Document in Normal view

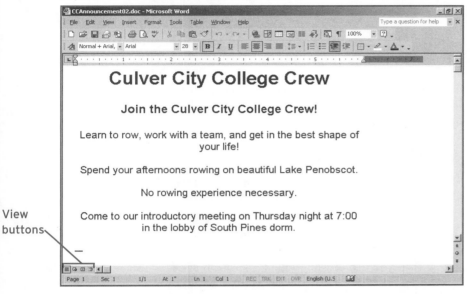

View
buttons

Figure GS-13: Document at Whole Page zoom in Print Layout view

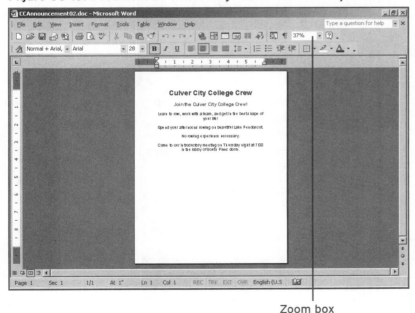

Zoom box

extra!

**Splitting a document
window into two parts**
When you work with a
long document, it can
sometimes be helpful to
split the document
window into two panes,
allowing you to jump
back and forth quickly
between two parts of
the document. The easi-
est way to do this is to
position the pointer on
top of the thin split
box, just above the
up scroll arrow in the
vertical scroll bar, so
that the pointer changes
to ⬍. Drag the split
box down to create two
panes in the document
window. To close the
second window, double-
click the split box.

Getting Started

Getting Started with Word 2002

Save the Files You Create

As you work through the activities in this book, you might want to save your completed files. You will learn more about saving files in Skill Set 4, but in the meantime, you can save your files in one of two ways. If you want to leave the original files that you open unchanged, you can save your completed files with a new name by using the Save As command on the File menu. If you don't care if the original file changes, you can save the changes that you make when you complete the steps to the same file that you opened by clicking the Save button 🖫.

Activity Steps

 open CCMemo01.doc

1. Make sure that you opened the **CCMemo01** file as indicated above, click **File** on the menu bar, then click **Save As** to open the Save As dialog box

2. Click the **Save in list arrow,** then select the drive or folder where you want to store your files

3. If you are storing your files within another folder, double-click that folder in the list to display its contents

4. Select the text in the **File name box** if it's not already selected, then type **Intro Letter** in the Filename box
   See Figure GS-14.

5. Click **Save** to save the document with the new name and leave the original document unchanged

6. Type **Culver,** then press the **[Spacebar]**

7. Click the **Save button** 🖫 to save the changes to the document with the same filename
   See Figure GS-15.

8. Make sure that you close the **Intro letter** document as indicated below

 close Intro Letter.doc

tip

Copy all of the project files before you use them to complete the skills in this book. This will allow you to repeat the steps for any skills that you want to review.

 **extra!**

Closing without saving
If you do not want to save the changes you made to the documents as you work through the activities, you can simply close the files without saving them first. When you do this, a warning box will appear asking if you want to save the changes to the file. If you click No, the file closes without saving your changes. If you click Yes, the changes you made are saved, then the file closes.

Figure GS-14: Save As dialog box

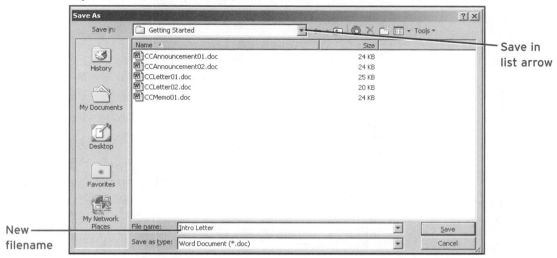

Save in list arrow

New filename

Figure GS-15: Using the Save button

filename

button

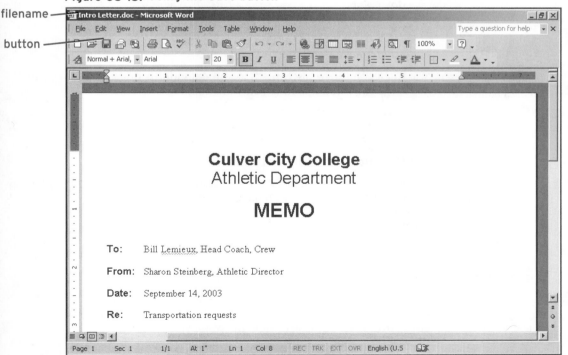

Getting Started

Getting Started with Word 2002

Use Smart Tags

A **smart tag** is a button that appears on screen when Word recognizes a word or phrase as belonging to a certain category, for example, names, addresses, and dates. When you click the button, you can choose to add the name or address to your electronic address book, or you can choose to add the date to your electronic scheduler. Some smart tags do not appear until you position the pointer over their locations, which are identified by a dotted red line under a word or phrase.

Step 4
If the Outlook 2002 startup wizard screen appears, you will need to use it to set up Outlook before you can complete Steps 4 and 5. Follow the wizard steps, or click Cancel in the wizard, then continue with Step 6.

Activity Steps

open CCLetter02.doc

1. Make sure that you opened the **CCLetter02** file as indicated above, then move the pointer over the **date** in the first line to see the smart tag ⊕ appear
See Figure GS-16.

2. Point to the **smart tag** to make the Smart Tag Actions button ⊕ ▾ appear

3. Click the **Smart Tag Actions button** ⊕ ▾ to open the drop-down list
See Figure GS-17.

4. Click **Schedule a Meeting** on the drop-down list to open your electronic calendar

5. Click the **Close button** ☒ in the calendar program window, then click **No** when asked if you want to save changes

6. Move the pointer over the **street address** in the inside address to display the smart tag, move the pointer over the **smart tag** ⊕, then click the **Smart Tag Actions button** ⊕ ▾

7. Click **Remove this Smart Tag**

8. Make sure that you close the **CCLetter02** document as indicated below, clicking **No** when asked if you want to save changes

close CCLetter02.doc

Changing smart tag options
You can change what type of text is labeled by Word with smart tags. Click Smart Tag Options on the Smart Tag Actions button drop down list, or click AutoCorrect Options on the Tools menu, then click the Smart Tags tab. Click the check boxes in the Recognizers list to select or deselect the types of text you want to be recognized. If you are connected to the World Wide Web, you can also click More Smart Tags on the Smart Tags tab in the AutoCorrect Options dialog box. This will connect you to a Microsoft Web site, where you can find more Smart Tags you can download.

Figure GS-16: Displaying a smart tag

Smart tag ——

Pointer——

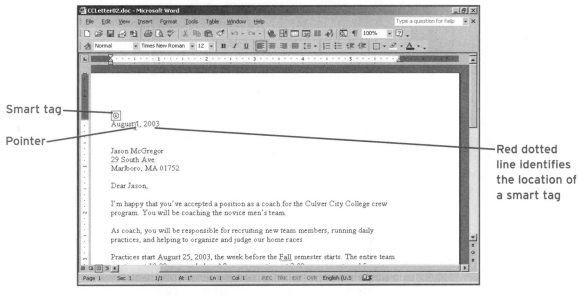

Red dotted
line identifies
the location of
a smart tag

Figure GS-17: Using the Smart Tag Actions button

Smart Tag
Actions
button

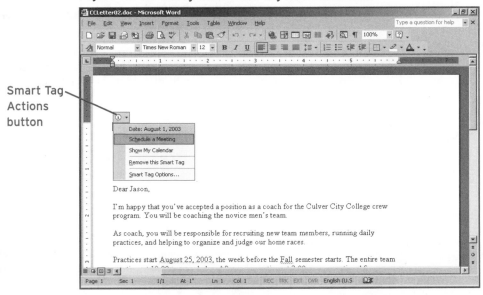

Getting Started

Getting Started with Word 2002

Get Help

Word provides an online Help system to help you find information about Word and instructions on how to use Word commands and features. The easiest way to access the Help system is to type a question in the Ask a Question box in the menu bar in the program window. You can also open the Help window by pressing [F1] or by clicking the Microsoft Word Help button ⑦.

Step 6
If the topics shown in Figure GS-19 do not appear on your screen, click the plus sign next to Microsoft Word Help in the Contents tab, then click the plus sign next to Viewing and Navigating Documents.

Activity Steps

1. Click in the **Ask a Question box** [Type a question for help] in the menu bar

2. Type **Look at two parts of a document**, then press **[Enter]**
   See Figure GS-18.

3. Click the **See more link** at the bottom of the drop-down list

4. Click the **View two parts of a document simultaneously link** to open a Help window displaying this information

5. If the Help window is not expanded as shown in Figure GS-19, click the **Show button** ⊞ in the Help window toolbar to expand the Help window

6. Click the **Contents tab** in the pane on the left of the Help window, if necessary, then click **Move around in a document** as shown in Figure GS-19

7. Click the **plus sign** next to **Getting Started with Microsoft Word** in the Contents tab to expand that topic list

8. Click the **Back button** ⇐ at the top of the Help window to return to the previous Help screen, then click the **Close button** ✕ in the Help window title bar to close the Help window

Figure GS-18: Selecting a Help topic from the Ask a Question box drop-down list

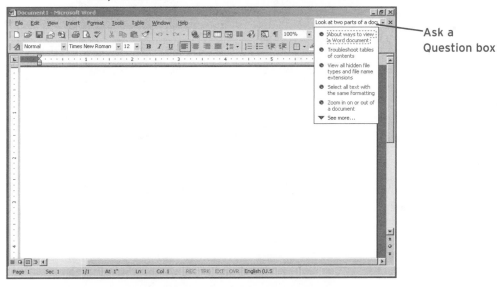

Ask a Question box

Figure GS-19: Contents tab in the Help window

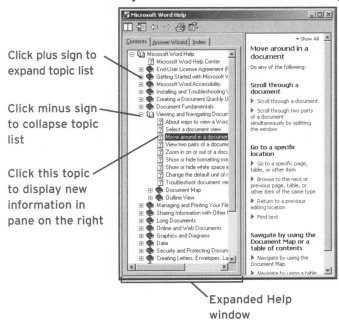

Click plus sign to expand topic list

Click minus sign to collapse topic list

Click this topic to display new information in pane on the right

Expanded Help window

Target Your Skills

Getting Started with Word 2002

Target Your Skills

If you know the answers to the following questions, then you are ready to move ahead to the rest of the chapters in this book. If you have trouble with any of the questions, refer to the page listed next to the question to review the skill.

1. How do you start Word? How do you exit Word? (p. 2)

2. What is the three-letter filename extension for Word documents? Name two other filename extensions that Word recognizes. (p. 3)

3. Describe a toolbar. How are toolbars positioned in the window? Describe two ways to close a toolbar. (p. 4)

4. Define **toggle**. (p. 5)

5. Describe task panes. How do you open a task pane? Describe three ways to close a task pane. (p. 6)

6. How do you open a new, blank document? How do you open an existing document? Describe two ways to close a document. (p. 8)

7. Define **active document**. Describe two ways to switch between open documents. Explain how to display two open documents on the screen at the same time. (p. 10)

8. to the beginning of a document? (p. 12)

9. Describe the four views in Word. Explain what the Zoom command does. (p. 14)

10. How do you split a document window in two? (p. 15)

11. How do you save changes to a document? How do you save a document with a new name? How do you save a new document for the first time? (p. 16)

12. Can you close a document without saving changes that you made? (p. 17)

13. Define **smart tag**. How are smart tags identified in a document? (p. 18)

14. How do you access Word's online Help system? (p. 20)

Skill List

1. Insert, modify, and move text and symbols
2. Apply and modify text formats
3. Correct spelling and grammar usage
4. Apply font and text effects
5. Enter and format date and time
6. Apply character styles

In Skill Set 1, you will learn how to create a document in Microsoft Word 2002. A **document** is any file that you create using Word. You can create many kinds of documents, including memos, letters, newsletters, resumes, brochures, and multi-page reports.

Once you insert text into a document, you can modify that text in several ways. You can change the words or the word order. If you want, you can change the way the text looks by modifying the format of the text. You can also use Word to check your spelling and grammar and to automatically insert the current date and time.

Skill Set 1

Inserting and Modifying Text

Insert, Modify, and Move Text and Symbols
Insert Text

The first thing you do when you create a document is insert text. To do this, you simply start typing using the keyboard. The blinking **insertion point** on the screen indicates where the text will appear. When you reach the end of a line, the insertion point automatically moves to the next line—you do not need to press [Enter]. This is called **word-wrap**. You press [Enter] when you want to start a new paragraph. To add a blank line between paragraphs, you can press [Enter] twice.

You do not need to type two spaces after any punctuation, because Word adjusts the space automatically.

Activity Steps

1. Create a new, blank document

2. Type **November 3, 2003**, then press **[Enter]** twice
   See Figure 1-1.

3. Type **Ms. Patsy Madison**, then press **[Enter]**

4. Type **503 Shore Drive**, then press **[Enter]**

5. Type **Charleston, SC 29407**, then press **[Enter]** twice

6. Type **Dear Ms. Madison:**, then press **[Enter]** twice

7. Type the body of the letter shown in Figure 1-2, then press **[Enter]** twice at the end of the paragraph

8. Type **Sincerely**, press **[Enter]** four times, then type your name

    close file

Figure 1-1: Text entered in a new document

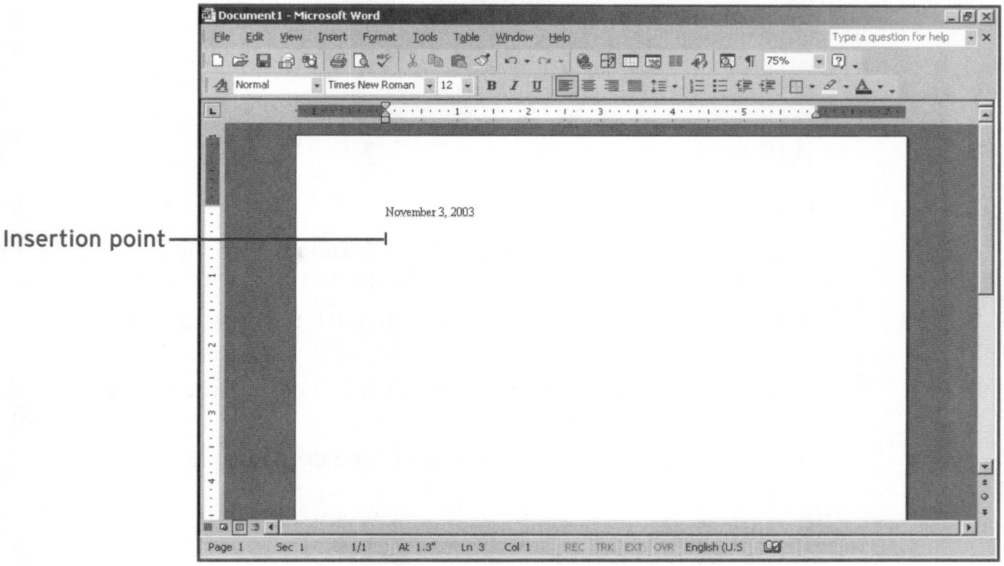

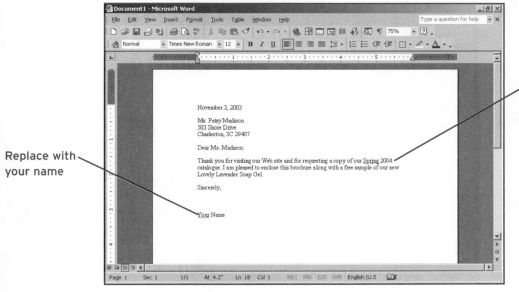

Insertion point

Figure 1-2: Document with paragraphs

Your text may wrap at a different point

Replace with your name

Skill Set 1
Inserting and Modifying Text

Insert, Modify, and Move Text and Symbols
Insert Symbols

In addition to letters and numbers, you can enter symbols in a document. A **symbol** is a character not included in the standard English alphabet or set of Arabic numbers. You enter symbols using the Symbol dialog box.

Click the Special Characters tab in the Symbol dialog box to see a short list of common symbols.

Activity Steps

 open EWLetter01.doc

1. Click Ⲓ immediately after the word **Soap** in the third line, so that the insertion point blinks to the left of the period

2. Click **Insert** on the menu bar, then click **Symbol** to open the Symbol dialog box

3. Click the **Font list arrow**, then click to select **Times New Roman**, if necessary

4. Drag the **scroll box** to the top of the scroll bar, then click the **down scroll arrow** three times

5. Click ©, the copyright symbol
   See Figure 1-3.

6. Click **Insert**, then click **Close**
   See Figure 1-4.

 close EWLetter01.doc

Figure 1-3: Symbol dialog box

Copyright symbol

Description of selected symbol

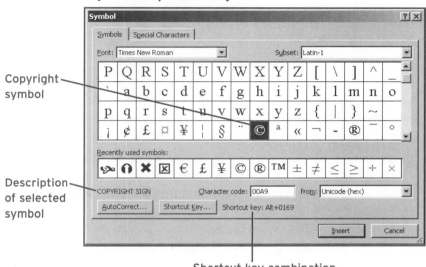

Shortcut key combination
to insert selected symbol

Figure 1-4: Symbol inserted in document

Copyright symbol inserted

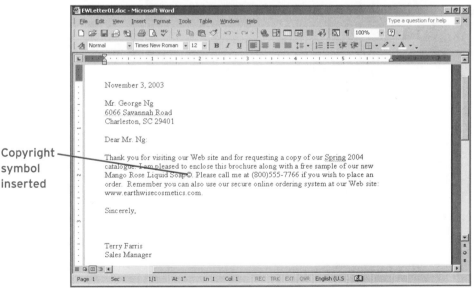

Skill Set 1
Inserting and Modifying Text

Insert, Modify, and Move Text and Symbols
Edit Text

With a word processor, you do not need to retype an entire document when you want to change a word or delete a sentence. The easiest way to edit text is to use the [Backspace] and [Delete] keys. When you press [Backspace], you delete the character immediately to the left of the insertion point. When you press [Delete], you delete the character immediately to the right of the insertion point. You can also **select**, or highlight, the text you want to change and then start typing, and the characters you type will replace all of the selected text.

If you make a mistake, you can "undo" it by clicking the Undo button. Undo any number of previous actions by clicking the list arrow next to the Undo button, then selecting as many actions as you want.

Activity Steps

 open EWMemo01.doc

1. Click immediately to the right of **Seaview** in the first paragraph in the body of the memo

2. Press **[Backspace]** seven times, then type **Riverside**

3. Click immediately to the left of **20** (after **June**) in the first paragraph

4. Press **[Delete]** twice, then type **19**

5. Double-click the word **three** in the first line in the first paragraph to select it

6. Type **four**
   See Figure 1-5.

 close EWMemo01.doc

Figure 1-5: Document with edited text

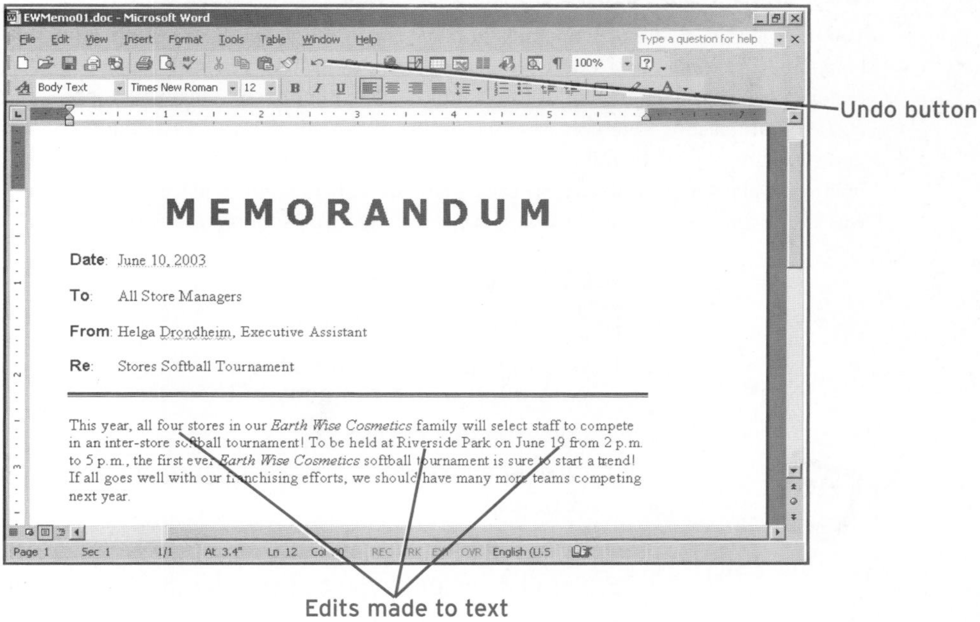

Undo button

Edits made to text

extra!

Selecting text

There are several ways to select text. You can position the pointer to one side of the text you want to select, press and hold the mouse button, drag the pointer across the text to select it, then release the mouse button. To select a word quickly, double-click it. To select a line of text, position the pointer in the blank area on the left side of the document to the left of the line, so that the pointer changes to ⤹, then click. To select a large body of text, click at the beginning of the text you want to select, press and hold [Shift], then click at the end of the text. You can also use the keyboard to select text. Position the pointer to the left or right of the text you want to select, press and hold [Shift], then press [➡] or [⬅] as many times as necessary to select the word or phrase. To select a word at a time, press and hold [Shift] and [Ctrl] while you press [➡] or [⬅].

Skill Set 1
Inserting and Modifying Text

Insert, Modify, and Move Text and Symbols
Cut and Paste Text

You use the Cut and Paste commands to move text from one place in a document to another, or even from one document to another. When you **cut** text, it is removed from the document and stored in the system **clipboard**. When you **paste** text, you are pasting whatever is stored on the clipboard. You can paste the text you stored on the clipboard as many times as you like. The system clipboard can hold only one thing at a time, so each time you cut text, you replace whatever was stored there before. The clipboard is cleared when you shut off your computer.

Activity Steps

 open EWLetter02.doc

1. Double-click the word **online** in the first sentence of the second paragraph within the body of the letter

2. Click the **Cut button**

3. Click between the words **completed** and **that** in the second paragraph

4. Click the **Paste button**

5. Scroll down until you can see the third paragraph

6. Click to position the insertion point before the word **Again** in the third paragraph, press and hold the mouse button, drag to highlight the entire first sentence including the space after the period, then release the mouse button

7. Point to the selected sentence and hold down the mouse button

8. Drag down so that the vertical indicator line attached to the pointer appears after the last sentence in the paragraph
   See Figure 1-6.

9. Release the mouse button to position the dragged sentence at the end of the paragraph
   See Figure 1-7.

 close EWLetter02.doc

tip

Click the Paste Options button that appears on the screen after you perform the Paste command or drag and drop text to choose options for changing the format of the pasted text.

Understanding the Office Clipboard
With Office XP you can use the standard system clipboard or the Office Clipboard. The system clipboard can store only the most recently cut or copied item. The Office Clipboard which opens as a task pane, can store up to 24 items. To activate it, click Office Clipboard on the Edit menu or perform several cut, copy, and paste commands in succession. To paste an item from the Office Clipboard, click the item in the Clipboard task pane. (When you use the Paste command, you paste only the last item placed on the system clipboard.)

Figure 1-6: Document with moved text and sentence being dragged and dropped

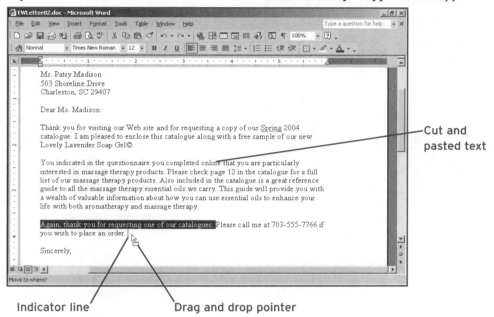

Cut and
pasted text

Indicator line   Drag and drop pointer

Figure 1-7: Document after sentence is dropped in new location

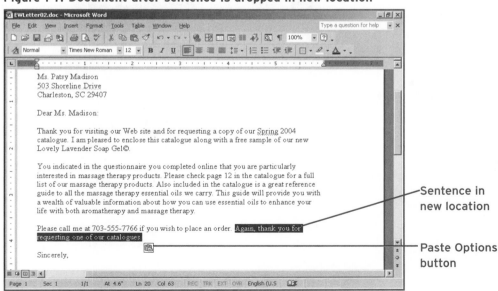

Sentence in
new location

Paste Options
button

Skill Set 1

Inserting and Modifying Text

Insert, Modify, and Move Text and Symbols
Copy and Paste Text

Copying is similar to cutting, but when you copy text, you don't remove it from its original location. As with cutting, whatever you copy is placed on the clipboard for you to paste as many times as you want, until you replace it with new cut or copied text.

Right-click selected text, then click Cut or Copy. Right-click where you want to paste the text, then click Paste.

Activity Steps

 open EWLetter03.doc

1. Select **Mr. Ng** in the salutation (do not select the colon)

2. Click the **Copy button** 📇

3. Click immediately after **thank you** in the first line in the last paragraph, type **,** (a comma), then press the **[Spacebar]**

4. Click the **Paste button** 📇, then type **,** (a comma)
   See Figure 1-8.

5. Double-click **catalogue** in the second line in the first paragraph

6. Press and hold **[Ctrl]**, then drag **catalogue** between **the** and **for** in the second line in the second paragraph
   See Figure 1-9.

 close EWLetter03.doc

Figure 1-8: Text copied to new location

Copied text

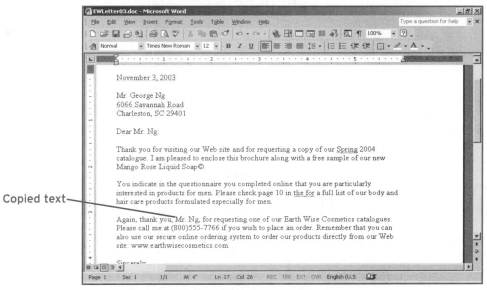

Figure 1-9: Copied text being dragged and dropped

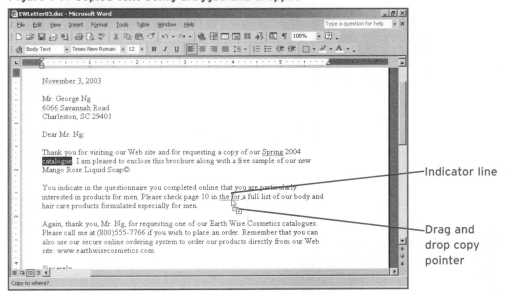

Indicator line

Drag and drop copy pointer

Skill Set 1
Inserting and Modifying Text

Insert, Modify, and Move Text and Symbols
Use the Paste Special Command

The Paste Special command allows you to control how information is pasted by giving you a variety of paste options. You can use it when you cut or copy something from one place in a Word document to another place in the same document, when you cut or copy between Word documents, or when you cut or copy from a file created in another program to a Word document. You can also use it to copy formatted text—text with a specific appearance—to another paragraph that is formatted differently, and have the pasted text pick up the formatting of its destination paragraph.

Activity Steps

 open **EWBrochure01.doc**
EWLetter04.doc

Another way to paste copied text so that it picks up the formatting of the destination paragraph is to use the Paste command, click the Paste Options button that appears on screen, then click Match Destination Formatting.

1. Click **Window** on the menu bar, then click **EWBrochure01.doc**

2. Select the entire paragraph under the heading **Lavender Soap Gel** (do not select the heading or the blank line below the paragraph) *See Figure 1-10.*

3. Click the **Copy button** 📋

4. Click **Window** on the menu bar, then click **EWLetter04.doc**

5. Click at the end of the first paragraph, after the period

6. Click **Edit** on the menu bar, click **Paste Special**, then click **Unformatted Text** in the list in the Paste Special dialog box

7. Click **OK** to paste the copied text so it picks up the formatting of the destination paragraph *See Figure 1-11.*

 close **EWBrochure01.doc**
EWLetter04.doc

Figure 1-10: Formatted text selected in a document

EWBrochure01 is the active file

Selected text

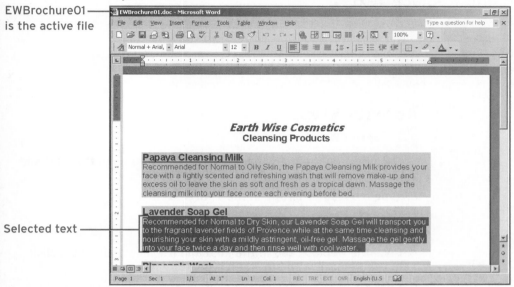

Figure 1-11: Pasted text with the formatting of the destination paragraph

EWLetter04 is the active file

Inserted text picks up formatting of this paragraph

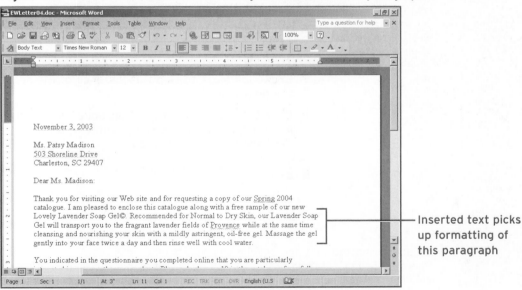

Skill Set 1
Inserting and Modifying Text

Insert, Modify, and Move Text and Symbols
Find and Replace Text

In a long document, you may need to locate a specific word or phrase. You may also want to replace that word or phrase with another. The Find and Replace commands in Word let you do this easily and quickly. Enter the word or words for which you are searching, and then tell Word to find them. If you want to replace the words you find, you can enter the new words and tell Word to replace the search terms.

Activity Steps

 open EWLetter05.doc

1. Click **Edit** on the menu bar, then click **Find** to open the Find and Replace dialog box

2. Type **massage therapy** in the Find what box

3. Click **Find Next**
   See Figure 1-12.

4. Click the **Replace tab** in the Find and Replace dialog box, click in the Replace with box, then type **aromatherapy**

5. Click **Replace** to replace the search term with the replacement term and to find the next instance of the search term in the document

6. Click **Replace** two more times to replace the next two instances of the search term
   See Figure 1-13.

7. Click **Find Next** to skip this instance of the search term and find the next one

8. Click **OK** in the dialog box that appears telling you that Word has finished searching the document, then click **Close** in the Find and Replace dialog box

 close EWLetter05.doc

If you are sure that you want to replace all instances of the text for which you are searching, click Replace All on the Replace tab in the Find and Replace dialog box.

---

extra!

Finding formatted text and special characters
You can search for text with specific formatting as well as special characters. Click More in the Find and Replace dialog box, then click Format or Special. For example, if you wanted to find all the words with bold formatting, click in the Find what box, click Format, click Font, click Bold, then click OK. When you click Find Next, Word searches for words with bold formatting. To remove formatting options from the search criteria, click No Formatting.

Figure 1-12: Using the Find command

Text found in document

Find what box

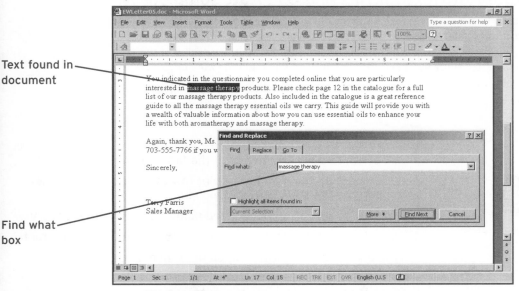

Figure 1-13: Replacing text

Replaced text

Don't replace this instance

Click to see more options

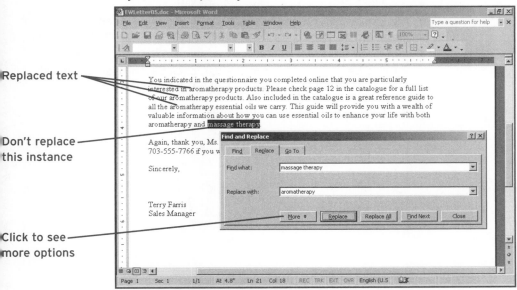

Skill Set 1
Inserting and Modifying Text

Insert, Modify, and Move Text and Symbols
Create AutoText Entries and Use AutoComplete

You can store frequently used words or phrases as AutoText, text that Word automatically enters. When you type the first few characters of an AutoText entry, a ScreenTip appears identifying it as AutoText. You can then use the AutoComplete feature by pressing [Enter] to insert the rest of the word or phrase automatically.

Activity Steps

 open EWAnnouncement01.doc

1. Select **Earth Wise Cosmetics** in the first line in the document

2. Click **Insert** on the menu bar, point to **AutoText**, then click **New** to open the Create AutoText dialog box

3. Click **OK** to accept the suggested name for the AutoText entry

4. Click immediately before the word **Softball** in the last paragraph

5. Type **eart** to see the AutoComplete ScreenTip
   See Figure 1-14.

6 Press **[Enter]** to complete the AutoText entry
   See Figure 1-15.

7. Click **Insert** on the menu bar, point to **AutoText**, then click **AutoText** to open the AutoText tab in the AutoCorrect dialog box

8. Type **e** in the Enter AutoText Entries here box to jump to the entries beginning with **e** in the list, click **Earth Wise** in the list, click **Delete**, then click **OK** to close the dialog box

 close EWAnnouncement01.doc

To see the predefined AutoText entries, click Tools on the menu bar, click AutoCorrect Options, then click the AutoText tab and scroll down the list.

Figure 1-14: AutoComplete ScreenTip

AutoComplete screen tip

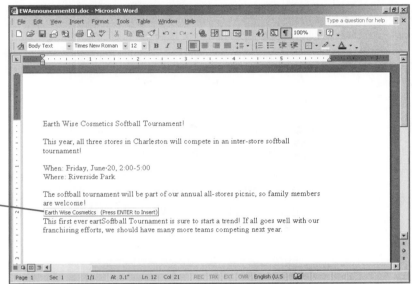

Figure 1-15: Completed AutoText entry in document

Completed AutoText

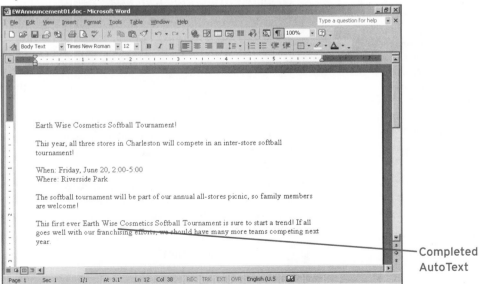

Skill Set 1
Inserting and Modifying Text

Insert, Modify, and Move Text and Symbols
Use AutoCorrect

AutoCorrect automatically detects and corrects frequently misspelled words, and it checks for and corrects incorrect capitalization. It also replaces text with symbols. For example, if you type *teh*, as soon as you press the [Spacebar] or [Enter], AutoCorrect replaces the mistyped word with *the*. You can add your own frequently typed words to the AutoCorrect list to cut down on the number of keystrokes you need to make.

To change the types of words automatically corrected, open the AutoCorrect tab in the AutoCorrect dialog box, and deselect any check boxes you wish.

Activity Steps

 open EWBrochure02.doc

1. Click below the **Lavender Soap Gel** heading, then type **We reccommend** with two *c*s exactly as shown

2. Press the **[Spacebar]**, watching the screen as you do to see AutoCorrect correct the spelling of **recommend**

3. Move the pointer over the word **recommend** to see the AutoCorrect Options button ▭
   See Figure 1-16.

4. Move the pointer over the **AutoCorrect Options button** ▭ to change it to a button icon ⬛

5. Click the **AutoCorrect Options button** ⬛, click **Control AutoCorrect Options** in the drop-down menu to open the AutoCorrect tab in the AutoCorrect dialog box, scroll down the list to see the AutoCorrect entries, then click **OK**

6. Type **this gle for** and observe the red, squiggly line under **gle** that indicates the word is misspelled

7. Right-click the misspelled word **gle**, point to AutoCorrect on the shortcut menu, then click **gel** as shown in Figure 1-17 to add this misspelling to the AutoCorrect list and correct the word in the document

8. Click **Tools** on the menu bar, click **AutoCorrect Options**, type **gl** in the Replace box to scroll the list, click **gle** in the list, click **Delete**, then click **OK** to delete the word you added from the AutoCorrect list

 close EWBrochure02.doc

Figure 1-16: AutoCorrect box in document

AutoCorrect box indicates the word was corrected

Pointer

Figure 1-17: Adding a word to the AutoCorrect list automatically

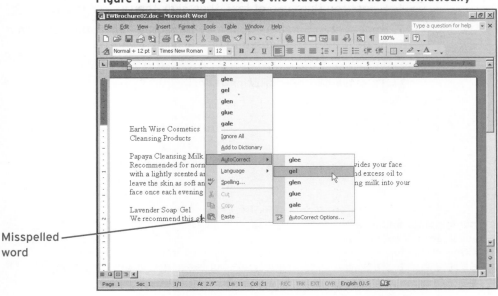

Misspelled word

Skill Set 1
Inserting and Modifying Text

Apply and Modify Text Formats
Apply Character Formats

Format refers to the way something looks. Specifically, you can add formatting to text by changing the **font** (the design of letters and numbers), the **font size**, and the **font style** (for example, adding boldface or italics). Judicious use of text formatting commands can make a document easier to read. Most text formatting can be accomplished using the buttons on the Formatting toolbar.

If unexpected changes occur as you type, click the AutoFormat As You Type tab in the AutoCorrect dialog box, then deselect the check boxes next to the items you want to stop formatting automatically.

Activity Steps

file open EWCoDescription01.doc

1. Select the first line of text, then click the **Bold button** **B**

2. Click the **Font box list arrow** , scroll, if necessary, then click **Arial**

3. Click the **Font Size box list arrow** `12 ▾`, click **16**, then click in a blank area of the screen to deselect the text
   See Figure 1-18.

4. Select the second line of text, click the **Bold button** **B**, click the **Italic button** *I*, then change the font size to **14**

5. Click the **Bold button** **B** again to turn bold formatting off for the selected text

6. Select the third line of text, then click the **Underline button** **U**

7. Repeat step 6 for the **Company Background** line, then click in a blank area of the screen to deselect the text
   See Figure 1-19.

file close EWCoDescription01.doc

Understanding points and picas

Points and picas are units of measurement for text. A **point** (pt) is approximately 1/72 of an inch, and a **pica** is equivalent to 12 points. Typically, fonts are measured in points, space between paragraphs is measured in points and picas, and margins and paragraph indents are measured in inches.

Figure 1-18: Document after formatting first line of text

Format of text changed

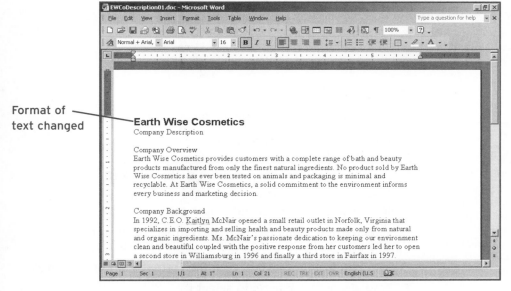

Figure 1-19: Document after formatting headings

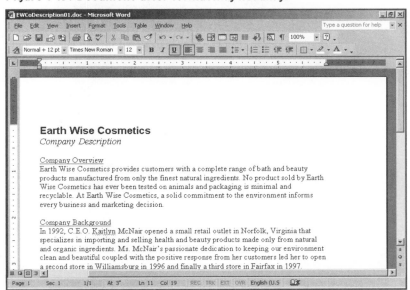

Skill Set 1

Inserting and Modifying Text

Apply and Modify Text Formats
Modify Character Formats

After you have applied formatting to characters, you can change it in any way you wish. Once you have formatted text the way you want, you can copy that formatting to other text in your document by using the Format Painter button.

tip

To format text in different areas of the document with Format Painter, select the text whose format you want to copy, then double-click the Format Painter button. It will remain active until you click it again.

Activity Steps

 open EWAnnouncement02.doc

1. Select the first line of text
   See Figure 1-20.

2. Click the **Font size list arrow** 22, then click **18**

3. Click the **Font Color list arrow** , then click the **Lavender color box** (last row, second to last column)

4. Select **When:**, click the **Bold button** B to turn the bold formatting off, then click the **Underline button** U

5. With **When:** still selected, click the **Format Painter button**

6. Drag across **Where:** to select it
   See Figure 1-21.

7. Click in a blank area of the screen to deselect the text

 close EWAnnouncement02.doc

Figure 1-20: Formatted text selected

Buttons reflect the formatting of the selected text

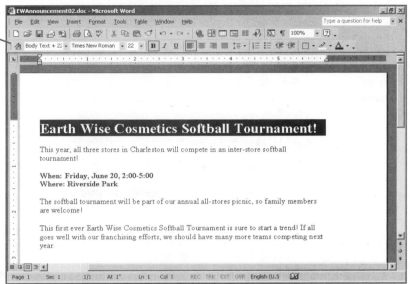

Figure 1-21: Reformatted text in document

Format Painter selected

Pointer

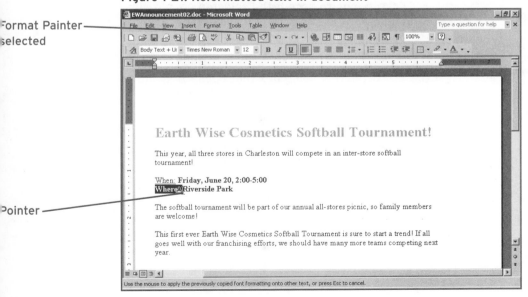

Skill Set 1

Inserting and Modifying Text

Correct Spelling and Grammar Usage

Correct Spelling Errors

When you click the Spelling command, Word scans the document and compares the words against its built-in dictionary. When it finds a word that isn't in its dictionary, it flags it as a possible misspelled word and offers a list of suggested corrections. You can choose one of the corrections from the list, correct the word yourself, or tell Word to ignore the word (in other words, that it is spelled correctly). If automatic spell checking is turned on, you will see red, squiggly lines under the words that Word is flagging as misspelled.

Activity Steps

 open EWLetter06.doc

1. Click the **Spelling and Grammar button**
   See Figure 1-22.

2. Click **catalog** in the Suggestions list, then click **Change All** to change all instances of the flagged word and search for the next possible misspelling

3. Click **Ignore All** to ignore all instances of the word **Provence** (a proper noun) and continue searching

4. Click **Change** to accept the selected entry **twice** in the Suggestions list and continue searching

5. Click **Change** to accept the selected entry **catalogs** in the Suggestions list and continue searching

6. Click **OK** in the dialog box that appears telling you that the spelling and grammar check is complete

 close EWLetter06.doc

Right-click a word with a red, squiggly underline to open a shortcut menu containing a list of suggested corrections. Click a suggested correction or click Ignore All.

Figure 1-22: Spelling dialog box

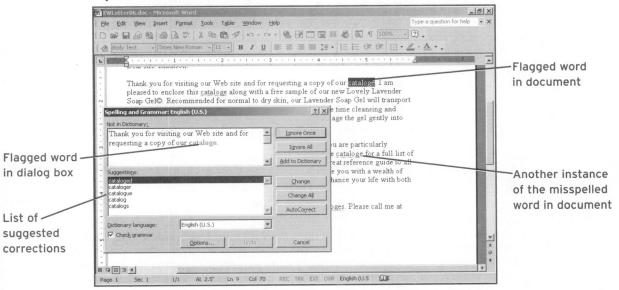

Flagged word in document

Flagged word in dialog box

List of suggested corrections

Another instance of the misspelled word in document

extra!

Changing Spelling and Grammar options

To change Spelling and Grammar checker options, click Options in the Spelling and Grammar dialog box or click Tools on the menu bar, click Options, then click the Spelling & Grammar tab. To hide the red and green squiggly lines in your document, deselect the check boxes next to Check spelling as you type and Check grammar as you type. To check style as well as grammar, click the arrow under Writing style and select Grammar and Style in the list. To change the Grammar checker rules, click Settings, then deselect the check boxes next to the items you don't want to check. If you have already checked the document for spelling and grammar errors but you want to recheck it, click Recheck Document to reset all of the items that you previously had told the Spelling and Grammar checker to ignore.

Skill Set 1
Inserting and Modifying Text

Correct Spelling and Grammar Usage
Correct Grammar Errors

The grammar checker is part of the spell checker. If the Check grammar check box in the Spelling and Grammar dialog box is selected, the grammar in your document will be checked at the same time as the spelling.

Activity Steps

 open EWLetter07.doc

1. Click the **Spelling and Grammar button**
   See Figure 1-23.

2. Click **Explain**, then read the explanation that appears when the Office Assistant appears

3. Click **Ignore Once** to ignore this rule (*Spring* is a title in the document, not a season) and continue the search

4. Click in the document behind the Spelling and Grammar dialog box, position the insertion point immediately after the **e** in **guide** in the highlighted sentence, press the **[Spacebar]**, then type **will**
   See Figure 1-24.

5. Click **Resume** in the Spelling and Grammar dialog box

6. Click the second suggestion in the Suggestions list, then click **Change**

7. Click **OK** in the dialog box that appears telling you that the spelling and grammar check is complete

 close EWLetter07.doc

> **tip**
>
> The grammar checker is not perfect. It compares sentences against a built-in set of rules, but it may miss errors or identify something that is correct as an error, so use your common sense.

Figure 1-23: Grammar problem flagged by Spelling and Grammar checker

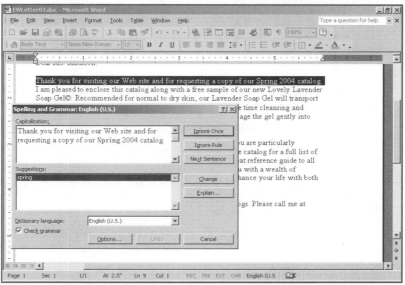

Figure 1-24: Fixing an error in the document

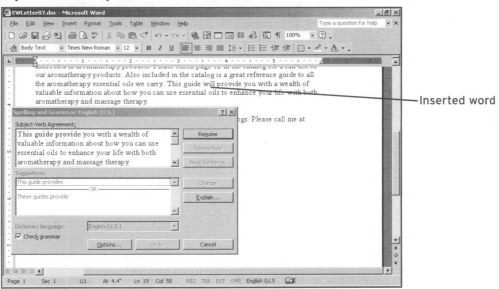

Inserted word

Skill Set 1
Inserting and Modifying Text

Correct Spelling and Grammar Usage
Use the Thesaurus

Word has a built-in thesaurus to help you when you need to find a synonym or an antonym for a word. You can access the thesaurus by right-clicking the word you want to replace or by using a command on the Tools menu.

If none of the Thesaurus suggestions is exactly the word you want, click Look Up in the dialog box to look up the synonym in the Replace with Synonym box to see more suggestions.

Activity Steps

 open EWLetter08.doc

1. Select **asking** in the first line in the body of the letter

2. Click **Tools** on the menu bar, point to **Language**, then click **Thesaurus**

3. Click **Look Up** to look up the infinitive form of the verb, which appears in the Replace with Related Word box
   See Figure 1-25.

4. Click **Replace** to replace the selected word in the document with the selected word in the Replace with Synonym box

5. Press **[Backspace]**, then type **ing**

6. Right-click **talk** in the last paragraph, point to **Synonyms** on the shortcut menu, then click **chat**, as shown in Figure 1-26

 close EWLetter08.doc

Figure 1-25: Thesaurus dialog box

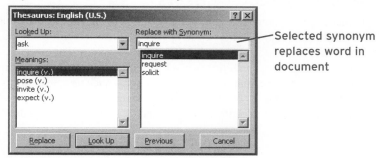

Selected synonym replaces word in document

Figure 1-26: Looking up synonyms

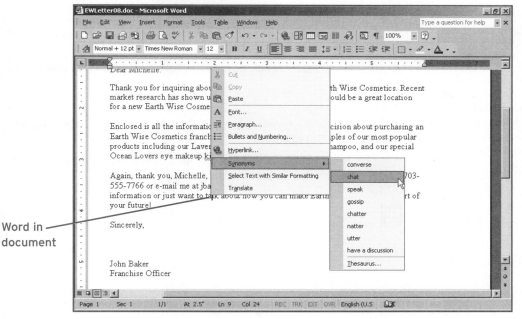

Word in document

Skill Set 1
Inserting and Modifying Text

Apply Font and Text Effects
Apply Character Effects

Formatting commands like Bold, Italic, and Underline are common and appear on the Formatting toolbar. You can apply additional formatting effects to your text if you use the Effects section in the Font dialog box. For example, you can add a line through text, shift text up or down for super- and subscripts, change text to all uppercase, and add interesting effects, such as a shadow, to text. In addition to the buttons on the Formatting toolbar, you can also open the Font dialog box and take advantage of a few additional formatting options.

Activity Steps

 open EWCoDescription02.doc

1. Select **Earth Wise Cosmetics** in the first line

2. Click **Format** on the menu bar, then click **Font** to open the Font dialog box

3. Click the **Outline check box**, then click the **Small caps check box**
   See Figure 1-27.

4 Click **OK**

5. Select © in the fourth line in the paragraph under the heading **Company Background**

6. Open the Font dialog box, click the **Superscript check box**, click **OK**, then click in a blank area of the screen to deselect the text
   See Figure 1-28.

 close EWCoDescription02.doc

Right-click selected text, then click Font on the shortcut menu to open the Font dialog box.

Figure 1-27: Font dialog box with text effects selected

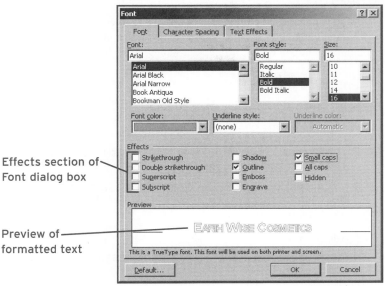

Effects section of
Font dialog box

Preview of
formatted text

Figure 1-28: Document with text effects applied

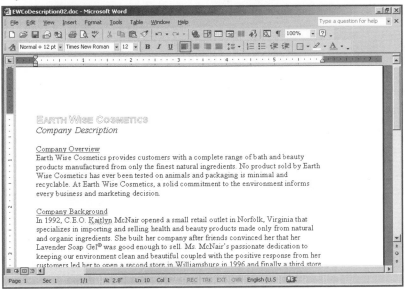

Skill Set 1

Inserting and Modifying Text

Apply Font and Text Effects
Apply Text Animation

If you create a document that is going to be read primarily onscreen rather than in printed form, you can add text animations. Animations are special text effects that move onscreen. You add animation effects in the Font dialog box.

tip

Do not use too many text animations in a document because they can distract the reader from your message.

Activity Steps

 open EWAnnouncement03.doc

1. Select the first line in the document

2. Right-click the selected text, click **Font** on the shortcut menu, then click the **Text Effects tab**

3. Click **Sparkle Text** in the Animations list, then watch the Preview box
   See Figure 1-29.

4. Click **OK**

5. Click anywhere in the document to deselect the text
   See Figure 1-30.

close EWAnnouncement03.doc

Figure 1-29: Text Effects tab in the Font dialog box

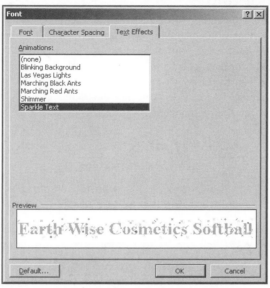

Figure 1-30: Text animation effect applied

Text with
Sparkle Text
animation

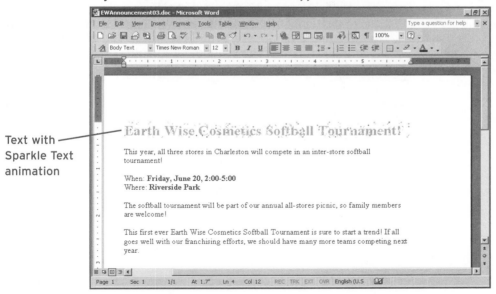

Skill Set 1
Inserting and Modifying Text

Apply Font and Text Effects
Apply Highlighting

Just as you would use a highlighting marker on paper documents, you can add highlighting to a Word document. Highlighting is easy to see when you are reading a document onscreen. If you want to print a document with highlighting, it's a good idea to use a light color for the highlight so that you can see the text underneath. To apply highlighting, you can select the text, then click the Highlight button list arrow and choose a highlight color, or you can click the Highlight button, and then drag it across the text you want to highlight.

Activity Steps

 open EWMemo02.doc

1. Select the phrase **wealth of valuable information** in the second paragraph in the body of the memo

2. Click the **Highlight button list arrow**

3. Click the **Yellow color box** to highlight the selected text

4. Click the **Highlight button** to activate it, then drag to highlight the phrase **you can use _____ to enhance your life** in the last line of the second paragraph
   See Figure 1-31.

5. Click the **Highlight button list arrow**, click **None**, then drag to remove the highlighting from the words **you can use _____ to** in the last line of the second paragraph

6. Click the **Highlight button** to deselect it
   See Figure 1-32.

close EWMemo02.doc

Step 6
You can also press [Esc] to turn the Highlighter off.

Figure 1-31: Highlighted text

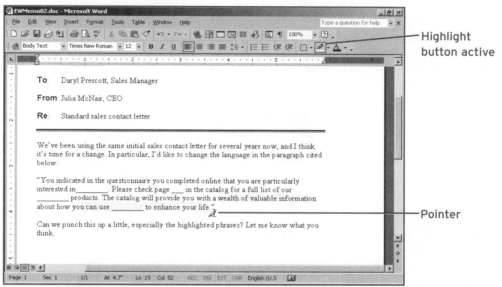

Highlight
button active

Pointer

Figure 1-32: Highlight button deselected

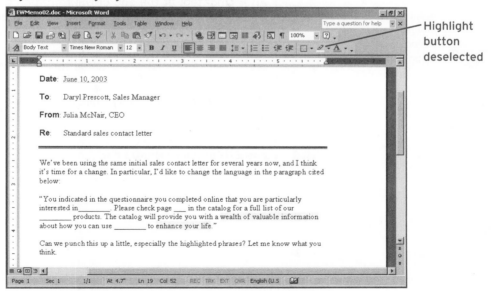

Highlight
button
deselected

Skill Set 1
Inserting and Modifying Text

Enter and Format Date and Time
Insert the Current Date and Time

Word makes it easy to insert the current date and time. You can insert them in two ways: either as static text that will not change, or as a date and time field that updates every time you open the document. A **field** is a placeholder for something that might change in a document. Fields are usually updated as the document changes.

To insert the current date using AutoText, type the first four characters of the current month, press [Enter], press the [Spacebar], then press [Enter] again.

Activity Steps

 open EWCoDescription03.doc

1. Click after **on:** in the third line (make sure there is a space between the colon and the insertion point)

2. Click **Insert** on the menu bar, click **Date and Time** to open the Date and Time dialog box, then click the third format in the list of Available formats
   See Figure 1-33.

3. If the **Update automatically check box** is selected, click it to deselect it so that the date in the document will not change, then click **OK**

4. Click after **Updated:** at the end of the third paragraph, immediately before the close parenthesis (make sure there is a space between the colon and the insertion point)

5. Click **Insert** on the menu bar, click **Date and Time**, then click the first format in the list of Available formats that shows the date and time (12th in the list)

6. Click the **Update automatically check box** to select it, then click **OK**
   See Figure 1-34.

 close EWCoDescription03.doc

Figure 1-33: Date and Time dialog box

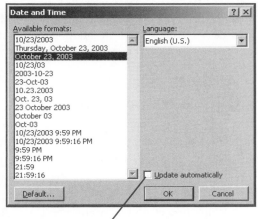

Select to update field
when file is opened

Figure 1-34: Date and time field in document

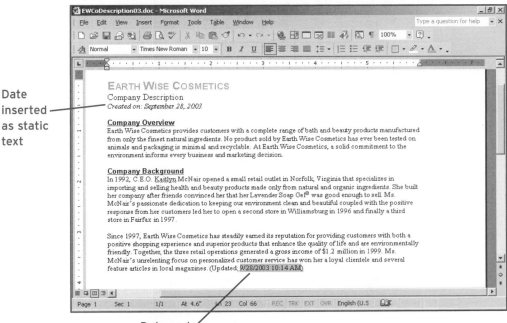

Date
inserted
as static
text

Date and
Time field

Skill Set 1
Inserting and Modifying Text

Enter and Format Date and Time
Modify Date and Time Field Formats

Once you've inserted a date or time, you can change it to a different format. For instance, if you inserted the date to be displayed in the format mm/dd/yy (for example, 06/04/03), you can change it to be displayed as text (for example, June 4, 2003).

Activity Steps

 open EWCoDescription04.doc

Once you've inserted the date and time, you can format it as you would any other text.

1. Position the insertion point so that it is immediately before the first number in the date at the end of the document

2. Press and hold **[Shift]**, then press **[➡]** to select the entire field
   See Figure 1-35.

3. Click **Insert** on the menu bar, then click **Date and Time**

4. Click the fourth format in the list of Available formats

5. If the **Update automatically check box** is not selected, click it to select it

6. Click **OK** to update the field with the new format

 close EWCoDescription04.doc

Figure 1-35: Selecting an entire field

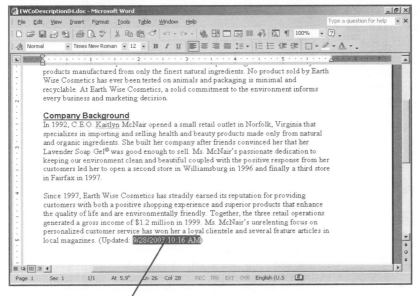

Entire field selected

extra!

Changing the date and time field codes

When the Date and Time is inserted into a document as a field instead of just simple text, you can modify the field codes to change how the date is displayed. Right-click the field, then click Toggle Field Codes to view the field codes instead of the result. Click anywhere in the code and make your changes. For example, if the date code contains the code M, the month number will display without a leading zero for single digit months (for example, 6 for June). You could change this to MM to display two digits for the month (06 for June), MMM to display a three letter abbreviation for the month (Jun), or MMMM to display the entire month name. Once you've made your changes, right-click the field again, then click Update Field to update the field and toggle back to the results.

Skill Set 1

Inserting and Modifying Text

Apply Character Styles

A **style** is a defined set of formats that is applied to text. If you want all the headings in your document to be 24 point, bold Arial, instead of selecting all of the text and then applying each of these formatting changes one at a time, you can apply a heading style that sets all three of these formats at once. Styles can be applied to characters and to paragraphs. When you apply a style, it overrides any formatting that was there previously. Word provides pre-defined styles from which you can choose.

Activity Steps

 open EWAnnouncement04.doc

1. Select the text **Earth Wise Cosmetics Softball Tournament** in the last paragraph

Don't forget that to apply a character style, you must first select all the text to which you want to apply it.

2. Click the **Style button list arrow** `Normal`, then click **More** to open the Styles and Formatting task pane
   See Figure 1-36.

3. Click the **Show box list arrow** `Available formatting` at the bottom of the Styles and Formatting task pane, then click **All styles** in the list

4. Scroll down the **Pick formatting to apply list** in the task pane, then click **Strong**

5. Select the text **first ever** in the last paragraph, scroll up the **Pick formatting to apply list**, then click **Emphasis**
   See Figure 1-37.

6. Click the **Styles and Formatting button** to close the Styles and Formatting task pane

 close EWAnnouncement04.doc

Figure 1-36: Styles and Formatting task pane open

Click to open and close Styles and Formatting task pane

Style button arrow

Task pane

Format for selected text

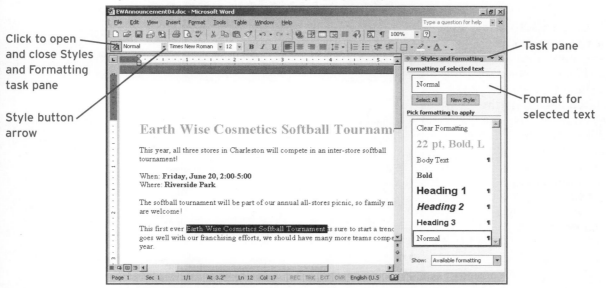

Figure 1-37: Applying a character style

"a" indicates this is a character style

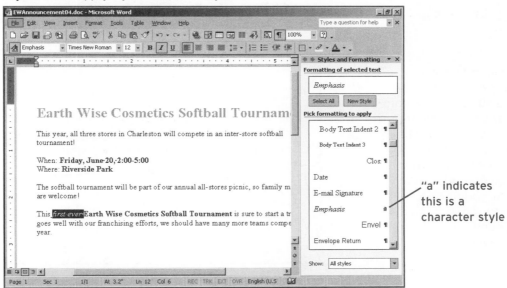

Skill Set 1

Inserting and Modifying Text

Target Your Skills

1 Use Figure 1-38 as a guide to create a new letter. Make sure you insert the current date as a field that will be updated each time the file is opened. Use the [Backspace] and [Delete] keys if you make any typing errors. Remember, don't worry if the lines don't wrap exactly as in the figure.

Figure 1-38

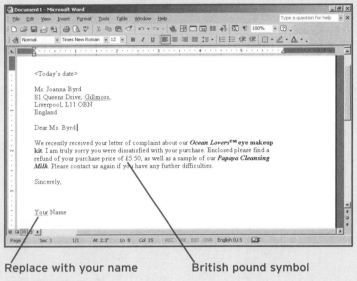

Replace with your name   British pound symbol

 EWBrochure03.doc

2 Use Figure 1-39 as a guide to create a final document. Use the spelling and grammar checker to get rid of any errors in the document. Note that the pargraph order is changed. Also note that you need to move, copy, or find a synonym for some of the words.

Figure 1-39

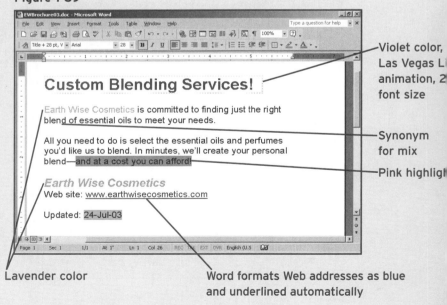

Lavender color   Word formats Web addresses as blue and underlined automatically

Skill List

1. Modify paragraph formats
2. Set and modify tabs
3. Apply bullet, outline, and numbering format to paragraphs
4. Apply paragraph styles

In Skill Set 2, you learn how to work with paragraphs. Word provides many commands to format paragraphs. Most of the paragraph formatting commands are available on the toolbars, although a few can be accessed only from within dialog boxes. Using good paragraph formatting results in neat, professional-looking documents.

Once you've formatted a paragraph, the formatting remains even if you make modifications to the paragraph text. Using paragraph formatting allows you to avoid a lot of tedious adjusting with the [Spacebar] every time you change the text.

Skill Set 2

Creating and Modifying Paragraphs

Modify Paragraph Formats
Apply Paragraph Formats

To select a paragraph, place the insertion point anywhere within the paragraph. If you want to apply a format to more than one paragraph, you must select each paragraph. Once you have set a paragraph format, that format is applied to subsequent paragraphs when you press [Enter].

Activity Steps

 open EWMemo03.doc

1. Position the insertion point anywhere in the second paragraph in the body of the memo

2. Click the **Line Spacing (1) button list arrow**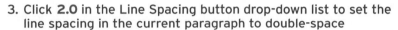
   See Figure 2-1.

3. Click **2.0** in the Line Spacing button drop-down list to set the line spacing in the current paragraph to double-space

4. Position the insertion point after the period at the end of the second paragraph, then press **[Enter]** twice to start a new paragraph with the same formatting as the previous one

5. Type **The essential oils used in our new line of aromatherapy products will bring pleasure to your senses while nourishing and revitalizing your skin.**

6. Drag to select the second and third paragraphs, click the **Line Spacing button list arrow** , then click **1.5** in the drop-down list

7. Click anywhere in the document to deselect the text
   See Figure 2-2.

 close EWMemo03.doc

> **tip**
>
> To insert blank space above and below individual paragraphs without pressing [Enter] twice, select the paragraphs, click Format on the menu bar, click Paragraph, then adjust the numbers in the Before and After boxes.

Figure 2-1: Setting paragraph line spacing

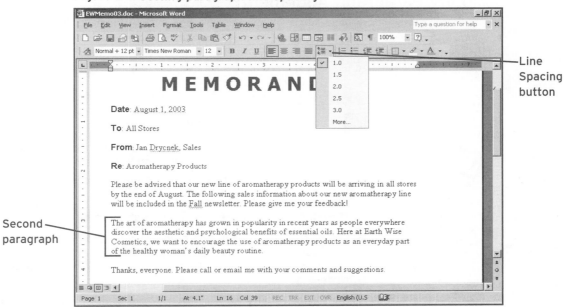

Line Spacing button

Second paragraph

Figure 2-2: Paragraphs formatted differently

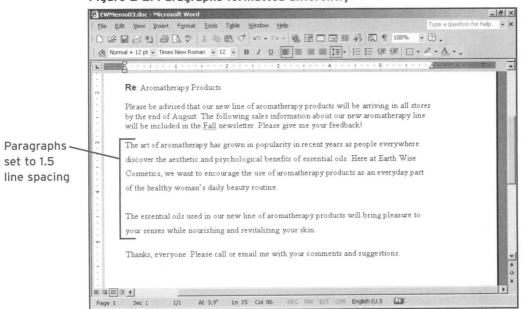

Paragraphs set to 1.5 line spacing

Skill Set 2
Creating and Modifying Paragraphs

Modify Paragraph Formats
Modify Paragraph Alignment

Paragraphs can be **left-aligned** (aligned along the left margin), **right-aligned** (aligned along the right margin), **centered**, or **justified** (aligned along both the left and right margins). Left-aligned paragraphs are the easiest to read. Justified paragraphs are often used in books and newspapers because they look neater.

Activity Steps

file open EWNewsletter01.doc

1. Make sure that the Insertion point is in the title line, **Earth Wise Cosmetics**, then note that the Align Left button is selected

2. Click the **Center button** to center the paragraph

3. Click anywhere in the second line on the page, **Fall 2003 Newsletter**, then click the **Align Right button**

4. Select the two paragraphs below the heading **Aromatherapy Products**, press and hold **[Ctrl]**, then drag to select the paragraphs below **Franchise Opportunities** and below **Online Ordering**

5. Click the **Justify button** to justify all of the selected paragraphs
See Figure 2-3.

6. Click anywhere in the document to deselect the text

file close EWNewsletter01.doc

tip

A paragraph that is left-aligned is sometimes called ragged right, because the right side of the paragraph is not aligned.

Figure 2-3: Paragraphs justified in document

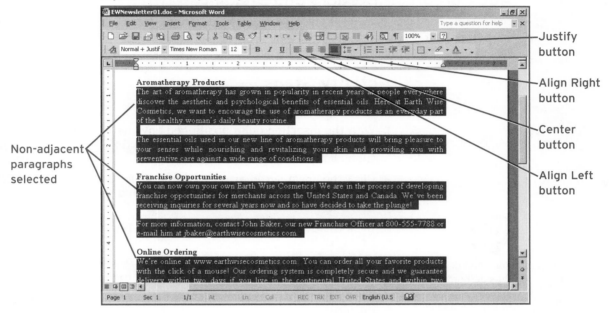

Justify button

Align Right button

Center button

Align Left button

Non-adjacent paragraphs selected

extra!

Figure 2-4: Paragraph dialog box

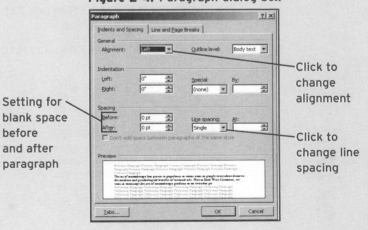

Using the Paragraph dialog box

To open the Paragraph dialog box click Paragraph on the Format menu (see Figure 2-4). The Paragraph dialog box contains the paragraph formatting commands available on the Formatting toolbar, as well as additional commands for formatting paragraphs. For example, to set the alignment from within the Paragraph dialog box, click the Alignment list arrow, then select an alignment option from the list.

Setting for blank space before and after paragraph

Click to change alignment

Click to change line spacing

Skill Set 2
Creating and Modifying Paragraphs

Modify Paragraph Formats
Add Paragraph Borders and Shading

You may want to make a paragraph stand out from the rest of the paragraphs on the page. You can do this by adding a border or shading. You can also add borders to blank paragraphs to separate sections of a document visually.

Activity Steps

 open EWAnnouncement04.doc

1. With the insertion point positioned anywhere in the first line of text, click **Format** on the menu bar, click **Borders and Shading**, then click the **Borders tab**, if necessary

2. Click the **down scroll arrow** in the Style list six times, then click the line style that shows a thick line with a thin line above and below it

3. Click the **Color list arrow**, then click the **Dark Teal square** (first row, fifth box)

4. Click the **left, right**, and **top lines** in the Preview box so they disappear and the only remaining line is the bottom line
See Figure 2-5.

5. Click **OK**

6. Scroll to the bottom of the page, select the paragraph that starts with **For more information**, click **Format** on the menu bar, click **Borders and Shading**, click the **Shading tab**, then click the **last gray square** in the top row below No Fill so that the indicator box to the right displays **Gray-30%**

7. Click **OK**, click anywhere in the document to deselect the text, click the **Zoom box list arrow** `100%`, then click **75%**
See Figure 2-6.

 close EWAnnouncement04.doc

> **tip**
>
> You can click the Outside Border button list arrow to apply a border.

Figure 2-5: Borders tab in the Borders and Shading dialog box

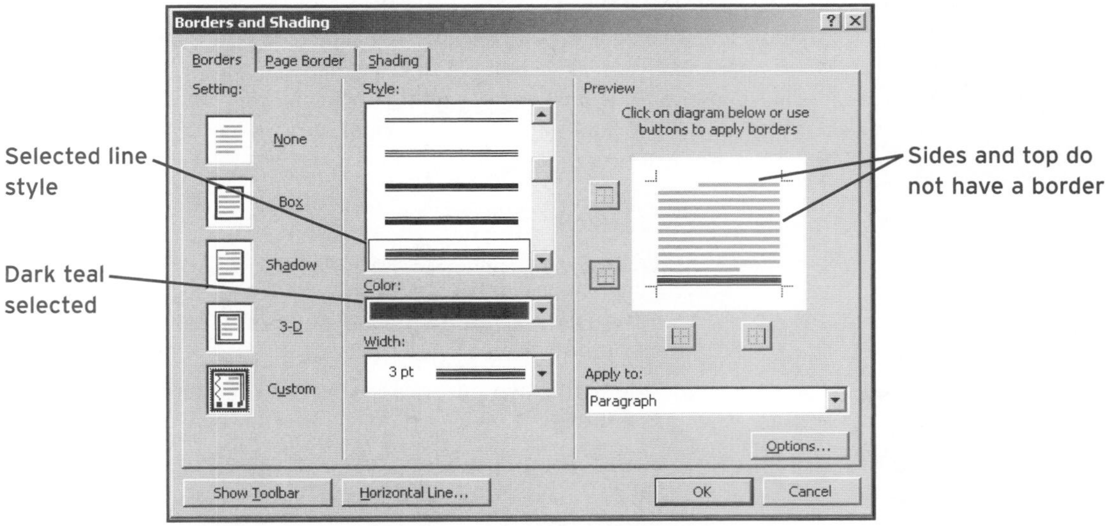

Selected line style

Dark teal selected

Sides and top do not have a border

Figure 2-6: Paragraphs with a border and shading

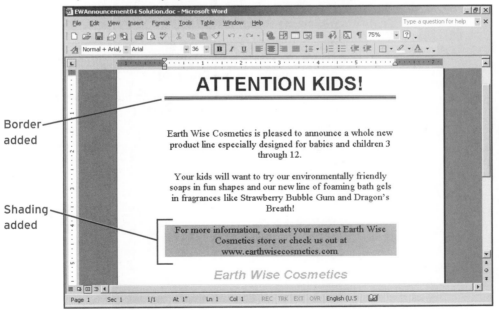

Border added

Shading added

Skill Set 2
Creating and Modifying Paragraphs

Modify Paragraph Formats
Set First-line Indents

To visually indicate a new paragraph, you typically press [Enter] twice or set the line space after a paragraph so that there is a blank line between paragraphs. You can, of course, also indicate a new paragraph by indenting the first line. (Note: It's not good practice to both skip a line between paragraphs and indent the first line; do one or the other.)

Activity Steps

 open EWNewsletter02.doc

1. If the ruler is not displayed on your screen, click **View** on the menu bar, then click **Ruler**

2. Select the two paragraphs below the heading **Aromatherapy Products**

Step 5
You may need to click the ¼" mark on the ruler a second time to format all of the selected text.

3. Click the **square** to the left of the ruler as many times as necessary to cycle through the selections until you see the **First Line Indent icon** ▽
See Figure 2-7.

4. Click the **¼" mark** on the ruler to place the First Line Indent marker at that point

5. Select the two paragraphs below the heading **Franchise Opportunities**, press and hold **[Ctrl]**, then select the two paragraphs below **Online Ordering**

6. Click the **¼" mark** on the ruler to indent the first line of these selected paragraphs to ¼" as well
See Figure 2-8.

7. Click anywhere in the document to deselect the text

 close EWNewsletter02.doc

Figure 2-7: Selecting a different ruler icon

First Line
Indent icon

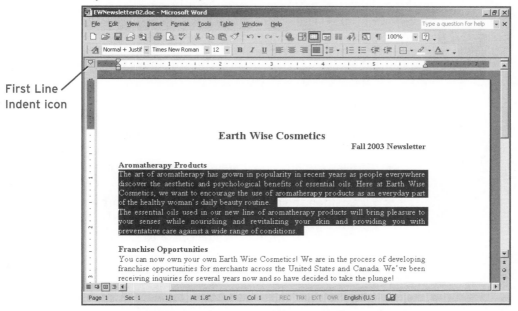

Figure 2-8: Document with first-line indents set

First Line
Indent
marker at
¼" mark

First lines
indented

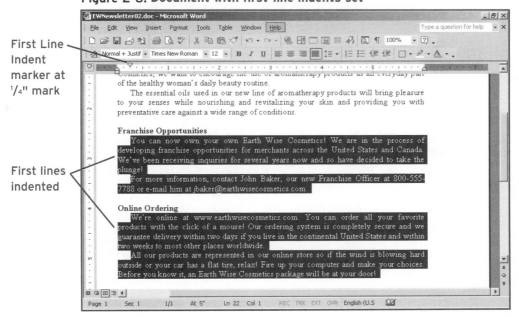

Skill Set 2
Creating and Modifying Paragraphs

Modify Paragraph Formats
Indent Entire Paragraphs

There may be times when you want to indent an entire paragraph in a document. You can click the Increase Indent button, or you can drag the Left and Right Indent Markers on the ruler.

Step 2
Click the Decrease Indent button to decrease the left indent by ¹/₂".

Activity Steps

 open EWMemo04.doc

1. Select the three paragraphs in the body of the memo listing the promotion dates

2. Click the **Increase Indent button** 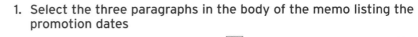 to increase the indent by ¹/₂"
   See Figure 2-9.

3. Position the pointer over the **Right Indent marker** △ on the right side of the ruler so that the ScreenTip appears

4. Drag the **Right Indent marker** △ to the left to the 5¹/₂" mark on the ruler as shown in Figure 2-10

5. Click anywhere in the document to deselect the text

 close EWMemo04.doc

Figure 2-9: Paragraphs indented ¹/₂"

Selected paragraphs indented to ¹/₂" mark

Increase Indent button

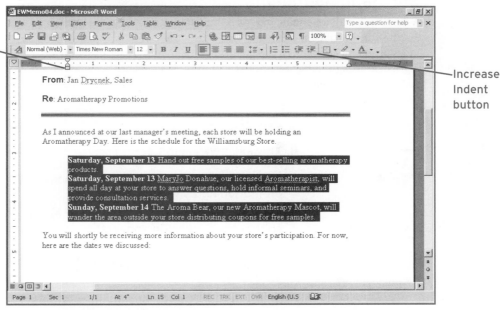

Figure 2-10: Dragging Right Indent marker to the 5¹/₂" mark

Right Indent marker

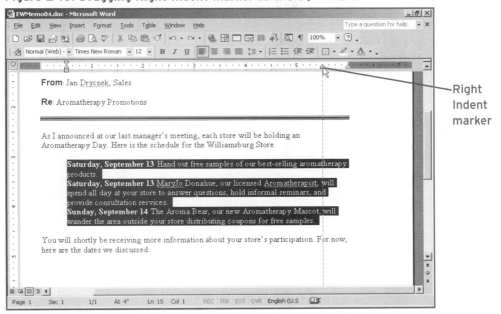

Skill Set 2
Creating and Modifying Paragraphs

Modify Paragraph Formats
Set Hanging Indents

A paragraph with a **hanging indent** is formatted so that all of the lines after the first line are indented more than the first line. You can set up a hanging indent by using the ruler or the Paragraph dialog box. Avoid trying to set up a hanging indent using the [Spacebar] and [Enter]. Any subsequent changes that you make to the document or to its format will alter the spacing you created by using the [Spacebar].

If you accidentally drag the Left Indent marker, either drag it back to the 0" mark on the ruler or click the Undo button.

Activity Steps

 open EWMemo05.doc

1. Select the three paragraphs in the body of the memo listing the promotion dates

2. Point to the **Hanging Indent marker** 📑 on left side of the ruler so that the ScreenTip appears
   See Figure 2-11.

3. Drag the **Hanging Indent marker** 📑 to the 2¼" mark on the ruler
   See Figure 2-12.

4. Click anywhere in the document to deselect the text

 close EWMemo05.doc

Figure 2-11: Finding the hanging indent marker

Hanging
Indent
marker

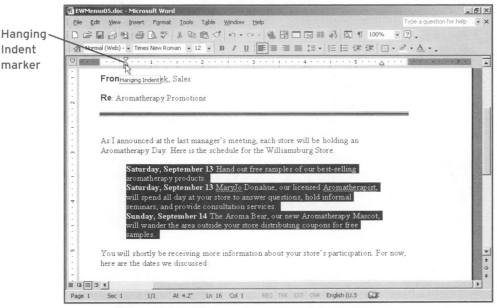

Figure 2-12: Paragraphs with hanging indents set

Hanging
Indent set at
2¹/₄" mark

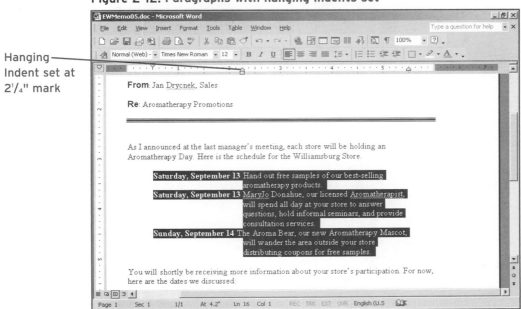

Skill Set 2
Creating and Modifying Paragraphs

Set and Modify Tabs
Set Tabs

You use tabs to align text to the same point in different paragraphs. Default **tab stops**, the location on the ruler where the text moves when you press [Tab], are set every half-inch across the page.

Activity Steps

 open EWMemo06.doc

1. Click immediately before **August** in the Date line, then press **[Backspace]** to delete the space after the colon

2. Press **[Tab]** to move the text over to the default tab stop at ¹/₂"

3. Replace the spaces after the colons in the next three memo header lines with tabs
   See Figure 2-13.

If you accidentally click the ruler and place a new tab stop on it, just drag it off the ruler.

4. Click the **square** to the left of the ruler as many times as necessary to cycle through the selections until you see the **Left Tab icon** [L]

5. Select the four memo header lines, starting with the Date line

6. Click the ³/₄" **mark** on the ruler to place a Left Tab stop and override the default tab setting in the selected paragraphs
   See Figure 2-14.

7. Click anywhere in the document to deselect the text

 close EWMemo06.doc

Figure 2-13: Tabs inserted in memo header paragraphs

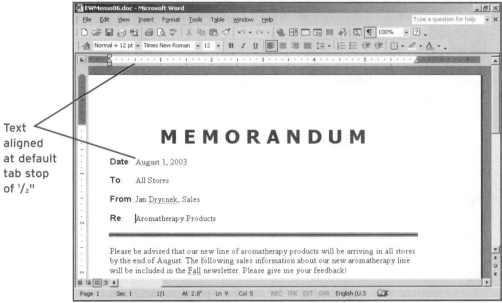

Text aligned at default tab stop of ¹/₂"

Figure 2-14: New tab stops set in memo header paragraphs

Inserted Left Tab stop overrides the default tab stop at ¹/₂"

Text aligned at new tab stop

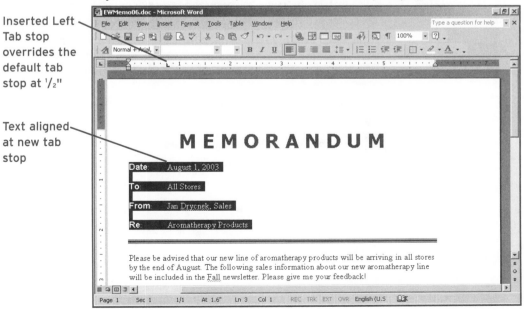

Skill Set 2
Creating and Modifying Paragraphs

Set and Modify Tabs
Modify Tabs

Once you have set tab stops, you can change them or delete them. You can also change the type of tab you set. For example, you can change from a left tab stop to a right tab stop.

Step 1
If tab markers don't appear when you click the Show/Hide ¶ button, click Options on the Tools menu, then click the Tab characters check box or the All check box to select it.

Activity Steps

 open EWAnnouncement05.doc

1. Click the **Show/Hide ¶ button** ¶ if necessary to display paragraph symbols and tab markers, then select the last four lines in the document

2. Drag the **Left Tab stop** L at the 3½" mark on the ruler off the ruler to delete it

3. Click the **square** to the left of the ruler as many times as necessary to cycle through the selections until you see the **Decimal Tab icon**

4. Click the 3³/₄" **mark** on the ruler to place a Decimal Tab stop

5. Drag the **Left Tab stop** L at the 4³/₄" mark off the ruler, then click the 5¼" **mark** on the ruler to place a Decimal Tab stop

6. Click anywhere in the first line of text, then click the **square** to the left of the ruler as many times as necessary to cycle through the selections until you see the **Right Tab icon**

7. Click just to the left of the **Right Indent marker** △ on the ruler to place the Right Tab stop, then drag the **Right Tab stop** to the right so it is directly on top of the Right Indent marker
   See Figure 2-15.

8. Click the **Show/Hide ¶ button** ¶ to turn off paragraph symbols and tab markers

 close EWAnnouncement05.doc

Figure 2-15: Tabs modified

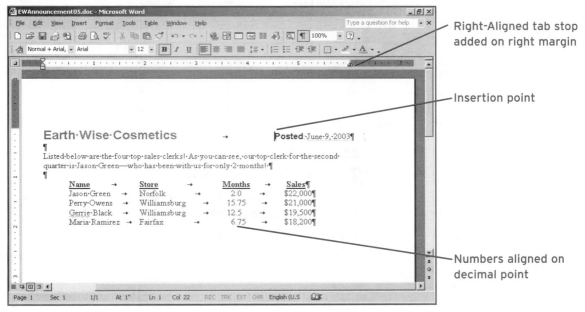

Right-Aligned tab stop added on right margin

Insertion point

Numbers aligned on decimal point

extra!

Using tab leaders

You can set a tab leader, a dotted, dashed, or solid line before a tab stop, by using the Tabs dialog box. Select the paragraphs in which you want to set the tab leaders, click Format on the menu bar, then click Tabs (see Figure 2-16). In the Tab stop position list, select the tab stop for which you want to set a leader, then click the leader style you want to use.

Figure 2-16: Tabs dialog box

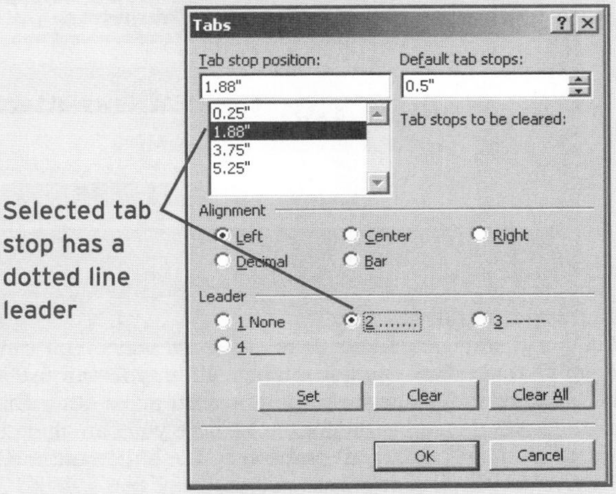

Selected tab stop has a dotted line leader

Skill Set 2
Creating and Modifying Paragraphs

Apply Bullet, Outline, and Numbering Format to Paragraphs
Create a Bulleted List

You can use bulleted lists for lists in which the order is not important, and no one item in the list is any more important than another. To create a bulleted list in Word, you can type the items in the list and then click the Bullets button, or you can click the Bullets button first, then start typing your list. A new bullet will be created every time you press [Enter] until you click the Bullets button again to turn the feature off.

Activity Steps

 open EWNewsletter03.doc

1. Select the five lines listing products, above the heading **Franchise Opportunities**

2. Click the **Bullets button**

3. Right-click the selected list, then click **Bullets and Numbering** on the shortcut menu

4. Click **Customize**, then click **Character** to open the Symbol dialog box

5. Click the **Font list arrow**, scroll down the list, then click **Wingdings**

6. Scroll through the list, then click the bullet style shown in Figure 2-17

7. Click **OK**, click **OK** in the Customize Bulleted List dialog box, then click anywhere in the document to deselect the list
See Figure 2-18.

 close EWNewsletter03.doc

Step 3
You can also click Bullets and Numbering on the Format menu to open the Bullets and Numbering dialog box.

extra!

Customizing bulleted lists
You can customize bulleted lists in several ways. You can change the bullet itself by choosing a different character, as you did in this skill, or, you can use a picture as a bullet by clicking Picture in the Bullets and Numbering dialog box. To make other changes, click Customize to open the Customize Bulleted List dialog box. There you can change the size of the bullet by clicking Font, and you can change the indent position of the bullet and the text by adjusting the measurements in the Indent at and Tab space after boxes.

Certification Circle

Figure 2-17: Symbol dialog box

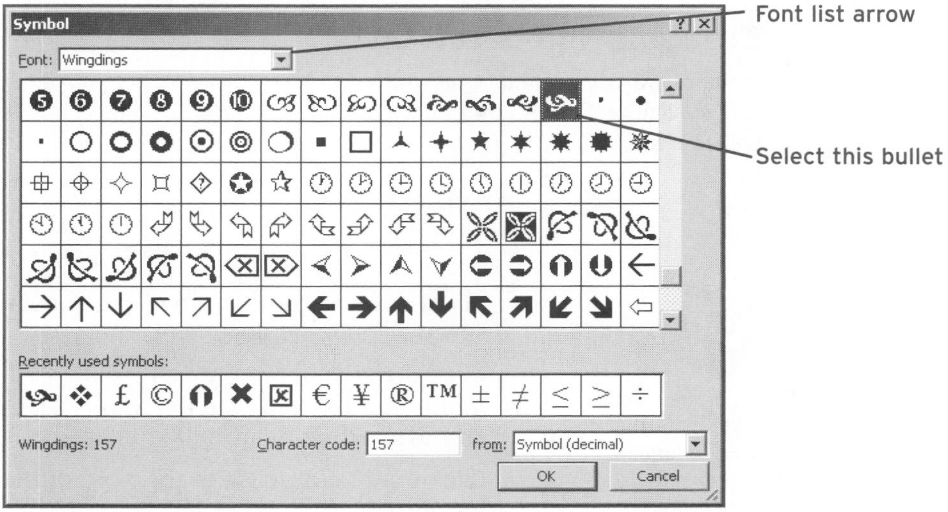

Font list arrow

Select this bullet

Figure 2-18: Bullets added to list

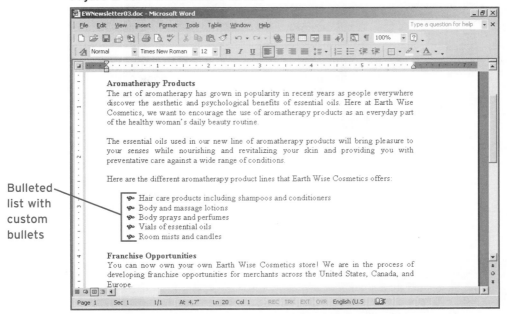

Bulleted list with custom bullets

Skill Set 2

Creating and Modifying Paragraphs

Apply Bullet, Outline, and Numbering Format to Paragraphs

Create a Numbered List

If you are working with a list in which the order is important or you need to be able to identify the items by a number, a numbered list is a better choice than a bulleted list.

tip

Click the Number style list arrow in the Customize Numbered List dialog box to select another style of numbering, such as A, B, C or I, II, III.

Activity Steps

 open EWNewsletter04.doc

1. Scroll down to the bottom of the document, then select the last seven lines in the document
2. Click the **Numbering button**
3. Right-click the **selected list**, then click **Bullets and Numbering** on the shortcut menu
4. Click **Customize**, click to the right of the entry in the **Number format box**, then press **[Backspace]** to delete the period after the number 1
   See Figure 2-19.
5. Click **Font**, click **Bold** in the Font style list, then click **OK** in the Font dialog box
6. Click **OK** in the Customize Numbered List dialog box, then click anywhere in the document to deselect the list
   See Figure 2-20.

 close EWNewsletter04.doc

extra!

Working with multiple numbered lists
If you have more than one numbered list in a document, Word assumes in the second list that you want to continue numbering where you left off in the first list. If this is not your intent, open the Bullets and Numbering dialog box and click the Restart numbering option button. You can also click Customize, and in the Customize Numbered List dialog box, change the Start at number.

Figure 2-19: Customize Numbered List dialog box

Period deleted

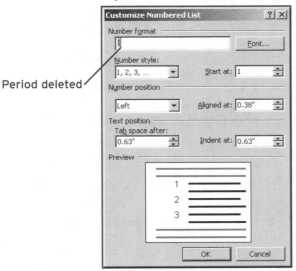

Figure 2-20: Numbers added to list

Formatted numbered list

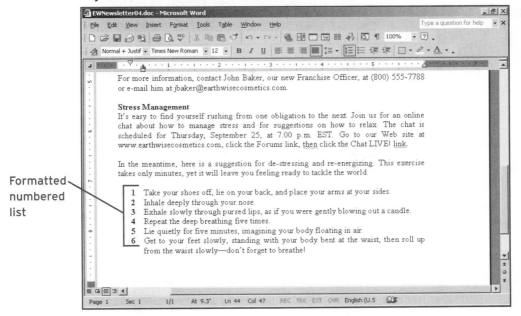

Skill Set 2

Creating and Modifying Paragraphs

Apply Bullet, Outline, and Numbering Format to Paragraphs
Create a Numbered List in Outline Style

A numbered list can be set up in standard outline style: a list of topics and sub-topics with each topic numbered according to its position in the outline and its level. You can create an automatically numbered outline using the Numbering command.

You can press [Tab] to increase the indent of an existing outline item and indent it to the next level, or you can press [Shift][Tab] to decrease the indent level of an existing outline item.

Activity Steps

 open EWProposal01.doc

1. Select all of the text except the two title lines

2. Click **Format** on the menu bar, click **Bullets and Numbering**, then click the **Outline Numbered tab**

3. Click the second style in the first row
   See Figure 2-21.

4. Click **OK**

5. Click anywhere in the **Benefits** line in the middle of the list, then click the **Increase Indent button** to move it down a level

6. Click anywhere in the **Financial Considerations** line in the last line, then click the **Decrease Indent button** to move it up a level

7. Click after the word **Considerations** in the last line, press [Enter], press [Tab], type **Projected Revenues**, press [Enter], then type **Liabilities**

8. Press [Enter], press [Shift][Tab], then type **Conclusion**
   See Figure 2-22.

close EWProposal01.doc

Figure 2-21: Outline Numbered tab in the Bullets and Numbering dialog box

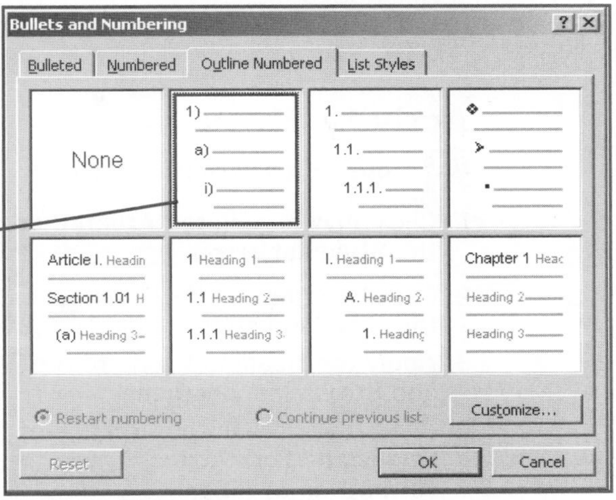

Select this style (it may be in a different spot on your screen)

Figure 2-22: Numbered outline

Skill Set 2
Creating and Modifying Paragraphs

Apply Paragraph Styles

To make it easier to apply consistent formatting throughout a document, you can use paragraph styles. Remember, a style is a defined set of formats. Just as character styles are applied to selected text, paragraph styles are applied to entire paragraphs.

Activity Steps

 open EWNewsletter05.doc

1. Click anywhere in the **Aromatherapy Products** line, then click the **Style list arrow** `Normal`

2. Click **Heading 1** in the Style list as shown in Figure 2-23 to apply the Heading 1 style to the paragraph

3. Apply the Heading 1 style to the lines **Franchise Opportunities** and **Stress Management**

4. Click anywhere in the first line of the document, then click the **Styles and Formatting button** to open the Styles and Formatting task pane

5. Click the **Show list arrow** `Available formatting` at the bottom of the task pane, click **All Styles**, scroll to the bottom of the **Pick formatting to apply list** in the task pane, then click **Title**

6. Click anywhere in the **Fall 2003 Newsletter** line, then apply the **Heading 3 style** using either the task pane or the toolbar

7. With the Fall 2003 Newsletter line still selected, click the **Align Right button**
   See Figure 2-24.

8. Click the **Close button** in the Styles and Formatting task pane title bar

 close EWNewsletter05.doc

Step 7
When you modify a style with manual formatting, the formats you add are listed after the style name in the Style list box.

Figure 2-23: Style list on the Formatting toolbar

Style list arrow

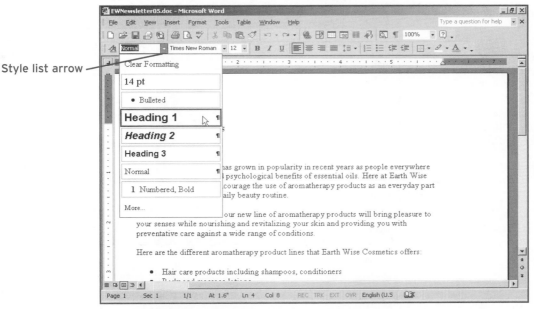

Figure 2-24: Document with styles applied

Styles and
Formatting
button

Current
paragraph
style

Insertion
point

Style of
selected
paragraph
with
modified
formatting

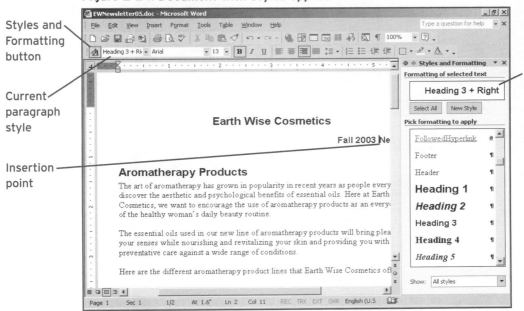

Skill Set 2

Creating and Modifying Paragraphs

Target Your Skills

 EWAnnouncement06.doc

1 Modify the file **EWAnnouncement06** to create the document shown in Figure 2-25. Paragraph marks are turned on to help you format the document correctly.

Figure 2-25

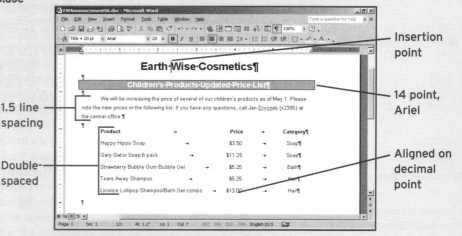

Insertion point

14 point, Ariel

1.5 line spacing

Double-spaced

Aligned on decimal point

 EWBrochure04.doc

2 Revise the **EWBrochure04** file to create the document shown in Figure 2-26. Paragraph marks are turned on to help you format the document correctly.

Figure 2-26

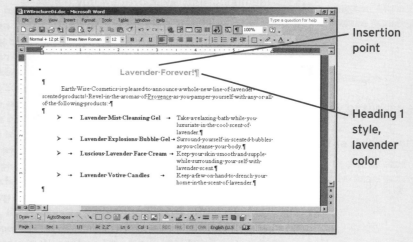

Insertion point

Heading 1 style, lavender color

Skill List

1. Create and modify a header and footer
2. Apply and modify column settings
3. Modify document layout and page setup options
4. Create and modify tables
5. Preview and print documents, envelopes, and labels

Once you've formatted the words and paragraphs in a document, you can think about the document as a whole. Adding headers and footers to a document can help the reader keep printed documents organized. You will learn how to add the filename, date, page numbers, and custom text to the header or footer. Sometimes a document is best laid out in more than one column, as in a newsletter. You will also learn how to set up a document with more than one column.

If you have quite a bit of information that would look better in multiple rows and columns, a table might be the best way to present it. You will learn how to insert a table into your document and modify it to fit your needs. Finally, you will learn to preview and print your document, as well as envelopes and labels.

Skill Set 3
Formatting Documents

Create and Modify a Header and Footer
Create a Header

A **header** is text that appears at the top of every page in a document. Headers can be very useful in a multiple-page document. You can insert **fields**, placeholders that will update automatically to match specific information like a page number or a date, or you can insert text that you type directly. Text in a header can be formatted just as any other text in a document.

You must be in Print Layout view or Print Preview to see headers and footers on the page.

Activity Steps

 open GCMemo01.doc

1. Click **View** on the menu bar, then click **Header and Footer**

2. Type **Draft Copy**, then click the **Align Right button**

3. Press **[Enter]**

4. Click the **Insert Date button** on the Header and Footer toolbar
   See Figure 3-1.

5. Select the two lines of text you entered, click the **Bold button** **B**, then click anywhere in the header area to deselect the text

6. Click the **Close button** on the Header and Footer toolbar
   See Figure 3-2.

 close GCMemo01.doc

Figure 3-1: Creating a header and using the Header and Footer toolbar

Header area

Insert Date
button

Align Right
button

Date field
(the format
of the date
on your
screen may
differ)

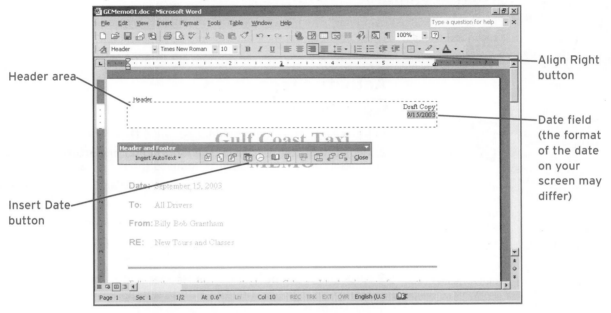

Figure 3-2: Header displays in Print Layout view

Header in
Print
Layout view

Print Layout
view selected

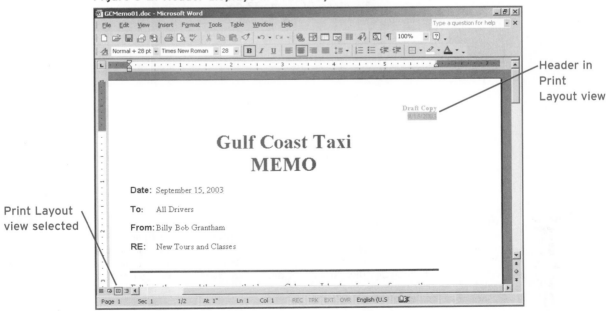

Skill Set 3
Formatting Documents

Create and Modify a Header and Footer
Create a Footer

A **footer** is text that appears at the bottom of every page in a document. Footers are identical to headers, except that they appear at the bottom of a page instead of the top.

To insert the current page number and the total number of pages quickly, click the Insert AutoText button on the Header and Footer toolbar, then click Page X of Y.

Activity Steps

 open GCMemo02.doc

1. Click **View** on the menu bar, then click **Header and Footer**
2. Click the **Switch Between Header and Footer button** 🖹 on the Header and Footer toolbar to jump to the Footer area
3. Click the **Insert AutoText button** `Insert AutoText ▾` on the Header and Footer toolbar
4. Click **Filename** to insert the filename in the footer
5. Press **[Tab]** twice, then type **Gulf Coast Taxi Company Memo**
   See Figure 3-3.
6. Click the **Close button** on the Header and Footer toolbar, then scroll down to see the footer on the page
   See Figure 3-4.

 close GCMemo02.doc

extra!

Skipping a header or footer on the first page
Sometimes you may not want a header or footer to appear on the first page of a document, for example, when you create a report with a title page. To suppress headers or footers on the first page of a document, click the Page Setup button 📖 on the Header and Footer toolbar, or click File on the menu bar, click Page Setup, then make sure the Layout tab is on top. Click the Different first page check box to select it.

Figure 3-3: Inserting the Filename field in a footer

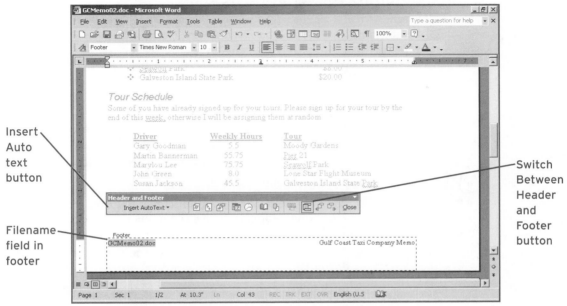

Insert Auto text button

Filename field in footer

Switch Between Header and Footer button

Figure 3-4: Viewing headers and footers on two pages in Print Layout view

Footer in Print Layout view

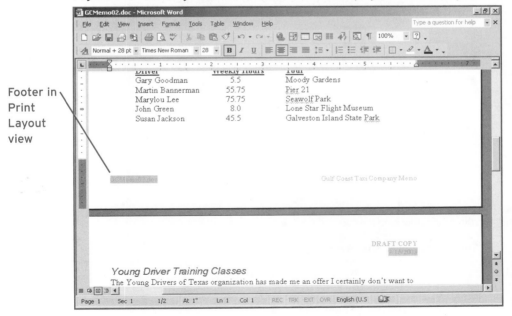

Skill Set 3
Formatting Documents

Apply and Modify Column Settings
Create Columns for Existing Text

Text in a document normally appears in one column. You may decide that the text would be easier to read or that you could fit more text if you used two or more columns. Newsletters are frequently set up in this way. The easiest way to create columns is to enter your text, then use the Columns command. You can choose to apply as many columns as you want.

Activity Steps

 open GCBrochure01.doc

1. Select all of the text below the line **Spring 2003**
2. Click the **Columns button** 🔲
3. Point to the **second column icon** in the drop-down list so that **2 Columns** appears below the icons
   See Figure 3-5.
4. Click the **second column icon** in the Columns button drop-down list
5. Click anywhere in the document to deselect the text
6. Click the **Zoom button list arrow** `100%` then click **Whole Page** to see the columns on the page
   See Figure 3-6.

 close GCBrochure01.doc

If you want to format the entire document with multiple columns, click Select All on the Edit menu before you click the Columns button.

Understanding sections
When you apply the Columns command to selected text, you created a second section in the GCBrochure01 document. **Sections** are parts of a document with separate page formatting options. If you turn on paragraph marks, you can see a double-dotted line labeled **Section Break (Continuous)** next to the heading line **Spring 2003**. Everything after that break—everything in the second section of the document—has a different page format from the text in the first section in the document. You can have as many sections as you want in a document.

Figure 3-5: Using the Columns button

Columns button

Figure 3-6: Document formatted with two columns

Formatted as single column

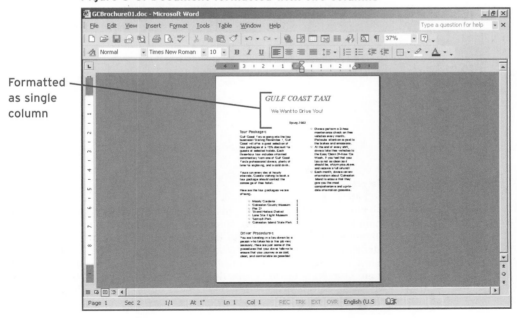

Skill Set 3

Formatting Documents

Apply and Modify Column Settings
Modify Text Alignment in Columns

Once you have created columns, you need to adjust them so that they look balanced on the page; in other words, so that you don't have one column that fills the length of the page and a second column that contains only a few lines.

To insert a vertical line between columns, make sure the insertion point is anywhere within the columns, click Columns on the Format menu, then click the Line between check box to select it.

Activity Steps

 open GCBrochure02.doc

1. Click the **Zoom button list arrow** 100% on the menu bar, then click **Whole Page** to see the columns

2. Click below the text in the second column (the insertion point will seem to appear between the columns)

3. Click **Insert** on the menu bar, then click **Break** to open the Break dialog box

4. Click the **Continuous option button**

5. Click **OK** to balance the columns on the page
   See Figure 3-7.

 close GCBrochure02.doc

extra!

Using the Columns dialog box

In addition to using the Columns button, you can click Columns on the Format menu to open and use the Columns dialog box to set and modify columns. See Figure 3-8. If you want to format the document with one column in one section and two columns in another, position the insertion point in the document at the point where you want to start the new column layout, open the Columns dialog box, select the number of columns you want, then click the Apply to list arrow at the bottom of the dialog box and select This point forward. You can also precisely adjust the column width and space between each column by typing measurements (in inches) in the Width and Spacing boxes. Deselect the Equal column width check box if you want columns of different widths.

Figure 3-7: Balanced newsletter columns

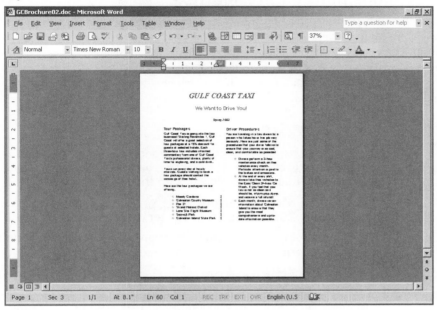

Figure 3-8: Columns dialog box

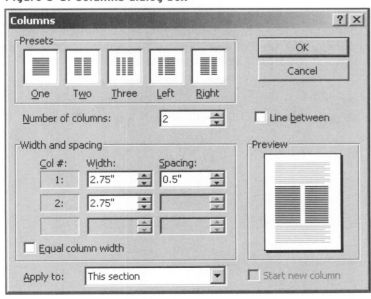

Skill Set 3
Formatting Documents

Apply and Modify Column Settings
Create Columns before Entering Text

If you know before you enter text that you want it to appear in two or more columns, you can use the Columns command before you enter the text. Note that if you start with a blank document, choosing the Columns command applies to all of the text in the document, even if you type a few lines first for a headline. So after you finish typing the text for your columns, you need to select the headline and format it with one-column layout.

To force a new column to start, position the insertion point at the point in the document where you want to start the new column, click Break on the Insert menu, then click the Column break option button.

Activity Steps

1. Open a new, blank document, change the zoom to 100% if necessary, click the **Style list arrow** [Normal ▼], click **Heading 1**, type **Gulf Coast Taxi Newsletter**, then press **[Enter]**

2. Click the **Style list arrow** [Normal ▼], click **Heading 3**, type **Summer 2003**, then press **[Enter]**

3. Click the **Columns button** [▦], then click the **second column icon** to format the text in two columns

4. Click the **Style list arrow** [Normal ▼], click **Heading 1**, type **Employee News**, then press **[Enter]**

5. Type **Elisa Newcomb was married last weekend to Frank Jessup. Believe it or not, the happy couple met in Elisa's cab!** *See Figure 3-9.*

6. Select the first two paragraphs (everything above **Employee News**), click the **Columns button** [▦], then click the **first column icon** to format the selected text in one column

7. Click the **Center button** [▦] to center the title over the two columns

8. Click anywhere in the document to deselect the text *See Figure 3-10.*

 close file

Figure 3-9: Text filling in first column in two-column format

Second column not yet filled

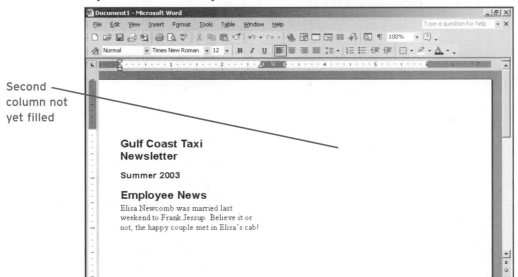

Figure 3-10: Headline spanning two columns

Paragraphs formatted as single column

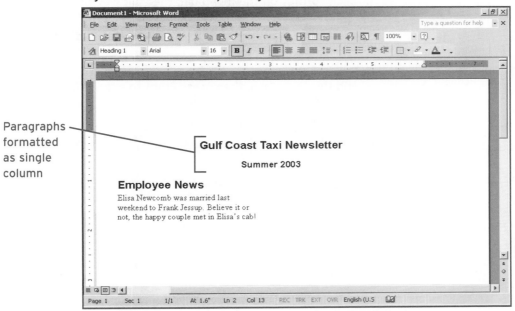

Skill Set 3
Formatting Documents

Apply and Modify Column Settings
Revise Column Layout

The default space between columns in a Word document is $1/2$". The column widths change depending on how many columns are on a page. You can adjust both the column width and the space between columns. If you want to see the columns as you change the width, drag the Move Column markers on the ruler. To adjust columns precisely, you should use the Columns dialog box.

Activity Steps

 open GCBrochure03.doc

1. Scroll down until you can see the bulleted list of tour packages in the first column, then click anywhere in the first column

2. Position the pointer over the **Move Column dotted box marker** between the 2" and 3" markers on the ruler so that the pointer changes to ↔

3. Drag the **Move Column dotted box marker** to the right until it's approximately over the 3.25" mark on the ruler and the list of tours and the fees charged in the first column appears with each fee on the same line as the tour name
See Figure 3-11.

4. Click **Format** on the menu bar, then click **Columns** to open the Columns dialog box

5. Drag to select all of the text in the **Col # 2 Width box**, then type **1.6**

6. Press **[Tab]**, type **.3** to decrease the space between the second and third columns, then press **[Tab]** to adjust the width in the Col # 3 Width box automatically

7. Click **OK** to close the Columns dialog box

8. Click the **Zoom button list arrow** [100% ▼], then click **Whole Page**
See Figure 3-12.

 close GCBrochure03.doc

To create two columns quickly with one of the columns twice as wide as the other, select the text, click Columns on the Format menu, then click Left or Right at the top of the dialog box.

Figure 3-11: Widening a column using the ruler

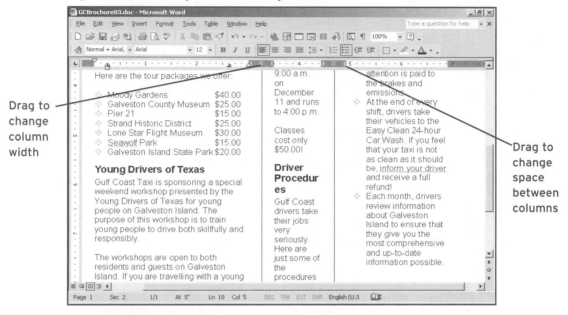

Drag to change column width

Drag to change space between columns

Figure 3-12: Newsletter with column widths adjusted

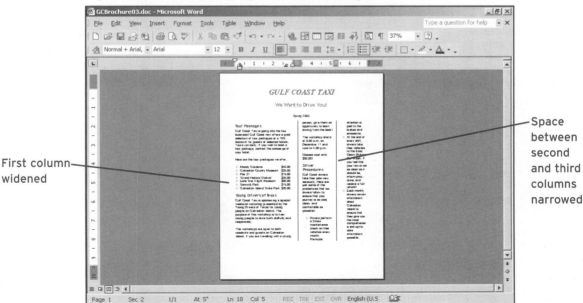

First column widened

Space between second and third columns narrowed

Skill Set 3
Formatting Documents

Modify Document Layout and Page Setup Options

Insert Page Breaks

Word automatically inserts page breaks in a document when the text will no longer fit on one page. You can insert page breaks manually if you want to start the next page at a different point in the document. In Print Layout view, manual page breaks look the same as automatic page breaks unless you turn on paragraph marks.

To delete a manually inserted page break, turn on paragraph marks, select the dotted line page break indicator, then press [Delete].

Activity Steps

 open GCProposal01.doc

1. Click the **Show/Hide ¶ button** ¶ to display paragraph marks, if necessary

2. Scroll down so that you can see the heading **Introduction**

3. Click at the beginning of the **Introduction** line to position the insertion point at the top of the new page you want to create

4. Click **Insert** on the menu bar, then click **Break** to open the Break dialog box

5. Make sure that the **Page break option button** is selected, then click **OK** to insert a manual page break
   See Figure 3-13.

6. Scroll down until you see the heading **Conclusion**

7. Click at the beginning of the **Conclusion** line, then press **[Ctrl][Enter]** to insert a manual page break

 close GCProposal01.doc

Figure 3-13: Manual page break

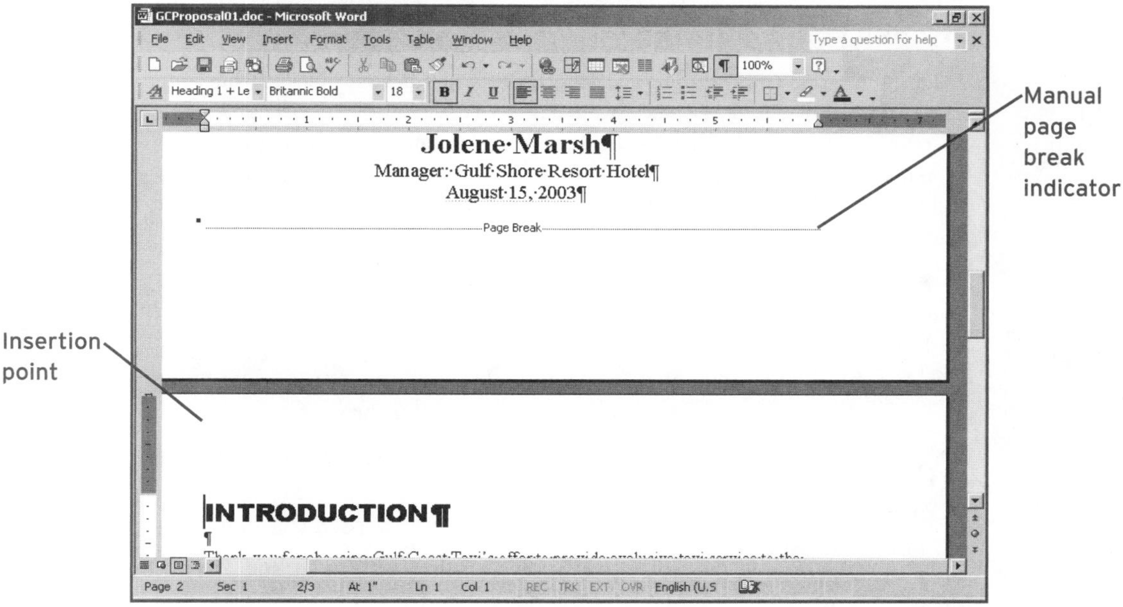

Manual page break indicator

Insertion point

extra!

Inserting section breaks

To create manual section breaks, click Break on the Insert menu, then select one of the option buttons under Section break types in the Break dialog box. See Figure 3-14. Clicking the Next page option button forces the new section to start on a new page. Clicking the Continuous option button creates a new section but keeps it on the same page. Clicking the Even and Odd page option buttons creates a new section that begins on the next even or odd-numbered page.

Figure 3-14: Break dialog box

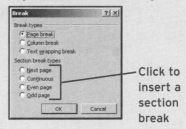

Click to insert a section break

Skill Set 3
Formatting Documents

Modify Document Layout and Page Setup Options
Insert Page Numbers

When you work with multiple-page documents, it's a good idea to add page numbers so that you don't mix up the pages when you print the document. To insert page numbers, you insert a field, and Word automatically updates the field to reflect the correct page number. You can insert page numbers using the Insert Page Number button on the Header and Footer toolbar or you can use the Page Numbers command on the Insert menu.

To format the page number, make the footer area active, then select the page number field and format it as you like.

Activity Steps

 open GCProposal02.doc

1. Click **Insert** on the menu bar, then click **Page Numbers** to open the Page Numbers dialog box

2. Make sure that **Bottom of page (Footer)** is selected in the Position list box

3. Click the **Alignment list arrow**, then click **Left**

4. Click the **Show number on first page check box** to deselect it
   See Figure 3-15.

5. Click **OK**

6. Scroll down to the bottom of the first page to see that there is no page number in the footer

7. Scroll down to the bottom of the second page to see the page number in the footer
   See Figure 3-16.

 close GCProposal02.doc

Figure 3-15: Page Numbers dialog box

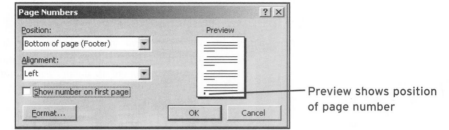

Preview shows position of page number

Figure 3-16: Page number in footer of page 2

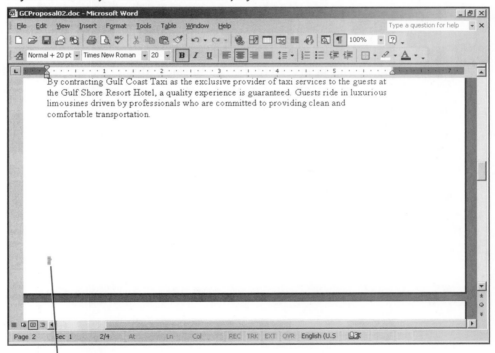

Page number in footer of page 2

Skill Set 3
Formatting Documents

Modify Document Layout and Page Setup Options
Modify Page Margins

The default page margins in a Word document are 1" at the top and bottom of the page and 1¹/₄" at the right and left of the page. Headers and footers print ¹/₂" from the top and bottom of the page. You can change the default page margins to suit your needs.

To adjust text to fit on a page quickly, click the Print Preview button, then click the Shrink to Fit button on the Print Preview toolbar.

Activity Steps

 open GCLetter01.doc

1. Click **File** on the menu bar, then click **Page Setup**
2. Click the **Margins tab**, if necessary
3. Type **1.25** in the Top box
4. Press **[Tab]** twice to select the text in the Left box, then type **1.5**
5. Click the **Right box down arrow** three times to change the right margin to **1"**
   See Figure 3-17.
6. Click **OK**
   See Figure 3-18.

 close GCLetter01.doc

Figure 3-17: Margins tab of the Page Setup dialog box

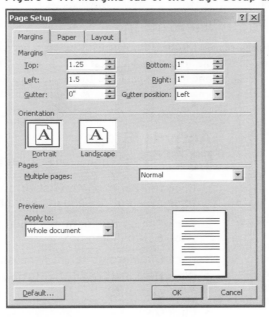

Figure 3-18: Margins changed in document

Top margin increased to 1.25"

Left margin increased to 1.5"

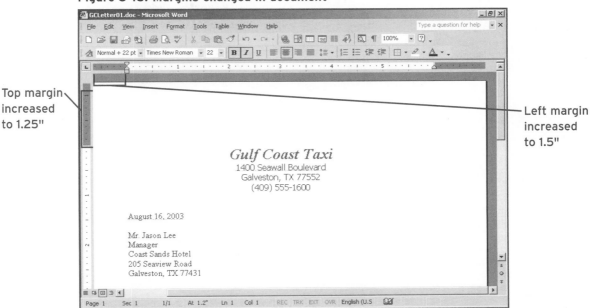

Skill Set 3

Formatting Documents

Modify Document Layout and Page Setup Options

Modify Page Orientation

Most documents are meant to be printed lengthwise on a page. This is called **portrait** orientation. Some documents look best if they are printed sideways on the page. This is called **landscape** orientation. The default for Word documents is portrait, but you can change the orientation to landscape in the Page Setup dialog box.

To set different orientations in a document, select the text to which you want to apply the new orientation, open the Margins tab in the Page Setup dialog box, select the orientation, then click Selected text in the Apply to list.

Activity Steps

 open GCAnnouncement01.doc

1. Click the **Zoom button list arrow** `100%`, then click **Whole Page** to see the entire page in portrait orientation

2. Click **File** on the menu bar, then click **Page Setup** to open the Page Setup dialog box

3. Click the **Margins tab**, if necessary

4. Click the **Landscape orientation box**
   See Figure 3-19.

5. Click **OK**
   See Figure 3-20.

 close GCAnnouncement01.doc

Figure 3-19: Margins tab in Page Setup dialog box

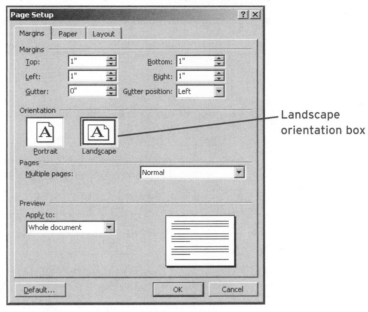

Landscape
orientation box

Figure 3-20: Document in landscape orientation

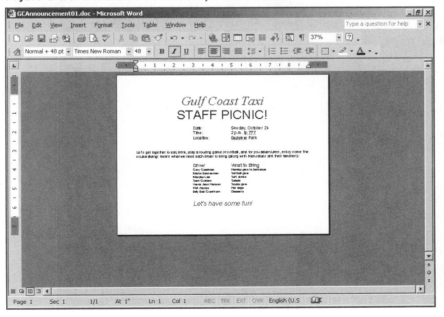

Skill Set 3

Formatting Documents

Create and Modify Tables

Create Tables

You can use tabs to arrange text in rows and columns, but when you have a lot of information to present in that format, a table is usually a better choice. A table sets up a grid of rows and columns. Each intersection of a row and column is called a **cell**. To move from one cell to another, you press [Tab] or an arrow key.

Activity Steps

 open GCBrochure04.doc

1. Press **[Ctrl][End]** to position the insertion point at the end of the document, then press **[Enter]**

2. Click the **Insert Table button** 🔲

3. Move the pointer over the grid to create a **4 × 3 Table**
   See Figure 3-21.

4. Click to create the table

5. Type **Destination**, press **[Tab]**, type **Average Time**, press **[Tab]**, type **Average Fare**, then press **[Tab]**

6. Type the rest of the information in the table as shown in Figure 3-22 in the same manner

 close GCBrochure04.doc

Step 6
If you press [Tab] after the last entry and accidentally insert a new row, click the Undo button.

Figure 3-21: Using the Table button

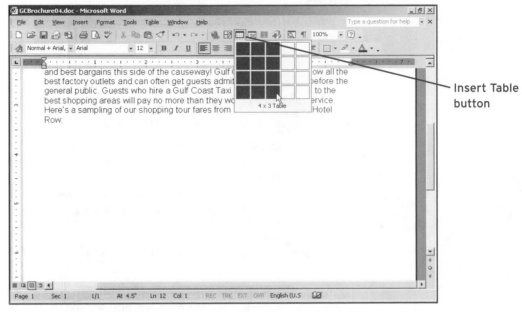

Insert Table button

Figure 3-22: Completed table

Tables and Borders toolbar may not appear on your screen

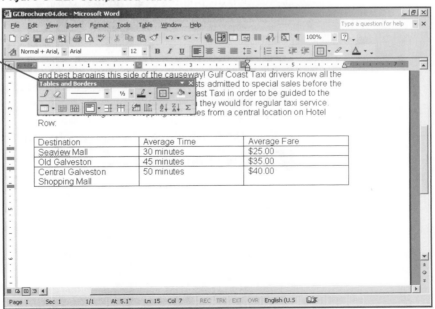

Skill Set 3
Formatting Documents

Create and Modify Tables
Modify Tables

Once you have created a table, you can modify it in several ways. You can resize the table to fit better on the page. You can merge several cells to form one cell, or you can split one cell to form several cells. You can also rotate text in a cell. These are only a few of the changes you can make to a table.

To make several columns or rows the same size, select them, then click the Distribute Columns Evenly button or the Distribute Rows Evenly button on the Tables and Borders toolbar.

Activity Steps

 open GCBrochure05.doc

1. Scroll down until you can see the table, then move the pointer anywhere over the table to see the table move and resize handles *See Figure 3-23.*

2. Position the pointer over the **table resize handle** ⊞ so that the pointer changes to ⊞, then drag the resize handle to the left until the dotted outline indicates that the table is approximately 4.5" wide

3. Drag the **table move handle** ⊞ to center the table horizontally on the page

4. If the Tables and Borders toolbar is not open, right-click any toolbar, then click **Tables and Borders**

5. Position the pointer over the first column so that the pointer changes to ↓, then click to select the entire first column

6. Click the **Merge Cells button** 🔲 on the Tables and Borders toolbar

7. With the first column still selected, click the **Change Text Direction button** 🔳 twice to rotate the text to read vertically up the page, then click anywhere in the table to deselect the text *See Figure 3-24.*

8. Click the **Close button** ✕ on the Tables and Borders toolbar

 close GCBrochure05.doc

Figure 3-23: Table handles

Table move handle

Table resize handle

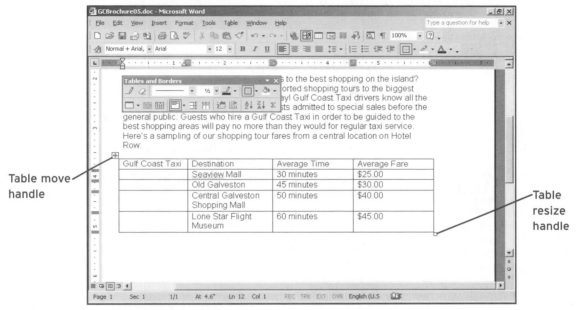

Figure 3-24: Modified table

Change Text Direction button

Merge Cells button

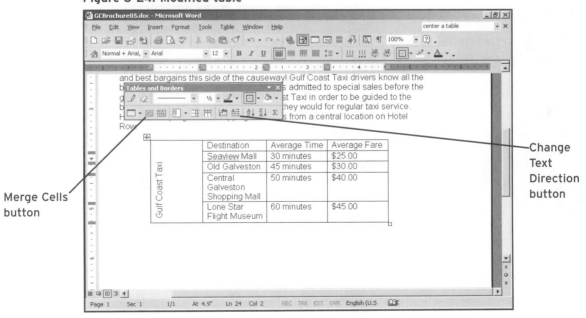

Skill Set 3
Formatting Documents

Create and Modify Tables
Apply AutoFormat to Tables

After you create a table, you can format it to make it look better. The quickest way to format a table is to use the Table AutoFormat command on the Table menu.

Activity Steps

 open GCMemo03.doc

1. Scroll down until you can see the table, then click anywhere within the table
2. Right-click any toolbar, then click **Tables and Borders** to open the Tables and Borders toolbar, if necessary
3. Click the **Table AutoFormat button** 📇 on the Tables and Borders toolbar to open the Table AutoFormat dialog box
4. Scroll up the Table styles list, then click **Table Classic 3**
5. Click the **Last row** and **Last column check boxes** to deselect them
   See Figure 3-25.
6. Click **Apply**
7. Click the **table move handle** ⊞ to select the entire table, click the **Center button** ▥ to center the table on the page, then click anywhere in the document to deselect the table
   See Figure 3-26.
8. Click the **Close button** ⊠ on the Tables and Borders toolbar

 close GCMemo03.doc

Step 7
You can drag the table move handle to position the table anywhere you like.

Figure 3-25: Table AutoFormat dialog box

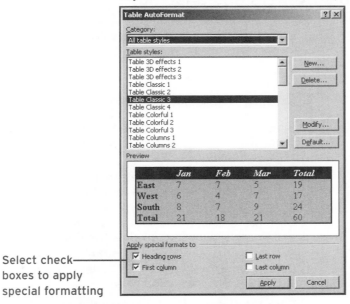

Select check boxes to apply special formatting

Figure 3-26: Table with AutoFormat applied

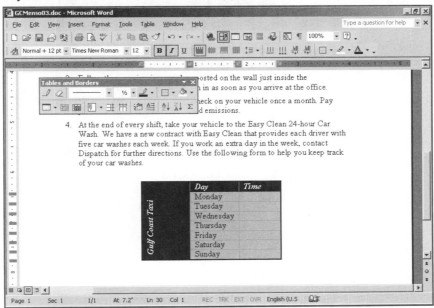

Skill Set 3

Formatting Documents

Create and Modify Tables
Modify Table Borders and Shading

You can manually change table borders and the shading in cells by changing the options in the Borders and Shading dialog box. You can make changes to these properties even after you've applied a table AutoFormat.

Activity Steps

 open GCBrochure06.doc

1. Scroll down until you can see the table, right-click any toolbar, then click **Tables and Borders** to open the Tables and Borders toolbar, if necessary

2. Move the pointer into the left margin to the left of the top row of the table so that it changes to ⇗, then click to select the top row
   See Figure 3-27.

3. Click the **Shading Color button list arrow** 🖌▾ on the Tables and Borders toolbar, then click the **Blue box**

4. Select the bottom four rows in the table, click the **Shading color button list arrow** 🖌▾ on the Tables and Borders toolbar, then click the **Light Turquoise box**

5. Click the **Outside Border button list arrow** ▭▾ on the Tables and Borders toolbar, click the **All Borders button** ⊞, then click anywhere in the table to deselect the text

6. Click the **Line Style button list arrow** ▭▾ on the Tables and Borders toolbar, then click the thick line with thin lines above and below it

7. Drag the pointer, which changes to ✐, across the line below the top row, then click the **Draw Table button** ✐ on the Tables and Borders toolbar to deselect it
   See Figure 3-28.

8. Click the **Close button** ✕ on the Tables and Borders toolbar

 close GCBrochure06.doc

Make sure the Line Style button displays the line style you want before you click one of the Borders buttons or draw a border.

Figure 3-27: Selecting a row in a table

Pointer

Top row selected

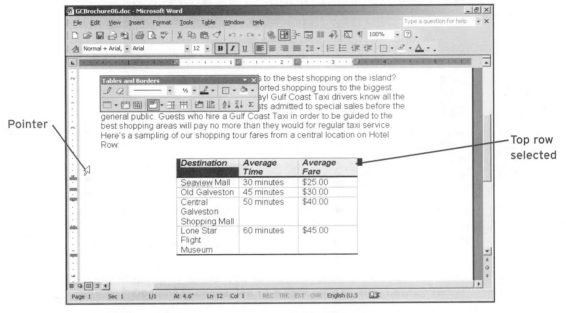

Figure 3-28: Table with modified borders and shading

Line Style button list arrow

Outside Border button

Shading Color button

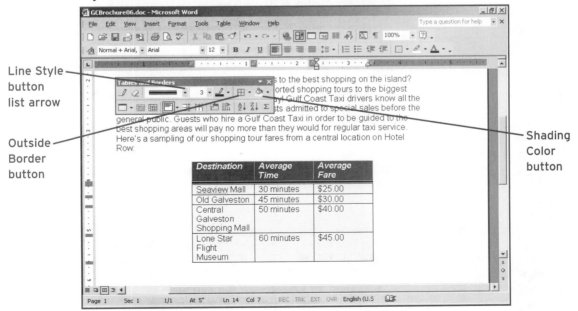

Skill Set 3
Formatting Documents

Create and Modify Tables
Insert and Delete Columns and Rows in a Table

You can add additional columns and rows to a table by using the Insert command on the Table menu. You can delete extra columns and rows from a table by using the Delete command on the Table menu.

If you want to prevent a table that flows onto a second page from breaking in the middle of a row, position the insertion point in the table, click Table Properties on the Table menu, click the Row tab, then click the Allow row to break across pages check box to deselect it.

Activity Steps

 open GCMemo04.doc

1. Scroll down so you can see the entire table, then click anywhere in the **Weekly Hours column**

2. Click **Table** on the menu bar, point to **Insert**, then click **Columns to the Right** to insert a new column to the right of the current column

3. Select the row with **Gary Goodman** in the **Driver column**

4. Click **Table** on the menu bar, point to **Insert**, then click **Rows Above** to insert a row above the selected row
   See Figure 3-29.

5. Select the row with **Verna Graham** in the **Driver column**

6. Right-click the selected row, then click **Delete Rows** on the shortcut menu
   See Figure 3-30.

 close GCMemo04.doc

Figure 3-29: Column and row inserted in table

Inserted column

Inserted row

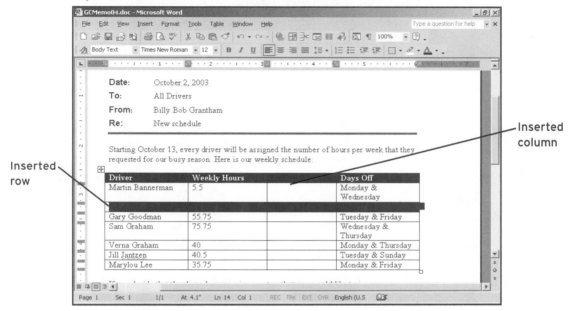

Figure 3-30: Table with row deleted

Row deleted

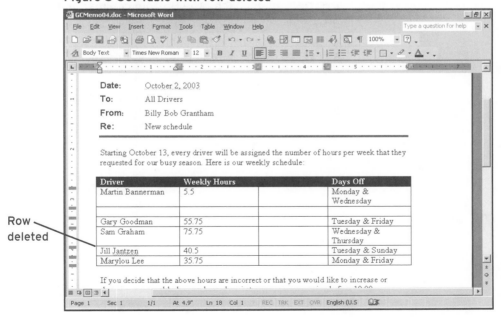

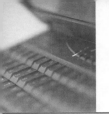

Skill Set 3
Formatting Documents

Create and Modify Tables
Modify Cell Format in a Table

You can format the text in cells just as you format regular text. For example, you can change the alignment of text within a cell, or you can add additional blank space around the entry in a cell.

Activity Steps

 open GCMemo05.doc

1. Scroll down until you can see the table, right-click any toolbar, then click **Tables and Borders** to open the Tables and Borders toolbar, if necessary

2. Drag to select all of the cells except those in the top row, then click the **Align Top Left button list arrow** on the Tables and Borders toolbar

3. Click the **Align Center Left button**

4. Click **Table** on the menu bar, click **Table Properties**, then click the **Table tab**, if necessary

5. Click **Options** on the Table tab to open the Table Options dialog box

6. Click the **Top up arrow** six times to change the Top cell margin to **0.06"**, then change the Bottom cell margin to **0.06"**
   See Figure 3-31.

7. Click **OK**, click **OK** in the Table Properties dialog box, then click anywhere on the screen to deselect the cells
   See Figure 3-32.

8. Click the **Close button** on the Tables and Borders toolbar

 close GCMemo05.doc

tip

To repeat the heading rows of a table automatically if a table occupies more than one page, select the header row (or rows), click Table, then click Heading Rows Repeat.

Figure 3-31: Table Options dialog box

Cell margins

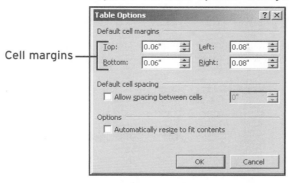

Figure 3-32: Table with modified cell formats

Increased space above and below text in cells

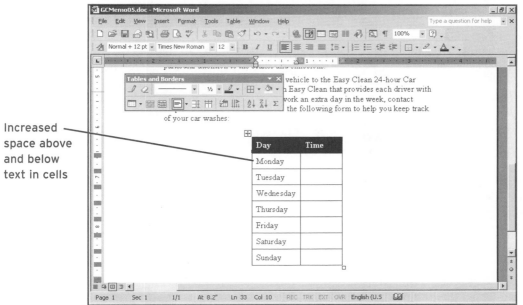

Skill Set 3
Formatting Documents

Preview and Print Documents, Envelopes, and Labels
Preview a Document

Before you print a document, you should look at it in Print Preview to make sure that it will print the way you expect it to.

Activity Steps

 open GCLetter02.doc

1. Click the **Print Preview button** 🔍

2. Click below the scroll box in the vertical scroll bar to move to the second page

3. Position the pointer over the page so that it changes to 🔍, click the line of text on page 2 to zoom in, and observe that the pointer changes to 🔍
   See Figure 3-33.

4. Click the screen again to zoom back out

5. Click the **Shrink to Fit button** 🔲 on the Print Preview toolbar
   See Figure 3-34.

6. Click the **Close button** on the Print Preview toolbar

 close GCLetter02.doc

tip

You can print from Print Preview by clicking the Print button or using the Print command on the File menu.

extra!

Adjusting text in Print Preview
You can enter and edit text in Print Preview. Click the Magnifier button 🔍 on the Print Preview toolbar to deselect it and change the pointer to I. Click the screen at the point where you want to insert or edit text, then start typing. When you are finished editing, click the Magnifier button again, and the pointer changes back to 🔍 or 🔍.

Figure 3-33: Document magnified in Print Preview

Pointer

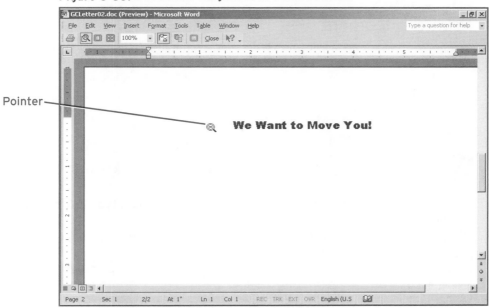

Figure 3-34: Text shrunk to fit on one page in Print Preview

Shrink to
Fit button

Pointer

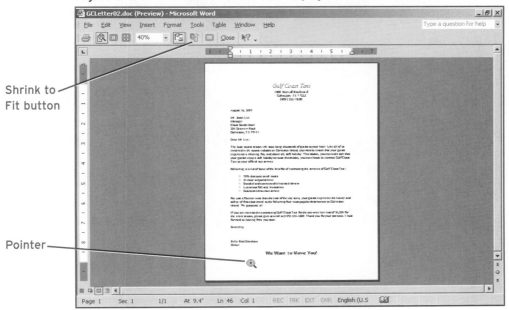

Skill Set 3
Formatting Documents

Preview and Print Documents, Envelopes, and Labels
Print a Document

Once you've created a document, you usually want to print it. To print a document, you can click the Print command on the File menu to change print settings (like the number of copies to print), or you can click the Print button to print your document with the current print settings.

Activity Steps

 open GCProposal03.doc

When you click the Print button, the Print dialog box does not open, and the document prints using the current print settings.

1. Click **File** on the menu bar, then click **Print** to open the Print dialog box
2. Click the **Pages option button**, then type **2-3** to print only the last two pages
3. Click the **Number of copies up arrow** to change the number of copies to **2**
4. Make sure the **Collate check box** is selected
   See Figure 3-35.
5. Click **OK**

 close GCProposal03.doc

Figure 3-35: Print dialog box

Select pages to print

Select number of copies

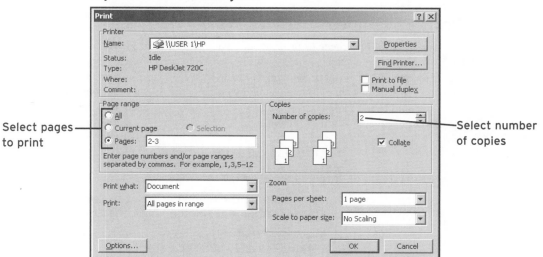

extra!

Print dialog box options

To change your printer's options, click Properties at the top of the Print dialog box. To print several document pages on one piece of paper, select one of the options from the Pages per sheet list in the Print dialog box. To scale the document to fit on a specific paper size, click the Scale to paper size list arrow in the Print dialog box.

Skill Set 3
Formatting Documents

Preview and Print Documents, Envelopes, and Labels
Print Envelopes

You can set up a document to print as an envelope. With the Envelopes and Labels command, you simply type the address, tell Word what size envelope you are using, and Word formats the address to fit in the proper position on the envelope. After you create your envelope, you can print it directly from the Envelopes and Labels dialog box, or you can click Add to Document to add it to the current document as a new section.

Step 2
You can change the Delivery address from the one suggested by typing a different one or by clicking the Insert Address button to insert a name and address from your electronic address book.

Activity Steps

 open GCLetter03.doc

1. Click **Tools** on the menu bar, point to **Letters and Mailings**, click **Envelopes and Labels**, then click the **Envelopes tab**, if necessary

2. Make sure that the Delivery address is the address for **Anna Perkins**, as shown in the letter
   See Figure 3-36.

3. Click in the **Return address box**, type **Gulf Coast Taxi**, press **[Enter]**, type **1400 Seawall Blvd.**, press **[Enter]**, then type **Galveston, TX 77552**

4. Click the **Feed box** to open the Printing Options tab in the Envelope Options dialog box, note the selected direction to feed the envelope into the printer, then click **OK**

5. Click the **Preview box** to open the Envelope Options tab in the Envelope Options dialog box, click the **Envelope size list arrow**, read through the list of envelope sizes, make sure that **Size 10** (the standard business size envelope) is selected in the list, then click **OK**

6. Click **Add to Document** to add the envelope as a new section in the current document, then if necessary, click **No** in the dialog box that opens asking if you want to save the return address as the default return address

7. Click the **Print Preview button** 🔍
   See Figure 3-37.

8. Click below the scroll box in the vertical scroll bar to move to the second page

9. Click **File** on the menu bar, click **Print**, click the **Pages option button**, type **1**, insert your envelope into the printer, then click **OK**

 close GCLetter03.doc

Figure 3-36: Envelopes tab in the Envelopes and Labels dialog box

Delivery address picked up from inside address in letter

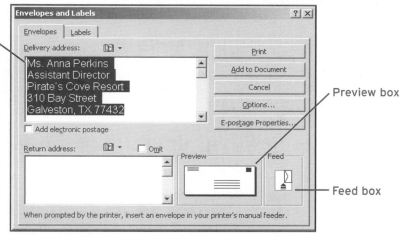

Preview box

Feed box

Figure 3-37: Envelope in Print Preview

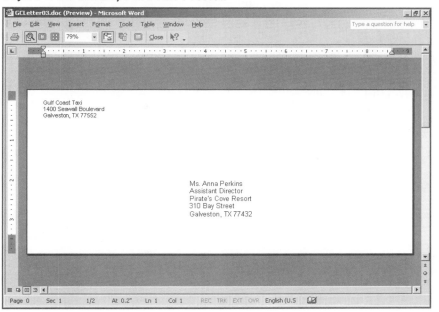

Skill Set 3
Formatting Documents

Preview and Print Documents, Envelopes, and Labels
Printing Labels

Labels are as easy to print as envelopes. Click the Labels tab in the Envelopes and Labels dialog box and select the options for the size of labels you are using. Word automatically formats the address to fit on the labels. After you create your label, you can print it directly from the Envelopes and Labels dialog box, or you can click New Document to create a new document so you can see how the labels will print.

Step 5
If your label is not in the Product number list in the Label Options dialog box, click New Label and specify the dimensions of your label.

Activity Steps

1. Open a new, blank document

2. Click **Tools** on the menu bar, point to **Letters and Mailings**, click **Envelopes and Labels**, then click the **Labels tab** if necessary

3. Click in the **Address box**, type **Mr. Jason Lee**, press **[Enter]**, then continue typing the address in the Address box, as shown in Figure 3-38

4. Click the **Label box** to open the Label Options dialog box, then examine the list of labels in the Product number list

5. Click the label that you are using in the Product number list (if you do not have a label, choose any label in the list), then click **OK**

6. Click **New Document**, click the **Zoom button list arrow** , then click **Whole Page**
   See Figure 3-39.

7. Click the **Print button**

   file close file

Figure 3-38: Labels tab in Envelopes and Labels dialog box

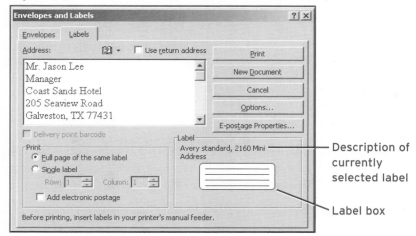

Description of
currently
selected label

Label box

Figure 3-39: Labels in document

Temporary
filename

Your layout
may look
different
depending
on the label
you chose

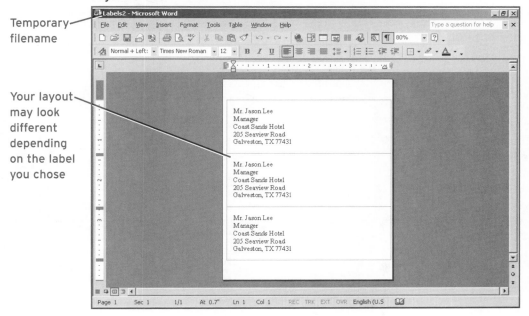

Skill Set 3

Formatting Documents

Targeting Your Skills

 GCNewsletter01.doc

1 Create the document shown in Figure 3-40. Insert a footer that identifies the page number and the total number of pages. Position this text so it is on the right side of the footer. Finally, make sure the columns are balanced. Preview your completed document and print it.

Figure 3-40

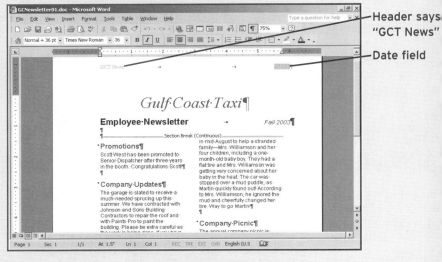

Header says "GCT News"

Date field

 GCAnnouncement02.doc

2 Create the document shown in Figure 3-41. Note that you need to insert page numbers and change the margins. Preview your completed document and print it.

Figure 3-41

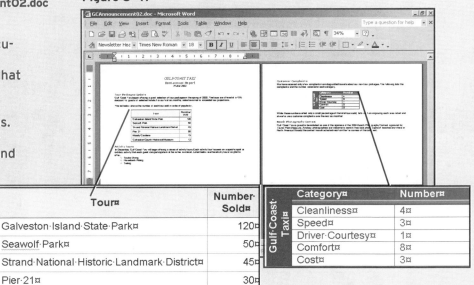

Tour¤	Number Sold¤
Galveston·Island·State·Park¤	120¤
Seawolf·Park¤	50¤
Strand·National·Historic·Landmark·District¤	45¤
Pier·21¤	30¤
Moody·Gardens¤	15¤
Galveston·County·Historical·Museum·¤	12¤

	Category¤	Number¤
Gulf·Coast· Taxi	Cleanliness¤	4¤
	Speed¤	3¤
	Driver·Courtesy¤	1¤
	Comfort¤	8¤
	Cost¤	3¤

Skill List

1. Manage files and folders for documents
2. Create documents using templates
3. Save documents using different names and file formats

In Skill Set 4, you will learn about managing documents. First, you will learn how to create folders within Word. Folders make it easy to organize your files so that you can quickly locate them when you want them. Then you will learn how to create a document from a template, which is a pre-designed document. Finally, you will learn how to save your documents with different names and in different file formats.

Learning how to manage your documents will save you time. If you master these skills, you will always be able to locate, organize, and store your documents quickly.

Skill Set 4

Managing Documents

Manage Files and Folders for Documents

Using the Open and Save As dialog boxes in Word, you can create new folders. To create a new folder, you click the Create New Folder button in the dialog box, then type a name for the folder. The folder is created as a new folder within the current folder, and the new folder becomes the current folder. Specifically, the Look in box at the top of the Open dialog box or the Save in box at the top of the Save As dialog box changes to display the new folder name.

Activity Steps

1. Create a new, blank document

2. Click **File** on the menu bar, then click **Save As** to open the Save As dialog box

3. Click the **Create New Folder button** on the toolbar at the top of the Open dialog box

4. Type **My New Folder** in the Name box

5. Click **OK**
   See Figure 4-1.

6. Click the **Up One Level button** 🔼 on the toolbar at the top of the Save As dialog box to see your new folder in the folder list
   See Figure 4-2.

7. Click **Cancel** to close the Save As dialog box without saving the file

   📄 **close file**

Step 3
The Create New Folder button is also available on the toolbar at the top of the Open dialog box.

Figure 4-1: New folder created in Save As dialog box

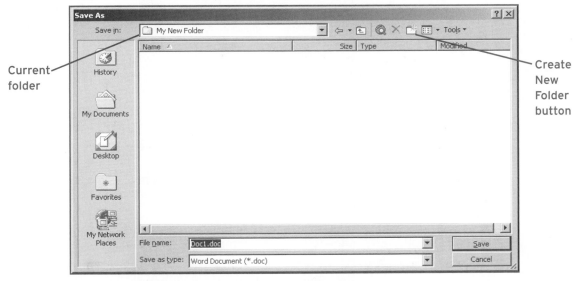

Current folder

Create New Folder button

Figure 4-2: New folder listed in Save As dialog box

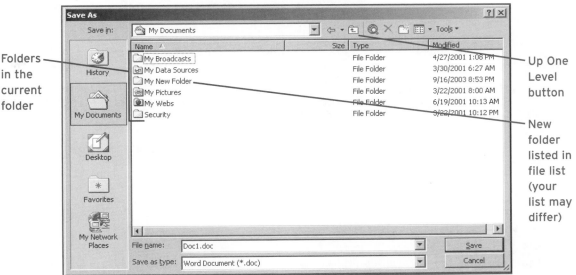

Folders in the current folder

Up One Level button

New folder listed in file list (your list may differ)

Skill Set 4
Managing Documents

Create Documents Using Templates

A **template** is a set of styles and formats that determines how a document will look. Every document is based on the Normal template, a template that is available to all documents. Word provides additional templates to make it easier for you to create specially formatted documents, like memos and resumes. Most templates provided with Word include **placeholders**, items you click once to select all of the existing text, then type to substitute your replacement text. When you save a document created from a template, it is saved as an ordinary Word document.

Activity Steps

To use any existing document as a template for a new document, click the Choose document link in the New Document task pane to open a copy of the document.

1. If the task pane is not open, click **View** on the menu bar, then click **Task Pane**

2. If the New Document task pane is not visible, click the **Other Task Panes list arrow** 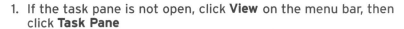 in the task pane title bar, then click **New Document**

3. Click the **General Templates link** in the New Document task pane to open the Templates dialog box

4. Click the **Other Documents tab**, click **Contemporary Resume**, then make sure that the **Document option button** is selected under Create New
   See Figure 4-3.

5. Click **OK**

6. Click the **[Click here and type address] placeholder**, type **4598 Main Street**, press **[Enter]**, then type **Charleston, SC 29407**

7. Drag to select the name **Deborah Greer**, then type **Mark Rodriguez**
   See Figure 4-4.

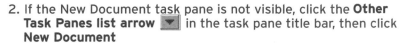 **close file**

Figure 4-3: Templates dialog box

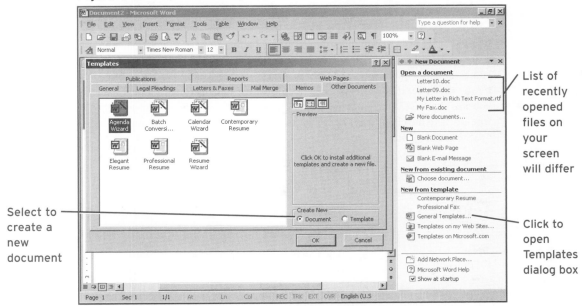

Select to create a new document

List of recently opened files on your screen will differ

Click to open Templates dialog box

Figure 4-4: Resume template with text selected

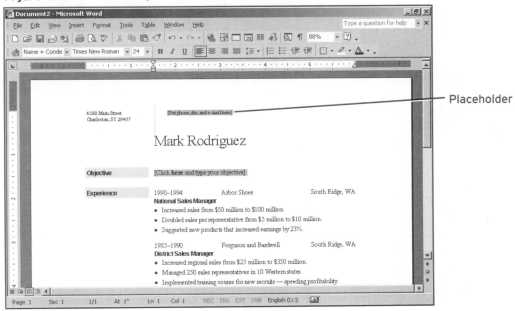

Placeholder

Skill Set 4
Managing Documents

Save Documents Using Different Names and File Formats
Save a Document

When you create a new document, you will probably need to save it. When you save a new document for the first time, you use the Save As dialog box, where you can change the drive and folder to which you are saving the file and specify the filename. If you want to save a copy of the document with a new name, you use the Save As command. If you make changes to a document and then want to save the changes without creating a new copy of the document, you use the Save command.

Step 3
If you want to save your document to the My Documents folder, you can click My Documents in the Places bar on the left in the Save As dialog box.

Activity Steps

 open EWLetter09.doc

1. Click **File** on the menu bar, then click **Save As**

2. Type **My Saved Letter** in the File name box

3. Click the **Save in list arrow**, then select the folder or drive to which you want to save your document

4. Double-click the folder name in which you want to save your document
   See Figure 4-5.

5. Click **Save** in the Save As dialog box
   See Figure 4-6.

6. Select **August 15** in the first paragraph in the body of the letter, then type **September 8**

7. Click the **Save button** 🖫 to save the change to the document

 close My Saved Letter.doc

Figure 4-5: Save As dialog box

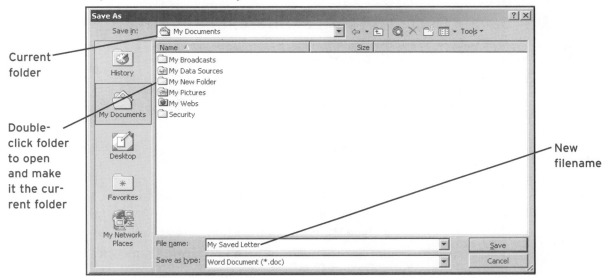

Current folder

Double-click folder to open and make it the current folder

New filename

Figure 4-6: File saved with a new name

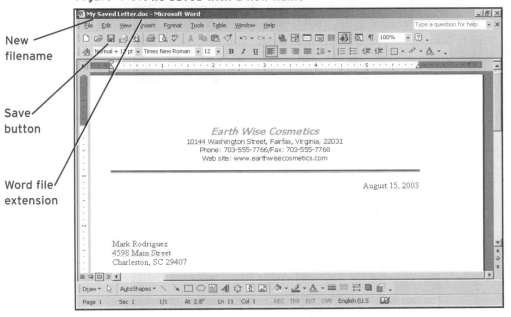

New filename

Save button

Word file extension

Skill Set 4
Managing Documents

Save Documents Using Different Names and File Formats
Save a Document with a Different File Format

When you save a document, you save it in the default Word file format. The file extension is .doc. If you are sending the file to someone who doesn't have Word, you can save the file with a different file format. For example, rich text format is a format that most word processors can read and will allow you to save most of your formatting. To save a document with a different file format, you need to use the Save As command.

Step 3
Select the file type Document Templates (*.dot) to save the file as a Word template that appears on the General tab in the Templates dialog box.

Activity Steps

 open EWMemo07.doc

1. Click **File** on the menu bar, then click **Save As** to open the Save As dialog box

2. Type **My Memo in Rich Text Format** in the File name box

3. Click the **Save as type list arrow**, then click **Rich Text Format (*.rtf)**

4. Click the **Save in list arrow**, then select the folder or drive to which you want to save your document
   See Figure 4-7.

5. Click **Save** in the Save As dialog box
   See Figure 4-8.

 close My Memo in Rich Text Format.rtf

Figure 4-7: Save As dialog box with Rich Text Format selected

Save As
Save in: My Documents
Name
Size
My Broadcasts
My Data Sources
My New Folder
My Pictures
My Webs
Security
History
My Documents
Desktop
Favorites
My Network Places
File name: My Memo in Rich Text Format.rtf
Save as type: Rich Text Format (*.rtf)
Save
Cancel
Rich text format file extension
Save as type list arrow

Figure 4-8: File saved in rich text format

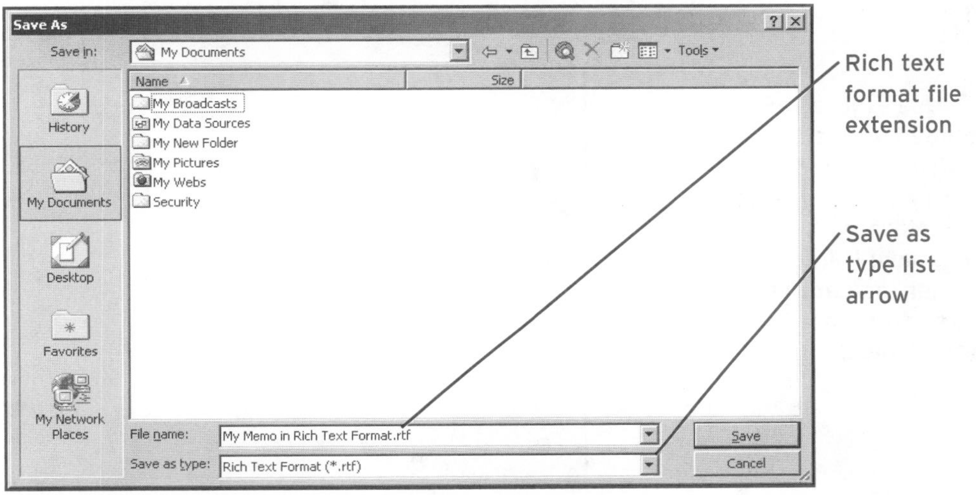

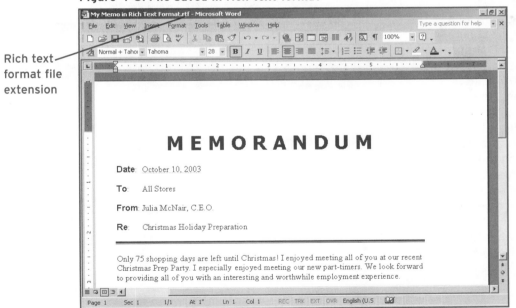

Rich text format file extension
My Memo in Rich Text Format.rtf - Microsoft Word
File Edit View Insert Format Tools Table Window Help
MEMORANDUM
Date: October 10, 2003
To: All Stores
From: Julia McNair, C.E.O.
Re: Christmas Holiday Preparation
Only 75 shopping days are left until Christmas! I enjoyed meeting all of you at our recent Christmas Prep Party. I especially enjoyed meeting our new part-timers. We look forward to providing all of you with an interesting and worthwhile employment experience.
Page 1 Sec 1 1/1 At 1" Ln 1 Col 1

Skill Set 4
Managing Documents

Target Your Skills

EWNewsletter06.doc

1 Use Figure 4-9 as a guide to save the EWNewsletter06 file with a new name as a template. Make sure you save it in the folder indicated (you'll need to create the folder first).

Figure 4-9

2 Use Figure 4-10 as a guide for creating a fax cover sheet from the Professional Fax template. (*Hint*: To insert a checkmark in a box, double-click the box. To delete the **Company Name Here** box, position the pointer above it so that it looks like a down-ward-pointing arrow, click to select the entire box, then click the Cut button.) Save the file as **My Fax**.

Figure 4-10

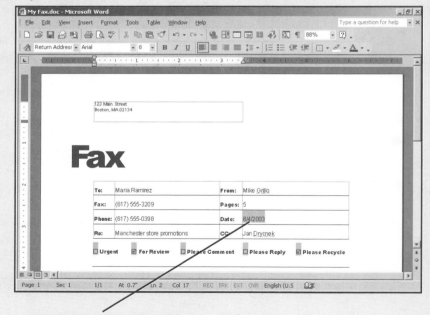

Current date will appear here

Skill List

1. Insert images and graphics
2. Create and modify diagrams and charts

Pictures, diagrams, and charts can make your documents more interesting and informative. For example, you might want to insert a company logo or an image into a newsletter. You can insert clip art or other pictures stored on your hard drive or on the Web.

You can use the Insert Diagram command to insert a variety of diagrams, including an organizational chart diagram or a pyramid diagram. Diagrams can help get your point across visually. You can also use a program built into Word called Microsoft Graph to insert a graph of numerical data.

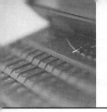

Skill Set 5
Working with Graphics

Insert Images and Graphics
Insert Clips Using the Clip Organizer

A **clip**, sometimes called **clip art**, is a drawing, photograph, sound, or movie that you can insert into a document. Clips are organized in the Clip Organizer in collections, or groups on the basis of keywords stored with the file. You can find clips appropriate to your subject by searching for a keyword you type in the Insert Clip Art task pane.

Activity Steps

file > open GCAnnouncement03.doc

1. If the Drawing toolbar is not visible, click the **Drawing button**, then position the insertion point between the headline and the paragraph

2. Click the **Insert Clip Art button** on the Drawing toolbar to open the Insert Clip Art task pane

3. If a dialog box appears asking if you want to catalog your clips, click **Later**

4. Click in the **Search text box** in the task pane, if necessary delete any text that is already there (from a previous search), type **wedding**, then click **Search**

5. Click the **clip** indicated in Figure 5-1 (if you don't have this clip, select another), then click the **Close button** × in the Insert Clip Art task pane

6. Click the clip to select it, then drag the **lower-right sizing handle** down and to the right until the dotted outline indicates that the clip extends to the right margin of the paragraph as shown in Figure 5-2

7. Click anywhere in a blank area of the document to deselect the clip

file > close GCAnnouncement03.doc

tip

To add your own clips to the Clip Organizer, on the File menu in the Clip Organizer, point to Add Clips to Gallery, click On My Own, click the clip you want to add, click Add to, click the collection in which you want to store the clip, then click Add.

Browsing the Clip Organizer
Click the Clip Organizer link at the bottom of the Insert Clip Art task pane to open the Microsoft Clip Organizer. You can click the various folders in the Collection List on the left to see the contents of each category. If there is a plus sign next to a folder, click it to see the list of folders within that folder. To insert clips into a document from the Clip Organizer, simply drag the clip to your document.

Figure 5-1: Insert Clip Art task pane

Select this clip

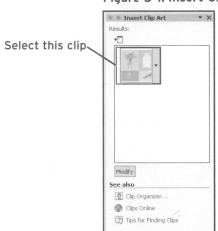

Figure 5-2: Resizing a clip

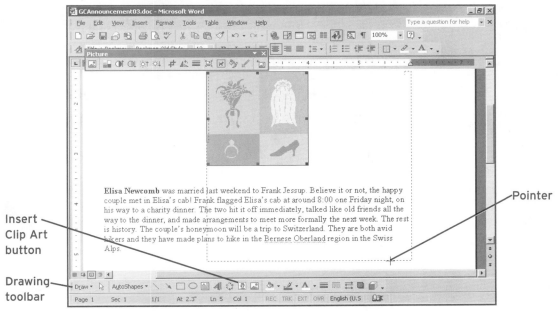

Pointer

Insert
Clip Art
button

Drawing
toolbar

Skill Set 5
Working with Graphics

Insert Images and Graphics
Insert Images Not Stored in the Clip Organizer

In addition to clips from the Clip Organizer, you can insert graphic images stored on your hard drive, another disk, or on the Web. Graphic images are saved in many file formats. Common file formats for graphics include .bmp, .tif, .jgp (also called JPEG), and .wmf.

Activity Steps

 open GCProposal04.doc

1. If the Drawing toolbar is not visible, click the **Drawing button** , click the **Zoom button list arrow** 100% ▼, then click **Whole Page**

2. With the insertion point at the beginning of the document, click the **Insert Picture button** 🖾 on the Drawing toolbar to open the Insert Picture dialog box

3. Locate the **GCTaxiLogo01.bmp** project file, then click it to select it
   See Figure 5-3.

4. Click **Insert** to insert the image at the insertion point

5. Click the image to select it, then drag the **bottom-right sizing handle** down and to the right until the dotted line indicates that the right edge of the image will be aligned with the **T** in **Taxi**

6. With the image still selected, click the **Center button** 🗮

7. Click anywhere in the document to deselect the image
   See Figure 5-4.

 close GCProposal04.doc

> **tip**
>
> To insert a picture directly from a scanner or a digital camera, point to Picture on the Insert menu, then click From Scanner or Camera.

Figure 5-3: **Logo selected in the Insert Picture dialog box**

Figure 5-4: **Picture resized and centered in document**

Insert Picture button

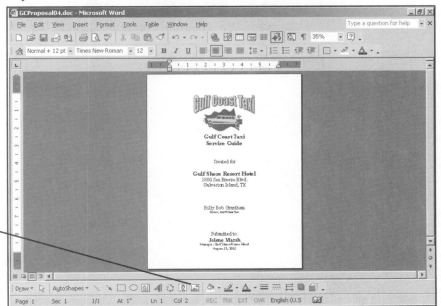

Skill Set 5
Working with Graphics

Create and Modify Diagrams and Charts
Create an Organizational Chart

Sometimes diagrams can convey information more clearly than a written description. You can insert a variety of diagrams into a Word document using the Insert Diagram or Organization Chart button. An **organizational chart** is a graphical representation of a hierarchical structure.

Right-click the edge of a chart box to see commands you can use to format or change the organizational chart.

Activity Steps

1. Open a new, blank document, then, if the Drawing toolbar is not visible, click the **Drawing button** 🔲

2. Click the **Insert Diagram or Organization Chart button** 🔲 on the Drawing toolbar to open the Diagram Gallery dialog box

3. Make sure the **Organization Chart button** is selected
   See Figure 5-5.

4. Click **OK** to insert an organizational chart into the document

5. Click in the top box in the chart, type **Billy Bob Grantham**, press **[Enter]**, type **Owner**, then click outside the box but inside the drawing canvas to automatically resize the box

6. Click in the first box on the left in the second row, type **Scott West**, press **[Enter]**, then continue filling in the boxes as shown in Figure 5-6

 close file

Figure 5-5: Diagram Gallery dialog box

Thick blue square indicates button is selected

Description of selected diagram type

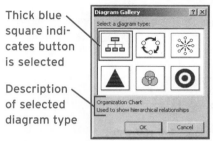

Figure 5-6: Completed organizational chart

Organization Chart toolbar

Drawing canvas

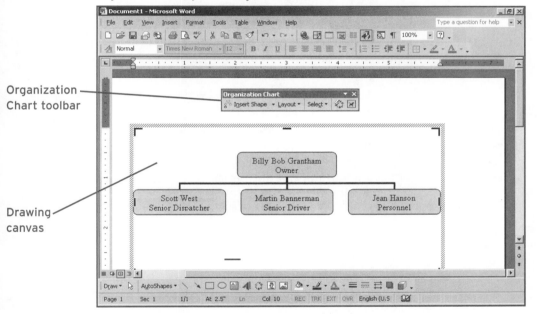

Skill Set 5

Working with Graphics

Create and Modify Diagrams and Charts

Modify an Organizational Chart

Once you have created a diagram or organizational chart, you can add elements to it and change their formatting. You can also rearrange the layout of the parts of the diagram.

Click the Layout button on the Organization Chart toolbar to change the arrangement of the boxes in the organizational chart.

Activity Steps

 open GCOrgChart01.doc

1. Click the **Jean Hanson box**, click the **Insert Shape button list arrow** ⬚ Insert Shape ▾ on the Organization Chart toolbar, click **Assistant**, click in the new Assistant box, then type **Mary Lou Lee**

2. Click the **Martin Bannerman box**, click the **Insert Shape button list arrow** ⬚ Insert Shape ▾ , click **Subordinate**, then with the Martin Bannerman box still selected, add another Subordinate box

3. Click the edge of the **Mary Lou Lee box** with ⬚, then drag the box on top of the Scott West box

4. Click the edge of the **Subordinate box** on the left under the Martin Bannerman box, then press **[Delete]**
   See Figure 5-7.

5. Click the **Autoformat button** ⬚ on the Organization Chart toolbar, click **Beveled** in the list in the Organization Chart Style Gallery dialog box, then click **Apply**

6. Right-click the edge of one of the boxes, then click **Use AutoFormat** to turn off the AutoFormat option so you can add manual formats

7. If the Drawing toolbar is not visible, click the **Drawing button** ⬚ , click the edge of the **Scott West box**, click the **Select button** Select ▾ on the Organization Chart toolbar, click **Level**, click the **Fill Color button list arrow** ⬚ ▾ on the Drawing toolbar, then click the **Turquoise box**

8. Click the edge of the **Billy Bob Grantham box**, click the **Fill Color button list arrow** ⬚ ▾ on the Drawing toolbar, click the **Blue box**, click the **Font Color button list arrow** ⬚ ▾, click the **White box**, click the **Bold button** ⬚ , then click in a blank area of the document to deselect the chart and the drawing canvas (you may need to click twice)
   See Figure 5-8.

    close GCOrgChart01.doc

Figure 5-7: Moving a box in an organizational chart

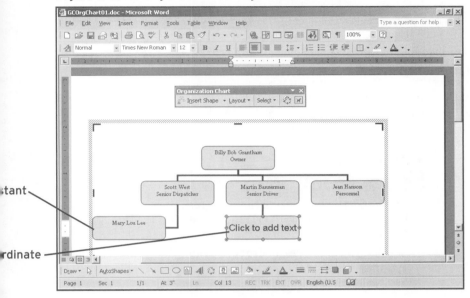

tant

rdinate

Figure 5-8: Formatted organizational chart

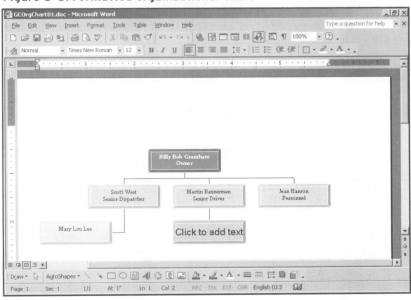

extra!

Understanding diagram types
In addition to organizational charts, you can create cycle, radial, pyramid, Venn, and target diagrams and flowcharts. Each diagram conveys information in a particular way by illustrating how a process works or by showing the relationship between parts of something larger. To create any of these diagrams except the flowchart, select the digram type in the Diagram Gallery dialog box. To create a flowchart, click the AutoShapes button on the Drawing toolbar, point to Flowchart, select the shape you want to insert, then drag to draw it in the document. Connect the flowchart shapes with lines from the Connectors or Lines categories on the AutoShapes menu.

Skill Set 5
Working with Graphics

Create and Modify Diagrams and Charts
Create a Chart

Graphs are a good way to communicate numerical information visually; for example, they can show at a glance how much sales have increased or whether one item is selling significantly more than another. You can add a graph to a document by using the built-in program Microsoft Graph. A graph consists of two parts: a **datasheet**, similar to a table or a spreadsheet, in which you enter the data you want to graph, and a **chart**, in which the data from the datasheet is graphed. When you start Microsoft Graph, the Word menu bar and toolbars are replaced with the Graph menu bar and toolbars.

Activity Steps

 open GCReport01.doc

1. Press **[Ctrl][End]** to position the insertion point at the end of the document, click **Insert** on the menu bar, then click **Object** to open the Object dialog box

2. Scroll down and click **Microsoft Graph Chart** in the Object type list, then click **OK**
   See Figure 5-9.

3. Click the **1st Qtr cell**, type **Airport**, press **[Tab]**, type **Tours**, press **[Tab]**, then type **Shopping**

4. Double-click the **column D header** to eliminate this column from the chart

5. Click the **East cell**, type **October**, press **[Enter]**, type **November**, then double-click the **row 3 header** to eliminate this row from the chart

6. Click in the first cell below the Airport column heading, type **140**, then continue filling in the datasheet as shown in Figure 5-10

7. Drag the datasheet by its title bar so you can see the chart, then click anywhere in the document to exit Microsoft Graph

 close GCReport01.doc

> **tip**
>
> If the labels on an axis in the chart do not all appear, drag a sizing handle on the chart to enlarge the chart object while Microsoft Graph is still active.

extra!

Understanding charts

Charts are made up of data markers grouped in series and data labels. A **data marker** represents a single piece of data—a number from the datasheet—in the chart. In this activity, the shorter bar over the Airport label in the chart is the data marker for the data in the first cell under the Airport column. A **data series** is the collection of all the data markers in a row or column in the datasheet. In this activity, the dark purple data markers make up the data series for the November data. A **data label** is text that identifies any part of the chart.

Figure 5-9: Graph and datasheet inserted into a document

Chart of placeholder data

Datasheet with placeholder data

Row 3 header

Column D header

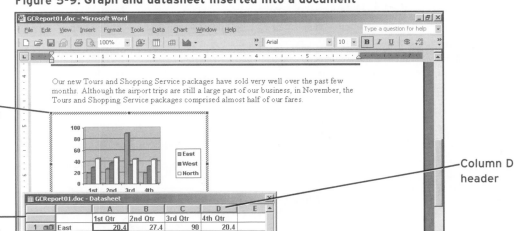

Figure 5-10: Completed datasheet

Airport data marker for October

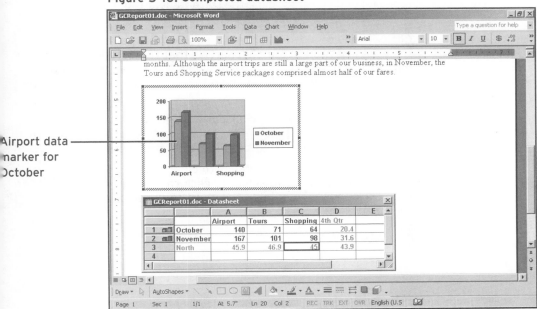

Skill Set 5
Working with Graphics

Create and Modify Diagrams and Charts
Modify a Chart

Once you have inserted a chart, you can modify it in several ways. For example, you can change the chart type, add labels, and resize the objects that make up the chart object. To format an object within a chart, make sure Microsoft Graph is open, click the chart to select it, then click the object in the chart that you want to format.

Activity Steps

 open GCReport02.doc

1. Scroll down to see the chart, then double-click the **chart** to open Microsoft Graph

2. Click the **Chart Type button list arrow** , then click the **Pie Chart button**

3. Double-click the **row 1 header** in the datasheet to exclude the October data and use only the November data in the pie chart *See Figure 5-11.*

4. Click **Chart** on the menu bar, then click **Chart Options** to open the Chart Options dialog box

5. Click the **Titles tab** if necessary, click in the **Chart title box**, type **November Fares**, click the **Data Labels tab**, click the **Percentage check box**, then click **OK**

6. Click anywhere in the chart area, position the pointer over the area just around the pie chart so that the ScreenTip says **Plot Area**, click to select the **Plot Area**, then drag the **sizing handles** to resize the pie chart so that it fills the left side of the chart object

7. Right-click the **Plot Area**, click **Format Plot Area** on the shortcut menu, click the **None option button** in the Border section to remove the border around the Plot Area, then click **OK**

8. Click outside of the **chart object** to close Microsoft Graph, click the chart object to select it, click the **Center button** , then click anywhere outside the chart to deselect the object *See Figure 5-12.*

 close GCReport02.doc

You can close the datasheet by clicking its Close button and reopen it by clicking Datasheet on the View menu.

Figure 5-11: Changing which data series is plotted in the pie chart

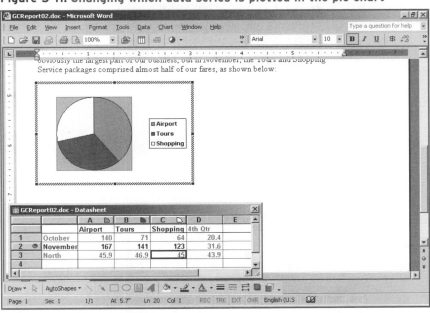

Figure 5-12: Modified chart

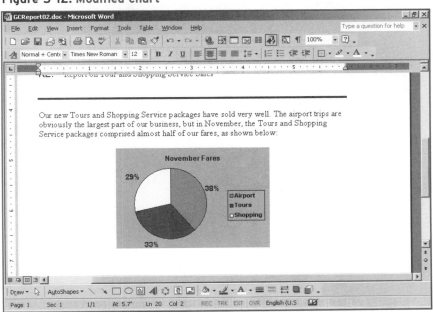

Skill Set 5
Working with Graphics

Create and Modify Diagrams and Charts
Add and Format Objects in a Chart

You can format almost any object in a chart individually. You can add labels to the axes, change the font of labels, add formatting to numbers on the chart, and add objects to your chart to enhance it.

Activity Steps

 open GCMemo06.doc

1. Scroll down to see the chart, double-click the **chart** to open Microsoft Graph, then click the **Close button** ⊠ in the datasheet title bar

2. Right-click any label on the vertical axis, click **Format Axis** on the shortcut menu, then click the **Number tab**

3. Click **Currency** in the Category list, click the **Decimal places down arrow** twice to change it to **0**, then click **OK**

4. Click **Chart** on the menu bar, click **Chart Options**, click the **Titles tab** if necessary, click in the **Value (Z) axis box**, type **Total Sales**, click the **Legend tab**, click the **Show legend check box** to deselect it, then click **OK**

5. Right-click **Total Sales**, click **Format Axis Title**, click the **Alignment tab**, double-click in the Degrees box, type **90**, then click **OK**

6. If the Drawing toolbar is not visible, click the **Drawing button** , click the **Arrow button** on the Drawing toolbar, then drag down to draw an arrow pointing to the top of the **Apr** data point as shown in Figure 5-13

7. Click the **Text Box button** on the Drawing toolbar, click above the **Apr** data point, click the **Font size list arrow** 11 ▾ , click **9**, then type **Easter sales increase**

8. Click anywhere in the document to close Microsoft Graph
See Figure 5-14.

 close GCMemo06.doc

Step 7
If the text box you inserted is in the wrong place, drag it by its edge. If the text box is not large enough, drag a sizing handle.

Figure 5-13: Adding an arrow object to a chart

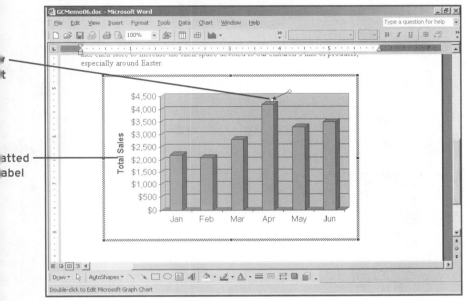

Figure 5-14: Chart with formatted objects

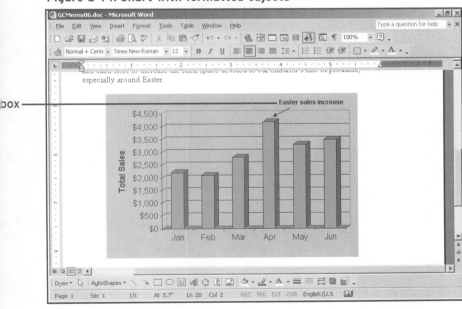

extra!

Understanding objects

An object is anything that can be manipulated—resized, dragged, recolored—as a unit. In this activity, once the chart was inserted into the document, it became a chart object, and Word treats it as one element. You can right-click the object, then use the Format Object command to change characteristics about the object, such as its fill color. Also, it's important to understand that many objects are made up of smaller objects. When you work with the chart in Microsoft Graph, you can manipulate individual components of the chart, such as the legend or the axis labels. Each of these components is an object.

Skill Set 5
Working with Graphics

Target Your Skills

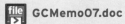 GCMemo07.doc

1 Modify the **GCMemo07** file to create the final document shown in Figure 5-15. To format the organizational chart, first choose a diagram style, then modify individual components as needed. (*Hint*: To format the connecting lines, click the Select button on the Organization Chart toolbar, then click All Connecting Lines.)

Figure 5-15

GCAnnouncement04.doc

2 Modify the **GCAnnouncement04** file to create the document shown in Figure 5-16. The image at the top of the document is in the **GCTaxiLogo02.bmp** file. Create the chart with the following tours and numbers of tours sold: **Galveston State Park, 120; Seawolf Park, 50; Moody Gardens, 45;** and **Pier 21, 30.**

Figure 5-16

Blue line color

Skill List

1. Compare and merge documents
2. Insert, view, and edit comments
3. Convert documents into Web pages

Word has several features and commands that make it easy to share information with others. For example, when you create a document, you might want to make changes based on someone else's input. In Skill Set 6, you will learn how to compare and merge two versions of the same document. You will also learn how to insert, view, and edit comments in your documents.

Posting a document on the Web is an easy way to make it available to others. You can do this easily by saving a Word document as a Web page. You will learn how to do this and how to preview the Web page before you save it.

Skill Set 6
Workgroup Collaboration

Compare and Merge Documents

Sometimes you need to get another person's opinion on a document you create. Someone else can open your document and make changes, then you can use the Compare and Merge command to see all the changes clearly shown on the screen. See Table 6-1 for a list of the three ways you can merge documents. Once you've created the merged document, you can display or print it with the changes showing or with all the changes made but hidden. You can also display or print the original document with the changes showing (which looks slightly different than the merged document, but the results are the same) or without any changes made at all.

Activity Steps

 open EWProductInfo01.doc, EWProductInfo02.doc

1. Make sure the **EWProductInfo02** project file, the edited document, is the current document, click **Tools** on the menu bar, then click **Compare and Merge Documents**

2. Locate and click the **EWProductInfo01** project file, then click the **Merge list arrow**
   See Figure 6-1.

3. Click **Merge into new document**

4. Click in the **Zoom box**, type **90**, press **[Enter]**, then scroll down, if necessary, so that all of the changes are visible on your screen

5. Position the insertion point over the word **Peppermint** in the first header to see the ScreenTip that identifies the person who made the change
   See Figure 6-2.

6. Click the **Display for Review list arrow** [Final Showing Markup] on the Reviewing toolbar that opened, then click **Final** to see the result of all the changes

7. Click the **Display for Review list arrow** [Final Showing Markup] on the Reviewing toolbar, then click **Original Showing Markup** to revert to the original marked-up document

8. Right-click any toolbar, then click **Reviewing** to close the Reviewing toolbar

 close EWProductInfo01.doc, EWProductInfo02.doc

Step 3
Another way to merge the documents into a new document is to click the Legal blackline check box in the Compare and Merge dialog box, then click Compare.

Figure 6-1: Compare and Merge Documents dialog box

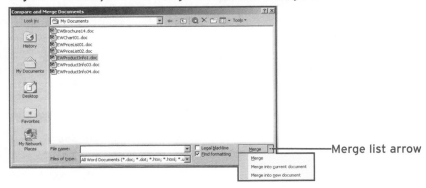

Merge list arrow

Figure 6-2: New document created by merging documents

Name of person who made changes and date and time edits were made

Pointer

Text inserted into original document

Identifies deletion to original document

Identifies formatting change to original document

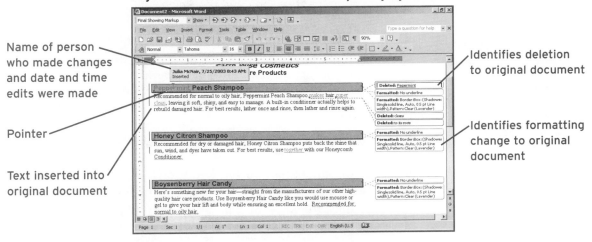

TABLE 6-1: Three ways to merge documents

command	best used for
Merge	Merges the changes into the original document and opens the original document if it's not already open
Merge into current document	Merges the changes into the edited (current) document
Merge into new document	Merges the changes into a new document and leaves the original and edited documents unchanged; clicking the Legal blackline check box and then clicking Compare produces the same result

Skill Set 6

Workgroup Collaboration

Insert, View, and Edit Comments

Insert and View Comments

Comments are notes that you add to a document. They are not printed with the document unless you specifically want them to be, but they are easily displayed on screen. In Print Layout and Web Layout view, comments are visible in Comment balloons, but you can hide them if you wish. You can also view comments in the Reviewing pane, a pane that you can open at the bottom of the window.

Activity Steps

open EWBrochure05.doc

1. Position the insertion point immediately before **and chemicals** in the first line under the first heading
2. Click **Insert** on the menu bar, then click **Comment** to open a Comment balloon and the Reviewing toolbar
   See Figure 6-3.
3. Type **Mention UV rays** in the Comment balloon
4. Drag the horizontal scroll bar to the left if necessary, position the insertion point after **over-worked** in the first paragraph, click the **New Comment button** on the Reviewing toolbar, then type **Delete "over-worked"** in the Comment balloon
   See Figure 6-4.
5. Click the **Show button** Show on the Reviewing toolbar, then click **Comments** to hide the Comment balloons
6. Click the **Show button** Show on the Reviewing toolbar, then click **Reviewing Pane** to display the Reviewing pane
7. Click the **Show button** Show on the Reviewing toolbar, click **Comments** to display the Comment balloons again, click the **Show button** Show, then click **Reviewing Pane** to close the Reviewing pane
8. Right-click any toolbar, then click **Reviewing** to close the Reviewing toolbar

close EWBrochure05.doc

tip

To see the names of all the people who have inserted comments in a document, click the Show button on the Reviewing toolbar, then point to Reviewers.

Figure 6-3: **Comment balloon and Reviewing toolbar opened**

Reviewing toolbar may be in a different position on your screen

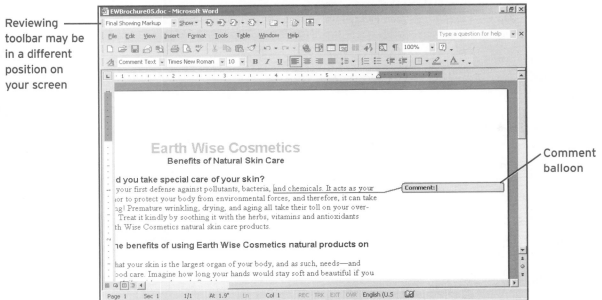

Comment balloon

Figure 6-4: **Comments entered in document**

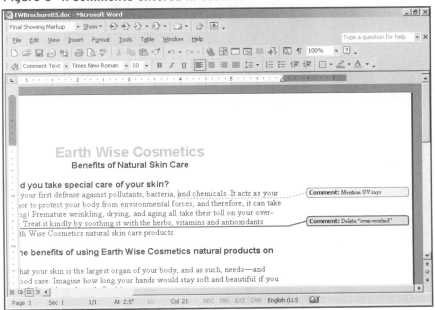

Skill Set 6
Workgroup Collaboration

Insert, View, and Edit Comments
Edit Comments

Once you've entered comments into a document, you can edit or delete them just like regular text. You can do this in each Comment balloon or in the Reviewing pane.

To print comments in a document, select Document showing markup in the Print what list in the Print dialog box. To print only comments, select List of markup in the Print what list.

Activity Steps

 open EWPriceList01.doc

1. Click **View** on the menu bar, point to **Toolbars**, then click **Reviewing** to open the Reviewing toolbar, if necessary

2. Click the **Next button** 🔁 on the Reviewing toolbar to move to the next comment in the document

3. Double-click **deluxe** in the selected comment, then type **luxury**

4. Click the **Next button** 🔁 on the Reviewing toolbar

5. Click the **Reject Change/Delete Comment button** 🔄 on the Reviewing toolbar
   See Figure 6-5.

6. Right-click any toolbar, then click **Reviewing** to close the Reviewing toolbar

 close EWPriceList01.doc

Figure 6-5: **Document with edited comments**

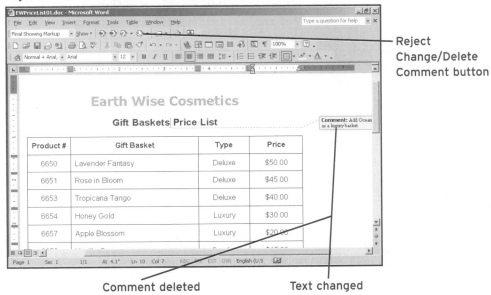

Reject
Change/Delete
Comment button

Comment deleted   Text changed

extra!

Changing the size and appearance of comments

You can change the way tracked comments look in the Comment balloons and in the Reviewing pane. To change the size of the text in the Comment balloons and in the Reviewing pane, click the Next button on the Reviewing toolbar to select a Comment balloon, open the Styles and Formatting task pane, click the list arrow next to Comment Text under Formatting of selected text, click Modify, then change the options in the dialog box. To change the size of the Comment balloons, click Options on the Tools menu, then click the Track Changes tab. Change the width in the Preferred width box under Use balloons in Print and Web Layout.

Skill Set 6
Workgroup Collaboration

Convert Documents into Web Pages
Preview and Save Documents as Web Pages

Publishing a document on the Web or a company intranet is an easy way to make it accessible to a wide audience. Before you save a document as a Web page, you should preview it to make sure that it looks the way you expect it to. After previewing the Web page, you use the Save as Web Page command to automatically save a copy of the document in the HTML file format, a file format that Web browsers use to display pages.

Step 5
The Web page title appears in the title bar of the browser window when the page is being viewed. It also appears in the browser's history list and would appear on a favorite or bookmark list if someone saves the link to the page.

Activity Steps

 open EWChart01.doc

1. Click **File** on the menu bar, then click **Web Page Preview**
2. Click the **Maximize button** in your Web browser window, if necessary
3. Click the **Close button** in your Web browser window
4. Click **File** on the menu bar, then click **Save as Web Page** to open the Save As dialog box
5. Click **Change Title**, press [➡], press the **[Spacebar]**, type **Aromatherapy Best Sellers**, then click **OK**
6. Select all of the text in the File name box, then type **My Web Page**
   See Figure 6-6.
7. Click **Save** to close the Save As dialog box, and view the HTML document in Web Layout view
   See Figure 6-7.

 close EWChart01.doc

Figure 6-6: Save As dialog box for saving a document as a Web page

Web page title

File type changes to HTML when Save as Web Page command is selected

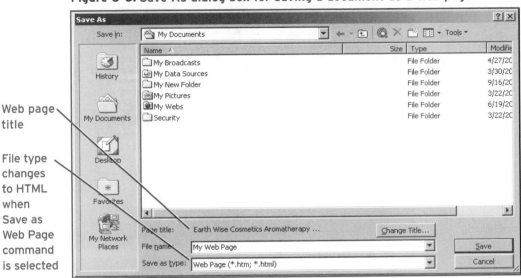

Figure 6-7: Document converted to a Web page in Web Layout view

File extension indicates document is saved as a Web page

Web Layout view selected

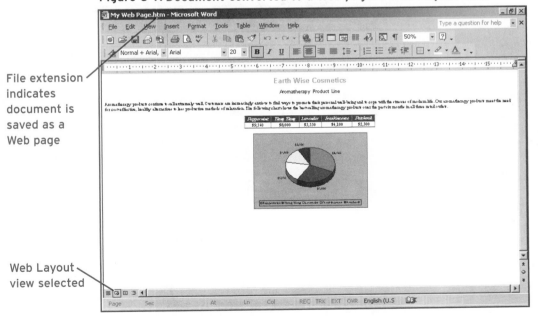

Skill Set 6

Workgroup Collaboration

Target Your Skills

file > EWProductInfo03.doc
EWProductInfo04.doc

1 Use Figure 6-8 as a guide for creating a new merged document. In addition to the changes in the figure, delete the comment **Will this be manufactured next year?** After you have created the final document, select Final in the Display for Review list. Close the Reviewing toolbar when you are finished.

Figure 6-8

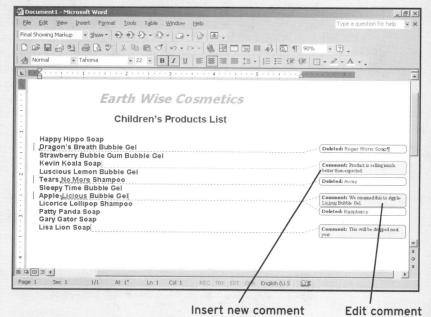

file > EWPriceList02.doc

2 Use Figure 6-9 as a guide to create the Web page shown. Note that the Web page in the figure is in a browser window, but you will end up with an HTML document displayed in Web Layout view in Word. Make sure you change the Web page title to match the one shown in the title bar in the figure.

Figure 6-9

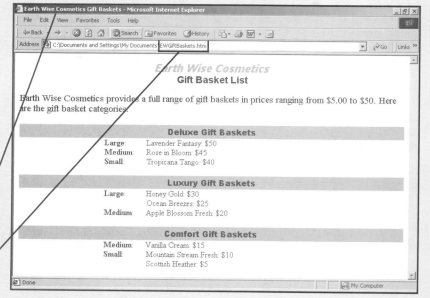

Skill List

1. Control pagination
2. Sort paragraphs in lists and tables

In Skill Set 7, you will learn more advanced commands for managing paragraphs. You will learn how to control pagination automatically. You can set paragraph formats so that page breaks occur only within a paragraph within certain parameters, do not occur within a paragraph at all, always occur after a paragraph, or never occur between two specific paragraphs.

You will also learn how to use Word's Sort feature. You can sort entries in a list or in a table. You can customize the sort in the Sort dialog box. Managing the pagination and sorting lists and paragraphs gives you more control of your documents so that you can achieve the look you want.

Skill Set 7
Customizing Paragraphs

Control Pagination
Control Page Breaks within Paragraphs

You can set options within paragraphs to make sure that a page break does not occur in an unexpected place. A **widow** is the last line of a paragraph printed at the top of a page or column. An **orphan** is the first line of a paragraph printed at the bottom of a page or column. It's generally considered to be bad page layout to have widows and orphans. The default in Word is for widow and orphan control to be turned on, preventing paragraphs from breaking with only one line of the paragraph printed on a page or in a column. You can also format a paragraph so that a page or column break does not occur in the middle of the paragraph at all.

A manual page break overrides paragraph formatting.

Activity Steps

 open CCNewsletter02.doc

1. Scroll down, then select the three paragraphs below the heading **Head of the Penobscot**

2. Click **Format** on the menu bar, click **Paragraph** to open the Paragraph dialog box, then click the **Line and Page Breaks tab**

3. Notice that the **Widow/Orphan control check box** is selected by default

4. Click the **Keep lines together check box** to select it and prevent a page or column break from occurring within the selected paragraphs
   See Figure 7-1.

5. Click **OK**

6. Click anywhere in the document to deselect the paragraphs
   See Figure 7-2.

 close CCNewsletter02.doc

Figure 7-1: Line and Page Breaks tab in the Paragraph dialog box

Select to prevent a page break in the middle of a paragraph

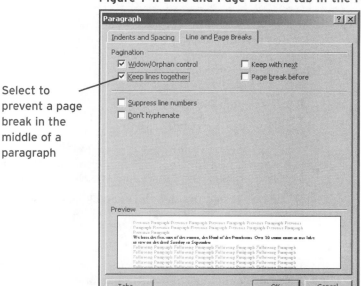

Figure 7-2: Formatted paragraphs

Column break no longer occurs within paragraph

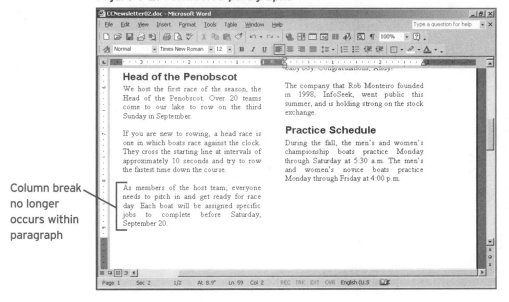

Skill Set 7
Customizing Paragraphs

Control Pagination
Control Page Breaks between Paragraphs

You can format a paragraph so that it will always appear at the top of a page; in other words, so that a page break will always occur before it. You can also format a paragraph so that a page break never occurs after it and so it will always appear on the same page as the paragraph following it.

Activity Steps

 open CCHistory01.doc

1. Scroll down and right-click in the heading **The Beginning**, click **Paragraph** on the shortcut menu to open the Paragraph dialog box, then click the **Line and Page Breaks tab**

2. Click the **Page break before check box** to select it so that the heading will always appear at the top of a new page

3. Click **OK**
   See Figure 7-3.

4. Scroll down to the bottom of the second page so that you can see the heading **The Boathouse and Lake**

5. Right-click in the heading **The Boathouse and Lake**, then click **Paragraph** to open the **Line and Page Breaks tab** in the Paragraph dialog box

6. Click the **Keep with next check box** to select it so that the heading will never appear at the bottom of a page

7. Click **OK**
   See Figure 7-4.

 close CCHistory01.doc

To prevent rows in a table from breaking across pages, click Table Properties on the Table menu, click the Row tab, then click the Allow row to break across pages check box to deselect it.

Figure 7-3: Paragraph formatted to start at top of page

Page break
inserted
before
paragraph

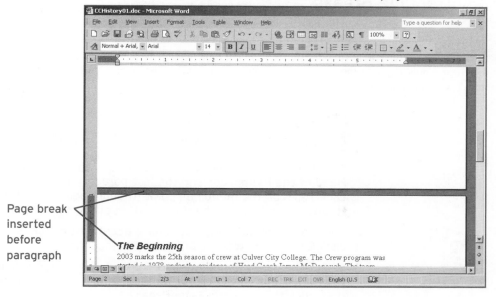

Figure 7-4: Paragraph formatted to appear on same page as following paragraph

Page break
no longer
occurs
between
pargraphs

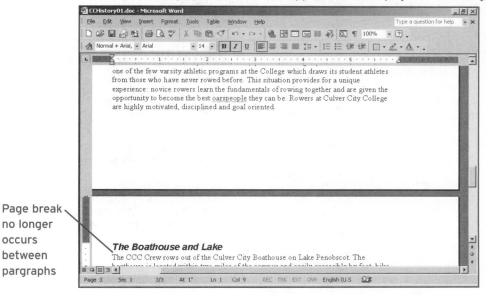

Skill Set 7
Customizing Paragraphs

Control Pagination
Control Line Breaks

By default, Word does not hyphenate words at the ends of lines. You may decide that the text would look better if words were hyphenated; for example, justified paragraphs that have hyphenation turned off might have too much space added between words to force the justification. You can also manually force a line break without creating a new paragraph.

Activity Steps

 open CCNewsletter03.doc

1. Scroll down so you can see the paragraph above the heading **Head of the Penobscot** and the last paragraph in that column, click **Tools** on the menu bar, point to **Language**, then click **Hyphenation** to open the Hyphenation dialog box

2. Click the **Automatically hyphenate document check box**, then click **OK** to have Word hyphenate the document

3. Select the paragraph immediately above the heading **Head of the Penobscot**, click **Format** on the menu bar, click **Paragraph**, then click the **Line and Page Breaks tab**

4. Click the **Don't hyphenate check box** to select it and override the automatic hyphenation for the selected text, then click **OK**
See Figure 7-5.

5. Click immediately before **September** in the last paragraph in the first column, then press **[Shift][Enter]** to insert a manual line break without creating a new paragraph

6. Drag to select the entire paragraph above the heading **Practice Schedule**, click **Tools** on the menu bar, point to **Language**, click **Hyphenation**, then click **Manual**

7. Press **[←]** three times to reposition the insertion point at the first suggested hyphenation location (between the **s** and the **t**), then click **Yes**

8. Click **No** in the dialog box that appears asking if you want to continue checking the rest of the document, then click **OK** in the dialog box that appears telling you that hyphenation is complete
See Figure 7-6.

 close CCNewsletter03.doc

If you do not want a word that has a hyphen in it to break at the end of a line (for example, a phone number), press [Ctrl][Shift][-] to insert the hyphen, and the entire word will shift to the next line if necessary.

Figure 7-5: Hyphenated document

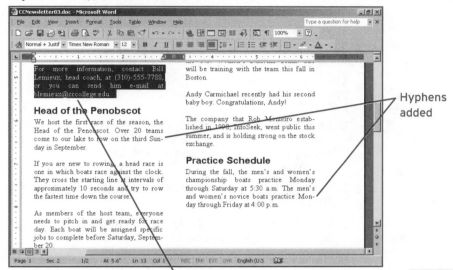

Hyphens added

Hyphens removed from paragraph

Figure 7-6: Document with some paragraphs manually hyphenated

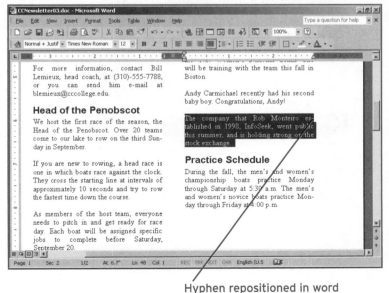

Hyphen repositioned in word

extra!

Using manual hyphenation

If you want to approve each suggested hyphenation, click Manual in the Hyphenation dialog box. The Manual Hyphenation dialog box then appears with the first suggestion for a hyphenated word, and the word appears in the document with the hyphen already inserted. Click Yes to accept the suggested hyphen, click No to reject it, or reposition the insertion point to another position in the word, and then click Yes to accept the changed hyphenation.

Skill Set 7

Customizing Paragraphs

Sort Paragraphs in Lists and Tables

A long list of data can be easier to interpret if it is sorted in some order. You can sort a list or a column in a table using the Sort command. Word can sort data as text, numbers, or dates. When the data is text, Word sorts words that begin with punctuation marks or symbols first, then numbers, then letters.

Activity Steps

 open CCLists01.doc

1. Select the list under the heading **Team List** (do not select the **Team List heading** or the three **column headings**), stopping before the page break above **GPA List**
   See Figure 7-7.

2. Click **Table** on the menu bar, then click **Sort** to open the Sort Text dialog box

3. Click the **Sort by list arrow**, click **Field 1** or **Word 1**, then make sure that the **Ascending option button** is selected

4. Make sure that the **No header row option button** is selected, then click **OK** to sort the list of names in alphabetical order

5. Scroll down and click in the **GPA List table**, click **Table** on the menu bar, then click **Sort** to open the Sort dialog box

6. Click the **Sort by list arrow**, click **GPA**, then click the **Descending option button**

7. Click the **Then by list arrow** in the middle of the dialog box, then click **Name**
   See Figure 7-8.

8. Make sure that the **Header row option button** is selected, then click **OK** to sort the table first in descending order by GPA then in ascending order by Name

 close CCLists01.doc

To sort only one column in a table, select the column, open the Sort dialog box, click Options, then click the Sort column only check box.

Figure 7-7: List to be sorted

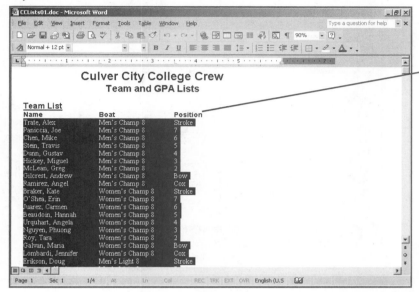

Header row not selected

Figure 7-8: Sort dialog box

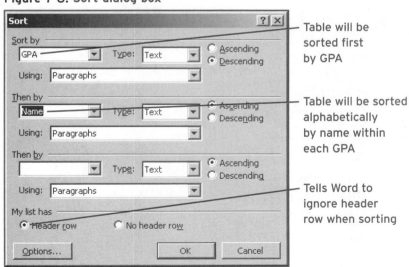

Table will be sorted first by GPA

Table will be sorted alphabetically by name within each GPA

Tells Word to ignore header row when sorting

extra!

Sorting a column with more than one word in each cell

If a column in a table contains items consisting of more than one word, for example a list of first and last names, you can sort by any word in the column. Select the column, then open the Sort dialog box and click Options. If the words are separated by something other than a comma or a tab, click the Other option button, then type the character that separates the words in the column (you can type a space). Click OK to close the Sort Options dialog box, then click the Using list arrow and select the word or field that you want to sort on.

Skill Set 7

Customizing Paragraphs

Target Your Skills

 CCPressRelease01.doc

1 Use Figure 7-9 as a guide for formatting the project file **CCPressRelease01**. First, hyphenate the document. After formatting the document as directed by the callouts, format the heading **From points south** so that there is no page break between it and the directions under it, then format the paragraph containing the directions from points south so that a page break does not occur in the middle of that paragraph.

 CCBrochure01.doc

2 Use Figure 7-10 as a guide for formatting the project file **CCBrochure01**. Hyphenate the document then format any paragraphs as needed to ensure that page 2 automatically starts with the Senior Program heading.

Figure 7-9

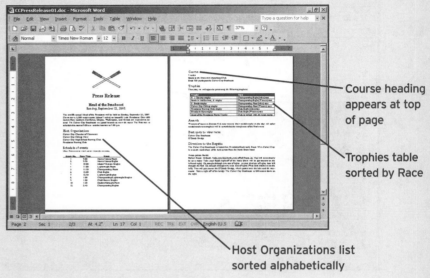

Course heading appears at top of page

Trophies table sorted by Race

Host Organizations list sorted alphabetically

Figure 7-10

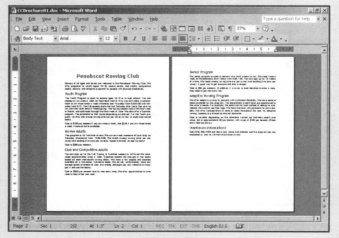

Skill List

1. Create and format document sections
2. Create and apply character and paragraph styles
3. Create and update document indexes and tables of contents, figures, and authorities
4. Create cross-references
5. Add and revise endnotes and footnotes
6. Create and manage master documents and subdocuments
7. Move within documents
8. Create and modify forms using various form controls
9. Create forms and prepare forms for distribution

As you work with longer documents, you can take advantage of Word's many formatting commands to make managing your documents easier. Working with document sections allows you to format parts of a document separately. You can create indexes, tables of contents, tables of figures, cross-references, and footnotes with little effort. You can create a master document and subdocuments to make working with a long document easier. You'll also find navigating in a long document becomes much easier when you use bookmarks or the Document Map.

You can also use Word to create and format electronic and printed forms. You can then prepare the forms for electronic distribution. If you learn to take advantage of the many advanced formatting capabilities in Word, you will find it easier to manage and work with longer, more complicated documents.

Skill Set 8
Formatting Documents

Create and Format Document Sections
Use Page Setup Options to Format Sections

Sections are parts of a document with separate page formatting options. For example, when you select some of the text in a document and format it with multiple columns, you actually create a new section. You can have as many sections as you want in a document. You can also decide where you want the new section to begin. If a section break is labeled as continuous, the new section will start on the same page as the paragraph before it. A section break labeled as next, even or odd page means that the new section starts at the top of a new page. When a section starts on a new page, it can have different page setup options (orientation, margins, etc.) applied to it than to other sections in the document.

Activity Steps

 open EWMemo08.doc

1. Click the **Print Preview button** , click the **down scroll arrow** if necessary to view the second page, then click on the right side of the table to zoom in and see that the table is cut off on the right

2. Click the **Close button** on the Print Preview toolbar, scroll down and click to position the insertion point immediately before the heading **Earth Wise Cosmetics**, then click the **Show/Hide ¶ button** to display paragraph marks, if necessary

Step 5
To apply the page setup options to the entire document, click the Apply to list arrow in the Page Setup dialog box, then select Whole document.

3. Click **Insert** on the menu bar, click **Break** to open the Break dialog box, click the **Next page option button** under Section break types, then click **OK** to insert a section break and start a new page
See Figure 8-1.

4. Click the **Show/Hide ¶ button** to hide paragraph marks, make sure the insertion point is still positioned in the new section, click **File** on the menu bar, click **Page Setup**, then click the **Margins tab**

5. Click the **Landscape orientation box**, then make sure that **This section** appears in the Apply to list

6. Click the **Layout tab**, click the **Vertical alignment list arrow**, click **Center**, then make sure that **This section** appears in the Apply to list

7. Click **OK**, click the **Print Preview button** , click the **Multiple Pages button** , then click the second icon in the top row to display **1 x 2 Pages**, if necessary
See Figure 8-2.

 close EWMemo08.doc

Figure 8-1: Section break inserted

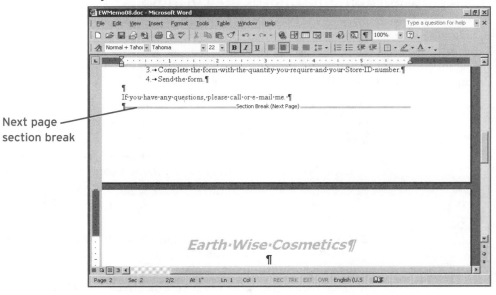

Next page
section break

Figure 8-2: Sections formatted differently in document

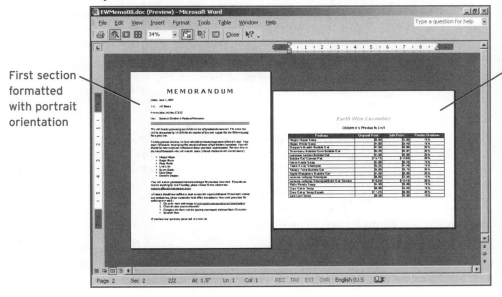

First section
formatted
with portrait
orientation

Second
section
formatted
with
landscape
orientation

Skill Set 8
Formatting Documents

Create and Format Document Sections
Verify Paragraph and Character Formats

Sometimes it can be helpful to know exactly what formatting is applied to text in a document. To see the formatting of selected text, you can use the Reveal Formatting task pane. When you open this task pane, the font and paragraph formats of the selected text are listed. You can click the links above each format description to open a dialog box to modify that format.

Activity Steps

 open EWBrochure06.doc

1. Select the first line of text, click **Format** on the menu bar, then click **Reveal Formatting** to open the Reveal Formatting task pane

2. Click the **Font link** in the Reveal Formatting task pane to open the Font dialog box, click **Arial Black** in the Font list as shown in Figure 8-3, then click **OK**

3. Click anywhere in the paragraph beginning with **Earth Wise Cosmetics**, and note the styles for the selected text in the Reveal Formatting task pane

4. Click the **Distinguish style source check box** at the bottom of the Reveal Formatting task pane to select it and see on which style the current paragraph format is based

5. Point to the box under **Selected text** at the top of the Reveal Formatting task pane, click the **list arrow** that appears, then click **Select All Text With Similar Formatting**

6. Click the **Alignment link** under Paragraph in the Reveal Formatting task pane to open the Paragraph dialog box, click the **Indents and Spacing tab**, click the **Alignment list arrow**, click **Centered**, then click **OK**
   See Figure 8-4.

7. Click the **Distinguish style source check box** to deselect it, click the **Close button** ⊠ in the task pane title bar to close the task pane, then click anywhere in the document to deselect the text

 close EWBrochure06.doc

> **tip**
>
> To check for formatting inconsistencies as you type, click Options on the Tools menu, click the Edit tab, then select the Keep track of formatting and Mark formatting inconsistencies check boxes.

Comparing formats with Reveal Formatting

To compare two formats in the Reveal Formatting task pane, click the Compare to another selection check box in the Reveal Formatting task pane to open a second box under Selected text at the top of the task pane. Then select new text in the document window. The format descriptions for the text in the second Selected text box will appear after the symbol -> .

Figure 8-3: Using the Reveal Formatting task pane

Selected text in document

View of selected text

Font link

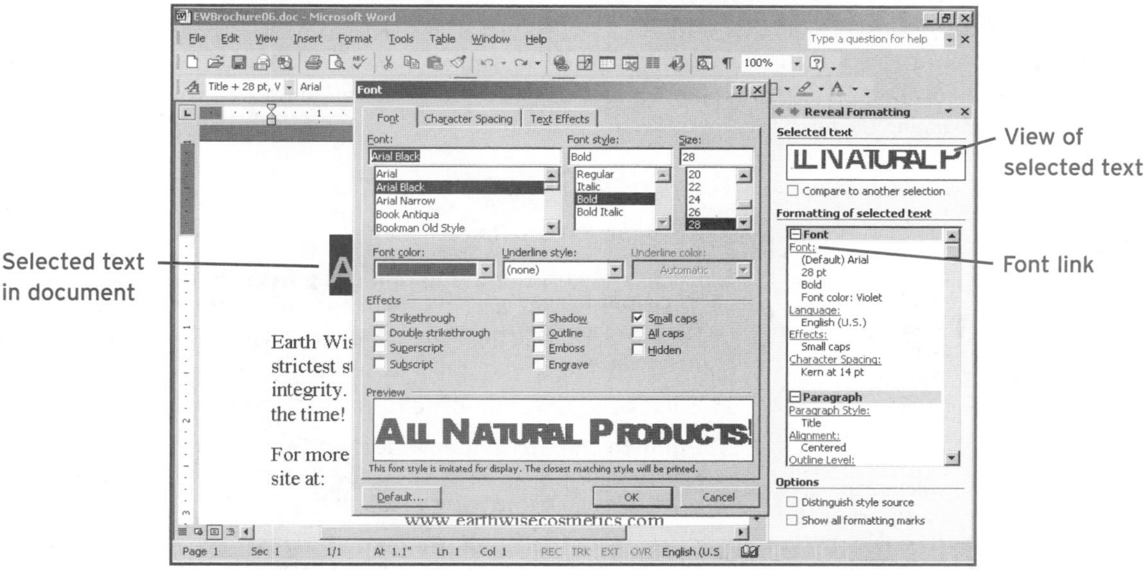

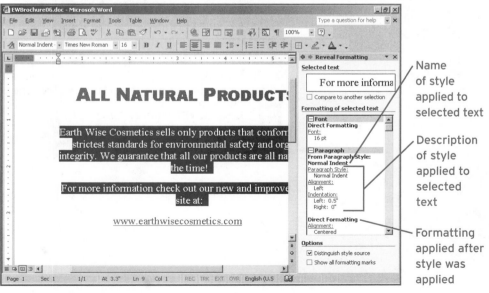

Figure 8-4: Paragraph format modified in the Reveal Formatting task pane

Name of style applied to selected text

Description of style applied to selected text

Formatting applied after style was applied

Skill Set 8
Formatting Documents

Create and Format Document Sections
Clear Formatting

Once you have applied formats to paragraphs and characters in a document, you can clear them quickly with the Clear Formatting command in the Reveal Formatting or the Styles and Formatting task panes. This can be faster than changing the formatting of one element at a time.

To format a document automatically, click Format on the menu bar, click AutoFormat, select a document type, then click OK. Open the Reveal Formatting task pane to see exactly what formats were applied.

Activity Steps

 open EWBrochure07.doc

1. Click **View** on the menu bar, click **Task Pane**, click the **Other Task Panes list arrow** in the task pane title bar, then click **Reveal Formatting**, if necessary, to open the Reveal Formatting task pane

2. Select the first line of text in the document

3. Point to the box under **Selected text** at the top of the Reveal Formatting task pane, click the **list arrow** that appears, then click **Clear Formatting** as shown in Figure 8-5

4. Click the **Other Task Panes list arrow** in the task pane title bar, then click **Styles and Formatting**

5. Click **Edit** on the menu bar, then click **Select All** to select all of the text in the document

6. Click **Clear Formatting** in the Pick formatting to apply list in the task pane
See Figure 8-6.

7. Click the **Close button** in the task pane title bar, then click anywhere in the document to deselect the text

 close EWBrochure07.doc

**Figure 8-5: Using the Clear Formatting command in the Reveal
Formatting task pane**

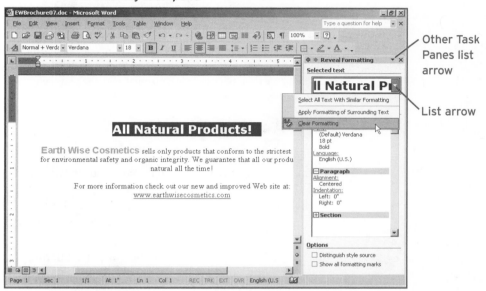

Other Task
Panes list
arrow

List arrow

Figure 8-6: Clear Formatting command in the Styles and Formatting task pane

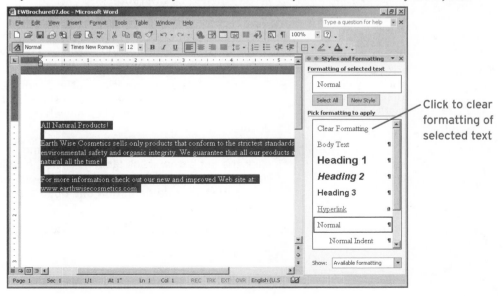

Click to clear
formatting of
selected text

Skill Set 8
Formatting Documents

Create and Apply Character and Paragraph Styles
Create and Apply Character Styles

You will quickly see the real advantage to using styles when you work with longer documents or with the same type of text over and over again. You can create a new style based on your needs, then apply that style wherever you want. The easiest way to create a new style is to format text the way you want, select it, then define a new style based on the selected text.

Activity Steps

 open EWBrochure08.doc

1. Select the text **Earth Wise Cosmetics** in the first paragraph in the document

2. Click the **Font list arrow** , click **Arial**, click the **Bold button** B, click the **Font Color list arrow** A⁻, then click the **Lavender box**

3. Click the **Styles and Formatting button** to open the Styles and Formatting task pane, then click **New Style** in the task pane to open the New Style dialog box

4. Type **Company Name** in the Name box, click the **Style type list arrow**, then click **Character**
   See Figure 8-7.

5. Click **OK** to complete the styles definition, then click **Company Name** in the Pick formatting to apply list in the task pane to apply the new style to the selected text

6. Select **Earth Wise Cosmetics** in the second paragraph in the document, click **Company Name** in the Pick formatting to apply list in the task pane, then click anywhere in the document to deselect the text

7. Point to **Company Name** in the Styles and Formatting task pane, click the **list arrow**, click **Modify**, click the **Bold button** B to turn off bold formatting, click the **Italic button** I, then click **OK** to change the style definition and update the document
   See Figure 8-8.

8. Click the **Close button** ✕ in the Styles and Formatting task pane

 close EWBrochure08.doc

Click the Add to template check box in the New Style or Modify Style dialog box to make your new style available to all documents based on the template you are using (including the Normal template).

Figure 8-7: New Style dialog box

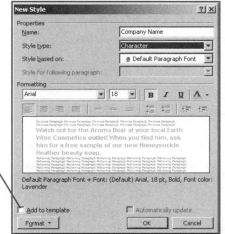

Click to make available to other documents that are based on this template

Figure 8-8: Format changed after modifying style

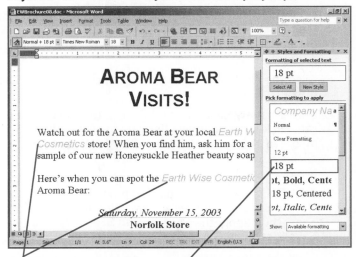

Format changed automatically to reflect modifications to style definition

Selected style on your screen will differ depending on where you clicked to deselect the text

Skill Set 8
Formatting Documents

Create and Apply Character and Paragraph Styles
Create and Apply Paragraph Styles

Paragraph styles are applied to entire paragraphs. As with character styles, one way to create a paragraph style is to format a paragraph the way you want, then define a new paragraph style based on this format. Another easy way to define a style is to modify the definition of a style that already exists.

Activity Steps

 open EWPriceList03.doc

1. Click the **Styles and Formatting button** to open the Styles and Formatting task pane, then click **New Style** to open the New Style dialog box

2. Type **My Heading Style** in the Name box, then make sure that **Paragraph** is selected in the Style type box

3. Click the **Style based on list arrow**, scroll up the list, then click **Heading 1** to base your new style on the existing Heading 1 style

4. Click the **Style for following paragraph list arrow**, then click **Main Text** to automatically apply the Main Text style to a new paragraph created by pressing [Enter] after a My Heading Style paragraph

5. Click the **Font Size list arrow** `18 ▾`, click **14**, then click the **Italic button** *I*

6. Click **Format**, click **Paragraph**, click the **Indents and Spacing tab**, click the **Alignment list arrow**, click **Left**, click the **After up arrow** to change the spacing after the paragraph to **6 pt**, then click **OK**
   See Figure 8-9.

7. Click **OK**, select the heading **Papaya Cleansing Milk**, click **My Heading Style** in the Pick formatting to apply list in the task pane, then apply the **My Heading Style style** to the heading **Lavender Soap Gel**

8. Click the **Close button** `✕` in the task pane title bar, scroll down and select the heading **Pineapple Wash**, click the **Style list arrow** `Normal + 12 pt ▾`, click **My Heading Style**, position the insertion point immediately after the word **Wash**, press **[Enter]**, then type **Recommended for oily skin.**
   See Figure 8-10.

 close EWPriceList03.doc

> **tip**
>
> To change the list of styles displayed in the Styles and Formatting task pane or on the Style list on the toolbar, click the Show list arrow in the Styles and Formatting task pane, click Custom to open the Format Settings dialog box, then select the check boxes of the styles you want to display.

Figure 8-9: New Style dialog box after creating paragraph style definition

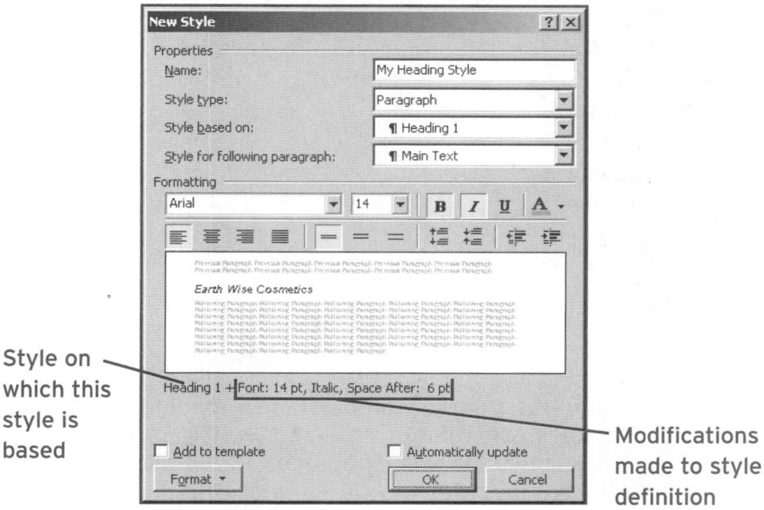

Style on which this style is based

Modifications made to style definition

Figure 8-10: Document with new paragraph style applied

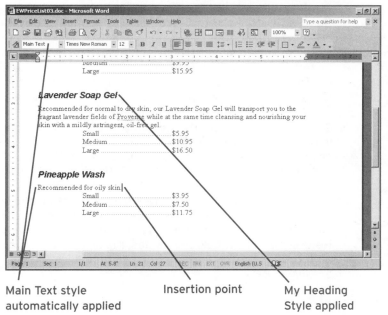

Main Text style automatically applied

Insertion point

My Heading Style applied

extra!

Using the Style Organizer

Click Styles in this dialog box to open the Style dialog box, then click Organizer; or click Tools on the menu bar, click Templates and Add-ins, then click Organizer to open the Styles tab in the Organizer dialog box. To copy styles from one template or document to another, click Close File on either side, then click Open File and open the document or template from which you want to copy a style. Click Close File then click Open File on the other side, and open the document or template to which you want to copy the style. Select the style in the list, click Copy, then click Close to close the Organizer.

Skill Set 8
Formatting Documents

Create and Update Document Indexes and Tables of Contents, Figures, and Authorities
Create an Index

To create an index, you first mark words in the document as **index entries**. Word inserts an **index field** for each entry. The index field is inserted between braces and is labeled *XE*. You can see index fields only if paragraph marks are turned on. After you mark all the index entries, you compile them into an index. Word automatically sorts the entries alphabetically, adds the page references, and removes any duplicate entries.

Activity Steps

 open EWReport01.doc

1. Click the **Show/Hide ¶ button** to display paragraph marks, if necessary, scroll down to page 2 and select the words **Naturally Yours** in the paragraph below the heading **Marilyn Arnold, Mobile Store**, then press **[Alt][Shift][X]** to mark the selected text as an index entry and open the Mark Index Entry dialog box

2. Make sure **Naturally Yours** appears in the Main entry box and that the **Current page option button** is selected, then click **Mark**

3. With the Mark Index Entry dialog box still open, select the words **massage therapist** in the paragraph below the heading **Sandra Grant, Atlanta Store**, click in the Main Index Entry dialog box to make it active, then click **Mark**

4. Scroll down and select **Mobile** in the heading below **Franchise Locations**, click in the Mark Index Entry dialog box, select all of the text in the Main entry box, type **Franchise Locations**, press **[Tab]**, type **Mobile, Alabama** in the Subentry box, then click **Mark All** to mark all instances of **Mobile** in the text as an index entry

5. Scroll down and select the word **Atlanta** in the next heading, click in the Mark Index Entry dialog box, replace the text in the Main entry box with **Franchise Locations**, press **[Tab]**, type **Atlanta, Georgia** in the Subentry box, click **Mark All**, then click **Close**
   See Figure 8-11.

6. Press **[Ctrl][End]**, click the **Show/Hide ¶ button** to hide paragraph marks and the field entries so the document will be paginated correctly, click **Insert** on the menu bar, point to **Reference**, click **Index and Tables**, make sure the **Index tab** is on top, click the **Formats list arrow**, then click **Classic**
   See Figure 8-12.

7. Click **OK** to create the index
   See Figure 8-13.

 close EWReport01.doc

To insert a cross-reference instead of the page number for an index entry, click the Cross-reference option button in the Mark Index Entry dialog box, and type the cross-reference after the word "See" in the Cross-reference box.

Figure 8-11: Index entries marked in document

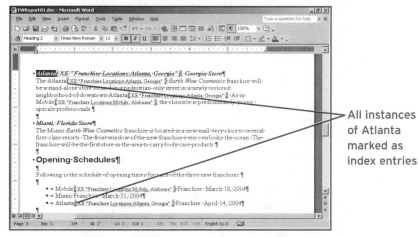

All instances of Atlanta marked as index entries

Figure 8-12: Index tab in Index and Tables dialog box

Index will appear in two columns

Click to change index format

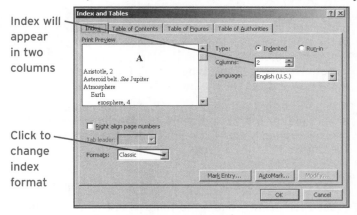

extra!

Customizing the index format

To customize the format of your index, click From template on the Formats list in the Index and Tables dialog box, then click Modify to open the Style dialog box. Select an index style, click Modify to open the Modify Style dialog box, then make whatever changes you want. If you want to format entries with the page number in bold or italics, click the Bold or Italic check boxes in the Mark Index Entry dialog box when you mark the index entry.

Figure 8-13: Index in document

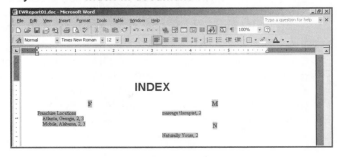

Skill Set 8
Formatting Documents

Create and Update Document Indexes and Tables of Contents, Figures, and Authorities
Update an Index

The index that Word creates is actually a field, and you can update it if you make changes to the document. You modify the index by marking new entries in the document, deleting an index field, or changing the format of the index.

Activity Steps

 open EWReport02.doc

1. Press **[Ctrl][End]** to see the current index
   See Figure 8-14.

2. Click the **Show/Hide ¶ button** ¶ to display paragraph marks, if necessary, scroll up to the last paragraph on page 3, select the words **opening day events**, press **[Alt][Shift][X]**, then click **Mark** in the Mark Index Entry dialog box to mark a new entry for the index

3. With the Mark Index Entry dialog box still open, scroll up to the paragraph above the heading **Opening Schedules**, select **Miami** in the heading, click in the Mark Index Entry dialog box to make it active, replace the text in the Main entry box with **Franchise Locations**, press **[Tab]**, type **Miami, Florida**, click **Mark All** to mark new entries for the index, then click **Close**

Step 7
You can also click anywhere in a field and press [F9] to update it.

4. Scroll up to the middle of page 2, click immediately before the index field for **marketing** below the **Marilyn Arnold, Mobile Store** heading, press and hold **[Shift]**, then press **[➡]** to select the entire field
   See Figure 8-15.

5. Press **[Delete]** to delete the field from the index

6. Press **[Ctrl][End]** to jump to the end of the document

7. Click the **Show/Hide ¶ button** ¶ to hide paragraph marks and the field entries so the document will be paginated correctly, right-click anywhere on the index, then click **Update Field** on the shortcut menu to update the index

8. Click anywhere in the index, click **Insert** on the menu bar, point to **Reference**, click **Index and Tables**, click the **Formats list arrow**, click **Modern**, click **OK**, then click **OK** in the dialog box that appears asking if you want to replace the selected index to reformat the index
   See Figure 8-16.

 close EWReport02.doc

Figure 8-14: Original index in document

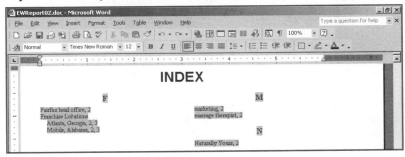

Figure 8-15: Entire index field selected

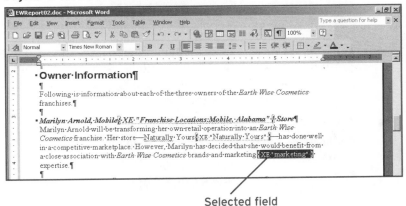

Selected field

Figure 8-16: Modified index in document

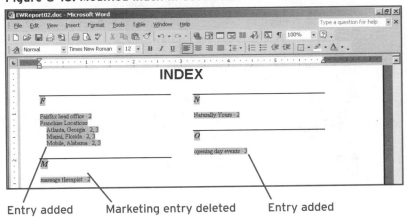

Entry added   Marketing entry deleted   Entry added

Skill Set 8
Formatting Documents

Create and Update Document Indexes and Tables of Contents, Figures, and Authorities
Insert and Update a Table of Contents

The easiest way to create a table of contents is to use the built-in heading styles for the headings in a document, then tell Word how many levels of headings you want to include in the table of contents. (If you did not use the built-in heading styles in your document, you need to assign the styles you used to a heading level, as explained in the extra! box on the following page.) When you create the table of contents, you can choose a number of formatting options, including whether to show page numbers, whether to right-align the page numbers, and whether to format the entries as hyperlinks.

Activity Steps

 open EWReport03.doc

1. Scroll down to page 2, then position the insertion point in the empty paragraph below the heading **Table of Contents**

2. Click **Insert** on the menu bar, point to **Reference**, click **Index and Tables**, then click the **Table of Contents tab**

3. Click the **Formats list arrow**, then click **Distinctive**

4 Click the **Tab leader list arrow**, then click the **dotted line** below **(none)** in the list

5. Click the **Show levels down arrow** to change the number of levels shown to **2**
   See Figure 8-17.

6. Make sure the **Use hyperlinks instead of page numbers check box** is selected, then click **OK** to insert the table of contents

7. Press **[Ctrl][End]**, scroll up a little and select the heading **Wrap-up**, type **Conclusion**, scroll up, select the heading **January Information Meeting**, click the **Style list arrow** `Heading 3`, then click **Heading 2**

8. Scroll back up to the table of contents and right-click anywhere on it, then click **Update Field** on the shortcut menu to update the table of contents
   See Figure 8-18.

 close EWReport03.doc

Step 6
If you format the entries as hyperlinks, you can position the insertion point over an entry, press and hold [Ctrl], and then click the mouse button to jump to that heading in the document.

Figure 8-17: Table of Contents tab in the Index and Tables dialog box

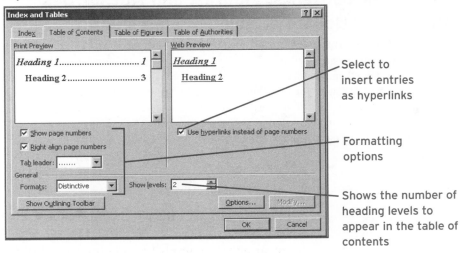

Select to insert entries as hyperlinks

Formatting options

Shows the number of heading levels to appear in the table of contents

Figure 8-18: Updated table of contents

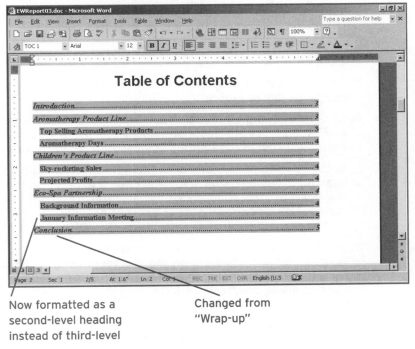

Now formatted as a second-level heading instead of third-level

Changed from "Wrap-up"

extra!

Creating a table of contents using custom heading styles
You can create a table of contents even if you did not use the built-in heading styles. Open the Table of Contents tab in the Index and Tables dialog box, then click Options to open the Table of Contents Options dialog box. The styles you used in your document will be listed on the left, and you can assign each of your styles a level in your table of contents.

Skill Set 8
Formatting Documents

Create and Update Document Indexes and Tables of Contents, Figures, and Authorities
Insert and Update a Table of Figures

A **table of figures** is a list of all the illustrations in a document. You can have Word create one as an updateable field. First, you select each figure, then you use the Caption command to add a numbered caption. After you create the figure captions, you position the insertion point at the place in the document where you want the table of figures to appear, and then have Word create the table. As with a table of contents or an index, you can make changes to the figure captions or add or delete captions, and then update the table field.

Activity Steps

 open EWReport04.doc

1. Scroll down and click the **pie chart** on page 4, click **Insert** on the menu bar, point to **Reference**, then click **Caption**

2. Make sure that **Figure** is listed in the Label list box and **Below selected item** is listed in the Position list box

3. Type **:** (a colon) in the Caption box after **Figure 1**, press **[Spacebar]**, then type **Top-selling Essential Oils**
   See Figure 8-19.

4. Click **OK**

5. Scroll up to page 3 and position the insertion point below the heading **Table of Figures**

6. Click **Insert** on the menu bar, point to **Reference**, click **Index and Tables**, click the **Table of Figures tab**, make sure that **Figure** is listed in the Caption label list box, then click **OK**

7. Scroll down to page 5 and click the **worksheet chart** below the heading **Projected Profits** to select it, click **Insert** on the menu bar, point to **Reference**, click **Caption**, type **:** (a colon), click in the Caption box after **Figure 2**, press **[Spacebar]**, type **Children's Line Projected Sales**, then click **OK**

8. Scroll back up to page 3, right-click anywhere on the table of figures, click **Update Field** on the shortcut menu, click the **Update entire table option button** in the Update Table of Figures dialog box, then click **OK**
   See Figure 8-20.

 close EWReport04.doc

To add a new label to the available labels in the Label list, click New Label in the Caption dialog box. To customize the caption numbering, click Numbering in the Caption dialog box.

Figure 8-19: Caption dialog box

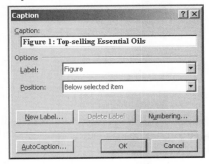

Figure 8-20: Updated table of figures

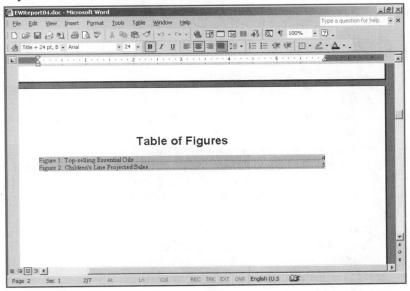

extra!

Creating a table of figures using custom styles

You can create a table of figures even if you added captions to your figures first. Make sure you assign a style to the captions, then open the Table of Figures tab in the Index and Tables dialog box. Click Options to open the Table of Figures Options dialog box. Click the Style check box, click the Style list arrow, then select the style you applied to the captions.

Skill Set 8

Create Cross-references

A **cross-reference** is a reference to a figure, table, or other element that appears somewhere else in the document. You can add a cross-reference as a field that changes to reflect an item's new position in the document whenever the document changes. Cross-references are inserted as hyperlinks.

Activity Steps

 open EWReport05.doc

1. Scroll to page 3, click to position the insertion point immediately before the **)** (close parenthesis) in the line below the heading **Top Selling Aromatherapy Products**

2. Click **Insert** on the menu bar, point to **Reference**, then click **Cross-reference** to open the Cross-reference dialog box

3. Click the **Reference type list arrow**, then click **Figure**

4. Click the **Insert reference to list arrow**, click **Only label and number**, then make sure the first caption in the list is selected
   See Figure 8-21.

5. Click **Insert**

6. With the Cross-reference dialog box still open, click immediately before the last **)** (close parenthesis) in the paragraph, after the word **page**

7. Click the **Reference type list arrow** in the Cross-reference dialog box, click **Heading**, click the **Insert reference to list arrow**, click **Page number**, click **Eco-Spa Partnership** in the For which heading list, click **Insert**, then click **Close**
   See Figure 8-22.

8. Press and hold **[Ctrl]**, position the pointer over the page number **4** in the cross-reference, then click to jump to the cross-referenced **Eco-Spa Partnership** heading

 close EWReport05.doc

If you don't want a cross-reference to be inserted as a hyperlink, click the Insert as hyperlink check box to deselect it in the Cross-reference dialog box.

Figure 8-21: Cross-reference dialog box

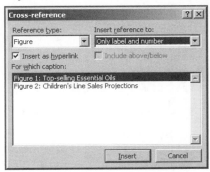

Figure 8-22: Cross-references in document

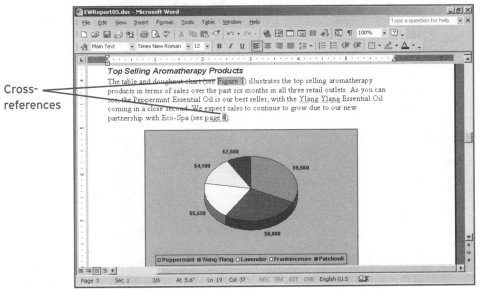

Cross-references

Skill Set 8

Formatting Documents

Add and Revise Endnotes and Footnotes

Footnotes are notes at the bottom, or foot, of a page. **Endnotes** are footnotes that are listed at the end of a document instead of at the bottom of each page. When you insert a footnote, a number or symbol appears at the insertion point, then you type your note. You can insert custom marks to denote a footnote, or you can have the footnotes numbered automatically.

Activity Steps

 open EWSummary01.doc

1. Scroll to the bottom of the page, then double-click the number **1** in the footnote that appears in the footer area to jump to the place in the document where the note reference mark is located, after **Williamsburg**

2. Position the insertion point immediately after the , (comma) after the word **Norfolk** in the first paragraph, click **Insert** on the menu bar, point to **Reference**, then click **Footnote** to open the Footnote and Endnote dialog box

3. Make sure that the **Footnotes option button** is selected and that **Bottom of page** appears in the Footnotes list box

4. Click **Insert** to insert a note reference mark next to the text and move the insertion point down to the number **1** in the footer area at the bottom of the page
See Figure 8-23.

5. Type **The Norfolk outlet is located at 1602 Federal St.**, then scroll back up so you can see that the note reference mark was added in the document and that the note reference mark next to Williamsburg automatically changed to **2**

6. Position the pointer directly over the note reference mark **1** so that the note text appears in a ScreenTip

7. With the insertion point anywhere in the current section, click **Insert** on the menu bar, point to **Reference**, click **Footnote**, click the **Number format list arrow**, click **A, B, C, ...**, then click **Apply**
See Figure 8-24.

8. Double-click directly on the note reference mark **A** to jump down to the note text at the bottom of the page, double-click **1602** in the footnote numbered A, then type **3502**

 close EWSummary01.doc

To insert a character such as an asterisk instead of a number for a note reference mark, click in the Custom mark box in the Footnote and Endnote dialog box, then type the character you want to use, or click Symbol and select the character you want to use.

Figure 8-23: Entering note text in a footnote

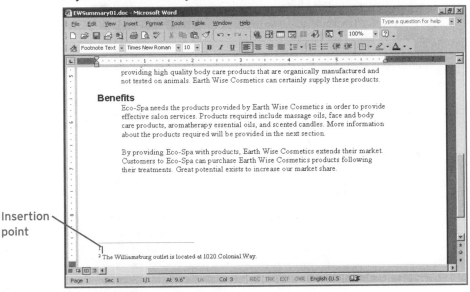

Insertion point

Figure 8-24: Note reference marks reformatted

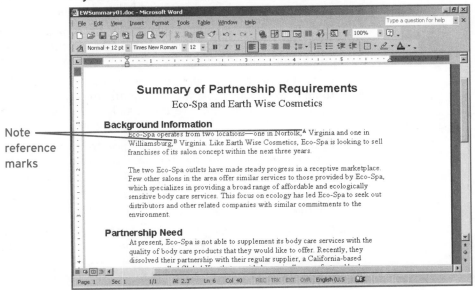

Note reference marks

Skill Set 8
Formatting Documents

Create and Manage Master Documents and Subdocuments
Create and Open Master Documents and Subdocuments

You can convert a document into a main document—the **master document**—that contains shorter documents—**subdocuments**. You can either designate a document as a master or sub document as you create it, or you can convert an existing document into a master or sub document. To work with master and sub documents, you must be in Outline view.

Activity Steps

 open EWProposal02.doc

1. Click the **Outline View button** to see the heading styles displayed as outline levels and to open the Outlining toolbar

2. Click the **Show Level list arrow** Show All Levels ▾ on the Outlining toolbar, then click **Show Level 1**

3. Select all of the text in the outline, then click the **Create Subdocument button** on the Outlining toolbar to create a subdocument from every level 1 heading as shown in Figure 8-25
   A separate file was created for each subdocument.

4. Click **File** on the menu bar, click **Save As**, type **My Master Document** in the File name box, navigate to the drive and folder where you are storing your project files, then click **Save**

5. Click the **Collapse Subdocuments button** on the Outlining toolbar to collapse the subdocuments into hyperlinks, then scroll down so you can see the links to the subdocuments
   See Figure 8-26.

6. Press and hold [Ctrl], position the pointer over the **Introduction subdocument link** so that the pointer changes to ⟨🖑⟩, then click to open that subdocument and open the Web toolbar

7. Click the **Back button** on the Web toolbar to jump back to the master document

8. Click the **Expand Subdocuments button** on the Outlining toolbar to display the content of the documents as part of the master document, click the **Print Layout View button**, right-click any toolbar, then click **Web** to close the Web toolbar

 close My Master Document.doc
Introduction.doc

Step 7
When you click the Back button to jump back to the Master document, the subdocument remains open.

Figure 8-25: Subdocuments listed in the master document

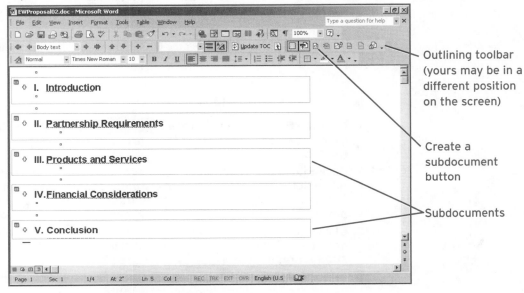

Outlining toolbar (yours may be in a different position on the screen)

Create a subdocument button

Subdocuments

Figure 8-26: Subdocuments collapsed to links

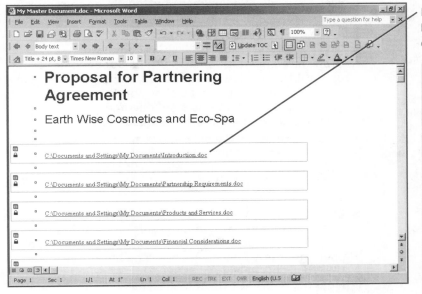

Introduction subdocument link (path to file may differ on your screen)

extra!

Printing master and sub documents

You can print subdocuments from the master document. Expand the subdocuments in the master document, click the Show Level list arrow [Show All Levels ▾] on the Outlining toolbar, then click Show All Levels. Switch to Print Layout view, then print the document as you normally would.

Skill Set 8
Formatting Documents

Create and Manage Master Documents and Subdocuments
Manage Master Documents and Subdocuments

You can add, delete, and rename subdocuments, combine several subdocuments into one subdocument, or remove a subdocument so that it becomes part of the master document again. Subdocuments must remain stored in the same folder in which they were created, so that the links in the master document will remain connected.

Activity Steps

file
open EWProposal03.doc

1. Click the **Show Level list arrow** on the Outlining toolbar, click **Show Level 1**, select all of the text in the outline, then click the **Create Subdocument button** 🗐 on the Outlining toolbar

2. Click **File** on the menu bar, click **Save As**, navigate to the location where your project files are stored, double-click the folder **EWProposal03 Folder**, select all of the text in the File name box, type **EWProposal03 Master Document**, then click **Save**

3. Click the **Introduction subdocument icon** 🗐, press and hold **[Shift]**, then click the **Partnership Requirements subdocument icon** 🗐

4. Click the **Merge Subdocument button** 🗐 on the Outlining toolbar to combine these two subdocuments into one

5. Click the **plus sign** ✛ next to **Partnership Requirements**, then click the **Split Subdocument button** 🗐 on the Outlining toolbar to split that outlining level into its own subdocument again
   A new subdocument named PartnershipRequirement1 is created. The Partnership Requirements subdocument created in step 1 still exists.

6. Drag the **Financial Considerations subdocument icon** 🗐 up until the vertical line indicator is below the **Partnership Requirements** heading, as shown in Figure 8-27, to make Financial Considerations a subdocument within the Partnership Requirements subdocument

7. With the **Financial Considerations subdocument** still selected, click the **Remove Subdocument button** 🗐 on the Outlining toolbar to remove that subdocument and combine the text into its master document (the Partnership Requirements subdocument) *See Figure 8-28.*

8. Click above the **Conclusion subdocument box** to the right of the small squares to position the insertion point there, click the **Insert Subdocument button** 🗐 on the Outlining toolbar to open the Insert Subdocument dialog box, make sure that **EWProposal03 Folder** is listed in the Look in box, click **January Meeting**, then click **Open** to insert a new subdocument

file
close EWProposal03 Master Document.doc

To rename a subdocument or to change its location, collapse the subdocuments in the master document, press and hold [Ctrl] and then click the subdocument link, then use the Save As command in the subdocument window that opens.

Figure 8-27: Repositioning a subdocument

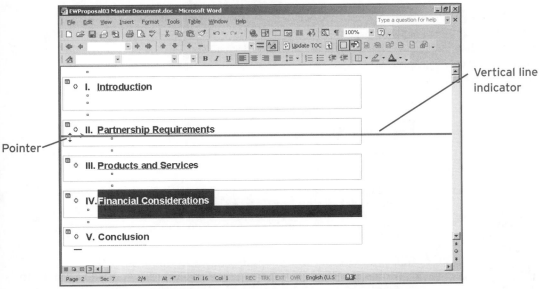

Vertical line indicator

Pointer

Figure 8-28: Subdocument removed as a subdocument and combined with its master document

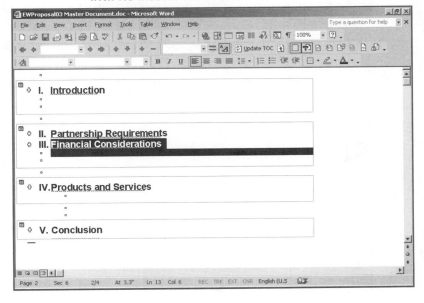

Skill Set 8
Formatting Documents

Move within Documents
Use Bookmarks

When you are navigating in a longer document, it can be time-consuming to scroll through it looking for a specific section. You can insert a **bookmark**, a named location in a document, and use it to jump to a frequently accessed part of the document. You must use a letter as the first character in a bookmark name, and the bookmark name cannot contain any spaces.

To see bookmarks in your document, click Options on the Tools menu, click the View tab, then click the Bookmarks check box to select it.

Activity Steps

 open EWMemo09.doc

1. Scroll down and position the insertion point immediately before the heading **Aromatherapy Day**

2. Click **Insert** on the menu bar, then click **Bookmark** to open the Bookmark dialog box

3. Type **AromatherapyDay** in the Bookmark name box, then click **Add**

4. Click **Insert** on the menu bar, click **Bookmark**, click **OnlineOrderingInfo** in the list of bookmarks, then click **Go To** to scroll the document to the location of the OnlineOrderingInfo bookmark
   See Figure 8-29.

5. With **OnlineOrderingInfo** still selected in the bookmark list, click **Delete** to delete that bookmark, then click **Close**

6. Click **Edit** on the menu bar, then click **Go To** to open the Go To tab in the Find and Replace dialog box

7. Click **Bookmark** in the Go to what list, click the **Enter bookmark name list arrow**, click **StockLevels**, then click **Go To**
   See Figure 8-30.

8. Click **Close**

 close EWMemo09.doc

Figure 8-29: Using the Bookmark dialog box to jump to a location in a document

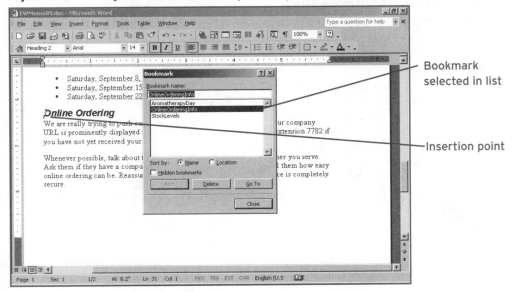

Bookmark selected in list

Insertion point

Figure 8-30: Go To tab in the Find and Replace dialog box

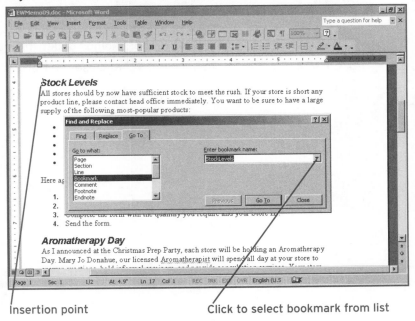

Insertion point

Click to select bookmark from list

extra!

Using the Go To command

You can use the Go To command to quickly jump to many elements in a document, not only to bookmarks. Click Edit on the menu bar, then click Go To to open the Go To tab in the Find and Replace dialog box. Select the element you want to jump to in the Go to what list, finalize your selection in the option box that appears on the right, then click Go To.

Skill Set 8
Formatting Documents

Move within Documents
Use the Document Map

The **Document Map** is a pane that lists the headings in your document in outline form. Word recognizes the headings in your document if they are formatted with the built-in heading styles. If you use other styles, Word attempts to find headings and applies an outline level to the headings it finds. If you don't use the built-in heading styles, Word may not represent your outline accurately in the Document Map. You can click headings in the Document Map to jump to that section of the document.

To change the width of the Document Map, drag the right edge of the Document Map pane.

Activity Steps

 open EWReport06.doc

1. Click the **Document Map button** 🔍 to open the Document Map
See Figure 8-31.

2. Click **Sky-rocketing Sales** in the Document Map to jump to that location in the document

3. Right-click in the Document Map, then click **Show Heading 1** in the shortcut menu

4. Click the **plus sign** ➕ next to **Eco-Spa Partnership** in the Document Map to display the headings under this heading
See Figure 8-32.

5. Click the **minus sign** next to **Eco-Spa Partnership** in the Document Map to collapse the subheadings under this heading

6. Click the **Document Map button** 🔍 to close the Document Map

 close EWReport06.doc

Figure 8-31: Document Map open

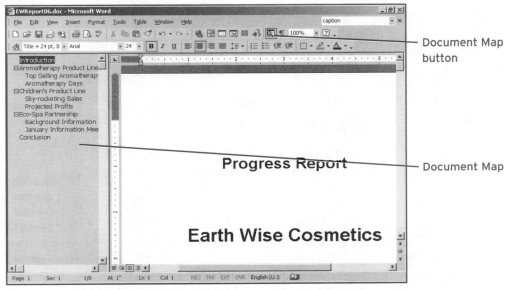

Document Map button

Document Map

Figure 8-32: Using the Document Map to see the document structure

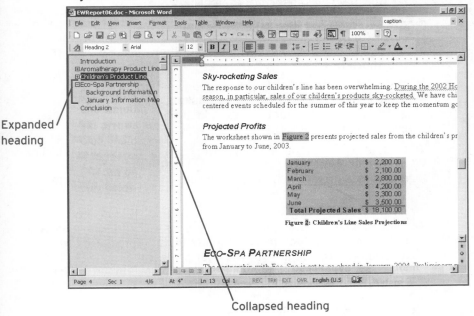

Expanded heading

Collapsed heading

Skill Set 8
Formatting Documents

Create and Modify Forms Using Various Form Controls
Create Forms

Forms are used to collect information in a structured format. To create a form, you add **form controls** that display or request information. An easy way to design a form is to start with a table. You save a form as a template, so that each user who opens the form can save their filled-in form as a document.

Activity Steps

 open EWForm01.doc

1. Right-click any toolbar, then click **Forms**

2. Click in the third column in the top row in the table, then click the **Text Form Field button** [abl] on the Forms toolbar to enter a text field form control

3. Click the **Form Field Options button** [icon] on the Forms toolbar

4. Click the **Type list arrow**, click **Current date**, click the **Date format list arrow**, then click **M/d/yy** (the fourth style in the list)
See Figure 8-33.

5. Click **OK**, press [↓], click the **Text Form Field button** [abl], click the **Form Field Options button** [icon] to verify that a regular text field was inserted, then click **OK**

6. Press [↓], click the **Drop-Down Form Field button** [icon] on the Forms toolbar to enter a drop-down list field form control, right-click the field you just inserted, then click **Properties** on the shortcut menu

7. Type **Choose from list** in the Drop-down item box, press [Spacebar], click **Add**, type **Gift Baskets**, click **Add**, type **Aromatherapy Products**, click **Add**, type **Children's Products**, click **Add**, then click **OK**

8. Click after **Yes** in the last cell in the table, press [Ctrl][Tab], click the **Check Box Form Field button** [icon] on the Forms toolbar, press [↓], press [Ctrl][Tab], then click the **Check Box Form Field button** [icon]
See Figure 8-34.

9. Click **File** on the menu bar, click **Save As**, click the **Save as type list arrow**, click **Document Template (*.dot)**, navigate to the location where you are storing your project files, select all of the text in the File name box, type **My Form Template**, click **Save**, then click the **Close button** [×] on the Forms toolbar

 close My Form Template.dot

If you want to print a form, click the Print Preview button to see how it will look when printed. Note that only the first item in a drop-down list will print.

Figure 8-33: Adding a current date field

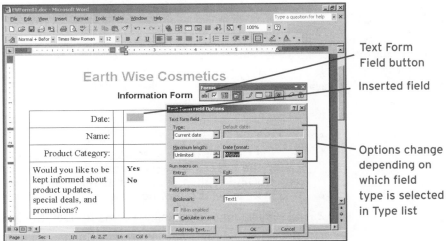

Text Form
Field button

Inserted field

Options change
depending on
which field
type is selected
in Type list

Figure 8-34: Completed form

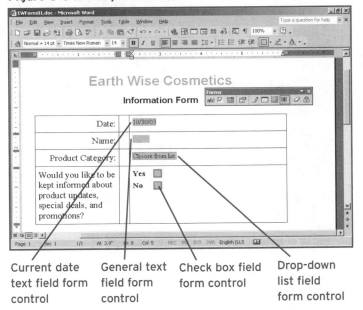

Current date
text field form
control

General text
field form
control

Check box field
form control

Drop-down
list field
form control

Skill Set 8
Formatting Documents

Create and Modify Forms Using Various Form Controls
Modify Forms

As with other types of Word documents, you can modify a form once you have created it. You can add or delete field form controls, or you can modify the properties of existing controls. You can also change the static text in the form. You must open the form template as a template, not as a new document to make and save changes to it.

You can change the format of the form field results by selecting the entire field and using font formatting commands.

Activity Steps

1. Click the **Open button** 📂 to open the Open dialog box, navigate to the folder where your project files are stored, click **EWForm02.dot**, then click **Open** to open the template as a template instead of as a new document

2. Right-click any toolbar, click **Forms** to open the Forms toolbar

3. Click anywhere in the row in the table containing **Name**, click **Table** on the menu bar, point to **Insert**, then click **Rows Below**

4. Click in the first cell in the newly inserted row, type **E-mail Address:**, then press **[Tab]** twice

5. Click the **Text Form Field button** 🔲 on the Forms toolbar to insert a regular text form field

6. Right-click the **check box field** after **Yes**, click **Properties** on the shortcut menu, click the **Checked option button** under Default value
   See Figure 8-35.

7. Click **OK**, click anywhere in the document window to deselect the field, then click the **Form Field Shading button** to turn shading off in the form fields
   See Figure 8-36.

8. Right-click any toolbar, then click **Forms** to close the Forms toolbar

 close EWForm02.dot

Figure 8-35: Check Box Form Field Options dialog box

Figure 8-36: Modified form

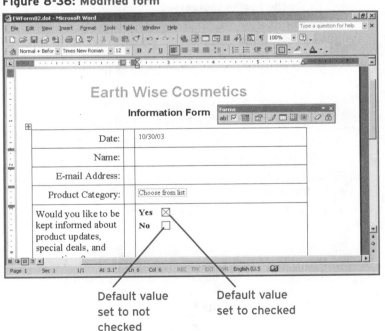

Default value set to not checked

Default value set to checked

extra!

Preparing a form to be used on the Web

You prepare a form to be used on the Web in essentially the same manner as you do for use in Word, but instead of creating controls by using commands on the Forms toolbar, you use commands on the Web Tools toolbar. The controls you insert appear between Top and Bottom of Form boundaries. To change the properties of a control, you click the Properties button on the Web Tools toolbar to open the Properties dialog box. You can change the values of each property individually by selecting or typing a new value in the box next to the property you want to change. The Web Tools toolbar includes a Submit button and a Submit with Image button. You should always include one of these buttons so that the person who fills out your form on the Web has a means for sending the completed form back to you.

Skill Set 8
Formatting Documents

Create Forms and Prepare Forms for Distribution
Protect Forms and Prepare for Distribution

You cannot enter any information into form fields until you protect the form. Conversely, you cannot change the field properties or the form itself when a form is protected. You can protect the form with a password before you distribute it, so that users cannot turn protection off and change the form structure. Note that passwords are case sensitive, so that *PASSWORD* is not the same as *password* or *Password*. Once you have protected a form, it is ready to be distributed.

Activity Steps

1. Open a new, blank document, click the **Open button**, navigate to the folder where your project files are stored, click **EWForm03.dot**, click **Open**, right-click any toolbar, click **Forms** to open the Forms toolbar, then click the **Protect Form button** on the Forms toolbar
   See Figure 8-37.

2. Type **Graham Long** in the Name form field, press **[Tab]** to move to the next unprotected field, then type **glong@earthwisecosmetics.com** in the E-mail Address form field

3. Press **[Tab]**, click the **Choose from list list arrow**, then click **Children's Products** as shown in Figure 8-38

4. Click the **No check box** to select it, then click the **Yes check box** to deselect it

5. Click in the **Name: cell** to see the insertion point jump to the Name form field because the form is protected

6. Click the **Protect Form button** to unprotect the form so you can set a password

7. Click **Tools** on the menu bar, click **Protect Document** to open the Protect Document dialog box, click the **Forms option button** if necessary, type **password** (all lowercase) in the Password (optional) box, click **OK**, type **password** in the Reenter password to open box, then click **OK**

8. Click the **Protect Form button** on the Forms toolbar to see that protection cannot be turned off without entering the password, click **Cancel** in the Unprotect Document dialog box, then click the **Close button** on the Forms toolbar

Step 7
If the form is in a separate section in the document, click Sections in the Protect Document dialog box, then click the form's section number.

close EWForm03.dot

Figure 8-37: Protected form

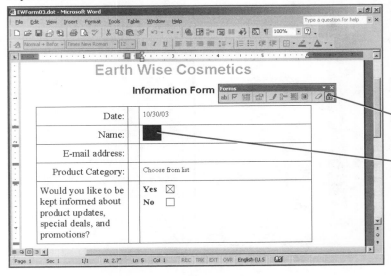

Protect Form button

First available field is selected automatically

Figure 8-38: Filling out a form

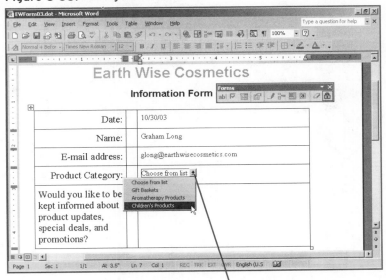

Drop-down list arrow becomes available when field is selected in protected form

extra!

Add Help information to form fields

You can add instructions for filling in the required information in a field. In the Options dialog box that opens when you modify a form field's properties, click Add Help Text to open the Form Field Help Text dialog box. Text you add on the Status Bar tab will appear in the document window status bar when the field is selected in the protected form. Text you add on the Help Key (F1) tab will appear when the user presses [F1] when a field is selected in a protected form.

Skill Set 8
Formatting Documents

Target Your Skills

 EWMemo11.doc

1 Create the document shown in Figure 8-39 by formatting the Aromatherapy Day flyer as a separate section that starts on a new page. Apply a new character style named Headline to the Aromatherapy Day title, then apply a new paragraph style named Flyer Body to the body text in the flyer. Verify the formats used when you are finished.

Figure 8-39

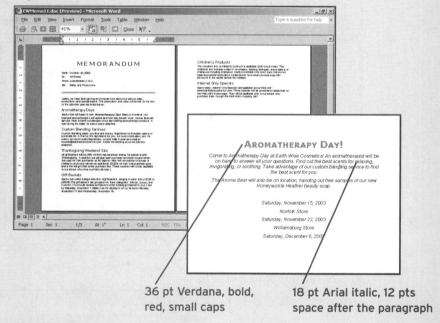

36 pt Verdana, bold, red, small caps

18 pt Arial italic, 12 pts space after the paragraph

2 Create the form shown in Figure 8-40. Insert the same drop-down list in each of the Scent fields. Insert Date type text fields for the Pickup date and Pickup time fields. Format the Pickup date field as **MMMM d, yyyy,** and format the Pickup time field as **HH:mm.** Save the form as a template named **Custom Blend Form.dot.** (*Hint:* Don't forget to lock the form.)

Figure 8-40

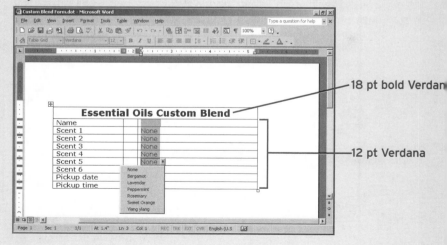

18 pt bold Verdana

12 pt Verdana

Skill List

1. Use Excel data in tables
2. Perform calculations in Word tables

Tables are an easy way to organize data in rows and columns in a document. If you want to include data that already exists in an Excel workbook, you can copy and paste the data from an Excel worksheet directly into a Word table. You can link the data so that if the Excel worksheet changes, the table will update automatically. If you want to be able to modify the worksheet directly from within the Word document, you can embed the worksheet, and Excel will open when you double-click the embedded worksheet object. You can also use simple formulas to perform calculations within a table.

If the structure of a table needs to be modified, you can merge or split cells. For example, you can merge two or more cells to create one cell that spans the columns if a table has a heading that spans several columns. If you need to create two or more cells from one existing cell, you can split the cell. Tables are a versatile way to display and manipulate data in columns and rows.

Skill Set 9
Customizing Tables

Use Excel Data in Tables
Linking Excel Data Using the Paste Command

You can copy data from an Excel worksheet (the **source file**), and then paste it into a Word document (the **destination file**). When you paste the data, the Paste Options button appears so that you can choose whether the data will be pasted or linked and the format of the data. When you **link** data, the data is represented in the destination file as fields. The fields are updated automatically when the data in the source file changes.

Activity Steps

 open GCMemo08.doc

1. Click the **Start button** on the taskbar, point to **Programs,** click **Microsoft Excel**, click the **More workbooks link** in the New Workbook task pane, navigate to the location where your project files are stored, click **GCProjections01.xls**, then click **Open**

2. Click the **Word program button** on the taskbar, right-click an empty part of the taskbar, then click **Tile Windows Vertically** Note that all open windows tile when you execute this command, so close all windows except the two used in this activity.

3. Click in the **GCProjections01.xls window**, drag to select **cells A4:C11**, then click the **Copy button** in the Excel window

4. Click in the **GCMemo08.doc window**, press **[Ctrl][End]**, then click the **Paste button** on the Word Standard toolbar to insert the data with the source formatting (the default option)

tip

If the linked data in the destination file does not update when you make a change in the source file, right-click the linked data, then click Update Link on the shortcut menu.

5. Click the **Paste Options button** below the pasted data, then click **Match Destination Table Style and Link to Excel** to link the Excel data to the document in the default Word table style *See Figure 9-1.*

6. Right-click anywhere in the table, point to **Linked Worksheet Object** on the shortcut menu, then click **Edit Link** to jump to the linked data in the source file

7. Click the **Maximize button** in the GCProjections01.xls window if necessary, click **cell B9**, type **45**, then press **[Enter]** to accept that entry and update the link in the Word window *See Figure 9-2.*

8. Click the **Save** button on the Excel toolbar to save the changed data, then click the Close button in the Excel program window

 close GCMemo08.doc

Figure 9-1: Excel data linked to a new Word table

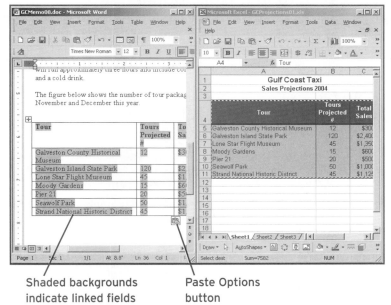

Shaded backgrounds
indicate linked fields

Paste Options
button

Figure 9-2: Linked data automatically updated in document

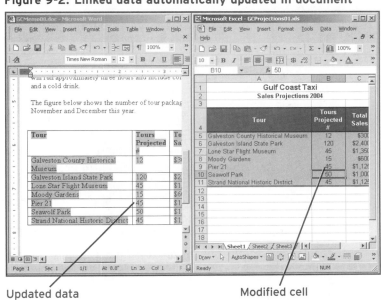

Updated data
in linked table

Modified cell
in worksheet

extra!

Using the Links dialog box

To open the Links dialog box, right-click the linked data, point to Linked Worksheet Object, then click Links; or click anywhere in the document, click Edit on the menu bar, then click Links. The default is for links to be updated automatically, but you can change this if you want. First, make sure the link is selected in the Source file list, then click the Manual update option button. If you move the source file to a new location, you can click Change Source, then navigate to the new location of the source file and click the source filename. You can also click the Locked check box to lock a link and prevent it from updating when the source data changes.

Skill Set 9

Customizing Tables

Use Excel Data in Tables
Embedding Excel Data in a Word Document

When you **embed** data, a copy of the source data becomes part of the destination file, and it contains a link to the source program. To edit embedded data, double-click the embedded object. The source program and the embedded file open in a new window. The original source file does not change when you edit embedded data.

Activity Steps

 open GCMemo09.doc

1. Position the insertion point between the two body paragraphs, click **Insert** on the menu bar, click **Object** to open the Object dialog box, then click the **Create from File tab**

2. Click **Browse**, navigate to the location where your project files are stored, click **GCSales01.xls**, then click **Insert**
   See Figure 9-3.

3. Click **OK** to embed a copy of the GCSales01 workbook

4. Double-click the **embedded worksheet object** to open the workbook in an Excel window in the document, click the **Next Sheet button** ▶ to the left of the worksheet tabs, click the **Oct & Nov Sales sheet tab**, click **cell C6**, type **150**, then press **[Enter]**
   See Figure 9-4.

5. Drag the **bottom middle sizing handle** up to just below row 9, then click anywhere in the document window outside the object

6. Click the **Start button** [Start] on the taskbar, point to **Programs**, click **Microsoft Excel**, click the **More workbooks link** in the task pane, navigate to the location where your project files are stored, click **GCSales01.xls**, click **Open** to open the original GCSales01 workbook file, then click the **Oct & Nov Sales sheet tab** and notice that the value in cell C6 has not changed

7. Click the **Dec & Jan Projections sheet tab**, select **cells A1:C12**, click the **Copy button** [copy], click the **Word program button** on the taskbar, position the insertion point below the last paragraph, click **Edit** on the menu bar, then click **Paste Special**

8. Click **Microsoft Excel Worksheet Object** in the list, make sure the **Paste option button** is selected, then click **OK**

9. Click the **Excel program button** on the taskbar, then click the **Close button** ✕ in the Excel program title bar

 close GCMemo09.doc

Step 1
To embed a new Excel worksheet in a document, click the Insert Microsoft Excel Worksheet button, or click the Create New tab in the Object dialog box, then click Microsoft Excel Object in the Object type list.

Figure 9-3: Object dialog box ready to embed existing data

Click to insert a new file

Path name on your screen may differ

Click to link file instead of embed it

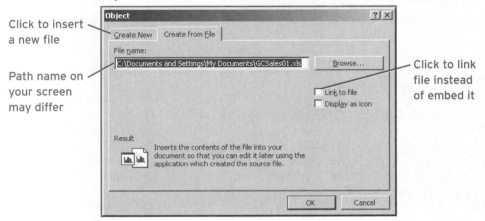

Figure 9-4: Embedded data's source program opened in window

Next Sheet button

Selected sheet tab

Edited value

Sizing handle

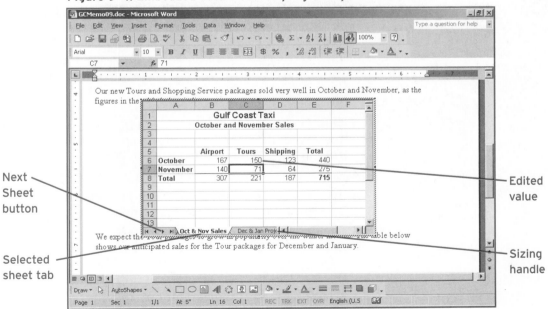

Skill Set 9

Customizing Tables

Perform Calculations in Word Tables
Use Formulas in Tables

You can use formulas in a Word table to perform simple calculations. When you click the AutoSum button on the Tables and Borders toolbar, it automatically checks for data in the cells above; if the cells above do not contain any data, it checks in the cells to the left. It then adds the data and displays the total. Every cell must contain data, so if a cell is empty, you must enter a zero in it. You can insert other formulas by using the Formula dialog box. Formulas always begin with an equal sign. When you insert a formula, you refer to the table cells in the same manner as in a Microsoft Graph data sheet or an Excel worksheet: the columns are labeled A, B, C, D, etc., and the rows are labeled 1, 2, 3, 4, etc., so the first cell—the cell in the upper-left corner—is cell A1, the cell just below it is cell A2, and the cell just to the right of the first cell is cell B1. When a formula is calculated, the result is displayed as a field.

Activity Steps

 open GCMemo10.doc

1. Right-click any toolbar, then click **Tables and Borders** if necessary to display the Tables and Borders toolbar

2. Scroll down so you can see the first table, click in the cell to the right of **Average Cost** (cell B9), then click the **AutoSum button** Σ on the Tables and Borders toolbar to insert a formula that adds the values in the cells above the current cell
   See Figure 9-5.

3. With the insertion point still in cell B9 (the cell to the right of the **Average Cost** cell), click **Table** on the menu bar, then click **Formula** to open the Formula dialog box

4. Select the contents of the Formula box, then press **[Delete]**

5. Type = (equal sign), click the **Paste function list arrow**, then click **AVERAGE** to insert the Average function in the Formula box

6. Type **b2:b8** between the parentheses in the Formula box to calculate the average of the values in cells B2 through B8, inclusive (in other words, the cells directly above the current cell)
   See Figure 9-6.

7. Click **OK** to insert the new formula into the cell and calculate the average cost

8. Click **View** on the menu bar, point to **Toolbars**, then click **Tables and Borders** to close the Tables and Borders toolbar

 close GCMemo10.doc

It is not necessary to click the AutoSum button if you know you want to insert a different formula.

Figure 9-5: Adding numbers using the AutoSum button

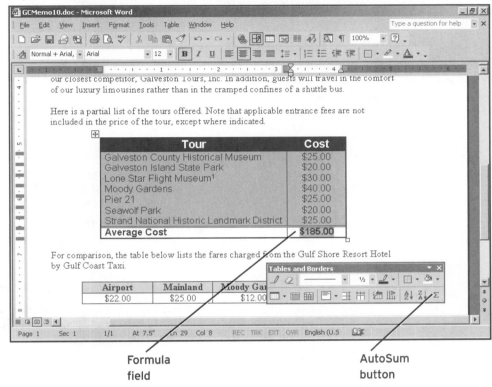

Formula
field

AutoSum
button

Figure 9-6: Formula dialog box

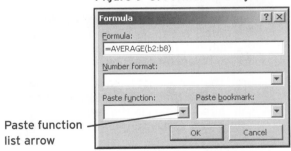

Paste function
list arrow

Skill Set 9
Customizing Tables

Perform Calculations in Word Tables
Merge and Split Table Cells

Some tables are more complex than others. You might, for example, need to combine cells to create a table with secondary headings. To do this, you can use the Merge Cells command. Conversely, you may need to split a cell into two or more cells. This is easy to do with the Split Cells command. When you split cells, you may need to reformat the table—or at least the cells you just split—to adjust the widths of the new cells.

Step 7
If you can't get the borders to align, press and hold [Alt] while you are dragging.

Activity Steps

 open GCAnnouncement05.doc

1. Right-click any toolbar, click **Tables and Borders** if necessary to display the Tables and Borders toolbar, scroll down so that you can see the table, then select the three cells in the **Malls row**

2. Click the **Merge Cells button** 🔳 on the Tables and Borders toolbar to merge the three cells into one cell, then click anywhere in the document to deselect the cells
See Figure 9-7.

3. Merge the cells in the **Factory Outlets** and **Outdoor Markets rows**

4. Click in the top row in the table, then click the **Split Cells button** 🔳 on the Tables and Borders toolbar to open the Split Cells dialog box

5. Click the **Number of columns up arrow** so that it changes to **3**, then click **OK**

6. Press [Delete], type **Destination**, press [Tab], type **Average Time**, press [Tab], then type **Average Fare**

7. Position the pointer over the border between **Destination** and **Average Time** so that it changes to ⁺‖⁺, then drag the border to the right, so that the border aligns with the border between the first and second columns in the table as shown in Figure 9-8

8. Drag the border between **Average Time** and **Average Fare** to the right so that it aligns with the border between the second and third columns in the table, right-click any toolbar, then click **Tables and Borders** to close the Tables and Borders toolbar

 close GCAnnouncement05.doc

Figure 9-7: Cells merged in table

Merged cells

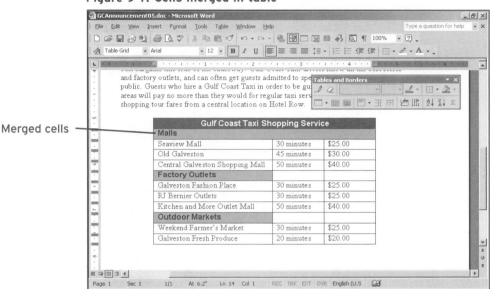

Figure 9-8: Table with merged and split cells

Cell split into three cells

Merged cells

Pointer

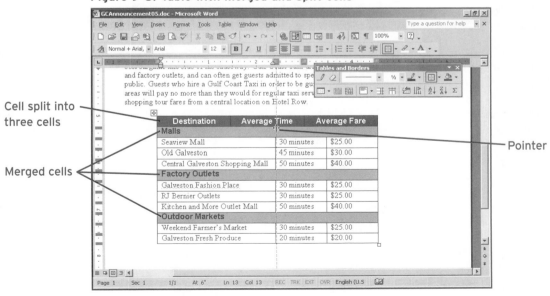

Skill Set 9
Customizing Tables

Target Your Skills

 GCMemo11.doc

1 Create the finished document shown in Figure 9-9. First paste the data from the Excel worksheet **GCChart01.xls** as a link formatted to match the destination file. Then change both the **Driver Courtesy** and **Cost** numbers to **2** in the Excel workbook. Save the revised workbook, then close it. In the document, modify the table as shown in Figure 9-9.

Figure 9-9

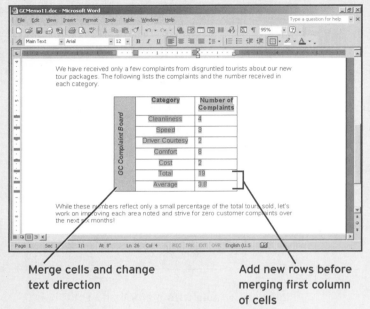

Merge cells and change text direction

Add new rows before merging first column of cells

 GCBrochure07.doc

2 Use Figure 9-10 as a guide for creating the table shown. Use the merge and Split Cells commands.

Figure 9-10

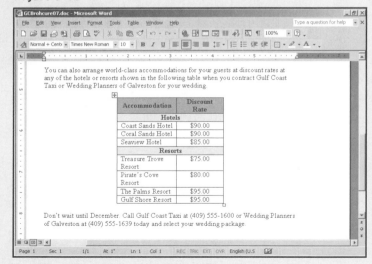

Skill Set 10
Creating and Modifying Graphics

Skill List

1. Create, modify, and position graphics
2. Create and modify charts using data from other applications
3. Align text and graphics

In this skill set, you will learn how to create and add graphics to your documents. You will use a variety of tools on the Drawing toolbar to draw and color graphics. To avoid re-creating existing data, you will also learn how to import data from other programs to a Microsoft Graph chart. Finally, you will learn advanced methods for positioning graphics in a document.

Skill Set 10
Creating and Modifying Graphics

Create, Modify, and Position Graphics
Create and Insert Graphics in a Document

You use the tools on the Drawing toolbar to create and insert graphics into a document. When you click a button on the Drawing toolbar, the drawing canvas appears. The **drawing canvas** is the name for the area on which you draw shapes. When you click a drawing tool on the Drawing toolbar, the pointer changes to ╫ and you can drag it to draw the shape you selected. After you draw a shape, **sizing handles**, small white circles, appear around the edge of the drawn object. You can drag a sizing handle to resize the object. You can also drag entire objects to reposition them.

To draw a freeform shape, click the AutoShapes button, point to Lines, then click Curve to draw curved line segments, click Freeform to draw curved or straight line segments, or click Scribble to use the pointer like a pencil.

Activity Steps

1. Create a new, blank document, then click the **Drawing button** 🖌 to open the Drawing toolbar, if necessary

2. Click the **Rectangle button** ▢ on the Drawing toolbar
   Note that the drawing canvas appears.

3. Position the ╫ pointer on the drawing canvas at approximately the intersection of the ½" marks on the rulers, then drag to create a rectangle about 4" wide and ⅛" high (refer to Figure 10-1)

4. Click the **AutoShapes button** AutoShapes ▾ on the Drawing toolbar, point to **Flowchart** on the menu, then click the **Flowchart: Manual Input button** ▱ (third row, third column)

5. Drag below the rectangle shape to create a shape approximately 1" wide and ¼" long
   See Figure 10-1.

6. With the second drawn shape still selected, click the **Fill Color list arrow** 🎨▾ on the Drawing toolbar, then click the **Sea Green box** (third row, fourth column)

7. Press and hold [Alt] so that you can position the graphic exactly, then drag the **second shape** on top of the right end of the rectangle shape, as shown in Figure 10-2, to create an oar shape

8. Click in a blank area of the document outside of the drawing canvas to deselect the object and hide the drawing canvas

 close file

Figure 10-1: Rectangle shape drawn on the drawing canvas

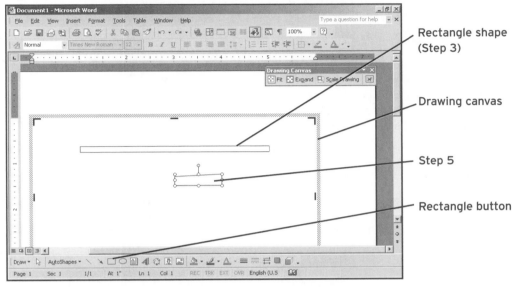

Rectangle shape (Step 3)

Drawing canvas

Step 5

Rectangle button

Figure 10-2: Oar shape created by combining two drawn shapes

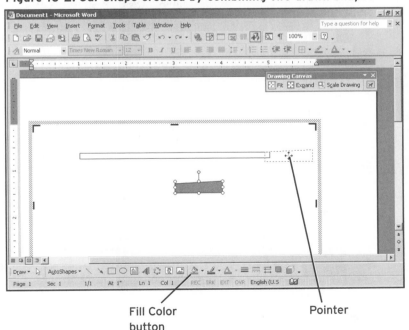

Fill Color button

Pointer

extra!

Understanding the drawing grid

When you position an object in a document, it snaps to an invisible grid. This is useful when you need to align objects, but it can be troublesome if you try to position an object and it keeps snapping to the grid. To override the grid, press and hold [Alt] while you drag the object you want to position.

Skill Set 10
Creating and Modifying Graphics

Create, Modify, and Position Graphics
Modify Graphics in a Document

You can modify the graphics that you create in a document. You can draw one object on top of another, and then rearrange the order of the objects so that an object that appeared to be behind another object can be brought forward and appear to be in front. You can group objects together so they are treated as a unit, you can rotate them, and you can copy and paste or reposition them. When you place shapes on the drawing canvas, you can move and resize the shapes as a single unit by dragging the white circle sizing handles on the drawing canvas. You can also resize the drawing canvas around an object.

Step 7
If the Drawing Canvas toolbar is not visible, right-click on the edge of the drawing canvas, then click Show Drawing Canvas Toolbar on the shortcut menu.

Activity Steps

 open CCLogo01.doc

1. Click the **handle section** of the oar shape, drag it approximately ½" to the left, then click the **Undo button** 🔙

2. With the handle section still selected, click the **Draw button** `Draw ▾` on the Drawing toolbar, point to **Order**, then click **Send to Back** to send the handle drawn object behind the blade object

3. Press and hold **[Shift]**, click the **blade section** of the oar shape to select both drawn objects, click the **Draw button** `Draw ▾` on the Drawing toolbar, then click **Group** to combine the two shapes into a single object

4. Position the pointer over the **rotate handle** so that it changes to 🔄, then drag the handle to the left so that the dotted outline of the grouped object rotates approximately 45 degrees
See Figure 10-3.

5. With the object still selected, click the **Copy button** 📋, then click the **Paste button** 📋

6. Click the **Draw button** `Draw ▾` on the Drawing toolbar, point to **Rotate or Flip**, click **Flip Horizontal**, then press **[⬆]** twice to cross the oars approximately at their centers

7. Click the **Fit Drawing to Contents button** 🔲 on the Drawing Canvas toolbar to shrink the drawing canvas so it fits exactly around the object

8. Click the **Scale Drawing button** 🔲 on the Drawing Canvas toolbar, position the pointer over the **lower-right sizing handle** of the drawing canvas so that the pointer changes to ↘, then drag up and to the left so that the object is approximately 2" wide, as shown in Figure 10-4

 close CCLogo01.doc

Figure 10-3: Object rotated 45 degrees

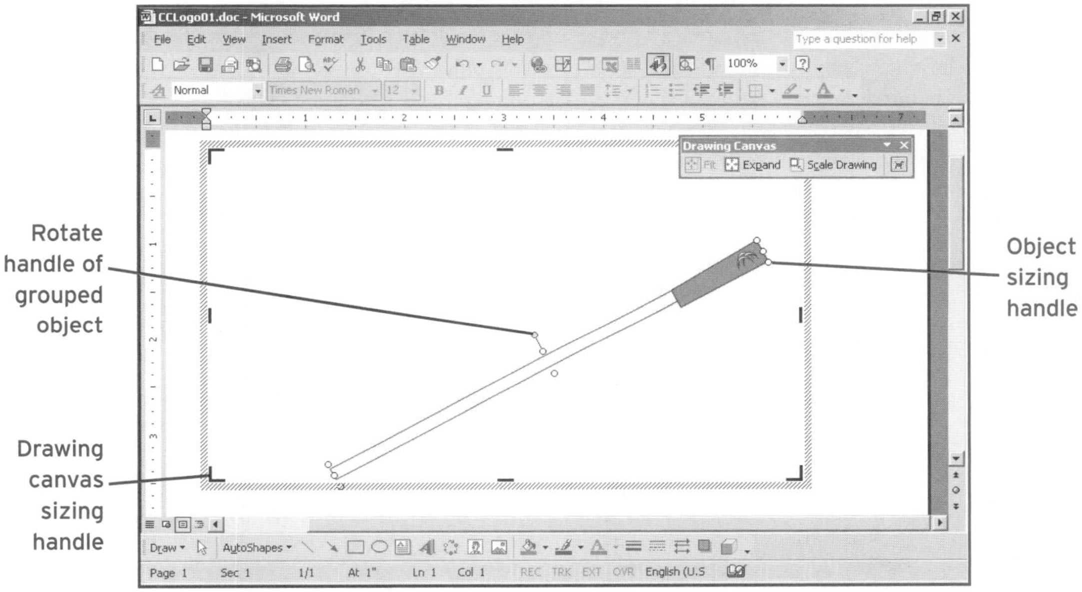

Rotate handle of grouped object

Object sizing handle

Drawing canvas sizing handle

Figure 10-4: Drawing canvas tight around the object

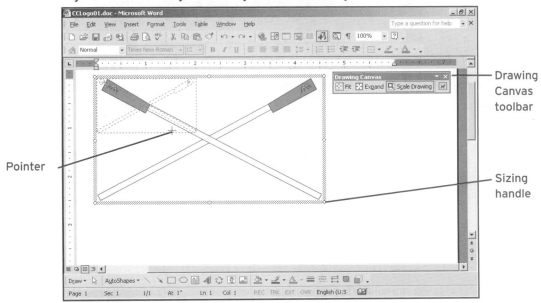

Drawing Canvas toolbar

Pointer

Sizing handle

Skill Set 10
Creating and Modifying Graphics

Create, Modify, and Position Graphics
Add Text to Graphics in a Document

You can add text to graphics or other objects. To do this, you use the Text Box button on the Drawing toolbar to create a text object. When you add a text box, the border of the text box is composed of slanted lines, which indicates that the text box is ready to accept any text you type. If you want to format the entire text box, you select the entire object by clicking the slanted line border so that it changes to a border composed of dots. When the border is the dotted line border, all formatting commands apply to the entire object.

To add text to an AutoShape object quickly, right-click the object, then click Add Text on the shortcut menu.

Activity Steps

 open CCDrawing01.doc

1. Click the **Text Box button** 🖼 on the Drawing toolbar

2. Scroll down below the new drawing canvas so you can see the T-shirt graphic

3. Position the pointer inside the T-shirt just under the left sleeve, then drag down and to the right to create a text box approximately ½" high and 1 ½" wide
   See Figure 10-5.

4. Type **Property of CCC Crew**

5. Click the **slanted line border** of the text box so that it changes to a dotted line border, click the **Font list arrow** Times New Roman, click **Arial**, click the **Font Size list arrow** 12, click **9**, then click the **Bold button** B

6. With the entire text object still selected, click the **Line Color list arrow** ✏ on the Drawing toolbar, then click **No Line** on the pop-up menu

7. Click in a blank area of the document to deselect the text object and hide the drawing canvas
   See Figure 10-6.

 close CCDrawing01.doc

Figure 10-5: Creating a text box in a drawn object

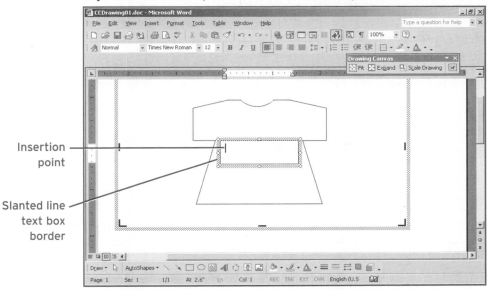

Insertion point

Slanted line text box border

Figure 10-6: Formatted text box

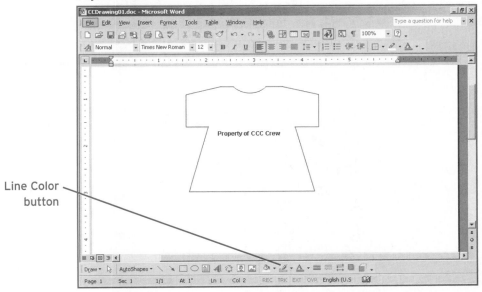

Line Color button

Skill Set 10
Creating and Modifying Graphics

Create, Modify, and Position Graphics
Position Graphics in a Document

The default position for graphics in a document is **inline** with the text; that is, objects are positioned at the insertion point and moved with the text around them. They are part of the paragraph in which they are positioned. This is usually the easiest way to work with graphics. To reposition an inline graphic, you drag it by its border or by the border of the drawing canvas. A vertical line follows the pointer to indicate where the inline graphic will be positioned when you release the mouse button.

To add color behind a drawn object, select the drawing canvas, click the Fill Color list arrow on the Drawing toolbar, then select a color.

Activity Steps

 open CCLetterhead01.doc

1. Click the **Show/Hide ¶ button** to display paragraph marks, if necessary

2. Click the graphic to select it, then drag it by the drawing canvas border to position it immediately in front of the word **Culver** in the first line in the document, as shown in Figure 10-7

3. Click anywhere in the document to deselect the graphic, then click between the inline graphic and the word **Culver** to position the insertion point

4. Press **[Enter]** twice

5. Drag to select the graphic, the blank paragraph below the graphic, and all four lines of the address

6. Click the **Center button** to center the graphic and the text on the page
   See Figure 10-8.

7. Click in a blank area of the document to deselect the text and the object, then click the **Show/Hide ¶ button** to hide paragraph marks

 close CCLetterhead01.doc

Figure 10-7: Inline graphic and text selected

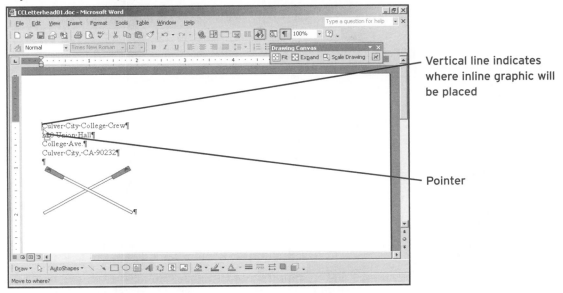

Vertical line indicates where inline graphic will be placed

Pointer

Figure 10-8: Inline graphic and text centered on page

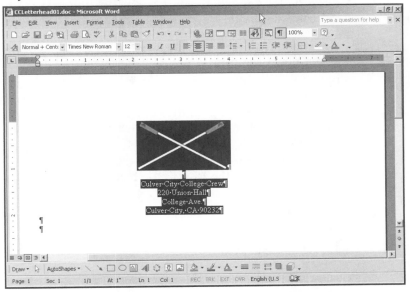

extra!

Editing wrap points
You can change the way text wraps around the shape of an object by editing its wrap points. **Wrap points** are the vertexes of the object, the point where two line segments meet or the highest point in a curved line. Select the drawing canvas, click the Text Wrapping button on the Drawing Canvas toolbar, then click Edit Wrap Points to display the vertexes. Drag any wrap point to change the invisible border around which the text wraps.

Skill Set 10

Creating and Modifying Graphics

Create and Modify Charts Using Data from Other Applications

If you want to include a chart in a document, and the data already exists in an Excel worksheet or in an Access table, you can import the data and then use Graph to display the chart. You can then change the data or the chart to suit your needs.

Activity Steps

 open CCMemo02.doc

1. Press [Ctrl][End], click **Insert** on the menu bar, click **Object** to open the Object dialog box, scroll down and click **Microsoft Graph Chart** in the Object type list, then click **OK**

2. Click the **top-left gray box** in the datasheet to select all of the cells in the datasheet as shown in Figure 10-9, then click the **Import File button** to open the Import File dialog box

3. Navigate to the location where your project files are stored, click **CCBudget01.xls**, then click **Open**

4. In the Import Data Options dialog box that opens, make sure **Budget** is selected in the list of worksheets, make sure the **Overwrite existing cells check box** is selected, then click **OK**

5. Click the **By Column button** to switch the data plotted on the chart so that it represents the data in the data sheet's columns, not its rows, click the **Close button** in the datasheet, then drag the lower-right sizing handle of the chart object down and over to the right margin of the document

6. Right-click one of the labels on the x-axis, click **Format Axis** on the shortcut menu to open the Format Axis dialog box, click the **Font tab**, click **Regular** in the Font style list, click **8** in the Size list if necessary, then click **OK** to resize the x-axis labels so that all six are visible

7. Click **Chart** on the menu bar, click **Chart Options**, click the **Titles tab**, click in the **Chart title box**, type **Crew Budget**, then click **OK**

8. Click in a blank area of the document to exit Graph
   See Figure 10-10.

 close CCMemo02.doc

Step 2
It is not always necessary to select all the existing cells before importing data, because the default is for the data you import to start at the upper-left corner of the datasheet.

Figure 10-9: All the cells in the datasheet selected

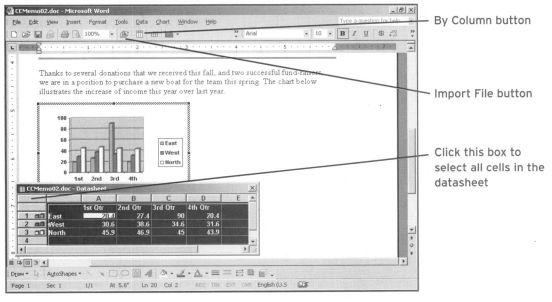

By Column button

Import File button

Click this box to select all cells in the datasheet

Figure 10-10: Chart created with imported data

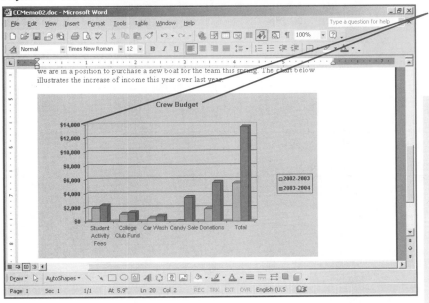

Font sizes may vary depending on how you resized the chart

extra!

Using Access data in a chart

You can also use data from an Access table in a chart. Open the table in Access, copy the table to the clipboard, then paste the data into the Graph datasheet. The chart will update as soon as you paste the new data.

Skill Set 10
Creating and Modifying Graphics

Align Text and Graphics

You can choose to have a drawn object or a graphic **float** in the document so that you can position it on the page by dragging it. If you choose to make an object a floating object, you need to select the way you want the text to wrap around the object. See Table 10-1 for a list of wrapping styles available.

Activity Steps

 open CCNewsletter01.doc

1. Click the **inline graphic** to select it, then drag it by the edge of the drawing canvas to just before the word **News** in the heading **Alumni News**, using the vertical line that follows the pointer to identify exactly where the graphic will be positioned

2. With the drawing canvas still visible, click the **Text Wrapping button** 🖾 on the Drawing Canvas toolbar, then click **Square**

3. Drag the **floating graphic** by the drawing canvas border to the middle of the page, using the dotted outline of the graphic to help position it as shown in Figure 10-11
   Note that the text wraps around the square edge of the drawing canvas.

4. With the graphic still selected, click the **Text Wrapping button** 🖾 on the Drawing Canvas toolbar, click **Tight** to wrap the text around the object's shape, then click in a blank area of the document
   See Figure 10-12.

5. Click the **graphic** to select it and display the drawing canvas, click the edge of the drawing canvas to select it, click **Format** on the menu bar, click **Drawing Canvas**, then click the **Layout tab**

6. Click **Advanced** on the Layout tab, then click the **Text Wrapping tab**

7. Click the **Right only option button**, click **OK**, then click **OK** again

 close CCNewsletter01.doc

> **tip**
>
> **Step 1**
> When you drag the graphic, make sure you drag the edge of the drawing canvas, not the graphic itself.

Table 10-1: Wrapping styles for floating objects

wrapping style	description
Square	text wraps around the object in a square
Tight	text wraps around the object in the shape of the object, but does not fill in any white space within the object itself
Behind Text	text does not wrap around the object at all; instead the object is placed behind the text
In Front of Text	text does not wrap around the object at all; instead the object is placed on top of the text
Top and Bottom	text wraps around the top and bottom of the object, but does not wrap on the sides
Through	text wraps around the object in the shape of the object, but also fills in any white space in the object itself

Figure 10-11: Floating graphic with text wrapped square around it

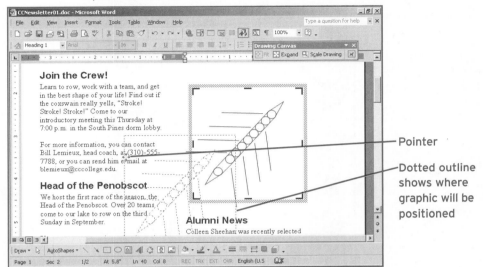

Pointer

Dotted outline shows where graphic will be positioned

Figure 10-12: Floating graphic with text wrapped tight only on the right

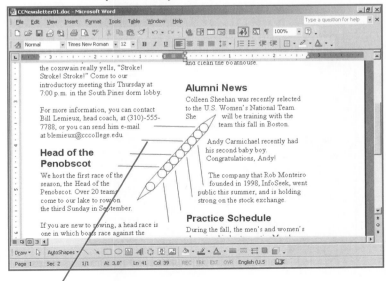

Text wraps around shape of graphic

extra!

Additional layout options

On the Text Wrapping tab in the Advanced Layout dialog box, you can customize the distance that is maintained between the graphic and the text that wraps around it. A distance of 0" means that no text will appear on that side of the graphic. You can also precisely adjust the position of the graphic by specifying exactly where it will go on the page. Click the Picture Position tab in the Advanced Layout dialog box, then specify the horizontal and vertical positions.

Skill Set 10
Creating and Modifying Graphics

Target Your Skills

 CCAnnouncement03.doc

1 Use Figure 10-13 as a guide for creating and positioning the graphic shown. Use buttons on the AutoShapes menus to create the two graphics. (*Hint*: To change the color of the heart AutoShape, click the Fill Color list arrow, click More Colors, then select a very light gray.)

Figure 10-13

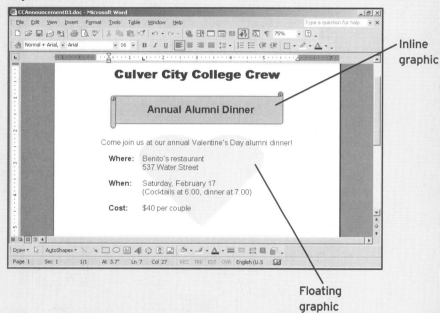

Inline graphic

Floating graphic

 CCMemo03.doc

2 Create the document shown in Figure 10-14. To create the chart, import the Expenses worksheet of the Excel file **CCExpenses01.xls**. Change the chart type to a pie chart, then plot the data series by columns. To add the values as data labels, right-click a pie slide, click Format Data Series, click the Data Labels tab, then click the Value check box. To change the font size of the data labels, right click one, click Format Data Labels, then click the Font tab.

Figure 10-14

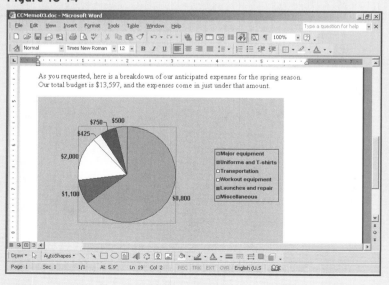

Skill List

1. Create, edit, and run macros
2. Customize menus and toolbars

You can customize Word in several ways to make it fit your work style. You can record a **macro**, a single command that you execute to perform a series of commands, to handle an often-repeated task. If you want to change a recorded macro, you can re-record it or edit it using Microsoft Visual Basic Editor.

You can add new custom menus to the current menu bar or to any toolbar. You can also add and remove buttons from toolbars to make it easier to perform tasks that you perform on a regular basis. Spending a few minutes customizing Word to suit your work habits will make you more efficient.

Skill Set 11

Customizing Word

Create, Edit, and Run Macros

Create Macros

A macro is a single command that you execute to perform a series of commands. Macros are useful because you can perform all of the steps necessary to execute a task by pressing a keyboard shortcut or clicking one command. To create a macro, you name the macro and start recording, execute the tasks, then stop recording. You must use a letter as the first character in a macro name, and the macro name cannot contain any spaces. You can store a macro in the Normal template (this is the default), any other open template, or in an open document. If you store a macro in a document, it is available only when that document is open. You can assign a keyboard shortcut to run the macro, or you can assign the macro to a toolbar or menu command.

Step 4
Click the Toolbars button to open the Customize dialog box and assign the macro to a toolbar button or menu command.

Activity Steps

1. Open a new, blank document, click **Tools** on the menu bar, point to **Macro**, then click **Record New Macro** to open the Record Macro dialog box

2. Type **SignatureLine** in the Macro name box

3. Click the **Store macro in list arrow**, then click the **document name** of the new document (for example, **Document1 (document)**) to store the macro in the current document instead of in the Normal template
See Figure 11-1.

4. Click the **Keyboard button** 🖳 to open the Customize Keyboard dialog box

5. Press **[Ctrl][Shift][Y]** to insert a shortcut key combination in the Press new shortcut key box, click the **Save changes in list arrow**, click the **document name** of the new document (for example, **Document1**) to store the shortcut key in the current document instead of in the Normal template, click **Assign**, then click **Close** to close the dialog box and open the Stop Recording toolbar

6. Type **Sincerely,** (including the comma), press **[Enter]** four times, type **Terry Farris**, press **[Enter]**, then type **Sales Manager**
See Figure 11-2.

7. Click the **Stop Recording button** ■ on the Stop Recording toolbar

8. Click **Tools** on the menu bar, point to **Macro**, click **Macros** to open the Macros dialog box, notice that the **SignatureLine** macro is listed, then click **Cancel** to close the dialog box

 close file

Figure 11-1: Record Macro dialog box

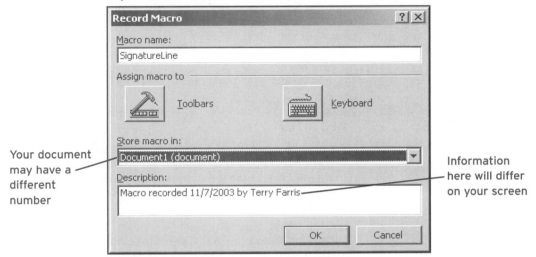

Your document may have a different number

Information here will differ on your screen

Figure 11-2: Recording a macro

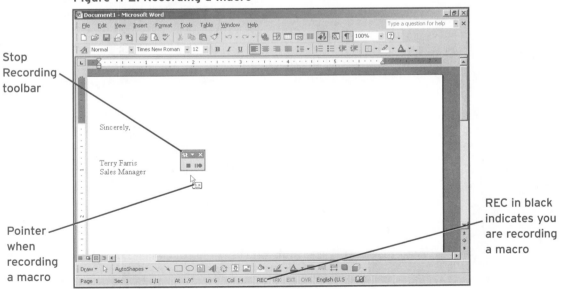

Stop Recording toolbar

Pointer when recording a macro

REC in black indicates you are recording a macro

Skill Set 11
Customizing Word

Create, Edit, and Run Macros
Run Macros

Once you have created a macro, you need to run it to test it. You can run macros stored in the current document or template. If macro security is set to High, Word automatically disables macros in the documents that you open. If you know that a document is from a trusted source, you can change the macro security setting to Medium and then choose to enable macros in documents or templates that you open, or to Low to enable macros automatically.

To copy a macro from one template or document to another, click Organizer in the Macros dialog box to open the Macro Project Items tab in the Organizer dialog box, select the macro you want to copy, then click Copy.

Activity Steps

1. Create a new, blank document, click **Tools** on the menu bar, click **Options** to open the Options dialog box, click the **Security tab**, click **Macro Security** to open the Security dialog box, make sure the **Security Level tab** is selected, note which option button is selected, then click the **Medium option button**, if necessary

2. Click **OK** to close the Security dialog box, click **OK** to close the Options dialog box, click the **Close button** ⊠ in the title bar of the document window, click the **Open button** 🖿, navigate to the location where your project files are stored, click **EWLetter10.doc**, click **Open**, then, in the dialog box that opens asking if you want to enable macros, click **Enable Macros**

3. Open the project file **EWLetter11**, enabling macros when asked, then press **[Ctrl][End]** to position the insertion point at the end of the document

4. Click **Tools** on the menu bar, point to **Macro**, then click **Macros** to open the Macros dialog box
   See Figure 11-3.

5. Make sure **TerrySignatureLine** is selected in the macro list, then click **Run** to insert a signature line

6. Click **Window** on the menu bar, click **EWLetter10.doc** to switch to that document, then press **[Ctrl][End]**

7. Press **[Ctrl][Shift][Y]** to run the SignatureLine macro by using the shortcut key assigned to it
   See Figure 11-4.

8. Click **Tools** on the menu bar, click **Options**, click **Macro Security** on the **Security tab**; *if* **High** was selected before you began this activity, click the **High option button**; *if* **Low** was selected before you began this activity, click the **Low option button**; then click **OK** twice

 close EWLetter10.doc
      EWLetter11.doc

Figure 11-3: Macros dialog box

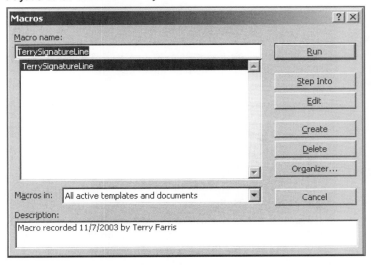

Figure 11-4: Signature line inserted in document

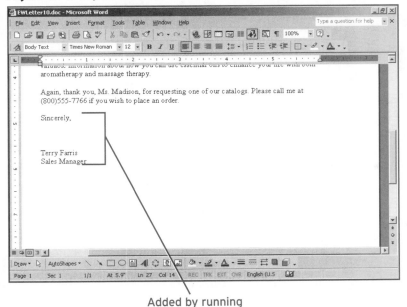

Added by running
TerrySignatureLine
macro

extra!

Understanding more about macros

If the name you assign to a macro is the same as the name assigned to a built-in command, your new macro will override the existing commands. To make sure that you don't create a macro with the same name as a built-in command, click the Macros in list arrow in the Macros dialog box, then click Word commands. Another thing to keep in mind when you are recording a macro is that, while the macro recorder will record mouse clicks on a menu command or toolbar button, it will not record the mouse actions in the document window, for example, dragging to select text or clicking to position the insertion point. Finally, not all formatting changes made using the buttons on the Formatting toolbar are recorded when you record a macro, so it's a good idea to open the appropriate formatting dialog box to change any character or paragraph formats.

Skill Set 11

Customizing Word

Create, Edit, and Run Macros
Edit Macros

If you make a mistake when you record a macro, or if you change your mind about any of the actions you included in the macro, you can re-record or edit the macro. For simple changes, it can be easier to edit the existing macro. Macros are recorded in Visual Basic for Applications, a programming language. If you know the steps you took to record a macro, it is fairly easy to figure out which line of code executes which step.

Note: This activity continues on page 248. Make sure you turn the page and complete all nine steps.

To re-record a macro, first delete it by opening the Macros dialog box, selecting the macro, then clicking Delete, then close the Macros dialog box and start the recording process again.

Activity Steps

1. Open a new, blank document, click **Tools** on the menu bar, click **Options**, click the **Security tab**, click **Macro Security**, note which option button is selected on the **Security Level tab**, click the **Medium option button** if necessary, click **OK** twice, close the blank document, open the project file **EWMemo10**, then click **Enable Macros**

2. Press **[Ctrl][End]**, click **Tools** on the menu bar, point to **Macro**, click **Macros**, make sure **MemoHeader** is selected, then click **Run** This macro created memo header lines, but made the name **Julia McNair** in the **From** line bold, added an extra **Re** line, and added a red border line.

3. Click **Tools** on the menu bar, point to **Macro**, click **Macros**, make sure **MemoHeader** is selected, then click **Edit** to open the Microsoft Visual Basic Editor window
   See Figure 11-5.

4. Click immediately after the quotation mark after **From:** in the eighth line of code after the comments, press **[Enter]**, press **[Delete]**, type **Selection.T**, click the down scroll arrow in the list that appeared when you typed the period, double-click **TypeText**, press the **[Spacebar]**, type **Text**, type : (a colon), type = (an equal sign), then press **[Delete]**

5. Click 🖫 to the left of the next line (**Selection.Font.Bold = wdToggle**) to select it, click the **Cut button** ✂, press **[↑]**, then click the **Paste button** 📋 to move the Bold toggle command so it comes before the line that inserts Julia's name
   See Figure 11-6.

Do not close the file. Continue with Step 6 on page 248.

Figure 11-5: Microsoft Visual Basic Editor window

Insertion point

Project window (may not be visible on your screen)

Comments

Eighth line of code below comments

Code window

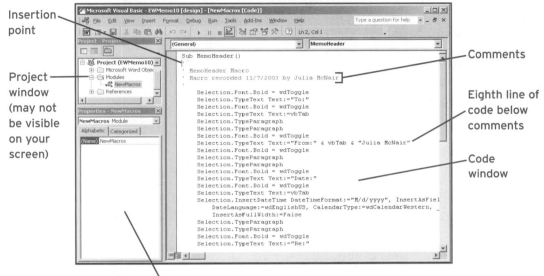

Properties window (may not be visible on your screen)

Figure 11-6: Edited macro program code in the Code window

Bold toggle command moved up

New line of code created

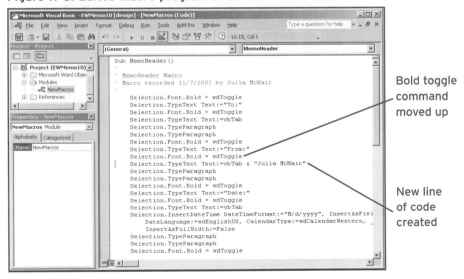

Skill Set 11
Customizing Word

Create, Edit, and Run Macros
Edit Macros (continued)

 In Steps 4 and 5 on page 246, you moved code so that the toggle command to turn off bold formatting now appears before Julia McNair's name. In the steps on this page, you will delete the extra Re line and change the color of the border line to dark blue.

Activity Steps

6. Click below the scroll box in the vertical scroll bar to scroll down a screen, position ⌐ to the left of the *second* line that inserts **Re: (Selection.TypeText Text:="Re:"**, about eight lines down), drag to select it and the next four lines (through the second **Selection.TypeParagraph** line as shown in Figure 11-7, then press **[Delete]** to delete the lines of code that inserted the *second* **Re** line in the memo header

7. Press **[↓]** six times, press **[End]** to position the insertion point at the end of the line (after **ColorRed**), press **[Backspace]** 12 times to delete **wdColorRed** and the equal sign, type **=** (equal sign), click the **down scroll arrow** in the list that appeared when you typed the equal sign, then double-click **wdColorDarkBlue**

8. Click **File** on the menu bar, click **Close and Return to Microsoft Word**, select everything in the document from the **To** line to the end, press **[Delete]**, click **Tools** on the menu bar, point to **Macro**, click **Macros**, make sure **MemoHeader** is selected in the list, then click **Run** to run the edited macro

9. Click **Tools** on the menu bar, click **Options**, click **Macro Security** on the **Security tab**, *if* **High** was selected before you began this activity, click the **High option button**, *if* **Low** was selected before you began this activity, click the **Low option button**, then click **OK** twice

 close EWMemo10.doc

Figure 11-7: Selecting lines that insert the second Re: line

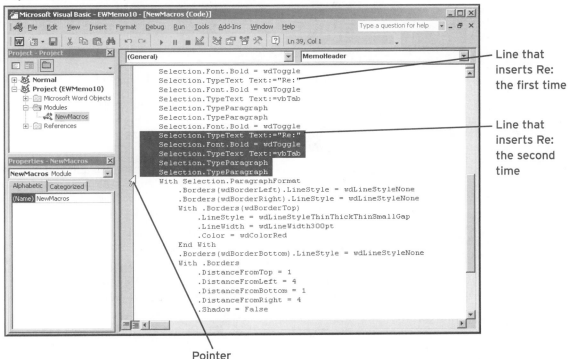

Line that inserts Re: the first time

Line that inserts Re: the second time

Pointer

extra!

Understanding the Visual Basic Editor

The Code window on the right side of the Visual Basic Editor window contains the macro program code. The lines of code are called programming **statements**. Statements that provide explanatory text but do not execute are called **comments**; comments are preceded by a quotation mark. A macro is a **subroutine**, a series of statements that executes a specific task. It begins with the keyword **Sub**, the macro name, and an empty set of parentheses and ends with the keywords **End Sub**. **Keywords** are words that have a specific meaning in Visual Basic. A macro can be composed of program statements and subroutines that contain their own programming statements. The other windows in the Visual Basic Editor window are the Project Explorer window at the top left, which contains a list of the current macro projects, and the Properties window at the bottom left, which lists the properties by macro name and category. If these windows are closed, you can open them by clicking the appropriate name on the View menu.

Skill Set 11

Customizing Word

Customize Menus and Toolbars

Create Menus

You can create a custom menu that contains commands that you use often. Custom menus can be added to a toolbar or to the menu bar. To create a new, custom menu, you open the Customize dialog box and click New Menu on the Toolbars tab. You can store a custom menu in the current document or template.

Activity Steps

1. Open a new, blank document, click **Tools** on the menu bar, click **Customize** to open the Customize dialog box, click the **Commands tab**, click the **Save in list arrow**, then click the **document name** of the new document (for example, **Document1**) so that your customizations are saved only in the current document

2. Scroll down to the bottom of the Categories list, click **New Menu**, then drag the **New Menu command** from the Commands list to the menu bar and position it to the right of the Help menu on the menu bar, as shown by the dark I-beam indicator

3. Scroll back to the top of the Categories list, click **Edit**, then scroll down the Commands list until you can see the **Go To command**

To delete a custom menu, open the Customize dialog box, then drag the menu name off of the menu bar or toolbar where it is located.

4. Drag the **Go To command** on top of New Menu on the menu bar so that a small box appears below New Menu, then release the mouse button when the dark I-beam indicator is in the box, as shown in Figure 11-8

5. Scroll down the Commands list so that you can see the next four **Go To commands**, drag the **Go To Next Page command** on top of New Menu on the menu bar, then drag down until the dark horizontal line indicates that the command will be positioned below the **Go To command**

6. Drag the **Go To Previous Page command** so that it is inserted below the Go To Next Page command on the New Menu

7. Click **New Menu** on the menu bar, click **Modify Selection** in the Customize dialog box, select all of the text in the Name box on the pop-up menu, then type **Go To Menu**
   See Figure 11-9.

8. Click anywhere in the Customize dialog box to close the pop-up menu and rename the new menu you added, click **Close**, click **Go To Menu** on the menu bar, click **Go To** to open the Go To tab in the Find and Replace dialog box, then click **Close**

 close file

Figure 11-8: Adding a command to a custom menu

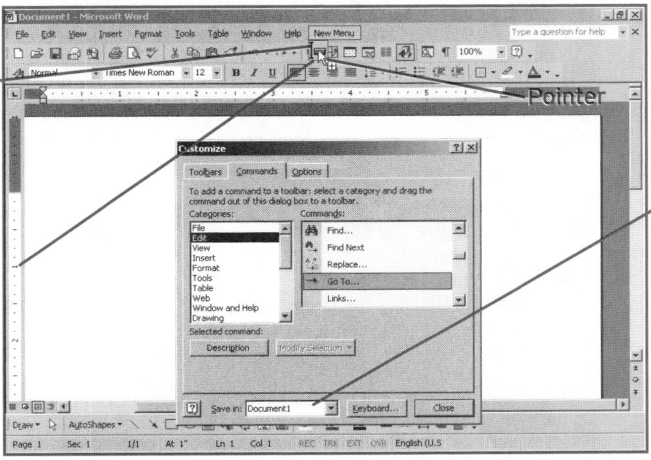

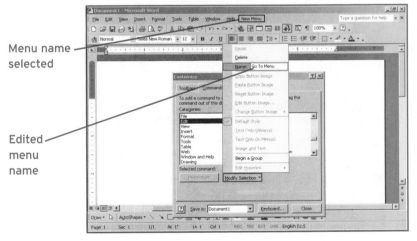

Indicates where button will be positioned
Pointer
Box below new menu
New menu will be stored in current document (your document may have a different number)

Figure 11-9: Menu name changed in the Modify Selection pop-up menu

Menu name selected
Edited menu name

extra!

Creating a new toolbar

You can also add menus and toolbar buttons to new, customized toolbars that you create. To do this, open the Customize dialog box, click the Toolbars tab, click New to open the New Toolbar dialog box, type a name for your new toolbar, then click OK. Drag the buttons that you want to add to the new toolbar. If you want the toolbar to be available only to the current document, click the Make toolbar available to list arrow in the New Toolbar dialog box, then click the current document name. To delete a custom toolbar, scroll down the list on the Toolbars tab in the Customize dialog box, select the new toolbar, then click Delete.

Skill Set 11

Customizing Word

Customize Menus and Toolbars
Add Buttons to and Remove Buttons from Toolbars

You can add buttons to and remove buttons from toolbars so that you can have one-click access to the commands that you frequently use. To add or remove toolbar buttons, you must open the Customize dialog box. You can store the customizations in the current document or template.

To assign a keyboard shortcut to a command, open the Customize dialog box, click Keyboard, select the command, click in the Press new shortcut key box, then press the shortcut key(s) you want to use.

Activity Steps

1. Open a new, blank document, right-click any toolbar, click **Customize** to open the Customize dialog box, click the **Commands tab**, click the **Save in list arrow**, then click the **document name** of the new document (for example, **Document1**)

2. Click **Edit** in the Categories list, then scroll down the Commands list until you can see the **Find**, **Find Next**, and **Replace commands**

3. Drag the **Find command** to the right end of the Standard toolbar, then release the mouse button when the dark I-beam indicator is positioned on the toolbar, as shown in Figure 11-10

4. Drag the **Find Next command** to the right of the Find button on the Standard toolbar

5. Drag the **Replace command** to the Standard toolbar so that it is between the Find and Find Next buttons you just added
   See Figure 11-11.

6. Drag the **Replace button** off the Standard toolbar, releasing the mouse button when the button is no longer on any toolbar

7. Click **Close** in the Customize dialog box

   file close file

Figure 11-10: Customize dialog box open

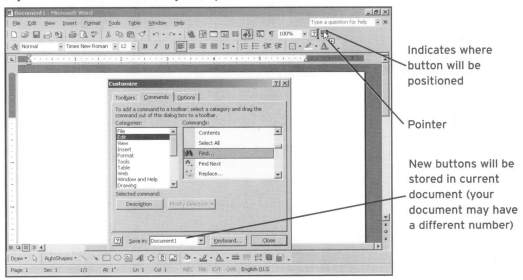

Indicates where button will be positioned

Pointer

New buttons will be stored in current document (your document may have a different number)

Figure 11-11: Command dragged to custom toolbar

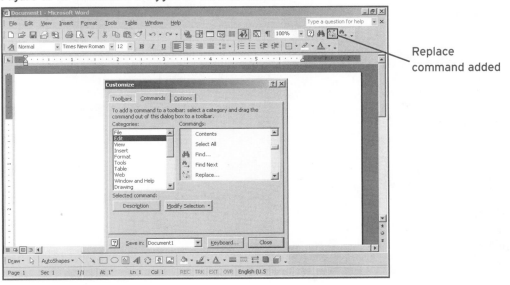

Replace command added

Skill Set 11

Customizing Word

Target Your Skills

1 Open a new, blank document and record a macro named **EarthWiseCoName** that inserts the text and blank paragraphs shown in Figure 11-12. Save the macro in the current document and not in the Normal template. Run the macro, then edit it so that the text is formatted as Lavender instead of Green, and is italicized as well as bold. (*Hint:* Set the value of italic to True.) Re-run the macro in the document below the second company heading.

Figure 11-12

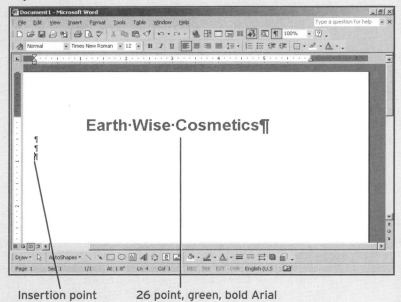

Insertion point   26 point, green, bold Arial

Figure 11-13

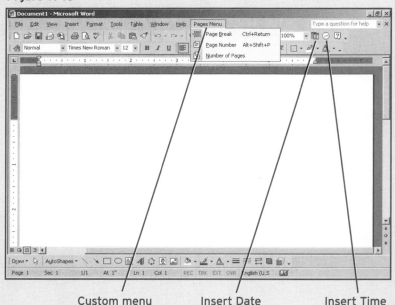

2 Open a new, blank document. Create the custom menu shown in Figure 11-13. Add the Insert Date and Insert Time custom toolbar buttons as shown. All of the menu commands and the two toolbar buttons are in the Insert category. Save your customizations in the current document and not in the Normal template.

Custom menu   Insert Date   Insert Time

Skill List

1. Track, accept, and reject changes to documents
2. Merge input from several reviewers
3. Insert and modify hyperlinks to other documents and Web pages
4. Create and edit Web documents in Word
5. Create document versions
6. Protect documents
7. Define and modify default file locations for workgroup templates
8. Attach digital signatures to documents

Being able to collaborate with others easily to finalize documents is one of the strengths of Word. Word offers several ways to share documents with others. You can edit documents and see the edits on screen. You can send a document to others to review and have their changes automatically marked so that you can decide whether to incorporate the changes. If you would rather not see the edits on screen, but you still want a record of them, you can save various versions of a document.

If you are sharing a document with others, you can protect it so that changes aren't made to it accidentally. You can also add a digital signature to a document so that anyone you send it to will know that it came from you and that it hasn't changed since you created it. You can also change the default location for document templates that are shared by a group.

To make it easy to move around in a document or from one document to another, you can add hyperlinks to your document that allow you to jump to another location. You can also add hyperlinks to jump to a Web page on the World Wide Web.

Word makes it easy to create a Web page using the Web Page Wizard. Once you have created a Web page, you can edit it as easily as any Word document.

Skill Set 12
Workgroup Collaboration

Track, Accept, and Reject Changes to Documents
Track Changes

You can see edits you make to a document on the screen when you use the Track Changes command. When Tracking Changes is turned on, text you add is in another color and underlined; text you cut or delete appears in a balloon to the right of the text in the same color as the insertions in Print layout view (the default), or with a line through it in Normal view. If you share a document with others, each person's changes are tracked in a different color.

Click the Reviewing Pane button on the Reviewing toolbar to see the changes in a pane at the bottom of the screen in addition to in the document and in the edit balloons.

Activity Steps

 open GCBrochure08.doc

1. Click **Tools** on the menu bar, click **Track Changes** to turn on tracking and open the Reviewing toolbar, then click the **Show/Hide ¶ button** ¶ to display paragraph marks, if necessary

2. Select the text **We at Gulf Coast Taxi recognize that the** in the first paragraph, type **Because**, then press the **[Spacebar]** if necessary to insert a space between **Because** and **seniors**
   See Figure 12-1.

3. Click immediately after the word **needs** at the end of the first sentence, press **[Delete]** to delete the period, type **,** (a comma), press **[➡]**, press **[Delete]**, then type **w**

4. Scroll down and select the entire **Details line**, then press **[Delete]**

5. Press **[⬅]** to position the insertion point immediately before the paragraph mark at the end of the first paragraph, press **[Delete]**, click immediately before **We** at the beginning of the last sentence in the combined first paragraph, then press **[Enter]**

6. Select the **three bulleted list items**, then click the **Bold button** B

7. Position the insertion point over the bottom edit balloon to see the registered user's name and the current date appear in a ScreenTip, along with a brief description of the change
   See Figure 12-2.

8. Click the **Track Changes button** on the Reviewing toolbar to turn tracking off, right-click any toolbar, click **Reviewing** to close the Reviewing toolbar, then click the **Show/Hide ¶ button** ¶ to hide paragraph marks

 close GCBrochure08.doc

Figure 12-1: Tracked change

Vertical line indicates a change in this line of text

Inserted text is underlined and in color

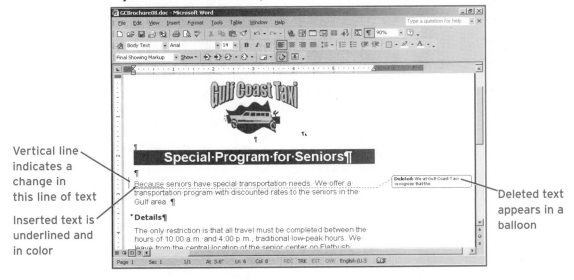

Deleted text appears in a balloon

Figure 12-2: ScreenTip identifying tracked change

Bold TRK indicates Track Changes is turned on

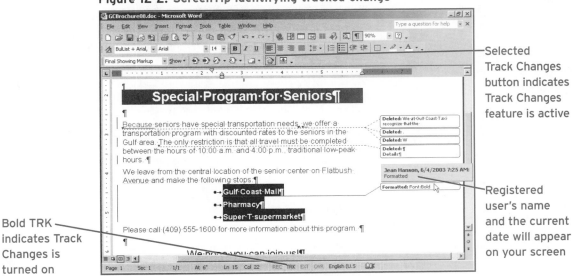

Selected Track Changes button indicates Track Changes feature is active

Registered user's name and the current date will appear on your screen

Skill Set 12
Workgroup Collaboration

Track, Accept, and Reject Changes to Documents
Review Changes

When you work with a document that contains edits made with Track Changes turned on, you can see all of the changes that were made to the document. If you position the pointer over a change, a ScreenTip appears identifying the reviewer who made the change, the date and time the change was made, and the type of change that was made (for example, a formatting change, an insertion, or a deletion). You can choose to display changes by only selected reviewers, only insertions and deletions, or only comments.

Activity Steps

 open GCBrochure09.doc

1. Click **View** on the menu bar, point to **Toolbars**, then click **Reviewing** to display the Reviewing toolbar, if necessary

2. Click the **Next button** on the Reviewing toolbar to jump to the first change made in the document, then position the pointer over the highlighted text to see the reviewer's name, the date the change was made, and a description of the change

3. Click the **Show button** Show ▾ on the Reviewing toolbar, point to **Reviewers**, notice that the registered user's name is listed as a reviewer, then click **Jean Hanson** to hide all of the changes made by that reviewer

To see the original document with all the changes (including insertions) noted in edit balloons, click the Display for Review list arrow on the Reviewing toolbar, then click Original Showing Markup.

4. Click the **Next button** to jump to the next displayed change in the document, then position the pointer over the balloon to see that Billy Bob Grantham made the change
See Figure 12-3.

5. Click the **Show button** Show ▾ on the Reviewing toolbar, point to **Reviewers**, then click **All Reviewers** to display changes by all the reviewers again

6. Click the **Show button** Show ▾ on the Reviewing toolbar, then click **Formatting** to hide all formatting changes

7. Scroll down so you can see the comment, click the **Show button** Show ▾ on the Reviewing toolbar, then click **Comments** to hide all comments, leaving only insertions and deletions displayed
See Figure 12-4.

8. Right-click any toolbar, then click **Reviewing** to close the Reviewing toolbar

 close GCBrochure09.doc

Figure 12-3: One reviewer's changes hidden

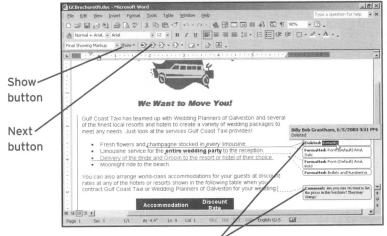

Show button

Next button

Only changes and comments made by Billy Bob Grantham are displayed

Figure 12-4: All changes hidden except insertions and deletions

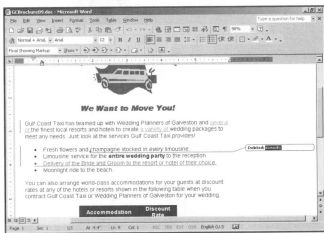

extra!

Changing options for the Track Changes command

To modify how changes are displayed on screen, click the Show button on the Reviewing tool-bar, then click Options to open the Track Changes dialog box. You can click the Color list arrow to assign a color to mark changes in the document, rather than having Word assign a different color to each reviewer. Click the Insertions and the Formatting list arrows to change the way that insertions and format-ting changes are dis-played. You can choose whether to use bal-loons, how large the balloons should be, whether to print in landscape with the bal-loons to the side, or whether to keep por-trait orientation if the document is in portrait. You can customize the appearance of the bal-loons by selecting options in the Balloons section in the dialog box. Finally, you can decide whether to mark all changes by adding a line to the left or right margin and what color that line will be.

Skill Set 12
Workgroup Collaboration

Track, Accept, and Reject Changes to Documents
Respond to Changes

After you review a tracked change, you can decide whether to accept it and incorporate it into the document, reject it and delete the suggested insertion, or re-insert the suggested deletion. You can also accept or reject all of the changes in a document at once. Finally, if the document contains any comments, usually you want to delete them before you finalize the document.

Activity Steps

 open GCBrochure10.doc

1. Right-click any toolbar, then click **Reviewing** to open the Reviewing toolbar, if necessary

2. Click the **Next button** on the Reviewing toolbar to highlight the first change in the document, the insertion of the text **several of**

If you track changes and add comments to a document and then save it as a Web page without accepting or rejecting the changes or deleting the comments, the tracked changes and comments will appear on the Web page.

3. Click the **Reject Change/Delete Comment button** on the Reviewing toolbar to reject this change, then click the **Next button**

4. Click the **Accept Change button** on the Reviewing toolbar to accept the insertion of **a variety of**, then click the **Next button** to highlight the next change
   See Figure 12-5.

5. Click the **Accept Change button** to accept the deletion of the word **domestic**, click the **Next button**, then click the **Accept Change button** to accept the formatting change

6. Click the **Next button**, click the **Show/Hide ¶ button** to display paragraph marks if necessary, then press **[←]**
   See Figure 12-6.

7. Click the **Accept Change button** to accept the insertion of a new paragraph, click the **Next button**, then click the **Reject Change/Delete Comment button** to delete the comment

8. Scroll to the bottom of the page, click the **Accept Change list arrow**, click **Accept All Changes in Document** to accept the rest of the suggested changes, click the **Show/Hide ¶ button** to hide paragraph marks, right-click any toolbar, then click **Reviewing** to close the Reviewing toolbar

 close GCBrochure10.doc

Figure 12-5: Suggested deletion highlighted in balloon

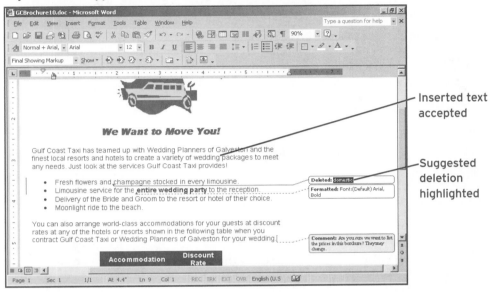

Inserted text accepted

Suggested deletion highlighted

Figure 12-6: Suggested insertion of new paragraph

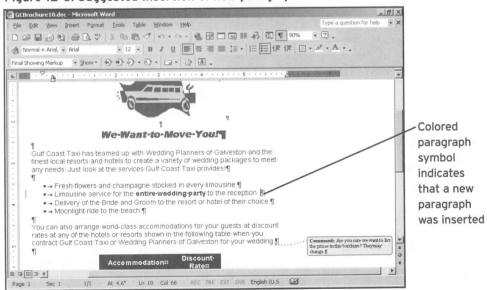

Colored paragraph symbol indicates that a new paragraph was inserted

Skill Set 12

Workgroup Collaboration

Merge Input from Several Reviewers
Distribute Documents for Review via E-mail

To send a document for review, you use the Send To Mail Recipient (for Review) command. When the reviewer receives the message and opens the document, tracking changes is turned on, and the Reply with Changes button appears on the Reviewing toolbar. The reviewer clicks the Reply with Changes button to send the reviewed document back to you.

Note: We assume you are using Microsoft Outlook as your e-mail program.

Activity Steps

  open GCReport03.doc

1. Make sure you are connected to the Internet, click **File** on the menu bar, point to **Send To**, then click **Mail Recipient (for Review)** *See Figure 12-7.*

2. Type your e-mail address in the **To box**, then click the **Send button** 📧 to send the message

3. Click the **Start button** 🏁Start on the taskbar, point to **Programs**, then click **Microsoft Outlook**

Step 1
If the document is stored in a location on a network, such as on a company intranet, the e-mail message will contain a link to the file rather than including it as an attachment.

4. If the message is in the Outbox, click the **Send/Receive button** 🔄 Send/Receive to send the message; then, if the message you sent is not yet in your Inbox, click the **Send/Receive button** 🔄 Send/Receive again to check for and retrieve the messages

5. Click **Outlook Today** in the Outlook Shortcuts bar, click the **Inbox link** under Messages on the right, then double-click the message **Please review 'GCReport03'**

6. Double-click **GCReport03.doc** in the Attachments line, if a dialog box opens asking if you want to open the document or save it, click the **Open it option button**, click **OK**, then click **No** in the dialog box asking if you want to merge changes *See Figure 12-8.*

7. Right-click the **Outlook program button** on the taskbar, click **Close**, then click **No** if asked if you want to save changes

8. Click **Window** on the menu bar, click **GCReport03.doc**, right-click any toolbar, click **Reviewing** to display the Reviewing toolbar if necessary, click the **End Review button** End Review... on the Reviewing toolbar, click **Yes** in the dialog box to end the reviewing cycle, then close the Reviewing toolbar, if necessary

  close GCReport03.doc
GCReport031.doc

Figure 12-7: E-mail message in Outlook with document attached

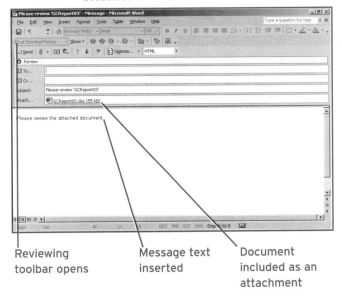

Reviewing toolbar opens

Message text inserted

Document included as an attachment

Figure 12-8: Reviewed document opened on sender's computer

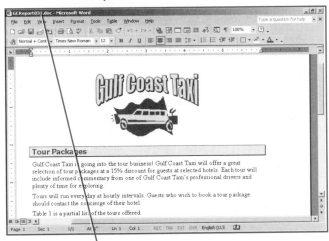

Number added to the end of the filename to indicate that it is a temporary file (may be a different number on your screen)

Skill Set 12
Workgroup Collaboration

Merge Input from Several Reviewers
Merge Revisions

If you sent a document for review and you receive the document back from several reviewers, you can merge all of the changes and comments into one document. To do this, you open the edited document, click the Compare and Merge Documents command, then select the original document. You can click the Merge list arrow in the Compare and Merge Documents dialog box to choose from three merge options: Merge; Merge into current document; and Merge into new document. If you click Merge, the changes are merged into the original document. Changes will be made whether or not the reviewer turned on Track Changes.

If reviewer changes conflict with one another, you may see a confusing markup on screen. Try clicking the Display for Review list arrow, then click Original Showing Markup; or click the Show button, point to Reviewers, and click each reviewer name to hide all reviewer comments except for the one whose change you want to see.

Activity Steps

 open GCReport04BG.doc

1. Scroll down to see the changes made in the document, then position the pointer over any change to see that Billy Bob Grantham made these changes

2. Click **Tools** on the menu bar, then click **Compare and Merge Documents** to open the Compare and Merge Documents dialog box

3. Navigate to the location where your project files are stored, click **GCReport04.doc** (the original document), then click **Merge** to merge the changes made in GCReport04BG into GCReport04
   See Figure 12-9.

4. Click the **Open button** , navigate to the location where your project files are stored, click **GCReport04JH.doc**, click **Open**, then scroll down and position the pointer over the inserted sentence under Table 1 to see that Jean Hanson made the change in this file

5. Click **Tools** on the menu bar, click **Compare and Merge Documents**, click **GCReport04.doc** (the original document), then click **Merge** to merge the changes into GCReport04

6. Scroll down and position the pointer to see that Jean Hanson's change was inserted

7. Open the project file **GCReport04SW**, position the pointer over the balloon to see that Scott West made the changes in this document, then merge the changes into the original document **GCReport04**
   See Figure 12-10.

8. Right-click any toolbar, then click **Reviewing** to close the Reviewing toolbar

 close GCReport04.doc   GCReport04JH.doc
GCReport04SW.doc   GCReport04BG.doc

Figure 12-9: Tracked changes merged into original document

Current document is original document

Reviewing toolbar opened automatically

Edited document is still open

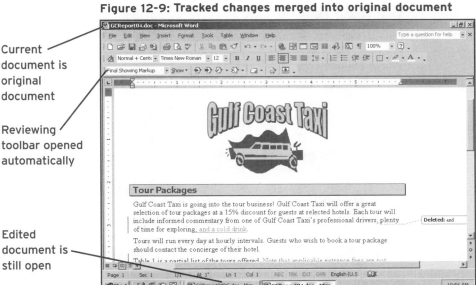

Figure 12-10: Tracked changes from three documents merged into original document

One of the changes made in Billy Bob Grantham's file

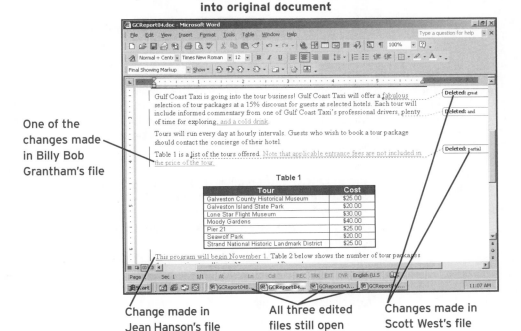

Change made in Jean Hanson's file

All three edited files still open

Changes made in Scott West's file

Skill Set 12
Workgroup Collaboration

Insert and Modify Hyperlinks to Other Documents and Web Pages
Insert Hyperlinks to Another Place in the Document or to Another Document

You can insert hyperlinks into your documents. A **hyperlink**, or **link**, is specially formatted text that, when clicked, moves you to another location in the document or opens another document or a Web page. To insert a link to another place in the current document or to another document, you select the text that you want to format as a link, then click the Insert Hyperlink button . Hyperlinks are formatted as blue underlined text. After you click a hyperlink, it changes to a **followed hyperlink**, and its color changes to purple.

Activity Steps
 open GCMemo11.doc

1. Scroll down and select the third bulleted item in the list, then click the **Insert Hyperlink button** to open the Insert Hyperlink dialog box

2. Click **Place in This Document** under Link to on the left, then click **Young Driver Training Classes** in the Select a place in this document list
   See Figure 12-11.

3. Click **OK**, position the pointer over the newly inserted hyperlink, press and hold **[Ctrl]**, then click to jump to the Young Driver Training Classes heading

4. Select the text **Young Driver Training Class Announcement** in the last paragraph, then click the **Insert Hyperlink button**

5. Click **Existing File or Web Page** under Link to on the left, click the Look in list arrow and navigate to the location where your project files are stored, click **GCAnnouncement06.doc** in the list, then click **OK**

6. Position the pointer over the newly inserted hyperlink, press and hold **[Ctrl]**, then click to open and jump to the file **GCAnnouncement06** and open the Web toolbar
   See Figure 12-12.

7. Click the **Back button** on the Web toolbar to return to the location of the hyperlink

8. Click **Window** on the menu bar, click **GCAnnouncement06.doc**, click the **Close button** in the title bar, if necessary click **No** in the dialog box that opens asking if you want to save changes, right-click any toolbar, then click **Web** to close the Web toolbar

 close GCMemo11.doc

To change the ScreenTip associated with a hyperlink, click ScreenTip in the Insert Hyperlink or in the Edit Hyperlink dialog box, then type the text you want to add as a ScreenTip.

Figure 12-11: Insert Hyperlink dialog box

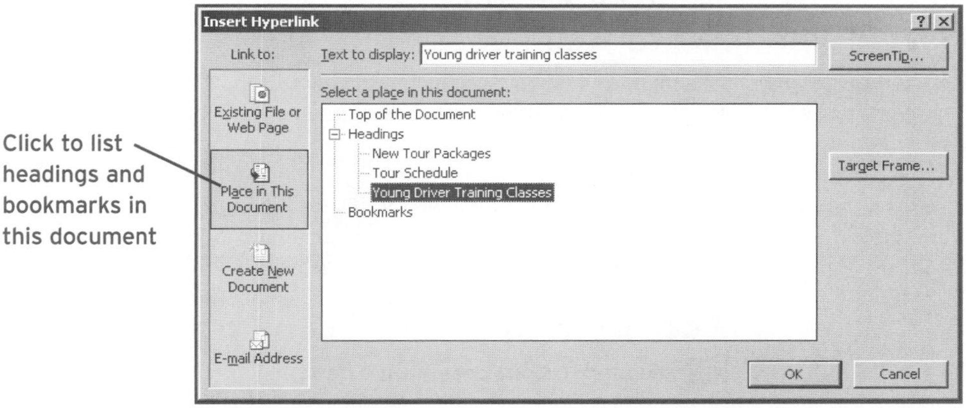

Click to list headings and bookmarks in this document

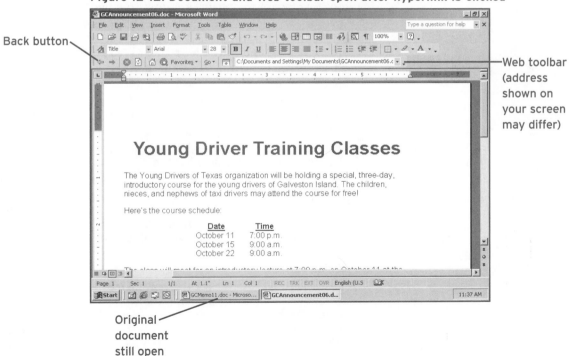

Figure 12-12: Document and Web toolbar open after hyperlink is clicked

Back button

Web toolbar (address shown on your screen may differ)

Original document still open

Skill Set 12
Workgroup Collaboration

Insert and Modify Hyperlinks to Other Documents and Web Pages

Insert Hyperlinks to Web Pages

You can insert hyperlinks to any location on an intranet or the Internet. In addition, Word recognizes URLs and e-mail addresses when you type them, so that when you press the [Spacebar] or [Enter], Word formats the text automatically as a hyperlink.

Note: In this activity, you are directed to go to two specific locations on the World Wide Web. These locations were active Web sites at the time of publication. If they are no longer active, link to any currently active Web site.

Step 1
To turn off automatic formatting of hyperlinks, click AutoCorrect Options on the Tools menu, click the AutoFormat As You Type tab, then click the Internet and network paths with hyperlinks check box to deselect it.

Activity Steps

 open GCAnnouncement07.doc

1. Click immediately before the word **if** in the last sentence in the paragraph below the table, type **www.mapquest.com**, then press the **[Spacebar]** to convert the text to a hyperlink

2. Make sure you are connected to the Internet, press and hold **[Ctrl]**, then click the newly inserted hyperlink to open your browser and jump to the MapQuest Web page

3. Click the **Back button** ⟵ Back to jump back to the Word document and close the browser window

4. Select the text **Drive Home Safe Web site** in the last sentence in the document, then click the **Insert Hyperlink button** to open the Insert Hyperlink dialog box

5. Click **Existing File or Web Page** under Link to on the left, then click the **Browse the Web button** to open your Web browser

6. Click in the Address or Location box, type **drivehomesafe.com**, press **[Enter]** to jump to that Web site, then click **Word program button** on the taskbar to switch back to your document and automatically insert the address of the current Web page in the Address box in the Insert Hyperlink dialog box
See Figure 12-13.

7. Click **OK**

8. Press and hold **[Ctrl]**, click the newly inserted hyperlink to open a new browser window displaying the Web page, click the **Back button** ⟵ Back to jump back to the Word document, click the **browser window program button** on the taskbar, click the **Close button** X in the title bar to switch back to the Word document, right-click any toolbar, then click **Web** to close the Web toolbar
See Figure 12-14.

 close GCAnnouncement07.doc

Figure 12-13: Inserting a hyperlink to a Web page

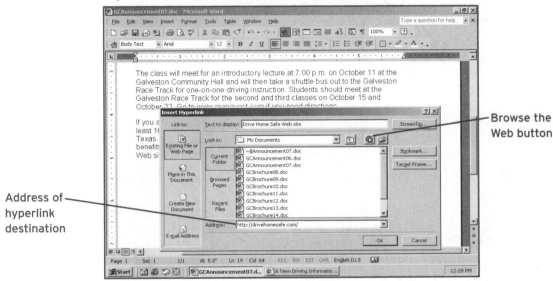

Browse the Web button

Address of hyperlink destination

Figure 12-14: Followed hyperlinks in a document

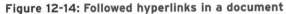

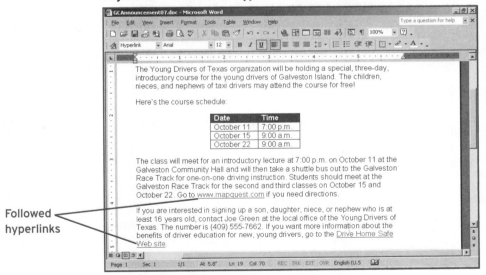

Followed hyperlinks

Skill Set 12
Workgroup Collaboration

Insert and Modify Hyperlinks to Other Documents and Web Pages
Modify hyperlinks

Once you've inserted a hyperlink, you can modify it. You can change the location of the link, the text displayed, or the ScreenTip displayed when you point to the link, or you can remove the link formatting altogether.

Activity Steps

 open GCMemo12.doc

1. Right-click any toolbar, click **Web** to open the Web toolbar, scroll down so you can see the bulleted list, press and hold **[Ctrl]**, then click the **Young driver training classes hyperlink** in the third bullet

2. Click the **Back button** ⇐ on the Web toolbar to return to the location of the hyperlink, right-click the **Young driver training classes hyperlink** in the third bullet, then click **Edit Hyperlink** on the shortcut menu to open the Edit Hyperlink dialog box and notice that the address of the hyperlink is to the file GCAnnouncement06.doc
See Figure 12-15.

Step 3
If you don't need to change the folder in which you are storing the new document you are creating, simply type the filename—with a filename extension—of the new document in the Name of new document box in the Insert Hyperlink or in the Edit Hyperlink dialog box.

3. Click **Create New Document** under Link to on the left, click **Change** to open the Create New Document dialog box, type **New Linked Document** in the File name box, click the **Save as type list arrow**, click **Documents (*.doc)**, navigate to the location where you are saving your project files, then click **OK**

4. Click the **Edit the new document later option button**, then click **OK**

5. Press and hold **[Ctrl]**, click the **Young driver training classes hyperlink** in the third bullet to open and jump to the new document file **New Linked Document**
See Figure 12-16.

6. Click the **Back button** ⇐ on the Web toolbar to return to the location of the hyperlink

7. Right-click the **Tour schedules hyperlink** in the second bullet, then click **Remove Hyperlink** on the shortcut menu to remove the hyperlink

8. Click **View** on the menu bar, point to **Toolbars**, then click **Web** to close the Web toolbar

 close GCMemo12.doc
New Linked Document.doc
GCAnnouncement06.doc

Figure 12-15: Edit Hyperlink dialog box

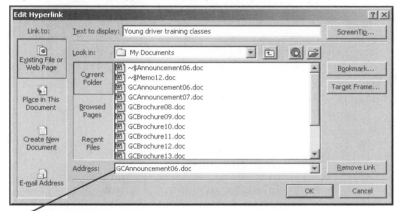

Hyperlink address
links to another file

Figure 12-16: New linked document open

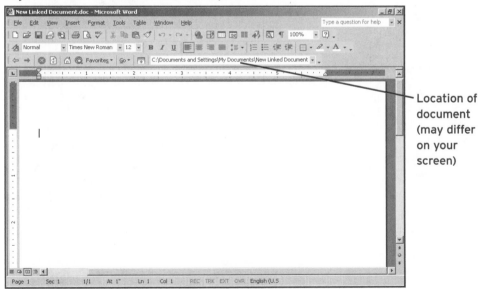

Location of
document
(may differ
on your
screen)

Skill Set 12
Workgroup Collaboration

Create and Edit Web Documents in Word
Create a Web Site in Word

When you create a Web site using a Web page template, you create a Web site with one page, no **theme** (a background design and set of colors for headings and other text) and no **frames** (a section of a Web page that acts as if it were a different window or pane on the screen). When you use the Web Page Wizard, the default is to create a Web site with a home page and two blank pages, along with a theme and a frame that contains links to jump to each page in the Web site.

Activity Steps

1. Click **File** on the menu bar, click **New** to open the New Document task pane, click the **General Templates link** in the task pane to open the Templates dialog box, click the **Web Pages tab**, click the **Web Page Wizard icon**, then click **OK**

2. Click **Next** to move to the Title and Location screen in the Web Page Wizard, type **Gulf Coast Taxi** in the Web site title box, click **Browse**, navigate to the location where you are saving your project files, click the **Create New Folder button** in the toolbar at the top of the Copy dialog box, type **Gulf Coast Taxi Web site**, click **OK**, then click **Open**
   See Figure 12-17.

3. Click **Next** to go to the Navigation screen, then make sure the **Vertical frame option button** is selected

4. Click **Next** to move to the Add Pages screen, click **Add Existing File**, navigate to the location where your project files are stored, click **GCBrochure11.htm**, then click **Open**

5. Click **Next** to move to the Organize Pages screen, make sure **GCBrochure11** is selected in the list, then click **Move Up** twice

6. Click **Next** to go to the Visual Theme screen, click **Browse Themes**, scroll down and click **Sumi Painting** in the Choose a Theme list, click **OK**, click **Next**, then click **Finish** to open a document in Web Layout view with the filename **default** and to open the Frames toolbar

7. Click **File** on the menu bar, click **Save As**, type **Gulf Coast Taxi Web site** in the File name box, note that **Web Page** is listed in the Save as type box, then click **Save**
   See Figure 12-18.

8. Click the **Close button** on the Frames toolbar to close it

   close Gulf Coast Taxi Web site.htm

Step 7
The file default.htm still exists in the folder where your Web page is stored.

Figure 12-17: Title and Location screen in the Web Page Wizard

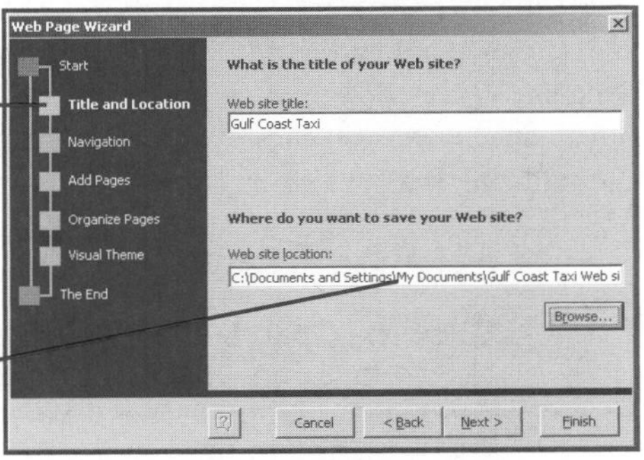

Green box highlights current screen name in wizard

Location on your screen may differ

Figure 12-18: Completed Web Page

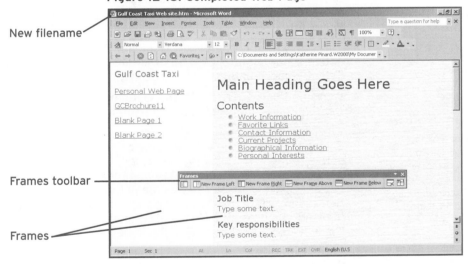

New filename

Frames toolbar

Frames

extra!

Understanding the files created by the Web Page Wizard

Each page in a Web site that you created using the Web Page Wizard is a separate HTML file. In this activity, you created the files default.htm, the original file for the entire Web site; Gulf Coast Taxi Web Site.htm, the renamed file for the entire Web site; Personal Web Page.htm, the default filename for the home page (the first page) of the Web site; Blank Page 1.htm, Blank Page 2.htm, and GCBrochure11.htm, the additional pages in the Web site that you added in the Add Pages screen in the Wizard; and TOCFrame.htm, the filename for the vertical frame that contains links to all the pages in the site. Each HTML file for an individual Web page has an associated folder with the same name as the file; for example, there is a folder named GCBrochure11_files. If you delete the HTML file, the associated folder is deleted automatically. If you copy the HTML file to a new location, you must also copy the associated folder.

Skill Set 12
Workgroup Collaboration

Create and Edit Web Documents in Word
Open and Edit Web Documents in Word

You can open a Web site in Word and edit it. Be aware of unexpected changes when you edit a Web site. Depending on how the Web site was created, a new document window may open when you click a link to a page, or edits may result in hyperlink formatting being removed so that the link no longer works.

Activity Steps

1. Click the **Open button** 📂 to open the Open dialog box, navigate to the location where your project files are stored, make sure the Files of type box lists **All Word Documents**, double-click the **GCWebSite01 folder**, click **GCWebSite01.htm**, then click **Open**

2. Select the text **Main Heading Goes Here**, type **Gulf Coast Taxi**, press **[Enter]**, click the **Italic button** 𝐼, then type **We Want to Move You!**

3. Click anywhere in the yellow frame on the left to make it the active frame, right-click the **Personal Web Page link**, click **Select Hyperlink** on the shortcut menu, then type **Home**

4. Press and hold **[Ctrl]**, click the **Wedding link**, which opens the wedding package brochure Web page in a new document
See Figure 12-19.

Step 5
If you make a typing mistake or press the [Spacebar] accidentally and the underline that indicates that this text is a hyperlink disappears, click the Undo button, then type the new link name again.

5. Click anywhere in the yellow frame on the left to make it the active frame, right-click the **Wedding link**, click **Select Hyperlink** on the shortcut menu, type **WeddingPackageInformation** (without any spaces), press **[◄]** as many times as necessary to position the insertion point between the **e** in **Package** and the **I** in **Information**, press the **[Spacebar]**, then insert a space between the **g** in **Wedding** and the **P** in **Package**

6. Click **Format** on the menu bar, point to **Frames**, click **Frame Properties** to open the Frame Properties dialog box, click the **Borders tab**, click the **Show all frame borders option button**, click the **Show scrollbars in browser list arrow**, click **Always**, then click **OK**
See Figure 12-20.

7. Press and hold **[Ctrl]**, click the **Home link**, click the **Close button** ☒ in the title bar to close the second document window (with **:2** after the filename in the title bar), click **No** when asked if you want to save changes, right-click any toolbar, then click **Web** to close the Web toolbar
To save your changes, you need to click the Save button, or to rename the file, you need to click Save As Web Page on the File menu.

📄 **close GCWebSite01.htm**

Figure 12-19: New document window opened after clicking link

Indicates that this is the second window open for this file

Renamed link

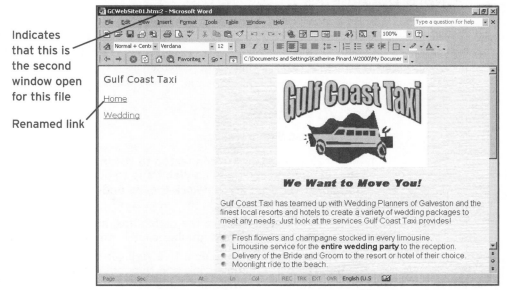

Figure 12-20: Web page with frame borders and scroll bars displayed

Border added between frames

Scroll bars added to both frames

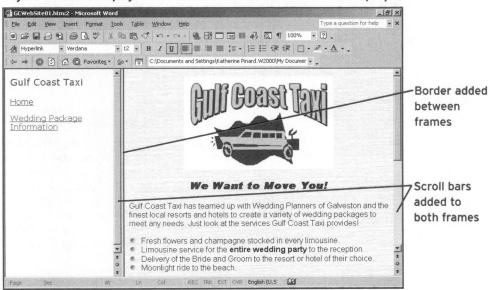

Skill Set 12
Workgroup Collaboration

Create and Edit Web Documents in Word
Save Word Documents to the Web

To post your Web site on the World Wide Web, you need permission from the server's owner to copy your files to a Web server and the exact address of a folder on that server. Then copy the files that are connected to the Web page by hyperlinks, and edit the hyperlinks so that they link to the new locations.

Note: We assume you are using Internet Explorer as your Web browser.

If you use the Web Page Wizard to create a Web site, when you click Browse in the Title and Location screen, you can click My Network Places in the Copy dialog box and select a location on a Web server.

Activity Steps

 open GCWebSite02.htm

1. Make sure that you are connected to the Internet, click **File** on the menu bar, click **Save as Web Page** to open the Save As dialog box, then click **My Network Places** under Save in on the left
   See Figure 12-21.

2. If a Web server is listed in the dialog box, and if you have permission to post files to it, double-click it, then skip to Step 5

3. If you have permission to post to a Web server but it is not listed in the dialog box, double-click **Add Network Place** to start the Add Network Place Wizard, make sure the **Create a shortcut to an existing Network Place option button** is selected, click **Next**, type the **URL** of the server in the Location box, press **[Tab]**, type a shortcut name for the server, click **Finish**, then skip to Step 5
   The folder should now be listed in the Save in box.

4. If you do not have permission to save files to a Web server, navigate to the location where you are saving your files

5. Select all of the text in the File name box, type **My Saved Web Site**, then click **Save**

6. Click the **Start button** [Start] on the taskbar, point to **Programs**, then click **Internet Explorer**

7. Click **File** on the menu bar, click **Open**, click **Browse**, navigate to the location on the Web server where you saved your Web site or to the location where you are saving your files, click **My Saved Web Site.htm**, click **Open**, then click **OK**
   See Figure 12-22. The Wedding Package Information hyperlink is linked to the Wedding.htm file in the folder where the file GCWebSite02.htm is stored. To copy the linked file, right-click the hyperlink, click Edit Hyperlink, then navigate to the file's new location.

8. Click the **Close button** [X] in the Internet Explorer program window

 close My Saved Web Site.htm

Figure 12-21: Save As dialog box after clicking My Network Places

Click to add the address for a Web server to the Save in list

List of folders and drives available on the network (your list will differ)

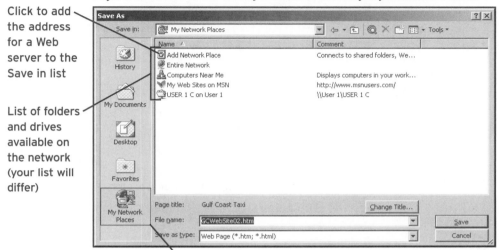

Click to display the list of folders and drives available on your network

Figure 12-22: Web site opened in Internet Explorer

File opened in Internet Explorer

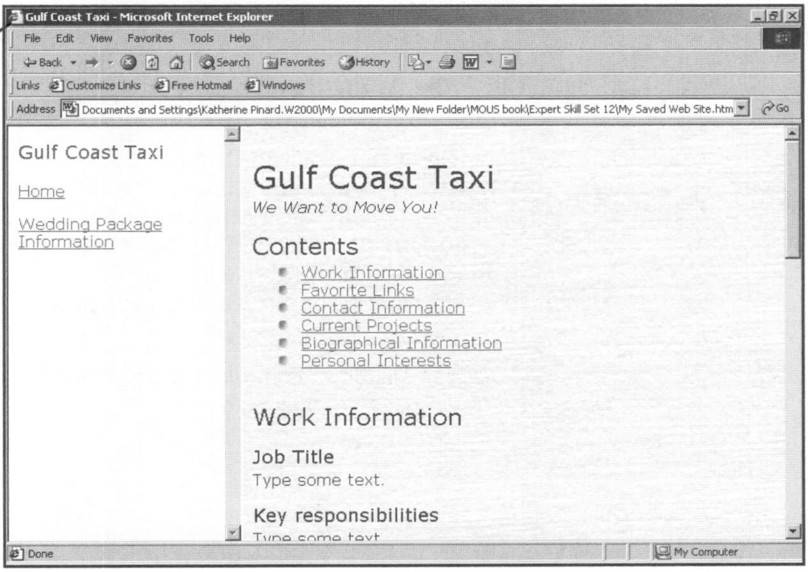

Skill Set 12
Workgroup Collaboration

Create Document Versions

If you don't want to use the Track Changes command but you still want to save a record of the changes you make to a document, you can save versions of your document. A **version** is the document saved at some point during its creation. When you are editing and you reach a point at which you would like to save the document, you use the Versions command on the File menu. Versions of a document are saved in the same file as the document file.

Activity Steps

  open GCBrochure12.doc

1. Click **File** on the menu bar, then click **Versions** to open the Versions in GCBrochure12.doc dialog box

2. Click **Save Now** to open the Save Version dialog box

3. Type **Original draft** in the Comments on version box
   See Figure 12-23.

You cannot save changes that you make to a document version unless you save that version as a separate document.

4. Click **OK**, select the entire **Details heading line**, press **[Delete]**, click **File** on the menu bar, then click **Versions**
   See Figure 12-24.

5. Click **Save Now**, type **Details heading deleted**, then click **OK**

6. Double-click **Special** in the title line, type **Transportation**, click **File** on the menu bar, click **Versions**, click **Save Now**, type **Title changed**, then click **OK**

7. Click **File** on the menu bar, click **Versions**, then click the last version in the list (with **Original draft** in the Comments column)

8. Click **Open** to open the Original draft version of the document in a new window arranged under the window containing the open document, click **File** on the menu bar of the Original draft version document window, click **Save As**, type **Original Transportation Brochure** in the File name box, navigate to the location where you are saving your project files, then click **Save**
   See Figure 12-25.

  close Original Transportation Brochure.doc
   GCBrochure12.doc

Figure 12-23: Save Version dialog box

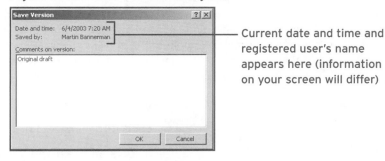

Current date and time and registered user's name appears here (information on your screen will differ)

Figure 12-24: Versions in GCBrochure12.doc dialog box

Original draft version

Figure 12-25: Original draft version open

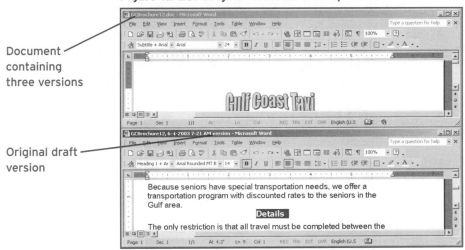

Document containing three versions

Original draft version

Skill Set 12
Workgroup Collaboration

Protect Documents

If you do not want others to make changes to a document, or if you want to be able to see those changes as tracked changes, you can protect the document. For extra security, you can protect it with a password. When you protect a document, you can choose to protect it so that users are allowed to make changes that are tracked with the Track Changes feature; or you can choose to prevent users from making any changes except to insert comments.

Activity Steps

 open GCBrochure13.doc

1. Click **Tools** on the menu bar, then click **Protect Document**

2. Make sure the **Tracked changes option button** is selected, then type **password** in the Password (optional) box
   See Figure 12-26.

3. Click **OK**, type **password** in the Confirm Password dialog box, then click **OK**

4. Select **every day** in the first line in the second paragraph, type **daily**, click **Insert** on the menu bar, click **Comment**, then type **Change this**

5. Click **Tools** on the menu bar, click **Unprotect Document**, type **password** in the Unprotect Document dialog box, then click **OK**

6. Click **Tools** on the menu bar, then click **Protect Document**, type **password** in the Password (optional) box, click the **Comments option button**, click **OK**, type **password**, then click **OK**

7. Select the number **3** in the first paragraph, type **three**, and note that the change is not recorded

8. Click the **New Comment button** on the Reviewing toolbar, type **Change to three**, right-click any toolbar, then click **Reviewing** to close the Reviewing toolbar
   See Figure 12-27.

 close GCBrochure13.doc

tip

Another way to protect your document from changes is to click Options on the Tools menu, click the Security tab, then click the Read-only recommended check box to select it.

Figure 12-26: Protect Document dialog box

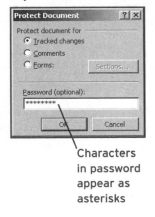

Characters
in password
appear as
asterisks

Figure 12-27: Protected document with tracked changes and comments

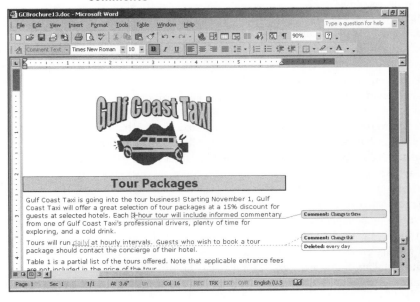

extra!

Using advanced protection options

In addition to the protection options discussed in this activity, you can also make it necessary to use a password to even open a document or to make any changes at all. To do this, click Options on the Tools menu, then click the Security tab. Type a password in the Password to open box to require users to type a password before they can open the document. Type a password in the Password to modify box to require users to enter a password to open the document normally rather than as read-only. When a document is opened as **read-only**, users cannot make changes or insert comments.

Define and Modify Default File Locations for Workgroup Templates

Define and Modify Default File Locations for Workgroup Templates

If you work on a network and want custom templates to be available to everyone on that network, you can change the default file location for workgroup templates. Basically, when you do this, you add tabs to the Templates dialog box that correspond to folders within the folder or on the drive that you specify.

The default setting is for the location or workgroup templates to be undefined so that only the standard tabs appear in the Templates dialog box. Once you have defined a location for workgroup templates, you cannot change it back to an undefined location; in other words, the change is permanent. You can modify the location, but you cannot reset it to its default undefined location.

WARNING: Do not attempt this on your computer unless you are sure you want to define the default location of workgroup templates permanently. If you are working on a network, do not attempt to do this at all. Ask your network support person for assistance.

To change the default location for workgroup templates and permanently add additional tabs to the Templates dialog box, click Tools on the menu bar, click Options to open the Options dialog box, then click the File Locations tab in the Options dialog box. Next, click Workgroup templates in the File types list. The default is that no location is specified in the Location column on the right; but if you are working on a network, your network administrator may have specified a location. See Figure 12-28.

Click Modify to open the Modify Location dialog box. The folder or drive listed in the Look in box at the top of the dialog box will become the location listed for workgroup templates on the File Locations tab. All folders in this folder or drive will appear as tabs in the Templates dialog box, and any files stored in those folders will appear on each tab. Click Cancel to leave the location of workgroup templates unchanged. For example, if you modify the location to be a folder named Group Templates, and that folder contains folders for the Development Group, the Production Group, and General Office Templates, those three folders will appear as tabs in the Templates dialog box. See Figure 12-29.

Note that if a folder in the new workgroup template location does not contain any documents or templates, it will not appear as a tab in the Templates dialog box.

Figure 12-28: File Locations tab in the Options dialog box

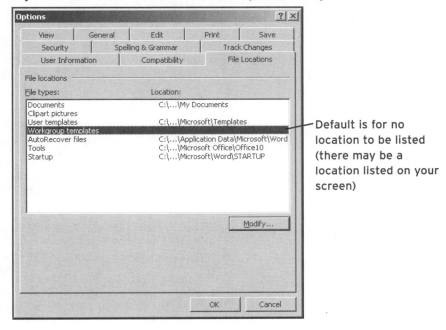

Default is for no location to be listed (there may be a location listed on your screen)

Figure 12-29: Templates dialog box with new tabs

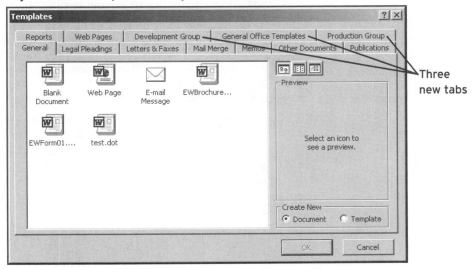

Three new tabs

Skill Set 12
Workgroup Collaboration

Define and Modify Default File Locations for Workgroup Templates
Modify and Re-post HTML Documents

You can open an HTML document in Internet Explorer, and then switch to Word to edit it. Then, you can repost a file or Web site to the Web.

Note: We assume you are using Internet Explorer as your Web browser.

Step 9
If you have already copied the file Wedding.htm to the location where you saved the Reposted Web Page file, right-click the Wedding Package Information hyperlink, click Edit Hyperlink, then click the Wedding.htm file in the location to which you saved your file.

Activity Steps

1. Click the **Start button** on the taskbar, point to **Programs**, then click **Internet Explorer**

2. Click **File** on the menu bar, click **Open**, click **Browse**, navigate to the location where your project files are stored, double-click the **GCWebSite03 folder**, click **GCWebSite03.htm**, then click **Open** *See Figure 12-30.*

3. Click **OK**, click **File** on the menu bar, then click **Edit with Microsoft Word** to open the HTML file in Word

4. Double-click **Work** below the list of links, then type **Company**

5. Make sure that you are connected to the Internet, click **File** on the menu bar, click **Save as Web Page** to open the Save As dialog box, then click **My Network Places** under Save in on the left *See Figure 12-31.*

6. If a Web server is listed in the dialog box, and if you have permission to post files to it, double-click it, then skip to Step 9

7. If you have permission to post to a Web server but it is not listed in the dialog box, double-click **Add Network Place** to start the Add Network Place Wizard, make sure the **Create a shortcut to an existing Network Place option button** is selected, click **Next**, type the **URL** of the server in the Location box, press **[Tab]**, type a shortcut name for the server, click **Finish**, then skip to Step 9

8. If you do not have permission to save files to a Web server, navigate to the location where you are saving your files

9. Select all of the text in the File name box, type **Reposted Web Page**, click **Save**, right-click the **Internet Explorer program button** on the taskbar, then click **Close** on the shortcut menu

close Reposted Web Page.htm

Figure 12-30: Open dialog box in Internet Explorer

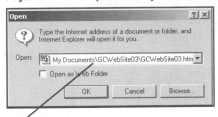

Your path may differ

Figure 12-31: Save As dialog box after clicking My Network Places

Click to add the address for a Web server to the Save in list

List of folders and drives available on the network (your list will differ)

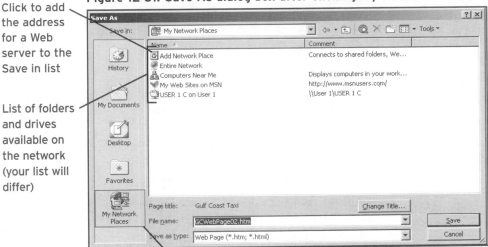

Click to display the list of folders and drives available on your network

Skill Set 12
Workgroup Collaboration

Attach Digital Signatures to Documents
Attach Digital Signatures

You can attach a **digital signature** to a document to verify that you created the document and prove that the file has not been modified since you attached the signature. A **digital certificate** is electronic verification that you actually created the digital signature by ensuring that the digital signature matches a special code in the software that created it. You can purchase a digital certificate from a company that sells them. If you don't have a digital certificate, you can still attach a digital signature to a document, but it will not be authenticated by any outside source, and when you view the certificate, you will see a warning that tells you this. When a document has a digital signature attached to it, **(Signed)** appears in the title bar, and a small red and yellow symbol appears in the status bar.

To remove a digital signature, open the Digital Signature dialog box, click the digital signature in the list, then click Remove.

Activity Steps

 open GCBrochure14.doc

1. Click **File** on the menu bar, click **Save As**, type **Signed Brochure** in the File name box, navigate to the location where you are saving your project files, then click **Save**

2. Click **Tools** on the menu bar, click **Options** to open the Options dialog box, then click the **Security tab**

3. Click **Digital Signatures** to open the Digital Signature dialog box

4. Click **Add** to open the Select Certificate dialog box, then if necessary click **Yes** in the dialog box to continue

5. Make sure the registered user's name is listed and selected, then click **View Certificate**
   See Figure 12-32.

6. Click **OK** to close the Certificate dialog box, then click **OK** to close the Select Certificate dialog box

7. Click **OK** to close the Digital Signature dialog box, click **OK** to close the Options dialog box, then click the **Save button** 🖫 to save the document with the digital signature you just created
   See Figure 12-33.

 close Signed Brochure.doc

Figure 12-32: Certificate dialog box

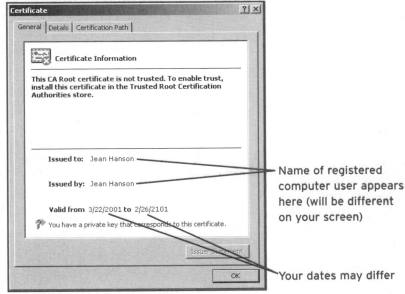

Name of registered computer user appears here (will be different on your screen)

Your dates may differ

Figure 12-33: Digitally signed document

Indicates document has a digital signature

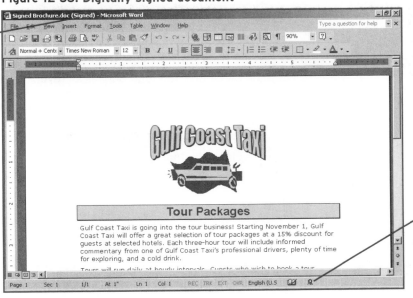

Indicates document has a digital signature

Skill Set 12
Workgroup Collaboration

Attach Digital Signatures to Documents
Use Digital Signatures to Authenticate Documents

If a digital signature is attached to a document, you can open and view the document to verify that it is from someone you trust. You can also view the digital certificate that accompanies it.

Activity Steps

 open GCBrochure15.doc

1. Note in the title and status bars that the project file GCBrochure15 is digitally signed, click **Tools** on the menu bar, click **Options**, click the **Security tab**, then click **Digital Signatures**

2. Make sure the certificate from **Course Technology** is selected, then click **View Certificate**

3. Note the names next to **Issued to** and **Issued by**, then make sure the certificate is still valid
   See Figure 12-34.

4. Click **OK** three times to exit out of all the open dialog boxes

5. Double-click **November** in the first line in the first paragraph, type **December**, then click the **Save button** 🖫
   See Figure 12-35.

6. Click **No** in the dialog box that opens asking if you want to remove all digital signatures in the document

7. Click **File** on the menu bar, click **Save As**, type **Unsigned Brochure** in the File name box, make sure the current folder is the folder where you are saving your project files, click **Save**, then click **OK** in the dialog box that opens warning you that a copy of this document will not contain any digital signatures

 close Unsigned Brochure.doc

Step 6
If you click Yes in the dialog box that asks if you want to remove all digital signatures, the change you made will be saved and the digital signatures will be removed from the current document.

Figure 12-34: **Certificate dialog box**

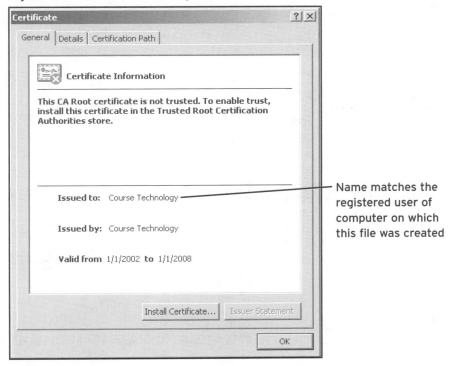

Name matches the registered user of computer on which this file was created

Figure 12-35: **Dialog box opens when trying to save changes to a digitally signed document**

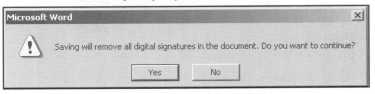

Skill Set 12
Workgroup Collaboration

Target Your Skills

 GCAnnouncement08.doc
GCAnnouncement08JH.doc
GCAnnouncement08SW.doc

1 Create the document shown in Figure 12-36. Start by merging the changes and comments from **GCAnnouncement08JH** and **GCAnnouncement08SW** into the original document, **GCAnnouncement08**, then turn on tracked changes and add the changes as noted in the figure. Accept all of the changes and delete all of the comments, save the final file as **Signed Announcement**, then add a digital signature and save your changes.

 GCBrochure16.doc

2 Create the document shown in Figure 12-37. First insert the hyperlink on the word **resorts** and link it to the heading **Hotels**. Save a version of the document at this point. Next, insert the hyperlink on the words **activity tours** and link it to the heading **Activity Tours**. Save another version of the document. Finally, protect the document so that only comments can be made. Use the password **GulfCoast**.

Figure 12-36

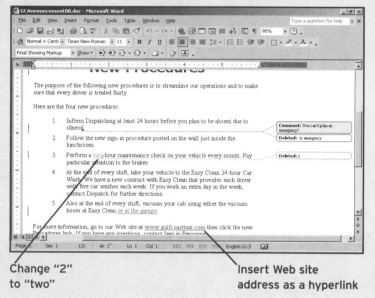

Change "2" to "two"

Insert Web site address as a hyperlink

Figure 12-37

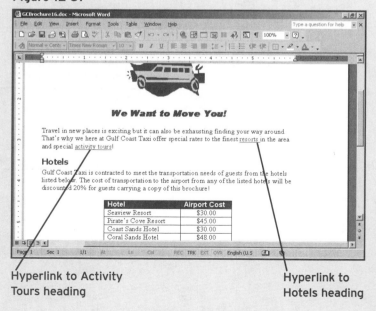

Hyperlink to Activity Tours heading

Hyperlink to Hotels heading

Skill List

1. Merge letters with a Word, Excel, or Access data source
2. Merge labels with a Word, Excel, or Access data source
3. Use Outlook data as a mail merge data source

When you need to send the same letter to many people, you can use the Mail Merge Wizard to merge names and addresses from a list with your form letter. The wizard takes you through a series of steps. First, you choose to use the current document as your form letter or to create the form letter as part of the process when you run the Mail Merge Wizard. You then choose the file that contains the list of names with which you want to merge the form letter. Finally, you merge the letter with a list of people in Word, Excel, Access, or Outlook. The Mail Merge Wizard can save you quite a bit of time.

Skill Set 13

Using Mail Merge

Merge Letters with a Word, Excel, or Access Data Source

The **Mail Merge Wizard** is a series of six steps that leads you through the process of merging a letter or other document (the **main document**) with a list of names and addresses from another document (the **data source**), such as a Word document, an Excel worksheet, or an Access database. Using the wizard, you first define or create the main document. Next, you select the data source, then you insert the merge fields into the main document. The **merge fields** are the placeholders for the data that you will use from the data source, for example, the inside address and the greeting line.

Note: This activity continues on page 294. Make sure you turn the page and complete all nine steps.

Activity Steps

 open CCLetter03.doc
CCMailList01.doc

1. Make sure **CCMailList01** is the active document, notice that the data is arranged in a table, click **Window** on the menu bar, click **CCLetter03.doc**, click **Tools** on the menu bar, point to **Letters and Mailings**, click **Mail Merge Wizard**, then position the insertion point in the main document below the date so that there is one blank line between it and the date
See Figure 13-1.

Step 3
You can use source data from a Word document, Excel worksheet, or Access table.

2. Make sure the **Letters option button** is selected in the Mail Merge task pane, click the **Next: Starting document link** at the bottom of the task pane, make sure the **Use the current document option button** is selected, then click the **Next: Select recipients link**

3. Make sure the **Use an existing list option button** is selected, click the **Browse link** to open the Select Data Source dialog box, navigate to the drive and folder where your project files are stored, click **CCMailList01.doc**, then click **Open** to open the Mail Merge Recipients dialog box
See Figure 13-2.

4. Click **OK**, click the **Next: Write your letter link** in the task pane, then click the **Address block link** to open the Insert Address Block dialog box

5. Make sure **Mr. Joshua Randall Jr.** is selected in the list at the top of the dialog box, click the **Only include the country/region if different than option button**, click in the text box below that option button, then type **US**

Do not close the files. Continue with step 6 on page 294.

Skill 1

Merge Letters with a Word, Excel, or Access Data Source

Figure 13-1: Starting the Mail Merge Wizard

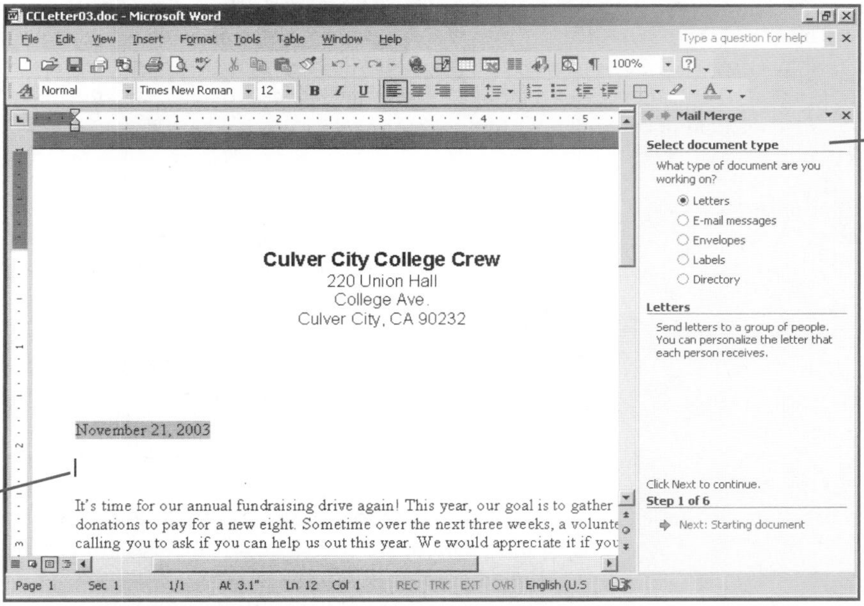

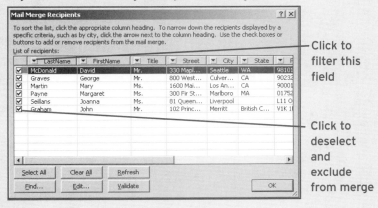

Mail Merge Wizard taskpane

Insertion point

extra!

Editing the recipient list

In Steps 3 and 5 of the Mail Merge Wizard, you can click the Edit recipient list link to open the Mail Merge Recipients dialog box and edit the list from the data source (see Figure 13-2). To exclude recipients from the merge, click the check box in the first column to deselect the person you want to exclude. To include only people that meet certain criteria, click the list arrow that appears next to each field name to filter the list.

Figure 13-2: Mail Merge Recipients dialog box

Click to filter this field

Click to deselect and exclude from merge

Skill Set 13

Using Mail Merge

Merge Letters with a Word, Excel, or Access Data Source (continued)

The Mail Merge Wizard will try to match the field names in your data source with its preset fields. You may need to specify any that the Wizard cannot assign. Finally, after reviewing your merged documents, you can save them as one document or send them directly to a printer.

Activity Steps

6. Click **Match Fields** to open the Match Fields dialog box, click the **Address 1 list arrow**, click **Street**, click the **Postal Code list arrow**, then click **Postal_Code**
   See Figure 13-3.

7. Click **OK** to close the Match Fields dialog box, then click **OK** again to close the Insert Address Block dialog box and insert the Address Block merge field into the main document

8. Press **[Enter]** twice, click the **Greeting line link** in the task pane to open the Greeting Line dialog box, click the list arrow next to **Mr. Randall**, scroll down and click **Joshua**, click **OK** to close the dialog box and insert the Greeting Line merge field into the main document, click the **Next: Preview your letters link**, then click the ⟫ in the task pane five times to scroll through the merged letters
   See Figure 13-4.

9. Click the **Next: Complete the merge link**, click the **Edit individual letters link**, make sure the **All option button** is selected in the Merge to New Document dialog box, then click **OK** to open a merged document containing all the form letters with the temporary filename **Letters** followed by a number

 close **Letters1.doc**
        CCLetter03.doc
        CCMailList01.doc

Figure 13-3: **Match Fields dialog box**

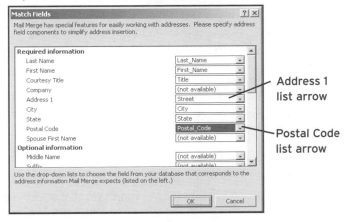

Address 1 list arrow

Postal Code list arrow

Figure 13-4: **Reviewing the merged letters**

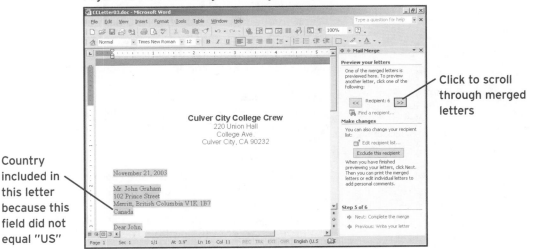

Click to scroll through merged letters

Country included in this letter because this field did not equal "US"

Skill Set 13

Using Mail Merge

Merge Labels with a Word, Excel, or Access Data Source

When you use the Mail Merge Wizard to merge letters and addresses, you still need a way to send those letters in the mail. You can use the Mail Merge Wizard to merge the names and addresses from the data source onto labels. Word has the dimensions and layouts of label sheets from over 14 companies, or you can create your own label format. The steps for merging the data source with a label's document are almost the same as those for merging a letter and a data source.

Note: This activity continues on page 298. Make sure you turn the page and complete all nine steps.

Step 3
If you don't have any labels, use the default selections of Avery standard in the Label products list and 2162 Mini - Address in the Product number list.

Activity Steps

1. Create a new blank document, click the **Show/Hide ¶ button** to display paragraph marks if necessary, click **Tools** on the menu bar, point to **Letters and Mailings**, click **Mail Merge Wizard**, click the **Labels option button** in the Mail Merge task pane, click the **Next: Starting document link**, make sure the **Change document layout option button** is selected, then click the **Label options link** to open the Label Options dialog box

2. Under Printer information, click the option button that corresponds to the printer attached to your computer, then, if you clicked the **Laser and ink jet option button**, click the **Tray list arrow** and click the tray used by your printer (**Default tray (Automatically Selected)** is a good choice)

3. Click the **Label products list arrow**, click the brand of labels you will be using, then click the type of label you are using in the **Product number list**
   See Figure 13-5.

4. Click **OK**, click the **Next: Select recipients link** in the task pane, click the **Browse link** to open the Select Data Source dialog box, navigate to the drive and folder where your project files are stored, click **CCMailList02.doc**, click **Open** to open the Mail Merge Recipients dialog box, then click **OK**
   See Figure 13-6.
   The number after the filename Document may be a number other than 1.

Do not close the files. Continue with the step 5 on page 298.

Figure 13-5: Label Options dialog box

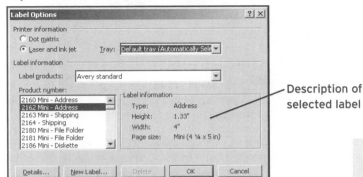

Description of selected label

Figure 13-6: Layout of labels

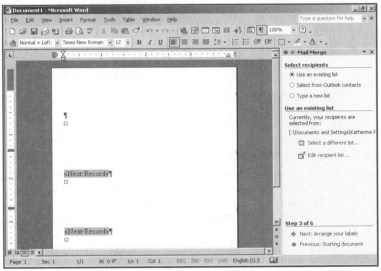

extra!

Creating labels or an envelope with one name

If you want to print just one name on a sheet of labels or on an envelope, point to Letters and Mailings on the Tools menu, then click Envelopes and Labels to open the Envelopes and Labels dialog box. Type the name and address in the Address box on either tab, or click the Insert Address button to insert a name and address from another source. Choose the dimensions of the envelope by clicking the Preview box on the Envelope tab and choose the label that you are using by clicking the Labels box on the Labels tab. Click Add to Document if you want to preview the label sheet or the envelope first; click Print to send the data directly to the printer.

Skill Set 13

Using Mail Merge

Merge Labels with a Word, Excel, or Access Data Source (continued)

Now that you've chosen your label format and your data source, you need to insert the merge fields and complete the merge.

Activity Steps

5. Click the **Next: Arrange your labels link** in the task pane, click the **Address block link**, click the **Only include the country/region if different than option button**, click in the text box below that option button, type **US**, click **Match Fields**, click the **Address 1 list arrow**, click **Street**, click the **Postal Code list arrow**, click **Postal_Code**, then click **OK** twice

6. Press **[Enter]**, click the **Postal bar code link** to open the Insert Postal Bar Code dialog box, then click **OK** to insert a bar code for US ZIP codes
   See Figure 13-7.

7. If the entire task pane is not visible on the screen, point to the **down arrow** in the thin bar at the bottom of the task pane to scroll down to the bottom of the task pane, click **Update all labels** to copy the format of the first label to the rest of the labels in the document, then click the **Next: Preview your labels link**

8. Click the **Next: Complete the merge link**, click the **Edit individual labels link**, make sure the **All option button** is selected in the Merge to New Document dialog box, then click **OK** to open a merged document containing all the form letters with the temporary filename **Labels** followed by a number

9. Scroll to the bottom of the document, click **Zip code not valid!** in the label addressed to England as shown in Figure 13-8, press **[Delete]**, click **Zip code not valid!** in the label addressed to Canada, press **[Delete]**, then click the **Show/Hide button** ¶

   file close Labels1.doc
   Document1.doc

Figure 13-7: Merge fields inserted in labels main document

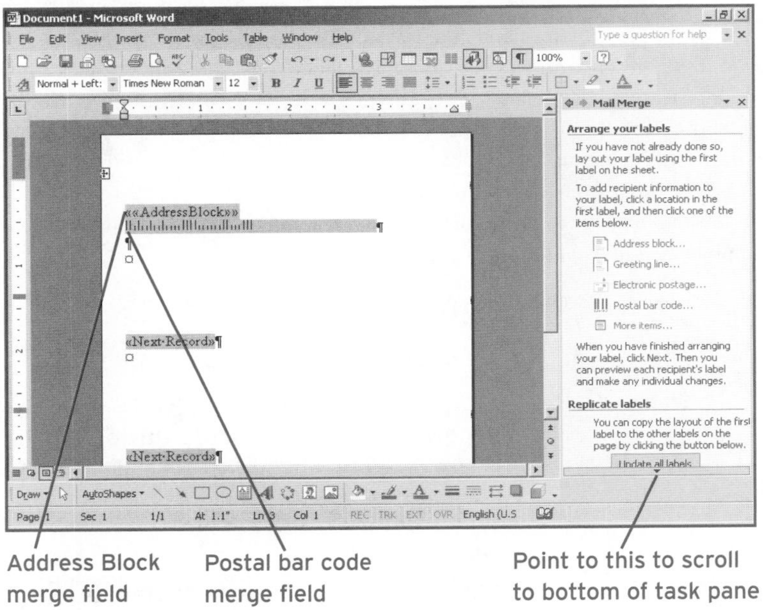

Address Block merge field

Postal bar code merge field

Point to this to scroll to bottom of task pane

Figure 13-8: Invalid Zip code field selected

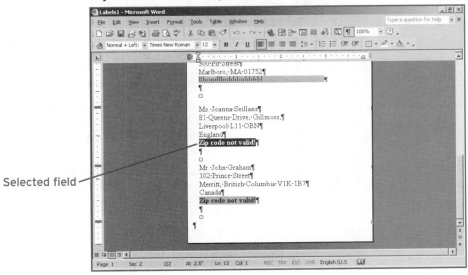

Selected field

Skill Set 13

Using Mail Merge

Use Outlook Data as a Mail Merge Data Source

Many people store names and addresses in the Contacts folder in Outlook. Using the Mail Merge Wizard, it is very simple to merge any names that you want with a main document. You can specify the Contacts folder or any folder within the Contacts folder as the data source. After you specify the data source and the Mail Merge Recipients dialog box opens, you can deselect any names in the list to exclude them from the merge.

Note: This activity continues on page 302. Make sure you turn the page and complete all nine steps.

Activity Steps

 open CCLetter04.doc

1. Click the **Start button** 🏁Start on the taskbar, point to **Programs,** click **Microsoft Outlook,** click the **New button list arrow** 📄 New ▾, click **Contact,** type **Mark Diaz,** click in the Address box, type **550 West Broad St.,** press **[Enter],** then type **Oakhurst, CA 93644**
See Figure 13-9.

Step 5
Any names with a check in the check box next to them will be merged with the main document letter.

2. Click the **Save and Close button** 💾 Save and Close, click the **New button list arrow** 📄 New ▾, click **Contact,** type **Lena Yee,** click in the Address box, type **24 Washington St.,** press **[Enter],** type **Phoenix, AZ 85001,** then click the **Save and Close button** 💾 Save and Close

3. Click the **Word program button** on the taskbar, click **Tools** on the menu bar, point to **Letters and Mailings,** click **Mail Merge Wizard,** click the **Next: Starting document link** in the task pane, then click the **Next: Select recipients link**

4. Click the **Select from Outlook contacts option button,** click the **Choose Contacts Folder link** to open the Select Contact List folder dialog box, then make sure **Contacts** is selected in the list
See Figure 13-10.

5. Click **OK** to open the Mail Merge Recipients dialog box, click **Clear All** to clear any check boxes that are selected, click the **check boxes** next to **Diaz, Mark** and **Yee, Lena** to select those two names to include them in the merge, then click **OK**

Do not close the files. Continue with step 6 on page 302.

Figure 13-9: Contact dialog box in Outlook

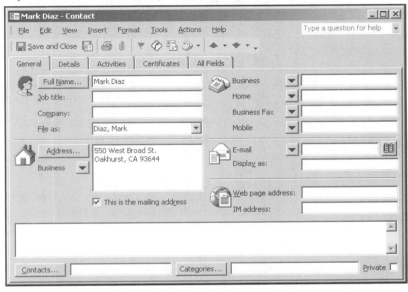

Figure 13-10: Select Contact List folder dialog box

Contacts folder
selected

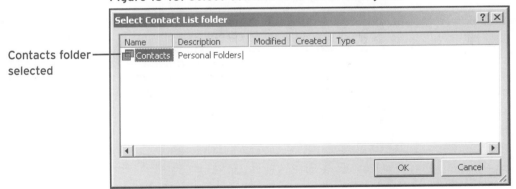

Skill Set 13

Using Mail Merge

Use Outlook Data as a Mail Merge Data Source (continued)

After you select the names from your Outlook contacts, you need to insert the merge fields as with an ordinary mail merge.

Activity Steps

6. Click the **Next: Write your letter link** in the task pane, position the insertion point in the main document below the date so that there is one blank line between it and the date, click the **Address block link**, click **Match Fields**, verify that each field in the Required information list contains a value except the Spouse First Name field, then click **OK** twice

7. Press **[Enter]** twice, click the **Greeting line link** to open the Greeting Line dialog box, click the list arrow next to **Mr. Randall**, scroll down and click **Joshua**, click **OK**, click the **Next: Preview your letters link**, then click in the task pane to see the second merged letter
   See Figure 13-11.

8. Click the **Next: Complete the merge link**, click the **Edit individual letters link**, make sure the **All option button** is selected in the Merge to New Document dialog box, then click **OK** to open a merged document containing all the form letters with the temporary filename Letters followed by a number
   See Figure 13-12.

9. Click the **Outlook program button** on the taskbar, click **Contacts** in the Outlook Shortcuts bar, click **Mark Diaz** in the Contacts list, click the **Delete button** ⊠, click **Lena Yee** in the Contacts list, click the **Delete button** ⊠, then click the **Close button** ⊠ in the Outlook program window

file ▷| close Letters1.doc
               CCLetter04.doc

Figure 13-11: Previewing the merged letters

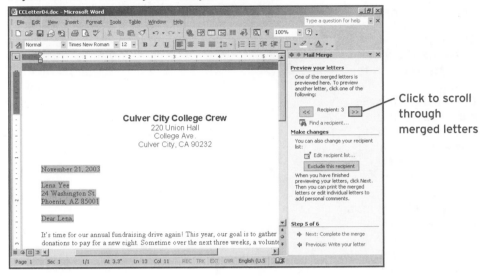

Click to scroll through merged letters

Figure 13-12: First merged letter after completing the merge process

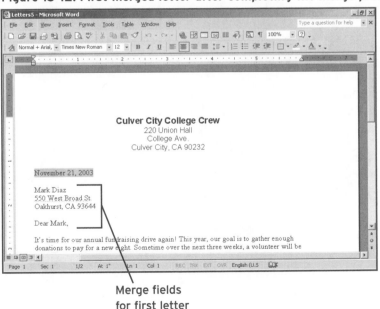

Merge fields
for first letter

Skill Set 13
Using Mail Merge

Target Your Skills

 CCLetter05.doc

1 Merge the file CCLetter05 with the mailing list in CCMailList03. Make sure you open the Match Fields dialog box and set each merge field to the correct field in the data source. In the Greeting line merge field, match the merge field Courtesy Title to the data source field Title. Figure 13-13 shows the last letter in the final merged document.

Figure 13-13

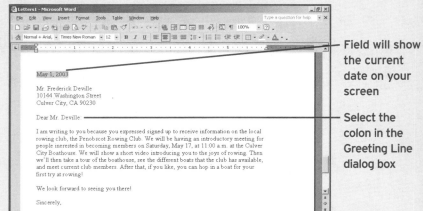

Field will show the current date on your screen

Select the colon in the Greeting Line dialog box

2 Create the merged labels document shown in Figure 13-14 by merging the data source CCMailList04 with a new, blank document. Use Avery standard 2160 Mini - Address labels. The figure shows the last three labels in the final merged document.

Figure 13-14

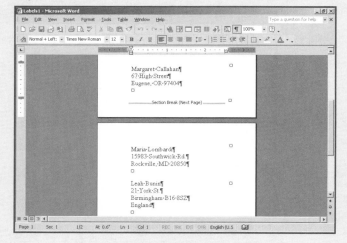

Getting Started

Getting Started with Excel 2002

Skill List

1. Start and exit the Excel program
2. Explore the Excel window
3. Open and close an Excel Workbook
4. Navigate an Excel Workbook
5. Explore task panes
6. Copy workbook files
7. Save a workbook
8. Preview and print a worksheet
9. Get Help

Microsoft Excel 2002 is a **spreadsheet** program, which is a program that lets you organize and analyze numeric information using a grid of columns and rows. Once you have entered your information into an Excel file, called a **workbook,** you can analyze it by having Excel perform calculations. Excel has many types of **charts** that let you portray your data in graphic form. But the real power of Excel lies in its ability to rapidly recalculate formulas when you change basic information; because you can easily explore different outcomes, Excel can be a powerful decision-making tool. This Getting Started Skill Set familiarizes you with the main parts of the Excel window and basic Excel skills; it also gives you information on the conventions in this book to help you complete the activities correctly.

Getting Started

Getting Started with Excel 2002

Start and Exit the Excel Program

Start and Exit Excel

In order to use Excel tools, you need to start the program. When you start Excel, your computer reads the program from your hard disk and displays it on the screen. You start Excel the same way you would start any other Microsoft Office program, by using the Start menu on the Windows taskbar at the bottom of the screen. After you start the program, you can open and work with Excel workbooks. When you are finished, you close your workbooks and **exit**, or close, the program. *In this book, we assume that Excel will be running on your computer before you proceed with lesson steps and that you will exit Excel at the end of your work session.*

Depending on your computer system, your startup procedure could differ from these instructions. If you are working on a networked computer, you may need to check with your technical resource person.

Activity Steps

1. Make sure your computer is on and that you can see the Windows desktop on your screen

2. Click the **Start button** 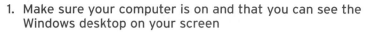 on the Windows taskbar

3. Point to **Programs**

4. Point to **Microsoft Excel**
   See Figure GS-1.

5. Click **Microsoft Excel**
   The Excel program starts, displaying the program window and a blank worksheet on the screen.

6. If your window is not maximized, click the **Maximize button** ▢ on the Excel title bar
   See Figure GS-2.
   The **New Workbook task pane** appears on the right side of the screen. The task pane window opens as you use the program to give you easy access to specific program features. In this case, it displays options for opening new Excel workbooks.

7. Click the **Close button** ☒ on the Excel program window title bar

8. If you see a dialog box asking if you want to save your changes, click **No**

Figure GS-1: Programs submenu

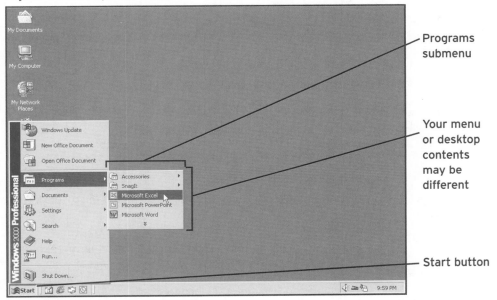

Programs submenu

Your menu or desktop contents may be different

Start button

Figure GS-2: Excel program window

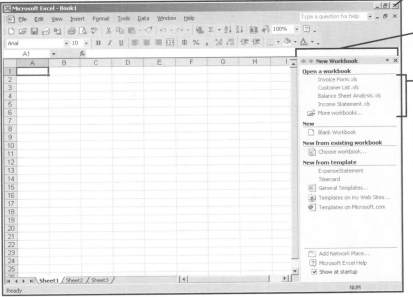

Program window Close button

New Workbook task pane

Your workbook list may vary

extra!

Another way to start Excel
You can also start Excel by opening a folder on the Windows desktop and double-clicking any Excel workbook icon, which will both start Excel and open that workbook.

Getting Started

Getting Started with Excel 2002

Explore the Excel Window
Explore Excel Window Elements

At the top of the Excel window you see the **title bar** containing the program and workbook name, as well as the **menu bar** and the **toolbars**, which you use to enter and work with information. The Excel program window contains the **worksheet**, which is the grid of columns and rows where you enter information. (Some people refer to a worksheet as a spreadsheet, although this also describes the software category.) An Excel workbook file can have multiple worksheets. In a worksheet, the intersection of each column and row is called a **cell**. One cell always has a black border surrounding it, which means it is the **active cell**; any numbers or words you type will appear in the active cell.

Step 1
The screens in this book show the Excel toolbars in two rows. If your screen shows only one toolbar instead of the two shown in the figure, click the Toolbar Options button on the right side of either toolbar, then click Show Buttons on Two Rows.

Activity Steps

1. **If you have not done so already, start the Microsoft Excel program**
   The program starts, and a new workbook automatically opens.

2. **Examine Figure GS-3 and Table GS-1 to identify the main parts of the Excel window and learn the function of each one**
   The cell at the intersection of column A and row 1 has a dark border around it, meaning that it is the active cell. The active cell is also called the **selected** or **highlighted cell**.

3. **Click the cell at the intersection of column D and row 15**
   Cell D15 is now the active cell. The column D heading and row 15 heading are now shaded. The Name box in the Formula bar reads "D15," which is the address of the active cell. A **cell address** is the combination of column number and row number that uniquely identifies each cell.

4. **Move the mouse to place the pointer over the toolbars, then slowly move the pointer, pausing over several buttons**
   As you point to each toolbar button, a yellow **ScreenTip** identifies it. While the steps in this book contain pictures of the buttons you click, you can use ScreenTips as you perform the steps to verify that you are selecting the correct button.

Figure GS-3: Excel window elements

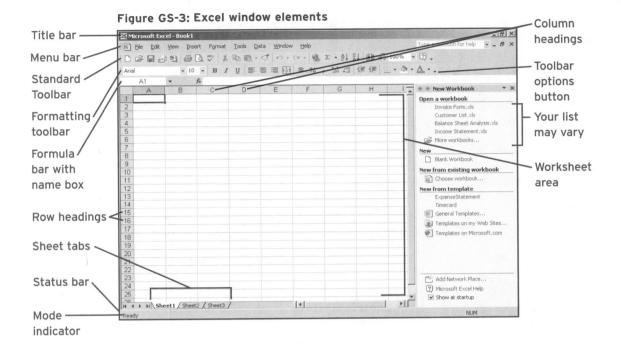

Title bar

Menu bar

Standard Toolbar

Formatting toolbar

Formula bar with name box

Row headings

Sheet tabs

Status bar

Mode indicator

Column headings

Toolbar options button

Your list may vary

Worksheet area

TABLE GS-1: Description of Excel window elements

element	description	element	description
Title bar	Displays program and workbook names	Column and row headings	Contain column letters and row numbers that identify worksheet cells
Menu bar	Contains names of menus with commands that let you interact with Excel	Worksheet area	Contains cells that will hold text and numbers you enter
Standard toolbar	Displays buttons you click to quickly open, save, and print worksheets	Sheet tabs	Let you display other worksheets in the workbook
Formatting toolbar	Displays buttons you click to change the appearance of worksheet text and numbers	Status bar	Gives information on status of program after certain actions
Formula bar with Name box	Formula Bar shows formula of active cell and buttons you use in creating formulas; Name box contains address of active cell or worksheet area	Mode indicator	Displays text such as "Enter" or "Edit" to indicate action taking place

Getting Started

Getting Started with Excel 2002

Open and Close an Excel Workbook
Open and Close an Excel Workbook

A **workbook** is an Excel file containing one or more worksheets. Worksheets contain information, usually a combination of text and numbers, that you analyze using Excel tools. After you start the Excel program, you either begin with a new workbook or open an existing one. When you open a workbook, your computer reads the file information from a disk, places it in your computer's temporary memory, and displays it on your screen. When you are finished with a workbook, you close it, which removes it from memory, but the workbook file remains on your disk. If you exit the Excel program while a workbook is open, the workbook will close also, but the program will ask if you want to save any changes you have made.

Activity Steps

Step 2
You can also click the More Workbooks hyperlink in the New Workbook task pane to display the Open dialog box.

1. If Excel is not already running, start it now

2. Click the **Open button** 📂 on the Standard toolbar

3. Click the **Look in list arrow**, then navigate to the location where your Project Files are stored
   See Figure GS-4.
   If your Project Files are stored in a folder, navigate to the folder by using the **Up One Level button** 📑 to move up in the disk structure, or by double-clicking folders to open them and move downward in the disk structure.

4. Click the filename **Income01**, then click **Open**
   See Figure GS-5.
   The Income01 workbook file opens on the screen. Its title appears in the title bar. The filename is Income01, and its file extension is .xls. A **file extension** contains a period followed by three letters and tells you what program created the file: .xls represents a Microsoft Excel file, .doc a Microsoft Word file, and .ppt a Microsoft PowerPoint file.

5. Click the **Close Window button** ☒ on the right side of the Menu bar to close the file but leave the Excel program open

Figure GS-4: Open dialog box

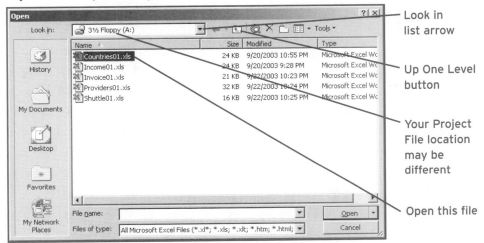

Look in
list arrow

Up One Level
button

Your Project
File location
may be
different

Open this file

Figure GS-5: Open document

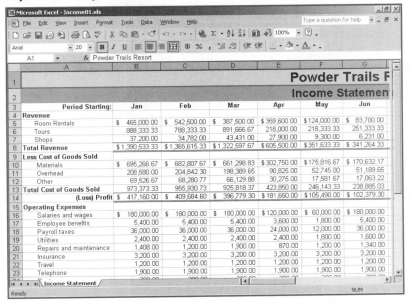

extra!

Displaying file extensions

This book assumes that your computer is set to display file extensions. To display them, go to the Windows desktop, then double-click any drive or folder icon. Click **OK**. Click **Tools**, click **Folder Options**, then click the **View tab**. Click to remove the check from **Hide file extensions for known file types**, then Click **OK**.

Getting Started

Getting Started with Excel 2002

Navigate an Excel Workbook

Navigate an Excel Workbook

As you enter and analyze data in an Excel workbook, you will need to move around the worksheet cells and, in many cases, switch among worksheets. You will save time if you use the most efficient ways of navigating in Excel. As you move the mouse pointer over different window areas, the pointer changes shape to indicate the type of action you can perform: the select pointer ⌀ lets you select open menus and click buttons; the normal pointer ✛ lets you select worksheet cells; the I-beam pointer Ⅰ lets you insert text and formulas; the column pointer ↓ and row pointer ➡ let you highlight an entire column or row. See Table GS-2 for a list of keyboard navigation tools.

Step 2
Scroll bars can help you navigate quickly, although they do not move the active cell. Click the scroll arrows to move one row or column at a time; click the gray areas on either side of the scroll box to move one screenful at a time; or drag the scroll box to move large distances.

Activity Steps

 open Countries01.xls

1. Click cell **B4**, press **[Tab]** five times, then look in the Formula bar
   The formula for the selected cell, cell G4, appears in the Formula bar; the selected cell address (G4) appears in the Name box.

2. Press **[↓]** three times, noticing that the cell addresses in the Name box change for each cell

3. Click the **down arrow** on the vertical scroll bar until the chart is visible on your screen
   See Figure GS-6.

4. Click the **Europe, Asia**, then the **North America sheet tabs**

5. Click the **International Guests sheet tab**, then press **[Pg Up]** (or **[Page Up]**)

6. Press **[Ctrl][Home]**
   The selected cell is now cell A1.

 close Countries01.xls

Figure GS-6: Chart on worksheet

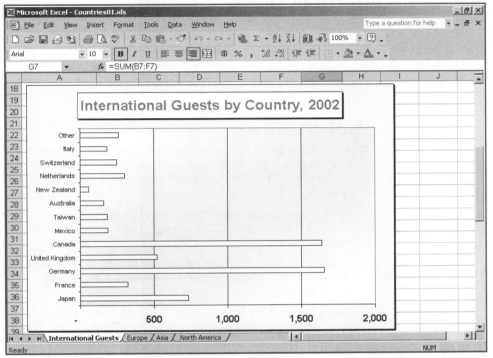

TABLE GS-2: Keyboard navigation tools

to move	press	to move	press
Up, down, left, or right by one cell	[↑] [↓] [←] [→]	Up one screen	[Pg Up] or [Page Up]
One cell to the right	[Tab]	Down one screen	[Pg Dn] or [Page Down]
One cell to the left	[Shift][Tab]	To beginning of a row	[Home]
One cell down	[Enter]	To cell A1 in the worksheet	[Ctrl][Home]

Getting Started

Getting Started with Excel 2002

Explore Task Panes
Explore the Excel Task Panes

As you perform Excel tasks, you will sometimes see **task panes**, windows that appear next to the worksheet to let you perform specific tasks. When you start Excel or when you select the New command from the File menu, the New Workbook task pane appears automatically. Table GS-3 describes the four Excel task panes. In the steps below, you learn how to display task panes and move among them.

Activity Steps

1. Make sure Excel is running and there is a blank workbook on the screen, if the New Workbook task pane is open on your screen, skip to Step 4; if a different task pane is open, skip to Step 3.

2. Click **View** on the menu bar, then click **Task Pane**
   The Task Pane command is a **toggle**, meaning that if you select it once, the task pane appears; if you select it again, the task pane closes.

3. Click the **Other Task Panes list arrow** ▼ on the New Workbook task pane title bar, then click **New Workbook**
   See Figure GS-7.

4. Move the pointer slowly down the task pane and watch how the pointer changes, depending on its location
   When the pointer turns to ⏚, the pointer is over a hyperlink that you can click to open that file.

5. Click the **Other Task Panes list arrow** on the New Workbook task pane title bar, then click **Clipboard**

6. Click the **Back arrow** ◀ on the task pane title bar

7. Click the **Other Task Panes list arrow** in the new **Workbook** task pane title bar, then click **Search**

8. Click the **Other Task Panes list arrow**, then click **Insert Clip Art**

9. Click the **Close button** ✖ on the task pane title bar

Step 2
If the task pane was open on your screen at the start of this activity, Step 2 will close it; repeating the step will redisplay it.

Figure GS-7: New Workbook task pane

Back arrow

Your list may vary

New Workbook task pane

Other Task Panes list arrow

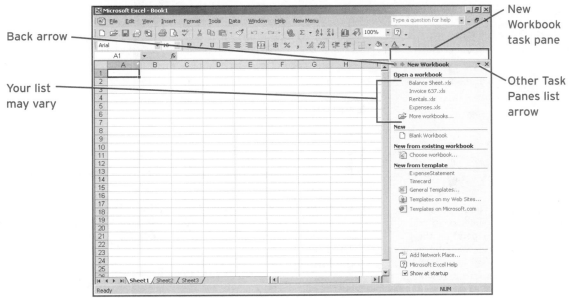

TABLE GS-3: Excel task panes

task pane	what it does
New Workbook	Shows hyperlinks you can click to open a new Excel workbook, which can be blank a copy of an existing workbook; or to open dialog boxes with more options for opening workbooks.
Clipboard	Shows items on the Office Clipboard, a temporary holding area in your computer's memory that holds up to 24 items you have cut or copied in any Office program; click a clipboard item to paste it in the active cell of the open worksheet.
Search	Search for Excel files on your disks by entering a file type, part of a name, and/or a location; has Basic and Advanced options
Insert Clip Art	Lets you search for graphics related to a topic you type, then insert a graphic into your worksheet
Document Recovery	In case the Excel program encounters problems and stops responding, this task pane appears automatically and lists the workbooks (also called **documents**) that were open at the time and the versions it has recovered; click the version you want to open. *The Document Recovery task pane appears only after you restart Excel due to program difficulties or an unexpected computer shutdown.*

Getting Started
Getting Started with Excel 2002

Copy Workbook Files
Copy Project Files

This book instructs you to open and close each project file without saving changes at the end of each activity. Before starting the activities in this book, you should copy all Excel Project Files so you have an original and intact set of files, in case you inadvertently accept your changes as you complete the activities. You can copy your workbooks to a folder, or you can copy them to another disk.

Activity Steps

The location of the folder copy will depend on the View menu option you have selected to arrange your files. You may need to scroll to see the folder copy. You can also use the Copy and Paste commands on the Edit menu to copy files or folders.

1. If the Excel program is running, click the **Minimize button** on the title bar to display the Windows desktop

2. If you have any other programs running, repeat Step 1 to minimize them

3. On the Windows desktop, double-click **My Computer**, then double-click folders and use the **Address list arrow** and the **Up arrow** to display the folder where your Project Files are stored
   The files may be stored in a folder named 5670-3, the last 5 digits of the ISBN number for this book.

4. Click **File** on the menu bar, point to **New**, then click **Folder**

5. Type **Backups**, then press **Enter**

6. Right-click the **Project Files folder**, then click **Copy**

7. Double-click the **Backups folder**, right-click in the folder window, then click **Paste**
   See Figure GS-8, which assumes that the Project Files folder is named for the last five digits of the ISBN number for this book. Windows places a copy of your Project Files folder in the Backups folder. You can use these Project File copies in case you should inadvertently save your changes as you work through the lessons. Then you can always return to the original versions of the files.

Figure GS-8: Copy of Project Files folder

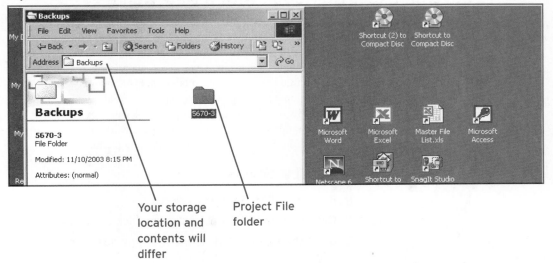

Your storage
location and
contents will
differ

Project File
folder

Getting Started
Getting Started with Excel 2002

Save Workbooks
Save an Excel Workbook with a New Name

Although this book assumes you will close your workbooks without saving at the end of each activity, you will usually want to save your Excel workbooks on a disk. (You will learn more about saving workbooks in Skill Set 2.) You can save your workbooks in the My Documents folder, but if you have many different workbooks, it might be difficult to find the one you need later on. It's good practice to save each workbook with a unique and descriptive name in a folder you name. To save a workbook using its existing name in its present location, you can use the Save button on the Standard toolbar. But to change a workbook's name or its save location, you use the Save As command on the File menu.

Step 1
To create a new Excel workbook, click the New button on the Standard toolbar or click File on the menu bar, then click New. Using the File menu command will open the New Workbook task pane; you then click Blank Workbook in the task pane.

Activity Steps

 open Shuttle01.xls

1. Click **File** on the menu bar, then click **Save As**

2. Click the **Save in list arrow**, then navigate to the drive or folder where you store your Project Files

3. Drag to select the text in the File name box (if it's not already selected), then type **Schedule**
   See Figure GS-9.

4. Click **Save** to save the workbook with the new name in the location you selected
   The saved file named Schedule remains open on the screen. The original file, Shuttle01, closes and remains unchanged on your disk.

5. Observe the total in cell **D18**, click cell **D14**, type **3**, then press **[Enter]**
   The total in cell D18 changes from 52 to 51.

6. Click the **Save button** 🖫 on the Standard toolbar
   See Figure GS-10.

 close Schedule.xls

Figure GS-9: Save As dialog box with new File name

Your storage location may differ

Save in list arrow

New File name

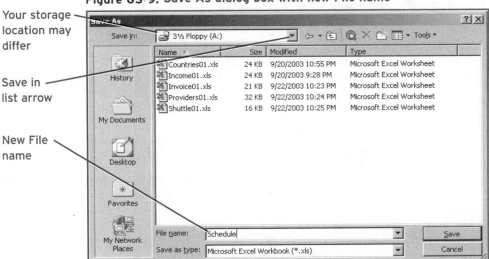

Figure GS-10: Saving the modified file

New filename in title bar

Save button

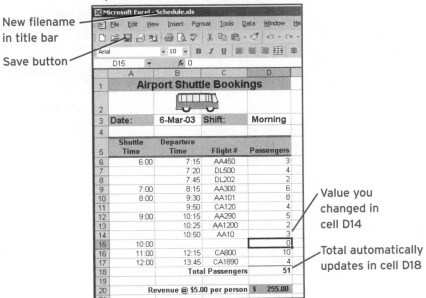

Value you changed in cell D14

Total automatically updates in cell D18

Getting Started
Getting Started with Excel 2002

Preview and Print a Worksheet
Preview and Print a Worksheet

The activities in this book do not instruct you to print your worksheets, but you can print a worksheet any time you want a hard copy. Before printing, you should always preview your worksheet to make sure it looks the way you want. That way you can make any necessary changes in its appearance without wasting paper and toner. If you print your workbooks at a shared printer, you may want to place your name in a worksheet cell to help you identify your copy.

Activity Steps

 open Invoice01.xls

1. Click cell **B6**, type your name, press **[Enter]**, then click the **Print Preview button** on the Standard toolbar
   The workbook appears in the Preview window, showing how the worksheet will look when you print it. When you move the pointer over the worksheet image, it becomes the **Zoom pointer** .
   See Figure GS-11.

2. Click near the word "invoice" at the top of the image, then click again
   You "zoom in" to get a closer look at the image, then "zoom out."

3. Click **Print** on the Preview toolbar
   See Figure GS-12.

4. Under Print what, click the **Active sheet(s) option button**, if it's not already selected

5. Make sure the Number of copies box reads **1**

6. Click **OK**

 close Invoice01.xls

Step 1
To print a worksheet without previewing, click the Print button on the Standard toolbar.

Figure GS-11: Worksheet in Print Preview with zoom pointer

Preview toolbar

Zoom pointer

Preview of printed document

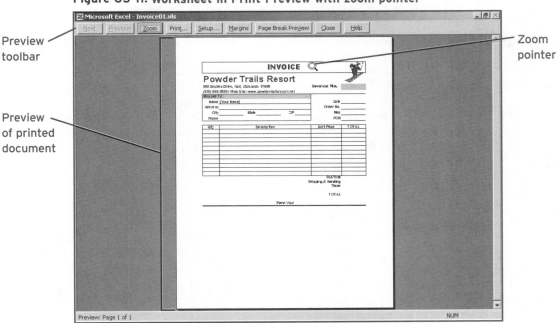

Figure GS-12: Print dialog box

Your printer information and options may be different

Indicate number of copies here

Select this option

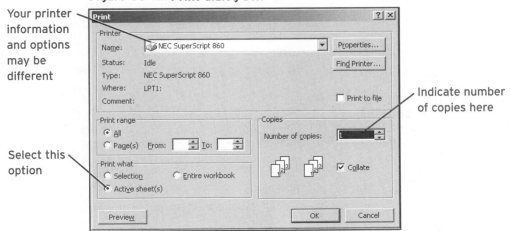

Getting Started

Getting Started with Excel 2002

Get Help

Use Online Help

Whenever you don't know how to proceed as you use Excel, you can always use its **online help system** to find answers to your questions. (The term "online" in "online help" means that you can find help on the screen instead of referring to a book.) There are several ways to get help in Excel. The fastest way is to use the "Type a question for help" box in the Excel menu bar, which will display topic hyperlinks. You click a hyperlink to open the help system and view help information on the topic you clicked. You can also use the Contents, Index, and Answer Wizard tabs in the Help window to search in different ways. You can use the **Print button** 🖶 at the top of the Help window to print any Help topic for future reference.

Step 1
To get help, you can also use the Office Assistant, an animated character in the shape of a paper clip that appears on your screen. Click Help, then click Show the Office Assistant; click the Assistant, type a question in the question balloon, then click a topic. The Help window opens.

Activity Steps

1. Make sure the Excel program is open with a blank workbook on the screen; to display a blank workbook, click the **New button** ▢ on the Standard toolbar

2. Click the **Type a question for help** box on the right side of the menu bar

3. Type **save workbooks**, press **[Enter]**, then click the **Save a workbook** hyperlink in the topic list that appears

4. Click **Show All** in the instructions window
   See Figure GS-13.

5. If your window does not display the tabs shown in Figure G-13, click the **Show button** ⮞ in the Help window toolbar

6. Click the **Index tab** in the Help window (if it's not already selected)

7. Click in the **Type keywords box**, type **print**, then press **[Enter]**

8. Under Choose a topic, click **About printing**, then click the **Show All link** in the information pane
   See Figure GS-14. Topics and terms that have definitions appear in blue text; when you click them or click Show All, the definition appears in green text.

9. Click the **Close button** ✖ on the Help window

Figure GS-13: Microsoft Excel Help dialog box

Show button becomes Hide button

Help information on saving a workbook

If necessary, drag this border to make your Help window size match this figure

This link is a toggle to show or hide details

Click this link to display only an outline of the Help information

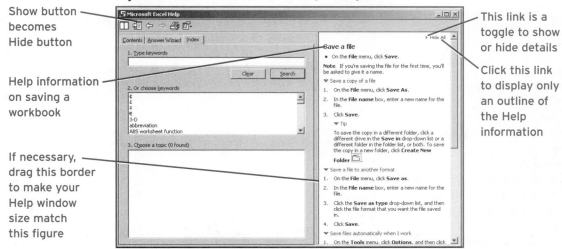

Figure GS-14: Help information on printing

Search text

Topics that relate to your search text

Click blue terms to see definitions; click again to hide definitions

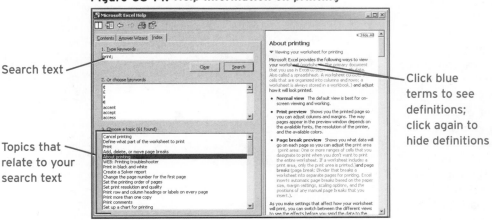

TABLE GS-4: Microsoft Excel Help window tabs

help window tab	how to use
Contents	Click plus signs next to topics to display further topics; click question mark icons to display help in right section
Answer Wizard	Type a question in the What would you like to do? Box, click Search, then click a topic to display information in right section
Index	Type text in Type keywords box, click Search, click topic at bottom, read explanation in right section

Getting Started

Getting Started with Excel 2002

Target Your Skills

 open Providers01.xls

Figure GS-15

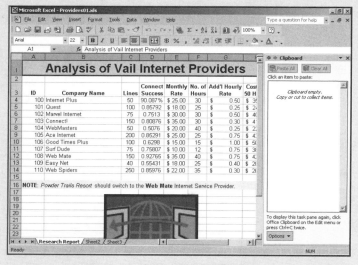

1 Refer to Figure GS-15. Use the navigation keys to move around the worksheet and examine the cells and cell contents. Display the first four task panes shown in Table GS-3, ending with the Clipboard. Preview the worksheet, zoom in and out, then print the worksheet. Save the workbook as Analysis in the drive and folder where you store your files.

2 Open a blank workbook. Use the Office Assistant to search on "help window." Select "About getting help while you work." Click the Assistant character to hide the balloon. Click the topic **"Ask a Question box,"** then click it again. Click Show All, then scroll the window contents. See Figure GS-16. Use the Index tab to search on the word "print," then click the topic of your choice.

Figure GS-16

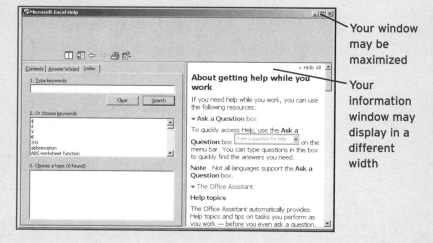

Your window may be maximized

Your information window may display in a different width

Skill List

1. Insert, delete, and move cells
2. Enter and edit cell data including text, numbers, and formulas
3. Check spelling
4. Find and replace cell data and formats
5. Work with a subset of data by filtering lists

In Skill Set 1, you learn how to enter and change cell data in Microsoft Excel 2002. Excel is an electronic spreadsheet program that lets you create and use workbooks. A **workbook** is an Excel file that contains **worksheets**, or electronic ledgers made up of rows and columns of cells. **Cells** are the intersections of worksheet rows and columns, and they can contain text, numbers, or formulas. You can add new data, delete, move, or edit existing data, or filter data to work on specific data in a large worksheet.

Skill Set 1

Working with Cells and Cell Data

Insert, Delete, and Move Cells
Insert and Delete Cells

As you build worksheets in Excel, you will need to add and delete information. You may find you forgot to add an item, or information may become obsolete. You can insert or delete cells, a block of cells, or entire rows or columns in any area of a worksheet. When you insert one or more cells, Excel adds them above the selected horizontal cell range or to the left of the selected vertical cell range. When you delete cells, Excel removes them from the worksheet. *After you insert or delete cells, be very careful to check the alignment of your data and the accuracy of your formulas. Also be sure columns or rows you want to delete don't contain any necessary data in an area not visible on the screen.*

Step 6
You can also right-click a selected range, or any row or column heading, then select Insert or Delete on the shortcut menu.

Activity Steps

 open Expenses01.xls

1. Select the range **B11:E11**

2. Click **Insert** on the menu bar, then click **Cells**
   See Figure 1-1.

3. Click **Shift cells down** (if it's not already selected), then click **OK**

4. Select cells **D7:D14**

5. Click **Edit** on the menu bar, then click **Delete**

6. Click the **Shift cells left** option button (if it's not already selected), then click **OK**
   See Figure 1-2.

 close Expenses01.xls

Figure 1-1: Insert dialog box

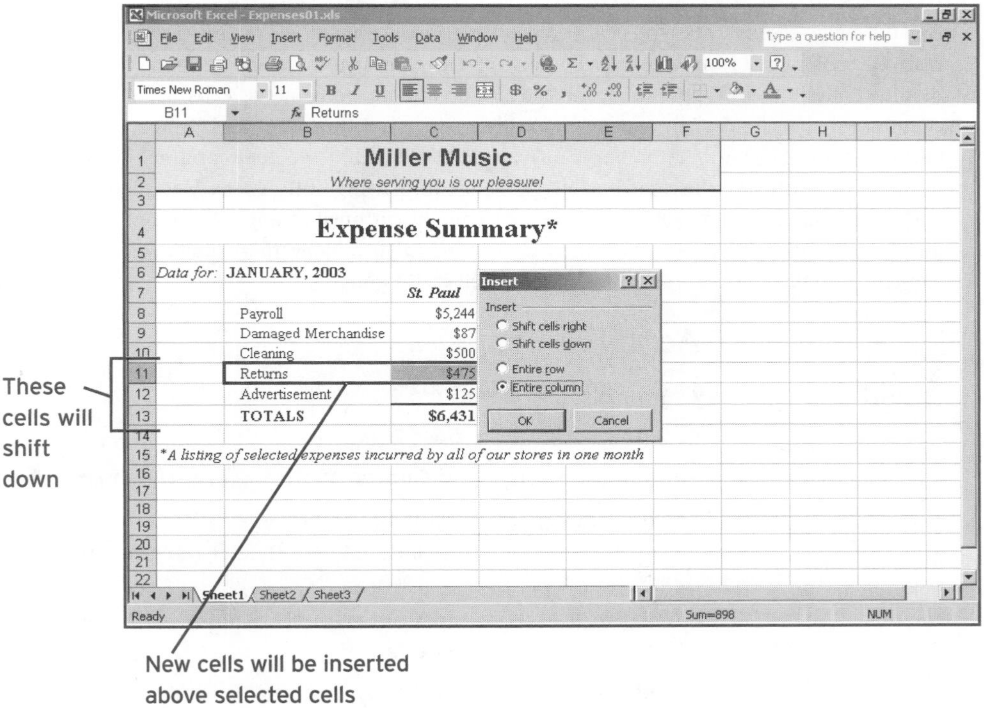

These cells will shift down

New cells will be inserted above selected cells

Figure 1-2: Worksheet after deleting cells

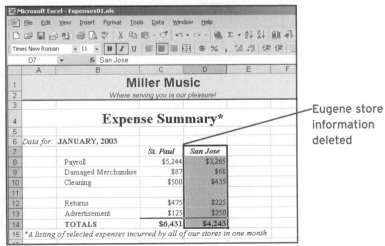

Eugene store information deleted

Skill Set 1

Working with Cells and Cell Data

Insert, Delete, and Move Cells
Merge and Split Cells

As you create worksheets, you will often want to create a title that spans several columns above your data. To do this, you can **merge**, or combine, contiguous cells into one large cell. You may also want to both merge cells and center a title in the new, larger cell. To do this you can use the Merge and Center button on the Formatting toolbar. You can **split** the cells into their original component cells using the same button. Like most formatting buttons, the Merge and Center button is a **toggle**, meaning that you click it once to apply the format to the selected cell or range, then click it again to remove the format. A merged cell takes the format of the leftmost cell in the range.

Step 2
To merge cells without centering, click Format on the menu bar, click Cells, click the Alignment tab, click to select the Merge Cells check box, then click OK.

Activity Steps

 open Update01.xls

1. Select the range **B6:E6**

2. Click the **Merge and Center button** on the Formatting toolbar

3. Click the heading **Miller Music**
   This is a merged and centered cell. Its cell reference in the Name Box is A1.

4. Click the **Merge and Center button** on the Formatting toolbar to split the cells

5. Click a blank area of the worksheet to deselect the cells
   See Figure 1-3.

close Update01.xls

Figure 1-3: Merged and centered text

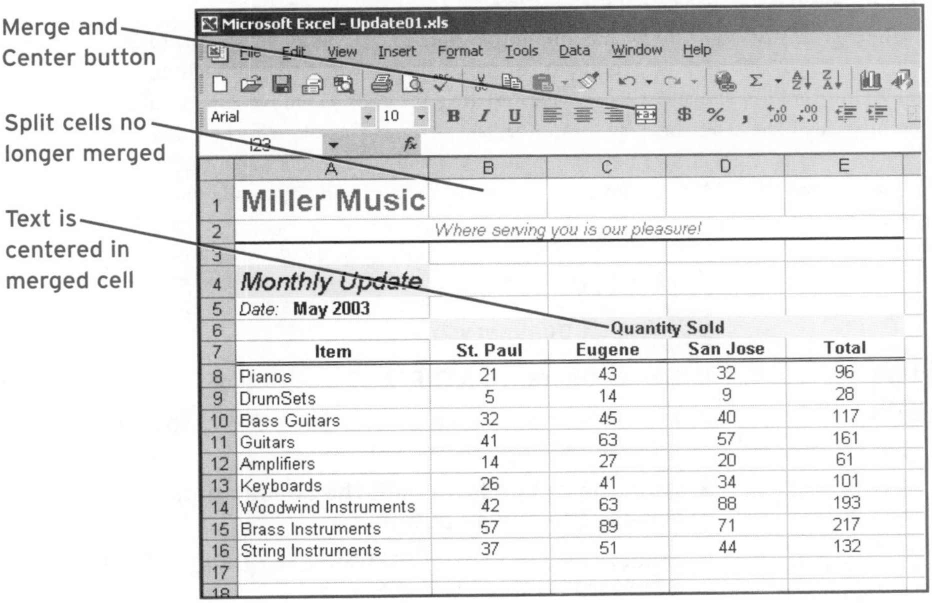

Merge and Center button

Split cells no longer merged

Text is centered in merged cell

	A	B	C	D	E
1	**Miller Music**				
2		*Where serving you is our pleasure!*			
3					
4	*Monthly Update*				
5	Date: **May 2003**				
6				Quantity Sold	
7	**Item**	**St. Paul**	**Eugene**	**San Jose**	**Total**
8	Pianos	21	43	32	96
9	DrumSets	5	14	9	28
10	Bass Guitars	32	45	40	117
11	Guitars	41	63	57	161
12	Amplifiers	14	27	20	61
13	Keyboards	26	41	34	101
14	Woodwind Instruments	42	63	88	193
15	Brass Instruments	57	89	71	217
16	String Instruments	37	51	44	132
17					
18					

extra!

Merging and centering cell data

You can change the alignment of a merged and centered cell by clicking the **Align Left**, **Center**, or **Align Right** buttons on the Formatting toolbar. You can merge and center only one row of data at a time.

Skill Set 1
Working with Cells and Cell Data

Insert, Delete, and Move Cells
Move Cells

You can easily move worksheet cells to another area of the same worksheet, to another worksheet in the same workbook, or to a different workbook altogether. To move information short distances, you can drag the cells. To move cells to a different part of the worksheet or to another sheet or workbook, use the Copy and Paste buttons. Pasted information replaces any cell data in the paste range. When you move cells, the cells' contents, formulas, format, and comments move with them.

Step 5
To move data to a different worksheet, cut the data, click the sheet tab of the destination worksheet, click the upper left cell of the paste range, then click the Paste button 📋 on the Standard toolbar.

Activity Steps

📄 **open Summary01.xls**

1. Select the range **A17:F17**

2. Place the mouse pointer over the edge of the selected range until it becomes

3. Drag the range down until the shaded outline is on row 19, then release the mouse button

4. Select the range **A6:F15**, then click the **Cut button** ✂ on the Standard toolbar
   See Figure 1-4.

5. Click cell **A8**
   You only need to select the upper left cell of the paste range.

6. Click the **Paste button** 📋 on the Standard toolbar, then click any blank cell
   The range you cut is now pasted in a new location: the range starting in cell A8.
   See Figure 1-5.

📄 **close Summary01.xls**

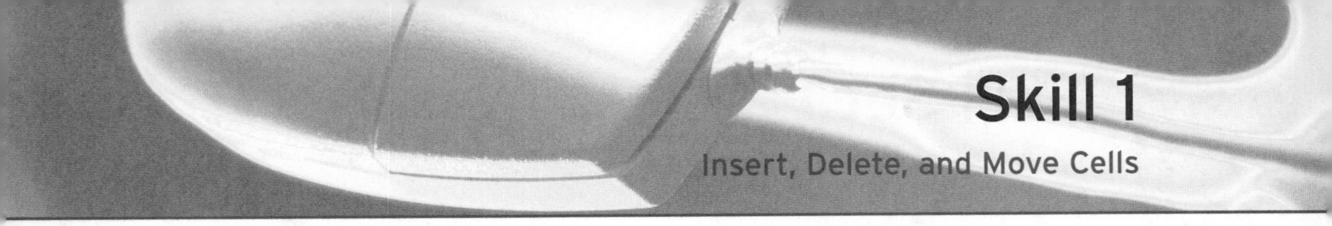

Figure 1-4: Cut range

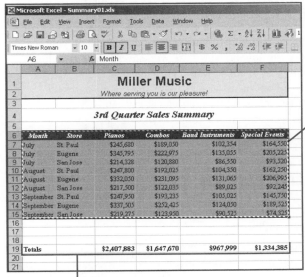

Dotted line around range
indicates information
has been cut

Range moved to
new location

Figure 1-5: Moved ranges

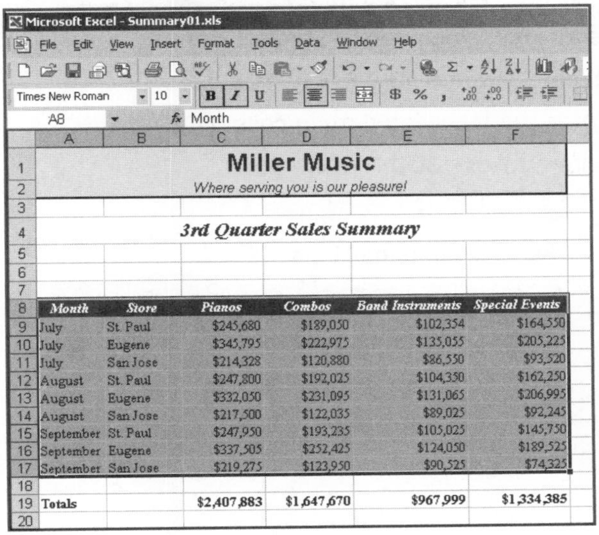

Using the Office Clipboard

When you cut information from an Office document, Office temporarily stores the data in the **Office Clipboard**, which appears in the task pane. The Office Clipboard stores up to 24 items in your computer's memory. All Clipboard items are available for you to paste as long as an Office program is open. To open the Clipboard task pane, click **View** on the menu bar, click **Task Pane**, click the **Other Task Panes list arrow** (the triangle in the Task Pane title bar), then select **Clipboard**. To paste any item, click the destination cell, then click the Clipboard item you want to paste.

Skill Set 1
Working with Cells and Cell Data

Enter and Edit Cell Data Including Text, Numbers, and Formulas
Enter Text and Numbers

You enter text and numbers in the **active cell**, which is the selected cell on your worksheet. You usually use text for **labels**, which are worksheet headings that identify the **values**, or numbers, that you may want to use in calculations. After you type a label or value, you can **enter**, or accept it, by using the mouse or the keyboard. Excel automatically left-aligns labels and right-aligns values. You can navigate around the worksheet using the mouse or the keyboard. See Table 1-1. To display other areas of a worksheet without moving the active cell, use the scroll bars.

Step 2
Occasionally you will want Excel to treat certain numbers (such as zip codes) as text instead of amounts to be used in calculations. To do this, place an apostrophe ('), also called the label prefix, before the number, as in '02174.

Activity Steps

 open Advertising01.xls

1. Click cell A10

2. Type **Newspapers**, then press **[Tab]**
   If you make a typing error, press [Backspace] and retype the character, or click the Cancel button ☒ on the Formula bar and begin again.

3. Type **1800**, press **[Tab]**, type **1300**, then press **[Tab]**

4. Type **1200**, then click the **Enter button** ☑ on the Formula bar

5. Enter the following data into the range **A11:D11**, using the same techniques you used in Steps 3 and 4:

   Radio Spots   600   800   700

6. Enter the following data in cells **A12:D12**:

   Subway Ads   300   400   250
   See Figure 1-6.

 close Advertising01.xls

Figure 1-6: Worksheet with labels and values entered

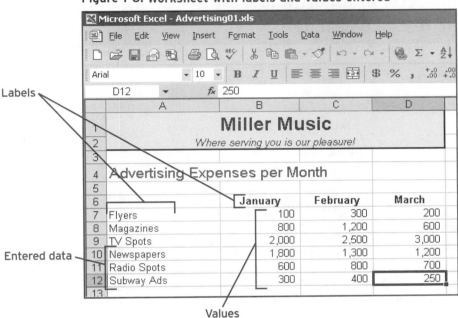

Labels

Entered data

Values

TABLE 1-1: Navigating within a worksheet using the keyboard

press	to move to	press	to move to
[Ctrl][Home]	Cell A1	[Page Up]	One screen up
[Tab]	Cell to right	[Page Down]	One screen down
[Enter]	Cell below	[Alt][Page Up]	One screen left
[up arrow], [down arrow], [left arrow] or [right arrow]	Cells above, below, to left or right	[Alt][Page Down]	One screen right

Skill Set 1

Working with Cells and Cell Data

Enter and Edit Cell Data Including Text, Numbers, and Formulas

Edit Text and Numbers

After you enter labels and values in a worksheet, you can easily edit them to correct errors or reflect new information. You can select a cell and edit data using the Formula bar, or you can use **in-cell editing**, which lets you modify the data directly in a selected cell.

Step 6
To activate in-cell editing, you can also press [F2].

Activity Steps

 open Advertising02.xls

1. Click cell **C11**

2. Click in the Formula bar after the number, then press **[Backspace]** three times

3. Type **750** then click the **Enter button** ☑ in the Formula bar

4. Click cell **D9**, then in the Formula bar drag to select the **3**
   See Figure 1-7.

5. Type **2**, then click ☑ in the Formula bar
   Next, you'll use in-cell editing.

6. Double-click cell **A9** to the left of TV, press **[Delete]** twice, type **Television**, then click ☑ in the Formula bar

7. Double-click cell **D11**, if necessary, use ← to move the insertion point before the 7, press **[Delete]**, then type **6**

8. Press **[Enter]**
   See Figure 1-8.

 close Advertising02.xls

Figure 1-7: Editing in the Formula bar

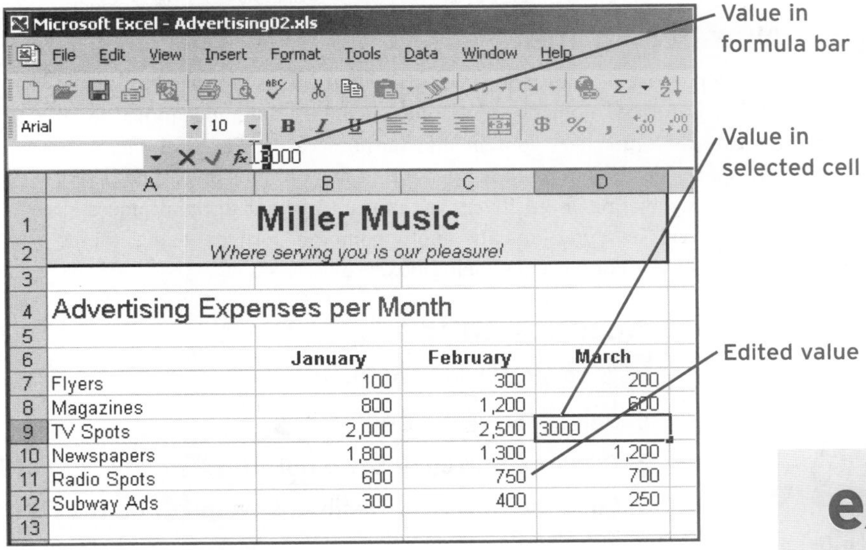

Value in formula bar

Value in selected cell

Edited value

Figure 1-8: Edited values

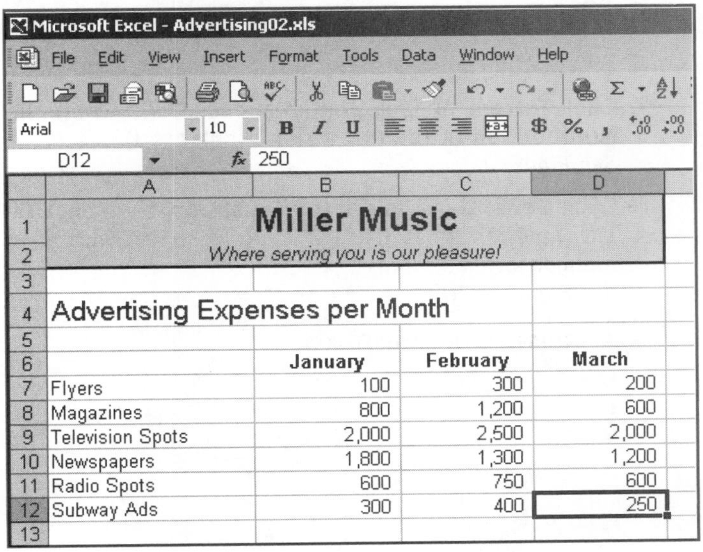

extra!

Editing automatically using AutoCorrect
To save you time, Excel can correct some errors automatically. It can capitalize days of the week, correct two capital letters at the beginning of a word, or convert (c) to ©. To control the corrections Excel makes, click **Tools** on the menu bar, click **AutoCorrect Options**, then click the **AutoCorrect tab**, where you can select or deselect correction options and add your own corrections. For example, if you tend to type "poeple" instead of "people," you can have Excel automatically change it to "people" every time you type it.

Skill Set 1

Working with Cells and Cell Data

Enter and Edit Cell Data Including Text, Numbers, and Formulas
Apply Number Formats

Depending on the purpose of your worksheet, your data values will need a specific look. When you **format** numeric values, you customize their appearance so they communicate the worksheet content and purpose easily. For example, a budget usually shows values with dollar signs; a timesheet often shows times of the day. Quantity information in an inventory appears without decimal places or dollar signs. Excel lets you quickly apply common formats using the Formatting toolbar or the Format Cells dialog box.

Step 8
You can use the Alignment, Font, Border, and Patterns tabs in the Format Cells dialog box to apply a wide array of formats to both labels and values.

Activity Steps

📁 open Markdowns01.xls

1. Select the range **E8:E14**

2. Click the **Currency Style button** on the Formatting toolbar

3. Click the **Decrease Decimal button** 📊 on the Formatting toolbar twice

4. Select the range **F8:F14**

5. Click the **Percent Style button** 📊 on the Formatting toolbar

6. Select the range **D8:D14**

7. Click **Format** on the menu bar, click **Cells,** then click the **Number tab** (if it's not already selected)
   See Figure 1-9.

8. Click **General** in the Category list box, then click **OK**
   The **General** format displays values centered, with no specific number format.
   See Figure 1-10.

 close Markdowns01.xls

Figure 1-9: Format Cells dialog box

Tabs allow detailed formatting of cell text

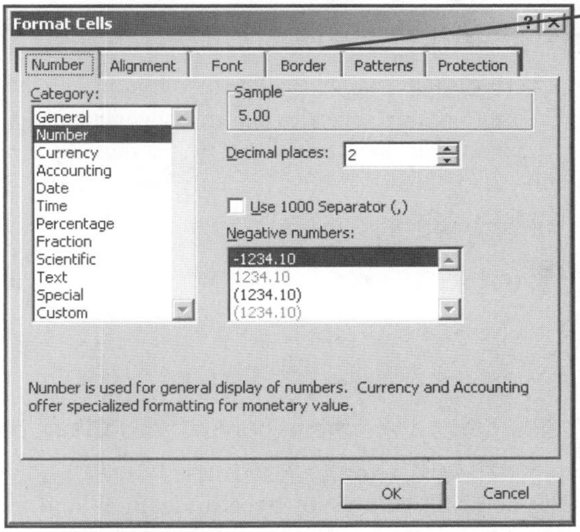

Figure 1-10: Cell formats applied to values

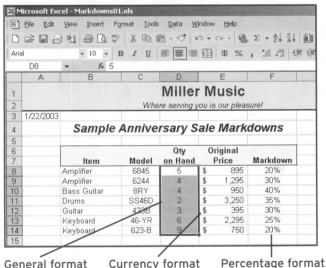

General format   Currency format   Percentage format

extra!

Using the Format Painter

If you need to apply formats to labels and values, you don't always have to use the Formatting toolbar or Format Cells dialog box. The **Format Painter** lets you copy only the formats from a formatted cell and apply them to other cells with just three mouse clicks. Click the cell containing the format you want to copy, click the **Format Painter button** on the Standard toolbar, then click the cell to which you want to apply the format. To apply the format to several cells, double-click the **Format Painter button**, click each cell you want to format, then press **[Esc]** to turn off the Format Painter.

Skill Set 1
Working with Cells and Cell Data

Enter and Edit Cell Data Including Text, Numbers, and Formulas
Clear Cell Contents and Formats

When you want to delete only cell contents while leaving the cell in place, you can **clear** the cell. You can choose to clear cell contents, formats, comments, or all of these. It's important to understand the difference between clearing and deleting cells: Clearing empties the cell of its contents only, while deleting removes both the cell and its contents from the worksheet.

Activity Steps

 open Sales01.xls

1. Click cell **B7**

Step 6
Pressing [Delete] is another way of clearing only cell contents while leaving the cell format intact.

2. Click **Edit** on the menu bar, point to **Clear**, then click **All**

3. Type **75000**, then press **[Enter]**
   The new value does not have the comma and font format because you cleared both contents and formats. It is now in General format, the Excel default.
   See Figure 1-11.

4. Select the range **C7:C13**

5. Click **Edit** on the menu bar, point to **Clear**, then click **Formats**
   The values remain, but their formatting is removed.

6. Click cell **D7**, click **Edit** on the menu bar, point to **Clear**, then click **Contents**

7. Type **7**, then press **[Enter]**
   The formatting remained because you cleared only the cell contents.
   See Figure 1-12.

 close Sales01.xls

Figure 1-11: Clearing formats displays values in General format

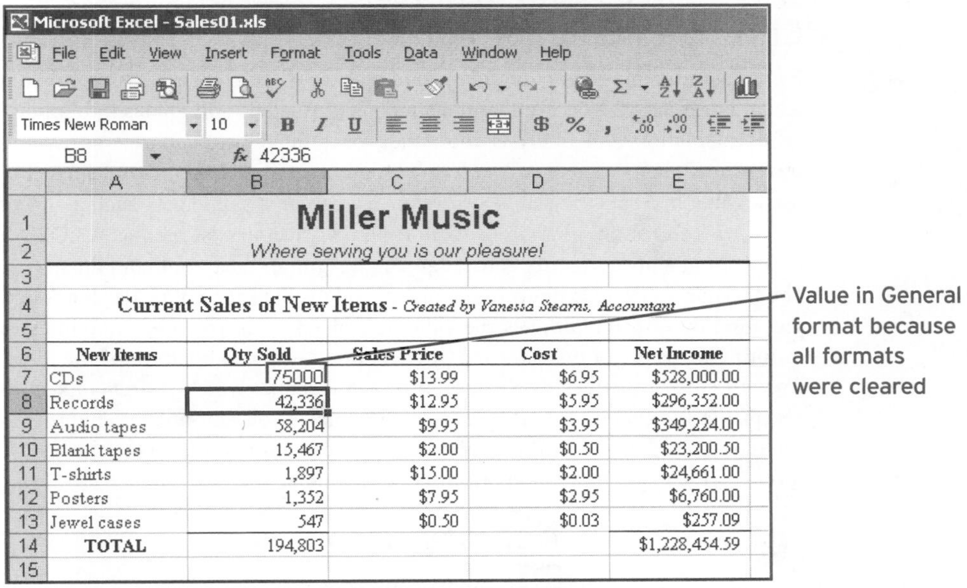

Value in General format because all formats were cleared

Figure 1-12: Clearing contents leaves format intact

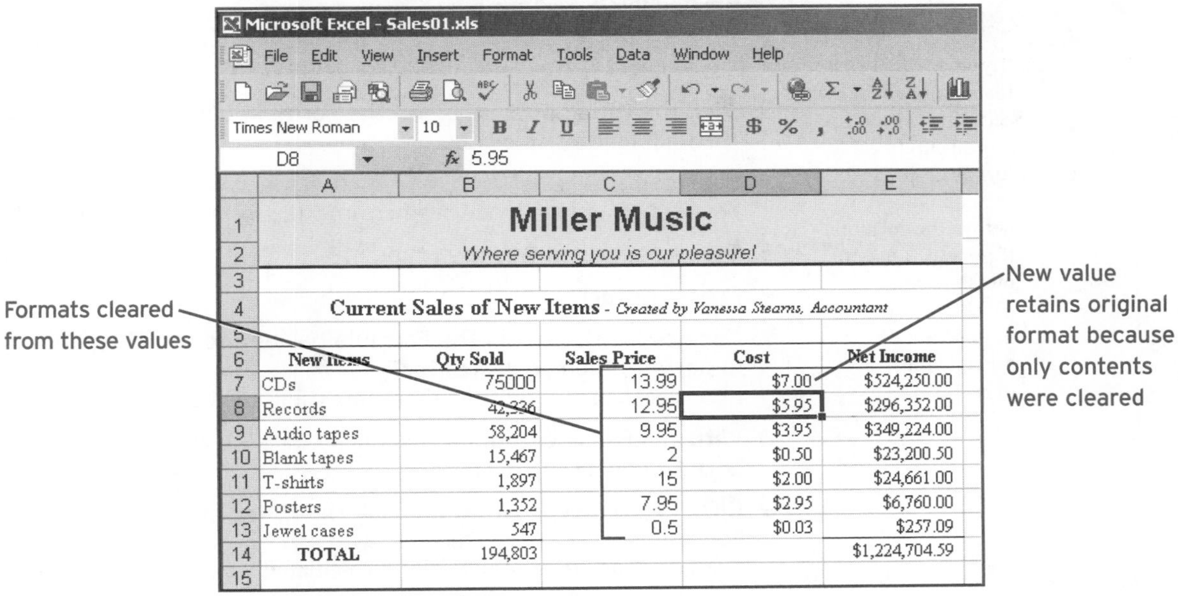

New value retains original format because only contents were cleared

Formats cleared from these values

Skill Set 1
Working with Cells and Cell Data

Enter and Edit Cell Data Including Text, Numbers, and Formulas
Enter and Edit Formulas

Formulas are equations containing values and cell references that calculate a result. Formulas let you transform a simple list of labels and values into a powerful calculation and analysis tool; they contain values, cell references and **operators**, such as + and -. A **cell reference** is a cell address that tells Excel to use a value in a specific cell. A cell reference can be a single cell, such as A6 or C13, or a **cell range**, a group of two or more adjacent cells, such as A3:C6. An Excel formula always starts with = (an equal sign) and may not contain spaces. The formula =1+2 adds the values 1 and 2, and displays the value 3 as the result. The formula =A4*6 multiplies the value in cell A4 by 6. To enter cell addresses in formulas, you can type, point and click, drag, or a combination of the three. As with entering values, you must **enter** the formula, which instructs Excel to accept the formula and perform the calculation. If you edit a cell value that is used in a formula, or edit the formula itself, Excel automatically recalculates the formula. Table 1-2 lists common formula operators.

If you see the formula itself in a cell after you enter it, you might have forgotten to type the equal sign before the formula. If you see an error message such as #VALUE, you might have mistyped an operator or a cell reference.

Activity Steps

   open Employee01.xls

1. Click cell **B9**

2. Type **=B7+B8**
   See Figure 1-13.

3. Click the **Enter button** ☑ on the Formula bar
   The total appears in cell B9.

4. Click cell **B10**
   You will intentionally enter an error in the formula, then correct it.

5. Type **=**, click cell **B9**, then type ***15**

6. Press **[Enter]**

7. Click cell **B10**, click in the Formula bar before the 15, type **.** (a period), then press **[Enter]**
   Excel recalculates the formula results using the edited formula.

8. With cell **B11** selected, type **=**, click cell **B9**, type **+**, click cell **B10**, then press **[Enter]**

9. Click cell **B7**, type **40**, then click the **Enter button** ☑ on the Formula bar
   The formulas are automatically recalculated using the new value.
   See Figure 1-14.

   close Employee01.xls

Figure 1-13: Formula cell references and operator before entering

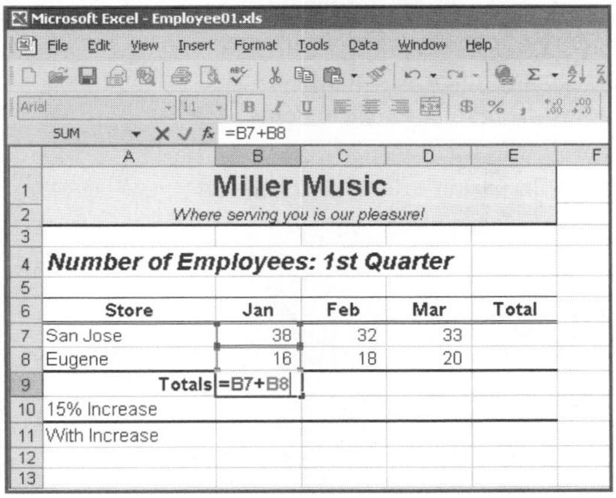

Figure 1-14: Recalculated formulas using edited values and formula

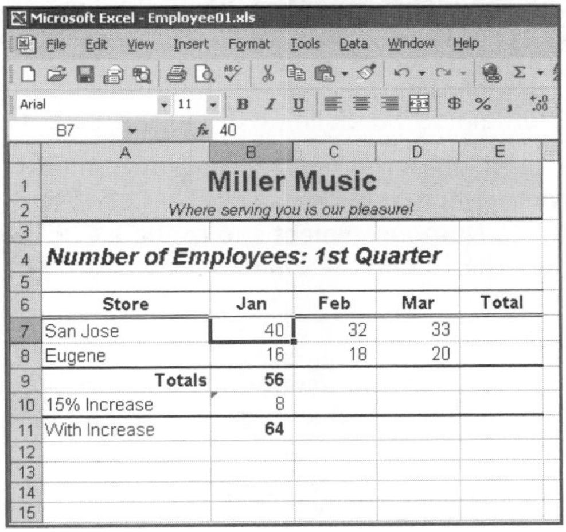

Table 1-2: Formula operators

operand	use to	operand	use to
=	Begin all formulas	*	Multiply values
+	Add values	/	Divide values
-	Subtract values	(and)	Enclose operations that should be performed first

Skill Set 1
Working with Cells and Cell Data

Enter and Edit Cell Data Including Text, Numbers, and Formulas
Add Functions to Formulas

Excel supplies many worksheet **functions**, which are presupplied formulas that calculate values. Some common functions are SUM, AVERAGE, and MAX. Each function has its own name and special **syntax**, or arrangement of elements. All functions start with = (an equal sign), followed by the function name, followed by **arguments**, which are cell or range references in parentheses that tell Excel which values to use to calculate the function result.

Activity Steps

 open Inventory01.xls

1. Click cell **E18**

2. Type **=4*(E8+E9+E10+E11)** then press **[Enter]**

3. Click cell **E21**

4. Type **=4*** and click the **Insert Function button** on the Formula bar to open the Insert Function dialog box and the Excel Function Wizard
   See Figure 1-15.

5. In the Insert Function dialog box, click **SUM** in the Select a function list, then click **OK**

6. In the Function Arguments dialog box, click the **Collapse dialog box button** next to Number1, select the range **E12:E15** on the worksheet, then click the **Redisplay dialog box button**
   See Figure 1-16.

7. Click **OK**
   An error button smart tip offers help, noting that the formula omits adjacent cells and flagging this possible error. The formula is correct as written.

8. Click the **Error button Smart Tip**, then click **Ignore Error**

 close Inventory01.xls

Step 8
To change the types of errors Excel checks for, click the smart tip list arrow, click Error Checking Options, select the options you want, then click OK.

Figure 1-15: Insert Function dialog box

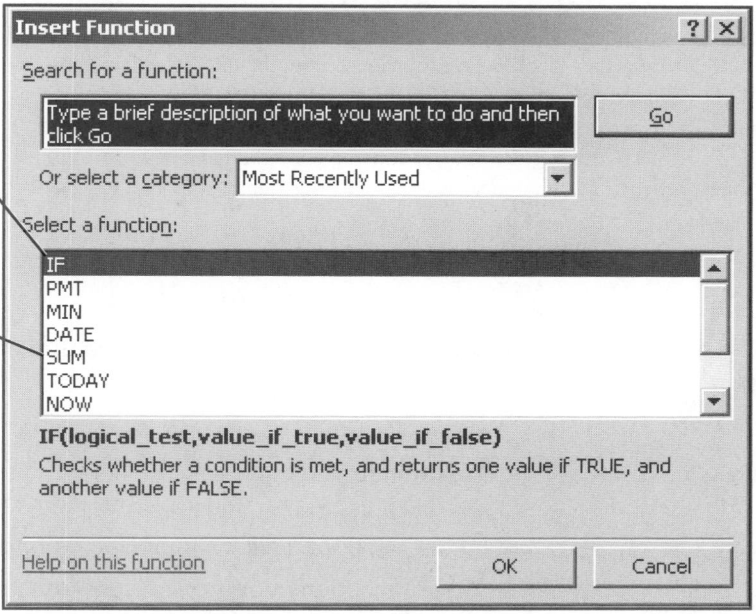

You might have a different function selected

Click this function

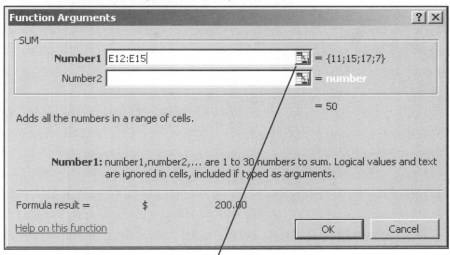

Figure 1-16: Function Arguments dialog box

Clicking Collapse dialog box button lets you drag to insert range

Skill Set 1
Working with Cells and Cell Data

Check Spelling
Check Worksheet Spelling

Even if you have a professional-looking spreadsheet with accurate data and attractive formatting, spelling errors can cast doubt on the reliability of your work. Excel provides a spelling checker that automatically compares each word in your worksheet against an internal spelling dictionary and flags errors. You can accept or reject suggested corrections or you can add the word in question to your own custom dictionary so Excel will not flag it again.

Step 1
Excel flags words that are not in its dictionary, such as your company name. You can click Add to Dictionary to include those words in your custom dictionary. Excel will recognize those words the next time you check spelling.

Activity Steps

 open Workshop01.xls

1. Click the **Spelling button** on the Standard toolbar
   Excel flags the incorrect spelling of "through" and suggests the correct spelling.
   See Figure 1-17.

2. Click **Change**
   Excel flags "perperson" and suggests a correction.

3. Click **Change**, then click **Change** again to correct "Beginning"

4. In the Suggestions box, click **Woodwinds**, then click **Change**
   The Spelling Checker flags "fture" and suggests only "future".

5. Click in the Not in Dictionary box to place the insertion point between the "f" and "t" of "fture", type **ea**, then click **Change**
   The Spelling Checker flags the name "Okimoto" and offers several suggestions.
   See Figure 1-18.

6. Click **Ignore All**

7. Click **OK**

 close Workshop01.xls

Figure 1-17: Incorrect spelling highlighted

Spell checker flags incorrect spelling

Spell checker suggests a possible correction

Click to accept displayed change

Click to change all occurrences in worksheet

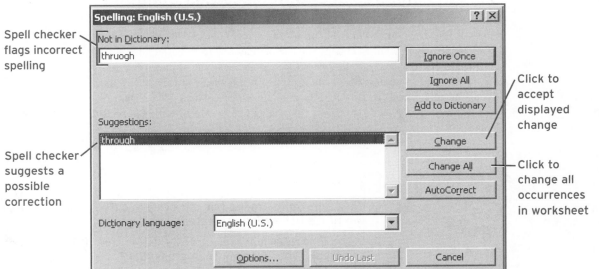

Figure 1-18: Corrected entry

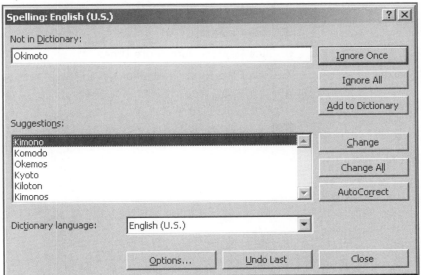

Skill Set 1
Working with Cells and Cell Data

Find and Replace Cell Data and Formats
Use Find and Replace to Replace Cell Contents

Correcting a few worksheet cells is not difficult, but if there are many occurrences of the same correction, you can use the Excel Find and Replace feature. For example, if you want to change the use of "Payroll" to "Salaries," the Find and Replace feature lets you do this quickly; it also lets you change only certain occurrences of an entry. You can also specify whether you want the found text or the replacement text to use upper- and lowercase letters. If you want to search only part of a worksheet, select the range before selecting the Find and Replace command.

Step 6
To have Excel search all sheets in a workbook, click Options in the Find and Replace dialog box, click the Within list arrow, then click Workbook.

Activity Steps

 open Report01.xls

1. Click **Edit** on the menu bar, click **Replace**, then click the **Replace tab** (if it's not already selected)

2. In the Find what box, select any existing text (if it's not already selected), type **Lodging**, then press **[Tab]**

3. In the Replace with box, type **Hotels**
   See Figure 1-19.

4. Click **Find Next**

5. Click **Replace**

6. Click **Replace** four more times

7. Click **Find Next**, then click **OK** in the message box

8. Click **Close**
   See Figure 1-20.

 close Report01.xls

Figure 1-19: Find and Replace dialog box

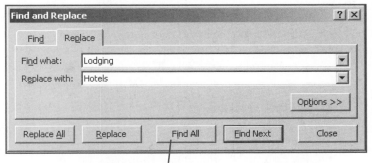

Click to view list of occurrences and their locations

Figure 1-20: Find and Replace results

	A	B	C	D
	Miller Music			
1				
2	*Where serving you is our pleasure!*			
3				
4	**Expense Report**			
5	*Dave Harris, Sales*			
6	*Date: Aug. 15, 2003*			
7				
8	**Begin Date**	**Destination**	**Item**	**Amount**
9	15-Jul	Portland	Airfare	$235.00
10	21-Jul	Dallas	Airfare	$368.00
11	15-Jul	Portland	Hotels	$255.00
12	15-Jul	Portland	Meals	$171.00
13	21-Jul	Dallas	Hotels	$325.00
14	21-Jul	Ft. Worth	Meals	$67.00
15	21-Jul	Dallas	Meals	$210.00
16	21-Jul	Dallas	Phone	$7.50
17	30-Jul	Salt Lake City	Hotels	$175.00
18	30-Jul	Salt Lake City	Meals	$159.00
19	8-Aug	LosAngeles	Phone	$17.20
20	8-Aug	LosAngeles	Hotels	$288.00
21	8-Aug	San Diego	Hotels	$98.00
22	8-Aug	LosAngeles	Meals	$152.00
23	8-Aug	LosAngeles	Airfare	$455.00
24				

Microsoft Excel - Report01.xls

All occurrences of "Lodging" replaced with "Hotels"

extra!

Using wildcards in your search

If you are not sure how to spell the word you are looking for, you can use wildcard characters in your search text. The wildcard character * can represent any letter or group of letters: mart* will find Marty, Martin, martial, or Martinelli. Use the wildcard character ? to represent any single character: cu? will locate cup, cut, or cub, but not cube or cutter.

Skill Set 1
Working with Cells and Cell Data

Find and Replace Cell Data and Formats
Go to a Specific Cell

When you work in large worksheets, you often need to find a specific area or a particular type of cell. Instead of scrolling through the worksheet and trying to find the cells visually, you can use the Excel **Go To** command. It lets you select (or "go to") any cell address, a range of cells, objects, all cells with formulas, and so forth.

Activity Steps

 open Projected01.xls

1. Click **Edit** on the menu bar, then click **Go To**

2. In the Reference box of the Go To dialog box, type **D14**, compare your screen to Figure 1-21, then click **OK**
   Cell D14 is selected.

3. Click **Edit** on the menu bar, click **Go To**, then click **Special**
   See Figure 1-22.

4. Click the **Last Cell option button**, then click **OK**
   The lower right worksheet cell is selected.

5. Click **Edit** on the menu bar, click **Go To**, then click **Special**

6. Click the **Formulas option button**, then click **OK**
   See Figure 1-23.

7. Click **Edit** on the menu bar, click **Go To**, then click **Special**

8. Click the **Objects option button**, then click **OK** to select the chart object

 close Projected01.xls

Step 1
You can also press [Ctrl][G] to open the Go To dialog box.

Figure 1-21: Go To dialog box

Cell address you want to go to

Figure 1-22: Go To Special dialog box

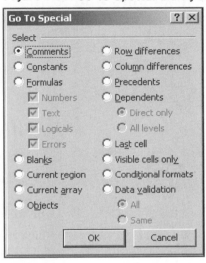

Figure 1-23: Worksheet with all formulas selected

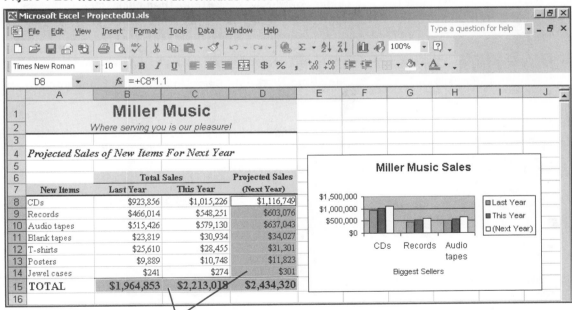

Cells with formulas highlighted

Skill Set 1
Working with Cells and Cell Data

Find and Replace Cell Data and Formats
Use Find and Replace to Change Cell Formats

You can use the Excel Find and Replace feature to replace not only cell contents but cell formats as well. This can save you a great deal of time in formatting worksheet headings and values, and it gives your worksheet a consistent look. For example, if you want to change all the worksheet values that are now in bold to unbolded italic, you could use the Find and Replace feature to do this in a few steps.

Step 8
If Excel does not find the format, clear any text from the Find what and Replace with text boxes. To clear any previously set formats, click the Format list arrow and click Clear Find Format and Clear Replace Format.

Activity Steps

 open Budget01.xls

1. Click **Edit** on the menu bar, then click **Replace**
2. If the Options button has » next to it, click **Options** to display the format options; if it does not, skip to Step 3
3. Click the topmost **Format button** (on the Find what line), then click the **Font tab**, if it's not already selected
   See Figure 1-24.
4. Under Font Style, click **Italic**, then click **OK**
5. Click the lower **Format button** (on the Replace with line)
6. Click **Bold** then click **OK**; select and delete any text in the "Find what" or "Replace with" boxes
7. Click **Find Next** until *Sales*, in cell A5, is highlighted, then click **Replace**
   See Figure 1-25.
8. Use the **Find Next** and **Replace buttons** to apply bold to only the indented italic labels, then click **Close**

 close Budget01.xls

Figure 1-24: Find Format dialog box

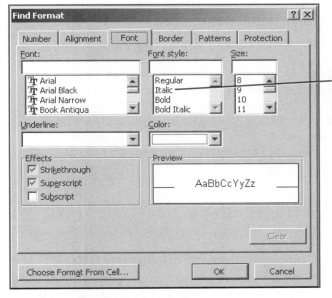

Click to specify that Excel should find italic text

Figure 1-25: Find and Replace Format dialog box

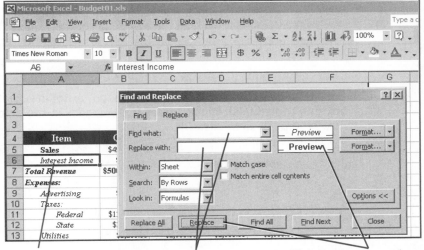

Excel has found italic text

To find and replace formats only, clear any text from these text boxes

Click Replace to replace the italic with bold text

extra!

Replacing by example
If there is a cell already formatted the way you want other cells to appear, you can use that as an example, rather than respecifying it in the Find Format or Replace Format dialog box. On the Format menu in the Find and Replace dialog box, choose Choose Format From Cell. When the pointer changes, and the dialog box temporarily closes, click the cell with the format you want to transfer. The Find and Replace dialog box reappears with the format of the cell you clicked selected.

Skill Set 1
Working with Cells and Cell Data

Work with a Subset of Data by Filtering Lists
Filter Lists using AutoFilter

In Excel, a collection of information is called a **list**. A list has columns with specific types of information, such as first name, address, or purchase amount, called **fields**. The individual items in each row are called **records**. You can easily **filter** the list to display only a **subset** of the data that matches certain conditions called **criteria**. For example, you could display only customers with "TX" in the State field, or sales reps with an amount greater than $50,000 in the Sales field. The simplest way to filter list information is to use the Excel **AutoFilter** feature, which displays list arrows for each field. After you filter on one field, you can click another list arrow to filter the list further. After filtering the list, you can print, chart, or analyze the information.

Step 5
To display all list records, click each blue list arrow, then click (All). To display all records in all fields, click Data on the menu bar, point to Filter, then click Show All.

Activity Steps

 open Report02.xls

1. Click any cell in the list range **A8:D23**

2. Click **Data** on the menu bar, point to **Filter**, then click **AutoFilter**
   A list arrow indicating that AutoFilter is on appears on each of the field names in the list.

3. Click the **Destination list arrow**, then click **Los Angeles**
   The Destination list arrow (and the row numbers where there is a sequence break) is now blue, indicating that a filter is in effect.
   See Figure 1-26.

4. Click the **Amount list arrow**, then click **Custom**

5. Click the **operator list arrow** in the Custom AutoFilter dialog box (next to equals), click **is greater than**, click in the amount box, type **200**, then click **OK**.
   See Figure 1-27.

 close Report02.xls

Figure 1-26: Filtered list

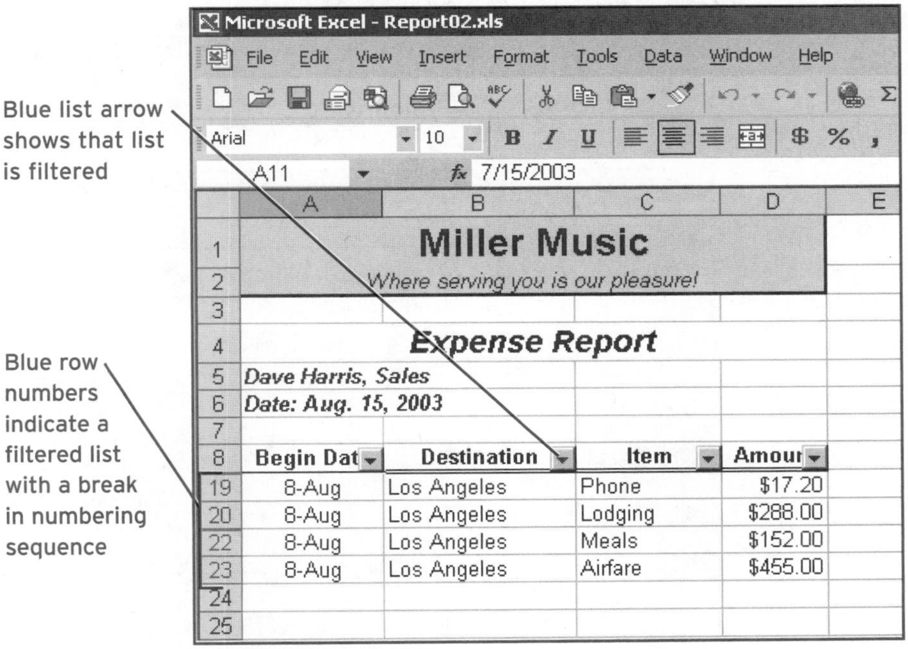

Blue list arrow shows that list is filtered

Blue row numbers indicate a filtered list with a break in numbering sequence

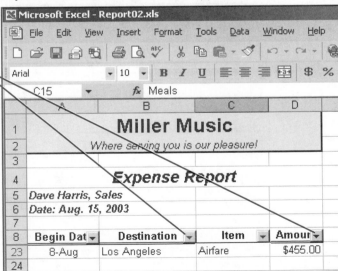

Figure 1-27: List with two filters applied

Destination and Amount list arrows are blue, indicating information is filtered on two fields

Skill Set 1

Working with Cells and Cell Data

Target Your Skills

 open Update02.xls

1 Use Figure 1-28 as a guide to modifying the Update02 worksheet file. Correct worksheet items as necessary, then spell check it. Format headings as shown. Create a formula in cell F9 that divides the total number of pianos by 3. Use a function in cell B17.

Figure 1-28

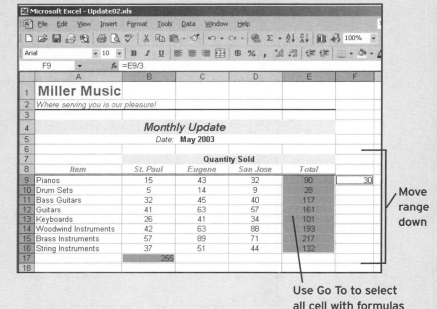

Move range down

Use Go To to select all cell with formulas

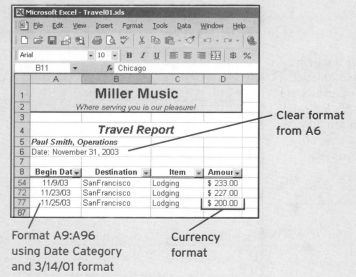 open Travel 01.xls

2 Use Figure 1-29 as a guide for modifying the Travel01 file. Clear the contents and formats from all cells containing travel data for 11/30/03. Lastly, filter the data to display only travel to San Francisco for Lodging.

Figure 1-29

Clear format from A6

Format A9:A96 using Date Category and 3/14/01 format

Currency format

Skill List

1. Manage workbook files and folders
2. Create workbooks using templates
3. Save workbooks using different names and file formats

As you know, a workbook is a collection of worksheets in a single file. As you use Excel to present and analyze data, you will store workbooks in different locations on your computer. To use them, you will need to understand the way files and folders are organized on your computer and how to move among them. Then, as you create new workbooks or use existing ones, you'll be able to find and save them easily, using names and file formats that will meet your needs.

Skill Set 2
Managing Workbooks

Manage Workbook Files and Folders
Locate and Open Existing Workbooks

When you open a workbook file, your computer reads the file information from your disk and places it into its temporary memory, allowing you to see it on the screen. To locate a file on your computer, you use the Look in list arrow and the Up One Level buttons in the Open dialog box. Files are usually stored in **folders**, which are named storage locations on your disk that let you group and organize files as you would the physical folders in your file cabinet.

Step 2
The New Workbook task pane lists recently-opened workbooks. If the workbook you want is listed there, click it once to open it. To open a blank workbook, click the New button on the Standard toolbar, or the Blank Workbook hyperlink in the New Workbook task pane.

Activity Steps

1. Start Excel
2. Click the **Open button** 🗁 on the Standard toolbar
3. Click the **Look in list arrow** in the Open dialog box
   See Figure 2-1.
   You can use the Look in list arrow to navigate between the levels and locations in the disk structure, or you can use the Up One Level button to move up in the disk structure. You can double-click a folder in the Open dialog box to move down in the disk structure.
4. Navigate to the location where your Project Files are stored
5. Click the filename **Staffing01**, then click **Open**
   See Figure 2-2.
   In the rest of the activities in this book, you will not see instructions for opening each workbook. Instead, each activity that requires a workbook file will display an Open File icon before its steps, with the name of the file you should open. After the last step, the Close File icon is your signal to close the file. Do not save your changes.

   close Staffing01.xls

Figure 2-1: Using the Open dialog box to locate files

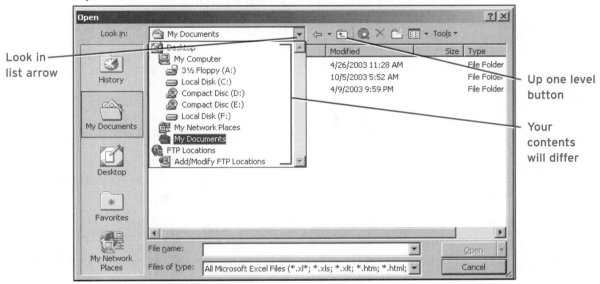

Look in list arrow

Up one level button

Your contents will differ

Figure 2-2: Open document

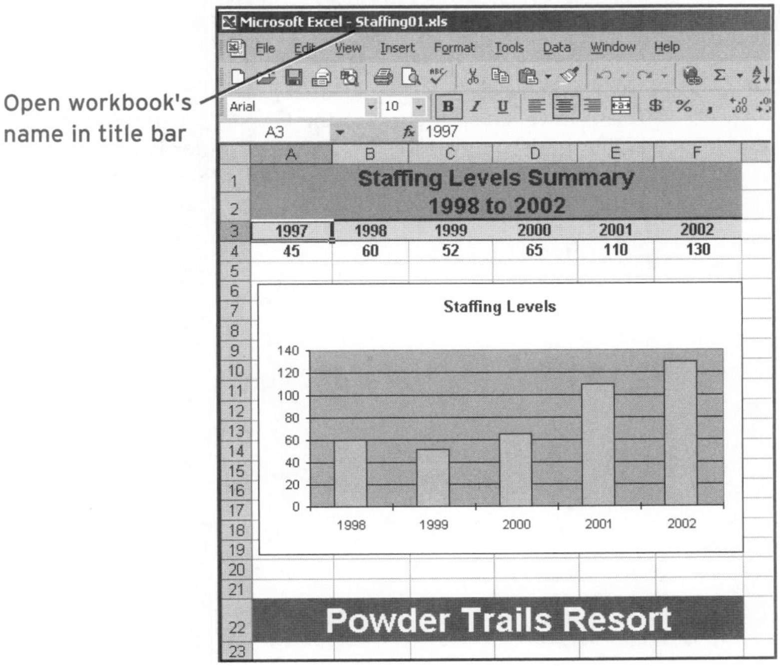

Open workbook's name in title bar

Skill Set 2
Managing Workbooks

Manage Workbook Files and Folders
Create Folders for Saving Workbooks

When you save files, you will often want to create a new folder for storing them. For example, your workbook may be the first file you create for a new project, so you might want to create a folder with that project's name to help you locate it later. You can create a new folder in the Save As dialog box, using the Create New Folder button.

Activity Steps

 open Guests01.xls

1. Click **File** on the menu bar, then click **Save As**

2. Click the **Save in list arrow**, then navigate to the drive and folder where your Project Files are stored
   See Figure 2-3.

3. Click the **Create New Folder button** in the Save As dialog box toolbar
   The new folder will be created and stored in the open folder where your Project Files are stored.

4. Type **Resort**, click **OK**, then compare your screen to Figure 2-4

5. Select the filename in the File Name box (if it's not already selected), then type **List**

6. Click **Save**
   You have saved a copy of the Guests01 workbook called List in the new folder named Resort. The new folder is in the Project File folder on your Project Disk. The Guests01 file closes automatically, leaving the List workbook open.

 close List.xls

tip

Step 6
You cannot have two files with the same name in one folder. However, you can have files with the same names in different folders.

Figure 2-3: Save As dialog box

Your storage location may be different

Create New Folder button

Your view may be different

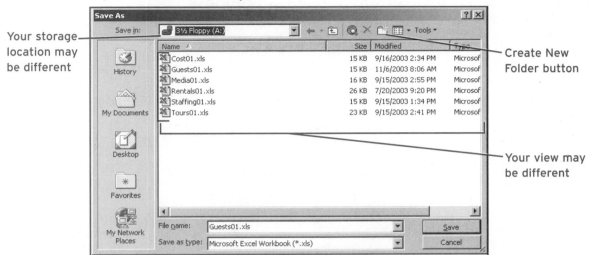

Figure 2-4: Save As dialog box showing new folder

New folder is open

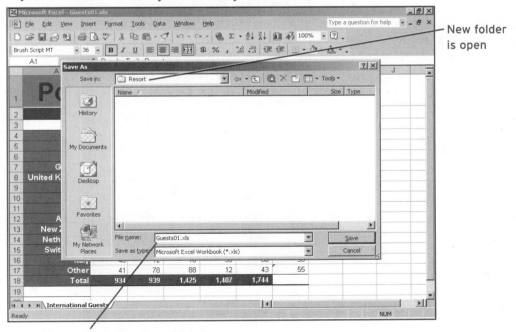

You will save a new version of this file

Skill Set 2
Managing Workbooks

Create Workbooks Using Templates
Create a Workbook from a Template

When you need to create workbooks for everyday use, such as an invoice or a balance sheet, you can save time by using a **template**, a workbook prepared for a specific use that can contain headings, formatting, and formulas. A template is an Excel file saved in a special format that has an .xlt file extension. Several templates are included with Excel; you can open a workbook using any template and customize it. When you use a template, you are not opening the template file itself, but a new workbook with the template's content and format that has an .xls file extension, like any Excel worksheet file. *If you have a standard Excel installation, the program may ask you to insert the Office CD to install the template files.*

Step 2
You can find hundreds more templates for all Office programs in the Template Gallery on the Microsoft Web site (Microsoft.com). In the New Workbook task pane, click Templates on Microsoft.com under New from template, then click any template name to see a preview.

Activity Steps

1. If the New Workbook task pane is not open, click **File** on the menu bar, then click **New**

2. In the New Workbook task pane, click **General Templates** in the New from template section

3. In the Templates dialog box, click the **Spreadsheet Solutions tab**
   See Figure 2-5.

4. Click **Timecard**, then click **OK**
   A workbook based on the Timecard template opens. Excel assigns it the temporary name Timecard1.

5. With cell E10 selected, type your name, press **[Tab]**, then use the horizontal and vertical scroll arrows to view the worksheet
   In this template, the cells in the Total Hours column and row are locked; you cannot place the insertion point in them. If you enter hours in the cells for each day, totals will appear, indicating that there are formulas in the locked cells.

6. Click **cell D19**, type **Bigelow**, press **[Tab]**, type **777**, press **[Tab]**, type **8**, press **[Tab]**, enter **8** in cells **K19, L19, M19, N19, O19**, and **P19**, then observe the total in cell **Q20**

7. Save the workbook as **Weekly** in the drive and folder where your Project Files are stored, then click the **Print Preview button**  on the Standard toolbar
   See Figure 2-6.

8. Click **Close** on the Print Preview toolbar

    close Weekly.xls

Figure 2-5: Excel templates available in Office XP

Template icons have yellow band

Templates supplied with Excel

Click to change view of template files

Preview of any selected template appears here

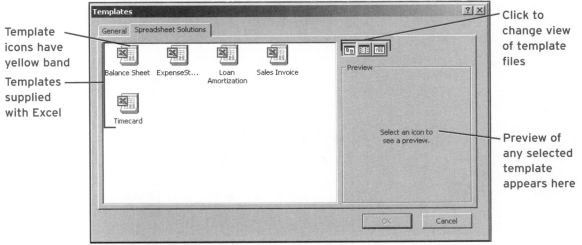

Figure 2-6: Workbook in Print Preview

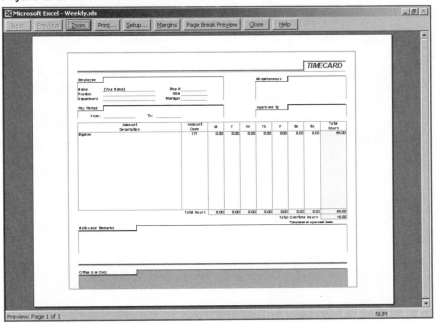

Skill Set 2
Managing Workbooks

Save Workbooks Using Different Names and File Formats
Open a Workbook from a Folder Created for Workbook Storage

As you create workbooks for different purposes using Excel, you will find it convenient to store them in folders. For example, you might want to group all your personal accounting workbooks in a folder named "Personal." You can also "nest" folders inside other folders.

Step 4
To copy a file from one folder to another, open the folder that contains the file you want to copy, right-click the filename, click Copy on the shortcut menu, open the folder where you want to place the file, right-click, then click Paste.

Activity Steps

1. If Excel is open, click the **Minimize button** on the title bar

2. At the Windows desktop, double-click **My Computer**, then navigate to the location where your Project Files are stored
   Depending on your computer and operating system, you may need to click Start on the Windows taskbar to find My Computer.

3. Click **File** on the disk window menu bar, point to **New**, then click **Folder**

4. Type **Site**, then press **[Enter]**
   See Figure 2-7.

5. Drag the **Cost01** file to the **Site folder**

6. Start Excel (or if Excel is running, click the Microsoft Excel button in the taskbar), then click the **Open button** 📂 on the Standard toolbar

7. Navigate to the folder where your Project Folders are stored

8. Double-click the **Site folder**, click the **Cost01** file, then click **Open**
   See Figure 2-8.

   📄 **close Cost01.xls**

Figure 2-7: New folder

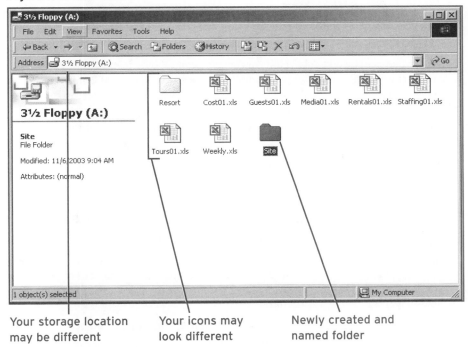

Your storage location
may be different

Your icons may
look different

Newly created and
named folder

Figure 2-8: File opened from newly created folder

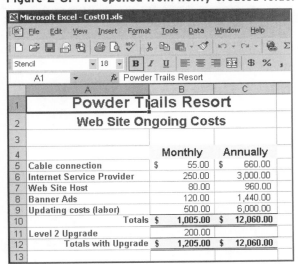

Skill Set 2
Managing Workbooks

Save Workbooks Using Different Names and File Formats
Use Save As to Store Workbooks Using Different Names and in Different Locations

After you open a workbook, you have complete control over its name and location. For example, you might want to save an alternative version of a workbook named Address List as Address List2 so you can always return to the original version. Or you might want to save a copy of a workbook on a network drive for others to open and use. You can perform both of these actions in the Save As dialog box.

Step 3
To move up in the file structure, click the Up One Level button in the Save As dialog box.

Activity Steps

 open Tours01.xls

1. Click **File** on the menu bar, then click **Save As**

2. Click the **Save in list arrow**

3. Navigate to the drive and folder where your Project Files are stored, then double-click the **Site folder**
   You have selected the storage location; next you'll change the filename.

4. Select the **File name**, then type **Tours**
   See Figure 2-9.

5. Click **Save**

 close Tours.xls

Figure 2-9: Save As dialog box showing new location and filename

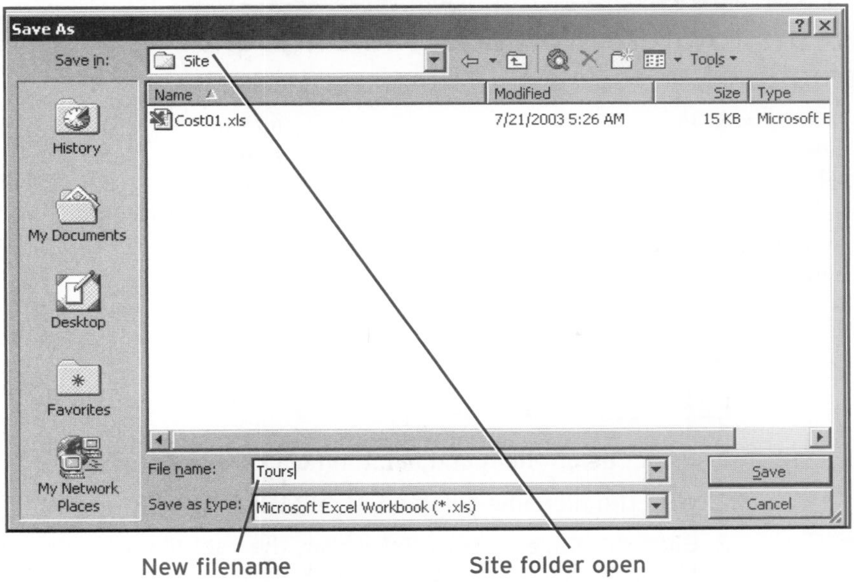

New filename   Site folder open

Skill Set 2

Managing Workbooks

Save Workbooks Using Different Names and File Formats

Use Save As to Store Workbooks in Different File Formats

You will sometimes need to save a workbook in a different file format. For example, a colleague may need a spreadsheet you created, but might be using an earlier version of Excel, such as version 4.0 or 5.0. You can save the workbook in an earlier file format using the Save As dialog box. Keep in mind that workbooks saved in earlier formats may not have all the features that you created in Excel 2002. Table 2-1 lists some common file formats in which you can save Excel 2002 files.

Step 4
Although earlier versions of Excel may not be able to open Excel 2002 files, Excel 2002 can open files created and saved in earlier versions of Excel.

Activity Steps

 open Media01.xls

1. Click **File** on the menu bar, then click **Save As**

2. With the filename selected, type **Media**

3. Click the **Save as type list arrow**, then scroll until you can see Microsoft Excel 5.0/95 Workbook (*.xls)

4. Click **Microsoft Excel 5.0/95 Workbook (*.xls)**
   See Figure 2-10.

5. Click **Save**, then click **Yes** in the dialog box warning that some features may be lost
   The file you created opens in Excel 2002 with the new name and the file extension in the title bar. The original Media01 file closes and remains unchanged on your disk.

 close Media.xls

Figure 2-10: Save As dialog box showing new filename and format

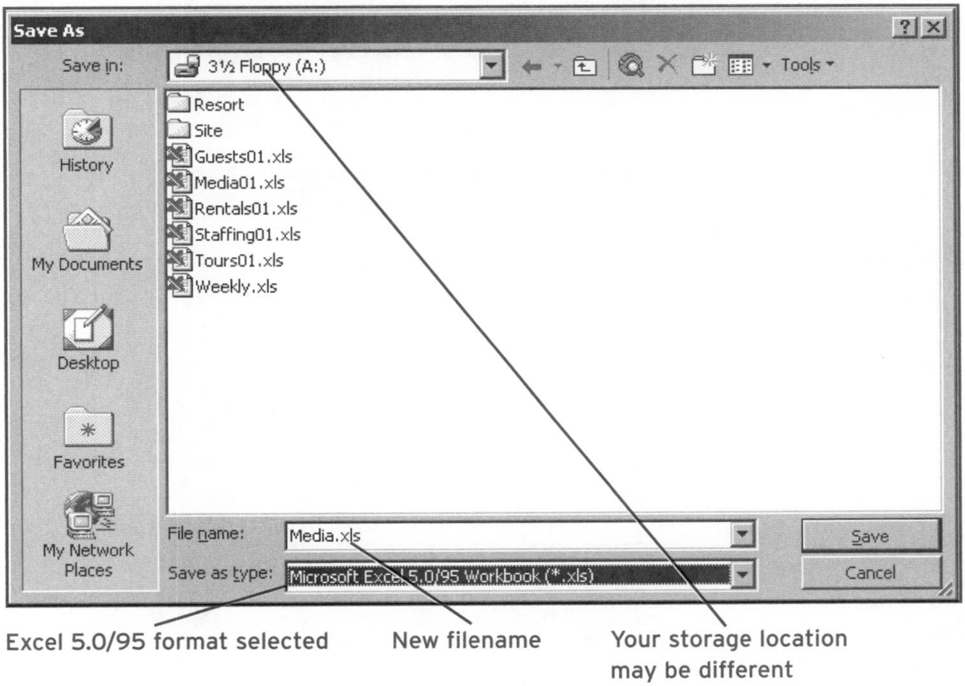

Excel 5.0/95 format selected   New filename   Your storage location may be different

TABLE 2-1: Selected file formats in which you can save Excel files

file format	file extension	what it is
Text (tab delimited)	.txt	Information only with no formatting and with columns separated by tabs; can be opened by many programs
WK3 (1-2-3)	.wk3	Format that can be opened by the Lotus 1-2-3 spreadsheet program
DBF 4	.dbf	Format that can be opened by the dBase IV database program
XML spreadsheet	.xml	XML (Extensible Markup Language) formatted documents can be opened by a variety of programs; program designers can create tags that let people define, transmit, and interpret data between programs

Skill Set 2
Managing Workbooks

Target Your Skills

 open Rentals01.xls

1 Open the file shown in Figure 2-11. At the Windows desktop, create a new folder called Ski in the drive and folder where your Project Files are stored, then save the file as Projection.xls in the Ski folder.

Figure 2-11

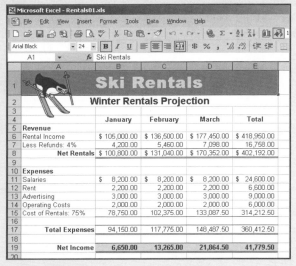

2 Create an Excel file based on the Expense Statement template on the Office XP Spreadsheets Solutions tab. Your screen should look like Figure 2-12. You may need to insert the Office XP CD to install the templates. Save the workbook as Expenses.xls in Excel 97-2002 & 5.0-95 Workbook format, in a new folder named Statements in the drive and folder where your Project Files are stored.

Figure 2-12

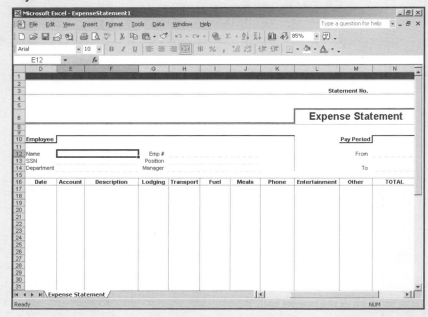

Skill List

1. Apply and modify cell formats
2. Modify row and column settings
3. Modify row and column formats
4. Apply styles
5. Use automated tools to format worksheets
6. Modify Page Setup options for worksheets
7. Preview and print worksheets and workbooks

A good worksheet communicates information clearly. You can format worksheets to add visual impact and to help readers understand your data quickly. Cell **formats** include type styles, sizes, and fonts you can use to make important information more prominent. Cell borders and **fills** (color that fills a cell) can help you visually separate your worksheet sections. For example, you might want to enclose totals in a shaded yellow box or with a heavy black border.

Rows and columns are your worksheet building blocks that you can modify to meet your needs. You can insert and delete rows and columns, as well as hide and redisplay them. In large worksheets, **freezing** rows and columns lets you keep labels visible as you scroll the rest of the worksheet. Changing row heights and column widths also help make your worksheet more readable.

Styles are combinations of number and cell formatting that you can apply to cells and ranges. Excel **AutoFormats** supply combinations of number and cell formats designed for different worksheet types, such as Accounting worksheets or lists.

When your worksheet is ready to print, you can change its layout, including its orientation on the page, its page titles, and which parts of the worksheet print.

Skill Set 3

Formatting and Printing Worksheets

Apply and Modify Cell Formats
Format Cells with Type Styles and Fonts

Readers of your worksheet should be able to distinguish general information from detail at a glance. One way to make this easier is to format column and row labels. To **format** cells, you can use typefaces (such as Arial) and **fonts**, which are the typefaces with formats such as bolding style and type style, to emphasize important text. Font size is measured in units called points; one point is equal to $1/72$ of an inch. You can apply cell formats from the Formatting toolbar or from the Format Cells dialog box.

To change font color, size, and style all at once, click Format on the menu bar, click Cells, then click the Font tab. The Preview box displays a sample of the options you have selected. Select the font, style, size, and color you want, then click OK.

Activity Steps

 open Addresses01.xls

1. Select the range **A3:F3**
2. Click the **Bold button** B on the Formatting toolbar
3. Select cell **A1**
4. Click the **Font list arrow** on the Formatting toolbar, then click **Arial**
5. Click the **Font Size list arrow** 10 on the Formatting toolbar, then click **24**
6. Click the **Font color list arrow** A on the Formatting toolbar, then click the **Red** color (third row, far left column)
   See Figure 3-1.

 close Addresses01.xls

Figure 3-1: Formatted text

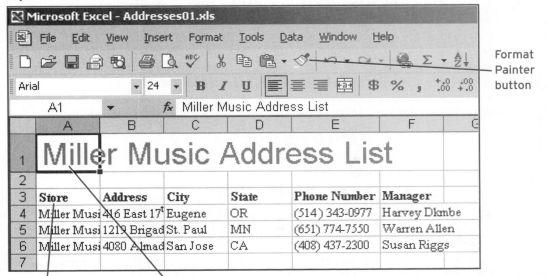

Format Painter button

Bolded text

Text enlarged and with red text color

Skill Set 3
Formatting and Printing Worksheets

Apply and Modify Cell Formats
Format Cells with Borders and Fills

You will often want to place borders around worksheet cells to call attention to their content. You might want to add a bottom border to cells just above a total, place a box around a cell or range containing important information, or place borders around every cell in a range. Borders can have varying lines, styles, and colors. You can also fill cells with a color, called a **fill color**, or pattern to separate worksheet sections. Make sure you preview your worksheets to ensure that fills won't obscure your text when you print.

Activity Steps

 open Projected02.xls

1. Select the range **A7:D7**

Step 2
For more line style and color choices, click Format on the menu bar, click Cells, then click the Border tab or the Patterns tab.

2. Click the **Borders list arrow** on the Formatting toolbar, click the **Bottom Border button** on the Borders palette, then click outside the range

3. Select the range **A10:D10**, click the **Borders list arrow** on the Formatting toolbar, click the **Thick Bottom Border button** on the Borders palette, then click outside the range

4. Select the range **A13:D13**, click the **Borders list arrow** on the Formatting toolbar, then click the **Thick Box Border button** on the Borders palette

5. Select the range **A1:D2**, press and hold **[Ctrl]**, then select the range **A13:D13**

6. Click the **Fill Color list arrow** on the Formatting toolbar, click the **Light Green color** (bottom row, fourth color from the left), then click outside the range
   See Figure 3-2.

close Projected02.xls

Figure 3-2: Worksheet formatted with borders and color

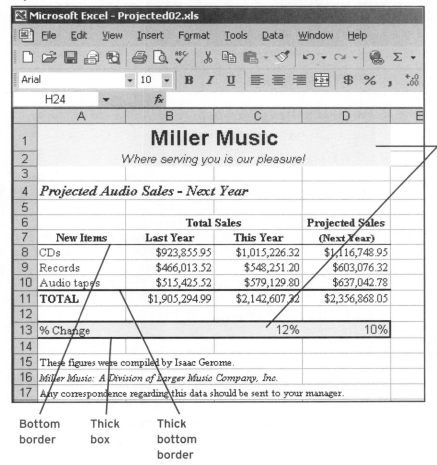

Light green fill color

Bottom border
Thick box
Thick bottom border

extra!

Using patterns
You can obtain a wider range of effects to set off worksheet cells by using patterns, either alone or with colors. Select a cell or range, click **Format** on the menu bar, click Cells, then click the **Patterns tab.** Click the color you want the pattern to be, then click the **Pattern list arrow.** Select a dot, crosshatch, or stripe pattern, then click **OK.** You may have to enlarge or bold the font in a patterned cell to make it visible over the pattern.

Skill Set 3
Formatting and Printing Worksheets

Modify Row and Column Settings
Insert Rows and Columns

After you have created a worksheet with labels, values, and formulas, you may find you need to add more data, often in the middle of existing data. To do this, you can insert one or more rows or columns. The Insert Options list arrow lets you specify whether you want the inserted rows or columns to have the same formatting as the rows or columns on either side.

Activity Steps

 open Instruments01.xls

1. Click cell **C8**
   You can click any cell in the row above which you want to add the new row. If you click a merged cell, the program will insert the same number of columns that the cell spans.

2. Click **Insert** on the menu bar, then click **Rows**
   A smart tag appears near the cell. A **smart tag** is an icon that appears after you modify worksheet cells. In this case the smart tag, an icon with a paintbrush on a white background, presents options for inserting the new row. When you point to the icon, a list arrow appears, along with a screen tip with the smart tag's name.

3. Click the **Insert Options smart tag**
   See Figure 3-3.

4. Click **Format Same As Below**, then click a blank cell

5. In the range A8:E8, enter the following data:
   Accordions [Tab] 3 [Tab] 8 [Tab] 3 [Enter]
   The new row takes on the formatting of the row below it.

6. Right-click cell **B14**, click **Insert**, click the **Entire Column option button**, then click **OK**
   See Figure 3-4.

 close Instruments01.xls

Step 1
To insert more than one row or column, select the number you want to insert. For example, to add four rows, select four rows before you click Insert on the menu bar.

Figure 3-3: Insert Options list

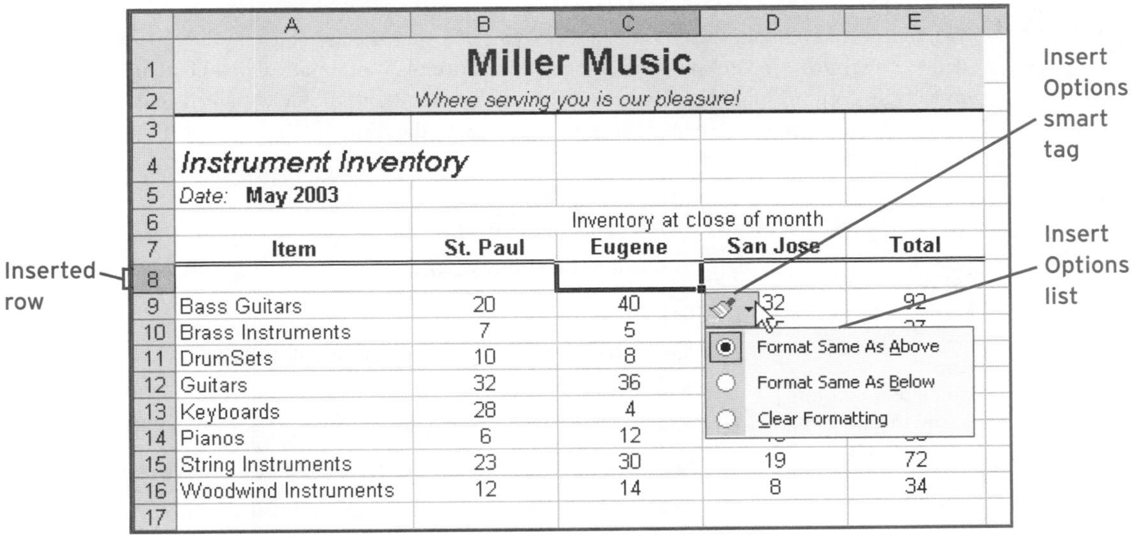

	A	B	C	D	E
1			**Miller Music**		
2			*Where serving you is our pleasure!*		
3					
4	*Instrument Inventory*				
5	*Date:* **May 2003**				
6			Inventory at close of month		
7	**Item**	**St. Paul**	**Eugene**	**San Jose**	**Total**
8					
9	Bass Guitars	20	40	32	92
10	Brass Instruments	7	5		
11	DrumSets	10	8	⦿ Format Same As <u>A</u>bove	
12	Guitars	32	36	○ Format Same As <u>B</u>elow	
13	Keyboards	28	4	○ <u>C</u>lear Formatting	
14	Pianos	6	12		
15	String Instruments	23	30	19	72
16	Woodwind Instruments	12	14	8	34
17					

Inserted row

Insert Options smart tag

Insert Options list

Figure 3-4: Worksheet with inserted row and column

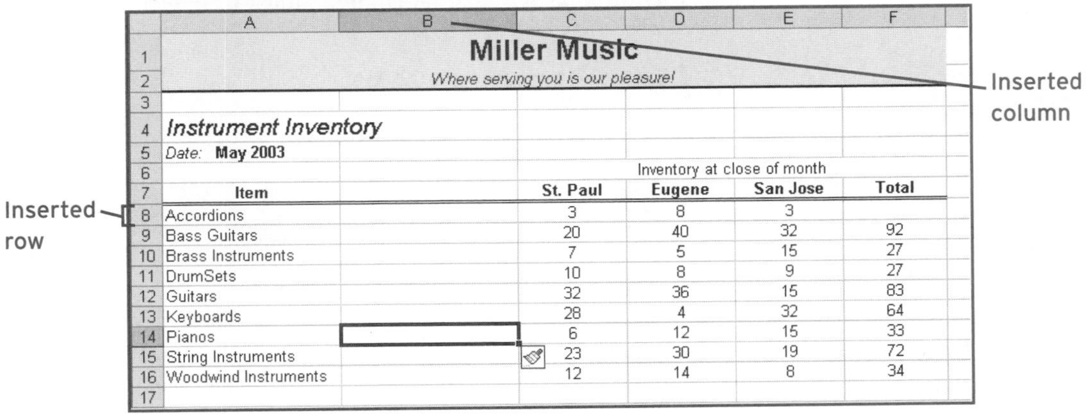

	A	B	C	D	E	F
1			**Miller Music**			
2			*Where serving you is our pleasure!*			
3						
4	*Instrument Inventory*					
5	*Date:* **May 2003**					
6			Inventory at close of month			
7	**Item**		**St. Paul**	**Eugene**	**San Jose**	**Total**
8	Accordions		3	8	3	
9	Bass Guitars		20	40	32	92
10	Brass Instruments		7	5	15	27
11	DrumSets		10	8	9	27
12	Guitars		32	36	15	83
13	Keyboards		28	4	32	64
14	Pianos		6	12	15	33
15	String Instruments		23	30	19	72
16	Woodwind Instruments		12	14	8	34
17						

Inserted column

Inserted row

Skill Set 3
Formatting and Printing Worksheets

Modify Row and Column Settings
Delete Rows and Columns

Worksheet data changes over time, and as you use worksheets, you may have to delete entire rows or columns of information. Formulas automatically adjust to reflect the reduced number of rows or columns in a range. If you delete a cell that a formula specifically refers to, however, the cell with the formula displays "#REF!", indicating that you need to modify the formula.

Step 1
To delete a column or row in one step, right click the column or row heading, then click Delete in the shortcut menu.

Activity Steps

 open Instruments02.xls

1. Click cell **B6**

2. Click **Edit** on the menu bar, then click **Delete**
   See Figure 3-5.

3. Click the **Entire row option button**, then click **OK**

4. Click any cell in column E, then observe the totals in column F

5. Click **Edit** on the menu bar, then click **Delete**

6. Click the **Entire column option button**, then click **OK**
   The formulas in the Total column adjust to reflect the deletion.
   See Figure 3-6.

 close Instruments02.xls

Figure 3-5: Delete dialog box

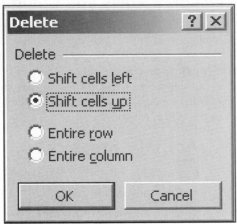

Figure 3-6: Worksheet after deleting row and column

Column deleted from here →

Row deleted from here →

Adjusted totals

	A	B	C	D	E
1	**Miller Music**				
2	*Where serving you is our pleasure!*				
3					
4	*Instrument Inventory*				
5	*Date:* **May 2003**				
6	**Item**	**Code**	**St. Paul**	**Eugene**	**Total**
7	Accordions	1000	3	8	**11**
8	Bass Guitars	2000	20	40	**60**
9	Brass Instruments	3000	7	5	**12**
10	DrumSets	4000	10	8	**18**
11	Guitars	5000	32	36	**68**
12	Keyboards	6000	28	4	**32**
13	Pianos	7000	6	12	**18**
14	String Instruments	8000	23	30	**53**
15	Woodwind Instruments	9000	12	14	**26**
16			**141**	**157**	**298**
17					

Skill Set 3
Formatting and Printing Worksheets

Modify Row and Column Settings
Hide and Redisplay Rows and Columns

Your worksheets may contain information that you don't want others to see, such as salaries or other personal data. You can hide these rows or columns. Hidden rows and columns are still in the worksheet, but are not visible; Excel reduces their column width or row height to zero. The row number or column letter of a hidden row or column does not appear; if you hide columns B through D, the column letters will appear as A, E, F, and so on. When you press [Tab], the selected cell skips the hidden column or row.

To hide a row, click any cell in the row, click Format on the menu bar, point to Row, then click Hide. To redisplay, or unhide, a row, select the rows above and below the hidden row, click Format on the menu bar, point to Row, then click Unhide. You can also redisplay rows by dragging the Row Height pointer , and you can redisplay columns by dragging the Column Width pointer ✛.

Activity Steps

📄 open Earnings03.xls

1. Click any cell in column F

2. Click **Format** on the menu bar, point to **Column**, click **Hide**, then click any blank worksheet cell
   Column F no longer appears in the worksheet, and the columns E and G are next to each other.
   See Figure 3-7.
   To redisplay a hidden column, you can select the columns on either side of it, or any two cells on either side of it.

3. Select the range E12:G12

4. Click **Format** on the menu bar, point to **Column**, click **Unhide**, then click any blank worksheet cell
   See Figure 3-8.

📄 close Earnings03.xls

Skill 2

Modify Row and Column Settings

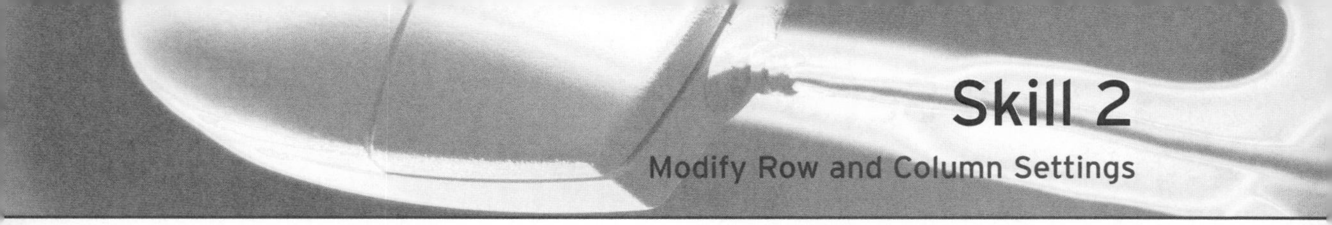

Figure 3-7: Worksheet with hidden column

	A	B	C	D	E	G
1	Miller Music					
2	*Where serving you is our pleasure!*					
3						
4	Employee Earnings for July 15-31					
5						
6				Gross Profit		Employee
7	Employee Name		Emp #	From Sales	Commission	Earnings
8	Davis	Jan	233	$4,568.00	$1,370.40	$1,493.74
9	Gibson	Carol	421	$2,321.00	$696.30	$731.12
10	Johnson	Chris	418	$1,588.00	$476.40	$495.46
11	Kniepp	Gordon	403	$2,790.00	$837.00	$887.22
12	Kramer	Joan	390	$1,265.00	$379.50	$390.89
13	McHenry	Bill	378	$2,576.00	$772.80	$819.17
14	Miller	George	347	$3,388.00	$1,016.40	$1,097.71
15	Wallace	Pat	262	$4,224.00	$1,267.20	$1,381.25
16	TOTAL				$6,816.00	$7,296.54
17						

Break in column letter sequence indicates hidden column

Figure 3-8: Worksheet with redisplayed column

Redisplayed column

	A	B	C	D	E	F	G
1	Miller Music						
2	*Where serving you is our pleasure!*						
3							
4	Employee Earnings for July 15-31						
5							
6				Gross Profit			Employee
7	Employee Name		Emp #	From Sales	Commission	Bonus	Earnings
8	Davis	Jan	233	$4,568.00	$1,370.40	9%	$1,493.74
9	Gibson	Carol	421	$2,321.00	$696.30	5%	$731.12
10	Johnson	Chris	418	$1,588.00	$476.40	4%	$495.46
11	Kniepp	Gordon	403	$2,790.00	$837.00	6%	$887.22
12	Kramer	Joan	390	$1,265.00	$379.50	3%	$390.89
13	McHenry	Bill	378	$2,576.00	$772.80	6%	$819.17
14	Miller	George	347	$3,388.00	$1,016.40	8%	$1,097.71
15	Wallace	Pat	262	$4,224.00	$1,267.20	9%	$1,381.25
16	TOTAL				$6,816.00		$7,296.54
17							

Skill Set 3
Formatting and Printing Worksheets

Modify Row and Column Settings
Freeze and Unfreeze Rows and Columns

When your worksheet contains so many columns or rows that the entire work-sheet is not visible on the screen at one time, you have to scroll to view it. However, when you do this, it can be difficult to remember which column and row labels line up with which values. The Excel Freeze Panes feature lets you **freeze** columns and rows so that the scroll bars display data below and to the right, while the labels stay in place.

Step 2
To freeze only rows, select the entire row below which you want data to scroll. To freeze only columns, select the entire column to the right of the one you want to scroll.

Activity Steps

 open Summary02.xls

1. Click cell **C7**, click **Window** on the menu bar, then click **Freeze Panes**
   Solid lines appear above and to the left of the selected cell, indicating that Excel has frozen the rows and columns above and to the left of the selected cell.
   See Figure 3-9.

2. Click the **Down vertical scroll arrow** twice
   The column labels remain in place as the row contents scroll upward.

3. Click the **Right horizontal scroll arrow** four times
   The row labels remain in place as the column contents scroll left.

4. Click **Window** on the menu bar, then click **Unfreeze panes**
   The solid lines disappear and all the worksheet data reappears.

 close Summary02.xls

Figure 3-9: Window with frozen panes

	A	B	C	D	E	F	G
1			**Miller Music**				
2			*Where serving you is our pleasure!*				
3							
4			*3rd Quarter Sales Summary*				
5							
6	*Month*	*Store*	*Pianos*	*Combos*	*Band Instruments*	*Special Events*	*Totals*
7	July	St. Paul	$245,680	$189,050	$102,354	$164,550	$701,634
8	July	Eugene	$345,795	$222,975	$135,055	$205,225	$909,050
9	July	San Jose	$214,328	$120,880	$86,550	$93,520	$515,278
10	August	St. Paul	$247,800	$192,025	$104,350	$162,250	$706,425
11	August	Eugene	$332,050	$231,095	$131,065	$206,995	$901,205
12	August	San Jose	$217,500	$122,035	$89,025	$92,245	$520,805
13	September	St. Paul	$247,950	$193,235	$105,025	$145,750	$691,960
14	September	Eugene	$337,505	$252,425	$124,050	$189,525	$903,505
15	September	San Jose	$219,275	$123,950	$90,525	$74,325	$508,075
16							
17	Totals		$2,407,883	$1,647,670	$967,999	$1,334,385	$6,357,937
18							

Lines indicate frozen columns and rows

extra!

Splitting the worksheet into scrollable panes

To divide the worksheet into two or four scrollable panes, place the pointer over the split box at the top of the vertical scroll bar until it changes to the Window split pointer ⬍, then drag downward. The scroll bar becomes two scroll bars, one for each pane. To remove the split, double-click it. You can split the worksheet horizontally in the same way using the split box to the right of the horizontal scroll bar.

Skill Set 3

Formatting and Printing Worksheets

Modify Row and Column Formats
Modify Row Height

Using fonts and rows of different heights can make your worksheet easier to read. When you change the font size of cell contents, the row height automatically adjusts. In other cases you will want to adjust the row height yourself. You can adjust the height of just one row or several rows; you can resize them to fit cell contents or to set them at a specific height.

Step 4
To adjust the height of several rows, select them, then drag to enlarge one of the selected rows; all of them will adjust to that height. To adjust the height of nonadjacent rows, select the first row, press and hold [Ctrl], select the remaining nonadjacent rows, then drag one to enlarge them all.

Activity Steps

 open Furniture01.xls

1. Position the mouse pointer over the bottom of the **row 4 heading** until the pointer becomes ✛

2. Drag downward to enlarge the row to approximately double its size
   See Figure 3-10.

3. Drag the bottoms of **rows 2** and **19** to approximately double their height

4. Click the **row 6 heading** to select the row

5. Click **Format** on the menu bar, point to **Row**, then click **Height**

6. Type **25**, then click **OK**

7. Click the Row 13 heading to select the row, press [F4], click any blank cell, then press **[PgUp]** or **[PageUp]**
   In Office, the [F4] key repeats the immediately preceding action.
   See Figure 3-11.

 close Furniture01.xls

Figure 3-10: Dragging a row border to change row height

ScreenTip shows height as you drag

Resize pointer

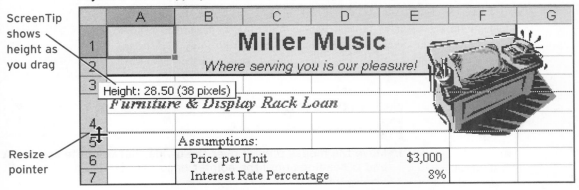

Figure 3-11: Worksheet with modified row height

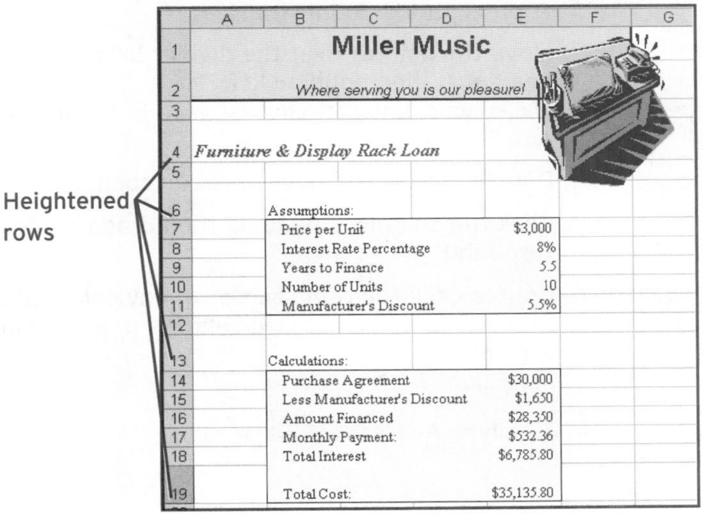

Heightened rows

Skill Set 3
Formatting and Printing Worksheets

Modify Row and Column Formats
Modify Column Width

Your worksheets will be easier to read if the data fits well into the worksheet columns. With a good fit, all the data will be visible and as much data as possible will fit on your screen at once, which is useful with large worksheets. Resizing one column in a group of selected columns resizes all the columns in the group.

To make a column the same width as another column in your worksheet, select the column of the desired width, click the Copy button on the Standard toolbar, right-click the destination column's heading, click Paste Special, click Column widths in the Paste Special dialog box, then click OK.

Activity Steps

 open Addresses02.xls

1. Move the mouse pointer over the divider between the **column A and B headings** until the pointer becomes ↔
   See Figure 3-12.

2. Drag the column divider to the right to widen the column to approximately double its size

3. Move the pointer over the divider between **columns B and C headings,** then double-click
   The column automatically resizes to fit its contents; this is called **AutoFit**.

4. Double-click the **divider** between columns D and E

5. Click the **column C heading** then drag to select **columns C through F**

6. Double-click the **right border** of any selected column heading
   AutoFit resizes the selected columns to accommodate their cell contents.
   See Figure 3-13.

 close Addresses02.xls

Figure 3-12: Dragging a column border to change column width

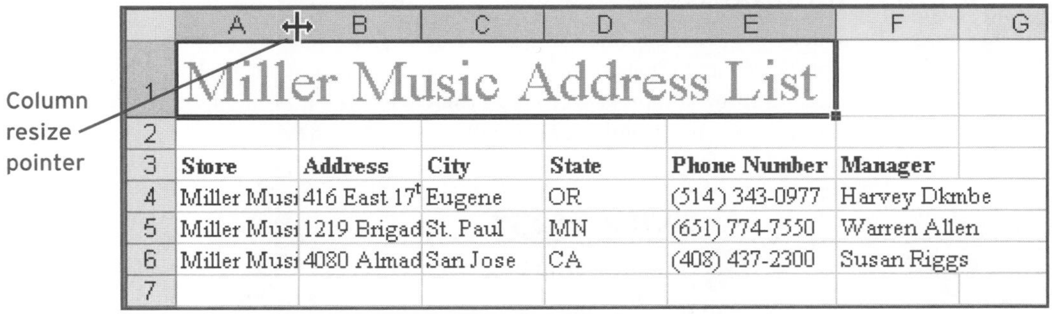

Column resize pointer

	A	B	C	D	E	F	G
1	Miller Music Address List						
2							
3	Store	Address	City	State	Phone Number	Manager	
4	Miller Musi	416 East 17ᵗ	Eugene	OR	(514) 343-0977	Harvey Dkmbe	
5	Miller Musi	1219 Brigad	St. Paul	MN	(651) 774-7550	Warren Allen	
6	Miller Musi	4080 Almad	San Jose	CA	(408) 437-2300	Susan Riggs	
7							

Column widths fit cell contents

Figure 3-13: Worksheet with modified column width

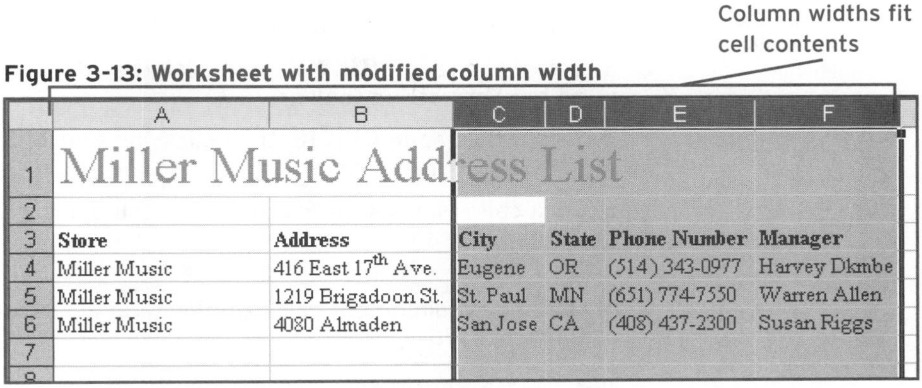

	A	B	C	D	E	F
1	Miller Music Address List					
2						
3	Store	Address	City	State	Phone Number	Manager
4	Miller Music	416 East 17th Ave.	Eugene	OR	(514) 343-0977	Harvey Dkmbe
5	Miller Music	1219 Brigadoon St.	St. Paul	MN	(651) 774-7550	Warren Allen
6	Miller Music	4080 Almaden	San Jose	CA	(408) 437-2300	Susan Riggs
7						
8						

Skill Set 3
Formatting and Printing Worksheets

Modify Row and Column Formats
Modify Alignment

When you type data into cells, Excel aligns the data according to its type: text on the left side of the cell and numbers on the right. Both text and numbers are automatically aligned at the bottom of a cell. You can change the horizontal or vertical alignment of any entry using the Formatting toolbar or the Alignment tab in the Format Cells dialog box.

Step 6
You can indent cell contents from the edge of a cell by one character width by clicking the Increase Indent and Decrease Indent buttons on the Formatting toolbar. You can also set a specific number of character widths on the Alignment tab of the Format Cells dialog box. Cell indents replace other horizontal alignment options.

Activity Steps

open Retire01.xls

1. Select the range A11:A18

2. Click the **Align Left button** on the Formatting toolbar

3. Select the range B11:B18, then click the **Align Right button** on the Formatting toolbar

4. Select the range C11:C18, then click the **Center button** on the Formatting toolbar

5. Click cell A4, click **Format** on the menu bar, click **Cells**, click the **Alignment tab**
   See Figure 3-14.

6. Under Text alignment, click the **Vertical list arrow**, click **Center**, then click **OK**

close Retire01.xls

Figure 3-14: Alignment tab in the Format Cells dialog box

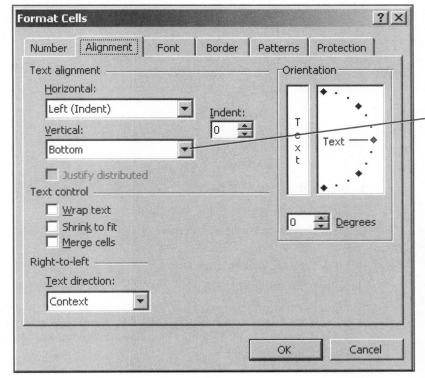

Click to change vertical alignment

extra!

Rotating cell contents
If you need to compress worksheet data columns, you can change the angle of selected cell text or numbers up to 90 degrees. Click **Format** on the menu bar, click **Cells**, then click the **Alignment tab** in the Format Cells dialog box. Under Orientation, drag the **red diamond** to the desired position, or click the **Degrees list arrow** to enter the number of degrees you want to rotate the contents of the selected cell or range. To have text read from top to bottom in a cell, click the text that is aligned that way under Orientation, then click **OK**.

Skill Set 3
Formatting and Printing Worksheets

Apply Styles

When you need to format a number of cells or ranges the same way, it can be tedious to select and format each one. Instead you can apply a **style** or collection of cell or number formats, such as bold, right-aligned, and red text. Styles help give your worksheets a consistent appearance. The Currency, Percent, and Number buttons on the Formatting toolbar are actually predefined styles that come with Excel. Until you apply another style, the Excel **Normal style** determines the default number format, alignment, and font for text and numbers you enter.

Step 2
To modify an existing style, click Font, click Style; in the Styles dialog box, select a style, then click Modify. Make changes in the Format dialog box. All text and numbers with that style applied will change. Style modifications only apply to the styles in that worksheet.

Activity Steps

 open Drums01.xls

1. Select the range C8 to D13

2. Click **Format** on the menu bar, then click **Style**

3. Click the **Style name list arrow**
   See Figure 3-15.

4. Click **Currency**, then click **OK**

5. Select the range F8:G15

6. Click **Format** on the menu bar, click **Style**, click the **Style name list arrow**, click **Currency [0]**, click **OK**, then click any blank cell
   The Currency [0] and Comma [0] styles display values with no decimal places.
   See Figure 3-16.

 close Drums01.xls

Figure 3-15: Style name list in the Style dialog box

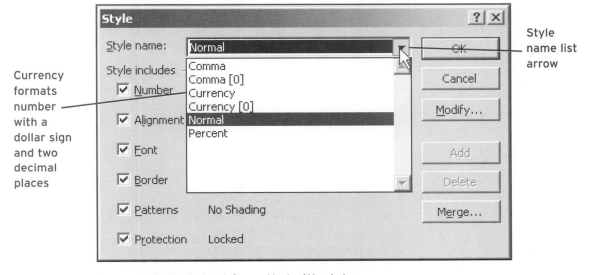

Currency formats number with a dollar sign and two decimal places

Style name list arrow

Figure 3-16: Worksheet formatted with styles

	A	B	C	D	E	F	G	H
1		**Miller Music**						
2		*Where serving you is our pleasure!*						
3								
4	*Drum Inventory*							
5	Date:		7/8/2003					
6					Quantity	Total	Retail	
7		Drum Type	Cost	Price	In Stock	Cost	Value	On Order
8		18" bass drum	$ 155.10	$ 310.20	10	$ 1,551	$ 3,102	21
9		6-1/2" snare drum	$ 115.25	$ 230.50	18	$ 2,075	$ 4,149	28
10		12" x 8" tom-tom	$ 125.95	$ 251.90	15	$ 1,889	$ 3,779	23
11		Small bongos	$ 62.95	$ 125.90	16	$ 1,007	$ 2,014	33
12		Piccolo snare drum	$ 103.45	$ 206.90	10	$ 1,035	$ 2,069	11
13		Timbales	$ 129.99	$ 259.98	15	$ 1,950	$ 3,900	0
14								
15		**Totals**			84	$ 9,506	$ 19,013	116
16								

Numbers formatted with dollar signs and no decimal places

Skill Set 3
Formatting and Printing Worksheets

Use Automated Tools to Format Worksheets

Apply AutoFormats to Worksheets

While Excel provides many formatting options that let you change the font, size, color, shading, and style of your worksheet content, you can also use the automatic formats supplied with Excel. **AutoFormats** contain distinctive combinations of shading, borders, fonts, fills, and alignment. You can apply an AutoFormat to an entire worksheet or to any selected range. If you click only inside a range, Excel will try to detect the correct range.

Step 3
If you don't want to use part of an AutoFomat, such as its alignment or border, click Options in the AutoFormat dialog box, then under "Formats to apply" at the bottom of the dialog box, select or deselect any formatting options.

Activity Steps

 open Drums02.xls

1. Select the range **B6:H15**

2. Click **Format** on the menu bar, then click **AutoFormat**

3. Click the picture of the **Classic 3 AutoFormat** (2nd row, right format)
   See Figure 3-17.

4. Click **OK**, then click any blank cell
   See Figure 3-18.

 close Drums02.xls

Figure 3-17: AutoFormat dialog box

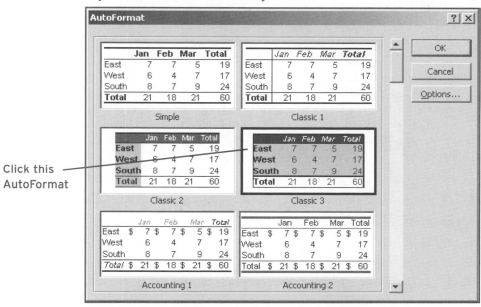

Click this AutoFormat

Figure 3-18: Worksheet with AutoFormat applied to a range

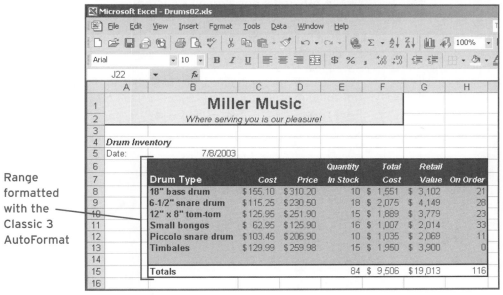

Range formatted with the Classic 3 AutoFormat

Skill Set 3
Formatting and Printing Worksheets

Modify Page Setup Options for Worksheets

Change Worksheet Orientation

Some printed worksheets fit on one 8-1/2" x 11" piece of paper that is taller than it is wide. This is called **portrait orientation**. Any information that does not fit on the page appears on page 2, making it difficult for a reader to see how headings and data line up. To fit data to one page that is wider than it is tall, you use **landscape orientation**. You set page orientation in the Page Setup dialog box, which you can open from the File menu or from the Print Preview window. To save paper and toner, always preview your worksheets before printing to see if you need to change the page orientation.

If your worksheet data does not appear to fit on a single page, you can scale the worksheet to fit the page. In the Page Setup dialog box, under Scaling, click the Fit to option, then enter the number of pages to which you want to fit the worksheet.

Activity Steps

 open Expenses02.xls

1. Click the **Print Preview button** on the Standard toolbar.

2. Click **Next**, then click **Close**
   A dotted line appears between columns G and H. The line is a **page break**, indicating that anything to its right will print on a second page.

3. Click **File** on the menu bar, click **Page Setup**, then click the **Page tab** (if it's not already selected)
   See Figure 3-19.

4. Under **Orientation**, click the **Landscape option button**, then click **Print Preview**
   See Figure 3-20.
   The Next button is dimmed, meaning that all the worksheet data now fits on one page.

5. Click **Close**

 close Expenses02.xls

Figure 3-19: Page Setup dialog box

Click to orient page sideways

Click to preview page before printing

Depending on your printer, text may appear here

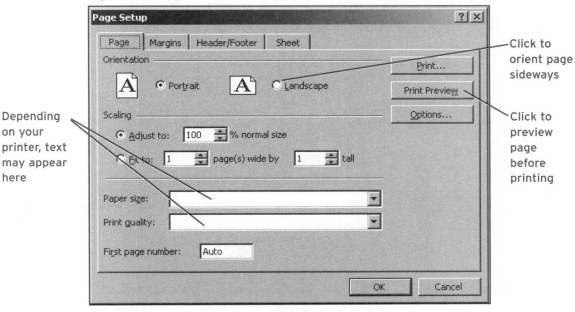

Figure 3-20: Worksheet in Print Preview

Next button is not active

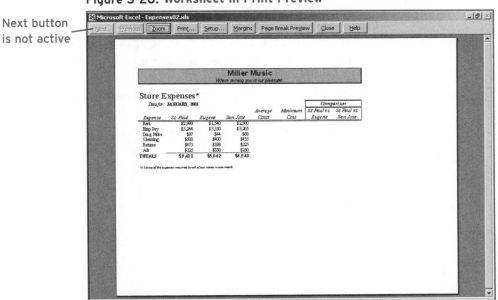

Skill Set 3
Formatting and Printing Worksheets

Modify Page Setup Options for Worksheets
Add Headers and Footers to Worksheets

When you print worksheets, you will frequently want to identify each page of your printout. You can do this easily with **headers**, text that prints at the top of each page, and **footers**, which print at the bottom of each page. A header or footer can contain text, a page number, the date, time, filename, or sheet name; it can also contain a picture you insert, such as a company logo. See Table 3-1 for icons you can use and the corresponding codes they insert.

Activity Steps

 open Markdowns02.xls

1. Click **View** on the menu bar then click **Header and Footer**

2. Click the **Header/Footer tab** (if it's not already selected)
   You could click the Header or Footer list arrow to select predefined headers or footers. To control their content and placement, you need to enter a custom header or footer.

3. Click **Custom Header**
   The word "Page" and the page number code "&[Page]" appear in the Center section.
   See Figure 3-21.

4. Click the **Left section box** (if the insertion point is not already there), click the **Date button** in the Header dialog box, click the **Right section box**, then click the **Sheet Name button**

5. Click **OK** in the Header dialog box, then click **Print Preview** in the Page Setup dialog box

6. Move the pointer across the top of the worksheet until it changes to ⭕, then click once
   See Figure 3-22.

7. Click **Close**

 close Markdowns02.xls

Step 1
To add headers or footers to more than one sheet in a workbook simultaneously, first select the sheets while holding down [Ctrl], then add the header or footer just as you would for a single sheet.

Figure 3-21: The Custom Header dialog box

Date button

Sheet name button

Code for page number

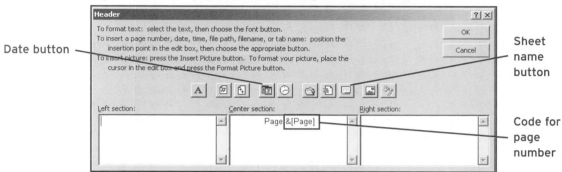

Figure 3-22: Worksheet Header

TABLE 3-1: Icons available in the Custom Header and Footer dialog boxes

click	to	code	click	to	code
A	Format font of selected header or footer text	--		Add path and file	&[Path]&[File]
	Add page number	&[Page]		Add filename	&[File]
	Add the total number of pages	&[Pages]		Add worksheet	&[Tab] tab name
	Add date	&[Date]		Insert a picture	&[Picture]
	Add time	&[Time]		Format picture	--

Skill Set 3

Formatting and Printing Worksheets

Modify Page Setup Options for Worksheets

Set Page Options for Printing

When printing worksheets, you can control exactly what parts of the worksheet should print, how the sheet should appear (including margins, row, and column headings), and where the worksheet cells should appear on the printed page. You set these features on the Margins and Sheet tabs in the Page Setup dialog box. As you change margins, you can view a worksheet sample with your new settings. When using Page Setup options, it's always a good idea to preview your worksheet to check its appearance before printing.

Step 4
In a multi-page worksheet, you can select any row to appear at the top of every printed page to help readers identify data. Click File on the menu bar, then click Page Setup. On the Sheet tab of the Page Setup dialog box, click the Collapse button next to Rows to Repeat at top, click the row, click the Redisplay button, then click Print Preview or OK.

Activity Steps

open Budget02.xls

1. Click **File** on the menu bar, then click **Page Setup**

2. Click the **Margins tab**, then click the **Left up arrow** once until 1 appears in the text box

3. Under Center on page, click the **Vertically** check box to select it
   See Figure 3-23.

4. Click the **Sheet tab**, then under Print, click the **Gridlines** and **Row and column headings check boxes** to select them

5. Click **Print Preview**, then click the preview window so you can see the full page
   See Figure 3-24.

6. Click **Close**

close Budget02.xls

Figure 3-23: Margins tab in the Page Setup dialog box

Set left
margin here

Select to
center
vertically
on page

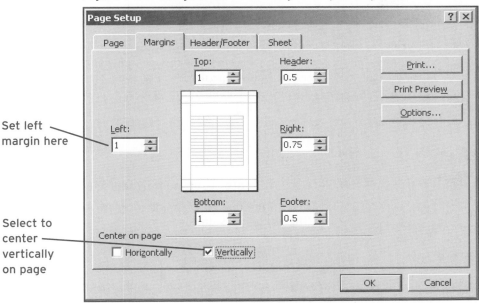

**Figure 3-24: Page in Print Preview centered vertically and showing
row and column headings**

Worksheet
centered
vertically
on page

Row and
column
headings

Gridlines

One-inch
left margin

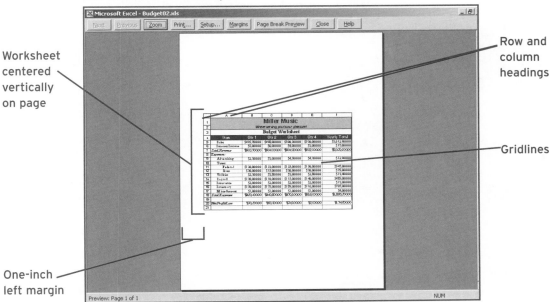

Skill Set 3

Formatting and Printing Worksheets

Preview and Print Worksheets and Workbooks

Set and Print Print Areas

If you are working on a large worksheet, you might want to print only a portion of it. To print a worksheet section once, you can use the Selection option button in the Print dialog box. To print an area repeatedly, you can set a **print area**, which is an area you designate; that area prints when you click the Print button on the Standard toolbar.

Step 2
You can set different print areas for each worksheet. To clear a print area, click File, point to Print Area, then click Clear Print Area.

Activity Steps

 open Earnings04.xls

1. Select cell A17, enter your name, then select the range **A4:G17**

2. Click **File** on the menu bar, point to **Print Area**, click **Set Print Area**, then click outside the range
   A dotted line surrounds the print area you set.
   See Figure 3-25.

3. Click the **Print Preview button** on the Standard toolbar
   Only the range you defined as the print area appears.
   See Figure 3-26.

4. Click **Print**, then click **OK** in the Print dialog box

 close Earnings04.xls

Figure 3-25: Print area in worksheet

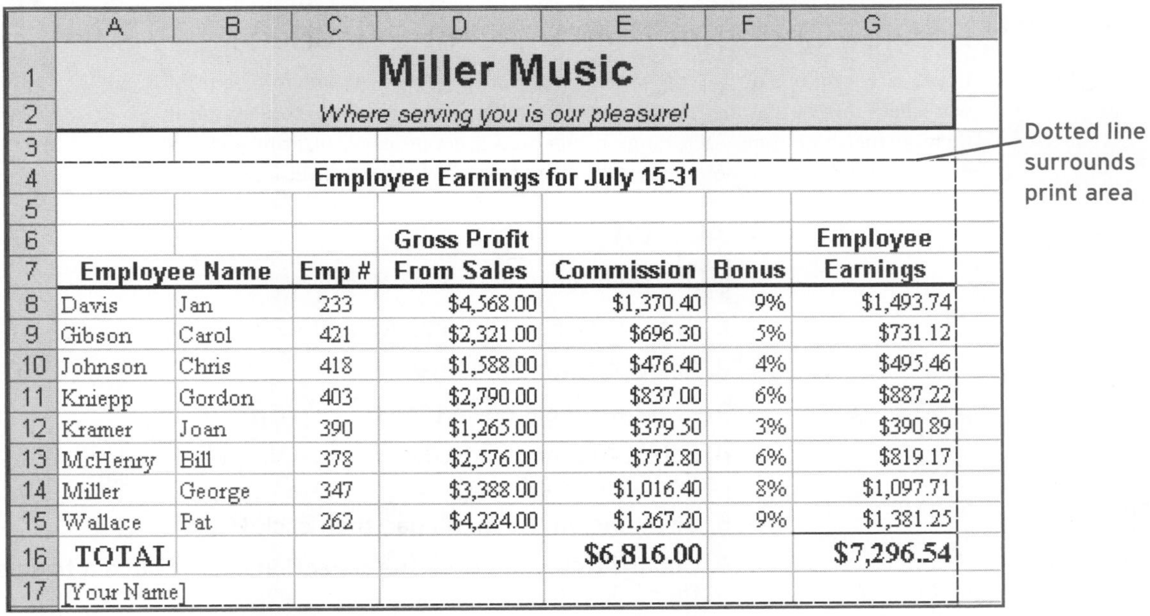

	A	B	C	D	E	F	G	
1				**Miller Music**				
2				*Where serving you is our pleasure!*				
3								Dotted line surrounds print area
4				**Employee Earnings for July 15-31**				
5								
6				**Gross Profit**			**Employee**	
7	**Employee Name**		**Emp #**	**From Sales**	**Commission**	**Bonus**	**Earnings**	
8	Davis	Jan	233	$4,568.00	$1,370.40	9%	$1,493.74	
9	Gibson	Carol	421	$2,321.00	$696.30	5%	$731.12	
10	Johnson	Chris	418	$1,588.00	$476.40	4%	$495.46	
11	Kniepp	Gordon	403	$2,790.00	$837.00	6%	$887.22	
12	Kramer	Joan	390	$1,265.00	$379.50	3%	$390.89	
13	McHenry	Bill	378	$2,576.00	$772.80	6%	$819.17	
14	Miller	George	347	$3,388.00	$1,016.40	8%	$1,097.71	
15	Wallace	Pat	262	$4,224.00	$1,267.20	9%	$1,381.25	
16	**TOTAL**				**$6,816.00**		**$7,296.54**	
17	[Your Name]							

Figure 3-26: Print area range in Print Preview

Only contents of Print Area will print

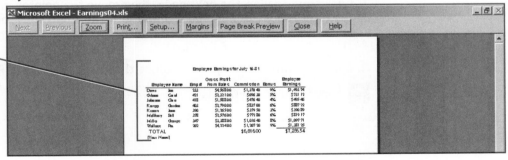

Skill Set 3
Formatting and Printing Worksheets

Preview and Print Worksheets and Workbooks
Preview and Print Non-Adjacent Selections

If you are working on a large worksheet, you may want to preview or print worksheet ranges that are not next to each other (non-adjacent). You can print them at the same time; each range prints on a separate page. In Print preview you can use the Zoom pointer to get a closer look at the worksheet image.

Activity Steps

 open Summary03.xls

1. Enter your name in cells A5 and A20

2. Select the range **A4:G9**

3. Press and hold down [Ctrl]

4. Select the range **A19:G24**
   See Figure 3-27.

5. Click **File** on the menu bar, then click **Print**

6. Under Print what, click the **Selection option button** to select it, then click **Preview**
   See Figure 3-28.

7. Click **Next** to view the next page, then move the pointer over the top part of the worksheet until the pointer becomes the Zoom pointer , then click once
   The worksheet view is magnified.

8. Click the worksheet again to reduce the image, then click **Print**

 close Summary03.xls

Step 2
The nonadjacent areas must be on the same worksheet.

Figure 3-27: Non-adjacent ranges selected

Selected non-adjacent ranges

	A	B	C	D	E	F	G
4			*3rd Quarter Sales Summary*				
5	[Your Name]						
6	*Month*	*Store*	*Pianos*	*Combos*	*Band Instruments*	*Special Events*	*Totals*
7	July	St. Paul	$245,680	$189,050	$102,354	$164,550	$701,634
8	July	Eugene	$345,795	$222,975	$135,055	$205,225	$909,050
9	July	San Jose	$214,328	$120,880	$86,550	$93,520	$515,278
10	August	St. Paul	$247,800	$192,025	$104,350	$162,250	$706,425
11	August	Eugene	$332,050	$231,095	$131,065	$206,995	$901,205
12	August	San Jose	$217,500	$122,035	$89,025	$92,245	$520,805
13	September	St. Paul	$247,950	$193,235	$105,025	$145,750	$691,960
14	September	Eugene	$337,505	$252,425	$124,050	$189,525	$903,505
15	September	San Jose	$219,275	$123,950	$90,525	$74,325	$508,075
16							
17	Totals		$2,407,883	$1,647,670	$967,999	$1,334,385	$6,357,937
18							
19			*4th Quarter Sales Summary*				
20	[Your Name]						
21	*Month*	*Store*	*Pianos*	*Combos*	*Band Instruments*	*Special Events*	*Totals*
22	October	St. Paul	$328,560	$195,400	$105,425	$172,778	$802,162
23	October	Eugene	$315,680	$220,550	$139,107	$215,486	$890,823
24	October	San Jose	$215,600	$115,880	$89,147	$98,196	$518,823
25	November	St. Paul	$213,452	$180,440	$107,481	$170,363	$671,735
26	November	Eugene	$435,770	$240,994	$134,997	$217,345	$1,029,106
27	November	San Jose	$220,335	$125,690	$91,696	$96,857	$534,578

Figure 3-28: Preview of first selected range

Indicates second range is on next page

First selected range

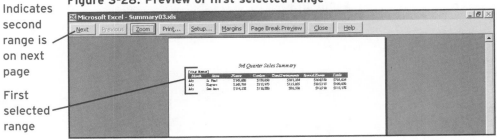

Skill Set 3

Formatting and Printing Worksheets

Target Your Skills

open Teaching01.xls

1 Format the work-sheet so it looks like Figure 3-29.

Add a custom footer with your name in the left section and the date in the right section. Print it centered vertically on the sheet, showing gridlines and row and column headings. Set a print area that includes only the data in rows 7 through 19, then print only the print area.

Figure 3-29

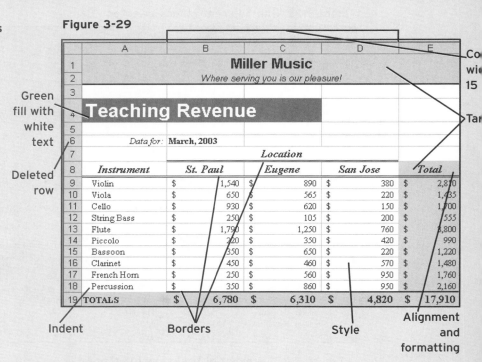

open Bonus01.xls

2 Refer to Figure 3-30. Freeze rows and columns above and to the left of cell B7. Change the work-sheet orientation so the data prints on one page. Then preview and print the two non-adjacent AutoFormatted ranges at the same time, then unfreeze the panes. Hide columns H and I, print the worksheet, then redis-play the hidden columns.

Figure 3-30

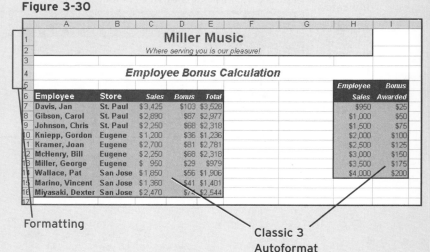

Skill List

1. Insert and delete worksheets
2. Modify worksheet names and positions
3. Use 3-D references

An Excel 2002 **workbook** is a file containing one or more worksheets. A **worksheet** is a grid of rows and columns you use to store and analyze data. On a worksheet, the intersection of every row and column is a **cell** into which you can insert labels, values, and formulas.

In some workbooks, you will only need one worksheet, but in others, you will need two or more. It's important to know how to organize worksheets in workbooks so you can quickly store, view, and use the data they hold. You can easily add, delete, move, and name worksheets. Formatting sheet tabs with color can make it easier to differentiate between sheets. When you have data in multiple worksheets, you can use **3-D references** in formulas to reference data from one or more worksheets.

Skill Set 4
Modifying Workbooks

Insert and Delete Worksheets
Insert a New Worksheet into a Workbook

A new Excel workbook contains three worksheets: Sheet1, Sheet2, and Sheet3. However, you can add as many sheets as you need. Excel inserts a new worksheet to the left of the selected worksheet and assigns it the next number in the sheet numbering sequence. The Insert command on the sheet tab shortcut menu lets you select the type of sheet to add. For example, you might want to add a chart sheet (a sheet that will contain a chart), or a sheet based on a **template**, a presupplied worksheet design. The worksheet command on the Insert menu automatically inserts one standard worksheet. Once you have added the worksheet, you cannot undo the action.

Step 2
Excel adds as many sheets as you have selected. To select more than two adjacent sheets, select the first worksheet tab in the sequence, press and hold [Shift], click the last worksheet tab in the sequence, click Insert on the menu bar, then click Worksheet.

Activity Steps

 open Payroll01.xls

1. **Right-click the June worksheet tab, then click Insert**
   The Insert dialog box lets you insert several different types of sheets, such as a standard worksheet, a chart sheet, or a sheet based on a template.
   See Figure 4-1.

2. **Click the Worksheet icon (if it's not already selected), then click OK**
   A new worksheet named Sheet1 appears to the left of the June worksheet.

3. **Click Insert on the menu bar, then click Worksheet**
   Another new worksheet, named Sheet2, appears to the left of Sheet1.
   See Figure 4-2.

 close Payroll01.xls

Figure 4-1: Insert dialog box

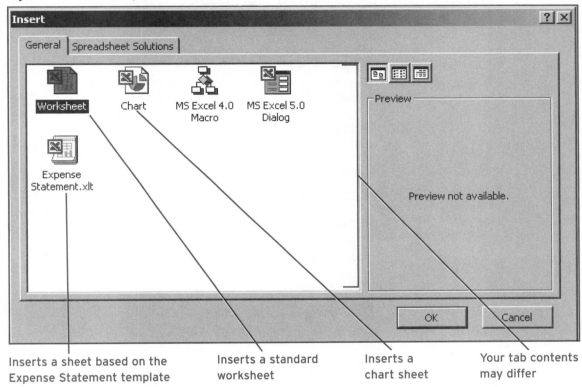

Inserts a sheet based on the Expense Statement template

Inserts a standard worksheet

Inserts a chart sheet

Your tab contents may differ

Figure 4-2: Workbook with two new worksheets

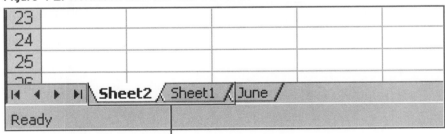

Newly inserted sheets

Skill Set 4
Modifying Workbooks

Insert and Delete Worksheets
Delete Worksheets from a Workbook

If you no longer need a particular worksheet in a workbook, you can delete it. You can also delete multiple selected worksheets. You cannot, however, delete all worksheets; a workbook must have at least one visible (unhidden) worksheet. *In workbooks that contain formulas using cell data from other sheets, recheck your formulas. Deleting a worksheet that has a value used in another sheet's formula can cause inaccurate formula results.*

Step 2
You can also right-click a sheet tab, click Delete, then click Delete again to confirm the deletion.

Activity Steps

 open Helicopters01.xls

1. Click the **2ⁿᵈ Quarter sheet tab**

2. Click **Edit** on the menu bar, then click **Delete sheet**
   A message tells you that the sheet contains data and asks you to confirm the deletion.
   See Figure 4-3.

3. Click **Delete**
   One sheet remains in the workbook.
   See Figure 4-4.

 close Helicopters01.xls

Figure 4-3: Confirmation dialog box

Microsoft Excel	☒
⚠ Data may exist in the sheet(s) selected for deletion. To permanently delete the data, press Delete.	
	Delete Cancel

Figure 4-4: Workbook with one remaining sheet

	A	B	C	D	E	F
1	**Powder Trails Resort Helicopter Ski Tours**					
2	*Projected Sales: First Quarter 2004*					
3				Helicopter		
4		Sky Master	Whirlygig	Big Bertha	Totals	
5	REVENUE					
6	Average Cost Per Guest	$ 140	$ 150	$ 220		
7	Total Number of Guests	4800	3000	7200	5672	
8	**Total Helicopter Trip Revenue**	$ 672,000	$ 450,000	$ 1,584,000	$ 2,706,000	
9						
10	EXPENSES					
11	Number of Tours Available	120	150	100		
12	Operating Cost per Helicopter	$ 4,300	$ 3,800	$ 7,400		
13	Total Operating Costs	$ 516,000	$ 570,000	$ 740,000	$ 1,826,000	
14	Advertising Costs	$ 8,500	$ 7,000	$ 8,000	$ 23,500	
15	**Total Expenses**	$ 524,500	$ 577,000	$ 748,000	$ 1,849,500	
16						
17	NET REVENUE	$ 147,500	$ (127,000)	$ 836,000	$ 856,500	
18						
19						
20						
21						
22						
23						
24						

|◀ ◀ ▶ ▶|\ **1st Quarter** /

Ready

One remaining sheet tab

Skill Set 4
Modifying Workbooks

Modify Worksheet Names and Positions
Moving Worksheets within a Workbook

In a workbook with multiple sheets, you may need to move a worksheet to make the workbook structure clear. You can drag sheets to a new position or use the sheet tab shortcut menu. A word of caution: *In workbooks where formulas contain references to other sheets, always recheck your formulas carefully after moving sheets. Moving sheets can make formula results inaccurate.*

Step 1
You may want to use one worksheet as the basis for another worksheet. To create a copy of a worksheet, click its sheet tab, then press and hold [Ctrl] as you drag the worksheet tab. Excel places a copy called [worksheet-name](2) in the new location.

Activity Steps

  open Commissions01.xls

1. Position the pointer over the **January sheet tab**

2. Press and hold down the mouse button, then drag the pointer left until the pointers ⬚ and ▼ are before the February sheet *See Figure 4-5.*

3. **Release the mouse button**
   The worksheet is repositioned before the February sheet tab.

  close Commissions01.xls

Figure 4-5: Dragging a sheet to a new location

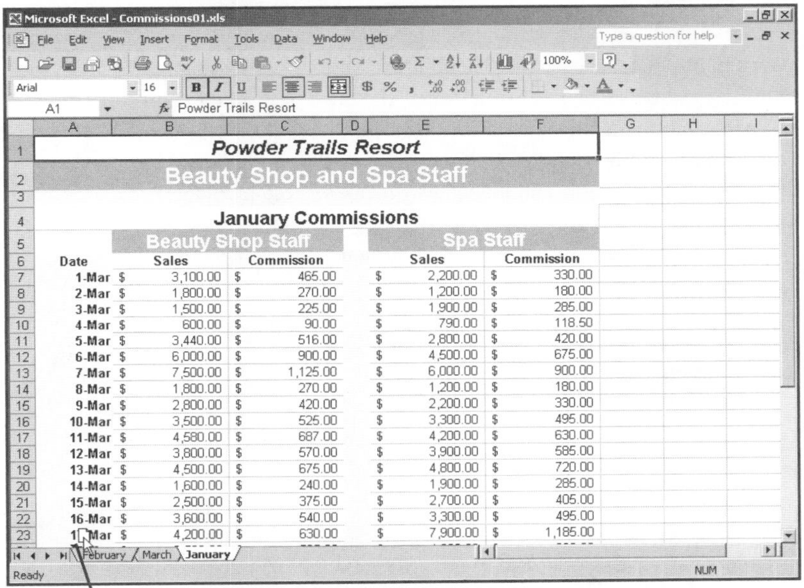

Triangle shows new worksheet location

extra!

Moving or copying worksheets from other workbooks

When you want to move or copy a worksheet from another workbook into the current workbook, you can use the Move or Copy dialog box. Open the destination workbook, then open the source workbook containing the sheet you want. Right-click the sheet you want to copy or move, then on the shortcut menu, click **Move or Copy**. Click the **To book list arrow**, click the name of the workbook where you want the sheet, click the sheet name before which you want the new sheet, then click **OK**. *If you have formulas that use values from other sheets, check them carefully after you move or copy sheets; their results may become inaccurate.*

Skill Set 4
Modifying Workbooks

Modify Worksheet Names and Positions
Name Worksheets

Excel worksheets have default names such as Sheet1, Sheet2, and so forth. In a workbook containing multiple worksheets, it is helpful to name sheets so you can easily find the data they contain. The worksheet name should reflect its content; for example, each sheet could have the name of the appropriate month, year, sales rep, or product. A name can contain up to 31 characters and must be unique. As you type the new name, the sheet tab automatically widens to accommodate it. While long sheet names are informative, they can make it necessary to use the sheet scroll buttons to display other sheets. In a workbook with many sheets, it's best to keep sheet names short.

Step 1
You can also click Format on the menu bar, point to Sheet, then click Rename to highlight the existing sheet name.

Activity Steps

 open Payroll02.xls

1. **Double-click the Sheet2 tab**
   See Figure 4-6.

2. **Type July**

3. **Press [Enter]**
   See Figure 4-7.

 close Payroll02.xls

Figure 4-6: Highlighted sheet name

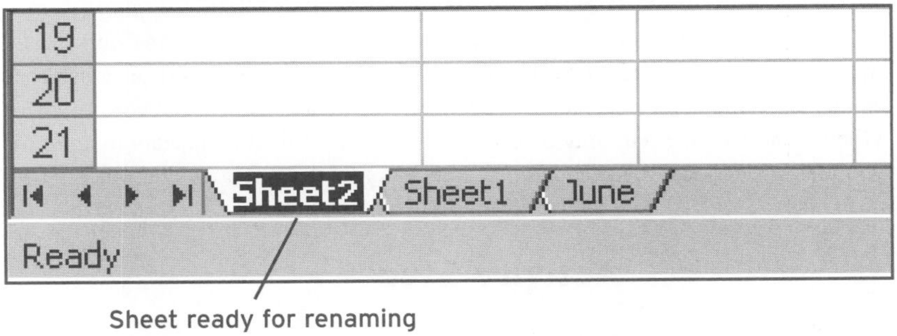

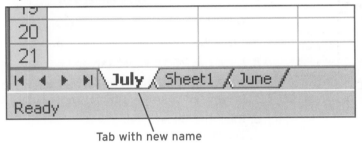

19
20
21
Sheet2
Sheet1
June
Ready
Sheet ready for renaming

Figure 4-7: Renamed sheet

20
21
July
Sheet1
June
Ready
Tab with new name

Skill Set 4

Modifying Workbooks

Modify Worksheet Names and Positions
Shading Worksheet Tabs

In a multi-sheet workbook, you might want to visually differentiate worksheets from one another. Excel lets you do so by adding color to worksheet tabs. You could, for example, shade income sheets one color and expense sheets another. When a sheet is selected, only a strip at the bottom of the tab appears in color. If you assign a dark color, Excel automatically changes the type to white so it is readable.

To remove color from a tab, right-click the tab, click Tab Color, click No Color, then click OK.

Activity Steps

 open Bikes01.xls

1. Right-click the **2003 sheet tab**
2. Click **Tab Color**
3. Click the **turquoise color** (4ᵗʰ row, 5ᵗʰ from the left), then click **OK**
4. Click the **2004 sheet tab** and observe the color of the 2003 tab
5. Right-click the **2004 sheet tab**, click **Tab Color**, then select the **bright red color** (3ʳᵈ row, leftmost color), then click **OK**
6. Click the **Sheet3 tab**
   See Figure 4-8.

 close Bikes01.xls

Figure 4-8: Tabs with color

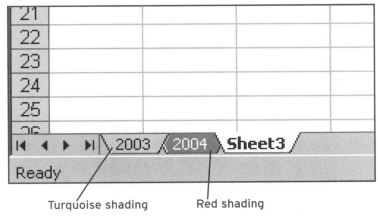

Turquoise shading   Red shading

extra!

Adding a picture as a worksheet background
You can create a sheet background from any graphic you have in electronic form. Click **Format** on the menu bar, point to **Sheet**, then click **Background**. Use the **Look in list arrow** and the **Up One Level arrow** to locate a graphic, select it, then click **Insert**. You may need to shade cells so their contents appear against the background. You can use a variety of picture file formats, including .jpeg, .wmf, and .gif. Background patterns do not print. If your background picture is small, Excel will insert multiple copies on the worksheet background.

Skill Set 4

Modifying Workbooks

Use 3-D References
Create Formulas using 3-D References to the Same Cell

Excel lets you analyze data using information from multiple worksheets in one formula. Because values from other sheets create a third "dimension" in workbooks, they are called **3-D references**; a formula that uses such references is called a **3-D formula**. You can use 3-D formulas to **consolidate**, or gather, data from multiple sheets. For example, a formula that sums the values in cell A6 on several sheets is preceded by a range of worksheet names separated by a colon, followed by the cell reference, as in =SUM(Sheet1:Sheet4!A6). The 3-D reference in parentheses adds the values in cell A6 on Sheets 1 through 4, including Sheets 2 and 3. The exclamation point (!) is called an **external reference indicator**; it separates the sheet name from the cell reference.

Activity Steps

 open Guests02.xls

1. Click cell **B3** then type **=SUM(**

2. Click the **Europe sheet tab**, press and hold [**Shift**], then click the **North America sheet tab**

Step 2
You can also click the first sheet, type : (a colon), then click the last sheet to enter the range that includes the first, last, and all sheets in between.

3. Click cell **B3**
   See Figure 4-9.

4. Type **)** (a closing parenthesis), then click the **Enter** button  on the Formula bar
   The formula in cell B3 of the Summary sheet sums the 1999 figures for the 0-5 years age group in Europe, Asia, and North America.

5. Drag the fill handle from cell **B3** on the Summary sheet through cell **F3**

6. Click cell **F3**, then read its formula
   See Figure 4-10.
   The formulas in the copied cells retain the references to the supporting worksheets.

 close Guests02.xls

Skill 3

Use 3-D References

Figure 4-9: Formula using a 3-D reference

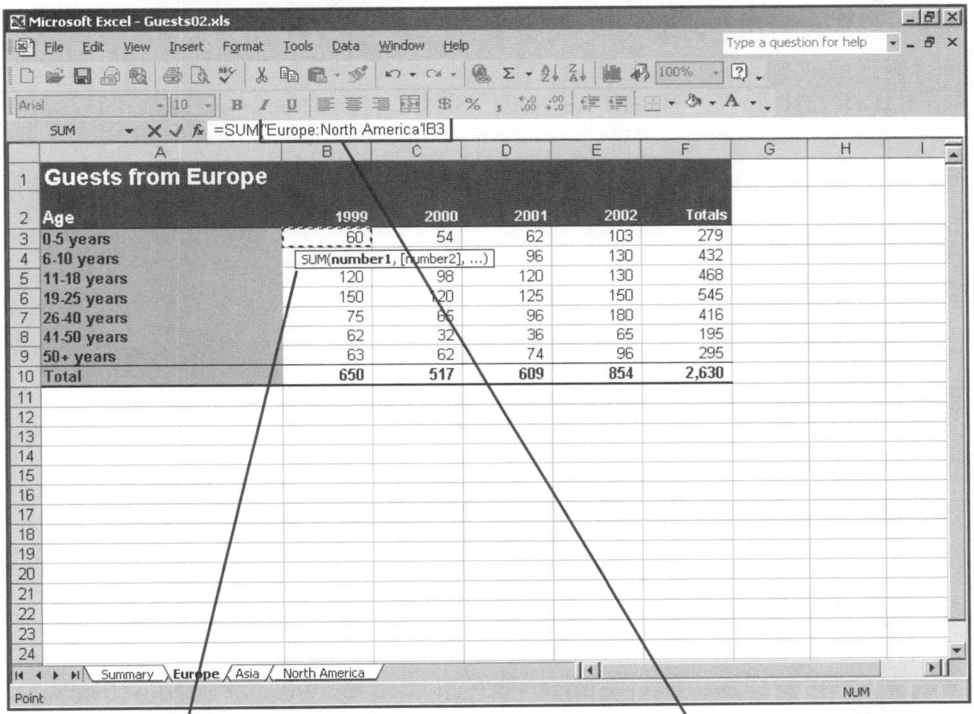

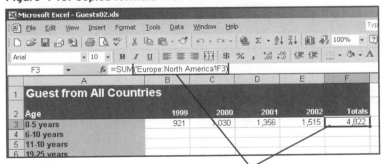

Screen tip shows function structure

3-D reference to cell B3 on three worksheets

Figure 4-10: Copied formula with 3-D references

Copied formula also contains 3-D reference

Skill Set 4
Modifying Workbooks

Use 3-D References
Create Formulas Using 3-D References to Different Cells

In Excel, **3-D references** are cell references that refer to a sheet other than the current sheet. A 3-D formula uses 3-D references to **consolidate**, or collect, data from other worksheets. A 3-D formula can use data from the same cell in different worksheets, but it can also use data from different cells in other worksheets. An example of such a reference might be =SUM(Sheet1!A5,Sheet2!B6,), which adds the values of cell A5 on Sheet1 and cell B6 on Sheet2. *If you delete sheets in the range you reference, be sure to recheck your formulas; a #REF! Error indicates a missing value in the formula.*

Step 5
To drag more than one sheet, press and hold [Ctrl], select the sheets you want to move, release [Ctrl], then drag the sheets.

Activity Steps

 open Guests03.xls

1. Click cell **B3** then type =SUM(
2. Click the **Europe sheet tab**, click cell **B10**, then type **,** (a comma)
   See Figure 4-11.
3. Click the **Asia sheet tab**, click cell **B7**, then type **,**
4. Click the **North America sheet tab**, click cell **B6**, then type **)**
5. Click the **Enter button** on the Formula bar
   See Figure 4-12.
6. With cell B3 selected, drag the fill handle to cell **G3** then click cell **E3**
   The formulas in the copied cells retain the references to the supporting worksheets.

 close Guests03.xls

Figure 4-11: Beginning the 3-D formula

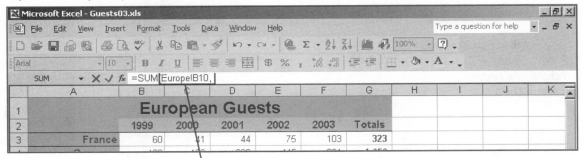

3-D reference to cell B10 on Europe sheet

Figure 4-12: Completed 3-D formula

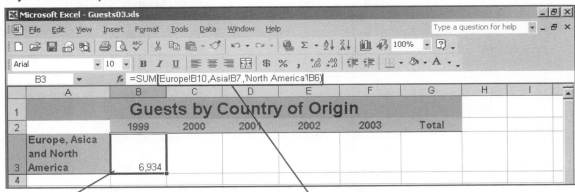

3-D formula result   3-D reference to different cells on different sheets

Skill Set 4

Modifying Workbooks

Target Your Skills

 open Rentals02.xls

1 Follow the instructions of Figure 4-13 to produce the results shown in the figure.

Figure 4-13

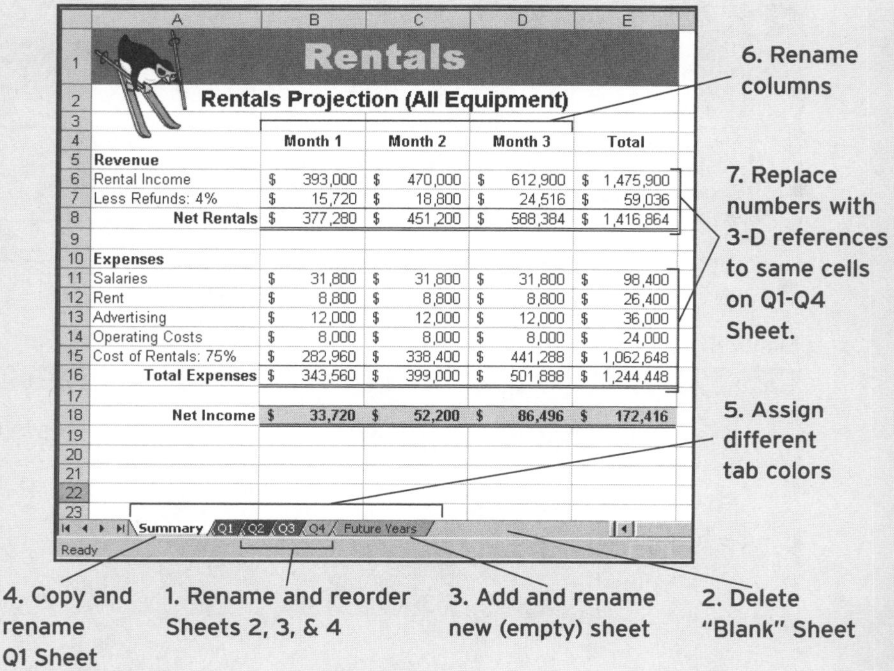

	A	B	C	D	E
1			**Rentals**		
2			**Rentals Projection (All Equipment)**		
3					
4		Month 1	Month 2	Month 3	Total
5	Revenue				
6	Rental Income	$ 393,000	$ 470,000	$ 612,900	$ 1,475,900
7	Less Refunds: 4%	$ 15,720	$ 18,800	$ 24,516	$ 59,036
8	Net Rentals	$ 377,280	$ 451,200	$ 588,384	$ 1,416,864
9					
10	Expenses				
11	Salaries	$ 31,800	$ 31,800	$ 31,800	$ 98,400
12	Rent	$ 8,800	$ 8,800	$ 8,800	$ 26,400
13	Advertising	$ 12,000	$ 12,000	$ 12,000	$ 36,000
14	Operating Costs	$ 8,000	$ 8,000	$ 8,000	$ 24,000
15	Cost of Rentals: 75%	$ 282,960	$ 338,400	$ 441,288	$ 1,062,648
16	Total Expenses	$ 343,560	$ 399,000	$ 501,888	$ 1,244,448
17					
18	Net Income	$ 33,720	$ 52,200	$ 86,496	$ 172,416
19					
20					
21					
22					
23					

Sheet tabs: Summary / Q1 / Q2 / Q3 / Q4 / Future Years

6. Rename columns

7. Replace numbers with 3-D references to same cells on Q1-Q4 Sheet.

5. Assign different tab colors

4. Copy and rename Q1 Sheet

1. Rename and reorder Sheets 2, 3, & 4

3. Add and rename new (empty) sheet

2. Delete "Blank" Sheet

 open Tours02.xls

2 Create formulas in cells B9:C10 that calculate the totals shown in Figure 4-14, using 3-D references to the appropriate figures on the Cross-Country sheet.

Figure 4-14

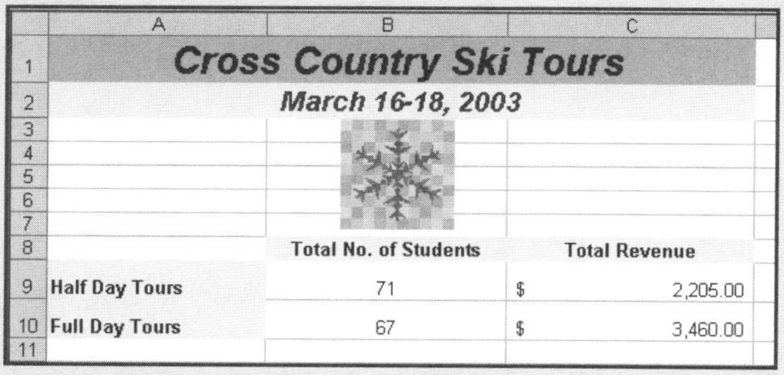

	A	B	C
1		**Cross Country Ski Tours**	
2		**March 16-18, 2003**	
3			
4			
5			
6			
7			
8		Total No. of Students	Total Revenue
9	Half Day Tours	71	$ 2,205.00
10	Full Day Tours	67	$ 3,460.00
11			

Skill List

1. Create and revise formulas
2. Use statistical, date and time, financial, and logical functions in formulas

The power of Excel lies in its ability to calculate results using the information you enter into a worksheet. You enter **formulas** that tell Excel what type of calculation to perform on which values. Formula results are "tied to" the values they use; when you change the underlying values, Excel instantly recalculates the results. Automatic recalculation saves time and lets you perform basic "what-if" analyses. For example, you can change a price that is used in a profit formula, and immediately see the effect of the new price on profits.

You can enter and edit formulas for any selected cell in the Formula bar. Cell references in formulas tell Excel which values to use; you can type cell references or you can click cells and drag across cell ranges. When you copy formulas to different cells, you can control whether you want the cell references to adjust to their new locations or always refer to the same cells.

You can create your own formulas or use built-in formulas called **functions** that help you perform more complex calculations easily. A series of dialog boxes called the Function Wizard helps you enter each part of the function. Excel contains functions for many common calculations, such as calculating totals, minimum or maximum values, and payments. You can even instruct Excel to enter one result if certain conditions are true and another result if they are not.

Skill Set 5
Creating and Revising Formulas

Create and Revise Formulas
Create Formulas Using the Formula Bar

Excel formulas contain numbers or values, **operators** such as +, -, *, or /, and **cell references**, which are addresses such as A6 or X11. Excel formulas must begin with an equal sign (=). You can enter a formula for a selected cell in the **Formula bar**, the white box above the worksheet column headings. As you enter formulas, you can either type cell references or you can click a worksheet cell to insert a reference. Excel calculates formulas with more than one operator, according to the **order of precedence**, in the following order: 1) calculations inside parentheses; 2) exponents; 3) multiplication and division; then 4) addition and subtraction.

Activity Steps

 open Markdowns03.xls

1. Click cell **G8**, then click in the Formula bar

2. Type **=**, click cell **E8**, type **-** (a minus sign), type **(**, click cell **F8**, type *****, click cell **E8**, then type **)**
   As you enter each cell reference, the cell becomes surrounded by a moving dotted line, called a **marquee**, so you can easily see the reference.
   See Figure 5-1.
   Your formula multiplies the Original Price by the Markdown percentage to obtain the markdown amount. Then it subtracts the markdown amount from the Original Price to calculate the Sale Price.

3. Click the **Enter button** on the Formula bar
   The formula result, $716, appears in cell G8.

4. Click cell **E8**, type **900**, then click the **Enter button** on the Formula bar
   See Figure 5-2.
   Excel automatically recalculates the formula with the new original price and changes the Sale Price from $716 to $720.

 close Markdowns03.xls

Step 3
You can also enter a formula or value by pressing [Enter] or [Tab] on the keyboard. Pressing [Enter] moves the active cell down one row, while pressing [Tab] moves it one cell to the right.

Figure 5-1: Markdown formula in Formula bar

Formula appears in Formula bar

Cell reference in formula matches cell outline color

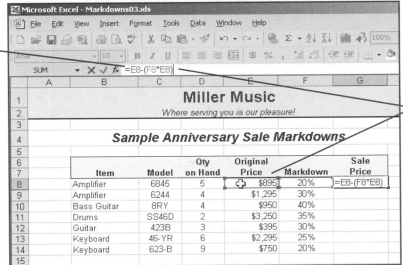

Figure 5-2: Recalculated formula after changing referenced value

Recalculated formula result

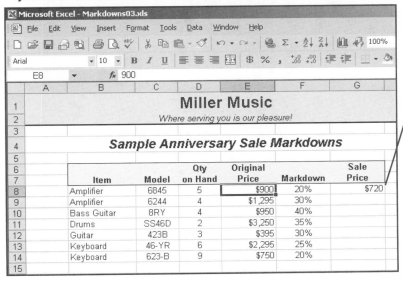

Skill Set 5
Creating and Revising Formulas

Create and Revise Formulas
Edit Formulas Using the Formula Bar

After you enter a formula, you can change it at any time. After selecting the cell containing the formula, you can edit values, cell references, or operators in the Formula bar. You can drag to select values, references, or operators, then type replacements; you can also use [Backspace] and [Delete]. To add to the formula, click the place in the formula where you want to add information, then type or click to enter the new data. In this activity you'll edit a cell to correct an error in a formula.

Activity Steps

 open Tickets01.xls

1. **Click cell E11**
   The formula in cell E11 has an error. Instead of multiplying the number of concert tickets in cell D11 by the Concert Ticket price in cell C6, the formula multiplies it by the Folk Festival price in cell C5.

2. **Move the pointer over the Formula bar until the pointer becomes the I-beam pointer**

3. **On the right side of the formula, drag to select the 5 in the C5 cell reference**
   See Figure 5-3.

4. **Type 6**

5. **Click the Enter button** ✓ **on the Formula bar**
   The formula now calculates the total sales of both ticket types for the first employee.
   See Figure 5-4.

 close Tickets01.xls

tip

Step 1
Instead of editing a formula in the Formula bar, you can edit it directly in its cell (called *in-cell editing*) by double-clicking the cell.

Figure 5-3: Incorrect cell reference selected in Formula bar

Incorrect reference selected in Formula bar

I-beam pointer

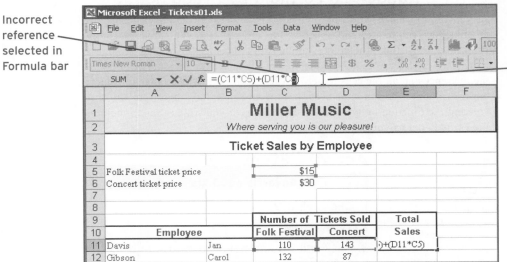

Figure 5-4: Corrected formula

Formula now contains correct references

Formula result now correct

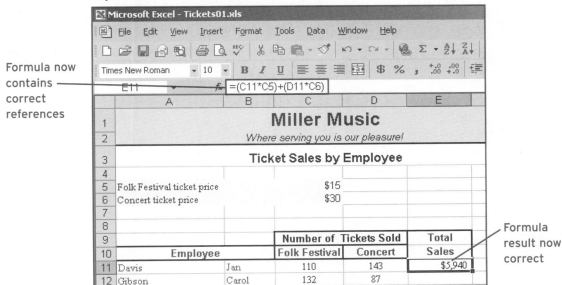

Skill Set 5
Creating and Revising Formulas

Create and Revise Formulas
Enter a Range in a Formula by Dragging

As you enter formulas, you will often enter references to cell ranges. Instead of entering each cell in a formula, such as =A6+A7+A8+A9, you can use a **range reference**, consisting of references to the first and last cell in a range separated by a colon, such as A6:A9. A range reference includes the first and last cells in the reference and all the cells in between them. You can type a range reference, but it is often easier and more accurate to drag across the range. You will start entering the function by typing directly in the cell; you will see the formula in the Formula bar as you type.

Step 4
You don't have to type the closing parenthesis at the end of a formula. After you click the Enter button on the Formula bar, or after you press [Enter] on the keyboard, Excel inserts the closing parenthesis automatically.

Activity Steps

 open Advertising03.xls

1. Click cell **C19**

2. Type **=SUM(**

3. Click cell **B8** and hold the mouse button, then drag to select the range **B8:D10**
   See Figure 5-5.

4. Type **)**

5. Click the **Enter button** on the Formula bar

6. Use the same techniques to enter the formula **=SUM(B12:D14)** in cell **C21**
   See Figure 5-6.

 close Advertising03.xls

Figure 5-5: Dragging to select the range for the SUM formula

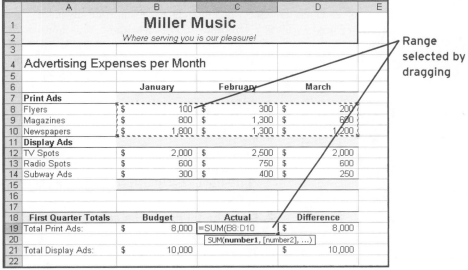

Range
selected by
dragging

Figure 5-6: Formula showing range reference you entered by dragging

	A	B	C	D
1	**Miller Music**			
2	*Where serving you is our pleasure!*			
3				
4	Advertising Expenses per Month			
5				
6		January	February	March
7	**Print Ads**			
8	Flyers	$ 100	$ 300	$ 200
9	Magazines	$ 800	$ 1,300	$ 600
10	Newspapers	$ 1,800	$ 1,300	$ 1,200
11	**Display Ads**			
12	TV Spots	$ 2,000	$ 2,500	$ 2,000
13	Radio Spots	$ 600	$ 750	$ 600
14	Subway Ads	$ 300	$ 400	$ 250
15				
16				
17				
18	**First Quarter Totals**	**Budget**	**Actual**	**Difference**
19	Total Print Ads:	$ 8,000	$ 7,600	$ 400
20				
21	Total Display Ads:	$ 10,000	$ 9,400	$ 600
22				

Completed
formulas

Skill Set 5
Creating and Revising Formulas

Create and Revise Formulas
Use Relative References in Formulas

When you enter a cell reference in a formula, Excel automatically makes it a relative reference. A **relative reference** adjusts when you copy and paste the formula in a new location. For example, if you enter =A1+B1 in cell C1, then copy the formula to cell C2, the copied formula will automatically read =A2+B2. Excel uses references to cells *relative to* the cell containing the formula.

Step 2
You could also copy the formula by using the Copy and Paste buttons on the Standard toolbar or by pressing [Ctrl][C] on the keyboard, then using the Paste or Paste Special commands on the Edit menu.

Activity Steps

open Tickets02.xls

1. Click cell **C19**
   See Figure 5-7.
   The Formula bar shows that the formula adds the values in the range C11:C18.

2. Drag the **fill handle** on cell **C19** to the right, across cell **D19**

3. Click cell **D19**
   The Formula bar now reads D11:D18, showing that Excel is using a relative reference to calculate the results of the copied formula. *See Figure 5-8.*

close Tickets02.xls

Figure 5-7: Original formula adds the values in column C

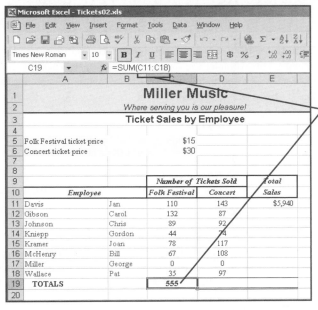

Formula in Formula bar calculates total of range in column C

Figure 5-8: Copied formula automatically adds the values in column D

Copied formula totals range in appropriate column because of relative referencing

Column letter automatically adjusted in copied formula

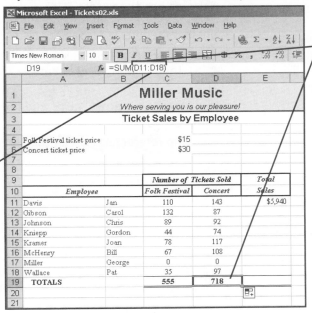

Skill Set 5
Creating and Revising Formulas

Create and Revise Formulas
Use Absolute References in Formulas

When you use cell references in copied formulas, you will sometimes want Excel to refer to a specific cell, regardless of the formula's location. In these cases, you use an **absolute reference**, which uses dollar signs before the row letter and column number. For example, the formula =A2*$A$1 will always multiply the first formula value by the value in cell A1, no matter where the formula is located. The [F4] key changes selected references to absolute references.

Activity Steps

 open Tickets03.xls

1. **Click cell E11**
   In the next step you will intentionally create incorrect formulas.

2. **Drag the fill handle on cell E11 down to cell E18 and observe the formula results**
   See Figure 5-9.
   The results are incorrect because Excel automatically made the references to cell C5 and C6 relative references. You want them always to refer to the ticket prices in cells C5 and C6, so you will make them absolute references.

3. **Click cell E11, then double-click the reference to cell C5 in the Formula bar, then press [F4]**
   Excel inserts dollar signs before the row and column number, indicating that they are now absolute references.

4. **Double-click the reference to cell C6 in the Formula bar, press [F4], then click the Enter button** **in the Formula bar**

5. **Drag the fill handle on cell E11 down to copy the corrected formula into the range E11:E18, then observe the results**

6. **Click cell E16 to deselect the range, then notice that the absolute references remain the same in the copied formulas**
   See Figure 5-10.

 close Tickets03.xls

> **tip**
>
> **Step 2**
> Repeatedly pressing [F4] cycles through the cell reference possibilities, from C5, $C$5, C$5, $C5, then back to C5.

Figure 5-9: Copied formulas are incorrect because ticket price references are relative

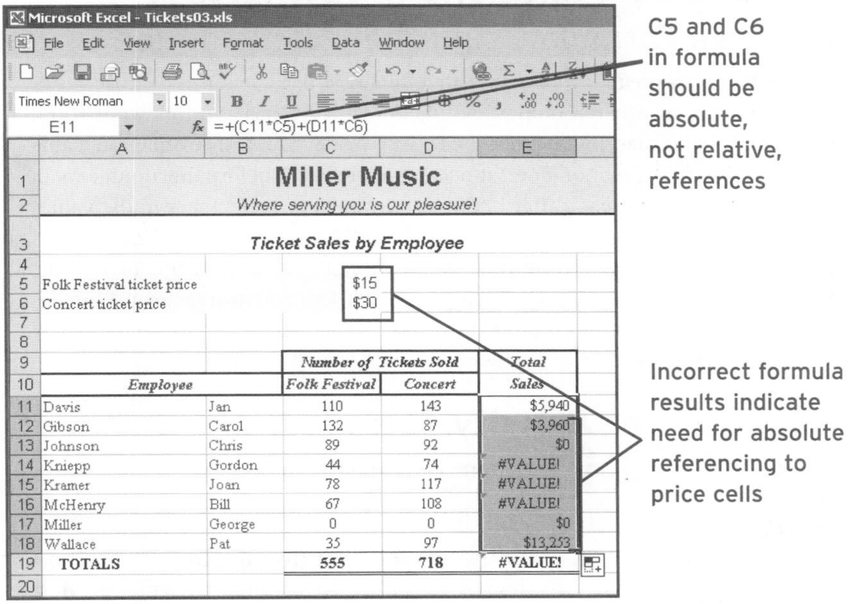

C5 and C6
in formula
should be
absolute,
not relative,
references

Incorrect formula
results indicate
need for absolute
referencing to
price cells

Figure 5-10: Copied formulas now correct with absolute references to ticket prices

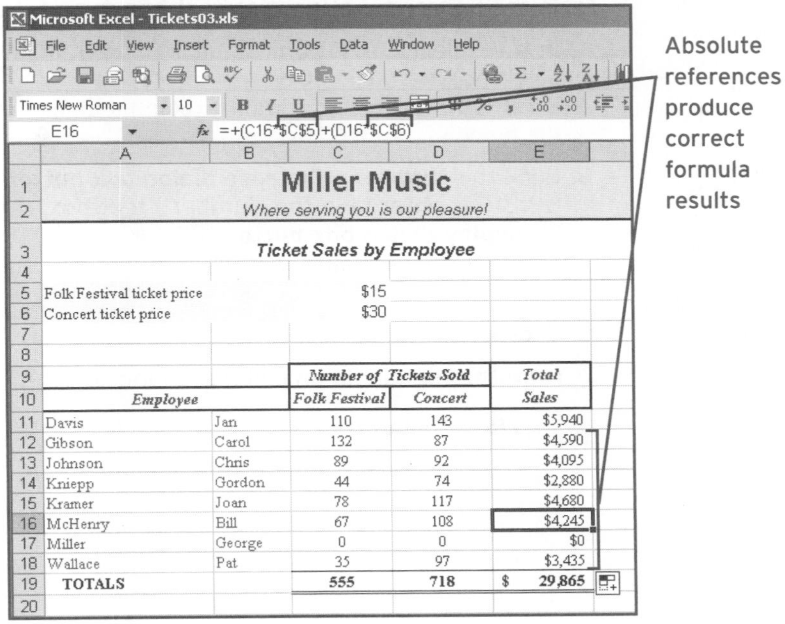

Absolute
references
produce
correct
formula
results

Skill Set 5
Creating and Revising Formulas

Use Statistical, Date and Time, Financial, and Logical Functions in Formulas
Create a Formula Using the SUM Function

A **function** is a predefined formula that comes with Excel. You can use functions alone or in other formulas. A function always has the following form: =[functionname](argument1,argument2...). The function name describes what the function does; it occurs immediately before the arguments in parentheses, with no space after it. The **arguments** are references to the values the function should act on. For example, the SUM function =SUM(A2,A3) totals the values in the cells A2 through A3. You can type a function or use the **Function Wizard**, a series of dialog boxes that lets you search for a function and then prompts you for each function argument. Table 5-1 shows an overview of Excel function categories and some of their related functions.

Step 2
Because the SUM function is so commonly used, Excel supplies an AutoSum button ∑ on the Standard toolbar; click it once to automatically insert the SUM function into the selected cell; drag to select another range, if necessary, then press [Enter].

Activity Steps

 open Update03.xls

1. Click cell **B17**

2. Click the **Insert Function button** _fx_ on the Formula bar
   In the "Search for a function" box, you can describe the task you want to complete, then Excel will search for an appropriate function.

3. In the Search for a function text box, type **total**, then click **Go**

4. In the Select a function list, click **SUM** (if it's not already selected), then click **OK**
   Excel "guesses" that you want to sum the range immediately above the function, B8:B16.

5. Click the **Number 1 Collapse dialog box button** 🔲, confirm that B8:B16 is entered in the Number 1 text box, then click the **Redisplay dialog box button** 🔲
   Excel places a preliminary result at the bottom of the dialog box. *See Figure 5-11.*

6. Click **OK**

7. Drag the **fill handle** on cell **B17** to include the range **C17:E17**

 close Update03.xls

Figure 5-11: Function Arguments dialog box

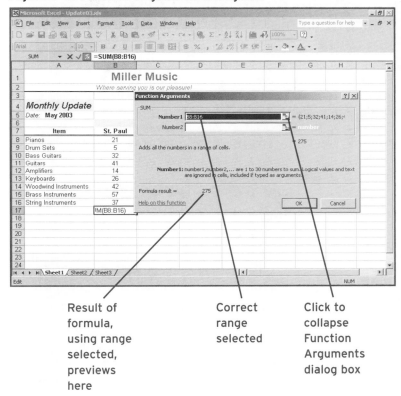

Result of
formula,
using range
selected,
previews
here

Correct
range
selected

Click to
collapse
Function
Arguments
dialog box

Table 5-1: Excel function overview

function category	examples of functions	use for
Financial	PMT, PV, FV	Analyzing purchases and investments
Date and Time	DATE, TODAY, WEEKDAY	Schedules and calculations based on time
Math and Trig	SUM, TAN, COS	Mathematical calculations
Statistical	AVER, COUNT, MEDIAN, MODE, CHITEST	Summarizing and analyzing numeric data
Logical	IF, AND, FALSE	Testing data against conditions

Skill Set 5

Creating and Revising Formulas

Use Statistical, Date and Time, Financial, and Logical Functions in Formulas

Create Formulas Using the MIN and MAX Functions

MIN and **MAX** are statistical functions. The MIN function finds and displays the lowest, or minimum, value in a range. The MAX function finds and displays the highest, or maximum, value in a range. You might use these functions to determine the highest or lowest price, salary, or grade in a worksheet column, row, or other range. These functions are especially useful in large worksheets, where you would have to scroll repeatedly and scan many numbers to locate such information.

Step 2
As you enter functions, you will sometimes see a Function ScreenTip containing the function name and the correct syntax. Click the function name in the tip to open a Help screen about that function.

Activity Steps

 open Practice01.xls

1. Click cell **H38**

2. Click the **Insert Function button** on the Formula bar
   Instead of searching for a function, you can display a list of function categories, then choose the one you want.

3. Click the **Or select a category list arrow**, then click **Statistical**

4. Scroll down the Select a function list, click **MIN**, then click **OK**

5. Click the **Number 1 Collapse dialog box button**, move the reduced dialog box so you can see the contents of column H, then use the vertical scroll arrow to view rows 38 through 40

6. Compare the range in the Function Arguments dialog box to the worksheet range
   See Figure 5-12.
   You need to adjust the range

7. In the Function Arguments dialog box, edit the reference to cell **H37** to **H36**, then press **[Enter]** twice

8. In cell H40, type **=MAX(H10:H36)**, then click the **Enter button** on the Formula bar
   See Figure 5-13.

 close Practice01.xls

Figure 5-12: Correcting a range in the Function Arguments dialog box

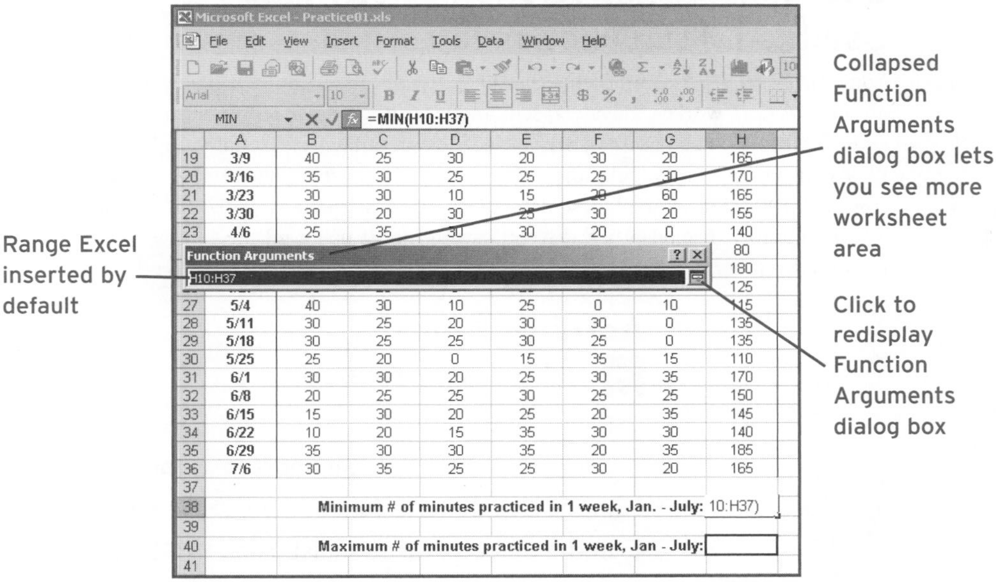
Microsoft Excel - Practice01.xls
=MIN(H10:H37)
Function Arguments
H10:H37
Minimum # of minutes practiced in 1 week, Jan. - July: 10:H37)
Maximum # of minutes practiced in 1 week, Jan - July:
Range Excel inserted by default
Collapsed Function Arguments dialog box lets you see more worksheet area
Click to redisplay Function Arguments dialog box

Figure 5-13: Worksheet with minimum and maximum statistics

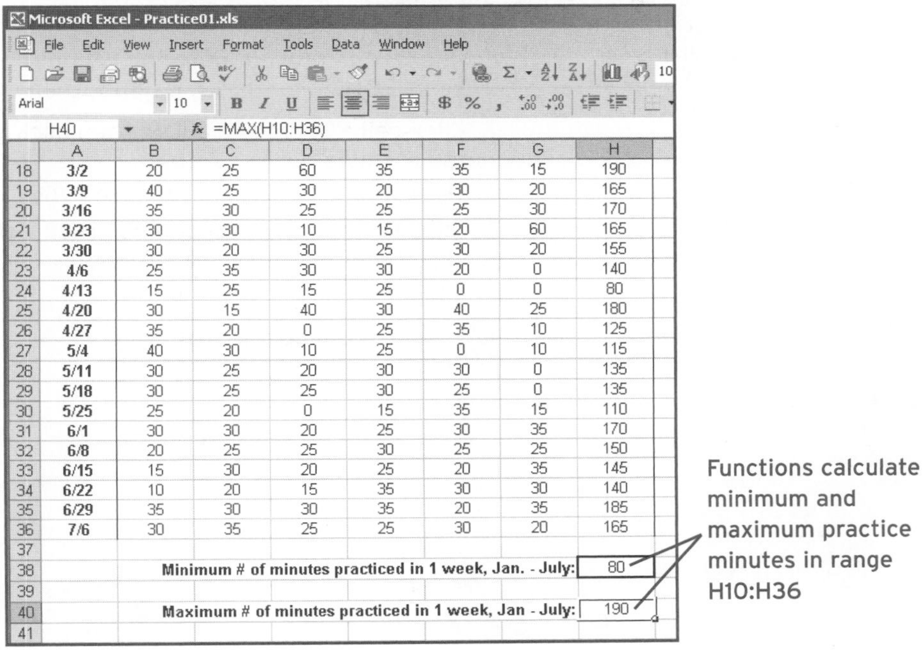
Microsoft Excel - Practice01.xls
H40
=MAX(H10:H36)
Minimum # of minutes practiced in 1 week, Jan. - July: 80
Maximum # of minutes practiced in 1 week, Jan - July: 190
Functions calculate minimum and maximum practice minutes in range H10:H36

Skill Set 5

Creating and Revising Formulas

Use Statistical, Date and Time, Financial, and Logical Functions in Formulas

Use the DATE Function in Formulas

You can use the DATE functions in calculations, for example, to calculate the amount of time worked, days elapsed, and so forth. The DATE function has the syntax DATE(year,month,day). Excel stores dates as serial numbers so they can be used in calculations. The numbers represent the number of days from 1/1/1900. For example, the date 12/15/2003 is stored as 37,970. If you see a serial number instead of a date, you can format it using a Date format to see the date itself.

If you type a date in a cell that has already been formatted using the General format, Excel will automatically format it as a date.

Activity Steps

 open Employment01.xls

1. Click cell **D8**

2. Click the **Insert Function button** on the Formula bar

3. In the Search for a function box, type **date**, then click **Go**

4. In the Select a function list, click **DATE**, then click **OK**

5. Type the following values in their respective text boxes, in the Function Arguments dialog box, pressing [**Tab**] after typing each value: Year: **2001**, Month: **12**, Day: **5**, then click **OK**

6. Repeat the procedure in cell **E8** but use the following values: Year: **2003**, Month: **10**, Day: **15**, then click **OK**

7. Click cell **F8**, type **=E8-D8**, then click the **Enter button** on the Formula bar
   The formula result is formatted as a date.

8. Click **Format** on the menu bar, click **Cells**, in the Category list, click **General**, then click **OK**
   See Figure 5-14.

 close Employment01.xls

Figure 5-14: Number of days calculated by subtracting two cells containing the DATE function

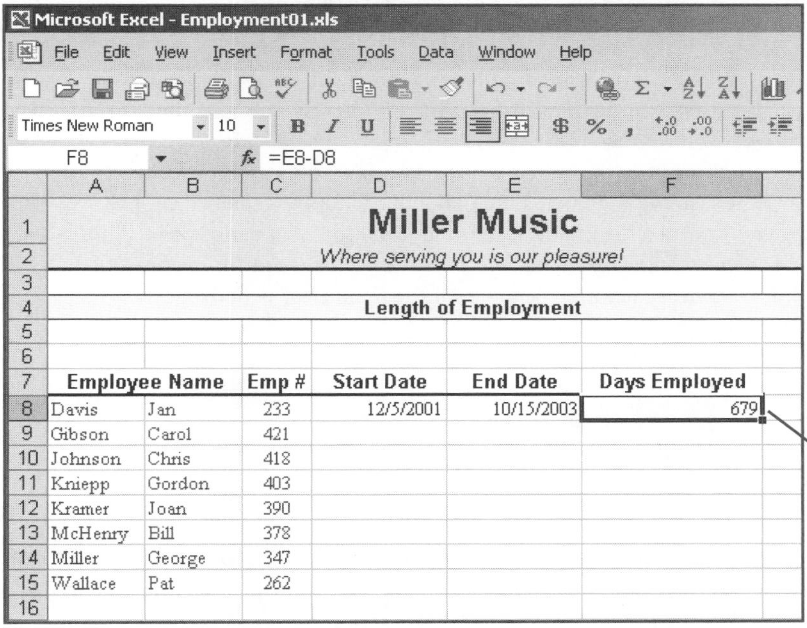

	A	B	C	D	E	F
1				**Miller Music**		
2				*Where serving you is our pleasure!*		
3						
4				**Length of Employment**		
5						
6						
7	**Employee Name**		**Emp #**	**Start Date**	**End Date**	**Days Employed**
8	Davis	Jan	233	12/5/2001	10/15/2003	679
9	Gibson	Carol	421			
10	Johnson	Chris	418			
11	Kniepp	Gordon	403			
12	Kramer	Joan	390			
13	McHenry	Bill	378			
14	Miller	George	347			
15	Wallace	Pat	262			
16						

Microsoft Excel - Employment01.xls

File Edit View Insert Format Tools Data Window Help

Times New Roman 10

F8 *fx* =E8-D8

Calculates number of days between Start Date and End Date

extra!

Using the NOW function
The NOW function is an Excel Date and Time function that inserts today's date and time in a worksheet cell. It has no arguments. In the Insert Function dialog box, select the **Date & Time category,** double-click **NOW,** then click **OK.** Excel inserts today's date and time in the selected cell. The NOW function date and time are updated when you reopen the worksheet or any time you press [F9].

Skill Set 5

Creating and Revising Formulas

Use Statistical, Date and Time, Financial, and Logical Functions in Formulas

Use the PMT Function in Formulas

The PMT (payment) function is a financial function that calculates the periodic payment on a loan of a given amount, using a given interest rate and time period. Its syntax is **PMT(rate,nper,pv,fv,type)**, where **rate** is the interest rate per period, **nper** is the number of periods, and **pv** is the present value of the loan. The last two arguments are optional: *fv* (future value) calculates the amount you want the loan to be at the end of the payment periods and *type* indicates whether payments occur at the beginning (1) or end (0) of the payment period. The interest rate, time period, and the number of periods must match. In other words, if you use a monthly interest rate, the number of periods must be months.

Step 5
You can show the payment as a positive amount by typing - (a minus sign) before the Pv amount in the function. Click the cell containing the function, then edit the function in the Formula bar or double-click the cell and edit directly in the cell.

Activity Steps

 open Computer01.xls

1. Click cell C11

2. Click the **Insert Function button** 🔊 on the Formula bar

3. In the Search for a function box, type **payment**, click **Go**, select **PMT** in the Select a function list, then click **OK**

4. Enter the following information in the Function Arguments dialog box:

Rate	.08/12
Nper	18
Pv	1825

   You leave the Fv (future value) box blank because you assume the future value will be zero—the loan will be completely paid off. You leave Type blank so Excel will assume a value of zero—payment at the end of each period.
   See Figure 5-15.

5. Click **OK**
   See Figure 5-16.
   You divide the yearly interest rate by 12 to make it a monthly rate, to match the 18-month loan term. The loan amount is $1,825. The monthly payment shows as a negative number, indicating an outflow of funds.

 close Computer01.xls

Figure 5-15: Insert Function dialog box for the PMT function

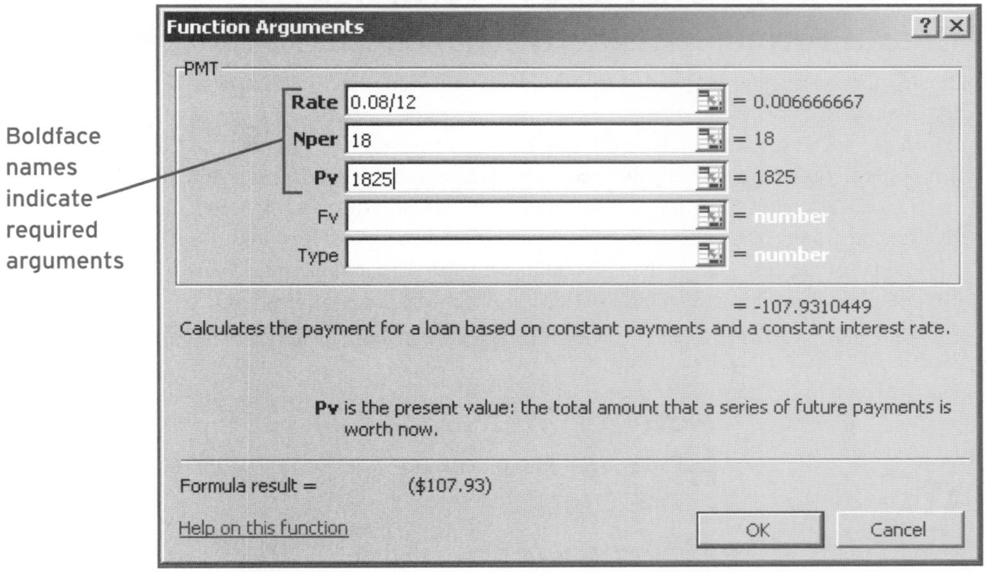

Boldface names indicate required arguments

Figure 5-16: Monthly loan payment calculated by the PMT function

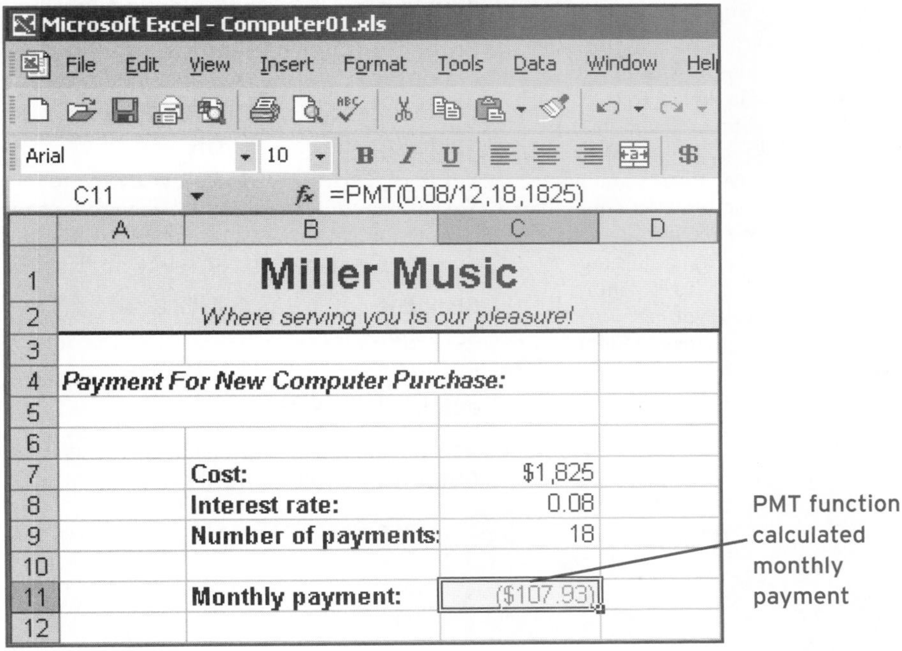

PMT function calculated monthly payment

Skill Set 5
Creating and Revising Formulas

Use Statistical, Date and Time, Financial, and Logical Functions in Formulas
Create Formulas Using the IF Function

The IF function is a logical function that evaluates conditions and calculates a result. Its syntax is `IF(logical_test, value_if_true, value_if_false)`, which you could restate by saying "If condition 1 is true, do X; if it is not, do Y." The **logical text** is the statement Excel uses to determine the function result. To have Excel calculate a 15% bonus if the sales figure in cell A3 exceeds $15,000, the IF function would read: `=IF(A3>15000,(A3*.15),0)`. This function says "If the value in cell A3 is greater than 15,000 (the logical test), multiply that value by .15 and place the calculated amount in this cell (value_if_true); if it does not exceed 15,000, place a zero in this cell (value_if_false)." You can use the comparison operators in Table 5-2 in the logical_test statement.

Step 4
The Function Wizard automatically places quotation marks around the Value_if_true and Value_if_false text, and it places parentheses around the function arguments. If you are typing an IF function directly into a cell, you need to type the quotation marks and opening parenthesis yourself.

Activity Steps
  open Practice02.xls

1. Click cell I10

2. Click the **Insert Function button** on the Formula bar

3. Click the **Or select a category list arrow**, click **Logical**, then double-click **IF** in the Select a function list

4. Enter the following information in the Function Arguments dialog box:

Logical_test	H10>120
Value_if_true	OK
Value_if_false	Below average

   You are saying, in effect, "If the student practiced more than 120 minutes during this week, place 'OK' in cell I11; if he practiced less than 120 minutes, place 'Below average' in cell I11."

5. Click **OK**
   See Figure 5-17.

6. Drag the **fill handle** on cell **I10** down through cell **I36**, then click outside the range

7. Double-click the right side of the column I **column heading** to AutoFit the cell contents

close Practice02.xls

Figure 5-17: Insert Function dialog box for the IF function

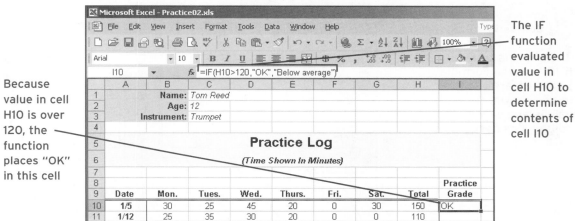

Because value in cell H10 is over 120, the function places "OK" in this cell

The IF function evaluated value in cell H10 to determine contents of cell I10

Table 5-2: Comparison operators for Logical_test statement

operator	meaning
=	Equals
>	Is greater than
<	Is less than
>=	Is greater than or equal to
<=	Is less than or equal to

Skill Set 5

Creating and Revising Formulas

Target Your Skills

open Comparison01.xls

1 Referring to Figure 5-18, use the Formula bar to create the formulas shown. Format values and widen columns as necessary.

Figure 5-18

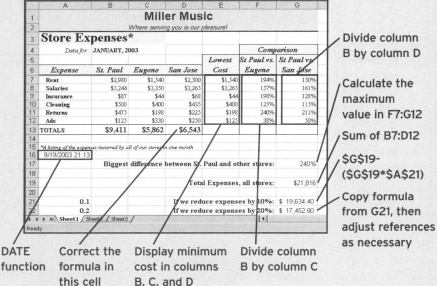

Divide column B by column D

Calculate the maximum value in F7:G12

Sum of B7:D12

$G$19-($G$19*$A$21)

Copy formula from G21, then adjust references as necessary

DATE function

Correct the formula in this cell

Display minimum cost in columns B, C, and D

Divide column B by column C

---

open Band01.xls

2 Modify the worksheet as shown in Figure 5-19.

Figure 5-19

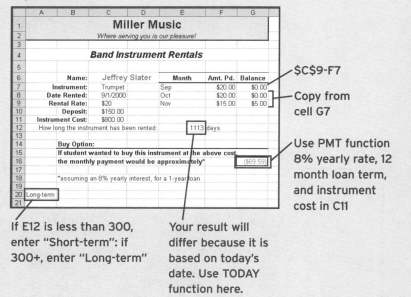

$C$9-F7

Copy from cell G7

Use PMT function 8% yearly rate, 12 month loan term, and instrument cost in C11

If E12 is less than 300, enter "Short-term"; if 300+, enter "Long-term"

Your result will differ because it is based on today's date. Use TODAY function here.

Skill List

1. Create, modify, position, and print charts
2. Create, modify, and position graphics

Excel worksheets provide powerful tools to help you analyze your data. To help you see trends and communicate your analyses to others, Excel lets you present your data as 2-dimensional or 3-dimensional charts (sometimes called **graphs**), which summarize your data in the form of a picture. The **Chart Wizard** is a series of dialog boxes that lets you choose from bar, line, pie, scatter, and other types of charts to create the most meaningful picture of your data.

Once you create a chart, you can readily change it to find the chart type that best communicates your information. For example, you might create a bar chart and then, on viewing it, decide that a column chart would be more appropriate. You can change the way your chart looks by adding or deleting labels, legends, or gridlines, or format chart text and graphics for a customized look.

You can place a chart on the worksheet containing the data you used to create it (also called the source data), or on its own worksheet, called a **chart sheet**. A chart is linked to the worksheet you used to create it, so if you change the underlying worksheet data, the chart changes automatically.

You can easily add and modify **graphics**, such as arrows, shapes, text blocks, and drawings to your worksheets and charts to enhance their appearance and draw attention to important trends.

Skill Set 6
Creating and Modifying Graphics

Create, Modify, Position, and Print Charts
Create and Modify a Pie Chart

A **pie chart** displays a data series as pieces of a pie. A **data series** is a group of related data, such as store sales for several departments. Each pie slice is a **data marker** that represents one worksheet cell. As a whole, the pie chart visually compares the contribution of each slice, or portion of data, which is called a **data point**. A pie chart is used only for a single data series.

Activity Steps

 open Sitecost02.xls

1. Drag to select the cell range **A4: B9**

2. Click the **Chart Wizard button** on the Standard toolbar, click the **Standard Types tab**, then under Chart type, click **Pie**

3. Click the middle Chart sub-type in the top row, then click and hold the **"Press and Hold to View Sample" button**
   See Figure 6-1.

4. Release the mouse button, click **Next**, verify that the data range is the range you selected, then click **Next**

5. Click after the text in the Chart title box, press **[Spacebar]**, type **Web Costs**, then Click **Next**

6. Click the **"As object in" option button**, then click **Finish**
   Excel places the chart on the current worksheet. *See Figure 6-2.* The chart toolbar appears at the bottom of the screen when the chart is selected. (If you don't see it there, click **View** on the menu bar, point to **toolbars**, then click **Chart**.) The "Monthly" column label becomes the chart title.

7. Move the pointer around on the chart, until the ScreenTip reads "Chart Area", click and hold the mouse button, drag the **chart** so its top border is under the data in cell B5, then release the mouse button

8. Click cell **B5**, type **200**, observe the "Cable connection" portion of the pie chart, then press **[Enter]**

9. Click cell **B5**, type **55**, then press **[Enter]**

 close Sitecost02.xls

If you don't see the chart toolbar on your screen, click View on the menu bar, point to Toolbars, then click Chart.

Figure 6-1: Chart Type dialog box in the Chart Wizard

Standard chart types you can create using Excel

Description of selected chart type

Preview of selected chart type showing your data

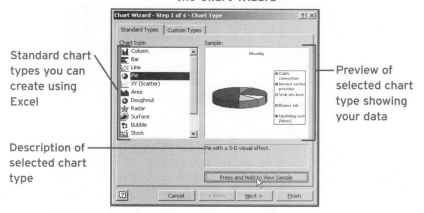

Figure 6-2: Pie chart

Chart object on worksheet

Range represented by selected chart is highlighted on worksheet

Text you added to title

Chart toolbar

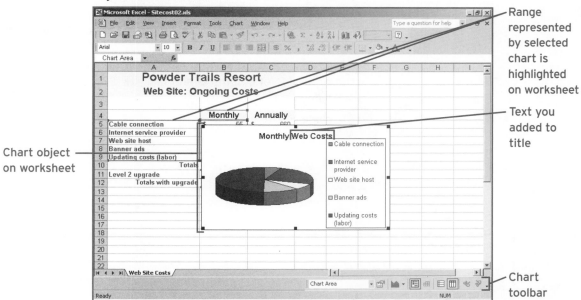

Skill Set 6
Creating and Modifying Graphics

Create, Modify, Position, and Print Charts
Move and Resize a Chart

A chart on a worksheet is an **object**, meaning that you can move and resize it separately from the worksheet. When you resize a chart object, all the chart elements, including text and data markers, automatically adjust to the new chart size. To resize a selected chart, you use its **sizing handles**, the small black squares that surround the selected chart. See Table 6-1 for common chart types.

Activity Steps

 open Staffing02.xls

1. Move the pointer slowly over different parts of the column chart, reading the ScreenTips that identify each element
See Table 6-2 for a description of major chart elements.

2. When the ScreenTip reads "Chart Area", click and hold the mouse button, then drag the chart so its top border is under the data, at the top of **row 7**, and its left border is on the left side of **column A**

3. Place the pointer over the chart's **lower right sizing handle** until the pointer becomes ⬊

4. Drag down and to the right, until the right side of the chart is at the right side of **column G** and fills row 22
See Figure 6-3.

 close Staffing02.xls

Step 4
To resize a chart in one direction only, drag the sizing handles on the sides, top, or bottom of the chart area.

TABLE 6-1: Common chart types

type	looks like	used to show
Column	🖼	Data in categories in vertical format
Bar	🖼	Data in categories in horizontal format
Line	🖼	Data trends over time
Pie	🖼	Portions of data in relation to the whole
XY Scatter	🖼	Data trends for value pairs
Area	🖼	Column changes over time

Figure 6-3: Resizing the chart

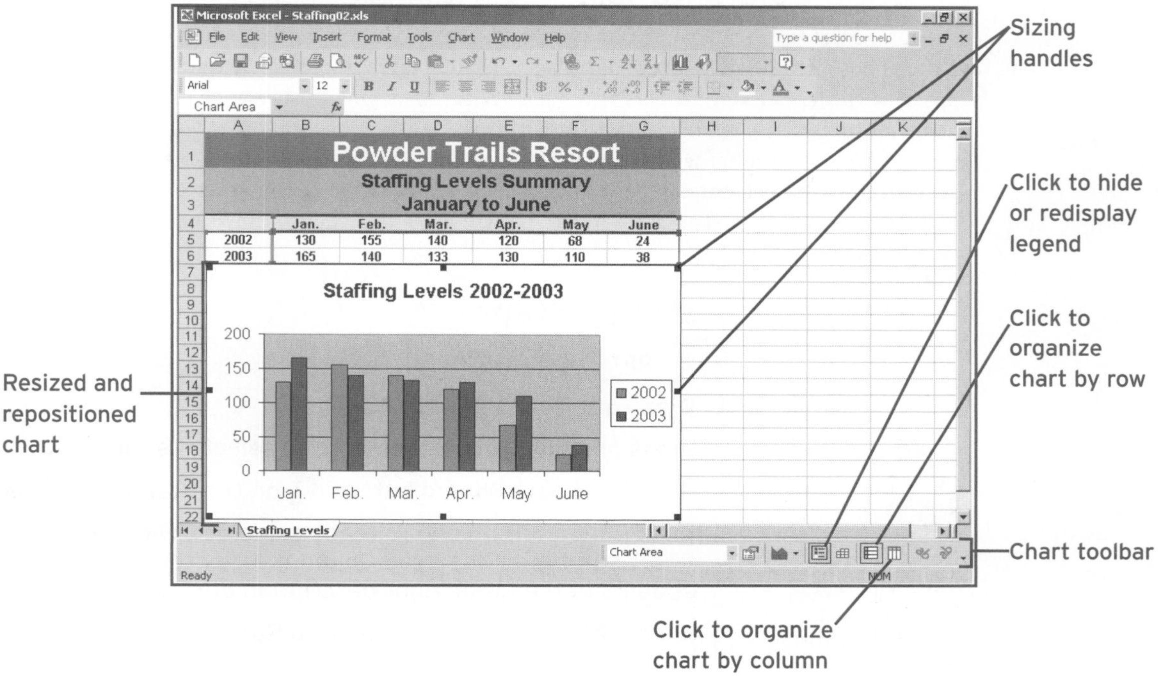

Sizing handles

Click to hide or redisplay legend

Click to organize chart by row

Resized and repositioned chart

Chart toolbar

Click to organize chart by column

TABLE 6-2: Common chart elements

element	what it is
Chart area	The entire chart and its surrounding area; drag this to move a chart
Plot area	The area within the chart axes, where data is plotted
Chart title	The chart name that describes chart content
Legend	Description of the colors assigned to each data point or series
Category axis	Axis that contains the categories being charted
Value axis	Axis that contains the numerical measurements for data points
Major gridlines	The lines behind a chart that help the viewer visually align data points with axis values
Tick marks	Small lines on axes denoting measurement intervals

Skill Set 6

Creating and Modifying Graphics

Create, Modify, Position, and Print Charts
Create a Column Chart

A column chart represents data points as vertical bars. While a pie chart allows you to chart only one series, a column chart lets you plot multiple series, which appear as clusters of vertical bars. The Chart Wizard lets you create the chart, change the data series reference, assign it a title, and specify its location as you create it. When you select worksheet cells to create a chart, you will often need to use [Ctrl] to select **nonadjacent** cells, which are cells located in rows or columns that are not next to each other. You will place this chart on the same sheet as the data.

Activity Steps

 open Resorts01.xls

1. Drag to select the range **A3:A12**

2. Press and hold **[Ctrl]**, then drag to select the range **G3:H12**

3. Click the **Chart Wizard button** on the Standard toolbar

4. Click **Column** (if it is not already selected), click the upper-left Chart sub-type, **Clustered Column**, verify that Clustered Column appears in the lower-right description box, then click **Next**

5. Verify that the ranges in the Data Range box are correct, then click **Next**
   With two columns of data, Excel does not add a default chart title.

6. Click the **Chart title box**, type **Resort Cost Comparison**, then click **Next**

7. Click the **As new sheet option button**, then type **Costs Chart** to name the chart sheet

8. Click **Finish**
   See Figure 6-4.

 close Resorts01.xls

tip

Step 1
When you use [Ctrl] to select nonadjacent rows or columns, the ranges you select must be the same size.

Figure 6-4: Completed column chart created from nonadjacent rows

Chart title —

Newly-
created
chart
sheet —

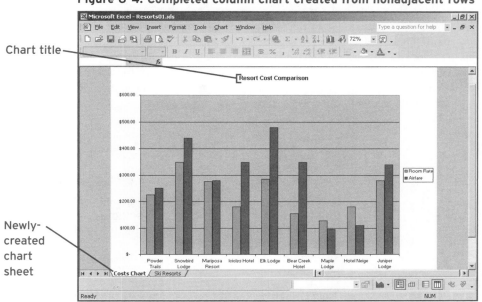

extra!

Creating a basic chart using the Chart toolbar

To create a basic chart on a worksheet quickly, you can use the Chart toolbar instead of the Chart Wizard. Click **View** on the menu bar, point to **Toolbars**, then click **Chart** to display the Chart toolbar. Select the worksheet range you want to chart, click the **Chart Type list arrow**, then click the button representing the chart type you want to create.

Skill Set 6
Creating and Modifying Graphics

Create, Modify, Position, and Print Charts
Change a Chart Type

After you create a chart, you may find that a different chart type would be more appropriate for your data. You can select from the many Excel standard chart types, or use Excel preformatted custom chart types. You can also create and save your own customized chart types. Make sure that the type of chart you select suits your data. Refer to Table 6-1 and the Chart Wizard dialog box for reminders on the best uses for each chart type.

Activity Steps

 open Guests04.xls

1. Click **Chart** on the menu bar, then click **Chart Type**

2. Click **Bar**, then under Chart sub-type, click the top-left subtype, **Clustered Bar** (if it's not already selected)
   The name and description appear in the lower-right box after you select a sub-type.
   See Figure 6-5.

3. Click **OK**

4. Click **Chart** on the menu bar, then click **Chart Type**

5. Click **Line**, then under Chart sub-type, click the bottom-left sub-type, **3-D Line**, then click **OK**

6. Click **Chart** on the menu bar, then click **Chart Type**

7. Click **Area**, under Chart sub-type, click the middle sub-type in the top row, **Stacked Area**, then click **OK**
   See Figure 6-6.

 close Guests04.xls

Step 2
To use preformatted custom chart types, click the Custom Types tab in the Chart Type dialog box.

Figure 6-5: Selecting a clustered bar chart

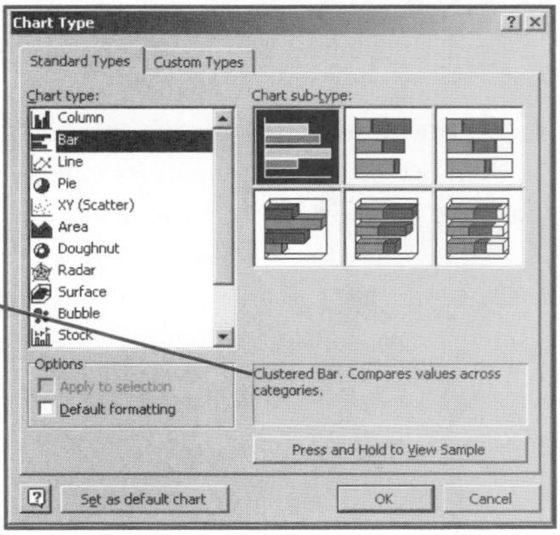

Description of chart sub-type selected above

Figure 6-6: Stacked area chart

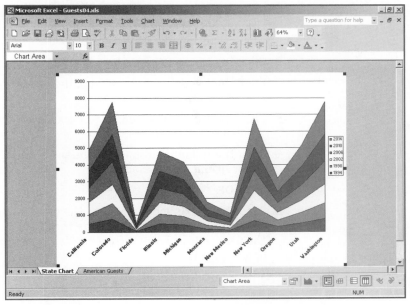

Skill Set 6
Creating and Modifying Graphics

Create, Modify, Position, and Print Charts
Modify Chart Options

Once you have created a chart, you will often want to change its appearance, such as adding or deleting a chart title, axis labels, a legend, or gridlines. You might also want to add **data labels**, which are text that appear next to each data point, such as its category or series name or its value. For certain charts, it is helpful to display a **data table**, a grid that appears under a chart and that contains the values on which the chart is based. A data table is most effective when a chart is on a chart sheet. You can set all of these options in the Chart Options dialog box. To delete any options you add, just click the title, label, legend or gridlines, then press [Delete].

Step 2
You can add labels to any or all data series. Double-click any data point. Click the Data Labels tab in the Format Data Series dialog box, select the label contents you want, then click OK. To change a label's position on the chart, double-click any data label, then use the Label Position scroll box on the Alignment tab in the Format Data Labels dialog box.

Activity Steps

 open Bikes02.xls

1. Click **Chart** on the menu bar, then click **Chart Options**
2. Click the **Titles tab** if it's not already selected, click the **Chart title box**, then type **Projected Income Q3 & Q4, 2003**
   After a moment, the preview displays the new title.
3. Click the **Value (Y) axis box**, then type **Projected U.S. $**
4. Click the **Legend tab**, then click the check mark next to **Show legend**, to remove it
5. Click the **Data Table tab**, then click **Show data table** to select it
   See Figure 6-7.
6. Click the **Gridlines tab**, then under Category (X) axis, click **Major gridlines** to select it
7. Click **OK**
8. Drag the **Y axis label** closer to the chart as shown in Figure 6-8, then click the gray area outside the chart
   The data table contains a color key for each data series, so there is no need for a legend.

 close Bikes02.xls

**Figure 6-7: Data Table tab in Chart
Options dialog box**

Value (Y) axis label

Data table contains
data and color key

New title
in preview

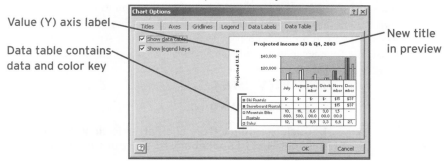

Figure 6-8: Modified chart

Major
gridlines
on X axis

Data points

Repositioned
Y axis label

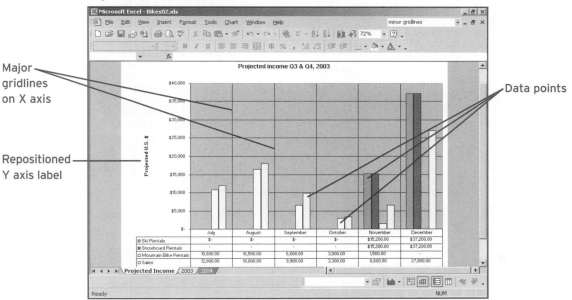

Skill Set 6
Creating and Modifying Graphics

Create, Modify, Position, and Print Charts
Print Charts

You can print a chart, whether it is on a worksheet with data or on its own chart sheet. If it's on a chart sheet, you print it as you would any worksheet. If the chart is on a worksheet, you can print it with the sheet data, or print it separately by selecting it first. The Page Setup dialog box lets you scale the chart on the page.

Step 2
You can click the Margins tab in the Print Preview window, then drag margins to new locations.

Activity Steps
 open Winter01.xls

1. Click the **chart title**, click after Helicopter, press **[Spacebar]-[Spacebar]**, type your name, then click any blank cell

2. Click the chart on the worksheet to select it, then click the **Print Preview button** on the Standard toolbar

3. Click **Setup**, then click the **Chart tab**

4. Click the **Scale to fit page option button**, then click **OK**
   See Figure 6-9.

5. Click **Print**, then click **OK** in the Print dialog box

6. Click the **Rev vs Exps Chart sheet tab**, then add your name to the chart title as you did in step 1 above

7. Click the **Print Preview button** on the Standard toolbar

8. Click **Print**, then click **OK** in the Print dialog box

 close Winter01.xls

Figure 6-9: Chart in Print Preview

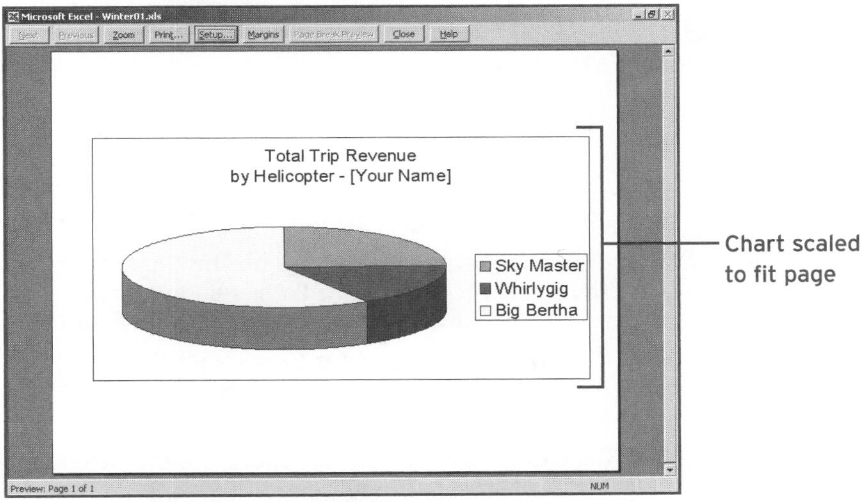

Chart scaled
to fit page

Skill Set 6

Creating and Modifying Graphics

Create, Modify, Position, and Print Charts
Format Chart Text

Once you create a chart, you can format any chart element. You can change the font, font size, style, alignment, or color of any text.

Activity Steps

 open Party01.xls

1. Click the chart title, **Winter Party Budget**, to select it

2. Click the **Format button** on the Chart toolbar
   The ScreenTip name of the Format button on the Chart toolbar reflects the selected object, in this case, the chart title.

3. Click the **Font tab**, under Size select **18**, click the **Patterns tab**, then click the **Shadow check box** to select it
   See Figure 6-10.

4. Click **OK**, then click in the Chart Area to deselect the title

5. Double-click any value on the Value (vertical, or Y) axis, click the **Number tab**, click the **Decimal places down arrow** twice, to display **0** (zero) decimal places, then click **OK**
   Double-clicking a chart object is often the fastest way to display the Format dialog box. The dialog box tabs present options appropriate to the object you select.

6. Double-click the **legend**, click the **Placement tab** in the Format Legend dialog box, click the **Bottom option button** to select it, then click **OK**

7. Drag the right sizing handle on the legend to the right about a half inch, then click in the Chart Area to deselect the legend

8. Double-click **Cost** (the vertical, or Y, axis title), click the **Alignment tab** in the Format Axis Title dialog box, drag the **red diamond** to the 12:00 mark (90 degrees) on the dial, then click **OK**

9. Click the gray area outside the Chart Area to deselect the axis and the chart
   See Figure 6-11.

 close Party01.xls

Step 2
You can also use the buttons on the Formatting toolbar to format a selected text object.

Figure 6-10: Patterns tab in Format
Chart Title dialog box

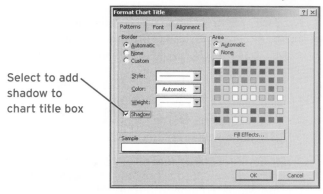

Select to add
shadow to
chart title box

Figure 6-11: Formatted chart text

Font now
18 point with
shadowed
box

Value axis
no longer
shows
decimals

Y axis title
vertically
aligned

Legend
appears
below chart

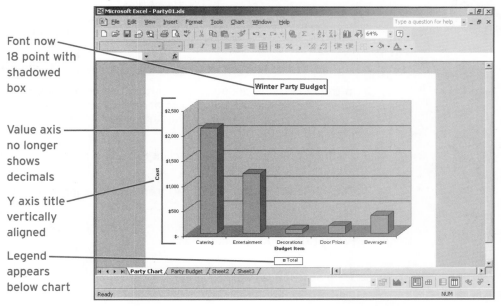

Skill Set 6
Creating and Modifying Graphics

Create, Modify, Position, and Print Charts
Format Chart Graphics

You can format any filled object, area, or line of a chart, including the fill color, pattern, style, or border. You can customize the data points, the chart background, or the plot area. The colors you choose should go well together, be appropriate for your audience, and should not detract from the message you want the chart to communicate. You can also add a picture to the chart area, the plot area, or a data point.

Step 2
If you add data labels to a chart and if your chart background is dark, click the Font color list arrow, then select a light color for the text.

Activity Steps

 open Holiday01.xls

1. Double-click the **legend**, click the **Patterns tab** (if it's not already selected), then click the **pale yellow fill color** (fifth row down, third color from the left)
   See Figure 6-12.

2. Click **OK**

3. Click anywhere on the pie chart to select it, click the largest slice, then double-click the slice

4. In the Format Data Point dialog box, under Area, click **Fill Effects**

5. In the Fill Effects dialog box, click the **Two colors option button** to select it; click the **Color 1 list arrow**, select the **light green color** (fifth row, fourth from the left), verify that Color 2 is white, then click **OK** twice

6. Double-click the **Chart Area**, click **Fill Effects**, then click the **Picture tab**

7. Click **Select Picture**, select **Ski** from the location where your Project Files are stored, then click **Insert**

8. Click **OK** in the Fill Effects dialog box, then click **OK** in the Format Chart Area dialog box
   See Figure 6-13.

 close Holiday01.xls

Figure 6-12: Format Legend dialog box

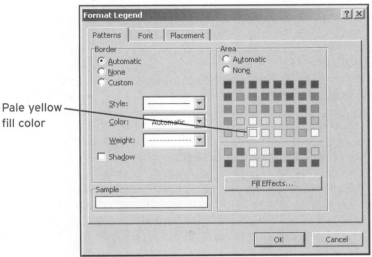

Pale yellow fill color

Figure 6-13: Chart with modified graphic elements

Chart area with picture

Guest Budget for Holiday Ski Weekend

Exploded pie slice with two-color shading

Legend with yellow fill

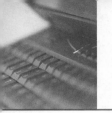

Skill Set 6
Creating and Modifying Graphics

Create, Modify, and Position Graphics
Create Graphics

A **graphic** is a shape, line, or block of text that you can add to any chart or worksheet. Add graphics by using tools on the Drawing toolbar. In addition to creating shapes such as squares, circles, lines and arrows, you can add predrawn shapes called **AutoShapes**, such as brackets, stars, banners, or arrows. You can also create **callouts**, which are text boxes with attached lines. When you drag callouts, their boxes and lines move together, making it easy to annotate screen items quickly. Use AutoShapes or callouts to create text annotations that call attention to worksheet features.

Activity Steps

 open Rentals03.xls

1. If the Drawing toolbar does not appear below the worksheet tabs (or elsewhere on your screen if a previous user has moved it), click the **Drawing button** on the Standard toolbar to display it

2. Click the **Oval button** on the Drawing toolbar

3. Position the ─┼─ pointer in the Chart Area above the value axis, press and hold down the mouse button, drag down and to the right to create an oval about an inch and a half wide, then release the mouse button

4. Type **Annotated by**, type your name, then click in the gray area outside the chart to deselect the object

5. Click **AutoShapes** on the Drawing toolbar, point to **Callouts**, then click **Line Callout 2** (second row, second callout from the left)

6. Click and hold the mouse button on the red Net Income bar portion for March, drag up and right into the chart area, then release the mouse button

7. Type **Net income is 16% of sales**, then click in the gray area to deselect the callout

8. Click the callout, press and hold [Shift], click the oval, then click the **Fill Color list arrow** on the Drawing toolbar

9. Click the **Light Yellow color** (fifth row, third from left), then click the gray area
See Figure 6-14.

 close Rentals03.xls

Use the Draw menu on the Drawing toolbar to change the alignment, grouping, or stacking order of any selected drawing objects.

Figure 6-14: Callout annotating chart data point and Oval AutoShape

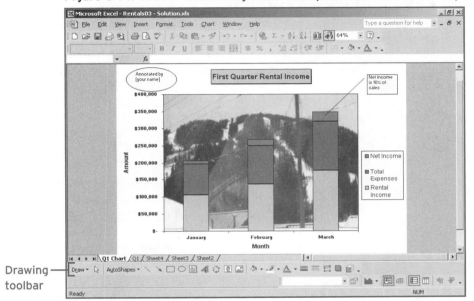

Drawing toolbar

extra!

Adding graphics to charts

You can enhance your chart's visual appeal by adding presupplied pictures called **clip art**, or shaped words called **WordArt**. To insert clip art, open the task pane, then display the **Clip Art pane**. Type a subject, then click **Go**. Click any graphic to insert it in the worksheet. To create WordArt, click the **Insert WordArt button** on the Drawing toolbar. Select a style, click **OK**, type the text you want to style, then click **OK**. You can drag any graphic object to a new location or resize it by dragging one of its round white sizing handles. If you have a dial-up Internet connection on your computer, your clip art collection will be smaller; if you are continually on line, Excel goes to the Web and makes a large collection available.

Skill Set 6
Creating and Modifying Graphics

Create, Modify, and Position Graphics
Modify and Position Graphics

Any graphic you create using the Drawing toolbar is an object that you can select, move, and resize separately from a worksheet or chart. You can format a graphic with fill colors, patterns, or shaded fill effects; you can modify the borders or add 3D or shadow styling. Before you modify or position a shape or an AutoShape, you must select it.

Step 3
If you select an AutoShape with the Move Cell Pointer, it highlights with a dotted outline, meaning that any change will apply to the entire graphic; if you select an AutoShape using the I-Beam pointer, it highlights with a striped outline, meaning that you can only add or edit text. You can rotate any selected shape by dragging the green circle attached to it.

Activity Steps

 open Quarters01.xls

1. Click the **large star shape** to select it

2. Position the pointer over the **lower-right sizing handle**, then drag the ↖ pointer up and left until the shape is about one inch across
   The sizing handles on AutoShapes are white circles, not black squares like those on a selected chart.

3. Position ↖ over the **dotted border** of the shape, then drag it left until it overlaps the Helicopter Skiing chart line
   See Figure 6-15.

4. Click ↖ on the edge of the callout AutoShape under the legend

5. Drag the **dotted border** up and to the left so it's just underneath the $800,000 gridline

6. Drag the **yellow diamond** on the AutoShape until it is at the **QTR 3 data point** for the Mountain Biking series

7. Click the **Fill Color list arrow** 🎨▾ on the Drawing toolbar, then click the **Light Yellow color** (fifth row, third from left)

8. Click the **3-D Style button** ▾ on the Drawing toolbar, click the **3-D Style 1 button** in the upper left, then click in the gray area outside the chart
   See Figure 6-16.

 close Quarters01.xls

Figure 6-15: Resizing a graphic

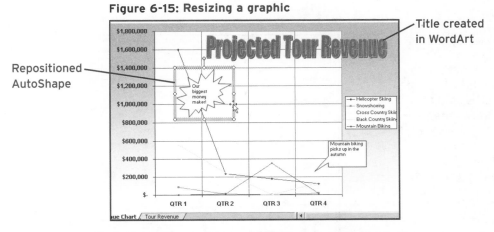

Title created in WordArt

Repositioned AutoShape

Figure 6-16: Callout AutoShape with fill color and 3-D effect

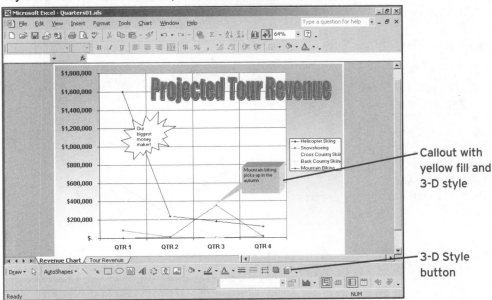

Callout with yellow fill and 3-D style

3-D Style button

Skill Set 6

Creating and Modifying Graphics

Target Your Skills

 open Statement01.xls

1 Use Figure 6-17 as a guide to chart the data in rows 3, 8, and 14 of the Income Statement (not including the totals in column N) as a line chart. Print the chart, using the Scale to Fit Page option.

Figure 6-17

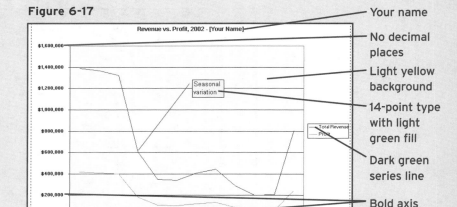

- Your name
- No decimal places
- Light yellow background
- 14-point type with light green fill
- Dark green series line
- Bold axis labels

Tab name

 open Payroll03.xls

2 Create the chart shown in Figure 6-18, using the data in F6:I6, and F13:I13. Use a Pie chart with a 3-D visual effect, place it on the worksheet, and size and position it as shown.

Figure 6-18

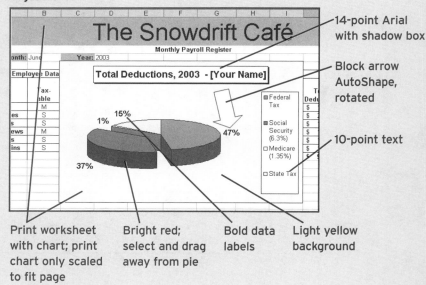

- 14-point Arial with shadow box
- Block arrow AutoShape, rotated
- 10-point text

Print worksheet with chart; print chart only scaled to fit page

Bright red; select and drag away from pie

Bold data labels

Light yellow background

Skill List

1. Convert Worksheets into Web Pages
2. Create Hyperlinks
3. View and Edit Comments

Computer users can now share information easily using the **Internet**, a world-wide network of computers and smaller networks, and company **intranets**, or networks within organizations. Users communicate over these networks using the **World Wide Web**, an interconnected collection of electronic documents called **Web pages**. **Workgroups**, people in an organization who exchange information, can now collaborate, or work together, on documents to make their work more efficient.

You can share your Excel worksheets or workbooks with others by saving them as specially-formatted files that you can place on the Web or an intranet. Before you save them, you can **preview** them in Excel to see how they will look as Web pages. Any worksheet can also have hyperlinks to other worksheets, other workbooks or documents, or locations on the World Wide Web. **Hyperlinks** consist of text or graphics that users click to display other documents. Hyperlinks are available to users of your worksheets in both Excel and Web versions.

As you communicate with others using Excel documents, perhaps by placing them on a centralized company computer, you can attach **comments** to worksheet cells that others can read and then respond to with their own comments.

You can also use **discussion comments** to communicate about an Excel document. This powerful feature lets you conduct continuous discussions with others about a workbook. Unlike workbook comments, discussion comments are not attached to a particular cell. You need to have access to an **Office-Extended discussion server** to use this feature. *This is a MOUS requirement; be sure you learn the steps covered in the box on page 167 on how to insert and answer discussion comments.*

Skill Set 7
Workgroup Collaboration

Convert Worksheets into Web Pages
Preview and Create Web Pages

You can place a worksheet or workbook on the Internet or on a company intranet for others to use. To do this, you need to save it in a special file format that other users can open in their **Web browsers**, which are programs that let you view documents on the Web; **Internet Explorer** is a commonly used Web browser. Before you resave the file and place it on the Web, you should preview it. When saving your file as a Web page, Excel saves it in a special file format called **Hypertext Markup Language**, or **HTML**. When saving your worksheet in HTML format, Excel creates a document with the file extension htm as well as a folder of supporting files in a folder called [filename]_files.

Activity Steps

 open Sales02.xls

1. Click **File** on the menu bar, click **Web Page Preview**, maximize the preview window

2. Close the preview window, make sure no worksheet objects are selected, click **File** on the menu bar, then click **Save as Web Page**

3. Click the **Save in list arrow**, navigate to the location where your Project Files are stored, then click the **Selection: Sheet option button** (If you have saved this sheet previously, the button will read "Republish: Sheet")

4. Highlight the existing filename, then type **newitems**

5. Click **Change Title**, type **Price vs. Cost for New Items at Miller Music**, then click **OK**
   The text you typed will appear in the Web page title bar.
   See Figure 7-1.

6. Click **Save**
   The Excel Workbook remains open.

7. Open your Web browser program, click **File** on the menu bar, then click **Open**

8. Click **Browse**, navigate to the location where your Project Files are stored, select **newitems.htm**, click **Open**, then click **OK**
   See Figure 7-2.

9. Click the **Close button** [X] on the Browser window

 close Sales02.xls

The newitems.htm file is saved in your Project File location, along with a folder called newitems_files that contains supporting graphics and other file infomation.

Figure 7-1: Completed Save As dialog box

Only current worksheet will be saved

Text will appear in Web page title bar

Some computer systems prefer 8-character htm filenames

Location where HTML file will be saved (your location may be different)

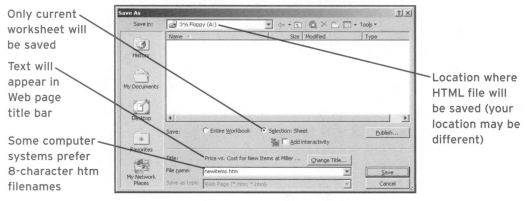

Figure 7-2: Web page opened in Internet Explorer browser

Your location may be different

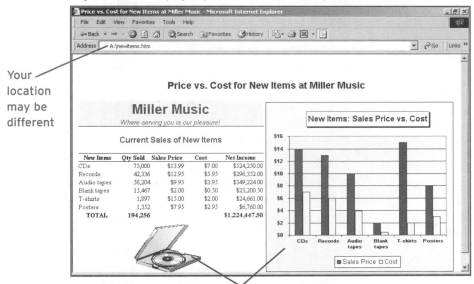

Depending on your browser and operating system, graphics may not be visible

Skill Set 7
Workgroup Collaboration

Create Hyperlinks
Create Hyperlinks

A **hyperlink** is a word or graphic that you click to display (or "jump to") another location in the document, another document, or a location on the Web, known as the **target** or **destination**. In an Excel workbook, a hyperlink might take you to another sheet in the same workbook, it might open another workbook containing more detailed information, or it might take you to a Web site that has additional information of interest. You can also use hyperlinks to display photos or other graphics that might not fit well in a worksheet cell. After you click a hyperlink, use the **Back button** on the Web toolbar to return to the original document.

Activity Steps

 open Checkbook01.xls

1. On the February worksheet, notice the beginning balance is in cell F8; click the March sheet tab, then notice the beginning balance is also in cell F8

2. Click the **Summary** sheet, click cell **C7**, then click the **Insert Hyperlink button** on the Standard toolbar

3. Under Link to, click **Place in This Document**
   See Table 7-1 for other options in the Insert Hyperlink dialog box.

4. In the Type the cell reference box, select any text, then type **F8**

5. In the Text to Display box, select any text, then type **Click here**

6. Click **Screen Tip**, type **Click here to see beginning monthly balance**, then click **OK**

7. In the Or select a place in this document list, click **February**, compare your screen to Figure 7-3, then click **OK**

8. Move the pointer over the hyperlink in cell **C7**, read the ScreenTip, shown in Figure 7-4, then click once with the ⁤ pointer; observe how the destination worksheet appears with the destination cell, F8, selected

9. If the Web toolbar does not appear on your screen, click **View** on the menu bar, point to **Toolbars**, click **Web**, then click the **Back button** on the Web toolbar
   When you return to the Summary worksheet, you will notice that the hyperlink has become purple, indicating that it has been used. It will remain purple until you close and reopen the workbook.

 close Checkbook01.xls

Step 9
To remove a hyperlink, right-click it, then click Remove Hyperlink. To select a cell with a hyperlink (instead of going to the hyperlink target), click the link and hold down the mouse button until you see the white cross pointer ✛ .

Figure 7-3: Insert Hyperlink dialog box

Indicates hyperlink will jump to a location in the current document

Place in This Document

The work-sheet the hyperlink will jump to

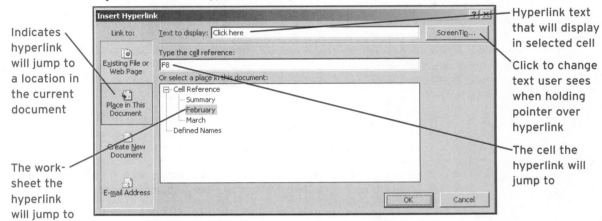

Hyperlink text that will display in selected cell

Click to change text user sees when holding pointer over hyperlink

The cell the hyperlink will jump to

Figure 7-4: ScreenTip

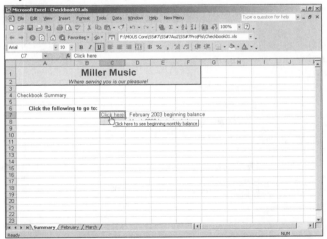

TABLE 7-1: Specifying other hyperlink destinations

to create a hyperlink that will display	click in Insert Hyperlink dialog box	then
Another file	Existing file or Web page	Navigate to file location
A Web page	Existing file or Web page	Click Browse the Web button, go to site
A new Excel document	Create New Document	Type name of document and specify storage location
A blank e-mail to a particular address	E-mail address	Type address and subject, or select address from list

Skill Set 7
Workgroup Collaboration

Create Hyperlinks
Modify Hyperlinks

After you create a hyperlink, you might want to edit it to change its destination, its ScreenTip, or the text that users click to display the hyperlink. If the destination is a Web site, you may want to change the site to a more current one; if it's a location in the current document, you might want to change it to another cell or worksheet. You make these changes using the same dialog box you used to create the hyperlink itself.

Activity Steps

 open Drums03.xls

1. Click the **drum graphic**, then notice that it displays the Brass Suppliers sheet, not the Drum Suppliers sheet

2. Click the **Back button**  on the Web toolbar

3. Point to the **drum graphic** until the pointer becomes 🖑

4. Right-click the graphic (the Picture toolbar also opens), then click **Edit Hyperlink**

5. Under Or select a place in this document, click **Drum Suppliers**
   See Figure 7-5.

6. Click **OK**

7. Click cell **A1** to deselect the graphic, then click the **drum graphic**
   The Drum Suppliers worksheet appears.
   See Figure 7-6.

8. Click the **Back button** on the Web toolbar

 close Drums03.xls

Step 2
To remove a hyperlink, right-click it, then click Remove Hyperlink.

Figure 7-5: Hyperlink destination selected

Correct worksheet name for hyperlink

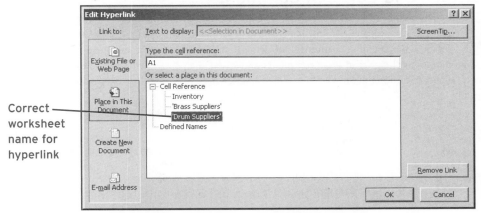

Figure 7-6: Hyperlink destination displayed

Skill Set 7
Workgroup Collaboration

View and Edit Comments
Attach and Edit Cell Comments

As part of collaborating with members of a workgroup, you will want to share your reactions to documents and have others respond to your ideas. Excel lets you attach notes called **comments** to any worksheet cell. Others who use a shared document can read your comments and insert their own. Each comment is preceded by the computer user's name, making it easy to identify who said what. You can also edit any worksheet comment.

Step 4
If you click a blank cell and the comment still appears, click Tools, click Options, click the View tab, then under Comment, click the Comment indicator only option button.

Activity Steps

 open Loan01.xls

1. Right-click cell **C6**

2. Click **Insert Comment** on the shortcut menu
   See Figure 7-7.

3. Type **Is this the quantity price we got from Groveland?**

4. Click a blank worksheet area
   Cell C6 displays a small red triangle called a **comment indicator**, indicating that it has an attached comment.

5. Move the pointer over cell **C6**, then read the comment in the comment balloon

6. Right-click, then click **Edit Comment** from the shortcut menu

7. Press ◄ , press **[Spacebar]**, type **in January**, then click on a blank worksheet area

8. Point to cell **C6** to review the edited comment
   See Figure 7-8.

 close Loan01.xls

Figure 7-7: New comment

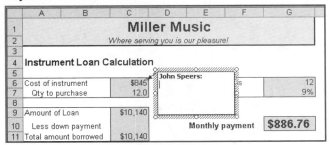

Figure 7-8: Edited comment

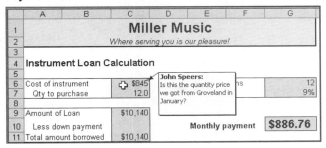

Responding to a Discussion

In any Excel document that will be saved in HTML format and placed on the Web, you can insert and respond to discussion comments relating to the document. All comments are **threaded**, or placed one after another, so you can follow the "thread" of the discussion. *You must have access to a discussion server to use this feature.* All comments are stored on the discussion server. Click **Tools** on the menu bar, point to **Online Collaboration**, then click **Web Discussions**. To insert a discussion comment, click the **Insert Discussion about the Workbook button** on the Web Discussions toolbar. Other users can reply by clicking the Discuss button on the Standard Buttons toolbar in Internet Explorer to display the Discussion toolbar. Then they click the Insert Discussion in the Document button and enter comments.

Skill Set 7

Workgroup Collaboration

Target Your Skills

 open Instruments03.xls

1 Make the changes shown on Figure 7-9, then preview the file as a Web page.

Figure 7-9

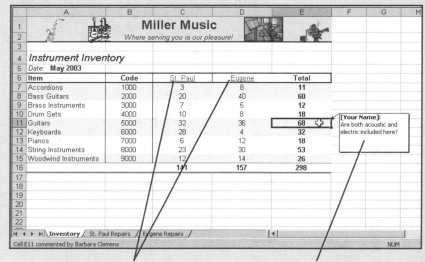

Create links to the appropriate worksheets

Insert comment shown, then insert "guitars" after "electric"

 open Markdowns04.xls

2 Make the changes shown in Figure 7-10. Preview the worksheet as a Web page. Save the worksheet as a Web page named specials.htm using the title "Special Instrument Markdowns," then open it in your browser.

Figure 7-10

Add a hyperlink here to any amplifier manufacturer's site

Add a comment that reads "You won't find a price like this anywhere else!"

Skill List

1. Import data to Excel
2. Export data from Excel
3. Publish worksheets and workbooks to the Web

If you have data that was created in another program, you don't have to retype it to use it in Microsoft Excel 2002. Excel lets you bring in, or **import**, a variety of information, including unformatted data files and data from the World Wide Web. The commands you use vary depending on the type of information you want to import. Similarly, you can **export** Excel workbook information to other programs. Exporting can include placing copies of entire worksheets or worksheet ranges in other documents, such as Microsoft PowerPoint presentation slides or Microsoft Word word processing documents.

You can export Excel workbooks and worksheets to the Web for users to view or to interact with using their Web browsers. You can also publish a Web page directly to a Web site, and have Excel automatically update and republish the page every time you save the workbook.

Skill Set 8
Importing and Exporting Data

Import Data to Excel
Import a Text File

You may have data created in another program that you want to analyze in Excel. Because that data is in the **source program's** file format, you cannot always open the file in Excel using the Open command on the File menu. Instead, many source programs let you save files as **text files** (also called **ASCII** files), which contain only data without formatting, formulas, or other information. Then you **import**, or bring in, the text file to an Excel worksheet for analysis using the Text Import Wizard. In a text file, data columns are separated by a character such as a tab, with a return character at the end of each line. Such a file is called a **tab-delimited text file**; a **delimiter** is a separator. Commas and spaces can also act as delimiters. The Text Import Wizard lets you specify how you want Excel to interpret the file.

Activity Steps

1. With Excel running and a blank worksheet open, select cell **A1** (if it's not already selected), click **Data** on the menu bar, point to **Import External Data**, then click **Import Data**

2. In the Select Data Source dialog box, navigate to the location where your Project Files are stored

3. Click the **Files of type list arrow**, then select **Text files (*.txt, *.prn, *.csv, *.tab, *.asc)**
   Now that you have selected the file type, only the text files appear.

4. Click **Rooms01.txt**, then click **Open**

5. In the Step 1 of 3 dialog box of the Text Import Wizard, make sure the **Delimited option** is selected, then examine the file preview at the bottom of the box

6. Click **Next**; in the Step 2 of 3 box, make sure the **Tab option** is selected, observe how the columns are divided by lines in the preview box, then click **Next**
   See Figure 8-1.

7. In the Step 3 of 3 box, make sure **General** is selected under Column data format, then click **Finish**

8. With the **Existing worksheet option** selected, then click **OK**
   The text file opens in the existing worksheet. The Total Revenue column and the Totals row display as values. The External Data toolbar opens.

9. Click **File** on the menu bar, click **Save As**; notice that in the **Save as type list, Microsoft Excel workbook (*.xls)** is already selected, type **Rooms02**, then click **Save**
   See Figure 8-2.

Step 7
You don't have to import all the text file columns. Select any column in the Step 3 of 3 dialog box, then click to select "Do not import (Skip)". Excel will not import that column.

 close Rooms02.xls

Figure 8-1: Step 3 of 3 of the Text Import Wizard

Text Import Wizard - Step 3 of 3

This screen lets you select each column and set the Data Format.

'General' converts numeric values to numbers, date values to dates, and all remaining values to text.

Column data format
- ◉ General
- ○ Text
- ○ Date: [MDY ▾]
- ○ Do not import column (skip)

[Advanced...]

Data preview

General	General	General	General
Powder Trails Resort Guest Rooms			
Revenues: 2002			
Month	Standard	Deluxe	Total Revenu
January	$120,450	$206,850	$327,300
February	$132,440	$208,550	$340,990

[Cancel] [< Back] [Next >] [Finish]

Preview of imported file

Figure 8-2: Imported text data in Excel

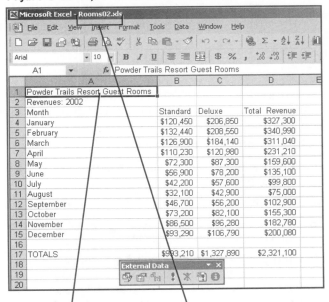

Microsoft Excel - Rooms02.xls

File Edit View Insert Format Tools Data Window Help

Arial ▾ 10

A1 ▾ fx Powder Trails Resort Guest Rooms

	A	B	C	D	E
1	Powder Trails Resort Guest Rooms				
2	Revenues: 2002				
3	Month	Standard	Deluxe	Total Revenue	
4	January	$120,450	$206,850	$327,300	
5	February	$132,440	$208,550	$340,990	
6	March	$126,900	$184,140	$311,040	
7	April	$110,230	$120,980	$231,210	
8	May	$72,300	$87,300	$159,600	
9	June	$56,900	$78,200	$135,100	
10	July	$42,200	$57,600	$99,800	
11	August	$32,100	$42,900	$75,000	
12	September	$46,700	$56,200	$102,900	
13	October	$73,200	$82,100	$155,300	
14	November	$86,500	$96,280	$182,780	
15	December	$93,290	$106,790	$200,080	
16					
17	TOTALS	$993,210	$1,327,890	$2,321,100	
18					
19					
20					

External Data ▾ ×

Make sure there is no data below and to the right of the selected cell; imported data will replace it

Text file saved in Excel format

extra!

Opening files created in other programs

Excel lets you open files created in many programs, including earlier versions of Excel, Web pages, and spreadsheets created in several other spreadsheet programs, such as Lotus 1-2-3. In the Open dialog box, click the **Files of type list arrow**, then select the file type you want to view. Double-click the filename to open it in Excel. Formatting and formulas created in the source program may be lost, but the data values will be intact.

Skill Set 8
Importing and Exporting Data

Import Data to Excel
Import Access Database Tables

Often you will want to import data that was created in a **database program**, a program that lets you organize and analyze large amounts of information. **Microsoft Access 2002** is the database program that is part of the Microsoft Office XP suite. A **database file** is similar to an Excel list in that it contains **records**, or rows of information for each item in the database. A record is information divided into **fields**, or columns of information; each field represents one piece of information about an item, such as Last Name or Age. Access files are organized into one or more **tables**, which contain all the information for a particular part of a database, such as a company's customers or suppliers. A database program like Access allows you to perform complex data manipulations not available in Excel. Yet sometimes you want to import Access information into Excel to perform statistical or graphical analyses not available in Access.

Activity Steps

 open Staff01.xls

1. Click **Data** on the menu bar, point to **Import External Data**, then click **Import Data**

2. In the Select Data Source dialog box, click the **Look in list arrow**, then navigate to your Project Files location

3. Click the **Files of type list arrow**, then select **All Data Sources (*.odc;*.mdb;*.mde...)** (if it is not already selected)

4. Click **Access01.mdb**, then click **Open**
   Because the database contains two tables, the Select Table dialog box opens, allowing you to choose the table you want to import. *See Figure 8-3.*

5. Click **Staff List**, then click **OK**

6. With the Import Data dialog box open, click the worksheet cell **A4** *See Figure 8-4.*

7. Click **OK**

8. Click the **Housekeeping Staff sheet tab**, repeat steps 1-4, click **Housekeeping**, then click **OK**

9. On the worksheet, click cell **A4**, then click **OK**
   You have imported the two Access tables in the Access01.mdb database to separate Excel worksheets. Each range is now an **external data range**, a range of worksheet data that originated outside of Excel, that you can analyze, format, and update.

 close Staff01.xls

Step 6
The Import Data dialog box also lets you import a table to a blank worksheet.

Figure 8-3: Select Table dialog box

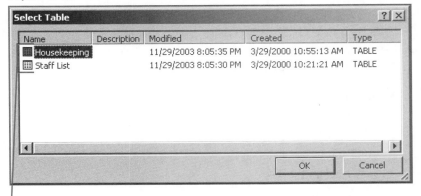

Tables in
Access01.mdb
database

Figure 8-4: Import Data dialog box with destination cell selected

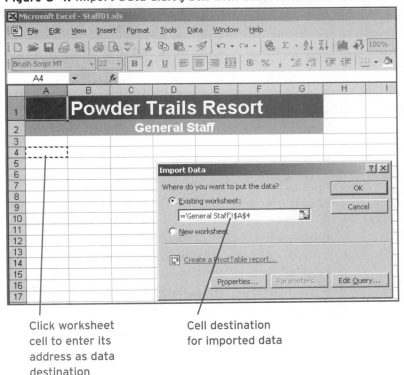

Click worksheet
cell to enter its
address as data
destination

Cell destination
for imported data

extra!

Refreshing an external data range

An external data range in Excel retains a connection to the location of its source file, which means that you can **refresh**, or update, the data in Excel at any time, so your range will reflect any changes to the source file since you imported it. To refresh an external data range, first display the External Data toolbar (if it is not already displayed): Click **View** on the menu bar, point to **Toolbars**, click **Customize**, select **External Data** on the Toolbars tab, then click **Close**. Click in the external data range, click the **Refresh Data button** on the toolbar.

Skill Set 8
Importing and Exporting Data

Import Data to Excel
Import Data Using a Query

When you import a database you may want to import only part of the data in a table; for example, only sales transactions above a certain amount. In these cases, you use a **query**, which is a specific request you make about the data. A query is a file with the .dqy file extension that you can save and use again. The external data can be an Access database, other databases, or another Excel file. To query an external data source, you use **Microsoft Query**, a program that comes with Excel. *Microsoft Query is not installed as part of a standard Excel installation, so you may need access to the Microsoft Office CD the first time you use it, or see your system administrator.*

Step 5
In the Filter dialog box, you can specify another filter and have Query apply it along with the first filter (an AND condition), or as an alternative to the first filter (an OR condition), such as Last Name >g AND Last name <p, which would choose people whose last names begin with G through O in the alphabet.

Activity Steps

1. With Excel running and a blank worksheet open, click **Data** on the menu bar, point to **Import External Data**, then click **New Database Query**

2. In the Choose Data Source dialog box, click **MS Access Database**, then click **OK** (a Connecting to data source message appears)

3. In the Select Database dialog box, display your Project Files location

4. Under Database Name, click **Access01.mdb**, then click **OK**
   The **Query Wizard** opens.

5. Click **Staff List**, then click **>** to select this table's fields
   See Figure 8-5.

6. In the columns in your query box, click **Status**, then click **<** to eliminate it from the query, then click **Next**
   Microsoft Query lets you **filter**, or screen out, data to include only the data you specify for any fields; you can also **sort**, or reorder, the data.

7. In the Query Wizard - Filter Data dialog box, click **Last Name** in the Column to filter list, click the **Last name list arrow**, then click **is greater than**
   See Figure 8-6.

8. Click the **top right text box**, type **g**, then click **Next**

9. Click the **Sort by list arrow**, click **Last Name**, click **Next**, click **Finish**, then click **OK**

10. Save the file as **Housekeeping01.xls**

    close Housekeeping01.xls

Figure 8-5: Selecting fields to import

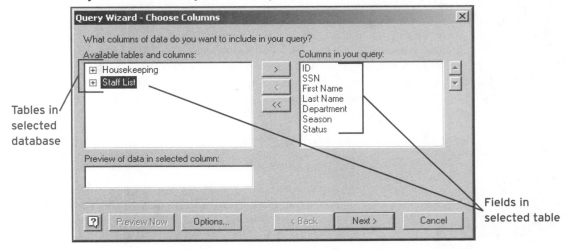

Tables in selected database

Fields in selected table

Figure 8-6: Filtering imported data

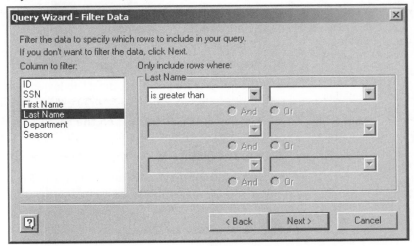

Skill Set 8
Importing and Exporting Data

Import Data to Excel
Import Graphics

You can import a variety of graphics to enhance your worksheets. A **graphic** is a picture or photograph file stored on disk. You can insert many common types of graphics (shown in Table 8-1) using the Picture/From File commands on the Insert menu. A picture you import from a file becomes a worksheet **object** that you can move or resize as you would a drawn shape you create using the Drawing toolbar. You can also **crop**, or clip off, any part of a selected picture using the cropping tool on the Picture toolbar.

Activity Steps

 open Resorts02.xls

1. Right-click any toolbar; if Picture does not have a check mark next to it, click **Picture** to display the Picture toolbar
   Your Picture toolbar may appear at the bottom of the screen or elsewhere if a previous user has moved it.

2. Click the **Insert Picture From File button** on the Picture toolbar

3. In the Insert Picture dialog box, click the **Look in list arrow**, then navigate to the location where your Project Files are stored
   See Figure 8-7.

4. Click the **Ski.jpg** picture, then click **Insert**

5. With the picture selected, drag the lower right **sizing handle** so the right side of the picture aligns with the right side of **column J**

6. Click the **Crop button** on the Picture toolbar, then drag the **lower left corner** of the picture to the right about an inch

7. Drag the picture to the right side of the data

8. Click the **Line Style button** on the Picture toolbar, click the bottom line style, then click any blank cell
   See Figure 8-8.

 close Resorts02.xls

Step 6
You can also use the buttons on the Picture toolbar to adjust a selected picture's brightness, contrast, or rotation. Click the Format Picture button for finer control of picture features.

Figure 8-7: Insert Picture dialog box

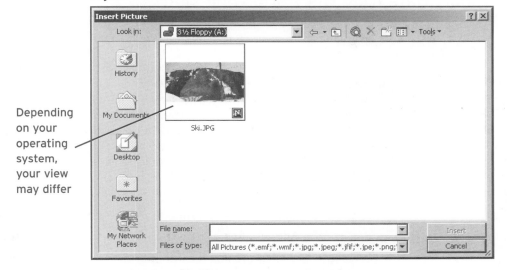

Depending on your operating system, your view may differ

Figure 8-8: Repositioned picture with border

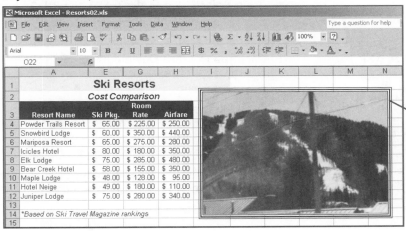

Cropped, resized, and repositioned picture with border

TABLE 8-1 Selected graphic formats you can import to Excel 2002			
file format	name	file format	name
.emf	Enhanced Metafile	.bmp	Microsoft Windows Bitmap
.jpg	Joint Photographic Experts Group	.gif	Graphics Interchange Format
.png	Portable Network Graphics	.wmf	Windows Metafile

Skill Set 8

Importing and Exporting Data

Import Data to Excel

Import Data from the World Wide Web

While you can easily import information from text, database, and graphics files into Excel, you are not limited to these. You may find information on the World Wide Web that you want to analyze in an Excel worksheet. Excel makes it easy to import data from Web pages. You can use the drag-and-drop or the cut-and-paste method to import data, text, and graphics. If the information you import contains **hyperlinks** ("live" areas you click to display other locations on the Web), they will still work when the data is in a worksheet. *In order to perform all the steps in this lesson, your computer needs to have access to the World Wide Web, and you must have Internet Explorer version 4.1 or later.*

Activity Steps

1. With Excel running and a blank workbook open, click **Start** on the taskbar, point to **Programs**, then click **Internet Explorer**

2. Click the **Address box**, type **www.goski.com**, then press **[Enter]**

3. Locate and click the link for **Canada**, click the link for **Alberta**, then click the **Lake Louise link**
   If the Web site has changed and you cannot locate the site or the links, use the site and links of your choice.

4. Scroll down until you see **Profile** information in a table format

5. Click the **Restore Down button** 🗗 in the title bar, make the window half the size of the screen, then drag it to the right side of your screen

6. Click **Microsoft Excel - Book 1 button** in the taskbar, click the program window's **Restore Down button** 🗗 in the title bar, then resize and drag it to the left side of your screen; scroll as necessary until your screen looks like Figure 8-9

7. In the Internet Explorer window, drag to select the **Profile information** from Vertical Drop down through the Web Site address

8. Position the **arrow pointer** ⬉ over the selected text, drag it over the Excel worksheet until the upper left corner of the outline is in cell A1, release the mouse button, then click a blank worksheet cell
   See Figure 8-10.

9. Save the file in Excel workbook format as **Profile01.xls** in the location where your Project Files are stored, then click the Browser window **Close button**

 close Profile01.xls

Step 8
You can also use the Copy and Paste commands from the Edit menu instead of dragging.

Figure 8-9: Worksheets positioned for importing data

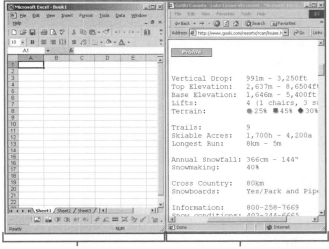

Excel window   Internet Explorer window

Figure 8-10: Data in worksheet after dragging from Web page

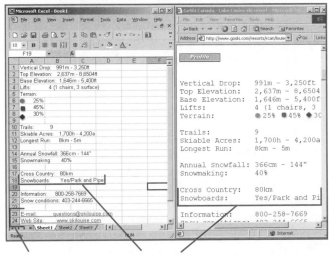

Hyperlinks work in Excel   Web information in Excel worksheet

extra!

Importing Web data
When you import Web data, check the Web page's legal statement, usually at the bottom of the page, to ensure that you are not violating any copyright or usage restrictions.

Skill Set 8
Importing and Exporting Data

Export Data from Excel
Embed an Excel Chart in a Word Document

To export Excel information to Microsoft Word documents, you don't need to save or convert the Excel file in a different format. Instead, you can place any chart or worksheet as an **object** that you can move and resize in the Word document using a process called **object linking and embedding (OLE)**. When you **embed** an Excel object (the **source object**) in a Word document (the **destination file**), you actually place a copy of the source object, which you can double-click to edit using source program tools. Although you can edit the object in Word using Excel tools, an embedded spreadsheet or graphic is not connected to the source workbook. Any changes you make to the copy in Word will not be made to the Excel source workbook.

Activity Steps

1. Click the **Start menu** on the Windows taskbar, point to **Programs**, then click **Microsoft Word**

2. In the New Document task pane, click **More documents**; click the **Look in list arrow**, then navigate to the location where your Project Files are stored

3. Double-click **Memo01.doc**; click in the blank area below the text line that reads "See the following:" to indicate where you want to place the embedded chart

4. Click **Insert** on the menu bar, click **Object**; in the Object dialog box, click the **Create from File tab**

5. Click **Browse**, double-click **Helicopters02.xls**
   See Figure 8-11.

6. Click **OK**
   The Excel chart appears at the location of the insertion point.

7. Click the **embedded chart** to select it, then, scrolling as necessary, drag the chart's **lower right sizing handle** until it is about as wide as the memo text

8. Double-click the **embedded chart**, click the **1st Quarter sheet tab**, then click the **Q1 Revenue per Guest sheet tab**
   See Figure 8-12.

9. Click in the memo outside the chart
   With the object deselected, the Word toolbars now appear.

    close **Memo01.doc**

Step 8
When you double-click an embedded object, the menu bar and toolbars above the memo change to Excel tools that you can use to modify the embedded copy of the chart or worksheet.

Figure 8-11: Locating the file to embed

Path to file you want to embed

Your path may be different

To embed a file, make sure this box is cleared

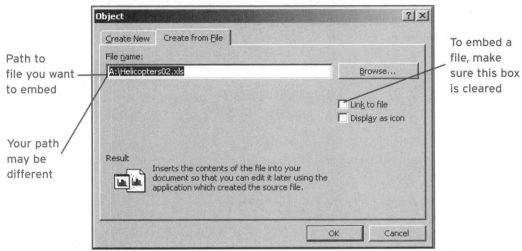

Figure 8-12: Excel chart embedded in a Word document

Word title bar

Excel menu bar and toolbars

Embedded chart in Word memo

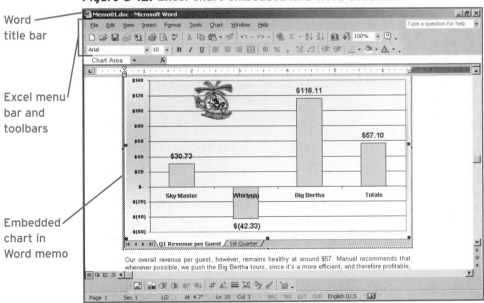

Skill Set 8

Importing and Exporting Data

Export Data from Excel
Link Excel Data to a PowerPoint Presentation

Using Microsoft Office programs—Word, Excel, Access, and PowerPoint—you can easily **integrate**, or combine, information created in one program in any of the other programs. For example, you can place an Excel chart in any Word document, or display any Word document in a PowerPoint slide. Sometimes, however, you want to paste information that will change over time, such as a sales report, and you want to make sure that the information in the **destination document** (the document that receives the data) contains the most recent information that you put in the source document. In these cases, you **link** the information using the Paste Link command on the Edit menu. Any changes to the source, or linked, information are automatically reflected in the destination document. You can link all or part of an Excel worksheet.

Step 7
To display the linked object as an icon, click the Display as icon check box in the Paste Special dialog box. Presentation users can double-click the icon to display the worksheet.

Activity Steps

1. With Excel open and a blank workbook displayed, click the **Start menu** on the Windows taskbar, point to **Programs**, then click **Microsoft PowerPoint**

2. In the New Presentation task pane, click **More presentations**, click the **Look in list arrow**, navigate to the location where your Project Files are stored, then double-click **Packages01.ppt**

3. Press [Page Down] three times to display slide #4, **Free Transportation**

4. Click the **Microsoft Excel - Book 1 button** on the taskbar, then open the file **Shuttle02.xls** from your Project File location

5. Drag to select the range A1:C14, click the **Copy button** 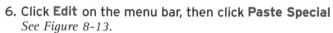 on the Standard toolbar, then click the Microsoft PowerPoint - **Packages01.ppt button** on the taskbar

6. Click **Edit** on the menu bar, then click **Paste Special**
   See Figure 8-13.

7. Click the **Paste link option button**, then click **OK**

8. Drag the **linked object** up and left, then drag its **lower right resizing handle** so it fills the area under the text

9. Click the **Microsoft Excel - Shuttle02.xls button** on the taskbar, change the time in cell B3 to 7:10, then press [Enter]; click the Microsoft PowerPoint - **Packages01.ppt button** on the taskbar, then observe that the departure time in the slide has been automatically updated
   See Figure 8-14.

 close Packages01.ppt
   Shuttle02.xls

Figure 8-13: Linking a file in the Paste Special dialog box

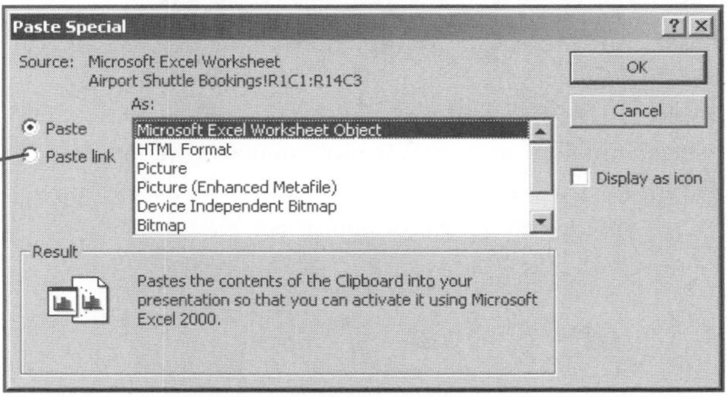

Click here to link file

Figure 8-14: Linked worksheet range on PowerPoint Slide

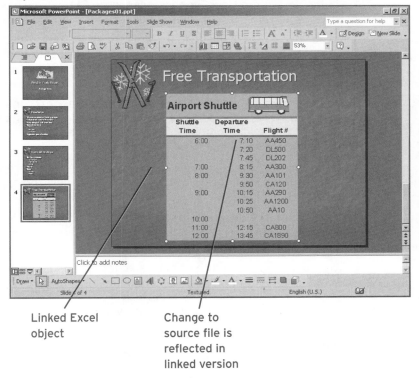

Linked Excel object

Change to source file is reflected in linked version

extra!

Updating linked information

You can have the destination program update your linked information automatically, or you can have it update only when you specify. In the destination program, click **Edit** on the menu bar, then click **Links**. In the Links dialog box, click the **Manual button.** To update a link, click to select the **link** in the list, then click **Update Now**. You can also use this dialog box to open the source document or to break the link.

Skill Set 8

Importing and Exporting Data

Export Data from Excel
Convert a List to an Access Table

To import Excel data into Microsoft Access to perform more sophisticated database tasks, you need to use the Import Spreadsheet Wizard in Access. An Excel list becomes an Access **table**, a collection of data about one subject, such as customers or suppliers. The Wizard asks you to indicate the sheet, the heading row, the sheet where you want to place the data, which columns you want, the **primary key** (the field that contains unique information for each record, or row), and the name of the new table.

Step 1
Be sure your list does not contain any extra characters or formats in surrounding columns or rows. Your Excel list field names cannot contain any spaces or any characters such as periods, exclamation points, or brackets. If Access sees that your field names do not meet its field name requirements, it offers to convert them to acceptable names.

Activity Steps

1. Click the **Start menu** on the Windows taskbar, point to **Programs**, then click **Microsoft Access**

2. Under New in the New File task pane, click **Blank Database**, then navigate to the location where your Project Files are stored

3. Select the **db1.mdb** in the File name box (if it's not already selected), type **Employees** to name the database, then click **Create**; click **File** on the menu bar, point to **Get External Data**, then click **Import**

4. Make sure your Project File storage location appears in the Look in box, click the **Files of type list arrow**, click **Microsoft Excel (*.xls)**, click **Rooms02.xls**, then click **Import**
   See Figure 8-15.

5. In the Import Spreadsheet Wizard dialog box, make sure the **Show Worksheets option button** is selected, view the sample data, then click **Next**

6. Click the **First Row Contains Column Headings check box** to select it, then click **Next**; make sure the **In a New Table option** is selected, then click **Next**

7. You want to import all the fields, so click **Next**; make sure **Let Access add primary key** is selected, click **Next**, type **Employees**, click **Finish**, then click **OK**
   Access has created a table named Employees.
   See Figure 8-16.

8. Double-click **Employees** to open the table
   See Figure 8-17.

9. Click the **Close button** ☒ on the Access program menu bar

Figure 8-15: Import Spreadsheet Wizard

Sample of
data you
are exporting

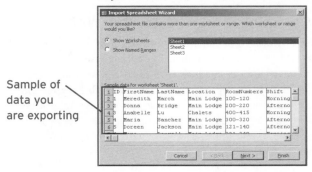

Figure 8-16: Table name in Access window

New Access
table created
from exported
Excel data

Figure 8-17: Exported Excel data in Access table

Access
assigned an ID
number field

Exported
Excel data in
Access table

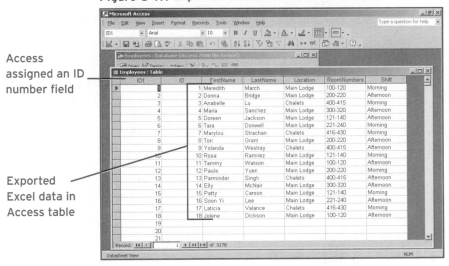

Skill Set 8

Importing and Exporting Data

Publish Worksheets and Workbooks to the Web

Publish a Worksheet Range to the Web

You can publish Excel worksheets and workbooks in HTML format for use on the Internet, World Wide Web, or an intranet. To save an entire workbook, you use the Save As command on the File menu. To publish a worksheet or worksheet range, you use the Publish option in the Save As Web Page dialog box. You can publish a worksheet or a workbook to a disk or directly to a Web or network server. When Excel publishes your data, it saves the data as an HTML file with the file extension .htm. It also creates a folder of supporting files in a folder called [filename]_files.

Activity Steps

 open Providers02.xls

1. Click **File** on the menu bar, click **Save As Web Page**, then click **Publish**

2. In the Publish as Web Page dialog box, click the **Choose list arrow**, then click **Range of cells**

3. Click the **Collapse dialog box button** , drag to select the range **A1:H16**, then click the **Expand dialog box button**

4. Click **Browse**, navigate to the location where your Project Files are stored, select the existing file name, type **analysis**, then click **OK**

   If you were publishing directly to a Web or network server, you would navigate to its online location. Also, it's best to name HTML files a maximum of eight characters, with no capital letters. Some networks do not handle long filenames well.

5. Click **Change**, type **Vail Internet Providers**, click **OK**, then click to select the check box next to **Open published web page in browser** if it's not already selected
   See Figure 8-18.

6. Click **Publish**
   After a moment, the file opens in your browser.

7. If your browser window is not already maximized, click its **Maximize button** on the title bar
   See Figure 8-19.

8. Close the Web browser window.

 close Providers02.xls

tip

Step 6
Once you have saved a workbook, you can open the HTML file in Excel to modify it. You do not have to modify the original .xls file and republish it.

Figure 8-18: Saving a worksheet

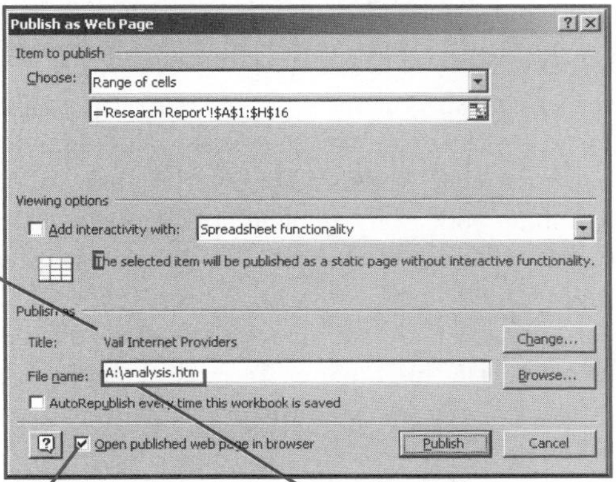

Users will see this text in Web page title bar

Automatically opens page in browser after you publish

Location and filename for HTML file (your location may be different)

Figure 8-19: Worksheet in HTML format in browser window

Your storage location may be different

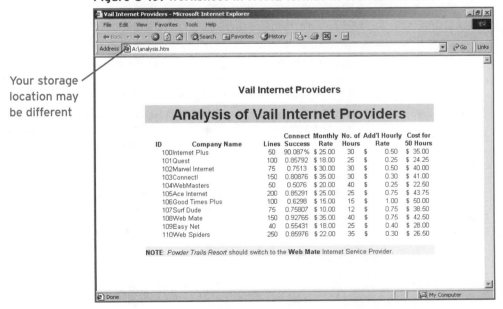

Skill Set 8
Importing and Exporting Data

Publish Worksheets and Workbooks to the Web
Publish an Interactive Workbook to the Web

When a workbook or worksheet is saved as an **interactive** HTML file, users can not only view it in their browsers, but they can also manipulate the information in it (provided they are using Microsoft Internet Explorer version 4.1 or later). They can switch among worksheets, manipulate data, and change formulas. For example, you could publish a worksheet that calculates net profit, and users could enter various sales numbers to see how the profit figure changes. Any changes users make, however, are not saved in the HTML document; the changes are lost when the user closes the browser. To retain modifications to an interactive worksheet you have already published, you have to modify the original Excel worksheet, then republish it.

Step 6
When you save a workbook with interactivity, it appears in a smaller window within your browser window, and wrapped text will no longer be wrapped. Be sure to test your files to make sure they look the way you want.

Activity Steps

 open Calculators01.xls

1. Click **File** on the menu bar, click **Save As Web Page**

2. Click to select the **Entire Workbook option button** (if it's not already selected), then click to select the **Add interactivity check box**
   See Figure 8-20.

3. Click **Publish**

4. Click **Browse**, navigate to the location where your Project Files are saved; in the File name box, select the existing file name if it's not already selected, type **mortgage**, then click **OK**

5. Deselect the **Open published page in Web browser** check box (if it's not already deselected); click to select the **AutoRepublish every time this workbook is saved check box**
   See Figure 8-21.

6. Click **Publish**
   The HTML file is saved as mortgage.htm. You could have previewed the file in your Web browser, but you will get a better view of the workbook if you open your browser first, then open the file, which you will do in the next lesson.

 close Calculators01.xls

Figure 8-20: Saving an interactive workbook

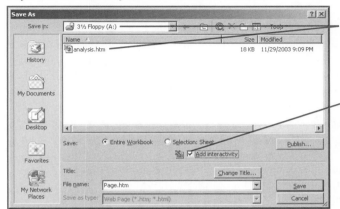

Your save location and folder contents may differ

Allows users to manipulate Web page using their browsers

Figure 8-21: Publish dialog box

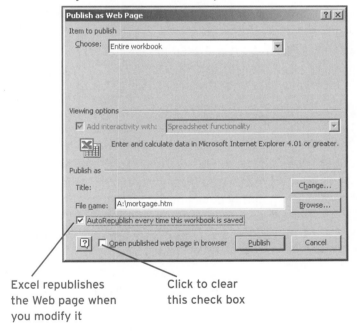

Excel republishes the Web page when you modify it

Click to clear this check box

extra!

Publishing worksheets with spreadsheet functionality
You can save worksheets with **spreadsheet functionality**, meaning that users can enter, format, calculate, analyze, and sort and filter all kinds of data. You can save the following with spreadsheet functionality: worksheets, external data ranges, PivotTable reports, cell ranges, filtered lists, and print areas. In the Publish as Web page dialog box, under Viewing options, select **Add interactivity with**, then make sure the box reads **Spreadsheet functionality**.

Skill Set 8
Importing and Exporting Data

Publish Worksheets and Workbooks to the Web

Use Interactive Workbooks

After you save a workbook or worksheet in HTML format, Excel saves the file with an .htm file extension and creates a folder containing any supporting files. Some objects will not appear in the htm file, such as embedded objects. You can view the HTML file in your browser at any time to see how it will look on the Web. To use an interactive workbook, you must use Internet Explorer version 4.1 or later. *Keep in mind that other users who do not have this software will not be able to view your worksheet at all; instead, they will see an error message, so you might not want to place an interactive worksheet on a public Web site.* Any changes you make to an interactive workbook using the browser are not saved to the HTML file or the original Excel file. After you close your browser, the file returns to its original state.

Activity Steps

Step 7
To change the appearance of the selected cell or range, click the Commands and Options button on the Interactive workbook toolbar, then use the options on the Formatting tab. The changes remain in effect until you close Internet Explorer.

1. Click **Start** on the Windows taskbar, point to **Programs**, then click **Internet Explorer**; if necessary, maximize the browser window

2. Click **File** on the menu bar, then click **Open**

3. Click **Browse**, click the **Look in list arrow**, then navigate to the location where your Project Files are stored

4. Click **calcs.htm**, then click **Open**
   See Figure 8-22.

5. Click **OK**

6. Click the **Condos sheet tab**, then click **Time Shares**

7. Click the **6.00%** figure after Interest Rate, type **5.00**, then watch the monthly payments as you press **[Enter]**
   See Figure 8-23.

8. Click **10** after # years, type **20**, then watch the monthly payments as you press **[Enter]**

9. Click the **Time Shares sheet tab**, click **Condos**, change the interest rate and loan term as you wish, then click the **Close button** ☒ on the Internet Explorer title bar

Figure 8-22: Internet Explorer Open dialog box

Your file location may differ

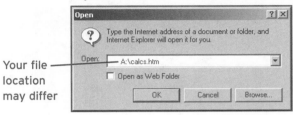

Figure 8-23: Monthly payments change after input cell is changed

Your file location may be different

Interactive workbook toolbar lets users manipulate and format worksheet data

Commands and Options button

Change rate and years to recalculate payments

Interactive workbooks have single sheet tab with list arrow

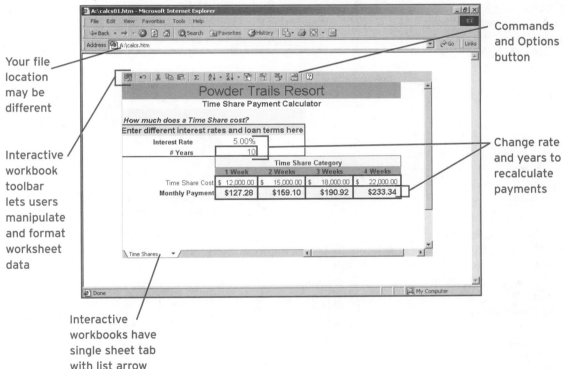

Skill Set 8
Importing and Exporting Data

Target Your Skills

1 Import the text file School01.txt to Excel, accepting default settings, then save the file as School02.xls. Then import and format the data shown in Figure 8-24. Save the worksheet as revenue.htm without automatic republishing, then preview it in your browser.

Figure 8-24

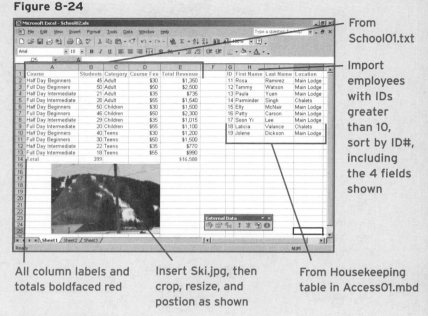

From School01.txt

Import employees with IDs greater than 10, sort by ID#, including the 4 fields shown

All column labels and totals boldfaced red

Insert Ski.jpg, then crop, resize, and postion as shown

From Housekeeping table in Access01.mbd

2 Import the text file Weather01.txt to a blank worksheet, accepting defaults, then save it as Weather02.xls. Make the changes shown in Figure 8-25. Save the file as an interactive workbook named "weather.htm". Open it in Internet Explorer. Add one formula, then format the cells using the Commands and Options button 🗐.

Figure 8-25

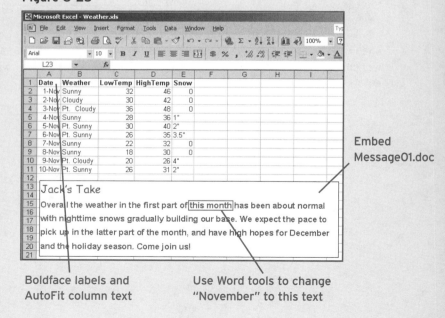

Embed Message01.doc

Boldface labels and AutoFit column text

Use Word tools to change "November" to this text

Skill List

1. Create, edit, and apply templates
2. Create workspaces
3. Use data consolidation

As you use Excel, you will find there are particular workbook types you use repeatedly. Instead of recreating the same workbook with the same column headings, formatting, and formulas, you can create an Excel **template** to duplicate workbooks with the same design.

You may also find that you often work with more than one workbook open at the same time, such as a customer list and a customer report. Instead of opening each one separately, you can create a **workspace** to open both at the same time, in an arrangement that suits the way you work.

Often, you will have data in multiple worksheets (or workbooks), such as sheets detailing individual sales rep sales totals, that you want to combine into one sales sheet detailing all sales reps' totals. Excel lets you do this quickly using **data consolidation**.

Workbook icon

Template icon

Workspace icon

Skill Set 9
Managing Workbooks

Create, Edit, and Apply Templates
Create a Workbook Template

As you use Excel, you will create workbooks that you want to use repeatedly, such as budgets, expense or sales reports, and invoices. You could open a previously created workbook and resave it, but you would need to delete the existing data and resave the workbook using a new name. You can save time by creating a **template**, a workbook file with an .xlt file extension, that you use as a basis for new workbooks with the same design. A template can contain text, formatting, formulas, macros, charts, or data. You usually store templates in the Templates folder created when you installed Excel, in C:\Documents and Settings\[your user name]\Application Data\Microsoft. Templates stored in the Templates folder appear on the General Templates tab in the Templates dialog box, which appears when you click New from template in the New Workbook task pane. *Because readers of this book might be using a shared computer and might not have access to the Templates folder, you will save the template to the location where you store Project Files.*

Activity Steps

 open Budget03.xls

1. Select the data in the range **B5:D6**, press and hold [Ctrl], select **B9:D17**, press [Delete], then click cell A1
   Although the data is no longer in the worksheet, the formulas and formatting remain.

2. Click **File** on the menu bar, then click **Save As**

3. Click the **Save as type list arrow**, then click **Template (*.xlt)**
   The Template folder opens automatically.

4. Navigate to the location where your Project Files are stored

5. Edit the file name so it reads **Budget Template01**
   See Figure 9-1.

6. Click **Save**
   See Figure 9-2.

7. Click **File** on the menu bar, click **Properties**, click the **Summary tab** (if it's not already selected), click the **Save Preview Picture check box** to select it, click **OK**, then click the **Save button** on the Standard toolbar
   An image of the first worksheet will now appear in the Preview section of the Templates dialog box when you create a workbook based on this template.

 close Budget Template01.xlt

Step 2
A template you create also contains a workbook's print areas, the number and type of sheets, hidden sheets, data validation settings, and any custom calculation options.

Figure 9-1: Saving a workbook as a template

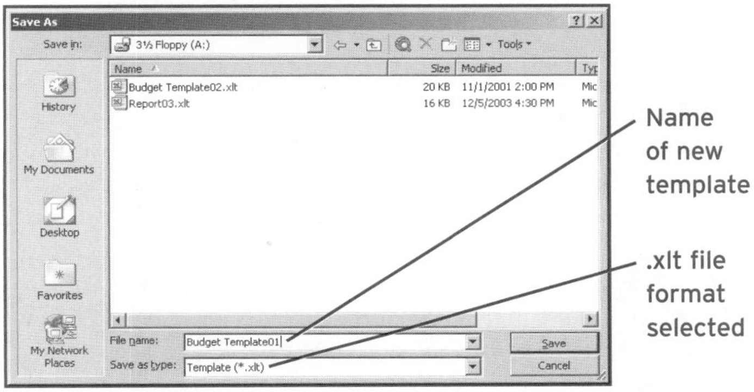

Name of new template

.xlt file format selected

Figure 9-2: Template file

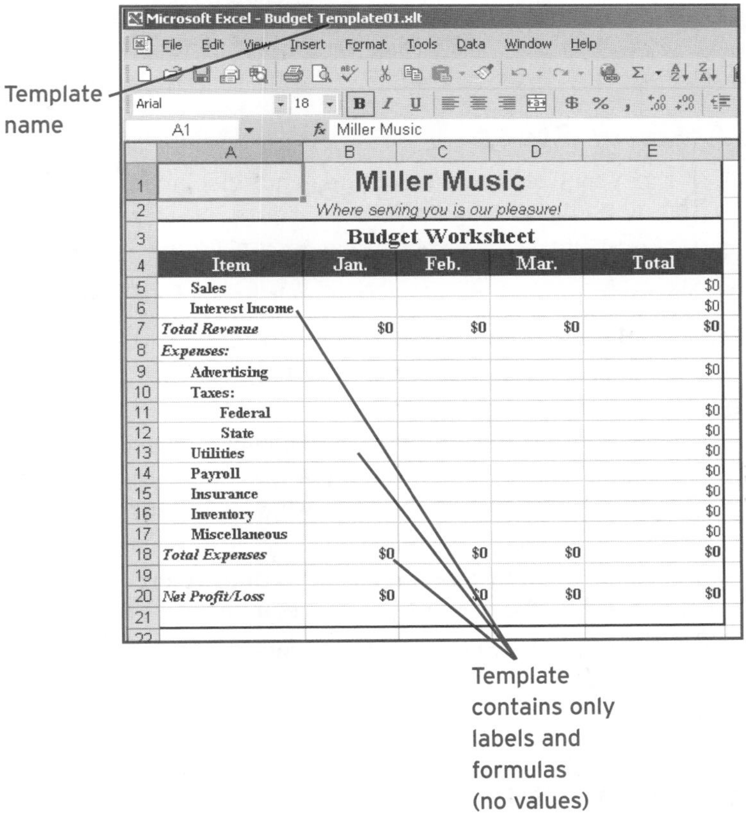

Template name

Template contains only labels and formulas (no values)

extra!

Creating worksheet templates

You can also create templates for the new worksheets you add to workbooks. For example, you might want all new worksheets to contain your company name, colors, font style, or logo in the footer. Create a workbook with one worksheet, then format it as you want all new worksheets to appear. Save it in the XLStart folder using the filename "sheet." The XLStart folder contains any items you want to open automatically every time you start Excel. Every new Excel worksheet will then have the features you added.

Skill Set 9

Managing Workbooks

Create, Edit, and Apply Templates
Create a New Workbook Based on a Template You Created

A workbook template is the basis for your future workbooks. Using a template is safer than resaving an older workbook because you are creating a fresh copy without the possibility of overwriting an older workbook. A workbook created from your template contains all the worksheets, formulas, formatting, styles, and macros in the template. You usually save your templates in the Templates folder created when you installed Excel, located at C:\Documents and Settings\[your user name]\Application Data\Microsoft. Templates stored in the Templates folder appear when you click General Templates in the New Workbook task pane. *Since you may be using a networked computer and may not have access to the Templates folder, you saved your template in the previous lesson in your Project File location. Therefore, this lesson has you open a workbook based on your template using the Choose workbook command in the New Workbook task pane. On the exam, however, the template you open and modify may be in the Templates folder. In this case, you should use the General Templates command under New from template in the New Workbook task pane to create the new workbook.*

Step 2
You can use the New from existing workbook command in the New Workbook task pane to open a workbook based on any Excel workbook, not just templates.

Activity Steps

1. If the New Workbook task pane is not displayed, click **File** on the menu bar, then click **New**

2. Under New from existing workbook, click **Choose workbook**

3. Navigate to the location where your Project Files are stored

4. Click **Budget Template02.xlt**
   See Figure 9-3.

5. Click **Create New**
   A new workbook opens based on the Budget Template02 workbook.

6. Enter the following information in the range B5:D5: **50,000, 40,000, 30,000**; enter the following information in the range B9:D9: **10,000, 8,000, 6,000**

7. Click each **chart tab**, then click the **Budget tab**
   The charts are based on the worksheet information you entered.

8. Click **File** on the menu bar, click **Save As**, change the filename to **Q1 Budget**

9. Click **Save**
   See Figure 9-4.

 close Q1 Budget.xls

Figure 9-3: Choosing a template

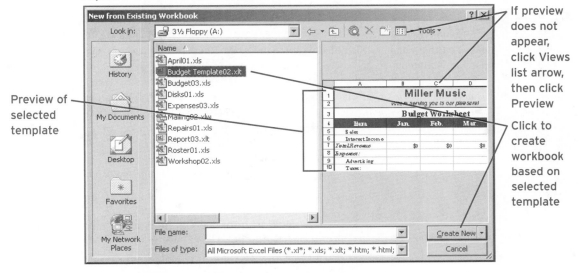

Preview of selected template

If preview does not appear, click Views list arrow, then click Preview

Click to create workbook based on selected template

Figure 9-4: Workbook based on a template

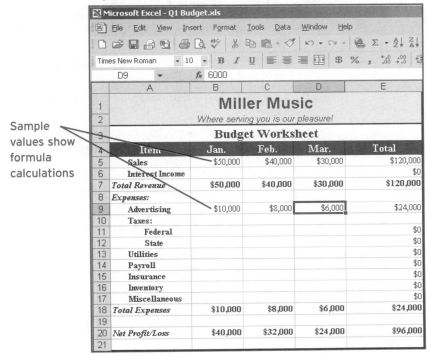

Sample values show formula calculations

Skill Set 9
Managing Workbooks

Create, Edit, and Apply Templates
Modify a Workbook Template

To modify a workbook template, you open the .xlt file from the Open dialog box. After modifying the file, you save the changes. All future workbooks you create based on the template will reflect your changes. Workbooks you created using the unrevised template, however, retain the original design. *Normally, templates are stored in the Templates directory folder created when you installed Excel, usually located at C:\Documents and Settings\[your user name]\Application Data\Microsoft. Templates stored in the Templates folder appear when you click General Templates in the New Workbook task pane. If you are using a networked computer you may not have access to the Templates folder in this activity you will open and save the template in your Project File location. On the exam, however, keep in mind that the template you open and modify may be in the templates folder.*

Activity Steps

1. If the New Workbook task pane is not visible, click **File** on the menu bar, then click **New**

2. Click **More workbooks** in the New Workbook task pane

3. In the Open dialog box, navigate to the location where your Project Files are stored

4. Make sure the Files of type box reads **All Microsoft Excel Files** to display workbooks and templates

Step 4
If you want to display only templates, you can select Templates (*.xlt) in the Files of type list.

5. If your files are not displayed in Preview view, click the **Views list arrow**, then click **Preview**

6. Click **Report03.xlt**, compare your screen to Figure 9-5, then click **Open**

7. Click the **column B heading** to select the column, click **Format** on the menu bar, point to **Column**, then click **Width**

8. Type **20**, then click **OK**

9. Click cell **A22**, then type **Original receipts must be submitted for all expenses**

10. Press **[Ctrl][Enter]**, then click the **Save button** 🖫 on the Standard toolbar
    The next time you or another user creates a document based on the template, it will have the wider column and the added text.
    See Figure 9-6.

 close Report03.xlt

Figure 9-5: Opening the template

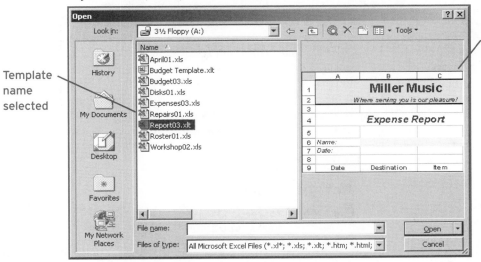

Template preview

Template name selected

Figure 9-6: Modified template

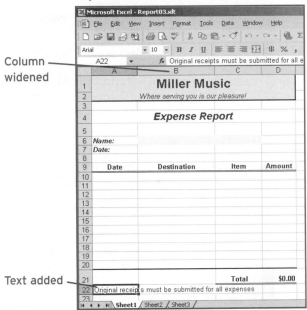

Column widened

Text added

Skill Set 9

Managing Workbooks

Create Workspaces

Create a Workspace File

If you frequently work with a particular set of workbooks that you need to have open at the same time, it can be time-consuming to open and reposition each one at the start of every work session. Using an Excel workspace file can help. A **workspace** is an Excel file with an .xlw file extension that contains the location, window sizes, and display settings of selected workbooks. Then, instead of opening each individual file, you open the workspace file, which automatically opens the workbooks in the arrangment and settings you specified. You can include two or more Excel workbooks in a workspace. The workspace file does not contain the workbooks themselves, so when you back up the files by copying them to another disk, be sure to copy the workbooks, not just the .xlw file.

Activity Steps

  open Roster01.xls
         Workshop02.xls

1. With Roster01 and Workshop02 open, click **Window** on the menu bar, then click **Arrange**

2. Click **Vertical**, then click **OK**

3. Click the **Roster01.xls** title bar, click the **Zoom list arrow** on the Standard toolbar, then click **75%**

4. Click **Tools** on the menu bar, click **Options**, click the **View tab** (if it's not already selected), under Window options click to deselect the **Row & column headers** check box, then click **OK**
   A workspace preserves most, but not all, of the settings you choose in the tabs of the Options dialog box.
   See Figure 9-7.

5. Click **File** on the menu bar, then click **Save Workspace**

6. Navigate to the location where your Project Files are stored, double-click **resume** (the default file name in the File Name box), then type **Mailing01**
   See Figure 9-8.

7. Click **Save**

8. Click **No** to close the Roster01 project file without saving your changes, then close both files without saving

  close Roster01.xls
         Workshop02.xls

Step 6
If you want to open the workbooks every time you start Excel, place the workspace file in your XLStart folder. The XLStart folder location can vary, depending on the way Excel was installed. Use the Search/For Files or Folders command on the Start menu to locate it.

Figure 9-7: Workbook arrangement

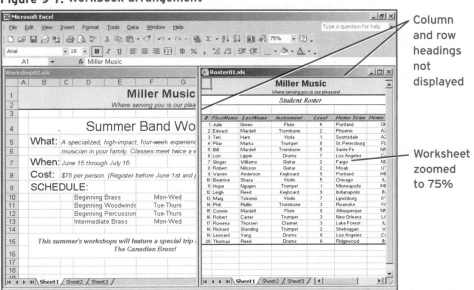

Column and row headings not displayed

Worksheet zoomed to 75%

Figure 9-8: Saving a workspace file

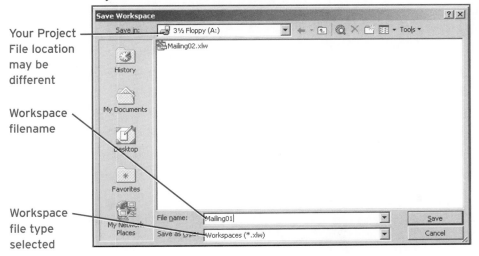

Your Project File location may be different

Workspace filename

Workspace file type selected

Skill Set 9

Managing Workbooks

Create Workspaces
Open a Workspace

Once you have created a workspace file, the file itself, named [filename].xlw, is stored in the location you specified. When you open the workspace file, Excel automatically opens the files that were open at the time you created the workspace, using the window arrangement, magnification settings, and options you specified.

Step 4
You can also select All Files (*.*) to display files of all types, including those created in other programs, or All Excel files to display all files created using Excel, including workbooks, templates, and workspaces.

Activity Steps

1. If the New Workbook task pane is not open, click **File** on the menu bar, then click **New**

2. Click **More workbooks** in the New Workbook task pane

3. In the Open dialog box, navigate to the location where your Project Files are stored (if it's not already displayed)

4. Click **Mailing02.xlw**, then compare your screen to Figure 9-9

5. Click **Open**
   The two workbooks referred to in the Mailing02.xlw workspace file open with the window arrangement and zoom settings that were saved at the time the Mailing02.xlw file was created. *See Figure 9-10.*

 close Roster01.xls
   Workshop02.xls

Figure 9-9: Opening a workspace file

All Microsoft
Excel files
displayed

Workspace
file

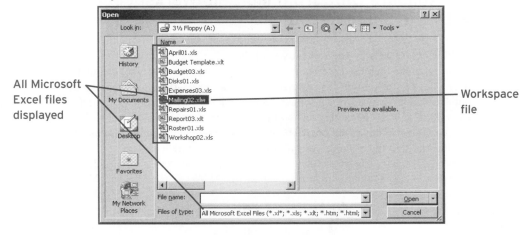

Figure 9-10: Workbooks open in workspace

Window
and zoom
settings
saved in
workspace
file

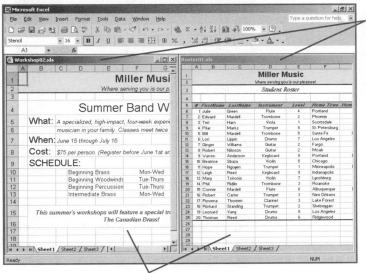

Depending on your
monitor, your screen may
look slightly different

Skill Set 9
Managing Workbooks

Use Data Consolidation
Consolidate Data from Multiple Worksheets with the Same Layout

As you use Excel, you may want to **consolidate**, or combine, information from multiple worksheets in one summary worksheet. For example, you might have monthly sales data on separate worksheets that you want to consolidate as quarterly sales figures on one summary sheet. You can use 3-D formula references, but Excel also features a Consolidate command that offers more options for combining data. If the worksheets you want to combine have an identical layout, you can consolidate **by position**, which combines data from the exact same cell locations. In the example you will use below, each store has CDs in the same categories, so you can consolidate the data by position. You can consolidate data using many standard functions, including SUM, AVERAGE, MIN, and MAX.

Step 4
If the range on the supporting worksheet has a name, you can enter it in the formula instead of selecting the range each time. Range names can save time and ensure accuracy when you are working with large worksheets.

Activity Steps

 open Disks01.xls

1. Maximize the Excel window if necessary; on the All Stores worksheet, select the range **C8:C16**, click **Data** on the menu bar, then click **Consolidate**

2. If necessary, move the dialog box right so you can see column C

3. Under Function, make sure **Sum** is selected

4. Click the **Eugene sheet tab**, (if the Consolidate dialog box is obscuring column C, drag the dialog box **title bar** so you can see the column contents), select the range **C8:C16**, then click **Add**
   See Figure 9-11.

5. Click the **St. Paul sheet tab**
   Because the worksheets have the same categories, the correct range is already selected.

6. Click **Add**

7. Click the **San Jose sheet tab**, then click **Add**

8. Click **OK**, then click any blank worksheet cell
   See Figure 9-12.

 close Disks01.xls

Figure 9-11: First consolidation range

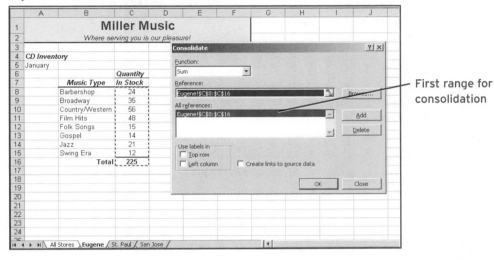

First range for consolidation

Figure 9-12: Consolidated data for three stores

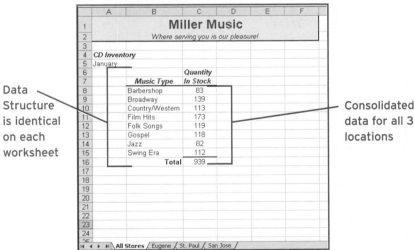

Data Structure is identical on each worksheet

Consolidated data for all 3 locations

extra!

Consolidating data from different workbooks

You can consolidate data from other workbooks as well as other worksheets. Make sure the supporting workbooks are open. References to cells in other workbooks have the filename in brackets before the sheet name, such as [Filename]Sheetname! Reference. You can also use range names in supporting workbooks.

Skill Set 9
Managing Workbooks

Use Data Consolidation
Consolidate Data from Multiple Worksheets with Different Layouts

You can consolidate by position when all sheets have an identical layout, but when sheets have different layouts, you must consolidate **by category**. To do this you use the Consolidation command, but you let Excel create the category listings from the supporting sheets. In the example you will use below, each store has identical expense categories in rows 10 to 15, but the San Jose and Eugene stores have additional distinct categories in rows 16 and 17.

Step 7
After you perform a consolidation, Excel saves the consolidation references in the All references list; you can repeat the consolidation by choosing Data/Consolidate, then clicking OK.

Activity Steps

 open Expenses03.xls

1. Maximize the Excel window if necessary

2. Click cell **B10**, click **Data** on the menu bar, click **Consolidate**, then move the dialog box to the right so you can see column C
   When you consolidate by category, you only select the upper left corner of the consolidation range.

3. Under Function, make sure **Sum** is selected; if there are references listed under All references, click each one, then click **Delete**

4. Click the **San Jose sheet tab**, select the range **A10:B18**, then click **Add**

5. Click the **Eugene sheet tab**, select the range **A10:B17**, then click **Add**

6. Click the **St. Paul sheet tab**, select the range **A10:B16**, then click **Add**

7. Under Use labels in, click the **Left column check box** to select it (if it's not already selected)

8. Click the **Create links to source data check box** to select it
   See Figure 9-13.

9. Click **OK**, then click any blank cell on the Consolidation sheet
   See Figure 9-14.

 close Expenses03.xls

Figure 9-13: **Completed Consolidation dialog box**

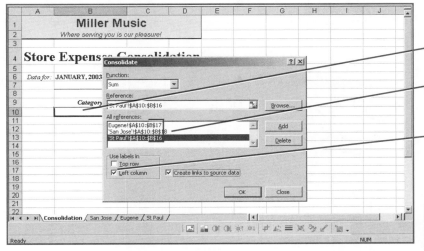

Select upper left corner of consolidation range

Ranges are different on each sheet

Tells Excel to use labels from left column in each range

Figure 9-14: **Consolidated data**

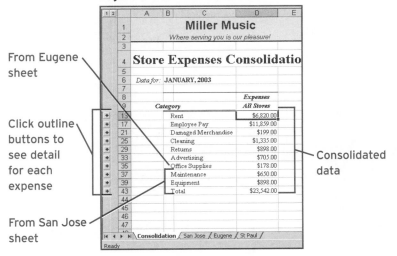

From Eugene sheet

Click outline buttons to see detail for each expense

From San Jose sheet

Consolidated data

extra!

Learning more about consolidation links

Unlike 3-D formulas, consolidation ranges are not automatically linked to the supporting data. This means that if you change data on the supporting sheets, you must repeat the consolidation. When you select the Create links to source data check box in the Consolidation dialog box, you link the source ranges to the consolidation sheet. When this option is selected, Excel creates an outline that links each source reference to the consolidation, along with a summary entry. Excel creates additional rows and columns for each unique entry and links formulas for each one.

Skill Set 9
Managing Workbooks

Target Your Skills

 Repairs01.xls

1 Create a template named Repairs.xlt containing only text and formulas from Repairs01.xls, then close the template. Create a workbook, enter data in the Accordions line, then save it as January.xls. Open both the template and the January workbook, tile the windows as shown in Figure 9-15, then save the workspace as Both.xlw. Close the workbooks, open the workspace, then close it. Reopen the template, then modify it as shown in Figure 9-15, saving your changes.

Figure 9-15

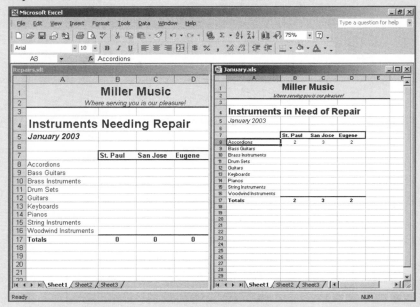

 April01.xls

2 Create the consolidation sheet shown in Figure 9-16, consolidating by category and linking the consolidation to the source.

Figure 9-16

	A	B	C	D	E	F
1			Miller Music			
2			Where serving you is our pleasure!			
3						
4	Sales					
5	April 2003					
6						
7	Category		Total Sales			
11	CDs		$ 160,490			
15	Audio Tapes		$ 54,950			
17	Scores		$ 1,650			
19	Videos		$ 25,860			
21	DVDs		$ 15,810			
24	Song Books		$ 8,570			

All Types / Classical / Rock / Folk /

Skill Set 10

Skill List

1. Create and apply custom number formats
2. Use conditional formats

You can apply many standard number formats (such as Currency and Percent) and cell formats (such as bolding and colors) to cell contents. As you become more proficient at using Excel and create more complex worksheets, you might want to format numbers in special ways. **Custom number formats** are formats that you create, usually by modifying existing formats. You can create a format that contains a specific number of decimal places not found in the standard formats, or a format that displays negative values in a particular color. You create custom formats in the Format Cells dialog box; they are then available for future use.

In other situations, you may want worksheet values to display with a specific format only if a particular condition is true. For example, if you want all the dates after January 1st to display in red, or all the values over 1,000,000 to display in bold, Arial type, you can specify these conditions using the Excel **conditional formatting** feature.

Skill Set 10
Formatting Numbers

Create and Apply Custom Number Formats
Create and Apply a Custom Number Format

You are not limited to the number formats Excel supplies. You can define your own formats to display text and values using the Custom category in the Format Cells dialog box. Excel supplies over 30 custom formats, but you can customize any of them to meet your needs. You use formatting codes to set custom formats: # represents any digit, and 0 represents a digit that will always be displayed, even if the digit is 0. The code #,### will display 3456 as 3,456. The code 0.000 will display .123 as 0.123. A number format can have four parts, each one separated by semicolons: [positive numbers];[negative numbers];[zeroes];[text]. You don't need to specify all four parts. If you specify only one part, your format will apply to anything you type in that cell. If you specify two parts, they will apply to positive and negative numbers. Always begin by selecting a cell with values in it before opening the Format Cells dialog box so that Excel will display a sample of the selected value using the format you have selected or created.

Activity Steps

 open Bikes03.xls

1. Click cell **B21**
   The formula calculates net profit or loss, and is currently in Accounting format with two decimal places, which displays negative values in parentheses.

Step 2
Custom formats apply to the workbook in which you created them. To make them available in another workbook, copy and paste a number with a custom format to the new workbook.

2. Click **Format** on the menu bar, click **Cells**, click the **Number tab** (if it's not already selected), then under Category, click **Custom**

3. Scroll the Type list until you see the last format that begins with a dollar sign (the 13th format): **$#,##0.00_);[Red]($#,##0.00)**, then click it once
   This custom format displays numbers with dollar signs and two decimal places. The _) inserts a space the width of a closing parenthesis after the number so that negative numbers in parentheses will align with positive numbers. The [Red] after the semicolon directs Excel to display negative numbers in red. The zeroes at the end limit the display to two decimal places.

4. In the Type box, click after the "d" in "Red", press **[Backspace]** three times, then type **Blue**
   See Figure 10-1.

5. Click **OK**

6. Drag the **cell B21 fill handle** to include cell **H21**, then click any blank cell
   See Figure 10-2.

 close Bikes03.xls

Figure 10-1: Customized format

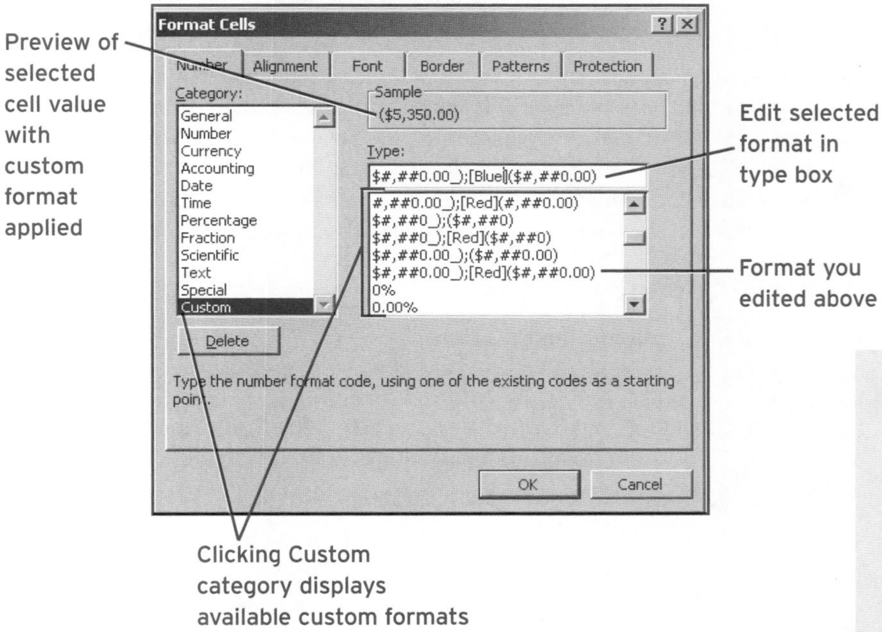

Preview of selected cell value with custom format applied

Edit selected format in type box

Format you edited above

Clicking Custom category displays available custom formats

Figure 10-2: Worksheet with custom format applied

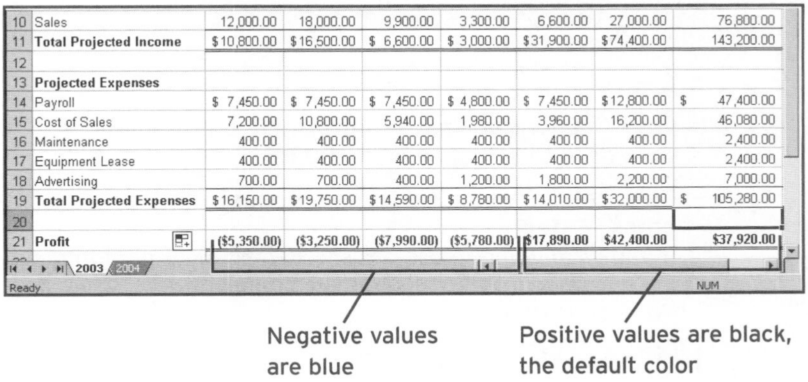

10	Sales	12,000.00	18,000.00	9,900.00	3,300.00	6,600.00	27,000.00		76,800.00
11	Total Projected Income	$10,800.00	$16,500.00	$ 6,600.00	$ 3,000.00	$31,900.00	$74,400.00		143,200.00
12									
13	Projected Expenses								
14	Payroll	$ 7,450.00	$ 7,450.00	$ 7,450.00	$ 4,800.00	$ 7,450.00	$12,800.00	$	47,400.00
15	Cost of Sales	7,200.00	10,800.00	5,940.00	1,980.00	3,960.00	16,200.00		46,080.00
16	Maintenance	400.00	400.00	400.00	400.00	400.00	400.00		2,400.00
17	Equipment Lease	400.00	400.00	400.00	400.00	400.00	400.00		2,400.00
18	Advertising	700.00	700.00	400.00	1,200.00	1,800.00	2,200.00		7,000.00
19	Total Projected Expenses	$16,150.00	$19,750.00	$14,590.00	$ 8,780.00	$14,010.00	$32,000.00	$	105,280.00
20									
21	Profit	($5,350.00)	($3,250.00)	($7,990.00)	($5,780.00)	$17,890.00	$42,400.00		$37,920.00

2003 2004
Ready   NUM

Negative values are blue

Positive values are black, the default color

extra!

Making conditions a part of a custom format

You can add conditions to a number format so that a number displays one way if the condition is met and another way if it is not met. To specify the level of conditions, use standard comparison operators, such as < for "less than," > for "greater than," <> for "not equal to," <= for "less than or equal to," and >= for "greater than or equal to." For example, the custom format [Green][>500];[Blue][<=500] will format values of 500 or less in blue and values above 500 in green. You can use the following colors in custom formats: black, cyan, magenta, white, blue, green, red, and yellow. Be sure to use a semicolon between the two conditions.

Skill Set 10

Formatting Numbers

Create and Apply Custom Number Formats

Create and Apply a Custom Date and Time Format

Excel supplies numerous date and time formats. To customize a date and time format on the Number tab of the Format Cells dialog box, you first select an existing custom format, then modify it. In date and time formats, Excel uses first letters to represent the month, date, year, hour, and minute (m, d, y, h, m). (The letter "m" can also stand for "month," but if you type it right after an "h", Excel interprets it as "minute.") Characters such as dashes and colons (-, :) appear as typed.

Activity Steps

 open Shuttle03.xls

1. Click **cell B6**

2. Click **Format** on the menu bar, click **Cells**, then click the **Number tab** (if it's not already selected)

3. Under Category, click **Custom**

4. Scroll through the Type list, then click **m/d/yyyy h:mm**
   The Sample above the Type box shows that this format displays an entered time as [month with 1 or 2 digits]/[day]/[year with 4 digits] [time in hours and minutes].

5. In the Type box, click after **mm** to place the insertion point there

6. Press **[Spacebar]**, then type **AM/PM**
   See Figure 10-3.

7. Click **OK**

8. Click the **Format Painter button** on the Standard toolbar, then drag to select the range **B7:B17**

9. Click cell **B6**, type **3/6**, press **[Spacebar]**, type **7:15**, then press **[Enter]**
   If you were going to use this sheet, you would need to enter dates in the remainder of the cells in the column.
   See Figure 10-4.

 close Shuttle03.xls

Step 9
Using this format, you would enter times after 11:59 am using a 24-hour clock, such as 13:15 for 1:15 p.m., and so forth.

Figure 10-3: Custom format in Format Cells dialog box

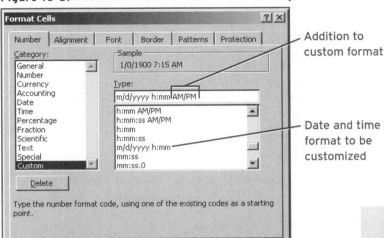

Addition to custom format

Date and time format to be customized

Figure 10-4: Custom format applied to worksheet cells

The year displayed on your screen may be different

For cells without dates entered yet, Excel displays earliest date available

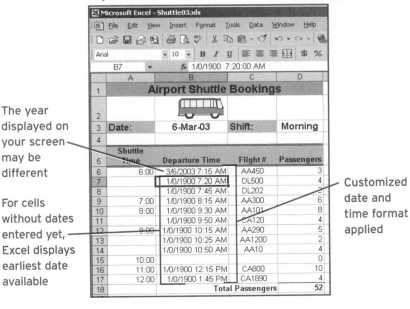

Customized date and time format applied

extra!

Specifying date and time codes

You can repeat date and time codes to indicate how you want the values to display. For example, mm displays the month as a 2-digit number, such as 03 for March. The code mmmm (the maximum number of month code letters) displays the full month name, such as December. The code dd displays the third day of the month as 03, and dddd displays the first day of the week as Monday. If the code "m" follows an "h" code, Excel will interpret it as minutes instead of months. Similarly, if the code "d" follows a month code, it will be interpreted as date instead of day.

Skill Set 10
Formatting Numbers

Create and Apply Custom Number Formats
Create and Apply a Custom Format with Text

When you create a custom number format, you can add text or symbols that will appear in the formatted cell. Certain symbols, such as $, _, !, < and the space character will appear as you type them, but you need to enclose words in quotation marks. For example, the codes $0.00" OK" will display 4.50 as $4.50 OK in the worksheet cell. The custom formats $0.00" OK";$-0.00" Under target" will display positive numbers as $4.50 OK but negative numbers as $-4.50 Under target.

Step 5
Custom formats you add appear at the bottom of the Type list on the Number tab of the Format Cells dialog box. To delete a format you created, scroll to display it, click it once, then click Delete.

Activity Steps

 open Providers03.xls

1. Click cell **D3**, click **Format** on the menu bar, then click **Cells**

2. Click the **Number tab** (if it's not already selected), then under Category, click **Custom**

3. Under Type, click **0.00%** (the 15th format)

4. In the Type box, click after %

5. Type **"**, press **[Spacebar]**, type **Rate**, then type **"**
   The format should read 0.00%" Rate".
   See Figure 10-5.

6. Click **OK**

7. Click the **Format Painter button** on the Standard toolbar, drag down the range **D4:D13**, then click any blank cell
   See Figure 10-6.

 close Providers03.xls

Figure 10-5: Specifying text in a custom format

Text will appear next to each percentage

Format being customized

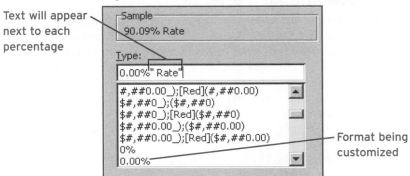

Figure 10-6: Custom format with text applied to cells

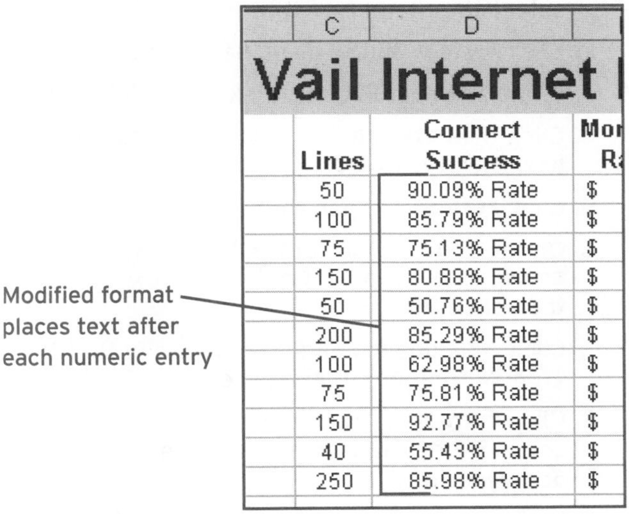

C	D	
Vail Internet		
Lines	Connect Success	Mor R:
50	90.09% Rate	$
100	85.79% Rate	$
75	75.13% Rate	$
150	80.88% Rate	$
50	50.76% Rate	$
200	85.29% Rate	$
100	62.98% Rate	$
75	75.81% Rate	$
150	92.77% Rate	$
40	55.43% Rate	$
250	85.98% Rate	$

Modified format places text after each numeric entry

Skill Set 10

Formatting Numbers

Use Conditional Formats

Apply Conditional Formats

A **conditional format** is a format you can have Excel apply only to cells whose values meet conditions you set. You can use any of the formats on the Fonts, Border, or Patterns tabs in the Format Cells dialog box. For example, in a schedule worksheet showing due dates, you can have Excel apply a bold, red format only to cells in which the date is later than a date you specify, such as >5/1 (which specifies dates later than May 1st). Or you could apply a shaded green format to values 20,000 and under (less than or equal to, or <=20,000). You can specify up to 3 conditional formats for a cell range.

Step 7
To delete a conditional format, select the range to which the formatting is applied, click Format, click Conditional Formatting, then click Delete. Click to place a check mark next to the format you want to delete, then click OK.

Activity Steps

 open Commissions02.xls

1. Select the range **C7:C37**, press and hold down [**Ctrl**], then select the range **F7:F37**

2. Click **Format** on the menu bar, then click **Conditional Formatting**

3. In the leftmost list box, make sure **Cell Value Is** is selected

4. Click the **between list arrow**, click **less than**, click the rightmost box, then type **500**

5. Click **Format** to open the Format Cells dialog box

6. On the Font tab, select the **Bold** Font style, click the **Color list arrow**, click the **Violet color** (3rd row, 2nd color from the right), then click **OK**

7. Click **Add**, under Condition 2, specify that the Cell Value Is **greater than or equal to**, then type **1000** in the text box

8. Click **Format** for condition 2, specify **Bold** Font style, click **Red** color (3rd row, leftmost color), then click **OK**
   See Figure 10-7.

9. In the Conditional Formatting dialog box, click **OK**, click any blank worksheet cell, then scroll to view the top of the list if necessary
   See Figure 10-8.

 close Commissions02.xls

Figure 10-7: Specifying two conditional formats

Cells with values under $500 will display violet text

Cells with values $1,000 or over will display red text

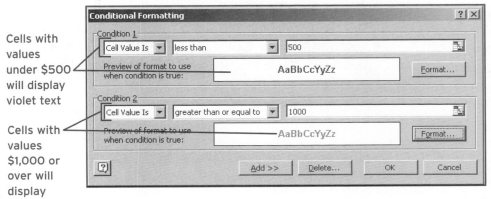

Figure 10-8: Worksheet values reflect conditional formats

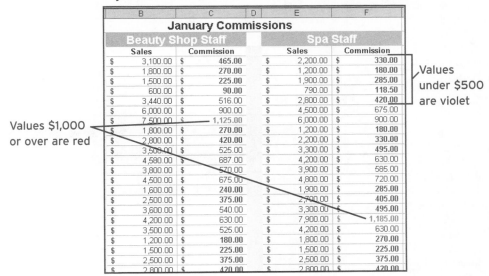

Values $1,000 or over are red

Values under $500 are violet

Skill Set 10

Formatting Numbers

Target Your Skills

 Water01.xls

1 Create four custom formats: for cell B3, modify the custom format mmm-yy as shown in Figure 10-9; for cell E7, modify the 0.00% format to delete the % sign, then add the word "HI" after the number, separated by a space; for cell E9, the same as E7 but have it add the word "LO" instead. Then in the range G7:G24, modify the 0.00% format so that negative numbers display in magenta.

Figure 10-9

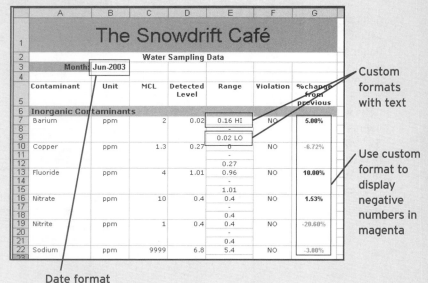

Date format

Custom formats with text

Use custom format to display negative numbers in magenta

 Guests05.xls

2 Using Figure 10-10 as a guide, create two conditional formats for the range B5:G15, one that displays numbers 1,000 and above in bold, italic, red, and another that displays numbers under 100 as bold, italic, blue.

Figure 10-10

	A	B	C	D	E	F	G
1		**Powder Trails Resort**					
2		American Guests: Top Ten States of Origin					
3		*Figures from 2006 until 2014 are projections based on 1994 to 2002.*					
4		**1994**	**1998**	**2002**	**2006**	**2010**	**2014**
5	California	490	588	706	847	*1,016*	*1,219*
6	Colorado	780	936	*1,123*	*1,348*	*1,617*	*1,941*
7	Florida	*52*	*62*	*75*	*90*	108	129
8	Illinois	485	582	698	838	*1,000*	*1,200*
9	Michigan	421	505	606	727	873	*1,048*
10	Montana	180	216	259	311	373	448
11	New Mexico	110	132	158	190	228	274
12	New York	678	814	976	*1,172*	*1,406*	*1,687*
13	Oregon	321	385	462	555	666	799
14	Utah	520	624	749	899	*1,078*	*1,294*
15	Washington	782	938	*1,126*	*1,351*	*1,622*	*1,946*
16	Total	4,819	5,783	6,939	8,327	9,987	11,984
17							

Skill List

1. Use named ranges in formulas
2. Use lookup and reference functions

Cell ranges, which are groups of adjacent cells, provide a convenient way of working with blocks of worksheet information. For example, if you want to total the values in the range E6 through E9, it's easier to refer to SUM(E6:E9), rather than to E6+E7+E8+E9. Excel simplifies the task of entering ranges further by allowing you to assign **range names**, which are names that represent groups of cells, such as "Sales" or "1997_Income." Once you name a cell range, you can use the name, instead of the range reference, in formulas.

You can name a range by typing, or you can direct Excel to use existing column or row labels as range names.

You can also use a range within a list to find list values. The VLOOKUP (vertical lookup) function searches down a list column and locates values, just as you would look down the names in a telephone book to locate a number. The HLOOKUP function looks across rows. These functions are especially useful in long lists of information.

Skill Set 11

Working with Ranges

Use Named Ranges in Formulas

Create a Cell or Range Name

Your Excel formulas usually contain references to other cells and ranges, such as =B5-C6 or =C2-SUM(C3:C10). While cell and range references will certainly do the job, formulas can become difficult to read in a large worksheet. You can simplify your formulas by using range names. A **range name** is a name that you assign to any cell or range; you can then use that name in formulas instead of the column and row references. For example, instead of =B6-B9, you could name cell B6 "Income" and cell B9 "Expenses", then create the formula =Income-Expenses. In a more complex example, you could assign the name "Salary" to range C3:C10, then use the name in the formula =C2-SUM(Salary). Range names you create are available on any worksheet in the workbook. You can assign names in the Name box on the left side of the Formula bar, or in the Define Name dialog box.

Step 3
You don't have to select a range before opening the Define dialog box. You can name the range, click the Collapse dialog box button , select the range, then click the Expand dialog box button .

Activity Steps

open Budget04.xls

1. Select the range **B10:D11**

2. Click the **Name box** on the left side of the Formula bar, type **Taxes**, then press **[Enter]**

3. Select the range **B12:D17**

4. Click **Insert** on the menu bar, point to **Name**, then click **Define**

5. Type **Other_Expenses**, check the range in the Refers to box, then click **Add**
   A range name cannot contain spaces, but it can contain letters, numbers, and the backslash (\) and underscore (_) characters.
   See Figure 11-1.

6. Click **Close**

7. Click the **Name list arrow**
   See Figure 11-2.

8. Click any blank worksheet cell

close Budget04.xls

Figure 11-1: Range name in the Define Name dialog box

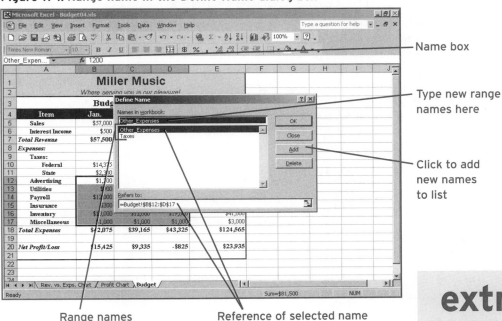

Name box

Type new range names here

Click to add new names to list

Range names appear here

Reference of selected name appears in bottom box

Figure 11-2: List of range names you created

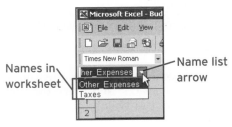

Names in worksheet

Name list arrow

extra!

Navigating with Range Names
In a large worksheet, you can use names to select worksheet sections. Click the **Name list arrow** in the Formula bar, then choose the name of the range you want to select. Excel displays and selects that range. This can be a convenient way of checking the cell references of existing names. Excel also automatically lists range names in the Go To dialog box, so you can click **Edit** on the menu bar, click **Go To**, then select any range to select it and click OK.

Skill Set 11
Working with Ranges

Use Named Ranges in Formulas
Use Labels to Create Range Names

You can use column or row labels as range names, which saves time by allowing you to name several ranges at once. You begin by selecting the range containing the column or row labels and the values in those columns or rows, then using the Create Names dialog box to indicate which cells contain the label names. Since the purpose of creating range names is to use them as references and in formulas, be sure that all the cells in the named range contain values you will want to use later. If the column or label name contains spaces, Excel automatically replaces them with an underscore character to make them "legal" range names.

Activity Steps

 open Instruments04.xls

1. Right-click the **column B heading** to select the column, then click **Delete**
   The column B information contains part numbers, which you don't want to include in your named range. When using cell labels to create range names, the labels and the data should be in contiguous columns.

2. Select the range **A7:C15**

3. Click **Insert** on the menu bar, point to **Name**, then click **Create**

4. Click the **Left column check box** to select it (if it's not already selected)
   See Figure 11-3.

5. Click **OK**, then click any blank worksheet cell

6. Click the **Name list arrow** in the formula bar, then click **Bass_Guitars**
   Excel has created a name for each row you selected, adding underscores in place of spaces. Notice that the name refers only to the cells containing values, not to the cells containing text.
   See Figure 11-4.

 close Instruments04.xls

Step 5
To delete a range name, click Insert on the menu bar, point to Name, then click Define. Select the range name in the list, then click Delete. Repeat as necessary for each name you want to delete, then click OK.

Figure 11-3: Specifying the location of labels that will become range names

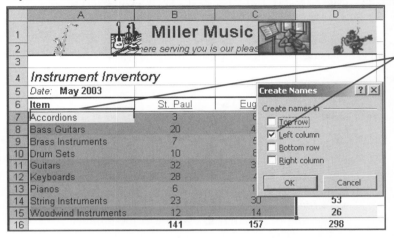

Excel will create range names for each row using item names in left column

Figure 11-4: Range names Excel created from row labels

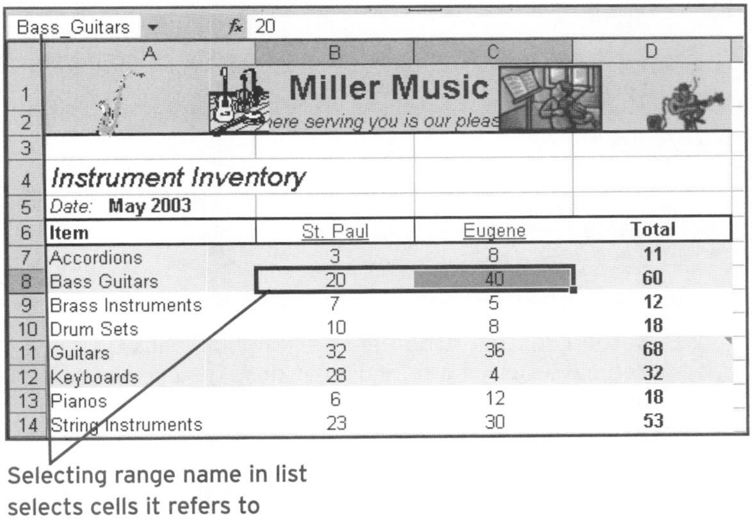

Selecting range name in list selects cells it refers to

Using range names for fixed values
Range names are also helpful when you have a value that doesn't change, called a **constant**, that you need to use repeatedly in a worksheet. For example, you might want to use a particular tax rate frequently in your formulas, such as a federal tax rate of 33%. In the Define Name dialog box, type a name, such as **Fed_Tax**, then type the constant, such as **=.33** in the Refers To box, then click **OK**. Then you can use the name Fed_Tax in formulas without having to recall the exact rate. Constant names do not appear in the Name list, but they do appear in the Define Name dialog box.

Skill Set 11
Working with Ranges

Use Named Ranges in Formulas
Use a Named Range Reference in One or More Formulas

After you have defined range names, you can use them in formulas so they are more readable. You can type the names or paste them using the Paste Names dialog box.

Activity Steps

 open Budget05.xls

1. Click cell **B22**

2. Type **=SUM(**

3. Type **taxes**, type **)**, notice that the range B10:D11 has a blue border, then press **[Ctrl][Enter]**
   Pressing [Ctrl][Enter] lets you enter the formula and leave the formula cell selected. The formula result uses the range name you entered— "taxes"—to calculate the total in cell B22. You don't have to type capital letters for Excel to recognize a range name.
   See Figure 11-5.

Step 5
Instead of pressing [F3] to display the Paste Name dialog box, you can click Insert on the menu bar, point to Name, click Paste, select the name you wish from the Paste name list, then click OK.

4. Click cell **B23**, then click the **Insert Function button** 𝑓𝑥 on the Formula bar
   If the Office Assistant appears, click "No, I don't need help right now."

5. Type **max**, press **[Enter]**, then double-click **MAX**

6. With the Number1 box highlighted, press **[F3]** to display the Paste Name dialog box
   See Figure 11-6.

7. Click **Other_Expenses**, then click **OK**

8. In the Function Arguments dialog box, click **OK**
   You have created a formula that finds the maximum, $19,000 value in the range named Other_Expenses.

 close Budget05.xls

Figure 11-5: Formula using typed range name

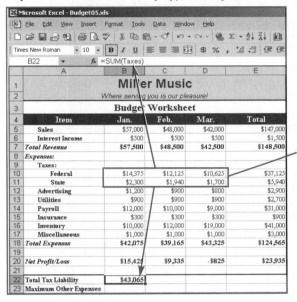

Formula uses range name to calculate total of B10:D11

Figure 11-6: Entering range name using the Paste Name dialog box

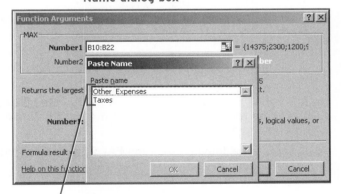

Click name to paste in Function Argument dialog box

Skill Set 11
Working with Ranges

Use Lookup and Reference Functions
Using VLOOKUP to Find Values in a List

You use an Excel **list** to record, manage, and analyze large amounts of data. In a list, if you need to search for a value, such as a customer number or a product price, you can save time by using the VLOOKUP function, which reads the list vertically and **returns** (finds and displays) a particular value based on information you enter. See Table 11-1 for an explanation of each of the VLOOKUP function arguments. The **comparison values**, the leftmost column in the search area, called the **table**, must be sorted in ascending order. The HLOOKUP function works just like the VLOOKUP function, but is used for tables arranged in rows. Instead of looking down a column to find comparison values, it reads across a row of information

Activity Steps

 open Roster02.xls

1. Copy the contents of cell **C4** and paste it in cell **H1**, then copy the contents of cell **F4** to cell **I1**

2. Type **Ramos** in cell **H2**, then press **[Tab]**
   You want to find the home town of the student with the last name of Ramos. Ramos is the lookup value.

3. Click the **Insert Function button** on the Formula bar, type **lookup**, press **[Enter]**, then double-click **VLOOKUP**

4. With the insertion point in the Lookup_value box, click cell **H2** on the worksheet, moving the dialog box as necessary, then press **[Tab]**

5. With the insertion point in the Table_array box, drag to select the range **C5:G29**, then press **[Tab]**

6. In the Col_index_num box, type **4** to indicate you want to know the home town (which is in column 4 of the table array) for the last name you type in, then press **[Tab]**

7. In the Range_lookup box, type **FALSE** to indicate you want an exact match
   See Figure 11-7.

8. Click **OK**, then scroll up so you can see row 1
   Excel has found the home town of Portland for the student named Ramos.
   See Figure 11-8.

9. Type the name **Marks** in cell **H2**, press **[Ctrl][Enter]**; then check the result against the list

 close Roster02.xls

Step 5
You can also assign a name to the table range C5:G29 and use the name in the function in place of the range reference.

Figure 11-7: VLOOKUP arguments

Location of value you want Excel to search for

Tells Excel to match lookup value exactly; a misspelled name will return an error value instead of a misleading one

Area of list to which the function applies

Tells Excel to return the value in 4th column of table

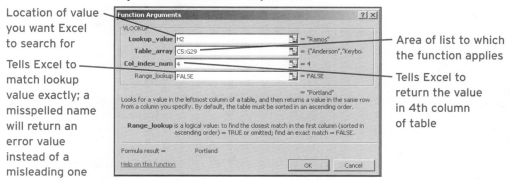

Figure 11-8: VLOOKUP function has located the home town for student named Ramos

List sorted by last name

Enter any other last name from table to display home town

Excel found correct home town for Ramos

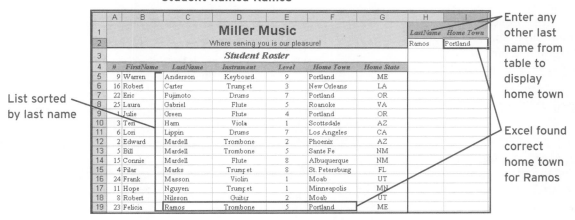

Table 11-1: VLOOKUP function arguments

argument	meaning
Lookup_value	the cell reference containing the value you want Excel to search for in the list
Table_array	the list range you want to search, known as a **table**
Col_index_num	the column number of the column you want Excel to look in, counted from the left side of the table
Range_lookup	value is either TRUE, to find the closest match to the lookup_value (TRUE is the default), or FALSE, to find an exact match

Skill Set 11

Working with Ranges

Target Your Skills

 Sales03.xls

1 Assign the range names shown in the boxed area of Figure 11-9. Use names (using the Paste Function command) to create the formulas in cells C16 and C17. (*Hint*: the first formula divides E13 by B13; C17 uses the AVERAGE function for the range C7:C12.) Paste the name list, add its heading, then format your results as shown.

Figure 11-9

	A	B	C	D	E	F
1			**Miller Music**			
2			*Where serving you is our pleasure!*			
3						
4			**Current Sales of New Items**			
5						
6	**New Items**	**Qty Sold**	**Sales Price**	**Cost**	**Net Income**	
7	CDs	75,000	$13.99	$7.00	$524,250.00	
8	Records	42,336	$12.95	$5.95	$296,352.00	
9	Audio tapes	58,204	$9.95	$3.95	$349,224.00	
10	Blank tapes	15,467	$2.00	$0.50	$23,200.50	
11	T-shirts	1,897	$15.00	$2.00	$24,661.00	
12	Posters	1,352	$7.95	$2.95	$6,760.00	
13	**TOTAL**	194,256			$1,224,447.50	
14						
15				**Range Names**		
16	Average income per item		$ 6.30	Cost	='New Items'!$D$7:$D$12	
17	Average Sales Price		$ 10.31	Net_Income	='New Items'!$E$7:$E$12	
18				Qty_Sold	='New Items'!$B$7:$B$12	
19				Sales_Price	='New Items'!$C$7:$C$12	
20				Total_Income	='New Items'!$E$13	
21				Total_Quantity	='New Items'!$B$13	

Pasted list of all worksheet names, showing worksheet name and cell references

Use Paste Function command to create formulas in these cells; use range names in formulas

 Roster03.xls

2 As shown in Figure 11-10, use the VLOOKUP function so that you can type a number in cell H2, then have Excel return the last name of the student with that number. (Specify an exact match, and remember to sort the list by number first. Select the range A5:G29 before sorting.)

Figure 11-10

	A	B	C	D	E	F	G	H	I
1				**Miller Music**				#	*LastName*
2				*Where serving you is our pleasure!*				5	Mardell
3				***Student Roster***					
4	#	*FirstName*	*LastName*	*Instrument*	*Level*	*Home Town*	*Home State*		
5	1	Julie	Green	Flute	4	Portland	OR		
6	2	Edward	Mardell	Trombone	2	Phoenix	AZ		
7	3	Teri	Harn	Viola	1	Scottsdale	AZ		
8	4	Pilar	Marks	Trumpet	8	St. Petersburg	FL		
9	5	Bill	Mardell	Trombone	5	Sante Fe	NM		
10	6	Lori	Lippin	Drums	7	Los Angeles	CA		

Skill List

1. Customize toolbars and menus
2. Create, edit, and run macros

Customizing Excel

While Microsoft Excel supplies numerous features for almost any spreadsheet need, you may still find that you want to customize the program to help you work more efficiently. You can change the appearance of toolbars and menus and place commands and buttons in more convenient locations. For example, you can add buttons to any toolbar or reposition existing ones; you can also create a custom menu, place it anywhere on the menu bar, and fill it with commands you use frequently.

You can also customize your Excel workbooks using **macros**, which are special command sequences that you can create, name, and save to quickly and automatically perform specific tasks. For example, if you download a particular set of data from the Web to a worksheet daily or weekly, you could instantly format the worksheet data using one macro instead of selecting data and applying various formats each time.

The easiest way to create a macro is to use the **macro recorder**, which records your command sequence for later use. Once you create a macro, you can edit it to customize its actions further.

Skill Set 12
Customizing Excel

Customize Toolbars and Menus
Add a Custom Menu

While Excel menus contain most of the commands you need for standard work-sheet tasks, you may find that commands you use frequently are not in conven-ient locations. For example, you might want to move a submenu command to a menu so you can display it more quickly. You can move commands to different menus or create an entirely new menu containing any Excel command, including some commands that do not appear on any standard menus. The Customize dia-log box must be open any time you work with custom menus, which will then appear each time you use Excel. *If you are using a shared computer, check with your instructor or technical resource person before customizing any menus. Your system may not allow you to make changes. If you do have permission to change menus, you should delete any custom menus you create at the end of the activity.*

Step 6
You can also drag a menu command onto any toolbar. The command name will appear on the toolbar along with the buttons.

Activity Steps

1. With a blank workbook open, click **Tools** on the menu bar, click **Customize**; in the Customize dialog box, click the **Commands tab**, scroll to the bottom of the Categories list, then click **New Menu**

2. In the Commands area on the right side of the dialog box, click **New Menu**, hold down the mouse button, drag **New Menu** upward until the **position indicator** and the **menu position pointer** are over the menu bar to the right of the Help menu, then release the mouse button

3. With the Customize dialog box still open, right-click **New Menu** in the menu bar, point to **Name: New Menu**, drag to select **New Menu**, then type **Special**
   See Figure 12-1.

4. Press **[Enter]**
   Your new menu is ready for you to add commands.

5. In the Categories list, click **Edit**, in the Commands list, drag the **Office Clipboard command** over the **Special menu** (you'll see a blank menu area appear under it), then down into the menu area to place the command on the menu
   See Figure 12-2.

6. Release the mouse button, drag the **Clear Contents command** onto the menu below the Office Clipboard command, then click **Close** in the Customize dialog box

7. Click **Special** on the menu bar, compare your screen to Figure 12-3, then click **Office Clipboard**

8. Click **Tools**, click **Customize**, drag the **Special menu** off the menu bar into the worksheet area, click **Close** in the Customize dialog box, then close the Office Clipboard

Skill 1

Customize Toolbars and Menus

Figure 12-1: Customizing the new menu name

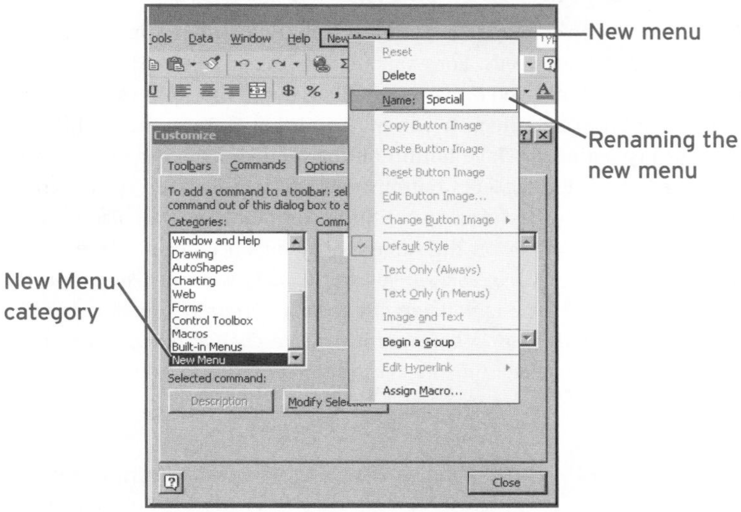

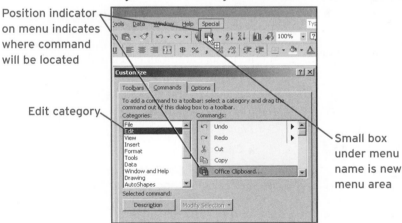

New menu
Renaming the new menu
New Menu category
Name: Special

Figure 12-2: Placing a command on the new menu

Position indicator on menu indicates where command will be located
Edit category
Small box under menu name is new menu area

Figure 12-3: New menu showing commands

Custom menu
Two commands on custom menu
Special
Office Clipboard...
Clear Contents

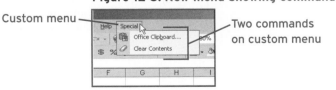

Skill Set 12
Customizing Excel

Customize Toolbars and Menus
Add and Remove Toolbar Buttons

Each Excel toolbar contains a default set of buttons, but you can add or delete buttons to suit your needs. For example, the Increase Font Size button does not appear by default on the Formatting toolbar, but if you want to use it frequently, you can add it to a toolbar. Or you may find that you use the [Ctrl][S] keyboard shortcut instead of the Save button on the Standard toolbar, so you could hide the Save button. Excel places buttons you add in a location the program determines, then hides a less-used button to make room. You can also move buttons to new locations, either on the same toolbar or on other displayed toolbars. *If you are using a shared computer, check with your instructor or technical resource person before customizing any toolbars. Your system may not allow you to make changes. If you do have permission to change them, return toolbars to their original arrangement at the end of the activity.*

Step 4
To return a toolbar to its default content and layout, click the Toolbar Options button ⏷ on the toolbar, point to Add or Remove Buttons, point to Formatting, move the pointer to the bottom of the menu, then click the Reset Toolbar command.

Activity Steps

1. With a blank workbook open, click the **Toolbar Options button** ⏷ on the right side of the Formatting toolbar

2. Point to **Add or Remove Buttons**, then point to **Formatting**

3. In the Formatting toolbar button list, click **Cells**, then compare your screen to Figure 12-4
   Any button image with a check mark next to it is currently displayed on the toolbar. You can check and uncheck any buttons to have them appear or not.

4. Click anywhere on the worksheet

5. Click the **Format Cells button** 🔲 on the Formatting toolbar
   See Figure 12-5.

6. Click **Cancel** in the Format Cells dialog box

7. Press and hold **[Alt]**, then drag the **Format Cells button** 🔲 from the Formatting toolbar to the worksheet area to remove it
   Pressing [Alt] is a shortcut for the "standard" way of removing toolbar buttons, which is to click Customize on the Toolbar Options/Add or Remove Buttons submenu. While the Customize dialog box is open, you can move buttons to new toolbar locations. You can also drag any button-and-command combination from the Customize dialog box onto any toolbar.

Figure 12-4: Buttons available for the Formatting toolbar

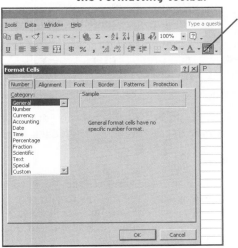

Check marks indicate buttons currently on toolbar

Format Cells button selected

Buttons available for the Formatting toolbar

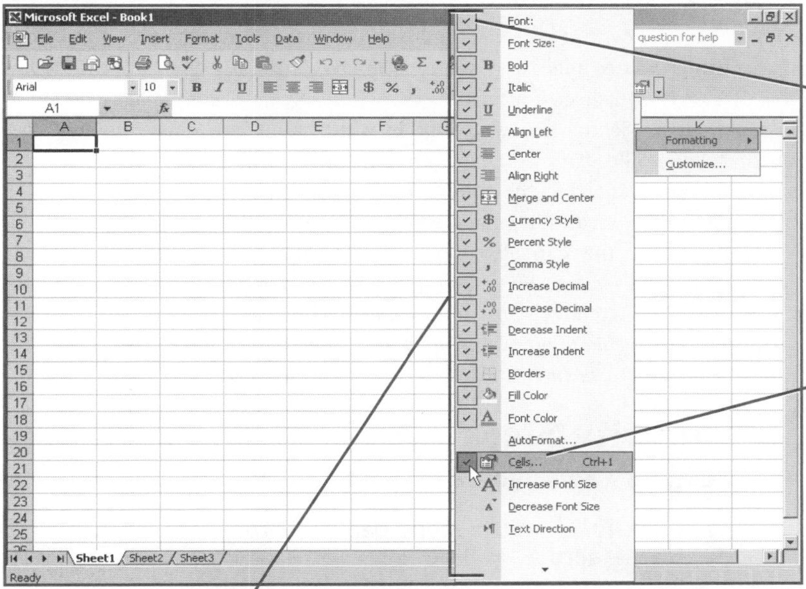

Figure 12-5: Format Cells button on the Formatting toolbar

Format Cells button on Formatting toolbar opens Format Cells dialog box

extra!

Customizing your toolbar display
To display or hide any toolbar, click **View** on the menu bar, point to **Toolbars,** then click next to any unchecked toolbar name to display it (clicking a checked toolbar name removes the check mark and hides the name). You can also open the Customize dialog box by clicking Customize at the bottom of the Toolbars submenu.

Microsoft Excel 2002   **EX-233**

Skill Set 12
Customizing Excel

Create, Edit, and Run Macros
Record a Macro

A **macro** is a series of commands that performs one or more tasks. For example, if your company wants you to place the company name, logo, and your name in the footer of every worksheet you create, you could create a simple macro to perform those tasks. Macros save you time by performing repetitive tasks more quickly than you could using standard program tools. You can create macros in two ways. You can have the **macro recorder** record the task sequence, which automatically creates a macro in the **Visual Basic for Applications (VBA)** language. You can also type macro commands in the Visual Basic window. Often it's easiest to record a macro, then modify the recorded commands in the VBA window. *After you create a macro, you should run it to make sure it performs the actions you intended. In this activity you only create a macro; you run the macro in the next activity.*

Activity Steps

 open Party02.xls

1. Click **Tools** on the menu bar, point to **Macro**, then click **Record New Macro**

2. Type **PowderTrails** to name the macro, then press **[Tab]**

3. Press **[Shift][N]** to assign a keyboard shortcut to run the macro, then compare your screen to Figure 12-6

4. Click **OK**
   The Stop Recording toolbar appears, meaning that every command you issue will now be recorded as part of the new macro.

5. Click cell **A1** (even though it's already selected), type **Powder Trails Resort**, press **[Enter]**, type **Vail, Colorado 81655**, press **[Enter]**, type **(970) 555-0888**, then press **[Enter]**

6. Click cell **A1**, click the **Font Size list arrow** [10 ▼], then click **18**

7. Click the **Bold button** [B] on the Formatting toolbar, click the **Font Color list arrow** [A ▼], then click **Blue** (2nd row, 3rd color from the right)
   See Figure 12-7.

8. Click the **Stop Recording button** [■] in the Stop Recording toolbar
   Although you can't see the macro you recorded, it is now attached to the Party02 workbook. In the next activity, you will open the Party03 workbook and run a PowderTrails macro that is identical to the one you created in this activity.

 close Party02.xls

Step 1
Clicking cell A1 at the beginning of the macro tells Excel that it should always place the company information there. Otherwise, the macro would place it in the high-lighted cell.

Figure 12-6: Assigning a macro name and keyboard shortcut

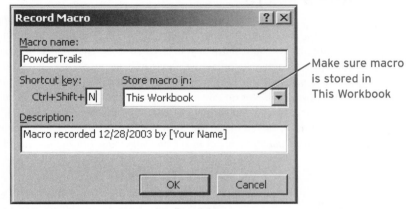

Make sure macro
is stored in
This Workbook

Figure 12-7: Recording the PowderTrails macro

Macro
includes
entry and
formatting of
this text in
this location

	A	B	C	D	E
1	**Powder Trails Resort**				
2	Vail, Colorado 81655				
3	(970) 555-0888				
4					
5		**Staff Winter Party**			
6	**Expense**	**Unit**	**Unit Cost**	**Number**	**Total**
7	Catering	Person	$ 42.00	50	$2,100.00
8	Entertainment	DJ	$1,200.00	1	$1,200.00
9	Decorations	Table	$ 5.00	15	$ 75.00
10	Door Prizes	Each	$ 15.00	10	$ 150.00
11	Beverages	Bottle	$ 9.00	40	$ 360.00
12					
13					
14				**Total Expense**	**$3,885.00**
15	**Scheduling:**				
16	Meet with Caterers	1/10/2003			
17	Set up room	1/12/2003			
18	Party date	1/13/2003			
19					

Stop button

Stop Recording toolbar (your toolbar might be in a different location)

Skill Set 12
Customizing Excel

Create, Edit, and Run Macros
Run a Macro

When you **run** a macro, Excel performs all the actions in the macro rapidly. You can run a macro by selecting it in the Macros dialog box and clicking Run, or by using the keyboard shortcut you specified when you created the macro. When you open a workbook containing a macro, Excel displays a dialog box explaining that macros can contain dangerous computer viruses and asking whether you want to enable or disable macros. If you are sure of the macro source, click Enable Macros. You will see this message only if your macro security level is set to Medium. *In this activity, you open the Party03 workbook, which contains a PowderTrails macro identical to the one you created in the last activity.*

Step 1
The Macros dialog box lists macros for all open workbooks. Macros from other open workbooks are listed with the workbook name first, followed by an exclamation point (which Excel uses to separate outside workbook sources), then the macro name.

Activity Steps

1. With Excel running, click the **Open button** 📂 on the Standard toolbar, navigate to the drive and folder where your Project Files are stored, click **Party03.xls**, then click **Open**

2. Click **Enable Macros**
   If you don't see a warning message, then your security level is set to high. To check, click Tools, point to Macro, click Security, click the medium option button, then click OK.

3. Click **Tools** on the menu bar, point to **Macro**, then click **Macros**
   See Figure 12-8.

4. Click the **PowderTrails macro** (if it's not already selected), then click **Run**
   The macro places the company information in the range A1:A3, then formats it.
   See Figure 12-9.

5. Select cells **A1:A3**, click **Edit** on the menu bar, point to **Clear**, click **All**, then click any cell outside the selected range

6. Press **[Ctrl][Shift]N**
   The assigned keyboard shortcut runs the macro. When you use a keyboard shortcut to run a macro, the Macro dialog box does not open.

    close Party03.xls

Figure 12-8: Macro dialog box

Commands in the selected macro are executed when you click Run

Figure 12-9: Company information inserted by the PowderTrails macro

Macro entered and formatted text

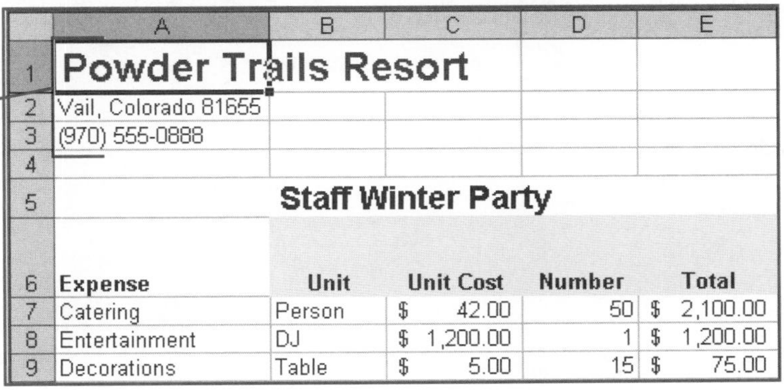

	A	B	C	D	E
1	**Powder Trails Resort**				
2	Vail, Colorado 81655				
3	(970) 555-0888				
4					
5	**Staff Winter Party**				
6	**Expense**	**Unit**	**Unit Cost**	**Number**	**Total**
7	Catering	Person	$ 42.00	50	$ 2,100.00
8	Entertainment	DJ	$ 1,200.00	1	$ 1,200.00
9	Decorations	Table	$ 5.00	15	$ 75.00

Skill Set 12
Customizing Excel

Create, Edit, and Run Macros
Run a Header and Footer Macro

You can also use macros to insert custom text and formatting in document headers and footers. As a macro runs, the screen may flicker slightly; the status bar will display "Ready" when the macro is finished running.

Step 1
In the Macro dialog box, the Macros in list arrow lets you choose and run macros from other open workbooks. It also lets you store macros in a workbook called Personal.xls, which will then open and make these macros available every time you start Excel. To hide the Personal workbook, click **Window** on the menu bar, then click **Hide**.

Activity Steps

open Quarters02.xls (Enable Macros)

1. Click the **Print Preview button** on the Standard toolbar
   You can see in the Preview window that the worksheet does not contain a header or footer.

2. Click **Close**

3. Click **Tools** on the menu bar, point to **Macro**, then click **Macros**
   See Figure 12-10.

4. Click the **HeaderFooter macro** (if it's not already selected), then click **Run**

5. Click the **Print Preview button** on the Standard toolbar
   See Figure 12-11.

6. Click the **Zoom pointer** at the top of the worksheet, then scroll down to view the bottom of the worksheet

7. Click **Close**

close Quarters02.xls

Figure 12-10: Macro dialog box

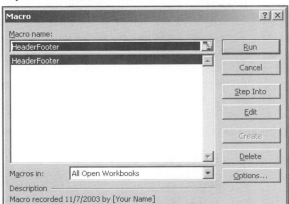

Figure 12-11: Macro results in Print Preview

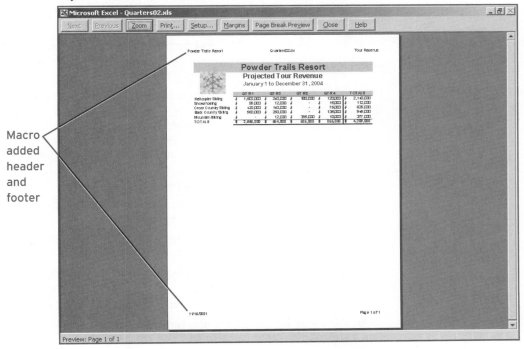

Macro added header and footer

Skill Set 12

Customizing Excel

Create, Edit, and Run Macros
View Macro Code

While you would need an entire book to learn macro programming details, you can learn about a macro's general structure by viewing its **code**, or programming commands. **Visual Basic for Applications**, called **VBA**, is a programming language that runs in its own program window, called the **Visual Basic Editor**. When you record a macro, VBA interprets each command you issue and converts it to VBA program lines. The code for each macro is stored in a separate storage area in your workbook called a **module**. Each line in VBA code is called a **statement**; a sequence of statements that performs an action is called a **procedure**.

Activity Steps

 open Party04.xls (Enable Macros)

1. Click **Tools** on the menu bar, click **Macro**, then click **Macros**

2. Click **PowderTrails** if it's not already selected, then click **Edit**

3. In the Project – VBAProject window, click **Module1** if it's not already selected
   See Figure 12-12.

Step 6
There are over 100 kinds of **objects** (items that are acted upon) in VBA. An object called *range* is followed by an action, in this case, *select*, which is called a **method**. An object is like the noun in a sentence, and a method is like the verb. The Range lines illustrate a common type of statement.

4. Click the **Project Explorer button** on the Visual Basic toolbar
   The Project Explorer window becomes highlighted, showing the project, which is the VBA name for a workbook.

5. Click the **Properties Window button** on the Visual Basic toolbar
   The name of the selected module is Module1, the default name. The code window on the right shows the code. The first line begins with Sub, which stands for Sub procedure, a series of statements that performs an action. The last line, End Sub, is the end of the procedure.

6. Click in the line that begins ' **Macro recorded**
   Lines with green text that begin with apostrophes are comments, which are notes that describe the code; they do not perform actions.

7. Click anywhere in the first line that reads **Range("A1").Select**
   This statement selects cell A1.

8. Click anywhere in the line that reads **ActiveCell.FormulaR1C1 = "Powder Trails Resort"**
   This line enters the text "Powder Trails Resort" in the selected cell.

9. Click **File** on the menu bar, then click **Close and Return to Microsoft Excel** to return to the worksheet

 close Party04.xls

Figure 12-12: Visual Basic Editor window

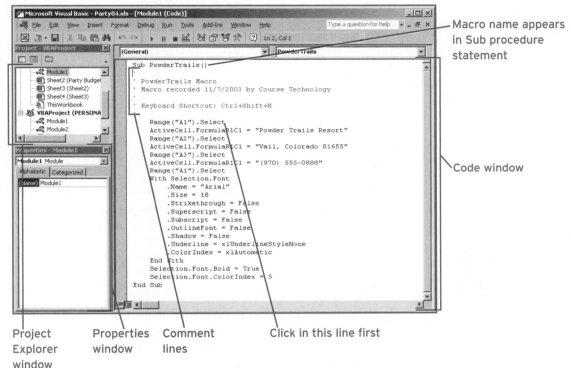

Macro name appears in Sub procedure statement

Code window

Project Explorer window

Properties window

Comment lines

Click in this line first

Skill Set 12
Customizing Excel

Create, Edit, and Run Macros
Edit a Macro

You can modify any macro in the Visual Basic for Applications window by editing the program code. When you edit a macro, it's good practice to **document** your changes by inserting a comment line with your name and the date so other users will know whom to contact if they have questions. *Make sure your comment line begins with an apostrophe, or your macro will not run correctly.* Be careful when you edit macros; if you alter the syntax (the exact arrangement and structure of statements) the macro may not run.

Activity Steps

 open Rentals04.xls (Enable Macros)

1. Click **Tools** on the menu bar, click **Macro**, then click **Macros**

2. With the FormatLogo macro name highlighted, click **Run**
   The macro formats the company name in 14-point type, bolds the text in cell A2, shades the range A1:E2, then selects cell A1. You will edit the macro to change the point size and the cell the macro selects. *See Figure 12-13.*

3. Click **Tools** on the menu bar, click **Macro**, then click **Macros**

4. With the FormatLogo macro name highlighted, click **Edit**

5. Click in the comment line under Macro Recorded, then type **Edited by [Your Name]** followed by the **date**

6. In the Size line, double-click **14**, then type **18**; in the second-to-last line (which selects cell A1), double-click **A1**, then type **B8** *See Figure 12-14.*

7. Click **File** on the menu bar, then click **Close and Return to Microsoft Excel**

8. Select the range **A1:E2**, click **Edit** on the menu bar, point to **Clear**, then click **Formats**

9. Click any worksheet cell, then press **[Ctrl][Shift][F]** *See Figure 12-15.*

 close Rentals04.xls

Step 7
You could also return to the workbook by clicking the **Microsoft Excel - Rentals04.xls button** on the taskbar. Saving the workbook would also save the edited version of the macro.

Figure 12-13: Results of macro before editing

FormatLogo macro applied formatting to A1:E2

FormatLogo macro made company name 14-point bold green Arial

Macro selected cell A1 after formatting A1:E2

Figure 12-14: Edited macro

Your documentation

Font size increased from 14 to 18 points

The macro will select cell B8 after it enters and formats text

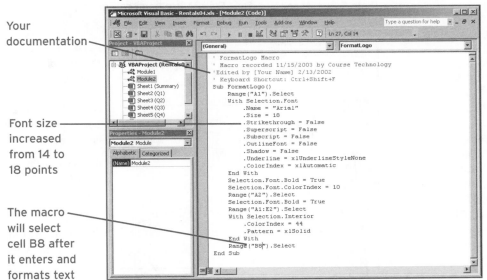

Figure 12-15: Results of edited macro

Title now 18-point type

Cell B8 selected

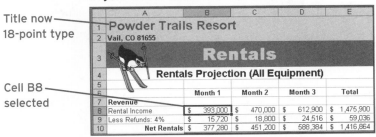

Skill Set 12

Customizing Excel

Target Your Skills

1 Create the custom menu and display the toolbar buttons shown in Figure 12-16. Then reset the toolbars and remove the custom menu.

 Revenues01.xls

2 Create a macro called FormatRooms that formats the worksheet as shown in Figure 12-17, using the keyboard shortcut [Ctrl][Shift][R]. Edit the macro to make the modifications shown to cell A1. Clear the formats from the data, then run your revised macro.

Figure 12-16

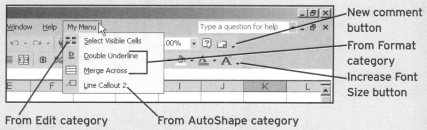

New comment button

From Format category

Increase Font Size button

From Edit category

From AutoShape category

Figure 12-17

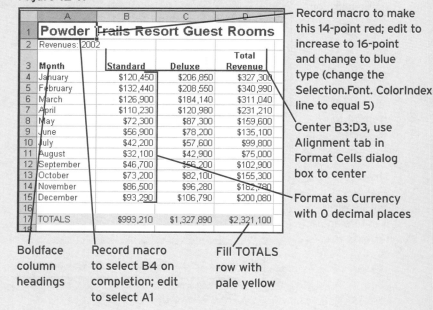

Record macro to make this 14-point red; edit to increase to 16-point and change to blue type (change the Selection.Font. ColorIndex line to equal 5)

Center B3:D3, use Alignment tab in Format Cells dialog box to center

Format as Currency with 0 decimal places

Boldface column headings

Record macro to select B4 on completion; edit to select A1

Fill TOTALS row with pale yellow

Skill Set 13

Skill List

1. Audit formulas
2. Locate and resolve errors
3. Identify dependencies in formulas

Most of the formulas that you create in Microsoft Excel contain cell references. When a formula refers to another cell, you can say it *depends on* that cell. While this interconnected relationship adds power to your worksheets, it also adds complexity. If you build a worksheet that has many "layers" of formulas and references, you will need a way to check them easily.

Excel provides several **auditing** features that can help you analyze your worksheet and formula structure to trace relationships between cells and formulas. You can find all the cells that formulas refer to, or you can locate all the formula cells that use a particular cell.

Worksheet auditing is most useful when your worksheet contains an error and you need to find its source. Excel recognizes several types of errors and helps you identify their cause.

Skill Set 13

Auditing Worksheets

Audit Formulas

Find Cell Dependents

In a complex worksheet, it can be difficult to keep track of the flow of data among cells. For example, a profit formula might use a total expenses figure, which might, in turn, use individual expenses figures, which themselves use values from other cells. This chain effect creates "levels" of dependency. To understand a worksheet's structure and find errors, you will often need to know what cells a formula uses, either directly or indirectly. In such cases, you will find it helpful to **trace**, or find, dependents. A **dependent** is a cell that uses the values in the selected cell(s). For example, if cell B6 contains the formula =B4+B5, cell B6 is a dependent of those cells. You can trace cells that are **direct dependents** of the selected cell (those which use the cell's value in a formula) and those that are **indirect dependents** (which depend on the cell, but only via other cells). The Formula Auditing toolbar lets you find dependents quickly by displaying blue **tracer arrows** between a selected cell and any dependents.

Activity Steps

 open Advertising04.xls

1. If the Formula Auditing Toolbar is not already displayed, click **Tools** on the menu bar, point to **Formula Auditing**, then click **Show Formula Auditing Toolbar**
2. Click cell **B8**
3. Click the **Trace Dependents button** on the Formula Auditing Toolbar
   Blue tracer arrows point to the cells that use the selected cell in its formulas; they are the dependents of cell B8.
4. Click the **Trace Dependents button** on the Formula Auditing Toolbar again
   Another tracer arrow appears, from cell C19 to D19, showing another dependency level.
   See Figure 13-1.
5. Double-click the **blue tracer arrow** between cells B8 and C19
   The cell at the other end of the tracer arrow becomes selected.
   See Figure 13-2.
6. Double-click the **blue tracer arrow** again
7. Verify that cell B8 is selected, click the **Remove Dependent Arrows button** on the Formula Auditing Toolbar to remove the arrow to the indirect dependent of the selected cell
8. Click the **Remove Dependent Arrows button** on the Formula Auditing Toolbar again to remove the arrows to the direct dependents of the selected cell

 close Advertising04.xls

Step 5
Double-clicking a line to change the active cell is especially useful in large worksheets, where dependent cells may not be visible on the screen. This feature can save you a lot of time because the worksheet will automatically scroll to the location of the other cell.

Figure 13-1: Dependent arrows show relationships among cells

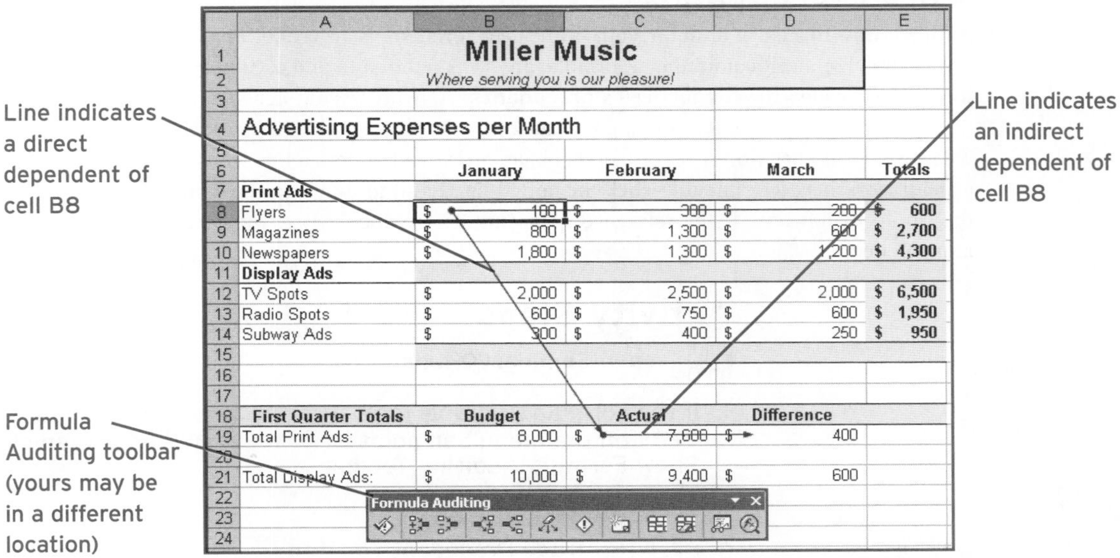

Line indicates a direct dependent of cell B8

Line indicates an indirect dependent of cell B8

Formula Auditing toolbar (yours may be in a different location)

Figure 13-2: Changing the selected cell using the tracer arrow

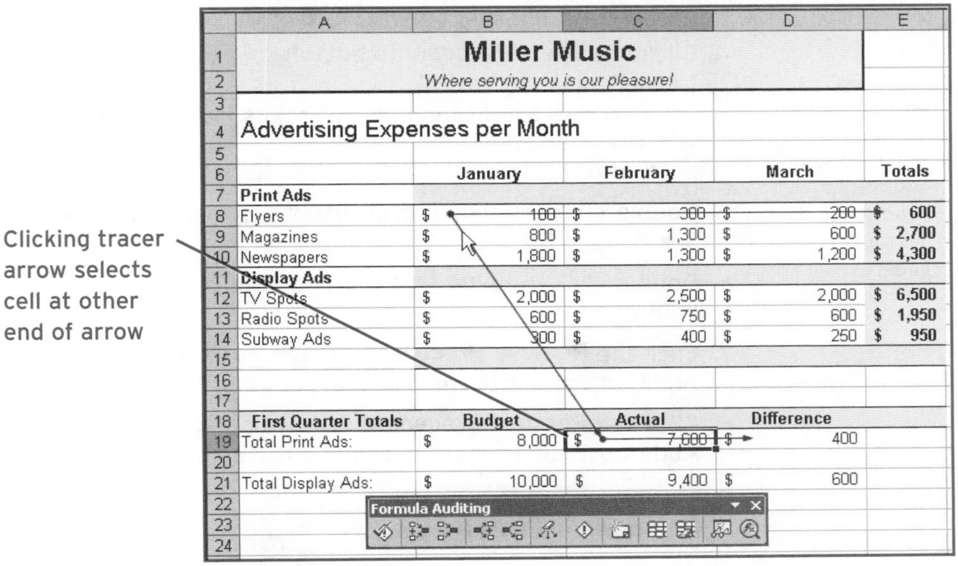

Clicking tracer arrow selects cell at other end of arrow

Skill Set 13

Auditing Worksheets

Audit Formulas

Trace Precedents

Another way to help you audit your worksheet formulas is to **trace**, or find, precedents. For a cell containing a formula, any cells referred to and used in that formula are called the formula cell's **precedents**. As with tracing dependents, tracing precedents is useful in finding the cause of worksheet errors. If a precedent is located in another worksheet or workbook, an arrow with a dotted line leads to a small worksheet icon; double-click the dotted line to go to that location using the Go To dialog box. If the reference is to another workbook, that workbook must be open.

Activity Steps

 open Summary04.xls

1. If the Formula Auditing Toolbar is not already displayed, click **Tools** on the menu bar, point to **Formula Auditing**, then click **Show Formula Auditing Toolbar**

2. Click cell **G17**

3. Click the **Trace Precedents button** on the Formula Auditing toolbar
   Excel displays a blue tracer arrow and outlines the entire range of cells that are precedents of cell G17.

4. Click the **Trace Precedents button** on the Formula Auditing toolbar again
   Tracer arrows appear from the other cells that are precedents of the selected range.
   See Figure 13-3.

5. Double-click the **blue tracer arrow** between cell G7 and G17
   See Figure 13-4.

6. Double-click the **blue tracer arrow** again to move the cell highlight again

7. Click the **Remove Precedent Arrows button** on the Formula Auditing Toolbar to remove the arrows to the indirect precedents

8. Click the **Remove Precedent Arrows button** on the Formula Auditing Toolbar again to remove the arrows to the direct precedents

 close Summary04.xls

Step 4
Each time you click the Trace Precedents button or the Remove Precedent Arrows button , you move to the next level of precedence.

Figure 13-3: Precedent arrows

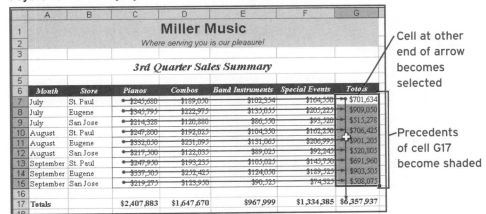

Arrows from indirect precedents of cell G17

Arrows from direct precedents of cell G17

	A	B	C	D	E	F	G
1			**Miller Music**				
2			*Where serving you is our pleasure!*				
3							
4			*3rd Quarter Sales Summary*				
5							
6	*Month*	*Store*	*Pianos*	*Combos*	*Band Instruments*	*Special Events*	*Totals*
7	July	St. Paul	$245,680	$189,050	$102,354	$164,550	$701,634
8	July	Eugene	$345,795	$222,975	$135,055	$205,225	$909,050
9	July	San Jose	$214,328	$120,880	$86,550	$93,520	$515,278
10	August	St. Paul	$247,800	$192,025	$104,350	$162,250	$706,425
11	August	Eugene	$352,050	$231,095	$131,065	$206,995	$901,205
12	August	San Jose	$217,500	$122,035	$89,025	$92,245	$520,805
13	September	St. Paul	$247,950	$193,235	$105,025	$145,750	$691,960
14	September	Eugene	$337,505	$252,425	$124,050	$189,525	$903,505
15	September	San Jose	$219,275	$123,950	$90,525	$74,325	$508,075
16							
17	Totals		$2,407,883	$1,647,670	$967,999	$1,334,385	$6,357,937

Figure 13-4: Changing the selected cell using the tracer arrow

Cell at other end of arrow becomes selected

Precedents of cell G17 become shaded

	A	B	C	D	E	F	G
1			**Miller Music**				
2			*Where serving you is our pleasure!*				
3							
4			*3rd Quarter Sales Summary*				
5							
6	*Month*	*Store*	*Pianos*	*Combos*	*Band Instruments*	*Special Events*	*Totals*
7	July	St. Paul	$245,680	$189,050	$102,354	$164,550	$701,634
8	July	Eugene	$345,795	$222,975	$135,055	$205,225	$909,050
9	July	San Jose	$214,328	$120,880	$86,550	$93,520	$515,278
10	August	St. Paul	$247,800	$192,025	$104,350	$162,250	$706,425
11	August	Eugene	$352,050	$231,095	$131,065	$206,995	$901,205
12	August	San Jose	$217,500	$122,035	$89,025	$92,245	$520,805
13	September	St. Paul	$247,950	$193,235	$105,025	$145,750	$691,960
14	September	Eugene	$337,505	$252,425	$124,050	$189,525	$903,505
15	September	San Jose	$219,275	$123,950	$90,525	$74,325	$508,075
16							
17	Totals		$2,407,883	$1,647,670	$967,999	$1,334,385	$6,357,937

Skill Set 13
Auditing Worksheets

Locate and Resolve Errors
Locate and Resolve Formula Errors

In a complicated worksheet, you may have formulas that contain errors. Excel helps you find and correct those errors. If a cell contains an error that Excel recognizes, you will see a green triangle in the upper left corner of the cell and a code that describes the type of error. See Table 13-1 for a summary of the most common formula errors. See the online help topic "Find and Correct Errors in Formulas" for a more complete description. If you select the cell with the error, you will see a smart tag that you can click to display options for diagnosing and correcting the problem.

Step 1
You can have Excel select each error consecutively by clicking the Error Checking button on the Formula Auditing Toolbar. The Error Checking dialog box offers the same options as the Smart Tag actions menu, and contains Previous and Next buttons to move from one error to another.

Activity Steps

 open Drums04.xls

1. If the Formula Auditing Toolbar is not already displayed, click **Tools** on the menu bar, point to **Formula Auditing**, then click **Show Formula Auditing Toolbar**

2. Click cell I18, which shows #DIV/O!

3. Move the pointer over the **smart tag** ⧫, then, when the smart tag changes to ⧫▾, click once
   See Figure 13-5.

4. In the Smart Tag actions menu, click **Help on this error**

5. Read the instructions, then click the Help window **Close button** ✕

6. Click the **Trace Error button** ⧫ in the Formula Auditing toolbar
   As shown in Figure 13-6, tracer arrows show that the formula precedents include cell I16, which is correct, and cell H17, which is blank. This produces an error because division by zero (a cell with no value) is impossible.

7. In the Formula bar, double-click the reference to cell **H17**, click cell **H16** on the worksheet, then click the **Enter button** ☑ on the Formula bar

   close Drums04.xls

Figure 13-5: Smart tag actions menu

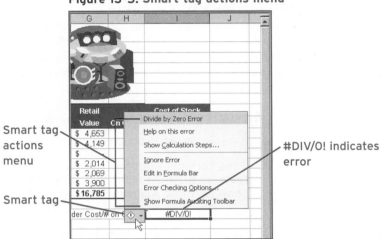

Smart tag actions menu

Smart tag

#DIV/0! indicates error

Figure 13-6: Tracer arrows point out error

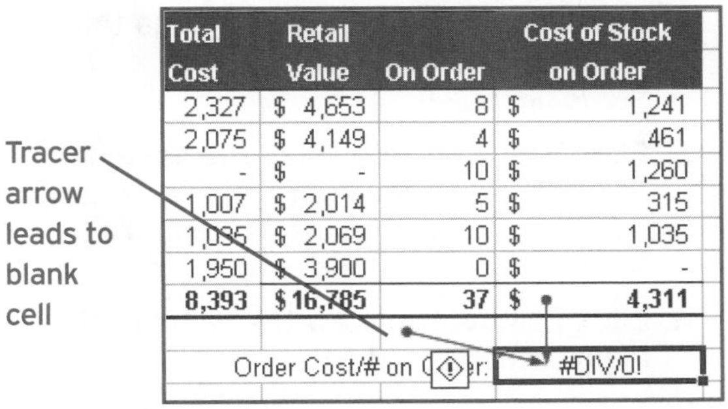

Tracer arrow leads to blank cell

Total Cost	Retail Value	On Order	Cost of Stock on Order
2,327	$ 4,653	8	$ 1,241
2,075	$ 4,149	4	$ 461
-	$ -	10	$ 1,260
1,007	$ 2,014	5	$ 315
1,035	$ 2,069	10	$ 1,035
1,950	$ 3,900	0	$ -
8,393	$ 16,785	37	$ 4,311

Order Cost/# on Order: #DIV/0!

Table 13-1: Common formula errors

error	meaning	example
#VALUE	Incorrect operand, value, or argument	Entering range in a function that requires one value
#DIV/O!	Value is divided by zero, which is impossible	Divisor refers to a blank cell
#NAME	Excel does not recognize text	Name used in formula does not exist
#N/A	Value is not available to formula	Function argument is missing
#REF	Incorrect cell reference	Deleting cells a formula refers to
#NUM	Incorrect formula numbers	Function requires number argument, not text

Skill Set 13
Auditing Worksheets

Identify Dependencies in Formulas
Locate Dependencies in Formulas

In a complex worksheet, your formulas may become long and difficult to analyze. The Evaluate Formula dialog box lets you step through the formula levels to help you understand the formula's structure. You can click the Evaluate button to display the results of a function or a function argument; clicking Evaluate repeatedly cycles through the levels of your formula so you can analyze each one.

Activity Steps

 open Practice03.xls

1. If the Formula Auditing Toolbar is not already displayed, click **Tools** on the menu bar, point to **Formula Auditing**, then click **Show Formula Auditing Toolbar**

2. Click cell I11

3. Click the **Evaluate Formula button** on the Formua Auditing toolbar
   See Figure 13-7.

4. Click **Step In** to view the formula that calculates the highlighted argument
   See Figure 13-8.

5. Click **Step Out** to display the value in cell I11
   The Step In and Step Out buttons are useful when part of a formula refers to another formula. The buttons let you evaluate the parts of a "nested" formula in the order in which they are calculated.

6. Click **Evaluate** to view the value of the second underlined argument, which is FALSE

7. Click **Evaluate** again to display the final value in the cell, which is Below average

8. Click **Close** to close the Evaluate Formula dialog box

 close Practice03.xls

Step 7
To begin the analysis again, click Restart. To proceed directly through the arguments without viewing the underlying formula, do not click Step In.

Figure 13-7: Evaluate dialog box showing "top level" formula

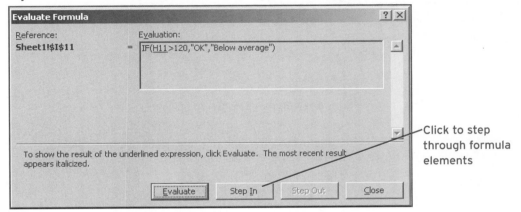

Click to step through formula elements

Figure 13-8: Revealing formula underlying function argument

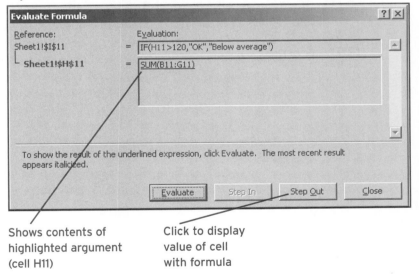

Shows contents of highlighted argument (cell H11)

Click to display value of cell with formula

extra!

Watching formulas
In a large or complex worksheet or workbook, you may want to monitor the status of one or more formulas. Instead of repeatedly clicking the cell to display it, you can keep it visible at all times by using the Watch Window. Click the cell you want to watch, click the **Show Watch Window button** on the Formula Auditing toolbar. Click **Add Watch**, then click **Add** in the Add Watch dialog box. The Watch Window displays the cell address, its value, and its formula. Any changes you make to the formula will be reflected in the window.

Skill Set 13

Auditing Worksheets

Identify Dependencies in Formulas
Remove All Tracer Arrows

Although you can remove the most recent level of tracer arrows using Remove Precedent Arrows and Remove Dependent Arrows buttons, you may want to remove all arrows at once.

Step 3
Tracer arrows are not saved when you close a worksheet.

Activity Steps

 open Budget06.xls

1. If the Formula Auditing Toolbar is not already displayed, click **Tools** on the menu bar, point to **Formula Auditing**, then click **Show Formula Auditing Toolbar**

2. Click cell **E20**

3. Click the **Trace Precedents button** [icon] on the Formula Auditing toolbar four times
   See Figure 13-9.

4. Click the **Remove All Arrows button** [icon] on the Formula Auditing toolbar
   See Figure 13-10.

 close Budget06.xls

Figure 13-9: All precedents' arrows displayed

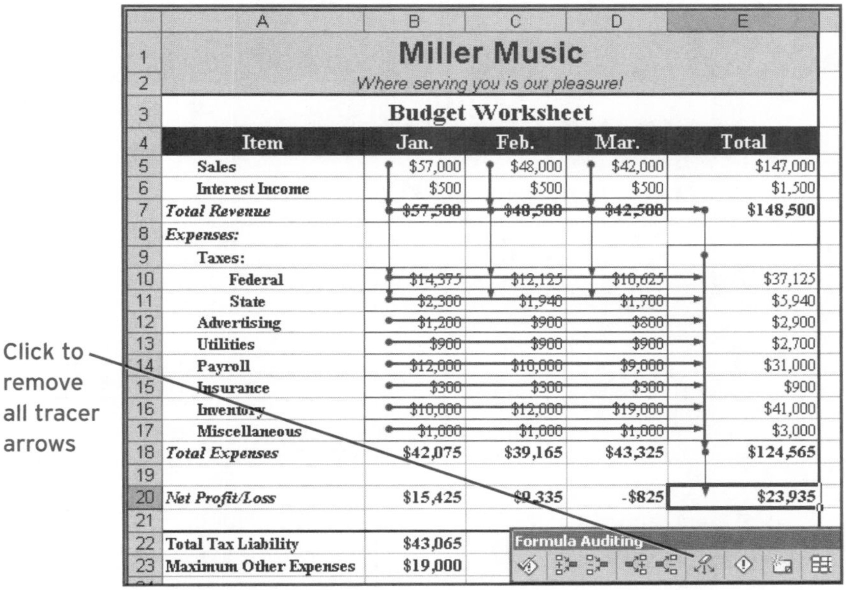

	A	B	C	D	E
1		**Miller Music**			
2		*Where serving you is our pleasure!*			
3		**Budget Worksheet**			
4	**Item**	**Jan.**	**Feb.**	**Mar.**	**Total**
5	Sales	$57,000	$48,000	$42,000	$147,000
6	Interest Income	$500	$500	$500	$1,500
7	*Total Revenue*	$57,500	$48,500	$42,500	$148,500
8	*Expenses:*				
9	Taxes:				
10	Federal	$14,375	$12,125	$10,625	$37,125
11	State	$2,300	$1,940	$1,700	$5,940
12	Advertising	$1,200	$900	$800	$2,900
13	Utilities	$900	$900	$900	$2,700
14	Payroll	$12,000	$10,000	$9,000	$31,000
15	Insurance	$300	$300	$300	$900
16	Inventory	$10,000	$12,000	$19,000	$41,000
17	Miscellaneous	$1,000	$1,000	$1,000	$3,000
18	*Total Expenses*	$42,075	$39,165	$43,325	$124,565
19					
20	*Net Profit/Loss*	$15,425	$9,335	-$825	$23,935
21					
22	Total Tax Liability	$43,065			
23	Maximum Other Expenses	$19,000			

Click to remove all tracer arrows

Formula Auditing

Figure 13-10: Worksheet without precedents' arrows

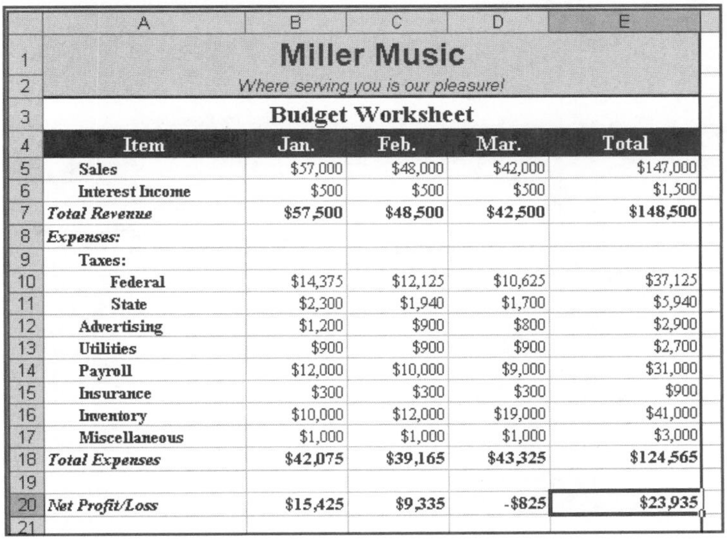

	A	B	C	D	E
1		**Miller Music**			
2		*Where serving you is our pleasure!*			
3		**Budget Worksheet**			
4	**Item**	**Jan.**	**Feb.**	**Mar.**	**Total**
5	Sales	$57,000	$48,000	$42,000	$147,000
6	Interest Income	$500	$500	$500	$1,500
7	*Total Revenue*	$57,500	$48,500	$42,500	$148,500
8	*Expenses:*				
9	Taxes:				
10	Federal	$14,375	$12,125	$10,625	$37,125
11	State	$2,300	$1,940	$1,700	$5,940
12	Advertising	$1,200	$900	$800	$2,900
13	Utilities	$900	$900	$900	$2,700
14	Payroll	$12,000	$10,000	$9,000	$31,000
15	Insurance	$300	$300	$300	$900
16	Inventory	$10,000	$12,000	$19,000	$41,000
17	Miscellaneous	$1,000	$1,000	$1,000	$3,000
18	*Total Expenses*	$42,075	$39,165	$43,325	$124,565
19					
20	*Net Profit/Loss*	$15,425	$9,335	-$825	$23,935
21					

Skill Set 13

Auditing Worksheets

Target Your Skills

 Sales04.xls

1 Locate and resolve the errors in cells B13 and B17 so that the results appear as in Figure 13-11. (*Hint*: For the error in cell C17, examine the range names.) Then display the tracer arrows shown to each cell's precedents and dependents. Remove all tracer arrows.

Figure 13-11

	A	B	C	D	E	F
1		**Miller Music**				
2		*Where serving you is our pleasure!*				
3						
4		**Current Sales of New Items**				
5						
6	**New Items**	**Qty Sold**	**Sales Price**	**Cost**	**Net Income**	
7	CDs	75,000	$13.99	$7.00	$524,250.00	
8	Records	42,336	$12.95	$5.95	$296,352.00	
9	Audio tapes	58,204	$9.95	$3.95	$349,224.00	
10	Blank tapes	15,467	$2.00	$0.50	$23,200.50	
11	T-shirts	1,897	$15.00	$2.00	$24,661.00	Formula Au
12	Posters	1,352	$7.95	$2.95	$6,760.00	
13	**TOTAL**	194,256			$1,224,447.50	
14						
15				**Range Names**		
16	Average income per item	$	6.30	Cost	='New Items'!$D$7:$D$12	
17	Average Sales Price	$	10.31	Net_Income	='New Items'!$E$7:$E$12	
18				Qty_Sold	='New Items'!$B$7:$B$12	
19				Sales_Price	='New Items'!$C$7:$C$12	
20				Total_Income	='New Items'!$E$13	
21				Total_Quantity	='New Items'!$B$13	

 Tickets04.xls

2 See Figure 13-12. Use the Step In button in the Evaluate Formula dialog box to evaluate the formula in cell F11. Use the Smart Tag action menu, the Formula Auditing toolbar, and tracer arrows to locate and resolve the problem in cell F21.

Figure 13-12

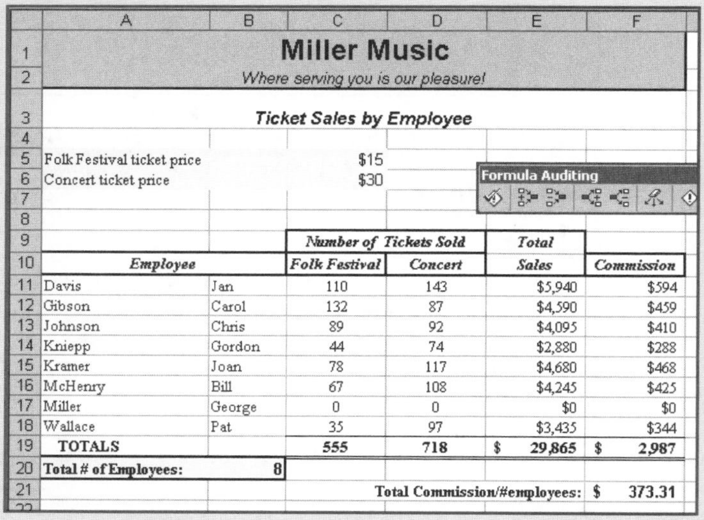

	A	B	C	D	E	F
1			**Miller Music**			
2			*Where serving you is our pleasure!*			
3			*Ticket Sales by Employee*			
4						
5	Folk Festival ticket price		$15			
6	Concert ticket price		$30		Formula Auditing	
7						
8						
9			**Number of Tickets Sold**		**Total**	
10		**Employee**	**Folk Festival**	**Concert**	**Sales**	**Commission**
11	Davis	Jan	110	143	$5,940	$594
12	Gibson	Carol	132	87	$4,590	$459
13	Johnson	Chris	89	92	$4,095	$410
14	Kniepp	Gordon	44	74	$2,880	$288
15	Kramer	Joan	78	117	$4,680	$468
16	McHenry	Bill	67	108	$4,245	$425
17	Miller	George	0	0	$0	$0
18	Wallace	Pat	35	97	$3,435	$344
19	**TOTALS**		555	718	$ 29,865	$ 2,987
20	**Total # of Employees:**	**8**				
21					Total Commission/#employees:	$ 373.31

Skill Set 14

Skill List

1. Use subtotals with lists and ranges
2. Define and apply filters
3. Add group and outline criteria to ranges
4. Use data validation
5. Retrieve external data and create queries
6. Create extensible markup Language (XML) Web queries

An Excel spreadsheet lets you analyze lists of data. A **list** consists of labeled columns and rows of organized data. When information is in list format, you can use the Excel Data menu commands to work with it.

You can **sort**, or reorder, the information based on the contents of any text or numeric column. You can also subtotal numeric list information to view selected group totals, or **filter** a list to display only selected information. Lists that have the same information in more than one record (for example, a list with several sales rep names listed with many sales transactions) can easily be grouped and used to view summary information.

If other people will enter data in your list, you may want to use **data validation** to limit cell entries to acceptable values.

Though you can type list data into Excel, you will often want to import it from another source, such as the World Wide Web. You can use one of the Web queries Excel supplies or create your own query to a Web site or Extensible Markup Language **(XML)** data (a universal file standard), on the Web or on a network. You can also share list information by saving files in XML format to send to others.

Skill Set 14
Summarizing Data

Use Subtotals with Lists and Ranges
Sort a List by One Field

An Excel **list** consists of columns and rows of related information with column labels in the first row. For example, a customer list might consist of names and addresses along with related sales information for each customer. A **field** is a column that contains one type of information (such as Last Name); a **record** is a row that contains the information for one item (such as one customer). See Table 14-1 for guidelines to follow when creating a list. You can **sort**, or change the order of, list data. An **ascending sort** orders column information beginning with the letter A or the number 0; a **descending sort** starts with the letter Z or with the highest number in a column.

Step 1
Excel recognizes your range as a list when it has formatted column labels and contains no blank rows or columns within the range.

Activity Steps

 open Packages01.xls

1. Click any cell in the list range **A5:H14**

2. Click **Data** on the menu bar, then click **Sort**

3. Click the **Sort by list arrow**, then click **Customer**

4. Click the **Ascending option button** (if it's not already selected)
   See Figure 14-1.

5. Click **OK**
   The list is sorted by Customer name. In a list, the data in each row stays together when you sort it.

6. Click **Data** on the menu bar, then click **Sort**

7. Click the **Sort by list arrow**, then click **Revenue**

8. Click the **Descending option button**, then click **OK**
   See Figure 14-2.

 close Packages01.xls

Figure 14-1: Specifying an ascending sort by Customer

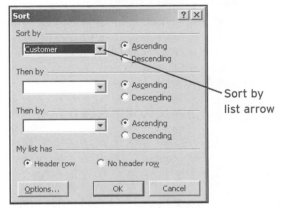

Sort by list arrow

Figure 14-2: List sorted in descending order by Revenue amount

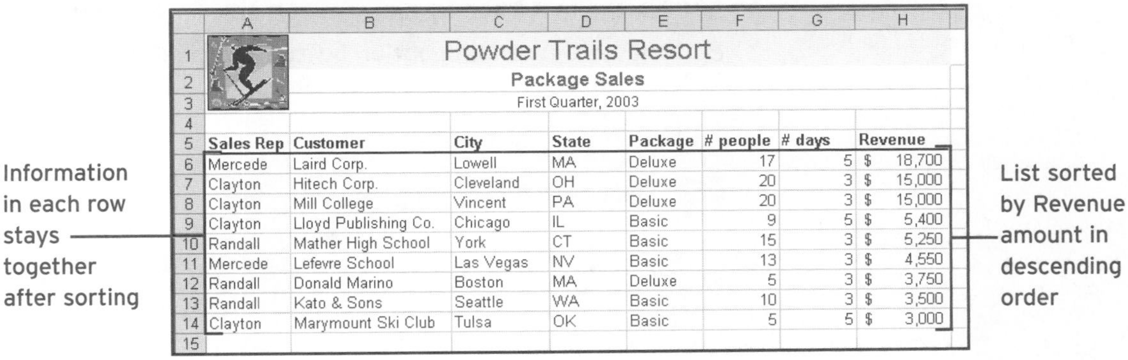

Information in each row stays together after sorting

List sorted by Revenue amount in descending order

	A	B	C	D	E	F	G	H
1			Powder Trails Resort					
2			Package Sales					
3			First Quarter, 2003					
4								
5	Sales Rep	Customer	City	State	Package	# people	# days	Revenue
6	Mercede	Laird Corp.	Lowell	MA	Deluxe	17	5	$ 18,700
7	Clayton	Hitech Corp.	Cleveland	OH	Deluxe	20	3	$ 15,000
8	Clayton	Mill College	Vincent	PA	Deluxe	20	3	$ 15,000
9	Clayton	Lloyd Publishing Co.	Chicago	IL	Basic	9	5	$ 5,400
10	Randall	Mather High School	York	CT	Basic	15	3	$ 5,250
11	Mercede	Lefevre School	Las Vegas	NV	Basic	13	3	$ 4,550
12	Randall	Donald Marino	Boston	MA	Deluxe	5	3	$ 3,750
13	Randall	Kato & Sons	Seattle	WA	Basic	10	3	$ 3,500
14	Clayton	Marymount Ski Club	Tulsa	OK	Basic	5	5	$ 3,000
15								

TABLE 14-1: Guidelines for creating lists

elements	guideline
Worksheet	Only include one list on a worksheet
Labels	Format column headings to help Excel separate them from the data
Rows	Do not include blank rows or columns within a list; do separate your list from other worksheet data using blank columns and rows
Spaces	Don't add extra spaces in data that could interfere with sorting
Columns	Place the same type of data in each column

Skill Set 14
Summarizing Data

Use Subtotals with Lists and Ranges
Sort a List by Two Fields

Excel lets you sort list information by more than one field at once. For example, you might want to sort a Supplier list by State, then within each state by the amount you ordered. You can think of each sort field as a level: the first sort field is the highest level, followed by the second field, which sorts data within each of the higher-level fields.

Step 5
You can specify up to three sort levels in a list.

Activity Steps

 open Packages02.xls

1. Click any cell in the range **A5:H14**

2. Click **Data** on the menu bar, then click **Sort**

3. Click the **Sort by list arrow**, then click **Package**

4. Click the **Ascending option button** (if it's not already selected)

5. Click the first **Then by list arrow**, then click **Revenue**

6. Click the **Descending option button** for the Revenue sort field
   See Figure 14-3.

7. Click **OK**
   See Figure 14-4.

 close Packages02.xls

Figure 14-3: Sorting by two fields

Sort within each Package type in descending order by Revenue

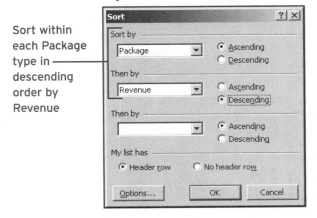

Figure 14-4: List sorted by Package type and Revenue

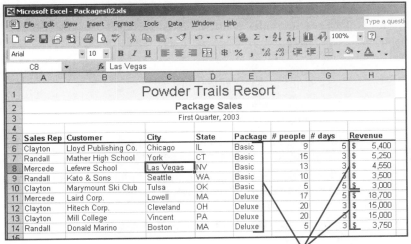

List sorted first by Package then in descending order by Revenue within each Package type

extra!

Sorting by multiple fields

When you sort by multiple fields, make sure that the first sort field occurs often enough to make the other sort levels meaningful. For example, if your list has many entries for each state, then you can sort by name or amount within each state. But if you only have one entry for each state, don't make State your first sort field; it won't group data in a way that is easily sorted on another field.

Skill Set 14
Summarizing Data

Use Subtotals with Lists and Ranges
Subtotal a List

An Excel list usually contains numeric data, such as budget or invoice amounts. You can use the Excel **subtotal** feature to calculate the total of each budget category or each region's invoices. Before you subtotal a list, you must first sort the list by the same category you want to subtotal. For example, if you want to calculate the amount of sales per store, first sort the list by the Store Name field. When Excel subtotals a list, it also outlines the list by placing brackets on the left side of the data. You can click the plus and minus signs on the brackets to hide or display list data. (For more information on outlining, see the Group and Outline Structured Data activity later in this skill set.)

Activity Steps

 open Tours03.xls

Step 5
You can subtotal a list using one of 11 standard functions, including COUNT, MAX, MIN, and AVERAGE. You can subtotal lists with nonnumeric data using the COUNT function.

1. Click anywhere in the list range **A4:E12**, click **Data** on the menu bar, then click **Sort**

2. Click the **Sort by list arrow**, click **Course Title**, make sure the **Ascending option button** is selected, then click **OK**

3. Click **Data**, then click **Subtotals**

4. Click the **At each change in list arrow**, then click **Course Title** (if it's not already selected)

5. Click the **Use function list arrow**, then click **Sum** (if it's not already selected)

6. In the Add subtotal to list, click to place a check next to **Total Revenue** (if it's not already selected)

7. Check the **check boxes** shown in Figure 14-5 (if they're not already selected), then click **OK**
   See Figure 14-6.

8. Click **Data**, click **Subtotals**, then click **Remove All**

 close Tours03.xls

Figure 14-5: Subtotaling the list by Course Type using the SUM function

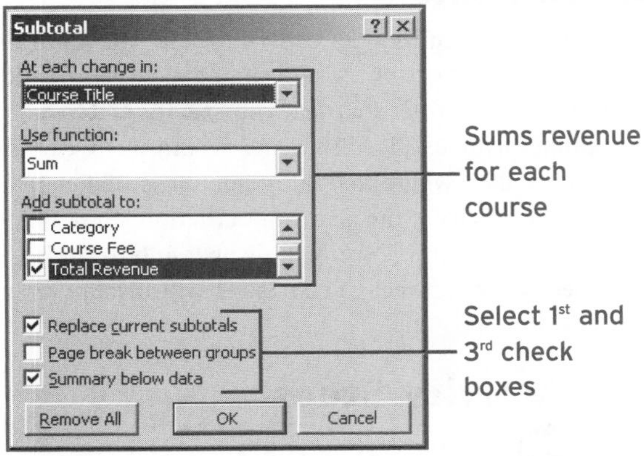

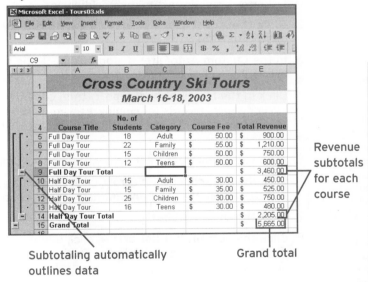

Sums revenue for each course

Select 1st and 3rd check boxes

Figure 14-6: Subtotaled list

Revenue subtotals for each course

Grand total

Subtotaling automatically outlines data

extra!

Modifying a subtotaled list

To modify a subtotaled list, click in the list, click **Data** on the menu bar, click **Subtotals**, then select a different function or field name. To display more than one subtotal (for example, a subtotal and an average of the same field), deselect the **Replace current subtotals check box**. To make subtotals stand out, click **Format**, click **Autoformat**, then choose a format with contrasting subtotal lines.

Skill Set 14
Summarizing Data

Define and Apply Filters
Create a Custom Filter

In a long Excel list, it can be difficult to view only the data you want. Excel lets you **filter** lists to display only a **subset**, or portion, of the data. In addition to AutoFilter, you can use a custom filter that lets you specify **criteria**, or conditions, you want the program to use in displaying records. For example, you might want to display only data where the Sales amount is higher than a certain number. You can also specify more than one criterion for a field: if you specify AND between the two criteria, Excel will display only records that meet both criteria. If you specify OR between them, Excel will display records that meet either criterion.

Step 4
To display all records for a field after a custom filter, click its AutoFilter list arrow, then click All. If you have filtered on more than one field, click Data on the menu bar, point to Filter, then click Show All. To clear all AutoFilter arrows, click Data on the menu bar, point to Filter, then reselect AutoFilter.

Activity Steps

 open Wages01.xls

1. Click **Data** on the menu bar, point to **Filter**, then click **AutoFilter**
   List arrows appear next to each field name.

2. Click the **AutoFilter list arrow** next to **Hourly Wage**, then click **(Custom)**

3. In the Custom AutoFilter dialog box, click the **Hourly Wage list arrow**, then click **is greater than**

4. Click in the top right box, type 7, then click **OK**
   Excel displays records for employees who make over $7 an hour. The Hourly Wage list arrow is blue, indicating that an AutoFilter is in effect.

5. Click the **Department list arrow**, then click **(Custom)**

6. Click the **Department list arrow**, click **equals** (if it's not already selected), click the **top right list arrow**, then choose **Housekeeping**

7. Click the **Or option button**

8. Click the **bottom left list arrow**, click **equals**, click the **bottom right list arrow**, then click **Front Desk**
   See Figure 14-7.

9. Click **OK**
   Excel displays employees who make more than $7 per hour and who work in either Housekeeping or at the Front Desk.
   See Figure 14-8.

 close Wages01.xls

Figure 14-7: Specifying two criteria using Or

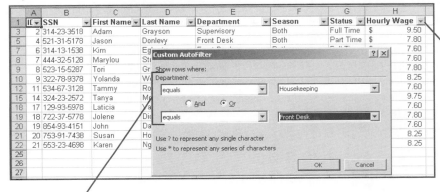

Current AutoFilter will be in addition to Hourly Wage filter

Displays rows where Department is Housekeeping or Front Desk

Figure 14-8: List filtered on two fields

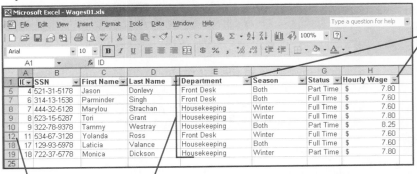

Blue arrows indicate sort on two fields

Blue row numbers indicate filter is in effect

Employees who work in Housekeeping or at Front Desk and who make more than $7.00 per hour

extra!

Using wildcards in a custom filter
You can use the wildcard characters * and ? in the Custom AutoFilter dialog box. Use * to represent any number of characters and use ? to represent any one character. To display all records beginning with the letter c, you could create a filter where "Last Name is equal to C*".

Skill Set 14
Summarizing Data

Define and Apply Filters
Create an Advanced Filter

While AutoFilter is useful for many types of data, it does not let you specify more complex criteria. An **advanced filter** lets you have three or more criteria for one field. In an advanced filter, you place criteria on the worksheet in a range above the list. Then in the Advanced Filter dialog box, you indicate the **criteria range**, which is the location where Excel should look for the criteria when filtering the list range. In the criteria range, you place criteria for AND conditions (where both criteria are true) on the same row, and criteria for OR conditions (where one criterion or the other is true) on different rows.

Activity Steps

 open Wages02.xls

1. Right-click the **row 1 heading**, click **Insert**, then press **[F4]** twice to repeat the action and insert another 2 rows

2. Right-click the **row 4 header**, click **Copy**, right-click the **row 1 header**, then click **Paste**

3. Click cell **E2**, type **Housekeeping**, click cell **H2**, type **>7**
   You have created a criteria range in A1:H2, asking Excel to display only employees who are in Housekeeping *and* who make more than $7 an hour.

4. Click anywhere in the list range (A4:H27), click **Data** on the menu bar, point to **Filter**, then click **Advanced Filter**

5. Verify that the List Range box contains **$A$4:$H$27**, click the **Criteria range box**, then drag across the range **$A$1:$H$2** on the worksheet
   See Figure 14-9.

6. Click **OK**, then press **[Ctrl][Home]** to select cell A1
   See Figure 14-10.

7. Click cell **H2**, then move its contents to cell **H3** to create an Or condition

8. Click anywhere in the list range A4:H27, click **Data** on the menu bar, point to **Filter**, then click **Advanced Filter**

9. Verify that the List range box contains **$A$4:$H$27** and modify the Criteria range to read **$A$1:$H$3**, click **OK**, then press **[Ctrl][Home]**
   The list displays those who work in Housekeeping or who earn more than $7 per hour.

 close Wages02.xls

Step 8
After you filter your data using Advanced Filter, you don't need to display all data again before your next filter. Excel will automatically refilter the entire list. But if you need to clear all filters, click Data on the menu bar, point to Filter, then click Show All.

Figure 14-9: Creating an Advanced Filter

Inserted rows for criteria

Criteria range

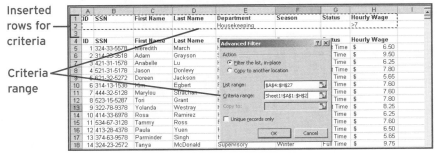

Figure 14-10: Results of Advanced Filter with AND criteria

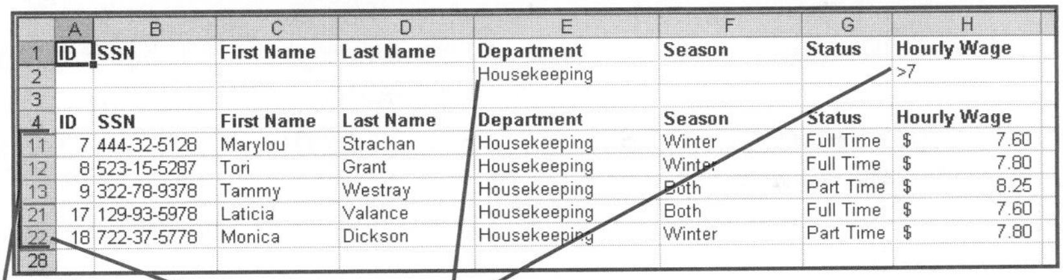

	A	B	C	D	E	F	G	H
1	ID	SSN	First Name	Last Name	Department	Season	Status	Hourly Wage
2					Housekeeping			>7
3								
4	ID	SSN	First Name	Last Name	Department	Season	Status	Hourly Wage
11	7	444-32-5128	Marylou	Strachan	Housekeeping	Winter	Full Time	$ 7.60
12	8	523-15-5287	Tori	Grant	Housekeeping	Winter	Full Time	$ 7.80
13	9	322-78-9378	Tammy	Westray	Housekeeping	Both	Part Time	$ 8.25
21	17	129-93-5978	Laticia	Valance	Housekeeping	Both	Full Time	$ 7.60
22	18	722-37-5778	Monica	Dickson	Housekeeping	Winter	Part Time	$ 7.80
28								

Records that meet above criteria

Blue row numbers indicate filter is in effect

Criteria range specifies Housekeeping employees earning over $7 per hour

Skill Set 14
Summarizing Data

Add Group and Outline Criteria to Ranges
Group and Outline Structured Data

An Excel list is an example of structured data: it contains column labels in the top row, followed by data rows containing similar types of information. If a list spans several screens or pages, it can be difficult to get the overall "picture" of your data. Excel lets you **group and outline** your list data to show summary information and hide detail. You can use the Hide and Show Details buttons to hide or expand rows or columns in any data grouping. The Row and Column Level buttons will hide or show particular levels on the entire worksheet.

Step 2
To use grouping and outlining, your data must be organized like a list, with no blank columns or rows. You may need to sort your data as well, so that rows with similar types of information are next to each other.

Activity Steps

 open Marketing01.xls

1. **Click anywhere in the list range A5:I13**
   The data is in list format: it has formatted column headings, no blank rows, and has similar data (sales figures) in each column.

2. **Click Data on the menu bar, point to Group and Outline, then click Auto Outline**
   Excel displays the worksheet in outline view, as shown in Figure 14-11.

3. **Click the Hide Detail button** ▬ **(above column E), which then becomes the Show Detail button**

4. **Click the Show Detail button** ✚ **above column E**

5. **Click the Row Level 1 button** ①
   See Figure 14-12.
   Only Level 1, summary information, is visible.

6. **Click the Row Level 2 button** ② **to redisplay the row details**

7. **Click the Column Level 1 button** ①

 close Marketing01.xls

Figure 14-11: Worksheet with outlining brackets

Row Level
1 button

Outline
indicators
for
columns

Outline
indicators
for rows

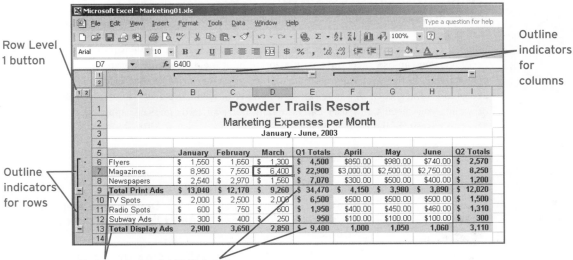

Data organized with totals for
each media type and quarter

Figure 14-12: Row summary information only

Column
Level 1
button

Hide Detail
buttons

Row Level 1
button
displays
highest
level
(Total)
rows

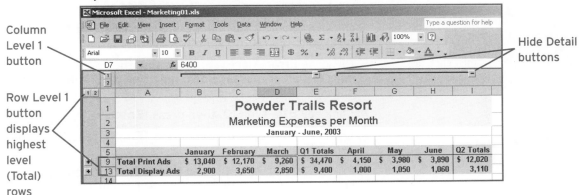

Skill Set 14
Summarizing Data

Use Data Validation
Validating Entered Data

When you create an Excel list, you usually want each column to contain a particular type of data. For example, a Price column should contain only values under $100, or a Customer column should contain only text. To help ensure list accuracy, you can use Excel **data validation** to limit the data users enter in any cell or range. In the Data Validation dialog box, you enter **criteria** that describe acceptable values, such as a date range, a number of decimal places, or a series of values you specify. If a user enters invalid data, an error message appears. You can customize the error message.

Activity Steps

 open Reservations01.xls

1. Select the range **B14:B18**, click **Data** on the menu bar, then click **Validation**; click the **Allow list arrow**, then click **Whole number**

2. Click the **Minimum box**, type **1**, click the **Maximum box**, type **10**, then click **OK**

3. Select the range **H14:H18**, click **Data** on the menu bar, then click **Validation**

4. Click the **Allow list arrow**, then click **List**

5. Click the **Source box**, type **Check, Charge, Not Paid**, then compare your screen to Figure 14-13

6. Click the **Error Alert tab**, make sure the check box is selected, click the Error message box, type **Use the list arrow to enter allowable entries**, then click **OK**

7. Click cell **B14**, type **10**, then press **[Enter]**

8. Click cell **H14**, type **15**, then press **[Enter]**, read the error message, then click **Retry**

9. Press **[Delete]**, click the **cell H14 list arrow**, compare your screen to Figure 14-14, click **Check**, then press **[Enter]**
   When you have limited data to a specific list, users can either use the list arrow or type an acceptable entry. The AutoComplete feature will enter the rest of the item after the user types enough characters to distinguish it from other acceptable entries.

 close Reservations01.xls

Step 9
If the acceptable values are listed on the worksheet, you can click the Collapse dialog box button [ ], drag across the range to enter it, then click the Redisplay dialog box button [ ].

Figure 14-13: Entering data validation criteria

Selected cells will only allow values from this list

Click to remove validation criteria from selected cells

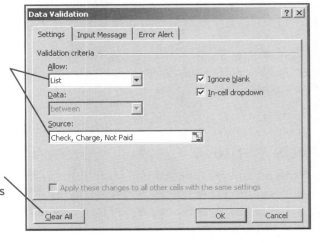

Figure 14-14: Limiting data to a list of entries

Cell entries limited to values in list

	A	B	C	D	E	F	G	H
1			**Powder Trails Resort**					
2			Banquet to Benefit the Hogarth Food Pantry					
3			Reservations					
4					Order			
5	**Name**	**Table #**	**# Adults**	**Veg.**	**Fish**	**Beef**	**Amount**	**Payment**
6	Bonwell, Irene	2	4	1	3		$ 200	Check
7	Muzzati, Dana	2	2		1	1	$ 100	Charge
8	Omura, Samuel	2	2		1	1	$ 100	Check
9	Lemonde, Francois	2	2		1	1	$ 100	Check
10	Nunez, Robert & Cheryl	3	2	1		1	$ 100	Charge
11	Gordon, Judy & Maxwell	3	1		1		$ 50	Check
12	Frazier, Michael	3	2	1	1		$ 100	Not Paid
13	Myers, Frederick	3	2		1	1	$ 100	Check
14		10						Check
15								Charge
16								Not Paid
17								
18								
19	**Totals**		17	3	9	5	$ 850	
20								

Value limited to numbers between 1 and 10

extra!

Adding screen tips
You can also add screen tip messages that users see after they select cells. Select a cell or range, click **Data** on the menu bar, click **Validation**, then click the **Input Message tab**. Select the **Show input message when cell is selected check box**, type a message title and a message, then click **OK**. You can use screen tips to tell users the type of data they should enter.

Skill Set 14

Summarizing Data

Retrieve External Data and Create Queries

Import Web Data Using an Existing Web Query

Just as you retrieve data from an external database, you can use a **query**, a reusable request saved in .iqy file format, to retrieve data from the World Wide Web. You can use the saved query to **refresh**, or update, imported Web data, also called the **external data range**. You can use one of the existing Excel queries to retrieve a variety of information. *In order to perform all the steps in this lesson, your computer needs to have access to the World Wide Web.*

Step 4
In the Import Data dialog box, you can click Properties to set refresh options; you can have Excel refresh the query every time you open the file or after a specified number of minutes.

Activity Steps

1. With a blank workbook open, click **Data** on the menu bar, point to **Import External Data**, then click **Import Data**

2. In the Select Data Source dialog box, click **MSN MoneyCentral Investor Currency Rates.iqy**
   See Figure 14-15.

3. Click **Open**
   See Figure 14-16.

4. Click **OK**
   The name of each country and its currency unit appears in column A in the form of a **hyperlink**, specially formatted text you can click to display more information on the subject from the Web.

5. Click the **Save button** 🖫 on the Standard toolbar, navigate to the location where your Project Files are saved, change the filename in the File name text box to **Currency01**, then click **Save**

6. If you do not see the External Data toolbar, right-click any toolbar, then click **External Data**
   See Figure 14-17.

7. Click the **Refresh Data button** 🛈 on the External Data toolbar, then watch the Status bar at the bottom of the screen
   Text and a rotating globe appear briefly to inform you that the program is going to the Web to refresh the worksheet data. *When you import Web data, check the Web page's legal statement to ensure that you are not violating any copyright restrictions.*

8. Click cell **A2, Click here to visit MSN MoneyCentral Investor**, scroll to the bottom of the page, click **Terms of Use**, then click the **Close button** ✕ on your browser window

    close Currency01.xls

Figure 14-15: Queries supplied with Microsoft Excel

My Data Sources folder opens automatically

Your dialog box contents may differ

Select this query

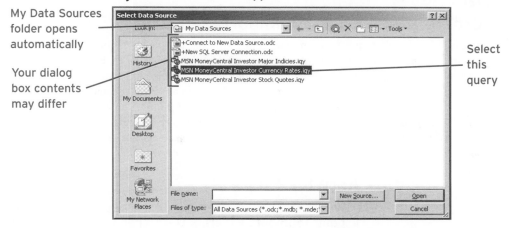

Figure 14-16: Specifying the destination of imported data

Retrieved data will be placed in the range starting in cell A1

Existing worksheet is default destination

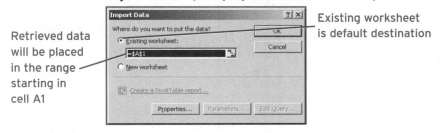

Figure 14-17: Imported data saved in Excel workbook format

External Data toolbar lets you manipulate and refresh data

Your query results will differ because data is updated regularly

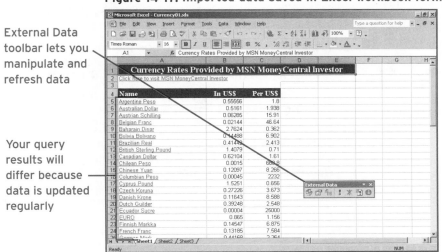

Skill Set 14

Summarizing Data

Retrieve External Data and Create Queries

Create a Web Query to Import Web Data

You can create a **Web query**, a reusable request with an .iqy file extension, to import information from the Internet and the World Wide Web into an Excel worksheet. You might use a Web query to obtain updated information on stocks, the weather, or the books a company currently publishes on a particular subject. As with any query, you can **refresh**, or update, the imported information at any time. *To perform all the steps in this lesson, your computer needs access to the World Wide Web. If the Web page in this lesson has become unavailable since this book was printed, use any other Web address, such as www.course.com.*

Activity Steps

1. With a blank workbook open, click **Data** on the menu bar, point to **Import External Data**, then click **New Web Query**
   The New Web Query dialog box displays your current home page.

2. In the Address box, select the current address if it isn't already highlighted, then type **http://weather.noaa.gov/weather/ current/KASE.html**
   See Figure 14-18.
   Because this service is not on the World Wide Web, you do not need to type www in the address.

3. Click **Go**

4. Move the pointer over any yellow arrow box and observe the ScreenTip and the heavy outline that surrounds the area

5. Click the yellow arrow box next to **Current Weather Conditions**
   See Figure 14-19.

6. In the New Web Query dialog box toolbar, click the **Save Query button** 📇, navigate to the location where your Project Files are saved, change the filename to **Weather Query**, then click **Save**

7. In the New Web Query dialog box, click **Import**, make sure the **Existing worksheet option button** is selected, then click **OK**
   The current weather conditions for Aspen, Colorado, appear.

8. Click **File** on the menu bar, click **Save**, navigate to the location where your Project Files are stored, change the filename to **Weather01**, then click **Save**
   When you import Web data, be sure to check the Web page's legal statement so that you are not violating any copyright or usage restrictions.

Step 1

If your browser is Internet Explorer, you can also right-click any Web page, then click Export to Microsoft Excel, which starts a new Excel session and creates a new Web Query.

 close Weather01.xls

Figure 14-18: Specifying Web address for the query

Type Web address from which you want to import data

Click to display page whose address you typed

Your home page may differ

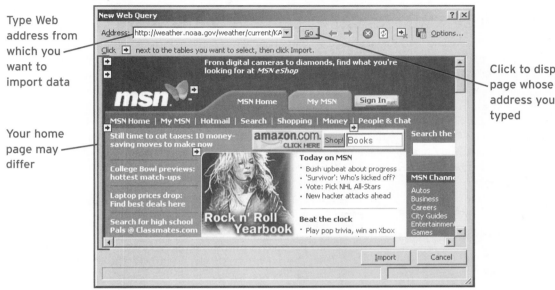

Figure 14-19: Specifying the information to include in the query

Click this arrow to include all page areas

Click any yellow arrow box to include area in query

Yellow arrow box becomes green check box after you click it

Page content will differ depending on when you access this site

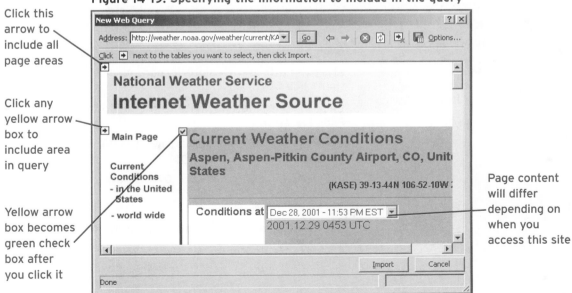

Skill Set 14

Summarizing Data

Retrieve External Data and Create Queries

Use XML to Share Excel Data on the Web

Extensible Markup Language, or **XML**, is a file standard that Web designers and organizations use for structured data, such as the data in Excel spreadsheets. XML is a universal format for sharing data. XML files are text files that can be easily exchanged either over the the Internet or an Intranet. Unlike text files, however, XML files are "marked up" with **tags** that describe the type of data they contain. The files do not contain formatting. Formatting is placed in **stylesheets** that Web developers apply to the XML file. Excel lets you save workbook files in XML format. You cannot see the XML code unless you open the file in a program designed for that purpose, called an **XML parser**, such as the parser in Internet Explorer 5.5.

Activity Steps

 open Media04.xls

1. Click **File** on the menu bar, click **Save As**, click the **Save in list arrow**, then if necessary navigate to the location where your Project Files are stored

2. Click the **Save as type list arrow**, then click **XML Spreadsheet (*.xml)**

3. Select the filename, then type **Media05**
   See Figure 14-20.

4. Click **Save**

5. Start the **Internet Explorer** program, click **File** on the menu bar, then click **Open**

6. Click **Browse**, then navigate to the location where your Project Files are stored

7. Click the **Files of type** list arrow, click **All Files**, click **Media05.xml**, then click **Open**

8. In the Open dialog box, click **OK** to view the XML file in Internet Explorer
   See Figure 14-21.

9. Click the **Close button** ☒ on the Internet Explorer title bar

 close Media05.xls

Step 3
When you save an Excel file in XML format, certain features are lost, including graphic objects, charts, and custom views.

Figure 14-20: Saving a worksheet in XML format

Your save location and file list may differ

XML file type

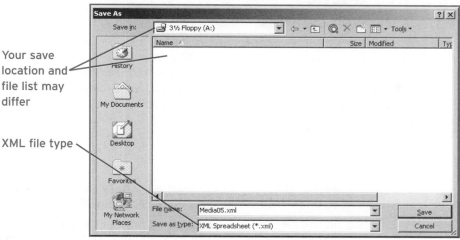

Figure 14-21: XML code for the Media04.xml file

XML code

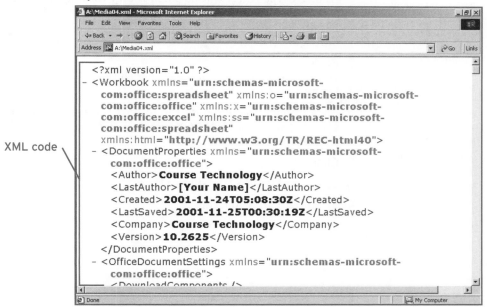

Skill Set 14
Summarizing Data

Create Extensible Markup Language (XML) Web Queries
Create XML Web Queries

You may want to retrieve XML data regularly from the Web or from a network. To do this, you can create a query to an XML file on the Web using the same techniques you would use to query a database file. *Web sites with XML data exist, but it would be difficult to supply a stable Web site that users can access months after this book is published. In this activity, you will create a Web Query to an existing XML file in your Project Files location. The procedure is the same as if you were going to a Web site.*

Step 4
Unlike most Web pages you would view in the New Web Query dialog box, the XML file contains only one arrow, which selects the entire page. You don't need to click the arrow; clicking Import will automatically import the entire page.

Activity Steps

1. With a blank workbook open, click **Data** on the menu bar, point to **Import External Data**, then click **New Web Query**

2. In the Address box of the New Web Query dialog box, type the path to your Project File location, followed by **Providers04.xml**
   For example, if your Project Files are stored on a floppy disk in the A: drive, type A:\Providers04.xml. If they are on your hard drive, designated C: in a folder called Project Files, type C:\Project Files\Providers04.xml.
   See Figure 14-22.

3. Click **Go**
   The XML code appears in the New Web Query window, as shown in Figure 14-23.

4. Click **Import**, making sure the Import Data dialog box has the **Existing worksheet option** selected and cell **$A$1** designated as the destination

5. Click **OK**

6. Save the file as **XML Query.xls**

   close XML Query.xls

Figure 14-22: XML Query

Type path to XML file (normally this would be a Web or intranet site address)

Click to display XML code

Figure 14-23: XML code in New Web Query window

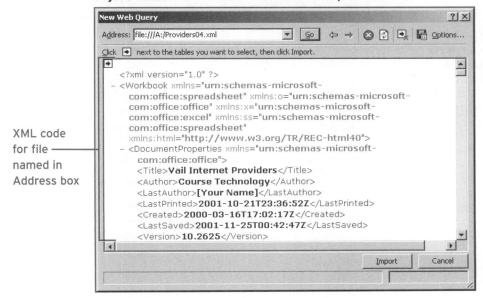

XML code for file named in Address box

Skill Set 14
Summarizing Data

Target Your Skills

 Wages03.xls

1 Sort the list by Department and Last Name in ascending order. Use a Custom Filter to display employees who make more than $6 *and* less than $8. Clear the AutoFilter, then create an Advanced Filter above the data as shown in Figure 14-24. Save the file in XML format as Wages04.xml. Close the file, then open it in your Web browser.

Figure 14-24

	A	B	C	D	E	F	G	H
1	ID	SSN	First Name	Last Name	Department	Season	Status	Hourly Wage
2				>f	Housekeeping	Winter	Full	<7
3								
4	ID	SSN	First Name	Last Name	Department	Season	Status	Hourly Wage
12	10	414-33-6978	Adam	Grayson	Housekeeping	Winter	Full Time	$ 6.25
14	3	421-31-1578	Anabelle	Lu	Housekeeping	Winter	Full Time	$ 6.25
20	12	413-28-4378	Paula	Yuen	Housekeeping	Winter	Full Time	$ 6.50
28								

2 Use a Web Query to import the information in School02.xml from your Project File location, then save the file as School02.xls. Format it as shown in Figure 14-25. Use Data Validation to restrict data entered in cells C2:C13 to the three options that appear in the column, then create the Category subtotals shown. Collapse then expand the outline levels.

Figure 14-25

	A	B	C	D	E
1	Course	Students	Category	Course	Total Revenue
2	Half Day Beginners	45	Adult	30	$ 1,350
3	Full Day Beginners	50	Adult	50	$ 2,500
4	Half Day Intermediate	21	Adult	35	$ 735
5	Full Day Intermediate	28	Adult	55	$ 1,540
6			Adult Total		$ 6,125
7	Half Day Beginners	50	Children	30	$ 1,500
8	Full Day Beginners	46	Children	50	$ 2,300
9	Half Day Intermediate	29	Children	35	$ 1,015
10	Full Day Intermediate	20	Children	55	$ 1,100
11			Children Total		$ 5,915
12	Half Day Beginners	40	Teens	30	$ 1,200
13	Full Day Beginners	30	Teens	50	$ 1,500
14	Half Day Intermediate	22	Teens	35	$ 770
15	Full Day Intermediate	18	Teens	55	$ 990
16			Teens Total		$ 4,460
17	Total	399			$ 16,500
18			Grand Total		$ 33,000
19					

Skill List

1. Create PivotTable reports and PivotChart reports
2. Forecast values with what-if analysis
3. Create and display scenarios

Excel worksheets let you track large amounts of information; Excel analysis tools let you explore data relationships in your worksheets. **What-if analysis** lets you explore how a change in worksheet values affects formula results.

In a long data list with many fields, simple column totals or subtotals only tell part of the story. **PivotTable reports** let you drag list fields in a special table layout to create automatic grouping and totals quickly. **PivotChart reports** let you use the same technique to create charts that summarize your data. These easy-to-use features let you explore data relationships quickly and efficiently.

While changing formula values is a simple type of what-if analysis, chart **trend-lines** help you project data based on past trends. Excel scenarios are another type of what-if analysis. **Scenarios** let you create and save named sets of formula input values so you can apply them to your worksheet and view their effect on formula results.

Skill Set 15
Analyzing Data

Create PivotTable Reports and PivotChart Reports
Create a PivotTable Report

In a long Excel list, it can be difficult to see trends in your data. A **PivotTable report** is an interactive grid that lets you quickly rearrange data fields to combine and analyze list data. For example, you could create a PivotTable report from a long list of sales figures for each sales rep and district, then drag fields to "pivot" that data and see totals for each rep and district. This flexibility makes PivotTable reports a useful analysis tool, especially for long lists of information. The PivotTable and PivotChart Wizard helps you set up a report in three steps.

Step 6
As you drag fields over drop areas, the pointer displays a miniature PivotTable with the current drop area highlighted. For example, if the pointer is over the row area, the leftmost area of the pointer is blue.

Activity Steps

 open Report04.xls

1. Click anywhere within the list range **A7:E29**

2. Click **Data** on the menu bar, then click **PivotTable and PivotChart Report**
   If the Office Assistant appears, click **No, I don't need help now**.

3. In the Step 1 of 3 dialog box, make sure that the **Microsoft Excel list or database** and the **PivotTable option buttons** are selected, then click **Next**

4. In the Step 2 of 3 dialog box, make sure that the list range **$A$7:$E$29** appears in the Range box, then click **Next**

5. In the Step 3 of 3 dialog box, make sure the **New worksheet option** is selected, then click **Finish**
   A new worksheet appears, containing PivotTable **drop areas** surrounded by blue lines and a **PivotTable Field List** showing all of the list fields. The PivotTable toolbar appears on the worksheet.

6. Drag the **Begin Date field** from the Field List to the **Drop Row Fields Here area**, releasing the mouse button when the pointer becomes ↓
   See Figure 15-1.

7. Drag the **Item field** from the Field List to the **Drop Column Fields Here area**

8. Drag the **Amount field** from the Field List to the **Drop Data Items Here area**
   You can see expense totals by date and totals for each expense item.
   See Figure 15-2.

 close Report04.xls

Figure 15-1: Begin Date in row fields area

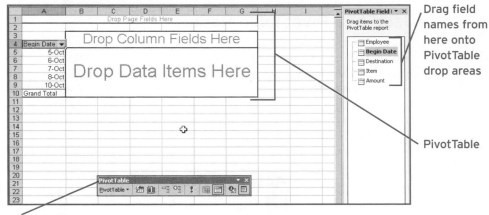

Drag field names from here onto PivotTable drop areas

PivotTable

Your PivotTable toolbar may be in a different position

Figure 15-2: Completed PivotTable

Item field in column area

Begin Date in row area

Amount field in data area

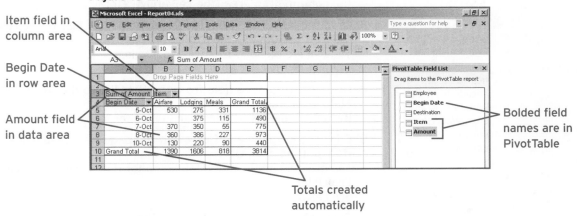

Bolded field names are in PivotTable

Totals created automatically

Skill Set 15
Analyzing Data

Create PivotTable Reports and PivotChart Reports
Modify a PivotTable Report

Once you have created a PivotTable report, you will want to use it to explore relationships in your data, which is the real power of a PivotTable. To do this, you drag fields to row, column, data, and page field "drop areas" and view the results. Excel immediately recalculates the summary information. A **page field** is the area at the top of the PivotTable report where you can place any field to filter the PivotTable data. For example, if you have data for different years, you could place a Year field in the page field area, then select a particular year to show only data for that year.

Activity Steps

 open Report05.xls

1. Drag the **Item field** from the column area on the left side of the PivotTable to any blank worksheet area outside the PivotTable, releasing the mouse button when the pointer becomes

2. Drag the **Destination field** from the row drop area on the left to the **column drop area** (the cell above "Total")

3. Drag the **Item field** from the PivotTable Field List to the **row area** (below the Sum of Amount field)
   You can see the total for each expense item for each city.
   See Figure 15-3.

4. Drag the **Employee field** from the field list to the **Drop Page Fields Here** area
   By default, the PivotTable displays data for all employees.

5. Click the **Employee list arrow** in the page field area, click **Harris**, then click **OK**
   The item and destination information for Harris appears in the PivotTable.
   See Figure 15-4.

6. Click the **Employee list arrow** in the page field area, click **(All)**, then click **OK**

 close Report05.xls

Step 4
In the PivotTable field list window, fields that have already been placed in the PivotTable are boldfaced; unused fields are in light type.

Figure 15-3: Rearranged PivotTable

Item field in row area

Totals for each item by destination

Destination field in column area

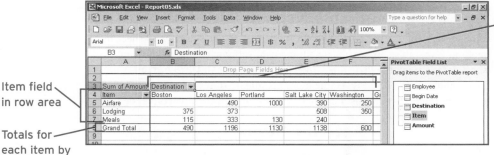

Figure 15-4: Page field filters PivotTable data

Selecting one name shows expenses for only that employee

Employee field in page area

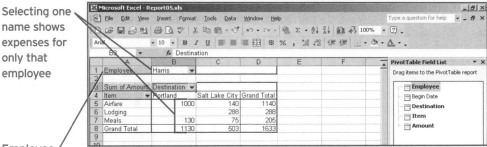

Skill Set 15
Analyzing Data

Create PivotTable Reports and PivotChart Reports
Update a PivotTable Report

While Excel charts automatically reflect changes to the source worksheet information, PivotTables do not update automatically. If you change underlying worksheet data, display the PivotTable, then click the **Refresh Data button** on the PivotTable toolbar. The PivotTable amounts update to include the new information. See Table 15-1 for a summary of the buttons on the PivotTable toolbar.

To remove the Field List from your screen, click the Hide Field List button on the PivotTable toolbar. This button is a toggle, meaning that you click it once to display the Field List and click it again to hide the Field List.

Activity Steps

 open Songbooks01.xls

1. On the PivotTable, notice that the sales total for Educators, Inc. is $1,046.00
   See Figure 15-5.

2. Click the **Sales Data sheet tab**

3. Click cell **H8**

4. Type **15**, then press **[Enter]**

5. Click the **PivotTable sheet tab**, then notice that the Educators, Inc. total has not changed

6. Watch the sales amounts for Educator's Inc., then click the **Refresh Data button** on the PivotTable toolbar
   See Figure 15-6.

 close Songbooks01.xls

Table 15-1: Selected PivotTable toolbar buttons

button	name	use to
	Format Report	Apply one of 21 table and report formats
	ChartWizard	Create a PivotChart report from your PivotTable
	Refresh Data	Update PivotTable report after changing source data
	Field Settings	Change summary function of selected fields
	Show/Hide Field List	Close Field List window

Figure 15-5: PivotTable before editing worksheet

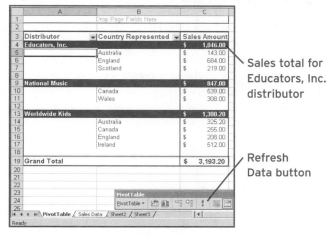

Sales total for Educators, Inc. distributor

Refresh Data button

Figure 15-6: PivotTable after updating

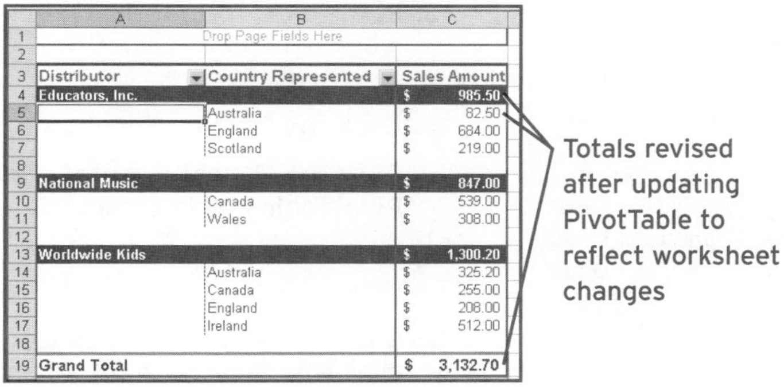

Totals revised after updating PivotTable to reflect worksheet changes

Skill Set 15

Analyzing Data

Create PivotTable Reports and PivotChart Reports

Format a PivotTable Report

The default PivotTable report contains minimal formatting, but you can apply AutoFormats to enhance its appearance. You can choose from **table formats**, which apply shading and fonts, or **report formats** (also called **indented formats**). Indented formats apply shading and fonts and move column fields to the row area; they also indent each row field and show data in a single column. To format PivotTable numbers, you use the Field Settings button on the PivotTable toolbar.

Step 3
To remove all formatting from a PivotTable, click None at the bottom of the AutoFormat dialog box, then click OK. To restore a previous format, click the Undo button immediately after applying a format.

Activity Steps

open Classes01.xls

1. Click any cell inside the PivotTable
    The PivotTable field list appears.

2. Click the **Format Report button** on the PivotTable toolbar
    See Figure 15-7.

3. In the AutoFormat dialog box, scroll down and click the format labeled **Table 2**, click **OK**, then click any PivotTable cell
    See Figure 15-8.

4. Click the **Format Report button** on the PivotTable toolbar

5. Click the **Report 6** AutoFormat, click **OK**, then click any PivotTable cell in column C

6. Click the **Field Settings button** on the PivotTable toolbar, then click **Number**

7. Click **Currency**, verify that the Decimal places box contains 2, click **OK**, then click **OK** again
    See Figure 15-9.

close Classes01.xls

Figure 15-7: PivotTable formats

Format
Report button

Figure 15-8: Table 2 AutoFormat applied

AutoFormat
adds fonts
and fills

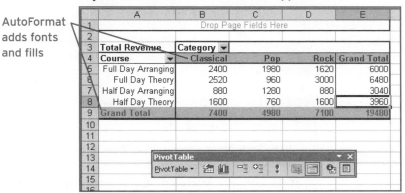

Figure 15-9: Report 6 AutoFormat applied

Row fields
indented

Column
fields move
to row area

Summary
figures
appear in
one column

Numbers
formatted
as currency

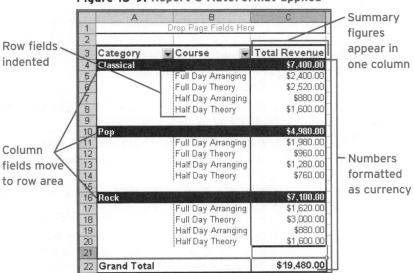

Skill Set 15

Analyzing Data

Create PivotTable Reports and PivotChart Reports

Create and Modify a PivotChart Report

PivotChart reports are useful for creating graphical representations of list data. You can pivot the data the same way you would in a PivotTable report, by dragging fields to different locations to explore data relationships. Like an Excel chart, a PivotChart report has data markers, series, categories, and axes, as well as a field representing each element. It also has a page field area. When you use the Wizard to create a PivotChart report, Excel creates the corresponding PivotTable on a separate sheet. *When you create a PivotTable, carefully check the range that Excel suggests. If there is no space between your worksheet title information and the column headings, the suggested range may be incorrect.*

Step 9
To view a chart of selected series data, click the Course list arrow, click the (Show All) box to deselect it, click one or more of the Course types to select them, then click OK.

Activity Steps

 open Classes02.xls

1. Click **Data** on the menu bar, then click **PivotTable and PivotChart Report**

2. Make sure the **Microsoft Excel list or database option button** is selected, click the **PivotChart report (with PivotTable report) option button**, then click **Next**

3. On the worksheet, drag to select the correct range, **A3:E15**
   If you include the worksheet title or any information outside the list range, the PivotChart report will not appear.
   See Figure 15-10.

4. Click **Next**

5. Make sure the **New worksheet option button** is selected, then click **Finish**

6. Drag the **Type field** to the **Drop Category Fields** Here area at the bottom of the chart area (you may need to move the PivotTable toolbar)

7. Drag the **Course Fee field** to the **Drop Page Fields Here** area

8. Drag the **Total Revenue field** to the **Drop Data Items Here** area

9. Drag the **Course field** to the **Drop Series Fields Here** area (depending on how your system is set up, you may need to move the PivotTable Field List box to the far right in order to view the Drop Series Fields Here area)
   See Figure 15-11.

 close Classes02.xls

Figure 15-10: Selecting the list range

Headings not included in list range

Drag to insert sheet name and correct range reference

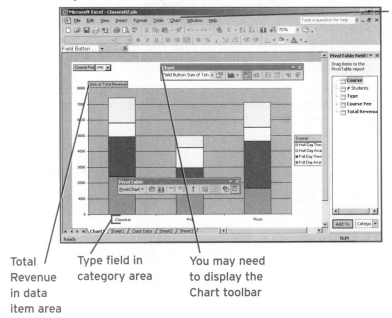

Figure 15-11: Completed PivotChart report

Use Chart type command on Chart menu to choose a different chart type

Total Revenue in data item area

Type field in category area

You may need to display the Chart toolbar

Skill Set 15

Analyzing Data

Forecast Values with What-If Analysis
Create a Trendline

In an Excel chart, you might want to display not only a graphical representation of the data but also of the overall tendency in one or more series. To do this, you can display a **trendline**, which is used to make mathematical predictions about data trends using the principles of **regression analysis**, a statistical measure. When you add a trendline to a chart, Excel uses the data in your selected series and the mathematical formula for the trendline you chose to calculate the trendline position. You can use trendlines to project data levels based on existing trends. A **linear trendline** assumes that the trend will continue at a steady rate. An **exponential trendline** is curved, indicating that the series will increase or decrease at an increasing rate over time. You format a trendline by double-clicking it and selecting options, as you would any chart data series.

Activity Steps

 open Projection01.xls

1. Click the **Lesson Revenue Chart sheet tab**

2. Click **Chart** on the menu bar, then click **Add Trendline**

3. In the Add Trendline dialog box, click the **Type tab** (if it's not already selected), then, under Trend/Regression type, click **Linear** (if it's not already selected)
   See Figure 15-12.

4. Click **OK**

5. Click **Chart** on the menu bar, then click **Add Trendline**

6. In the Add Trendline dialog box, click **Exponential**, then click **OK**
   If the sales increase trend follows the same pattern it did in the first six months, December lesson revenues are projected to be about $37,000. If revenues are expected to increase exponentially, December revenues are projected to be about $43,000.
   See Figure 15-13.

 close Projection01.xls

Step 3
To delete a trendline, select it on the chart, then press [Delete].

Figure 15-12: Choosing a trendline

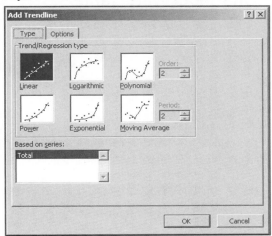

Figure 15-13: Chart showing linear and exponential trendlines

Exponential trendline

Linear trendline

Projected Revenue figures based on previous trend

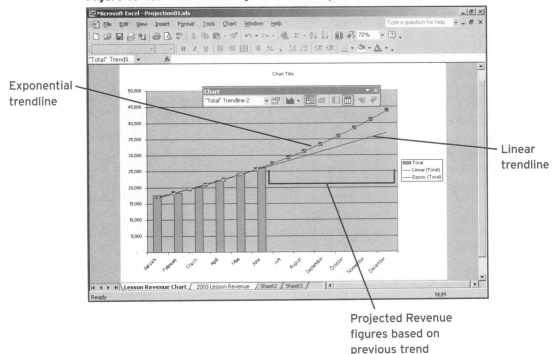

Skill Set 15

Analyzing Data

Forecast Values with What-If Analysis
Create a One-Input Data Table

When performing what-if analysis using Excel, you might want to investigate many different levels of an **input value** (a value that is used in a formula) on a formula result. For example, for a car payment calculation, you might want to substitute many different interest rates in the payment formula and examine the payment for each rate. It would be time-consuming to type each rate in a cell and see its effect on the payment. An Excel **data table** lets you quickly examine the effect of many levels of a changing value (often called a **variable**) on formula results. You create a table that contains the varying rates in a column and the formula, which you usually hide to make the table easier to read. The Data Table command uses the formula to calculate results for each input value level you list.

Step 7
A custom format has four sections representing positive numbers, negative numbers, zero values, and text, separated by semicolons. Entering only the semicolons means that nothing will display for any value, effectively hiding the cell value.

Activity Steps

 open Computer02.xls

1. Click cell **C11** and view its formula, noting that the input value for the interest rate is in cell C8

2. Click cell **F6**, type **6.25%**, press **[Enter]**, type **6.50%**, then press **[Enter]**

3. Drag to select the range **F6:F7**, then drag its fill handle to cell **F17** until the screen tip reads **9.00%**

4. Click cell **F5**, then type **Rate**

5. Click cell **G5**, type **=**, click cell **C11**, click the **Enter button** ☑ on the Formula bar, then compare your screen to Figure 15-14

6. With cell G5 selected, click **Format** on the menu bar, then click **Cells**

7. Click the **Number** tab (if it's not already selected), under Category click **Custom**, double-click the **Type** box, type **;;;** (three semicolons) to indicate no format and hide the formula, then click **OK**

8. Drag to select the range **F5:G17**, click **Data** on the menu bar, then click **Table**

9. Click the **Column input cell box**, click cell **C8** on the worksheet, click **OK**, then click any blank cell
   See Figure 15-15.

 close Computer02.xls

Figure 15-14: Setting up a data table

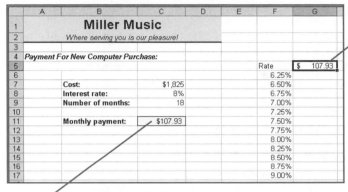

Reference to cell C11 formula; will be hidden

Formula the data table uses to compute values

Figure 15-15: Completed data table

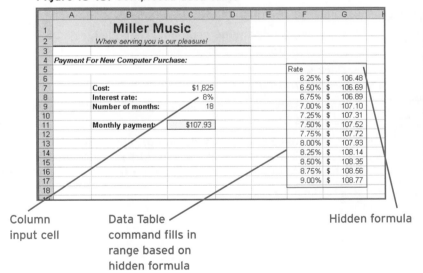

Column input cell

Data Table command fills in range based on hidden formula

Hidden formula

extra!

Creating a two-input data table

To create a two-input data table, place the values of a second variable, such as months, across the top of the table, and place the formula reference at the intersection of the variable 1 column and the variable 2 row (which now reads "Rate"). Select the entire table, click **Data** on the menu bar, then click **Table**. The Row input cell would contain the months cell reference, and the Column input cell would contain the rate cell reference.

Skill Set 15

Analyzing Data

Forecast Values with What-If Analysis
Use Goal Seek

When using trendlines and data tables, you work with given input values in order to calculate an end result in a dependent formula cell. But when you want to determine the input level that will create a known result, you can use an Excel feature called **Goal Seek**. For example, you might want to determine an item's inventory level that will produce a profit of $10,000. With Goal Seek, Excel rapidly substitutes different input values until it reaches the result you want.

Activity Steps

 open Tickets05.xls

1. Click cell **E19**
   Cell E19 is an indirect dependent of the ticket price, $30, in cell C6. You use Goal Seek to see what concert ticket price would produce $35,000 in total sales.

2. Click **Tools**, then click **Goal Seek**

3. Verify that the Set Cell box contains **E19**

4. Click the **To value box** then type **35000**

5. Click the **By changing cells box**, then click cell **C6**
   See Figure 15-16.

6. Click **OK**
   See Figure 15-17.

7. If necessary, drag the Goal Seek Status dialog box so you can see cells C6 and E19

8. In the Goal Seek Status dialog box, click **OK**
   Goal Seek found that a ticket price of $37 would produce your goal of $35,000 in Total Sales. It substitutes these values in the worksheet.

 close Tickets05.xls

Step 6
Instead of replacing worksheet values with the Goal Seek result, you could click Cancel to return to the original values.

Figure 15-16: Goal Seek dialog box

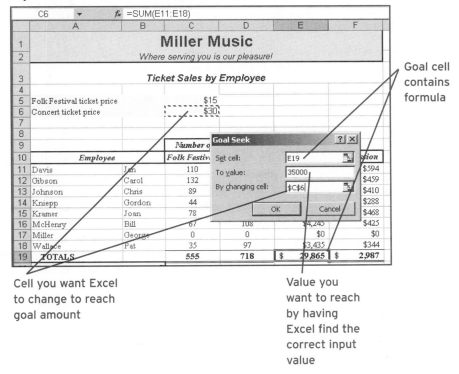

Goal cell contains formula

Cell you want Excel to change to reach goal amount

Value you want to reach by having Excel find the correct input value

Figure 15-17: Goal and modified input value substituted in worksheet

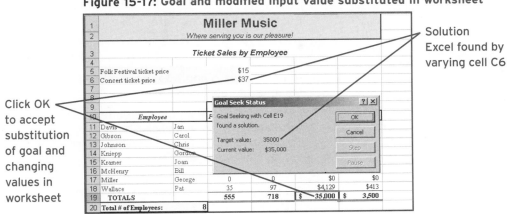

Solution Excel found by varying cell C6

Click OK to accept substitution of goal and changing values in worksheet

Skill Set 15

Analyzing Data

Create and Display Scenarios
Create Two or More Scenarios

In a **what-if analysis**, you can manually change formula input values, then view the effect of your change on formula results. This analysis method, however, can be slow and difficult to manage. To keep track of varying values, you can use an Excel **scenario**, which is a named set of values that Excel will substitute in your worksheet. For example, you might want to create a scenario where revenues are $10,000 per month higher than their current values. You could save this value in a scenario called "High Revenue," then show the scenario in a worksheet to see its effect on profit formula results.

Activity Steps

 open Band02.xls

1. Click cell **E15**, click **Tools**, then click **Scenarios**
   The Formula bar shows that cell E15 calculates the monthly payment based on the amount in B9 and the rate in B18. You will create scenarios for two interest rates and see their effect on the payment.

2. Drag the Scenarios dialog box as necessary so you can see the worksheet range **A1:E15**

3. Click **Add**, click the **Scenario name box**, then type **High Rate**

4. Click the **Changing cells box**, delete any text there, click cell **B18**, see Figure 15-18, then click **OK**
   You now define the new value that this scenario will substitute in cell B19.

5. Type **.12**, see Figure 15-19, then click **OK**

6. Click **Add**, type **Low Rate**, make sure the Changing cells box contains **B18**, then click **OK**

7. In the $B$18 box, type **.05**, then click **OK**

8. Repeat steps 6 and 7 to enter a Scenario called **Current Rate**, using a rate of **.08**

9. In the Scenario Manager dialog box, click **High Rate**, then watch cell E15 as you click **Show**
   The value of the High Rate scenario is inserted in the worksheet, and the formula output in cell E15 changes to reflect the higher rate. *See Figure 15-20.*

10. Click **Low Rate**, click **Show**, click **Current Rate**, click **Show**, then click **Close**

 close Band02.xls

Step 8
The worksheet values will display the values of whichever scenario you last selected.

Skill 3

Create and Display Scenarios

Figure 15-18: Creating a scenario

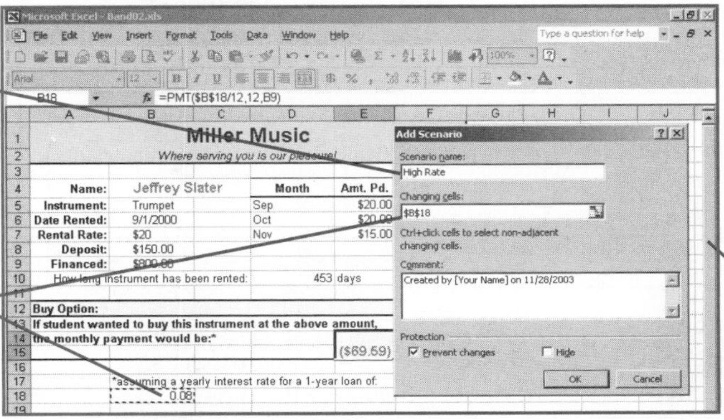

Name for first scenario
First scenario will "try out" a higher value in cell B18
Formula result will be affected by higher interest rate scenario

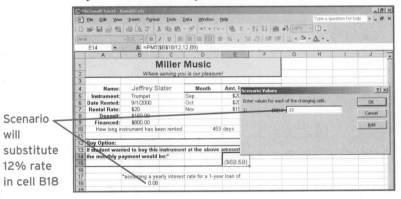

Figure 15-19: Defining a scenario value

Scenario will substitute 12% rate in cell B18

Figure 15-20: Worksheet with High Rate Scenario values displayed

High Rate scenario substituted higher rate and shows effect on payment

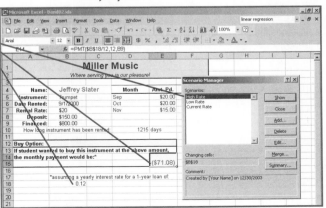

extra!

Creating a scenario summary

Often you will want to see the results of all your scenarios at the same time. In the Scenario Manager dialog box, click **Summary**. Click the **Scenario summary option button**, make sure the Results cells box contains the location of the formula, then click **OK**. Excel creates a new worksheet displaying the results of all scenarios that relate to the formula you indicated.

Skill Set 15
Analyzing Data

Target Your Skills

 Instruction01.xls

1 Create and format the PivotTable shown in Figure 15-21, using the Table 4 AutoFormat. Change the Data Items from "Paid" to "Minutes." Create a PivotChart report from the table, then position the fields using the instructions on the figure.

Figure 15-21

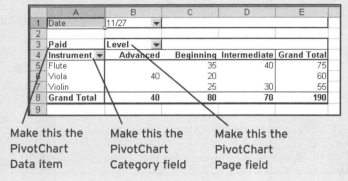

Make this the PivotChart Data item

Make this the PivotChart Category field

Make this the PivotChart Page field

 Budget07.xls

2 On the Projection chart, click the Total Revenue series, then create an Exponential trendline. Create a Linear trendline for Total Expenses series. Double-click the Exponential trendline and select a heavier line weight. On the Budget worksheet, create the three scenarios for cell B5 shown in Figure 15-22.

Figure 15-22

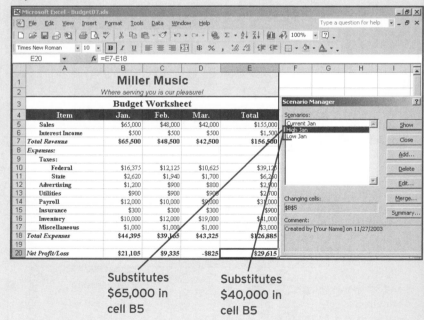

Substitutes $65,000 in cell B5

Substitutes $40,000 in cell B5

Skill Set 16
Workgroup Collaboration

Skill List

1. Modify passwords, protections, and properties
2. Create a shared workbook
3. Track, accept, and reject changes to workbooks
4. Merge workbooks

Working collaboratively on spreadsheets used to be a laborious undertaking. You could distribute workbook copies on a floppy disk, then examine each co-worker's changes and type them into your master. Like all Microsoft Office programs, Microsoft Excel is designed to help you work efficiently in a workgroup.

In a shared work environment, it is important to think about the types of information you want to share with users. Sensitive payroll information, for example, should be available only to those who have approval to access it. Excel lets you protect cells, worksheets, and entire workbooks, depending on your needs. You can hide information and use passwords to customize the amount of information available to others.

When you work with many shared documents, it is often helpful to catalog information by using document properties.

You can share workbooks to solicit feedback and changes from other users, using either a shared file on a central file server or multiple copies of the same shared workbook. Then you can keep track of feedback and accept or reject suggested changes. You can also merge user changes into one master copy, then choose which to accept or reject.

Skill Set 16
Workgroup Collaboration

Modify Passwords, Protections, and Properties

Protect Worksheet Cells

While workbook sharing can speed your work, it also offers two challenges: protecting confidential information and preventing unauthorized changes. You might not want all users to see all your data, formulas, or worksheets, or you might want them to see data but not change it. Excel protection commands let you **hide** information from view and **lock** cells to prevent changes. Locking and hiding only take effect if you also **protect** the worksheet from changes using the Protection command on the Tools menu. By default, Excel locks all worksheet cells. In an unprotected workbook, you are not aware of this. But you can unlock any cells you want, such as an area reserved for data entry. See Table 16-1 for other hiding and protecting options.

Step 3
To hide a worksheet formula, click the cell containing the formula, click Format on the menu bar, click Cells, click the Protection tab, then select the Hidden check box. As with cell locking, formulas are hidden only if you then protect the worksheet using the Protection command on the Tools menu.

Activity Steps

 open Helicopters03.xls

1. Drag to select the range **B7:D7**, press and hold down **[Ctrl]**, then select the range **B11:D11**

2. Click **Format** on the menu bar, click **Cells**, then click the **Protection tab**

3. Click the **Locked check box** to remove the check mark and unlock the selected cells
   See Figure 16-1.

4. Click **OK**

5. Click **Tools** on the menu bar, point to **Protection**, then click **Protect Sheet**

6. Click to select the **Protect worksheet and contents of locked cells check box** (if it's not already selected)
   You don't need to enter a password. Other users, however, will still be able to unprotect the sheet.

7. Click **OK**

8. Click cell **B11**, type **110**, then press **[Enter]** to edit the unlocked cell

9. Click cell **B14** (which is still locked), press any key, then read the message that appears
   See Figure 16-2.

10. Click **OK**

 close Helicopters03.xls

Figure 16-1: Unlocking selected cells

Removing
check mark
unlocks
selected cells

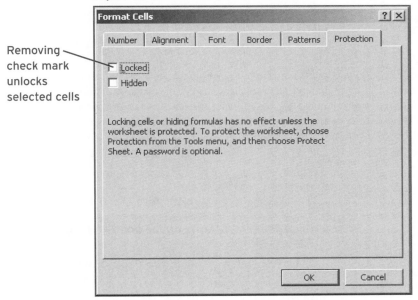

Figure 16-2: Attempting to modify a locked cell

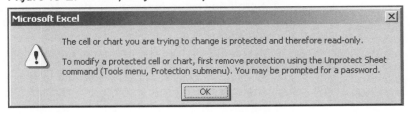

TABLE 16-1: Selected options for hiding and protecting

to	click
Hide a worksheet	Format/Sheet/Hide
Hide a row	Format/Row/Hide
Hide a column	Format/Column/Hide
Hide a formula	Format/Cells/Protection tab, select Hidden, click OK

Skill Set 16

Workgroup Collaboration

Modify Passwords, Protections, and Properties

Protect Worksheets

Excel lets you protect an entire worksheet from changes by others. You can also assign a **password**, a confidential sequence of letters and/or numbers that will unprotect the sheet. Password-protecting a sheet blocks unauthorized users from using locked cells. (By default, all worksheet cells are locked; you can unlock them using the Protection tab in the Format Cells dialog box.) *But be sure to keep track of any passwords you assign. If you lose a password, you will not be able to use the worksheet.* If you want finer control over the types of changes users can make, you can allow or prevent use of specific worksheet features.

Step 3
You must type passwords exactly as they were created, including upper- and lower-case letters. Excel passwords can contain up to 255 letters, numbers, or characters. For added security, use a combination of letters and numbers.

Activity Steps

 open Wages04.xls

1. Click **Tools** on the menu bar, point to **Protection**, then click **Protect Sheet**

2. Click to place a check in the **Protect worksheet and contents of locked cells check box** (if it's not already selected)

3. In the Password to unprotect sheet box, type **bluedog**
   Excel masks the characters you type with asterisks as added protection.

4. Scroll down the feature list, click to place a check mark next to **Use AutoFilter**, compare your screen to Figure 16-3, then click **OK**

5. In the Confirm Password dialog box, type **bluedog**, then click **OK**

6. Click any worksheet cell, press any letter or number key, read the message shown in Figure 16-4, then click **OK**

7. Click the **Department list arrow**, then click **Front Desk**

8. Click **Tools** on the menu bar, point to **Protection**, then click **Unprotect sheet**

9. Type **bluedog**, then click **OK**

 close Wages04.xls

Figure 16-3: Allowing access to selected worksheet features

Password masked with asterisks

Allows users to use AutoFilter lists

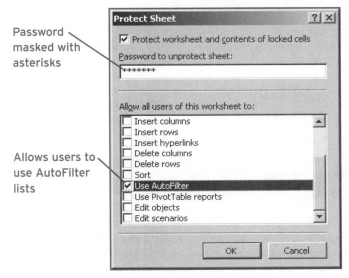

Figure 16-4: Worksheet protection message

Skill Set 16
Workgroup Collaboration

Modify Passwords, Protections, and Properties
Protect Workbooks

When you share your workbooks with others, Excel lets you assign varying protection levels. You can protect entire workbooks to prevent others from opening or editing them or changing their structure.

Activity Steps

 open Bikes03.xls

1. Click **File** on the menu bar, click **Save As**

2. On the Save As dialog box toolbar, click **Tools**, then click **General Options**

3. In the Password to open box, type **icebox**, then press **[Tab]** twice

4. In the Password to modify box, type **redhouse**

5. Compare your screen to Figure 16-5, click **OK**, reenter **icebox**, click **OK**, then reenter **redhouse** in the next two dialog boxes

6. Click the **Save in list arrow**, then navigate to the location where your Project Files are stored, if it is not already visible

7. In the File name text box, edit **Bikes03.xls** to read **Bikes04.xls**

8. Click **Save**, then click the **Close Window button** ⊠ on the menu bar

9. Click the **Open button** 🗁 on the Standard toolbar, double-click **Bikes04.xls**, in the Password dialog box shown in Figure 16-6, type **icebox**, press **[Enter]**, type **redhouse**, then press **[Enter]**
   See Figure 16-7.

 close Bikes04.xls

Step 9
Be sure to type passwords exactly as you entered them, including upper- and lower-case letters, or the workbook will not open. Write down your passwords and keep them in a secure location.

Figure 16-5: Setting workbook passwords

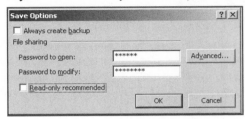

Figure 16-6: Using a password to open a workbook

Type **icebox**

Figure 16-7: Opened workbook after entering passwords

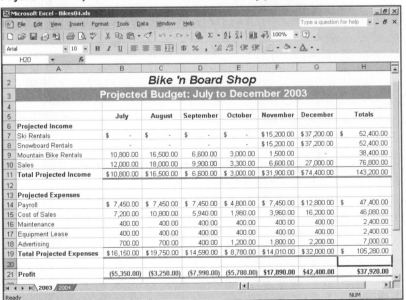

Skill Set 16
Workgroup Collaboration

Modify Passwords, Protections, and Properties
Protect Workbook Elements

Instead of protecting an entire workbook from all changes, you can protect particular aspects of the workbook, such as its structure, window size, and position. When you protect a workbook's *structure*, users cannot add, delete, move, rename, or insert worksheets. When you protect a workbook's *windows*, the workbook window is the same size every time you open it. To prevent others from deleting workbook protection, you can enter a password.

Activity Steps

 open Reservations02.xls

1. Click **Tools** on the menu bar, point to **Protection**, then click **Protect Workbook**

2. In the Protect Workbook dialog box, make sure there is a check next to **Structure**, then click to place a check mark next to **Windows**

3. Click the **Password box**, type **apple**, compare your screen to Figure 16-8, then click **OK**

4. Type **apple**, then click **OK**
   The title bar only displays Minimize, Maximize, or Close buttons for the program. There is no extra set of buttons for the workbook.

5. Right-click any **sheet tab**, and note that the worksheet commands are unavailable
   See Figure 16-9.

6. Click **Tools**, point to **Protection**, click **Unprotect Workbook**, type **apple**, then click **OK**

 close Reservations02.xls

Step 4
To assign a password to a shared workbook, you must first unshare the workbook. You learn more about workbook sharing in the next lesson.

Figure 16-8: Protecting workbook elements

Figure 16-9: Workbook with protected structure and windows

Sheet manipulation commands not available

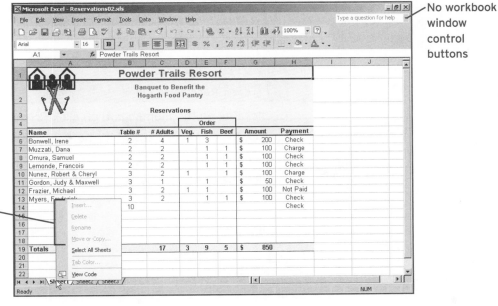

No workbook window control buttons

Skill Set 16

Workgroup Collaboration

Modify Passwords, Protections, and Properties

Modify Workbook Properties

Every Excel workbook has **properties**, which include identifying features such as the author and when it was created and last modified. Excel updates some properties automatically, such as the modification date, every time you save a file. You can set some properties, including the Author and Company, and add detailed information about the document that will help others who might use your workbook later. Some properties apply to all workbooks you open in Excel, while others apply only to an individual workbook. Companies that keep file libraries for employees to share on an intranet or the Internet can use properties to help users find and organize files.

If you are working on a shared computer on a network, you may not have permission to change Excel or workbook properties. Check with your technical resource person.

Step 1
You can also display the Properties dialog box from the Tools menu in the Open and Save As dialog boxes. At the Windows desktop, you can right-click any filename, then click Properties.

Activity Steps

 open Rentals05.xls

1. Click **File** on the menu bar, then click **Properties**

2. Click the **Summary tab** (if it's not already selected)

3. Click the **Category box**, then type **Forecasts**

4. Click the **Comments box**, then type Q1 **Rental and Profit Projections**
   See Figure 16-10.

5. Click **OK**

 close Rentals05.xls

Figure 16-10: Properties dialog box

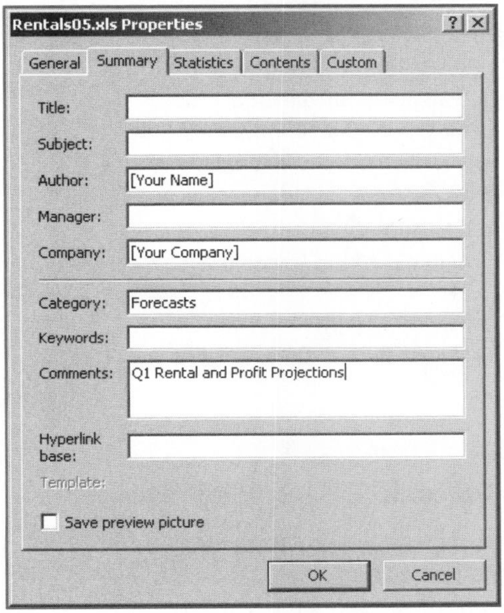

extra!

Viewing properties
You can also view selected properties for any document in the Open or Save dialog box. Click **File** on the menu bar, click **Open** or click **Save As**, click the **Views list arrow** on the dialog box toolbar, then click **Properties**. The properties of any filename you click in the dialog box will appear in the Preview pane.

Skill Set 16
Workgroup Collaboration

Create a Shared Workbook
Create Workbooks for Shared Use

Shared workbooks offer users a way of working together on the same project. For example, you may have a financial analysis worksheet where various accounting employees contribute and update different pieces of data, such as payables or receivables. You can resave any workbook as a shared workbook, then place it on a network for others to access. See Table 16-2 for a summary of features that you cannot change after you save a workbook as shared. Also, if you want to track changes by other users later on, be sure Change tracking is turned on before saving it as a shared workbook. (Change tracking is covered in the next lesson.)

Be sure you are working on a copy of the Statement02.xls file in case you want to repeat this activity. Saving a workbook in shared format automatically overwrites the original shared workbook.

Step 4
After you save a workbook as shared, you can use the Save As command on the File menu to save it to a network server, but not a Web server.

Activity Steps

 open Statement02.xls

1. Click **Tools** on the menu bar, click **Share Workbook**, then click the **Editing tab** if it's not already selected

2. Click to select the **Allow changes by more than one user at the same time. This also allows workbook merging. check box**
   See Figure 16-11.

3. Click **OK**

4. In the dialog box that asks if you want to continue by saving the workbook, click **OK**
   See Figure 16-12.

 close Statement02.xls

TABLE 16-2: Features to set before sharing a workbook

graphics	Web	data & analysis	formatting & layout
Charts	Hyperlinks	Scenarios	Conditional formats
Pictures		Outlines & subtotals	Merged cells
Drawing objects		PivotTable Reports	Cell block changes
		Data validation	Delete sheets

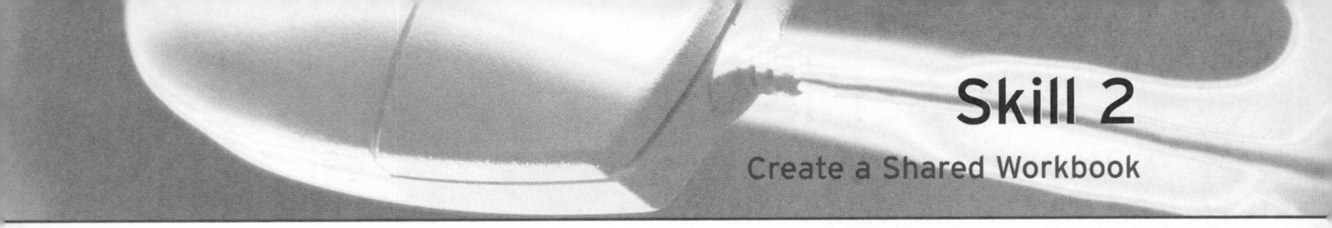

Figure 16-11: Saving a workbook as shared

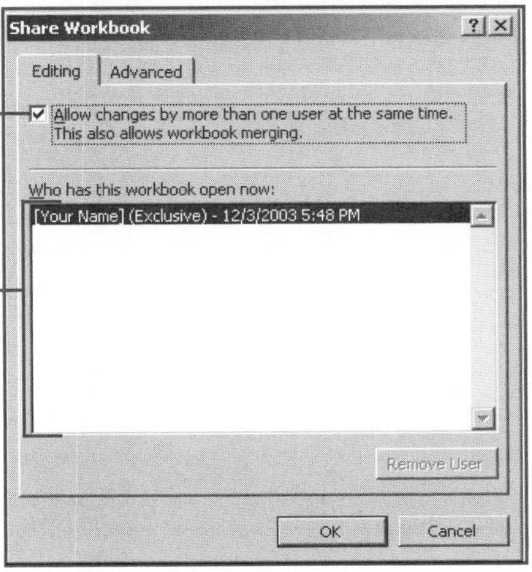

Select to create shared workbook

Lists people using this workbook now

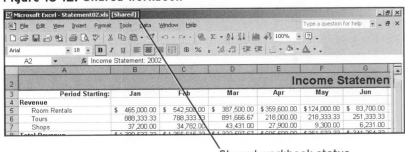

Figure 16-12: Shared workbook

Shared workbook status appears in title bar

Sharing workbooks

After you save a workbook as shared and place it on a network server, others can open the workbook, change it, then save it. All users have their own settings for viewing, filtering, and printing the workbook. When a user saves, the shared workbook is automatically upated with changes others have made. If your changes conflict with changes another user has made to the same cell, Excel opens a conflict resolution dialog box, in which you indicate changes you want to keep.

Skill Set 16

Workgroup Collaboration

Track, Accept, and Reject Changes to Workbooks

Track Worksheet Changes

When sharing workbooks with others, it is often helpful to automatically **track**, or keep a record of, changes that each person makes to a workbook. Tracked changes are highlighted on the worksheet with a different color representing each user. You can display a list of tracked changes that Excel creates on a separate worksheet called a **change history**. You can also decide which changes to accept and reject, either individually or in a dialog box that will display each change for your evaluation. When you turn on change tracking, Excel automatically resaves the workbook as shared.

If you want to repeat the steps in the activity, be sure you are working on a copy of the Party03.xls file, because you must save your changes for change tracking to take effect.

Step 8
The History sheet tab will disappear after you save your workbook again, but the workbook is still tracking changes. Reopen the Track Changes dialog box, deselect the When option, then select List changes on a new sheet again to redisplay the sheet.

Activity Steps

 open Party03.xls

1. Click **Tools** on the menu bar, point to **Track Changes**, then click **Highlight Changes**

2. In the Highlight Changes dialog box, click to select **Track changes while editing. This also saves your workbook.** to share your workbook

3. Click the **When option** to deselect it, then make sure the **Who option** is deselected and reads **Everyone**
   See Figure 16-13.

4. Click to select the **Highlight changes on screen** (if it's not already selected), click **OK**, then click **OK** again
   To appear in the change history, changes must first be saved.

5. Click cell **C9**, type **10**, press **[Enter]**, then click the **Save button** 🖫 on the Standard toolbar

6. Point to cell **C9**, then view the screen tip

7. Click **Tools** on the menu bar, point to **Track Changes**, then click **Highlight changes**

8. Click to select **List changes on a new sheet**, then click **OK**
   See Figure 16-14.

   close Party03.xls

Figure 16-13: Setting change tracking

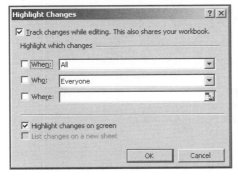

Figure 16-14: Change History sheet

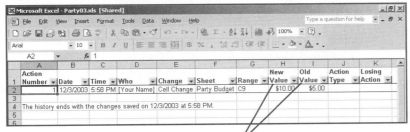

Change history sheet
shows new and old values

extra!

Learning more about change tracking

Change history does not record formatting changes. You can specify that you want to track changes only in a particular range if you select the **Where option** in the Highlight Changes dialog box, click the **Where box**, then drag to select the range. To set the number of days to track changes, click **Tools** on the menu bar, click **Share Workbook**, click the **Advanced tab**, then, under **Track changes**, set the number of days.

Skill Set 16

Workgroup Collaboration

Track, Accept, and Reject Changes to Workbooks

Review, Accept, and Reject Changes

If you activate change tracking when you save a workbook for sharing, you can review user changes to accept or reject each one. To have Excel automatically display a dialog box with each change for your evaluation, you specify that you want to see all changes "not yet reviewed." The dialog box summarizes the change, its author, and when the change was made. After you have accepted or rejected all changes, you cannot review them again, but you can still view them on the Change History worksheet.

If you want to repeat this activity, make sure you are working on a copy of the Holiday02.xls file, because you can only accept or reject changes once.

Step 7
Remember that Excel erases change history items older than the number of days in effect the last time you saved the workbook. For example, if you are keeping 10 days of change history and you open the workbook after 30 days, you'll be able to view the changes from 30 days before, but when you close the workbook, the history from 11 to 30 days is deleted.

Activity Steps

 open Holiday02.xls

1. Click **Tools** on the menu bar, point to **Track Changes**, then click **Accept or Reject Changes**
   The Select Changes to Accept or Reject dialog box opens.

2. In the When box, make sure **Not yet reviewed** is selected, then click **OK**
   See Figure 16-15.

3. Click **Accept**
   See Figure 16-16.

4. Click **Reject**

5. Accept the remainder of the changes in the workbook, then click the **Save button** 🖫 on the Standard toolbar

6. Click **Tools** on the menu bar, point to **Track Changes**, then click **Highlight Changes**

7. Under Highlight which changes, make sure **When** is checked and that the When box says **All**, click to select **List changes on a new sheet**, then click **OK**
   Notice that any rejected changes appear under a line on the change history.
   See Figure 16-17.

 close Holiday02.xls

Figure 16-15: Evaluating the first tracked change

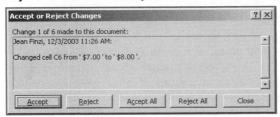

Figure 16-16: Evaluating the second tracked change

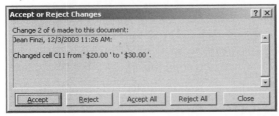

Figure 16-17: Change history shows all changes

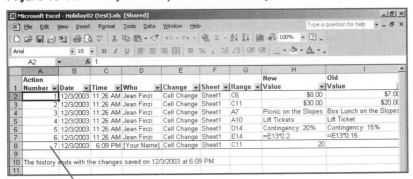

Rejected change (scroll right
to see accept/reject status)

extra!

**What changes
Excel tracks**
When tracking changes,
Excel records changes
to cell contents, as well
as row and column
changes. It does not
track sheet name
changes, formatting,
cell comments, formula
result changes, or any
changes unavailable in
shared workbooks (see
Table 16-2).

Skill Set 16
Workgroup Collaboration

Merge Workbooks
Merge Workbook Revisions

In workgroups without a shared file server, not everyone can work on one file at the same time. In these cases, you can save a workbook as shared, then distribute copies to people you want to review it. Reviewers edit the workbook and return their copies to you. You then open the original workbook and **merge**, or combine, all their changes into your copy. You can accept or reject any merged change. When you save the workbook as shared, make sure you allow enough days on the Advanced tab of the Share Workbook dialog box for all users to return their changes. To be safe, use a large number such as 300.

If you want to repeat this activity, make sure you are working on a copy of the Early01.xls file, because the merged information will remain in the master file even if you don't save changes. If you are using Excel 2002 version 1.0, you may see an error message regarding a sharing violation. If you do, click Save Temporary file and continue with the unit. To avoid this error, you must download and install Office XP Service Pack 1.

Activity Steps

 open Early01.xls

1. Click **Tools** on the menu bar, then click **Compare and Merge Workbooks**

2. In the Select Files to Merge Into Current Workbook dialog box, navigate to the location where your Project Files are stored, click **Early02.xls**, press and hold down [Ctrl], click **Early03.xls**, then click **Early04.xls**
   See Figure 16-18.

3. Click **OK**
   After a moment, the new information appears in the Early01.xls file.

4. Click **Tools** on the menu bar, point to **Track Changes**, then click **Highlight Changes**

5. Click the **When list arrow**, then click **All**

6. Click to select the **List changes on a new sheet check box**, then click **OK**
   See Figure 16-19.

7. Click the **Sheet 1 sheet tab**, then move the pointer over each cell with a triangular change marker, observing how changes appear in a different color for each reviewer
   See Figure 16-20.

 close Early01.xls

Step 1
You can only merge workbooks that you saved while file sharing was turned on.

Figure 16-18: Selecting workbooks to merge into the master workbook

Three files to merge with Early01.xls

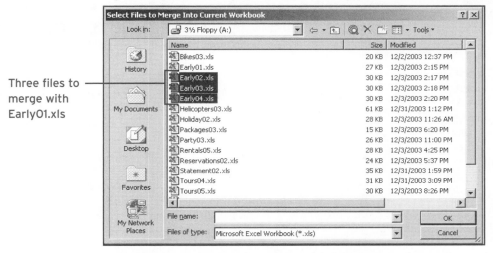

Figure 16-19: Change history sheet shows all reviewers' changes

Changes by user #1

Changes by user #2

Changes by user #3

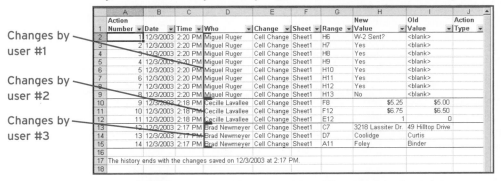

Figure 16-20: Review changes display in different colors

Brad Newmeyer's changes in yellow

Another reviewer's changes in turquoise

Third reviewer's changes in gray

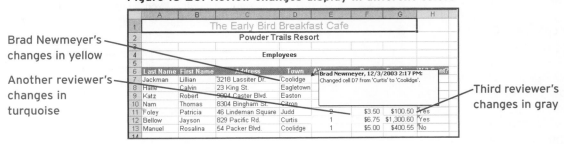

Skill Set 16
Workgroup Collaboration

Target Your Skills

 Packages03.xls

1 Unlock the range shown, then protect the worksheet, using the password "packages." Save the workbook as Packages04, but specify the password "desktop" to open it and "picture" to edit it. Add a comment in the workbook properties that reads "First quarter group sales." Share the workbook and make sure change tracking is turned on.

Figure 16-21

	A	B	C	D	E	F	G	H
1			Powder Trails Resort					
2			Package Sales					
3			First Quarter, 2003					
4								
5	Sales Rep	Customer	City	State	Package	# people	# days	Revenue
6	Clayton	Lloyd Publishing Co.	Chicago	IL	Basic	9	5	$ 5,400
7	Randall	Mather High School	York	CT	Basic	15	3	$ 5,250
8	Mercede	Lefevre School	Las Vegas	NV	Basic	13	3	$ 4,550
9	Randall	Kato & Sons	Seattle	WA	Basic	10	3	$ 3,500
10	Clayton	Marymount Ski Club	Tulsa	OK	Basic	5	5	$ 3,000
11	Mercede	Laird Corp.	Lowell	MA	Deluxe	17	5	$ 18,700
12	Clayton	Hitech Corp.	Cleveland	OH	Deluxe	20	3	$ 15,000
13	Clayton	Mill College	Vincent	PA	Deluxe	20	3	$ 15,000
14	Randall	Donald Marino	Boston	MA	Deluxe	5	3	$ 3,750
15								

Unlock this range

 Tours04.xls

2 With Tours04.xls open, merge the workbook revisions in the files Tours05.xls, Tours06.xls, and Tours07.xls. Save your changes, then review all changes, accepting all changes. Create the change history shown in Figure 16-22. Remove the workbook from shared status, then protect the workbook's structure and windows, using the password "merged."

Figure 16-22

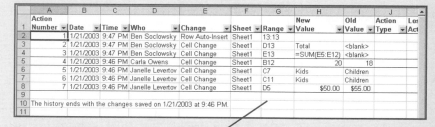

If you are using Excel 2002 version 1.0, you may see an error message regarding a sharing violation. If you do, click Save Temporary file and continue with the unit. To avoid this error, you must download and install Office XP Service Pack 1.

Getting Started

Getting Started with Access 2002

Skill List

1. What you need to know before you start
2. Start Access and open a database
3. Identify the parts of the Database window
4. Understand database terminology
5. Understand the benefits of using a relational database
6. Manage toolbars and understand views
7. Use the Help system
8. Close a database and exit Access

This book will help you prepare for the Access 2002 Microsoft Office User Specialist (MOUS) exams and learn more about Access 2002. An Access database provides an efficient way to enter and maintain data, as well as fast and flexible ways to report and analyze information. Also, by relating several lists of data, an Access database can minimize data redundancy, which decreases the possibility of errors in your database. To enjoy the benefits of an Access database, you must be comfortable with the terminology specific to Access databases and be able to navigate through Access.

This Skill Set will introduce you to database terminology and will outline the benefits of using an Access database. It will provide information that you'll use throughout the book to open and close databases and to manage various Access screen elements, such as toolbars, menu bars, and windows. It will also introduce you to the Access Help system so that you can find and troubleshoot problems.

Before you get started, you need to store a copy of the Project Files on your computer to complete the exercises (or **Activities**) in this book. If you store the Project Files on floppy disks, use one floppy disk for each chapter (or **Skill Set**) to avoid running out of room. Within each activity, you are not usually instructed to specifically open, close, or save your files, so to get the correct results, use the specific file(s) listed at the beginning of the activity to the right of the floppy disk icon. If you want to practice an activity more than once, use a new, unmodified copy of the file each time.

Getting Started

Getting Started with Access 2002

Start Access and Open a Database

The Windows desktop is often customized to show icons that you can use to start commonly used programs quickly. But whether or not your computer has a desktop icon for Access, you can start the program by clicking the Start button on the taskbar, then clicking Microsoft Access on the Programs menu. Once you've started Access, you can open an existing database or create a new one. You can also open an existing database from either the My Computer or Windows Explorer windows by double-clicking the database file, which will automatically open both Access and the database.

Step 1
If you don't see Microsoft Access on the Programs menu, point to the Microsoft Office group icon to see if the Microsoft Access icon appears there.

Activity Steps

1. Click the **Start button**  on the taskbar, point to **Programs**, then click **Microsoft Access**
   See Figure GS-1. The **task pane** displays links that allow you to open an existing file or start a new database.

2. Click the **More files link,** click the **Look in list arrow,** then navigate to the drive and folder where your Project Files are stored
   See Figure GS-2. Access database files have an **mdb** file extension. A file **extension** consists of one to three characters attached to the end of a filename, and it tells the computer what type of information is stored in that file. Typically, file extensions are three characters and are always separated from the filename by a period. Depending on your Windows settings, you might not see the file extensions for the files on your computer.

3. Click **Employees01,** then click **Open**
   See Figure GS-3. The Employees01 Database window appears. Since you can only work on a single database in an Access window, once you open or start a new database, the task pane closes.

Figure GS-1: Task pane

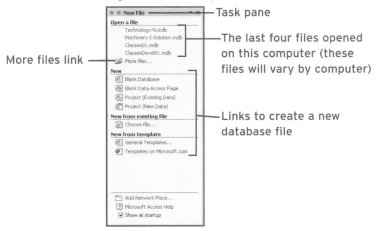

Task pane

The last four files opened on this computer (these files will vary by computer)

More files link

Links to create a new database file

Figure GS-2: Open dialog box

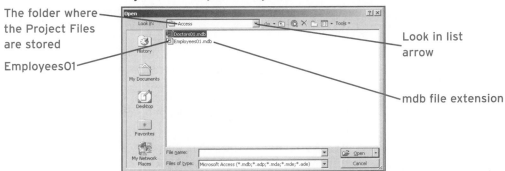

The folder where the Project Files are stored

Employees01

Look in list arrow

mdb file extension

Figure GS-3: Employees01 Database window

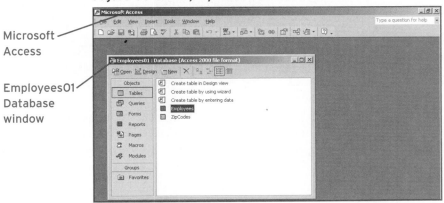

Microsoft Access

Employees01 Database window

Getting Started

Getting Started with Access 2002

Identify the Parts of the Database Window

Access contains the same screen elements as other Microsoft Office programs: a title bar, a menu bar, one or more toolbars, and Minimize, Maximize/Restore, and Close buttons. Access also contains other elements that are specific to managing a database. One such element is the Database window, the first window you see after you open a database. The **Database window** displays the name of the current database in its title bar. Icons that represent existing database objects (as well as shortcuts to create new objects) appear in the body of the Database window. On the left side of the Database window is the **Objects bar**, which you use to access the seven types of database **objects**, the major parts of the database file. The **Database window toolbar** contains buttons to help create a new database object or modify an existing one. Table GS-1 describes some of the elements of the Database window.

Activity Steps

file▷ **Employees01.mdb**

1. Click **File** on the menu bar, then point to **Edit**, **View**, **Insert**, **Tools**, **Window**, and **Help** on the menu bar to view menu options

2. Press **Esc** twice

3. Point to the **New button** ☐ on the Database toolbar, then point to the other buttons on the Database toolbar to view their ScreenTips
   A **ScreenTip** is descriptive information that automatically appears in a small box by the pointer when you point to a toolbar button.

Step 6
The first and most important Access object is the table because it contains all the data.

4. Point to the **Open button** 🗁 Open on the Database window toolbar, then point to the other buttons on the Database window toolbar to view their ScreenTips

5. Click the **Queries button** 🗗 Queries on the Objects bar
   See Figure GS-4. The Database window displays the new object shortcut links as well as any existing objects of that type.

6. On the Objects bar, click the **Forms button** 🖽 Forms, click the **Reports button** 🖩 Reports, click the **Pages button** 🖺 Pages, click the **Macros button** ⧉ Macros, click the **Modules button** ⤳ Modules, then click the **Tables button** ▥ Tables

7. Click the **Maximize button** ☐ on the Database window
   The Maximize button is a toggle that resizes a window.

8. Click the **Restore Window button** 🗗 on the Database window

Figure GS-4: Elements of the Access window and Database window

Access title bar — Access Minimize, Restore/Maximize, and Close buttons

Menu bar

ScreenTip — Database toolbar

Objects bar

Queries button is selected — Database Minimize, Maximize/Restore, and Close buttons

Existing query objects

New object shortcuts

TABLE GS-1: Access window and Database window elements

element	description
Access title bar	Contains the name of the active program: Microsoft Access.
Access Minimize, Maximize, Restore Down, and Close buttons	Minimizes, resizes, or closes the entire Microsoft Access program and an opened database. When the Access window is maximized, the Restore Down button appears and can be used to restore the window to a smaller size.
Menu bar	Contains menus with options that are appropriate for the current view.
Database toolbar	Contains buttons for commonly performed tasks that affect the entire database (such as New, Open, or Relationships) or are common to all database objects (such as Print, Copy, or Spelling).
Database Minimize, Maximize, Restore Window, and Close buttons	Minimizes, resizes, or closes the current database. The Database Close button will close the current database, but Access will still be open.
Database title bar	Contains the filename of the active database.
Database window toolbar	Contains buttons to open, modify, create, or delete the selected database object. The view buttons (Large Icons, Small Icons, List, and Details) on the Database window toolbar are used to display the icons in different sizes and arrangements.
Database window	Allows you to work with the individual objects stored within the database.
Objects bar	Contains one button for each database object type.
Status bar	Displays messages regarding the current database operation.

Getting Started

Getting Started with Access 2002

Understand Database Terminology
Understand Fields, Records, and Tables

At the most basic level, a database is a list of structured data. The "structure" is a column and row grid in which each piece of data is stored. Data organized in this type of structure is very easy to find, update, and analyze. In database terminology, a column of the structure is called a **field** and represents one category or type of information. For example, a database storing information about employees might contain the three fields FirstName, LastName, and HireDate. Each item of data that you enter into each field, such as Mark in the FirstName field or 1/1/2003 in the HireDate field, is called a **value**. All the fields for one employee compose a **record**. Therefore, you'd have as many records in your database as you have employees. The records for a single subject, such as all employee records, are collectively called a **table**. When you open a table, the data that it stores is displayed in a spreadsheet-like grid called a **datasheet**.

Step 5
Be sure to click the Close button for the Employees table rather than the Close button for the Access window, or you'll close the entire Employees01 database and Access.

Activity Steps

 Employees01.mdb

1. Click the **Tables button** ⊞ Tables on the Objects bar (if it's not already selected), click **Employees** (if it's not already selected), then click the **Open button** 📂 Open on the Database window toolbar
   See Figure GS-5. Field names are displayed on the first row of the datasheet.

2. Press **Enter** or **Tab** several times to move through the fields of the first record

3. Press **[Down Arrow]** several times to move through the records of the table

4. Press **[Ctrl][Home]** to return to the first field of the first record

5. Close the Employees table

Figure GS-5: Employees table

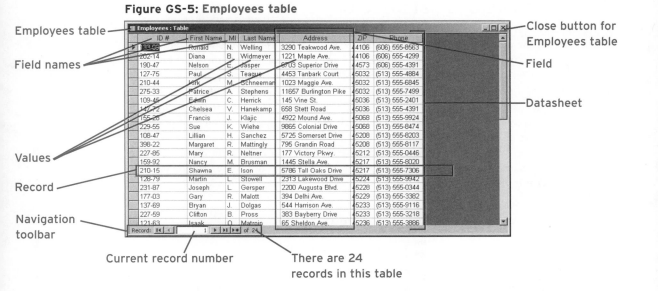

Employees table

Field names

Values

Record

Navigation toolbar

Current record number

Close button for Employees table

Field

Datasheet

There are 24 records in this table

extra!

Using relational databases

In Access, you can create multiple tables of data and link them together. When two tables are linked, or related, your database becomes a **relational database.** The purpose of creating multiple tables of data is to eliminate duplicate data entry. For example, by providing a ZipCodes table in the Employees01 database, you can enter each ZipCode record (each containing a ZIP, City, and State value) only once, but reuse those records if multiple employees live in the same ZIP code.

Getting Started

Getting Started with Access 2002

Understand Database Terminology
Understand Database Objects

Access includes seven types of database objects that represent the major pieces of the database and correspond with the seven buttons on the Objects bar. The most important objects are tables, because tables contain all the data in an Access database. All object types are described in Table GS-2. You can enter data into a database using the table, query, form, or page objects. However, all data that you enter is stored only in the table objects. This means that no matter where you enter or edit data, the data will be updated throughout all objects and views of the data at all times. For example, if you create a report that displays a company name and change the company name later using a form, the report will automatically show the updated company name the next time that you open or print it.

Step 4
A form typically displays the fields of only one record at a time. Often the fields of a form are are displayed in a vertical arrangement (unlike the horizontal arrangement of fields on a datasheet).

Activity Steps

 Employees01.mdb

1. Click the **Queries button** [Queries] on the Objects bar (if it's not already selected), click **Employees in KY** (if it's not already selected), then click the **Open button** [Open] on the Database window toolbar
   See Figure GS-6.

2. Double-click **Ronald** in the First Name field of the first record for Ronald Welling, then type **Jack**

3. Close the Employees in KY query
   Entries to a record are automatically saved when you move to another record or when you close the window.

4. Click the **Forms button** [Forms] on the Objects bar, click **Employee Entry Form** (if it's not already selected), then click the **Open button** [Open] on the Database window toolbar
   See Figure GS-7. The name "Jack" appears in the first record even though you entered "Jack" into a query object.

5. Double-click **Welling** in the Last Name field of the form, type **Goodspeed** then close the Employee Entry Form

6. Click the **Tables button** [Tables] on the Objects bar, click **Employees** (if it's not already selected), then click the **Open button** [Open] on the Database window toolbar
   Jack Goodspeed (formerly Ronald Welling) is listed as the first record in the Employees table.

7. Close the Employees table

Figure GS-6: Employees in KY query

Employees in KY query

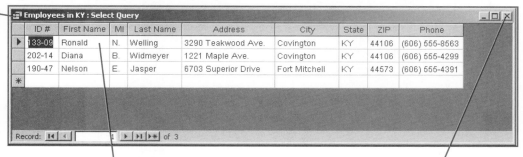

The value "Ronald" in the First
Name field of the first record

Close button for the
Employees in KY query

Figure GS-7: Employee Entry Form

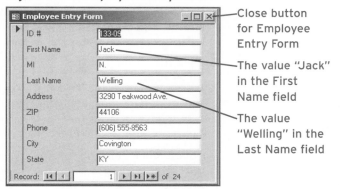

Close button
for Employee
Entry Form

The value "Jack"
in the First
Name field

The value
"Welling" in the
Last Name field

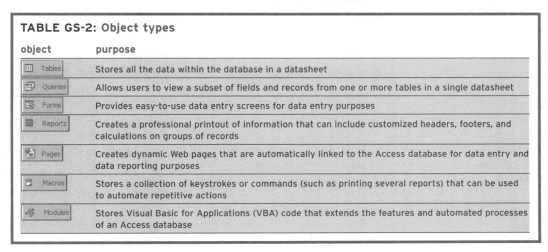

object	purpose
TABLE GS-2: Object types	
Tables	Stores all the data within the database in a datasheet
Queries	Allows users to view a subset of fields and records from one or more tables in a single datasheet
Forms	Provides easy-to-use data entry screens for data entry purposes
Reports	Creates a professional printout of information that can include customized headers, footers, and calculations on groups of records
Pages	Creates dynamic Web pages that are automatically linked to the Access database for data entry and data reporting purposes
Macros	Stores a collection of keystrokes or commands (such as printing several reports) that can be used to automate repetitive actions
Modules	Stores Visual Basic for Applications (VBA) code that extends the features and automated processes of an Access database

Getting Started

Getting Started with Access 2002

Understand the Benefits of Using a Relational Database

You've already used databases even if you've never used Access before. Any structured list of information that is stored in electronic or paper format can be considered a database, such as a telephone book, collection of business cards, or address book. Many people choose to create an electronic database in Microsoft Excel, because an Excel spreadsheet provides a tabular grid, making it easy to enter fields and records. However, if you manage your lists in Access, which can link multiple tables of data to create a relational database, you'll enjoy several additional benefits that single-list management systems such as Excel cannot provide. See Table GS-3 for a list of these benefits.

Activity Steps

 Employees01.mdb

1. Click the **Tables button** 🔲 Tables on the Objects bar (if it's not already selected), click **ZipCodes**, then click the **Open button** 🔲 Open on the Database window toolbar

2. Click the **expand button** ➕ to the left of the third record for ZIP 45032
   See Figure GS-8. Three related records that also contain the value 45032 in the ZIP field from the Employees table appear in a **sub-datasheet**, a datasheet within a datasheet. The presence of a sub-datasheet indicates that the tables of your database are related.

3. Double-click **Fairfield** in the City field of the third record, then type **Bridgewater**

4. Close the ZipCodes table

5. Click the **Reports button** 🔲 Reports on the Objects bar, click **Employees Listed by City** (if it's not already selected), then click the **Preview button** 🔲 Preview on the Database window toolbar

6. Maximize the report in the Print Preview window, then click the report to zoom to 100%
   See Figure GS-9. When a relational database is working properly, changes made to a record in one object are automatically updated in all other views of that information.

7. Click the **Restore Window button** 🔲 on the Employees Listed by City report window

8. Close the Employees Listed by City report

Step 6
You use reports to view and print data. You cannot enter data into a report object.

Figure GS-8: ZipCodes table

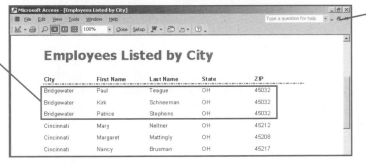

Expand button becomes a collapse button

Close button for ZipCodes table

Subdatasheet

Figure GS-9: Employees Listed by City report

"Bridgewater" entry appears as the City value for ZIP 45032

Restore Window button for Employees Listed by City report

Employees Listed by City

City	First Name	Last Name	State	ZIP
Bridgewater	Paul	Teague	OH	45032
Bridgewater	Kirk	Schneeman	OH	45032
Bridgewater	Patrice	Stephens	OH	45032
Cincinnati	Mary	Neltner	OH	45212
Cincinnati	Margaret	Mattingly	OH	45208
Cincinnati	Nancy	Brusman	OH	45217

TABLE GS-3: Benefits of using Access to manage data

feature	benefit
Relational tables	Storing tables in multiple tables and linking them versus storing information in one large table reduces redundant data, which improves data accuracy.
Querying capabilities	Being able to query the database using **SQL (Structured Query Language)** makes the data available to other programs.
Data entry screens	Creating data entry screens (forms) makes it easier to enter and find data in the database.
Advanced reporting tools	Using the advanced reporting tools of an Access database allows you to quickly summarize and analyze data in many ways. You can save the reports that you build so that you can quickly view data in multiple arrangements without recreating the report.
Web page connectivity	Connecting an Access database to a Web page means that you can provide data entry, editing, and reporting capabilities to users through World Wide Web technologies.
Multi-user file	An Access database is inherently **multi-user**; multiple people can enter and update data in the same database at the same time.

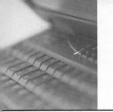

Getting Started

Getting Started with Access 2002

Manage Toolbars and Understand Views

Access displays different toolbars and menu bar options depending on the object you are working with. Furthermore, each object has multiple views, each of which displays a different default toolbar and menu bar. A **view** is a presentation of an object that allows you to perform certain tasks. Most objects have two views. Table GS-4 contains more information on object views. The toolbars that are displayed in each view show the buttons for the commands that are most common to that view. But since it's easy to accidently reposition or remove toolbars, it's also important that you know how to redisplay and move toolbars to the screen location that works best for you.

Activity Steps

 Employees01.mdb

1. Click the **Tables button** ▦ Tables on the Objects bar (if it's not already selected), click **Employees**, then click the **Open button** ▦ Open on the Database window toolbar

2. Click **View** on the menu bar, point to **Toolbars**, click **Formatting (Datasheet)** (if it's not already checked) to toggle the Formatting (Datasheet) toolbar on, point to the left edge of the Formatting (Datasheet) toolbar so that your pointer changes to ↔, then drag the toolbar to move it just below the Table Datasheet toolbar (if it's not already positioned there)
   See Figure GS-10. The Formatting (Datasheet) toolbar contains buttons that apply formatting characteristics such as font size, bold, and text color. After you toggle on a toolbar, it will appear each time you open the view that you displayed it in.

3. Close the Employees table, click **ZipCodes** in the Database window, then click the **Open button** ▦ Open on the Database window toolbar

4. Click **View** on the menu bar, point to **Toolbars**, then click **Formatting (Datasheet)** to toggle the Formatting (Datasheet) toolbar off

5. Click the **View button** ▨ on the Table Datasheet toolbar
   See Figure GS-11. The View button icon acts as a toggle to help you quickly switch between the "open" and "design" views of an object. When you are in Table Design View, the View button displays a datasheet icon ▦, and when you are in Table Datasheet View, the View button displays a designer's tools icons ▨.

6. Click the **View button** ▦ on the Table Design toolbar

7. Close the ZipCodes table

Step 2
Two toolbars can also be positioned on the same row, which hides some of the buttons on each toolbar. If this happens, point to the left edge of one of the toolbars so that your pointer changes to ↔, then drag the toolbar to reposition it in the way that works best for you.

Figure GS-10: Table Datasheet toolbar and Formatting (Datasheet) toolbar

Figure GS-11: Table Design toolbar and Table Design View

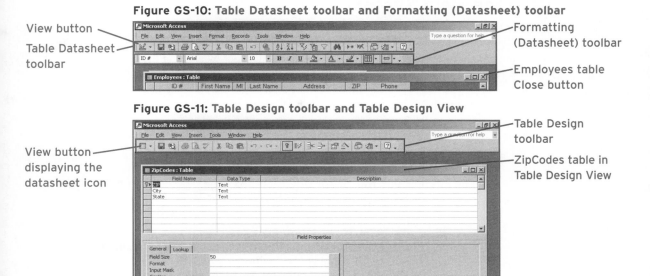

View button

Table Datasheet toolbar

Formatting (Datasheet) toolbar

Employees table Close button

View button displaying the datasheet icon

Table Design toolbar

ZipCodes table in Table Design View

TABLE GS-4: Object views

object	view displayed if you click the object, then click the Open button 🗁 Open on the Database Window toolbar	view displayed if you click the object, then click the Design button 🖍 Design on the Database toolbar
Table	**Table Datasheet View** is used to view, enter, edit, and delete data.	**Table Design View** is used to enter, modify, and delete fields from a table.
Query	**Query Datasheet View** is used to view, enter, edit, and delete data.	**Query Design View** is used to define the fields and records displayed by Query Datasheet View.
Form	**Form View** is used to view, enter, edit, and delete data.	**Form Design View** is used to define the layout and formatting characteristics of the form.
Report	Reports do not have an "Open" view. If you double-click a report object in the Database window, you'll open it in Print Preview.	**Report Design View** is used to define the layout and formatting characteristics of a report.
Page	**Page View** is used to view, enter, edit, and delete data; shows you how the Web page will appear when opened in Internet Explorer.	**Page Design View** is used to define the layout and formatting characteristics of a Web page.
Macro	Macros do not have an "Open" view. If you double-click a macro object in the Database window, you'll run the macro.	**Macro Design View** is used to define macro actions.
Module	Modules do not have an "Open" view. If you double-click a module object in the Database window, you'll run the VBA code that the module stores.	Modules contain VBA code. When you design a module, you work in the **Microsoft Visual Basic window**.

Getting Started

Getting Started with Access 2002

Use the Help System

Access provides an extensive **Help system** that you can use to learn more about Access or to troubleshoot problems. You can open the Access Help window through the Help menu, Ask a Question box, toolbar buttons, or by pressing the F1 key. Help menu options are further described in Table GS-5. Once the Help window is open, you can search for information by scanning a table of contents, by searching through an index of keywords, or by typing a question.

Activity Steps

 Employees01.mdb

1. Click the **Ask a Question box** [Type a question for help ▼] on the menu bar, type **create a table**, then press **Enter**
   See Figure GS-12. Based on your entry, the Help system displays a list of topics for you to choose from.

2. Click the **About creating a table link**, then maximize the Microsoft Access Help window
   The Help page contains information about creating a table.

3. Click the **fields** link on the Help page
   Glossary words appear as blue links on a Help page. Definitions appear in green text.

4. Click the **Contents tab** (if it's not already selected), click the **Microsoft Access Help expand button** ⊞, click the **Tables expand button** ⊞, click the **Creating Tables expand button** ⊞, click **Create a table** in the Contents window, then click the **Create a table by using the Table Wizard link** on the Help page to expand that section of the page
   See Figure GS-13.

5. Click the **Show All link** on the Help page to show all sections and glossary words on the Help page

6. Click the **Answer Wizard tab**, type **How do I create a table?**, then click **Search**
   The topics that address that question are displayed in the Select topic to display list. You can click any entry in the list to show that page of the Help system.

7. Click the **Index tab**, type **table** in the Type keywords box, then click **Search**
   All the topics for this keyword are displayed in the Choose a topic list. You can click any entry in the list to show that page of the Help system.

8. Close the Microsoft Access Help window

Step 4
If the Contents, Answer Wizard, and Index tabs are not visible, click the Show button ⊞ on the Microsoft Access Help toolbar.

Figure GS-12: Using the Ask a Question box

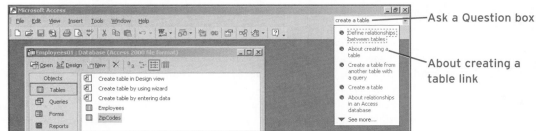

Ask a Question box

About creating a table link

Figure GS-13: Using the Contents window to find information in the Help system

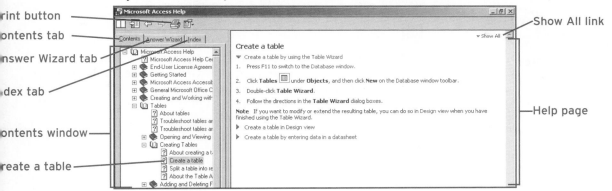

Print button
Contents tab
Answer Wizard tab
Index tab
Contents window
Create a table

Show All link
Help page

TABLE GS-5: Help menu options

Help menu option	description
Microsoft Access Help	Opens the Office Assistant, which prompts you for a keyword search of the Help manual
Show the Office Assistant	Displays the **Office Assistant**, an automated character that provides tips and interactive prompts while you are working
Hide the Office Assistant	Temporarily closes the Office Assistant for the working session
What's This	Changes the pointer to and provides a short description of an area, icon, or menu option that you click using this special pointer
Office on the Web	If you are connected to the Web, displays the Microsoft Web site, which provides additional Microsoft information and support articles
Sample Databases	Provides easy access to the sample databases installed with Access 2002
Detect and Repair	Analyzes a database for possible data corruption and attempts to repair problems
About Microsoft Access	Provides the version and product ID of Access

Close a Database and Exit Access

You can close a database and exit Access by clicking the Access Close button in the upper-right corner of the screen at any time. Since data is automatically saved in an Access database, you don't need to worry about saving data before you close a window or exit Access. However, if you make any structural or formatting changes to an object (such as add a new field to a table or change the font in a datasheet), you will be prompted to save those changes when you close the object. Therefore, it's a good idea to close each object window when you are finished working in it to make sure you've saved the changes you intend to save. When all object windows are closed, you are returned to the Database window. From there, you can close the database and exit Access.

Step 2
If your database is stored on a floppy disk, do not eject the floppy disk from the disk drive until the Access window (not just the Database window) is closed.

Activity Steps

 Employees01.mdb

1. Click the **Close button** ☒ on the Database window
   See Figure GS-14. When the Access window is open without an open database, you can still use the Access Help system and many Access tools (such as those used to compact or convert existing databases). You can also open a new database.

2. Click the **Close button** ☒ on the Access window

Figure GS-14: Access window Close button

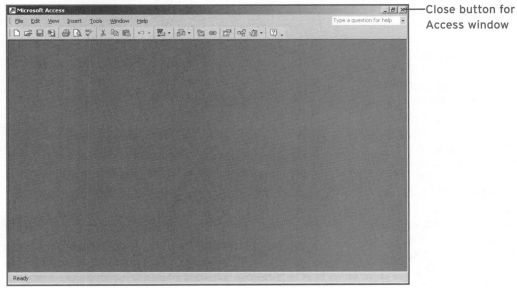

Close button for Access window

extra!

Compacting on Close

The **Compact on Close** feature compacts and repairs your database each time you close it. To activate the Compact on Close feature, click **Tools** on the menu bar, click **Options**, click the **General tab** in the Options dialog box, select the **Compact on Close check box,** and click **OK**. While the Compact on Close feature works well if your database is stored on a hard drive, it can cause problems if you are working from a floppy disk. This is because the Compact on Close process creates a temporary file that is just as large as the original database. This temporary file is deleted after the compact process finishes. If you are working on a floppy disk and do not have enough room on the disk to complete the compact process successfully, an error occurs that might result in an error message, or, in the worst case, a corruption of the database. Therefore, you shouldn't compact a database unless you know that you have plenty of room to accommodate the temporary file that is created during the process.

Target Your Skills

 Doctors01.mdb

1 Answer the following questions on a separate sheet of paper: What tables are stored in this database? How many fields and records are in each table? What queries are stored in this database? How many fields and records are in each query? What form is stored in this database? How many fields are displayed on the form? How many records are in the form? What reports are stored in this database? Open the Zips table, then display the subdatasheet as shown in Figure GS-15. What is the relationship between the Zips and Doctors tables?

Figure GS-15

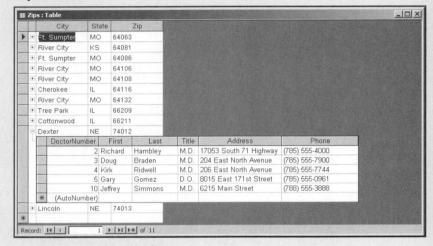

 Doctors01.mdb

2 Start Access, but do not open a database. Enter "toolbar" in the Ask a Question box, then click the Troubleshoot toolbars link to display the Help page shown in Figure GS-16.

Figure GS-16

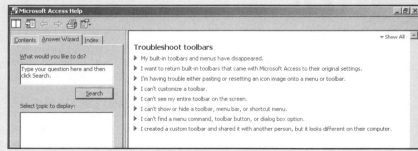

Skill Set 1

Skill List

1. Create Access databases
2. Open database objects in multiple views
3. Move among records
4. Format datasheets

In Skill Set 1, you will learn how to use an Access database wizard to build a database quickly, and you will explore many database objects, such as tables, queries, forms, and reports. You'll also learn how to navigate through a database to find information and how to format information to enhance your printouts.

Skill Set 1

Creating and Using Databases

Create Access Databases

Access provides many **templates**, or sample databases, such as inventory, event, contact, and expense management, which you can use to create your own database quickly. Some Access templates are also **database wizards**, which provide a series of dialog boxes that guide you through a process for creating a database. Whether you create a database using a template or a database wizard, you can further modify it to meet your needs.

Step 1
If Access is running, but the task pane is not visible, click the New button 🗋 on the Database toolbar.

Activity Steps

1. Start Access, then click **General Templates** in the task pane

2. Click the **Databases tab** in the Templates dialog box
   See Figure 1-1.

3. Click **Contact Management**, then click **OK**

4. Click **Create** to save the database with the name Contact Management1 in the My Documents folder
   If a database with the name Contact Management1 already exists, the new database will be named Contact Management2, and so on.

5. Click **Next**, click **Next** again to accept all of the suggested fields in the three sample tables, click **SandStone** for the screen display style, click **Next**, click **Soft Gray** for the printed report style, click **Next**, click **Next** again to accept "Contact Management" as the database title, then click **Finish** to instruct the wizard to build the database using these choices

6. Click the **Enter/View Contacts button**, click the **Close button** ☒ on the Contacts form, then click other buttons on the Main Switchboard form to explore the Contact Management database
   See Figure 1-2.

7. When finished exploring, click the **Exit this database button** on the Main Switchboard form to close the Contact Management1 database

Figure 1-1: Access database wizards and task pane

New button

Templates dialog box

Databases tab

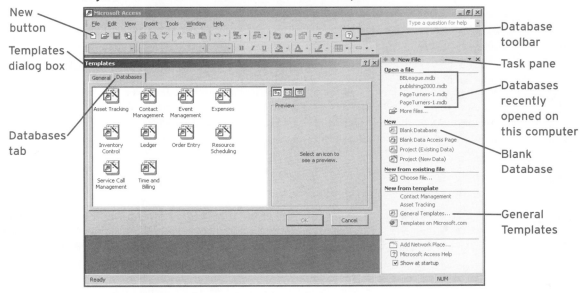

Database toolbar

Task pane

Databases recently opened on this computer

Blank Database

General Templates

Figure 1-2: Contact Management database

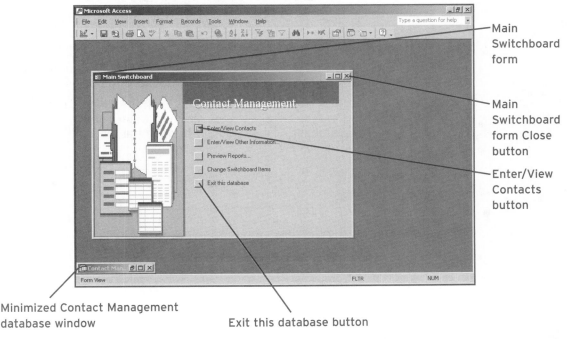

Main Switchboard form

Main Switchboard form Close button

Enter/View Contacts button

Minimized Contact Management database window

Exit this database button

Microsoft Access 2002   **AC-21**

Skill Set 1

Creating and Using Databases

Open Database Objects in Multiple Views

Database objects, such as tables, queries, forms, and reports, have different **views**, or presentations of an object that support different database activities. Every object has a **Design View**, which you use to modify the structure of the object. For example, in Table Design View, you add or delete fields; in Report Design View, you change the layout and format of the report. **Datasheet View** of a table and query displays data in a spreadsheet-like arrangement in which the fields are in columns and the records are in rows. You use Datasheet View to view, find, edit, and enter records. **Form View** of a form presents information in a layout that you create, and you use it to edit and enter data. **Preview** allows you to view a report on the screen before you print it.

Activity Steps

 PageTurners01.mdb

1. Click the **Tables button** ⊞ Tables on the Objects bar (if it's not already selected), click **Employees**, then click the **Open button** 🔓 Open on the Database window toolbar to open the table in Datasheet View
   See Figure 1-3.

2. Click the **View button** 🔍 to view Table Design View, then click the table's **Close button** ✕ to close the Employees table

3. Click the **Queries button** ⊞ Queries on the Objects bar, click **Sales List**, then click the **Open button** 🔓 Open on the Database window toolbar to open the query in Datasheet View

4. Click the **View button** 🔍 to view Query Design View, then click the query's **Close button** ✕ to close the Sales List query

5. Click the **Forms button** ⊞ Forms on the Objects bar, click **Customer Orders**, then click the **Open button** 🔓 Open on the Database window toolbar to open the form in Form View
   See Figure 1-4.

6. Click the **View button** 🔍 to view Form Design View, then click the form's **Close button** ✕ to close the Customer Orders form

7. Click the **Reports button** ⊞ Reports on the Objects bar, click **Books by Category**, then click the **Preview button** 🔍 Preview on the Database window toolbar to open the report in Preview

8. Click the **View button** 🔍 to view Report Design View, then click the report's **Close button** ✕ to close the Books by Category report

Step 1
Double-clicking an object in the Database window has the same effect as clicking an object in the Database window, then clicking the Open button on the Database window toolbar.

Skill 2

Open Database Objects in Multiple Views

Figure 1-3: Employees Datasheet View

Employees table

Employees : Table

ID #	First Name	MI	Last Name	Address	City	State	ZIP	Phone	Start [
108-47	Lillian	H.	Sanchez	5725 Somerset Drive	Cincinnati	OH	45208	(513) 555-8203	7/8/
109-45	Edwin	C.	Herrick	145 Vine St.	Lebanon	OH	45036	(513) 555-2401	8/12/
121-63	Isaak	O.	Matroin	65 Sheldon Ave.	Norwood	OH	45236	(513) 555-3886	7/15/
127-75	Paul	S.	Teague	4453 Tanbark Court	Fairfield	OH	45032	(513) 555-4884	3/10/
128-79	Martin	L.	Stowell	2313 Lakewood Drive	Cincinnati	OH	45224	(513) 555-9942	3/28/
133-09	Ronald	N.	Welling	3290 Teakwood Ave.	Covington	KY	44106	(606) 555-8563	5/19/
137-69	Bryan	J.	Dolgas	544 Harrison Ave.	West Chester	OH	45233	(513) 555-9116	2/11/
147-72	Chelsea	V.	Hanekamp	658 Stett Road	Lebanon	OH	45036	(513) 555-4391	6/21/
155-28	Francis	J.	Klajic	4922 Mound Ave.	Milford	OH	45068	(513) 555-9924	11/19/
159-92	Nancy	M.	Brusman	1445 Stella Ave.	Mt. Healthy	OH	45217	(513) 555-8020	7/17/
177-03	Gary	R.	Malott	394 Delhi Ave.	Cincinnati	OH	45229	(513) 555-3382	5/27/
190-47	Nelson	E.	Jasper	6703 Superior Drive	Fort Mitchell	KY	44573	(606) 555-4391	12/1/
202-14	Diana	B.	Widmeyer	1221 Maple Ave.	Covington	KY	44106	(606) 555-4299	1/30/
210-15	Shawna	E.	Ison	5786 Tall Oaks Drive	Cincinnati	OH	45217	(513) 555-7306	12/1/
210-44	Kirk	M.	Schneeman	1023 Maggie Ave.	Fairfield	OH	45032	(513) 555-6845	4/4/
213-33	Raymond	A.	Franklin	912 Wilma Court	Montgomery	OH	45244	(513) 555-7520	6/23/
227-59	Clifton	B.	Pross	383 Bayberry Drive	Cincinnati	OH	45233	(513) 555-3218	8/10/
227-85	Mary	R.	Neltner	177 Victory Pkwy.	Cincinnati	OH	45212	(513) 555-0446	9/15/
229-55	Sue	K.	Wiehe	9865 Colonial Drive	Milford	OH	45068	(513) 555-8474	2/21/
231-87	Joseph	L.	Gersper	2200 Augusta Blvd.	Cincinnati	OH	45228	(513) 555-0344	9/29/
256-81	Jessica	B.	Kindig	5417 Fairfax Ave.	Evanston	OH	45238	(513) 555-7743	10/17/

Record: 1 of 24

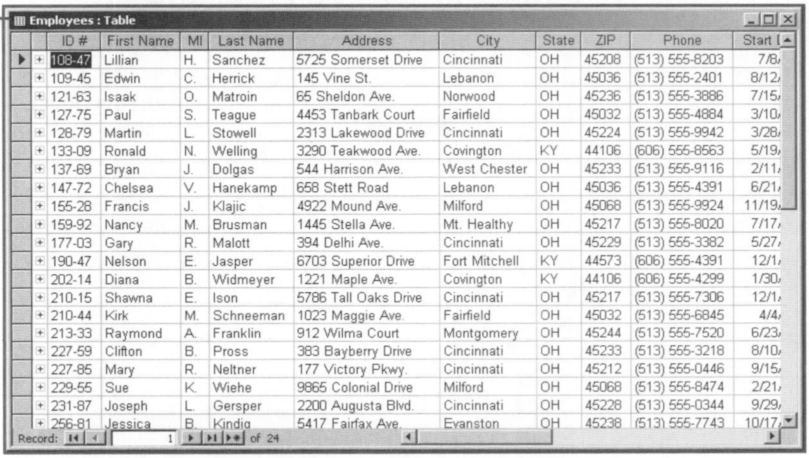

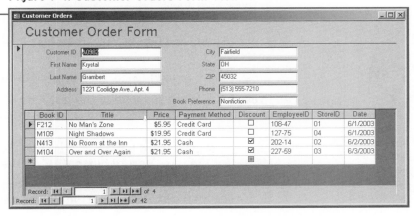

Figure 1-4: Customer Orders Form View

Customer Orders form

Book ID	Title	Price	Payment Method	Discount	EmployeeID	StoreID	Date
F212	No Man's Zone	$5.95	Credit Card	☐	108-47	01	6/1/2003
M109	Night Shadows	$19.95	Credit Card	☐	127-75	04	6/1/2003
N413	No Room at the Inn	$21.95	Cash	☑	202-14	02	6/2/2003
M104	Over and Over Again	$21.95	Cash	☑	227-59	03	6/3/2003

Skill Set 1
Creating and Using Databases

Move Among Records
Navigate Through Datasheet View and Form View

To view or find specific records or to add or edit data, you must be able to move around in a database. You can use the navigation buttons on the **navigation toolbar** in the Database View and Form View windows to navigate through records. The navigation toolbar also displays the number of the current record and the total number of records. You can also use keys, such as [Tab] and [Up Arrow], to navigate through records and individual fields. Table 1-1 summarizes the navigation buttons and common navigation keys that you can use to navigate through data in Datasheet View or Form View.

Activity Steps
 PageTurners01.mdb

1. Click the **Tables button** ▦ Tables on the Objects bar (if it's not already selected), then double-click **Inventory** to open the table in Datasheet View
   See Figure 1-5.

2. Press **[Enter]** or **[Tab]** as many times as it takes to move to the second record

3. Press **[Down Arrow]** twice, then press **[Up Arrow]** twice

4. Press **[Ctrl][End]** to move to the last field of the last record, then press **[Ctrl][Home]** to move to the first field of the first record

5. Click the **Next Record button** ▶ on the navigation toolbar, then click the **Last Record button** ▶| on the navigation toolbar

6. Click the **Previous Record button** ◀ on the navigation toolbar, then click the **First Record button** |◀ on the navigation toolbar

7. Close the Inventory table, click the **Forms button** ▦ Forms on the Objects bar, then double-click **Inventory Entry** to open the form in Form View
   See Figure 1-6.

8. Repeat steps 2 through 6 to observe how the same quick keystrokes and navigation buttons work in Form View

9. Close the Inventory Entry form

Select the record number in the Specific Record box on the navigation toolbar, type any other record number, then press [Enter] to move directly to that record.

Skill 3

Move Among Records

Figure 1-5: Navigating in Datasheet View

Inventory table
Navigation toolbar
Inventory : Table

Figure 1-6: Navigating in Form View

Inventory Entry form
Current record number
Specific Record box
Total number of records
Inventory Entry

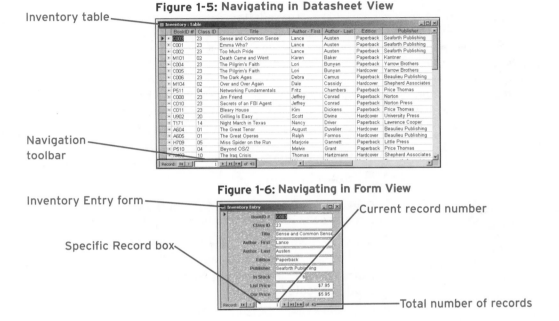

TABLE 1-1: Common navigation techniques

navigation button	navigation button name or key	moves to the following place
I◀	First Record	first record
◀	Previous Record	previous record
▶	Next Record	next record
▶I	Last Record	last record
▶*	New Record	new record (for data entry purposes)
	[Enter]	next field
	[Tab]	next field
	[Up Arrow]	previous record (Datasheet View)
	[Up Arrow]	previous field (Form View)
	[Down Arrow]	next record (Datasheet View)
	[Down Arrow]	next field (Form View)
	[Ctrl][Home]	first field of the first record
	[Ctrl][End]	last field of the last record

Skill Set 1
Creating and Using Databases

Move Among Records
Navigate Through Subdatasheets

A **subdatasheet** is a datasheet within a datasheet that contains records from a related table. Subdatasheets are available when a one-to-many relationship exists between two tables. For example, suppose that a one-to-many relationship exists between the tables Customers and Sales. If you expand a record in the Customers table datasheet, a subdatasheet (from the Sales table) containing records of what the customer purchased will appear. After you expand the subdatasheet, you navigate through a subdatasheet the same way you navigate through a datasheet.

Step 2
You can expand all subdatasheets at the same time by clicking the Selector button in the upper-left corner of the table in Datasheet View, then clicking any expand button.

Activity Steps

 PageTurners01.mdb

1. Click the **Tables button** `Tables` on the Objects bar (if it's not already selected), then double-click **Customers**

2. Click the **expand button** `+` to the left of the first record
   See Figure 1-7.

3. Press [Enter] several times to move through the fields of the subdatasheet

4. Click the **expand button** `+` to the left of the second record, click the date entry in the first record of the second subdatasheet, then click the **Next Record button** `▶` on the navigation toolbar
   See Figure 1-8.

5. Click the **collapse button** `-` to the left of the first record, then click the **collapse button** `-` to the left of the second record

6. Close the Customers table

Figure 1-7: Navigating through a subdatasheet

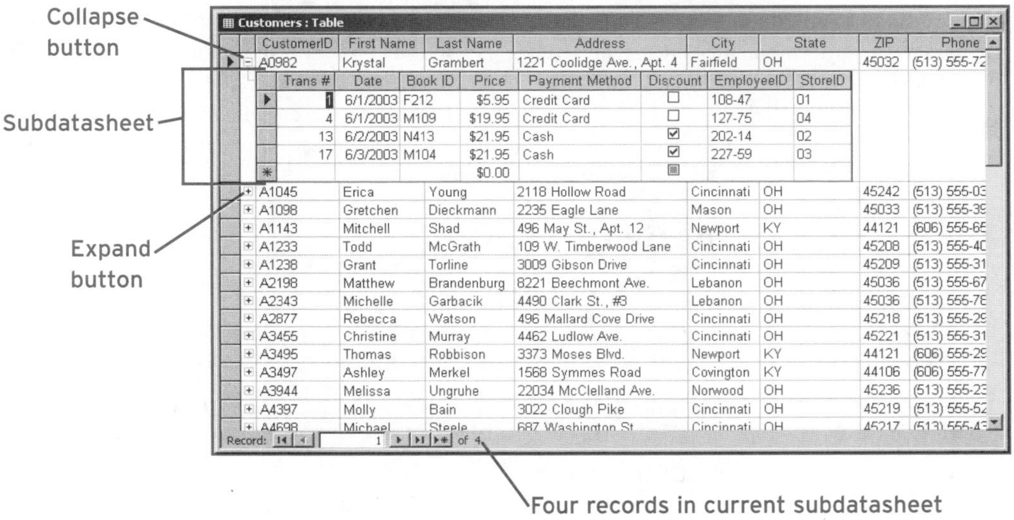

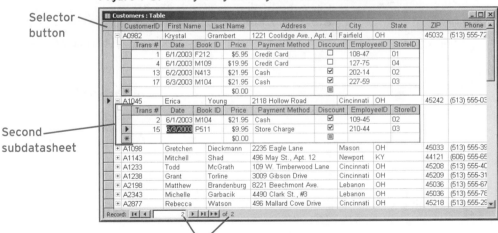

Collapse button
Subdatasheet
Expand button
Customers : Table
Four records in current subdatasheet

Figure 1-8: Navigating through a second subdatasheet

Selector button
Second subdatasheet
Customers : Table
Record 2 of 2 in current subdatasheet

Skill Set 1

Creating and Using Databases

Format Datasheets

You can format datasheets in a variety of ways to enhance the presentation of information on the screen and on printouts. The most common formatting enhancement commands are represented as buttons on the Formatting (Datasheet) toolbar. You can use these buttons to change the type, size, and colors of a datasheet. These buttons are described in Table 1-2. You can access other formatting and datasheet modification commands, such as hiding, resizing, and renaming columns, from the Format menu.

Step 5
To unhide a column in a datasheet, click Format on the menu bar, click Unhide Columns, select the check boxes beside those columns (fields) that you want to unhide, then click Close.

Activity Steps

 PageTurners01.mdb

1. Click the **Tables button** 🔲 Tables on the Objects bar (if it's not already selected), then double-click **Inventory**

2. Click the **Font list arrow** [Arial ▾] on the Formatting (Datasheet) toolbar, press **[v]**, then click **Verdana**

3. Click the **Font/Fore Color button list arrow** [A ▾] on the Formatting (Datasheet) toolbar, then click the **Blue box** in the sixth column in the second row

4. Click the **Gridlines button list arrow** [⊞ ▾] on the Formatting (Datasheet) toolbar, then click **Gridlines: Horizontal**

5. Click any entry in the Edition field, click **Format** on the menu bar, then click **Hide Columns**
   See Figure 1-9.

6. Close the Inventory table without saving changes

Figure 1-9: Formatting a datasheet

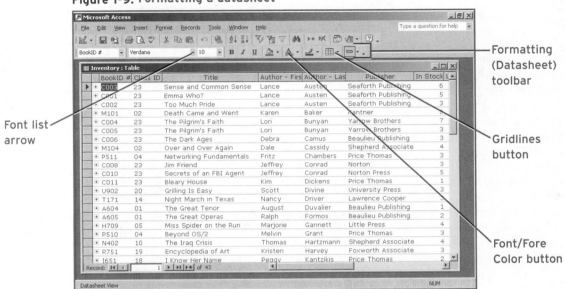

Formatting (Datasheet) toolbar

Font list arrow

Gridlines button

Font/Fore Color button

TABLE 1-2: Formatting buttons

button	name	description
Arial	Font	Applies a new font face
10	Font Size	Applies a new font size
B	Bold	Toggles the bold font style on and off
I	Italic	Toggles the italic font style on and off
U	Underline	Toggles the underline font style on and off
🖌	Fill/Back Color	Changes the background color of the datasheet
A	Font/Fore Color	Changes the text color of the datasheet
🖋	Line/Border Color	Changes the gridline color of the datasheet
▦	Gridlines	Determines which gridlines appear on the datasheet
▭	Special Effect	Changes the effect (flat, raised, or sunken) of the cells in a datasheet

Skill Set 1

Creating and Using Databases

Target Your Skills

 PageTurners01.mdb

1 Use Figure 1-10 as a guide to open the Datasheet View of the Stores table with one expanded sub-datasheet. Using the Next Record naviga-tion button and key-board, navigate to the field that is selected in the subdatasheet so that your datasheet matches the figure.

Figure 1-10

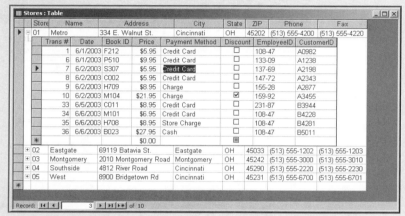

 PageTurners01.mdb

2 Use Figure 1-11 as a guide to format the Categories table datasheet. Use the information shown on the Formatting (Datasheet) toolbar to help you determine what formatting changes need to be applied.

Figure 1-11

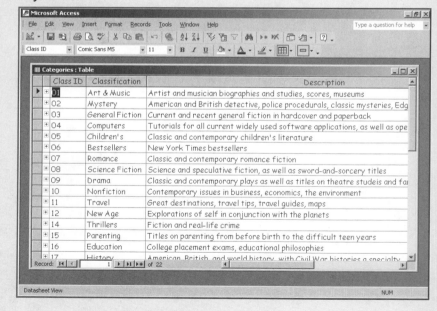

Skill Set 2

Skill List

1. Create and modify tables
2. Add a pre-defined input mask to a field
3. Create lookup fields
4. Modify field properties

In Skill Set 2, you will learn how to create and modify tables. Tables are the most important object in the database because they store data. Access provides several different techniques and tools for creating tables. You can create a table by using Table Design View, by importing data from an external data source (such as a Microsoft Excel workbook), or by using the Table Wizard. The primary task in creating a table is defining **fields**, the categories of information that determine what data can be entered for each record. You can also add, delete, or modify fields within an existing table by using Table Design View.

Skill Set 2
Creating and Modifying Tables

Create and Modify Tables
Create Tables Using the Table Wizard

You can create a table by using the **Table Wizard**, which lists sample tables and fields that you can use to quickly build a new table. The Table Wizard also helps you choose a field that will make each record in the table unique (the primary key field) and helps you connect the new table to existing tables in the database.

tip

Step 1
You can click the New button on the Database window toolbar to display the New Table dialog box, which provides several techniques for creating a new table (including the Table Wizard).

Activity Steps

📄 **MedSchool01.mdb**

1. Click the **Tables button** 🔳 Tables on the Objects bar (if it's not already selected), then double-click **Create table by using wizard**

2. Scroll down to the bottom of the Sample Tables list, then click **Students**
   See Figure 2-1.

3. Click the **Select All Fields button** ▸▸

4. Click **ParentsNames** in the Fields in My New Table list, then click the **Remove Single Field button** ◂

5. Click **MiddleName** in the Fields in My New Table list, click **Rename Field**, type **MiddleInitial**, then click **OK**

6. Click **Next**, click **Next** to accept Students as the table name and to allow the wizard to set the primary key

7. Click **Next** to avoid setting any table relationships at this time, click the **Modify the table design option button**, then click **Finish** to open the table in Design View
   See Figure 2-2.

8. Close the Students table, then click **Yes** (if prompted) to save it

Figure 2-1: Table Wizard dialog box

Business and Personal categories

Students

Sample fields in the Students table

Select All Fields button

Remove Single Field button

Rename Field

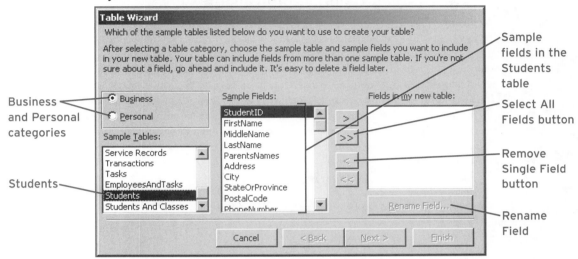

Figure 2-2: Students table in Design View

Primary key field symbol indicating that StudentID is the primary key

Fields selected using the Table Wizard

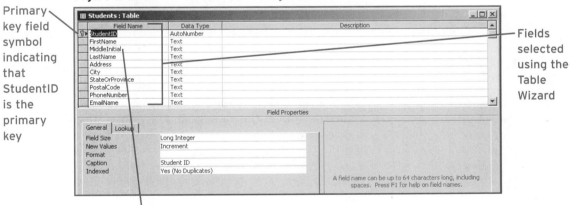

MiddleInitial field renamed using the Table Wizard

Skill Set 2

Creating and Modifying Tables

Create and Modify Tables

Create Tables Using Table Design View

You can use Table Design View to create a new table. Unlike the Table Wizard, which helps you make decisions about field names and other characteristics of a table, Table Design View requires that you plan and enter each new field by yourself. In Table Design View, you enter field names, field data types, and field **properties** (individual characteristics of a field, such as Field Size). The **data type** of the field determines what types of values you can enter into the field, such as numbers, dates, or text. (See Table 2-1 for more information on data types.) Regardless of the technique you use to build a table, you use Table Design View to add, delete, or modify the fields in an existing table.

Step 4
The Primary Key button works as a toggle, so if you set the wrong field as the primary key field, click the field, then click the Primary Key button to remove the primary key field designation from the incorrect field.

Activity Steps

 MedSchool01.mdb

1. Click the **Tables button** on the Objects bar (if it's not already selected), then double-click **Create table in Design view**

2. Type **InstructorID**, press [Down Arrow], type **InstructorFirst**, press [Down Arrow], type **InstructorLast**, press [Down Arrow], then type **Specialty**

3. Click **Text** in the Data Type cell for the InstructorID field, click the **list arrow**, then click **AutoNumber**

4. Click the **Primary Key button** on the Table Design toolbar to set the InstructorID field as the primary key field for this table

5. Click the **Save button** on the Table Design toolbar, type **Instructors** in the Table Name box, then click **OK**
   See Figure 2-3.

6. Close the Instructors table

Figure 2-3: Creating and Modifying the Instructors table in Design View

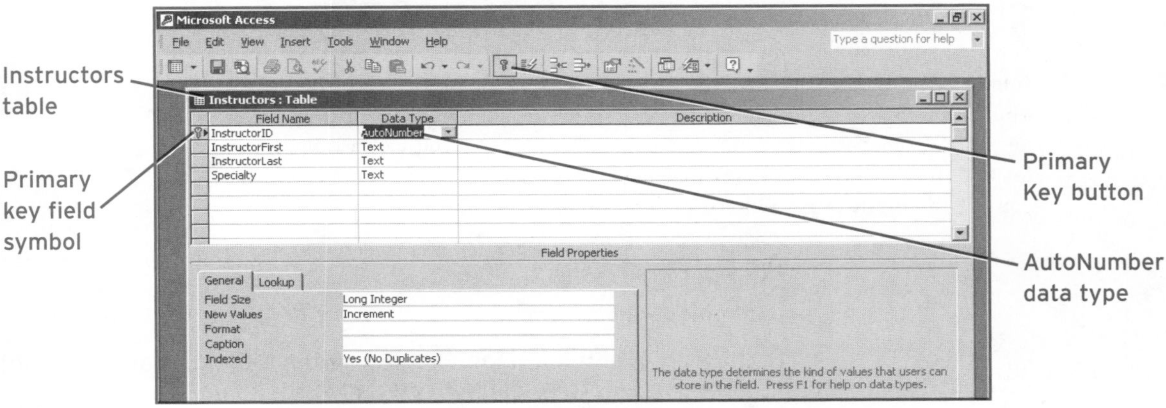

Instructors table

Primary key field symbol

Primary Key button

AutoNumber data type

TABLE 2-1: Data types

data type	description of data	field examples
Text	Text or combinations of text and numbers	FirstName, City
Memo	Lengthy text over 255 characters	Comments, Notes
Number	Numeric information used in calculations	Quantity, Rating
Date/Time	Dates and times	BirthDate, InvoiceDate
Currency	Monetary values	PurchasePrice, Salary
AutoNumber	Integers assigned by Access to sequentially order each record added to a table	InvoiceID, CustomerID
Yes/No	Only one of two values (Yes/No, On/Off, True/False)	Veteran, Tenured
OLE Object	Files created in other programs	Resume, Picture
Hyperlink	Web page addresses	HomePage, CompanyWebPage

Skill Set 2

Creating and Modifying Tables

Add a Pre-defined Input Mask to a Field

You can use the **Input Mask** property to specify the number and types of characters that can be entered into a field and to display a visual guide as data is entered. For example, you might apply an input mask to a Social Security Number field so that the only characters allowed are the numbers 0 through 9. You could also set the input mask to enter dashes automatically as the Social Security Number is entered (for example 123-12-1234). You can use the Input Mask property only with fields that have Text and Date/Time data types. You can use the **Input Mask Wizard** to enter Input Mask properties.

Activity Steps

 MedSchool01.mdb

1. Click the **Tables button** ⊞ Tables on the Objects bar (if it's not already selected), click **Physicians**, then click the **Design button** ⌐ Design on the Database window toolbar to open the table in Design View

2. Click the **Input Mask property box** (for the selected field, SocialSecurityNumber), click the **Build button** ..., then click **Yes** (if prompted) to save the table

3. Click **Social Security Number** in the Input Mask list, press **[Tab]**, then type **111223333** to test the new input mask
   See Figure 2-4.

4. Click **Next**, click **Next** to accept the suggested input mask (000-00-000) and the placeholder character (_)
   In the input mask 00-000-0000, 0 represents a required number, which means that only numbers (not letters or symbols) are allowed as valid characters for the SocialSecurityNumber field.

5. Click **Finish** to store the data without the symbols in the input mask
   See Figure 2-5.

6. Click the **Save button** 🖫 on the Table Design toolbar, click the **View button** ⊞ on the Table Design toolbar, type **333224444**, then press **[Tab]** to test the new Input Mask property
   The Input Mask property guides the entry of the numbers in the SocialSecurityNumber field.

7. Close the Physicians table

You can press F6 to switch between the upper and lower panes of Table Design View.

Figure 2-4: Input Mask Wizard dialog box

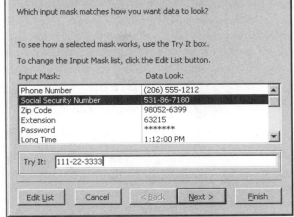

Figure 2-5: Input mask entry in Table Design View

SocialSecurity Number field

Selected field symbol

Input Mask property box displaying input mask

Build button

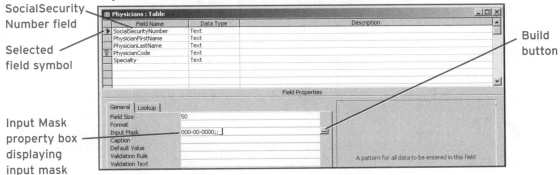

Skill Set 2

Creating and Modifying Tables

Create Lookup Fields

To make data entry easier, faster, and more accurate, you can provide a **lookup field**, a field that contains a list of values from which you can choose an entry. This data appears in a combo box (sometimes called a drop-down list) for a lookup field on either a datasheet or form. To create a lookup field, you must specify **Lookup properties**, which will provide the list of values for the field. You can use the **Lookup Wizard** to enter Lookup properties for a field.

Activity Steps

 MedSchool01.mdb

1. Click the **Tables button** ▦ Tables on the Objects bar (if it's not already selected), click **Insurance**, then click the **Design button** ▨ Design on the Database window toolbar to open the table in Design View

2. Click **Text** in the Data Type cell for the ZipCode field, click the **list arrow**, then click **Lookup Wizard**

3. Click **Next** to accept the option for the lookup column to look up values in a table or query

4. Click **Table: Zip** to choose the table that will provide the values for the combo box, then click **Next**

5. Double-click **ZipCode**, then double-click **City**
   See Figure 2-6.

6. Click **Next**, deselect the **Hide key column check box**
   A **key column** refers to the primary key field column.

7. Click **Next**, then Click **Next** to accept the option that the ZipCode field uniquely identifies each row, click **Finish** to accept "ZipCode" as the label for the lookup column, then click **Yes** when prompted to save the table

8. Click the **View button** ▦ on the Table Design toolbar, click the **ZipCode** field for the first record, click the **list arrow**, then click **64014** in the combo box list

9. Close the Insurance table

You can click any property box to display a short description of it in the lower right corner of Table Design View. Click any property box, then press F1 to display a longer description of the property in the Help system.

Figure 2-6: Lookup Wizard dialog box

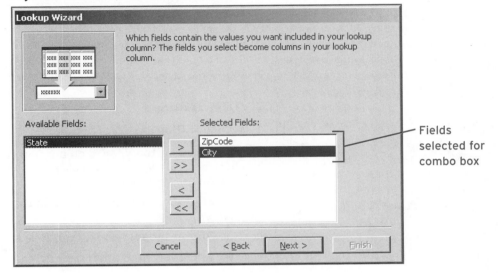

Fields
selected for
combo box

Skill Set 2
Creating and Modifying Tables

Modify Field Properties

You modify field properties in Table Design View. Field properties vary among field data types. For example, fields with a Text data type have a Field Size property that you can use to change the number of characters allowed for entries stored in that field. However, fields with a Date/Time data type do not have a Field Size property, because the size of a Date/Time field is controlled by Access. A list of common field properties for various data types is shown in Table 2-2.

Activity Steps

 MedSchool01.mdb

1. Click the **Tables button** ⊞ Tables on the Objects bar (if it's not already selected), click **Zip**, then click the **Design button** ⬚ Design on the Database window toolbar to open the table in Design View

2. Click the **State** field, double-click **50** in the Field Size property box, then type **2**

3. Click the **Format property box**, then type **>**

4. Click the **Validation Rule property box**, then type **CO or WY**

5. Click the **Validation Text property box**, then type **Must be CO or WY**
   See Figure 2-7.

6. Click the **Save button** 🖫 on the Table Design toolbar, click **Yes** when prompted to continue, click **Yes** when prompted to test the rules, then click the **View button** ⊞ on the Table Design toolbar

7. Press **[Tab]** to move to the State field, type **MDD** (note that the third character is not allowed), then press **[Down Arrow]**

8. Click **OK** when prompted with the Validation Text message, then press **[Esc]** to undo the edit to the current record

9. Close the Zip table

Step 4
Access automatically enters quotation marks around text typed into the Validation Rule property box.

Figure 2-7: Modifying other properties

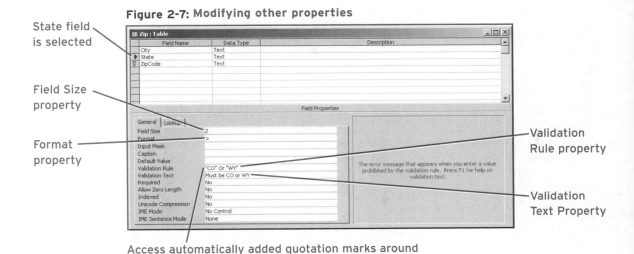

State field is selected

Field Size property

Format property

Validation Rule property

Validation Text Property

Access automatically added quotation marks around text criteria for the Validation Rule property

---

TABLE 2-2: Common Field Properties

property	description	typical value
Field Size (Text data type)	Determines how many characters can be entered into a field	1 through 255
Field Size (Number data type)	Determines the size and type of numbers that can be entered into a field	Integer
Format	Determines how data will appear on the datasheet	> (display values in uppercase) < (display values in lowercase)
Caption	Overwrites the actual field name in the first row of the datasheet	First Name (if the field name is FName, for example)
Default Value	Automatically provides a value for a field in a new record	CO (for a State field in which the majority of records contained the CO entry)
Validation Rule	Provides a list of valid entries for a field	"CO" OR "WY" or "MT"
Validation Text	Provides a descriptive message in case a user attempts to enter data into a field that doesn't meet the criteria specified in the Validation Rule property box	Valid entries are CO, WY, or MT
Decimal Places	Determines the number of digits that are displayed to the right of the decimal point	0, 2
Input Mask	Determines the number and type of characters that can be entered in a field and provides a visual guide for data entry	00000-9999;;_

Skill Set 2

Creating and Modifying Tables

Target Your Skills

 MedSchool01.mdb

1 Create a new table in Table Design View and save it with the name Hospitals. Use Figure 2-8 to determine the fields to create. Be sure to designate the HospitalNumber field as the primary key field. Use the Input Mask Wizard to apply the Input Mask property to the HospitalPhone field.

 MedSchool01.mdb

2 Open the Physicians table in Design View and add a new field named Title, as shown in Figure 2-9. Modify the Field Size, Format, Validation Rule, and Validation Text properties as shown in the figure.

Figure 2-8

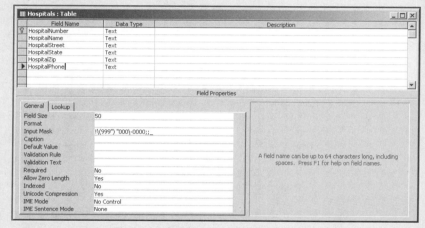

Figure 2-9

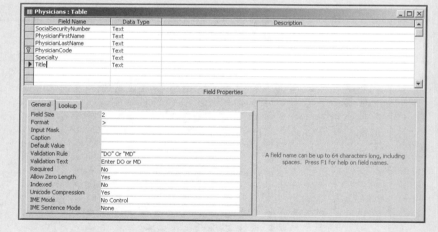

Skill List

1. Create and modify select queries
2. Add calculated fields to select queries

In Skill Set 3, you will work with the **select query**, a database object that collects fields from one or more tables into a single datasheet. You build a query when you have a question about the data. For example, you could use a query to determine which customers bought a particular product. You can build a select query by using either the Simple Query Wizard or Query Design View. Once a query is created, you open it in Datasheet View to find, filter, and edit data. You can also use a select query to create **calculated fields**, fields whose contents depend on the values in other fields. For example, you could multiply a numerical value in a field, such as Sales, by a percentage to obtain a numerical value for a different field, such as Tax.

Skill Set 3
Creating and Modifying Queries

Create and Modify Select Queries
Create Select Queries Using the Simple Query Wizard

You can use the **Simple Query Wizard** to build a select query. The Simple Query Wizard prompts you to choose the fields you want in the query, asks you how the final records should be presented (as individual or summarized records), and asks you to enter a title for the query. Your selections determine how the data is presented and organized in the final Datasheet View of the query.

Step 4
You can also use the Select Single Field button $\boxed{>}$, Select All Fields button $\boxed{>>}$, Remove Single Field button $\boxed{<}$, or Remove All Fields button $\boxed{<<}$ to add fields to or remove fields from the Selected Fields list.

Activity Steps

 Team01.mdb

1. Click the **Queries button** [⊞ Queries] on the Objects bar (if it's not already selected), then double-click **Create query by using wizard**

2. Click the **Tables/Queries list arrow**, then click **Table: Players** (if it's not already selected)

3. Double-click **FName**, then double-click **LName**

4. Click the **Tables/Queries list arrow**, click **Table: Pledges**, double-click **Amount**, then double-click **Date**
   See Figure 3-1.

5. Click **Next**, then click **Next** again to accept the Detail option
   The Detail option will show every record.

6. Type **Pledges To Date** as the title for the query, then click **Finish** to view the query in Datasheet View
   See Figure 3-2.

7. Close the **Pledges to Date** query

Figure 3-1: Building a select query with the Simple Query Wizard

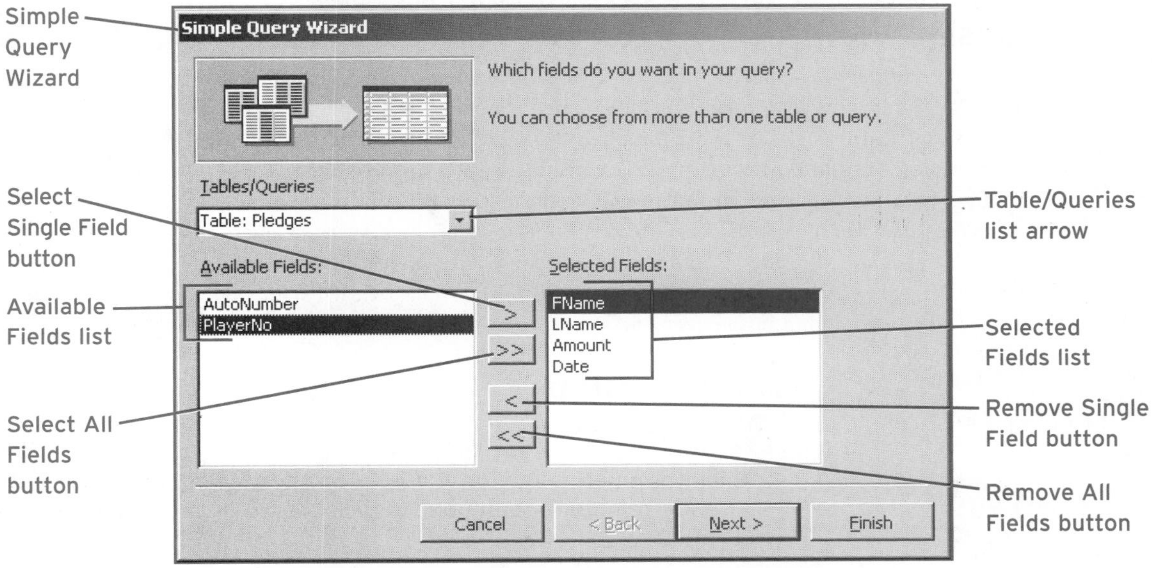

Simple Query Wizard
Simple Query Wizard
Which fields do you want in your query?
You can choose from more than one table or query.
Tables/Queries
Table: Pledges
Available Fields:
AutoNumber
PlayerNo
Selected Fields:
FName
LName
Amount
Date
>
>>
<
<<
Cancel
< Back
Next >
Finish
Select Single Field button
Available Fields list
Select All Fields button
Table/Queries list arrow
Selected Fields list
Remove Single Field button
Remove All Fields button

Figure 3-2: Datasheet View for the Pledges To Date query

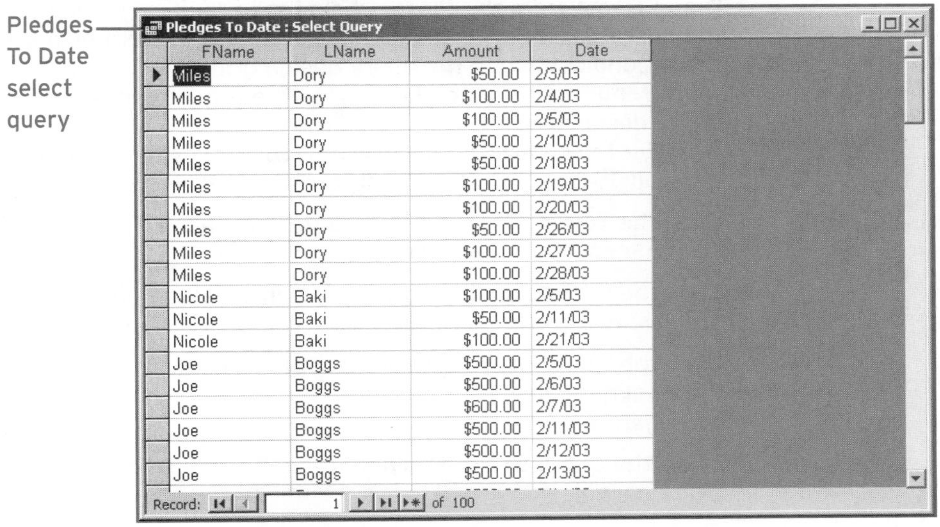

Pledges To Date select query
Pledges To Date : Select Query
Record: 1 of 100

FName	LName	Amount	Date
Miles	Dory	$50.00	2/3/03
Miles	Dory	$100.00	2/4/03
Miles	Dory	$100.00	2/5/03
Miles	Dory	$50.00	2/10/03
Miles	Dory	$50.00	2/18/03
Miles	Dory	$100.00	2/19/03
Miles	Dory	$100.00	2/20/03
Miles	Dory	$50.00	2/26/03
Miles	Dory	$100.00	2/27/03
Miles	Dory	$100.00	2/28/03
Nicole	Baki	$100.00	2/5/03
Nicole	Baki	$50.00	2/11/03
Nicole	Baki	$100.00	2/21/03
Joe	Boggs	$500.00	2/5/03
Joe	Boggs	$500.00	2/6/03
Joe	Boggs	$600.00	2/7/03
Joe	Boggs	$500.00	2/11/03
Joe	Boggs	$500.00	2/12/03
Joe	Boggs	$500.00	2/13/03

Skill Set 3
Creating and Modifying Queries

Create and Modify Select Queries
Create Select Queries Using Query Design View

You can use Query Design View to create or modify a select query. Query Design View is separated into two parts: the upper and lower panes. The upper pane displays table field lists, which show the fields available for the query. The lower pane displays the **query design grid**, which contains rows that you use to specify field name, table name, sort order, and **criteria**, rules that limit the number of records that will appear in Query Datasheet View. To create a query in Query Design View and to specify the order in which you want the fields to appear in Query Datasheet View, you can drag the desired field from a field list in the upper pane to a column in the query design grid.

Step 2
To add field lists to the upper pane of Query Design View, click the Show Table button on the Query Design toolbar, then double-click the desired table. To delete field lists, click the title bar of the extra list and press [Delete].

Activity Steps
file Team01.mdb

1. Click the **Queries button** ⊞ Queries on the Objects bar (if it's not already selected), then double-click **Create query in Design view**

2. Click **Players** (if it's not already selected), click **Add**, click **Teams**, click **Add**, then click **Close** in the Show Table dialog box

3. Drag **FName** from the Players field list to the first column in the query design grid, drag **LName** from the Players field list to the second column in the query design grid, then drag **TeamName** in the Teams field list to the third column of the query design grid
   You added three fields to the query design grid by dragging. You can also double-click a field to add it to the next available column.

4. Click the **Sort cell** for the Lname field, click the **list arrow**, then click **Ascending**

5. Click the **Criteria cell** for the TeamName field, then type **sharks**
   See Figure 3-3.

6. Click the **View button** ▦ on the Query Design toolbar to view the final datasheet
   See Figure 3-4.

7. Close the query without saving it

Figure 3-3: Building a select query with Query Design View

View button

Players field list

Teams field list

Sort cell for LName field

Show Table button

Query design grid

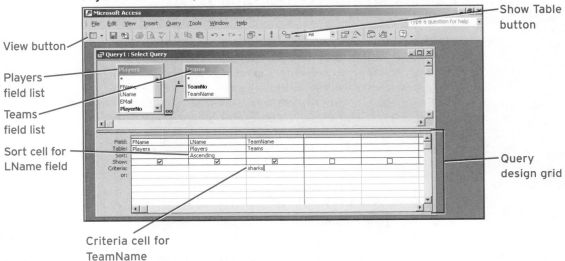

Criteria cell for TeamName

Figure 3-4: Query Datasheet View

Records are in ascending order based on the LName field

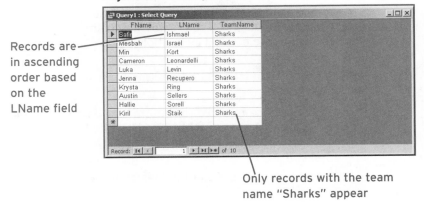

Only records with the team name "Sharks" appear

Skill Set 3

Creating and Modifying Queries

Add Calculated Fields to Select Queries

Add a Calculated Field Using Query Design View

A **calculated field's** contents are created by an **expression**: any combination of field names, **constants** (such as the number 5 or word "Page"), and **operators** (such as add, subtract, multiply, and divide) used to calculate a value. Table 3-1 shows examples of expressions you can use to define new calculated fields. A calculated field built in Query Design View will automatically calculate the field value, guaranteeing that the new field will always contain accurate, up-to-date information. Therefore, if you can calculate field values, you shouldn't define the field in Table Design View the way you'd define the other fields. Rather, build the field in Query Design View so that it will automatically calculate the correct value.

In an expression, field names need to be referenced (but not capitalized) exactly the same way they are defined in Table Design View.

Activity Steps

 Team01.mdb

1. Click the **Queries button** 📋 Queries on the Objects bar (if it's not already selected), click **50% of Pledges**, then click the **Design button** 📐 Design on the Database window toolbar

2. Click in the fourth Field cell column in the query design grid, then type **Half:[Amount]*0.5** to create a calculated field named Half, whose values are created by multiplying the Amount field by 0.5. *See Figure 3-5.*

3. Click the **View button** 🔲 on the Query Design toolbar to view the datasheet

4. Press **[Tab]** twice to move to the Amount field for the first record, type **150**, press **[Tab]** twice to move to the next record, then view the calculated value in the Half field *See Figure 3-6.*

5. Save and close the 50% of Pledges query

Figure 3-5: **Creating a calculated field in Query Design View**

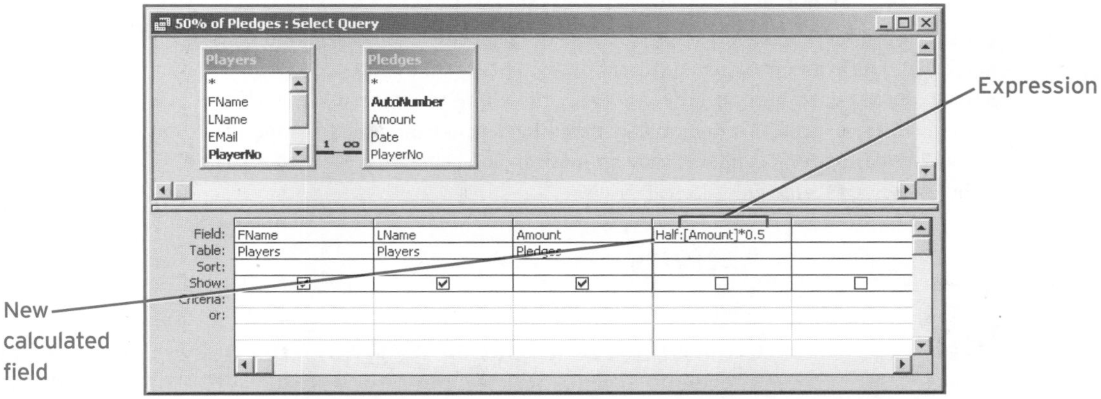

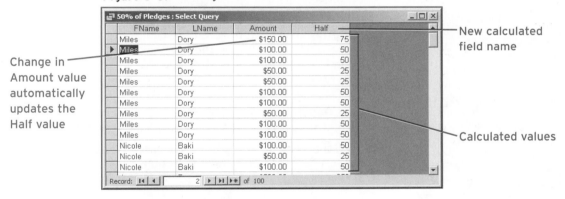

New calculated field

Expression

Figure 3-6: **Viewing a calculated field in Datasheet View**

Change in Amount value automatically updates the Half value

New calculated field name

Calculated values

TABLE 3-1: Common Access expressions

category	sample expression	description
Arithmetic	=[Retail]/[Wholesale]	Divides the Retail field by the Wholesale field to calculate the markup percentage
Page Number	="Page "&[Page]	Displays the word "Page," a space, and the current page number, such as Page 2, Page 6, or Page 10
Text	=[FirstName]&" "&[LastName]	Displays the value of the FirstName field and LastName field separated by a space

Skill Set 3
Creating and Modifying Queries

Add Calculated Fields to Select Queries
Format Values in a Calculated Field

Formatting a value means changing the way it appears but not changing the value itself. For example, you can format the number 5000 as $5,000, $5,000.00, or 5,000.0000, depending on how you want the value to appear on the screen and on printed reports. To format a calculated field, you change field properties, such as the Format or Decimal Places properties, using the Field Properties dialog box accessed from Query Design View.

Step 3
Choosing the Currency option for the Format property automatically displays values with two digits to the right of the decimal point. You can override this default by entering a specific value such as 0 in the Decimal Places property box.

Activity Steps

 Team01.mdb

1. Click the **Queries button** on the Objects bar (if it's not already selected), then double-click the **Corporate Match** query to open it in Datasheet View
   View the formatting characteristics of the calculated field named Double.

2. Click the **View button** on the Query Datasheet toolbar, click the **Double** field name in the fourth column, then click the **Properties button** on the Query Design toolbar to open the field property sheet (if it's not already open)
   See Figure 3-7.

3. Click **General Number** in the Format property box, click the **Format property list arrow**, then click **Currency**

4. Click the **View button** on the Query Design toolbar to view the formatting change for the Double field
   See Figure 3-8.

5. Save and close the Corporate Match query

Figure 3-7: Formatting a calculated field

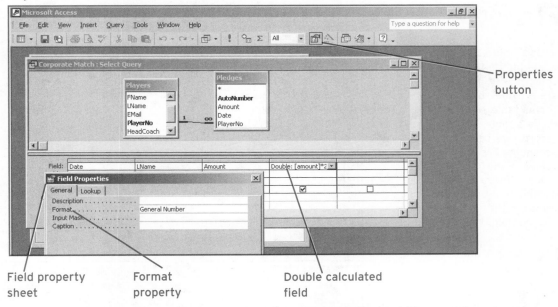

Properties button

Field property sheet

Format property

Double calculated field

Figure 3-8: Viewing a formatted calculated field in Datasheet View

Date	LName	Amount	Double
2/10/03	Armani	$100.00	$200.00
2/10/03	Banka	$500.00	$1,000.00
2/10/03	Beebe	$50.00	$100.00
2/10/03	Buzikcy	$600.00	$1,200.00
2/10/03	Carley	$500.00	$1,000.00
2/10/03	Cerda	$100.00	$200.00
2/10/03	Chen	$90.00	$180.00
2/10/03	Cho	$100.00	$200.00
2/10/03	Dory	$50.00	$100.00
2/10/03	Mazon	$500.00	$1,000.00
2/10/03	Mikelson	$100.00	$200.00
2/10/03	Robar	$100.00	$200.00
2/10/03	Shahzaib	$90.00	$180.00

Record: 1 of 100

Calculated field values appear with currency symbols

Skill Set 3

Creating and Modifying Queries

Target Your Skills

 Team01.mdb

1 Use Figure 3-9 as a guide to create a new select query. The fields are provided by the Teams table and the Players table. The records are sorted in ascending order by the values in the TeamName field, followed by an ascending order by the values in the LName field.

Figure 3-9

TeamName	FName	LName	HeadCoach
Angels	Paige	Cahill	☐
Angels	Kelsey	Land	☐
Angels	Cici	Lapoint	☐
Angels	Ananias	Marcus	☐
Angels	Gina	Noack	☐
Angels	Marco	Polo	☐
Angels	Monserrat	Toby	☐
Angels	Riley	Toloza	☐
Angels	Tyler	Vandewalle	☑
Angels	Cornelius	Washington	☐
Eggheads	Sevana	Buzikcy	☑
Eggheads	Peter	Cerda	☐
Eggheads	Jimmy	Chen	☐

Record: 1 of 40

 Team01.mdb

2 Use Figure 3-10 as a guide to create a select query. The records are sorted in descending order by the values in the Amount field. The Points calculated field is created by dividing the Amount field by three, Points:[Amount]/3. The Points field is formatted with the Standard option for the Format property and 0 for the Decimal Places property. (Hint: If you're having trouble opening the property sheet for the Point field, switch to Datasheet View, then return to Query Design View.)

Figure 3-10

TeamName	LName	Date	Amount	Points
Angels	Cahill	2/17/03	$600.00	200
Sharks	Kort	2/13/03	$600.00	200
Sharks	Kort	2/14/03	$600.00	200
Eggheads	Merlo	2/11/03	$600.00	200
Sharks	Staik	2/11/03	$600.00	200
Angels	Cahill	2/13/03	$600.00	200
Sharks	Ring	2/14/03	$600.00	200
T-Bones	Boggs	2/25/03	$600.00	200
Eggheads	Buzikcy	2/10/03	$600.00	200
Angels	Marcus	2/13/03	$600.00	200
T-Bones	Boggs	2/7/03	$600.00	200
Angels	Marcus	2/17/03	$600.00	200
T-Bones	Boggs	2/11/03	$500.00	167
Angels	Vandewalle	2/17/03	$500.00	167
T-Bones	Boggs	2/6/03	$500.00	167
T-Bones	Boggs	2/13/03	$500.00	167

Record: 1 of 100

Skill List

1. Create and display forms
2. Modify form properties

In Skill Set 4, you will learn how to create, view, and modify forms. An Access database **form** provides an easy-to-use data entry screen. While you can also enter or edit data using the Datasheet View of a table or query, a datasheet is not always the fastest or easiest way to view, enter, or edit existing data. For example, if a record has many fields, you might not be able to see all the fields for one record on a datasheet without scrolling left or right. Using a form, however, you can rearrange the fields on the screen and present them in any layout that you design, or you can model an Access form after an existing paper form. You can also add graphical items, such as images and buttons, to forms to make your database easy to use.

Skill Set 4

Creating and Modifying Forms

Create and Display Forms
Create Forms Using AutoForms

You can use the AutoForm tool to create a new form quickly. First you need to choose a record source, a table or query upon which a form is to be based. After you select a record source, you start the AutoForm process by using the New Object: AutoForm button on the Database toolbar. The AutoForm process creates the new form using all the fields and records from the record source, organizes the fields in a Columnar layout, and automatically displays the new form in Form View. To apply form layouts other than the Columnar layout to a new form, you can use the Form Wizard or design the form yourself in Form Design View. Form layouts are described in Table 4-1.

Step 2
If the New Object button displays the AutoForm icon , you can click the button to create a form using the AutoForm tool instead of clicking the New Object button list arrow and clicking AutoForm.

Activity Steps

file▷ RecycleO1.mdb

1. Click the **Tables button** 🔳 Tables on the Objects bar (if it's not already selected), then click **Clubs**

2. Click the **New Object button list arrow** 🗗 ▾ on the Database toolbar, then click **AutoForm**
   See Figure 4-1. The AutoForm tool automatically created a form in a Columnar layout using the Clubs table as the record source. Since the Clubs table is related to the Deposits table in a one-to-many relationship, associated records from the Deposits table also were added automatically. Deposits records appear as a subform in datasheet layout.

3. **Close the Clubs form without saving it**

Figure 4-1: Clubs form created by the AutoForm tool

Fields from the Clubs table

Fields and records from the Deposits table

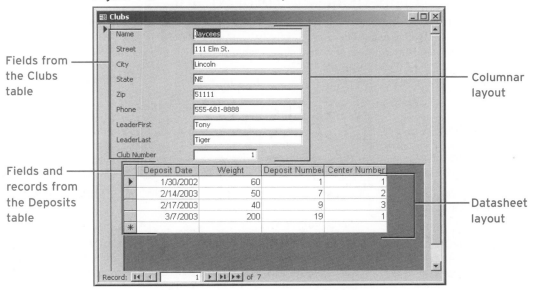

Columnar layout

Datasheet layout

TABLE 4-1: Form layouts

layout	description
Columnar	Fields are positioned in a column (or multiple columns, if needed), each with a descriptive label to its left
Tabular	Fields are organized in columns with all the fields of one record on one row; descriptive field labels are positioned at the top of each column
Datasheet	Fields are organized in columns with all the fields of one record in one row just as they appear in the datasheet of a table or query; descriptive field labels are positioned at the top of each column
Justified	Fields are organized in columns, but if all the fields of one record do not fit on one row (as defined by the width of the screen), additional fields are positioned on a second (or third) row
PivotTable	Opens the form in PivotTable View; to add fields to the form, drag them from the Field List to the PivotTable field areas
PivotChart	Opens the form in PivotChart View; to add fields to the form, drag them from the Field List to the PivotChart field areas

Skill Set 4
Creating and Modifying Forms

Create and Display Forms
Create Forms Using the Form Wizard

You can use the **Form Wizard** to quickly create a form. The Form Wizard prompts you with several questions to specify many aspects of the final form, including the fields you want to use and the layout, style, and title of the form. If you want to modify a form that was created using the Form Wizard, you use Form Design View.

Step 4
Forms created with the Form Wizard are automatically saved as form objects within the database. They are given the same name as the form title specified in the last step of the Form Wizard.

Activity Steps

file ⎋ **Recycle01.mdb**

1. Click the **Forms button** on the Objects bar (if it's not already selected), then double-click **Create form by using wizard**

2. Click the **Tables/Queries list arrow**, click **Table: Clubs**, then click the **Select All Fields button** >>
   See Figure 4-2.

3. Click **Next**, click the **Columnar option button** (if it's not already selected) for the layout, click **Next**, click **Blends** (if it's not already selected) for the style, click **Next**, then click **Finish** to accept "Clubs" as the form title
   See Figure 4-3. The form is created with the specific fields, layout, style, and name that you specified in the steps of the Form Wizard.

4. Close the Clubs form

Figure 4-2: Form Wizard dialog box

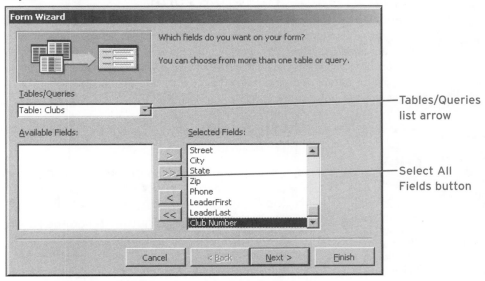

Tables/Queries list arrow

Select All Fields button

Figure 4-3: Clubs form created by the Form Wizard

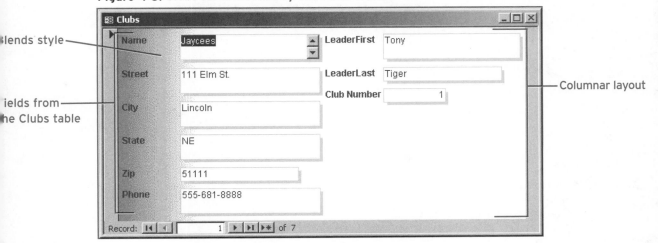

Blends style

fields from the Clubs table

Columnar layout

Skill Set 4
Creating and Modifying Forms

Modify Form Properties
Apply an AutoFormat to a Form

An **AutoFormat** is a collection of formatting characteristics and design elements, such as background colors and images, text color and styles, and border colors and styles, that you can quickly apply to a form. Access provides ten AutoFormats from which you can choose while using the Form Wizard, or you can apply an AutoFormat to any existing form in Form Design View using the AutoFormat dialog box.

Step 2
To create your own AutoFormat, click Customize in the AutoFormat dialog box. You will be given options to create your own AutoFormat, or update or delete the existing AutoFormat.

Activity Steps

 Recycle01.mdb

1. Click the **Forms button** ⊞ Forms on the Objects bar (if it's not already selected), **click Center Contact Info**, then click the **Design button** ⊠ Design on the Database window toolbar

2. Click the **AutoFormat button** 🗐 on the Form Design toolbar to display the AutoFormat dialog box
   See Figure 4-4.

3. Click **Industrial**, then click **OK**

4. Click the **View button** 🗐 on the Form Design toolbar to display the Center Contact Info form with the new AutoFormat properties in Form View
   See Figure 4-5.

5. Save and close the Center Contact Info form

Figure 4-4: AutoFormat dialog box

Industrial

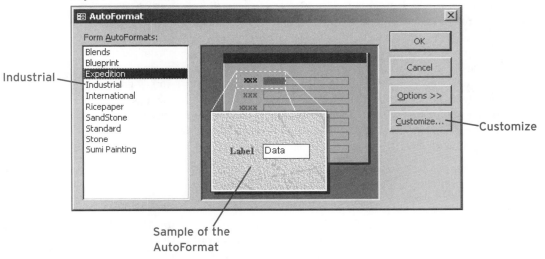

Customize

Sample of the
AutoFormat

Figure 4-5: Centers form with the Industrial AutoFormat

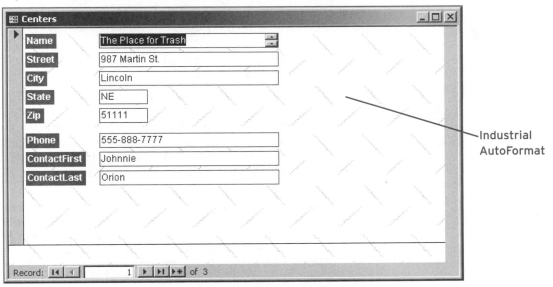

Industrial
AutoFormat

Skill Set 4
Creating and Modifying Forms

Modify Form Properties
Modify a Control on a Form

A **control** is any item on a form, such as a label, text box, or command button. You modify the properties of a control in Form Design View. **Properties** refer to all of the characteristics of the control including its color, size, and position. You can modify control properties in many ways. For example, you can apply a new formatting property (such as text color) to a selected control using the Formatting (Form/Report) toolbar. You can change a form's properties by using its **property sheet**, a window used to view and modify an object's properties. You can also modify a control's location and size properties by using pointers and dragging move or sizing handles. See Table 4-2 for information on pointers.

Activity Steps

 Recycle01.mdb

1. Click the **Forms button** 🔲 Forms on the Objects bar (if it's not already selected), click **Center Designation**, then click the **Design button** 📐 Design on the Database window toolbar

2. Click the 1-inch mark on the horizontal ruler to select all the labels in the first column, click the **Font Size list arrow** 10 ▾ on the Formatting (Form/Report) toolbar, then click **11**
   See Figure 4-6.

3. Click **Format** on the menu bar, point to **Vertical Spacing**, then click **Make Equal**

4. Point to any **sizing handle** of any of the selected labels so that the pointer changes to a double-headed arrow, then double-click to resize each label automatically to display all text

5. Point to the edge of any selected control so that the pointer changes to , then drag the controls to the right so that the right edge of the labels are positioned at about the 2-inch mark on the horizontal ruler

6. Click the **Designation text box**, click the **Properties button** 🗐 on the Form Design toolbar to display the property sheet, click the **Other tab**, scroll down, click the **ControlTip Text property box**, type **Federal size designation number**, then click the **Properties button** to toggle off the property sheet

7. Click the **View button** 📼 on the Form Design toolbar, then point to the **Designation text box**
   See Figure 4-7.

8. Save and close the Center Designation form

tip

Step 5
You use the move handle in the upper-left corner of a selected control to move only that control.

Figure 4-6: Modifying control properties

Format menu

1" mark on horizontal ruler

Move handles

Labels

Properties button

Formatting (Form/Report) toolbar

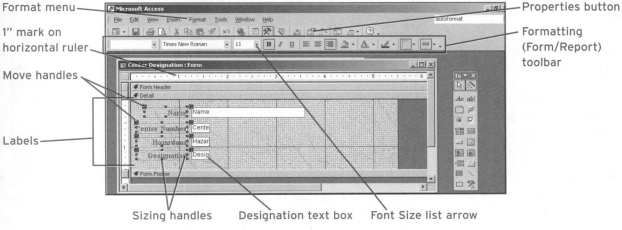

Sizing handles Designation text box Font Size list arrow

Figure 4-7: Final form

Label controls are formatted, resized, and moved

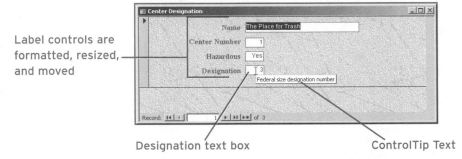

Designation text box ControlTip Text

TABLE 4-2: Form Design View pointer shapes

shape	when does this shape appear?	action
▷	When you point to any nonselected control on the form (the default pointer)	Single-clicking with this pointer *selects* a control
🖐	When you point to the edge of a selected control (but not when you are pointing to a sizing handle or the move handle)	Dragging this pointer moves all selected controls
☝	When you point to the move handle in the upper-left corner of a selected control	Dragging this pointer *moves only the single control* where the pointer is currently positioned, not other controls that might also be selected
↔ ↕ ⤢ ⤡	When you point to any sizing handle	Dragging one of these pointers *resizes* the control; double-clicking one of these pointers *resizes* the control to be as large as required to display the text

Skill Set 4

Creating and Modifying Forms

Target Your Skills

 Recycle01.mdb

1 Use the Form Wizard to create a new form. Use all of the fields from the Centers table, apply a Columnar layout, apply a Ricepaper style, and title the form "Center Information." In Form Design View, change the font size for all labels to 11, then move and resize the controls as necessary to display all text. The final form is shown in Figure 4-8.

Figure 4-8

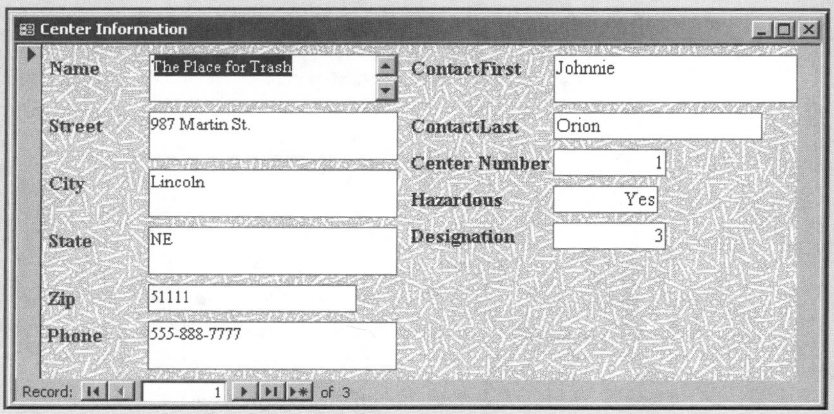

Center Information				_ □ ×
Name	The Place for Trash	ContactFirst	Johnnie	
Street	987 Martin St.	ContactLast	Orion	
City	Lincoln	Center Number	1	
State	NE	Hazardous	Yes	
Zip	51111	Designation	3	
Phone	555-888-7777			

Record: ◀ ◀ 1 ▶ ▶I ▶* of 3

 Recycle01.mdb

2 Use the AutoForm tool to create a form based on the Deposit List query. In Form Design View, apply a SandStone AutoFormat, then display the form in Form View as shown in Figure 4-9. Save the form with the name "Deposit List."

Figure 4-9

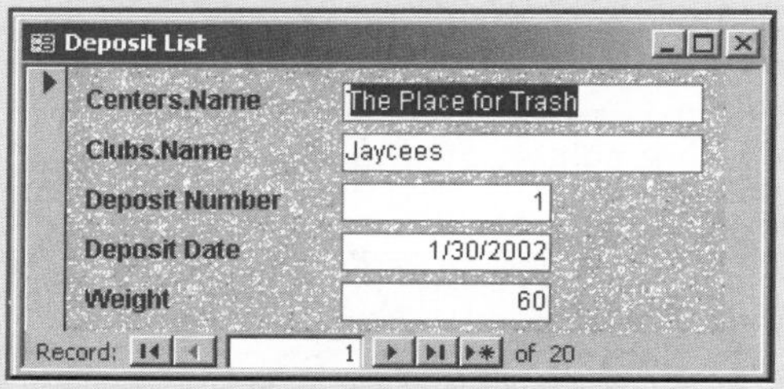

Deposit List		_ □ ×
Centers.Name	The Place for Trash	
Clubs.Name	Jaycees	
Deposit Number	1	
Deposit Date	1/30/2002	
Weight	60	

Record: I◀ ◀ 1 ▶ ▶I ▶* of 20

Skill List

1. Enter, edit, and delete records
2. Create queries
3. Sort records
4. Filter records

In Skill Set 5, you will study ways to enter, edit, and delete information using the Datasheet View of a table or query and the Form View of a form. You'll use the Crosstab Query Wizard to create a datasheet that summarizes groups of records. You'll learn how to sort records in the Datasheet View of a table or query and how to specify multiple sort orders in Query Design View. Finally, you'll use two filter tools, Filter by Selection and Filter by Form, to display a subset of records within Datasheet View.

Skill Set 5

Viewing and Organizing Information

Enter, Edit, and Delete Records
Enter, Edit, and Delete Records in Datasheet View

In Datasheet View, you enter a new record by clicking the New Record button on either the Table (or Query) Datasheet toolbar or navigation toolbar, then typing the new data in the new record that opens as the last record in the datasheet. To delete a record, you click any value in the record that you want to delete, then click the Delete Record button on the Table (or Query) Datasheet toolbar. You edit a record by selecting the data that you want to change, then typing the new information. You can also use several special keystrokes to enter and edit data in a datasheet, as listed in Table 5-1.

Activity Steps

 PatientsO1.mbd

1. Click the **Tables button** [Tables] on the Objects bar (if it's not already selected), then double-click **Employees** to open it in Datasheet View

2. Click the **New Record button** ▶* on the Table Datasheet toolbar

3. Type **Brothers**, press **[Tab]**, type **Gina**, press **[Tab]**, type **A**, press **[Tab]**, then type **17**
   See Figure 5-1. When you are editing a record, the edit record symbol ✎ appears in the **record selector**, the square button to the left of the record.

Step 7
You cannot undo the deletion of a record.

4. Click the **record selector** for the Jefferson, Sara record, click the **Delete Record button** ✖ on the Table Datasheet toolbar, then click **Yes** to confirm the deletion

5. Double-click **Cooper** in the Cooper, Paula record, then type **Langdon**

6. Double-click **Paula** in the Langdon, Paula record, then type **Jordan**

7. Press **Esc** once to undo the change to the current field, then press **Esc** again to undo all changes to the current record
   While you are editing a record, use the Esc key to undo changes. As soon as you move to a different record, however, the edits you made to the previous record are automatically saved to the database and the Esc key cannot undo them. To undo the changes to a saved record, click the Undo button ↺ on the Table (or Query) Datasheet toolbar. You can undo only your last action in Datasheet View.

8. Close the Employees table

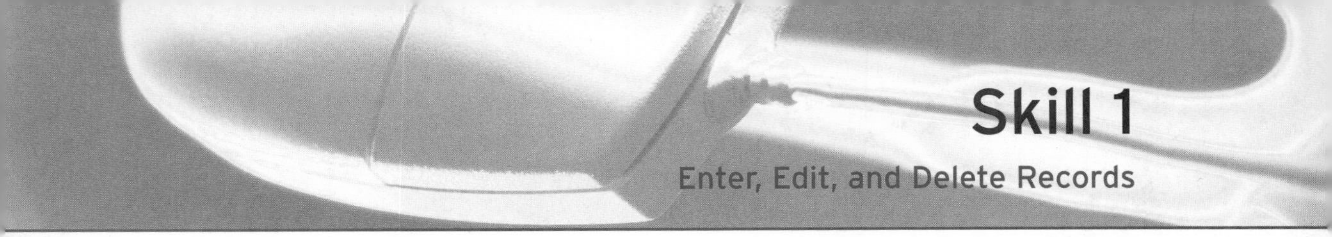

Figure 5-1: Adding a new record to the Employees table using Datasheet View

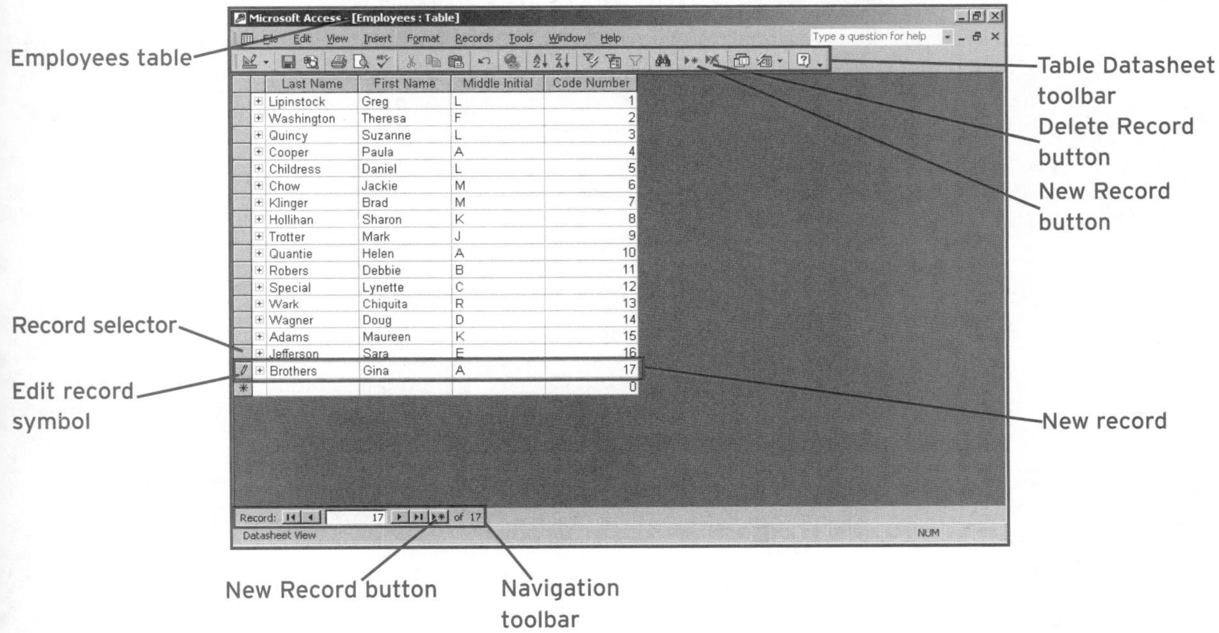

Employees table

Record selector

Edit record symbol

Table Datasheet toolbar

Delete Record button

New Record button

New record

New Record button   Navigation toolbar

TABLE 5-1: Special keystrokes to enter and edit data

keystroke	action
[Backspace]	Deletes one character to the left of the insertion point
[Delete]	Deletes one character to the right of the insertion point
[F2]	Switches between Edit and Navigation mode
[Esc]	Undoes the change to the current field
[Esc][Esc]	Undoes all changes to the current record
[F7]	Starts the spell check feature
[Ctrl][']	Inserts the value from the same field in the previous record into the current field
[Ctrl][;]	Inserts the current date in a date field

Skill Set 5

Viewing and Organizing Information

Enter, Edit, and Delete Records
Enter, Edit, and Delete Records in Form View

You use the Form View of a form object to enter, edit, and delete records in a database. Since you can arrange fields in any layout on a form, using Form View is generally preferable to using the Datasheet View of a table or query object when entering, editing, or deleting data in a database. Because a form usually displays only one record at a time, you will use the navigation toolbar to move between the records of a form. The buttons on the navigation toolbar are listed in Table 5-2.

Activity Steps

 Patients01.mbd

1. Click the **Forms button** [≡ Forms] on the Objects bar (if it's not already selected), double-click **Patients** to open it in Form View, then maximize the Patients form

2. Click the **New Record button** [▶*] on the Form View toolbar

3. Type **333224444**, press **[Tab]**, type **9/6/81**, press **[Tab]**, type **Winger**, press **[Tab]**, then type **Travis**
   See Figure 5-2. The edit record symbol [✎] appears in the record selector, the button to the left of the record.

4. Click the **First Record button** [◀] on the navigation toolbar to move to the first record for Alvin Patterson

5. Double-click **Alvin** to select it (if it's not already selected), then type **Aaron**

6. Click the **Next Record button** [▶] on the navigation toolbar to move to the second record for Andre Quantie

7. Click the **Delete Record button** [▶✗] on the Form View toolbar, then click **OK** when notified that the record cannot be deleted
   By default, Access will not allow you to delete a record that has related records in another table.

8. Close the Patients form

Step 3
You can also press [Enter] to move between the fields of a record.

Figure 5-2: Adding a new record to the Patients table using Form View

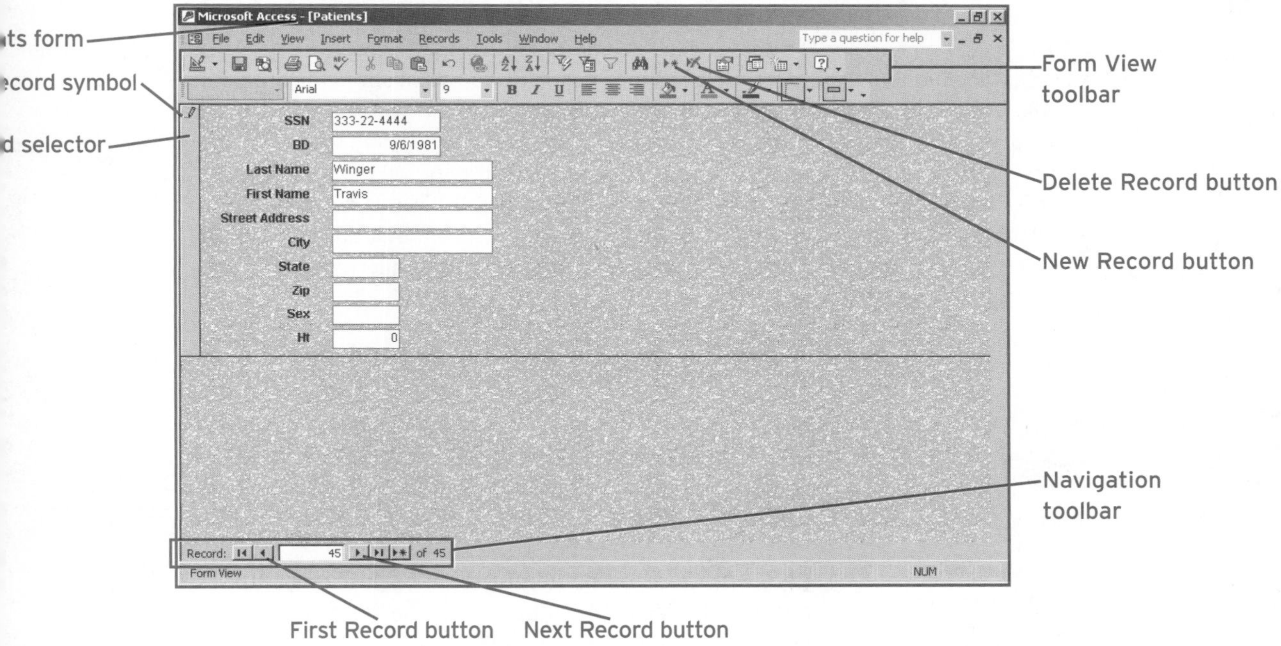

ts form

ecord symbol

d selector

Form View
toolbar

Delete Record button

New Record button

Navigation
toolbar

First Record button   Next Record button

TABLE 5-2: Navigation toolbar buttons

button	name
I◄	First Record button
◄	Previous Record button
►	Next Record button
►I	Last Record button
►*	New Record button

Skill Set 5

Viewing and Organizing Information

Create Queries

A **crosstab query** calculates a sum, average, count, or other type of statistic for data that is grouped by at least two other fields. You use this type of query to obtain statistics on groups of records. A crosstab query typically uses three fields: one as a column heading, one as a row heading, and one to be summarized (that is, subtotaled, counted, or averaged) within the intersection of each column and row. For example, you might use a crosstab query to subtotal a company's sales values by product and by country. For this example you'd use the values in the Country field as row headings, the values in the ProductName field as column headings, and the summarized values in the Sales field as subtotals within the body of the crosstab query datasheet. You can create a crosstab query using the **Crosstab Query Wizard**.

Step 1
To start the Crosstab Query Wizard, you must click the New button on the Database window toolbar. If you double-click Create query by using wizard in the Database window, you'll start the Simple Query Wizard, which creates a select query rather than a crosstab query.

Activity Steps

📁 **Patients01.mbd**

1. Click the **Queries button** on the Objects bar (if it's not already selected), click the **New button** on the Database window toolbar, then double-click **Crosstab Query Wizard** in the New Query dialog box

2. Click the **Queries option button**, click **Query: Visit Stats** to choose the Visit Stats query as the record source for the new crosstab query, then click **Next**

3. Double-click **Last Name** to choose the Last Name values as row headings, then click **Next**

4. Click the **Gender** field (if it's not already selected) to choose the Gender values as column headings, click **Next**, then click **Count** in the Functions list (if it's not already selected)
   See Figure 5-3.

5. Click **Next**, then click **Finish** to accept **Visit Stats_Crosstab** as the query name, and to create the query
   See Figure 5-4. The second column, the Total Of Visit Date column, calculates a total for each row. In this case, the Total Of Visit Date column totals the F and M values for each last name.

6. Close the Visit Stats_Crosstab query

Figure 5-3: Crosstab Query Wizard dialog box

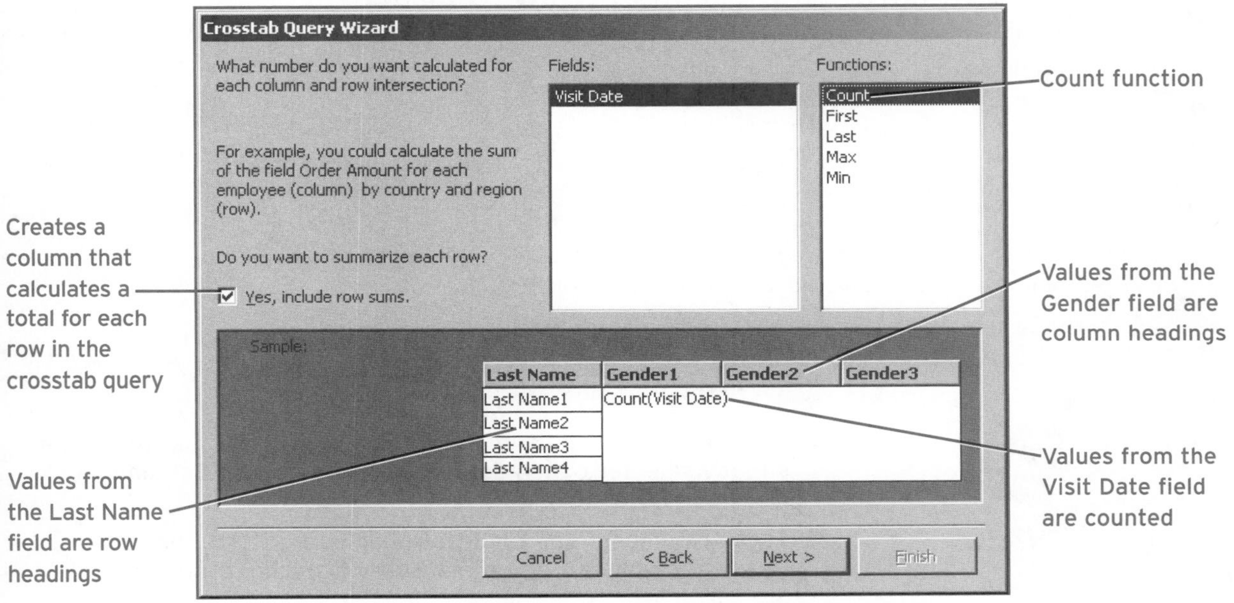

Count function ────── Count function

Creates a column that calculates a total for each row in the crosstab query

Values from the Gender field are column headings

Values from the Last Name field are row headings

Values from the Visit Date field are counted

Crosstab Query Wizard

What number do you want calculated for each column and row intersection?

Fields:
Visit Date

Functions:
Count
First
Last
Max
Min

For example, you could calculate the sum of the field Order Amount for each employee (column) by country and region (row).

Do you want to summarize each row?

☑ Yes, include row sums.

Sample:

Last Name	Gender1	Gender2	Gender3
Last Name1	Count(Visit Date)		
Last Name2			
Last Name3			
Last Name4			

Cancel | < Back | Next > | Finish

Figure 5-4: Visit Stats_Crosstab query in Datasheet View

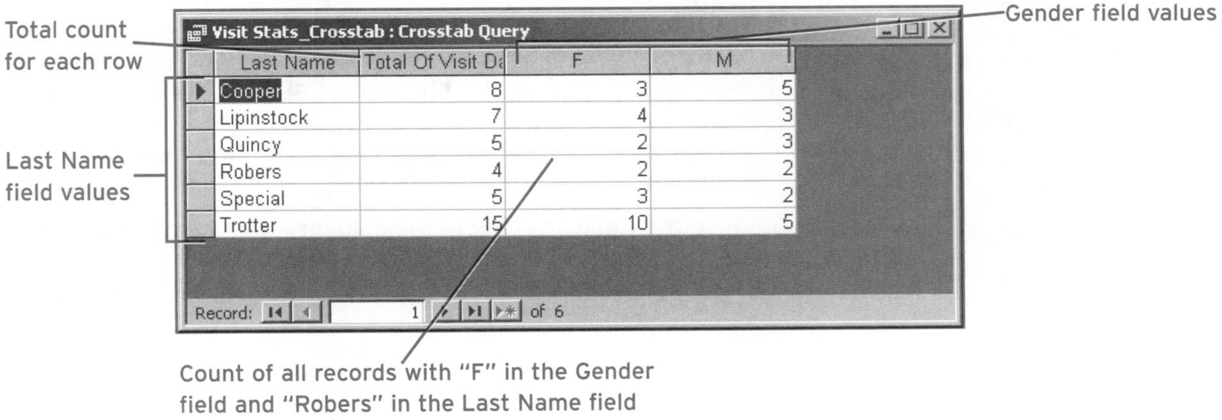

Total count for each row

Gender field values

Last Name field values

Visit Stats_Crosstab : Crosstab Query

Last Name	Total Of Visit Da	F	M
Cooper	8	3	5
Lipinstock	7	4	3
Quincy	5	2	3
Robers	4	2	2
Special	5	3	2
Trotter	15	10	5

Record: 1 of 6

Count of all records with "F" in the Gender field and "Robers" in the Last Name field

Skill Set 5

Viewing and Organizing Information

Sort Records

Sort Records in Datasheet View

Sorting means arranging records in an ascending or descending order based on the values in a field. An ascending sort on a field with a Text data type arranges the values from A-Z, with numbers appearing before letters (for example, 1ABC appears before ABC). An ascending sort on fields with a Number or Currency data type arranges the values from smallest to largest. An ascending sort on a field with a Date/Time data type arranges the values from the past to the future. To sort records in Datasheet View, click any value for the field that you want to base the sort on, then click either the Sort Ascending button or the Sort Descending button on the Table Datasheet toolbar.

Step 3
When you sort in ascending order, null values (fields that contain nothing) appear before fields with any value, even the value of 0 in a Number field.

Activity Steps

 Patients01.mdb

1. Click the **Queries button** [Queries] on the Objects bar (if it's not already selected), then double-click **Cholesterol Screenings** to open it in Datasheet View

2. Click any value in the Cholesterol field, then click the **Sort Descending button** on the Query Datasheet toolbar
   See Figure 5-5.

3. Click the **Sort Ascending button** on the Query Datasheet toolbar

4. Click any value in the Last Name field, then click the **Sort Ascending button** on the Query Datasheet toolbar

5. Click any value in the BD field, then click the **Sort Ascending button** on the Query Datasheet toolbar
   See Figure 5-6.

6. Close the Cholesterol Screenings query without saving changes

Figure 5-5: Sorting in descending order on a Number field

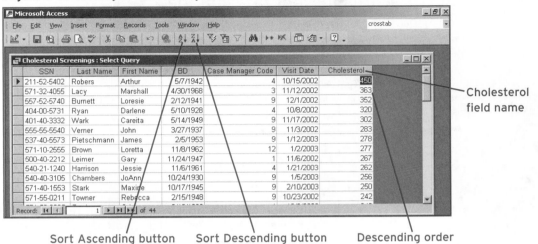

Sort Ascending button   Sort Descending button   Descending order

Cholesterol field name

Figure 5-6: Sorting in ascending order on a Date/Time field

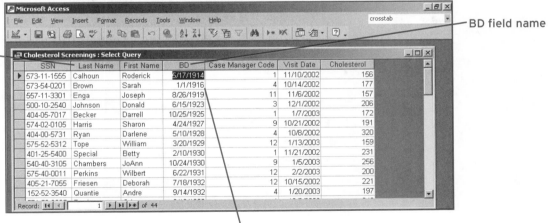

BD field name

Last Name field name

Ascending order

Skill Set 5

Viewing and Organizing Information

Sort Records

Sort Records in Query Design View

You use Query Design View to sort records using more than one sort field. For example, the records in a telephone book are sorted by at least three fields: LastName, FirstName, and MiddleInitial. The second sort field is not needed unless multiple records contain the same value in the first sort field. Using the telephone book as an example, if two records with the last name "Gomez" exist, the values of the FirstName field will determine which record appears first. If two records with the last name "Gomez" *and* the first name "Anthony" exist, the value in the third sort field, MiddleInitial, will determine which record appears first.

Activity Steps

 Patients01.mdb

1. Click the **Queries button** [Queries] on the Objects bar (if it's not already selected), click **Cholesterol Screenings**, then click the **Design button** [Design] on the Database window toolbar

2. Click the **Sort cell** for the Last Name field, click the **list arrow**, then click **Ascending**

3. Click the **Sort cell** for the First Name field, click the **list arrow**, then click **Ascending**
   See Figure 5-7. Sort orders entered in Query Design View are evaluated in a left-to-right order. Therefore, the Last Name field is the first sort order and the First Name field will not be used to sort the records unless the same value is in the Last Name field for more than one record.

4. Click the **View button** [⊞] on the Query Design toolbar
   See Figure 5-8.

5. Close the Cholesterol Screenings query without saving changes

Step 3
Fields used to specify sort orders do not have to be side-by-side in the query design grid.

Figure 5-7: **Using two sort fields in Query Design View**

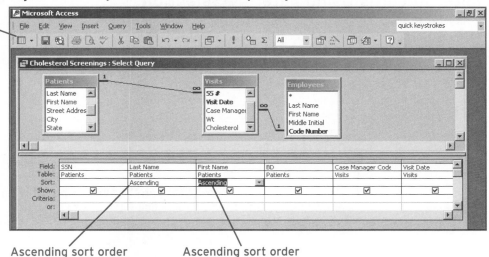

iew button

Ascending sort order
for Last Name field

Ascending sort order
for First Name field

Figure 5-8: **Datasheet View of a query with two sort fields**

SSN	Last Name	First Name	BD	Case Manager Code	Visit Date	Cholesterol
404-05-7017	Becker	Darrell	10/25/1925	1	1/7/2003	172
571-22-5401	Bellard	Lou	7/16/1957	9	2/25/2003	221
571-10-2555	Brown	Loretta	11/8/1962	12	1/2/2003	277
573-54-0201	Brown	Sarah	1/1/1916	4	10/14/2002	177
401-52-1140	Brown	Toni	3/10/1950	1	1/14/2003	158
557-52-5740	Burnett	Loresie	2/12/1941	9	12/1/2002	352
573-11-1555	Calhoun	Roderick	5/17/1914	1	11/10/2002	156
540-40-3105	Chambers	JoAnn	10/24/1930	9	1/5/2003	256
572-31-5211	Edmundson	Richard	11/30/1962	9	11/4/2002	218
557-11-3301	Enga	Joseph	8/26/1919	11	11/6/2002	157
405-21-7055	Friesen	Deborah	7/18/1932	12	10/15/2002	221
407-11-5520	Fulkerson	Delora	8/21/1971	11	11/21/2002	229
407-40-3140	Fulton	Dimple	2/21/1953	9	10/7/2002	219

Record: 1 of 44

Records with
"Brown" in the
Last Name field
are ordered by
values in the
First Name
field: Loretta,
Sarah, Toni

Skill Set 5

Viewing and Organizing Information

Filter Records
Filter Records Using Filter by Selection

A **filter** is a tool you can use to temporarily isolate a subset of records that matches a limiting condition. For example, you could display only those records that contain the value "Madison" in the City field. The **Filter by Selection** tool lets you quickly display a subset of records that matches a value you choose in a single field. You can use the Filter by Selection tool in both Datasheet View and Form View. Since both filters and queries are used to show subsets of records, some similarities exist between these tools. Table 5-3 compares filters and queries.

Activity Steps

 PatientsO1.mdb

1. Click the **Tables button** [Tables] on the Objects bar (if it's not already selected), then double-click **Patients** to open it in Datasheet View

2. Click any **F** value in the Gender field, then click the **Filter By Selection button** on the Table Datasheet toolbar
   See Figure 5-9.

3. Click the **Remove Filter button** on the Table Datasheet toolbar to redisplay all records
   The Remove Filter button toggles between two buttons: Apply Filter and Remove Filter. Once the filter is removed, you can use the Apply Filter button to quickly reapply the last filter used on the datasheet.

4. Click the **Apply Filter button** on the Table Datasheet toolbar to reapply the filter that displays records with "F" in the Gender field

5. Close the Patients table without saving changes

Step 5
Filters are temporary and are not saved with the object, even if you click "Yes" to save the changes.

Figure 5-9: Using the Filter by Selection tool

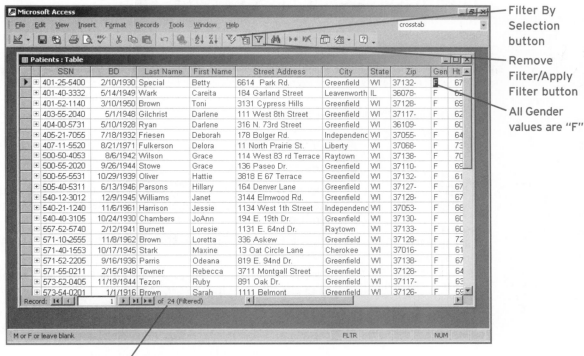

— Filter By Selection button

— Remove Filter/Apply Filter button

— All Gender values are "F"

24 records are filtered

TABLE 5-3: Queries versus filters

characteristics	filters	queries
Are saved as an object in the database	No	Yes
Can be used to select a subset of records in a datasheet	Yes	Yes
Can be used to select a subset of fields in a datasheet	No	Yes
Its resulting datasheet can be used to enter, edit, and delete data	Yes	Yes
Its resulting datasheet can be used to sort, filter, and find records	Yes	Yes
Can be used as the record source for a form or report	No	Yes
Can calculate sums, averages, counts, and other types of summary statistics across records	No	Yes
Can be used to create calculated fields	No	Yes

Skill Set 5

Viewing and Organizing Information

Filter Records

Filter Records Using Filter by Form

You use the **Filter by Form** tool to specify more than one limiting condition within a filter. For example, you could display only those records that contain the value "Spain" in the Country field *and* the value "Barcelona" in the City field. Or you might want to use the Filter by Form tool to define the limiting condition using **comparison operators**, such as less than (<) or greater than (>). For example, you could filter for all orders with an OrderDate field entry greater than 1/1/2002. Common comparison operators are described in Table 5-4.

Activity Steps

 PatientsO1.mdb

1. Click the **Queries button** [≡ Queries] on the Objects bar (if it's not already selected), then double-click **Cholesterol Screenings** to open it in Datasheet View

2. Click the **Filter By Form button** [▣] on the Query Datasheet toolbar

3. Click the **Cholesterol cell**, type **>300**, click the **Case Manager Code cell**, click the **list arrow**, then click **4**
   See Figure 5-10.

4. Click the **Apply Filter button** [▽] on the Filter/Sort toolbar
   See Figure 5-11. Two records matched the >300 and Case Manager Code equals 4 criteria for the Cholesterol field.

5. Close the Cholesterol Screenings query without saving changes

tip

Step 3
Click the Clear Grid button [✗] on the Filter/Sort toolbar to clear all entries in the Filter by Form window.

Figure 5-10: Filter by Form window

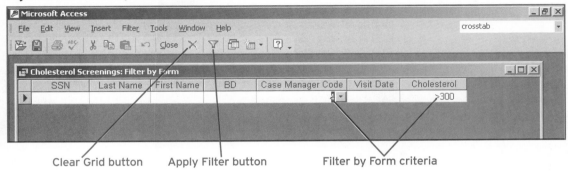

Clear Grid button   Apply Filter button   Filter by Form criteria

Figure 5-11: Filtered datasheet

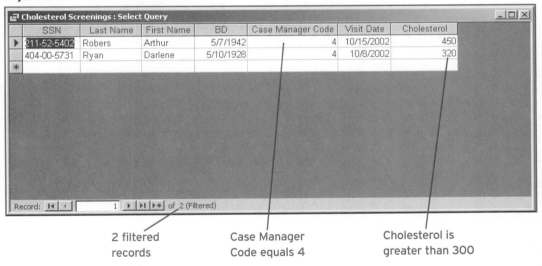

2 filtered records   Case Manager Code equals 4   Cholesterol is greater than 300

TABLE 5-4: Comparison operators

operator	description	expression	meaning
>	Greater than	>500	Numbers greater than 500
>=	Greater than or equal to	>=500	Numbers greater than or equal to 500
<	Less than	<"Braveheart"	Names from A through Braveheart, but not Braveheart
<=	Less than or equal to	<="Bridgewater"	Names from A through, and including, Bridgewater
<>	Not equal to	<>"Cyclone"	Any name except for Cyclone

Skill Set 5

Viewing and Organizing Information

Target Your Skills

 Patients01.mdb

1 Open the Cholesterol Screenings query in Datasheet View. Filter for all records with a Visit Date earlier than 1/1/2003, then sort the records in descending order based on the value in the Cholesterol field. The resulting datasheet should look like Figure 5-12.

Figure 5-12

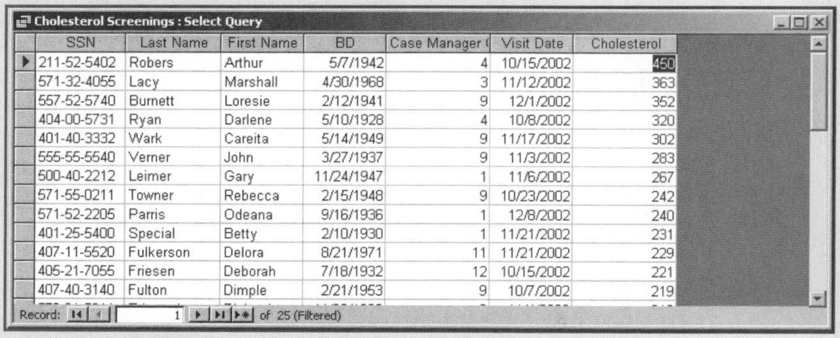

SSN	Last Name	First Name	BD	Case Manager (	Visit Date	Cholesterol
211-52-5402	Robers	Arthur	5/7/1942	4	10/15/2002	450
571-32-4055	Lacy	Marshall	4/30/1968	3	11/12/2002	363
557-52-5740	Burnett	Loresie	2/12/1941	9	12/1/2002	352
404-00-5731	Ryan	Darlene	5/10/1928	4	10/8/2002	320
401-40-3332	Wark	Careita	5/14/1949	9	11/17/2002	302
555-55-5540	Verner	John	3/27/1937	9	11/3/2002	283
500-40-2212	Leimer	Gary	11/24/1947	1	11/6/2002	267
571-55-0211	Towner	Rebecca	2/15/1948	9	10/23/2002	242
571-52-2205	Parris	Odeana	9/16/1936	1	12/8/2002	240
401-25-5400	Special	Betty	2/10/1930	1	11/21/2002	231
407-11-5520	Fulkerson	Delora	8/21/1971	11	11/21/2002	229
405-21-7055	Friesen	Deborah	7/18/1932	12	10/15/2002	221
407-40-3140	Fulton	Dimple	2/21/1953	9	10/7/2002	219

Record: 1 of 25 (Filtered)

 Patients01.mdb

2 Open the Employees form in Form View. Enter a new record with the following data:
Last Name: Quincy
First Name: Kia
Middle Initial: A
Code Number: 20
Use the Filter by Selection tool to filter all records with the last name equal to Quincy, and sort by first name in ascending order as shown in Figure 5-13.

Figure 5-13

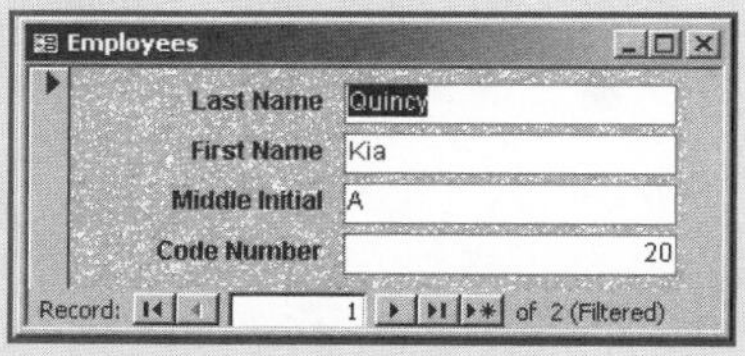

Employees

Last Name	Quincy
First Name	Kia
Middle Initial	A
Code Number	20

Record: 1 of 2 (Filtered)

Skill List

1. Create one-to-many relationships
2. Enforce referential integrity

In Skill Set 6, you will use the Relationships window to create one-to-many relationships between two database tables. A **one-to-many relationship** ties or relates one table to another. By using multiple tables to store your data, you can minimize redundant data in your database. For example, suppose you enter all the information for a customer purchase into a single table. One problem with this scenario becomes apparent when the customer makes a second purchase; you must reenter all the customer fields, such as name and address, into a second record of the same table. Duplicating data in a single table is unproductive and can cause data entry errors. If you put the customer fields in a Customers table and the fields that are determined at the time of the purchase in a Purchases table, you won't need to reenter all the customer information a second time. Instead, you can create a one-to-many relationship between the Customers and Purchases tables to tie "one" customer to "many" purchases. You'll also learn about referential integrity, a set of rules that, when applied to a one-to-many relationship, helps maintain the integrity of the data in the database.

Skill Set 6

Defining Relationships

Create One-To-Many Relationships

A one-to-many relationship between two tables in an Access database ties the tables together; a one-to-many relationship lets a record in one table look up information in another. To create a one-to-many relationship, the same field must be present in both tables so that "one" record in the first table knows how to connect or relate to "many" records in the second table. The field common to both tables is called the **linking field**, and is often the primary key field for the table on the "one" side of the relationship. The linking field is called the **foreign key field** in the table on the "many" side of the relationship. You create one-to-many relationships using the Relationships window.

Activity Steps

 Clients01.mdb

1. Click the **Relationships button** on the Database toolbar to open the Relationships window

2. Click the **Show Table button** on the Relationship toolbar, click **ZipCodes**, click **Add**, click **Contacts**, click **Add**, then click **Close** in the Show Table dialog box

3. Drag the **bottom border** of the Contacts field list down so that all fields are visible

4. Drag the **ZIPCODE** field from the ZipCodes field list to the ZipCode field in the Contacts field list
See Figure 6-1.

5. Click **Create**
See Figure 6-2. The bold field in a field list is the primary key field for a table.

6. Click the **Save button** on the Relationship toolbar, then close the Relationships window

7. Click the **Tables button** on the Objects bar (if it's not already selected), then double-click **ZipCodes** to open it in Datasheet View
When a one-to-many relationship is established between two tables, the datasheet for the table on the "one" side of the relationship will display expand buttons to the left of each record in Datasheet View. You click an expand button to see a subdatasheet of related records from the table on the "many" side of the relationship.

8. Click the **expand button** to the left of the first record to show related records from the Contacts table
See Figure 6-3.

9. Close the ZipCodes table

Step 5
To edit a relationship, double-click the relationship line to open the Edit Relationships dialog box and make desired changes. To delete a relationship, right-click the line, then click Delete on the shortcut menu.

Figure 6-1: Edit Relationships dialog box

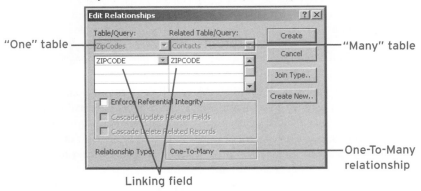

"One" table — · · · "Many" table

One-To-Many relationship

Linking field

Figure 6-2: Final Relationships window

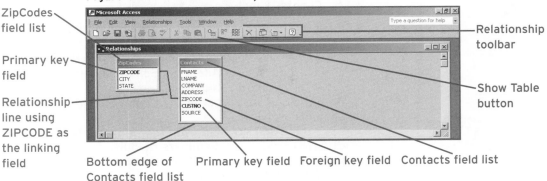

ZipCodes field list

Primary key field

Relationship line using ZIPCODE as the linking field

Relationship toolbar

Show Table button

Bottom edge of Contacts field list   Primary key field   Foreign key field   Contacts field list

Figure 6-3: Datasheet View and subdatasheet showing one-to-many relationship between the ZipCodes table and Contacts table

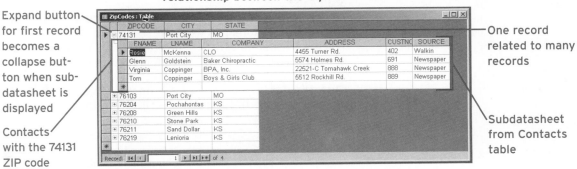

Expand button for first record becomes a collapse button when subdatasheet is displayed

Contacts with the 74131 ZIP code

One record related to many records

Subdatasheet from Contacts table

Skill Set 6

Defining Relationships

Enforce Referential Integrity

Referential integrity is a set of rules imposed on a one-to-many relationship. The rules help to ensure that no orphan records are entered or created in a database. An **orphan record** is a record in the "many" table that doesn't have a matching entry in the linking field of the "one" table. For example, if you apply referential integrity to the link between a Sales and Customers table, all records entered in the Sales table must have a matching record in the Customers table. In this scenario, applying referential integrity will prevent you from entering a customer's order without first entering important customer information, such as a billing and shipping address. When you apply referential integrity to a one-to-many relationship, a one (1) symbol will appear next to the table on the "one" side of the relationship, and an infinity (∞) symbol will appear next to the table on the "many" side of the relationship.

Activity Steps

 Clients02.mdb

1. Click the **Relationships button** on the Database toolbar to open the Relationships window
2. Click the **Show Table button** on the Relationship toolbar, click **Contacts**, click **Add**, click **Seminars**, click **Add**, then click **Close** in the Show Table dialog box
3. Drag the **bottom border** of the Contacts field list down so that all fields are visible
4. Drag the **CUSTNO** field from the Contacts field list to the CUSTNO field in the Seminars field list, then select the **Enforce Referential Integrity check box** in the Edit Relationships dialog box
   See Figure 6-4.
5. Click **Create**
   See Figure 6-5.
6. Click the **Save button** on the Relationship toolbar, then close the Relationships window
   When referential integrity is enforced on a relationship, Access will not allow you to enter or create an orphan record in the table on the "many" side of the relationship.
7. Click the **Tables button** on the Objects bar (if it's not already selected), then double-click **Seminars** to open it in Datasheet View
8. Type **222** as the CUSTNO entry for the first record, then press the down arrow key
   An alert box appears indicating that there is no related record in the Contacts table. (There is no record in the Contacts table with 222 in the CUSTNO field.) *See Figure 6-6.*
9. Click **OK**, press **Esc** to undo the last edit, then close the Seminars table

To create a report that shows the table relationships, click File on the menu bar in the Relationships window, then click Print Relationships.

Figure 6-4: Enforcing referential integrity

"One" table

Enforce Referential Integrity check box

"Many" table

Linking field

"Many" table

One-To-Many relationship

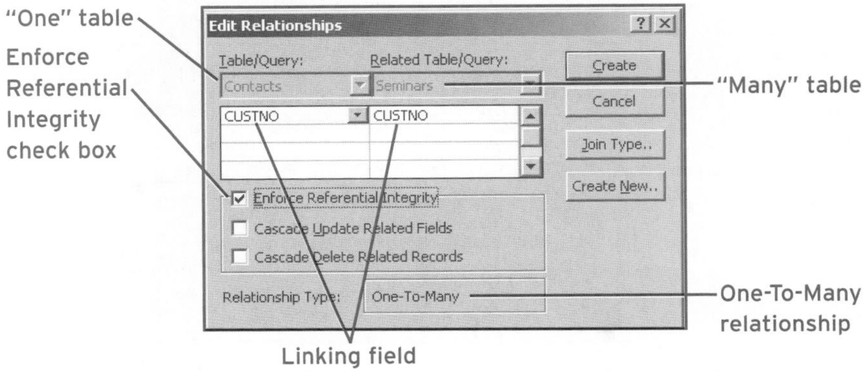

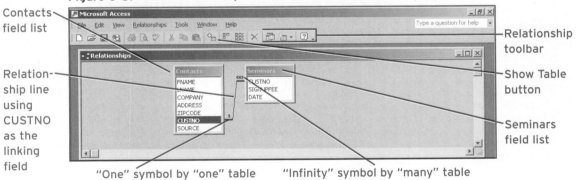

Figure 6-5: Final Relationships window with referential integrity enforced

Contacts field list

Relationship line using CUSTNO as the linking field

Relationship toolbar

Show Table button

Seminars field list

"One" symbol by "one" table

"Infinity" symbol by "many" table

Figure 6-6: Referential integrity alert box

Skill Set 6

Defining Relationships

Target Your Skills

 Members01.mdb

1 Build one-to-many relationships between the Activities, Names, and Zips tables as shown in Figure 6-7.

Figure 6-7

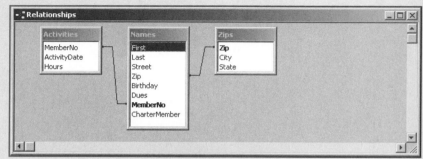

 Members02.mdb

2 Build one-to-many relationships with referential integrity enforced between the Activities, Names, and Zips tables as shown in Figure 6-8.

Figure 6-8

Skill List

1. Create and format reports
2. Add calculated controls to reports
3. Preview and print reports

In Skill Set 7, you will work with **reports**, the Access object used to create professional printouts. While you can print the Datasheet View of a table or query, the report object provides important printing benefits. For example, you can customize the header and footer on a report to include any type of information, but you cannot modify the header or footer of a datasheet printout. Also, a report allows you to show both detail and summary information in one printout, which is not possible on a datasheet printout. For example, you might want to show all the individual sales records as well as the subtotaled sales for each customer. Finally, with a report, you can specify many formatting options, such as multiple colors, graphics, and font choices for different fields and sections of the report. You cannot choose different formats for different areas of a datasheet, nor can you add graphics, such as logos, lines, or clip art, to a datasheet printout.

Skill Set 7

Producing Reports

Create and Format Reports
Create Reports Using the Report Wizard

The **Report Wizard** is a tool you can use to quickly create a report. Using the wizard, you can specify several aspects of a report, such as the fields you want to use and how you want to group and sort the report's records. You can also use the wizard to specify the layout, style, and title of a report. You can later modify a report created by the Report Wizard using **Report Design View**, the view in which you modify or format the items on the report or the report itself.

Activity Steps

 ClinicO1.mdb

1. Click the **Reports button** 🔳 Reports on the Objects bar (if it's not already selected), then double-click **Create report by using wizard**

2. Click the **Tables/Queries list arrow**, click **Table: Patients**, click the **Select All Fields button** >> , then click **Next**
   See Figure 7-1.

3. Click **Next** to accept the Doctor field as the grouping field, click the first sort order **list arrow**, click **PtLastName** as the first sort field, then click **Next**
   The **grouping field** determines the primary sort order of the records on the report. The sort fields determine the order of records *within* each group. In this case, the records are sorted by the values in the PtLastName field (the sort field) within the Doctor field (the grouping field).

4. Click the **Outline 2 option button** for the layout, click **Next**, click **Corporate** for the style, click **Next**, type **Patient Visits by Doctor** as the title for the report, then click **Finish**

5. Maximize the report, then scroll to view information for the first three doctors
   See Figure 7-2.

6. Close the Patient Visits by Doctor report

Step 6
Reports created with the Report Wizard are automatically saved as report objects in the database. They are given the name that you entered as the report title while using the Report Wizard.

Figure 7-1: Report Wizard dialog box

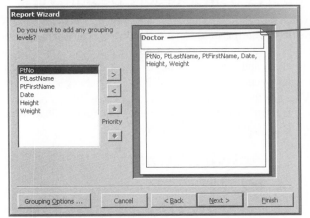

Records will be grouped
by the Doctor field

Figure 7-2: Patient Visits by Doctor report

Records are
grouped by the
Doctor field

Within each
Doctor field
value, records
are in ascend-
ing order based
on PtLastName

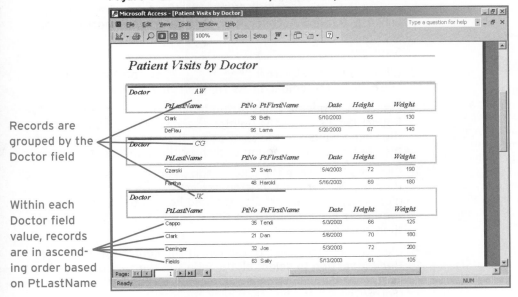

Skill Set 7
Producing Reports

Create and Format Reports
Format Reports Using Report Design View

Formatting a report means to customize its appearance by changing the fonts, colors, or borders of the controls on the report. A **control** is any item on a report, such as a label, line, or text box. Report controls are placed in report **sections**, which determine where and how often controls print. See Table 7-1 for more information on report sections. You make all formatting changes to a report in Report Design View. To format a control in Report Design View, you first select the control(s) you want to change, then make the formatting change using the buttons on the Formatting (Form/Report) toolbar.

Activity Steps

 Clinic01.mdb

1. Click the **Reports button** [Reports] on the Objects bar (if it's not al-ready selected), click **Patient Activity Report**, click the **Design button** [Design] on the Database window toolbar, maxi-mize Report Design View (if it's not already maximized), then click the **Patient Activity Report label** in the Report Header section
   See Figure 7-3.

2. Click the **Font list arrow** [Times New Roman] on the Formatting (Form/Report) toolbar, press [i], then click **Impact**

3. Point to the **middle-right sizing handle** of the Patient Activity Report label so that the pointer changes to ↔, then drag the sizing handle to the right about 0.5 inches to ensure that the control is wide enough to display the label's text

4. Click the **line** above the label in the Report Header section, click the **Line/Border Color button list arrow** ∠▾ on the Formatting (Form/Report) toolbar, click the **Red box** (in the first column, third row), click the **Line/Border Width button list arrow** ▯▾, then click **4**

5. Click the **vertical ruler** to the left of the controls in the Page Header section to select all the labels in the section, click the **Font/Fore Color button list arrow** A▾ on the Formatting (Form/Report) toolbar, then click the **Red box** (in the first column, third row)

6. Click the **View button** 🔍 on the Report Design toolbar
   See Figure 7-4.

7. Save and close the Patient Activity Report

Step 3
If you make a mistake, click the Undo button ↺ on the Report Design toolbar to undo your last action. You can undo up to 20 actions in Report Design View.

Figure 7-3: Formatting the Patient Activity Report in Report Design View

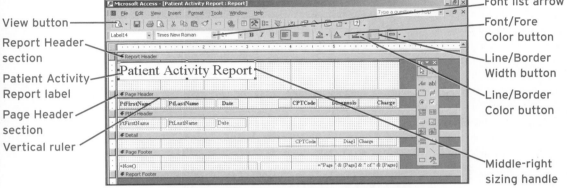

View button

Report Header section

Patient Activity Report label

Page Header section

Vertical ruler

Font list arrow

Font/Fore Color button

Line/Border Width button

Line/Border Color button

Middle-right sizing handle

Figure 7-4: Formatted Patient Activity Report

Thick red line

Impact font

Red text

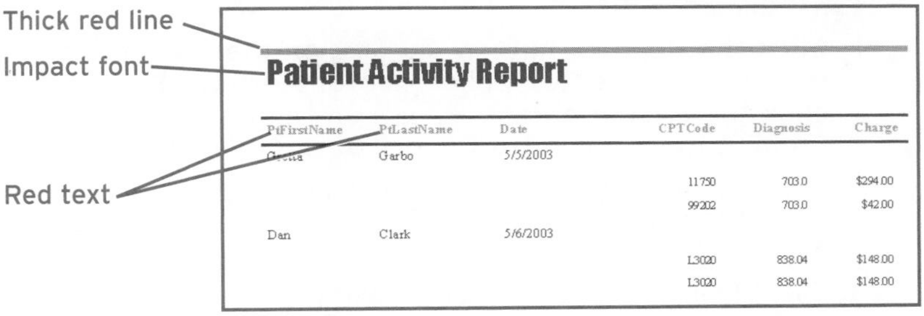

TABLE 7-1: Report sections

section	where does this section print?	what type of information does this section typically display?
Report Header	At the top of the first page of the report	Report title
Page Header	At the top of every page (but below the report header on page one)	Page number, current date, clip art
Group Header	Before every group of records	Value of the current group
Detail	Once for every record	Values for the rest of the fields in the report
Group Footer	After every group of records	Subtotal or count of the records in that group
Page Footer	At the bottom of every page	Page number or current date
Report Footer	At the end of the entire report	Grand total or count for all of the records in the entire report

Skill Set 7
Producing Reports

Add Calculated Controls to Reports
Add Subtotals for Groups of Records

To produce a subtotal for a group of records, you create a calculated control. A **calculated control** is a text box control that contains an expression that calculates a value. Expressions can contain **functions**, built-in formulas that help you build an expression quickly. Not all expressions contain functions, but the Sum, Avg, and Count functions are commonly used to create subtotals for groups of records. See Table 7-2 for more examples of common Access expressions used with reports. To make a calculated control work as a subtotal, you add it to the Group Footer section of the report. When you preview or print the report, a subtotal will appear immediately after each group of records. To add controls to a report, you use Report Design View.

Activity Steps

file
> Clinic01.mdb

1. Click the **Reports button** 🔲 Reports on the Objects bar (if it's not already selected), click **Doctor Activity Report**, click the **Design button** 🔲 Design on the Database window toolbar, then maximize Report Design View

2. Click the **Sorting and Grouping button** 🔳 on the Report Design toolbar
   See Figure 7-5.

3. Click **No** in the Group Footer property box, click the **list arrow**, then click **Yes** to display the Group Footer section for the DocCode field

4. Click the **Sorting and Grouping button** 🔳 to close the Sorting and Grouping window

5. Click the **Text Box button** 🔲 on the Toolbox toolbar, then click in the DocCode Footer section just below the Charge text box

6. Click **Unbound** in the new text box, then type **=Sum([Charge])**
   In expressions, the arguments for a function (the pieces of information expressions need to calculate a value) are always surrounded by parentheses. When an argument is a field name, the name is surrounded by brackets. In the =Sum([Charge]) expression, the Sum function will subtotal the values in the Charge field.

7. Click **Text16** in the label to the left of the new text box to edit the text, double-click **Text16** to select it, type **Subtotal**, click the vertical ruler to the left of the label to select it, double-click one of the label's sizing handles to automatically resize it to display all text, then click the **View button** 🔲
   See Figure 7-6.

8. Save and close the Doctor Activity Report

Step 7
If you double-click the edge of the label instead of the text within a selected label, you'll open the label's property sheet instead of selecting the label's text.

Figure 7-5: Sorting and Grouping window

DocCode field is selected

Grouping symbol

Group Header property

Group Footer property

Sorting and Grouping button

Text Box button

Charge text box in Detail section

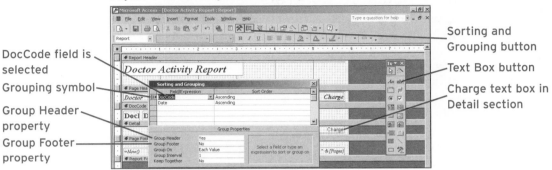

Figure 7-6: Final Doctor Activity Report with subtotal calculation

Subtotal label

=Sum([Charge]) calculates the sums for the charges for each doctor

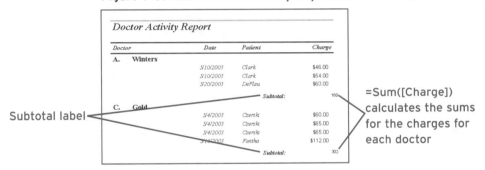

TABLE 7-2: Sample expressions

sample expression	description
=[Price]*1.05	Multiplies the Price field by 1.05 (adds 5% to the Price field)
=[Subtotal]+[Shipping]	Adds the value of the Subtotal field to the value of the Shipping field
=[Page]	Displays the current page number, such as 5, 6, or 10
="Page "&[Page]	Displays the word Page, a space, and the current page number, such as Page 5, Page 6, or Page 10
=[FirstName]& " "&[LastName]	Displays the value of the FirstName and LastName fields separated by a space
=Avg([Freight])	Uses the **Avg** function to display an average of the values in the Freight field
=Count([FirstName])	Uses the **Count** function to display the number of records that contain an entry in the FirstName field
=Sum([Tracks])	Uses the **Sum** function to display the total value from the Tracks field
=Date()	Uses the **Date** function to display the current date in the form of m/d/yyyy, such as 10/23/2002 or 11/14/2003

Skill Set 7
Producing Reports

Add Calculated Controls to Reports
Add Date Calculated Controls

A **date calculated control** is a text box control that uses an Access function to calculate and display today's date on a report. Two date functions are commonly used: Date and Now. The **Date function** displays today's date in the m/d/yyyy format, for example, 6/15/2003. The **Now function** displays both today's date as well as the current time, for example, 6/15/2003 2:37:22 PM. You can add a date calculated control to any report section, but they are most commonly added to the Report Header, Page Header, or Page Footer sections. To add controls to a report, you use Report Design View.

Activity Steps
 Clinic01.mdb

Step 3
In an expression, the function name is not case-sensitive, so =date() is the same as =Date().

1. Click the **Reports button**  on the Objects bar (if it's not already selected), click **Doctor List**, click the **Design button** on the Database window toolbar, then maximize Report Design View (if it's not already maximized)

2. Click the **Text Box button** [ab] on the Toolbox toolbar, then click in the middle of the Report Header section

3. Click **Unbound** in the new text box, then type **=Date()**
   See Figure 7-7. The Date function does not have any arguments, but the parentheses are still required.

4. Click **Text11** in the label to the left of the new text box, double-click **Text11**, type **Today's Date**, then click the **View button**
   See Figure 7-8. The date calculated control reads the current date from your computer's battery, so if you open this report tomorrow, the date will automatically change to tomorrow's date.

5. Save and close the Doctor List report

Figure 7-7: Adding a date calculated control to the Report Header section

w label

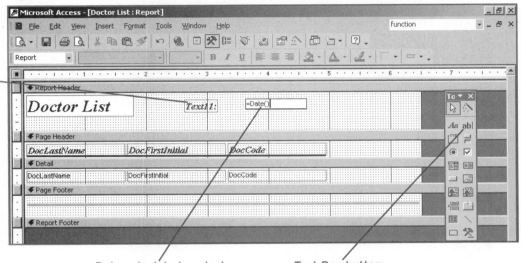

Date calculated control
in new text box

Text Box button

Figure 7-8: Final Doctor List report with today's date
created from a calculated control

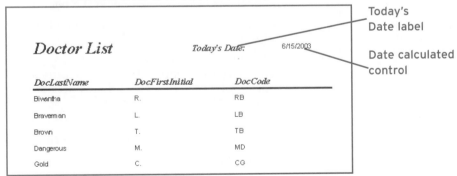

Today's
Date label

Date calculated
control

Skill Set 7
Producing Reports

Preview and Print Reports

You use **Print Preview** to see how your report will appear before you actually print it. This gives you an opportunity to fix printing problems (crowded data, for example) or change the layout of a report (add or modify a footer, for example) before printing. You use the buttons on the Print Preview toolbar to change the magnification of the report on the screen (called zooming) so that you can see more or less text or more or fewer pages. Any object view that you can print, such as Table Datasheet, Query Datasheet, or Form View, has an associated Print Preview window. However, Print Preview is most commonly used to preview reports, because reports are specifically created for the purpose of producing printouts.

Activity Steps

 Clinic01.mdb

1. Click the **Reports button** [Reports] on the Objects bar (if it's not already selected), double-click **Patient List**, then maximize Report Preview (if it's not already maximized)
   See Figure 7-9.

2. Click the **Two Pages button** [] on the Print Preview toolbar

3. Click the last record on the second page with the Zoom In pointer to zoom in to read that record
   The pointer changes to a Zoom Out pointer.

4. Click the last record with the Zoom Out pointer to restore the two-page view

5. Click the **Zoom button list arrow** [Fit ▾], click **200%** to magnify the printout to twice as large as it'll appear on the printout, scroll to view various parts of the report, click the **Zoom button list arrow** [200% ▾], then click **Fit,** which "fits" full pieces of paper in the Print Preview window

6. Click the **Print button** [] on the Print Preview toolbar

7. Close the Patient List report

Step 2
In Print Preview, the navigation buttons are not available when all pages of a report are currently displayed.

Figure 7-9: Patient List report in Print Preview

Two Pages button

Setup button

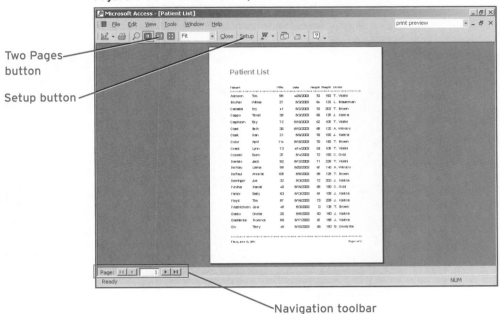

Navigation toolbar

Skill Set 7

Producing Reports

Target Your Skills

 Seminar01.mdb

1 In Report Design View of the Attendee List report, create the report shown in Figure 7-10. Format the labels in the Page Header section with an Arial, bold, italic, 12-point font. Set the line below the labels in the Page Header section to a 1 line/border width. Format the Attendee List label in the Report Header section with an Arial, red, 24-point font.

Figure 7-10

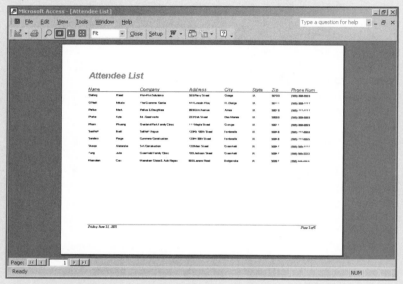

 Seminar01.mdb

2 Add calculated controls to the Event Registration Report to create the report shown in Figure 7-11. Open the EventID Footer section, then add a calculated control to this section to subtotal the RegistrationFee field. (Use the expression =Sum([RegistrationFee]).) Change the label to the left of the calculated control in the EventID Footer section to "Subtotal:". Add a date calculated control to the Report Header section. (Use the expression =Date().) Delete the date calculated control's label.

Figure 7-11

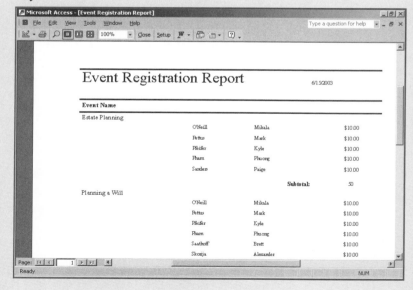

Skill List

1. Import data to Access
2. Export data from Access
3. Create a simple data access page

In Skill Set 8, you will work with other software programs, including Microsoft Excel and Internet Explorer, to import data into and export data out of an Access database. **Import** means to convert data from an external data source, such as an Excel workbook, into an Access database. **Export** means to convert data from an Access database to an external file, such as a Word document. Both processes are fast ways to copy data from one file format to another without having to reenter the data. Another way to make Access data available to others who prefer a different file format is to create a data access page. A **data access page** is a special type of Web page that maintains a connection with the database and gives other users the ability to edit and view up-to-date Access data using Internet Explorer.

Skill Set 8
Integrating with Other Applications

Import Data to Access
Import Data from an Excel Workbook

You can import data into an Access database from several file formats, including an Excel workbook or another Access, FoxPro, dBase, or Paradox database. It is not uncommon for a user to enter a list of data into Excel and later decide to convert that data into an Access database, because the user wants to use Access's extensive form or report capabilities or wants multiple people to be able to use the data at the same time. (An Access database is inherently **multi-user**; many people can enter and update data at the same time.) Since the data in an Excel workbook is structured similarly to data in an Access table datasheet, you can easily import data from an Excel workbook into an Access database by using the **Import Spreadsheet Wizard**.

Activity Steps

 Classes01.mdb

1. Click **File** on the menu bar, point to **Get External Data**, then click **Import**

2. Navigate to the drive and folder where your Project Files are stored, click the **Files of type list arrow**, click **Microsoft Excel**, click **Instructors**, then click **Import** to start the Import Spreadsheet Wizard
   See Figure 8-1.

3. Select the **First Row Contains Column Headings check box**, then click **Next**

4. Click **Next** to indicate that you want to create a new table, then click **Next** to not specify field changes

5. Click the **Choose my own primary key option button** to set InstructorID as the primary key field, then click **Next**

6. Type **Instructors** in the Import to Table box, click **Finish**, then click **OK**

7. Double-click **Instructors** to open it in Datasheet View
   See Figure 8-2. Imported data works the same way as any other table of data in a database.

8. Close the Instructors table

Step 4
You can also import Excel workbook data into an existing table if the field names used in the Excel workbook match the field names in the Access table.

Figure 8-1: Import Spreadsheet Wizard dialog box

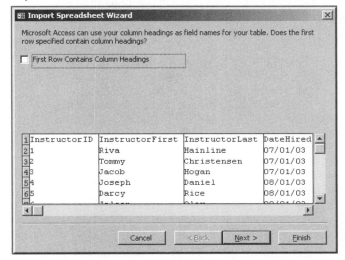

Figure 8-2: Imported Instructors table in Datasheet View

Seven records were imported

extra!

Using delimited text files

You can import data from a **delimited text file**, a file of unformatted data where each field value is delimited (separated) by a common character, such as a comma or a tab. Each record is further delimited by a common character, such as a paragraph mark. A delimited text file usually has a **txt** (for text) file extension. You can use delimited text files to convert data from a proprietary software system (such as an accounting, inventory, or scheduling software system) into a format that other programs can import. For example, most accounting software programs won't export data directly into an Access database, but they can export data to a delimited text file, which can then be imported by Access.

Skill Set 8

Integrating with Other Applications

Import Data to Access

Import Objects from Another Access Database

As a **database developer**, one who creates new database objects such as queries, forms, and reports, you should know how to import objects from one Access database to another. This skill will allow you to do your development work in a test database (often called the **development database**). When you're finished testing the new objects and are ready to make them accessible to others, you can import them into the database that's used on a regular basis by database users (often called the **production database**). (A **database user** is anyone who enters, edits, views, or uses database information, but doesn't design or create new database objects.) For example, you might use the development database to create and test a new data entry form that accommodates sales entries for a new product. Then you could import the new form into the production database on the day the new product is officially announced.

Activity Steps

Classes01.mdb

1. Click the **Queries button**  on the Objects bar (if it's not already selected), then click the **Reports button** on the Objects bar to view the existing queries and reports

2. Click **File** on the menu bar, point to **Get External Data**, then click **Import**

3. Navigate to the drive and folder where your Project Files are stored, click the **Files of type list arrow**, click **Microsoft Access**, click **ClassesDevel01**, then click **Import** to display the Import Objects dialog box

4. Click the **Queries tab**, click **Class Rosters Query** to select it, click the **Reports tab**, then click **Class Rosters Report** to select it
   See Figure 8-3.

5. Click **OK** to import the Class Rosters query and the Class Rosters report from the ClassesDevel01 database
   You imported both the query and the report because a report cannot be displayed without a data source (in this case, the query defines what data from the tables are displayed in the report).

6. Click the **Queries button** on the Objects bar to see that the Class Rosters Query was imported successfully, then click the **Reports button** on the Objects bar to see that the Class Rosters Report was also imported successfully

7. Double-click the **Class Rosters Report**, maximize the Print Preview window, then click the report to zoom to 100% magnification
   See Figure 8-4.

8. Close the Class Rosters Report

Step 4
To select all objects of the same type, click the Select All button in the Import Objects dialog box.

Figure 8-3: Import Objects dialog box

Queries tab

Reports tab

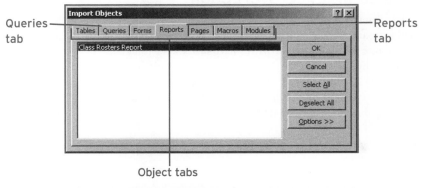

Object tabs

Figure 8-4: Previewing the imported Class Rosters Report

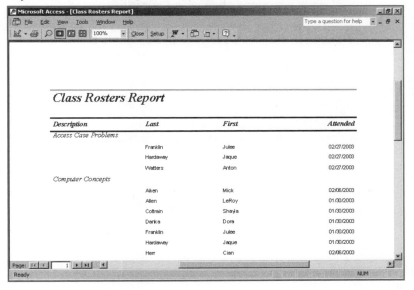

extra!

Creating a development database

If you want to develop a database outside the office, one way is to copy the production database, then delete all but a few records in each table. (Leaving some data helps you know what data is typically entered in each field in case the field names are not self-explanatory. It also gives you some sample data from which to create new forms and reports.) These steps create a development database that contains all the table definitions that you need to develop new queries, forms, and reports (which will later be imported back into the production database). These steps also minimize problems associated with copying and moving large amounts of sensitive data, which isn't required for development work.

Skill Set 8

Integrating with Other Applications

Export Data from Access
Export Data to an Excel Workbook

You can export data from an Access database to a variety of file formats, including a Word document, an Excel workbook, or another Access database. Access provides a special tool called **Analyze It with Microsoft Excel** to export the set of records defined by an Access table, query, form, or report to an Excel workbook. The Analyze It with Microsoft Excel feature is one of three special **OfficeLinks** tools for exporting Access data to other Microsoft Office file formats. The OfficeLinks tools are described in Table 8-1

Step 2
If an OfficeLink tool doesn't work with the selected object, the button and text for that option will be dim.

Activity Steps

 ClassesO1.mdb

1. Click the **Tables button** ⊞ Tables on the Objects bar (if it's not already selected), then click **Courses**

2. Click the **OfficeLinks button list arrow** 🄦 on the Database toolbar, then click **Analyze It with Microsoft Excel**
   This process automatically creates an Excel workbook with the name Courses in the C:\My Documents folder. If a file with this name is already stored in that location, you'll be prompted to replace it.

3. **If prompted to replace an existing file, click Yes**
   See Figure 8-5.

4. **Close the Courses workbook, then exit Excel**

Figure 8-5: Courses Excel workbook

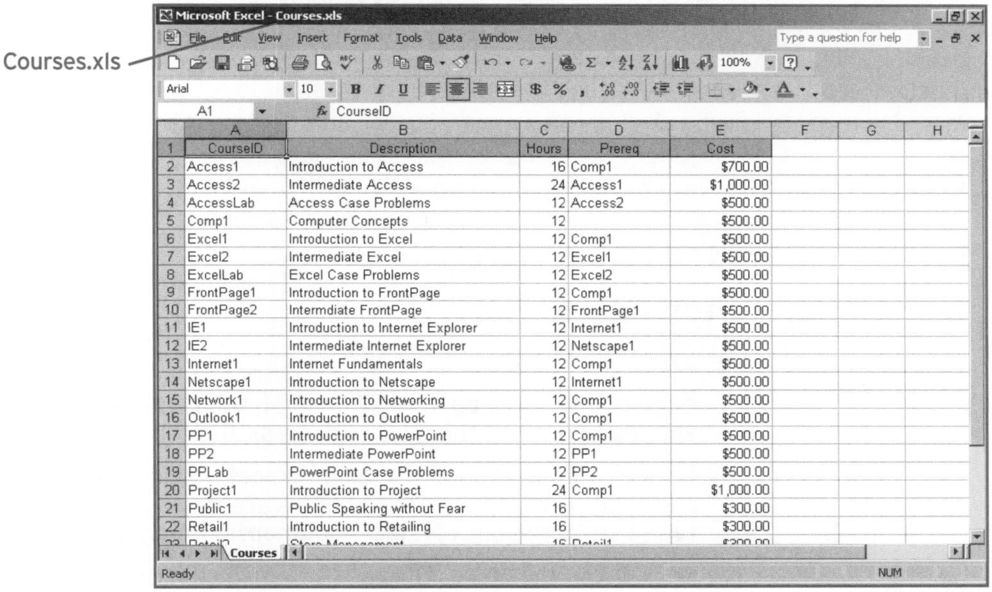

Courses.xls →

	A	B	C	D	E	F	G	H
1	CourseID	Description	Hours	Prereq	Cost			
2	Access1	Introduction to Access	16	Comp1	$700.00			
3	Access2	Intermediate Access	24	Access1	$1,000.00			
4	AccessLab	Access Case Problems	12	Access2	$500.00			
5	Comp1	Computer Concepts	12		$500.00			
6	Excel1	Introduction to Excel	12	Comp1	$500.00			
7	Excel2	Intermediate Excel	12	Excel1	$500.00			
8	ExcelLab	Excel Case Problems	12	Excel2	$500.00			
9	FrontPage1	Introduction to FrontPage	12	Comp1	$500.00			
10	FrontPage2	Intermdiate FrontPage	12	FrontPage1	$500.00			
11	IE1	Introduction to Internet Explorer	12	Internet1	$500.00			
12	IE2	Intermediate Internet Explorer	12	Netscape1	$500.00			
13	Internet1	Internet Fundamentals	12	Comp1	$500.00			
14	Netscape1	Introduction to Netscape	12	Internet1	$500.00			
15	Network1	Introduction to Networking	12	Comp1	$500.00			
16	Outlook1	Introduction to Outlook	12	Comp1	$500.00			
17	PP1	Introduction to PowerPoint	12	Comp1	$500.00			
18	PP2	Intermediate PowerPoint	12	PP1	$500.00			
19	PPLab	PowerPoint Case Problems	12	PP2	$500.00			
20	Project1	Introduction to Project	24	Comp1	$1,000.00			
21	Public1	Public Speaking without Fear	16		$300.00			
22	Retail1	Introduction to Retailing	16		$300.00			
23	Retail2	Store Management	16	Retail1	$300.00			

TABLE 8-1: OfficeLinks tools

name	icon	description
Analyze It with Microsoft Excel		Sends a selected table, query, form, or report object's records to Excel
Publish It with Microsoft Word		Sends a selected table, query, form, or report object's records to Word
Merge It with Microsoft Word		Helps merge the selected table or query with a Word document

Skill Set 8

Integrating with Other Applications

Export Data from Access

Export Data to a Web Page

You can export data from Access tables, queries, forms, and reports to a variety of file formats, including Microsoft Office files, text files, and **Hypertext Markup Language** (**HTML**) documents, commonly called Web pages. Because Web pages can be distributed using the Internet, information provided on a Web page is more accessible to a larger audience than information provided as an Access report. Like all exported data, the data you export to an HTML document is no longer connected to the Access database, so the data is only as up-to-date as it was the moment you exported it.

Activity Steps

 Classes01.mdb

1. Click the **Reports button** on the Objects bar (if it's not already selected), then click **Progress Report**

2. Click **File** on the menu bar, click **Export**, navigate to the drive and folder where your Project Files are stored, click the **Save as type list arrow**, click **HTML Documents**, then click **Export**

3. Click **OK** in the HTML Output Options dialog box
   The export process finishes but doesn't automatically open the Progress Report Web page. You can open the Progress Report Web page from Windows Explorer.

4. Click **Start** on the taskbar, point to **Programs**, then click **Internet Explorer**

5. Maximize the Internet Explorer window (if it's not already maximized), click **File** on the menu bar, click **Open**, click **Browse**, navigate to the drive and folder where your Project Files are stored, click **Progress Report**, click **Open**, then click **OK**
   See Figure 8-6. The Progress Report Web page opens in Internet Explorer. The export progress created eight Web pages from the report and linked them with **hyperlinks** (text or images that, when clicked, open another Web page). Four hyperlinks appear in the bottom-left corner of the Web page.

6. Scroll to the bottom of the Progress Report Web page, then click the **Last** hyperlink
   See Figure 8-7. The last page of the report, converted into the Web page Progress Report8, opens in Internet Explorer.

7. Close Internet Explorer

Step 3
An HTML template contains formatting characteristics, such as font sizes and colors, that you can apply to Web pages to give them a consistent appearance.

Figure 8-6: First page of Progress Report, Progress Report.html

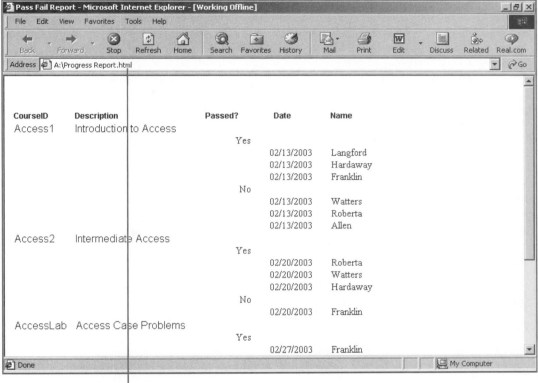

Progress Report.html

Figure 8-7: Last page of Progress Report, Progress Report8.html

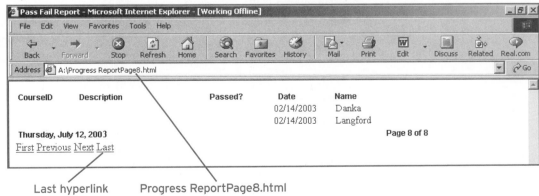

Last hyperlink   Progress ReportPage8.html

Skill Set 8

Integrating with Other Applications

Create a Simple Data Access Page
Create a Data Access Page for Data Entry

You use the **page** object, also called a **data access page** (**DAP**), to create a dynamic Web page. **Dynamic** means that the Web page is automatically linked to the database; every time the Web page is opened or refreshed, it reconnects with the database to display up-to-date data. You can use data access pages to enter and edit data in the database (like a form) or display current data in a Web page format (like a report). You can use the **Page Wizard** to create a data access page or build one by yourself using **Page Design View**. You view a data access page in **Page View**, which displays the final Web page just as it will appear in Internet Explorer. You modify a data access page in Page Design View.

Activity Steps

 Classes01.mdb

1. Click the **Pages button** [Pages] on the Objects bar (if it's not already selected), then double-click **Create data access page by using wizard**

2. Click the **Tables/Queries list arrow**, click **Table: Courses**, click the **Select All Fields button** [>>], then click **Next**

3. Click **Next** to not specify any grouping levels, click the first sort order **list arrow**, click **CourseID**, then click **Next**

4. Type **Course Entry Form** as the title for the page, click the **Open the page option button**, then click **Finish**
   See Figure 8-8. You can enter and edit data using a data access page opened in Page View or in Internet Explorer, and it will automatically update the database just as if you were using a database form object. You use the buttons on the navigation toolbar to move through the data access page.

5. Double-click **$700.00** in the Cost box, then type **750**

6. Click the **Sort Descending button** [⬇] on the navigation toolbar to sort the records in descending order based on the Cost values, then click the **Next button** [▶] twice to move to the third record for the Access1 CourseID to make sure that the records were sorted correctly

7. Click the **Save button** [💾] on the Page View toolbar, navigate to the drive and folder where your Project Files are stored, type **cform** in the File name box, click **Save**, then click **OK** when notified about the connection string

8. Close the Course Entry Form

Step 6
The Sort Ascending, Sort Descending, and Filter by Selection buttons work the same way on the navigation toolbar as they do on the Form View, Table Datasheet, or Query Datasheet toolbars.

Figure 8-8: Course Entry Form in Page View

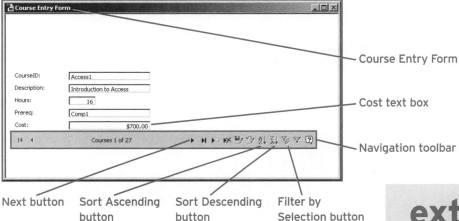

Course Entry Form

Cost text box

Navigation toolbar

Next button   Sort Ascending   Sort Descending   Filter by
button   button   Selection button

Figure 8-9: Deleting a data access page

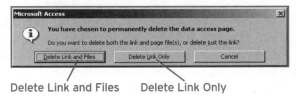

Delete Link and Files   Delete Link Only

extra!

**Understanding the
two parts of a data
access page**
When you create a data
access page, you really
create two things: the
Web page itself (which
is saved and given a
filename with an HTML
extension) and the link
to the Web page (which
is displayed as a page
object in the Database
window). If you click a
page object icon in the
Database window, then
press **[Delete]**, the
message shown in
Figure 8-9 will appear.
This message helps
clarify that a data
access page is really
composed of two
parts, and also points
out that you can delete
the link in the Access
database and the asso-
ciated Web page files,
or just the link within
the Access database.

Skill Set 8

Integrating with Other Applications

Create a Simple Data Access Page
Create a Data Access Page for Data Reporting

The two main purposes for building a data access page are to allow users to enter and edit data from a Web page, and to dynamically report up-to-date database activity through a report on a Web page. Your data access page will function as either a form or a report, depending on the choices you make while using the Page Wizard. All data access pages are automatically connected to the original database, so they will display up-to-date data when the Web page is opened or refreshed in the browser.

Activity Steps

 Classes01.mdb

1. Click the **Pages button** 🗐 Pages on the Objects bar (if it's not already selected), then double-click **Create data access page by using wizard**

2. Click the **Tables/Queries list arrow**, click **Table: Courses**, click **Description**, then click the **Select Single Field button** >

3. Click the **Tables/Queries list arrow**, click **Table: Customers**, click **First**, click the **Select Single Field button** > , click **Last**, click the **Select Single Field button** > , then click **Next**

4. Click **Description**, click the **Select Single Field button** > to use the Description field as the grouping level, then click **Next**

5. Click **Next** to bypass the sort order options and not specify a particular sort order, type **Course Attendee Report** as the title for the page, click the **Open the page option button**, then click **Finish**
   See Figure 8-10. As specified in the Page Wizard, the records are grouped by the Description field.

6. Click the **expand button** + to the left of the Description label
   See Figure 8-11. The Web page expands to show you the First and Last field values for each person who took that course. The upper navigation toolbar tells you that there are three records within this course description (three people have taken this course).

7. Click the upper navigation bar's **Next button** ▶ twice to move to the third record for Anton Watters
   You use the upper navigation toolbar to work with the records within each group and the lower navigation toolbar to work with the groups themselves.

8. Double-click **Watters**, then try to type **Winters**
   If you group records on a data access page, the Web page can be used only for data reporting, not for data entry.

9. Close the data access page without saving it

Step 1
If you open the page in Page Design View instead of Page View, click the View button 🖼 on the Page Design toolbar to switch to Page View.

Figure 8-10: Course Attendee Report in Page View

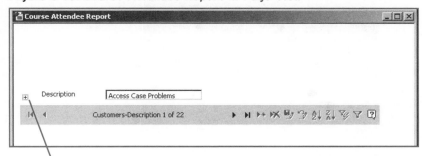

Expand button

Figure 8-11: Expanding records on a data access page

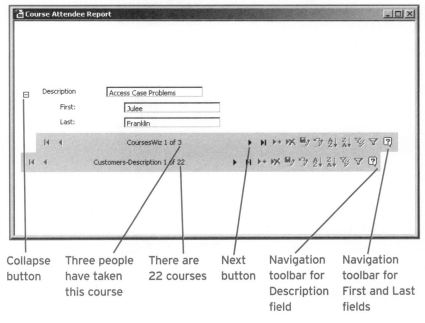

Collapse button

Three people have taken this course

There are 22 courses

Next button

Navigation toolbar for Description field

Navigation toolbar for First and Last fields

extra!

Understanding data access page browser requirements

When you create a data access page, special codes are added to the Web page to connect to the Access database, query the database for the latest data, and return that information to the Web page. You use **browser software** to find, download, and display Web pages. Because the codes placed in data access pages contain proprietary Microsoft technologies, the only browser that will display a data access page successfully is Microsoft's Internet Explorer version 5.0 or later. This means that data access pages are most useful in environments where you control users' browser software, such as corporate intranets or local area networks.

Skill Set 8

Integrating with Other Applications

Target Your Skills

 Classes01.mdb

1 Export the Customers table as an HTML document to the drive and folder where your Project Files are stored. Use the default name, Customers, as the filename, and do not apply an HTML template if given the choice to do so. Open the Customers file in Internet Explorer as shown in Figure 8-12.

Figure 8-12

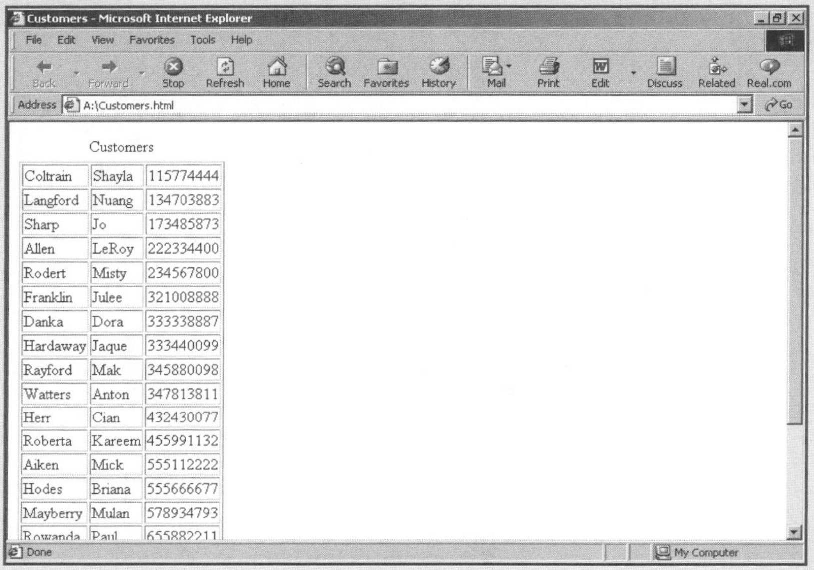

Coltrain	Shayla	115774444
Langford	Nuang	134703883
Sharp	Jo	173485873
Allen	LeRoy	222334400
Rodert	Misty	234567800
Franklin	Julee	321008888
Danka	Dora	333338887
Hardaway	Jaque	333440099
Rayford	Mak	345880098
Watters	Anton	347813811
Herr	Cian	432430077
Roberta	Kareem	455991132
Aiken	Mick	555112222
Hodes	Briana	555666677
Mayberry	Mulan	578934793
Rowanda	Paul	655882211

Customers - Microsoft Internet Explorer

Address: A:\Customers.html

 Classes01.mdb

2 Create a data access page based on the fields in the Customers table. Do not add grouping levels or sort orders, and title the page Customer Entry Form. Navigate to the second record, then change the last name from Langford to Adams. Sort the records in ascending order based on the value in the Last field as shown in Figure 8-13. Close the page without saving it.

Figure 8-13

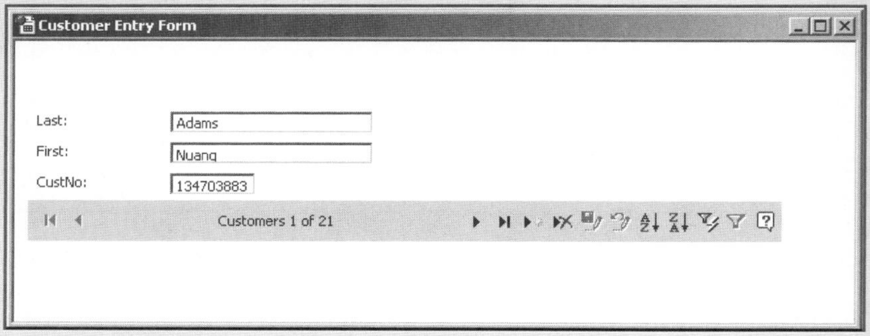

Customer Entry Form

Last: Adams

First: Nuang

CustNo: 134703883

Customers 1 of 21

Skill List

1. Use data validation
2. Link tables
3. Create lookup fields and modify Lookup field properties
4. Create and modify input masks

In Skill Set 9, you will use advanced tools to modify tables and fields to maximize fast and accurate data entry. Specifically, you will learn how to link tables to make use of data that is stored and maintained in another Access database. You'll also use the Field Validation and Input Mask properties, which help prevent inaccurate data from being accepted into the database. In addition, you will create and modify lookup fields, which support fast, easy, and accurate data entry.

Skill Set 9

Creating and Modifying Tables

Use Data Validation

Data validation is a process that compares a field entry with criteria that define a set or range of acceptable entries for a field. For example, you might limit a Gender field to only two possible entries, "Female" or "Male." However, for a DateofService field, you might allow any date after the date a business started. You use the **Validation Rule** property to set the criteria for data entry. You use the **Validation Text** property to display a message if a user attempts to enter a value that is outside the acceptable entries. By using the Validation Rule and Validation Text properties, you can minimize some types of data entry errors.

Activity Steps

 Basketball01.mdb

1. Click the **Tables button** [Tables] on the Objects bar (if it's not already selected), click **Games**, then click the **Design button** [Design] on the Database window toolbar

2. Click the **Home-Away** field, click the **Validation Rule property box**, type **A or H**, then click the **Validation Text property box**
   See Figure 9-1. Access helps you make a valid criteria entry in the Validation Rule property box by adding quotation marks around the possible text entries and by automatically capitalizing the word *Or*.

3. Type **Enter A for Away or H for Home** in the Validation Text property box

4. Click the **Date** field, click the **Validation Rule property box**, type **>=11/1/03**, then click the **Validation Text property box**
   This validation rule will require that all entries in the Date field are November 1, 2003 or later.

5. Type **Season starts November 1, 2003** in the Validation Text property box

6. Click the **Save button** [ ] on the Table Design toolbar, click **Yes** when prompted to test the existing data against the new rules, then click the **View button** [ ] on the Table Design toolbar

7. Press **[Tab]** three times to select the value in the Home-Away field, type **B**, then press **[Tab]**
   See Figure 9-2. The text that you entered in the Validation Text property appears in an alert box.

8. Click **OK**, press **[Esc]** to undo the unacceptable "B" entry in the Home-Away field, press **[Tab]** three times to select the value in the Date field, type **10/1/03**, then press **[Tab]**

9. Click **OK**, press **[Esc]** to undo the unacceptable 10/1/30 entry in the Date field, then close the Games table

Step 3
If you enter a Validation Rule property but not a Validation Text property, Access still displays an error message if you attempt to enter data outside the criteria defined by the Validation Rule. By using the Validation Text property, though, you can customize the error message.

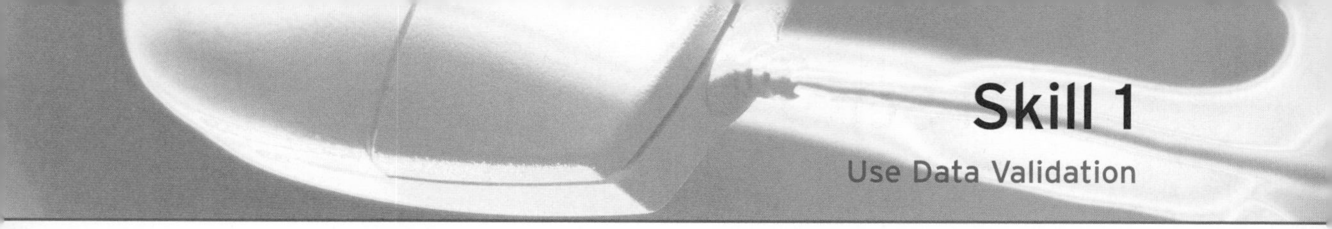

Figure 9-1: Entering a Validation Rule property

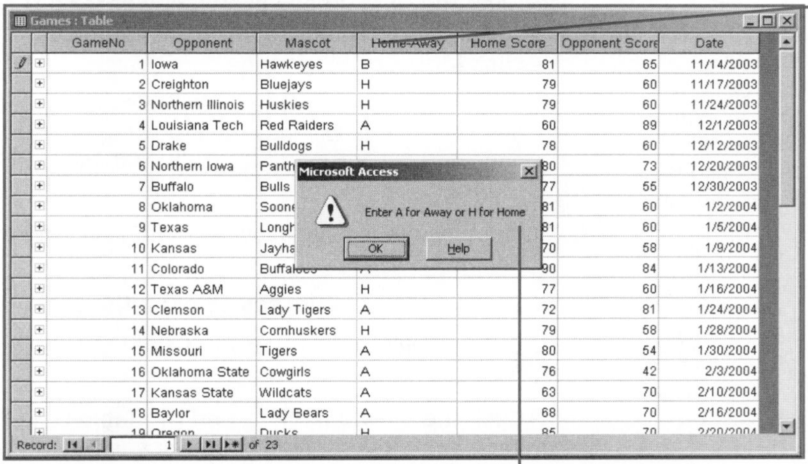

Home-Away field is selected

Validation Rule entry

Validation Text property box

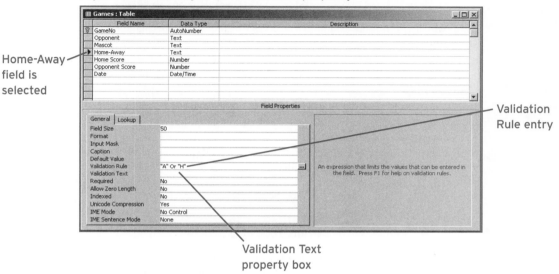

Figure 9-2: Testing the Validation Text property

B entry

Validation Text property entry

Skill Set 9

Creating and Modifying Tables

Link Tables

If you have a table that you can use in two or more databases, you don't need to create a copy of the table for each database. Instead, you can use a **linked table**, which is a link to data stored in a "real" table in another database. The advantage of using a linked table is that updates made in either database are automatically reflected in both databases. For example, if you have a database that tracks employee projects and another that tracks employee benefits, both databases could use a single table containing employee information. To ensure that changes to the employee data made from one database are automatically updated in the other, you would create the employee table in one database and use a linked table in the other. You can use a linked table to enter, modify, or delete data (just like you would in the original table), but you cannot save any changes in Table Design View of a linked table.

Activity Steps

 Benefits01.mdb
Projects01.mdb

1. In the Benefits01 database, click the **Tables button** ▦ Tables on the Objects bar (if it's not already selected), click **File** on the menu bar, point to **Get External Data**, then click **Link Tables**

2. Click the **Look in list arrow**, navigate to the drive and folder where the Projects01 database is stored, click **Projects01**, then click **Link**

3. Click **Employees** in the Link Tables dialog box
   See Figure 9-3. The Link Tables dialog box shows all the tables that you can link to from the Projects01 database.

4. Click **OK**
   The Employees table appears as an object in the tables list with a linking table icon.

5. Double-click **Employees** to open the table in Datasheet View

6. Double-click **Jeff** in the First field of the second record, then type **Jeffrey**

7. Click the **View button** ⊠ on the Table Datasheet toolbar, then click **Yes** after reading the message about linked table limitations

8. Read the message in the lower-right corner of the Field Properties pane that clarifies that you are working in a linked table and therefore cannot modify the current property, then close the Employees table

Step 2
You can link to data in multiple file formats including dBASE, Excel, Outlook, and HTML files. Click the Files of type list arrow in the Link dialog box to view a list of files that an Access database will link to.

Figure 9-3: Link Tables dialog box

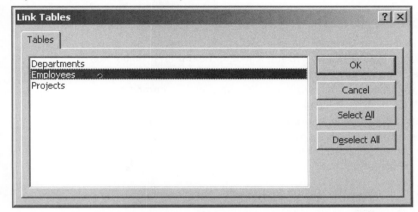

extra!

Using the Linked Table Manager

You use the Linked Table Manager to change the path between an original and linked table if one of the databases is moved. You also use the Linked Table Manager to refresh the linked copy of the table if the original table's structure (field names and properties) has been modified. While a linked table contains no data, it does store a copy of the structure of the original table, so you should refresh the linked table after you add or modify field properties in the original table. To access the Linked Table Manager, right-click a linked table, then click **Linked Table Manager** on the shortcut menu to open the Linked Table Manager dialog box.

Skill Set 9

Creating and Modifying Tables

Create Lookup Fields and Modify Lookup Field Properties

Create Lookup Fields

You create a lookup field by entering Lookup properties directly into Table Design View or by using the Lookup Wizard. A **lookup field** uses a combo box (sometimes called a drop-down list), which displays values for a field in either Datasheet View (of a table or query) or Form View of a form. A **combo box** is a "combination" of a list and a text box, so it allows you to choose a value from a drop-down list or type a value into a field. Choosing from a list of common entries improves data entry ease-of-use, speed, and accuracy. To create the combo box's list of values, you can enter your own values or use an existing list of values from a table in the database.

Step 2
The Lookup Wizard isn't a data type even though it's listed in the Data Type list. After using the Lookup Wizard, the data type will return to Text because the field values are text entries.

Activity Steps

 Basketball01.mdb

1. Click the **Tables button** ⊞ Tables on the Objects bar (if it's not already selected), click **Players** (if it's not already selected), then click the **Design button** ▨ Design on the Database window toolbar

2. Click **Text** in the Data Type cell for the Year field, click the **list arrow**, then click **Lookup Wizard**

3. Click the **I will type in the values that I want option button**, then click **Next**

4. Click the first cell for the **Col1** column, type **Fr**, press **[Tab]**, type **So**, press **[Tab]**, type **Jr**, press **[Tab]**, type **Sr**, then press **[Tab]**
   See Figure 9-4. These values will appear in the combo box list for the Year field.

5. Click **Next**, then click **Finish** to accept Year as the label for the lookup column

6. Click the **View button** ⊞ on the Table Design toolbar, click **Yes** to save the table, click the **Year** field for the first record, then click the **list arrow**
   See Figure 9-5. The values that you entered in the Lookup Wizard are displayed in the combo box list, and can be used to enter and edit data in the Year field.

7. Close the Players table

Figure 9-4: Creating a list of values for a lookup field

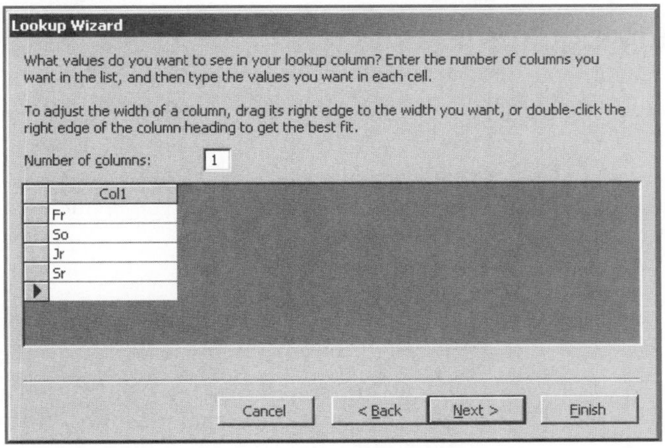

Figure 9-5: Viewing a list of values for a lookup field

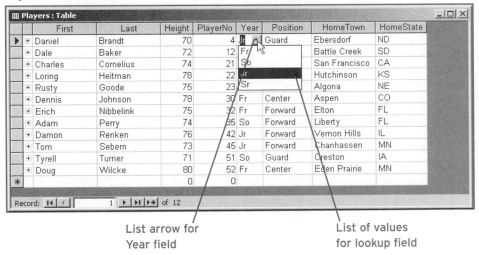

List arrow for
Year field

List of values
for lookup field

Skill Set 9
Creating and Modifying Tables

Create Lookup Fields and Modify Lookup Field Properties

Modify Lookup Properties

You can modify a lookup field by using the Lookup Wizard or by changing the Lookup properties in Table Design View. While the Lookup Wizard is an excellent tool for creating a new lookup field, modifying a lookup by directly changing individual Lookup field properties can be faster. You modify Lookup properties using Table Design View, as you would modify any other properties.

Activity Steps

 Basketball01.mdb

1. Click the **Tables button** [⊞ Tables] on the Objects bar (if it's not already selected), click **Players** (if it's not already selected), then click the **Design button** [🔲 Design] on the Database window toolbar

2. Click the **Position** field, then click the **Lookup tab** in the Field Properties pane

3. Click the **Row Source property box**, then modify the entry to display the following text: "Point Guard";"Off Guard";"Forward";"Center"
   See Figure 9-6. These will appear in the combo box list for the Position field.

4. Click the **View button** [⊞] on the Table Design toolbar, click **Yes** to save the table, click the **Position** field for the first record, then click the **list arrow**
   See Figure 9-7. Even though the existing value in the field, "Guard," isn't in the current drop-down list, it's still an acceptable entry for this field. By default, lookup fields give you a list of values to choose from, but they don't limit your ability to store or enter another value that is not in the list.

5. Close the Players table

Step 3
If you want to limit the choices for a lookup field to those in the list, change the Limit To List lookup property to Yes in the Field Properties pane in Table Design View.

Figure 9-6: Modifying a list of values for a lookup field

Position field is selected

Lookup tab

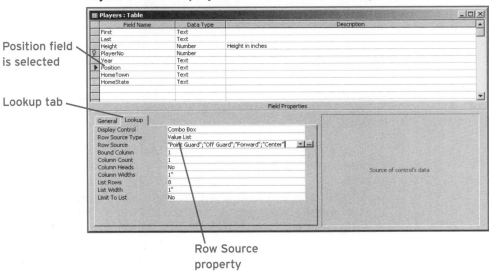

Row Source property

Figure 9-7: Using a list of modified values for a lookup field

List arrow for Position field

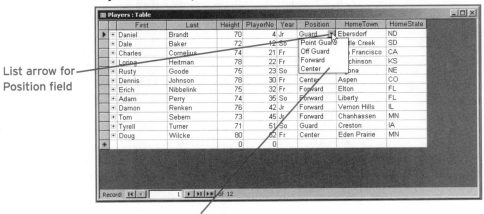

List of modified values for lookup field

Skill Set 9
Creating and Modifying Tables

Create and Modify Input Masks

You can use the Input Mask property to specify the number and types of characters that can be entered into a field, and also to display a visual guide as data is
entered into a field. For example, you could apply an input mask to a Telephone
field that allows only 10 digits and automatically enters dashes at the appropriate places as a user types the entry. You can use the Input Mask property only
with fields that have Text and Date/Time data types. A complete Input Mask
property has three parts (separated by semicolons) as described in Table 9-1. You
can use the Input Mask Wizard to apply existing or create custom Input Mask
properties, or you can modify Input Mask properties in Table Design View.

Activity Steps

 Basketball01.mdb

1. Click the **Tables button** ▦ Tables on the Objects bar (if
   it's not already selected), click **Games**, then click the
   Design button ✏ Design on the Database window toolbar

2. Click the **Date** field, click the **Input Mask property box** in the
   Field Properties pane, click the **Build button** […], then click
   Yes if prompted to save the table
   By default, the Input Mask Wizard lists five common input masks for
   a field with a Date/Time data type. You will create an input mask that
   requires a two-digit month, two-digit day, and four-digit year entry,
   each separated by dashes. Since none of the existing input mask
   options meets this requirement, you'll create a custom input mask.

3. Click **Edit List**, type **Two-Two-Four** in the Description box, press
   [Tab], type **00/00/0000**, press **[Tab]**, type ***** (an asterisk), press
   [Tab], type **11/22/2004**, click the **Mask Type list arrow**, and
   then click **Date-Time**
   See Figure 9-8. This custom input mask will be available each time
   you use the Input Mask Wizard.

4. Click **Close**, click **Two-Two-Four**, click **Next**, click **Next** to accept
   the input mask options, then click **Finish**

5. Click the **View button** ▦ on the Table Design toolbar, click **Yes**
   when prompted to save the table, then press **[Tab]** six times to
   select the Date value for the first record

6. Type **1114**
   See Figure 9-9. The Input Mask property guides your entry by displaying asterisks for each number of the date. The slashes are automatically entered for you. Without the Input Mask property, you
   would have to type the slashes.

7. Type **2003** to finish the entry, then close the Games table

Step 4
If you use only two
digits for the year,
numbers you enter
from 0 to 29 are
assumed to be
2000 through 2029
and numbers from
30 to 99 are
assumed to be
1930 through 1999.

Figure 9-8: Customize Input Mask Wizard dialog box

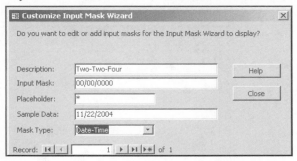

Figure 9-9: Entering a date in a field with a custom input mask

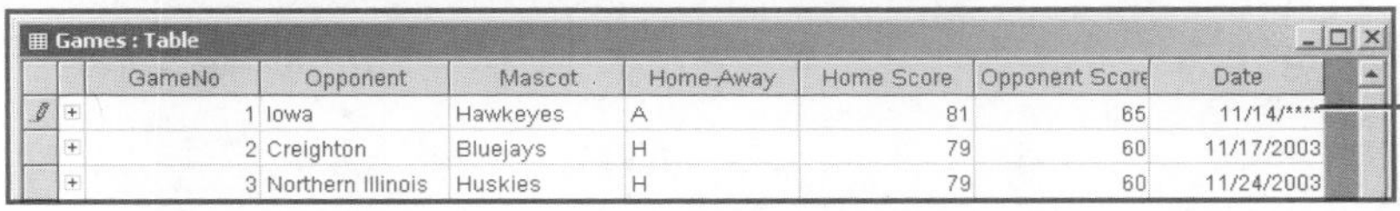

		GameNo	Opponent	Mascot	Home-Away	Home Score	Opponent Score	Date
∅	+	1	Iowa	Hawkeyes	A	81	65	11/14/****
	+	2	Creighton	Bluejays	H	79	60	11/17/2003
	+	3	Northern Illinois	Huskies	H	79	60	11/24/2003

— Entering a date using an input mask

TABLE 9-1: The parts of the input mask entry

part	description	options	examples (parts appear in bold)	how a sample entry appears in Datasheet View or Form View
first	Controls what type of data can be entered and how it will be displayed.	**9** represents an optional number **0** represents a required number **?** represents an optional letter **L** represents a required letter **** causes the next character to be displayed as entered	Telephone Number \\(**999**\\)\\-**000**\\-**0000**;1;*	(123)-456-7899
second	Determines whether all displayed characters (such as dashes in the SSN field) are stored in a field, or just the part you enter.	**0** stores all characters **1** stores only the entered characters	ZIP Code 00000\\-9999;**0**;_	12345 or 12345-7777
third	Determines which character Access will display as a placeholder for the space where a character will be typed in a field.	***** (asterisk) **_** (underscore) **#** (pound sign)	Social Security Number 000\\-00\\-0000;0;**#**	987-65-4321

Skill Set 9

Creating and Modifying Tables

Target Your Skills

 Basketball01.mdb
States01.mdb

1 In the Basketball01 database, create a linked table that links to the States table in the States01 database. In the Players table, create a new field using "Major" as the field name. Use the Lookup Wizard to add the values shown in Figure 9-10 to the Major field. Then use the combo box in the Major field to add the value "Business" to the first record in the Players table.

Figure 9-10

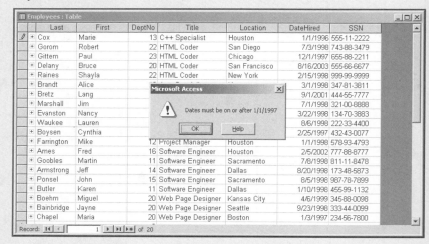

 Projects01.mdb

2 Set the Validation Rule property of the DateHired field in the Employees table so that values must be on or after 1/1/1997. Set the Validation Text property of the DateHired field to display the message shown in Figure 9-11. Create an input mask for the SSN field. Specify that all nine digits are required and separated by dashes in a 3-2-4 digit pattern. Use the asterisk (*) character for the place-holder, and store only the digits in the field.

Figure 9-11

Skill Set 10

Skill List

1. Create a form in Design View
2. Create a switchboard and set startup options
3. Add subform controls to Access forms

In Skill Set 10, you will use advanced tools to create and modify forms. For example, you'll use Form Design View to modify a form using a property sheet, and you'll work with advanced controls such as subforms. You will also create a special type of form called a **switchboard**, which is used to help users navigate through a database rather than help them enter or edit data (which is the purpose of most forms). Finally, you'll learn about Access startup options that help make your database easy to use and more secure.

Skill Set 10

Creating and Modifying Forms

Create a Form in Design View

You can use Form Design View to create a new form without the aid of a form creation tool, such as AutoForm or the Form Wizard. You also use Form Design View to modify an existing form. When you create a form in Form Design View, you need to set the **Record Source property** for the form, which determines which fields and records the form will display. You select either a table or a query as the Record Source property for the form. After you set the Record Source property, you specify where you want each field to appear on the form.

Activity Steps

 Jobs01.mdb

1. Click the **Forms button** 🔲 Forms on the Objects bar (if it's not already selected), then double-click **Create form in Design view**

2. Click the **Properties button** 🖺 on the Form Design toolbar to open the Form property sheet (if it's not already open), click the **Data tab** (if it's not already selected), click the **Record Source list arrow**, then click **Project Summary**
   See Figure 10-1. Project Summary is a query in this database that contains five fields from three different tables. When you choose a table or query for the Record Source property, the **field list** opens, which displays the fields from the record source that you specify.

3. Click the **Properties button** 🖺 to toggle off the Form property sheet

4. Double-click the **title bar** of the field list to select all the fields, then drag the selected fields to the middle of the form
   You can drag an individual field or several selected fields to a specific location on the form. You can also move, resize, and format fields after they have been added to a form.

5. Click the **View button** 🖺 on the Form Design toolbar
   See Figure 10-2. This form shows the five fields of the Project Summary query. The navigation toolbar indicates that there are 13 records in this query.

6. Close the new form without saving it

Step 2
If the field list doesn't open when you set the Record Source property, click the Field List button 🔲 on the Form Design toolbar to toggle it on. Drag a border of the Field List to expand it to see all the fields or view the entire query or table name on the title bar.

Figure 10-1: Setting the Record Source property

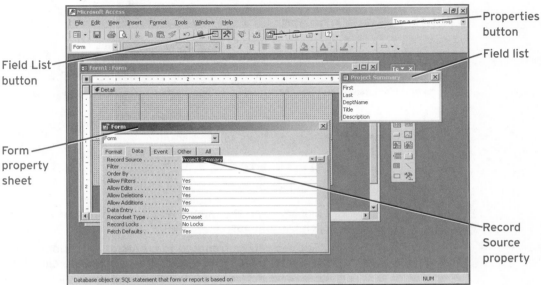

Properties button

Field list

Field List button

Form property sheet

Record Source property

Figure 10-2: Form created in Form Design View

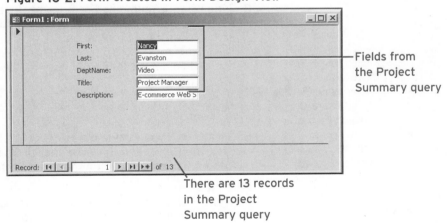

Fields from the Project Summary query

There are 13 records in the Project Summary query

Skill Set 10

Creating and Modifying Forms

Create a Switchboard and Set Startup Options

Create a Switchboard

You can create a special form called a **switchboard**, which is used to find, open, and use various parts of the database. A switchboard displays one command button for each object so that users don't have to use the Database window to find the parts of the database that they need. If you create more than one switchboard, you must designate a switchboard as the **default switchboard**. Typically, you add command buttons to the default switchboard to open the other switchboards. You use the **Switchboard Manager** to create all switchboards.

Activity Steps

 Jobs01.mdb

1. Click **Tools** on the menu bar, point to **Database Utilities**, then click **Switchboard Manager**

2. Click **Yes** when prompted to create a switchboard, click **Edit** in the Switchboard Manager dialog box, double-click **Main** and type **Jobs** in the Switchboard Name box to name the switchboard "Jobs Switchboard," then click **New** in the Edit Switchboard Page dialog box

3. Type **Open Employees Form** in the Text box, click the **Command list arrow**, click **Open Form in Edit Mode**, click the **Form list arrow**, then click **Employees**
   See Figure 10-3. The Edit Switchboard Item dialog box identifies the text and command for each button on the final switchboard.

4. Click **OK**
   The Edit Switchboard Page dialog box lists the existing commands on the switchboard.

5. Click **New**, type **Preview Assignments Report** in the Text box, click the **Command list arrow**, click **Open Report**, click the **Report list arrow**, click **Assignments**, then click **OK**

6. Click **Close** in the Edit Switchboard Page dialog box, click **Close** in the Switchboard Manager dialog box, click the **Forms button** ⊞ Forms on the Objects bar (if it's not already selected), then double-click **Switchboard**
   See Figure 10-4. The Jobs Switchboard form displays the two command buttons you specified in the Switchboard Manager.

7. Click the **Open Employees Form button**, close the Employees form, click the **Preview Assignments Report button**, close the Assignments report, then close the Jobs Switchboard

If you delete a switchboard form, you must also delete the Switchboard Items table (which is automatically created by the Switchboard Manager) before you can create a new switchboard form.

Figure 10-3: Using the Switchboard Manager

Switchboard Manager dialog box

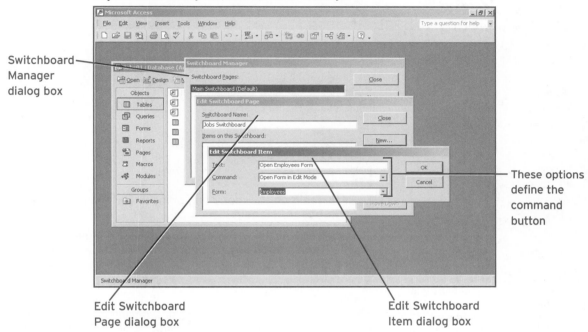

These options define the command button

Edit Switchboard Page dialog box

Edit Switchboard Item dialog box

Figure 10-4: A switchboard with two command buttons

Switchboard command buttons

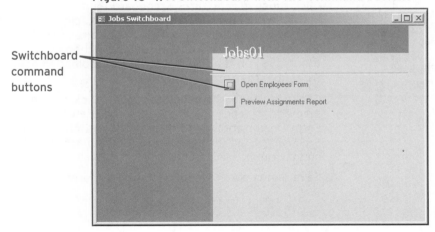

Skill Set 10
Creating and Modifying Forms

Create a Switchboard and Set Startup Options
Modify a Switchboard

After you create a switchboard form, you might want to modify it by adding, deleting, or changing the existing command buttons, or by formatting the form. To modify the command buttons (or the text to the right of the command buttons), you must use the Switchboard Manager. To format or modify any control other than the command buttons (for example, labels or clip art), you use Form Design View.

Step 5
The default teal color on a switchboard is created with two teal-colored rectangles. To change this color, click a rectangle, then choose a new color using the Fill/Back Color button in Form Design View.

Activity Steps

 Health01.mdb

1. Click **Tools** on the menu bar, point to **Database Utilities**, click **Switchboard Manager**, then click **Edit**

2. Click **View Activity Report**, then click the **Move Up button** three times to change the command button from the last position to the first position

3. Click **Edit**, change "View" to "Preview" in the Text box, then click **OK**
   See Figure 10-5. Any change to the command buttons or command button text of a switchboard *should* be made using the Switchboard Manager.

4. Click **Close** in the Edit Switchboard Page dialog box, click **Close** in the Switchboard Manager dialog box, click the **Forms button** on the Objects bar (if it's not already selected), click **Switchboard** in the Database window, then click the **Design button** on the Database window toolbar to open the Switchboard form in Design View

5. Click the **Medical Associates label**, click the **Font Size list arrow**, click **20**, then click the **View button** on the Form Design toolbar to display the switchboard in Form View
   See Figure 10-6. Changes to any control *other* than the command buttons can be made in Form Design View.

6. Save and close the Main Switchboard form

Figure 10-5: Modifying switchboard command buttons with the Switchboard Manager

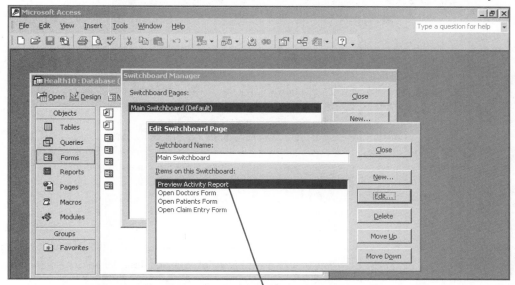

Item moved up and "View" is
changed to "Preview"

Figure 10-6: Switchboard formatted in Form Design View

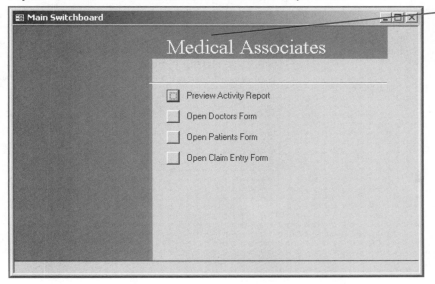

Font size
of label
has been
increased

Skill Set 10
Creating and Modifying Forms

Create a Switchboard and Set Startup Options
Set Startup Options

Startup options are commands that are automatically applied to the database when you open it. Some startup options help make the database easier to use. For example, you can use the Display Form/Page startup option to display a form or page object as soon as the database is opened. (If your database includes a switchboard form, you can use the Display Form/Page startup option to automatically display the switchboard when the database is opened.) You can also use startup options to increase database security. For example, some startup options allow you to disable the user's ability to modify Access toolbars and menus or hide the database window. Table 10-1 describes many popular startup options.

Activity Steps

 Health01.mdb

1. Click **Tools** on the menu bar, then click **Startup**

2. Click the **Display Form/Page list arrow**, then click **Switchboard**

3. Deselect the **Display Database Window check box**, then deselect the **Allow Toolbar/Menu Changes check box**
   See Figure 10-7.

4. Click **OK**, Close the Health01 database, then reopen the Health01 database
   The Main Switchboard form is automatically opened when you open the Health01 database. The Database window is hidden.

5. Right-click any toolbar or menu bar
   Since the startup options specify that you are not allowed to modify toolbars and menu bars, nothing happens when you right-click a toolbar or menu bar.

6. Close the Main Switchboard form and exit Access

Step 4
To bypass the startup options, press and hold [Shift] while opening a database.

Figure 10-7: Startup dialog box

Startup dialog box —

Display Form/Page option

Allow Toolbar/Menu Changes check box

Display Database Window check box

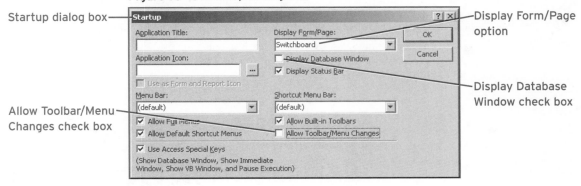

TABLE 10-1: Startup options

option	description
Application Title	Displays text (that you specify) on the Database title bar instead of the name of the database
Application Icon	Displays a bitmap or an icon file (that you specify) to the left of the text on the Database and application title bars
Menu Bar	Specifies which menu bar appears when the database is opened
Allow Full Menus	Toggles on or off the ability to work with full menus
Allow Default Shortcut Menus	Toggles on or off the ability to work with shortcut menus
Use Access Special Keys	Toggles on or off the ability to work with Access special keys such as F11, which opens the Database window
Display Form/Page	Specifies which form or page object automatically opens when you open the database
Display Database Window	Works as a toggle to hide or display the Database window when you open a database
Display Status Bar	Toggles on or off the ability to display the status bar
Shortcut Menu Bar	Specifies which shortcut menu bar appears when you right-click a menu bar
Allow Built-in Toolbars	Toggles on or off the ability to display Access toolbars
Allow Toolbar/Menu Changes	Toggles on or off the ability to modify Access toolbars and menu bars

Skill Set 10

Creating and Modifying Forms

Add Subform Controls to Access Forms

A **subform** is a form within a form. The form that contains the subform is called the **main form**. If two tables are joined in a one-to-many relationship, you can create a form and a subform by using data from the tables. For example, if you have two tables, Customers and Sales, that are joined in a one-to-many relationship, you can use a form and a subform to show information for one customer in the main form and the many related records of what the customer purchased in the subform.

Activity Steps

 Jobs01.mdb

1. Click the **Forms button** 📇 Forms on the Objects bar (if it's not already selected), click **Employees**, click the **Design button** 📐 Design on the Database window toolbar, then maximize the Employees form in Form Design View

2. Click the **Toolbox button** 🛠 on the Form Design toolbar to toggle it on (if it's not already visible), click the **Subform/Subreport button** 📧 on the Toolbox toolbar, then click under the **Dept No label** on the form
   The SubForm Wizard appears and assists you with the process of adding a subform. Each employee is related to many projects, so the subform should contain fields from the Projects table. You can also use an existing query or form as the source of data for the subform control.

3. Click **Next** to accept the option to use existing tables or queries, click the **Tables/Queries list arrow**, click **Table: Projects**, click the **Select All Fields button** >>, click **Next**, click **Next** to accept the suggested link between the main form and subform, then click **Finish** to accept the name "Projects subform" for the subform

4. Maximize the Employees form, point to the **lower-right sizing handle** of the subform so that the resize pointer ⬊ appears, then drag down and to the right to expand the size of the subform to fill the screen
   See Figure 10-8.

5. Click the **View button** 📧 on the Form Design toolbar to display the Employees form with the new subform in Form View, then click the **Next Record button** ▶ on the main form navigation toolbar several times to display the record for Marie Cox
   See Figure 10-9.

6. Save and close the Employees form

Step 2
If the SubForm Wizard doesn't automatically appear, delete the subform control, make sure that the Control Wizards button 🔧 on the Toolbox toolbar is selected, then repeat Step 2.

Figure 10-8: Adding a subform to a main form in Form Design View

Toolbox button

Main form

Subform

Project table fields

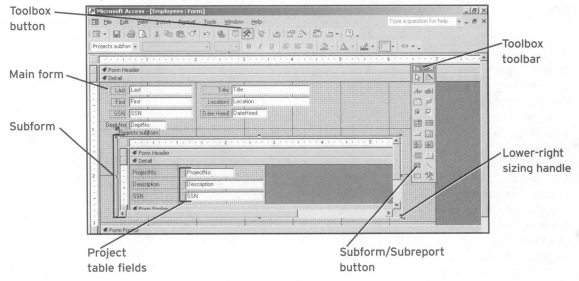

Toolbox toolbar

Lower-right sizing handle

Subform/Subreport button

Figure 10-9: Working with a form and subform in Form View

Subform

Next Record button

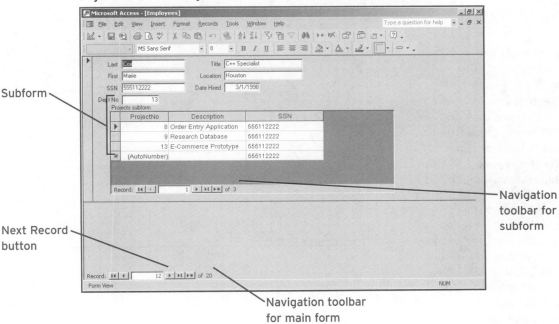

Navigation toolbar for subform

Navigation toolbar for main form

Skill Set 10

Creating and Modifying Forms

Target Your Skills

 Jobs01.mdb

1 Use Form Design View to create the form and subform displayed in Figure 10-10. Use the Departments table for the main form's Record Source property, and use all the fields of the Employees table for the subform. Use the DeptNo field to link the main form and subform. Adjust the subform's columns in Form View.

Figure 10-10

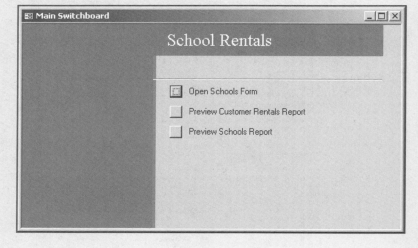

 Rentals01.mdb

2 Create the Switchboard form shown in Figure 10-11. The first button opens the Schools form in edit mode, the second opens the Customer Rentals report, and the third opens the Schools report. In Form Design View, change the "Rentals01" label to "School Rentals," move it up, and delete the gray "Rentals01" label. Set the switchboard to automatically open when you open the database.

Figure 10-11

Skill List

1. Specify multiple query criteria
2. Create and apply advanced filters
3. Create and run parameter queries
4. Create and run action queries
5. Use aggregate functions in queries

In Skill Set 11, you will use advanced query functions that help you find, display, and analyze data. For example, you will apply advanced filters to quickly find and display specific data. You will use parameter criteria to customize a query to prompt a user to enter criteria. You'll also use action queries that change data, including the make-table, append, update, and delete queries. Finally, you'll use aggregate functions to help you analyze data by creating summary statistics for groups of records.

Skill Set 11

Refining Queries

Specify Multiple Query Criteria
Use AND Conditions

An **AND condition** consists of two or more criteria entered in Query Design View, where *each* criterion must be true for a record to appear in Query Datasheet View. For example, in a personnel database, you could create a query to show employees who are from a particular department *and* have a particular job code. In this example, both conditions must be true for a record to appear. Adding more AND conditions to a query decreases the number of records in a resulting datasheet. You enter AND conditions in the same row of the query design grid.

Step 5
Text criterion is not case sensitive, so "laptop," "Laptop," and "LAPTOP" all work the same way.

Activity Steps

 Computers01.mdb

1. Click the **Queries button** ⊞ Queries on the Objects bar (if it's not already selected), then double-click **Create query in Design view**

2. Click **Categories**, click **Add**, click **Equipment**, click **Add**, then click **Close**

3. Drag **CategoryDesc** from the Categories field list to the first column of the query design grid, then double-click **Description**, **PurchaseDate**, and **InitialValue** in the Equipment field list to add them to the query design grid

4. Click the **View button** ▦ on the Query Design toolbar to view the datasheet before adding criteria to the query design grid
   53 records appear in the datasheet.

5. Click the **View button** ◹ on the Query Datasheet toolbar to return to Query Design View, click the **Criteria cell** for the CategoryDesc field, type **laptop**, then click the **View button** ▦ on the Query Design toolbar
   17 records match the criterion.

6. Click the **View button** ◹ on the Query Datasheet toolbar, click the **Criteria cell** for the InitialValue field, then type **>2000**
   See Figure 11-1. Access automatically applied quotation marks around the criterion for the CategoryDesc field because it is a Text field.

7. Click the **View button** ▦ on the Query Design toolbar
   See Figure 11-2. 10 records appear in the datasheet. Each record has both "laptop" in the CategoryDesc field and a value greater than 2000 in the InitialValue field.

8. Close the query without saving changes

Figure 11-1: AND condition in Query Design View

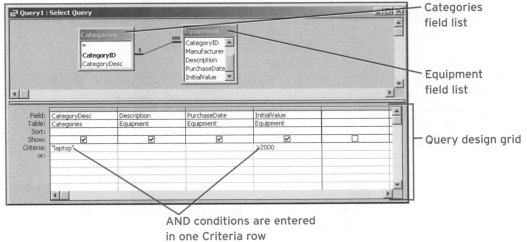

Categories field list

Equipment field list

Query design grid

AND conditions are entered in one Criteria row

Figure 11-2: Query Datasheet View with an AND condition applied

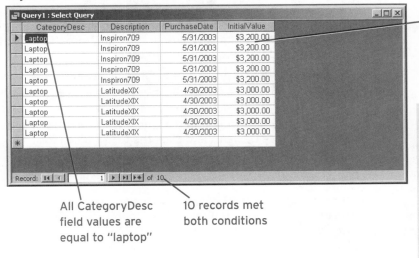

All InitialValue field values are greater than 2000

All CategoryDesc field values are equal to "laptop"

10 records met both conditions

extra!

Adding an AND condition to one field
If two or more criteria must be true for the same field, (for example, the values in a PurchaseDate field must be greater than 1/1/2003 *and* less than 12/31/2003) you use the AND operator in one Criteria cell of the query design grid. For this example, the Criteria cell for the PurchaseDate field would contain >1/1/2003 AND <12/31/2003.

Skill Set 11

Refining Queries

Specify Multiple Query Criteria
Use OR Conditions

An **OR condition** consists of two or more criteria entered in Query Design View, where only *one* criterion must be true for a record to appear in Query Datasheet View. For example, in a product inventory database, you could create a query to show records for all products that are categorized as fragile *or* those that require refrigeration. In this example, *either* criterion needs to be true for a record to appear. Because only one criterion in an OR condition must be true for a record to appear in a datasheet, adding more OR conditions to a query increases the number of records in a resulting datasheet. You enter OR conditions in different rows of the query design grid.

Activity Steps

 Computers01.mdb

1. Click the **Queries button** ⊞ Queries on the Objects bar (if it's not already selected), then double-click **Create query in Design view**

2. Click **Categories**, click **Add**, click **Equipment**, click **Add**, then click **Close**

3. Drag **CategoryDesc** from the Categories field list to the first column of the query design grid, then double-click **Description**, **PurchaseDate**, and **InitialValue** in the Equipment field list to add each field to the query design grid

4. Click the **View button** ▦ on the Query Design toolbar to view the datasheet before adding criteria to the query design grid
   53 records appear in the datasheet.

5. Click the **View button** ⊠ on the Query Datasheet toolbar to return to Query Design View, click the **Criteria cell** for the CategoryDesc field, type **laptop**, then click the **View button** ▦ on the Query Design toolbar
   17 records match the criterion.

6. Click the **View button** ⊠ on the Query Datasheet toolbar, click the **or cell** for the InitialValue field, then type **>2000**
   See Figure 11-3. Access automatically applied quotation marks around the criterion for the CategoryDesc field because it is a Text field.

7. Click the **View button** ▦ on the Query Design toolbar, then press **[Ctrl][End]** to quickly navigate to the last field of the last record
   See Figure 11-4. 19 records appear in the datasheet. Each record has either "laptop" in the CategoryDesc field, a value greater than 2000 in the InitialValue field, or both.

8. Close the query without saving changes

Step 6
You can add as many OR conditions as desired by using additional rows of the query design grid. If you run out of rows, click Insert on the menu bar, then click Rows.

Figure 11-3: OR condition in Query Design View

Equipment field list
Categories field list
or row
Query design grid
OR conditions are entered on two rows
Query1 : Select Query
Categories
CategoryID
CategoryDesc
Equipment
CategoryID
Manufacturer
Description
PurchaseDate
InitialValue
Field: CategoryDesc Description PurchaseDate InitialValue
Table: Categories Equipment Equipment Equipment
Sort:
Show:
Criteria: "laptop"
or: >2000

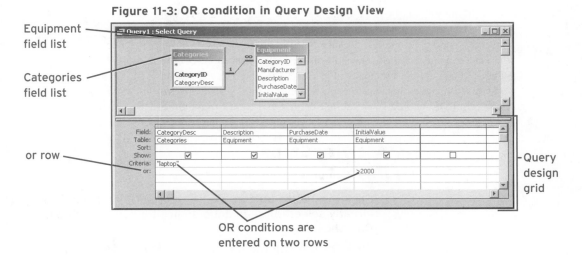

Figure 11-4: Query Datasheet View with an OR condition applied

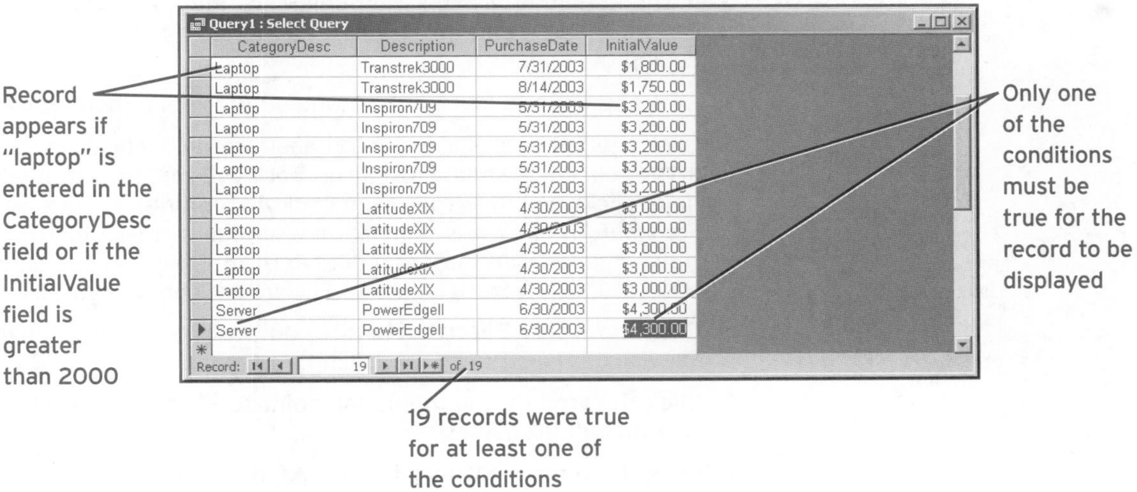

Record appears if "laptop" is entered in the CategoryDesc field or if the InitialValue field is greater than 2000
Only one of the conditions must be true for the record to be displayed
19 records were true for at least one of the conditions
Query1 : Select Query
CategoryDesc Description PurchaseDate InitialValue
Laptop Transtrek3000 7/31/2003 $1,800.00
Laptop Transtrek3000 8/14/2003 $1,750.00
Laptop Inspiron709 5/31/2003 $3,200.00
Laptop LatitudeXIX 4/30/2003 $3,000.00
Server PowerEdgeII 6/30/2003 $4,300.00
Record: 19 of 19

Skill Set 11
Refining Queries

Create and Apply Advanced Filters

You can apply filters in Table Datasheet View, Query Datasheet View, or Form View to isolate a subset of records based on criteria that you specify. Advanced filters are similar to queries, because both are used to answer questions about the data in your database, and both use a design grid to enter criteria. Unlike queries, filters are not automatically saved as an object in the database, so they are typically applied for one-time questions that arise while working with data. However, if you build a filter and decide that you want to save the criteria you specified, you can save the filter as a query object in the database.

Activity Steps

 Computers01.mdb

1. Click the **Tables button** 🔲 Tables on the Objects bar (if it's not already selected), then double-click **Equipment** to open it in Datasheet View

2. Click **Records** on the menu bar, point to **Filter**, then click **Advanced Filter/Sort**

3. In the Equipment field list, double-click **Manufacturer**, **PurchaseDate**, and **InitialValue** to add each field to the filter design grid

4. Click the **Criteria cell** for the Manufacturer field, then type **Micron**

5. Click the **Sort cell** for the PurchaseDate field, click the **list arrow**, click **Ascending**, click the **Sort cell** for the InitialValue field, click the **list arrow**, then click **Ascending**
   See Figure 11-5. Access automatically surrounds criteria in a Text field with quotation marks just as it does in Query Design View. Sort orders are evaluated left-to-right just as they are in Query Design View.

6. Click the **Apply Filter button** 🔽 on the Filter/Sort toolbar
   See Figure 11-6. 15 records match the criteria.

7. Click **Records** on the menu bar, point to **Filter**, then click **Advanced Filter/Sort**

8. Click the **Save As Query button** 🔲 on the Filter/Sort toolbar, type **Micron equipment** in the Query Name box, then click **OK**

9. Close the Filter window, close the Equipment table without saving changes, then click **Queries button** 🔲 Queries on the Database window toolbar to confirm that the filter has been saved as a query

Step 5
You can enter more AND conditions to the same Criteria row or more OR conditions to multiple rows of the filter design grid just as you can in Query Design View.

Figure 11-5: Filter Design View

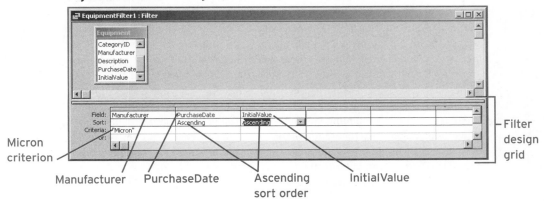

Micron criterion

Manufacturer | PurchaseDate | Ascending sort order | InitialValue

Filter design grid

Figure 11-6: Table Datasheet View with filter applied

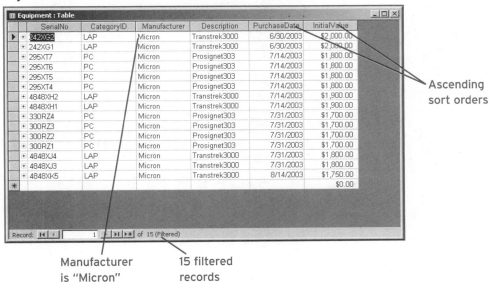

Manufacturer is "Micron"

15 filtered records

Ascending sort orders

Skill Set 11
Refining Queries

Create and Run Parameter Queries

A **parameter query** is a query that contains parameter criteria. **Parameter criteria** prompt you to enter actual criteria each time you run the query. (You **run** a query by opening it in Query Datasheet View.) For example, if you create a query based on an Employees table and enter parameter criteria for the table's Department field, the parameter criteria will prompt you to enter a department name each time you run the query. The department name that you enter determines the records that appear in Query Datasheet View. If you base a form or report on a parameter query, each time you open the form or report, the parameter query will run, prompting you for criteria. You create a parameter query by entering parameter criteria in the Criteria row of the query design grid. You create parameter criteria by typing the text that you want to use as a prompt inside brackets. The text you enter in the brackets appears in a dialog box each time you run the query. You enter the actual criteria entry into a dialog box.

Activity Steps

 Computers01.mdb

1. Click the **Queries button** Queries on the Objects bar (if it's not already selected), click **Inventory Parameter**, then click the **Design button** Design on the Database window toolbar

2. Click the **Criteria cell** for the CategoryDesc field, then type **[Enter category:]**
   See Figure 11-7.

Step 4
If you enter more than one parameter criterion in the query design grid, an Enter Parameter Value dialog box will appear for each parameter criterion entry you add.

3. Click the **View button** on the Query Design toolbar
   See Figure 11-8. The same text you entered in the Criteria cell is displayed in the dialog box.

4. Type **server** in the Enter Parameter Value dialog box, then click **OK**
   See Figure 11-9. Only two records appear (records with "Server" in the CategoryDesc field).

5. Save and close the Inventory Parameter query

6. Click the **Reports button** Reports on the Objects bar, double-click **Inventory Listing**, type **laptop** in the Enter Parameter Value dialog box, click **OK**, then zoom in as necessary to read the category value
   The Inventory Listing report was previously created from the Inventory Parameter query. Therefore, when you open the Inventory Listing report, you also run the Inventory Parameter query, which prompts you to specify a criterion for the CategoryDesc field.

7. Close the Inventory Listing report

Figure 11-7: Entering parameter criteria in the query design grid

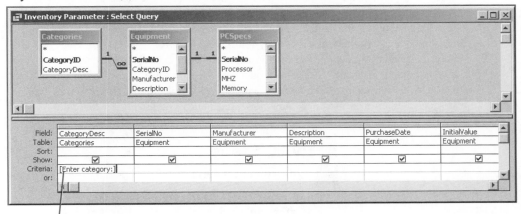

Parameter criteria

Figure 11-8: Enter Parameter Value dialog box

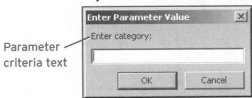

Parameter criteria text

Figure 11-9: Query Datasheet View

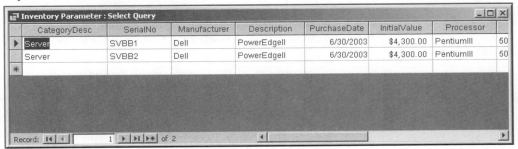

Skill Set 11

Refining Queries

Create and Run Action Queries

An **action query** helps you create, update, or delete data in the database. Unlike a select query, which simply displays a customized view of records in the database, an **action query** actually changes data in the database. There are four types of action queries: **make-table**, **append**, **delete**, and **update**. Table 11-1 provides more information on action queries. You can change an existing select query to an action query or create a new action query. You use the Query Type button on the Query Design toolbar to choose the action query you want, and then you use the query design grid to specify how you want data to be modified when you run the query.

Step 3
To display a long criteria entry in its entirety, position the pointer on the right edge of a column in the query design grid so that a resize pointer ↔ appears, then drag the column to widen it. You can also double-click the right edge of the column while the resize pointer ↔ is displayed to automatically widen the column to the width of the widest entry.

Activity Steps

 Instruments01.mdb

1. Click the **Queries button** ⊞ Queries on the Objects bar (if it's not already selected), verify that Sales Log is selected, then click the **Design button** ☑ Design on the Database window toolbar

2. Click the **Query Type button list arrow** ⊞ ▾ on the Query Design toolbar, click **Make-Table Query**, type **1Qtr Sales Log** in the Table Name box, then click **OK**
   You will create a table called 1Qtr Sales Log based on the data defined by the Sales Log query, which selects records from the Sales table.

3. Click the **Criteria cell** for the Date field, type **Between 1/1/03 and 3/31/03**, then click the **Run button** ⚡ on the Query Design toolbar
   See Figure 11-10. Notice that Access added pound signs around the criteria in the Date field. The alert box tells you that you are about to create a table that contains 6 rows and that you cannot undo this.

4. Click **Yes** in the alert box
   You created a table that stores the first quarter sales records, so you no longer need those records in the Sales table. You can run a delete query using the same criteria you used for the make-table query to delete the records between 1/1/03 and 3/31/03 in the Sales table.

5. Click the **Query Type button list arrow** ⊞ ! ▾, then click **Delete Query**

6. Click the **Run button** ⚡ on the Query Design toolbar, then click **Yes** when prompted that you are about to delete 6 rows

7. Close the Sales Log query without saving changes, then click the **Tables button** ⊞ Tables on the Objects bar

8. Verify that six records appear in the 1Qtr Sales Log table and that these six records were deleted from the Sales table, then close the tables

Figure 11-10: Creating a Make-Table query

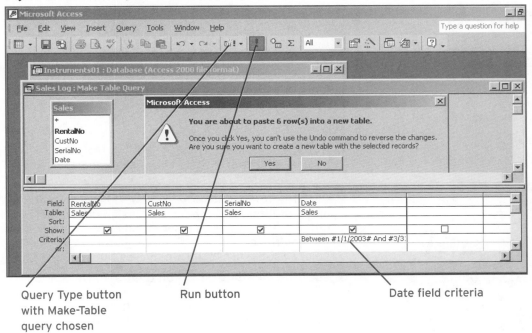

Query Type button
with Make-Table
query chosen

Run button

Date field criteria

TABLE 11-1: Action queries

type of action query	query icon	description	example
Delete		Deletes a group of records from one or more tables	Remove products that are discontinued
Update		Makes global changes to a group of records in one or more tables	Raise prices by 10 percent for all products
Append		Adds a group of records from one or more tables to the end of a table	Add an employee address table from one company to an address table for another
Make-Table		Creates a new table from data in one or more tables	Export records to another Access database or make a backup copy of a table

Skill Set 11

Refining Queries

Use Aggregate Functions in Queries

You use **aggregate functions**, such as Sum, Count, and Avg (average) to calculate summary statistics on groups of records. For example, suppose your database tracks sales. You could use an aggregate function to subtotal the revenue for each country, region, or product, or you could calculate the total sales for each sales representative. See Table 11-2 for a list of aggregate functions that you can use. You specify aggregate functions in Query Design View.

Activity Steps

 ComputersO1.mdb

1. Click the **Queries button** [Queries] on the Objects bar (if it's not already selected), double-click **Create query in Design view**, click **Equipment**, click **Add**, then click **Close**

2. Click the **Totals button** Σ on the Query Design toolbar to display the Total row in the query design grid, double-click **InitialValue** in the Equipment field list to add it to the query design grid, click **Group By** in the Total row for the InitialValue field, click the **list arrow**, then click **Sum**

3. Click the **View button** on the Query Design toolbar
   All the values in the InitialValue field for each record have been summed into a single value, $110,450.00. However, when using an aggregate function such as Sum, another field is usually used as the Group By field so that you can view subtotals for groups of records rather than a grand total for all records.

4. Click the **View button** on the Query Datasheet toolbar

5. Click the **Show Table button** on the Query Design toolbar, verify that Categories is selected, click **Add**, then click **Close**
   You'll group the records by the values in the CategoryDesc field so that you can view subtotals for each category.

6. Drag **CategoryDesc** from the Categories field list to the first column, double-click **InitialValue** in the Equipment field list twice, click **Group By** in the Total row for the second InitialValue field, click the **list arrow**, click **Count**, click **Group By** in the Total row for the third InitialValue field, click the **list arrow**, then click **Avg**
   See Figure 11-11.

7. Click the **View button** on the Query Design toolbar, then widen each column in Query Datasheet View to display all the text in the field names
   See Figure 11-12. The InitialValue field is summed, counted, and averaged for each group of records.

8. Close the query without saving it

Step 7
The field names created by aggregate functions that appear at the top of each column in Datasheet View are somewhat long. To create a new field name, insert the desired name followed by a colon in front of the existing entry in the Field cell of the query design grid.

Figure 11-11: Entering an aggregate function in Query Design View

Show Table button

Totals button

Total row

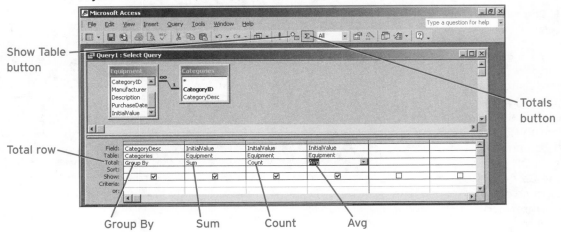

Group By   Sum   Count   Avg

Figure 11-12: Summarized records grouped by CategoryDesc

Group By CategoryDesc field values

Average of InitialValue field values

Sum of InitialValue field values

Count of InitialValue field values

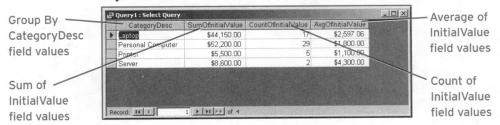

TABLE 11-2: Aggregate functions

aggregate function	calculates
Sum	Total of values in a field
Avg	Average of values in a field
Min	Minimum value in a field
Max	Maximum value in a field
Count	Number of values in a field (not counting null values)
StDev	Standard deviation of values in a field
Var	Variance of values in a field
First	Field value from the first record in a table or query
Last	Field value from the last record in a table or query

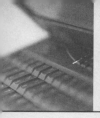

Skill Set 11

Refining Queries

Target Your Skills

Computers01.mdb

1 Create a query to select the fields and records shown in Figure 11-13. The query's fields come from the Categories and Equipment tables. Use an OR criteria in the CategoryDesc field to select only the printer and server records.

Figure 11-13

Query1 : Select Query

CategoryDesc	Manufacturer	Description	PurchaseDate	InitialValue
Printer	Lexmark	Optra2000	1/4/2003	$2,000.00
Printer	Lexmark	Optra2000	1/4/2003	$2,000.00
Printer	HP	Deskjet 900XJ2	1/4/2002	$500.00
Printer	HP	Deskjet 900XJ2	1/4/2001	$500.00
Printer	HP	Deskjet 900XJ2	1/4/2002	$500.00
Server	Dell	PowerEdgeII	6/30/2003	$4,300.00
Server	Dell	PowerEdgeII	6/30/2003	$4,300.00

Record: 1 of 7

Computers01.mdb

2 Create a query using aggregate functions to select the fields and records shown in Figure 11-14. Base the query on the Equipment table. Group the records by the Manufacturer field and apply both the Sum and Count statistics to the InitialValue field.

Figure 11-14

Query2 : Select Query

Manufacturer	SumOfInitialValue	CountOfInitialValue
Compaq	$28,200.00	16
Dell	$49,600.00	17
HP	$1,500.00	3
Lexmark	$4,000.00	2
Micron	$27,150.00	15

Record: 1 of 5

Skill List

1. Create and modify reports
2. Add subreport controls to Access reports
3. Sort and group data in reports

In Skill Set 12, you will create and modify reports in Report Design View. You will build a new report and customize an existing report by adding, moving, and formatting controls. You'll also work with the subreport control, which allows you to preview or print multiple reports from one report object. In addition, you'll use sorting and grouping options to determine the order in which records are printed and how records are subtotaled and summarized on a report.

Skill Set 12
Producing Reports

Create and Modify Reports
Create a Report in Report Design View

Instead of using a report creation tool, such as AutoReport or the Report Wizard, you can use Report Design View to create a new report. When you create a report in Report Design View, you need to specify a table or query for the report's Record Source property. After you set the Record Source property, you specify where you want fields from the record source to appear on the report by dragging fields from the field list to the report.

Activity Steps

 Baseball01.mdb

1. Click the **Reports button** on the Objects bar (if it's not already selected), double-click **Create report in Design view**, then maximize Report Design View

2. Click the **Properties button** on the Report Design toolbar to open the Report property sheet, click the **Data tab**, click the **Record Source list arrow**, then click **TeamStandings**
   As soon as you choose a table or query for the Record Source property, the field list opens showing the fields in the table or query.

3. Close the property sheet

4. Double-click **TeamStandings** on the title bar of the field list to select all of the fields, then drag them to the middle of the Detail section of the form
   Controls in the Detail section will print once for every record.

5. Click the **Label button** on the Toolbox toolbar, click the left side of the Page Header section, then type **Team Standings Report**
   Controls in the Page Header section will print at the top of each page.

6. Click the **Text Box button** on the Toolbox toolbar, click the middle of the Page Footer section, click **Unbound** in the text box, type **=[Page]**, click the label to select it, then press **[Delete]**
   See Figure 12-1. Controls in the Page Footer section will print at the bottom of each page. The =[Page] expression adds the page number.

7. Click the **View button** on the Report Design toolbar, then click the report twice to zoom out and in to view the page header and page footer sections
   See Figure 12-2. This report shows the four fields of the TeamStandings query.

8. Close the report without saving it

tip

Step 6
It's generally more difficult to distinguish between text box and label controls in Report Design View (as compared to Form Design View) because the controls are formatted similarly. To determine what type of control is currently selected, click the Properties button. The title bar of the property sheet identifies the type of control that is selected.

Figure 12-1: Creating a report in Report Design View

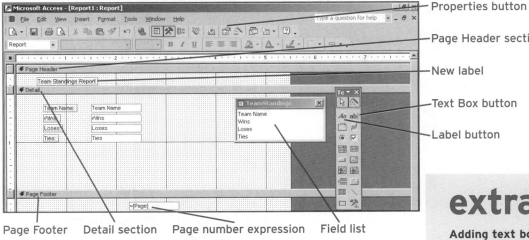

— Properties button

— Page Header section

— New label

— Text Box button

— Label button

Page Footer section

Detail section

Page number expression in a text box

Field list

Figure 12-2: Previewing a report created in Report Design View

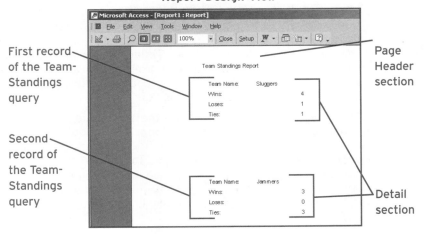

First record of the Team-Standings query

Second record of the Team-Standings query

Page Header section

Detail section

extra!

Adding text box controls without accompanying labels

When you add a text box control to a report, an accompanying label control is also created. The label appears to the left of the text box and describes its contents. If you do not want to automatically create a label control every time you add a text box to a report, you need to change the default properties for the text box control. To change the default properties for a text box, click the **Text Box button** on the Toolbox toolbar, click the **Properties button** on the Report Design toolbar, click the **Format tab** in the property sheet, click the **Auto Label list arrow**, click **No**, and then close the Default Text Box property sheet.

Skill Set 12
Producing Reports

Create and Modify Reports
Modify Report Sections Using Report Design View

You can modify report sections in many ways. For example, you can use the Report Header section to add a descriptive title to the first page of the report. Or, you can use the Report Footer section to add a concluding comment or calculation to the last page of the report. Also, you can move, resize, or format report controls in any section to make a report easier to read or look more professional. You make all modifications to a report in Report Design View. For more information about report sections, see Table 12-1.

Activity Steps
 Baseball01.mdb

1. Click the **Reports button** on the Objects bar (if it's not already selected), click **Player Listing**, click the **Design button** on the Database window toolbar, then maximize the report (if it's not already maximized)

2. Click **View** on the menu bar, then click **Report Header/Footer** to open the Report Header and Report Footer sections of the report

3. Click the **Label button** on the Toolbox toolbar, click the left side of the Report Header section, type **Player Listing**, and then press **[Enter]**
   Controls that you add to the Report Header section print once at the top of the first page of the report. Controls in the Page Header section print just below the Report Header section on the first page and at the top of the report's subsequent pages.

4. Click the **Text Box button** on the Toolbox toolbar, click the middle of the Report Footer section, click **Unbound** in the text box, type **=Count([LName])**, click the label to select it, double-click the text in the label, then type **Total Players**
   See Figure 12-3. Controls that you add to the Report Footer section print once at the end of the report. The =Count([LName]) expression will count the number of values in the LName field for every record in the report.

5. Click the **View button** on the Report Design toolbar, then click the **Last Page button** on the navigation toolbar
   See Figure 12-4. The last page of the report shows the Total Players label and the result of the =Count ([LName]) expression, because those controls are in the Report Footer section. There are 36 players in this report.

6. Save and close the Player Listing report

Step 4
To count the number of players in the report, you can use any field that contains a value for each player, such as FName, LName, or TeamName. Be sure to surround a field name in an expression with brackets.

Figure 12-3: Modifying a report in Report Design View

Report Header section —

New label —

Report Footer section —

New label —

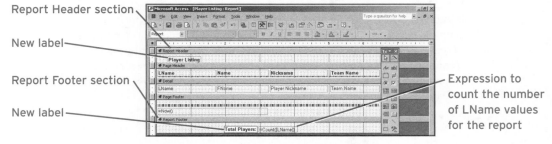

— Expression to count the number of LName values for the report

Figure 12-4: Previewing the Report Footer section of a report

Page Header section —

Detail section —

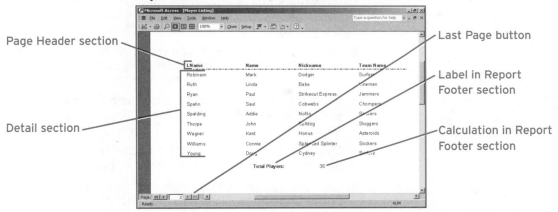

— Last Page button

— Label in Report Footer section

— Calculation in Report Footer section

TABLE 12-1: Report sections

section	where does this section print?	what type of information does this section typically present?
Report Header	At the top of the first page of the report	Report title
Page Header	At the top of every page (but below the report header on page one)	Page number, current date, clip art
Group Header	Before every group of records	Value of the current group
Detail	Once for every record	Values for the rest of the fields in the report
Group Footer	After every group of records	Subtotal or count of the records in a group
Page Footer	At the bottom of every page	Page number or current date
Report Footer	At the end of the entire report	Grand total or count for all of the records in the entire report

Skill Set 12

Producing Reports

Add Subreport Controls to Access Reports

A **subreport** is a report within a report. You can use subreports to preview or print multiple reports as a single report object. The report that contains the subreport is called the **main report**. You add a subreport to a main report by adding a **subreport control** in Report Design View. You can add a subreport control by using the **SubReport Wizard**.

Activity Steps

 BaseballO1.mdb

1. Click the **Reports button** Reports on the Objects bar (if it's not already selected), then double-click **Team Listing** to preview the report

2. Click the **View button** on the Print Preview toolbar to display the Team Listing report in Report Design View, then maximize the report (if it's not already maximized)

3. Using the resize pointer ⊥, drag the bottom edge of the Report Footer section down about 1 inch so that you can add controls to it

4. Click the **Subform/Subreport button** on the Toolbox toolbar, then click the left side of the Report Footer section

5. Click the **Use an existing report or form option button**, click **Player Standings** in the list, then click **Next**

6. Click **None** in the list that determines which fields will be used for the link, click **Next**, click **Finish** to accept "Player Standings" as the name for the subreport, then maximize the Team Listing report (if it's not already maximized)
   See Figure 12-5. You can't see the entire Player Standings subreport in Report Design View; however, because you added it as a subreport to the Report Footer section of the Team Listing report, you can preview and print the subreport immediately after the Team Listing report.

7. Click the **View button** on the Report Design toolbar, then click the **Next Page button** on the navigation toolbar
   See Figure 12-6. The Player Standings report appears as the last page of the Team Listing report.

8. Save and close the Team Listing report

Step 4
If the SubReport Wizard doesn't appear, delete the existing subreport control, click the Control Wizards button on the Toolbox toolbar, then redo Step 4.

Figure 12-5: Adding a subreport to a main report

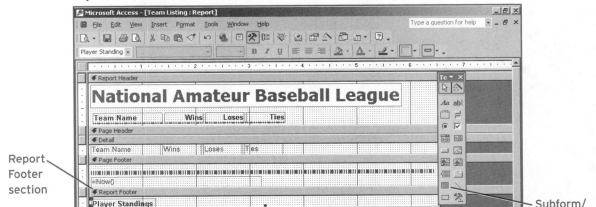

Report Footer section

Subreport control

Subform/ Subreport button

Figure 12-6: Previewing a subreport added to the Report Footer section of a main report

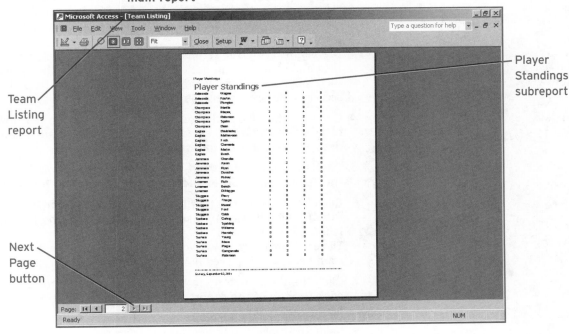

Team Listing report

Next Page button

Player Standings subreport

Skill Set 12

Producing Reports

Sort and Group Data in Reports

Grouping means sorting records in ascending or descending order based on the value of a field. When you group records, you add either the **Group Header** section or the **Group Footer** section, or both. For example, if your database contains records for several international clients, you can group client records by a Country field so that a country name appears before each group of clients. You use the Sorting and Grouping window to specify grouping and sorting orders.

Activity Steps

 Baseball01.mdb

1. Click the **Reports button** 🖹 Reports on the Objects bar (if it's not already selected), then double-click **Player Information**
   The records are sorted in ascending order based on the Team Name field.

2. Click the **View button** 🔍 on the Print Preview toolbar, maximize the report (if it's not already maximized), then click the **Sorting and Grouping button** [≡ on the Report Design toolbar
   The Sorting and Grouping window shows that the records are currently sorted in ascending order based on the Team Name field.

3. Click the Group Header property box, click the **list arrow**, click **Yes**, click the Group Footer property box, click the **list arrow**, click **Yes**, click the **second Field/Expression cell**, click the **list arrow**, then click **LName**
   See Figure 12-7. The records will be grouped by the Team Name field and sorted within each Team Name group by the values in the LName field. The Team Name Header and Team Name Footer sections appeared when you changed the properties to Yes.

4. Close the Sorting and Grouping window, click the **Team Name text box** in the Detail section, then using the move pointer 🖑, drag the text box up into the Team Name Header section

5. Click the **Text Box button** ⓐⓑ on the Toolbox toolbar, then click the Team Name Footer section below the Home Runs text box

6. Click **Unbound** in the text box control, type **=Sum([Home Runs])**, click the label to select it, double-click the text in the label, then type **Total**
   The calculated control will total the number of Home Runs for each team because it is placed in the Team Name Footer section.

7. Click the **View button** 🔍 on the Report Design toolbar and click the top of the report to zoom in on the first group
   See Figure 12-8.

8. Save and close the Player Information report

A grouping field is really just a sorting field with its Group Header and/or Group Footer properties set to Yes.

Figure 12-7: Setting grouping and sorting properties for a report

Grouping symbol

Team Name Header section

Team Name Footer section

Group Footer property

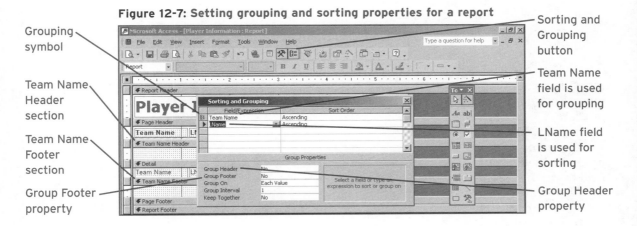

Sorting and Grouping button

Team Name field is used for grouping

LName field is used for sorting

Group Header property

Figure 12-8: Previewing a report that uses a Group Header and Group Footer section

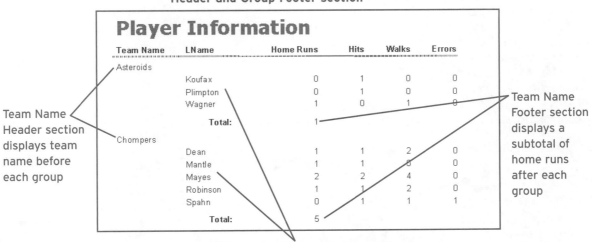

Team Name Header section displays team name before each group

Team Name Footer section displays a subtotal of home runs after each group

Records within each group are further sorted in ascending order by the LName field

Skill Set 12

Producing Reports

Target Your Skills

 Baseball01.mdb

1 Use the Schedule report to create the report shown in Print Preview in Figure 12-9. Set the Group Header and Group Footer properties for the Ballpark field to Yes, and sort the Game Date field in ascending order within the Ballpark groups. Move the Ballpark text box into the Ballpark Header section and add a text box control to the Ballpark Footer section to count the number of Team Name values for each group. Label the new text box control "Total."

Figure 12-9

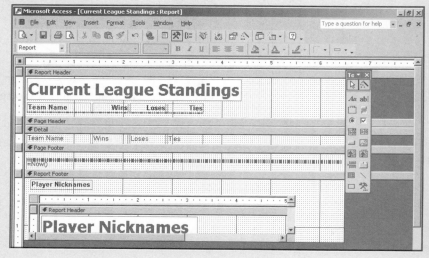

 Baseball01.mdb

2 Add the Player Nicknames report as a subreport to the Current League Standings report as shown in Figure 12-10. Use the SubReport Wizard to make your selections, and select None when prompted to specify a field to create a link. Accept "Player Nicknames" as the name for the subreport.

Figure 12-10

Skill Set 13

Skill List

1. Establish one-to-many relationships
2. Establish many-to-many relationships

In Skill Set 13, you will use the Relationships window to create relationships between database tables. Relationships allow tables to share information, which minimizes redundant data in your database. The process of determining how tables should be organized and related is called **database normalization**. A properly normalized database provides increased data entry productivity and accuracy, increased reporting flexibility, and decreased storage requirements. You'll also work with **referential integrity**, a set of rules that, when applied to a one-to-many relationship, helps maintain the integrity of the data in the database.

Skill Set 13

Defining Relationships

Establish One-To-Many Relationships

A one-to-many relationship links two tables in an Access database. For example, you can connect a Students table to an Enrollment table using a one-to-many relationship to relate one student to many classes. The fields that define the student (such as StudentID, FirstName, LastName, and Address) need to be entered only once in the Students table. As a student enrolls in additional classes, only one field that uniquely identifies the student, such as StudentID, needs to be entered in the Enrollment table. This field serves as the link between the two tables. It is called the foreign key field in the Enrollments table and the primary key field in the Students table. If you apply referential integrity to the one-to-many link, you ensure that no records are entered in the Enrollment table before the corresponding student is established in the Students table. You create one-to-many relationships and enforce referential integrity using the Relationships window.

Activity Steps

 EastCollege01.mdb

1. Click the **Relationships button** on the Database toolbar to open the Relationships window

2. Click the **Show Table button** on the Relationship toolbar, click **Students**, click **Add**, click **Enrollment**, click **Add**, click **Courses**, click **Add**, then click **Close** in the Show Table dialog box

3. Drag the **StudentNo** field from the Students field list to the StudentNo field in the Enrollment field list
   See Figure 13-1.

4. Select the **Enforce Referential Integrity check box**, then click **Create**
   The bold field in a field list is the primary key field for that table. It is always the "one" side of a one-to-many relationship. The foreign key field is the "many" side (indicated by an infinity symbol) of a one-to-many relationship.

5. Drag the **CourseID** field from the Courses field list to the CourseID field in the Enrollment field list

6. Select the **Enforce Referential Integrity check box**, then click **Create**
   See Figure 13-2.

7. Save and close the Relationships window

tip

Step 2
If you accidentally add a field list to the Relationships window twice, click the title bar of one of the duplicate field lists, then press [Delete].

Figure 13-1: Edit Relationships dialog box

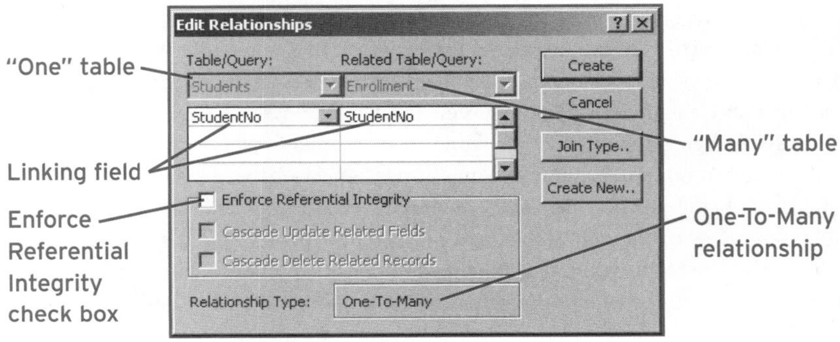

"One" table

Linking field

Enforce Referential Integrity check box

"Many" table

One-To-Many relationship

Figure 13-2: Final Relationships window

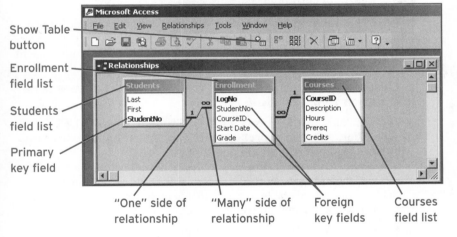

Show Table button

Enrollment field list

Students field list

Primary key field

"One" side of relationship

"Many" side of relationship

Foreign key fields

Courses field list

extra!

Understanding enforce referential integrity options

When you select the Enforce Referential Integrity check box, the Cascade Update Related Fields and Cascade Delete Related Records check boxes become available. These options should be used with caution because they both make automatic changes to the "many" table when you are working in the "one" table. If you select the **Cascade Update Related Fields** check box and change the linking field in the "one" table, all matching entries in the linking field in the "many" table will be automatically updated. (For example, if the CustomerNumber field is the linking field between the Customers and Sales tables, and you change the CustomerNumber entry in the Customers table, all matching records in the Sales table will be automatically updated.) Similarly, if you select the **Cascade Delete Related Records** check box and you delete a record in the "one" table, all related records in the "many" table will also be automatically deleted.

Skill Set 13

Defining Relationships

Establish Many-To-Many Relationships

A **many-to-many** relationship exists between two tables when one record in the first table relates to many records in the second table, and one record in the second table relates to many records in the first table. For example, in a school database, one class relates to many students and one student can take many classes. To make a many-to-many relationship possible, you must create a third table, called a **junction table**. Each original table has a one-to-many relationship with the junction table, which produces the many-to-many relationship between the two original tables. In the school database example, you could use an Enrollments table to serve as the junction table between the Students and Classes tables. One student would relate to many enrollments and one class would relate to many enrollments. Table 13-1 has more information on table relationships.

Activity Steps

 WestCollege01.mdb

1. Click the **Relationships button** on the Database toolbar to view the Relationships window
   In this database, one course relates to many students and one student can take many courses. A junction table will join the tables.

2. Close the Relationships window, then double-click **Create table in Design view**

3. Type **EnrollmentID**, press [↓], type **StudentID**, press [↓], type **CourseID**, click **EnrollmentID**, then click the **Primary Key button** on the Table Design toolbar
   See Figure 13-3. In this junction table, the EnrollmentID field will serve as the primary key field, the StudentID field as the foreign key field to connect this table to the Students table, and the CourseID field as the foreign key field to connect this table to the Courses table.

4. Click the **Save button** on the Table Design toolbar, type **Enrollment** in the Table Name box, click **OK**, then close Table Design View

5. Click the **Relationships button** on the Database toolbar

6. Drag the **StudentID** field from the Students field list to the StudentID field in the Enrollment field list, select the **Enforce Referential Integrity check box**, then click **Create**

7. Drag the **CourseID field** from the Courses field list to the CourseID field in the Enrollment field list, select the **Enforce Referential Integrity check box**, then click **Create**
   See Figure 13-4.

8. Save and close the Relationships window

Step 3
Access does not require you to have a primary key field in each table, but since primary key fields uniquely identify each record, it's good database practice to add a primary key field to each table.

Figure 13-3: Creating a junction table

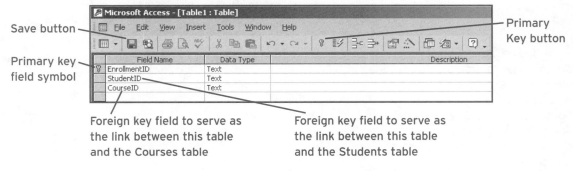

Save button

Primary Key button

Primary key field symbol

Foreign key field to serve as the link between this table and the Courses table

Foreign key field to serve as the link between this table and the Students table

Figure 13-4: Final Relationships window with junction table

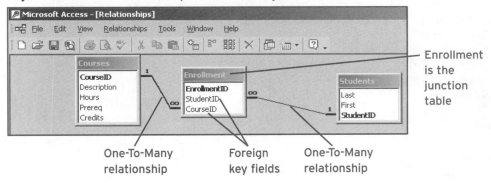

Enrollment is the junction table

One-To-Many relationship

Foreign key fields

One-To-Many relationship

TABLE 13-1: Relationship types			
relationship	description	example	notes
One-to-One	A record in Table X is related to only one record in Table Y	The Students table has only one matching record in the Graduation table (which tracks the student's graduation date and final major)	This relationship is not common, because all fields related this way could be stored in one table
One-to-Many	A record in Table X is related to many records in Table Y	One product in the Products table is related to many records in the Sales table	The one-to-many relationship is the most common relationship
Many-to-Many	A record in Table X is related to many records in Table Y, and a record in Table Y is related to many records in Table X	One record in the Teachers table is related to several records in the Courses table, and one course in the Courses table is related to several records in the Teachers table	To create a many-to-many relationship in Access, you must establish a junction table between two original tables

Skill Set 13

Defining Relationships

Target Your Skills

 Metro01.mdb

1 In this database, one doctor can practice at many clinics, and one clinic can support many doctors. Therefore, a many-to-many relationship exists between the Clinics and Doctors tables. Create a junction table named Assignments with the fields and relationships shown in Figure 13-5. Enforce referential integrity on the relationships.

Figure 13-5

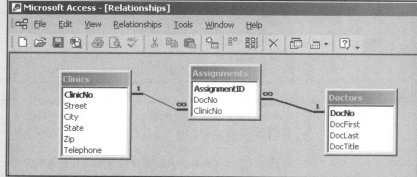

 City01.mdb

2 In this database, one doctor accepts many insurance companies, and one insurance company is used by many doctors. Therefore, a many-to-many relationship exists between the Insurance Companies and Doctors tables. Create a junction table named Authorizations with the fields and relationships shown in Figure 13-6. Enforce referential integrity on the relationships.

Figure 13-6

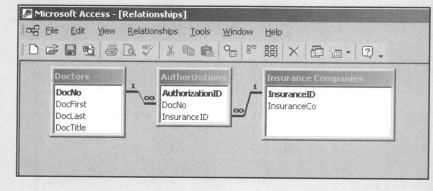

Skill Set 14

Skill List

1. Create and modify a data access page
2. Save PivotTable and PivotChart views to data access pages

In Skill Set 14, you will build **data access pages**, dynamic Web pages that are created using the page object. A **dynamic** Web page reflects current data when it is opened or refreshed because it retains a connection to the database. You can use data access pages for data entry and reporting. You will also add PivotTables and PivotCharts to data access pages. A **PivotTable** allows you to sort, filter, and analyze data. A **PivotChart** is a graphical representation of data, and like the PivotTable, allows you to analyze data by sorting, filtering, and using other data analysis features.

Skill Set 14

Operating Access on the Web

Create and Modify a Data Access Page

You can use Page Design View to create a new data access page or to modify an existing one. When you create a data access page in Page Design View, you determine what data will be displayed by using the fields from the **Field List**, a window that shows fields from the tables and queries in the database. In Page Design View, you can also modify the size and position of the fields, formatting characteristics (such as fonts, colors, and themes), and the title of the data access page.

Activity Steps

 Cars01.mdb

1. Click the **Pages button** Pages on the Objects bar (if it's not already selected), double-click **Create data access page in Design view**, click **OK** if an alert box appears informing you about Access 2000, then maximize Page Design View

2. Click the **Field List button** on the Page Design toolbar to toggle on the Field List, then click the **plus sign** to the left of Inventory in the Field List to view all the fields of the Inventory table
   Expanding a table or query in the Field List shows the object's fields.

3. Drag each field from the Inventory table in the Field List to the "Drag fields from the Field List and drop them on the page" section as shown in Figure 14-1
   When you are adding a field to the data access page, a blue rectangle indicates the border of the section.

4. Click in the **Click here and type title text** placeholder, then type **Car Inventory**

5. Click **Format** on the menu bar, click **Theme**, click **Capsules** in the Choose a Theme list, then click **OK**

6. Click the **View button** on the Page Design toolbar to display the data access page in Page View
   See Figure 14-2. Page View shows you how the Web page would appear if saved and opened in Internet Explorer.

7. Close the data access page without saving it

Step 3
If your data access page doesn't look like Figure 14-1, you can move controls in the body by dragging them to a new location, just as if you were working in Form Design View or Report Design View.

Figure 14-1: Adding fields to a data access page in Page Design View

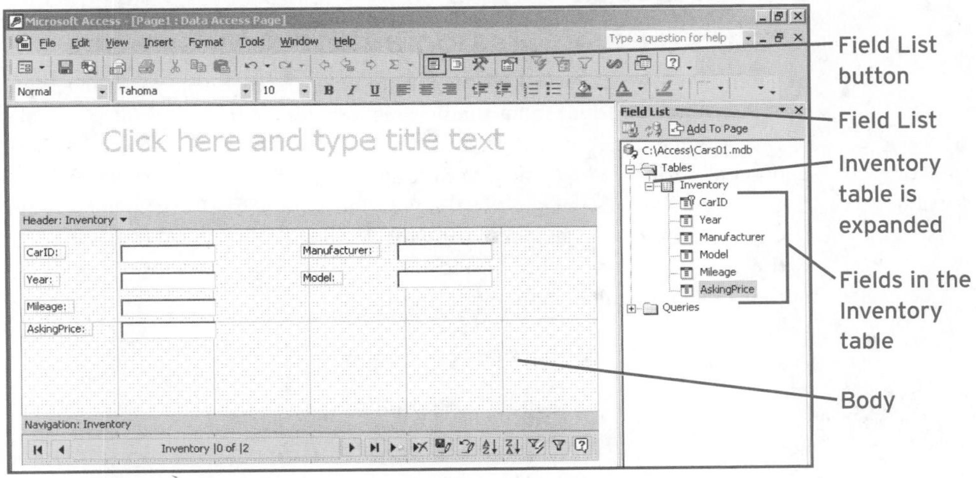

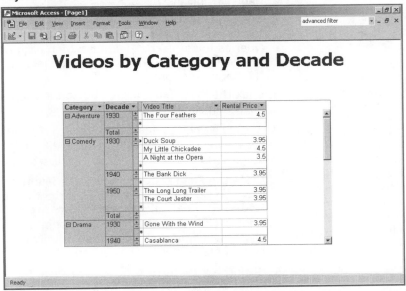

Figure 14-2: The final data access page in Page View

Skill Set 14
Operating Access on the Web

Save PivotTable and PivotChart Views to Data Access Pages
Create a PivotTable on a Data Access Page

You can add a **PivotTable List control** to a data access page to arrange data in a PivotTable. A **PivotTable** summarizes data by columns and rows to make it easy to analyze. A typical PivotTable uses one field as a column heading, another as a row heading, and a third to summarize data (usually subtotal, average, or count) within the body of the PivotTable. To add a PivotTable List control to a data access page, you must work in Page Design View. If you drag an entire table or query object to a data access page, the **Layout Wizard** will appear to help you determine the layout for the fields.

Activity Steps

 Cars01.mdb

1. Click the **Pages button** [Pages] on the Objects bar (if it's not already selected), double-click **Create data access page in Design view**, click **OK** if an alert box appears, then maximize Page Design View

Step 4
You cannot move the fields in a PivotTable List control unless the PivotTable displays a hashed border, which indicates that you're editing the control. Click a PivotTable List once to select it. Click a selected PivotTable to edit it.

2. Click the **Field List button** on the Page Design toolbar to toggle on the Field List, click the **plus sign** to the left of the Queries folder in the Field List, then drag the **Inventory Value** query to the "Drag fields from the Field List and drop them on the page" section

3. Click the **PivotTable option button** in the Layout Wizard dialog box, then click **OK**

4. Click the **PivotTable List control** to display a hashed border
See Figure 14-3. You will determine the total inventory value (based on the AskingPrice field) for all cars based on manufacturer and year.

5. Close the Field List, right-click the **Manufacturer field**, click **Move To Column Area** on the shortcut menu, right-click the **ModelYear field**, click **Move To Row Area** on the shortcut menu, right-click the **AskingPrice field**, point to **AutoCalc** on the shortcut menu, click **Sum**, then drag the **sizing handles** on the PivotTable List control to expand it

6. Click the **View button** on the Page Design toolbar, click the **Manufacturer list arrow**, deselect the **(All) check box**, select the **Ford check box**, select the **Toyota check box**, then click **OK**

7. Click the **collapse button** in the Ford column, then click the **collapse button** in the Toyota column
See Figure 14-4.

8. Close the page without saving it

Figure 14-3: Creating a PivotTable in Page Design View

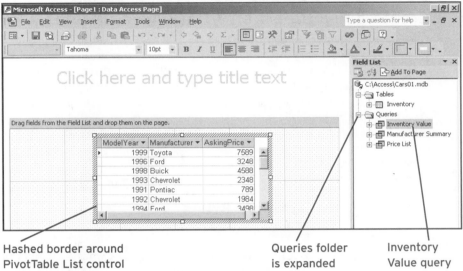

Hashed border around
PivotTable List control

Queries folder
is expanded

Inventory
Value query

Figure 14-4: Using a PivotTable in Page View

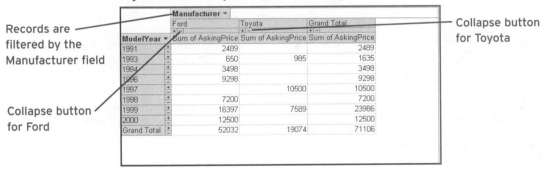

Records are
filtered by the
Manufacturer field

Collapse button
for Toyota

Collapse button
for Ford

Skill Set 14

Operating Access on the Web

Save PivotTable and PivotChart Views to Data Access Pages

Create a PivotChart on a Data Access Page

You can add a **PivotChart control** to a data access page to arrange data in a PivotChart. A **PivotChart** graphically summarizes data. A typical PivotChart uses one field as an x-axis label (the **Category field**), another field for the legend area (the **Series field**), and a third to summarize data (usually subtotal, average, or count) within the body of the PivotChart. For example, you could use a PivotChart to graph the total value of your products summarized by two fields, such as Supplier and Product. To add a PivotChart control to a data access page, you must work in Page Design View. Dragging an entire table or query object to a data access page displays the Layout Wizard, which you use to determine the layout for the fields.

The PivotChart and PivotTable List controls that you add to a data access page work similarly to the PivotChart and PivotTable views you can display for tables, queries, and forms.

Activity Steps

 Cars01.mdb

1. Click the **Pages button** ⬛ Pages on the Objects bar (if it's not already selected), double-click **Create data access page in Design view**, click **OK** if an alert box appears informing you about Access 2000, then maximize Page Design View

2. Click the **Field List button** 🔲 on the Page Design toolbar to toggle on the Field List, click the **plus sign** to the left of the Queries folder in the Field List, then drag the **Inventory Value** query to the "Drag fields from the Field List and drop them on the page" section

3. Click the **PivotChart option button** in the Layout Wizard dialog box, click **OK**, then drag the **sizing handles** on the PivotChart control to expand it within the borders of the "Drag fields from the Field List and drop them on the page" section
   See Figure 14-5.

4. Click the **plus sign** to the left of Inventory Value in the Field List to display the fields within that query

5. Drag the **ModelYear** field to the "Drop Category Fields Here" section, drag the **Manufacturer** field to the "Drop Series Fields Here" section, then drag the **AskingPrice** field to the "Drop Data Fields Here" section

6. Click the **View button** 🔲 on the Page Design toolbar, click the **Manufacturer list arrow**, deselect the **(All) check box**, select the **Chevrolet check box**, then click **OK**
   See Figure 14-6. You can filter the data in a PivotChart.

7. Close the data access page without saving it

Figure 14-5: Creating a PivotChart in Page Design View

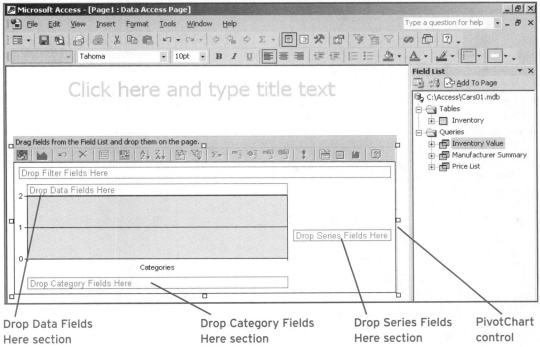

Drop Data Fields
Here section

Drop Category Fields
Here section

Drop Series Fields
Here section

PivotChart
control

Figure 14-6: Using a PivotChart in Page View

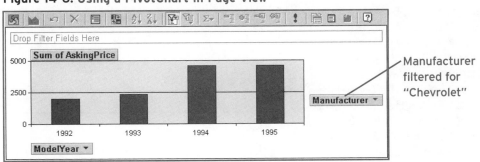

Manufacturer
filtered for
"Chevrolet"

Skill Set 14
Operating Access on the Web

Target Your Skills

 Government01.mdb

1 Use Page Design View to create the PivotTable shown in Figure 14-7. Base the PivotTable on the State Analysis query. Move the State field to the Row Area and the Party field to the Column Area of the PivotTable. Resize the PivotTable to fill the screen, and add the title "PivotTable of State Representatives."

 Government01.mdb

2 Use Page Design View to create the PivotChart shown in Figure 14-8. Base the PivotTable on the State Analysis query. Resize the PivotChart to fill the screen. Add the Last field to the Drop Data Fields Here section, the Party field to the Drop Series Fields Here section, and the State field to the Drop Category Fields Here section. Use the State field to filter the data so that only the data for Alabama and Colorado appears.

Figure 14-7

PivotTable of State Representatives

State	Party ▾			Grand Total
	D	I	R	
	Last ▾	Last ▾	Last ▾	No Totals
Alabama	Aderholt		Everett	
	Bachus		Hilliard	
	Callahan			
	Cramer			
	Riley			
Alaska			Young	
American Samoa	Faleomavaega			
Arizona	Flake		Hayworth	
	Shadegg		Kolbe	
	Stump		Pastor	
Arkansas	Hutchinson		Berry	
	Ross		Snyder	
California	Baca		Becerra	

Figure 14-8

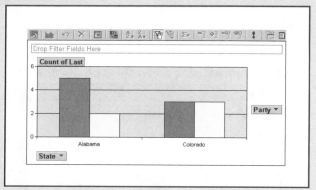

Skill Set 15

Skill List

1. Import XML documents into Access
2. Export Access data to XML documents
3. Encrypt and decrypt databases
4. Compact and repair databases
5. Assign database security
6. Replicate a database

In Skill Set 15, you'll work with Access tools to secure and protect a database. Using encryption, you'll convert database objects and data into a format that is indecipherable to other programs. Using compact and repair tools, you'll organize and compress a database to help it run as efficiently as possible. You'll use passwords to protect a database from unauthorized use, and you'll learn about replication tools that allow you to give remote or traveling users the ability to use and update a database, even when they do not have a physical connection to the database. You'll also import and export XML files into and out of a database.

Skill Set 15

Using Access Tools

Import XML Documents into Access

Using **XML (Extensible Markup Language)** you can deliver data from one application to another over an intranet or the World Wide Web. The XML file format allows you to share data with many other software applications. An **XML document** is a text file that contains data and Extensible Markup Language tags that identify field names and field values. You can import an XML file as a new table of data into Access. An **XSD (Extensible Schema Document)** file accompanies the XML file to further define the structure of the data.

Activity Steps

  Service01.mdb
zips.xml
zips.xsd

Step 2
Access can import many types of files, as listed in the Files of type list in the Import dialog box.

1. Click **File** on the menu bar, point to **Get External Data,** then click **Import**

2. Click the **Look in list arrow,** navigate to the drive and folder where your Project Files are stored, click the **Files of type list arrow,** click **XML Documents,** click **zips.xml,** then click **Import**

3. Click **OK** in the **Import XML** dialog box, then click **OK** when the import process is finished

4. Double-click the **Zips** table to open it in Table Datasheet View
   See Figure 15-1. Twenty-one records with three fields, Zip, City, and State, are imported into the database.

5. Close the Zips table

Figure 15-1: The imported Zips table

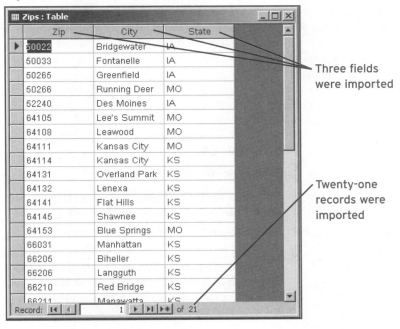

Three fields were imported

Twenty-one records were imported

extra!

Defining the World Wide Web Consortium The **World Wide Web Consortium**, also known as **W3C**, is an international league of companies and associations that supports initiatives to sustain the growth and health of the World Wide Web. W3C recommended XML as a standard way to describe and organize data so that it can be used by multiple programs consistently.

Skill Set 15

Using Access Tools

Export Access Data to XML Documents

The **recordset** consists of the fields and records that are displayed when you open an object. Access can export the recordset of a table to many different file formats, including an XML document. Once your data is in an XML file format, it can be transferred to and used by other software applications that are written to read XML data. When you export Access data to an XML document, you also have the option to export an XSD (Extensible Schema Document) file, which contains structural information about the fields (such as field properties), and an **XSL (Extensible Style Language)** file, which contains formatting information about the data (such as font size and color).

Activity Steps

 Service01.mdb

1. Click the **Tables button** 	▦ Tables	 on the Objects bar (if it's not already selected), then click **Names**

2. Click **File** on the menu bar, then click **Export**

3. Click the **Save in list arrow**, navigate to the drive and folder where your Project Files are stored, click the **Save as type list arrow**, click **XML Documents**, then click **Export**
   The Export XML dialog box appears, prompting you for information about what you want to export. *See Figure 15-2.*

4. Click **OK** in the Export XML dialog box to export both the data as an XML document and the schema as an XSD document
   A **schema** contains structural information about the data in an XSD file.

5. Start Internet Explorer, click **File** on the menu bar, click **Open**, then click **Browse**

6. In the Microsoft Internet Explorer dialog box, click the **Look in list arrow**, navigate to the drive and folder where your Project Files are stored, click the **Files of type list arrow**, click **All Files**, click **Names.xml** in the files list, click **Open**, then click **OK**
   See Figure 15-3. The XML document opens in the browser window and shows you both the data and tags in an XML document.

7. Close Internet Explorer

Step 6
Another way to view an XML document is to locate it within Windows Explorer and then double-click the filename to automatically open it in Internet Explorer.

Figure 15-2: Export XML dialog box

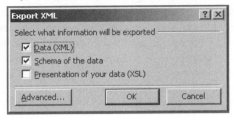

Figure 15-3: Names.xml file displayed in Internet Explorer

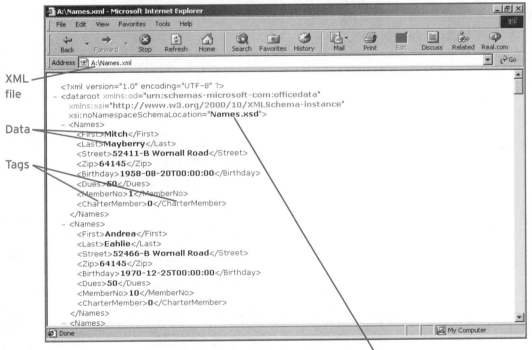

XML file

Data

Tags

Reference to an accompanying XSD file

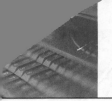

Skill Set 15

Using Access Tools

Encrypt and Decrypt Databases

Encrypting means making database objects and data indecipherable to other programs (such as a word processor or a utility program used to read data). **Decrypting** reverses encryption. Because you can open an encrypted database within Access itself, encryption is usually used in conjunction with other security measures, such as setting user IDs, passwords, and user permissions. Using both encryption and another form of security protects your database from anyone who might attempt to open it within Access and from anyone who might attempt to read the data using other types of programs. Additional threats to your database are described in Table 15-1.

Step 1
If you are using a floppy disk to complete this activity, please copy Service01.mdb to a new floppy disk before doing these steps so that you have plenty of space to complete the encryption and decryption processes.

Activity Steps

 Service01.mdb

1. **Close any open databases, but leave Access running**
   To encrypt a database, Access must be running, but the database that you want to encrypt must be closed.

2. **Click Tools on the menu bar, point to Security, then click Encrypt/Decrypt Database**

3. **In the Encrypt/Decrypt Database dialog box, click the Look in list arrow, navigate to the drive and folder where your Project Files are stored, click Service01, then click OK**

4. **Type Service01E (for "encrypted") in the File name box, then click Save**

5. **To decrypt a database, click Tools on the menu bar, point to Security, then click Encrypt/Decrypt Database**

6. **Click Service01E in the Encrypt/Decrypt Database dialog box**
   See Figure 15-4.

7. **Click OK, type Service01D (for "decrypted") in the File name box, then click Save**
   You can also encrypt and decrypt a database without renaming it. The encrypted or decrypted database will replace the existing database. However, it's always a good idea to have a backup of any file that you are overwriting, should anything go wrong during the encryption or decryption process.

Figure 15-4: Encrypt/Decrypt Database dialog box

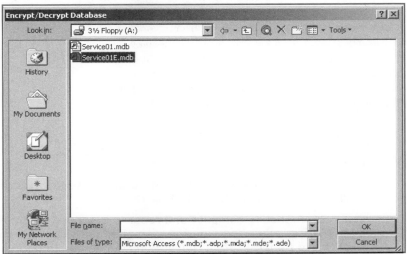

TABLE 15-1: Database security threats

incident	what can happen	appropriate actions
Virus	Viruses can cause many kinds of damage, ranging from profane messages to destruction of files	Purchase the leading virus-checking software for each computer, and keep it updated
Power outage	Power problems such as **brown-outs** (dips in power often causing lights to dim) and **spikes** (surges in power) can cause damage to the hardware, which can render the computer useless	Purchase a **UPS** (Uninterruptible Power Supply) to maintain constant power to the file server (if networked) and **surge protectors** (power strip with surge protection) for each user
Theft or intentional damage	Theft or intentional damage of computer equipment or data destroys valuable assets	Place the file server in a room that can be locked after hours, use network drives for user data files that are backed up on a daily basis, use off-site storage for backups, set database passwords and encryption so that files that are stolen cannot be used, and use computer locks for equipment that is at risk, especially laptops

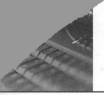

Skill Set 15

Using Access Tools

Compact and Repair Databases

When you delete data or objects in an Access database, the disk space formerly occupied by the deleted information remains unused. This means that as you work with a database over time, it becomes fragmented, using more disk space and running slower. **Compacting** a database rearranges the database on your disk, and reuses the space formerly occupied by the deleted objects. A compacted database minimizes disk storage requirements and improves performance. The compacting process also automatically repairs damaged databases, which can help you find and correct structural problems before they become bigger issues.

Activity Steps

  Service01.mdb

1. Click **Tools** on the menu bar, point to **Database Utilities**, then click **Compact and Repair Database**

2. To automatically compact and repair a database each time it is closed, click **Tools** on the menu bar, click **Options**, then click the **General tab** in the Options dialog box (if it is not already selected)
   See Figure 15-5.

3. If the Service01 database is stored on your hard drive, select the **Compact on Close check box**, then click **OK**

4. If the Service01 database is stored on a floppy disk, click **Cancel**
   The Compact on Close option can corrupt your database if it is stored on a floppy disk that doesn't have sufficient room to complete the process. For more information on the Compact on Close option, see the Extra! on page 17 of the Getting Started Skill Set.

Changes that you make in the Options dialog box affect every database. So if you are using a shared computer, it is best to use the default options rather than customizing the Access environment for all databases.

Figure 15-5: Options dialog box

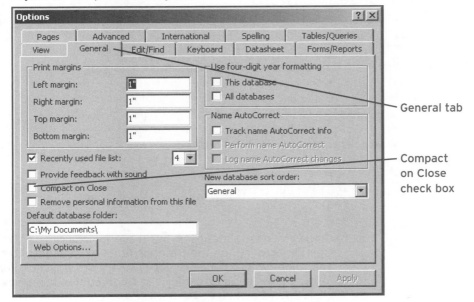

General tab

Compact
on Close
check box

Skill Set 15
Using Access Tools

Assign Database Security
Set a Database Password

You can secure an Access database in many ways, as described in Table 15-2. Setting passwords is a common method to secure information. You can set three types of passwords for an Access database: database, security account, and Visual Basic for Applications (VBA) passwords. If you set a **database password**, all users must enter a password before they can open the database file. Once they open it, users have full access to the database. **Security account passwords** act at the user level rather than at the file level. Setting this type of password enables you to limit what a user can do to the database, such as read, delete, or edit data. **VBA passwords** prevent unauthorized users from modifying VBA code.

Activity Steps

 Service02.mdb

1. Close any open databases, but leave Access running, click the Open button on the Database toolbar, navigate to the drive and folder where your Project Files are stored, click **Service02** in the Open dialog box, click the **Open button list arrow**, then click **Open Exclusive**

   To set or change a database password, the database must be opened in **Exclusive Mode**, an environment that doesn't allow users to work in the database simultaneously.

2. Click **Tools** on the menu bar, point to **Security**, then click **Set Database Password**

3. Type **ames4321** in the Password box, press **[Tab]**, then type **ames4321** in the Verify box
   See Figure 15-6.

4. Click **OK**, then close the database

5. To test the password, open the **Service02** database

6. Type **ames4321** in the Password Required dialog box, then click **OK**

7. To unset the database password, close the database, click the Open button on the Database toolbar, click **Service02** in the Open dialog box, click the **Open button list arrow**, click **Open Exclusive**, type **ames4321** in the Password Required dialog box, then click **OK**

8. Click **Tools** on the menu bar, point to **Security**, click **Unset Database Password**, type **ames4321** in the Unset Database Password dialog box, then click **OK**

Step 4
Passwords are case sensitive and harder to guess if they contain both characters and numbers.

Figure 15-6: Set Database Password dialog box

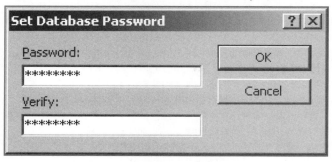

TABLE 15-2: Methods to help secure an Access database

method	description
passwords	Protects the database from unauthorized use, and can be implemented at the database, workgroup, or VBA level
encryption	Compacts the database and makes the data indecipherable to other programs
startup options	Hides or disables certain functions when the database is opened
show/hide objects	Shows or hides objects in the Database window, which can prevent users from unintentionally deleting objects
split a database	Separates the data (table objects) from the rest of the objects (such as forms and reports) into two databases that work together; splitting a database allows you to give each user access to only those specific database objects that they need, instead of all the objects in the database

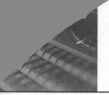

Skill Set 15
Using Access Tools

Assign Database Security
Create Workgroups and Permissions

You can set permissions to restrict user activities in a database and add a level of security. **Permissions** specify the activities that users are allowed to complete, such as modifying or entering new data. You assign permissions to a user by assigning permissions to a **workgroup**, a list of database users who have the same needs. See Table 15-3 for a list of permissions. To set up workgroups, you create a workgroup information file or add users to an existing one. A **workgroup information file** defines users, passwords, and user permissions. Only the workgroup's administrator (Admin), the user who has all permissions, can set permissions. If you create a new workgroup information file, you must join the workgroup as the administrator. If your database has never been secured, you are automatically the administrator of a default workgroup information file, so you can bypass the steps to join a workgroup as an administrator and then set up users, workgroups, and permissions.

Step 1
As the administrator, you can set up a new workgroup information file for a database. Click Tools on the menu bar, point to Security, click Workgroup Administrator, then click Create to create a new workgroup information file for a database.

Activity Steps
  ServiceO3.mdb

1. Click **Tools** on the menu bar, point to **Security**, then click **User and Group Accounts**

2. Click **New** in the User and Group Accounts dialog box, type **Joe** in the Name box, type **swim50** in the Personal ID box, then click **OK**
   You can add users and workgroups (group accounts) because you are the administrator of the default workgroup information file.

3. Click the **Groups tab**, click **New**, type **Accounting** in the Name box, type **money121** in the Personal ID box, then click **OK**

4. Click the **Users tab**, click **Accounting** in the Available Groups list, click the **Name list arrow**, click **Joe**, then click **Add**
   See Figure 15-7.

5. Click **OK** in the User and Group Accounts dialog box
   Now you can set permissions within a database file.

6. Click **Tools** on the menu bar, point to **Security**, then click **User and Group Permissions**

7. Click the **Groups option button**, click **Accounting** in the User/Group Name list, click the **Object Type list arrow**, click **Query**, click the **Member Activity** query in the Object Name list, select the **Read Data check box** as shown in Figure 15-8, then click **OK**

8. To delete the new group and user, click **Tools** on the menu bar, point to **Security**, click **User and Group Accounts**, click the **Users** tab, click **Joe** in the Name list, click **Delete**, click the **Groups** tab, click **Accounting** in the Name list, click **Delete**, then click **OK**

Figure 15-7: User and Group Accounts dialog box

New Accounting group

Default groups

Add

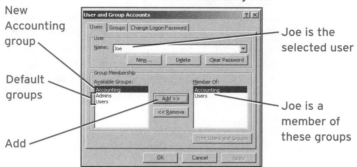

Joe is the selected user

Joe is a member of these groups

Figure 15-8: User and Group Permissions dialog box

Accounting group is selected

Groups option button

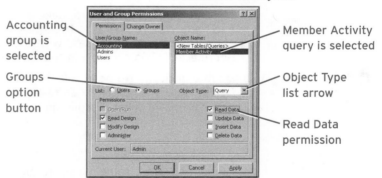

Member Activity query is selected

Object Type list arrow

Read Data permission

TABLE 15-3: Workgroup permissions

permission	description
Open/Run	Open the specified database, form, or report, or run the specified macro
Open Exclusive	Open a database in Exclusive Mode
Read Design	View objects (tables, queries, forms, reports, or macros) in Design View
Modify Design	View, modify, and delete objects (tables, queries, forms reports, or macros)
Administer	For a database, set a database password, replicate a database, or change start properties; For objects (tables, queries, forms, reports, macros), have full access including the ability to assign permissions
Read Data	View data in tables and queries
Update Data	View and modify, but not insert or delete, records in tables and queries
Insert Data	View and insert, but not modify or delete, data in tables and queries
Delete Data	View and delete, but not modify or insert, data in tables and queries

Skill Set 15

Using Access Tools

Replicate a Database

If you want to copy a database to another computer, such as a home computer or a laptop that you use when traveling, you can create a replica of the database. A **replica** is a special copy that keeps track of changes made in both the original database (called the **Design Master**) and the copy so that the files can be reconciled and updated at a later date. The Design Master and all replicas created from the Design Master are called the **replica set**. The process of making the copy is called **replication**, and the process of reconciling and updating changes between the replica and the master is called **synchronization**.

Activity Steps

 Service04.mdb

1. Click **Tools** on the menu bar, point to **Replication**, click **Create Replica**, then click **Yes** in the alert box informing you that the database will be closed and converted into the Design Master

2. Click **No** when prompted to make a backup, navigate to the drive and folder where you want to store your replica, click **OK** to create a replica of the database with the filename "Replica of Service04," then click **OK** in the alert box that appears

3. Double-click the **Names** table, then change Daniels in the Last field of the first record to **Zamboni**
   See Figure 15-9. Replica icons appear to the left of the tables within a replicated database, and "Design Master" appears on the title bar. Data entered or edited in the Design Master can be resynchronized with replica databases (or vice versa).

Replication works well when the Design Master is located on a file server and replicas are located in a Briefcase folder on a laptop.

4. Close the Names table, close the Service04 database, click the **Open button** 🖼 on the Database toolbar, double-click **Replica of Service04** to open the replica database, double-click the **Names** table to observe that the first record still shows "Daniels," then close the Names table

5. Click **Tools** on the menu bar, point to **Replication**, click **Synchronize Now**, click **OK**, click **Yes** to temporarily close the database, then click **OK** when informed that the synchronization was successful

6. Double-click the **Names** table
   See Figure 15-10. Note that the edit to the first record, originally entered in the Design Master, was synchronized with the replica.

7. Close the Names table

Figure 15-9: Changing an entry in the Design Master

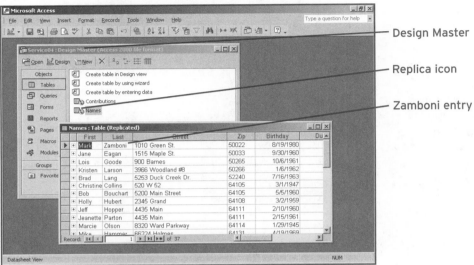

Design Master

Replica icon

Zamboni entry

Figure 15-10: Viewing the change in the replica after synchronization

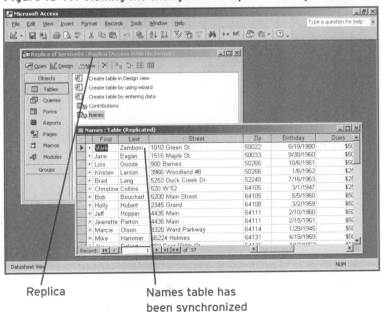

Replica

Names table has been synchronized

extra!

Replicating with the Briefcase folder

A **Briefcase** is a special type of folder designed to help keep files that are used on two computers synchronized. If you copy an Access database to a Briefcase folder, you create a replica of it, so you can synchronize the replica with the Design Master. By default, the desktop displays a single Briefcase icon called "My Briefcase." If there is no Briefcase icon on the desktop, you can create one. Right-click the desktop, point to **New**, then click **Briefcase**.

Skill Set 15

Using Access Tools

Target Your Skills

 Travel01.mdb

1 Import the countries.xml file into the Travel01 database, then open the Countries table in Table Datasheet View as shown in Figure 15-11. Compact and repair the Travel01 database.

Figure 15-11

 Travel01.mdb

2 Export the Cities table in the Travel01 database to an XML file named Cities. Export both the XML data as well as the schema of the data. View the Cities.xml file in Internet Explorer as shown in Figure 15-12.

Figure 15-12

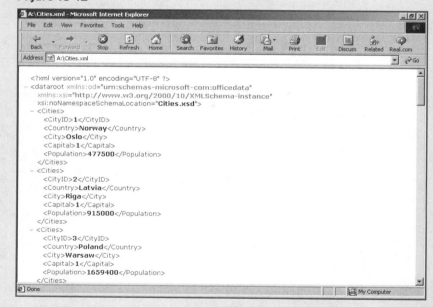

Skill Set 16

Creating Database Applications

Skill List

1. Create Access modules
2. Use the Database Splitter
3. Create an MDE file

In Skill Set 16, you will work with tools that help you transform an Access database into a full application. In this context, **application** refers to an Access database that has been customized to meet the needs of a specific audience. For example, you could add command buttons that perform specific actions to make a form and a database easier to use. You could also split a database into multiple parts to improve its overall performance and to add a level of security. Or, you could create an **MDE** database, a special copy of a database that is used both to improve database performance and to restrict users from making changes in Design View of most objects.

Skill Set 16
Creating Database Applications

Create Access Modules
Create a Class Module in a Form Using the Command Button Wizard

Modules store **Visual Basic for Applications (VBA)** programming code. **VBA** is a programming language packaged within each program of the Microsoft Office suite. VBA enables you to customize a program. For example, you might use VBA to help users navigate through various forms, making the database easier to use. Access has two types of modules: **global modules**, which contain VBA code used throughout an entire database, and **class modules**, which contain VBA code used only in the specific form or report object in which the code is stored. For example, when you use the **Command Button Wizard** to create a custom command button, you create VBA code, which is stored in a class module in the form.

Activity Steps

 Inventory01.mdb

1. Click the **Forms button** [Forms] on the Objects bar (if it's not already selected), verify that **Equipment Entry Form** is selected, click the **Design button** [Design] on the Database window toolbar, then maximize Form Design View

Step 5
Even if you delete a command button in Form Design View, the associated VBA code remains. To delete the VBA code, open the Code window, then delete every line from the Sub statement to the End Sub statement for that button.

2. Click the **Toolbox button** [ ] on the Form Design toolbar to toggle on the Toolbox toolbar (if it's not already displayed), click the **Command Button button** [ ] on the **Toolbox** toolbar, then click about 1 inch to the right of the Processor text box on the form
The Command Button Wizard includes six different categories of command buttons. Each category contains several common actions that you can assign to a command button.

3. Click **Record Operations** in the Categories list, then click **Print Record** in the Actions list
See Figure 16-1.

4. Click **Next**, click **Next** to accept the image, type **PrintRecord** as a meaningful button name, then click **Finish**
See Figure 16-2.

5. Click the **Code button** [ ] on the Form Design toolbar to view the class module that you created by using the wizard
See Figure 16-3. You can enter and edit VBA statements in this window. The **Sub statement** marks the beginning of the VBA code, and the **End Sub statement** marks the end.

6. Close the Microsoft Visual Basic window, then click the **View button** [ ] on the Form Design toolbar

7. Click the **PrintRecord button** to test it, then save and close the Equipment Entry Form

Figure 16-1: Command Button Wizard dialog box

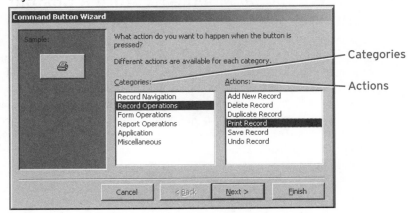

Categories

Actions

Figure 16-2: A new command button in Form Design View

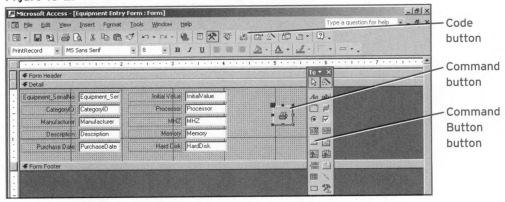

Code button

Command button

Command Button button

Figure 16-3: Viewing the VBA code in a class module

Sub statement

Button name

End Sub statement

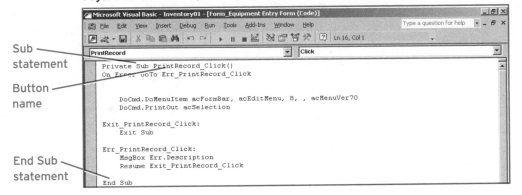

Skill Set 16
Creating Database Applications

Create Access Modules
Create a Global Module to Store a Custom Function

When you click the Modules button on the Objects bar, global modules are displayed in the Database window. It's common to use global modules to store custom functions, VBA code that performs calculations in queries, forms, and reports. Although Access provides many built-in functions such as Sum, Count, and Avg (average), you might want to create a new function that simplifies a custom calculation. For example, you might use VBA to create a custom function called YearsOfService that calculates the number of years an employee has worked for a company.

Activity Steps
 Personnel01.mdb

1. Click the **Modules button** [Modules] on the Objects bar, then click the **New button** [New] on the Database window toolbar

2. Create the VBA function named **YearsOfService** by entering the VBA code as shown in Figure 16-4
   The Option Compare Database statement is provided automatically in new modules. It sets rules for how text is sorted in a Text field.

3. Click the **Save button** [ ] on the Standard toolbar, type **Custom Functions** in the Module Name box, then click **OK**
   You defined the YearsOfService function using two existing Access functions, Int and Now. The value of the DateOfHire argument is subtracted from Now(). (Now() represents the current date.) This subtraction results in the number of days that the employee has worked. The number is then divided by 365 to calculate the number of years. The Int function determines the integer portion of the answer.

4. Close the Microsoft Visual Basic window, click **Queries** [Queries] on the Objects bar, then double-click **Create query in Design view**

5. Click **Add** in the Show Table dialog box to add the Employees field list to Query Design View, then click **Close**

6. Scroll down, double-click the DateHired field to add it to the first column of the query design grid, click the **Field cell** in the second column, then type **Service:YearsOfService([DateHired])**
   See Figure 16-5. You created a new calculated field named Service that uses the YearsOfService custom function you previously created in a global module.

7. Click the **View button** [ ] on the Query Design toolbar
   See Figure 16-6. The Service field calculates the years of service.

8. Save the query using the name Years of Service, then close it

Step 2
VBA is not case sensitive, but using uppercase and lowercase characters in the function name helps clarify the code.

Figure 16-4: Defining a custom function in the Microsoft Visual Basic window

Enter this VBA code

Automatically entered

Figure 16-5: Creating a calculated field using the custom function in Query Design View

Calculated field name

Expression using the new YearsOfService function

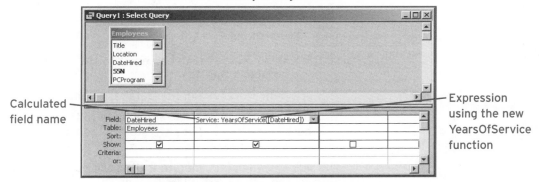

Figure 16-6: Query Datasheet View of calculated field

New calculated field named Service

Answer is calculated using the new YearsOfService function

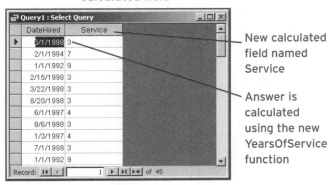

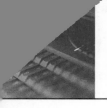

Skill Set 16

Creating Database Applications

Use the Database Splitter

The **Database Splitter** feature splits a database into two files: the **back-end database**, which contains tables (all the data) typically stored on a shared file server, and the **front-end database**, which contains other database objects, such as queries, forms, and reports, stored on user computers. You can copy and customize the front-end database for as many users as needed. Each front-end database contains linked tables that connect it to the data stored in the back-end database. Front-end database users share a single copy of data stored in the back-end database and have fast access to all other objects stored on their own computer. A split database adds a level of customization, because a database administrator can customize each front-end database to contain only the queries, forms, and reports that each user needs. A split database also adds a level of security, because users can't modify a table's design from a front-end database.

Activity Steps

 Derby01.mdb

1. Click **Tools** on the menu bar, point to **Database Utilities**, then click **Database Splitter**

2. Click **Split Database** in the Database Splitter dialog box

3. Click the **Save in list arrow**, navigate to the drive and folder where your Project Files are stored, then click **Split** to save the back-end database with the name Derby01_be

Step 3
You can give a back-end database any valid filename, but "be" in the default filename can remind you that it is the "back-end" database.

4. Click **OK** when informed that the split was successful, then click the **Tables button** 📖 Tables on the Objects bar (if it's not already selected)
See Figure 16-7. The original Derby01 database is now a front-end database and contains no data. Instead, it contains a link to the Stats table, which is stored in the Derby01_be back-end database. Therefore, front-end database users can view, edit, and enter data in tables, but they cannot modify table objects in Table Design View.

5. Click the **Forms button** 📧 Forms on the Objects bar
A front-end database retains the original query, form, and report objects that it had before it was split.

6. Right-click the **Start button** on the taskbar, click **Explore**, navigate to the folder that contains your Project Files, then double-click Derby01_be
The back-end database contains the Stats table. Normally, the back-end database would be on a server, so everyone using a front-end database could access the data stored in the back-end database.

7. Click the **Forms button** 📧 Forms on the Objects bar
The back-end database contains no other objects.

Figure 16-7: Front-end database

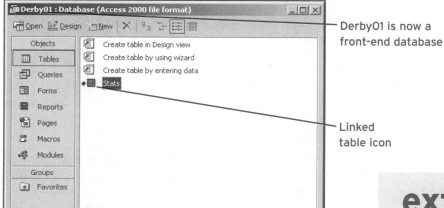

Derby01 is now a front-end database

Linked table icon

Skill Set 16

Creating Database Applications

Create an MDE File

An Access **MDE file** is a special copy of a database that prevents others from opening or editing form, report, or module objects in Design View. Users can still enter data in the MDE file just like they can in the original database, but they can't view or copy the development work of the form, report, and module objects. An MDE file is much smaller than an **MDB file** (a regular database file), making it easier to distribute and run faster than the original MDB file. To create an MDE file using Access 2002, your database must be in an Access 2002 file format.

Activity Steps

 Technology01.mdb

1. Click **Tools** on the menu bar, point to **Database Utilities**, point to **Convert Database**, then click **To Access 2002 File Format**

2. Type **Technology2002** in the File name box, click the **Save in list arrow**, navigate to the drive and folder where your Project Files are stored, click **Save**, then click **OK** when informed about Access 2000

3. Close the database, but leave Access running

4. Click **Tools** on the menu bar, point to **Database Utilities**, then click **Make MDE File**

5. Click **Technology2002**, then click **Make MDE**

6. Type **TechnologyMDE** in the File name box, click **Save**, then close Access

7. Right-click the **Start button** on the taskbar, click **Explore**, navigate to the folder that contains your Project Files, then double-click **TechnologyMDE**

8. Click the **Forms button** [≡⊟ Forms] on the Objects bar
See Figure 16-8.

9. Click each object button on the Objects bar
The Design button is not available for any database object in an MDE file except for tables and queries.

Step 1
By default, databases created in Access 2002 are Access 2000 version databases so that they can be opened in Access 2000 without going through any conversion process. Access file format version information appears on the Database window title bar.

Figure 16-8: Using an MDE file

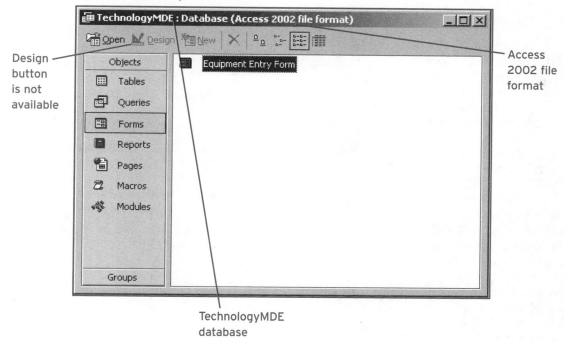

Design
button
is not
available

Access
2002 file
format

TechnologyMDE
database

Skill Set 16

Creating Database Applications

Target Your Skills

1 In Form Design View of the Patient Entry Form, use the Command Button Wizard to add three command buttons to the form as shown in Figure 16-9. Use the Go To First Record action, the Go To Last Record action, and the Close Form action for the command buttons. Use the default pictures for each button, and use the meaningful button names of GoToFirst, GoToLast, and CloseForm. Test the buttons in Form View.

 WellVisits01.mdb

2 Create an MDE file from the WellVisits01 version Access 2000 database by converting it to an Access 2002 version database with the name WellVisits2002, and then making an MDE file named WellVisitsMDE from the WellVisits2002 database. The final WellVisitsMDE file is shown in Figure 16-10.

Figure 16-9

Figure 16-10

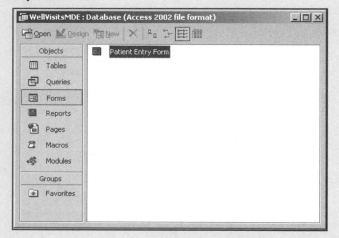

Skill List

1. Start Outlook
2. Understand Outlook folders and items
3. Work with items and views
4. Get Help

Outlook 2002 is a powerful personal information manager and communication tool that is part of Microsoft Office XP. You can use Outlook to send and receive e-mail messages, schedule appointments, keep track of people, manage your to-do list, and much more. In this skill set, you become familiar with the basics of using Outlook. You will learn how to start and exit the program and how to view the different program components. You will copy the Project Files that accompany this book to the appropriate Outlook folders so that you will be able to complete the steps in the other skill sets. You will also learn how to view information in Outlook in different ways. Finally, you will learn how to access the Help system so that you can take full advantage of all the powerful tools and functionality that Outlook provides.

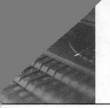

Getting Started

Getting Started with Outlook 2002

Start Outlook

Start and Exit Outlook

To start using the many useful features of Outlook, you need to start the program. Like any other Windows program, you can start Outlook using the Start menu on the taskbar. You can also start Outlook by double-clicking its program icon on the Windows desktop. If many people use Outlook on your computer, then you might need to enter a profile name in the Choose Profile dialog box before the Outlook program window opens. A **profile** is a group of e-mail accounts and address books set up for a particular user. Separate profiles are handy if you share your computer with others. By default, the Outlook setup program sets up only one profile on a computer. You close Outlook using the Exit command on the File menu.

Step 2
Your screen might look different than Figure GS-2, depending on how Outlook is set up on your computer.

Activity Steps

1. Click the **Start button** on the taskbar, then point to **Programs**
   See Figure GS-1.

2. Click **Microsoft Outlook** on the Programs menu (If you have profiles set up on your computer, then the Choose Profile dialog box will appear. Click the **Profile Name list arrow**, click your **Profile name**, enter your **password**, then click **OK**)
   The Outlook Program window opens.
   See Figure GS-2.

3. Click **File** on the menu bar, then click **Exit**

Figure GS-1: Programs menu

Click to
open the
Programs
menu

Start button

Click to start
Outlook

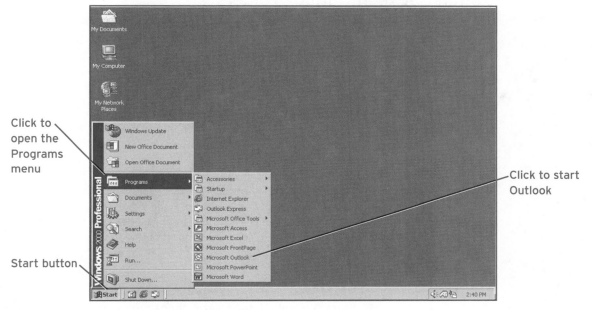

Figure GS-2: Outlook program window

File menu

Close button

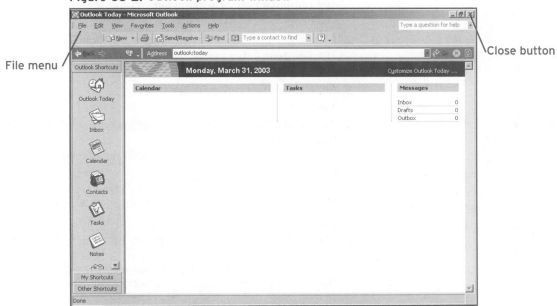

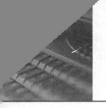

Getting Started

Getting Started with Outlook 2002

Understand Outlook Folders and Items

Switch Between Outlook Folders

Outlook is composed of several different **folders** that let you perform particular tasks and that store different kinds of information. The primary folders in Outlook are the **Inbox**, which you can use to send and receive e-mail, the **Calendar**, which you can use to manage your schedule, the **Contacts folder**, where you store information about people, such as their addresses and phone numbers, and the **Tasks folder**, where you keep track of your to-do list items. The **Outlook Today folder** shows you an at-a-glance view of items in your Calendar, Tasks, and Inbox folders. See Table GS-1 for a description of the other default Outlook folders. An **item** is a basic piece of information that is stored in an Outlook folder, such as an e-mail message or a Calendar appointment. To open a folder and view the items it contains, you click its icon on the **Outlook Bar**, located along the left edge of the Outlook window. The contents of the folder are displayed in the **View pane**, which is the large area to the right of the Outlook Bar. You can also open a folder by clicking its icon on the **Folder list**, which you can open using the View menu. The name of the open folder appears in the **Folder banner**, just above the Outlook Bar.

When you first start Outlook, the Outlook Bar displays the icons for the Outlook Shortcuts group. You can display other icons on the Outlook Bar by clicking My Shortcuts or Other Shortcuts on the Outlook Bar.

Activity Steps

1. Start **Outlook**, if necessary, choose your **Profile name**, type your **password**, then click **OK**
   The Outlook program window opens, and the View pane displays the contents of the current folder.

2. Click the **Calendar icon** 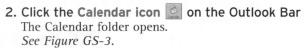 on the Outlook Bar
   The Calendar folder opens.
   See Figure GS-3.

3. Click **Calendar** in the Folder banner
   The Folder List opens.

4. Click the **push pin** in the upper-right corner of the Folder List to keep the Folder List open
   The Calendar resizes itself so that both the Calendar and the Folder List appear in the Outlook window.

5. Click the **Inbox folder** in the Folder List
   The Inbox folder opens, and the Folder List remains open. *See Figure GS-4.*

6. Click the **Folder List Close button**, then click **My Shortcuts** on the Outlook Bar
   The icons on the Outlook Bar change to show the icons for Drafts, Outbox, Sent Items, Journal, and Outlook Update.

Figure GS-3: Calendar folder open in Outlook window

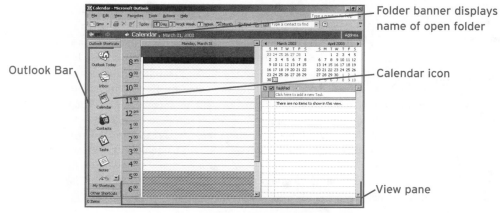

Folder banner displays name of open folder

Outlook Bar

Calendar icon

View pane

Figure GS-4: Inbox folder open with Folder List open

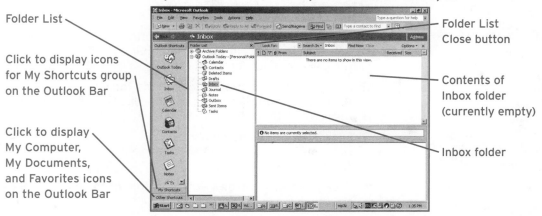

Folder List

Click to display icons for My Shortcuts group on the Outlook Bar

Click to display My Computer, My Documents, and Favorites icons on the Outlook Bar

Folder List Close button

Contents of Inbox folder (currently empty)

Inbox folder

TABLE GS-1: Other Outlook folders and the type of information they store

folder	stores this type of information
Notes	Electronic "sticky notes" for recording thoughts, notes, ideas, and reminders
Journal	Log entries that describe completed tasks or events that have occurred
Drafts	In-progress e-mail messages
Outbox	Completed e-mail messages that have not yet been sent to the server for delivery to the recipients
Sent Items	E-mail messages that have been delivered to the recipients
Deleted Items	Items that have been removed using the Delete command
Outlook Update	Opens the Microsoft Office Web site where you can access resources, tools, and assistance

Getting Started

Use Toolbars, Menus, and Dialog Boxes

As in other Windows applications, you perform actions in Outlook using commands on menus or buttons on toolbars. The **menu bar** is located at the top of the Outlook window, just below the **title bar**. To execute a menu command, click a menu name on the menu bar to open the menu, then click a command on the open menu. When you first click a menu name on the menu bar, a short list of menu items opens. If you click the double arrows at the bottom of a menu, the **full menu** will open, displaying the complete list of commands for that menu. If more information is required to complete a command, a dialog box will open. A **dialog box** is a window from which you need to make selections or in which you need to type information in order for a task to be completed. You can also use toolbar buttons to perform actions. The **toolbar** is located directly above the Folder banner and contains buttons that you can click to perform tasks appropriate for the current folder. By default, the Standard toolbar is open. The toolbar buttons and menu commands that are available at any given time change depending on which folder is open.

Activity Steps

You can reposition the toolbar by dragging it to a different location anywhere in the Outlook window.

1. Click **Outlook Shortcuts** on the Outlook Bar, then click the **Calendar icon** on the Outlook Bar
   The Calendar folder opens, showing time slots for today.

2. Click the **Week button** Week on the toolbar
   The Calendar format changes to show the days of the current week. Today's date is highlighted.

3. Click **View** on the menu bar
   The short version of the View menu opens.
   See Figure GS-5.

4. Click the **double arrows** at the bottom of the menu, if necessary
   The full menu opens.

5. Point to **Go To** on the menu, then click **Go to Date** on the submenu that appears
   The Go To Date dialog box appears.
   See Figure GS-6.

6. Click the **Date list arrow** to open a small calendar for the current month, click the **date for tomorrow** on the calendar, then click **OK**
   Tomorrow's date is highlighted on the Calendar.

7. Click **Today** on the toolbar, then click the **Day button** Day on the toolbar
   The Calendar now shows today's date in Day format.

Figure GS-5: View menu

Click to display full menu

Calendar icon

Week button

Partial View menu

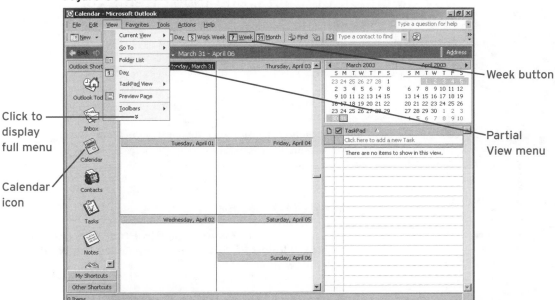

Figure GS-6: Go To Date dialog box

Date list arrow

extra!

Displaying other toolbars

Outlook has three toolbars. By default, only the Standard toolbar is displayed. You might also want to display the Advanced toolbar, which contains buttons for performing additional Outlook tasks, or the Web toolbar, which contains buttons to help you view Web pages. To display the Advanced toolbar or the Web toolbar, point to the Standard toolbar, right-click, then click the name of the toolbar you want to display.

Getting Started

Getting Started with Outlook 2002

Work with Items and Views

Copy Calendar, Contacts, and Inbox Items to Outlook Folders

This book comes with a large number of Project Files, most of which are Outlook items that you will use for practice. In order to complete the steps in the remaining activities in this book, you need to copy the Project Files from Windows Explorer to the appropriate Outlook folder. For instance, to copy a Calendar item located in Windows Explorer to the Calendar folder, you drag the item from its folder in Windows Explorer over to the Calendar icon on the Outlook Bar. Before you begin the steps in this activity, make sure that you close all other applications so that only Outlook is running. You need to complete both this activity and the following one in order to copy all the files needed for the activities in this book.

Step 1
If you are using Microsoft Windows 98, click Start, click Programs, then click Windows Explorer.

Activity Steps

1. Click the **Start button**, point to **Programs**, point to **Accessories**, click **Windows Explorer**, then maximize the Windows Explorer window if necessary
   Windows Explorer opens.

2. Locate and then click the **Outlook MOUS Cert Circle Project Files folder** in the Folders pane of Windows Explorer
   Six folders appear in the right pane of Windows Explorer, along with three other files.
   See Figure GS-7.

3. Right-click **the taskbar**, then click **Tile Windows Vertically** on the shortcut menu
   The Outlook program window and the Windows Explorer window now appear side by side on your screen.

4. Double-click the **Calendar Items folder** in the right pane of the Windows Explorer window, click **Edit** on the Windows Explorer menu bar, then click **Select All**
   See Figure GS-8.

5. Drag all the selected files to the **Calendar icon** on the Outlook Bar
   The selected items are copied to your Calendar folder in Outlook.

6. Click the **Contacts Items folder** in the Folders pane of the Windows Explorer window, click **Edit** on the Windows Explorer menu bar, click **Select All**, then drag all the selected files to the **Contacts icon** on the Outlook Bar

7. Click the **Inbox Items folder** in the Folders pane of Windows Explorer, click **Edit** on the menu bar, click **Select All**, then drag the selected items to the **Inbox icon** on the Outlook Bar

Figure GS-7: Project Files in Windows Explorer

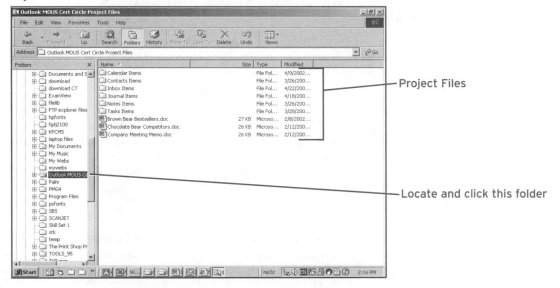

Project Files

Locate and click this folder

Figure GS-8: Windows Explorer and Outlook side by side

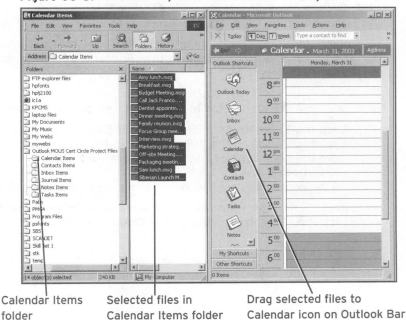

Calendar Items folder

Selected files in Calendar Items folder

Drag selected files to Calendar icon on Outlook Bar

extra!

Changing the default folder that opens when Outlook starts
When you first start Outlook, the Outlook Today folder opens by default. To specify that a different folder should open when Outlook starts, click Tools on the menu bar, click Options, click the Other tab, click Advanced Options, click the Startup in this folder list arrow, click a folder of your choice, then click OK twice.

Getting Started

Getting Started with Outlook 2002

Work with Items and Views

Copy Journal, Notes, and Tasks Items to Outlook Folders

This activity is a continuation of the previous activity, "Copy Calendar, Contacts, and Inbox Items to Outlook Folders." Make sure you complete the previous activity before starting this one. In the steps below, you will copy the Journal, Notes, and Tasks items from your Project Files folder to the appropriate Outlook folder.

You can use Outlook to browse for any file on your computer, network, or the Web. To do this, click Other Shortcuts on the Outlook Bar to display the My Computer, My Documents, and Favorites icons. Click any of these icons as appropriate to locate the file you want.

Activity Steps

1. Make sure that both Windows Explorer and Outlook are open on your screen, and that the **Outlook MOUS Cert Circle Project Files folder** is selected in the Folders pane of Windows Explorer

2. Click **My Shortcuts** on the Outlook Bar
   The icons in the Outlook Bar change.
   See Figure GS-9.

3. Click the **Journal Items folder** in the left pane of the Windows Explorer window, click **Edit** on the Windows Explorer menu bar, click **Select All**, then drag the **selected items** from the right pane of Windows Explorer to the **Journal icon** on the Outlook Bar
   The items are copied to your Journal folder in Outlook.

4. Click **Outlook Shortcuts** on the Outlook Bar
   The icons on the Outlook Bar change again.

5. Click the **Notes Items folder** in the left pane of the Windows Explorer window, click **Edit** on the Windows Explorer menu bar, then click **Select All**
   See Figure GS-10.

6. Drag the selected items to the **Notes icon** on the Outlook Bar

7. Click the **Tasks Items folder** in the left pane of Windows Explorer, then drag the **Write monthly status report.msg** item from the right pane of Windows Explorer to the **Tasks icon** on the Outlook Bar
   All the Project Files are now copied to the appropriate Outlook folders.

8. Click **File** on the Windows Explorer menu bar, click **Close**, then click the **Maximize button** on the Outlook window

Figure GS-9: Outlook Bar with My Shortcuts icons displayed

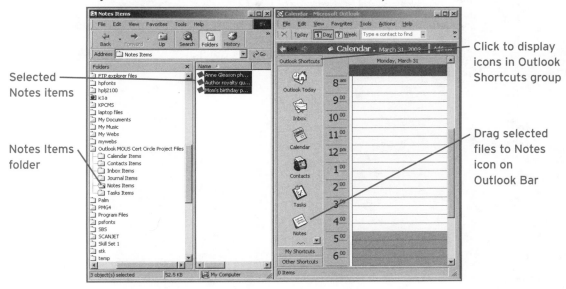

Journal icon

Journal Items folder

My Shortcuts icon group button

Icons in My Shortcuts icon group

Figure GS-10: Selected Notes items in Windows Explorer

Selected Notes items

Notes Items folder

Click to display icons in Outlook Shortcuts group

Drag selected files to Notes icon on Outlook Bar

Getting Started

Getting Started with Outlook 2002

Work with Items and Views
Understand Views

A **view** is a particular way to display the items in an Outlook folder. When you click a folder icon on the Outlook Bar, the items contained in that folder appear in the default view for that folder. Each folder has many different views available so that you can see the same information in different ways. For instance, the default view for the Calendar folder is Day/Week/Month view, which shows your appointments for the current day. You might want to change this view to show only active appointments, so that you can see all of your active appointments in a table. You can change a view by choosing a view type on the Current View menu. The available views for each folder are unique to that folder; however, the method for changing views is the same no matter what folder you are using.

Step 3
Your active appointments might be different from the ones shown in figure GS-12, depending on the date you complete these steps.

Activity Steps

1. Click the **Calendar icon** , if necessary, on the Outlook Bar

2. Click **View** on the menu bar, then point to **Current View**
   A list of available views appears on the Current View menu.
   See Figure GS-11.

3. Click **Active Appointments**
   All your active appointments appear in table format.
   See Figure GS-12.

4. Click **View** on the menu bar, point to **Current View**, then click **Day/Week/Month**
   The default view is restored.

Figure GS-11: Current View menu

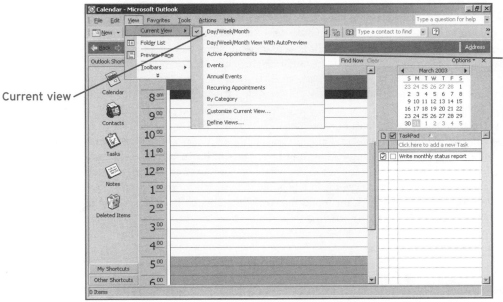

Current view

Click to display appointments in table format

Figure GS-12: Calendar in Active Appointments view

Subject column heading

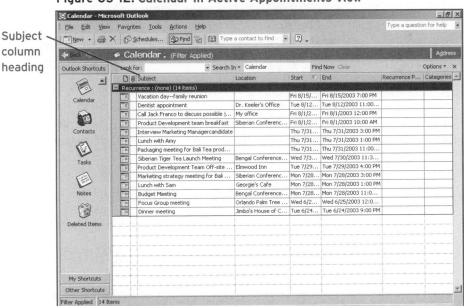

Getting Started
Getting Started with Outlook 2002

Get Help
Access the Help System

Outlook is a powerful program packed with an impressive array of features. As you use Outlook you will probably need help completing certain tasks and will probably also have questions about how to take full advantage of all of its functionality. Fortunately, like all the other applications in Microsoft Office XP, Outlook comes with a powerful Help system. There are many ways to access Help. You can type a question or keywords in the **Ask a Question box**, located at the right end of the menu bar. Once you enter a question or keywords, the Ask a Question box presents a list of related topics. Clicking a topic opens the Microsoft Outlook Help window, where you can view additional topics and perform additional topic searches, using one of three tabs. The **Contents tab** shows a comprehensive listing of all the Help topics available. The **Answer Wizard tab** lets you type a question or keywords in a box and then search for related topics. The **Index tab** lets you search for topics that contain particular keywords. Some of the topics listed in the Help window are actually stored on the Web. Clicking one of these topics will open the relevant Web page on the Microsoft Web site.

Activity Steps

Step 4
You can resize the panes in the Help window by dragging the split bar that divides the two panes.

1. Click in the Ask a Question box, type How do I hide a toolbar?, then press [Enter]
A list of Help topics related to the question appears.
See Figure GS-13.

2. Click Show or hide a toolbar
The Microsoft Outlook Help window opens, with the topic you selected in the right pane.
See Figure GS-14.

3. Click Show All in the upper-right corner of the Help window, then read all the text in the right pane of the Help window

4. Click the Contents tab in the left pane of the Help window, click the (+) next to Getting Started with Microsoft Office, then click the (+) next to Getting Help

5. Click About getting help while you work, click Show All in the right pane, then read the topic in the right pane

6. Click the Index tab, type toolbar in the Type keywords box, click Search, then view the list of topics that appears below 3 Choose a topic

7. Click the Answer Wizard tab, type change views, then click Search

8. View the topics that appear, then click the Microsoft Outlook Help Close button

Figure GS-13: Ask a Question box topics

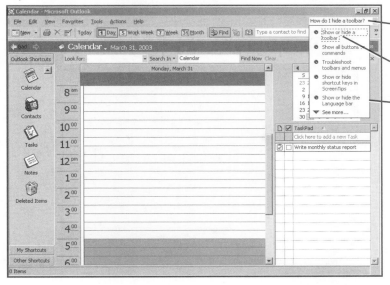

— Ask a Question box

— Click this topic

— Related Help topics

Figure GS-14: Microsoft Outlook Help window

Contents tab

Answer Wizard tab

Index tab

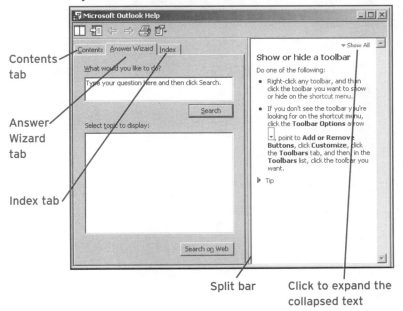

Split bar

Click to expand the collapsed text

extra!

Using the Office Assistant and getting help on the Web

You can access Help at any time by pressing [F1] to open the Office Assistant, an animated character that lets you type a search word or question in its yellow bubble to get help. The Office Assistant also appears as you work to offer context-sensitive help. You can hide the Office Assistant by clicking Help on the menu bar, then clicking Hide the Office Assistant or right-clicking the Office Assistant and choosing Hide from the shortcut menu. You can also get help and find valuable technical resources on the Microsoft Office Web site, which you can access directly from Outlook. To do this, click Help on the menu bar, then click Office on the Web.

Getting Started

Getting Started with Outlook 2002

Target Your Skills

1 Use Figure GS-15 as a guide. Start Outlook, open the Calendar folder, then use the Month button on the toolbar to make your screen look like the figure. Open the Folder List as shown. Change the view to Active Appointments view, then close the Folder List. Open each folder on the Outlook Bar and notice the Project Files that you copied. Exit Outlook.

2 Use Help to display the topic shown in Figure GS-16. Locate the topic shown by typing appropriate keywords in the Ask a Question box. Once you locate the topic shown, follow the on-screen instructions to take a tour of Outlook. Then use the Index tab of the Help window to learn how to add a new user profile to Outlook. Finally, use the Contents tab to learn about the new features of Outlook 2002, then use the Answer Wizard to learn how to hide the Outlook Bar.

Figure GS-15

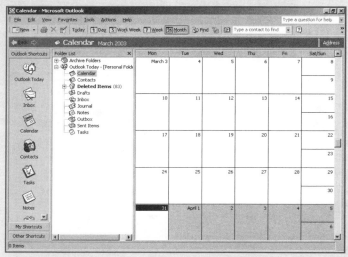

Figure GS-16

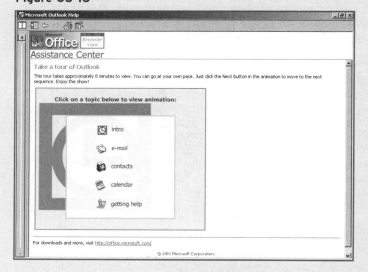

Skill List

1. Display and print messages
2. Compose and send messages
3. Insert signatures and attachments
4. Customize views

You can use Outlook to send and receive electronic messages, or **e-mail**, over a network or the Internet. In this skill set, you will learn how to open and print a message you receive, and also how to reply to, forward, compose, and send messages. You will also learn how to add personalized information, called a **signature**, to the end of a message. Finally, you will learn how to view, group, and sort the items in your Inbox in various ways to make it easier to find and manage messages.

Skill Set 1

Creating and Viewing Messages

Display and Print Messages

View a Message

To view your e-mail messages in Outlook, you need to open the Inbox folder. When you open the Inbox folder, a list of your messages appears in the order you received them, with the most recent messages listed first. Unread messages appear in bold, marked with a closed envelope icon. Below the list of messages is the **Preview pane**. When you click a message header in the Inbox, the text of the message appears in the Preview pane. If a message is short, you can view all of it in the Preview pane without scrolling. If it is long, you can open it in its own window, called the **Message form**. You open and close the Preview pane using the Preview Pane command on the View menu. If you need to find a particular message in your Inbox, but don't want to click each message individually to view it in the Preview pane, you can use the **AutoPreview** feature to display the first three lines of each message in the Inbox.

Steps 3 and 5
If you have trouble locating the messages in Steps 3 or 5, click the From column heading to sort the messages by the name of the sender, then scroll to locate the messages from Linda Miller or Muriel Baldwin.

Activity Steps

1. Start **Outlook,** then if necessary, choose your **Profile name,** click **OK,** type your **password,** then click **OK**

2. Click the **Inbox icon** 🖳 on the Outlook bar, if necessary, to view the contents of your Inbox folder

3. Scroll up or down in your Inbox to locate the **Meeting attendees message** from Linda Miller, then click this message to view it in the Preview pane
   See Figure 1-1.

4. Click **View** on the menu bar, then click **Preview Pane**
   The Preview pane closes, and you can see more of your messages.

5. Double-click the **Summer reunion message** from Muriel Baldwin to open the Message form
   See Figure 1-2.

6. Read the message, click the **Message form Close button,** click **View** on the menu bar, then click **AutoPreview**
   The first three lines of each message now appear under each message heading.

7. Click **View** on the menu bar, click **AutoPreview,** click **View** on the menu bar, then click **Preview Pane**
   AutoPreview is now turned off, and the Preview pane is open at the bottom of your screen.

Figure 1-1: Selected message open in Preview pane

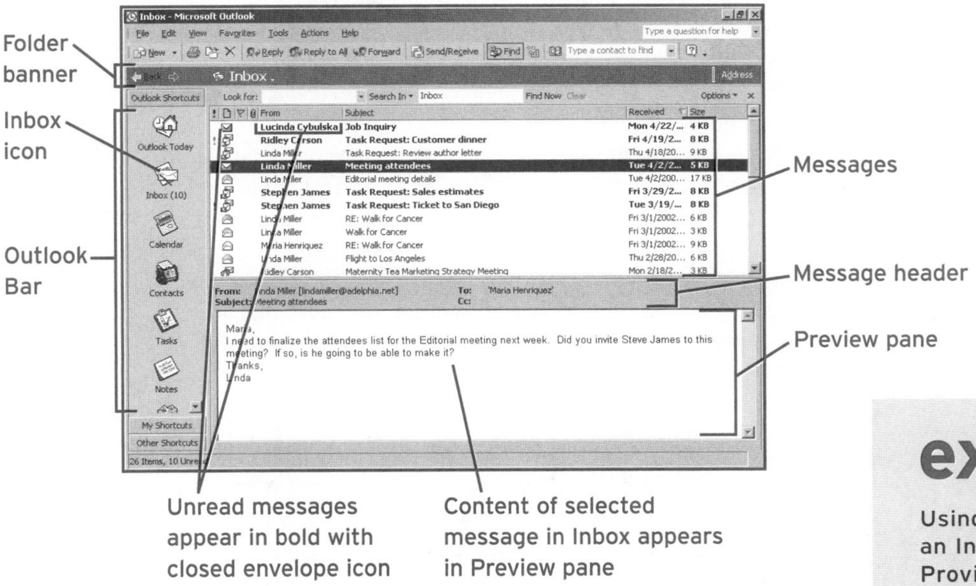

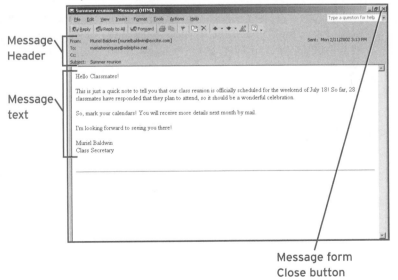

Folder banner

Inbox icon

Outlook Bar

Messages

Message header

Preview pane

Unread messages appear in bold with closed envelope icon

Content of selected message in Inbox appears in Preview pane

Figure 1-2: Open message in Message form

Message Header

Message text

Message form Close button

extra!

Using Outlook with an Internet Service Provider

If you are using an Internet Service Provider with Outlook, then you will see a Send/Receive button on your toolbar. Clicking this button transfers any new messages that you have received from the server to your Inbox. Therefore, if you are using an Internet Service Provider, you must click the Send/Receive button to check for new e-mail messages. The figures in this book show the Send/Receive button. If you are using Outlook on a corporate network, any new messages you receive will automatically be transferred to your Inbox from the server.

Skill Set 1
Creating and Viewing Messages

Display and Print Messages
Open an Attachment

Though you can include a lot of information in an e-mail message, sometimes it's more efficient to send a brief message and attach a file with additional information. For example, a colleague might attach an Excel spreadsheet to a message about your department's budget. To open and view an attachment, you must have the software in which the attachment was created, or else have another software program that is able to open the file. Messages that have attachments appear with a paper clip icon next to them in the Inbox. You can open an attachment either from the Preview pane or from the Message form. You can choose to save an attachment to a folder on a disk, or you can open an attachment without saving it first. To avoid harming your computer, never open or save an attachment unless you are completely confident that the file is free of viruses.

Activity Steps

To open an attachment from the Preview pane, double-click the attachment filename in the Preview pane message header.

1. Click the Inbox icon 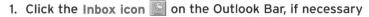 on the Outlook Bar, if necessary

2. Double-click the Company meeting message from Linda Miller (you might have to scroll to locate it)

3. In the message header, right-click the filename Company Meeting Memo.doc, then click Open
   The Opening Mail Attachment dialog box opens.
   See Figure 1-3.

4. Click the Open it option button, then click OK (if a dialog box opens asking if you want to merge changes, click No)
   A document opens in the Word program window.
   See Figure 1-4.

5. Read the memo, click File on the menu bar, then click Exit
   The Word program window closes and you return to the Outlook window.

6. Click the Message form Close button

Figure 1-3: Opening Mail Attachment dialog box

Click to open the attached file from its current location

Message warns about the danger of getting a virus from an attached file

Figure 1-4: Attachment opened in Word program window

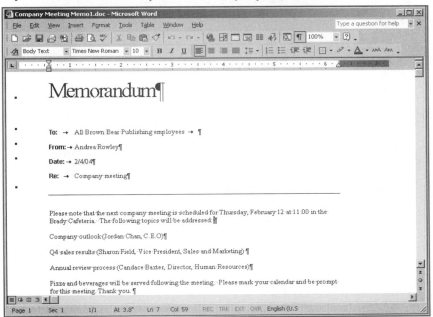

Skill Set 1

Creating and Viewing Messages

Display and Print Messages

Print a Message

If a message is particularly long or contains important information, you might decide to print it so that you have a hard copy to file or read. You can print an e-mail message with the default settings using the Print button on the Standard toolbar. However, you can make changes to the default print settings using the Page Setup and Print dialog boxes. The Page Setup dialog box lets you choose the orientation of the paper, change margin settings, or add a customized header or footer. A **header** is specified text that prints at the top of every page, and a **footer** is specified text that prints at the bottom of every page. You can use the Print dialog box to change other settings, such as which printer to use, how many copies to print, whether to print with a wide (**landscape**) or tall (**portrait**) orientation, or whether to print the message in color or in black and white. You can also specify to use fewer pages to print an e-mail message that is several pages long.

If you don't have Windows 2000 installed, you might not see the Print dialog box shown in Figure 1-6. If this is the case, skip steps 4, 5, and 6 and click the Print button on the Message toolbar to print the message with the current print settings.

Activity Steps

1. Click the **Inbox icon** 🖳, if necessary, then double-click the **Editorial meeting details message** from Linda Miller

2. Click **File** on the menu bar, point to **Page Setup**, then click **Memo Style**
   The Page Setup dialog box opens.
   See Figure 1-5.

3. Select the text in the Left margin box, type **1**, select the text in the Right margin box, type **1**, then click **OK**

4. Click **File** on the menu bar, click **Print**, then click the **Layout tab**
   See Figure 1-6.

5. Click the **Pages Per Sheet list arrow**, then click **2**

6. Click **Print**
   The two pages of the message print on one page.

7. Close the **Editorial meeting details Message form**

Figure 1-5: Page Setup dialog box

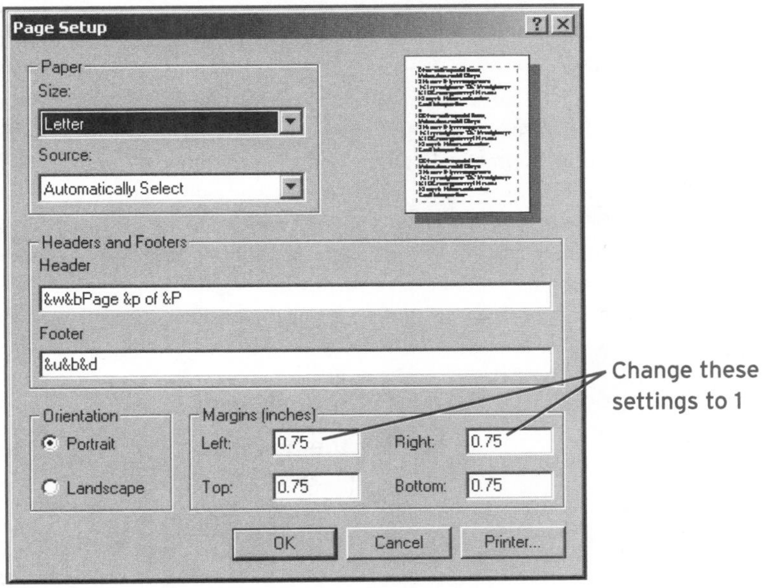

Figure 1-6: Layout tab of the Print dialog box

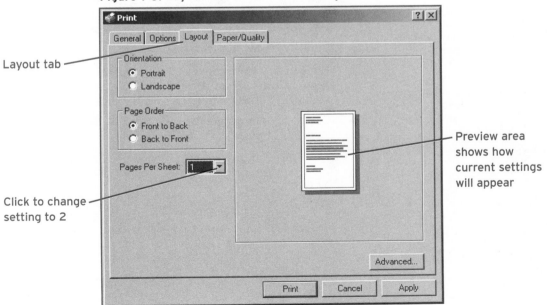

Skill Set 1

Creating and Viewing Messages

Compose and Send Messages
Reply to a Message

One of the most common e-mail tasks is responding to messages sent to you by others. You can use the Reply button to reply to only the sender, or you can use the Reply to All button to address your response to everyone who received the message. When you click the Reply or Reply to All button, a new Message form opens that is automatically addressed to the sender. If you use the Reply to All button, the sender is listed in the To: box and all recipients of the original message are listed in the Cc: box. The insertion point is in the message body, ready for you to start typing your message. If you have Microsoft Word 2002 installed on your computer, the message form will actually open in Word, providing you with a powerful array of tools to use to format and edit your message. By default, Outlook uses Word as its editor.

You can also use keyboard shortcuts to reply to messages. To reply only to the sender, press [Ctrl][R]. To reply to all recipients of the original message, press [Ctrl][Shift][R].

Activity Steps

1. Click the **Inbox icon** , if necessary, then click the **From column heading**
   The messages are sorted by sender in alphabetical order, making it easier to find messages sent by a particular sender.

2. Double-click the **Job Inquiry message** from Lucinda Cybulska
   See Figure 1-7.

3. Read the message, then click the **Reply button** on the toolbar
   The Reply form opens. The insertion point is already in the message box, above the text of the Job Inquiry message.

4. Type the following text:

   Thanks for your message. I would be happy to meet with you on June 18 at 10:00 in my office. Please contact my assistant, Linda Miller, if you need directions.

5. Compare your screen with Figure 1-8, then click **Send** on the Message toolbar

6. Click the **Job Inquiry Message form Close button**, then click the **Received column heading** in the Inbox to sort the messages by date

Figure 1-7: Open message in Message form

Click to reply to the sender only and not other recipients of the original message

Click to reply to the sender and all recipients of the original message

Cc: line shows no other recipients

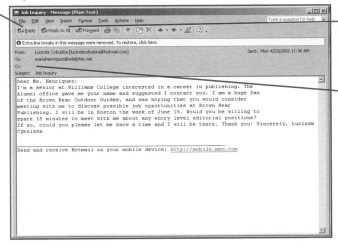

Figure 1-8: Completed message in Reply form

Original sender automatically appears in To: box

Type reply text here

Original message automatically appears in message body

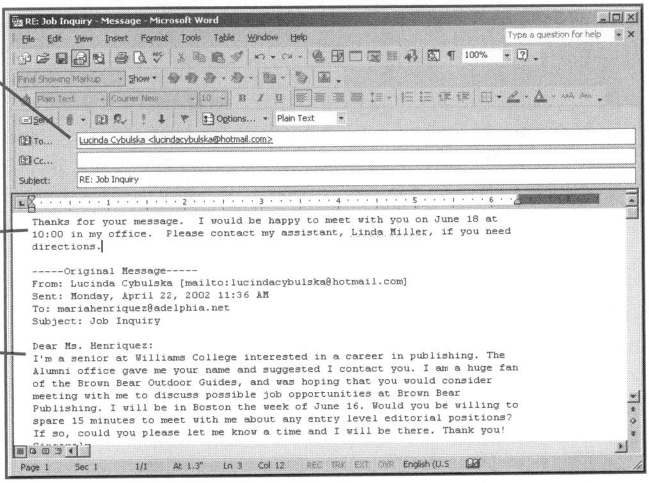

extra!

Using the Send/Receive button

If you are using Outlook on a corporate network, then clicking the Send button in the Message form automatically transfers your reply or new message to the server so it can be delivered to your recipient. However, if you are using Outlook with an Internet Service Provider, and if you are working off-line, then clicking Send in the Message form only transfers your message to your Outbox folder. In order to transfer your message from your Outbox folder to the ISP's server, you must click the Send/Receive button on the Standard toolbar in the Outlook window.

Skill Set 1
Creating and Viewing Messages

Compose and Send Messages
Forward a Message

If you receive a message that is important for others to read, you can forward the message to them using the Forward button on the toolbar. When you click the Forward button, a Message form opens, with the insertion point in the To: box and a copy of the message displayed in the message body. In the To: box, type the addresses of the people to whom you want to forward the message. You can type additional text above the message to explain why you are forwarding it, or you can forward the message by itself. If Word is installed on your computer, the Message form will open in Microsoft Word, the default editor for Outlook.

You can also forward a message by clicking Actions on the menu bar, then clicking Forward, or by pressing [Ctrl][F].

Activity Steps

1. Click the Inbox icon [icon], then click the Reunion attendees message from Muriel Baldwin

2. Click the Forward button on the Standard toolbar
   The Message form opens, with the insertion point in the To: box.

3. Type your e-mail address

4. Click at the top of the message area, then type FYI
   See Figure 1-9.

5. Click Send on the Message toolbar

6. If you are using Outlook with an Internet Service Provider, click the Send/Receive button on the Message toolbar, wait a minute or two, then click the Send/Receive button again (If you are using Outlook on a corporate network, skip to Step 7)
   The message that you forwarded appears in the Inbox, with the letters FW preceding the Subject title.
   See Figure 1-10.

7. Click the FW: Reunion attendees message, then press [Delete]

Figure 1-9: Forward Message form with To: address and text added

Type your
e-mail address
here

Type additional
text here

Forwarded
message
appears here
automatically

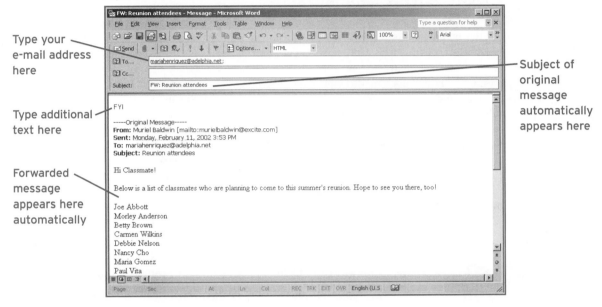

Subject of
original
message
automatically
appears here

Figure 1-10: Inbox with new forwarded message

Your e-mail
address will
appear here

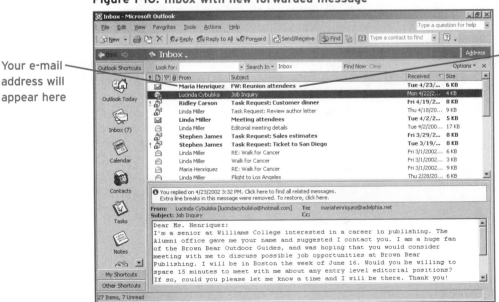

Forwarded
message in
Inbox

Skill Set 1

Creating and Viewing Messages

Compose and Send Messages

Create a New Mail Message

You can create new messages in Outlook and send them to recipients who are part of your corporate work group, or to recipients with an Internet e-mail address. When you create a new e-mail message, a new Message form opens. If Microsoft Word 2002 was installed on your computer at the same time as Outlook, then your Message form will open in Microsoft Word, providing you with a powerful array of formatting and editing tools to make your message more visually compelling. Otherwise, Outlook will be your editor. No matter which editor you have, you complete the message header in the same way. You first type the addresses of the recipients in the To: and Cc: boxes, then type a title for your message in the Subject box. You then type your message into the message body, then use the Send button to place the message in your Outbox. If you are using an Internet Service Provider, you need to use the Send/Receive button on the Standard toolbar to transmit the message from the Outbox folder to your mail server.

If Word is not currently your editor and you would like it to be, click Tools on the menu bar, click Options to open the Options dialog box, click the Mail Format tab, then click the Use Microsoft Word to edit e-mail messages check box, then click OK.

Activity Steps

1. Click the **Inbox icon**, 🖳, if necessary, then click the **New Mail Message button** 📧 New ▾ on the Standard toolbar

2. Type **lucindacybulska@hotmail.com**, then click in the **Cc: box**

3. Type your e-mail address, then press **[Tab]** twice to move the insertion point to the Subject box

4. Type **June 18 meeting**, then press **[Tab]** to move the insertion point to the message body

5. Type **I need to change the time of our meeting on June 18 to 11:00. Please let me know if this is a problem for you. Thanks.** *See Figure 1-11.*

6. Click **Send** on the Message toolbar, then if you are using an Internet Service Provider, click **Send/Receive** on the Standard toolbar as needed until the message appears in your Inbox Depending on the speed of your mail server, the new message should appear in your Inbox.

7. Click the **June 18 meeting message**, read the message in the Preview pane, then click the **Delete button** ☒ on the Standard toolbar The message is deleted.

Figure 1-11: Completed message in Message form

Click to place message in Outbox folder

Type your e-mail address here

Message body

Type meaningful subject for your message here

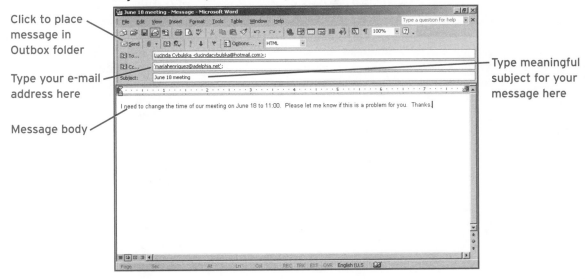

extra!

Creating a new Office document from within Outlook

You can create a new Word document, Excel worksheet, or PowerPoint presentation from within Outlook. To do this, click the New list arrow on the Standard toolbar, then click Office Document. The New Office Document dialog box opens, as shown in Figure 1-12. Click the program icon you want to use, then click OK. The program opens. To return to Outlook, click the Outlook program icon on the taskbar.

Figure 1-12: New Office Document dialog box

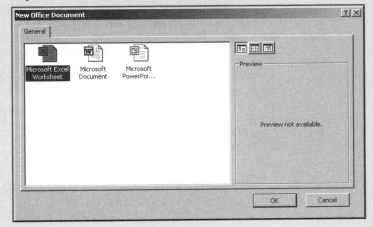

Skill Set 1

Creating and Viewing Messages

Compose and Send Messages
Use the Address Book

If you exchange frequent e-mails with particular people, you might want to store their e-mail addresses and other information in the Address Book to save time and ensure accuracy. The **Address Book** stores names, addresses, phone numbers, and other information about people you know. Entries in the Address Book are called **contacts**, and are stored in the Contacts folder in Outlook. You enter each new e-mail address and other information, such as address and phone number, in the **Contact form**. To access e-mail addresses for all the contacts in your Contacts folder, click the To: button in the message header and choose the recipients.

Unless you specify otherwise, the full name and e-mail address of each contact will appear in the message header when you select it from the Select Names dialog box. You can control how the name of the contact appears by entering the name precisely as you want it to appear in the Display as box in the Contact form.

Activity Steps

1. Click the **Inbox icon** 🖳, click **Tools** on the menu bar, then click **Address Book**
   The Address Book dialog box opens.

2. Verify that **Contacts** is selected in the Show Names from the box, then click the **New Entry button** 🖳 on the toolbar

3. In the New Entry dialog box, verify that **New Contact** is selected, then click **OK**
   The Contact form opens.

4. Maximize the Contact form, if necessary, type **Muriel Baldwin** in the Full Name box, click in the E-mail box, then type **murielbaldwin@excite.com**
   See Figure 1-13. Notice that Baldwin, Muriel automatically appeared in the File as box when you clicked in the E-mail box.

5. Click the **Save and Close button** on the toolbar, then click the **Close button** in the Address Book dialog box

6. Click the **New Mail Message button** 🖳 New ▼ on the toolbar to open the Message form, then click the **Address book button** 🖳 To... to the left of the To: box
   The Select Names dialog box opens. Muriel Baldwin now appears in the Name list. *See Figure 1-14.*

7. Click **Muriel Baldwin** in the Name list, click the **To button**, click **OK**, click in the Subject box, type **Reunion**, press **[Tab]**, type **I plan to attend this summer's reunion.**, then click the **Send button**

Figure 1-13: Contact form

Save and
Close button

Automatically
entered; based
on Full Name
box contents

Type contact's
e-mail
address here

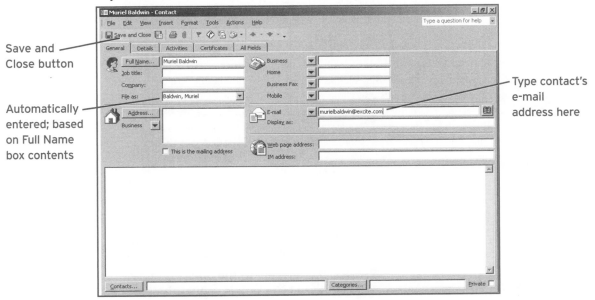

Figure 1-14: Select Names dialog box with new name

To button

Your list of names
might be different

Muriel Baldwin
appears in the list

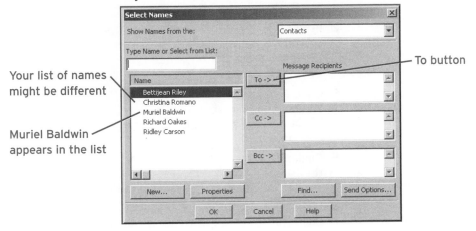

Skill Set 1

Creating and Viewing Messages

Insert Signatures and Attachments

Insert and Remove Signatures

If you want the same information to appear at the end of all your messages, you can save time by inserting a signature. A **signature** is a block of text that you can specify to appear at the end of a message. Usually a signature includes your name, job, title, address, and phone number, although you can create signatures that include anything you want, such as a motto or favorite saying. You can create several different signatures and choose an appropriate one for a specific message. To create a new signature, you use the Signatures command on the Mail Format tab of the Options dialog box. You can apply formatting to signatures using any of the formatting or special effects tools available with Word. Once you create a new signature, it will be inserted automatically at the end of your new messages. You can choose a different signature or specify that no signature appear by adjusting the settings in the Signature section of the Mail Format tab of the Options dialog box.

Activity Steps

1. Click the Inbox icon 🔲, click Tools on the menu bar, click Options, then click the Mail Format tab

2. Click Signatures (to the bottom right of the dialog box), then click New in the Create Signature dialog box

3. Type Maria Henriquez in the Enter a name for your new signature box, verify that the Start with a blank signature option button is selected, then click Next

4. In the Edit Signature dialog box, type Best wishes, press [Enter], type Maria Henriquez, press [Enter], type Editorial Director, press [Enter], then type Brown Bear Publishing
   See Figure 1-15.

5. Click Finish, then click OK
   The Mail Format tab of the Options dialog box appears. Notice that Maria Henriquez now appears in the Signature for new messages list box. *See Figure 1-16.*

6. Click OK, then click the New Mail Message button 🔲 New ▾ on the toolbar
   The Message form opens. The Maria Henriquez signature appears in the message body.

7. Click the Message form close button, click the Outlook program button on the taskbar, click Tools on the menu bar, click Options, click the Mail Format tab, click Signatures, verify that the Maria Henriquez signature is selected, click Remove, click Yes, then click OK twice

Figure 1-15: Edit Signature dialog box

Use these buttons to format the text of a signature

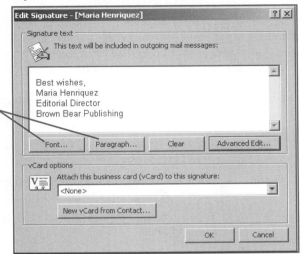

Figure 1-16: Mail Format tab of the Options dialog box

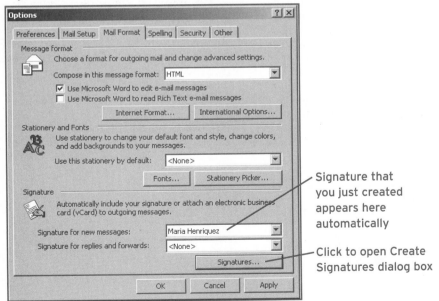

Signature that you just created appears here automatically

Click to open Create Signatures dialog box

Skill Set 1
Creating and Viewing Messages

Insert Signatures and Attachments
Insert Message Attachments

Though you can include a lot of information in an e-mail message, sometimes it is more efficient to send a message with a file attached to it. For instance, rather than writing a message that summarizes the contents of a memo, you could simply attach the memo file to the message so that the recipients can view it for themselves. You can attach any kind of file you want to an e-mail message; however, keep in mind that the recipient must have the appropriate software to view the file. You attach a file using the Insert File button on the Message form toolbar.

Step 8
If you are using Outlook with an Internet Service Provider, you also need to click the Send/Receive button on the toolbar to upload your message to the server. Your message will remain in your Outbox folder until you click Send/Receive on the toolbar.

Activity Steps

1. Click the **Inbox icon** , then click the **New Mail Message button** on the Standard toolbar

2. Type **lindamiller@adelphia.net** in the To: box, then click in the **Subject box**

3. Type **Bestseller list** in the Subject box, then press **[Tab]**

4. Type **Please make 25 copies of the attached bestseller list for the Editorial meeting. Thanks.**

5. Click the **Insert File button** on the Message toolbar

6. Navigate to the folder where your Project files are stored, then click **Brown Bear Bestsellers** in the file list
   See Figure 1-17.

7. Click **Insert**
   See Figure 1-18.

8. Click **Send** on the toolbar

Figure 1-17: Insert File dialog box

Your files might be located in a different folder

Your file list might be different

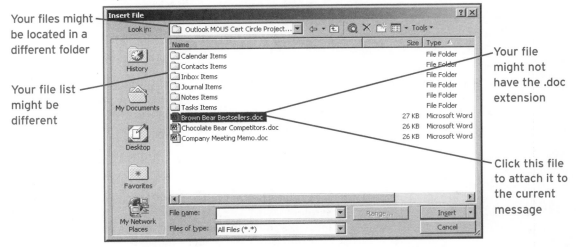

Your file might not have the .doc extension

Click this file to attach it to the current message

Figure 1-18: Message with file attachment

Click to send message

Attachment icon indicates type of file, Word in this case

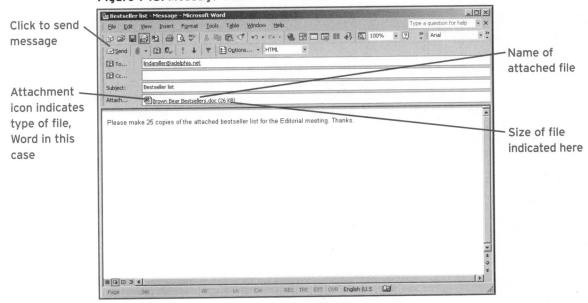

Name of attached file

Size of file indicated here

Skill Set 1
Creating and Viewing Messages

Customize Views
Changing Outlook Views

If you use e-mail frequently, and regularly receive a large number of messages, it can sometimes be difficult to locate a particular message. You can view your Outlook folders in a variety of ways to make it easy to locate particular messages or items. First, open the folder you want to view by clicking the down arrow next to the folder name in the Folder banner, then click the name of the folder you want to open. You can then use the commands on the Current View submenu to change how the information is displayed in the Outlook window. For instance, you can choose to group your messages by sender, or to show only unread messages.

tip

You can sort the contents of any folder by clicking a gray column header. For instance, to sort the messages in your Inbox by sender in ascending alphabetical order, click the From gray header box at the top of the column. Click it again to sort in descending order.

Activity Steps

1. Click **View** on the menu bar, point to **Current View**, then click **By Sender**
   The messages in the Inbox are no longer visible; instead you see a list of headings of each sender's name, with a plus sign (+) next to each one.
   See Figure 1-19.

2. Click the **+ sign** next to Linda Miller
   Ten messages appear under the From: Linda Miller heading.

3. Click the **down arrow** next to Inbox in the Folder banner, then click **Sent Items**
   Sent Items now appears in the Folder banner, indicating that this folder is open. A list of all the messages you have sent appears below.

4. Click the **Inbox icon** on the Outlook Bar, click **View** on the menu bar, point to **Current View**, then click **Unread Messages**
   Notice that (Filter Applied) appears in the Folder banner, indicating that some of the messages in this folder might not be showing. (In this case, the messages you have already read are not showing.)
   See Figure 1-20.

5. Click **View** on the menu bar, point to **Current View**, then click **Messages**

Figure 1-19: Inbox with messages grouped by Sender

Click plus
sign to view
messages
from that
sender

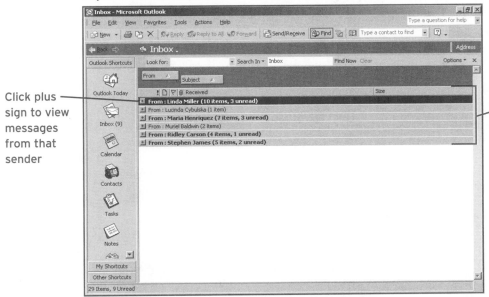

Messages are
grouped by
sender

Figure 1-20: Inbox with Unread Messages filter applied

Folder banner

Current folder
name appears
in Folder
banner

Unread
messages in
Inbox folder
(you might
have a
different
number)

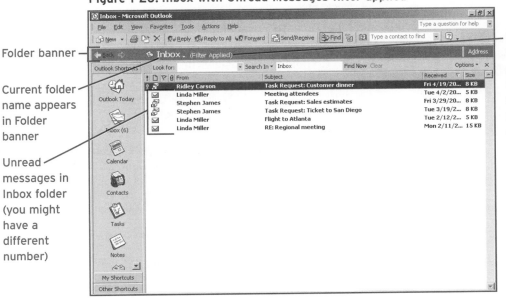

Indicates that
filter is applied
and some
messages in
open folder
might not
appear

Skill Set 1
Creating and Viewing Messages

Customize Views
Customize Outlook Views

You can customize the way the information in Outlook appears on your screen. For instance, you can change the way messages appear in your Inbox. By default, the Inbox shows fields for your messages that indicate the sender, the date you received the message, the size of the message, and the Subject. It also includes fields that convey other information, such as the importance of each message, or whether or not the message has an attachment. You can hide any of these fields, change their order, or add new fields using the Customize Views dialog box. You can also use this dialog box to specify that messages be grouped or sorted in a certain way, or to apply a filter to show only messages that contain certain information, such as the word "reunion" in the Subject field. Finally, you can change the way fonts appear for various parts of the Outlook window, and specify whether to include gridlines in the message header list. If you create a customized view and decide you prefer the original settings, you can use the Reset button in the Define Views dialog box to restore the defaults.

Step 4
You can also change the order of fields in the Show these fields in this order list by dragging them to a different position.

Activity Steps

1. Click **View** on the menu bar, point to **Current View**, then click **Customize Current View**
   The View Summary dialog box opens.
   See Figure 1-21.

2. Click **Fields**

3. Click **Cc** in the Available fields list, then click **Add**

4. With the Cc field selected, click **Move Up** three times to move the Cc field to just below the From field, then click **OK**

5. Click **Other Settings** in the View Summary dialog box, click the **Grid line style list arrow**, click **Dashes**, click the **Grid line color list arrow**, scroll up, click the **red rectangle**, then click **OK** twice
   See Figure 1-22.

6. Click **View** on the menu bar, point to **Current View**, click **Define Views**, click **Reset**, click **OK** in the dialog box that appears, then click **Close**
   The Inbox appears with its default view settings.

Figure 1-21: View Summary dialog box

Click to change
the way fields are
ordered on screen
in current view

Click to enhance
or change the
appearance of
elements in the
current view

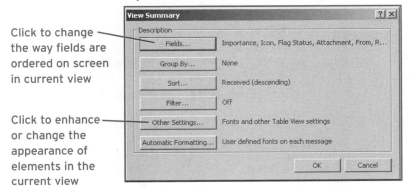

Figure 1-22: Inbox with dashed grid lines

Colored
gridlines
now
appear

Cc field now
appears in
this view,
after the
From field

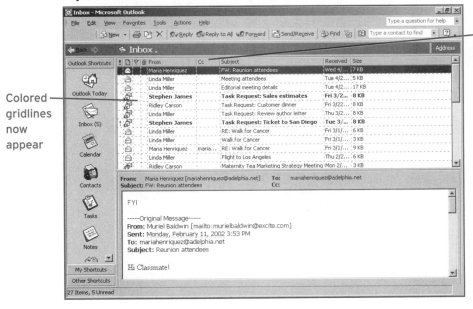

Skill Set 1
Creating and Viewing Messages

Target Your Skills

1 Use Figure 1-23 as a guide. Create three messages to yourself with the subject headings shown. Write the message text shown for the Travel schedule message; make up text for the other two messages. Use the Customize current View dialog box to change the fields so that they appear as shown. Add a blue gridline with the large dots style.

Figure 1-23

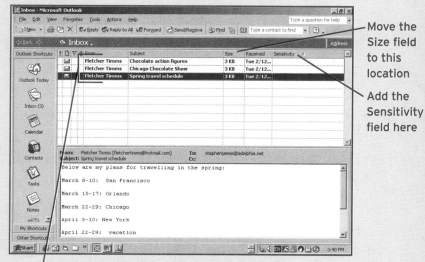

Move the Size field to this location

Add the Sensitivity field here

Your e-mail address should appear here

2 Use Figure 1-24 as a guide. Create the message shown, and attach the Project File Chocolate Bear Competitors. Create a new signature named Sugar Bear Productions with the text shown in the figure. (Include the text from "Regards" to the end of the message in the signature.) Send the message to yourself, then view the message and the attachment.

Figure 1-24

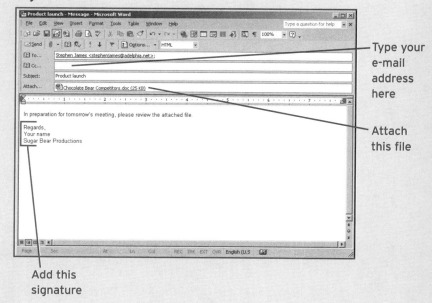

Type your e-mail address here

Attach this file

Add this signature

Skill List

1. Add appointments, meetings, and events to the Calendar
2. Apply conditional formats to the Outlook Calendar
3. Respond to meeting requests
4. Use categories to manage appointments
5. Print Calendars

Managing your time can be a huge challenge, but fortunately, the Calendar in Outlook has powerful tools that can help. In this skill set, you will learn to use the Calendar to manage your schedule by adding single appointments, as well as appointments that recur at regular intervals, to your Calendar. You will learn ways to apply color-coded labels to your appointments so you can quickly identify the type of appointments you have scheduled. You will learn how to categorize appointments so you can view related appointments together. You will also learn how to use the Calendar to schedule meetings and invite participants, as well how to respond to meeting requests sent by others. Finally, you'll learn how to print your Calendar in a format that works best for a particular circumstance.

Skill Set 2

Scheduling

Add Appointments, Meetings, and Events to the Calendar

Add Appointments to the Calendar

You can use the Calendar in Outlook to manage your schedule just like you would a paper-based date book, by entering appointments for particular dates and times. In Outlook, an **appointment** is an activity, such as a meeting, that takes place on a specific day at a specific time. When you first open the Calendar, it opens in Day view, showing today's date. You can switch to a different date by clicking that date on the **Date Navigator**, a small calendar in the upper right of the Calendar window. You view your appointments for a particular day by looking at the **Appointment area**, the section of the Calendar that resembles a yellow pad of paper divided into time slots. You also use the Appointment area to enter new appointments. To enter a new appointment, double-click a time slot to open the **Appointment form**, where you provide information about the appointment. If your appointment recurs regularly, you can use the Recurrence button of the Appointment form to set a specific recurring time. When you do this, **recurring appointments** are automatically added to the Calendar.

To move a non-recurring appointment to a different time, drag it to a new time slot in the Appointment area. To move a non-recurring appointment to the same time on a different day, drag it to a new date on the Date Navigator.

Activity Steps

1. Start Outlook, then if necessary, choose your **Profile name**, click **OK**, enter your **password**, then click **OK**

2. Click the **Calendar icon** on the Outlook Bar
   See Figure 2-1.

3. Use the Date Navigator to navigate to June 2003, then click **June 16** on the Date Navigator

4. Double-click the **8:00 am time slot** to open the Appointment form, type **Staff meeting** in the Subject box, press [Tab], type **Siberian Conference Room**, click the **second End time list arrow** (in the time section), then click **9:00 AM (1 hour)**
   See Figure 2-2.

5. Click **Recurrence** on the toolbar to open the Appointment Recurrence dialog box, select the **Monthly option button** in the Recurrence pattern section, select **the third Monday of every 1 month(s) option button**, then click **OK**

6. Click **Save and Close** on the toolbar
   The bell icon indicates that an alarm is set for this appointment, and the circular arrows icon shows that the appointment recurs.

7. Click **Today** on the toolbar

Figure 2-1: Calendar showing today's date in Day view

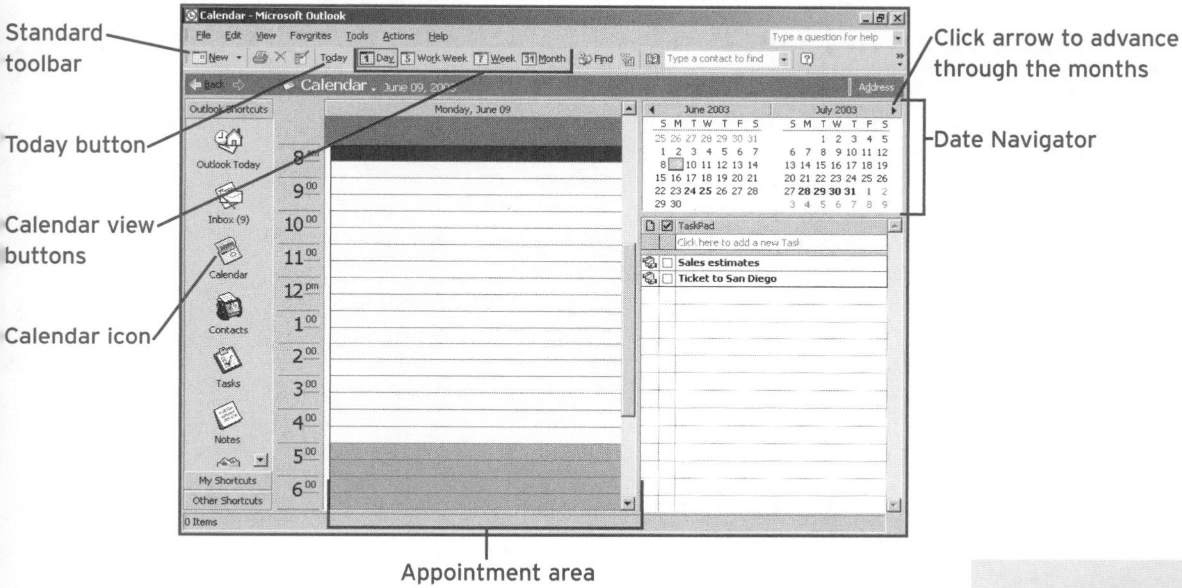

Standard toolbar

Today button

Calendar view buttons

Calendar icon

Click arrow to advance through the months

Date Navigator

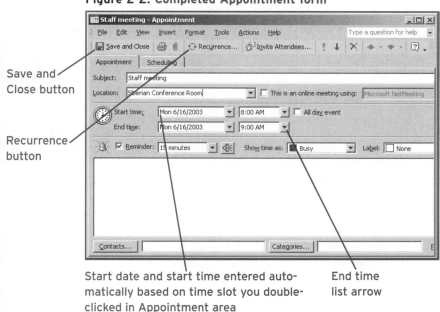

Appointment area

Figure 2-2: Completed Appointment form

Save and Close button

Recurrence button

Start date and start time entered auto-matically based on time slot you double-clicked in Appointment area

End time list arrow

extra!

Changing Calendar views

The default view for the Calendar is Day view, which lets you view your appointments for a particular day. If you need a broader look at your schedule, you can use one of the View buttons on the Standard toolbar to change to a different view. Click the Work Week button to view Monday through Friday of the current week. Click the Week button to see a seven-day view of the current week. Click the Month button to view the current month in a grid format.

Skill Set 2
Scheduling

Add Appointments, Meetings, and Events to the Calendar
Add Events to the Calendar

Sometimes you need to schedule full-day activities, called **events**, in Outlook. Entering a new event in the Calendar is much like entering a new appointment. You use the Appointment form to specify the subject and location of the appointment, as well as other information. To save yourself the trouble of setting start and end times, you can use the All day event check box to specify that the event will take up an entire day. You can also set a reminder alarm or specify that the Calendar visually highlight the event in a particular way so that colleagues who view your Calendar can see whether you are free, busy, out of the office, or have a tentative appointment. You can even color-code events so that you can see at a glance which events are personal, business-related, or require preparation. You can also use the Appointment form to specify that an appointment is private, which will make it visible only to you, not to others who have access to your Calendar.

To enter appointments in the Calendar without opening the Appointment form, click a time slot in the Appointment area, then type the subject for the appointment.

Activity Steps

1. Click the **Calendar icon** on the Outlook Bar, if necessary, then click the **New Appointment button** on the toolbar
   The Appointment form opens with the Appointment tab displayed.

2. Maximize the Appointment form, if necessary, type **Vacation day** in the Subject box, press **[Tab]**, then type **Peace and Tranquility Day Spa** in the Location box

3. Click the **Start time list arrow**, then click **next Wednesday's date** on the Start time Calendar

4. Click the **All day event check box**

5. Verify that there is a check mark in the Reminder check box, click the **Reminder list arrow**, click **1 day**, click the **Show time as list arrow**, click **Out of Office**, click the **Label list arrow**, then click **Personal**

6. Type the following in the text box below the Reminder check box: **Package includes massage, yoga class, spa lunch, and sea salt body scrub.**, then click the **Private check box** in the lower-right corner of the form
   See Figure 2-3.

7. Click **Save and Close** on the toolbar, then click **next Wednesday's date** on the Date Navigator
   A green shaded box shows the All day event. See Figure 2-4.

8. Click **Today** on the toolbar

Figure 2-3: Completed Appointment form for All day event

Save and Close button

Reminder list arrow

Choose this label to apply green shading to appointment

Click to mark appointment as private

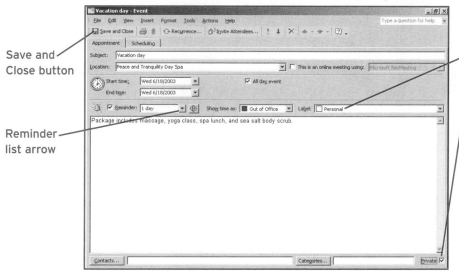

Figure 2-4: Calendar showing All day event

Today button

New All day event

Bell icon indicates alarm will sound as a reminder

Key icon indicates appointment is private

TaskPad

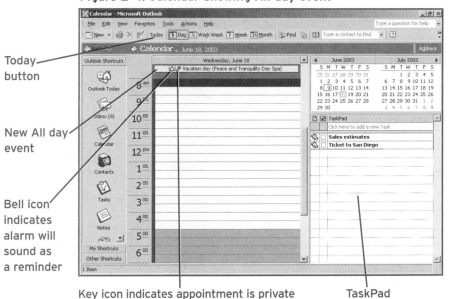

extra!

Viewing tasks in the TaskPad

Below the Date Navigator in the Calendar window is the TaskPad, which shows a list of the tasks stored in your Tasks folder. The tasks shown in Figure 2-4 are the task item Project Files that you copied in the Getting Started skill set. If you have additional tasks in your Tasks folder, then they will appear in the list, too. To change the way tasks appear in the TaskPad, click View on the menu bar, point to TaskPad view, then click a selection from the submenu.

Skill Set 2
Scheduling

Add Appointments, Meetings, and Events to the Calendar
Schedule Meetings and Invite Attendees

Trying to schedule a meeting with a large group of busy people can be both frustrating and time-consuming. It often seems impossible to find a meeting time that works for everyone. Outlook has tools that can help save you time and make scheduling meetings much easier. To invite attendees to a meeting you use the **Meeting Request form** available in the Calendar. You use the **Appointment tab** of this form to enter details such as the subject and location for the meeting and to select attendees you want to invite to the meeting. You can also add additional notes for the attendees and set a label color for the meeting so that attendees know what type of meeting it is. You use the **Scheduling tab** to view the schedules of all the attendees, and then set a meeting time that works for all. You can manually set a meeting time or specify that Outlook automatically schedule a meeting at the next available time that works for everyone. Once you've filled in all the necessary information in the Meeting Request form, you send it to the attendees.

Activity Steps

1. Click the **Calendar icon** 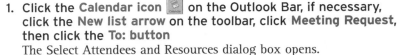 on the Outlook Bar, if necessary, click the **New list arrow** on the toolbar, click **Meeting Request**, then click the **To: button**
   The Select Attendees and Resources dialog box opens.

2. Click **Bettijean Riley** in the Name list, click **Required**, click **Ridley Carson** in the Name list, click **Optional**, then click **OK**

3. Type **Product launch planning meeting** in the Subject box, press **Tab**, type **Bengal Conference Room** in the Location box, then click the **Scheduling tab** (If a dialog box opens asking if you want to join the Microsoft Office Internet Free/Busy Service, click **Cancel**)

4. Use the horizontal scroll bar on the time grid to navigate to **tomorrow's date**

5. Click the **11:00 time slot** anywhere on the grid, then drag the **red border** of the time slot box to **12:00**
   See Figure 2-5.

6. Click the **Appointment tab**, then type **Bettijean, please prepare a competitive analysis for this meeting.** in the large text box in the bottom half of the screen

7. Click the **Label list arrow**, click **Needs Preparation**, compare your screen with Figure 2-6, then click **Send** on the toolbar

Click the Importance: High button on the toolbar to let attendees know that a particular meeting is a crucial one. Click the Importance: Low button on the toolbar to communicate that a meeting is not that important.

Figure 2-5: Scheduling tab of Meeting Request form

Your name should appear here

Icon indicates attendee is required

Icon indicates attendee is optional

Drag red border to here

Pattern shows that you have no information about these attendees' schedules at this time

Use this scroll bar to view the schedule for different days

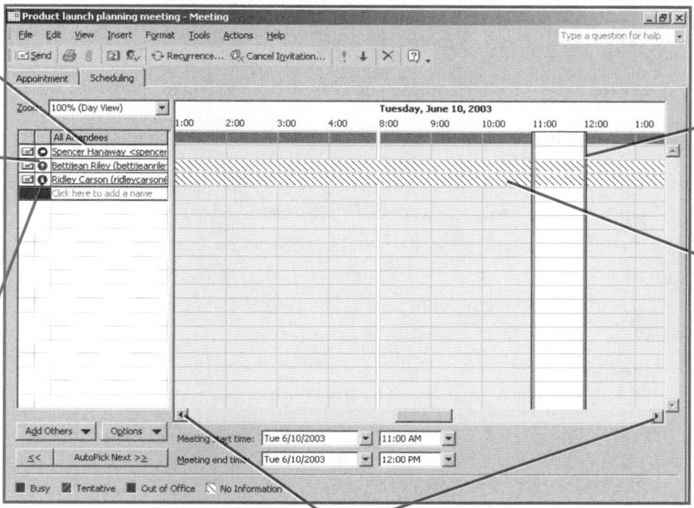

Figure 2-6: Completed Appointment tab of Meeting Request form

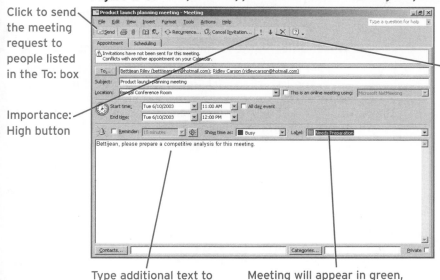

Click to send the meeting request to people listed in the To: box

Importance: High button

Importance: Low button

Type additional text to attendees here

Meeting will appear in green, indicating preparation is needed

extra!

Scheduling a meeting time automatically
Click the AutoPick Next button in the Scheduling tab to have Outlook automatically set the meeting for the next available time slot that works for all invitees.

Skill Set 2

Scheduling

Add Appointments, Meetings, and Events to the Calendar

Schedule Resources for Meetings

Sometimes a meeting requires special equipment, such as a flip chart, a projector, or a monitor. You can use Outlook to reserve this kind of item, called a **resource**, for a meeting. To do this, you invite the resource you need to the meeting, just as you would invite a person. However, this feature is not available to everyone using Outlook. In order to schedule resources for a meeting, you must have Outlook running on a Microsoft Exchange Server. In addition, each resource you want to invite must have its own e-mail box on the server. If both these requirements are met, then you can schedule resources. To schedule a resource, you use the Plan a Meeting form to set a time for your meeting, and then use the Select Attendees and Resources dialog box to choose the resources you want. You then use the Meeting Request form to invite all the attendees and resources to the meeting.

Sometimes, certain resources are restricted so that only a select group of people have the right to use them. If you try to schedule a resource you do not have permission to use, the resource will automatically reject your meeting request.

Activity Steps

1. Click the **Calendar icon** on the Outlook Bar, if necessary, click **Actions** on the menu bar, then click **Plan a Meeting**

2. Click **Add Others**, then click **Add from Address Book**
   If your school or company is connected to a Global Address List, you will see a list of resources in the Name list. *See Figure 2-7.*

3. Click **Bettijean Riley** in the Name list, then click **Required**

4. If you see a list of Resources in the Name list, click **one of the Resources in the list**, then click **Resources** (If you don't see a list of resources, click one of the names, then click **Resources**)
   The e-mail address of the person responsible for the resource you clicked appears in the Resources box.

5. Click **OK** (If a dialog box opens asking if you want to join the Microsoft Office Internet Free/Busy Service, click **Cancel**)

6. Use the horizontal scroll bar so that 3:00 tomorrow appears on the time grid, click **3:00**, then click **Make Meeting** at the bottom of the Plan a Meeting form

7. Type **Brainstorming meeting** in the Subject box, type **Siberian Conference Room** in the Location box, then click **Send**
   The Meeting form closes. The Plan a Meeting form shows the day of your newly planned meeting with the 3:00 time slot shaded in blue. *See Figure 2-8.*

8. Click **Close**, click **tomorrow's date** on the Date Navigator to view the new meeting, then click the **Today button** on the toolbar

Figure 2-7: Select Attendees and Resources dialog box

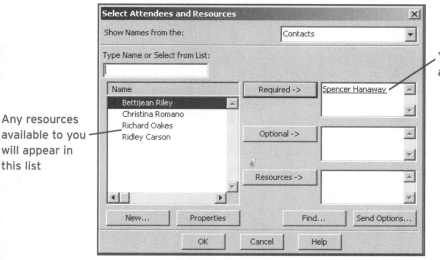

Your name should appear here

Any resources available to you will appear in this list

Figure 2-8: Plan a Meeting form with new meeting

Any resources you scheduled will be listed here

Click to select additional attendees and resources for the meeting

Your name should appear here

New meeting

extra!

Using the Microsoft Office Free/Busy Service

If you have Internet access and would like to let others know when you have free blocks of time, you can publish your available and busy times to the Microsoft Office Internet Free/Busy Service, a Web-based service offered through Microsoft. Doing this service lets other users plan meetings and schedule a time that works for you. For more Information, visit *http://freebusy. office.microsoft.com/ freebusy/freebusy.dll on the Web.*

Skill Set 2
Scheduling

Apply Conditional Formats to the Outlook Calendar
Apply Conditional Formats to the Calendar

If your Calendar is packed with appointments, it can be overwhelming to look at your schedule for a particular day and see everything you have to do. You can ease your mind and help make sense of your day by applying color-coding labels to each appointment. Color coding lets you see at a glance what kind of appointments are ahead for the day or week. For instance, you could label an appointment as Personal, Important, or Travel Required. You can assign a label to an appointment when you first create it, using the Appointment form. However, if your Calendar already contains lots of different appointments that are not color-labeled, you can apply labels to them using the Automatic Formatting dialog box. In this dialog box, you create rules for labeling a particular type of appointment. For instance, you could create a new rule called Dance Class and specify that the Personal label be applied to all appointments that have the words "dance class" in the Subject box.

Step 4
You can also open the Automatic Formatting dialog box by clicking View on the menu bar, pointing to Current View, clicking Customize Current View, then clicking Automatic Formatting in the View Summary dialog box.

Activity Steps

1. Click the **Calendar icon** on the Outlook Bar, if necessary, then click **next Thursday's date** on the Date Navigator

2. Click the **New Appointment button** , type **Board of Directors Meeting** in the Subject box, press **Tab**, type **Bengal Conference Room**, set the Start time at **10:00 AM**, set the End time at **12:00 PM**, then click **Save and Close**

3. Click the **Calendar Coloring button** on the toolbar, then click **Automatic Formatting**

4. Click **Add**, type **Board of Directors** in the Name box, click the **Label list arrow**, then click **Important**
   See Figure 2-9.

5. Click **Condition**, type **Board of Directors** in the Search for the words text box, then click **OK** two times
   The Board of Directors appointment that you created now appears in red with the conditional formatting applied, indicating it is an important meeting.
   See Figure 2-10.

6. Click the **Today button** on the toolbar

Figure 2-9: Automatic Formatting dialog box with new rule added

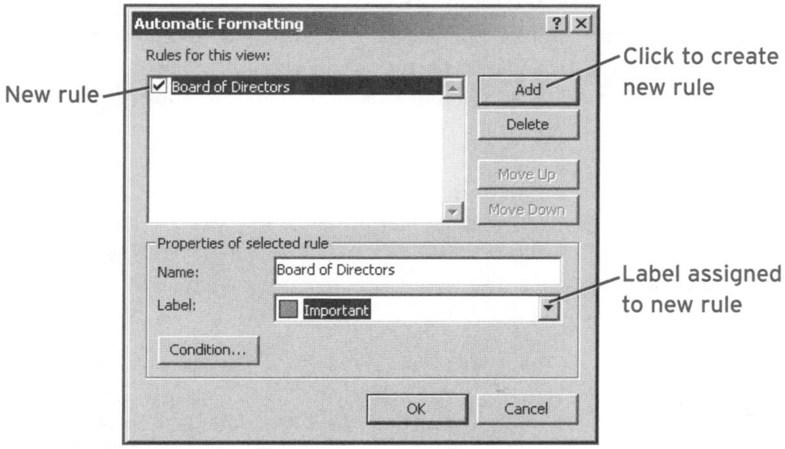

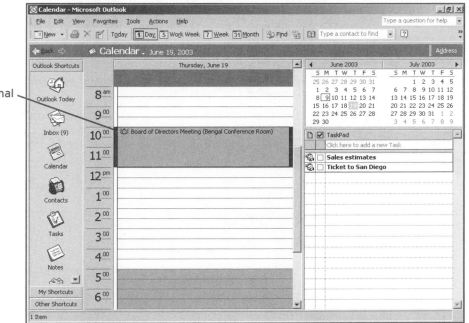

New rule

Click to create new rule

Label assigned to new rule

Figure 2-10: Calendar showing appointment with conditional formatting applied

Color-coded appointment with conditional formatting applied

Skill Set 2
Scheduling

Respond to Meeting Requests
Accept Meeting Requests

If you are involved in many projects, you will likely be asked to many meetings. If someone using Outlook needs you at a meeting, they will send a **meeting request** to your Inbox. A meeting request tells you the subject and location of the meeting as well as the date and time. You can quickly check your availability for a particular meeting by using the Calendar button on the Meeting Request form toolbar. This button opens your Calendar to the date of the meeting with the meeting inserted in the proposed time slot. You accept a meeting using the Accept button on the toolbar. When you accept, the meeting is automatically added to your Calendar. You can also include an additional message with your acceptance.

If you are not sure you can attend a particular meeting, you can accept it on a tentative basis by clicking the Tentative button on the Meeting form toolbar. Doing this tells the meeting organizer that you might not be able to attend. It also automatically enters the meeting in your Calendar.

Activity Steps

1. Click the **Inbox icon** on the Outlook Bar, then double-click the **Annual Review Meeting message** from Ridley Carson
   The Meeting form opens.

2. Maximize the Meeting form, if necessary, read the message, then click the **Calendar button** [⬚ Calendar...] on the toolbar
   The Calendar opens on top of the Meeting form, showing the date of the proposed meeting.
   See Figure 2-11.

3. Click the **Close button** in the Calendar window, then click **Accept** on the Meeting form toolbar

4. Click the **Edit the response before sending option button**, then click **OK**
   The Meeting Response form opens, with the insertion point in the response text box.

5. Type **I look forward to meeting with you.**
   See Figure 2-12.

6. Click **Send**

Figure 2-11: Calendar window open on top of Meeting form

Click to accept meeting

Click to accept meeting on a tentative basis

Calendar button on Meeting form toolbar

Time for proposed meeting (this time may be different for you, depending on your time zone)

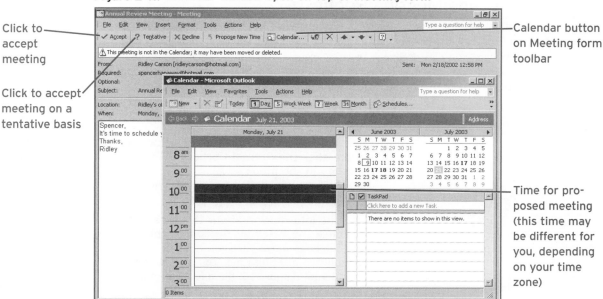

Figure 2-12: Accepted Meeting Response form with edited reply

Click to accept meeting and send reply message

Type additional text here

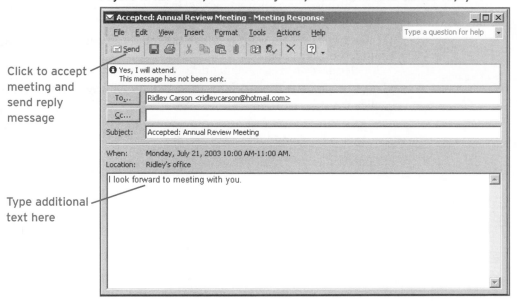

Skill Set 2
Scheduling

Respond to Meeting Requests
Decline Meeting Requests

If you receive a large number of meeting requests, or if you have a full schedule, you will probably not be able to attend all meetings to which you are invited. You can decline a meeting request using the Decline button in the Meeting form. You also have the option of including an additional message. When you decline, Outlook does not add the meeting to your Calendar.

Step 1
If you have many messages in your Inbox and can't find this particular message, click the From column heading to sort by the name of the Sender, then scroll to find the messages from Ridley Carson.

Activity Steps

1. Click the **Inbox icon** 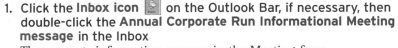 on the Outlook Bar, if necessary, then double-click the **Annual Corporate Run Informational Meeting message** in the Inbox
   The message information appears in the Meeting form.
   See Figure 2-13.

2. Read the information about this meeting in the Meeting form, then click the **Calendar button** on the Meeting form toolbar
   Your Calendar shows that you have no meetings that conflict with the proposed meeting time. You also need to check to see if you have a conflict on August 15, the day of the race.

3. Use the Date Navigator to navigate to August 2003, click **August 15, 2003** on the Date Navigator, then scroll to view 12 am in the Appointment area
   The Calendar shows that you are taking a vacation day on August 15.
   See Figure 2-14.

4. Click the Calendar window **Close button**, then click the **Decline button** on the toolbar
   An alert box opens containing three option buttons.

5. Click the **Edit the response before sending option button**, then click **OK**

6. Type **Sorry, I will be on vacation on August 15 so I cannot run in this race. Good luck!**

7. Click **Send**

Figure 2-13: Meeting Request form

Decline button

Subject of
proposed
meeting

Message
from
sender

Calendar
button

Time and
location of
proposed
meeting

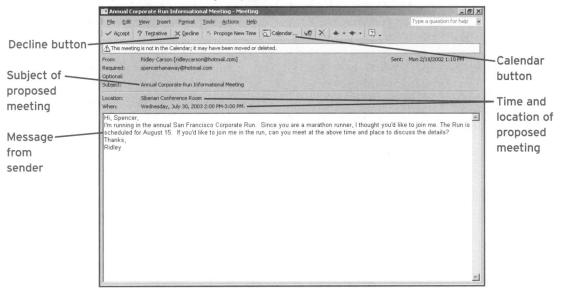

Figure 2-14: Calendar showing all-day event

All day event conflicts
with proposed subject
of meeting

Selected day

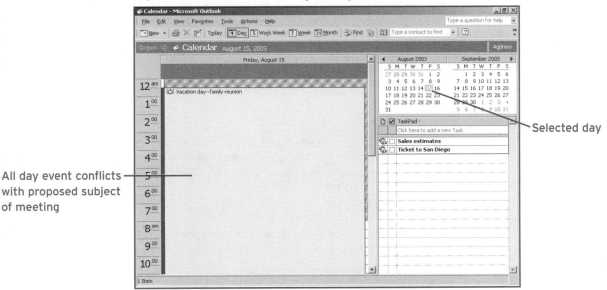

Skill Set 2

Scheduling

Respond to Meeting Requests

Propose New Meeting Times

You might get invited to an important meeting that you need to attend, but the proposed time conflicts with another previously scheduled appointment. When you receive such a meeting request in Outlook, you have the option of proposing new times for the meeting. To propose new times for a meeting, you use the Propose New Time button on the Meeting form toolbar. You can then view the schedules of the other attendees (if available to you), specify a different start and end time, and then use the Propose Time button to communicate your proposed new times to the sender. When you do this, the meeting is entered into your Calendar at the originally proposed time and is marked as tentative.

Step 4
You can also adjust the time in the Propose New Time form by dragging the red and green lines in the grid area.

Activity Steps

1. Click the **Inbox icon** on the Outlook Bar, if necessary, then double-click the **Maternity Tea Marketing Strategy Meeting message** from Ridley Carson

2. Click **Calendar** on the Meeting form toolbar
   If your computer clock is set to Eastern Standard Time, the Calendar shows that you have a dentist appointment that conflicts with the meeting.

3. Click the **Calendar Close button**, then click **Propose New Time** (If a dialog box opens asking if you want to join the Microsoft Office Internet Free/Busy Service, click **Cancel**)

4. Click the **second Meeting start time list arrow**, then click **11:00 AM**
   See Figure 2-15.

5. Click **Propose Time**
   The New Time Proposed form opens with text in the Subject box automatically included.

6. Type your e-mail address in the Cc: box, then click **Send** (If you are using an ISP, click **Send/Receive** two times to transfer your messages from your Outbox to the ISP's server and then to your Inbox)
   The message you just wrote should appear in your Inbox, with the new proposed time in the text area.

7. Double-click the **New Time Proposed message** in your Inbox
   See Figure 2-16.

8. Close the message form

Figure 2-15: Propose New Time form with new proposed start and end times

Yellow color indicates current time of meeting

Blue color indicates you are busy between 9:30 and 11:00 (your screen might not show this time as busy)

New proposed time

Figure 2-16: New Time Proposed Meeting Response form

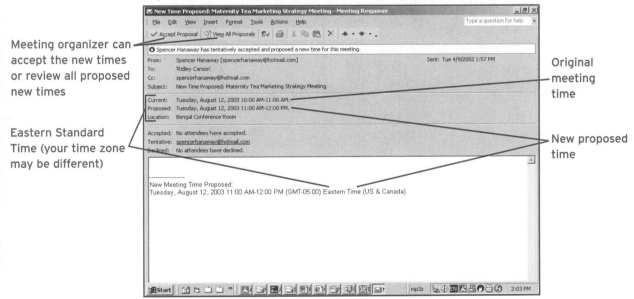

Meeting organizer can accept the new times or review all proposed new times

Eastern Standard Time (your time zone may be different)

Original meeting time

New proposed time

Skill Set 2

Scheduling

Use Categories to Manage Appointments
Assign Categories to Appointments

When your Calendar is jammed with appointments, it's helpful to group them into different categories so that you can look at related appointments together. Outlook comes with a variety of predefined categories that you can assign to any appointment, including Personal, Business, Ideas, and many others. You can also create your own categories. For instance, if you are organizing a food drive, you could create the category Food Drive and assign this name to all the appointments related to it. You can also assign multiple categories to a single appointment. You assign, view, and add categories using the Categories dialog box, which you open from the Appointment form.

To view your appointments by category, click View on the menu bar, point to Current View, then click By Category.

Activity Steps

1. Click the **Calendar icon** 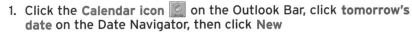 on the Outlook Bar, click **tomorrow's date** on the Date Navigator, then click **New**

2. Type **Competitive analysis for Bali Tea product line** in the Subject box, press **Tab**, then type **My office** in the Location box

3. Set the Start time at **2:00 PM** and the End time at **3:00 PM**

4. Click **Categories** to open the Categories dialog box

5. Type **Bali Tea Product Development** in the Item(s) belong to these categories text box, then click **Add to List**
   The new category is added to the list and is automatically selected. *See Figure 2-17.*

6. Click the **Competition** check box, then click **OK**
   The two categories you selected appear in the Categories box. *See Figure 2-18.*

7. Click **Save and Close** on the Appointment form toolbar

Figure 2-17: Categories dialog box with new category added

Type new category here

New category added to list and selected

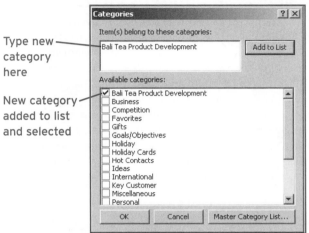

Figure 2-18: Appointment form showing selected categories in Categories box

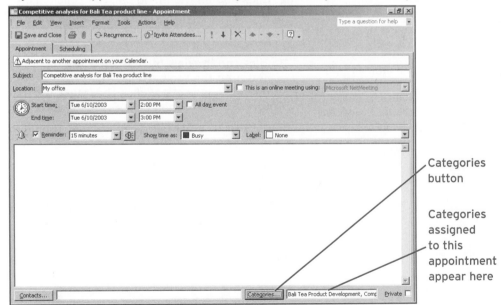

Categories button

Categories assigned to this appointment appear here

Skill Set 2
Scheduling

Print Calendars
Print the Calendar in Different Views

Because carrying your computer around with you is not always practical, you will probably find it helpful to print your Calendar on occasion, so that you can keep track of your appointments while on the go. Just as you can view your Calendar in different ways, you can also print it in a variety of formats. The format you choose is called a **print style**, and these include Daily, Weekly, and Monthly, among others. You use the Print dialog box to select a print style and a date range. For each print style, you can choose from a variety of formatting options using the Page Setup dialog box, accessible from the Print dialog box. For instance, you can choose to print a lined area for writing notes, or you can change the font for headings. To save paper, it's a good idea to preview your Calendar with your chosen settings before printing.

To print an entire month of the Calendar, click Monthly Style in the Print style area of the Print dialog box, then click OK.

Activity Steps

1. Click the **Calendar icon** on the Outlook Bar, if necessary, then use the Date Navigator to navigate to **July 28, 2003**

2. Click **File** on the menu bar, then click **Print**
   The Print dialog box opens, with the Daily Style selected in the Print style list.
   See Figure 2-19.

3. Click the **Preview button**, view the daily schedule, click **Page Setup** on the toolbar, click the **Notes area (lined) check box** in the Options section, click the **Paper tab**, click the **Landscape option button**, then click **Print Preview**

4. Click **Print** on the Preview toolbar, then click **OK** in the Print dialog box

5. Click **File** on the menu bar, click **Print** to open the Print dialog box, click **Weekly Style** ☐ in the Print style list box, click **Preview**, then click in the upper-left (Monday) square
   The top half of the Calendar is magnified, making it possible to read the appointments for Monday and Thursday.
   See Figure 2-20.

6. Click **Print** on the Preview toolbar, then click **OK** in the Print dialog box

Figure 2-19: Print dialog box

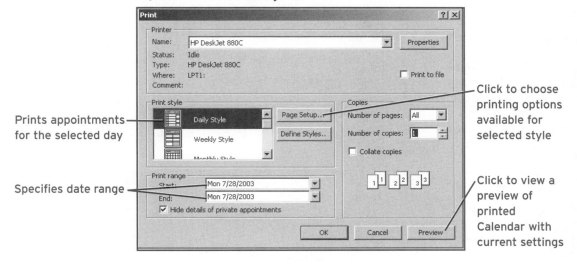

Prints appointments for the selected day

Specifies date range

Click to choose printing options available for selected style

Click to view a preview of printed Calendar with current settings

Figure 2-20: Print Preview window showing top half of weekly calendar

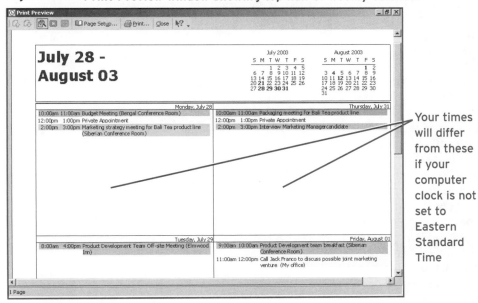

Your times will differ from these if your computer clock is not set to Eastern Standard Time

Skill Set 2
Scheduling

Target Your Skills

1 Use Figure 2-21 as a guide. Send a meeting request to Ridley Carson, Bettijean Riley, and yourself for the date, time, and location shown. Mark the meeting as private. Send the meeting request. Open the meeting request in your Inbox.

2 Using Figure 2-22 as a guide, enter the following appointments in your Calendar on the date shown:
9:00 Inventory Meeting
12:00 Lunch with Joe (mark as private)
3:00 Write inventory report
5:00 Farewell party
Specify a location and apply appropriate labels for each. Create a category called Inventory that has the Important label. Then, use conditional formatting to apply the Important label to all appointments that have "inventory" in the subject line. Print the Calendar using the settings shown.

Figure 2-21

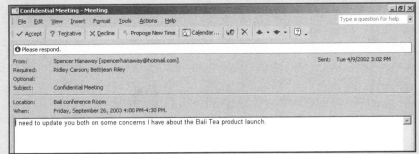

Figure 2-22

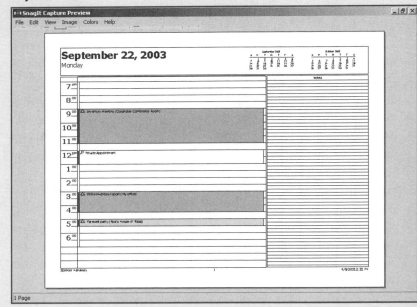

Skill List

1. Move messages between folders
2. Search for messages
3. Save messages in alternate file formats
4. Use categories to manage messages
5. Set message options

If you rely on e-mail for many of your daily communications, you might find yourself getting overwhelmed by a huge volume of messages. To avoid having an overcrowded Inbox, it's important that you organize the messages you want to save so that they are easy to retrieve. Outlook provides many tools for managing your messages. In this skill set, you'll learn to create folders to help you organize your messages into logical groups. You'll also learn to move messages between folders and to find messages by specifying search text or assigning categories. You'll learn how to save message files in different formats so they can be viewed on computers where Outlook is not installed, and how to archive old messages to free up space in your Inbox and other folders. Finally, you'll learn to modify the settings for delivering messages.

Skill Set 3
Managing Messages

Move Messages Between Folders
Move a Message to a Different Folder

If you receive a large amount of e-mail on a regular basis, your Inbox can fill up quickly. You will probably delete many old messages, but you may also want to keep some. To help you quickly locate the messages you need, you can create folders in which to store related messages. For instance, if you are coordinating all the arrangements for an upcoming sales meeting, you could create a folder called Sales Meeting and place all the messages related to the sales meeting in this folder. You use the Move Items dialog box to move messages to an existing folder or to create a new folder. If you create a new folder, that folder will be contained by the selected folder in the Move Items dialog box.

Activity

To move a message using the mouse, drag the message from the Inbox to the desired folder in the Folder List.

1. Start Outlook, then if necessary, choose your **Profile name**, click **OK**, enter your **password**, click **OK**, click the **Inbox icon** on the Outlook Bar, then click the **Subject column heading** to sort your messages by the Subject field

2. Click the **RE: Regional meeting message from Linda Miller**, press and hold **[Shift]**, then click the original **Regional meeting message** from Stephen James so that a total of four messages with Regional meeting in the Subject line are selected (You might have to scroll to see all four messages)

3. Click the **Move to Folder button** on the Standard toolbar, then click **Move to Folder**
   The Move Items dialog box opens.
   See Figure 3-1.

4. Click **Inbox**, if necessary, click **New** to open the Create New Folder dialog box, type **Regional Meeting**, then click **OK**

5. Click **No** in the dialog box that opens asking if you would like to add a shortcut to this folder to your Outlook Bar, then click **OK**

6. Click the **plus sign** next to the Inbox icon in the Folder List, if necessary, then click the **Regional Meeting folder** in the Folder list
   See Figure 3-2.

7. Click the **Inbox icon** on the Outlook Bar, click the **Folder List Close button**, then click the **Received column heading** to sort your messages by date

Figure 3-1: Move Items dialog box

New folder will be contained in the Inbox folder

Available folders

Click to create new folder

The number of unread items in your folders might be different

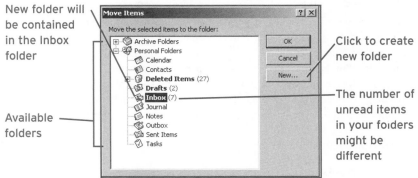

Figure 3-2: Messages moved to new folder

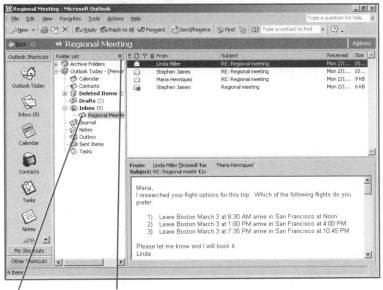

Selected new folder

Folder List Close button

Skill Set 3
Managing Messages

Search for Messages
Search for a Message

If you have a large number of messages in your Inbox or another folder and want to find one message in particular, it's not very practical to look for the message by scanning the contents of a folder. The **Find bar** makes it fast and easy to locate messages. You can use the Find bar to specify the text you want to locate and the folder where you want to look. The search text you specify is not case-sensitive and can be located in the message body or in the subject field. This means that you can find a particular message even if the only characteristic you remember about it was a specific word used in the message body. To open the Find bar, you use the Find button on the Standard toolbar.

Step 2
You can also open the Find bar by pressing [Ctrl][E], or by clicking Tools on the menu bar, then clicking Find.

Activity

1. Click the **Inbox icon** on the Outlook Bar, if necessary

2. Click the **Find button** on the Standard toolbar
   The Find bar appears above your list of messages.

3. Type **Denver** in the Look for box, then click **Find Now**
   All of the messages in the Inbox that have Denver in the Subject line or message body appear.
   See Figure 3-3.

4. Click the **Clear button** on the Find bar
   You could do another search, or close the Find bar.

5. Click the **Find button**
   The Find bar closes.

Figure 3-3: Messages in Inbox that contain the word "Denver"

Find button

Find bar

Type search
words here

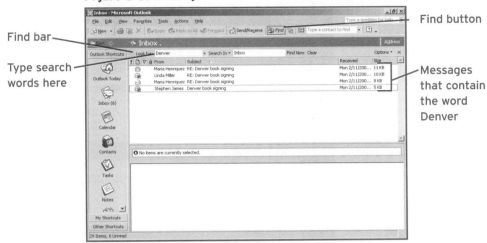

Messages
that contain
the word
Denver

extra!

Using the Advanced Find feature

You can use the Advanced Find dialog box, shown in Figure 3-4, to refine your search for a particular message or other Outlook item. For instance, you can search for messages from a particular sender or to a recipient. You can also specify that the search results contain only items sent, received, created, or modified in a particular time frame. If you assign categories to your messages or items, you can also set the search criteria for a specified category. You can also specify that the search results contain only read or unread messages, attachments or no attachments, or have a specific Importance level assigned to them. To open the Advanced Find dialog box, click Options on the Find bar, then click Advanced Find.

Figure 3-4: Advanced Find dialog box

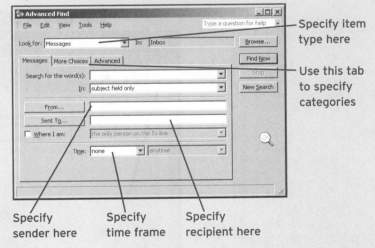

Specify item
type here

Use this tab
to specify
categories

Specify
sender here

Specify
time frame

Specify
recipient here

Skill Set 3
Managing Messages

Save Messages in Alternate File Formats
Save Messages as HTML files

By default, messages and all other items created in Outlook are saved with a .msg file extension. There might be times when you want to save an e-mail message in a different file format. For instance, if you need to view your message files on a computer that is not running Outlook, and want to preserve the formatting of the message, you can save it as an .htm file. When you save a file as an htm file, all the formatting is preserved. To save a file in .htm format, you use the Save As dialog box. When you open a message file in .htm format, it opens in your default browser.

Activity Steps

1. Click the **Inbox icon** on the Outlook Bar, if necessary, click the **Flight to Atlanta message** from Linda Miller, click **File** on the menu bar, then click **Save As**
   See Figure 3-5.

2. Verify that **HTML (*.htm; *.html)** is selected in the Save as type list box, then navigate to the folder where your Project Files are stored

3. Click **Save**

4. Click **Other Shortcuts** on the Outlook Bar, click **My Computer**, then navigate to the folder where your Project Files are stored

5. Double-click the **Flight to Atlanta.htm file** you just saved
   The message opens in Internet Explorer.
   See Figure 3-6.

6. Click the **Internet Explorer Close button**, then click the **Outlook program button** on the taskbar

7. Click the **Outlook Shortcuts** on the Outlook Bar

Figure 3-5: Save As dialog box

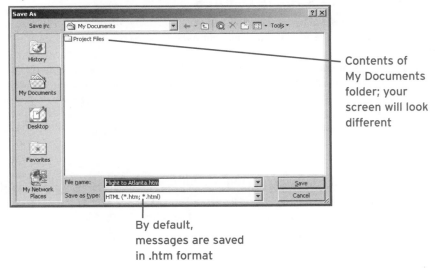

Contents of
My Documents
folder; your
screen will look
different

By default,
messages are saved
in .htm format

Figure 3-6: Saved message in .htm format in Internet Explorer

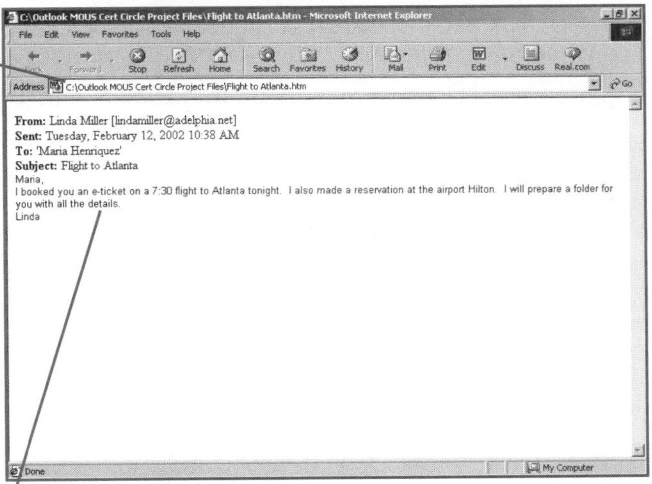

Location of file
appears here

Formatting of
original message
is preserved

extra!

Deleting messages
To delete messages that
you no longer want,
select the unwanted
messages in the Inbox
or any other folder, then
press [Del] or click the
Delete button on the
toolbar. Messages that
you delete are not
permanently removed
from your computer,
however; they are
moved to the Deleted
Items folder. To clear
the Deleted Items
folder, right-click the
Deleted Items folder in
the Folder List, click
Empty "Deleted Items"
Folder on the shortcut
menu, then click Yes.

Skill Set 3

Managing Messages

Save Messages in Alternate File Formats
Save Messages as Text Files

There might be times when you would like to save a message file in **Text Only format**, which saves the text of a message but does not preserve the formatting of the original message. Saving a message as a text file in Text Only format is often a good idea if you need to view a message on another computer that does not have Outlook installed, and if you are not concerned about preserving the original formatting. To save a message file as a text file, you use the Save As dialog box. Files saved as text files have a .txt extension. When you open a message file that has been saved as a text file, it opens in Notepad by default.

By default, all messages you create in Outlook are in HTML format. To change the default message format, click Tools on the menu bar, click Options, click the Mail Format tab, click the Compose in this message format list arrow, then click the format you want.

Activity

1. Click the **Inbox icon** on the Outlook Bar, if necessary

2. Click the **Flight to Atlanta message from Linda Miller**, click **File** on the menu bar, then click **Save As**

3. Click the **Save as type list arrow**, click **Text Only (*.txt)**, then navigate to the folder where your Project Files are stored
See Figure 3-7.

4. Click **Save**

5. Click **Other Shortcuts** on the Outlook Bar, click **My Computer**, then navigate to the folder where your Project Files are stored

6. Double-click the **Flight to Atlanta.txt file** you just saved
The message opens in Notepad. Only part of the message text fits in the NotePad window because Word Wrap is turned off.

7. Click **Format** on the menu bar, then click **Word Wrap**
All the message text now fits in the Notepad window.
See Figure 3-8.

8. Click the **Notepad Close button**, click the **Outlook program button** on the taskbar, then click **Outlook Shortcuts** on the Outlook Bar

Figure 3-7: Save As dialog box

Save as type
list arrow

Figure 3-8: Message saved as text file opened in Notepad

Message
retained
none of the
formatting of
the original
.msg file

Message opens
in Notepad

extra!

Understanding where items are stored

Unless you use the Microsoft Exchange Server, any Outlook items you create or receive or any folders you create in Outlook are saved to a data file known as a **Personal Folders file** on your computer's hard drive. The default data file to which items are stored is Outlook.pst. If you use a Microsoft Exchange Server, your Outlook items are stored on the server.

Skill Set 3

Managing Messages

Use Categories to Manage Messages
Assign Categories to Messages

To make finding messages or other items easier, you can assign categories to them. A **category** is a keyword or phrase that helps you organize items so you can sort them in meaningful ways. Outlook comes with a variety of predefined categories that you can assign to messages and other items, including Business, Personal, Miscellaneous, and many others. You can assign predefined categories to your messages, or you can create new categories appropriate for your specific needs. For example, you might want to create a category called Company Meeting and assign all the messages relating to the company meeting to it. You could then search for all the messages that have the Company Meeting category assigned to them. You use the Advanced Find dialog box to search for messages assigned to a particular category.

Step 5
You can also open the Advanced Find dialog box by clicking Find on the Standard toolbar to open the Find bar, clicking Options on the Find bar, then clicking Advanced Find.

Activity

1. Click the Inbox icon 📧 on the Outlook Bar, if necessary, then click the **Subject column heading** in the Inbox to sort the messages by subject

2. Scroll to locate the four messages that contain the words **Denver book signing**, then select all four of these messages

3. Click **Edit** on the menu bar, then click **Categories**
   A list of available categories appears. You can add a new one. *See Figure 3-9.*

4. Click the **Item(s) belong to these categories text box**, type **Book Signings**, then click **Add to List**
   The Book Signings category now appears in the list and is checked. You can use this new category to search for related messages.

5. Click **OK**, click **Tools** on the menu bar, then click **Advanced Find**

6. Click the **More Choices tab**, click **Categories**, click **Book Signings** in the Available Categories list, click **OK**, then click **Find Now**
   The four messages to which you applied the Book Signings category appear at the bottom of the dialog box.
   See Figure 3-10.

7. Click the **Advanced Find dialog box Close button**, then click the **Received column heading** to sort the messages by date

Figure 3-9: Categories dialog box

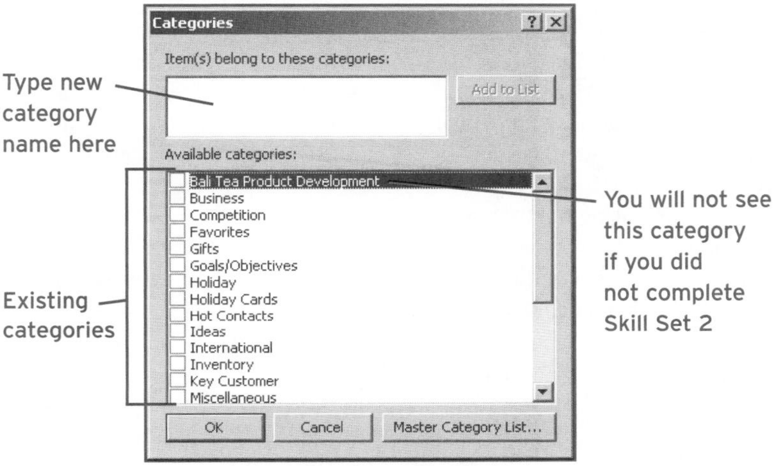

Type new category name here

Existing categories

You will not see this category if you did not complete Skill Set 2

Figure 3-10: Advanced Find dialog box

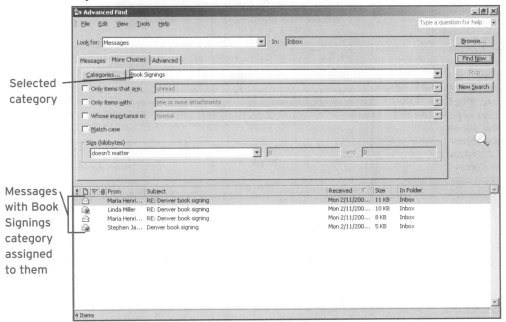

Selected category

Messages with Book Signings category assigned to them

Skill Set 3
Managing Messages

Set Message Options
Modify Message Settings

Unless you specify otherwise, messages you write are sent with default settings indicating a normal level of importance and sensitivity. Sometimes you might want to communicate a higher level of urgency to your recipient or mark a particular message as confidential so the recipient handles it with care. You can change these and other message settings using the Message Options dialog box. You can use this dialog box to set the level of importance and sensitivity, and to include **voting buttons**, which are buttons that appear in the recipients' message form to streamline their response. Voting buttons are useful if you need a quick yes/no or accept/decline response. You can also set delivery options using this dialog box and assign a category to a message.

To add your own voting buttons to a message, click the Use voting buttons check box in the Options dialog box, select the voting button names that appear in the Use voting buttons text box, then type new button names, separating each name with a semicolon.

Activity

1. Click the **Inbox icon** on the Outlook Bar, click the **New Mail Message button** , type **stephenjames@adelphia.net** in the To: box, type your e-mail address in the Cc: box, type **New series** in the Subject box, then press **[Tab]**

2. Type **Do you think we should move forward with the Children's Adventure Guide series?**

3. Click **Options** on the toolbar
   See Figure 3-11.

4. Click the **Importance list arrow**, click **High**, click the **Sensitivity list arrow**, then click **Confidential**

5. Click the **Use voting buttons check box**, click the **Use voting buttons list arrow**, then click **Yes; No**

6. Click the **Request a delivery receipt for this message check box**, click **Close**, then click **Send** on the Message form toolbar

7. Click the **Send/Receive button** on the toolbar, if necessary, then wait until the New series message appears in the Inbox
   When the New series message appears, notice that a red exclamation point indicates this message has a high level of importance.

8. Double-click the **New series message**, compare your screen to Figure 3-12, then click the **Message form Close button**

Figure 3-11: Message Options dialog box

Click to change the level of importance

Click to change Sensitivity setting to Confidential

Click to specify that voting buttons appear in recipients' message form

Click to receive acknowledgment of delivery

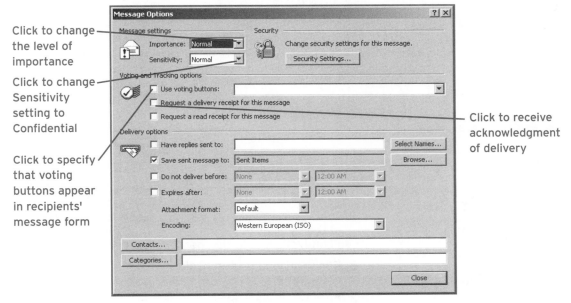

Figure 3-12: Message marked as Confidential with voting buttons

Voting buttons

Yellow banner items indicate message has high importance and is confidential

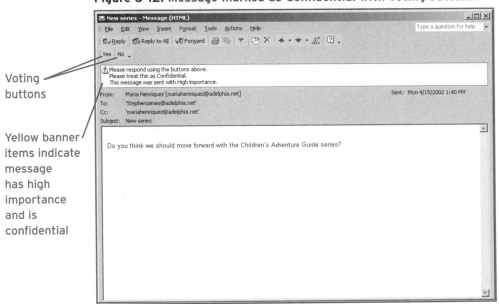

Skill Set 3
Managing Messages

Set Message Options
Modify Delivery Options

Sometimes it might be important to have a message delivered according to set specifications. For instance, you might want to choose a window of time when you want a message to be delivered, or to specify that the replies to a certain message be sent to another person. If you are the President of a company, you might send out a message to your employees asking for input on a particular issue. Rather than receiving all the replies yourself, you could specify that replies get sent to your assistant. You set message delivery options using the Delivery options section of the Message Options dialog box.

If you would like to receive a message notifying you that the recipient has opened your message, click the Request a read receipt for this message check box in the Message Options dialog box.

Activity

1. Click the **Inbox icon** on the Outlook Bar, if necessary, then click **the New Mail Message button**

2. Type your e-mail address in the To: box, type **Special Message** in the Subject box, press **[Tab]**, then type **Happy Company Founders' Day!** in the message body

3. Click **Options** on the toolbar to open the Message Options dialog box

4. Click the **Have replies sent to: check box**, then verify that your name appears in the text box

5. Click the **Do not deliver before check box**, then set the date box to the date of your next birthday, and set the time to 8:00 AM
   See Figure 3-13.

6. Click **Close**

7. Click **Send**

Figure 3-13: Message Options dialog box with modified delivery options

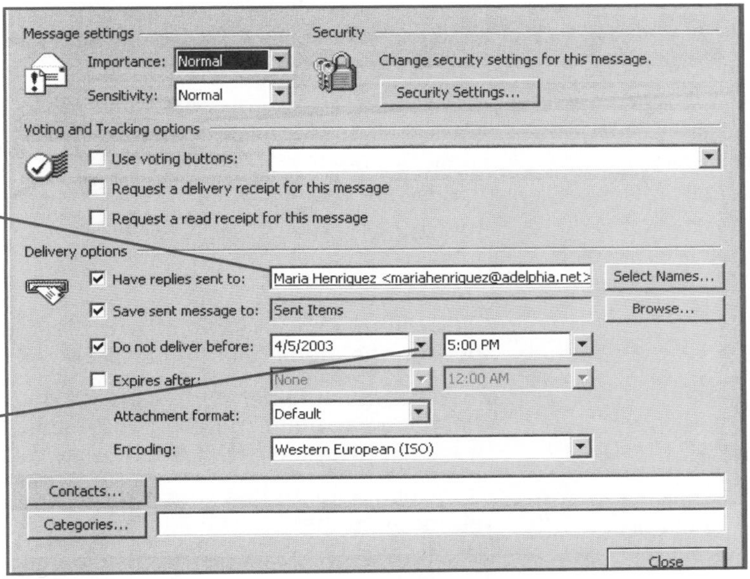

Specify e-mail address of person you want to receive replies

Click to choose delivery date

extra!

Setting other message options

In addition to specifying a window of time for delivering a message, you can also set a number of other options in the Message Options dialog box. To set an expiration date for a message, click the Expires after check box, then enter a date in the Expires after text box. To associate a contact with a message, click the Contacts button, then choose a contact name from the list. When you do this, the message will appear as an e-mail item in the Activities tab of the Contact form for that contact. To assign a category to a message, click Categories to open the Categories dialog box, click one or more categories from the list, then click OK.

Skill Set 3

Managing Messages

Set Message Options
Archive Messages Manually

After having an e-mail account for a long time, you might find it helpful to **archive**, or store, your old messages. The Outlook **AutoArchive feature** automatically removes files from your Inbox and other folders that you specify and stores them in an archive file, where they are still accessible but out of the way. By default, AutoArchive is always on. At specific times, it removes old items from folders and places them in the archive file. If you want to archive items from a particular folder earlier or later than the time that is specified for AutoArchive, you can use the Archive dialog box to archive these items manually.

To change the settings for how your Outlook items are automatically archived, right-click the folder whose AutoArchive settings you want to change, click Properties, click the AutoArchive tab, then specify the time interval that you want for archiving these items.

Activity

1. Click the **Inbox icon** on the Outlook Bar, if necessary, click **View** on the menu bar, then click **Folder List**

2. Click the **Inbox folder** in the Folder List, if necessary, click **File** on the menu bar, point to **New**, click **Folder**, type **Travel** in the Name box, click **OK**, then click **No** in the dialog box that appears

3. Drag the **Flight to Los Angeles message** from Linda Miller from the Inbox to the Travel folder in the Folder List, then click the **Travel folder**
   The Travel folder now contains the Flight to Los Angeles message.

4. Click **File** on the menu bar, then click **Archive**
   See Figure 3-14.

5. Click the **Archive items older than list arrow**, then click **Today**

6. Click **OK**
   After a few seconds, the Flight to Los Angeles message is removed from the Travel folder in the Inbox and is placed in a new Travel folder located in the Archive Folders folder.

7. In the Folders list, click the **+ sign** next to Archive Folders, click the **+ sign** next to Inbox, then click the **Travel folder**
   See Figure 3-15.

8. Click the **Inbox icon** on the Outlook Bar, then click the **Folder List Close button**

Figure 3-14: Archive dialog box

Selected folder

Files contained in selected folder will be archived to file specified in this path (yours will be different)

Click to open Calendar to set date

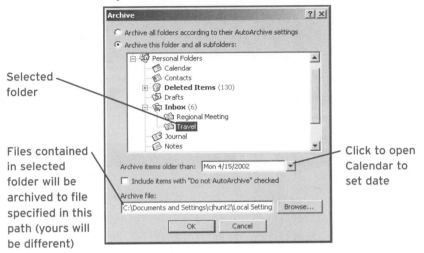

Figure 3-15: Folder List showing archived item

Travel folder that was automatically created, listed under Archive Folders

Travel folder

Message item is now archived

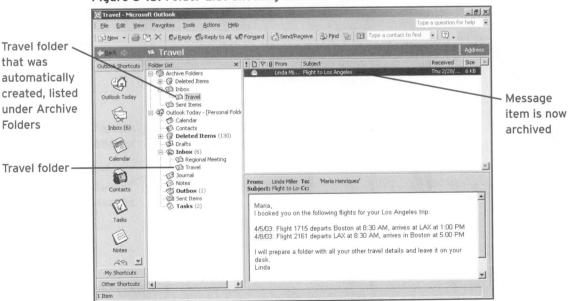

Skill Set 3
Managing Messages

Target Your Skills

1 Use Figure 3-16 as a guide. Write a message to yourself explaining that you just won two tickets for a Carribbean Cruise. Include Yes/No voting buttons, set the Importance level at High, the Sensitivity level to Personal, and specify that replies be sent to you. Send the message, then when you receive it, move it to a new folder you create called Vacation. Finally, save the message first as an .htm file and then as a text file.

Figure 3-16

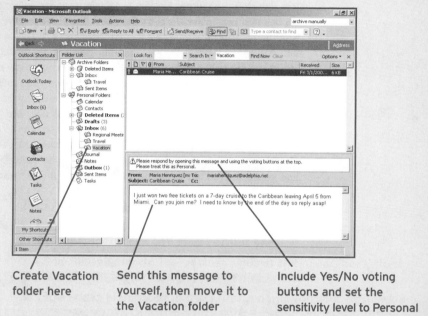

Create Vacation folder here

Send this message to yourself, then move it to the Vacation folder

Include Yes/No voting buttons and set the sensitivity level to Personal

2 Use Figure 3-17 as a guide. Use the Find bar to locate all the messages in your Inbox that have the word cancer in them. Assign a new category to these messages called Cancer Walk. Finally, archive these files.

Figure 3-17

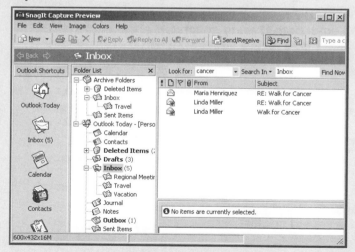

Skill List

1. Create and edit contacts
2. Organize and sort contacts
3. Link contacts to activities and Journal entries

Keeping track of all the people in your work and personal life can be a daunting task and is often more than a paper-based address book or Rolodex can handle. In this skill set, you will learn to use the Contacts component of Outlook to keep track of names, addresses, phone numbers, and other information for the people with whom you interact. You will start by creating new contact entries and editing existing ones. You will then learn ways to organize your contacts by viewing and sorting them in various ways, and grouping them by categories. Finally, you will learn to link other Outlook items to contacts so that you can keep track of the activities associated with a particular contact.

Skill Set 4

Creating and Managing Contacts

Create and Edit Contacts

Add Contacts

You can use the Contacts folder in Outlook to store information about your business associates, friends, and family. In Outlook, a **contact** is a person whose phone numbers, as well as e-mail, home, and business addresses, you want to keep track of. You open the Contacts folder using the Contacts icon on the Outlook Bar. When you first open the Contacts folder, all your contacts appear in **Address Cards view**, which displays a partial listing of each contact's information on what looks like a Rolodex card. To add a new contact, you use the **Contact form**. You use the General tab of the Contact form to enter the name, job title, company, address, phone numbers, and e-mail addresses of a contact. You can use the Details tab to enter additional information about a contact's job as well as personal information such as nickname, birthday, or spouse's name. The other tabs on the Contact form let you keep track of a contact's activities, send an encrypted message to a contact using a digital certificate, and view selected fields about a contact. Table 4-1 describes the Contact form toolbar buttons.

Step 2
You can enter up to three different addresses for a single contact. Click the list arrow next to the Address text box, click Business, Home, or Other to identify the type of address it is, then type the new address. You can add multiple e-mails, phone, and fax numbers as well.

Activity Steps

1. Start Outlook, if necessary, choose your **Profile name**, click **OK**, enter your **password**, then click the **Contacts icon** 📇 on the Outlook Bar
    The Contacts window opens in Address Cards view.

2. Click the **New Contact button** 📇 New ▾ on the toolbar
    The Contact form appears.
    See Figure 4-1.

3. Type **Spencer Hanaway** in the Full Name text box, then press **[Tab]**
    Notice that Hanaway, Spencer automatically appears in the File as box. Outlook will file this name with the last name listed first.

4. Type **Senior Product Manager** in the Job title text box, then press **[Tab]**

5. Type **Tiger Tea Company** in the Company text box, click in the Address text box, type **1445 Pacific Way**, press **[Enter]**, type **San Francisco, CA 94115**, then verify that there is a check mark in the This is the mailing address check box

6. Click in the Business phone text box, type **(415) 555-4563**, click in the E-mail text box, type **spencerhanaway@hotmail.com**, then press **[Tab]**
    The Display as text box shows how the e-mail address will appear.

7. Click the **Details tab**, type **Product Development** in the Department text box, then click **Save and Close** on the toolbar

Figure 4-1: Blank Contact form

Details tab

Type first and last name here

Address text box

Business phone box

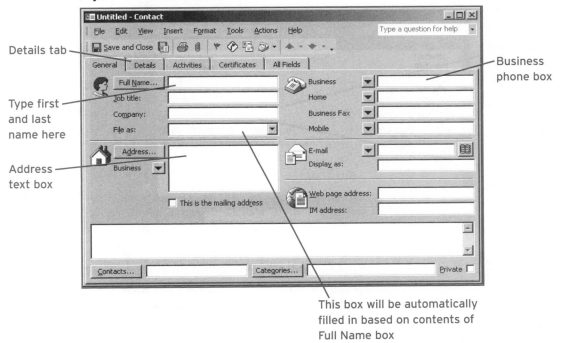

This box will be automatically filled in based on contents of Full Name box

Table 4-1: Contact form toolbar buttons

button	button name	what it does
Save and Close	Save and Close	Saves the current contact and closes the Contact form
	Save and New	Saves the current contact and opens a new, blank Contact form
	Print	Prints all Contact form information for the current contact
	Insert File	Opens the Insert File dialog box, where you select a file to attach to the contact
	Follow Up	Lets you identify a follow-up action and due date for the current contact and adds it to the Calendar
	Display Map of Address	Displays a geographic map of contact's address
	New Message to Contact	Opens the Message form with the current contact's e-mail address in To: box
	AutoDialer	Automatically dials a phone number you select or specify
	Previous Item	Opens a Contact form containing information for the previous contact
	Next Item	Opens a Contact form containing information for the next contact

Skill Set 4
Creating and Managing Contacts

Create and Edit Contacts
Edit Contacts

Because people move, get promoted, get married, and take new jobs, you will likely need to make changes to the contacts in your Contacts folder from time to time. To edit the information for a contact, you need to open the Contact form. You make editing changes just as you would in a word processor such as Word: you select the text you want to change, and then type the new text. You can also use the tools on the toolbar to enhance the information about a contact. For instance, you could attach a photograph of the contact using the Attach File button. You could also use the Follow Up button to insert a reminder to yourself to call, arrange a meeting, or respond to the contact in some way.

To remove a follow up flag, click Clear Flag in the Flag for Follow Up dialog box. When you have completed a follow up action, click the Completed check box.

Activity Steps

1. Click the **Contacts icon** on the Outlook Bar, if necessary, then double-click the **Riley, Bettijean** address card

2. Click to the left of **Product Manager** in the Job title text box, type **Associate**, then press **[Spacebar]**

3. Click in the Company box, then type **Tiger Tea Company**

4. In the Address section, click the **Business list arrow, click Home**, click in the Address box, type **2305 California Street, #3B**, press **[Enter]**, then type **San Francisco, CA 94123**
   See Figure 4-2.

5. Click the **Details tab**, type **Product Development** in the Department box, click in the **Manager's name box**, then type **Spencer Hanaway**

6. Click the **Follow Up button** on the toolbar, click the **Flag to: list arrow**, click **Arrange Meeting**, then click the **first Due by list arrow**
   See Figure 4-3.

7. Click **Today**, click the **second Due by list arrow**, click **5:00 PM**, click **OK**, then click **Save and Close** on the toolbar
   Notice that a Follow Up Flag note appears just below Riley, Bettijean.

Figure 4-2: Edited General tab of Contact form

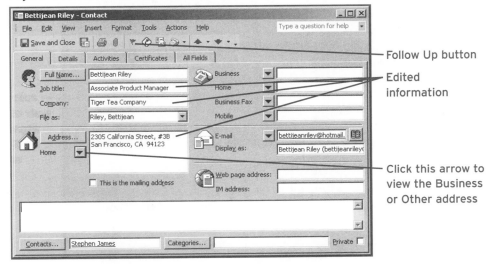

Follow Up button

Edited information

Click this arrow to view the Business or Other address

Figure 4-3: Flag for Follow Up dialog box

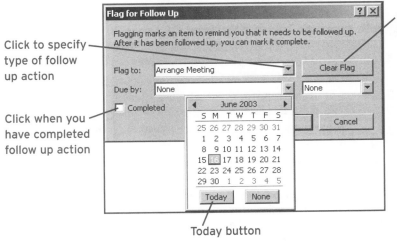

Click to specify type of follow up action

Click when you have completed follow up action

Click to remove flag from contact

Today button

extra!

Adding a contact based on an existing contact

If you need to add a contact who works at the same company as another contact in your Contacts folder, select the address card of the original contact, click Actions on the menu bar, then click New Contact from Same Company. The Contact form opens with the company, address, and phone boxes filled in.

Skill Set 4

Creating and Managing Contacts

Organize and Sort Contacts
Organize Contacts Using Categories

You can organize the contacts in your Contacts folder by assigning different categories to them. A **category** is a word or phrase you use to keep track of items so you can easily find or sort them into related groups. For instance, you might want to assign the VIP category to all the senior executives at your company. Outlook provides a number of predefined categories, from which you can choose, and you can also create your own. You can use the **Ways to Organize pane** to assign new or existing categories to your contacts. You can also assign more than one category to a contact. Once you assign categories to all your contacts, you can view all the contacts in a particular category using By Category view.

Activity Steps

1. Click the **Contacts icon** on the Outlook Bar, if necessary, then click the **Organize button** on the toolbar
   The Ways to Organize Contacts pane appears.
   See Figure 4-4.

2. Click **Oakes, Richard**, press and hold **[Ctrl]**, click **Romano, Christina**, release **[Ctrl]**, click the **Add Contacts selected below to list arrow**, scroll down until you see **Key Customer**, click **Key Customer**, then click **Add**

3. Click **Carson, Ridley**, press and hold **[Ctrl]**, click **Hanaway, Spencer**, click **Riley, Bettijean**, then release **[Ctrl]**

4. Click in the **Create a new category called box**, type **Product Development Team**, then click **Create**

5. Click **Add** to assign the Product Development Team category to the three selected contacts

6. Click **View** on the menu bar, point to **Current View**, then click **By Category**
   The two categories you assigned to your contacts appear in a table. You need to expand each category to view its associated contacts.

7. Click the **+ sign** next to Categories: Key Customer (2 items), if necessary, then click the **+ sign** next to Categories: Product Development Team (3 items), if necessary
   All the contacts appear under their assigned categories.
   See Figure 4-5.

8. Click **View** on the menu bar, point to **Current View**, then click **Address Cards**

---

tip

To view all the categories assigned to a contact, double-click an address card in Address Cards view, then click Categories to open the Categories dialog box.

Figure 4-4: Ways to Organize pane open in Contacts folder

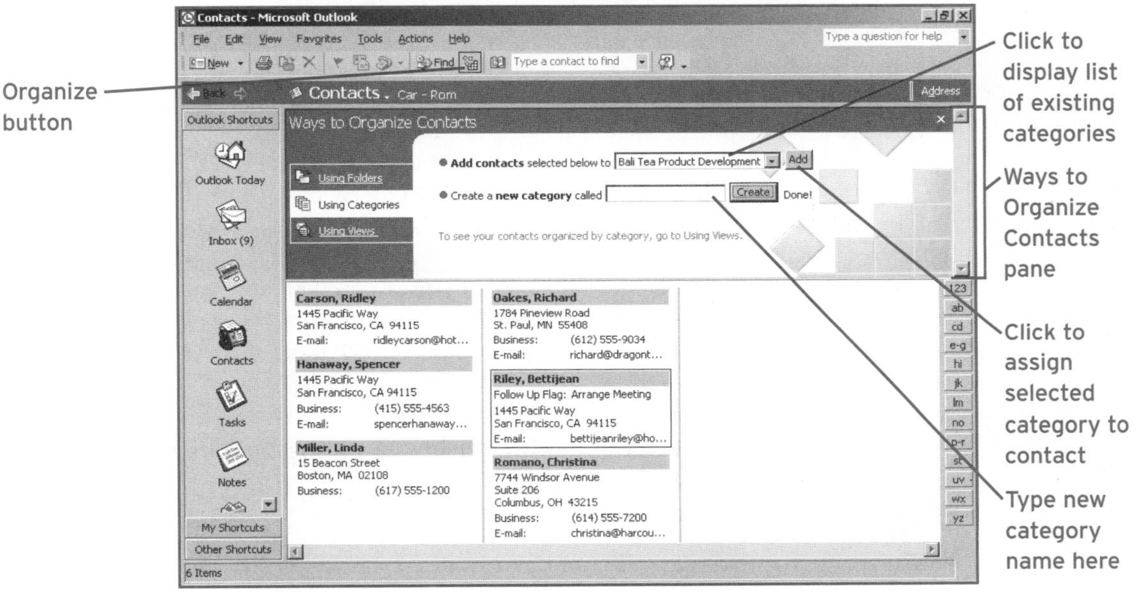

Organize button —

Click to display list of existing categories

Ways to Organize Contacts pane

Click to assign selected category to contact

Type new category name here

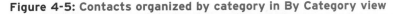

Figure 4-5: Contacts organized by category in By Category view

Contacts assigned to Key Customer category

Contacts assigned to Product Development Team category

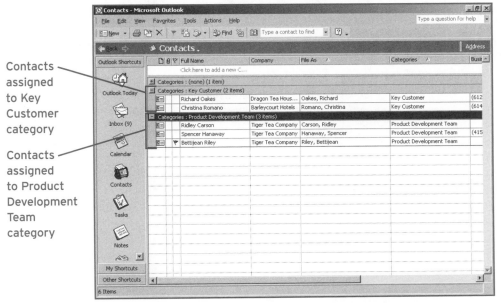

Skill Set 4

Creating and Managing Contacts

Organize and Sort Contacts

Sort Contacts

The default view for the Contacts folder is Address Cards view. If you have only a few contacts in your Contact list, you will be able to see all of them in this view. However, if you have a lot of contacts and are having trouble finding the one you need, you can use the View menu to switch to a more appropriate view. For instance, if you forget the name of a contact but know that she is employed by Barleycourt Hotels, you can use By Company view to view the contacts by Company. You can use Phone List view to view your contacts in a table. Phone List view is a good view to use if you want to sort your contacts in various ways. You can easily change the sort order in Phone List view by clicking the column heading by which you want to sort. For instance, to sort your contacts by last name in alphabetical order, you click the File As column heading.

To display expanded information for each contact on address cards, click View on the menu bar, point to Current View, then click Detailed Address Cards.

Activity Steps

1. Click the **Contacts icon** on the Outlook Bar, if necessary

2. Click **View** on the menu bar, point to **Current View**, then click **By Company**
   The contacts appear in a table, sorted by company.
   See Figure 4-6.

3. Click **View** on the menu bar, point to **Current View**, then click **Phone List**
   The contacts appear in a table.

4. Click the **Full name column heading**
   The contacts are sorted alphabetically by first names, in ascending order.
   See Figure 4-7.

5. Click the **File As column heading**
   The contacts are now sorted by last names in ascending order.

6. Click the **Company column heading**
   The contacts are now sorted by company names in ascending order.

7. Click **View** on the menu bar, point to **Current View**, then click **Address Cards**

Figure 4-6: Contacts in By Company view

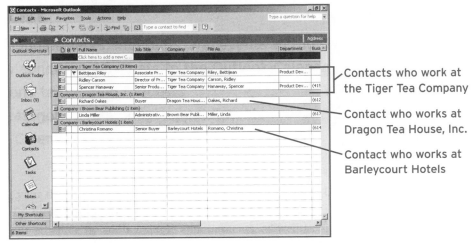

Contacts who work at the Tiger Tea Company

Contact who works at Dragon Tea House, Inc.

Contact who works at Barleycourt Hotels

Figure 4-7: Contacts in Phone List view, sorted by first names

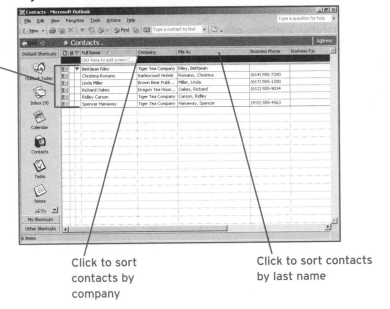

Contacts are sorted by first name

Click to sort contacts by company

Click to sort contacts by last name

extra!

Sorting by more than one field

Sometimes you might want to sort contacts by more than one field. For instance, you might want to sort your contacts first by Company, and then by last name. To do this, click View on the menu bar, point to Current View, then click Customize Current View to open the View Summary dialog box. Click Sort to open the Sort dialog box, specify the fields by which you want to sort (you can choose up to four fields), then click OK twice.

Skill Set 4

Creating and Managing Contacts

Link Contacts to Activities and Journal Entries

Assign Categories to Contacts

If the contacts in your Contacts list are involved in separate aspects of your working or personal life, you can organize them into related groups by assigning categories to them. For instance, you might want to group all your friends into the Personal category, and all your co-workers into the Business category. The activity titled "Organize contacts using Categories" explains how to assign categories to contacts using the Ways to Organize pane. You can also use the Categories dialog box to assign a contact to a category. You can choose from predefined categories or you can create your own.

Step 4
If you did not complete the activity called "Organize Contacts Using Categories," Product Development Team will not appear in the Items belong to these categories text box. In this case, type Direct Reports and ignore the other Step 4 instructions.

Activity Steps

1. Click the **Contacts icon** on the Outlook Bar, if necessary, click **Oakes, Richard**, press and hold **[Ctrl]**, then click **Romano, Christina**

2. Click **Edit** on the menu bar, click **Categories** to open the Categories dialog box, click the **Hot Contacts check box** in the Available categories list, then click **OK**

3. Click **Riley, Bettijean**, right-click to open the shortcut menu, then click **Categories**
   The Categories dialog box opens.

4. Click to the left of **Product Development Team** in the Item(s) belong to these categories box, type **Direct Reports**, type **,** (a comma), then press **[Spacebar]**

5. Click **Add to List**
   Direct Reports appears as a checked item in the Available categories list.
   See Figure 4-8.

6. Click **OK**, click **View** on the menu bar, point to **Current View**, then click **By Category**

7. Click the **+ (plus sign)** next to Categories: Direct Reports (1 item), then click the **+ (plus sign)** next to Categories: Hot Contacts (2 items)
   The contacts assigned to the Direct Reports category and the Hot Contacts category appear.
   See Figure 4-9.

8. Click **View** on the menu bar, point to **Current View**, then click **Address Cards**

Figure 4-8: Categories dialog box

New category

New category automatically checked

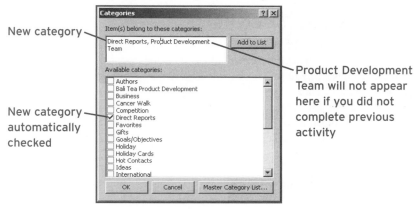

Product Development Team will not appear here if you did not complete previous activity

Figure 4-9: Contacts in By Category view with two new category assignments

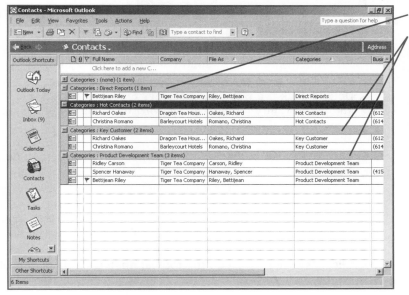

New category

You will not see these categories if you did not complete previous activity

extra!

Removing categories
If you find that you have categories that are no longer relevant, you can remove them. To delete a category, open the Categories dialog box, click Master Category List, click the Category you want to delete, click Delete, then click OK twice. To remove all categories that you have created and revert to the original categories list, open the Categories dialog box, click Master Category List, click Reset, then click OK twice.

Skill Set 4

Creating and Managing Contacts

Link Contacts to Activities and Journal Entries

Track All Activities for Contacts

If you deal with a large number of contacts, you might find it helpful to keep track of the various tasks, appointments, meetings, and conversations associated with each one. You can do this easily in Outlook by linking any item to a contact. For instance, you can link a Calendar appointment, meeting request, or e-mail message to a contact. You can also create Journal items that are linked to a contact. The **Journal** is a folder in Outlook that you can use to store information about activities and interactions with people. For instance, you can create a Journal entry that summarizes a task you completed or a phone conversation you had. Keeping track of such activities is very helpful if you need to show a manager or a client how you have spent your time. You can view all activities associated with a contact in the Activities tab of the Contact form.

Step 3
Be aware that it might take a few seconds for Outlook to find all the activities associated with Richard Oakes.

Activity Steps

1. Click the **Contacts icon**  on the Outlook Bar, if necessary

2. Double-click the **Richard Oakes address card**

3. Click the **Activities tab** on the Contact form
   All the activities assigned to Richard Oakes appear in a list.
   See Figure 4-10.

4. Double-click the **Bali Tea customer feedback item**
   The Journal Entry form opens, showing the summary of a phone conversation on May 28.
   See Figure 4-11.

5. Click the **Close button** on the Journal Entry form, then double-click the **Dinner meeting item**
   The Dinner meeting-Appointment form opens, showing the details of this Calendar item.

6. Click the **second Start time list arrow**, then click **6:00 PM**
   The meeting start time is now set to 6:00. The meeting end time automatically adjusts to end at 8:00.

7. Click **Save and Close** on the toolbar, then click **Save and Close** on the Richard Oakes-Contact form toolbar

Figure 4-10: Activities tab of Contacts form

Journal entries

Calendar appointments

Phone call Journal entry

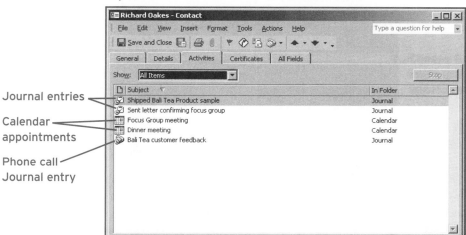

Figure 4-11: Journal Entry form linked to contact

Date and time of phone call

Indicates type of Journal entry

Summary of phone call

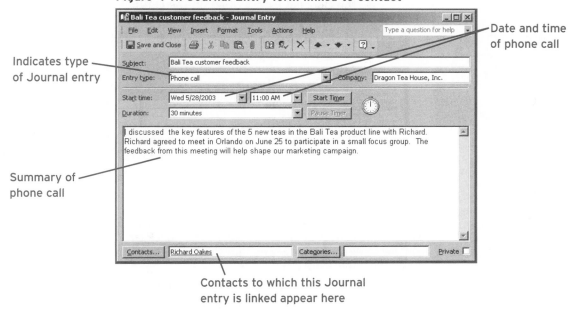

Contacts to which this Journal entry is linked appear here

Skill Set 4

Creating and Managing Contacts

Link Contacts to Activities and Journal Entries

Assign Journal Entries to Contacts

If you need to keep track of how you spend your time, then using the Journal is a good idea. For example, you can track your activities to help you write your annual review or to demonstrate to a client how you have billed for your time. You can create **Journal entries** to keep track of any activity, such as summarizing a meeting or a phone call, or sending a contract to a customer. You can also attach files to Journal entries. For instance, you could create a Journal entry about sending a memo and then attach the memo to the Journal entry. You can also record the duration of a Journal entry, either by using a timer or by entering the time yourself. To create a Journal entry, you open the Journal folder and use the New Journal Entry button on the toolbar to open the Journal Entry form. To link a Journal entry to a contact, you use the Select Contacts dialog box. Any Journal entries linked to a contact will appear in the Activities tab of the Contact form for that contact.

By default, your Journal timeline shows seven days. To change the view to a single day, click the Day button on the toolbar. To change the timeline to show a whole month, click the Month button on the toolbar.

Activity Steps

1. Click the **My Shortcuts button** on the Outlook Bar, then click the **Journal icon** [Journal] on the Outlook Bar (If a dialog box opens, click No)

2. Click the **New Journal Entry button** [New ▾] on the toolbar
   The Journal Entry form opens.
   See Figure 4-12.

3. Type **Thank you gift in the Subject line, press [Tab], click the Entry type list arrow, then click Task**

4. Click in the large text box in the bottom half of the form, then type **Sent Tiger Tea mug set to Richard Oakes and Christina Romano as a thank you gift for participating in focus group.**

5. Click the **Contacts button**
   The Select Contacts dialog box opens.
   See Figure 4-13.

6. Click **Oakes, Richard, press and hold [Ctrl], click Romano, Christina, release [Ctrl], then click OK**
   Richard Oakes and Christina Romano appear in the Contacts box in the Journal Entry form.

7. Click **Save and Close on the toolbar, then click the + sign next to Entry Type: Task, if necessary**
   The Thank you gift task appears under the current time on the timeline in the Journal window.

8. Click **Outlook Shortcuts on the Outlook Bar**

Figure 4-12: Journal Entry form

Type a subject for your Journal entry here

Click to see a list of available entry types

Click to start a timer which will automatically record the duration of the activity

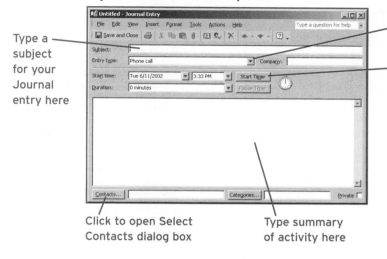

Click to open Select Contacts dialog box

Type summary of activity here

Figure 4-13: Select Contacts dialog box

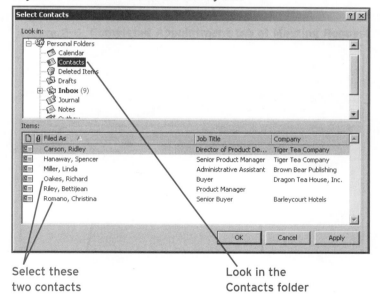

Select these two contacts

Look in the Contacts folder

extra!

Recording items automatically in the Journal

You can set up Outlook so that particular items for certain contacts are automatically recorded. For instance, you can specify that all e-mail messages sent to your boss are automatically recorded as Journal entries. You can also specify that Office XP files be automatically recorded as Journal entries. To do this, click Tools on the menu bar, then click Options to open the Options dialog box. Click Journal Options to open the Journal Options dialog box, specify which items or types of Office files you want the Journal to record and for which contacts, then click OK twice.

Skill Set 4

Creating and Managing Contacts

Target Your Skills

1 Use Figure 4-14 as a guide. Add the four contacts shown. Edit the Carson Lawrence contact form to change the company to Looking Good Times, Inc. and change the address, phone number, and e-mail entries with information you make up. Assign the Hot Contacts category to Carson Lawrence and Marcia Hammond. Assign a new category called Sales Team to Marianne O'Neill and Roxanne Waters. Sort the contacts in Phone List view by Company.

Figure 4-14

Hammond, Marcia		
Full Name:	Marcia Hammond	
Job Title:	Buyer	
Company:	Knock Out Beauty Supply	
Business:	1414 Oakwood Drive Rockville, MD 20850	
Business:	(301) 555-3200	
E-mail:	marcia@knockoutbeauty.com	
Categories:	Hot Contacts	

Lawrence, Carson		
Full Name:	Carson Lawrence	
Job Title:	Columnist	
Company:	Beauty Tips Newsletter	
Business:	15672 N.E. 29th Place Suite 404 Bellevue, WA 98007	
Business:	(425) 555-9876	
E-mail:	carson@beautytips.com	
Categories:	Hot Contacts	

O'Neill, Marianne		
Full Name:	Marianne O'Neill	
Job Title:	Sales Manager	
Company:	All Natural Cosmetics, Inc.	
Business:	6200 Lakeview Drive Houston, TX 77008	
Business:	(713) 555-2300	
E-mail:	marianne@naturalcosmetics.com	
Categories:	Sales Team	

Waters, Roxanne		
Full Name:	Roxanne Waters	
Job Title:	Vice President, Sales and Marketing	
Company:	All Natural Cosmetics, Inc.	
Department:	Sales	
Business:	6200 Lakeview Drive Houston, TX 77008	
Business:	(713) 555-2300	
E-mail:	roxanne@naturalcosmetics.com	
Categories:	Sales Team	

2 Use Figure 4-15 as a guide. Create a new contact for Melanie Wu. Melanie has signed up for a Day of Beauty at the Better Living Spa, where you work. Add the six appointments shown in the list (pick your own day and times). Then add the two Journal entries shown, making up your own information. Link Melanie Wu to each item. View all the items in the Activities tab as shown.

Figure 4-15

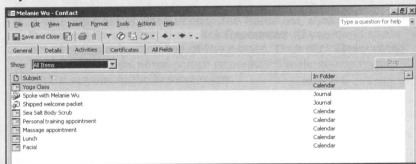

Skill List

1. Create and update tasks
2. Modify task organization and Task view
3. Accept, decline, or delegate tasks
4. Create and modify notes
5. Use categories to manage tasks and notes

If you are a busy person, you probably need a system to help keep track of all the tasks you need to accomplish. You could keep track of such tasks using an old fashioned to-do list. However, you can also take advantage of the powerful task-management features of Outlook. In this skill set, you will learn to use the Tasks component of Outlook to keep track of the tasks that you need to complete. You will create and update tasks, assign tasks to other people, and respond to task requests sent to you by others. You will also learn to use the Notes component of Outlook to record your thoughts and ideas. You will learn how to create, edit, and organize notes, as well as how to associate a note with a contact.

Skill Set 5
Creating and Managing Tasks and Notes

Create and Update Tasks
Create Tasks

You can use the Tasks folder in Outlook to keep track of **tasks**, which are errands or activities you need to perform and that you can track through their completion. By default, tasks appear in Simple List view in the Tasks window, which displays tasks in a grid format showing the completion status, subject, and due date for each task. To create a new task, you use the **Task form**, which contains two tabs. You use the Task tab to enter basic information, such as the subject, due date, and start date of the task. You can also use the Task tab to indicate the completion status and completion percentage, set a priority level, and enter descriptive information about the task. You use the Details tab of the Task form to indicate the completion date of the task, and enter information about the number of hours it took to complete the task. You use the Save and Close button to save new tasks to the Tasks folder. You can use the Delete button on the toolbar to delete a task.

To enter a new task quickly in Simple List view, click Click here to add a new task at the top of the grid, type the subject for the new task, enter a due date, then press [Enter].

Activity

1. Start Outlook, if necessary, choose your Profile name, click OK, enter your password, then click the Tasks icon 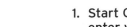 on the Outlook Bar
   The contents of the Tasks folder appear in Simple List view.

2. Click the **New Task button** on the toolbar
   The Task form appears.
   See Figure 5-1.

3. Type **Write memo to Steve James** in the Subject text box

4. Click the **Due date list arrow**, click the date for tomorrow, click the **Start date list arrow**, then click **Today**

5. Click the **Status list arrow**, then click **In Progress**

6. Click the large text box below the Reminder check box, then type **Summarize feedback on marketing plan for Brown Bear Adventure Guides.**, then click the **Save and Close button** on the toolbar
   The new task appears as an item in Simple list view.
   See Figure 5-2.

7. Click the **Write memo to Steve James** task, then click the **Delete button** on the toolbar
   The task is deleted from the Tasks folder.

Figure 5-1: Task form

Type task title here

Type details about task here

Click to set due date

Click to set start date

Click to specify completion status

Click to set priority level

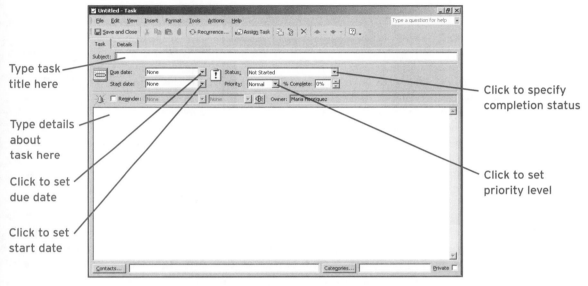

Figure 5-2: New task in Tasks folder in Simple List view

Delete button

New task

Your list may be different

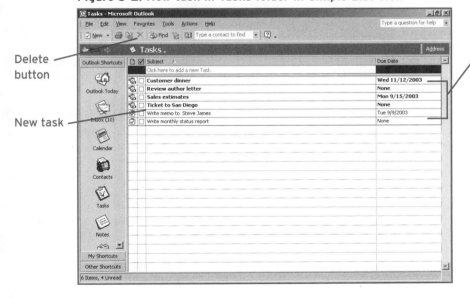

extra!

Viewing tasks on the TaskPad

Saved tasks appear in the Tasks window and also on the TaskPad. The **TaskPad** is a small window that shows a list of tasks and appears in the Calendar window. By default, the TaskPad shows tasks that are active for the current day.

Skill Set 5
Creating and Managing Tasks and Notes

Create and Update Tasks
Update Tasks

Once in a while, you will probably need to make changes to tasks to update them. For instance, you might need to change the priority level of a task from low to high, or move a due date earlier or later. To make changes to a task, you open the Task form and make edits just as you would in a word processor. You also might have some tasks that recur at certain intervals. For instance, perhaps you need to write a weekly status report for your boss. Instead of manually creating a new task every week, you can update a task so that it recurs. A **recurring task** is a task that occurs repeatedly at regular intervals. You use the Task Recurrence dialog box to specify a recurrence pattern for a task.

Activity

1. Click the Tasks icon on the Outlook Bar, if necessary, then double-click **Write monthly status report**

2. Click the Due date list arrow, then click the date for tomorrow

3. Click the Status list arrow, then click **In Progress**, then click the % Complete up arrow three times to change the setting to 75%

4. Click the Priority list arrow, then click **High**
   See Figure 5-3.

5. Click the Recurrence button on the toolbar
   The Task Recurrence dialog box opens.
   See Figure 5-4.

6. Click the Monthly option button, click the **Regenerate new task 1 month(s) after each task is completed** option button, then click OK

7. Click the Save and Close button on the Task form toolbar

Step 5
You can also open the Recurrence dialog box by clicking Actions on the Task form menu bar, then clicking Recurrence.

Figure 5-3: Edited task in Task form

Recurrence button

Click to change due date to tomorrow

Click to change start date to today

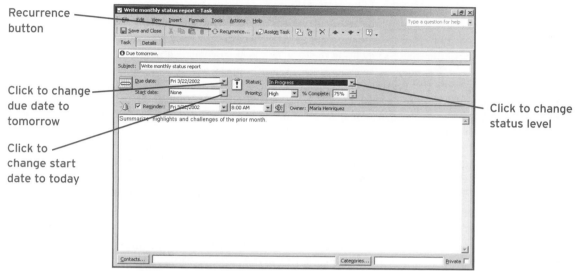

Click to change status level

Figure 5-4: Task Recurrence dialog box

Monthly option button

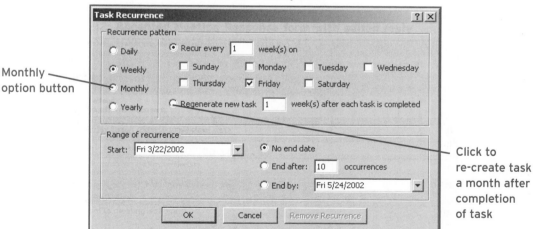

Click to re-create task a month after completion of task

Skill Set 5
Creating and Managing Tasks and Notes

Modify Task Organization and Task View
Assign Tasks to One or More Contacts

If you have administrative resources at your disposal, you might have the luxury of assigning the tasks in your task list to someone else to handle. You can assign a task to someone else by using the New Task Request command. When you use the New Task Request command, the Task form opens and contains a To: text box, where you can type the name of the contact to whom you want to assign the task. You use the Task form to complete the detailed information about the task, such as start date, due date, and priority level, and then you use the Send button on the toolbar to send the task request to the assigned person. The assigned person receives the task request as an e-mail message in their Inbox and can then accept, decline, or delegate the task. When you assign a task to someone else, the task still appears in your task folder. When the assigned person accepts your task, the task will show the assigned person as the task owner.

You can view additional task details in Simple List view by opening the Preview pane. To do this, click View on the menu bar, then click Preview Pane. To close the Preview pane, click View on the menu bar, then click Preview Pane again.

Activity

1. Click the **Tasks icon** ▨ on the Outlook Bar, if necessary, click the **New list arrow** on the toolbar, then click **Task Request**
   The Task form appears.

2. Click the **To: button**
   The Select Task Recipient dialog box opens.
   See Figure 5-5.

3. Click **Linda Miller** in the Name list, click **To**, then click **OK**
   Linda Miller appears in the To: box in the Task form.

4. Press **[Tab]** twice, then type **Handouts for Editorial Month-in-Review meeting** in the Subject box

5. Click the **Due date list arrow**, click the date for tomorrow, click the **Start date list arrow**, then click the date for tomorrow

6. Verify that both check boxes below the Start date list box are checked

7. Click in the large text box at the bottom of the form, then type **Please make 25 copies of my presentation for tomorrow's meeting.**
   See Figure 5-6.

8. Click the **Send button** ▭ Send

Figure 5-5: Select Task Recipient dialog box

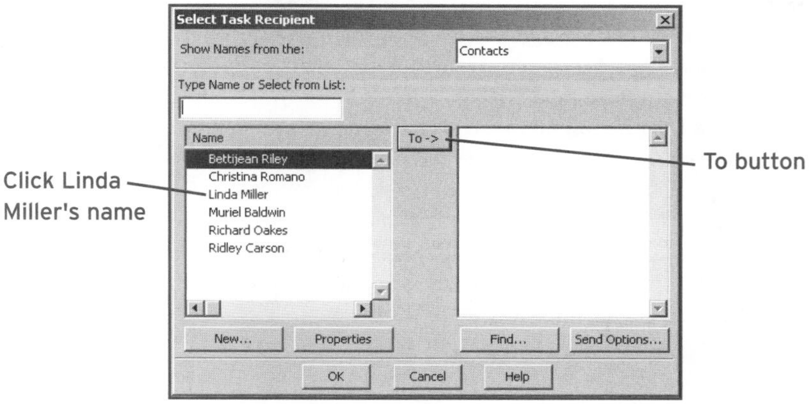

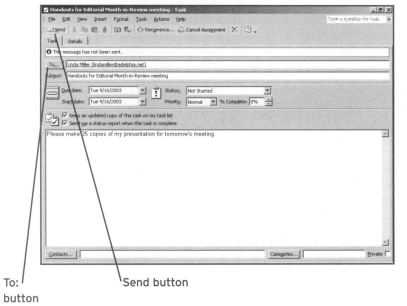

Click Linda
Miller's name

To button

Figure 5-6: Completed Task Request form

To:
button

Send button

Viewing and sorting tasks

If you find yourself getting overwhelmed by a huge number of tasks, you can organize your tasks by sorting and viewing them in different ways. You use the commands on the Current View menu to specify how to view your task list. For example, to view only the tasks that are due in the next week, click View on the menu bar, point to Current View, then click Next Seven Days. Some of the other views available on the Current View menu include Detailed List, which shows most of the details for each task in a grid format; Overdue Tasks, which shows only those tasks whose due date has passed; and Assignment, which shows all the tasks you've assigned to others. You can also sort your tasks quickly in any view by clicking the column heading by which you want to sort. For instance, to sort your tasks by the date they are due, click the Due Date column heading in Simple List view.

Skill Set 5

Creating and Managing Tasks and Notes

Accept, Decline, or Delegate Tasks
Accept Tasks

Just as you can assign tasks to other people to complete, you can also receive task assignments from others. You receive task requests from others in the form of e-mail messages delivered to your Inbox. If you agree to take ownership of the task, you can use the Accept button on the toolbar to send a message to the task sender informing them that you agree to see the task through to completion. You can provide a personalized message to the sender, or you can simply send a generic acceptance. If you send a personalized message, you can also attach a file. For instance, if a task request asks you to provide or prepare a particular file, you can attach the requested file to your acceptance message. Tasks for which you accept ownership are added to your Tasks folder.

To view only the tasks you have completed, click View on the menu bar, point to Current View, then click Completed Tasks. To view only tasks you have not yet completed, click View on the menu bar, point to Current View, then click Active Tasks.

Activity

1. Click the **Inbox icon** 🗐 on the Outlook Bar
2. Click the **From column heading** to sort the messages by sender, then double-click the message **Task Request: Sales estimates from Stephen James**
   The Sales estimates-Task form opens.
   See Figure 5-7.
3. Click the **Accept button**  on the toolbar
   The Task Request: Sales estimates message disappears from your screen and the next message in your Inbox appears.
4. Click the **Task Form Close button**, then Click the **Tasks icon** 🗐 on the Outlook Bar
   The Sales estimates task now appears in the Tasks folder.
5. Click the **check box** to the left of Sales estimates
   A strikethrough appears over the Sales estimates item, indicating that you have completed this task.
   See Figure 5-8.
6. Click the **Delete button** ⊠

Figure 5-7: Task form with task request

Accept button

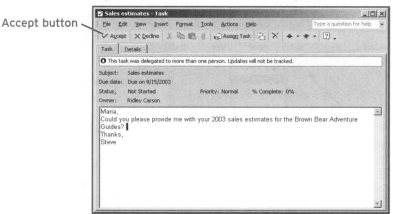

Figure 5-8: Completed task in Simple List view

Check mark
in box and
strikethrough
text indicate
task is
completed

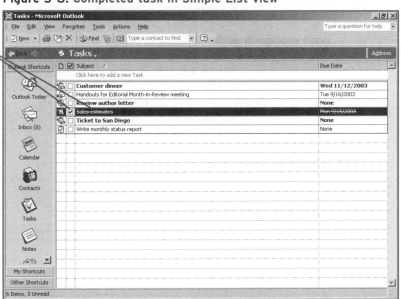

Skill Set 5
Creating and Managing Tasks and Notes

Accept, Decline, or Delegate Tasks
Decline Tasks

If you are a particularly capable person, others who appreciate your ability to get things done will probably send you task requests once in a while. For any number of reasons, you might need to decline a task request. You decline a task request using the Decline button on the Task form toolbar. You can choose to send a generic decline message, or you can send a personalized message to the requester that explains your reasons for rejecting the task request. Task requests that you decline do not get saved to your Tasks folder.

Activity

tip

You can also accept and decline tasks when your Inbox is in Messages view. To do this, click the Accept or Decline buttons in the Preview pane.

1. Click the **Inbox icon** 📧 on the Outlook Bar

2. Click the **From column heading** to sort the messages by sender, then scroll so you can see the messages from Linda Miller
   See Figure 5-9.

3. Double-click the message **Task Request: Review author letter** from Linda Miller
   See Figure 5-10.

4. Click the **Decline button**
   The Task Request: Review author letter message automatically closes. The task request disappears from your screen.

5. Click the **Message Window Close button,** then click the **Tasks icon** 📋 on the Outlook Bar
   The Review author letter task does not appear in your Tasks folder because you declined it.

Figure 5-9: Inbox sorted by sender

Click to sort messages by sender

Double-click this message

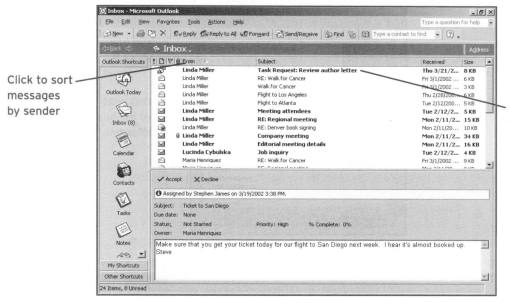

Figure 5-10: Task Request form

Decline button

You might see a different message here

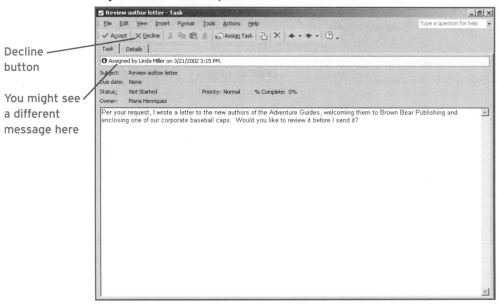

Skill Set 5

Creating and Managing Tasks and Notes

Accept, Decline, or Delegate Tasks
Delegate Tasks

Sometimes you might receive task requests that would be more appropriate for another person to handle. In such cases, you can delegate a task request to someone else. To delegate a task, you use the Assign Task button to open the Task form. You specify the name of the person to whom you want to assign the task, then use the Send button to send it to them. When you assign a task request to another person, a message is sent to the original requester that provides an update on the task. The task also is saved to your Tasks folder. Once you assign a task to someone, his or her name will appear as the temporary owner of the task. If the person to whom you assigned the task accepts the task, then that person becomes the permanent owner of the task. If he or she declines the task, then the task is returned to you and your name appears as the owner of the task.

The owner of a task is the only person who can make changes to the task. When the owner of a task makes changes to it, all copies of the task get updated.

Activity

1. Click the **Inbox icon** 📩 on the Outlook Bar

2. Click the **From column heading** to sort the messages by sender, if necessary, then scroll so you can see the messages from Stephen James

3. Double-click the **Task Request: Ticket to San Diego** message from Stephen James
   The Ticket to San Diego - Task form opens.

4. Click the **Assign Task button** 🗹 Assign Task on the toolbar
   A To: text box appears in the Task Request form. *See Figure 5-11.*

5. Click the **To: button** to open the Select Task Recipient dialog box, double-click **Linda Miller** in the Name list, then click **OK**
   Linda Miller appears in the To: box.

6. Click at the top of the large text box at the bottom of the form, type **Please book me a ticket to San Diego on that flight we discussed yesterday.**, then click the **Send button** 📧 Send on the toolbar

7. Click the **Tasks icon** 📋 on the Outlook Bar, then double-click the **Ticket to San Diego task**
   The Task form opens showing that Linda Miller now is the owner of this task and that she has not yet responded to your task request. *See Figure 5-12.*

8. Click the **Delete button** ✕ on the toolbar, then click the **Task form close button**

Figure 5-11: Task Request form with empty To: box for delegating to another person

Send button

To: button

You might see a different message here

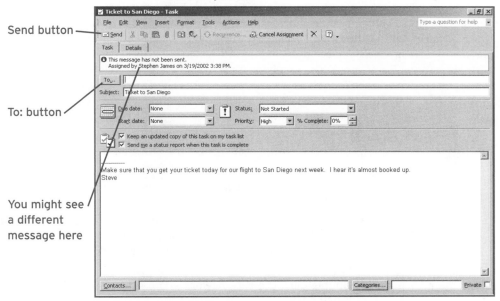

Figure 5-12: Task form showing Linda Miller as the task owner

Indicates Linda Miller has not yet responded to the task request (your message may be different)

Indicates Linda Miller is owner of this task

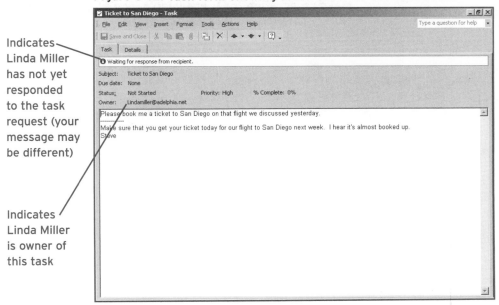

Skill Set 5

Creating and Managing Tasks and Notes

Create and Modify Notes
Create and Edit Notes

If you are the kind of person who jots down information about various things on sticky notes and posts them around your work area, then you will love the Notes feature of Outlook. Notes are computerized sticky notes that you can place anywhere on your screen. You can use Notes to write reminders, notes to yourself, inspirational words of wisdom, or anything you want. You use the **Note form** to write a new note. You use the Close button on the Note form to close the Note form and save a note to your Notes folder.

To change the default color, size, and font used for notes, click Tools on the menu bar, then click Options to open the Options dialog box. Click Note Options on the Preferences tab, make your selections for color, size and font, and then click OK.

Activity

1. Click the **Notes icon** [icon] on the Outlook Bar

2. Click the **New Note button** [New] on the toolbar
   A new note form appears with the date and time at the bottom. *See Figure 5-13.*

3. Type **Buy flowers and card today for Linda's birthday lunch**, then click the **Note Form Close button**
   The Note appears as an icon in the Notes folder. *See Figure 5-14.*

4. Double-click the **Buy flowers and card today for Linda's birthday lunch note**

5. Click to the right of lunch in the Note form, press **[Enter]**, type **Make reservation for 8 at Lillian's for 12:00**, then click the **Note form Close button**
   The changes are saved to the note.

Figure 5-13: Blank Note form

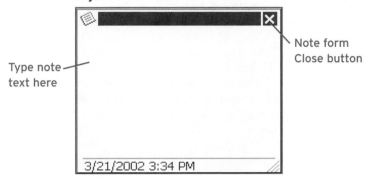

Type note text here

Note form Close button

3/21/2002 3:34 PM

Figure 5-14: Notes folder with new note

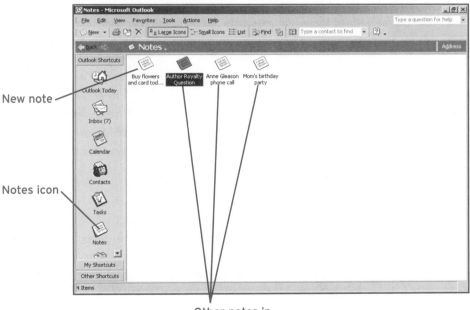

New note

Notes icon

Other notes in Notes folder

Skill Set 5

Creating and Managing Tasks and Notes

Create and Modify Notes
Assign Contacts to Notes

If you use the Notes feature frequently, your Notes folder will fill up fast with a large number of notes. Finding a particular note when your Notes folder is over-flowing with notes can be frustrating and time-consuming. One way to help you retrieve the notes you need is to associate each note with a particular person from your Contacts folder. For instance, perhaps you created a note during a phone call with your boss that contains critical information. So that you can quickly retrieve this note, you can link the note to your boss's name in your Contacts folder. When you need to locate the note again, you can open the Activities tab of your boss's Contact form and view all notes that are linked to your boss. To assign a contact to a Note, you use the Contacts command on the Note form menu. You open the Note form menu by using the menu button located in the upper-left corner of the Note form.

To forward a note to a contact, click the Note form menu button, click Forward, type the e-mail address of the person to whom you want to forward the note in the To: box, then click Send.

Activity

1. Click the **Notes icon** on the Outlook Bar, if necessary, then click the **New Note button** on the toolbar

2. Type **Editorial Summer Outing**, then press [Enter]

3. Type **Ask Linda to plan day of fun for editorial team**

4. Click the **menu button** in the upper-left corner of the Note form
   The Note form menu opens.
   See Figure 5-15.

5. Click **Contacts**
   The Contacts for Note dialog box opens.
   See Figure 5-16.

6. Click **Contacts**, click **Miller, Linda** in the Items list, click **OK**, click **Close** in the Contacts for Note dialog box, then click the **Note form Close button**

7. Click the **Contacts icon** on the Outlook Bar, double-click the **Miller, Linda address card** to open the Linda Miller Contact form, click the **Activities tab**, click the **Show list arrow**, then click **Notes**
   The Editorial Summer Outing Note appears, indicating this note is linked to Linda Miller.

8. Click the **Contact form Close button**

Figure 5-15: Note form menu

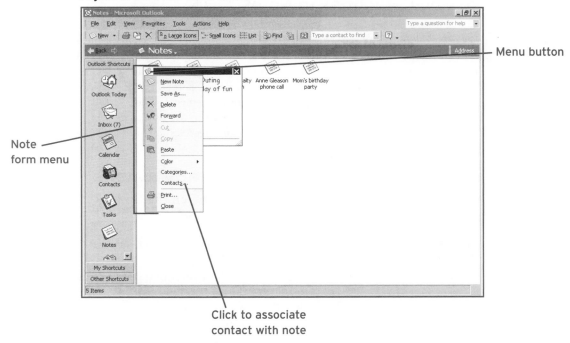

Menu button

Note
form menu

Click to associate
contact with note

Figure 5-16: Contacts for Note dialog box

Click to
select contact
from list

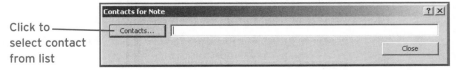

Skill Set 5

Creating and Managing Tasks and Notes

Use Categories to Manage Tasks and Notes
Assign Categories to Notes

If you use the Notes feature frequently, you will need to develop a system to keep your notes organized. Otherwise, you run the risk of accumulating hundreds of "unclassified" notes in your Notes folder, making it extremely difficult to find the one you want. To help keep your notes organized, you can assign categories to your notes so that you can look at related notes together. You can assign any of Outlook's predefined categories, or create new categories of your own. Once you assign categories to your notes, you can use By Category view to view the notes within each category. You assign categories to notes using the Categories command on the Note form menu.

Step 2
You can also assign categories to tasks. To do this, open the Task form for the task you want to categorize, click the Categories button, specify the category you want to assign, then click OK.

Activity

1. Click the **Notes icon** on the Outlook Bar, if necessary, click **View** on the menu bar, point to **Current View**, then click **Notes List**
The contents of your Notes folder appear in a list format.
See Figure 5-17.

2. Double-click the **Mom's birthday party note**, click the **menu button**, then click **Categories**
The Categories dialog box opens.

3. Scroll down, click the **Personal check box** in the Available categories list, click **OK**, then click the **Note form Close button**

4. Click the **Author Royalty Question note**, press and hold **[Ctrl]**, click the **Anne Gleason phone call note**, release **[Ctrl]**, click **Edit** on the menu bar, then click **Categories**

5. Click in the **Item(s) belong to these categories box**, type **Authors**, click **Add to List**, then click **OK**

6. Click **View** on the menu bar, point to **Current View**, then click **By Category**
The Categories you assigned to your notes appear.
See Figure 5-18.

7. Click the **plus sign (+)** next to Categories: Authors (2 items), then click **(+)** next to Categories: Personal (1 item)
The notes appear under their assigned categories.

Figure 5-17: Contents of Notes folder in Notes List view

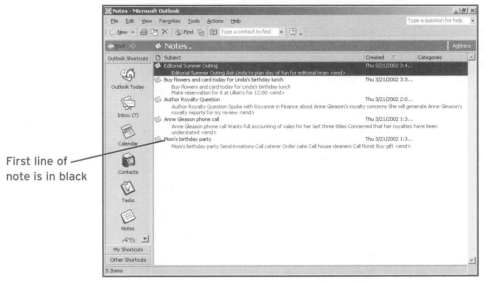

First line of note is in black

Figure 5-18: Contents of Notes folder in By Categories view

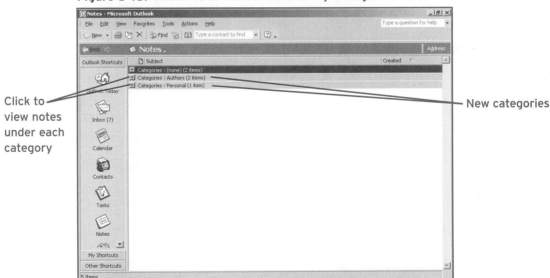

Click to view notes under each category

New categories

Skill Set 5

Creating and Managing Tasks and Notes

Target Your Skills

1 Create the tasks and note shown in Figure 5-19. Update the Finalize agenda task so that it shows a due date of tomorrow, and change its priority level to High. Create a new category called Spring Conference and assign it to the note and the tasks shown in the grid. Assign the Book airlines task and the Order luggage tags note to a contact in your Contacts folder. (Assign Linda Miller if you don't have any contacts of your own.)

2 Open the Task Request: Customer dinner message from Ridley Carson in your Inbox. Assign the task to Bettijean Riley, providing the information shown in Figure 5-20, then send the task request.

Figure 5-19

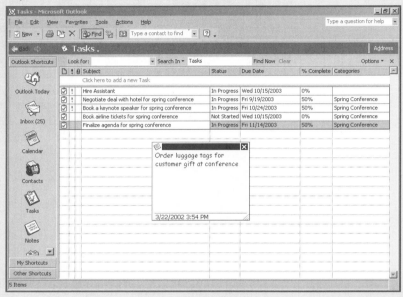

Figure 5-20

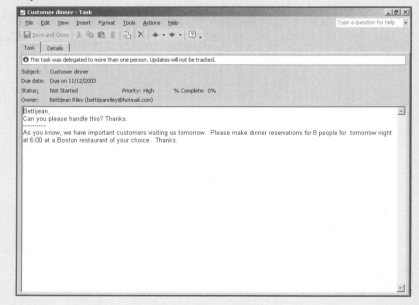

Skill List

1. Start PowerPoint
2. Understand PowerPoint views
3. Work with objects
4. Get Help
5. Save files

PowerPoint 2002 is the presentation graphics program that is part of Microsoft Office XP. You can use PowerPoint to create presentation materials, including computer-based slide shows, 35 mm slides, transparencies, handouts, and speaker notes. Using PowerPoint, you can create professional-looking presentations to teach concepts, advertise products, entertain an audience, or simply convey a message. Slides can contain static or animated text and graphics as well as video to help express your ideas. In this skill set, you will learn how to start and exit the program, open, save, and close files. You will learn the elements that comprise the PowerPoint window, many of which will look familiar to you if you have worked with other Microsoft Office applications. PowerPoint has several different views that you use for different purposes. You will learn how to switch among views and understand the type of work you can do in each one. You will also learn how to get help using the extensive PowerPoint Help system.

Getting Started

Getting Started with PowerPoint 2002

Start PowerPoint

Start and Exit PowerPoint

There are many ways to start PowerPoint. The way you choose will depend on your personal working style as well as the task at hand. You can click the Start button on the taskbar and then click PowerPoint from the Programs menu. You can also double-click the PowerPoint icon on the desktop if one was created. You can click the New Office Document command on the Start Menu to open the New Office Document dialog box and then click the Presentations tab to start a new presentation from the available templates. You also have several options for exiting the program, including the Close button on the title bar and the Exit command on the File menu.

Step 3
To exit PowerPoint, you can also click File on the menu bar, then click Exit.

Activity Steps

1. Click the **Start button** on the taskbar, then point to **Programs**
   See Figure GS-1.

2. Click **Microsoft PowerPoint** on the Programs menu
   PowerPoint opens, with a blank presentation open.
   See Figure GS-2.

3. Click the **Close button** on the title bar to exit the program

Figure GS-1: Programs menu

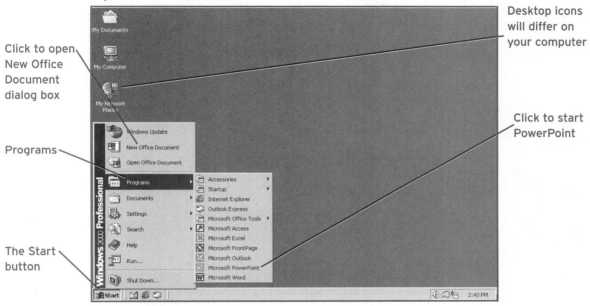

Desktop icons will differ on your computer

Click to open New Office Document dialog box

Programs

The Start button

Click to start PowerPoint

Figure GS-2: The PowerPoint window

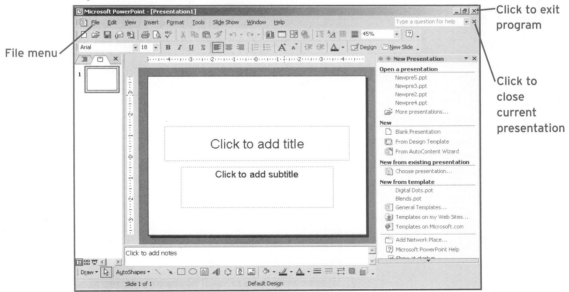

File menu

Click to exit program

Click to close current presentation

Getting Started

Getting Started with PowerPoint 2002

Understand PowerPoint Views
View the PowerPoint Window

Like other Office applications, PowerPoint has **menus** and **toolbars** from which you choose commands to perform actions. PowerPoint also has a **task pane**, which is a window that opens on the right side of your screen and gives you access to many commonly used commands. The task pane changes depending on what action you are performing. You can change task panes by clicking the Other Task panes arrow, or close the task pane if you want more room to work on the slide in the window. When you first open PowerPoint, a blank presentation opens in the **presentation window**.

Activity Steps

If your computer is not set up to show file extensions, you won't see ppt in the title bar after the filename. To change this setting, open the Control Panel in Windows, double-click Folder Options, click the View tab, then remove the check box from Hide file extensions for known file types.

1. **Start PowerPoint to open a blank presentation, then point to the title bar**
   The **title bar** has the Program name as well as the current filename on the left. Because this is a blank presentation, it has the temporary filename Presentation1. *See Figure GS-3.*

2. **Point to File on the menu bar**
   The **menu bar** includes the menus for accessing the PowerPoint commands. Click a menu name on the menu bar to open it and view the most commonly used menu commands. Double-click the menu item to view all the commands on that menu. The menu bar also has a **Close button** to close the presentation window and the **Ask a Question box** to get help.

3. **Point to but do not click the Open button on the Standard toolbar**
   A **ScreenTip**, a yellow box with the button name, appears to identify the command for each button. By default, the Standard and Formatting toolbars appear on two rows. You click a toolbar button to select the command.

4. **Point to the presentation window**
   The **presentation window** contains four work areas: the Slides tab, Outline tab, Slide pane, and Notes pane. The **ruler** helps you place objects on the slide.

5. **Point to the View buttons**
   The View buttons change the way you view your presentation; Normal (for working on individual slides), Slide Sorter (for arranging slide order), and Slide Show (for viewing your presentation as a slide show).

6. **Point to the Status bar**
   The **Status bar** displays several indicators to help you as you work, such as the title of the slide you are viewing and the total number of slides in the presentation.

Figure GS-3: Elements in the PowerPoint window

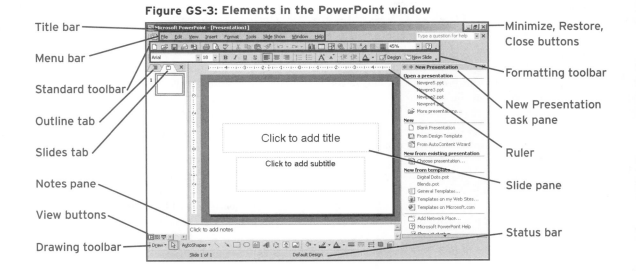

Title bar — Menu bar — Standard toolbar — Outline tab — Slides tab — Notes pane — View buttons — Drawing toolbar

Minimize, Restore, Close buttons — Formatting toolbar — New Presentation task pane — Ruler — Slide pane — Status bar

extra!

Minimizing, maximizing, and restoring Windows

On the far right end of the title bar are three control buttons for controlling the PowerPoint program window: the **Minimize button**, the **Restore button**, and the **Close button**. Minimized windows appear as buttons on the taskbar. If you click the Minimize button on the PowerPoint window title bar, the PowerPoint window will minimize and become a button on the taskbar. You can restore the window by clicking that taskbar button. If you click the Maximize button for any window, it will display as a full screen. If you click the Restore button on a window that you just maximized, the window will be restored to its previous size. You can also double-click the title bar of a window to maximize it or restore it to its previous size. To minimize all open windows, you can click the Show desktop button on the Quick Launch bar (if it is active) on the taskbar. To close a window, click the Close button on the taskbar. To close a window that has been minimized, you can right-click the taskbar button, then click Close.

Getting Started

Getting Started with PowerPoint 2002

Understand PowerPoint Views
Open and Close a Presentation

There are many ways to open a PowerPoint file, or **presentation**. Once again, the way you choose will depend on your personal working style and the task at hand. If you want to start with a blank presentation, you can just start PowerPoint from the Programs menu. If you have an existing file you want to open and continue working on, you can use the New Presentation task pane to open a file using the Open dialog box. If you are done with a specific file but want to keep PowerPoint open so you can work on another, you can close the file by using the Close command on the File menu.

NOTE: Understanding the file icons: In this activity you learn how to open a file. Most of the other activities in this book require that you open a file at the beginning of the steps in order to complete the steps for that activity. When an activity requires that you open a file to complete the steps, you will see 📄 above Step 1 with the filename of the file you need to open. 📄 will appear at the end of the steps to remind you to close the file. Unless your instructor tells you to do otherwise, you should close the file without saving your changes.

Before you begin to work though the activities in this book, it is recommended that you make a backup copy of all the Project Files that are supplied with this book and store them in a safe place.

Activity Steps

1. If the New Presentation task pane is not open, click **File** on the menu bar, then click **New** to open it

2. Click **More presentations** in the Open a presentation section of the task pane to open the Open dialog box
   See Figure GS-4.

3. Click the **Look in list arrow**, locate your Project Files, click **Newpre1.ppt**, then click the **Open list arrow**
   This menu gives you options for opening a file in special ways. Open as Read-Only protects the file from being overwritten. Open as Copy opens a copy of the file that you can rename so that the original file remains intact.

4. Click **Open**
   The Newpre1.ppt presentation file opens in the PowerPoint window.
   See Figure GS-5.

5. Click **File** on the menu bar, then click **Close**
   The presentation closes but PowerPoint is still running.

Step 2
You can also open the Open dialog box by clicking File on the menu bar, then clicking Open or by clicking the Open button on the toolbar.

Figure GS-4: The Open dialog box

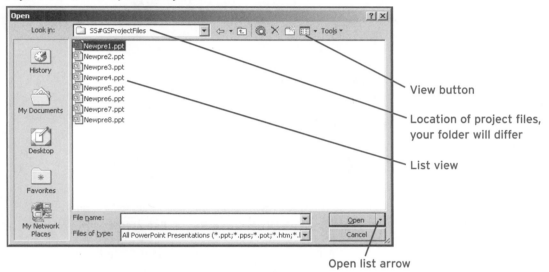

View button

Location of project files, your folder will differ

List view

Open list arrow

Figure GS-5: Presentation open in the PowerPoint window

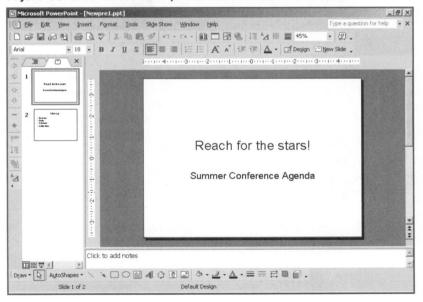

extra!

Changing views in the Open dialog box
The Open dialog box can display files in eight different views. Click the Views list arrow to select from Large Icons, Small Icons, List, Details, Properties, Preview, and Thumbnail views. Select Preview to see the first slide in a small preview window to help you locate the file you need.

Getting Started

Getting Started with PowerPoint 2002

Understand PowerPoint Views
Use Toolbars, Menus, and the Task Pane

Working on a presentation requires that you access the many commands available in PowerPoint to place, format, create, edit, and work with objects and slides. Commands are available through the menu bar, various toolbars, task panes, dialog boxes, and short-cut menus.

This activity requires that you open the file Newpre2.ppt. You can use the More presentations command on the task pane to locate and open this file.

Step 1
As you work, PowerPoint places the commands that you have used most recently on the short menu that displays when you click a menu name. To display all available commands on a menu, double-click the menu name or click the arrows at the bottom of the short menu. If you wait a few seconds, a short menu will automatically expand to the complete menu.

Activity Steps

 open Newpre2.ppt

1. Double-click **View** on the menu bar

2. Click **Task Pane**
   The New Presentation task pane opens. *See Figure GS-6.*

3. Click the **Other Task Panes list arrow** in the New Presentation task pane
   A list of the task panes available in PowerPoint opens. To open a specific task pane, click its name on the list.

4. Click **View** on the menu bar, notice that Task Pane has a shaded box with a check mark in it to indicate that it is open, then click **Task Pane** to close the task pane
   You can also close the task pane by clicking its Close button.

5. Double-click **Reach** on the slide, then click the **Bold button** [B]
   By default, the Formatting toolbar is located below the Standard toolbar and contains buttons for enhancing the appearance of your presentation. Some toolbars are **floating** and open when you need them. You can move toolbars to get them out of your way or you can **dock** toolbars to place them in a specific spot; the next time they open they will appear in that place. You can drag a toolbar to a new location, even after it is docked.

6. Click **Format** on the menu bar, then click **Font**
   The Font dialog box opens. You use dialog boxes to choose options for completing a particular task.

7. Click **Regular** in the Font style box to remove the bold, click **OK** to close the dialog box, then right-click **Reach**
   The shortcut menu has many commands that you might use at this time.

8. Right-click any toolbar
   See Figure G-7. Toolbars can be opened at any time by right-clicking the toolbar, then selecting the toolbar you need.

9. Press **[Esc]** to close the toolbar menu

 close Newpre2.ppt

Figure GS-6: Accessing commands

View menu

Open button

Format menu

New Presentation task pane

If the file you want to open is listed here, click the link

Click to close task pane

Other Task Panes list arrow

Click to open a new blank presentation

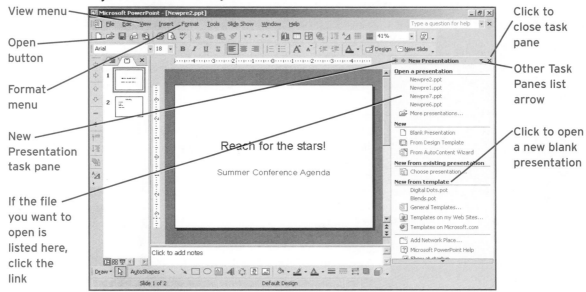

Figure GS-7: Viewing open toolbars

Bold button

Outlining toolbar is docked here

Drawing toolbar is docked here

Open toolbars have check marks

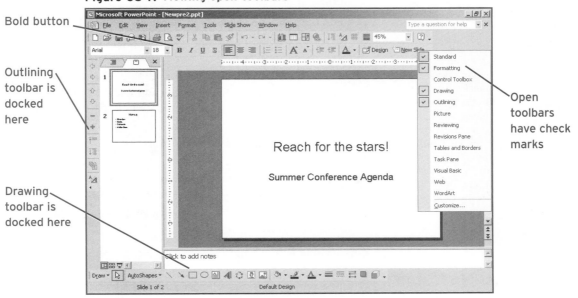

Getting Started

Getting Started with PowerPoint 2002

Understand PowerPoint Views
Change Views

PowerPoint has three views that you can use to create and modify presentations: The default view is **Normal view**, which you use to create and modify individual slides. Normal view has four work areas: the **Outline tab**, where you can work with the text on slides, the **Slides tab**, where you navigate among all your slides and get an overview of the entire presentation, the **Slide pane**, where you work with both text and graphic elements on an individual slide, and the **Notes pane** (located below the Slide pane), where you can enter speaker notes. You use **Slide Sorter view** for arranging the order of your slides, creating animation and transition effects (which you will learn about later), and for getting a bird's eye view of every slide in your presentation at once. You use Slide Show view to view the slides as a slide show. In Slide Show view, each slide fills the full screen. You can change from one view to another by clicking the View buttons, or using the commands on the View menu.

Activity Steps

 open Newpre3.ppt

1. **Double-click View on the menu bar to see all the view commands**
   See Figure GS-8. Normal is selected, indicating that you are in Normal view.

2. **Click outside the menu to close it, then click the Outline tab**
   The Outline tab displays the text on each slide in outline formatting.

3. **Click the Slides tab**
   The Slides tab shows thumbnails of the slides.

4. **Click Slide 2 on the Slides tab, then click Slide 1**
   You can move quickly to a specific slide by clicking it on the Slides tab or Outline tab.

5. **Click the Slide Sorter View button**
   See Figure GS-9.

6. **Click the Slide Show (from current slide) button**
   The slide show appears full screen on your computer.

7. **Press the [Spacebar] three times to view both slides and return to Normal view**

 close Newpre3.ppt

You can choose whether to view your slides in color, grayscale, or black and white. Click View on the menu bar, point to Color/Grayscale, then click either Color, Grayscale, or Pure Black and White.

Figure GS-8: Normal view

View Menu

Click to view Outline tab

Slides tab

Slide Sorter View button

Normal view is selected

Slide Show (from current slide) button

Current slide in Slide pane

Notes pane

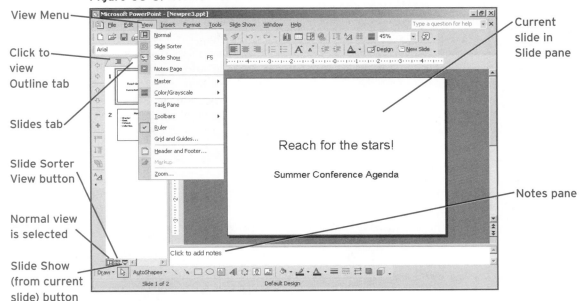

Figure GS-9: Slide Sorter view

Slide Sorter toolbar

Two slides in presentation

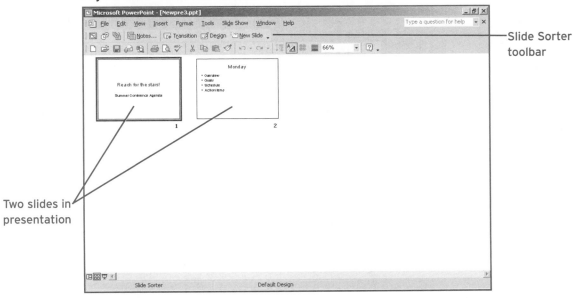

Getting Started

Getting Started with PowerPoint 2002

Understand PowerPoint Views
Work in Normal View

Depending on your work style and the task you are completing, you might find it helpful to rearrange parts of the Normal view window. For instance, if you want to see more of the slide on the screen but still want to use the Outline tab and Slides tab, you can reduce the width of the tabs by dragging the split bar. If you want to add a significant number of notes to the Notes pane, you could increase its height by dragging the split bar up. You can also close the Slides and Outline tabs by clicking the Close button on either tab. You can also move or resize the task pane as necessary to facilitate your work, or Zoom in and out to get a better view of your slides.

Activity Steps

 open Newpre4.ppt

1. If the Ruler does not appear in the Normal view window, click **View** on the menu bar, then click **Ruler**

2. Place the pointer on the bar between the Slides tab and the vertical ruler so that the pointer changes to ⊹‖⊹, then drag ⊹‖⊹ to the left ¹/₂ " so that the thumbnails turn into icons

3. Place the pointer on the bar between the Slides tab and the vertical ruler, press and hold the left mouse button, drag ⊹‖⊹ to the right of the vertical ruler, release the mouse button, place the pointer on the bar between the Notes pane and the Slide pane, then drag ⊹═⊹ up to the 2" mark on the vertical ruler
   See Figure GS-10.

Step 2
To move the task pane to another location, drag its title bar.

4. Click the **Close button** on the Slides tab
   Both the Slides tab and Notes pane close, giving you more room to work in the Slide pane.

5. Click **View** on the menu bar, then click **Normal (Restore Panes)**

6. Double-click **View** on the menu bar, then click **Zoom**
   See Figure G-11. You can change the Zoom percentage to see more or less detail on any slide by opening the Zoom dialog box or by clicking the Zoom list arrow on the toolbar.

7. Click **Cancel**

 close Newpre4.ppt

Figure GS-10: Changing the size of the panes

Close button

Vertical ruler

Drag split bars to resize panes

Zoom list arrow

Notes pane resized

Figure GS-11: Zoom dialog box

Getting Started

Work with Objects
Select and Move Objects

When you create a presentation, your slides will probably contain a combination of text and graphics. In PowerPoint, all graphics are objects that you can move or resize. All text is stored in **placeholders** or textboxes, which are also objects that you can move and resize. To move, resize, or make formatting changes to an object, you first have to select it. How you select an object determines whether you are working with the object or the contents of the object. To select a text placeholder so that you can edit or format the text contained in it, click in the placeholder so that the insertion point changes to an I-beam. To move or resize a placeholder, click in the placeholder to select it, then click its border so that the edge changes to a dot pattern.

Activity Steps

 open Newpre5.ppt

1. Click **Slide 2** on the Slides tab, then click **Overview**
   Round **sizing handles** appear on the edges of the left text placeholder, indicating that it is selected. The border of slanted lines indicates that you can edit, enter, or format the text now. The I-beam pointer will place the insertion point wherever you click. The blinking vertical line is the insertion point, where any keyboard action you complete will appear. *See Figure GS-12.*

2. Double-click **items** to select this word
   Text selecting and editing in PowerPoint is similar to how you might edit a document file in a word processor such as Microsoft Word.

3. Click the **placeholder border**
   The border is now a dotted border.

4. Place the pointer on the border so that the pointer changes to ⬚, then drag down slightly
   See Figure GS-13.

5. Click outside the object to deselect it, press **[Tab]** to select the **Monday** text placeholder, then press **[Tab]** three times to cycle through all the objects on the slide and to select the clip art
   The clip art is selected. Sizing handles surround the image, and a green rotation handle is at the top.

6. Press **[Esc]** to deselect the object and close the Picture toolbar

 close Newpre5.ppt

To select more than one object at a time, select an object, press and hold [Shift], then click another object.

Figure GS-12: Object selected for editing

Sizing handles

I beam pointer for editing, click to place insertion point in text

Diagonal border

Text placeholder object selected for editing

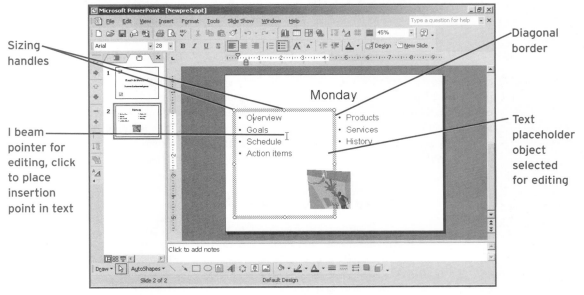

Figure GS-13: Moving or formatting an object

Move pointer

Dashed line shows new position of object

Object selected for formatting or moving

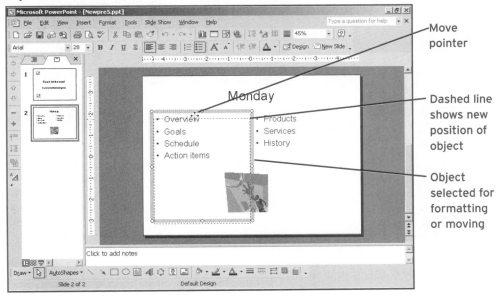

Getting Started

Getting Started with PowerPoint 2002

Get Help
Use the Help System

PowerPoint has a very impressive collection of features and tools. To take advantage of all it has to offer to create the best presentations possible, you will sometimes need help. The extensive Help system provided with PowerPoint is easy to access and can provide you with answers to your questions or give steps on how to complete tasks. You can access the Help system by typing a question in the Ask a Question box. You can search contents just as you would a table of contents in a book. You can also find out what specific items are on the screen by clicking Help on the menu bar, clicking What's This?, and then pointing to an item to get an explanation. Help is always available by pressing F1, which opens the Office Assistant. Help is available whether you are working on a presentation or you just have PowerPoint open.

If the Tabs window is not open, click the Show button on the Help Window toolbar.

Activity Steps

1. Click **Type a question for help** in the Ask a Question box on the menu bar, type **How do I create a presentation?**, press **[Enter]**, then click **About creating presentations**
   See Figure GS-14.

2. Click **Show All**
   All blue linked text is expanded to show green definitions.

3. Click the **Index tab** if necessary, type **view** in the Type keywords box, then click **Search** to see a list of topics

4. Click the **Contents** tab, click the **Expand button** to the left of Microsoft PowerPoint Help, click the **Expand button** to the left of Getting Started, click **What's installed with Microsoft PowerPoint 2002**, then click **Show All**

5. Click the **Answer Wizard tab**, type **Get Help**, press **[Enter]**, then click **Show All**
   See Figure GS-15.

6. Click the **Help window Close button**

Figure GS-14: The Help window

Type keyword for search then click Search

Topics will appear here

Click to display all content on page

Scroll to see more

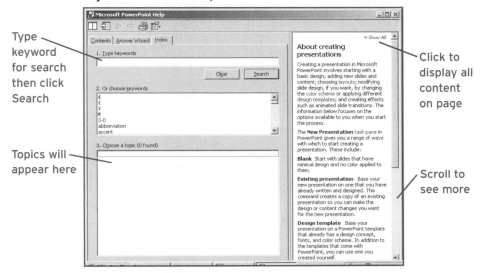

Figure GS-15: Results of get help search

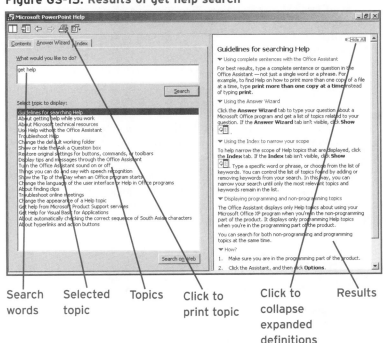

Search words

Selected topic

Topics

Click to print topic

Click to collapse expanded definitions

Results

extra!

Using the Office Assistant

The Office Assistant is an animated character that offers you access to help topics. A yellow bubble appears, into which you type a query or search words to get an answer. You can hide the Office Assistant at any time by right-clicking the character, then clicking Hide.

Save Files

Save a Presentation

After you work long and hard on your presentation, you want to be sure to save it in a secure place. When you save a file, you copy the version of the file that is currently in the computer's memory onto storage media. This could be a hard disk or a floppy disk. There are many different ways to save files. To save a file for the first time, you click the Save button on the Standard toolbar to open the Save As dialog box. You use this dialog box to give the file a filename and specify the folder where you want to save it. **Filenames** are names used to identify files on storage media. If you have been working on a presentation that was saved previously and decide that you want to save an updated version of it while retaining the original file, you can use the Save As command to save it with a new name. If you know before you begin to create your presentation that you want to base a new presentation on an existing one, you can use the Choose presentation command on the New Presentation task pane. This command lets you open a copy of an existing presentation and save it with a new filename. If you click the Save button after working on a file that was previously saved, the file will be saved using the current filename, and the existing file will be overwritten with the changes you made.

Activity Steps

 open Newpre6.ppt

1. Click **File** on the menu bar, then click **Save As**
   The Save As dialog box opens as shown in Figure GS-16.

2. To rename the file, click to the right of the 6 in the File name box, type **-new**, then click **Save**

3. Double-click **stars!**, click the **Bold button** B on the toolbar, then click the **Save button** on the toolbar
   The change is saved in the Newpre6-new presentation.

4. Click **View** on the menu bar, click **Task Pane**, click the **Other Task Panes list arrow**, click **New Presentation**, then click **Choose presentation** in the New from existing presentation section
   The New from Existing Presentation dialog box opens.
   See Figure GS-17.

5. Click **Newpre6.ppt**, then click **Create New**
   The presentation opens with the default name Presentation2.

6. Click the **Save button** to open the Save As dialog box

7. Click **Save** to save the file with the name **Reach for the stars!.ppt**

 close Reach for the Stars!.ppt
close Newpre6-new.ppt

PowerPoint presentation files have a .ppt file extension that is added to all saved presentation files by default.

Figure GS-16: Save As dialog box

Your folder will differ

Current filename

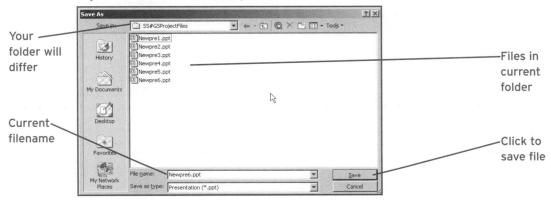

Files in current folder

Click to save file

Figure GS-17: New from Existing Presentation dialog box

Your folder will differ

Type new filename here

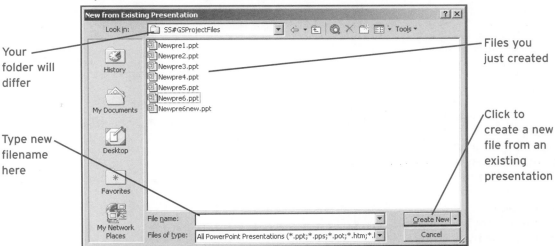

Files you just created

Click to create a new file from an existing presentation

Skill Set

Getting Started with PowerPoint 2002

Target Your Skills

1 Review Figure GS-18 to identify the 12 elements on the PowerPoint screen. Use a sheet of paper to name each element and write a short statement about the function of each.

Figure GS-18

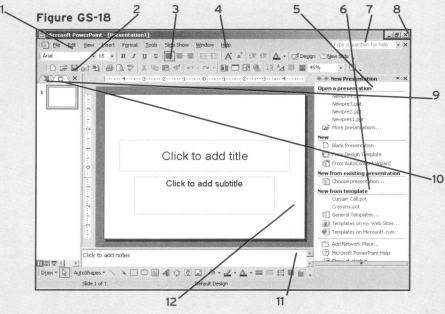

2 Figure GS-19 shows a Help screen that discusses the document recovery feature in PowerPoint. Use the Ask a question box to find this page about document recovery, and then read this screen. Then use the Answer wizard to find out about the new features in PowerPoint 2002. (*Hint*: Search on the keyword "new features".)

Figure GS-19

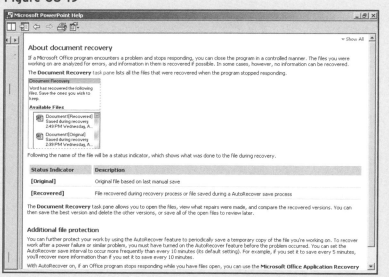

Skill List

1. Create presentations manually and using automated tools
2. Add slides to and delete slides from presentations
3. Modify headers and footers in the Slide Master

When you create a presentation in PowerPoint, you can start "from scratch" by opening a blank presentation, then enter content and create your own design. You can also choose to use the automated tools that come with PowerPoint to create presentations. These automated tools ask you a series of questions about the type of presentation you want to create, such as a marketing plan. Based on your answers, PowerPoint creates a designed presentation containing sample text that you can adapt to suit your needs.

If you're not the artistic type and wonder how you can make your presentations look professional, you can begin by having PowerPoint design the slides for you. PowerPoint can set up the background graphics, colors, and text styles for the presentation, and then you can add your own text. But you don't always need to start a new presentation; PowerPoint makes it easy to adapt existing presentations by deleting slides, creating new ones, or importing slides from other presentations.

When you create presentations, you might want the same text or graphic to appear on every slide. In PowerPoint, you only need to add this information once and indicate which slides you want it applied to.

Skill Set 1
Creating Presentations

Create Presentations Manually and Using Automated Tools
Create Presentations from a Blank Presentation

You can create a PowerPoint presentation by starting from a blank presentation. When you start PowerPoint, a new blank presentation opens. If PowerPoint is already running, you can use the Blank Presentation command in the New Presentation task pane to create a new presentation with one title slide. You can change the slide layout, add new slides, enhance slides with text and graphics, select a design template, animation schemes, or color scheme, then save the presentation.

Step 1
If a new blank presentation is not open, click the New button on the toolbar to open a new blank presentation.

Activity Steps

1. Start PowerPoint (if PowerPoint is already running, click **File** on the menu bar, click **New** to open the task pane, then click **Blank Presentation** on the New Presentation task pane)
   See Figure 1-1.

2. Click **Click to add title**, then type **Broadway Lights Theater**

3. Click **Click to add subtitle**, then type **Staging Broadway on Main Street**

4. Click the **New Slide button** on the toolbar

5. Click **Click to add title**, type **Broadway Lights Theater**, press **[Enter]**, type **Summer of Musicals**, then click **Click to add text**

6. Type **Pippin**, press **[Enter]**, type **A Chorus Line**, press **[Enter]**, type **Hello Dolly**, press **[Enter]**, type **Peter Pan**, press **[Enter]**, then type **Evita**
   See Figure 1-2.

   file close file

Figure 1-1: A new blank presentation

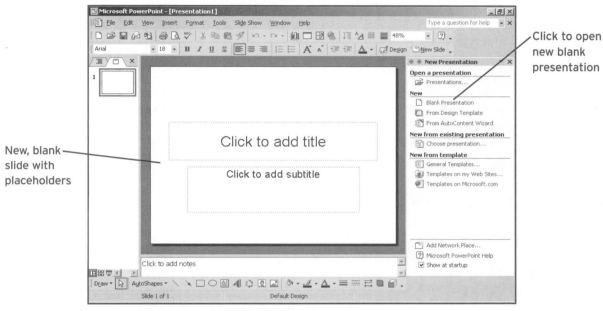

Click to open new blank presentation

New, blank slide with placeholders

Figure 1-2: Presentation with two slides

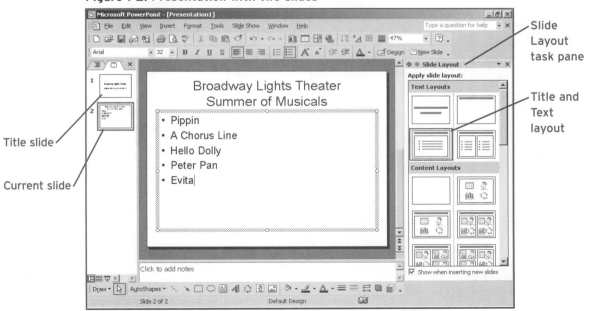

Slide Layout task pane

Title and Text layout

Title slide

Current slide

Skill Set 1

Creating Presentations

Create Presentations Manually and Using Automated Tools

Create Presentations using the AutoContent Wizard

If you are unsure how to begin creating your presentation, or if you are pressed to meet a deadline, PowerPoint comes with an automated tool that can help you get started. The **AutoContent Wizard** is a series of dialog boxes that asks you to choose your presentation purpose, such as selling a product or recommending a strategy, and how you plan to present it, such as on-screen or over the Web. Based on your answers, the Wizard creates a presentation with sample content and a professional-looking design. You can then adapt the sample text and design to meet your specific needs. While the AutoContent Wizard can save you time and help you create high-quality presentations, you have complete control over the final look and content.

The AutoContent Wizard has five categories of presentations: General, Corporate, Projects, Sales/Marketing, and Carnegie Coach. Click All to see all the presentations for all categories.

Activity Steps

1. Click **File** on the menu bar, then click **New**

2. Click **From AutoContent Wizard** in the New Presentation task pane
   The AutoContent Wizard opens, and the Office Assistant appears.

3. Click **No** on the Office Assistant, then click **Next**
   See Figure 1-3.

4. Click **Carnegie Coach**, click **Motivating A Team**, then click **Next**

5. Click the **On-screen presentation option button** (if not already selected), then click **Next**

6. Click the **Presentation title box**, then type **Teambuilding at Broadway Lights Theater**

7. Press **[Tab]**, type **Confidential** in the Footer box, click the **Slide number check box** to deselect it, then click **Next**

8. Click **Finish**
   The presentation contains 10 predesigned slides with content generated by PowerPoint. *See Figure 1-4.*

 close file

Figure 1-3: AutoContent Wizard Presentation Type dialog box

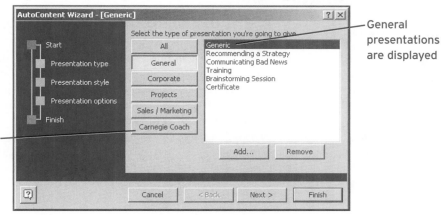

Click to select from Carnegie Coach presentations

General presentations are displayed

Figure 1-4: Presentation created by AutoContent Wizard

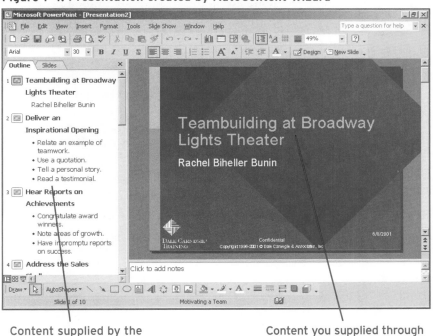

Content supplied by the AutoContent Wizard

Content you supplied through the AutoContent Wizard

Skill Set 1
Creating presentations

Create Presentations Manually and Using Automated Tools
Create Presentations Using Design Templates

A **design template** is a file that offers no suggested text, but does contain all the specifications for how a presentation looks, including background designs, color schemes, fonts, and layout. **Layout** is the organization of text and graphics on a slide. Though PowerPoint comes with more than 30 design templates that you can apply to some or all slides in your presentation, you can also create your own. For example, you could create a custom design template containing your company logo and company colors to be applied to every slide. You could then base future presentations on your customized design template. You can preview and select design templates in the Slide Design task pane.

Activity Steps

For your convenience, the Slide Design task pane organizes templates into areas called Recently Used and Used in This Presentation.

1. Click **File** on the menu bar, click **New**, then click **From Design Template** in the New Presentation task pane
2. In the Slide Design task pane, scroll if necessary until you see the Capsules design template in the Apply a design template area
   The name of each design template appears as a ScreenTip when you place the pointer over the thumbnail of each design template.
3. Click the **Capsules design template**
   See Figure 1-5.
4. Click **Click to add title**, type **Teambuilding at Broadway Lights Theater**, click **Click to add subtitle**, type **Staging Broadway on Main Street**, then click outside the text box to deselect it
5. Scroll the design template list, then click the **Kimono design template**
   See Figure 1-6.

 close file

Figure 1-5: Capsules design template

Slide Design task pane

Title slide for new presentation

Click to apply Capsules design template

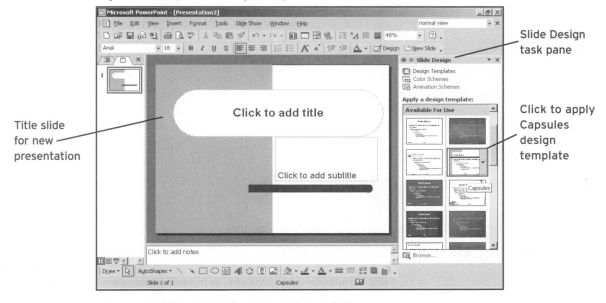

Figure 1-6: Kimono design template applied

Kimono design template

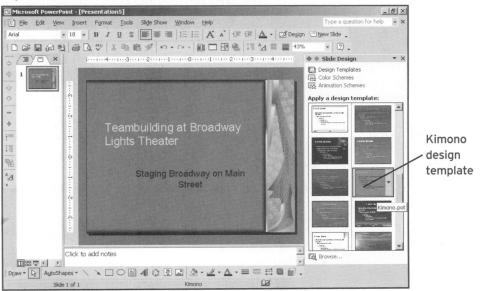

Skill Set 1
Creating Presentations

Add Slides to and Delete Slides from Presentations
Add Slides to Presentations

As you work on a presentation and add content, you will need to add slides. The New Slide button on the Formatting toolbar adds a new slide after the selected slide. It also displays the Slide Layout task pane, which allows you to choose a layout for the new slide. A layout contains **placeholders**, boxes with dotted or hatchmarked borders, for entering various types of information, such as images, bulleted lists, and charts. Text layouts contain placeholders for titles and bulleted lists. Content layouts contain placeholders for charts, graphics, diagrams, tables, and media clips.

Activity Steps

 open Present1.ppt

1. Click **Slide 3** on the Slides tab

2. Click the **New Slide button** 🖳 on the toolbar
   The new slide (slide 4) is inserted after slide 3, the slide you had selected.

3. Click the **Title and 2-Column Text layout** in the Slide Layout task pane to apply the layout to the new slide
   See Figure 1-7.

4. Click **Click to add title**, then type **Featured Actors**

5. Click **Click to add text** in the left text box, type **Michael Benjamins**, press [Enter], type **Emily Catalan**, press [Enter], type **Jennifer Laina**, press [Enter], then type **David Samuels**

6. Click **Click to add text** in the right text box, type **Pippin**, press [Enter], type **A Chorus Line**, press [Enter], type **Evita**, press [Enter], type **Peter Pan**, then click the slide to deselect the text box
   See Figure 1-8.

7. Click the **Close button** on the Slide Layout task pane

 close Present1.ppt

---

tip

Add a new slide by clicking a slide in the Outline or Slides tab then pressing [Enter]. To add a slide and specify its layout at the same time, click the list arrow next to a slide layout in the Slide Layout task pane, then click Insert New Slide.

 **extra!**

Creating new presentations from existing presentations
You can create a new presentation by using an existing presentation as a base, then adding or modifying slides to adapt the content and design for the new audience. Open the New Presentation task pane, click Choose presentation in the New from existing presentation area of the task pane, open the presentation you want to use, then save it with a new name. You can also use the Save As command on the File menu at any time to save a new version of a presentation with a different name.

Certification Circle

Figure 1-7: Inserting a slide

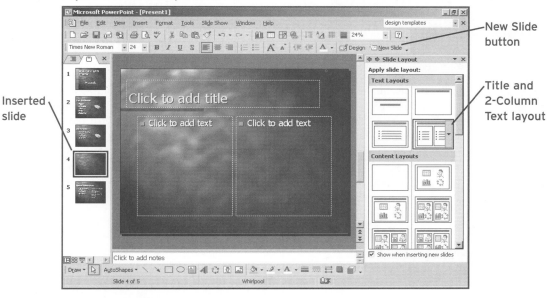

New Slide button

Inserted slide

Title and 2-Column Text layout

Figure 1-8: Completed slide

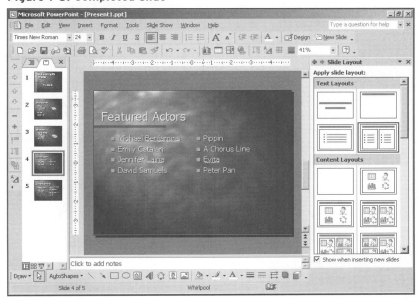

Skill Set 1

Creating Presentations

Add Slides to and Delete Slides from Presentations

Delete Slides from Presentations

There are frequently slides in a presentation that are no longer current, or that you no longer want. You can delete slides easily by selecting them on the Slides or Outline tab, or in Slide Sorter view, then clicking the Delete Slide command on the Edit menu. You can also press [Delete]. To select a group of contiguous slides, click the first slide in the group, press and hold [Shift], then click the last slide in the group. To select non-contiguous slides, press and hold [Ctrl] then click each one.

Often you will want to create a new presentation by deleting slides from an existing presentation. For example, you might have a new project proposal presentation you made for your marketing group that you now want to modify to present to prospective clients. The clients won't need to see the detail slides that an in-house group would need to see.

Step 2
If you delete a slide accidentally, you can retrieve it by immediately clicking the Undo button or pressing [Ctrl] [Z], or by clicking Edit on the menu bar, then clicking Undo Delete Slide.

Activity Steps

 open Present2.ppt

1. Click the **Slide Sorter View button** ⊞, then click **Slide 2** to select the slide you want to delete

2. Press **[Delete]**

3. Click the **Normal View button** ▣

4. Click **Slide 10** on the Slides tab, press and hold **[Ctrl]**, then click **Slide 7** on the Slides tab to select the two slides you want to delete

5. Click **Edit** on the menu bar, then click **Delete Slide** as shown in Figure 1-9

6. Click the **Outline tab**, click **Slide 3** to select the contents of the Mission slide, then press **[Delete]**

 close Present2.ppt

Figure 1-9: Deleting two non-contiguous slides

Delete Slide command

Selected slides to be deleted

Slide Sorter View button

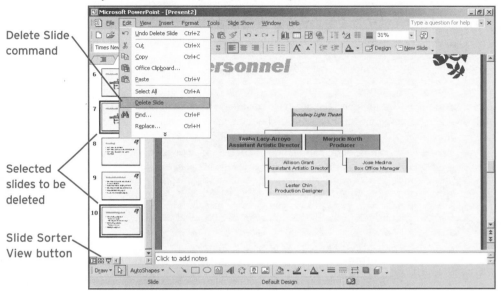

extra!

Copying slides from other presentations

The Slide Finder dialog box makes it possible to copy slides from one presentation to another without having to open the presentation from which you want to copy slides. Click Insert on the menu bar, then click Slides from Files to open the Slide Finder dialog box. Browse to locate the file you want to get the slides from, select the slides you want to copy by clicking the thumbnails in the Select slides area, then click Insert. Click Insert All to copy all the slides from a presentation. Click the Keep source formatting check box to retain the formatting of the source presentation; otherwise the template of the destination file will be applied to the slides. You can even add presentations to the List of Favorites tab if you select slides from a specific presentation often.

Skill Set 1
Creating Presentations

Modify Headers and Footers in the Slide Master
Add Information to the Slide Master

The **slide master** is the part of the presentation that specifies how text and graphics appear on each slide. You can use the slide master to make a global change to your presentation, such as changing the font or bullet style. The slide master stores information about the design template, including placeholder sizes, position, background design, and color schemes. The slide master can store text or graphics that you want to appear in the same place on each slide. To omit the graphics from the slide master from a particular slide, select the slide on the Slides tab, click Format on the menu bar, click Background, then click the Omit background graphics from master check box. There are also masters for the notes and handouts pages that work in the same way as the slide master. Your presentation can have more than one slide master. To insert a new slide master, view the slide master, then click Insert New Slide Master on the toolbar.

Activity Steps

 open Present3.ppt

1. Click **View** on the menu bar, point to **Master**, then click **Slide Master** to view the Slide Master
2. Click **Click to edit Master title style**, click the **Font Color list arrow** , click the middle **Custom Color Blue box** in the second row, click the **Font list arrow** `Times New Roman ▼`, type **BR** to display fonts beginning with Br, click **Broadway**, then click outside the selection
3. Click the **drama masks clip art**, press and hold **[Ctrl]**, then drag the copy of the clip art to the lower left corner of the Object Area for AutoLayouts placeholder
4. Click the **Format Picture button** 🖼 on the Picture toolbar (or double-click the image if the Picture toolbar is not open), click the **Size tab** on the Format Picture dialog box, select the number in the Scale Height box, type **20**, then click **OK**
   See Figure 1-10.
5. Click the **Normal View button** 🔲, click **Slide 5** on the Slides tab, click **Format** on the menu bar, click **Background**, click the **Omit background graphics from master check box**, then click **Apply**
6. Click the **Slide Sorter View button** 🔠
   See Figure 1-11.

 close Present3.ppt

step 2
If the Broadway font is not available to you, click any other font.

Figure 1-10: Changing slide master title, font, style, and type

Slide Master

Format Picture button on the Picture toolbar

Copied and resized image

Slide Master toolbar

Font style and color changed

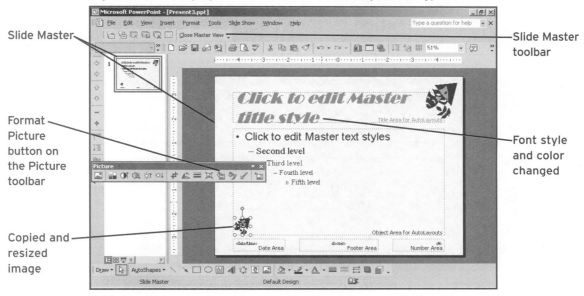

Figure 1-11: Slide showing changes from slide master edits

Graphics from the slide master

Background graphics from slide master not on Slide 5

Font style and color for title changed for all slides

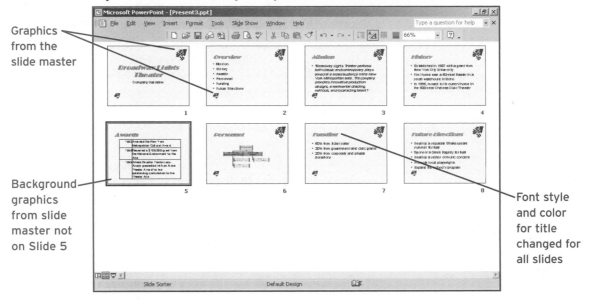

Skill Set 1
Creating Presentations

Modify Headers and Footers in the Slide Master
Add Information to the Footer area of the Slide Master

A **footer** is text information, such as the date, the presentation name, your company name, or the slide number, that appears at the bottom of every slide. You can display a footer on a single slide or on all slides in the presentation. If you display a footer on all slides, you can still exclude it from the title slide. You can add or delete a footer in the Header and Footer dialog box, which you can open from the View menu or from the Options menu in the Print Preview window. A footer automatically becomes part of the slide master.

Activity Steps

 open Present4.ppt

1. Click **View** on the menu bar, click **Header and Footer**, then click the **Slide tab** in the Header and Footer dialog box if it is not already selected

2. Verify that the **Date and time check box** has a check mark in it, then click the **Update automatically option button**

3. Click the **Update Automatically list arrow**, then select the date format **August 20, 2003** (today's date will appear in the list)

4. Make sure the **Slide number check box** is not selected, verify that the **Footer check box** has a check mark in it, then type **Broadway Lights Theater** in the footer box

5. Click the **Don't show on title slide check box** to select it
   See Figure 1-12.

6. Click **Apply to All**, then click **Slide 1** on the Slides tab if it is not already selected

7. Click the **Slide Show (from current slide) button** 🖳, then press **[Spacebar]** to display Slide 2
   See Figure 1-13.

8. Press **[Spacebar]** as many times as necessary to display the rest of the slides in the presentation, then click anywhere to exit the slide show

 close Present4.ppt

If you are using more than one slide master in your presentation, clicking Apply to All applies the footer to all the slide masters in your presentation.

Figure 1-12: Header and Footer dialog box

Current date will display as this date format

Footer will not appear on title slide

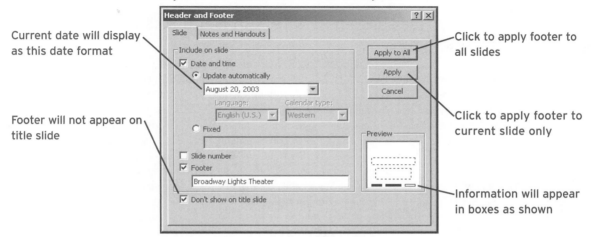

Click to apply footer to all slides

Click to apply footer to current slide only

Information will appear in boxes as shown

Figure 1-13: Footer on slide

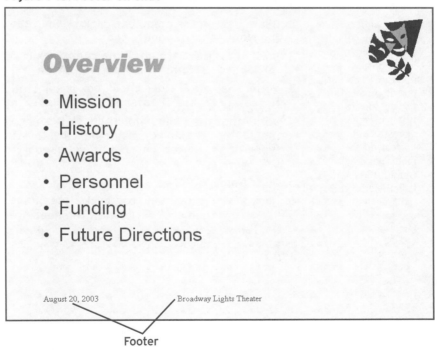

Footer

Skill Set 1
Creating Presentations

Modify Headers and Footers in the Slide Master
Modify Headers and Footers in Handouts and Notes Pages

While you can add only footers to slides, you can add either headers or footers to handouts and notes pages. **Handouts** are copies of your slides that you can provide your audience to help them follow the presentation. **Notes pages** contain a copy of the slides along with notes on what to say about each slide.

Slide numbers on printed notes pages and handouts are called **page numbers** and are contained in the header or footer. You can modify the headers and footers on handouts and notes pages using either Handout Master View or the Notes and Handouts tab in the Header and Footer dialog box. To open Handout Master View, click View on the menu bar, click Master, then click Handout Master. You must show the header or footer on all notes pages or handouts.

If you want to restore the default placeholders to the handout master, open the handout master, delete the placeholder if it has been removed or resized, click Format on the menu bar, click Handout Master Layout, then click the Placeholder check box to restore.

Activity Steps

 open Present5.ppt

1. Click **View** on the menu bar, click **Header and Footer**, then click the **Notes and Handouts tab**
2. Verify that the **Date and time check box** is selected, then click the **Update automatically option button**
3. Verify that the **Header check box** is selected, then type **Broadway Lights Theater Patrons' Dinner** in the Header box
4. Verify that the **Page number check box** is selected, verify that the **Footer check box** is selected, click the **Footer box**, then type **Thank you for your continued support!**
   See Figure 1-14.
5. Click **Apply to All**
6. Click **View** on the menu bar, click **Notes Page**, click the **Zoom list arrow**, then click **Fit** to view the header and footer
   See Figure 1-15.

 close Present5.ppt

Figure 1-14: Notes and Handouts tab of Header and Footer dialog box

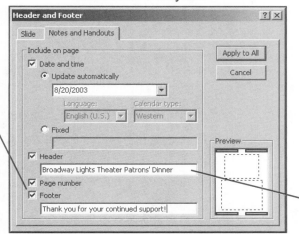

Footer will appear on notes pages and handouts

Header will appear on notes pages and handouts

Figure 1-15: Notes page with header and footer

Header

Date

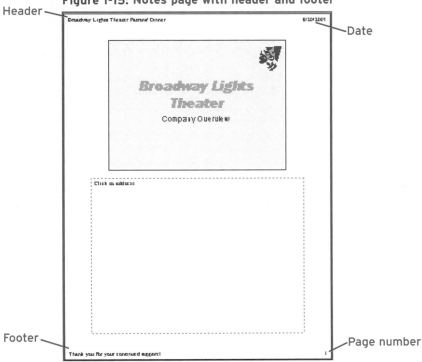

Footer

Page number

Skill Set 1

Inserting and Modifying Text

Target Your Skills

1 Use Figure 1-16 as a guide. Use the AutoContent Wizard to create a Brainstorming session on-screen presentation. Title it **Fundraising Event for Dumont District Band**, add a footer that contains your name, the slide number, and no date. Add your name to the footer in the handout master.

Figure 1-16

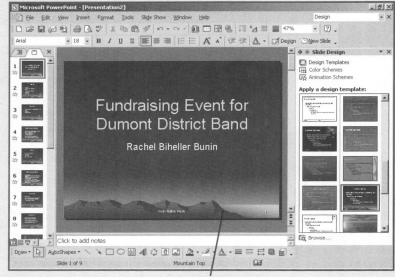

Mountain top design template

2 Use Figure 1-17 as a guide to create a presentation. Add a footer to all the slides containing the text **Broadway Lights Theater** and today's date, updated automatically. Add the text **Staging Broadway on Main Street** as a Header and your name as the Footer to the Notes and Handouts Master.

Figure 1-17

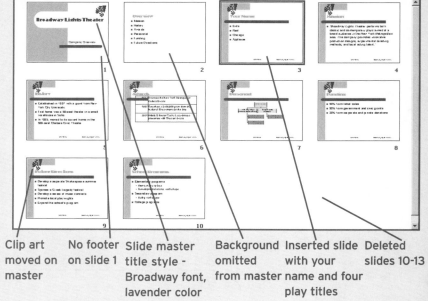

Clip art moved on master

No footer on slide 1

Slide master title style - Broadway font, lavender color

Background omitted from master

Inserted slide with your name and four play titles

Deleted slides 10-13

Skill List

1. Import text from Word
2. Insert, format, and modify text

In PowerPoint, there are many ways to add text and change the way it looks on a slide. You can manually enter text in placeholders, text boxes, as WordArt, or in AutoShapes on individual slides. If you want the same text to appear on every slide of your presentation, you can enter it on the slide master. You can type text directly in PowerPoint or import it from another program such as Word. If you are planning to create a presentation that includes a lot of text, you might want to use **Microsoft Word** or a text editor to write the text. PowerPoint makes it easy to insert Word documents (.doc files), files saved as Rich Text Format (.rtf files), and plain text files (.txt files) into your presentations. When you insert a Word or .rtf file, PowerPoint creates slides with titles and bulleted lists in text boxes based on the heading styles in the document.

Once you insert text in a presentation, you can modify it in several ways. You can edit it to make your message clearer and to correct grammatical or spelling errors. Formatting text helps you emphasize or deemphasize specific words or phrases as well as enhance the appearance of your slides.

Skill Set 2

Inserting and Modifying Text

Import Text from Word
Open a Word Outline as a Presentation

If you created a Word document using Outline formatting, it is very easy to create slides from it using the Insert Slides from Outline Command. When you insert a text file, Tab codes and heading styles define how the text appears on a slide. Text preceded by one tab appears as a slide title; text preceded by two tabs appears as a second level of text, and so on. Text with the Heading 1 style will appear as a title on a slide, text with the Heading 2 style will be the first level of text in a bulleted list, and so on. If the source document contains no styles, PowerPoint creates the outline based on paragraphs and gives each paragraph its own slide.

Activity Steps

1. Start PowerPoint with a blank new presentation on the screen

2. Click **Insert** on the menu bar, then click **Slides from Outline**

3. Click the **Look in list arrow**, navigate to the drive and folder where your Project Files are stored, click **Outline1.doc**, then click **Insert**

   The document file had two heading 1 text entries, each with four heading 2 lines of text. When brought into PowerPoint, two slides were created, as shown in Figure 2-1, one for each heading 1.

4. Close the task pane, click the **Outline tab**, click **View** on the menu bar, point to **Toolbars**, then click **Outlining** (if it's not already selected) to open the Outlining toolbar

5. Click the **Collapse button** on the Outlining toolbar to collapse the bullets beneath the November recipes head, then click the **Expand button** to display the bullets again

6. Click the **Collapse All button** on the Outlining toolbar

   The outlines collapse and you see only the heading 1 text for both slides. *See Figure 2-2.*

   close the open presentation

Step 3
If you get a message telling you that PowerPoint needs a converter to display this file correctly, click Yes to install it.

---

extra!

Promoting and Demoting text
You can work with the bullet items on a slide to create sub bullets or even create new slides by using the Promote and Demote buttons on the Outlining toolbar. If you have a bullet item in a placeholder that should be a subtopic, select the bullet, then click the Demote button to make it a second or third level item. Click the Promote button to bring the bullet back up to its original level. If you promote a top-level item, a new slide will be created with the item as the title style. Use the Move Down and Move Up buttons on the Outlining toolbar to change the order of bullet items within a slide.

Figure 2-1: Importing a Word outline

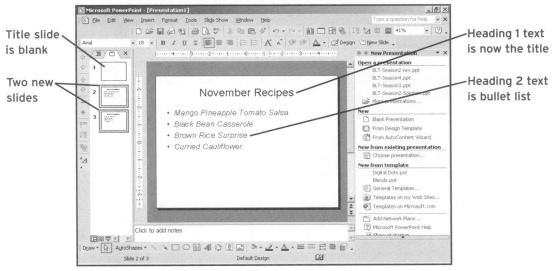

Title slide is blank

Two new slides

Heading 1 text is now the title

Heading 2 text is bullet list

Figure 2-2: Using the Outline tab

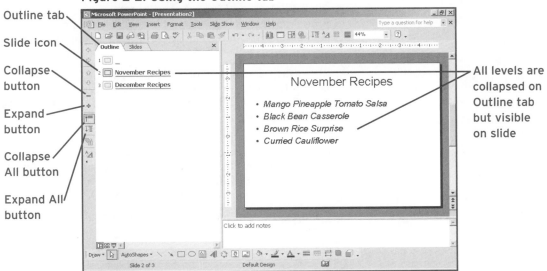

Outline tab

Slide icon

Collapse button

Expand button

Collapse All button

Expand All button

All levels are collapsed on Outline tab but visible on slide

Skill Set 2

Inserting and Modifying Text

Insert, Format, and Modify Text
Add Body or Title Text to Slides

Inserting text onto slides is a critical part of creating a presentation. There are many ways to insert text onto a slide, one of which is through slide layouts. PowerPoint provides four different slide layouts appropriate for text. To insert text, click the placeholder, then start typing. If your text won't fit into the current layout, you can choose a different layout that has additional text placeholders. When you change the slide layout to add a text placeholder, the text will have the formatting specified by the default placeholders.

Activity Steps

 open Recipes1.ppt

1. Click **Slide 2**, click **View** on the menu bar, click **Task Pane**, click the **Other Task Panes list arrow** on the task pane, click **Slide Layout** (if it is not already selected), then click the **Title and 2-Column Text** icon in the Text Layouts area of the task pane
   The existing text is now formatted in the left text placeholder, and a new placeholder with a bullet list appears on the right, ready for you to enter text.

2. Click **Click to add text**, type **Cherry compote**, press **[Enter]**, type **Apple crumble**, press **[Enter]**, type **Apple cobbler**, press **[Enter]**, type **Cucumber salad**, then click anywhere on the slide
   See Figure 2-3.

3. Click **Slide 3** on the Outline tab, click the **New Slide button** on the toolbar, click **Click to add title**, type **January Recipes**, click **Click to add text**, type **Baked Alaska**, press **[Enter]**, type **Black Bean Soup**, press **[Enter]**, then type **Manicotti**
   All text entered in placeholders appears on the Outline tab.

4. Click **Slide 1** on the Outline tab, click the **New Slide button** on the toolbar, click the **Title Slide layout** in the Text Layouts task pane, click **Click to add title**, type **Steven's favorite dishes**, click **Click to add subtitle**, then type **CJ says, "It's the best!"**

5. Collapse the outline for the November and December Recipes slides, then click **Slide 5**
   See Figure 2-4.

 close Recipes1.ppt

tip

You can delete, insert, cut, copy, and paste slides directly from the Outline tab; right-click any slide for a complete list of options.

Figure 2-3: Adding text by changing the slide layout

Second text box identified in Outline view

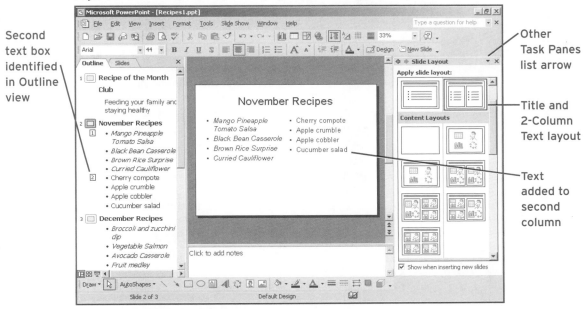

Other Task Panes list arrow

Title and 2-Column Text layout

Text added to second column

Figure 2-4: Adding two new slides with text layouts

New slides

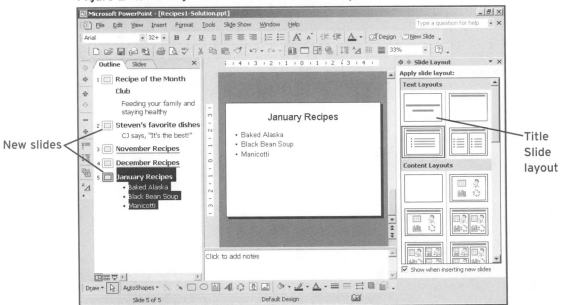

Title Slide layout

Skill Set 2
Inserting and Modifying Text

Insert, Format, and Modify Text
Add Text boxes to Slides

You can add text anywhere on a slide by using the Text Box button. However, keep in mind that text added with the Text Box button does not appear in the Outline tab, although you can see it on the Slide tab. If you want the text inside a text box to stay on one line, click the Text Box button, click where you want to place the text, then start typing. The text box will expand to fit the text until you press [Enter] or stop typing. If you want the text box to be a specific size, click the Text Box button, drag to create a text box to the size you want, then start typing. When the text reaches the end of a line, it will wrap to the next line.

Activity Steps

 open DecJan1.ppt

1. Click **December Recipes** in the Outline tab, then close the task pane if it is open

Step 3
To open the Ruler, click View on the menu bar, then click Ruler.

2. Click the **Text Box button** on the Drawing toolbar, click near the lower-right corner of the December Recipes slide, then type **Happy Holidays!**
   See Figure 2-5.

3. Click the **January Recipes slide**, click the **Text Box button** on the Drawing toolbar, then drag a text box under the M in Manicotti that is 4" wide using the horizontal ruler as a guide

4. Type **Happy New Year to all our gourmet friends. We will not be meeting in February but will meet again in March with more delicious recipes for you to learn how to cook!**
   See Figure 2-6.

 close DecJan1.ppt

Certification Circle

Figure 2-5: Adding a text box

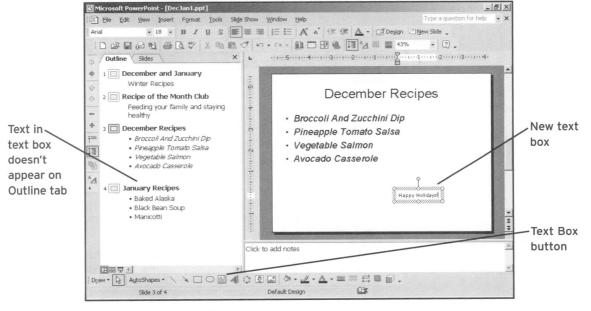

Text in text box doesn't appear on Outline tab

New text box

Text Box button

Figure 2-6: Text box with wrapped text

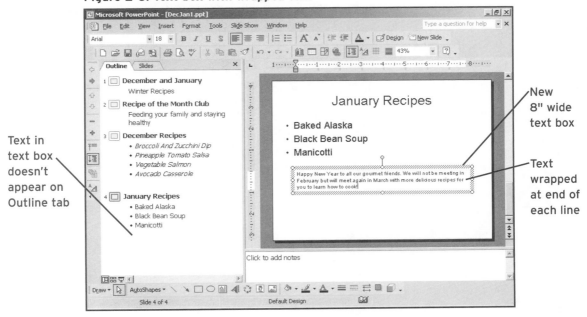

Text in text box doesn't appear on Outline tab

New 8" wide text box

Text wrapped at end of each line

Skill Set 2

Inserting and Modifying Text

Insert, Format, and Modify Text

Add Text to an AutoShape

If you want your words to have more visual impact, you can place them inside a graphic. **AutoShapes** are a group of ready-made graphics that come with PowerPoint, and include basic shapes such as squares and circles as well as elaborate shapes such as banners, stars, symbols, and connectors. To add text to a new AutoShape, begin typing as soon as you draw the shape. To add text to an existing AutoShape, click to select the AutoShape then type the text. Any text you add to an AutoShape automatically becomes part of the AutoShape. The image combined with the text helps emphasize your message.

Activity Steps

 open DecJan2.ppt

Double-click the AutoShape to open the Format AutoShape dialog box to change its colors and lines, size, position, and text box specifica-tions. If this slide is part of a Web page, you can also specify alternative text to display as the graphic is loading.

1. Click **December Recipes** in the Outline tab, click **AutoShapes** on the Drawing toolbar, point to **Stars and Banners**, then click **Explosion2** (the second icon)

2. Click slightly below and to the right of Casserole on the December Recipes slide, type **Happy Holidays!**, drag the corner handles of the AutoShape so the whole text is visible inside the shape, then click the slide to deselect the AutoShape
   See Figure 2-7.

3. Click **January Recipes** in the Outline tab, click **AutoShapes** on the Drawing toolbar, point to **Callouts**, then click **Rectangular Callout** (the first icon)
   Callouts have an additional yellow sizing handle that resizes the arrow part of the AutoShape.

4. Click to the right of Black Bean Soup, drag the shape up and to the right, stopping just under the word Recipes, type **Steven says, "Black Bean Soup is delicious!"**, then click outside the AutoShape to deselect the AutoShape callout
   Your screen should look like Figure 2-8.

 close DecJan2.ppt

Figure 2-7: Adding text with an AutoShape

AutoShape text is not on Outline tab

AutoShapes button

AutoShape with text

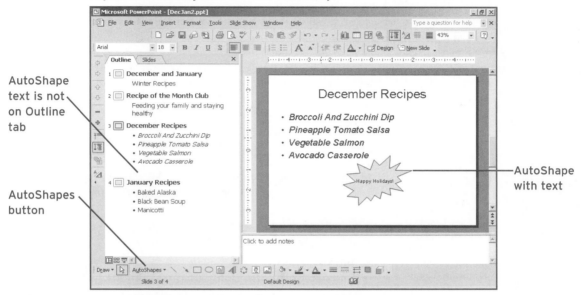

Figure 2-8: Adding a callout

AutoShape text is not on Outline tab

Callout AutoShape with text

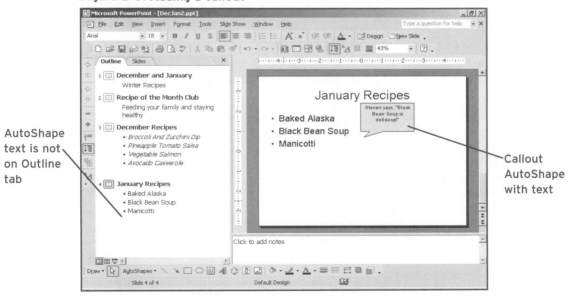

Skill Set 2

Inserting and Modifying Text

Insert, Format, and Modify Text
Add WordArt

Another way to give your words more visual impact is to transform them into **WordArt**. WordArt is a text object that has highly stylized effects, including color, outline, shape, shading, font, sizes, and fill. WordArt is best used for single words or short phrases on a slide. Text added as WordArt does not appear on the Outline tab. You insert WordArt using the WordArt button on the Drawing toolbar.

Selected WordArt has sizing handles as well as a green rotation handle at the top that you can drag to rotate the WordArt to any angle.

Activity Steps

 open DecJan3.ppt

1. Click **Slide 4**, then click the **Insert WordArt button** on the Drawing toolbar to open the WordArt Gallery
   See Figure 2-9.

2. Click **Rainbow WordArt style** in the third row in the fourth column, then click **OK**

3. Type **Happy New Year**, click the **Font list arrow**, click **Comic Sans MS**, click the **Bold button**, then click **OK**

4. Use the pointer to drag the **WordArt object** to below the text in the center of the slide
   See Figure 2-10.

 close DecJan3.ppt

Figure 2-9: WordArt Gallery dialog box

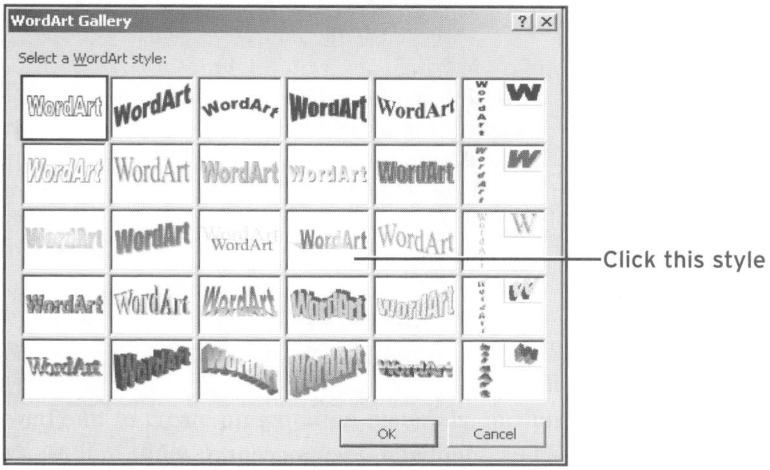

Figure 2-10: Adding text using WordArt

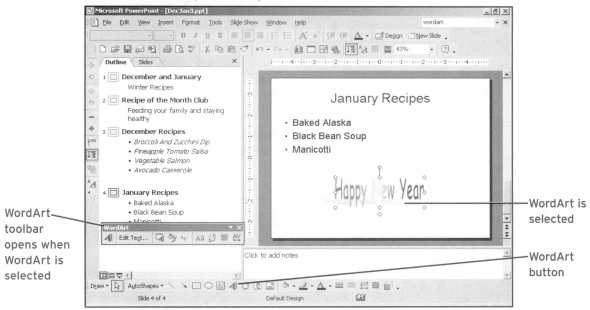

Skill Set 2

Inserting and Modifying Text

Insert, Format, and Modify text
Edit Text on Slides

Whether you insert a document file into PowerPoint to create slides or begin typing text directly in PowerPoint, you will probably want to make changes to the text to fix errors or make your message stronger. In Normal view you can edit directly on the slides or on the Outline tab.

You can add and delete words in bulleted lists, add new bullets, or move and rearrange the order of bulleted lists. You can change words or correct spelling errors. Using the copy and paste commands, you can copy words or phrases from one place to another on the same slide or to other slides.

Avoid putting too much text on a slide. Try to limit each slide to six bulleted items and a maximum of six words per bulleted item.

Activity Steps

📄 open Recipes2.ppt

1. Click the **November Recipes slide** on the Outline tab
2. Click to the right of the **c** in **compote** in the Outline tab, press **[Backspace]**, type **C**, click to the right of the **c** in **crumble** in the Outline tab, press **[Backspace]**, then type **C**
   You can also edit text directly on a slide.
3. Double-click **cobbler** on the slide, type **Pie**, click to the right of the **s** in **salad** on the slide, press **[Backspace]**, then type **S**
   The slide for November should look similar to Figure 2-11.
4. Place the pointer to the left of **Fruit medley** on slide 3 in the Outline tab so that the pointer changes to ⟷, click to select **Fruit medley**, then press **[Del]**
5. Place the pointer to the left of **Mango Pineapple** on slide 2 on the Outline tab, click to select the whole line, click the **Copy button** 📋 on the toolbar, click below **Avocado** on slide 3 on the Outline tab, then click the **Paste button** 📋 on the toolbar
   The line is copied from one slide to another.
6. Double-click **Mango** on slide 3 in the Outline tab, press **[Del]**, place the pointer to the left of **Pineapple** on slide 3 so that the pointer changes to ⟷, press and hold the left mouse button, then drag **Pineapple Tomato Salsa** up so that it is below **Broccoli**, as shown in Figure 2-12

Using Find and Replace

If there is a word that you want to change globally, click Edit on the menu bar, then click Replace to open the Replace dialog box. Type the word you want to find in the Find what box, then type the word you want to replace it with in the Replace with box. You can specify whether to search for whole words only or match the case for the text you want to find. Click Find Next to begin the operation. Click Replace if you want to confirm each replacement one by one. Click Replace All to replace all occurrences throughout the presentation.

extra!

Certification Circle

Figure 2-11: Editing text on a slide

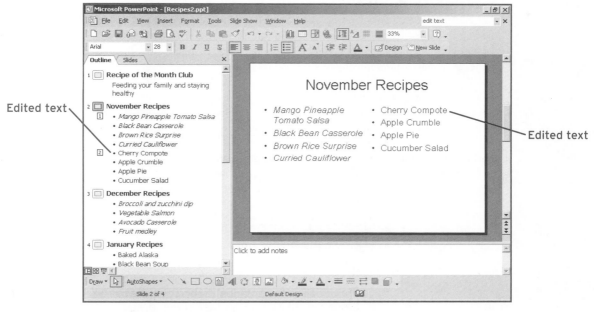

Figure 2-12: Moving text

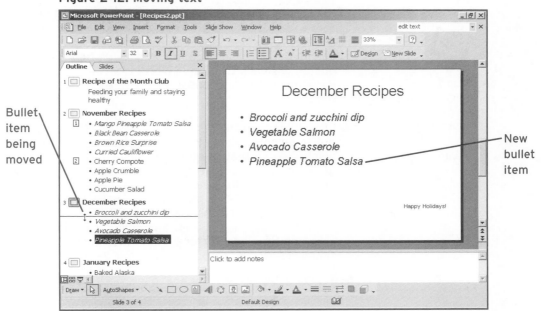

Skill Set 2

Inserting and Modifying Text

Insert, Format, and Modify Text
Format Text on Slides

You can take advantage of PowerPoint's many formatting features to enhance the appearance of text and help convey your message clearly. You can use bold formatting to emphasize certain words, bright colors to communicate a cheerful mood, or somber colors to convey a serious message.

You should use formatting wisely and with consideration for your audience. You can apply a design template to your presentation and then modify the formatting to meet your needs. Even though you have many choices, you should limit your use of font styles and formatting to avoid creating a presentation that is in poor taste or so busy that your message gets lost in the clutter. If possible, limit number of fonts to two and vary size, weight, and other attributes for subtle emphasis. PowerPoint provides design templates that offer preset fonts, color schemes, and layouts to ensure a unified look throughout your presentation.

Activity Steps

 open Recipes3.ppt

1. Click **View** on the menu bar, click **Task Pane**, click the **Other Task Panes list arrow**, click **Slide Design – Design Templates**, then click the **Capsules design template**
2. Close the **Slide Design** task pane, drag the pointer to select **Recipe of the Month Club** on slide 1, click the **Font list arrow** on the Formatting toolbar, click **Broadway**, click the **Font Size list arrow**, then click **40** (If Broadway is not available, choose another font)
3. Select **Feeding your family and staying healthy**, click the **Italic button**, click the **Font Color list arrow**, click the **lavender square** (the right-most square in the row), then click outside the selection
See Figure 2-13.
4. Click **Slide 3** on the Slides tab, click the **Happy Holidays text box** to select it, then click the **text box border** with the Move pointer ✛ so that the text box has a dotted border
5. Click the **Increase Font Size button** three times so that the font size is **28**, drag the text box to the left so it is positioned on the slide, click the **Shadow button**, then click the **Font Color button** to change the color to lavender
6. Click the **Slide Sorter View button**, click the **Zoom list arrow** on the Slide Sorter toolbar, then click **100%**
Your slides should look similar to Figure 2-14.

 close Recipes3.ppt

Step 1
You can also click the Slide Design button to open the Slide Design task pane.

Figure 2-13: Applying formatting, font styles, and font colors

Font Color list arrow

Increase Font Size button

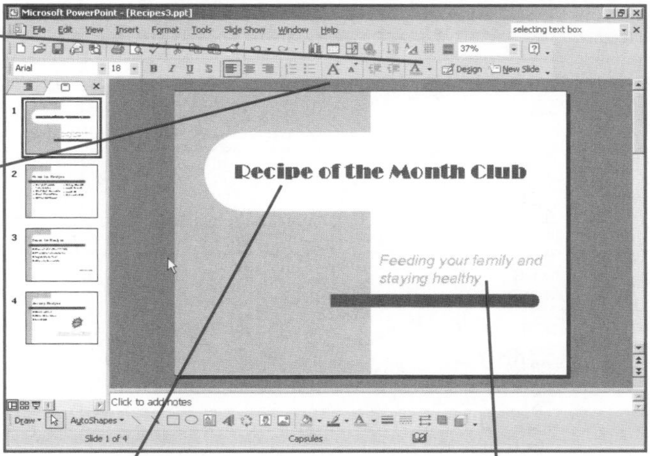

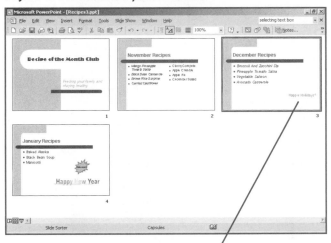

Text formatted with Broadway font, 40-point

Text formatted with italic and lavender color

Figure 2-14: Finished presentation

Reformatted text

extra!

Replacing fonts throughout a presentation

If you want to replace all text that is in one font with another font throughout a presentation, click Format on the menu bar, click Replace Fonts, click the Replace drop down list arrow, select the font to replace, click the With drop down list arrow to select the font you want to replace it with, then click Replace. You can select the text that is in the font you want to replace before clicking Format on the menu bar to have that font appear in the Replace text box automatically. All occurrences of the font throughout the presentation will be replaced. To change the case of selected text to Sentence, Lower, Upper, Title, or Toggle case, click Format on the menu bar, click Change Case, click the Case option button, then click OK.

Skill Set 2

Inserting and Modifying Text

Target Your Skills

1 Use Figure 2-15 as a guide to create a presentation. Start with a new blank presentation, then insert slides from the Outline file Outline2.doc. Save the presentation as Outline2.ppt. Apply the Blends design template to all the slides. **open**

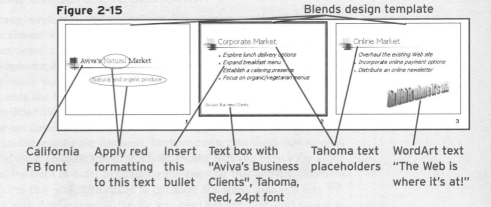

Figure 2-15

Blends design template

California FB font

Apply red formatting to this text

Insert this bullet

Text box with "Aviva's Business Clients", Tahoma, Red, 24pt font

Tahoma text placeholders

WordArt text "The Web is where it's at!"

file >] **open Aviva1.ppt**

2 Use Figure 2-16 as a guide to create a final presentation. Format the placeholder text as shown.

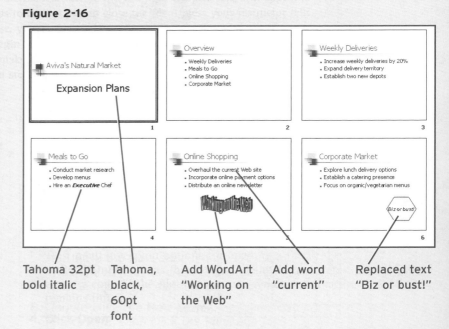

Figure 2-16

Tahoma 32pt bold italic

Tahoma, black, 60pt font

Add WordArt "Working on the Web"

Add word "current"

Replaced text "Biz or bust!"

Skill List

1. Add tables, charts, clip art, and bitmap images to slides
2. Customize slide backgrounds
3. Add OfficeArt elements to slides
4. Apply custom formats to tables

Most people absorb information and concepts better from a presentation when images are used to complement text. In this skill set, you will learn how to add photographs, images, and other graphic objects such as organization charts to slides. You will learn to apply slide backgrounds that contain textures, patterns, and images. You will learn to present numerical data in your presentation as a chart so that your audience can quickly grasp its meaning. PowerPoint uses a program called Microsoft Graph to create charts. A **chart** is a graphic presentation of data, useful for showing trends or comparisons. You will also learn to create **tables**, which are structures that organize data in columns and rows, and then learn how to format tables to make them visually interesting.

Skill Set 3
Inserting and Modifying Visual Elements

Add Tables, Charts, Clip Art, and Bitmap Images to Slides
Create Tables on Slides

Some text or graphic information is best presented as a **table**, which is made up of columns and rows. The basic unit of a table is a **cell**, the intersection of a column and row. In a PowerPoint slide, you can insert a table with any number of columns and rows and then enter text or insert images into the individual cells. Typically you use the first row of a table to identify the content of each column; these are the **column heads**. You can also insert **row labels** into each cell of the first column to identify the content of each row.

The Title and Table layout on the Slide Layout task pane makes it easy to add a table to a slide. You can also insert a table by clicking the Insert Table button on the Standard toolbar, or by clicking Insert on the menu bar, then clicking Table. You specify the number of columns and rows in the Insert Table dialog box.

You can divide an existing column or row by using the Draw Table button on the Tables and Borders toolbar. Click the Draw Table button, then draw a line between any two columns or rows. To create a new row at the bottom of the table, place the insertion point in the cell in the last row and column, then press [Tab].

Activity Steps

 open Bwayshk1.ppt

1. Click **View** on the menu bar, click **Task Pane** to open the task pane, click the **Other Task Panes** down arrow, then click **Slide Layout**
2. Click **Slide 2** to display the slide with the Title and Text layout, then scroll down the Slide Layout task pane until you see the Other Layouts section
3. Click the **Title and Table layout** in the Other Layouts section to change the layout of slide 2
   See Figure 3-1.
4. Double-click **Double click to add table**, type **4** in the Number of columns box, press [Tab], type **3** in the Number of rows box, then click **OK**
   The Tables and Borders toolbar opens.
5. Close the task pane, click **Click to add title**, then type **Ticket Prices**
6. Click the first cell in the upper left corner, press [Tab] to move to row 1 column 2, type **Child**, press [Tab], type **Student**, press [Tab], type **Adult**, then press [Tab] to move to row 2
7. Type **Afternoon**, press [Tab], type **$5**, press [Tab], type **$7**, press [Tab], type **$10**, press [Tab] to move to row 3, type **Evening**, press [Tab], type **$6**, press [Tab], type **$8**, press [Tab], type **$15** then click the slide outside the table
   The Tables and Borders toolbar closes and the table is complete. *See Figure 3-2.*

 close Bwayshk1.ppt

Figure 3-1: Title and Table layout applied

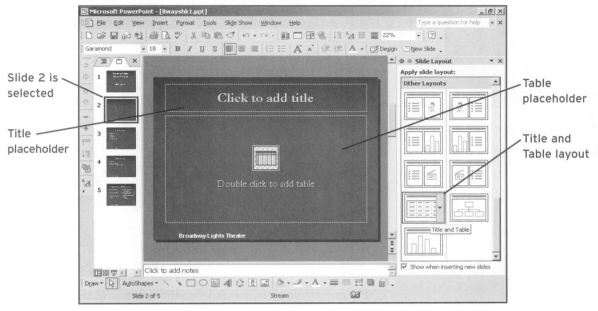

Slide 2 is selected

Title placeholder

Table placeholder

Title and Table layout

Figure 3-2: Table in slide

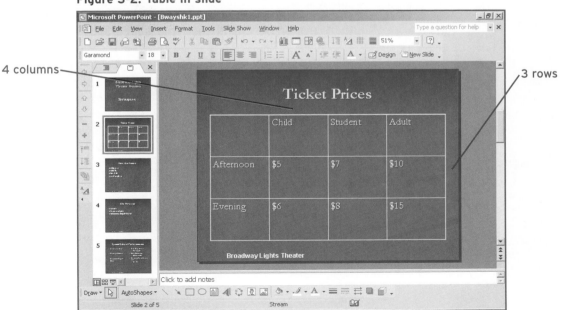

4 columns

3 rows

Skill Set 3

Inserting and Modifying Visual Elements

Add Tables, Charts, Clip Art, and Bitmap Images to Slides
Add Clip Art Images to Slides

A presentation would be pretty dull if it contained only words. Fortunately, Office XP comes with a large library of drawings, images, photographs, sounds, and other media files, all of which are called **clips**. Clips are stored and organized in a repository called the **Clip Organizer**. **Clip art** is a collection of images in the Clip Organizer that you can use to enhance your presentations. You can browse through the clip collections using the search feature in the Insert Clip Art task pane.

You can also use the Insert Clip Art task pane to browse for **AutoShapes**, which are ready-made shapes provided by Office XP that you can insert into your presentations.

When you insert a clip, you see an Automatic Layout SmartTag. If you click the Automatic Layout Options list arrow, you can stop the automatic layout and have the image appear in the middle of the slide, so you can place it wherever you want.

Activity Steps

 open Bwayshk2.ppt

1. Click Slide 3 on the Slides tab, click Insert on the menu bar, point to Picture, then click Clip Art (if the Add Clips to Organizer dialog box appears, click Later)

2. Type Shakespeare in the Search text box in the Insert Clip Art task pane, click Search, then click the image of William Shakespeare that appears in the Search results (if you don't see William Shakespeare, type Theater in the Search text box, then click one of the images that appears)
   See Figure 3-3.

3. Click Slide 4 on the Slides tab, click the AutoShapes button on the Drawing toolbar, then click More AutoShapes
   The Insert Clip Art task pane changes to display a selection of AutoShapes.

4. Click the Cloud image, then drag it to the lower right corner of the slide
   See Figure 3-4.

 close Bwayshk2.ppt

Figure 3-3: Insert Clip Art task pane search results

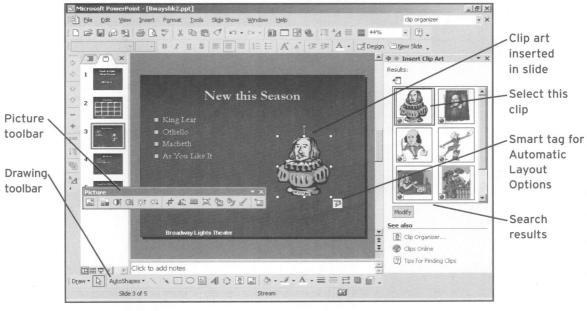

Clip art
inserted
in slide

Select this
clip

Picture
toolbar

Smart tag for
Automatic
Layout
Options

Drawing
toolbar

Search
results

Figure 3-4: AutoShapes in Clip Art task pane

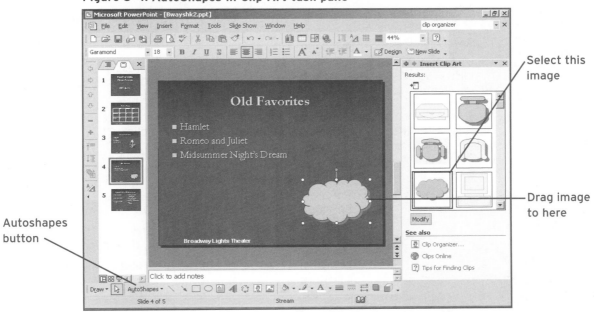

Select this
image

Drag image
to here

Autoshapes
button

Skill Set 3

Inserting and Modifying Visual Elements

Add Tables, Charts, Clip Art, and Bitmap Images to Slides
Add Charts to Slides

You can easily insert a chart into a slide by choosing one of the chart layouts on the Slide Layout task pane. When you insert a chart, Graph opens and displays a chart with a datasheet containing placeholder information. A **datasheet**, which looks like a spreadsheet, is made up of lettered columns and numbered rows, which intersect to form cells. You enter data for the chart by replacing the placeholder text and numbers in the datasheet. You enter the **data series**, or the information that is represented in the chart, in the datasheet rows. Each data series has a unique color. Pie charts have only one data series. The **categories** of data are represented along the horizontal or **X-axis** of the chart; the **values** of data are represented along the vertical or **Y-axis**.

Activity Steps

 open Bwayshk3.ppt

1. Click **Slide 2**, then click the **Insert Chart button** on the content layout placeholder
   See Figure 3-5.

2. Click the **East** cell, type **Classics**, press [Tab], type **125**, press [Tab], type **132**, press [Tab], type **150**, press [Tab], then type **250**

3. Click the **West** cell, type **Musicals**, press [Tab], type **175**, press [Tab], type **250**, press [Tab], type **295**, press [Tab], then type **310**

4. Click the **North** cell, type **Comedies**, press [Tab], type **160**, press [Tab], type **140**, press [Tab], type **210**, press [Tab], then type **285**

5. Close the datasheet, double-click **300** on the Value Axis, click the **Number tab**, click **Currency** in the Category list box, type **0** in the Decimal places list box, then click **OK**

6. Click **Chart** on the menu bar, click **Chart Type**, click **Line** in the Chart type list box, click **OK** to view the data as a line graph, click **Chart** on the menu bar, click **Chart Type**, click **Column**, click the **Stacked Column icon** (first row, second column) in the Chart Sub-type list box, then click **OK**

7. Double-click the **Legend**, click **Fill Effects**, click the **Texture tab**, click the **Paper Bag effect**, click **OK**, then click **OK** again

8. Click **Click to add title**, then type **Ticket Sales in Hundreds of Dollars**
   See Figure 3-6.

 close Bwayshk3.ppt

Step 7
The Chart Objects list box on the Standard toolbar tells you which object in the chart is selected. Click the Chart Objects list arrow to select any object in the chart.

Figure 3-5: Chart with sample data

Datasheet with sample data

Labels identify data series

Y-axis values

X-axis labels

Legend describes each data series

North data series

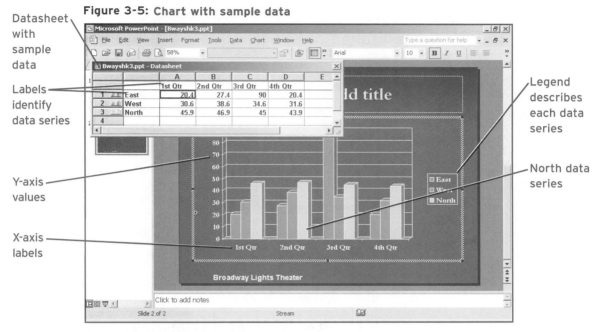

Figure 3-6: Completed chart slide

Value Axis formated in currency with no decimal places

Formatted legend

Stacked column chart

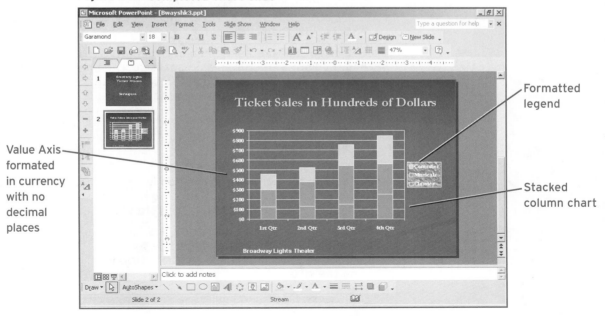

Skill Set 3

Inserting and Modifying Visual Elements

Add Tables, Charts, Clip Art, and Bitmap Images to Slides
Add Bitmap Images to Slides

Although PowerPoint comes loaded with a wide range of clip art images, you will sometimes want to insert other images in your presentation, such as a logo or photograph. A **bitmap image** is an image stored as a series of small dots. The most common bitmap image file format is .bmp, but others are .jpg, .tif, .png, and .gif. You can acquire photographs by taking them using a digital camera, scanning existing pictures using a scanner, or downloading them from a Web site or from a CD of photographs purchased from a commercial retailer. Always keep in mind that most images have some form of copyright protection; take care to honor those rights when you use photos or images in your presentations. To insert a picture that's stored on a disk, you use the Insert Picture command or click the Insert Picture button on the Drawing toolbar. Once you've inserted a picture, you can resize it by using the Format Picture dialog box or by dragging one of the sizing handles. You can move the picture on the slide by dragging it.

Activity Steps

 open Bwayshk4.ppt

1. Click **Slide 2**, click **Insert** on the menu bar, point to **Picture**, then click **From File**

2. Click the **Look in list arrow** to locate your Project Files, click **stars1.jpg**, then click **Insert**

3. Click **Format** on the menu bar, click **Picture**, click the **Size tab** in the Format Picture dialog box, select the number in the Size and rotate Height box, type **4.0**, verify that the Lock aspect ratio box has a check mark, then press **[Tab]**
   The Width measurement automatically changes in proportion to the height you specified so that the picture keeps the same scale.

You can double-click a picture to open the Format Picture dialog box.

4. Click **OK**, click the **Insert Picture button** 🖼 on the Drawing toolbar, click **stars2.jpg**, then click **Insert**

5. Position the pointer over the top left sizing handle of stars2.jpg until it changes to a ⤡, then drag it up and to the left so that the picture is slightly larger than stars1.jpg

6. Position the pointer over the stars2.jpg image until the pointer changes ⬚, drag the image to the far right of the slide, then drag the stars1.jpg image to the position shown in Figure 3-7 on the slide

 close Bwayshk4.ppt

Figure 3-7: Bitmap images inserted on slide

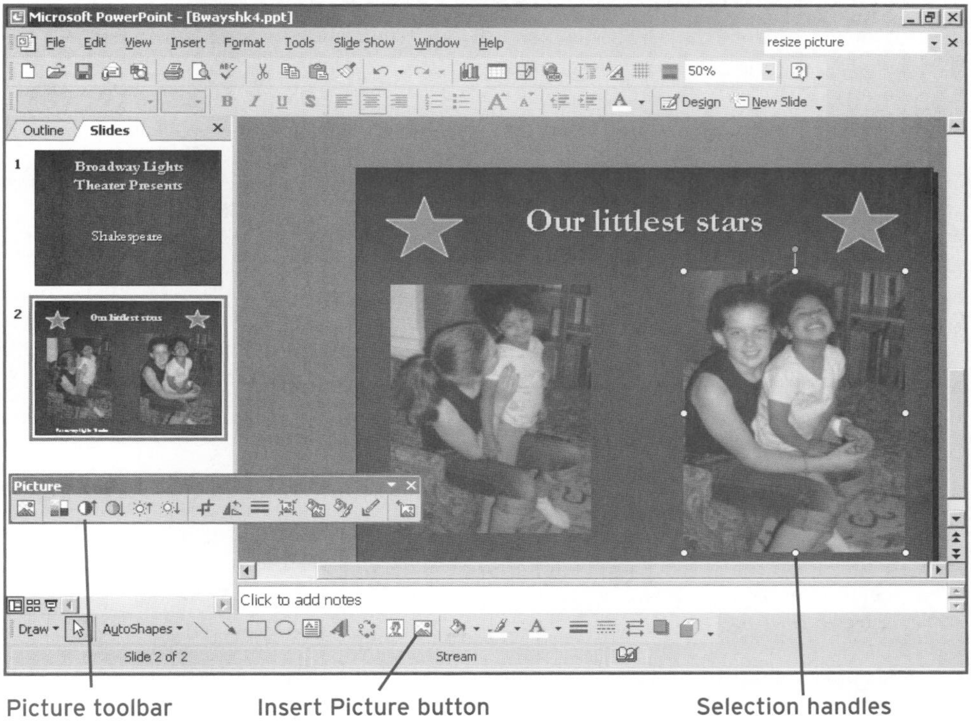

Picture toolbar   Insert Picture button   Selection handles

extra!

Compressing images

Image files are often large; a presentation that includes many images makes for an extremely large PowerPoint file. You can reduce the size of the image files in your PowerPoint presentation by clicking the Compress Pictures button 🖾 on the Picture toolbar. The Compress Pictures dialog box lets you specify whether to compress all the pictures in the presentation or just the selected pictures. You can also change the resolution or delete cropped areas. Compression does not reduce the image measurements, only the size of the image file.

Skill Set 3

Inserting and Modifying Visual Elements

Customize Slide Backgrounds
Add Fill Effects to Slide Backgrounds

You can enhance the way a slide looks by applying a **background**, which can apply to all the slides in a presentation or just to selected slides. You can have a solid color background or you can apply one of PowerPoint's special effects, called **fill effects**. You use the Format Background dialog box to apply backgrounds to your slides. You use the Fill Effects dialog box to apply special effects to your backgrounds.

To create customized fill effects on your slide background, click the Gradient tab of the Fill Effects dialog box, choose either one color or two colors in the color area, then select one of the six available shading styles.

Activity Steps

 open Bwayshk5.ppt

1. Click **Format** on the menu bar, click **Background**, click the **Background fill list arrow**, then click **Fill Effects**

2. Click the **Texture tab**, then click **Granite**
   See Figure 3-8.

3. Click **OK**, then click **Apply to all** in the Background dialog box
   See Figure 3-9.

 close Bwayshk5.ppt

Creating a photo album
If your presentation contains mostly photographs, PowerPoint can automatically create a presentation in the style of a photo album directly from the pictures you select. You can format the album with design templates and select attractive layouts to display your photographs to full advantage. Start a new presentation, click Insert on the menu bar, point to Picture, then click New Photo Album. The Photo Album dialog box lets you select the pictures, specify color values and brightness, choose whether you want black and white pictures, select a shape for the frame, and decide whether or not to rotate the images. You can apply any of the available design templates. You select the picture layout, which can either fit the pictures to the slide, or place as many pictures as you like on each slide. You put the selected pictures in the order you need for the album, decide if you want captions below the pictures, and then click Create. The photo album is created as a presentation you can then modify.

Figure 3-8: Fill effects dialog box

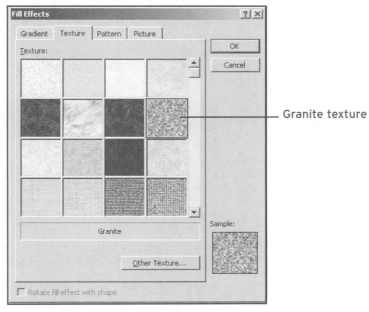

Granite texture

Figure 3-9: Granite texture applied to background

Fill effect applied to all slides

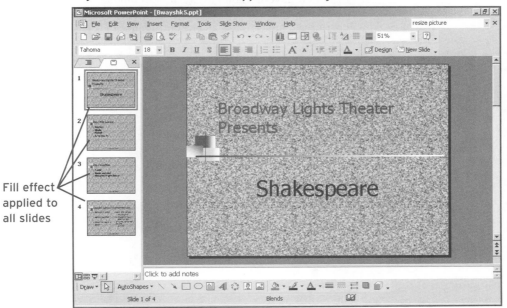

Skill Set 3

Inserting and Modifying Visual Elements

Customize Slide Backgrounds
Add Bitmap Graphics to Slide Backgrounds

You might have a particular image such as a logo that you want to feature prominently in your presentation. You can use any image as the background for all or some of the slides in the presentation. You can select a photograph that you created with a digital camera, an image that you made using graphics editing software, or any image stored as a file on your computer. You use the Picture tab of the Fill Effects dialog box to select a picture as a background image.

Step 3
Click the Lock aspect ratio check box in the Fill Effects dialog box to prevent the image from becoming distorted when it is resized to fit the slide.

Activity Steps

 open Bwayshk6.ppt

1. Click **Slide 3**, click **Format** on the menu bar, then click **Background**

2. Click the **Background fill list arrow**, click **Fill Effects**, then click the **Picture tab** in the Fill Effects dialog box

3. Click **Select Picture**, navigate to the folder where your Project Files are stored, click **flower1.jpg** in the Select Picture dialog box, then click **Insert**
   See Figure 3-10.

4. Click **OK**, then click **Apply**
   You often have to modify text to accommodate the characteristics of the image you selected for a background. This picture has a dark spot where the slide title text is currently placed.

5. Click **Old Favorites**, click the **Align Right button** ▤ on the toolbar, then click outside the slide to deselect it
   See Figure 3-11.

 close Bwayshk6.ppt

Figure 3-10: Fill Effects dialog box with flower1 selected

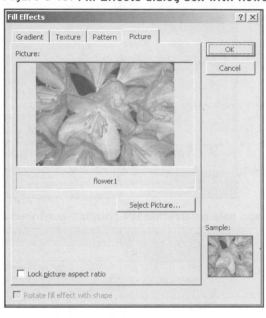

Figure 3-11: Graphic applied to slide background

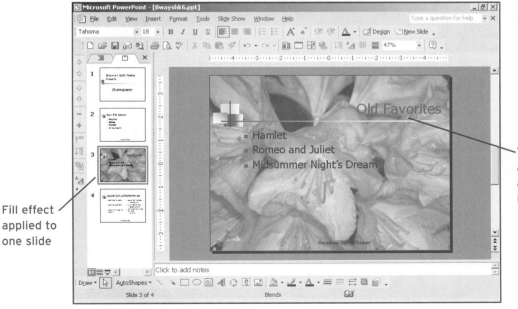

Fill effect applied to one slide

Title aligned to accommodate image

Skill Set 3

Inserting and Modifying Visual Elements

Add OfficeArt Elements to Slides
Add Freeform Objects and AutoShapes to Slides

You can use the various drawing tools available on the Drawing toolbar to create unique shapes and graphic elements to enhance your presentation. If you don't want to draw shapes yourself, you can choose from one of the many ready-made AutoShapes, also available on the Drawing toolbar. You can use the Drawing toolbar buttons to customize the shape with colors, line widths, and line styles to get the exact effect you want.

You can change the colors, line styles, position, and size of an AutoShape using the Format AutoShape dialog box. To open the Format AutoShape dialog box, double-click the AutoShape.

Activity Steps

 open Bwayshk7.ppt

1. Click **Slide 2**, click the **Oval button** ⬭ on the Drawing toolbar, place the ╋ pointer slightly above the bullet next to **Comedy of Errors**, then drag down and right to create an oval around Comedy of Errors

2. Click the **Fill Color button list arrow** on the Drawing toolbar, click **No Fill**, then click the **Line Style button** ▤

3. Point to the **3pt single line style** as shown in Figure 3-12, then click **3pt single line style**

4. Click the **Arrow button** ◤ on the Drawing toolbar, drag the ╋ pointer from the bottom middle sizing handle on the oval down and right to the middle of the two columns just below the last bullet

5. Click the **Line Style button** ▤, click the **3pt single line style**, click the **Arrow Style button** ⇄ on the Drawing toolbar, then click **Arrow Style 6** (the left facing arrow)

6. Click **AutoShapes** on the Drawing toolbar, point to **Stars and Banners**, then click **Vertical Scroll** (column 1 row 4)

7. Drag the ╋ pointer from the beginning of the arrow down and right to create a scroll 2½" wide and 1" tall, then type **Special Holiday Performance**
See Figure 3-13.

 close Bwayshk7.ppt

Figure 3-12: Drawing an oval

Oval drawn on slide

Fill Color list arrow

Oval button

Current line width

New line width

Line Style button

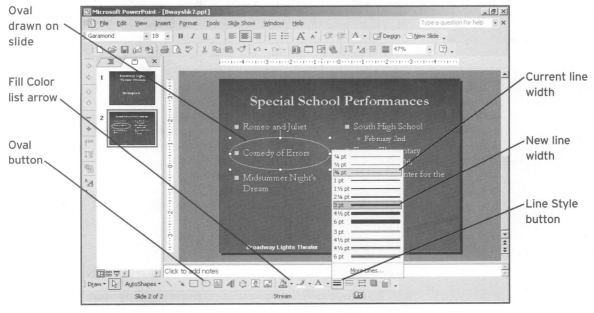

Figure 3-13: Slide with Autoshape and freeform objects

Arrow

Arrow button

AutoShape

Arrow Style button

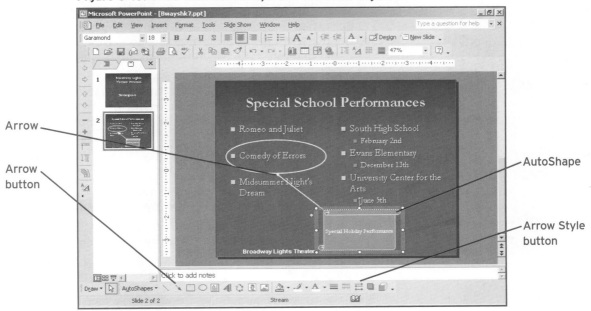

Skill Set 3

Inserting and Modifying Visual Elements

Add OfficeArt Elements to Slides
Add an Organization Chart to a Slide

Although you could use the drawing tools to create conceptual drawings, PowerPoint's diagramming tools let you create certain types of diagrams quickly. **Organization charts**, often called **org charts**, combine text and graphics to create a representation of how people or things are related to each other. They are often used to show the hierarchy of employees in a business. In an organization chart, shapes are connected by lines to show relationships. Items at a higher level in the hierarchy are known as **superior** shapes and feed into lesser items such as **assistant** shapes, **subordinate** shapes, and **coworker** shapes. Typically the most important item is at the top, although you can invert the chart. To insert an organization chart, you use the Insert Diagram or Organization Chart button, which is located on both the Drawing toolbar and the Content slide layout. The Organization Chart toolbar has buttons that let you change the chart layout, expand, scale, or fit the contents to the chart, and insert new subordinates, coworkers, or assistants.

Right-click a shape to open a shortcut menu with commands to help you create organization charts.

Activity Steps

 open Bwayshk8.ppt

1. Click Slide 2, click View on the menu bar, click Task Pane, click the Other Task Panes down arrow, click Slide Layout, then click the Title and Content layout in the Content Layouts area

2. Click the Insert Diagram or Organization Chart button 🔲 on the Content Layout template placeholder, click the Organization Chart diagram type 🔲 in the Diagram Gallery, then click OK
See Figure 3-14.

3. Click the top shape, click the Font Color list arrow ▲▾, click More Colors, click the Black cell, click OK, type Jennifer Laina, press [Enter], type Producer, then press [Esc]

4. Click the left subordinate shape, click the black Font Color button ▲, type Emily Michaels, press [Enter], type Director, then press [Esc]

5. Click the middle shape, click the black Font Color button ▲, type Rita Backer, press [Enter], type Staging, then press [Esc]

6. Click the right shape, click the black Font Color button ▲, type Karen Louie, press [Enter], type Casting, then press [Esc]

7. Click outside the chart to deselect it, then close the task pane
See Figure 3-15.

 close Bwayshk8.ppt

Figure 3-14: Organization chart on slide

Organization chart

Organization chart toolbar

Title and Content layout

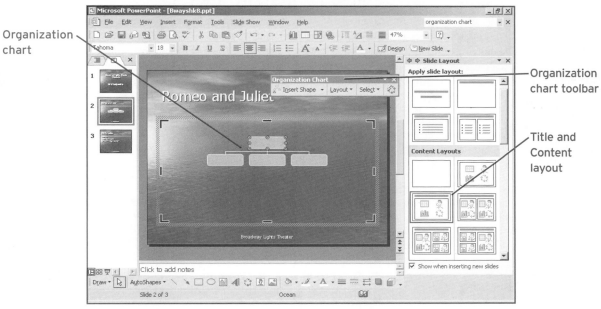

Figure 3-15: Completed organization chart

Subordinate shapes

Superior shape

Font Color button

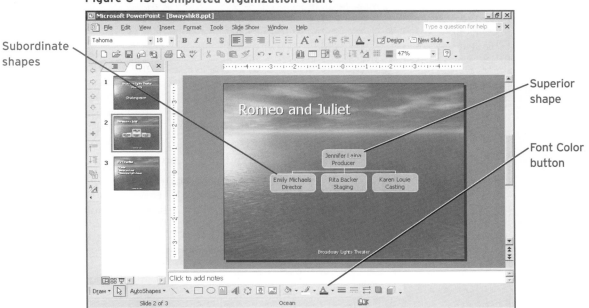

Skill Set 3

Inserting and Modifying Visual Elements

Apply Custom Formats to Tables
Apply User-Defined Formats to Tables

Tables organize information so that it is easier for an audience to understand. Formatting tables makes data even more visually comprehensible. For instance, applying different colors to each row or to column heads can help distinguish them from other elements of the table. Applying a decorative line style to your borders can also make your table more appealing. These and other formatting commands are available on the Tables and Borders toolbar and the Format menu.

Step 4
To get exact colors, you can enter the exact values. This is useful if you are trying to match colors.

Activity Steps

 open Bwayshk9.ppt

1. Click **Slide 2**, click the table to select it, then open the Tables and Borders toolbar

2. Drag the pointer to select the **Afternoon row**, click the **Center Vertically button** 🔲 on the Tables and Borders toolbar, click the **Fill Color list arrow** 🎨▾, then click the **Pink custom color square** in the second row of the palette

3. Drag to select the **Evening row**, click the **Center Vertically button** 🔲, click the **Fill Color list arrow** 🎨▾, then click **More Fill Colors**

4. Click the **Custom tab**, type **130** in the Red box, press **[Tab]**, type **56** in the Green box, press **[Tab]**, type **250** in the Blue box, click **OK**, then click in the first cell
   See Figure 3-16.

5. Double-click the **table border** to open the Format Table dialog box, scroll the **Borders Style list**, click the **long dash, dot line style** (the last one in the list), click the **three horizontal border buttons** off and then on again (top, middle, and bottom) to apply the new dashed border to all horizontal borders, then click **OK**

6. Drag the pointer to select the **Child, Student**, and **Adult cells**, then click the **Bold button** 🅱 on the toolbar

7. Click **cell 1**, click **Format** on the menu bar, click **Table**, click the **Fill tab**, click the **Fill color list arrow**, click **Fill Effects**, click the **Two colors option button**, click the **Color 1 list arrow**, click the **Pink color square** on the second row, click the **Color 2 list arrow**, click the **Blue color square** on the second row, click **OK**, click **OK** again, then click to deselect the table
   See Figure 3-17.

 close Bwayshk9.ppt

Figure 3-16: Changing table formats

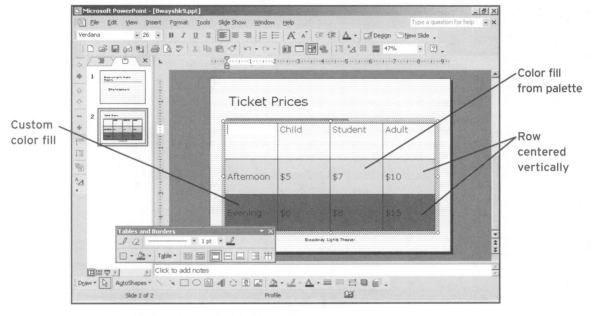

Custom color fill

Color fill from palette

Row centered vertically

Figure 3-17: Final formatted table

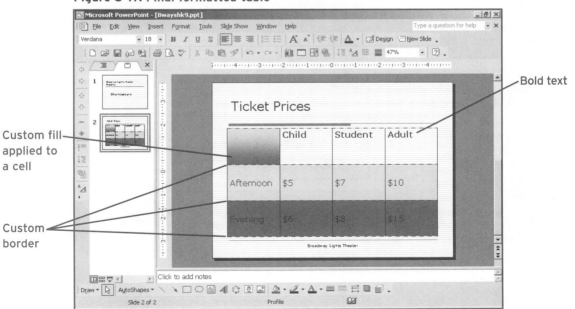

Custom fill applied to a cell

Custom border

Bold text

Skill Set 3

Inserting and Modifying Visual Elements

Target Your Skills

 open Pretzel1.ppt

1 Use Figure 3-18 to finish a presentation for the PerfectPretzel company. The column headings in the table are PA, CT, NJ, NY. The row labels are Manager and Assistant Manager.

Figure 3-18

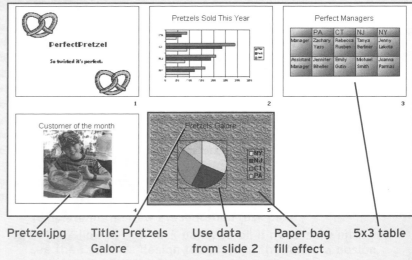

Pretzel.jpg — Title: Pretzels Galore — Use data from slide 2 — Paper bag fill effect — 5x3 table

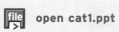 open cat1.ppt

2 Use Figure 3-19 as a guide to create a final presentation. Add an organization chart to slide 2 showing you as the Director and the four shelters as subordinate shapes. Click the Insert Shape button on the Organization Chart toolbar to insert a coworker.

Figure 3-19

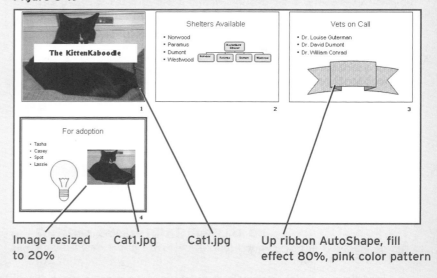

Image resized to 20% — Cat1.jpg — Cat1.jpg — Up ribbon AutoShape, fill effect 80%, pink color pattern

Skill List

1. Apply formats to presentations
2. Apply animation schemes
3. Apply slide transitions
4. Customize slide formats
5. Customize slide templates
6. Manage a Slide Master
7. Rehearse timing
8. Rearrange slides
9. Modify slide layout
10. Add links to a presentation

PowerPoint comes with a wide variety of tools to help you control and format your presentations. In this skill set, you'll learn how to make formatting changes to design templates, slide masters, and slide layouts to enhance your presentations. You'll also learn to add and customize color and animation schemes and apply transition effects for an entire presentation or individual slides. To help you prepare for a live audience, you'll also rehearse and change the timings for your presentation and rearrange slides as needed. Finally, you'll add hyperlinks to other slides within the presentation, other files on your computer, an intranet, or the Web.

Skill Set 4
Modifying Presentation Formats

Apply Formats to Presentations
Format Slides Differently in a Single Presentation

You do not have to be a graphic designer to create professional-looking presentations. You can apply any of the design templates that come with PowerPoint to some or all of your slides to take advantage of great-looking layouts, graphics, and colors that work well together. The Slide Design task pane contains all the available design templates. Once you apply a particular design template, you can easily make modifications to individual slides to create a unique look for background graphics, bullets, text, and color.

Use the Bullets and Numbering dialog box to change the bullet color, the numbering style, or the size of the bullet relative to the text. To use a picture as a bullet, click Picture, choose an available image or click Import to browse for one, then click OK.

Activity Steps

 open Hamlet1.ppt

1. Click the **Design button** 🖼 to open the Slide Design task pane, then click **Slide 4** on the Slides tab

2. Scroll the Slide Design task pane to view the Available For Use design templates, then click the **Digital Dots template icon**
See Figure 4-1.

3. Click the **left text box** on the slide, press and hold **[Shift]**, then click the **right text box** to select both text boxes

4. Click **Format** on the menu bar, click **Bullets and Numbering**, verify that the **Bulleted tab** is selected, click the **four dots in a diamond pattern** bullet design, then click **OK**

5. Click the **Font Size list arrow** on the toolbar, then click **28**

6. Close the Slide Design task pane, click **Slide 3** on the Slides tab to view the original formatting of the design template, then click **Slide 4** on the Slides tab to view the formatting modifications you made
See Figure 4-2.

 close Hamlet1.ppt

Figure 4-1: Design template applied

Digital Dots applied

Slide 4 is selected

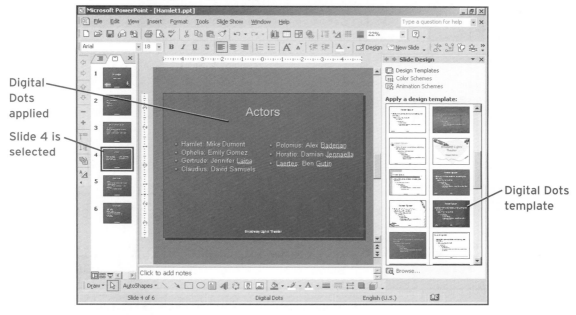

Digital Dots template

Figure 4-2: Formatting changes to slide

Font size changed for this slide

Bullet format changed for this slide

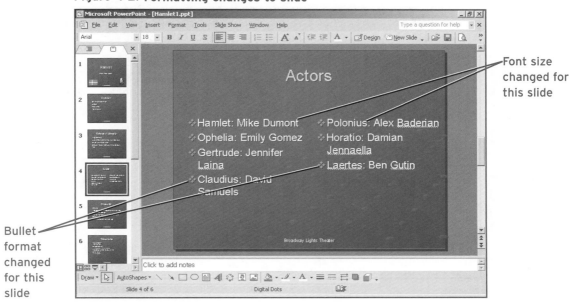

Skill Set 4
Modifying Presentation Formats

Apply Formats to Presentations
Modify Presentation Templates

Design templates contain text and bullet styles, background images, and color schemes that give your presentation a professional look. However, you might want to make formatting modifications to one or more of these elements to create a design that better meets the needs of your presentation. All the specifications for a design template are stored in the slide master, the part of the presentation that specifies how graphics and text appear on each slide. Formatting changes made to text, bullets, and other elements in the slide master will be applied to every slide in the presentation.

You can also open the slide master by pressing and holding [Shift], then clicking the Normal View button.

Activity Steps

 open Hamlet2.ppt

1. Click **Slide 5** on the Slides tab, click **View**, point to **Master**, then click **Slide Master**
   See Figure 4-3.

2. Click **Click to edit Master title style**, click the **Font Style list arrow**, then click **Algerian**, or another font if Algerian is not available

3. Right-click **Click to edit Master text styles**, click **Bullets and Numbering** on the shortcut menu, click **Customize**, type **150** in the Character code box to select the symbol **Wingdings 150**, click **OK**, then click **OK** again (Note: If you do not have the Wingdings 150 symbol, click another symbol)

4. Click the **Normal View button** 🔲

5. Click the **Slide Sorter View button** ▦, click the **Zoom list arrow** on the toolbar, then click **100%** to see the changes applied to all the slides
   See Figure 4-4.

 close Hamlet2.ppt

Figure 4-3: Slide Master view

Slide Master View toolbar

Text styles and placement from design template

Bullet format from design template

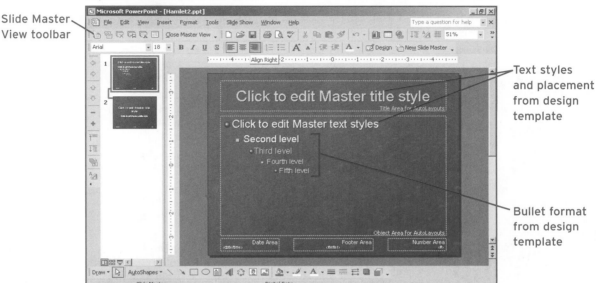

Figure 4-4: Slide Sorter view

Font change for Title text

Modified bullet style

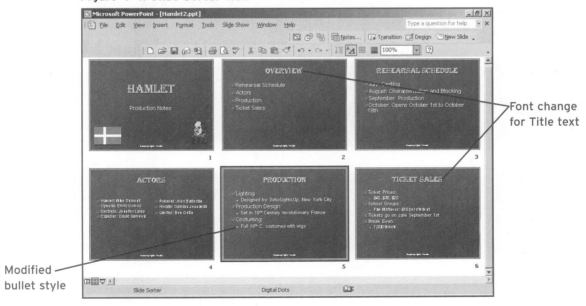

Skill Set 4

Modifying Presentation Formats

Apply Formats to Presentations
Modify the Format of Individual Slides

Choosing a design template applies set colors, fonts, and bullet styles to your presentation. Sometimes, you might want to make a change to an individual slide so that it is formatted differently from the rest of the slides in your presentation. For instance, you might want to change the color scheme for one slide so that it stands out from the rest. A **color scheme** is a set of eight colors that is consistently applied to fonts, accents, hyperlinks, backgrounds, and fills. PowerPoint comes with several color schemes that you can apply to all or selected slides. Each design template has a set color scheme that you can change for individual slides or the entire presentation, as needed. Changing the color scheme can alter the whole feel of a presentation; use the Slide Design task pane to change the color scheme.

Activity Steps

 open Hamlet3.ppt

You can override the slide master formatting for individual slides by using the Format menu.

1. Click the **Design button** ⊞ on the toolbar to open the Slide Design task pane, then click **Color Schemes**
   The selected color scheme is currently applied to the entire presentation.

2. Click **Slide 3** on the Slides tab, press and hold **[Shift]**, then click **Slide 6** on the Slide tab
   See Figure 4-5.

3. Click the **teal background color scheme list arrow** (the fourth color scheme in the first column), then click **Apply to Selected Slides**
   See Figure 4-6.

 close Hamlet3.ppt

Figure 4-5: Default color scheme applied to all slides

Modify the format of these selected slides

Color scheme currently applied

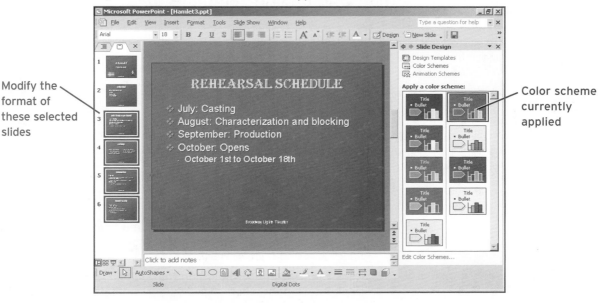

Figure 4-6: New color scheme applied to selected slides

Color scheme applied to selected slides

Color scheme list arrow

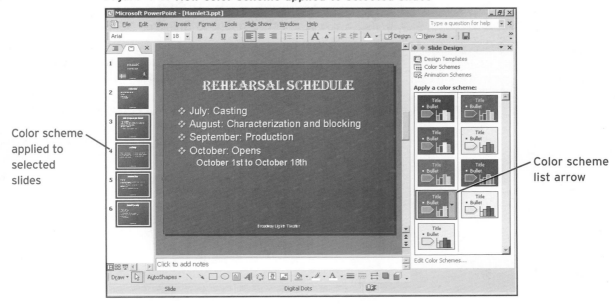

Skill Set 4

Modifying Presentation Formats

Apply Formats to Presentations
Apply More than One Design Template to Presentations

Design templates come with default color schemes as well as graphics, bullet, and font styles. You can enhance any presentation by applying more than one design template to it. When you apply a new design template to selected slides, the graphics and specifications for color and text are copied from the slide master in the new design template to a corresponding slide master for those selected slides. You can have more than one slide master in a presentation. Most design templates have slide master pairs: one master for the title slide and another for all other slides. To apply a new design template, use the Slide Design task pane.

Activity Steps

 open Hamlet4.ppt

1. Click **Slide 2** in the Slides tab, press and hold **[Ctrl]**, click **Slide 4**, press and hold **[Ctrl]**, then click **Slide 6**
   Slides 2, 4, and 6 are selected.

Not all design templates contain both a slide master and title master. To add a title master, click Insert on the menu bar, then click New Title Master.

2 Click the **Design button** on the toolbar to open the Slide Design task pane, then click **Design Templates** to display all available design templates

3. Scroll the list of templates, click the **Digital Dots.pot template list arrow**, then click **Apply to Selected Slides**

4. Scroll to the top of the Apply a design template list, then place the pointer on the **Digital Dots** template in the Used in This Presentation section to display the screen tip
   See Figure 4-7.

5. Click **View** on the menu bar, point to **Master**, then click **Slide Master**
   The presentation now contains two slide master pairs; each pair consists of a slide master for the title slide and a slide master for all other slides.

6. Close the Slide Design task pane
   See Figure 4-8.

 close Hamlet4.ppt

Figure 4-7: Digital Dots design template applied to selected slides

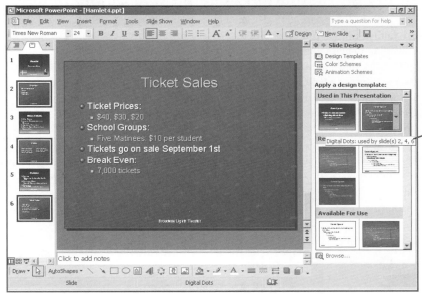

ScreenTip tells you which slides use the design template

Figure 4-8: Presentation with two slide master pairs

Original slide master and title master pair

Second slide master and title master added when Digital Dots template was applied to selected slides

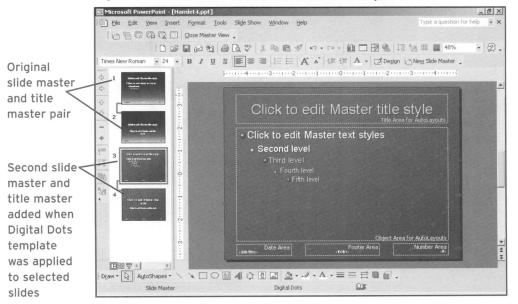

Skill Set 4

Modifying Presentation Formats

Apply Animation Schemes

Apply an Animation Scheme to a Single Slide

Animation is the motion of text and objects on a slide along with special visual and sound effects. You can bring life to your presentations by using animation. PowerPoint comes with an astounding array of ways to make text and graphics spin, swirl, and interact. You can choose from professionally designed **animation schemes**, which apply preset visual effects to text on a slide. Animation schemes are available in the Slide Design task pane, divided into three categories: Subtle, Moderate, and Exciting, to help you choose just the right animation for your presentation and audience. You can also apply preset **transitions** to your slides, which are effects that take the presentation from one slide to the next. Some animation schemes also include transitions. If both animation and transition effects are applied to a slide, transition effects occur first.

Select No Animation in the Slide Design task pane to remove animation from a slide.

Activity Steps

 open Hamlet5.ppt

1. Click the **Design button** 🖼 on the toolbar to open the Slide Design task pane

2. Click **Animation Schemes**

3. Click **Slide 4** on the Slides tab

4. Scroll through the list of subtle animation schemes, scroll through the list of Moderate animation schemes, then click **Credits** in the Exciting animation scheme list
   See Figure 4-9.

5. Click the **Slide Show (from current slide) button** 🖳 to view the animation

 close Hamlet5.ppt

Figure 4-9: Apply an animation scheme to one slide

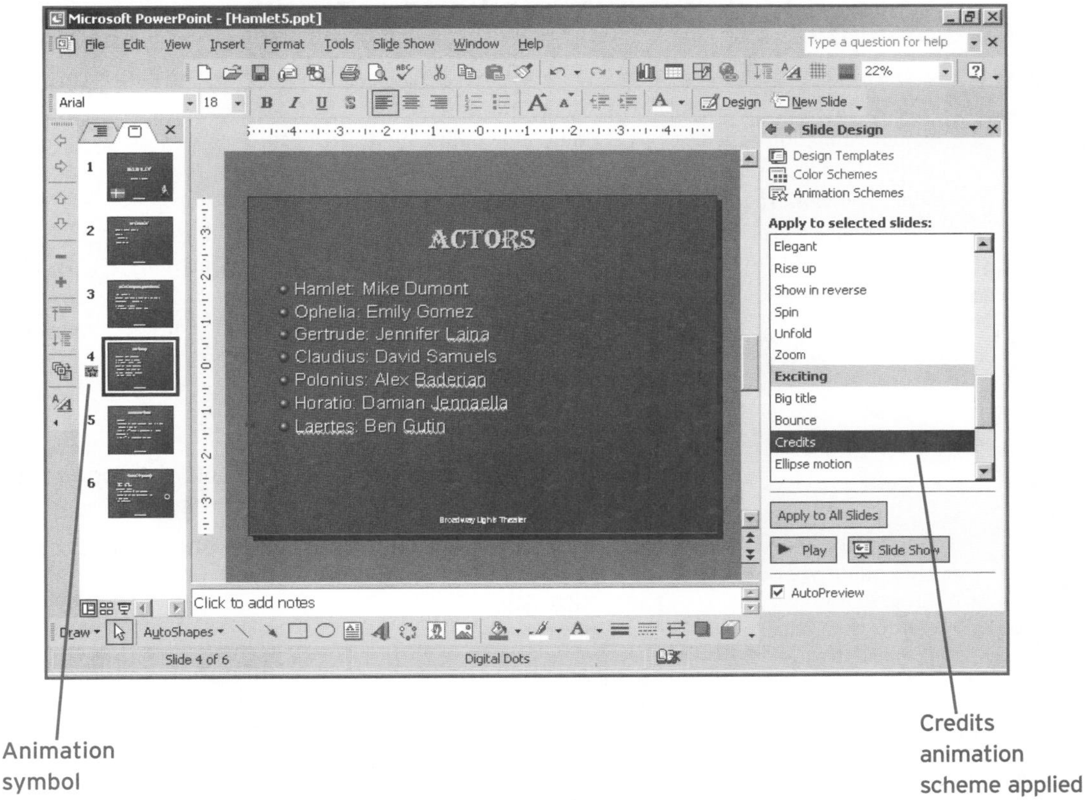

Animation symbol

Credits animation scheme applied

extra!

Viewing the slide show

The best way to get a sense of how the presentation is going to look with the animations you've chosen is by viewing the slide show during development. You can do this by clicking the slide from which you want to start and then clicking the Slide Show button on the Slide Design task pane or the Slide Show (from current slide) button. You can also view the show by clicking View on the menu bar, then clicking Slide Show, or by pressing [F5] at any time from any view. To stop the show at any time, press [Esc].

Skill Set 4
Modifying Presentation Formats

Apply Animation Schemes
Apply an Animation Scheme to a Group of Slides

You can apply animation schemes to a selected group of slides by selecting the slides you want and choosing an animation scheme from the Slide Design task pane. Animation schemes can include any combination of transition effects or title and body animations. If you want to animate only certain elements on your slide, you can use the Custom Animation task pane to select those elements and then choose a type of animation to apply to them. You should be careful as you apply animation schemes in a presentation; while selective use of animations can focus attention on a particular point, too much animation can detract from your message.

To select contiguous slides, click the first slide, press and hold [Shift] then click the last slide.

Activity Steps

 open Hamlet6.ppt

1. Click the **Design button** 🖾 on the toolbar to open the Slide Design task pane

2. Click **Slide 2** on the Slides tab, press and hold **[Ctrl]**, click **Slide 3**, press and hold **[Ctrl]**, click **Slide 5**, press and hold **[Ctrl]**, then click **Slide 6**
   See Figure 4-10.

3. Scroll through the list of subtle animation schemes, scroll through the list of Moderate animation schemes, then click **Pinwheel** in the Exciting animation scheme list

4. Click the **Slide Sorter View button** 🔲
   See Figure 4-11.

5. Click **Slide 1**, then click the **Slide Show (from current slide) button** 🖳 to view the show

 close Hamlet6.ppt

extra!

Creating Custom Animations
You can animate individual elements of a slide using the Custom Animation task pane. Click Slide Show on the menu bar, then click Custom Animation to open the Custom Animation task pane. To animate individual elements, select the element, click Add Effect in the task pane, then choose an animation style from the menu. You can also modify the start, property, and speed effects for each animation that you apply. You can also change the order in which text appears by clicking the Reorder arrows.

Certification Circle

Skill 2

Apply Animation Schemes

Figure 4-10: Apply an animation scheme to a group of slides

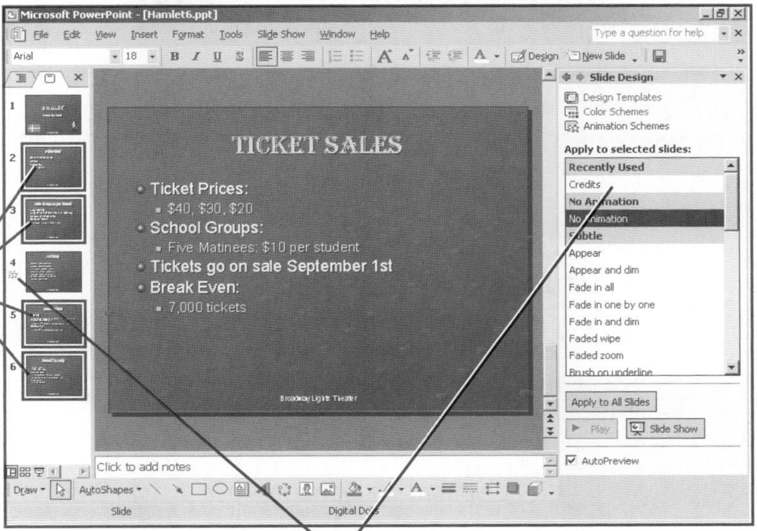

Slides 2, 3, 5, and 6 are selected

Credits animation scheme was recently used and applied to slide 4

Figure 4-11: Slide Sorter view showing animations

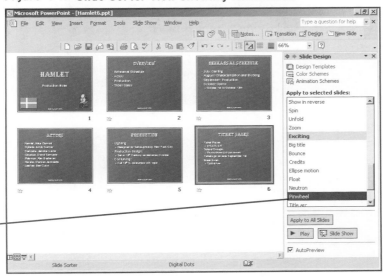

Pinwheel animation applied to slides 2, 3, 5, and 6

Skill Set 4

Modifying Presentation Formats

Apply Animation Schemes
Apply an Animation Scheme to an Entire Presentation

If you want the animations in your slides to have a consistent appearance, you can apply a single animation scheme to the entire presentation. If your presentation already contains several animation schemes, you can override the current schemes by applying a new scheme to the entire presentation.

Text or an object must have an animation applied to it before you can add a custom animation.

Activity Steps

 open Hamlet7.ppt

1. Click the **Normal View button**, Click **Slide 1** on the Slides tab, then click the **Slide Show (from current slide) button**

2. Press **[PgDn]** as many times as necessary to view the entire show and return to Normal view

3. Click the **Design button** to open the Slide Design task pane, click **Animation Schemes**, then click **Wipe** in the Subtle list

4. Click **Apply to All Slides** in the Slide Design task pane
   See Figure 4-12.

5. Click the **Slide Show (from current slide) button**, then press **[Enter]** as needed to view all slides with the new animation scheme

 close Hamlet7.ppt

Figure 4-12: Apply an animation scheme to all slides in a show

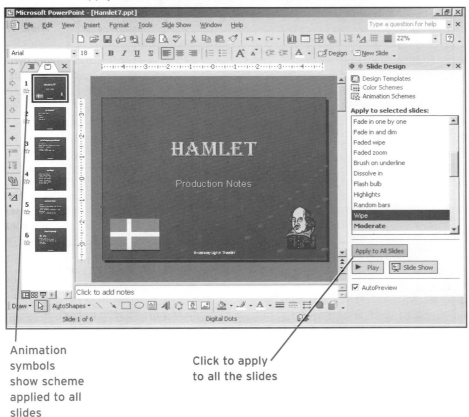

Animation symbols show scheme applied to all slides

Click to apply to all the slides

extra!

Understanding animation categories

PowerPoint organizes animation schemes into three categories in the Slide Design task pane: subtle, moderate, and exciting. Although somewhat subjective, these categories will help you choose the most appropriate animation for your presentation. In the Custom Animation task pane, animation effects are divided into four categories: Entrance (determines how text or object enters the slide), Emphasis (adds an effect to an object that is already on the slide), Exit (determines how the text or object leaves the slide at some point while the slide is displayed on the screen), and Motion paths (the path the object takes on a slide as part of the animation). You should view the effects before deciding which ones you will use. If you plan to use several effects in a show, you might want to select from the same group to keep the feel of the effects consistent.

Skill Set 4

Modifying Presentation Formats

Apply Slide Transitions
Apply Transition Effects to a Single Slide

The **transition** between slides occurs when the previous slide leaves the screen and a new slide appears. PowerPoint offers several **transition effects** you can use to liven up transitions. To apply a transition effect to selected slides, you use the Slide Transition task pane. Though you can apply only one transition effect to each slide, you can adjust the timing and the trigger for each effect. Transition effects may or may not be included in an animation scheme. You can add or change transition effects from any view.

A star symbol under a slide in Slide Sorter view, or under the slide number in the Slides tab, indicates that a transition effect or animation has been applied to the slide. Click the symbol to preview the transition or animation.

Activity Steps

 open Hamlet8.ppt

1. Click **Slide 3** on the Slides tab

2. Click **Slide Show** on the menu bar, then click **Slide Transition** to open the Slide Transition task pane
   See Figure 4-13.

3. Scroll the list of transitions, then click **Newsflash**

4. Click the **Speed list arrow** in the Modify transition section, then click **Slow**
   See Figure 4-14.

5. Click the **Slide Show button** in the Slide Transition task pane to view the show

 close Hamlet8.ppt

Figure 4-13: Slide Transition task pane

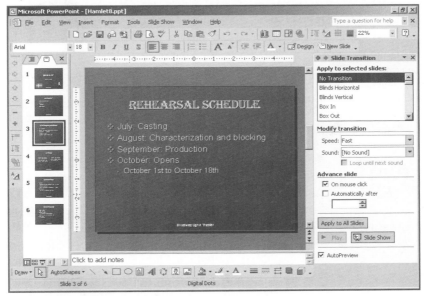

Figure 4-14: Newsflash transition

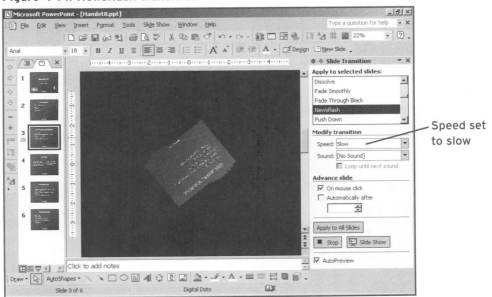

Speed set to slow

Skill Set 4
Modifying Presentation Formats

Apply Slide Transitions
Apply Transition Effects to a Group of Slides in a Presentation

To keep a presentation interesting, you might want to apply one transition to some of the slides and a different transition to others. Content may drive your decision. For example, a slide with important figures or facts can make a bold statement if you apply the Cut Through Black transition. Somber news can be introduced with a slow Dissolve transition. Adding sound such as a drum roll can highlight a specific slide. You can add or edit transition effects from Normal or Slide Sorter view using the Slide Transition task pane.

Many transition effects have descriptive names that tell you which direction they will progress, such as Wipe Left or Checkerboard Down. To change the direction of a transition effect, choose the appropriately named transition from the Slide Transition task pane.

Activity Steps

 open Hamlet9.ppt

1. Click the **Zoom list arrow**, then click **50%** to see all the slides in Slide Sorter view

2. Click **Slide 1**, press and hold **[Ctrl]**, click **Slide 4**, press and hold **[Ctrl]**, then click **Slide 6**

3. Click the **Transition button** 🖼, scroll through the Slide Transition task pane, click **Wheel Clockwise, 3 spokes** in the Slide Transition task pane
   See Figure 4-15.

4. Click **Slide 1**, click **Slide show** in the task pane, then press **[Enter]** as needed to view the entire show

 close Hamlet9.ppt

Figure 4-15: Transition applied to selected slides

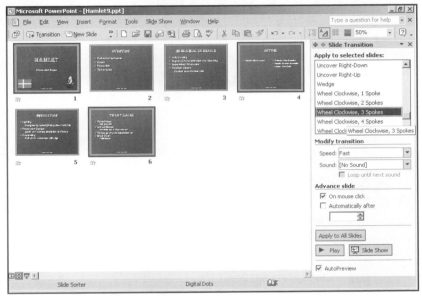

extra!

Specifying how to advance slides

The Slide Transition task pane offers options for how to advance from one slide to the next in a slide show. The On mouse click option makes it necessary for the presenter to click or press [Enter], [Tab], or [PgDn] to advance to the next slide. To make the show run without intervention, click the Automatically after check box, then specify a time interval in the box.

Skill Set 4

Modifying Presentation Formats

Apply Slide Transitions
Apply Transition Effects to an Entire Presentation

To keep a presentation professional-looking and cohesive, you might want to apply one transition to all the slides. You can do this from either Normal or Slide Sorter view, using the Slide Transition task pane.

Click the Play button in the Slide Transition task pane to view the transition effects in the selected slides.

Activity Steps

 open Hamlet10.ppt

1. Click the **Transition button** 🔲 on the toolbar to open the Slide Transition task pane

2. Click **Fade Through Black** in the Slide Transition task pane

3. Click **Apply to All Slides**
   See Figure 4-16.

4. Click **Slide Show** in the task pane, then press **[Enter]** as needed to view the entire presentation

 close Hamlet10.ppt

Figure 4-16: Transition effect applied to all the slides

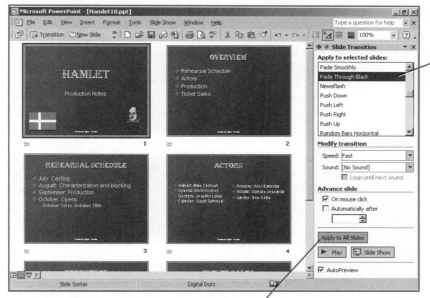

Fade Through Black transition effect

Click to apply transition to all slides

Skill Set 4
Modifying Presentation Formats

Customize Slide Formats
Customize Slides

A design template provides unique formatting specifications for text, bullets, graphics, and color that you can apply to any or all slides in a presentation. Every design template has a set **color scheme**, which is a group of specified colors applied consistently to the background, titles, fills, and bullets on slides. When you apply a design template to selected slides, all the formatting specifications for that design template are applied to the slide master. However, if you want certain slides to stand out from the others, you can override the design template formatting specified by the slide master. For instance, you can modify any of the elements of a color scheme and apply the revised color scheme to selected slides. Any edited color schemes will be available to you as new color schemes in the Slide Design task pane. The custom color schemes you create do not change the slide master formatting or color scheme for the rest of the slides in the presentation, and if you add a new slide it will take on the characteristics of the slide master.

If you inadvertently apply any color scheme to all the slides by mistake, click Edit on the menu bar, then click Undo.

Activity Steps

 open Bitpress1.ppt

1. Click the **Design button** [image] on the toolbar, then click **Slide 3** on the Slides tab

2. Click **Color Schemes** in the task pane
   The selected color scheme determined by the Crayons design template specifies a red title, small square bullet, black text, and yellow fill.

3. Click the **purple background color scheme list arrow (first column fourth scheme)**, then click **Apply to Selected Slides**
   See Figure 4-17.

4. Click **Edit Color Schemes** in the Slide Design task pane, click the **Standard tab**, click the **purple background color scheme** (third row first scheme), then click the **Custom tab**

5. Click the **Title text white color box**, click **Change Color**, click the **Bright yellow color box** as shown in Figure 4-18, then click **OK**

6. Click **Apply** to close the Edit Color Scheme text box
   The edited color scheme appears as a new option in the Apply a color scheme list.

7. Click **Slide 4** in the Slides tab, click the new **yellow title with purple background** color scheme list arrow (first column fifth scheme), then click **Apply to Selected Slides**

 close bitpress1.ppt

Figure 4-17: Slide Design task pane with color schemes displayed

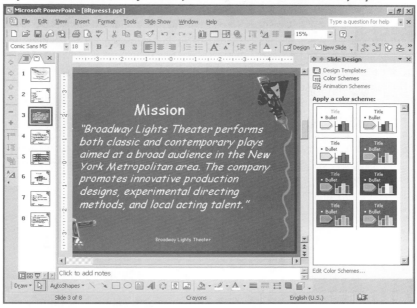

Figure 4-18: Creating a custom color scheme

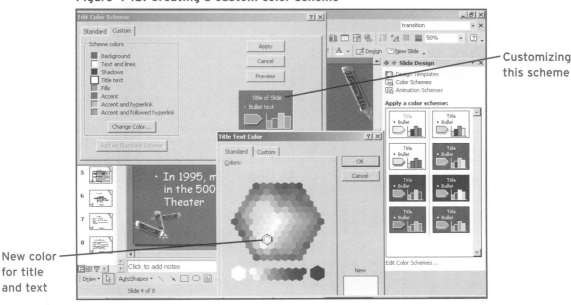

Customizing
this scheme

New color
for title
and text

Skill Set 4

Modifying Presentation Formats

Customize Slide Templates

Customize Templates

Every design template includes formatting for placeholders that contain text, graphics, and other types of content. All of the formatting specifications for these placeholders and their content are contained in the slide master. If you want to make global changes to fonts, bullets, or placeholders throughout your presentation, you make these changes to the slide master in Slide Master view. Many design templates contain two slides in Slide Master view: the **Title Master**, which contains the layout and formatting specifications for the title slide, and the **Slide Master**, which contains specifications for all non-title slides. A slide master and title master are referred to as **slide master pairs**. Titles can have different alignments, margins, tabs, font sizes, and styles from the body text. If you modify the default settings in the slide master for a design template, you can save it as a new template to use in any new presentation.

Step 6
Click View on the menu bar then click Ruler to display or hide the ruler.

Activity Steps

  open Bltpress2.ppt

1. Click View on the menu bar, point to Master, then click Slide Master
   Slide 1 is the slide master; slide 2 is the title master.
2. Click Slide 2 to select the title master, click Click to edit Master subtitle style, click the Font Color list arrow △▾, then click the blue box (eighth box on the right)
3. Click Slide 1, click Click to edit Master title style, then click the Shadow button on the toolbar
4. Click Click to edit Master text styles on the slide master, click Format on the menu bar, click Bullets and Numbering, click the open square boxes, click the Color list arrow, click the red box, then click OK
5. Right-click Second level, click Bullets and Numbering, click the solid square boxes, click the Color list arrow, click the blue box, then click OK
6. Drag the leftmost margin marker on the Horizontal Ruler 1/4" to the right on the ruler
   See Figure 4-19.
7. Click File on the menu bar, click Save As, click the Save as type list arrow, click Design Template (*.pot), then type Bltpress2-2 in the File name box
   See Figure 4-20.
8. Click Save

  close Bltpress2.ppt

Figure 4-19: Changes to slide masters

Margin marker moved 1/4"

Title master font color changed

Shadow style applied to title

Modified bullet styles

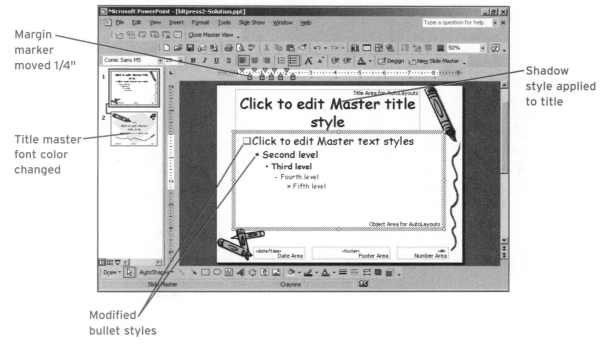

Figure 4-20: Saving a presentation as a design template

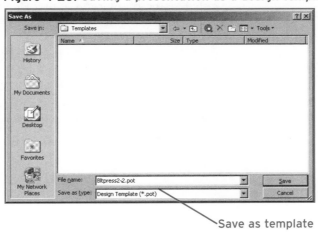

Save as template

Skill Set 4

Modifying Presentation Formats

Manage a Slide Master
Create and Manage a Slide Master

Global formatting changes to all the slides in your presentation are made to the slide master, the part of the presentation that specifies how text and graphics appear on each slide. You can use Slide Master view to change the arrangement of text placeholders or objects on the slide master, or make changes to font and bullet styles. Most design templates have two slide masters, known as a master pair; one master for the title slide and another for all other slides. You can have more than one master pair in any presentation. To insert a new slide master that uses PowerPoint default styles, click the Insert New Slide Master button on the Master View toolbar or begin a new blank presentation. To insert a new title master, click the Insert New Title Master button on the Slide Master View toolbar. To help manage slide masters, you can rename them by clicking the Rename Master button. If the presentation no longer uses a master, you can click the Delete Master button to delete both the slide master and title master.

Activity Steps

1. Click the **New button** on the toolbar, click **View** on the menu bar, point to **Master**, then click **Slide Master**

2. Click **Click to edit Master title style**, click the **Underline button** on the toolbar, then click to deselect the text

The Master toolbar may be docked on the top, bottom, left, or right side of the window.

3. Click the **Insert New Title Master button** on the toolbar, click the **Click to edit Master title style** placeholder on the new Title Master, then drag the placeholder up so the top of the box is at the 3" mark on the vertical ruler
   See Figure 4-21.

4. Click the **Rename Master button** on the toolbar, type **Underlined titles** in the Rename Master text box, click **Rename**, then click the **Normal View button**

5. Click **Click to add title**, type **American Pride**, click **Click to add subtitle**, type **Summer Meeting**, then click to deselect the placeholder
   See Figure 4-22.

 close the presentation

Figure 4-21: New slide title master with formatting changes

Slide Master
View toolbar

positioned
e
ceholder
h new
matting
titles

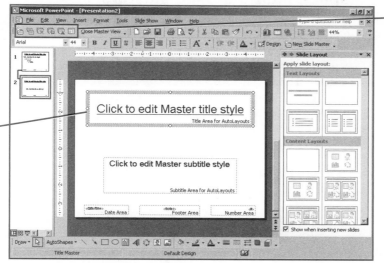

Figure 4-22: Using the new slide master

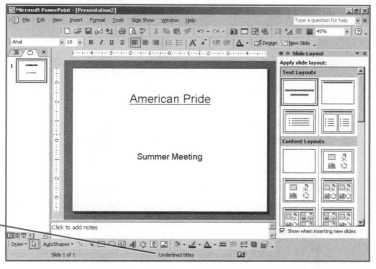

ew slide
aster is
plied

extra!

Restoring a layout
To restore a slide to its original formatting, click the Normal View button, click Format on the menu bar, click Slide Layout, locate the original layout from the task pane, click that layout list arrow, then click Reapply Layout.

Skill Set 4

Modifying Presentation Formats

Manage a Slide Master
Create and Manage Multiple Slide Masters

In PowerPoint 2002, a presentation can have more than one slide master. Applying a new slide master to different slides lets you add variety to your presentation while maintaining a consistent design for groups of slides. If for some reason you want to limit the number of masters to one per presentation, you can disable this feature by clicking the Multiple masters check box on the Edit tab in the Options dialog box. You can also choose to **preserve** a master, which keeps it from being deleted if no slides use it in the presentation. To preserve a master, click the Preserve Master button on the Slide Master toolbar. A pushpin icon next to a master indicates it is preserved.

Activity Steps

 open Bltpress3.ppt

1. Click **View** on the menu bar, point to **Master**, then click **Slide Master**

2. Click the **Insert New Slide Master button** on the toolbar, click **Format** on the menu bar, click **Background**, click the **Color list arrow**, click the **first blue square in the second row**, then click **Apply**
   The new master has a preserved icon next to it; new masters are preserved by default.

3. Click the **Design button** on the toolbar, then click the **Profile.dot** template in the Apply a design template task pane
   The presentation now contains three different masters, two of which are paired with title masters. *See Figure 4-23.*

4. Click the **Normal View button**, click **Slide 2** on the Slides tab, click the **Custom Design** Master design template list arrow in the Used in This Presentation section of the task pane, then click **Apply to Selected Slides**

5. Click **Slide 6** in the Slides tab, press and hold [Shift], click **Slide 8** to select slides 6-8, click the **Profile design template list arrow**, then click **Apply to Selected Slides**
   See Figure 4-24.

 close Bltpress3.ppt

> **tip**
>
> To delete a slide master that you no longer want in the presentation, select it in Slide Master View, then click the Delete Master button on the Slide Master View toolbar.

Figure 4-23: Presentation with three slide masters

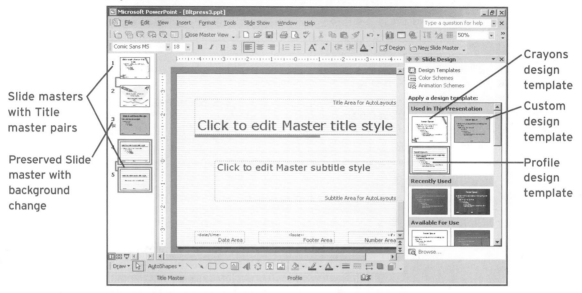

Slide masters with Title master pairs

Preserved Slide master with background change

Crayons design template

Custom design template

Profile design template

Figure 4-24: Slide masters applied to selected slides

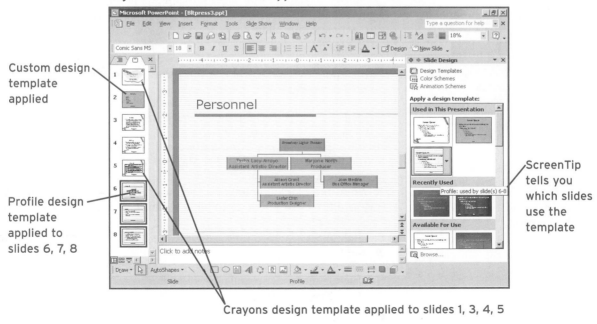

Custom design template applied

Profile design template applied to slides 6, 7, 8

ScreenTip tells you which slides use the template

Crayons design template applied to slides 1, 3, 4, 5

Skill Set 4

Modifying Presentation Formats

Rehearse Timing
Rehearse Presentations

If you are going to deliver your presentation to a live audience, you should be prepared. PowerPoint has many tools to help you rehearse your presentation. You can set the presentation to advance automatically from one slide to the next, or you can specify to advance manually by clicking the mouse or pressing a key on the keyboard. If you want your slides to advance automatically, you can specify the **Slide Timings** for the amount of time each slide appears on the screen in the Slide Transition task pane. You can specify the same or different timings for each or all the slides in the show. You can use the **Rehearse Timings** to help you determine the best amount of time to allot for each slide. To use this feature, click the Rehearse Timings button on the toolbar in Slide Sorter view, then set the timings for each slide on the Rehearse Timings bar that appears.

Activity Steps

 open Bitpress4.ppt

1. Click **Slide 1** in Slide Sorter view, press and hold [Shift], click **Slide 8**, then click the **Transition button** on the toolbar to open the Slide Transition task pane

2. Scroll the list of transition effects in the Apply to selected slides box, click **Fade Through Black**, click the **Automatically after check box**, click the **up arrow** twice to specify **00:02**, then click the Slide pane
   See Figure 4-25.

Click the Pause button on the Rehearsal toolbar while the timer is running if you need to take a break and want to save the timings.

3. Click **Slide 1**, click the **Slide Show button** in the Slide Transition task pane, view the show, then press any key to return to Slide Sorter view
   The Rehearse Timings button initiates a timer that begins counting immediately. You might want to read through step 4 and step 5 and then come back to complete the steps.

4. Click the **Rehearse Timings button** on the toolbar
   The first slide appears in Slide Show view, with the Rehearsal dialog box open in the upper left corner.

5. When the clock displays **12** seconds, click the **Next button** three times to advance to slide 2, then click the **Rehearsal dialog box close button**

6. Click **Yes** to keep the new slide timing for Slide 1 and return to Slide Sorter view
   See Figure 4-26. All the slides are set at 2 seconds except slide 1, which is set to 12 seconds.

7. Close the task pane

 close Bitpress4.ppt

Figure 4-25: Setting transition effects

Rehearse timings button

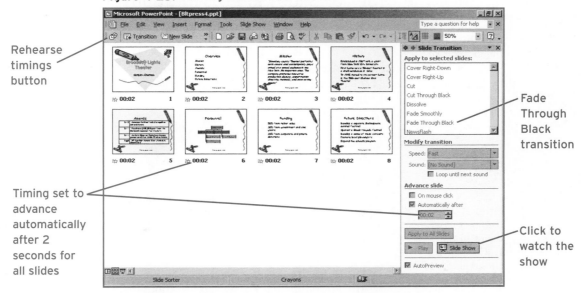

Fade Through Black transition

Timing set to advance automatically after 2 seconds for all slides

Click to watch the show

Figure 4-26: New timings after rehearsing the slide show

The new timing for slide 1

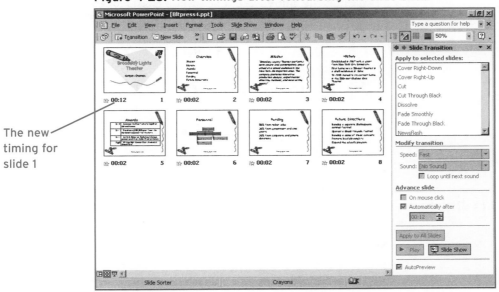

Skill Set 4

Modifying Presentation Formats

Rearrange Slides
Change the Order of Slides in Presentations

You can easily rearrange the order of slides in a presentation. You can work in Normal view using the Slides tab or in Slide Sorter view. To move a slide, drag it to the location you want. To create a copy of a slide and place it in a new location, press and hold [Ctrl] as you drag. You can also rearrange slides using the Outline tab by using the Move Up and Move Down buttons on the Outlining toolbar.

Step 3
You can move slides in the Outline tab by dragging the Slide icon. A horizontal line shows the new placement on the tab as you move the slide.

Activity Steps

open Bltpress5.ppt

1. Click **Slide 3-Future Directions** in Slide Sorter view, then drag it to after Slide 8-Personnel

2. Click the **Normal View button** , click **View** on the menu bar, click **Normal (Restore panes),** click the **Outline tab** if it is not already displayed, then click the slide icon for Slide 6-Funding on the Outline tab
   See Figure 4-27.

3. Click the **Move Down button** on the Outline toolbar to move the Funding slide below the Personnel slide

4. Click the **Slides tab**, click **Slide 5-History** in the Slides tab, then drag it up using the ⬚ pointer between slides 3 and 4

5. Click the **Slide Sorter View button**
   Compare your screen with Figure 4-28 to verify that the order is correct.

close Bltpress5.ppt

Figure 4-27: Moving slides using the Outline tab

Move buttons on Outlining toolbar

Funding slide selected

Future Directions moved to slide 8

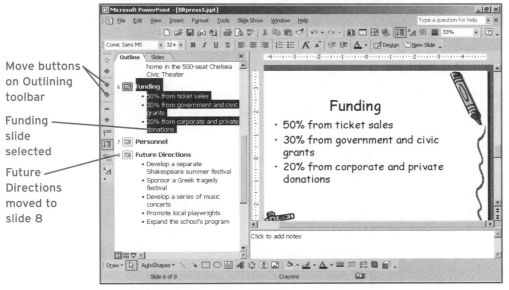

Figure 4-28: Final order after rearranging slides

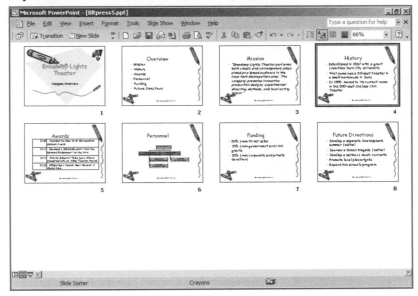

Skill Set 4
Modifying Presentation Formats

Modify Slide Layout
Change the Layout of Individual Slides

The Slide Layout task pane provides a wide array of layouts for different types of content. You may create a slide using one layout then decide another is more appropriate. You may determine that an image or chart is appropriate on a slide that currently only has text. Changing the layout does not affect the content but provides the new placeholders you need. Sometimes, though, you might want to make a formatting change to one of the sample layouts to accommodate the content for a particular slide. You can easily make changes to a layout by resizing or repositioning its placeholders or making another type of formatting change.

Activity Steps

 open Hamlet11.ppt

1. Click **Format** on the menu bar, click **Slide Layout**, then click **Slide 2**

2. Click the **Title, Text, and Content layout** in the Text and Content Layouts section of the Slide Layout task pane as shown in Figure 4-29

3. Click **Slide 6** on the Slides tab, then click the **Title and 2-Column Text Layout** in the Text Layouts section of the Slide Layout task pane

4. Click **Click to add text**, type **Specials**, press [Enter], then type **Seniors**

5. Click the Ticket Sales title placeholder, then use the ⬉ pointer to drag the lower-right sizing handle of the **Ticket Sales title placeholder** up and to the left to resize the placeholder so that the words appear on two lines and the first letters align with the words in the first bullet column
See Figure 4-30.

 close Hamlet11.ppt

If you resize a text placeholder so that text no longer fits in it, the AutoFit Options ⬍ button will appear next to the placeholder. Click this button to open its menu, then click AutoFit Text to Placeholder to resize the text automatically to fit.

Figure 4-29: Changing the slide layout

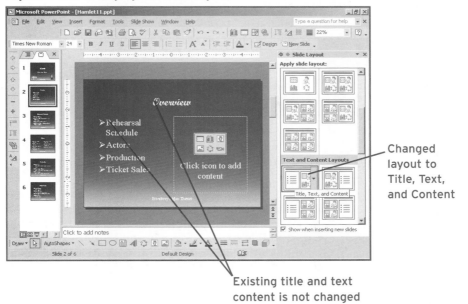

Changed
layout to
Title, Text,
and Content

Existing title and text
content is not changed

Figure 4-30: Reapplying a layout

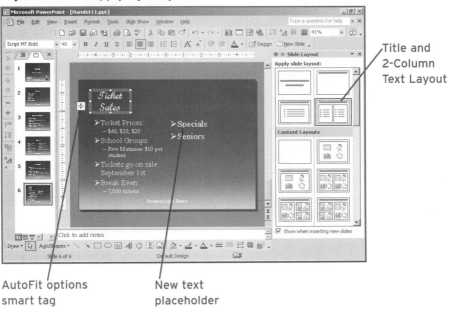

Title and
2-Column
Text Layout

AutoFit options
smart tag

New text
placeholder

Skill Set 4
Modifying Presentation Formats

Add Links to a Presentation
Add Hyperlinks to Slides

A **hyperlink** is text or an object on a slide that you click to connect to another location. In PowerPoint you can add hyperlinks on a slide to connect to another slide in the same presentation, a slide in another presentation, or a Web page on the Internet. A hyperlinked object can be a picture, graph, shape, or WordArt. If your hyperlink connects to another slide, the linked slide will display in PowerPoint. If your hyperlink connects to a Web page and your computer is connected to the Internet, the page will open in your default browser. You insert a hyperlink using the Insert Hyperlink button on the Standard toolbar.

Hyperlinks are active only when you run a presentation in Slide Show view.

Activity Steps

 open Hamlet12.ppt

1. Click **Slide 4** on the Slides tab, double-click **Shakespeare**, click the **Insert Hyperlink button** on the toolbar, click **Existing File or Web Page** in the Link to bar, type **www.shakespeare.org.uk/** in the Address box, click **OK**, then click the slide to deselect the text and see the hyperlink
See Figure 4-31.

2. Click **Slide 5-Actors** in the Slides tab, drag to select the text **Jennifer Laina**, click the **Insert Hyperlink button**, click **Place in This Document** in the Link to bar, then click **Slide 8 Jennifer** in the Select a place in this document box
See Figure 4-32.

3. Click **OK** to close the dialog box

4. Click **Slide 1**, click the **Show (from current slide) button**, press **[Spacebar]** three times, then click the **Shakespeare link**
If you were connected to the Internet, the page will open in your browser.

5. Close the browser to return to the PowerPoint slide show, press **[Spacebar]**, click the **Jennifer Laina** link, press **[Spacebar]**, then press **[ESC]**

 close Hamlet12.ppt

Figure 4-31: Linking to an address on the Web

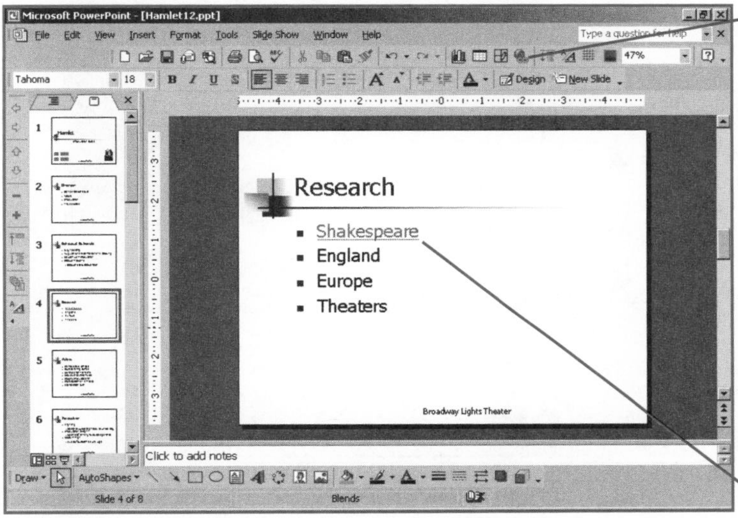

Insert Hyperlink button

Hyperlink

Figure 4-32: Linking to another slide in the presentation

extra!

Using Action Buttons

An action button is a premade button that you can use to create hyperlinks for commonly used activities such as navigating among slides and playing sounds or video. To create an action button, click Slide Show on the menu bar, point to Action Buttons, click the desired Action Button, then drag to create the action button on the slide. Specify what you want the button to do in the Action Settings dialog box that opens, then click OK. As with all hyperlinks, action buttons work only in Slide Show view.

Skill Set 4

Modifying Presentation Formats

Target Your Skills

 open Funding1.ppt

1 Use Figure 4-33 as a guide. Apply the Neutron Animation scheme to slide 1, and Grow and exit to slides 4 and 5. Set the transition for slide 1 to a slow Checkerboard Across, for slides 2-5 to Fast Newsflash. Rehearse, inserting appropriate timings for each slide. Verify that the links work.

Figure 4-33

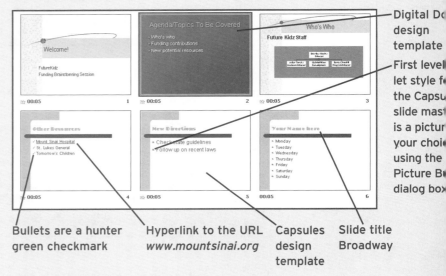

Digital D◌
design
template

First level◌
let style f◌
the Capsu◌
slide mast◌
is a pictur◌
your choi◌
using the
Picture B◌
dialog box◌

Bullets are a hunter green checkmark

Hyperlink to the URL www.mountsinai.org

Capsules design template

Slide title Broadway

 open Ppretzel1.ppt

2 Use Figure 4-34 as a guide. Delete the existing default template. Apply the Compress animation scheme to all slides. Set show to have a Fade Smoothly transition automatically after 3 seconds. Then set other transition times between each slide.

Figure 4-34

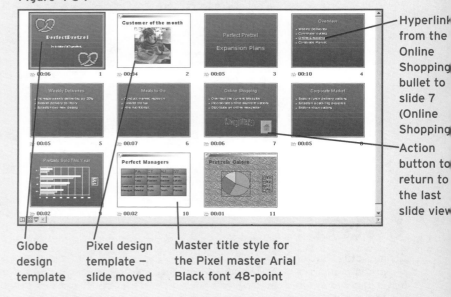

Hyperlink◌
from the
Online
Shopping◌
bullet to
slide 7
(Online
Shopping◌

Action
button to
return to
the last
slide view◌

Globe design template

Pixel design template – slide moved

Master title style for the Pixel master Arial Black font 48-point

Skill List

1. Preview and print slides, outlines, handouts, and speaker notes

Though you will often want to give a presentation by projecting your slides on a screen, you might also want to print them. In this skill set you will learn how to preview and print your PowerPoint slides as well as various support materials in the presentation, such as the outlines, notes, and comments. You will also learn how to create handouts for your audience and speaker notes for yourself.

Skill Set 5
Printing Presentations

Preview and Print Slides, Outlines, Handouts, and Speaker Notes
Preview Slides

It's a good idea to preview your slides before you actually print them. Your presentations can have many slides, and printing can use up a lot of paper. To see how the printout will look using the current print settings, click the Print Preview button on the Standard toolbar. You can also click Preview in the Print dialog box to see how the settings will affect your printout.

When you click the Print Preview command, the Preview window opens and displays a preview of your printed slides. You can use the Previous Page and Next Page buttons to view each slide, and you can use the Zoom list arrow to view your slides at any magnification. You can specify what you want to print, and can use the Options drop-down list to frame each slide.

You can view Slides, Handouts, Notes, and Outlines in the Preview window.

Activity Steps

 open Avivamkt1.ppt

1. Click the **Print Preview button**  on the toolbar
   See Figure 5-1. If your printer settings specify a black-and-white printer, the slides will appear in grayscale. If your printer settings specify a color printer, you will see the slides in color.

2. Click the **Next Page button** on the Preview toolbar

3. Click the **Previous Page button** on the toolbar, click the **Options list arrow**, then click **Frame Slides**

4. Click the **Next Page button** four times on the toolbar, click the on the **Working on the Web! WordArt**, click the **Zoom list arrow**, then click **Fit**
   See Figure 5-2.

5. Click the **Close button** on the toolbar.

 close Avivamkt1.ppt

Figure 5-1: Preview window

Next Page button

Zoom pointer

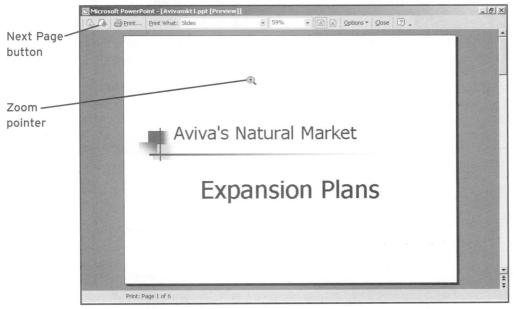

Figure 5-2: Preview window with framed slide

Zoom list arrow

Frame around slide

Zoom pointer

WordArt

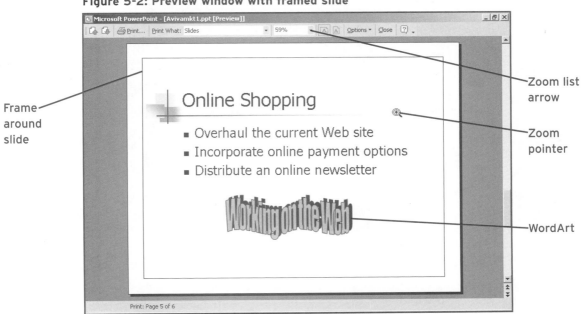

Skill Set 5
Printing Presentations

Preview and Print Slides, Outlines, Handouts, and Speaker Notes
Print Slides

To print a presentation, you can use the Print button on the Standard Toolbar to print the slides with the default settings. If you want to change the print settings before you print, use the Print command on the File menu to open the Print dialog box. This dialog box lets you specify whether to print slides, notes, handouts, or an outline of your presentation. You can also specify which slides to print, whether to print them in landscape or portrait orientation, how many copies to print, and whether to collate the copies or not. If you have a color printer you can also stipulate whether to print in color, grayscale, or black and white.

You can select specific slides and the order in which they print by clicking the Slides option button in the Print Range area of the Print dialog box. Type the slide numbers separated by commas in the Slides box. Consecutive slides can be entered with a dash.

Activity Steps

 open Avivamkt2.ppt

1. Click **File** on the menu bar, then click **Print**
   The Print dialog box opens.

2. Click the **Slides option button** in the Print range section, then type **1-2,4-6**

3. Click the **Color/grayscale list arrow**, then click **Grayscale**

4. Verify that **1** is in the Number of copies box, then verify that **Slides** is in the Print what box
   See Figure 5-3.

5. Click **OK**

6. Click **Slide 3**, click **File** on the menu bar, click **Print**, click the **Current slide option button**, click the **Color/grayscale list arrow**, click **Color**, then click **OK**
   If you have a printer connected to your computer, slide 3 will print in grayscale.

 close Avivamkt2.ppt

Figure 5-3: The Print dialog box

Your printer will probably be different

Specifies which slides will print

Specifies the slides will print in grayscale even if you have a color printer

Number of copies

Click to frame slides

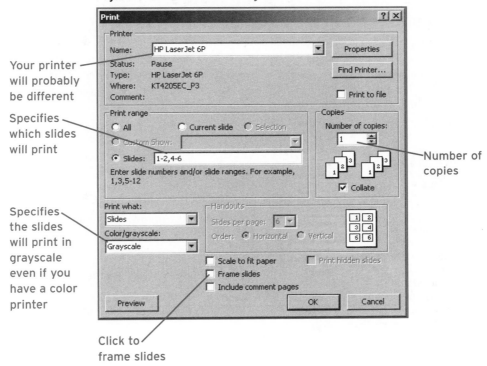

extra!

Creating a summary slide

You can create a summary slide that includes all the titles from a selection of slides as a bulleted list. When you want to present your slides, this slide can be very helpful in providing your audience with an overview of key points in your presentation. From Slide Sorter View, click to select the slides that you want included in the summary slide, then click the Summary Slide button on the toolbar. The slide is created automatically and placed at the beginning of your presentation. You can move or modify it as necessary.

Skill Set 5
Printing Presentations

Preview and Print Slides, Outlines, Handouts, and Speaker Notes
Preview and Print Outlines

Sometimes it's helpful to view and print only the text of your presentation without having to print every slide. The Outline tab displays all the text in your presentation, except for any text entered in text boxes or AutoShapes. Printing the outline is a good way to focus on the words of your presentation; it can save paper, too. You can print the outline at any time and control various factors that determine how it looks as a printed document.

To set up slide sizes for printing on special paper, click File on the menu bar, click Page Setup, then specify the paper size in the Slides sized for box, or enter sizing for a custom width and height.

Activity Steps

file > open Avivamkt3.ppt

1. Click **File** on the menu bar, then click **Print**
2. Click the **Print what list arrow**, then click **Outline View**
3. Click **Preview**
   See Figure 5-4.
4. Click the **Landscape button** on the toolbar
   See Figure 5-5.
5. Click the **Print button** , then click **OK** in the Print dialog box

file > close Avivamkt3.ppt

Figure 5-4: Outline in Preview window—portrait orientation

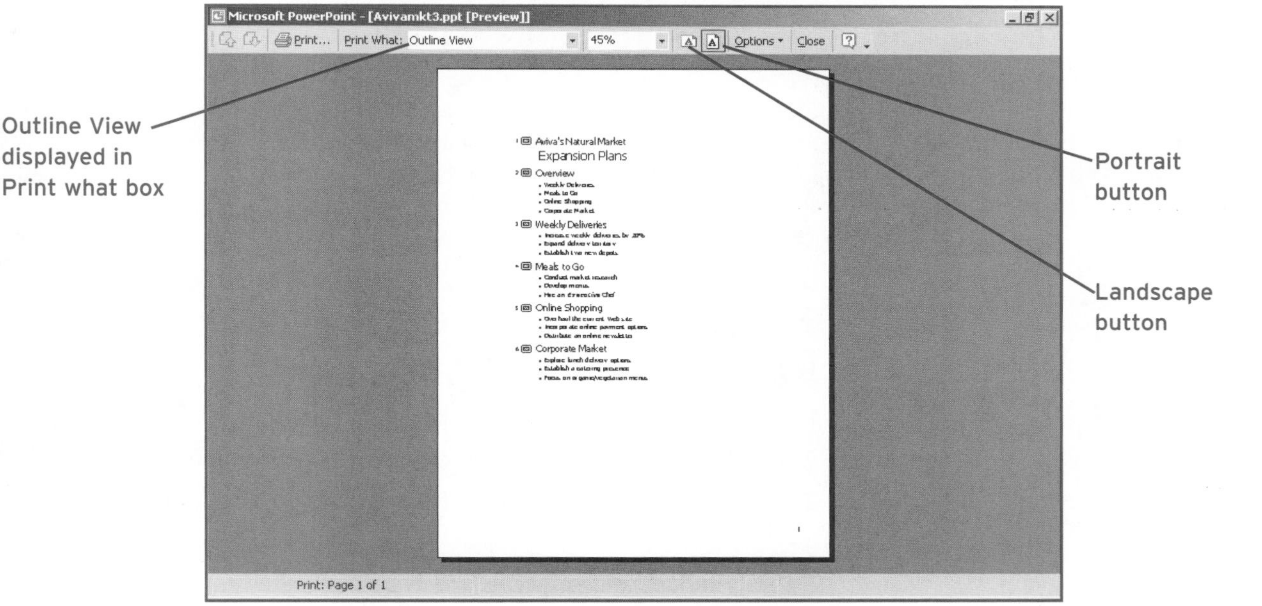

Outline View
displayed in
Print what box

Portrait
button

Landscape
button

Figure 5-5: Outline in Preview window—landscape orientation

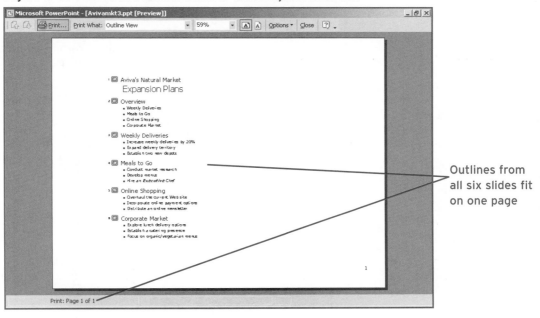

Outlines from
all six slides fit
on one page

Skill Set 5

Printing Presentations

Preview and Print Slides, Outlines, Handouts, and Speaker Notes

Preview and Print Handouts

Handouts are printed versions of your presentation that contain one or more slides on each page. You can use handouts to help your audience follow your presentation. You have many options for organizing the slides on the handout pages. You can print up to nine slides per page. If your presentation contains **hidden slides,** slides that you chose not to show or print for a particular audience, you can select whether or not to include them in the handouts. You can also select which slides print and the order in which they print.

The Handout Master shows how the slides will be positioned and lets you change the header and footer. To view the Handout Master, click View on the menu bar, click Master, then click Handout Master.

Activity Steps

 open Avivamkt4.ppt

1. Click **File** on the menu bar, then click **Print**

2. Click the **Print what list arrow,** then click **Handouts**

3. Click the **Slides per page list arrow** in the Handouts area, then click **3**

4. Click **Preview**
   See Figure 5-6.

5. Click the **Print What list arrow,** then click **Handouts (6 slides per page)**
   See Figure 5-7.

6. Click the **Options list arrow,** click **Frame slides** to remove the frames, review the difference, click **Options list arrow,** then click **Frame slides** to turn it on

7. Click the **Print button** , then click **OK** in the Print dialog box

 close Avivamkt4.ppt

Figure 5-6: Handouts with three slides per page in Preview window

Three slides on each page

Handout will be two pages

Portrait button

Lines for notes

Each slide is framed

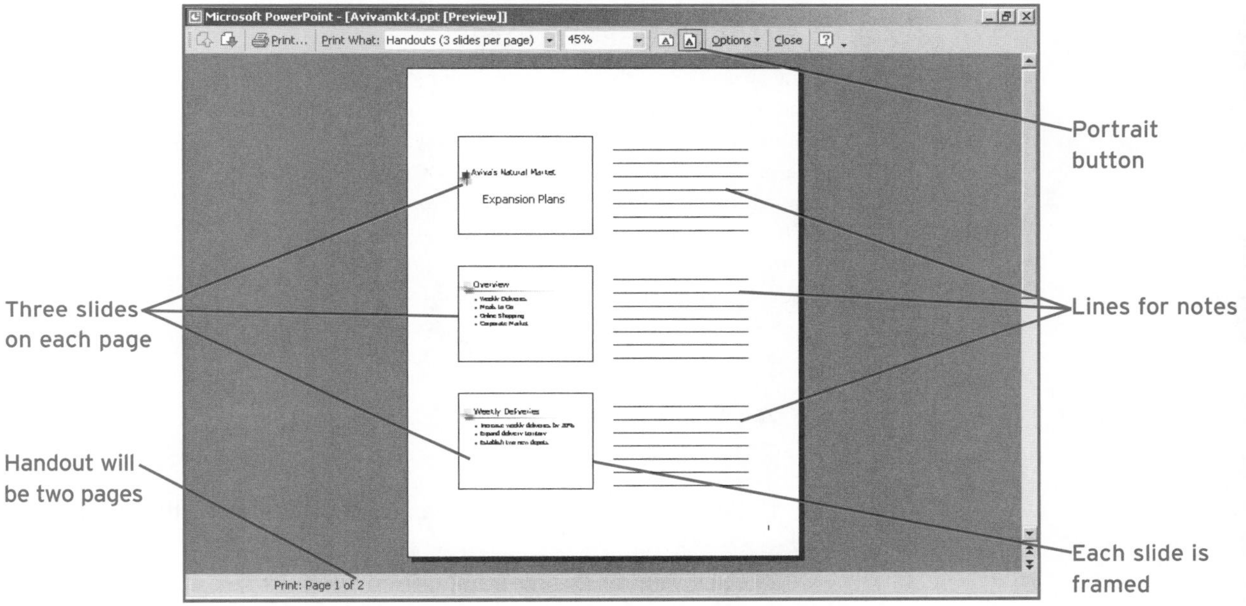

Figure 5-7: Handouts with six slides per page in Preview window

Print What list arrow

No lines for notes when six slides on a page

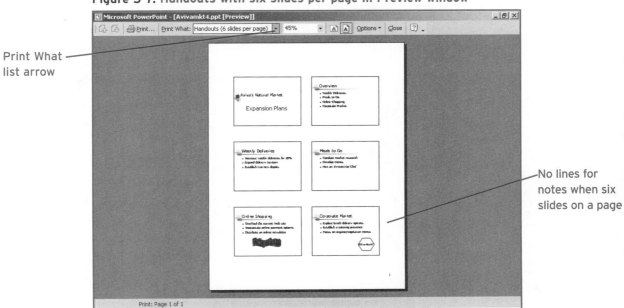

Skill Set 5
Printing Presentations

Preview and Print Slides, Outlines, Handouts, and Speaker Notes
Preview and Print Speaker Notes

When you're in front of an audience giving a presentation, it's helpful to have notes on hand to remind you what to say about each slide. In PowerPoint, notes pages contain a picture of the slide with your notes underneath. You enter your notes in the Notes pane in Normal view. You can view these on the computer as you deliver the presentation if you use multiple monitors, or print them out to help you or others prepare for the presentation. You can apply text formatting to notes to make them easier to read, and you can even add pictures or objects. To make global changes to the notes page layout or to add a logo or text that you want to appear on all the notes, add it to the notes master. You can specify the default formatting of your notes, such as font or bullet styles, on the master.

Use the Print dialog box to print on various sized paper, overheads, or banners. You can print to a file rather than to a printer, and you can also find a printer on the Web.

Activity Steps

open Avivamkt5.ppt

1. Click **View** on the menu bar, point to **Master**, then click **Notes Master**

2. Click **File** on the menu bar, then click **Print**

3. Click the **Print what list arrow**, then click **Notes Pages**

4. If you have a color printer, click the **Name list arrow** in the Printer section, select the color printer, click the **Color/grayscale list arrow**, then click **Color**
   See Figure 5-8.

5. Click **Preview**, then click the **Next Page button** four times to display slide 5
   See Figure 5-9.

6. Click the **Print button** 🖨, then click **OK** in the Print dialog box

close Avivamkt5.ppt

Figure 5-8: Print dialog box for printing notes pages on a color printer

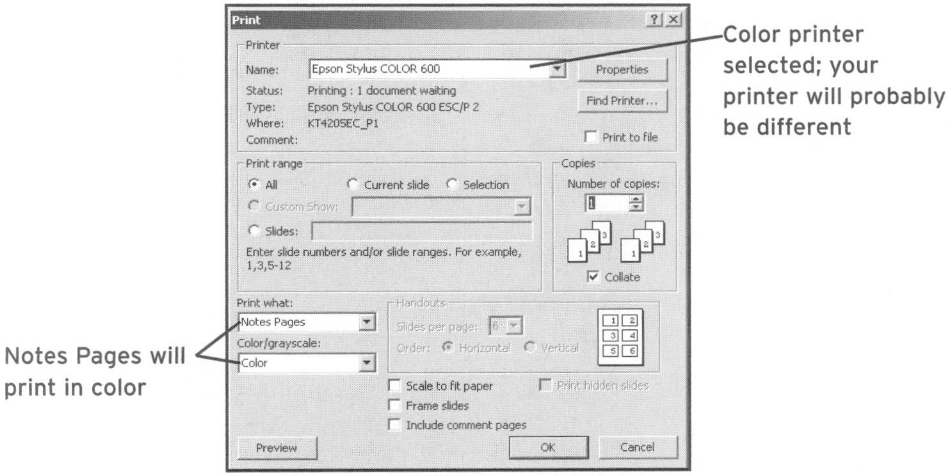

Color printer selected; your printer will probably be different

Notes Pages will print in color

Figure 5-9: Notes page in Preview window

Notes Pages will print

Slides in color for color printer

Notes area

Logo appears on each page because it is in Notes master

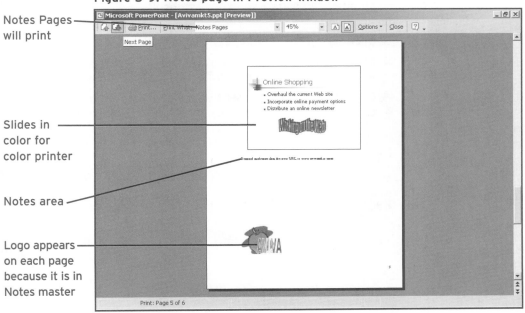

Skill Set 5

Printing Presentations

Preview and Print Slides, Outlines, Handouts, and Speaker Notes
Print Comments Pages

If you work with several people to create a presentation, you might want to insert comments to communicate your ideas or concerns about particular slides to the other people on the team. They, in turn, can add their own comments for you to review. Comments appear as yellow popup boxes on the slide with the reviewer's initials identifying each comment. If you point to the small box with the initials, a larger box will open to display the comment. You can print the comments as part of the slides, handouts, or notes.

Click the Insert Comment button on the Reviewing toolbar, then type any notes to add a comment to any slide.

Activity Steps

 open Avivamkt6.ppt

1. Click **Slide 3**, click **View** on the menu bar, point to **Toolbars**, then verify that there is a checkmark next to **Reviewing** (if there is no checkmark, click Reviewing to open the Reviewing toolbar)

2. Click outside the menu, then place the pointer over the **comment** in slide 3 to expand the comment
See Figure 5-10.

3. Click **File** on the menu bar, then click **Print**

4. Click the **Print what list arrow**, click **Slides**, then verify that the **All option button** in the Print range area is selected

5. Click the **Include comment pages check box**, click **Preview**, click the **Next Page button** to display the comments page for slide 1, then click **Options** on the toolbar
The Options list shows that Include Comments Pages is selected, as shown in Figure 5-11.

6. Click the **Print button** , then click **OK** in the Print dialog box

 close Avivamkt6.ppt

Figure 5-10: Viewing a comment

Reviewing toolbar

Comment

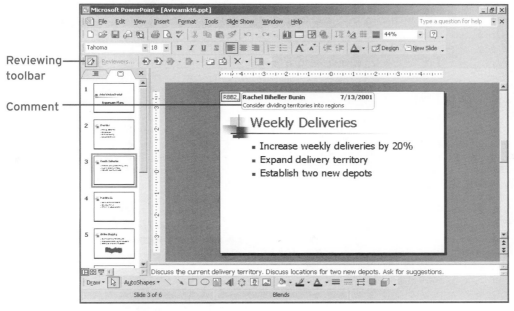

Figure 5-11: Comment page in Preview window

Comment for slide 1

Comments will print

Printout includes all comments pages

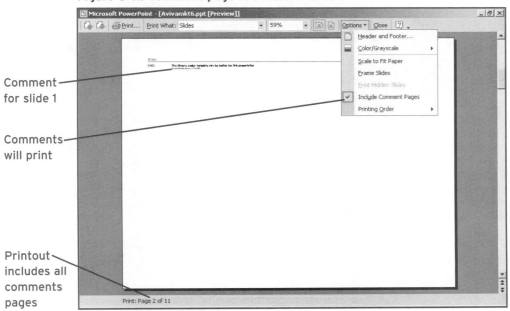

Skill Set 5

Printing Presentations

Target Your Skills

 open Jjewels1.ppt

1 Use Figure 5-12 as a guide. Preview and print handouts containing all the slides. First print the handouts with 6 slides per page, then print the handouts with three slides per page. Finally, preview and print one copy of Slides 1, 3, and 5.

Figure 5-12

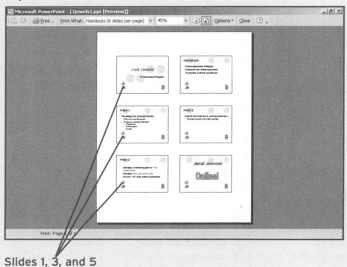

Slides 1, 3, and 5

 open Springrecipes1.ppt

2 Use Figure 5-13 as a guide to preview and print the Notes pages. Be sure to include Comments Pages and frame the slides. There are several comments throughout the presentation and each slide has a note. After you print the Notes pages, preview and print the outline for this presentation. Include all the slides in each of the printouts.

Figure 5-13

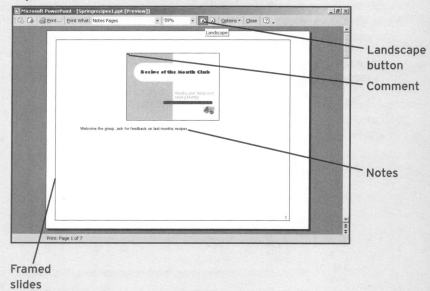

Landscape button

Comment

Notes

Framed slides

Skill Set 6

Skill List

1. Import Excel charts to slides
2. Add sound and video to slides
3. Insert Word tables on slides
4. Export a presentation as an outline

When you create a presentation, you often want to display data on your slides for discussion and analysis. For instance, you might want to insert a chart or table to show sales trends, budgets, marketing results, or projections. PowerPoint is a presentation tool, not an analysis tool, so it's best to create these objects in other programs and then insert them into your presentation. In this skill set, you will learn how to use PowerPoint to incorporate data from other sources. You will learn to insert Word tables, Excel charts, and video and sound files into your slides. You'll also learn how to save a presentation as an RTF file so that it can be opened in other programs, making it easier to collaborate with colleagues.

Skill Set 6
Working with Data from Other Sources

Import Excel Charts to Slides
Embed Excel Charts on Slides

A picture is worth a thousand words, especially when presenting numeric data. You can add an Excel chart to your presentation by embedding it as an object. **Embedding** means inserting an object created in another program, called a **source program**, into your presentation. Once you embed an object into a presentation, the object becomes part of the presentation file and no longer has a connection to the **source file**, where the object was originally created. The embedded object does stay connected to the source program, however. Clicking the embedded object activates the source program so you can make changes to the object using the source program's tools. Changes to the object in the presentation file (known as the **destination file**, because it contains the embedded object) are not reflected in the source file. Changes made to the object in the source file are not updated in the destination file. You embed an Excel chart using the Insert Object dialog box.

Activity Steps

 open Famfarm1.ppt

1. Click **Slide 7**, click **Insert** on the menu bar, then click **Object** to open the Insert Object dialog box
   See Figure 6-1.

To create an Excel chart in PowerPoint, click Insert on the menu bar, click Object, verify that the Create new option button is selected, select Microsoft Excel Chart, then click OK.

2. Click the **Create from file option button** in the Insert Object dialog box, click **Browse**, locate the folder containing your Project Files, click **Famfarm1.xls**, then click **OK**
   The path to the source file Famfarm1.xls appears in the Insert Object dialog box.

3. Click **OK**
   A worksheet and chart appear in the slide as an embedded object.

4. Use the ⬚ pointer to drag the chart to the right, as shown in Figure 6-2

5. Double click the **chart** to open the embedded chart and work-book in Excel, click the **Zoom list arrow** (you may have to click the Toolbar Options button ⬚ to display the Zoom button), then click **100%**

6. Click **WashDC** in cell E2 of the worksheet, type **MetroDC**, press **[Enter]**, type **8800** in cell E3, then click the slide
   The changes appear in the chart legend and in the data. Because this is an embedded chart, the changes will not appear in the source file.

 close Famfarm1.ppt

Figure 6-1: Insert Object dialog box

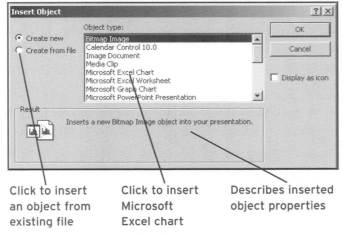

Click to insert an object from existing file

Click to insert Microsoft Excel chart

Describes inserted object properties

Figure 6-2: Slide with embedded Excel chart

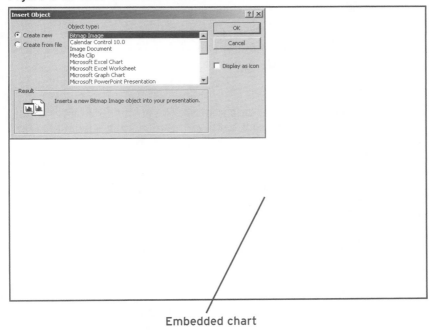

Embedded chart

extra!

Embedding part of a file

Using the Insert Object command embeds an entire Excel workbook into your presentation, which could contain multiple worksheets and charts. If you want to insert only a part of an Excel workbook (for instance only a chart), open the workbook in Excel, right-click the chart, then click Copy. Next, open your presentation in PowerPoint, select the slide where you want to insert the object, click Edit on the menu bar, click Paste Special, select the Paste option button, click Microsoft Excel Chart Object, then click OK.

Skill Set 6

Working with Data from Other Sources

Import Excel Charts to Slides

Link Excel Charts to Slides

If you want the Excel chart you have inserted into your presentation to be updated every time a change is made to the source file, you can link it to the source file. **Linking** an object means that you set up a connection between the inserted object and the source file; any changes made to the object in the source file are reflected in the object in the destination file. You link objects when you want updates in the source file to be reflected in the presentation or updates in the linked object to be reflected in the source file. To link a chart in Excel to a PowerPoint presentation, you first open the Excel worksheet and copy the chart you want to insert. Then you open the presentation and use the Paste Link command to insert the chart as a linked object. The linked object appears in the presentation and is a shortcut to the source file in the source program. If you work with active data that changes regularly, inserting linked objects in your slides will ensure that your presentation contains the most up-to-date numbers.

Step 5
To view all the linked objects in a presentation, click Edit on the menu bar, then click Links to open the Links dialog box. Use this dialog box to set the update to Automatic or Manual, to change a source, to update manual links, or to break a connection to a linked object.

Activity Steps

 open Famfarm2.ppt

1. Start **Microsoft Excel**, click **File** on the menu bar, click **Open**, navigate to the folder containing your Project Files, click **Famfarm2.xls**, then click **Open**
An Excel worksheet opens with data in cells A1:B6 and a pie chart below the data.

2. Click the **border of the chart** to select the chart and open the Chart toolbar, click **Edit** on the menu bar, then click **Copy**

3. Click the **Microsoft PowerPoint button** on the taskbar, click **Slide 5**, click **Edit** on the menu bar, click **Paste Special**, verify that **Microsoft Excel Chart Object** is selected in the As: box, then click the **Paste link** option button
See Figure 6-3.

4. Click **OK** (if the chart covers the text box, move it to the right)

5. Right-click the **chart**, point to **Linked Worksheet Object**, click **Open** on the shortcut menu to open the source file, click **300** in cell B2, type **700**, then press **[Enter]**

6. Click the **PowerPoint button** on the taskbar, click the **Zoom list arrow** on the toolbar, then click **100%**
The White and brown rice pie segment has changed to 700 corresponding to the changes you made in the source file. *See Figure 6-4.*

 close Famfarm2.ppt

Figure 6-3: Paste Special dialog box

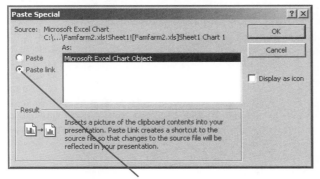

Click to paste Excel
chart as a linked object

Figure 6-4: Slide with linked Excel chart

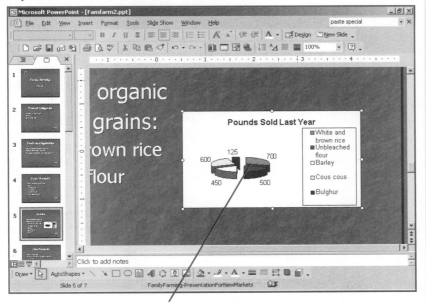

Linked chart shows
updated data

extra!

Linking Objects from within PowerPoint

You can also insert linked objects into a presentation without having to open the source file. To link a worksheet from within PowerPoint, click Insert on the menu bar, then click Object to open the Insert Object dialog box. Click the Create from file option button in the Insert Object dialog box, click Browse, locate the source .xls file, click the Link check box, then click OK. An image of the worksheet with the chart appears in the slide. It's important to note that inserting an object this way inserts the entire file into your presentation. If you want to link only a portion of a file, you need to copy the object from within the source program, then use the Paste Special command to paste it into the presentation.

Skill Set 6

Working with Data from Other Sources

Add Sound and Video to Slides
Add Sound Effects to Slides

There's nothing like sound to give life to your presentation. A **sound file** can be music, a speech, or a sound effect such as a train whistle, rocket noise, or bells. Sound can create a mood; you can insert a sound to make a point, amuse the audience, or demonstrate an effect. The sound file can play automatically when the slide appears or when you click the slide. PowerPoint has many ways to insert sound effects into a presentation. Most sound files have a .wav or an .mp3 file extension. You can create your own sounds if your computer is set up to record sound, or you can insert the many sound files that come with Office in the Clip Organizer.

Step 2
To select a sound file from the Clip Organizer, click Insert point to Movies and Sounds, then click Sound from Clip Organizer to open the Insert Clip Art task pane. You can also insert a sound file by applying a slide layout that includes a Media Clip, then clicking the Media Clip icon 🖼 and choosing a sound file from the Media Clip dialog box.

Activity Steps

 open Famfarm3.ppt

1. Click **Slide 3**, click **Insert** on the menu bar, point to **Movies and Sounds**, then click **Sound from File**

2. Locate the folder where your Project Files are stored, click **cheers.wav** in the Insert Sound dialog box, click **OK**, click **Yes** to play the sound automatically in the slide show, then drag the **sound icon** to the middle of the line below the last bullet item
   See Figure 6-5. If you get a message to install the feature for the instructions in step 2, follow the instructions to install it.

3. Click **Slide 6**, click **Slide Show** on the menu bar, click **Slide Transition** to open the Slide Transition task pane, click the **Sound list arrow** in the Modify transition section, click **Drum Roll**, click the **Automatically after** check box, then set the timer to **00:03**
   See Figure 6-6.

4. Click **Slide 1**, click the **Slide Show (from current slide) button** 🖳, then press **[Enter]** as many times as needed to advance through the slide show and return to Normal view
   If a sound card and speakers are attached to your computer, you will hear two sounds as you advance through the slides.

 close Famfarm3.ppt

Figure 6-5: Sound clip inserted in slide

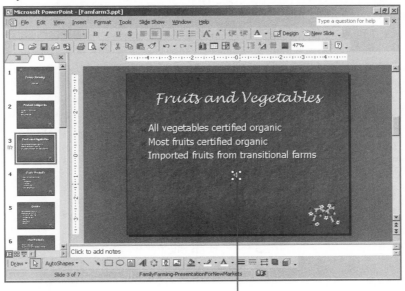

Icon for sound file

Figure 6-6: Sound specifications in Slide Transition task pane

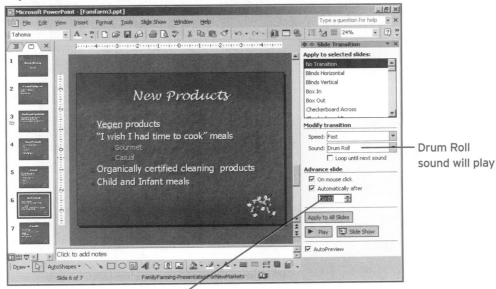

Drum Roll sound will play

Timer set for 3 seconds

Skill Set 6

Working with Data from Other Sources

Add Sound and Video to Slides

Add Video Effects to Slides

Static images go only so far when you need to illustrate certain concepts. **Video files** show motion and could be used to make your points stronger in a variety of ways. For instance, you might insert a video clip of your company president talking about a trend, one of your customers reacting to a product, or an animation that shows a process. You can insert a ready-made media clip from the Clip Organizer or you can record digital video using you own camera and then insert it into a presentation. Video formats include AVI, QuickTime, and MPEG. You can insert any file with an .avi, .mov, .qt, .mpg, or .mpeg file extension as a video in your presentation. You can also insert **animated gif files**, which contain multiple static images that stream to create an animated effect.

Step 4
Open the Custom Animation task pane to change the animation effects for the video, including the trigger and speed.

Activity Steps

  open Famfarm4.ppt

1. Click **Slide 2**, click **Insert** on the menu bar, point to **Movies and Sounds**, then click **Movie from File**
   The Insert Movie dialog box opens showing all the movie file types in the files of type box.

2. Navigate to the folder containing your Project Files, click the file **globe.avi**, click **OK**, then click **No** to specify that the movie not play automatically

3. Drag the **bottom left corner handle** of the globe.avi image down and to the left to increase the size of the clip to approximately 3" square, then drag the **globe image** to the position shown in Figure 6-7

4. Right-click the **globe image**, click **Action Settings**, click the **Mouse Over tab**, click the **Object action option button**, then click **OK**

5. Click the **Slide show (from current slide) button** 🖳, then place the pointer on the **globe** image to set it in motion
   See Figure 6-8.

  close Famfarm4.ppt

Figure 6-7: Video inserted on slide

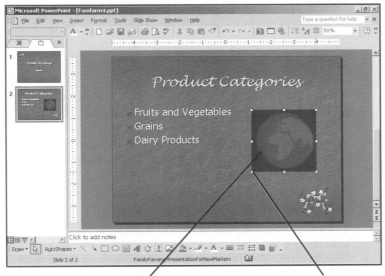

Globe.avi video in slide   Drag corner to resize

Figure 6-8: Video in motion

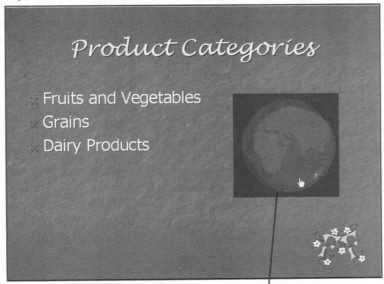

Video in motion with mouse positioned over it

extra!

Using the Media Clip Slide Layout

You can also insert a video on a slide by selecting a layout that includes the Media Clip icon. You'll find one of these in the Other Layouts section of the Slide Layout task pane. Double-click the Media Clip icon on the slide layout to open the Media Clip dialog box. To search for a particular clip, type a keyword in the Search box, then click Search. Click a clip to insert it into your presentation. To import a media clip, click the Import button, then click the file you want to import.

Skill Set 6

Working with Data from Other Sources

Insert Word Tables on Slides

Embed Word Tables on Slides

Even though PowerPoint has the ability to create native tables, it's sometimes easier to insert an existing Word table in your presentation. If you are not concerned about maintaining a connection between the table in the presentation and the source file (the Word file where it was created), you can embed the table. When you embed a table, changes to the table in the presentation are not reflected in the source file and vice versa. When you double-click the table in PowerPoint, you activate Word and can make changes to the table using Word's tools. To embed a Word table in a presentation, you use the Insert Object dialog box to specify the name and location of the Word file you want to embed.

Activity Steps

 open Famfarm5.ppt

1. Click **Slide 3**, click **Insert** on the menu bar, then click **Object** to open the Insert Object dialog box

2. Click the **Create from file option button** in the Insert Object dialog box, click **Browse**, navigate to the folder containing your Project Files, click **Famfarm5.doc**, then click **OK**
   The Insert Object dialog box shows the path to the file Famfarm5.doc in the File box. This file contains the Word table you want to insert.

3. Click **OK**, then resize the table so it is slightly larger and centered on the slide

4. Double-click the **embedded table** on the slide to activate Word
   See Figure 6-9.

5. Click the **Zoom list arrow** on the toolbar, click **100%**, select **WashDC**, type **Metro DC**, press **[Tab]** five times to select **$3,800**, type **$8,800**, click the slide, click the **Zoom list arrow** on the toolbar, click **50%**
   See Figure 6-10. The change is made only to the table on the slide. No change is made to the source file.

 close Famfarm5.ppt

Step 3
When you resize the table, be careful to drag a corner handle to retain the proportions for the height and width.

Figure 6-9: Embedded table in slide with Word activated

Your toolbars may be docked differently

Word table embedded in slide with Word activated

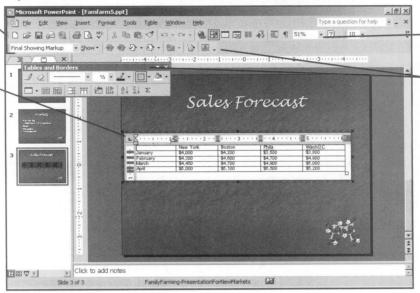

Zoom list arrow

Word toolbars are integrated in PowerPoint so you can edit the embedded object

Figure 6-10: Edited table in slide

Edited Word table

Changes to text

Skill Set 6

Working with Data from Other Sources

Insert Word Tables on Slides

Link Word Tables on Slides

Just as you can link an Excel chart to a slide in a presentation, you can also insert a Word table as a linked object on a slide. As outlined above, a **linked object** is one that maintains a connection with the source file where it was created, so that when changes are made in the source file, those changes are reflected in the linked object. You link Word tables when you want updates in the source file to be reflected in the presentation or updates in the linked object to be reflected back in the source file. To add a linked table to a PowerPoint slide, click Insert on the menu bar, then click Object to open the Insert Object dialog box. Specify the location of the document containing the table, click the Link check box, then click OK to insert the linked table. The table appears in the presentation. Double-clicking the table in the presentation opens the source file in Word, where you can make changes to it.

If the source document for a linked table has been moved, renamed, or deleted, click Edit on the menu bar, click Links, click Change Source, then click the new location of the source file.

Activity Steps

 open Famfarm6.ppt

1 Click **Slide 3**, click **Insert** on the menu bar, then click **Object** to open the Insert Object dialog box

2. Click the **Create from file option button** in the Insert Object dialog box, click **Browse**, navigate to the folder containing your Project Files, click **Famfarm6.doc**, then click **OK** in the Browse dialog box

   The Insert Object dialog box shows the path to the file Farmfarm6.doc in the File box. This file contains the Word table that you want to link.

3. Click the **Link check box**

4. Click **OK**, then resize the object so it is slightly larger and centered on the slide

5. Right-click the **table object**, point to **Linked Document Object**, then click **Edit**

   The source file Famfarm6.doc opens in Microsoft Word. *See Figure 6-11.*

6. Double-click **1000**, type **700**, double-click **6000**, then type **500**

7. Click the **PowerPoint button** on the taskbar, right click the **table**, then click **Update Link**

   The table is updated in the slide. *See Figure 6-12.*

 close Famfarm6.ppt

Figure 6-11: Document opens in Microsoft Word

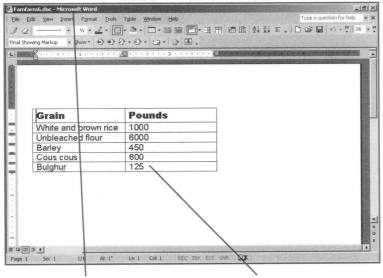

Source file open in Microsoft Word   Table

Figure 6-12: Linked table is updated

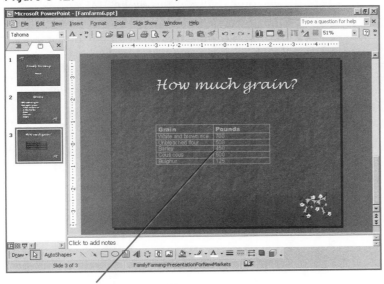

Linked data is updated in slide

extra!

Using Paste Special

To use Paste Special to link a Word table, select the table in Word, click Edit on the Word toolbar, click Copy, click the slide in PowerPoint, click Edit on the menu bar, then click Paste Special. Click the Paste Link option button in the Paste Special dialog box, click Microsoft Word Document Object, then click OK. Using Paste Special inserts just the copied object; using the Insert Object inserts the entire document.

Skill Set 6

Working with Data from Other Sources

Export a Presentation as an Outline
Saving Slide Presentations as RTF Outlines

If you work with colleagues who do not have access to Microsoft Office but would like to view the text from your presentation using another application, you can save the text as an RTF file. **Rich Text Format (RTF) files** can easily be imported or transferred between other application formats. However, when you save a presentation as RTF, you lose any graphics or media files that were part of the original file. The text does retain formatting such as font type and font style.

Step 5
If the Famfarm7.rtf file does not have a Word icon, rtf files are not associated with Word on your computer. Right-click Famfarm7.rtf in the Explorer window, click Open With, then click Microsoft Word in the Open With dialog box.

Activity Steps

 open Famfarm7.ppt

1. Click **File** on the menu bar, then click **Save As**

2. Click the **Save as type list arrow**, then click **Outline/RTF (*.rtf)**
   See Figure 6-13.

3. Click **Save**

4. Click the **Start button** on the task bar, point to **Programs**, point to **Accessories**, click **Windows Explorer**, then navigate to the folder where your Project Files are stored

5. Double-click **Famfarm7.rtf**
   The file opens in Word showing all the text with formatting from the original presentation.

6. Click **View** on the Word menu bar to be sure you are in Normal view
   See Figure 6-14.

7. Scroll to view both pages of the document file

 close Famfarm7.ppt

Figure 6-13: Save as RTF file

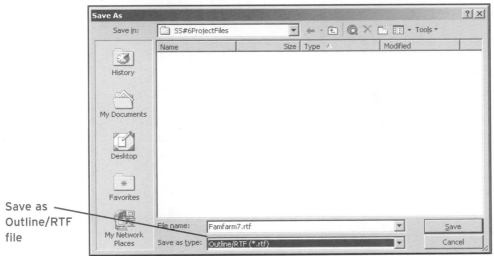

Save as Outline/RTF file

Figure 6-14: Famfarm7.rtf open in Word

Text formatting from presentation

Bullet formatting from presentation

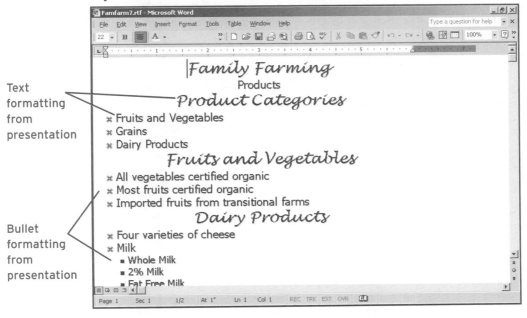

Skill Set 6

Working with Data from Other Sources

Target Your Skills

 open Pan1.ppt

1 Use Figure 6-15 as a guide to enhance the presentation. Edit the table in Microsoft Word so that the June matinee show begins at 2:30. Update the link in the presentation. Go back to the Pan1.doc file in Word, change the June matinee time back to 2pm, then use the Update Link command to update the table on the slide. Run the slide show.

Figure 6-15

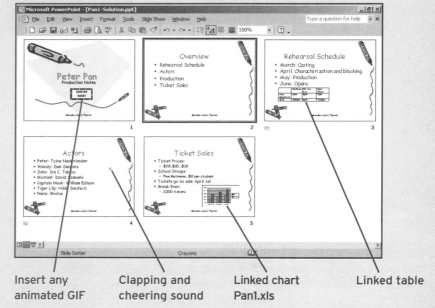

Insert any animated GIF

Clapping and cheering sound

Linked chart Pan1.xls

Linked table

 open Retreat1.ppt

2 Use Figure 6-16 as a guide to enhance the presentation. Save the presentation as an RTF outline. Run the slide show, making sure to place the pointer on the video image on slide 4 to view the animation. View the RTF file in Word.

Figure 6-16

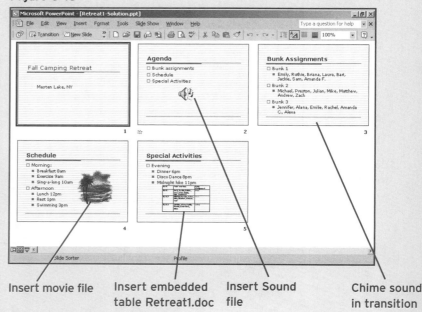

Insert movie file

Insert embedded table Retreat1.doc

Insert Sound file

Chime sound in transition

Skill Set 7

Skill List

1. Set up slide shows
2. Deliver presentations
3. Manage files and folders for presentations
4. Work with embedded fonts
5. Publish presentations to the Web
6. Use Pack and Go

Once you have completed a presentation, you are ready to set it up for delivery. Showing your finished slides to an audience is the goal of creating a presentation. You can run your slide show on your computer using one or two monitors. With special equipment, you can use your computer like a projector to show your presentation in a large room. In this skill set, you'll learn to use PowerPoint to accommodate almost any presentation situation. You'll learn how to set up a slide show so that it runs according to your specifications, embed fonts to make sure that all fonts appear on the slides, and create a custom slide show that displays only selected slides for a specific audience. You'll learn how to add discussion notes to slides in Slide Show view and how to use a drawing tool to highlight important points. You'll also learn how to save your presentation as an HTML file so that it can be viewed over the Web, and how to package your presentation so it can be delivered on a kiosk or a computer that may or may not have PowerPoint installed.

Skill Set 7

Managing and Delivering Presentations

Set Up Slide Shows
Set Up Presentations for Delivery

The hard work is done. All text and graphics are in place. Now it's time to get the presentation ready to deliver. You set the specifications for how you want to deliver the presentation in the Set Up Show dialog box. If you have the appropriate hardware and the option to use two or more monitors, you can set up the show for multiple monitors.

Activity Steps

 open Annie1.ppt

1. Click **Slide Show** on the menu bar, then click **Set Up Show** to open the Set Up Show dialog box

2. Click the **Browsed by an individual (window) option button**, verify that the **Show scrollbar check box** has a check mark, then click the **Manually option button** in the Advance slides section
   See Figure 7-1.

3. Click **OK**

4. Verify that **Slide 1** is selected, click the **Slide Show from current slide button** , then click the **down scroll arrow** on the vertical scroll bar as many times as necessary to watch the entire slide show and return to Normal view

5. Click **Slide Show** on the menu bar, click **Set Up Show** to open the Set Up Show dialog box, click the **Presented by a speaker (full screen) option button**, click the **Loop continuously until 'Esc' check box**, then click **Using timings, if present option button**

6. Click the **Use hardware graphics acceleration check box** to take advantage of any graphics card that may be in your computer, then click **OK**

7. Click the **Slide Show (from current slide) button** , press **[Pg Dn]** as many times as necessary until you loop back to Slide 1, then press **[Esc]** to end the show

 close Annie1.ppt

Step 4
Click the scroll box to display a ScreenTip that shows the current slide title and number out of the total number of slides in the presentation.

Figure 7-1: Set Up Show dialog box

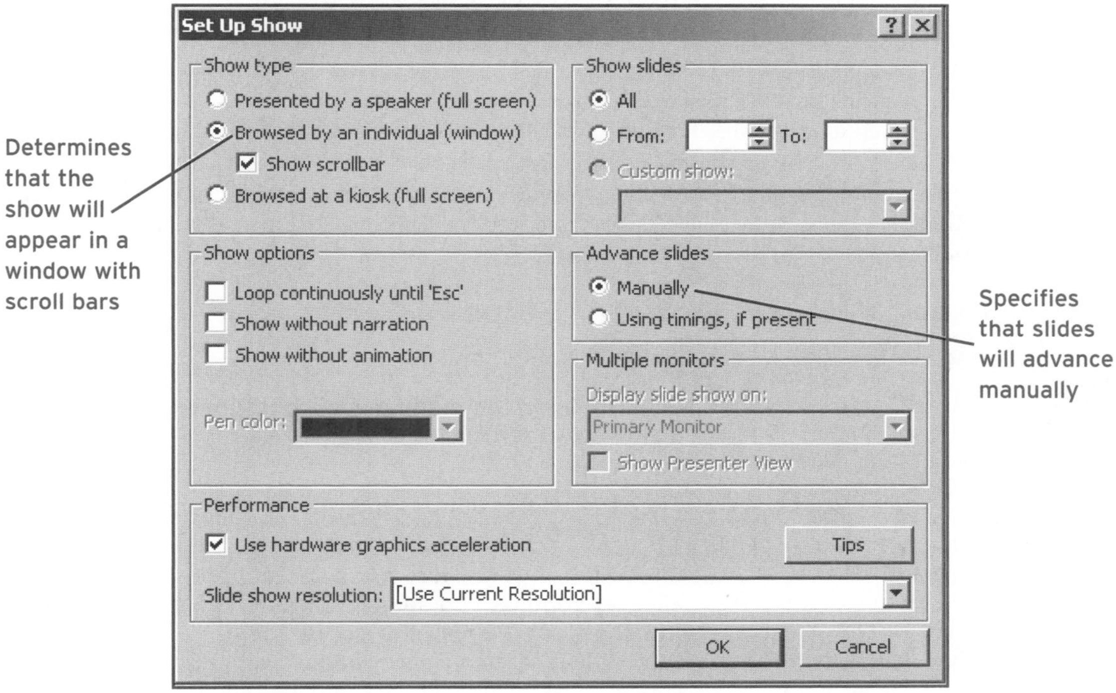

Determines that the show will appear in a window with scroll bars

Specifies that slides will advance manually

extra!

Hiding slides

For a particular audience, you might not want to show all the slides in a slide show. Rather than creating a new slide show that contains only selected slides, you can simply designate a slide (or several slides) in an existing presentation as hidden. **Hidden slides** are slides that do not display in Slide Show view. To hide selected slides, right-click any slide in Slide Sorter view or on the Slides tab in Normal view, then click Hide Slide. You can also select the slides you want to hide in Slide Sorter or Normal view, click Slide Show on the menu bar, then click Hide Slide. To hide slides using the toolbar, select the slides you want to hide, then click the Hide Slide button on the Slide Sorter toolbar. Hidden slides are marked with special icons in the Slides tab and in Slide Sorter view. The Hide Slide command is a toggle; click or select the command once to hide a slide, click it again to "unhide" a slide.

Skill Set 7
Managing and Delivering Presentations

Deliver Presentations
Prepare Slide Shows for Delivery

Before you run a slide show, you should make sure that the slide show specifications are set the way you want them. Refer to Table 7-1 for a list of ways to begin a slide show. The Show popup menu provides navigation commands and other tools to help you as the slide show is running. You use the View tab of the Options dialog box to specify whether to open the Show popup menu by right-clicking and whether to show the popup menu button on the lower left corner of the slides during the show. You can also specify whether to end the show with a black slide.

If you plan to make the slide show available on the Web or from a kiosk, you will probably want it to be self-running. To specify that the slide show will run automatically and continuously, check the Loop Continuously until 'Esc' check box in the Set Up Show dialog box.

Activity Steps

 open Annie2.ppt

1. Click **Tools** on the menu bar, click **Options** to open the Options dialog box, then click the **View tab**
See Figure 7-2.

2. Click the **Show popup menu button** to remove the check box, then click **OK**

3. Click **Slide 1**, if not already selected, press **[F5]**, then right-click as soon as you see the Characters slide appear to stop the show and display the popup menu
Each slide is set to advance automatically through transitions, although the popup menu button does not appear. The popup menu appears when you right-click during the show.

4. Click anywhere on the slide to continue the show
The slide show will run until a black screen appears, indicating the end of the show.

5. Press **[Esc]**

 close Annie2.ppt

Figure 7-2: Options dialog box

View tab

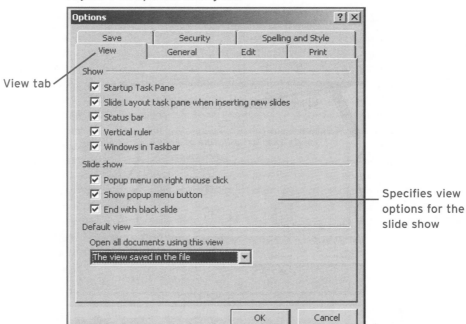

Specifies view options for the slide show

TABLE 7-1: Starting a slide show

From the...	To start the show....
My Computer	Right-click PPT file icon, then click Show
Windows Desktop	Right-click PPT file icon, then click Show
Windows Explorer	Right-click PPT file icon, then click Show
Power Point Normal View	• Click the Slide Show (from current slide) button • Click Slide Show on the menu bar, then click View Show • Press [F5]
Slide Transition task pane	Click the Slide Show button
Power Point Slide Sorter View	• Click the Rehearse Timings button (this is only to set the timings but will run the show) • Click Slide Show on the menu bar, then click View Show • Press [F5] • Click the Slide Show (from current slide) button
PowerPoint Show (pps file)	Double-click the pps filename

Skill Set 7

Managing and Delivering Presentations

Deliver Presentations
Run Slide Shows

There are many ways to run a slide show. If you are in Normal or Slide Sorter view, you can click the Slide Show (from current slide) button, or click View on the menu bar, then click Slide Show. You can also press [F5] from any view to start a slide show. Once you start the slide show, you can use the commands on the Show Popup menu to help you during the presentation. If you are giving a presentation during a meeting, you can use the Meeting Minder feature to keep track of meeting minutes or to record action items. You can also open Speaker Notes for individual slides to remind you about important points to make. Use the Slide Navigator to jump to a particular slide in your presentation. The Show Popup menu also lets you change Pointer Options, allowing you to end the show at any moment.

Activity Steps

 open Annie3.ppt

1. Click **Tools** on the menu bar, click **Options**, verify that the **Show popup menu button check box** has a check mark, click **OK**, verify that **Slide 1** is selected, click the **Slide Show (from current slide) button** 🖳, then press **[PgDn]** four times to display the **Characters slide**

2. Place the pointer in the lower-left corner of the slide, click the **Show popup menu button** that appears, then click **Speaker Notes** The Speaker Notes dialog box appears. *See Figure 7-3.*

You can set the color for the pen feature in the Set Up Show dialog box. Select a dark pen color for slides with light color backgrounds; select a light pen color for slides with dark backgrounds.

3. Click **Close** on the Speaker Notes window, click the **Show popup menu button**, click **Meeting Minder**, then type **Call EastSide Casting** *See Figure 7-4.*

4. Click **OK**, press **[PgDn]** to view the Production slide, click the **Show popup menu button**, point to **Pointer Options**, click **Pen**, then drag the mouse pointer to draw a circle around **Choreography** Because the pen color was changed in the Setup show dialog box, the pointer draws like a purple pen or crayon as you move it on the screen until you end the show or press [Esc].

5. Press **[PgDn]**, draw two horizontal lines under **2,000**, type the letter **E** to erase the lines on the slide, then press **[PgUp]** Lines you draw with the pen do not become part of the slide show.

6. Type **B** to blacken the slide, type **B** to view the slide, type **W** to whiten the slide, press any key, right-click the **slide**, then click **End Show**

 close Annie3.ppt

Figure 7-3: Speaker Notes dialog box

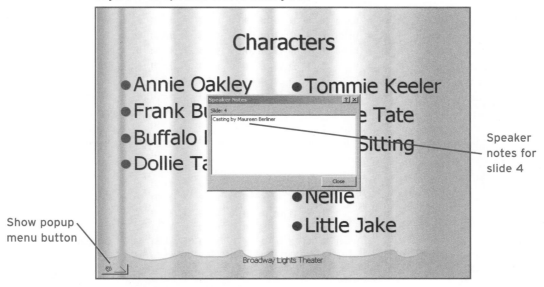

Show popup menu button

Speaker notes for slide 4

Figure 7-4: Meeting Minder dialog box

Note entered during presentation

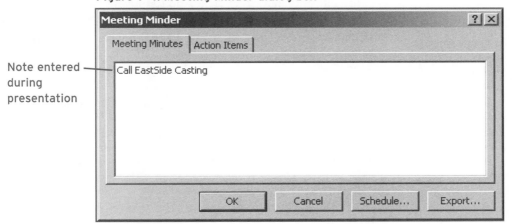

Skill Set 7

Managing and Delivering Presentations

Deliver Presentations
Setup a Custom Show

Often, you will need to deliver a presentation about a particular topic to several different audiences. For instance, you might wish to give a presentation on a particular project not only to a group of employees, but also to prospective clients and existing customers. Each audience will have slightly different interests, and you might want to show each audience only slides relevant to its needs. Fortunately, PowerPoint lets you do all your work in one presentation and then modify it for different audiences by creating a custom show. When you create a custom show, you first choose the slides you want, then give this selection a name. To run a custom show, you open the Custom Shows dialog box, then choose the custom show you want from the list.

Activity Steps

 open Annie4.ppt

1. Click **Slide Show** on the menu bar, click **Custom Shows**, then click **New** in the Custom Shows dialog box

2. Type **Singers** in the Slide show name box in the Define Custom Show dialog box, click **1. Annie Get Your Gun** in the Slides in presentation list, then click **Add** to move it to the Slides in custom show list

3. Add slides 2, 3, 4, 7, 8, 9, and 10 to create a custom show with 8 slides
See Figure 7-5.

4. Click **OK**
The custom show named Singers appears in the Custom Shows dialog box.

5. Click **Show** to view the entire Singers custom show

6. Click anywhere to exit the show and return to Slide Sorter view

 close Annie4.ppt

Click the up or down arrow buttons to reorder the slides in the Custom Show dialog box.

Figure 7-5: Defining a custom show

Lists slides in the presentation that are available for the custom show

Name of custom show

Click to reorganize slides in the custom show

Lists slides in custom show

extra!

Adding narrations

If you set your presentation to run automatically—without the benefit of your being there to deliver it—you might want to add voice narration that plays while the slides advance. To record your narration, you need a computer equipped with a microphone and sound card. Select the slide during which you want the narration to begin, click Slide Show on the menu bar, then click Record Narration. Set the microphone level, then click OK to embed the narration. **Embedding** the narration means that the sound files become part of the presentation and travel with it. If you want to minimize the size of your presentation file, you can link the narration instead. **Linking** stores the narration in a separate file in a location you specify. To link your narration to your presentation, click the link check box in the Record Narration dialog box, then specify a location for your narration sound file. If your presentation has a recorded narration and you want to run the show without it, click the Show without narration check box in the Set Up Show dialog box.

Skill Set 7
Managing and Delivering Presentations

Deliver Presentations
Use Onscreen Navigation Tools

When you give a presentation, you might need to locate and show a slide out of sequence. The Go by Title command and the Slide Navigator, both available on the Show Popup menu, let you quickly jump to any slide in your presentation. To open the Show popup menu, right click the screen or click the Show Popup menu button in the lower left corner of the slide. The Show popup menu also provides you with other helpful navigation tools. You can use it to go to the next or previous slide, select a custom show to run, make the screen go black, or end the show at any time.

Activity Steps

 open Annie5.ppt

1. Start the slide show, press **[Spacebar]** to advance to the **Rehearsal Schedule** slide, right-click the **slide** to open the Show popup menu, point to **Go**, then point to **By Title**
   See Figure 7-6.

2. Click **9. Act I song list**

3. Right-click the **Act I song list slide**, point to **Go**, point to **Custom Show**, click **Actors** to begin the Actors custom show, right-click the **Annie Get Your Gun** slide, click **Next**, right-click the **Overview slide**, point to **Go**, then click **Slide Navigator**
   See Figure 7-7.

4. Click **Story** in the Slide Navigator, then click **Go To** to display the Story slide

5. Press **[Esc]** to end the custom show and return to Slide Sorter view

 close Annie5.ppt

Step 5
To view a list of shortcut keys that can help you perform many tasks during a slide show, right-click any slide, then click Help.

Figure 7-6: Navigation options during a slide show

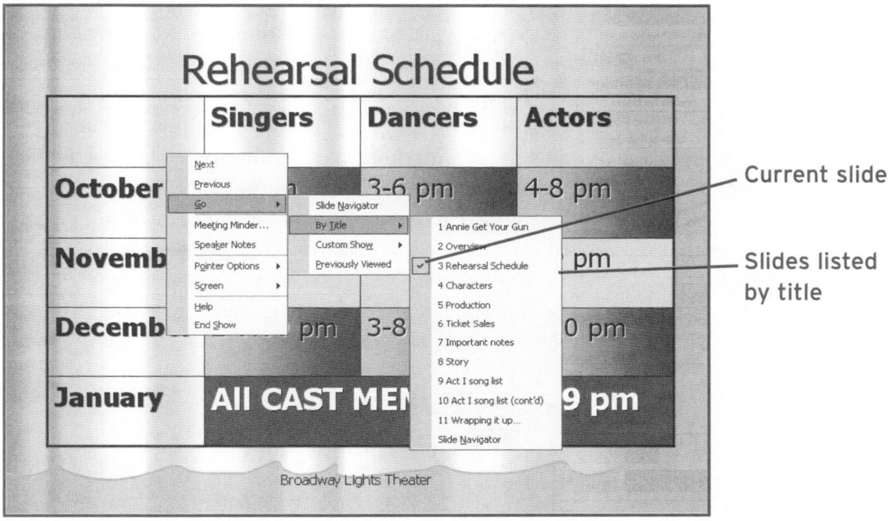

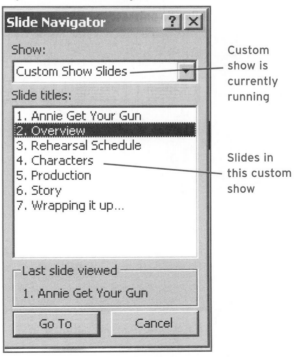

Current slide

Slides listed by title

Figure 7-7: Slide Navigator

Custom show is currently running

Slides in this custom show

Skill Set 7

Managing and Delivering Presentations

Manage Files and Folders for Presentations
Create Folders for Storing Presentations

When buying real estate, the mantra is "location, location, location." When working with presentations and creating files, the mantra is "organization, organization, organization." If you create folders on your computer that are set up in an organized way and save all your presentation files to these folders, you will be able to find your presentations quickly and easily. If your folders have logical names, whether by client, date, or purpose, you will not lose your files. If your files are systematically named, you won't copy older versions over newer ones, show outdated or incorrect presentations, or find yourself spending precious time trying to locate a particular file. You can create new folders from within PowerPoint using the Save As dialog box. You can also create new folders using My Computer or Windows Explorer.

Step 2
Click History in the Save As dialog box to see a list of all recently opened PowerPoint presentations.

Activity Steps

 open Annie6.ppt

1. Click **File** on the menu bar, then click **Save As** to open the Save As dialog box
   See Figure 7-8.

2. Click the **Create New Folder button** on the Save As dialog box toolbar, type **Annie Get Your Gun** in the Name box in the New Folder dialog box, then click **OK**
   The new folder is a subfolder of the current drive and folder. The Save in box shows the new folder name, and the Save As dialog box displays the contents of the new folder.

3. Type **NewAnnie6** in the File name box, then click **Save** to save the renamed file to the new **Annie Get Your Gun** folder

 close NewAnnie6.ppt

Figure 7-8: Save As dialog box

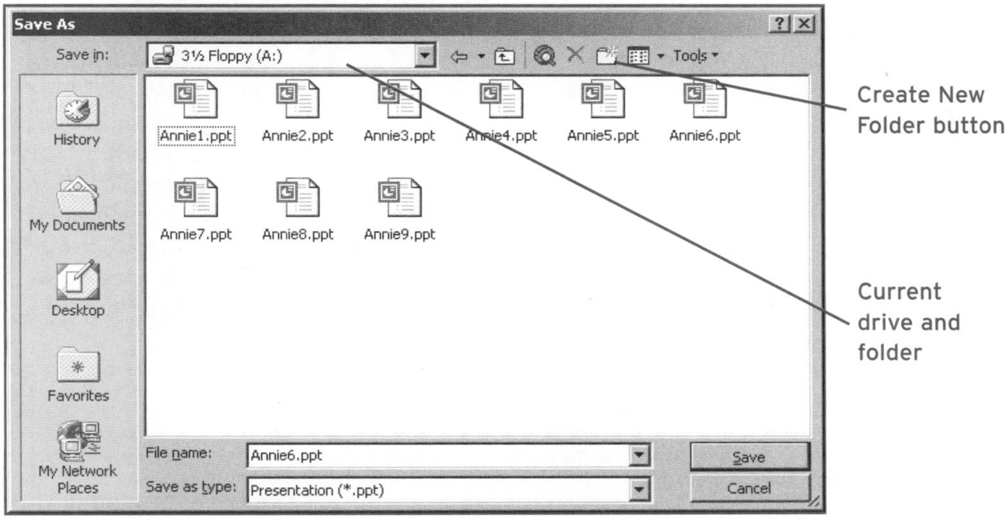

Create New Folder button

Current drive and folder

extra!

Understanding the My Documents folder

The My Documents folder is simply a default folder provided by Windows to help you organize your files. Windows includes shortcuts to this folder in the Save and Open dialog boxes of many applications to help you navigate there quickly. You should consider creating subfolders within My Documents to meet your file management needs. To change the way your files are displayed in the Save As dialog box, click the View button list arrow to select from Large Icons, Small Icons, List, Details, Properties, Preview, Thumbnails, or WebView views.

Skill Set 7
Managing and Delivering Presentations

Work with Embedded Fonts
Embed Fonts in Presentations

If you plan to show your presentation on another computer or have someone else show the presentation for you, you need to make sure that all the fonts you used travel with your file. If your presentation contains unusual fonts, they might not be installed on the computer used to deliver your presentation, and therefore won't appear in your slides. To make sure that all fonts used in your presentation travel with the file, you need to embed the fonts. **Embedding fonts** means including the font file that defines the fonts directly in the presentation file. You can choose to embed only the characters that you used in the presentation or the entire set. To embed fonts with your presentation, you use the Save tab of the Options dialog box, which is available from the Tools menu within PowerPoint or from the Tools menu in the Save As dialog box.

Activity Steps

 open Annie7.ppt

1. Press **[F5]**, then press **[Enter]** as needed to view the slide show and observe the fonts
   This presentation includes several special fonts such as Lucida Handwriting, Rockwell, Rockwell Extra Bold, ShowCard Gothic, and Broadway.

2. Click **Tools** on the menu bar, click **Options,** then click the **Save tab**

3. Click the **Embed TrueType fonts** check box
   See Figure 7-9.

4. Click **OK**
   When you save the file, the fonts will be saved along with it so you can continue to work on the presentation using all these fonts on any computer.

 close Annie7.ppt

tip

Too many fonts in a presentation can make it look busy and detract from your message. You should limit the number of fonts in any presentation to two or three.

Figure 7-9: Save tab of the Options dialog box

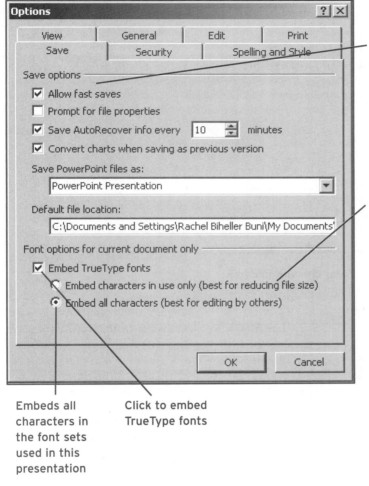

Save options

Only embeds those characters used in this presentation

Embeds all characters in the font sets used in this presentation

Click to embed TrueType fonts

extra!

Securing the file

PowerPoint offers several security options on the Security tab in the Options dialog box to restrict access to your files and help keep them secure. You can require that a password be used to open the file. You can also set a password to restrict access to modifying the file; this arrangement still allows those without the password to open and view the file. Other security measures include adding a Digital signature and setting macro security to help avoid viruses when you send and receive files from other users, particularly over the Web.

Skill Set 7
Managing and Delivering Presentations

Publish Presentations to the Web
Saving a Presentation as an HTML file

In order to make your presentation available to users on the Internet (known as **publishing** your presentation), you have to save the file as a Web page. Before files can be viewed in a **browser**, the special software used to view Web pages, they must be saved in **Hypertext Markup Language (HTML)**. To save a presentation as a Web page, you use the **Save As Web Page** command on the File menu to open the Save As dialog box, specify a name for the file, and then specify Web Page in the Files of type box to save the file with an .htm extension. PowerPoint creates a folder from the filename and places all the graphics and other required files in it. When you view the presentation as a Web page, each slide title appears on the left side of the browser as a link to a slide. Click the slide titles to view each slide as a Web page. When you save a presentation as a **Web Archive** you create one file that contains all the files required to display Web pages. Web archives can be sent via e-mail and are more easily transported between computers. Older browsers do not support this format.

Activity Steps

 open Annie8.ppt

1. Click **File** on the menu bar, click **Save as Web Page**, then click **Change Title**
   The Page Title, which will appear in the title bar of a Web page when you view the page in a browser, is determined by the Title name entered in the Properties for the presentation.

Click File on the menu bar, then click Properties to view or change the properties of any file, including the title, subject, author, manager, company, keywords, and comments.

2. Type **Annie Get Your Gun** as shown in Figure 7-10, click **OK** to change the page title, click in the **File name box**, select **Annie8**, type **blt-agyg**, then click **Save**
   This filename blt-agyg is used to create the folder to contain all the required files and graphics for the Web pages in that folder.

3. Click **File** on the menu bar, then click **Web Page Preview**
   The presentation displays as Web pages in the default browser for your computer. *See Figure 7-11.*

4. Click **Rehearsal Schedule** in the Navigation frame, click **Story** in the Navigation frame, click **File** on the browser menu bar, then click **Close**

5. Click **File** on the menu bar, click **Save As**, click the **Save as type list arrow**, click **Web Archive (*.mht; *.mhtl)**, click **Save**, then click **Yes** if asked about special characters displaying in some browsers

 close Annie8.ppt

Figure 7-10: Saving a presentation as a Web page and setting the page title

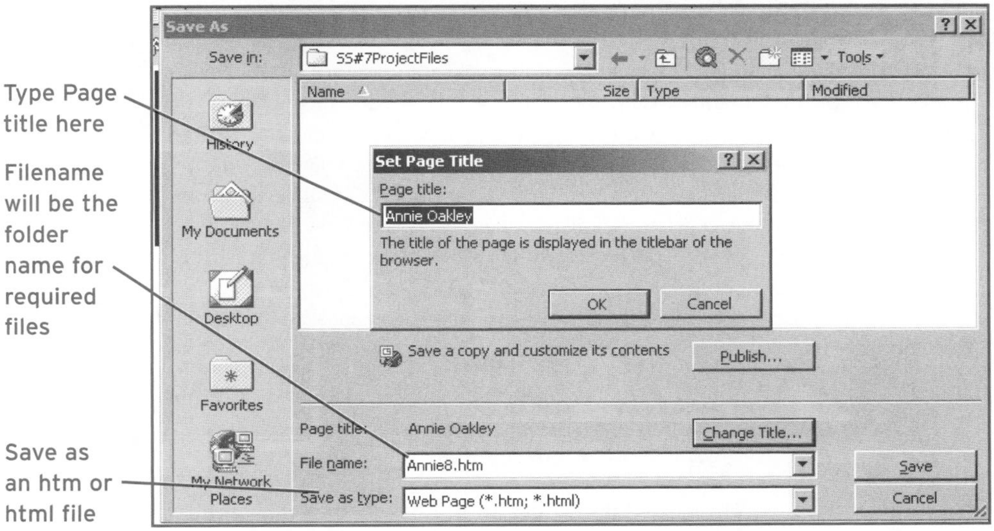

Type Page title here

Filename will be the folder name for required files

Save as an htm or html file

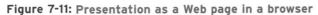

Figure 7-11: Presentation as a Web page in a browser

Internet Explorer browser

Page title

Link pointer

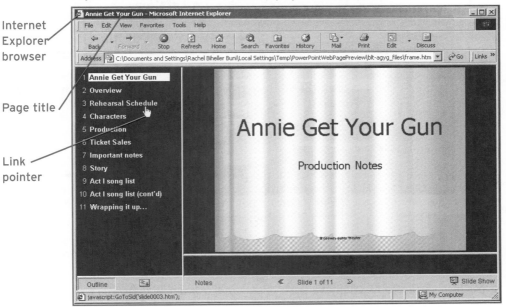

Skill Set 7

Managing and Delivering Presentations

Use Pack and Go
Prepare Presentations for Remote Delivery Using Pack and Go

You don't always have to be there to deliver the presentation in person. However, you do want the presentation to run smoothly whether you are there or not. The Pack and Go Wizard creates a neat package that includes all the required files to run your presentation on any remote computer. You can pack your presentation to a floppy disk, to your hard disk, or across a network to another computer. When you run the Pack and Go wizard, you need to decide whether or not to embed the fonts or to include the **PowerPoint Viewer**, a special program that will run the slide show even if PowerPoint is not installed. Pack and Go creates two files: Preso.ppz and Pngsetup.exe, which are used to unpack and show the presentation.

Step 1
If you get a "This feature is not currently installed..." message, click Yes, then follow the onscreen instructions to navigate to the packandgo folder in the Pack and Go Setup dialog box, then click OK. You will need your Office XP CD to install this feature.

Activity Steps

 open Annie9.ppt

1. Click **File** on the menu bar, click **Pack and Go** to start the Pack and Go Wizard, then click **Next**

2. Verify that the **Active presentation check box** has a check mark, then click **Next**

3. Place a blank formatted floppy disk in Drive A, verify that the **A:\drive option button** is selected, then click **Next**
   See Figure 7-12.

4. Click the **Embed TrueType fonts** check box, verify that the **Include linked files check box** has a check mark, then click **Next**

5. Click **Next** to specify not to include the Viewer, then click **Finish**
   The Pack and Go Status window will tell you how the process is progressing.

6. Click **File** on the menu bar, click **Exit**, double-click **My Computer** on the desktop, navigate to a folder where you can create a new folder, create a new folder called **PackandGoFiles**, navigate to the A: drive, then double-click **Pngsetup.exe**

7. Navigate to the **PackandGoFiles folder** in the Pack and Go Setup dialog box, click **OK**, then click **Yes** to run the presentation

 close Annie9.ppt

Figure 7-12: Pack and Go Wizard

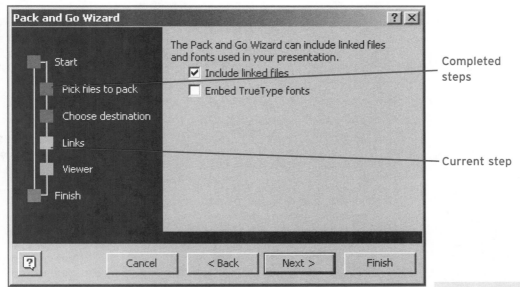

Completed steps

Current step

Skill Set 7

Managing and Delivering Presentations

Target Your Skills

 open Develop1.ppt

1 Use Figure 7-13 as a guide. Specify the show type as a presentation given by a speaker on a full screen, set the show to loop continuously until Escape, and set the pen color to red. Embed the TrueType fonts (only the characters in use.) Open the Meeting Minder, then type your name at the end of the notes.

 open Jewels1.ppt

2 Use Figure 7-14 as a guide. Save the presentation as a Web page Jewels.htm. Embed the fonts in the file. Use the navigation frame to click the links for all six slides. Save the file as a Web archive. Use the Pack and Go Wizard. Unpack and view the presentation file.

Figure 7-13

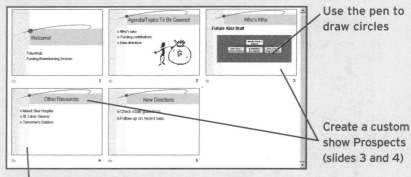

Use the pen to draw circles

Create a custom show Prospects (slides 3 and 4)

While the slide show is running, add speaker notes "Contact Michael Dumont at HUMDC"

Figure 7-14

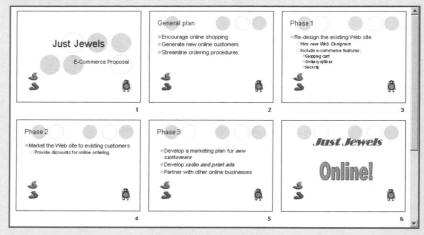

Skill List

1. Set up a review cycle
2. Review presentation comments
3. Schedule and deliver presentation broadcasts
4. Publish presentations to the Web

Collaborating on team-based projects lets you combine everyone's best skills to achieve a shared goal. PowerPoint provides powerful collaboration tools to facilitate working in groups. If you are creating a presentation with colleagues, or just want input from others on a presentation you are creating by yourself, you can easily get feedback by setting up a review cycle. A **review cycle** is the process of routing a file to specified reviewers, where each reviewer's comments are added to the file. You can send a presentation via e-mail or across a network to colleagues for review. If more than one person is working on the team, the first reviewer can enter any changes or comments into the presentation and then pass it to the next reviewer. All additional reviewer comments and changes are added to the file along with information about each review pass. Once all colleagues have seen and reviewed the file and the review cycle is complete, you can review, accept, or reject the contributions of your colleagues.

When you deliver a presentation, you and your audience do not have to be in the same room. You can schedule and deliver online broadcasts for viewing over an **intranet**, a network of interlinked computers that is restricted to a specific company or group of people. During the broadcast, you can use PowerPoint's tools to interact with your audience and gather feedback from them. You can also publish the presentation to a Web server so that the slide show can be viewed by anyone at any time on the Web.

Skill Set 8

Workgroup Collaboration

Set Up a Review Cycle
Set Up a Review Cycle and Send Presentations for Review

To set up a review cycle you need to send the file using your e-mail program. The steps in this activity assume you will use Outlook 2002. If you use another e-mail program, Outlook will still manage the review cycle for you. To send the file to more than one reviewer, use the **Send To Routing Recipient** command to open the Add Routing Slip dialog box. This lets you choose the addresses of the recipients and specify options, such as whether all recipients receive the file all at once, or one after the other so that each reviewer can see the previous reviewers' comments. A **routing slip** travels with the file and contains the e-mail addresses of the people who are on the list to receive the file. If a file has a routing slip attached to it, each reviewer has the chance to add a new address to the slip or just send the presentation to the next person on the list.

Activity Steps

 open BLT-Season1.ppt

1. Click **File** on the menu bar, point to **Send To**, then click **Routing Recipient** (if a dialog box opens asking you to allow access to addresses stored in Outlook, click **Yes**)

2. If the Choose Profile dialog box opens, select your **profile name**, then click **OK**
   The Add Routing Slip dialog box opens. *See Figure 8-1.*

3. Click **Address** to open your Outlook address book (if you are using another e-mail program, the address book for that e-mail program will open)

4. Choose the names of two people to whom you want to send the file, click **OK** to return to the Add Routing Slip dialog box, then verify that the **One after another option button** is selected in the Route to recipients section

5. Click **Route**, click **Yes** to access the e-mail addresses if the warning dialog box opens, then click **Yes** to send the e-mail
   The file is sent to the first recipient.

6. Click **File** on the menu bar, point to **Send To**, then click **Mail Recipient (for Review)**
   The Outlook new message window opens. *See Figure 8-2.* To send the file for review, you would fill in the recipients' e mail addresses, then click Send.

7. Click **File** on the new message window menu bar, click **Close**, then click **No** to return to PowerPoint

 close BLT-Season1.ppt

Step 2 and 3
If a warning dialog box opens telling you that a program is trying to access e-mail addresses stored in Outlook, click Yes.

Figure 8-1: Add Routing Slip dialog box

Lists all
addresses
in route

Click to select
addresses from
Contacts file

Click to choose
whether file is
sent in a loop
or to all recipients
at once

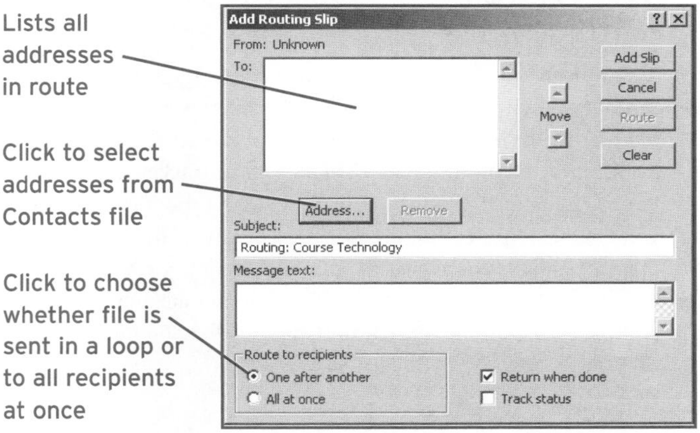

Figure 8-2: Message window in Outlook

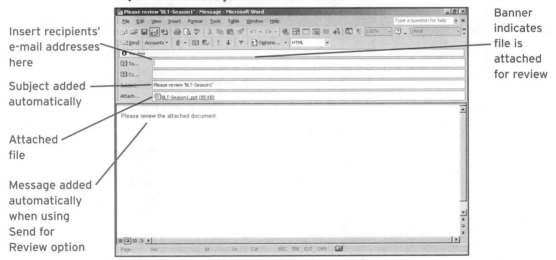

Insert recipients'
e-mail addresses
here

Subject added
automatically

Attached
file

Message added
automatically
when using
Send for
Review option

Banner
indicates
file is
attached
for review

extra!

Understanding different sending options

If you want to send the presentation to only one person, you can use the **Send To Mail Recipient (as Attachment)** command to attach the file to an e-mail message, so a recipient can open, view, and edit it. If you want a message to be included automatically in the e-mail requesting that the recipient review the attachment, you can use the **Send To Mail Recipient (for Review)** command. To make changes to the routing of a file, click File on the menu bar, point to Send To, then click Routing Recipient to open the Edit Routing Slip dialog box. This lets you change the order of recipients, add recipients, or change the routing for the file.

Skill Set 8
Workgroup Collaboration

Review Presentation Comments
Reviewing, Acccepting, and Rejecting Changes from Multiple Reviewers

If you send your presentation to more than one reviewer, you will get back several versions of the presentation with comments and tracked changes. Depending on the options specified by the original sender, the file will go to all recipients at once, or in sequence. The status of the file may or may not be tracked to allow the originator to see the progress. Fortunately, you can merge all the files so that you can review all the comments at once and accept or reject any of the changes. When the file arrives in your e-mail, you have the option of merging it with your original file or opening it for review as shown in Figure 8-3. Each reviewer's comments appear in a different color, tagged with the date of the comment and the reviewer's initials or name.

Each reviewer is assigned a different color to make it easy to distinguish among reviewers. To view a list of all the reviewers who have contributed to the file, click the Reviewers list arrow in the revisions pane.

Activity Steps

 open BLT-Season2.ppt

1. Click **Tools** on the menu bar, then click **Compare and Merge Presentations**
   The Choose Files to Merge with Current Presentation dialog box opens.

2. Click **BLT-Season2-rev.ppt**, click **Merge**, click **Continue**, then click **Next** in the Revisions Pane to go to Slide 2

3. Place the pointer over the **ECB1 colored box** on the slide to read the comment
   See Figure 8-4.

4. Click **Next** in the revisions pane to move to slide 3, view the comment, click **Next** to move to slide 4, then click **Text 2: Established in 1987** in the Revisions Pane to open a popup window listing the suggested changes
   See Figure 8-5. You can use the Reviewing toolbar or the Revisions Pane to apply suggested changes.

5. Click in the **Inserted paragraph separator check box** in the popup window to see the first change, then click the **Inserted "In 2004..." check box**

6. Click **Next** in the Revisions Pane, click **Text 2: 50% from ticket sales...**, click the **Apply button** [image] to view all the suggested slide changes, then click the **Unapply button** [image] to reject the changes

7. Click **Next** in the Revisions Pane, click **Text 2: Elementary programs...**, add check marks to each check box, view the changes, click **Next**, then view and apply the change to slide 11

 close BLT-Season2.ppt

Figure 8-3: Message dialog box to determine whether to merge or open file

Figure 8-4: Reviewing a comment

Reviewing toolbar

Revisions Pane

Reviewer's comment

Click to see next slide

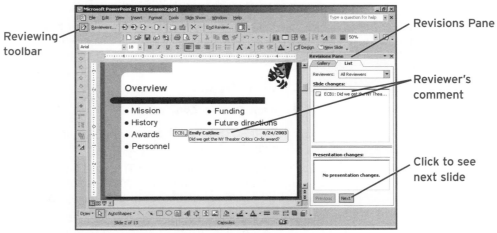

Figure 8-5: Comments in revisions pane

Apply button

Unapply button

Popup window shows text change suggested by reviewer

Click to add check marks to accept reviewers' changes

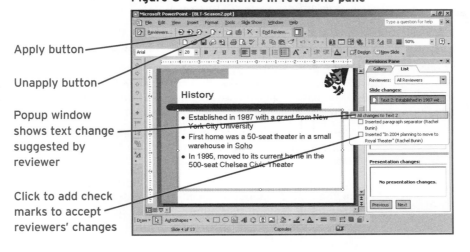

To delete a comment, click the comment on the slide, then click the Delete Comment button on the Reviewing toolbar.

Skill Set 8

Workgroup Collaboration

Schedule and Deliver Presentation Broadcasts

Set Up and Schedule Online Broadcasts

You can deliver a presentation over the Web, on the Internet, or over a network as an online broadcast. An **Online broadcast** is a live performance of your presentation that is captured and delivered over the Web or a network to viewers through a browser. Your audience must use Netscape Navigator 4.0 (or later) or Internet Explorer 5.1 (or later) to view an online broadcast. You also must have access to a shared network drive or a URL to be able to schedule an online broadcast.

When you set up an online broadcast, PowerPoint creates a **lobby page**, which contains information about the title, subject, host name, and time of the broadcast and appears in the viewer's browser before the broadcast begins.

If you get a dialog box that says the Online Broadcast feature isn't currently installed, click Install then follow the onscreen steps to install the feature.

Activity Steps

 open BLT-Season3.ppt

1. Click **Slide Show** on the menu bar, point to **Online Broadcast**, then click **Schedule a Live Broadcast**

2. Type the information in the Title and Description box in the Schedule Presentation Broadcast dialog box shown in Figure 8-6
The information will appear in the lobby page.

3. Click **Settings**, click **Browse** on the Presenter tab, then navigate to the location of the shared folder to save the broadcast
The File location must be a shared folder on a network server or a URL for a broadcast on the Web.

4. If you don't have a shared folder, click **OK** to close the error box, then click **Cancel** in the Broadcast Settings dialog box

5. If you are able to specify a shared folder on a network in the Broadcast Settings dialog box, click **OK**, then click **Schedule**
If you have a shared network folder and Outlook, the program will open a meeting request window. *See Figure 8-7.*

6. Close the Meeting window if one is open, do not save the changes, then click **Cancel** in the Schedule a Presentation Broadcast window

7. To broadcast the show at the scheduled time, click **Slide Show** on the menu bar, point to **Online Broadcast**, click **Start a Live Broadcast Now** (if you have Outlook, click **Yes** to allow access) to open the Live Presentation Broadcast dialog box

8. Click **Cancel**

 close BLT-Season3.ppt

Figure 8-6: Schedule Presentation Broadcast dialog box

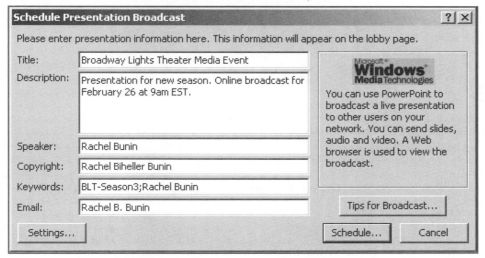

Figure 8-7: Meeting request window in Outlook

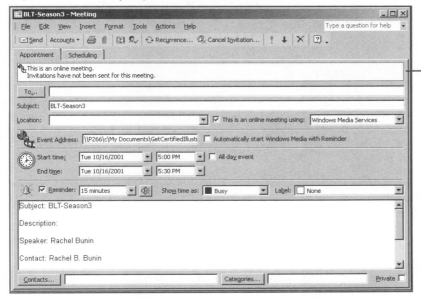

Fill in these boxes to specify the time and attendees for your presentation

Skill Set 8

Workgroup Collaboration

Publish Presentations to the Web
Save Presentations as Web Pages (Using the Publish Option)

If you want to allow others to view your presentation whenever they want, you can save the presentation as a Web page and publish it to the Web. **Publishing** a Web page means that you place it on a Web server so that users can view it through a browser any time they find convenient. This differs from an online broadcast, which you, the presenter, schedule for a specific time. To publish a presentation to the Web, you must first save it as a Web page in HTML Format. Once it is saved as a Web page, you can use the Publish option in the Save As dialog box to specify the location of your Web server. Once a file is published to a Web server, it is available to anyone with Internet access.

Activity Steps

 open BLT-Season4.ppt

1. Click **File** on the menu bar, then click **Save As Web Page** to open the Save as dialog box.
   See Figure 8-8.

The Web page title appears in the title bar of each page.

2. Navigate to the folder containing your Project Files, click **Change Title**, type **your name**, click **OK**, then click **Publish**
   The Publish as Web Page dialog box opens. *See Figure 8-9.*

3. Click the **Open published Web page in browser check box**, then click **Publish**
   The presentation opens in your default browser. Unless you specified a Web server location in the Publish as Web Page dialog box, the file will not be available on the Web to other viewers.

4. Click each link to view all 13 slides, click **File** on the browser menu bar, then click **Close** to return to PowerPoint

 close BLT-Season4.ppt

Figure 8-8: Save As dialog box

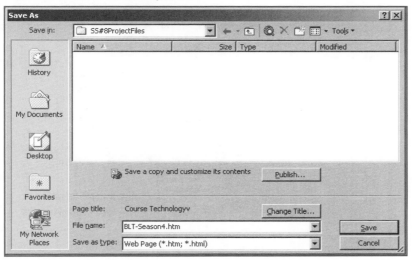

Figure 8-9: Publish as Web Page dialog box

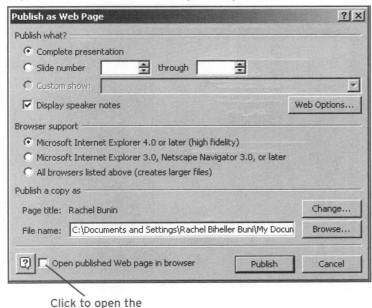

Click to open the presentation in a browser

Skill Set 8
Workgroup Collaboration

Target Your Skills

 open Shelter1.ppt

1 With Figure 8-10 as a guide, send the file Shelter1.ppt for review to two friends using the Send to Routing Recipient command. Compare and merge the Shelter1.ppt file with the file Shelter1-rev.ppt. Reject the change to add Angela on slide 5. Accept all the other changes to the presentation. Delete the comment on slide 4.

 open Shelter2.ppt

2 Use Figure 8-11 as a guide. Save the presentation as a Web page and use the Publish option to publish the presentation to a location on your hard drive. Change the title to your name. If you have access to a shared network folder or URL on a Web site, schedule an online broadcast for the presentation.

Figure 8-10

Figure 8-11

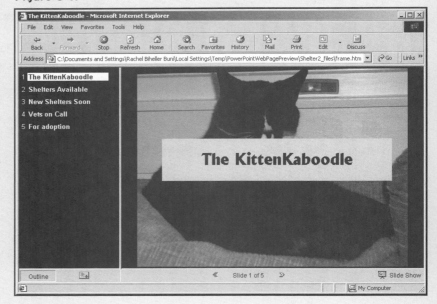

Word 2002 Core Projects Appendix

Projects List

Project 1 – Meeting Minutes for Mariposa Community Center

Project 2 – Advertising Bulletin for Skis 'n Boards

Project 3 – Newsletter for the Marine Educational Foundation

Project 4 – Memo for Lakeland Art Gallery

Project 5 – Information Sheet for Classic Car Races

Project 6 – Web Page for Allure Cosmetics

The Word Core skill sets cover a broad range of formatting and file management skills. Once you have mastered these skills, you can create many different document types. In the following projects, you will format a set of meeting minutes, an advertising bulletin, and a newsletter. You will also create a memo from one of Word's preset templates, add graphics to an information sheet, and save a Word document as a Web page that you can post to a Web site on the World Wide Web.

Project for Skill Set 1

Inserting and Modifying Text

Meeting Minutes for Mariposa Community Center

Each month a different staff member at the Mariposa Community Center in Carmel, California is responsible for recording the minutes of the monthly staff meeting. As the Office Manager at the Center, you receive and format each month's set of minutes before printing them for distribution to all staff. For this project, you will edit and format the minutes of the May 2004 meeting.

Activity Steps

 open WC_Project1.doc

1. Change **Mara Ramon** to **Darryl Cook** in the first bulleted item

2. Use the Find and Replace function to replace every instance of **Manjit Sidhu** with **Mitra Biazar**

3. Replace the second '**e**' in Hélene with **è** (in the bulleted item under "France Exchange Program")

4. Copy **report** in the first bullet under Fundraising Committee Report, use Paste Special to paste it after **Recreation Council** as unformatted text, capitalize **report**, then cut **Recreation Council Report** and its accompanying bulleted items and paste it below **Other Committee Reports**

5. Format the text **Mariposa Community Center** at the top of the page with **Bold**, then remove *Italics* from **Gym Fitness Program Builder** (in the first bulleted item below "Director's Report")

6. Use spell check to correct the spelling errors "**brekfast**" and "**oportunities**" and the grammatical error in the second bulleted item under Other Committee Reports
   Note that you should ignore the correction to "Mitra Biazar."

7. Enhance the text **May Meeting Minutes** with the Shadow font effect, then highlight the two names in the first bulleted item with **Turquoise**

8. Insert and center the current date below May Meeting Minutes; ensure the date is set to update automatically

9. Change the format of the date you just inserted to use the format that corresponds with **May 2, 2004**

10. Apply the Pacific character style to the text Pacific Marathon Boosters Association (under the Other Committee Reports heading)
    The completed minutes appear as shown in Figure WP 1-1.

 close WC_Project1.doc

Step 3
To insert the è symbol, click Insert on the menu bar, click Symbol, select the (normal text) font, click è, click Insert, then click Close.

Figure WP 1-1: Completed minutes for Mariposa Community Center

Mariposa Community Center
May Meeting Minutes
May 2, 2004

Approval of Minutes
- Minutes from the April 2004 meeting were approved by Darryl Cook and seconded by Mitra Biazar

Fundraising Committee Report – Barry Deville
- Barry circulated a report on fundraising activities. The report provided information about the following topics:
  - Organizing a large fund-raising committee for the summer of 2004
  - Organizing a bingo night in partnership with Mitra Biazar, the Director of Athletics
  - Learning about the Charitable You Club, a local charity fundraising company

Other Committee Reports

P.M.B.A. (***Pacific Marathon Boosters Association***)
- The next run event will be held on June 2 and will include a marathon, a 10K fun run, and a 5K walk/run. The cost of the run will be $30.00, which includes a T-shirt, a hat, OR a water bottle.
- Tim Simmons, a world champion marathoner, will hold a Marathon Clinic on May 20. All registrants for the June 2 marathon are encouraged to attend.
- The next P.M.B.A. meeting is June 5, 2004.

Recreation Council Report
- The breakfast held for fitness instructors on Instructor Appreciation Day was a success
- The gym equipment committee will be cleaning and restoring equipment during the week of May 24 to May 31. Volunteers are requested.

France Exchange Program
- Marie-Hélène Rousseau will host a meeting for parents and students interested in participating in the 9th Annual France-California Exchange. This year, students will spend three weeks in the Loire Valley.

Director's Report
- The Professional Development day on May 1 was successful. Recreation instructors learned how to use the new Gym Fitness Program Builder to upload fitness information to the Mariposa Community Center Web site.
- A new large group room will be located in the lower hallway on the 200 floor. Multimedia presentations can be given in the room to audiences of up to 75 people.
- The post-secondary evening held on May 5 was fully attended. Parents and students from the area's high schools attended a lively presentation about career and educational opportunities.

Project for Skill Set 2
Creating and Modifying Paragraphs

Advertising Bulletin for Skis 'n Boards

Skis 'n Boards is a ski and snowboarding shop with three outlets in the Vancouver area. To celebrate the start of the ski season, each outlet will host a snowboarding demonstration given by two world-class snowboarders from International Snowboarding, the premier manufacturer of snowboarding equipment. The demonstrations will take place on three consecutive Saturdays in November at each of the three Skis 'n Boards outlets. You've been given a Word document containing a bulletin that advertises the event. Now you need to format the bulletin attractively so that each Skis 'n Boards outlet can distribute copies to customers, media people, and local businesses. The completed bulletin appears as shown in Figure WP 2-1.

Activity Steps

 open WC_Project2.doc

1. Apply the **Heading 1** style to the document heading **Snowboard Demo!**, increase the font size to **28 pt**, then center the heading

2. Apply the **Heading 3** style to the entire first paragraph

3. Indent the first paragraph **.5"** from both the left and the right margins of the page, apply the **Justified** alignment, then select **1.5 line spacing** for the first paragraph
   You can make all these changes in the Paragraph dialog box.

4. Apply **Gray-10% shading** to the entire first paragraph

5. Select the paragraph that begins "Two awesome world-class boarders...", then apply the same formatting you applied to the first paragraph

6. Select the line containing Day, Date, and Location, open the Tabs dialog box, clear all the current tabs, set **Center tabs** at **.9"**, **2.6"**, and **4.6"**, click to the left of Day, press **[Tab]** to position the three headings, then enhance the three headings with **Bold**

7. Select the information about the three locations, use the ruler bar to set **Left tabs** at **.5"**, **2"**, and **4"**, then indent the three lines to the first tab stop
   The .5 stop appears halfway between the left margin and the 1 on the ruler bar.

8. Apply bullets in the style shown in Figure WP 2-1 to the text that describes the events at each Snowboarding Demo

9. Use the Increase Indent button to indent the bulleted text to the **1"** tab stop, then double-space the text

 close WC_Project2.doc

Step 6
To set tabs, click Format on the menu bar, click Tabs, click Clear All, type the required position, click the Center option button, then click Set. Type and set the remaining positions, then click OK.

Figure WP 2-1: Completed bulletin for Skis 'n Boards

Snowboard Demo!

Don't miss the Snowboard Demo at your local Skis 'n Boards outlet. You can also meet the Ski Bunny and win one of ten all-day lift tickets for Whistler-Blackcomb!

Day	Date	Location
Saturday	November 13, 2004	West Vancouver store
Saturday	November 20, 2004	Lonsdale Avenue store
Saturday	November 27, 2004	Kerrisdale store

Two awesome world-class boarders from International Snowboarding will be on hand to share tips and tricks while they perform an awesome series of stunts in our simulated half pipe. Each Snowboard Demo kicks off at noon. Here's an outline of events:

- Noon: The Ski Bunny mascot arrives to greet shoppers and pose for pictures
- 12:30: International Snowboarding experts Maury White and Adam Schreck arrive and sign autographs
- 1:00: First half pipe demo
- 1:30   Break; entertainment provided by the Powder Blues Band
- 2:00   Second half pipe demo
- 2:30   Maury and Adam sign autographs
- 3:00   Drawing for 10 discount lift tickets

Project for Skill Set 3

Formatting Documents

Newsletter for the Marine Educational Foundation

You work part-time in the administrative office of the Marine Educational Foundation, a non-profit educational organization that offers courses in marine ecology from its residential facility in Marathon, Florida. Your supervisor has just e-mailed you a copy of the Fall 2004 Newsletter and asked you to format it over two pages so it appears as shown in Figure WP 3-1 on pages 307 and 309.

Step 4
You will need to bold and center the text in Row 1, reduce the width of the columns, center the percentages in column 2, then center the table between the left and right margins of the newsletter column.

Activity Steps

 open WC_Project3a.doc

1. Change the orientation of the document to **Portrait**, then change the left and right margins to 1"

2. Format the text from **2004 Educational Programs** to the end of the document in **two columns** of equal width

3. Remove the current header, then create a footer containing **your name** at the left margin and a **page number** at the right margin

4. Click below the first paragraph in the 2004 Educational Programs topic, create a table containing **seven rows** and **two columns**, then enter and format the text as shown in Figure WP 3-1

5. Apply the **Table Contemporary** AutoFormat to the table in the Leadership Programs section, remove the row containing information about **Angus Marsh**, insert a new column to the left of **State**, then enter the column head **Age** in bold and the ages of the students in the column cells, as shown in Figure WP 3-1

Figure WP 3-1: Completed newsletter for Marine Educational Foundation

Marine Educational Foundation

Fall 2004 Newsletter

2004 Educational Programs

In 2004, the Marine Educational Foundation hosted 300 student groups from all over the United States in its marine educational programs. Over 1000 students learned about the history and ecology of the mangrove, coral reef, and grass bed systems of the Florida Keys. Most student groups were from the state of Florida, followed closely by students from California and then New York and Georgia. The following table shows the states from which the highest percentage of our student groups traveled in 2004.

State	Percent of Students
Florida	43%
California	19%
New York	13%
Georgia	13%
South Carolina	7%
New Jersey	5%

New Facility

In 2005, we will begin construction of a new facility near San Diego in California to provide our west coast students with an ecological experience more related to their home environment.

Our members recognize the benefits of combining travel with study. The students who attend the Marine Educational Foundation enjoy a unique travel experience, while gaining knowledge that they can apply directly to their Marine Science classes.

Web Presence

Increasingly, our Web site is attracting interest from students and educators outside the United States. In 2005, we plan to expand our program to include students from Canada, England, Germany, Japan, and Brazil. Check out our site at: www.marinedfoundation.com.

Leadership Programs

The table shown below lists the students who participated in a special leadership group that was run at the Marine Educational Foundation in June 2004. The students were chosen on the basis of their teamwork skills, leadership potential, and academic achievement. The three-day program was a great success.

Last Name	First Name	Age	State
Amin	Zahra	16	CA
Flynn	Kate	17	NY
Leblanc	Michel	16	NY
McGraw	Andy	16	NJ
Penner	Marike	18	PA
Ramirez	Teresa	18	FL
Sanchez	Juan	17	FL
Yeung	Martha	17	CA

[Your Name]

1

Project for Skill Set 3

Formatting Documents

Newsletter for the Marine Educational Foundation (continued)

6. In the table in the Upcoming Educational Program section, change the Green shading to **Light Green**, then change the font color of the text to **Black**

Step 7
To clear formatting, click the Styles list arrow on the Formatting toolbar, then click Clear Formatting.

7. Increase the width of column 1 to **3.2"**, insert a page break before the Upcoming Educational Programs section, clear the formatting to remove the Heading 1 style at the bottom of page 1, then balance the columns on Page 1

8. Insert a column break at the beginning of the second paragraph of the Annual Meeting section on Page 2, view the newsletter in Print Preview, then print a copy of the document

9. Create and print a sheet of labels containing the address of the Marine Educational Foundation shown on Page 2 of the newsletter, then save the labels as **WC_Project3b.doc**

   close WC_Project3a.doc
WC_Project3b.doc

Figure WP 3-1 (continued): Completed newsletter for Marine Educational Foundation

Upcoming Educational Programs

We are anticipating the best season ever in the Spring of 2000 as over five-hundred groups are scheduled to go through the program! Here's the list of programs offered in 2005:

Study	Price
Mangroves, Coral Reefs, and Grass Beds	$300
Mangroves 3-days	$100
Coral Reefs 3-days	$100
Grass Beds 3-days	$100
Coral Reefs, Dolphins Plus	$200
Save the Manatee	$75
Grass Beds and Coral Reefs	$200

All programs, except for those listed as 3-day, last for five days and do not include the cost of transportation from the student's home town to Marathon, Florida. The program price includes all meals, books, transportation, and dormitory-style accommodation while students are participating in the programs.

Annual Meeting

On October 23 at 5 p.m., the Marine Educational Foundation will host its annual meeting and member get-together! As always, we will hold the meeting at the Marine Educational Foundation site in Marathon, Florida. We hope to see some new faces this year, so bring along your friends. For out-of-town members, we're offering a special weekend rate at one of our local hotels of $180 for two nights. You can also enjoy the gourmet delights of our student cafeteria. It's a deal you just can't pass up! Check out the beautiful Florida Keys! If you want to take advantage of this special offer, please call Mark at (305) 872-6641.

Our agenda for this year's meeting is as follows:

- Welcome to New Members
- Budget Report
- Detailed Program Schedule for 2005
- Slide Presentation by Scott Smith on his 2004 Teaching Experience
- New Business
- Adjournment
- Party Time!

We're counting on seeing all the Marine Educational Foundation members this year!

Marine Educational Foundation
P.O. Box 41
Marathon, Florida 33051

[Your Name]

2

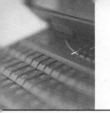

Project for Skill Set 4

Managing Documents

Memo for Lakeland Art Gallery

You've just been hired as an Administrative Assistant at the Lakeland Art Gallery on the shores of Georgian Bay in Ontario. One of your first duties is to create a memo describing the upcoming winter exhibition of gallery artists. You decide to base the memo on a template and then create a new folder to contain the memos you create for the gallery. You'll also save the memo in Text (.txt) format so you can distribute it to artists who use other word processing programs that may not be compatible with Word 2002.

Activity Steps

1. Click **General Templates** in the New Document task pane, click the **Memos tab** in the Templates dialog box, then select the **Contemporary Memo** template

2. Modify the template so the completed memo appears as shown in Figure WP 4-1

3. Open the Save As dialog box, then create a new folder called **Art Gallery Memos**

4. Save the document as **WC_Project4.doc** in the Art Gallery Memos folder

5. Modify the document by changing the name of **Flora Wong** to **Flora Leung**

6. Save the changes to the document, then close the document

7. Open **WC_Project4.doc**, save the document in Plain Text (.txt) format with the default settings, then close the document

8. Open the **WC_Project4.txt** file
   Note that you'll need to click the Files of type list arrow and select All Files to see the .txt file.

   close WC_Project4.txt

Project 4

Memo for Lakeland Art Gallery

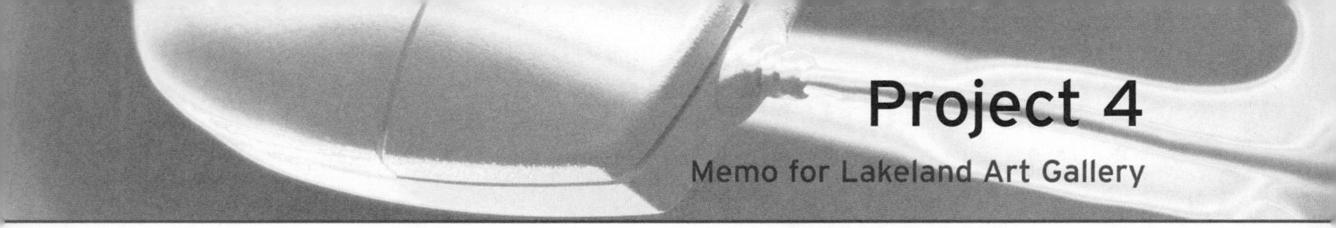

Figure WP 4-1: Completed memo for Lakeland Art Gallery

Memorandum

To: All Gallery Artists

From: [Your Name]

Date: [Current Date]

Re: Lakeland Art Gallery Winter Exhibition

From December 6 to January 5, the Lakeland Art Gallery will host its annual Winter Group Exhibition. We require a maximum of three pieces from each of you.

The Winter Group Exhibition attracts collectors from all over Ontario. As many of you already know, this exhibition is traditionally one of the Lakeland Art Gallery's most successful. Many of our artists sell at least one piece during the course of the exhibition.

Please bring the following items when you come to the gallery to help hang your pieces:

- Artwork
- List of titles
- Price list
- Curriculum vitae
- Brochures, postcards, posters, or prints, if available

If you have any questions about the setup schedule or any other concerns, please call Flora Wong at 555-2233. I am looking forward to making this Winter exhibition our most successful yet!

CONFIDENTIAL

1

Project for Skill Set 5

Working with Graphs

Information Sheet for Classic Car Races

The Adirondacks Raceway hosts a series of races for owners of classic sports racing cars of the 1950's and 1960's. As the Office Manager of the facility, you decide to create an information sheet for prospective racers. The sheet includes a pie chart, a clip art picture, a photograph of a classic car, and a diagram showing the steps required to register for a classic car race. The two pages of the completed information sheet appear in Figure WP 5-1 on pages 11 and 13.

Step 3
After you create the default column chart, click Chart on the menu bar, click Chart Type, click Pie, then click OK. You will then need to click Data on the Menu bar and then click Series in Columns.

Activity Steps

 open WC_Project5.doc

1. Insert the picture file called **Ferrari.jpg** at the beginning of paragraph 1, then change the layout to **Square**

2. Use your mouse to size and position the picture in paragraph 1 as shown in Figure WP 5-1

3. Create a **pie chart** that includes a legend from the data in the table, then delete the table

4. Increase the size of the pie chart and center it, as shown in Figure WP 5-1, double-click the **chart**, click just the **grey background** behind the pie, then press **[Delete]**

5. Insert, size, and position the **clip art image** shown in Figure WP 5-1
   Search for "racing car" in the Microsoft Clip Gallery. You will need to be online to access the full Microsoft Clip Gallery. If you are not able to go online, use another similar image of a car from the Microsoft Clip Gallery.

 close WC_Project5.doc

Figure WP 5-1: Completed information sheet for Classic Car Races

Adirondacks Raceway
Classic Sports Racing Car Competition

The Adirondacks Raceway located outside Saratoga Springs, New York hosts five classic sports racing car competitions each season. Drivers who own some of the most beautiful classic racing cars of the 1950's and 60's relive the glory days of racing, when the sleek design and ear-shattering power of front engine sports cars ruled the raceways. Famed drivers of the times make regular appearances to the delight of their many fans.

The pie chart shown below displays the breakdown of race winners over the past three years by car type.

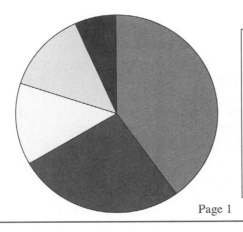

- 250 Testa Rosa Ferrari (1957)
- D Type Jaguar (1960)
- Tipo 61 Birdcage Maserati (1961)
- Lotus Eleven (1959)
- Aston Martin DBR 2/370

Page 1

Project for Skill Set 6

Workgroup Collaboration

Web Page for Allure Cosmetics

Allure Cosmetics owns several shops in New Zealand. The company's rich, multi-scented soaps, gels, lotions, and cosmetics have become justly famous throughout the country. Now you and your colleagues are working on transforming existing marketing documents for use on the company's new Web site. In this project you will work on a description of the company's three top-selling cleansing products and insert a comment for your colleague, Joanne Plaice. You will then merge the document with another version edited by Joanne to produce a final copy that incorporates your comment and Joanne's comments and changes. Finally, you will save the document as a Web page and view it in your browser. Figure WP 6-1 shows the merged version of the document with two sets of comments.

Activity Steps

 open WC_Project6A.doc
WC_Project6B.doc

1. In the WC_Project6A document, select **Mango Cleansing Milk**, insert a comment with the text **What do you think of changing the name to Mango Wash?**, then save and close the document

2. In the WC_Project6B document, view the two comments inserted by Joanne

3. Merge to a new document the WC_Project6B document with the WC_Project6A document

4. Save the new document as **WC_Project6C.doc**, then print a copy
   Figure WP 6-1 shows how the merged document appears when printed.

5. In response to the three comments, change the name of Mango Cleansing Milk to **Mango Wash** (two places), change tropical dawn to **tropical evening**, then change cool water to **warm water**

6. Use the appropriate buttons on the Reviewing toolbar to accept all the changes in the document, then delete all the comments in the document

7. Save the document as a Web page called **WC_Project6D.htm**, apply the Watermark theme, then view the document in your Web browser
   Figure WCP 6-2 shows how the document appears in the browser.

 close WC_Project6B.doc
WC_Project6C.doc
WC_Project6D.htm

Figure WP 6-1: Merged document

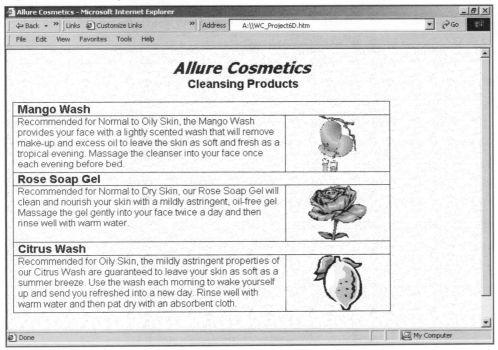

Word 2002 Expert Projects Appendix

Projects List

Project 7 – Architectural Heritage Campaign Information

Project 8 – TV Documentary Proposal

Project 9 – Ohio Teen Choir Trip Information

Project 10 – Flyer for Fascinatin' Rhythms Dance Studio

Project 11 – Phoenix Concert Society Posters

Project 12 – Short Story for Footloose Travel Magazine

Project 13 – Film Location Form Letter

The Word Expert skill sets include features for customizing Word, applying advanced formatting options, creating and working with complex tables and graphics, working with multiple-page documents and different versions of documents, collaborating with one or more colleagues on a document, and using Mail Merge. In the following projects, you will practice these skills by creating and managing a variety of documents.

Project for Skill Set 7

Customizing Paragraphs

Architectural Heritage Campaign Information

The Architectural Heritage Campaign in Vancouver, British Columbia is working to preserve buildings of architectural and historical significance in the downtown core. As part of their campaign to raise public awareness about the many buildings that need saving, the organizers of the campaign have produced an information sheet. For this project, you will format the information sheet over two pages and then use the Sort feature to organize information about the buildings. The formatted document is shown in Figure WP 7-1.

Activity Steps

 open WE_Project7.doc

1. Remove the line breaks between each of the three subtitle lines at the top of page 1, then use the [Shift][Enter] keys to add manual line breaks so that the space between each item is closed up

2. Sort the items in the table on page 1 in alphabetical order by the information in column 1

3. Turn on widow and orphan control for the second paragraph that appears below the table on page 1
   The first line of the paragraph should now appear at the top of page 2.

4. Sort the five paragraphs describing the five heritage buildings on page 2 in alphabetical order

5. On page 1 insert a manual page break to the left of **Five buildings are slated ..."**
   The document is formatted over two pages as shown in Figure WP 7-1.

 close WE_Project7.doc

Figure WP 7-1: Document formatted over two pages

Architectural Heritage Campaign

Prepared by the Heritage Advisory Board
Vancouver, BC
September 20, 2004

The City Planning Department, in cooperation with the Heritage Advisory Board, is currently in the process of identifying heritage structures throughout the Vancouver area. In 2003, the Board plans to focus on saving as many good examples of the Modernist style (1933-1973) as possible. Several structures now slated for demolition should be placed in the Class A heritage list as good examples of the West Coast Modern style, which Vancouver as a city is internationally renowned.

The following buildings will be discussed at with the exception of the B.C. Binning house Vancouver city limits.

Building Name	Street
B.C. Binning House	Mathers Aven
Commonwealth Building	West Pender S
Customs House	Hastings Stree
Downtown Branch	Denman Stree
Marwell Construction Building	West Georgia
Mayor's Residence	Cambie Street
St. Andrew's United Church	Point Grey Ro
Waterfront Building	Burrard Street

Five buildings are slated for special campaigns in 2004. All of these buildings face imminent development bids.

B.C. Binning House: In an era which is finally waking up to the value of 20th Century architecture, this fine example of an early west coast Modernist house has long been on Vancouver's architectural heritage list. Artist and university instructor B.C. Binning lived in the house for forty years. The house remains under the ownership of his widow who is working with the heritage committees to save it.

Mayor's Residence: This turn of the century mansion is one of the few remaining examples of Victorian architecture in the city. Its classical columns and domed roof make it a prime candidate for inclusion in the city's heritage list. Plans are underway to preserve the structure for use as a public museum.

St. Andrew's United Church: This wooden church is another building from the Modernist 1950's era. The A-frame design includes a steep angled shingle roof and an open design that is complemented by vertical mahogany siding, reminiscent of the forest. The congregation and management of the church are currently seeking heritage protection for the structure.

Vancouver Public Library: Main Branch: This low-rise building in the center of Vancouver was awarded a Governor General's silver medal for design in 1957. The building's clean lines and classical proportions illustrate the most appealing side of Modernist architecture. Features of note include louvered front façade, unique roof elements, and original murals.

Waterfront Building: This excellent example of the late 1920's art deco style must be preserved as a prime example of its period. This building was once the tallest structure in the British Empire. Used as offices by the Port Authority for decades, the building is lavishly decorated with relief sculptures of marine life and other detailing which makes it a singular example of the use of ornamentation in 20th Century architecture.

Project for Skill Set 8

Formatting Documents

TV Documentary Proposal

Art Seen Productions, which produces TV documentaries about art and artists has created a proposal for a documentary about three art foundations. At present, the proposal consists of four documents that you need to format and organize into one document. You also will create a form that readers complete to provide feedback about the proposal.

Step 4
You'll need to add a space after you insert the cross-reference text "below."
Step 6
You'll need to add the text "Table of Contents" and "Index" as titles on the two pages and enhance them with the Documentary Title style, as shown in Figure 8-1. The index entries appear in the Gallery History section of the Episode 1 subdocument.

Activity Steps

 open WE_Project8A.doc

1. Use the Document Map to go to the **Production Schedule** section, verify that the line spacing in the numbered list is 1.5, then select the three numbered items and clear the formatting

2. Create a paragraph style called **Documentary Title** that centers text and formats it as **Times New Roman, 22 point, Bold** and **Dark Blue**, apply the style to the title **Art Seen Productions**, then modify the **Galleries** character style so that it formats text with the **Blue** font color

3. At the end of the first sentence, add a footnote that reads **The episodes are created for public television and so will span the full thirty minutes.**, delete the first sentence from footnote 3, then change the format of all the footnotes to the A, B, C style

4. Go to the **Schedule** bookmark, click after the text **Figure 1** in paragraph 1, then insert a cross-reference to **Figure 1**, using **Above/below** as the reference text

5. Switch to Outline view, move to the end of the document, then add three sub-documents: **WE_Project8B.doc, WE_Project8C.doc,** and **WE_Project8D.doc**

6. In Print Layout view, add a new page on a new section at the beginning of the document, insert a Table of Contents in the **Formal** format, find and mark **André Malraux** and **Samuel Beckett** for inclusion in an index, insert a new page at the end of the document, then insert an Index in the **Classic** format

7. Change the margins for section 1 to 2", update the table of contents as shown in Figure WP 8-1, then save, print, and close the document

8. Open **WE_Project8E.doc**, add a check box form field where indicated, then add a drop-down form field that includes the items shown in Figure WP 8-2

9. Protect the form, then save the file as a form template called **WE_Project8E.dot** and close it

 close WE_Project8E.dot

Figure WP 8-1: Completed table of contents

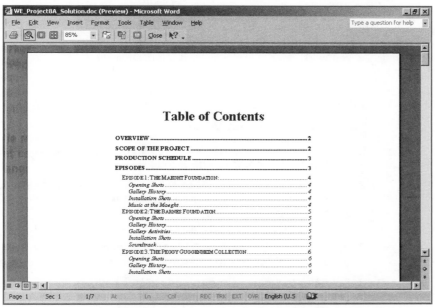

Figure WP 8-2: Items for the drop-down list

Project for Skill Set 9

Customizing Tables

Ohio Teen Choir Trip Information

The Ohio Teen Choir is California bound! During a 5-day tour of Los Angeles, the 60-person choir will perform at a variety of venues including Disneyland and Universal Studios. In this project, you need to add data to an information sheet that will be distributed to parents to inform them about the trip costs and performance schedule. As you work, refer to the completed information sheet shown in Figure WP 9-1.

Activity Steps

 open WE_Project9A.doc

1. Insert the Excel file **WE_Project9B.xls** as a linked worksheet object following paragraph 2

2. Enter a formula in cell **E9** of the worksheet object that adds the values in cells **E3** to **E8**, then center the worksheet object horizontally in the document
   The completed worksheet object appears as shown in Figure WP 9-1.

3. In the Concert Schedule Table that appears after the third paragraph in the document, merge the four cells in row 1 of the table

4. Split the last row of the table into two cells, then widen the first cell in that row so that it spans the first three columns

5. Enter the text **Total Performance Time** in the first cell of the last row, then format this text as shown in Figure WP 9-1

6. Enter a formula in the blank cell in the last row of the table that adds all the values in the rows above, then format the result as shown in Figure WP 9-1

 close WE_Project9A.doc
WE_Project9B.xls

Figure WP 9-1: Completed information sheet

Ohio Teen Choir
California Bound!

In 2004, the Ohio Teen Choir will embark on a seven-day, five-concert tour of sunny California! The choir will perform four solo concerts and then participate in a massed choir at a grand finale concert hosted by Disneyland! Each choir member should bring both the casual and the concert uniform, along with two pairs of casual pants, three shirts, seven pairs of socks and underwear, a bathing suit, and personal toiletries. The tour will be fully chaperoned with three assistants in addition to the conductor.

The table shown below breaks down costs for the tour. Please make sure your teen has sufficient funds for the extra meals, attractions, and spending money. The suggested amount is $460.00. The prepaid amount is $850.00 for hotels, fifteen meals, and air fare, and is due on February 1, 2004.

Cost per Choir Member				
Expense	Unit	Unit Cost	Number	Total
Airfare from Cleveland	Ticket	$ 350.00	1	$ 350.00
Hotel	Night	50.00	7	350.00
Meals (prepaid)	Meal	10.00	15	150.00
Meals (extra)	Meal	15.00	7	105.00
Entrance Fees	Attraction	45.00	4	180.00
Spending Money	Day	25.00	7	175.00
			Total Cost	$ 1,310.00

The schedule shown below lists the locations of each concert and the total duration. Two concert programs will be performed—the *Jazz in the City* program and the *Classical Nights* program.

Concert Schedule			
Date	Location	Time	Duration (minutes)
March 2	Anaheim Convention Center	8:00 PM	40
March 4	Disneyland (Fantasyland)	4:30 PM	60
March 5	Marineland	3:00 PM	60
March 7	Universal Studios	5:00 PM	45
March 9	Disneyland (Massed choir)	7:00 PM	90
Total Performance Time			295

Project for Skill Set 10

Creating and Modifying Graphics

Flyer for Fascinatin' Rhythms Dance Studio

The Fascinatin' Rhythms dance studio teaches a variety of popular dance styles to couples and singles in the Milwaukee area. You've been asked to enhance a new flyer with some interesting graphics. In this project, you will draw and modify some AutoShapes in the drawing canvas and create a chart that includes data from an Excel worksheet. As you work, refer to the completed flyer shown in Figure WP 10-1.

Step 4
You'll find the arrow shape in the Block Arrows category on the AutoShapes menu.

Step 8
To change the color of a data series, right-click the data series, click Format Data Series, then select the color required.

Activity Steps

 open WE_Project10A.doc

1. Use the [ALT] key to position the picture of the dancers floating over the first paragraph so that it appears as shown in Figure WP 10-1

2. In the space below paragraph 1, draw and format an arrow as shown in Figure WP 10-1, then copy it twice

3. Use flip and rotate commands to position the three arrows as shown in Figure WP 10-1

4. Add a text box containing the text **Step-by-Step** in Arial 14-point Bold below the three arrows as shown in Figure WP 10-1, then remove the line from around the text box

5. Fit the drawing canvas to the contents, then center the drawing canvas between the left and right margins of the document

6. In the space below paragraph 2, insert a **Column chart** containing data from the Excel file **WE_Project10B.xls**

7. Move the chart legend below the chart by right-clicking it and clicking **Format Legend, Placement, Bottom**

8. Change the color of the **Ballroom data series** to **pink** and the color of the **Jazz and Pop data series** to **bright green**, then size and position the chart as shown in Figure WP 10-1

 close WE_Project10A.doc
WE_Project10B.xls

Figure WP 10-1: Completed flyer

Fascinatin' Rhythm
Dance Studio

1600 Pine Drive, Milwaukee, WI 53223
www.fascinatinrhythm.com

Welcome to the *Fascinatin' Rhythm Dance Studio*. Here is the place where you can learn not only the new dances but also brush up on your mambo, waltz, and fox trot. We specialize in Latin and Jazz dance steps from samba to jive dancing. Learn from our accredited experts, who have had professional careers as performers and are also excellent instructors.

Step-by-Step

When you book your classes you can choose from three different series: Latin, Jazz and Pop, or Ballroom. Shown below is a chart of our classes.

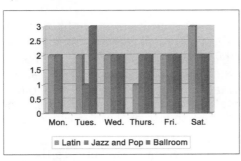

In the Latin classes, we teach Salsa, Mambo, Samba, Conga, and Cha-Cha. In the Jazz and Popular classes, we teach Jive dancing, Jitterbug, Swing Dancing, and Polka. In the Ballroom classes, we teach Waltz, Slow Dance, Tango, and Fox Trot.

Project for Skill Set 11

Customizing Word

Phoenix Concert Society Posters

Each month, the Phoenix Concert Society presents an evening of classical music. However, several members of the society usually take turns creating posters for each month's concert with the result that formatting is not always the same. You decide to create a macro and a toolbar that can be used to apply consistent formatting to each month's poster. You'll then use the macro and toolbar to format concert posters for the new two months.

Activity Steps

 open WE_Project11.doc

Step 2
You'll need to find the code line in the Visual Basic Editor that reads ".LineSpacingRule = wdLineSpace1pt5", then select 1pt5 and type Double.

Step 6
You will need to click the Grow Font 1 pt button twice to increase the font size to 18-point.

1. Create a macro called **Poster** that is saved in the current document, runs with the **Alt + P** keystrokes, and performs the steps shown in Figure WP 11-1

2. Open the Visual Basic Editor and edit the macro by changing the line spacing from 1pt5 to **Double**

3. Run the revised Poster macro

4. Customize the Formatting toolbar by adding the button for **Grow Font 1 pt** (in the Format category) and save the customized toolbar with the current document

5. Create a new menu called **Concert** that is saved with the current document, appears to the right of the Help menu, and contains both the Small Caps menu item and the Double Underline menu item (both in the Format category)

6. Select the title of the document, use the Grow Font button on the Formatting toolbar to increase the font size of the title to 18-point, then use the Double Underline command in the Concert menu to format the title with double underlining

7. Select all the text in the table, then use the Small Caps selection in the Concert menu to enhance the text with Small Caps
   The formatted document should appear as shown in Figure WP 11-2.

 close WE_Project11.doc

Figure WP 11-1: Macro steps

Macro Steps

1. Press [Ctrl][A] to select all the text in the document.

2. Open the Font dialog box, change the font to Arial, the font size to 16 point, and the font color to Blue, then click OK to close the Font dialog box.

3. Open the Paragraph dialog box, turn on 1.5 line spacing and centered alignment, then click OK to close the Paragraph dialog box.

4. Press the down arrow once to deselect the text.

5. Press [Ctrl][Home] to move to the top of the document.

6. Stop the macro recording.

Figure WP 11-2: Completed poster

An Evening of Beethoven

Be sure to catch the June performance by the Phoenix Concert Society at the Red Rock Theater on South Main Street. This month, you will be enveloped by the passion of Ludwig Von Beethoven. The all-Beethoven program includes two exquisite piano sonatas: the *Moonlight* and the **Pathetique** followed by the sublime 7th Symphony.

We are privileged this month to have the Four Corners Symphony as our special guest orchestra. Featured on the piano will be Gertrude Halliday, who has entertained Phoenix audiences for many years with her mesmerizing performances of the classics.

DATE	SATURDAY, NOVEMBER 27, 2004
TIME	8 P.M.
COST	$25.00

Project for Skill Set 12

Workgroup Collaboration

Short Story for Footloose Travel Magazine

As editor of a local travel magazine you collaborate with two other editors and an author to edit a short story. You use Word's collaboration features to edit a draft of the short story and then combine your changes with those made by two other editors (Melanie Reynolds and Florence Metz) and the author of the story (Lars Svensen). Finally, you open a document from Internet Explorer, edit it in Word, then upload it to a server.

Activity Steps

 open WE_Project12A.doc

1. Review the first formatting change made to the document, accept this change, review and accept the first change made by Melanie Reynolds, then reject her second change

2. With the Track Changes option turned on, enter a new line of text under the title that reads **By Lars Svensen**, press **[Enter]**, then save a version of the document with the comment **First version of the Print copy**

Step 3
Press [Enter] after typing the Web site address.
Step 8
If you do not have permission to save files to a Web server, navigate to the location where you are saving your project files, then click Save.

3. At the bottom of the document, add a centered hyperlink on a new line that goes to the top of the document and displays the text **Return to Top**, then save a new version with the comment **Print copy with hyperlink**

4. Use the **Compare and Merge Documents command** to merge the current document with **WE_Project12B.doc** and **WE_Project12C.doc**, so the first page of the merged version of WE_Project12C.doc appears as shown in Figure WP 12-1

5. View the changes made by the two other reviewers and your own changes, then accept all the changes

6. Add a digital signature to the document, if available, protect the document against tracked changes with the password **footloose**, save and close the document, then close the two other open documents without saving them

7. Open **WE_Project12D.htm** in Internet Explorer, edit the file in Word by editing the hyperlink at the bottom of the document so that it goes to the document top, then change the document title from Ocher to **Roussillon** as shown in Figure WP 12-2

8. Post the file to your Web server with the new name **RepostedStory.htm**

 close RepostedStory.htm

Figure WP 12-1: Merged document

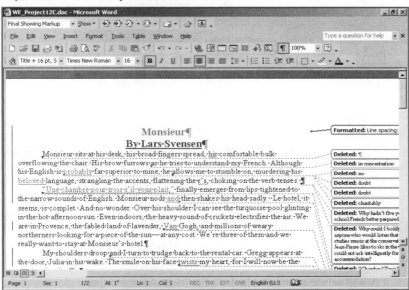

Figure WP 12-2: HTML document in Word

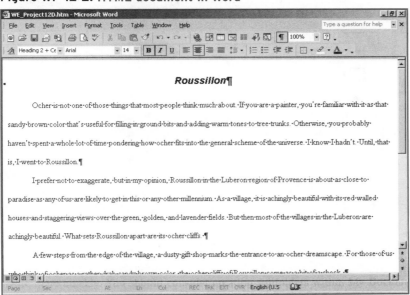

Project for Skill Set 13

Using Mail Merge

Film Location Form Letter

Pacific Drive is a Hollywood film production that plans to film on location in several residential neighborhoods throughout the Seattle area. As part of your job in the production office, you've been asked to create a form letter to send to homeowners in each of the neighborhoods where filming will occur. You will then merge the letter with an Access database containing the names and addresses of the homeowners and then you'll create a sheet of labels.

Activity Steps

 open WE_Project13A.doc

1. Set up the document as a form letter that uses the **Neighbors table** in the **WE_Project13B.mdb** file as the data source

2. Enter fields in the form letter as shown in Figure WP 13-1
   Make sure you enter the current date where indicated. Note that the fields are highlighted in Figure WP 13-1 so that you can easily see them. In your form letter, the fields will not appear highlighted.

3. Run the merge and print only letters to **Lara Drake** and **Ed Jefferson**

4. Save the form letter as **Neighbors Form Letter**, then close it

5. Create a sheet of labels using **3261R-Return Address** as the label type, the **Neighbors table** in the **WE_Project13b.mdb** file as the data source, and the Address Block field

6. Preview the sheet of labels, then compare it to WP 13-2

7. Save the labels as **Location Labels**, then print a copy

 close Location Labels.doc

Figure WP 13-1: Form letter with form fields

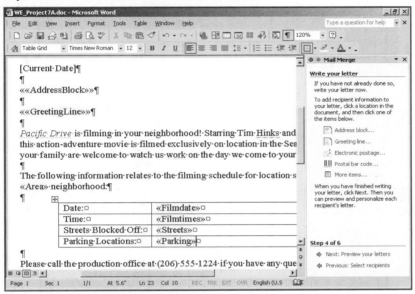

Figure WP 13-2: Form fields for label sheet

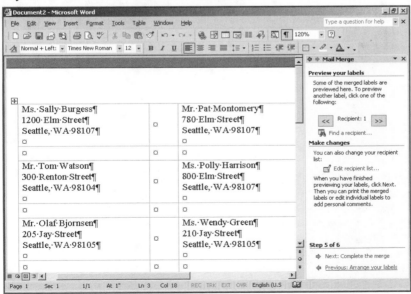

Excel 2002 Core Projects Appendix

Projects List

Project 1 – Sales Projection for Alaska Adventures

Project 2 – Invoice for Art Rentals to Movies

Project 3 – Budget for Into Thin Air Balloon Tours

Project 4 – Price Lists for Keeping the Beat Drum Shop

Project 5 – Maui Resorts Time Share Vacation Options

Project 6 – Sales Information for Fanfloratastic Flowers

Project 7 – Sales Report for Splashdown Rafting

The Excel Core skill sets include the features and functions you need to create and modify spreadsheets for a variety of purposes. In the following projects, you will format a sales projection, create an invoice, modify a budget, organize price lists, calculate mortgage options, present sales information with charts and graphics, and save a sales report created in Excel as a Web page.

Project for Skill Set 1

Working with Cells and Cell Data

Sales Projection for Alaska Adventures

You work for Alaska Adventures, a small company based in Juneau, Alaska, that offers sea kayaking, mountain biking, and hiking tours. You've received a workbook containing a sales projection for the sea kayaking tours that the company hopes to sell in the busy summer months of June, July, and August. In this project, you will complete and format this worksheet. The workbook also contains a second worksheet that includes a list of the guests who purchased sea kayaking tours on a single day during the previous summer. You'll use the AutoFilter features on this list to determine the number of customers who came from countries other then the United States and Canada.

Activity Steps

 open EC_Project1.xls

1. Clear the contents and formats of cell **A3**, drag cell **A4** up to cell **A3**, then delete cell **D14** and shift the cells left

2. Merge cell **A3** across cells **A3** to **E3**, then check the spelling in the worksheet and correct any errors

3. Enter **Total** in cell **E5**, use the **Go To** command to navigate to cell **C13**, then change the value in cell **C13** to **1200**

4. Use the **SUM** function in cell **E12** to add the values in cells **B12** through **D12**, then copy the formula to cells **E13** through **E15**

5. Select cells **B12** through **B16**, then use the **AutoSum button** to calculate the totals required for cells **B16** through **E16**

6. In cell **B18**, enter the formula required to subtract the value in cell **B16** from the value in cell **B9**, then copy the formula to cells **C18** through **E18**

7. Use **Find and Replace** to locate all instances of **1500** and replace them with **500**

8. Format cells **B7** through **E7**, **B9** through **E9**, **B12** through **E12**, **B16** through **E16**, and **B18** through **E18** with the **Currency style**, format cells **B8** through **E8** and cells **B13** through **E15** with the **Comma** style, then compare the completed worksheet to Figure EP 1-1

9. Switch to the **Customers worksheet**, then use AutoFilter to show only the **International** customers in the Category column
   The filtered list appears as shown in Figure EP 1-2.

 close EC_Project1.xls

Step 8
To save time, press and hold the [CTRL] key, select each group of cells, and then click the Currency Style button.

Figure EP 1-1: Completed Projections worksheet

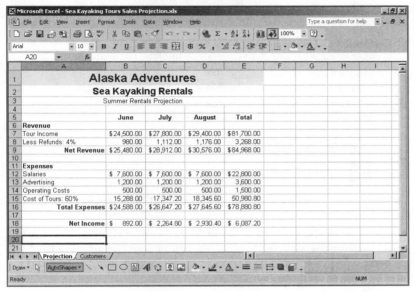

Figure EP 1-2: AutoFiltered list in Customers worksheet

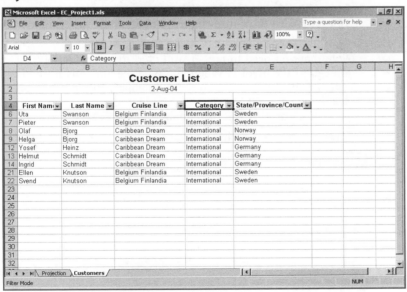

Project for Skill Set 2

Managing Workbooks

Invoice for Art Rentals to Movies

Max Brenner, an artist friend of yours, frequently rents his paintings, drawings, and sculptures to movie crews for use on film sets throughout Vancouver, British Columbia—the new "Hollywood North." Max has asked you to help him create and manage Excel workbooks he can use to track his rental contracts. In this project, you will first create a folder in which to store all of the files related to Max's rental contracts and then save an existing workbook listing information about Max's most recent rental contracts to the new folder. You will then create a workbook in Excel that Max can use to generate invoices. You will create this invoice form from an Excel template and save it into the new folder.

Activity Steps

  open EC_Project2.xls

1. Create a new folder called **Art Rentals** on your floppy disk or hard drive

2. Save the current workbook, **EC_Project2.xls**, as **Rentals List** into the Art Rentals folder, then close the workbook

3. Open the New Document task pane, click **General Templates**, then click the **Spreadsheet Solutions tab** in the Templates dialog box

4. Select the **Sales Invoice template**
    You may need to wait for a few minutes while the template is loaded.

5. Complete the invoice as shown in Figure EP 2-1
    Note that you need to press [Alt][Enter] to enter multiple lines in the top cell of the invoice. When you type the amounts in the Unit Price column, the totals will automatically appear in the Total column. To delete the Farewell Statement at the bottom of the page, click Edit, point to Clear, then click Contents.

6. Save the invoice as **Invoice101** to the Art Rentals folder

  close Invoice101.xls

Figure EP 2-1: Completed invoice

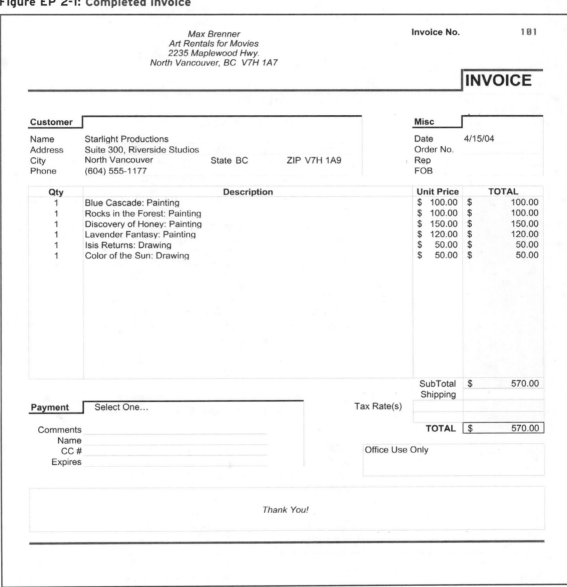

Max Brenner
Art Rentals for Movies
2235 Maplewood Hwy.
North Vancouver, BC V7H 1A7

Invoice No.   101

INVOICE

Customer

Name	Starlight Productions			
Address	Suite 300, Riverside Studios			
City	North Vancouver	State BC	ZIP V7H 1A9	
Phone	(604) 555-1177			

Misc

Date	4/15/04
Order No.	
Rep	
FOB	

Qty	Description	Unit Price		TOTAL
1	Blue Cascade: Painting	$ 100.00	$	100.00
1	Rocks in the Forest: Painting	$ 100.00	$	100.00
1	Discovery of Honey: Painting	$ 150.00	$	150.00
1	Lavender Fantasy: Painting	$ 120.00	$	120.00
1	Isis Returns: Drawing	$ 50.00	$	50.00
1	Color of the Sun: Drawing	$ 50.00	$	50.00

	SubTotal	$	570.00
	Shipping		

Payment   Select One…

Tax Rate(s)

TOTAL	$	570.00

Comments	
Name	
CC #	
Expires	

Office Use Only

Thank You!

Project for Skill Set 3

Formatting and Printing Worksheets

Budget for Into Thin Air Balloon Tours

You work for Into Thin Air Balloon Tours, a company based in Phoenix that takes tourists on spectacular hot air balloon tours over the deserts and canyons of Arizona. You've been asked to format the company's budget for January to June 2004 and then to print various views of the budget data. The printed budget appears as shown in Figure EP 3-1.

Activity Steps

 open EC_Project3.xls

1. Unhide **column E** (the totals for March), set the width of **columns B through I** to **15**, set the height of **row 1** to **30**, then format cell **A1** with **Bold**, the **Arial** font syle, and **24 pt**

2. Insert a new row following the first row, enter **Projected Budget: January to June 2004** in the new cell **A2**, center the text across cells A2 through I2, decrease the font size to **16 pt**, then remove the shaded fill

3. Delete **column B**, freeze panes at cell **B5**, then change the Equipment Rentals for June to **9000**

4. Click cell **B19**, create a style called **Profit** that formats cell contents with **Bold, Grey 25%** shading, a **Single top** border, and a **Double bottom** border, then apply the Profit style to cells **B19** through **H19**

5. Unfreeze the panes, apply the **Classic 2 AutoFormat** to cells **A4** through **H17**, then right-align the label in cell **A19**

6. In the Page Setup dialog box, change the orientation of the worksheet to **Landscape**, then set the worksheet to print on one page

7. Create a custom header containing the **current date** at the left margin, nothing in the center, and **your name** at the right margin, then create a custom footer containing the **tab name** in the center

8. Print a copy of the worksheet
   The printed worksheet appears in landscape orientation, as shown in Figure EP 3-1.

9. Set the print areas as cells **B4 through B19** and cells **G4 through G19**, then preview and print the two areas
   The two areas print on separate pages.

 close EC_Project3.xls

Figure EP 3-1: Printed budget worksheet in landscape orientation

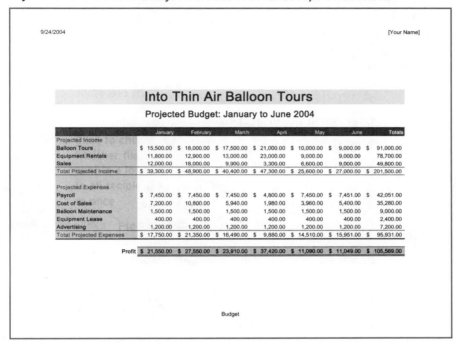

9/24/2004 [Your Name]

Into Thin Air Balloon Tours
Projected Budget: January to June 2004

	January	February	March	April	May	June	Totals
Projected Income							
Balloon Tours	$ 15,500.00	$ 18,000.00	$ 17,500.00	$ 21,000.00	$ 10,000.00	$ 9,000.00	$ 91,000.00
Equipment Rentals	11,800.00	12,900.00	13,000.00	23,000.00	9,000.00	9,000.00	78,700.00
Sales	12,000.00	18,000.00	9,900.00	3,300.00	6,600.00	9,000.00	49,800.00
Total Projected Income	$ 39,300.00	$ 48,900.00	$ 40,400.00	$ 47,300.00	$ 25,600.00	$ 27,000.00	$ 201,500.00
Projected Expenses							
Payroll	$ 7,450.00	$ 7,450.00	$ 7,450.00	$ 4,800.00	$ 7,450.00	$ 7,451.00	$ 42,051.00
Cost of Sales	7,200.00	10,800.00	5,940.00	1,980.00	3,960.00	5,400.00	35,280.00
Balloon Maintenance	1,500.00	1,500.00	1,500.00	1,500.00	1,500.00	1,500.00	9,000.00
Equipment Lease	400.00	400.00	400.00	400.00	400.00	400.00	2,400.00
Advertising	1,200.00	1,200.00	1,200.00	1,200.00	1,200.00	1,200.00	7,200.00
Total Projected Expenses	$ 17,750.00	$ 21,350.00	$ 16,490.00	$ 9,880.00	$ 14,510.00	$ 15,951.00	$ 95,931.00
Profit	$ 21,550.00	$ 27,550.00	$ 23,910.00	$ 37,420.00	$ 11,090.00	$ 11,049.00	$ 105,569.00

Budget

Project for Skill Set 4

Modifying Workbooks

Price Lists for Keeping the Beat Drum Shop

As the office manager of Keeping the Beat Drum Shop, you have decided to use Excel to organize some of your price lists into various worksheets within one workbook. You can then use 3-D cell references to calculate totals for data contained in the various worksheets.

Step 6
In each worksheet, the total to be used in the 3-D reference formula appears in cell D14.

Activity Steps

 open EC_Project4.xls

1. Delete the **Hardware** worksheet

2. Insert a new worksheet called **Summary**

3. Move the Summary worksheet so it is the first worksheet in the workbook

4. Change the name of the **Miscellaneous** worksheet to **World Percussion**

5. Set up the Summary sheet so it appears as shown in Figure EP 4-1

6. Enter a formula in cell B7 that uses **3D cell references** to calculate the total value of the Cymbals, World Percussion, and Drums price lists
   The total value of all three price lists is $5,944.00 in cell B7, as shown in Figure EP 4-2.

 close EC_Project4.xls

Figure EP 4-1: Summary sheet setup

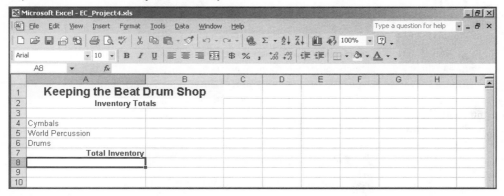

Figure EP 4-2: 3D total in cell B7

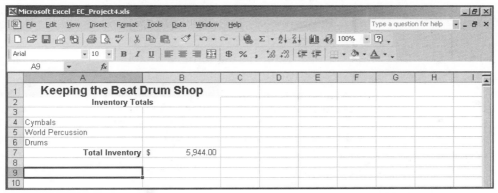

Project for Skill Set 5

Creating and Revising Formulas

Maui Resorts Time Share Vacation Options

You are thinking of purchasing a time share at a condominium resort complex in Maui, Hawaii. Several time share condos are available, so you decide to use Excel to help you determine which option best suits your budget. You'll also use formulas to help you calculate other vacation costs such as airfare, food, and recreation. The workbook you will use contains two worksheets. The Budget worksheet contains values related to your vacation budget and the Mortgage worksheet contains the calculations you'll use to determine the mortgage options on various time share condos.

Activity Steps

 open EC_Project5.xls

1. In the **Budget** worksheet, enter a formula in cell **E3** that multiplies the **Unit Cost** by the **Number**, copy the formula into cells **E4** through **E9**, then define cells **E3** through **E9** as a range called **Expenses**

2. In cell **E11** enter a **SUM** formula that adds all the values in the Expenses range

3. In the **Mortgage** worksheet, use the **PMT** function in cell C7 to calculate mortgage payments; use the value in cell **B4** as the Rate/12, the value in cell **B5** as the Nper*12, the value in cell **B7** as the PV (as a negative number), then make the **Rate** and **Nper** values absolute
   The PMT Argument Function dialog box should appear as shown in Figure EP 5-1.

4. Copy the PMT formula to cells **C8** through **C16**, then name cells **C7** through **C16** as a range called **Payments**

5. In cell **B18** enter the **MIN** function to determine which payment option is the lowest, then in cell **B19**, enter the **MAX** function to determine which payment is the highest

6. In cell **D7** enter an **IF** function that enters **YES** in cell D7 if the mortgage payment is less then $400 and **NO** if the mortgage payment is greater than or equal to $400
   Figure EP 5-2 shows how the IF function dialog box should appear.

7. Copy the formula from cell D7 to cells **D8** through **D16**, click cell **A3**, then use the **NOW** function to enter the current date and time
   The completed Mortgage worksheet appears as shown in Figure EP 5-3.

 close EC_Project5.xls

Figure EP 5-1: PMT function

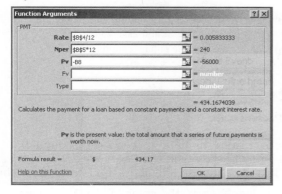

Figure EP 5-2: IF function

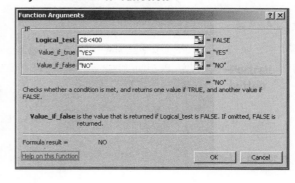

Figure EP 5-3: Completed Mortgage worksheet

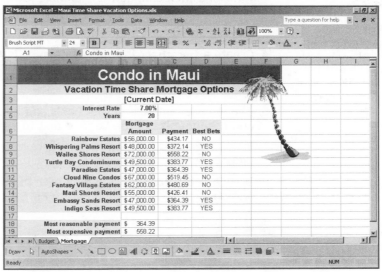

Project for Skill Set 6

Creating and Modifying Graphs

Sales Information for Fanfloratastic Flowers

Fanfloratastic is a small flower stall located at San Francisco's Fisherman's Wharf. The owner of the stall provides you with sales information and asks you to create a worksheet that includes two charts and some graphic enhancements. When printed, the worksheet appears as shown in Figure EP 6-1.

Activity Steps

 open EC_Project6.xls

1. Create a **Pie chart** from the data in cells **A6** through **B11**; accept all the default settings in the Chart Wizard except select the option to include a legend and show the Percentage labels

2. Modify the chart by changing the color of the **Roses wedge** to **Pink**, and then change the pie chart format to 3D format with an elevation of **45 degrees**

3. Re-size and position the chart as shown in Figure EP 6-1

4. Create a **Bar chart** from the data in cells **A24** through **F26**

5. Move the legend below the chart data, then size and position the chart as shown in Figure EP 6-1

6. Change the font size of the Y-axis and X-axis labels to **8-point** and the font size of the Legend text to **11-point**

7. Insert, size, and position the clip art picture of a rose shown in Figure EP 6-1

8. Draw a sun autoshape and fill it with Light Yellow, then size it and position it as shown in Figure EP 6-1

 close EC_Project6.xls

Step 7
Note that you must be connected to the Internet to insert this piece of clip art from the complete Microsoft Clip Gallery.

Figure EP 6-1: Completed sales information

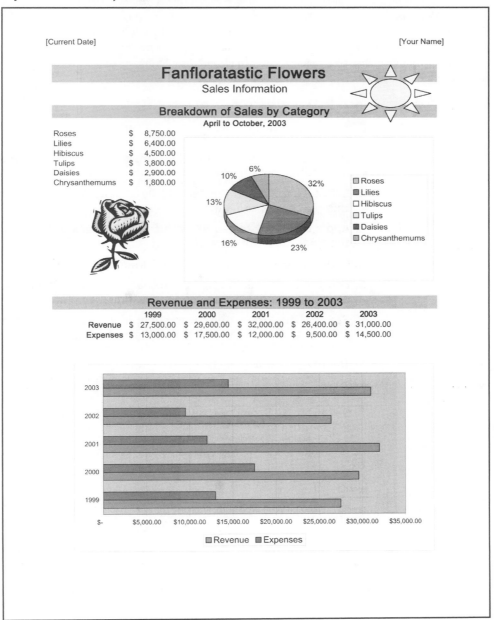

Project for Skill Set 7

Workgroup Collaboration

Sales Report for Splashdown Rafting

Splashdown Rafting takes thrill-seekers on wet-and-wild raft trips down the Snake River in Montana. You've agreed to help the company modify a Sales Report worksheet for viewing on the company intranet. The worksheet already includes a comment from the owner, Zack Barr. You respond to Zack's comment, add a comment of your own, insert a hyperlink to a second worksheet in the workbook, and then save the workbook for viewing on the intranet.

Activity Steps

 open EC_Project7.xls

1. Read Zack's comment in cell **E8**, make the change he requests, then delete his comment

2. Edit Zack's comment in cell **E12** by adding the sentence **I think this number is too low.**

3. Add a comment to cell **B9** with the text **Check out the chart in the Summary worksheet!**

4. Make cell **B9** a hyperlink to the **Summary** worksheet

5. Edit the hyperlink in cell **A19** so that it points to the company's new Web site at www.splashdownrafting.com

6. Preview the **2004 Tours** worksheet in your browser, test the link to the **Summary** worksheet, then click the **2004 Tours tab** to return to the 2004 Tours worksheet
   The Tours worksheet appears in the browser as shown in Figure EP 7-1 and the 2004 Summary worksheet appears in the browser as shown in Figure EP 7-2.

7. Save the EC_Project7.xls workbook as a Web page called **2004Tours.htm**

 close 2004Tours.htm

Figure EP 7-1: 2004 Tours worksheet displayed in the browser

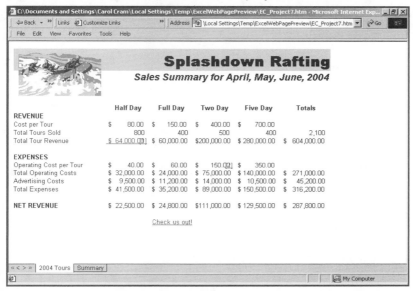

Figure EP 7-2: Summary worksheet displayed in the browser

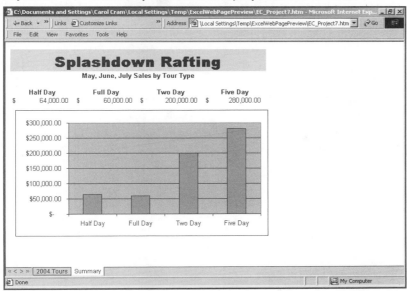

Excel 2002 Expert Projects Appendix

Projects List

The Excel Expert skill sets include the features and functions you use to perform advanced data analysis and summary functions, to apply custom features, and to collaborate with one or more other users. In the following projects, you will import and export data, manage workbooks, apply custom formats to numbers, work with ranges, automate Excel by creating macros, audit worksheets, summarize and analyze data, and finally use collaboration options to share workbooks between users.

Project for Skill Set 8

Importing and Exporting Data

E-Commerce Conference Itinerary

As the manager of a Web-based travel service, you've decided to attend a conference on E-Commerce issues being held in The Hague in the Netherlands. You need to compile a workbook that contains information about the trip and the conference. In this project, you will insert the trip itinerary from an existing text file and insert a picture file to enhance the appearance of the itinerary worksheet. You will then insert information about the conference sessions from an Access database table and obtain a map of the Netherlands from a Web site on the World Wide Web. Finally, you will save selected worksheets for use in other applications, including the Web browser and Access.

Activity Steps

 open EE_Project8A.xls

1. Import the **EE_Project8B.txt** file to cell **A7** in the **Itinerary worksheet**, accepting all defaults in the Text Import Wizard

2. Insert the picture file **Tulips.jpg** into the **Itinerary worksheet**, then size and position it as shown in Figure EP 8-1

3. Import the **E-Commerce Sessions table** from the Access database **EE_Project8C.mdb** into cell **A3** of the **Sessions worksheet**

4. Connect to the Internet, start your Web browser, type *http://www.maptown.com/geos/netherlands.html* in the Address text box, then press [**Enter**]
   If the Web site is not available, use the search engine of your choice to find a map of the Netherlands that you can copy without violating copyright restrictions.

5. Arrange the Excel workbook window and the browser window so they appear side by side on the desktop, then drag the map of the Netherlands from the Web page into the Map worksheet and position it as shown in Figure EP 8-2

6. Publish the **Itinerary worksheet** from the EE_Project8A.xls workbook as a Web page called **Itinerary.htm** that includes interactivity

7. Close the Web browser, then save and close the workbook

8. Start Access, open **EE_Project8C.mdb**, then import the **Costs worksheet** from **EE_Project8A.xls** into the database, accepting all defaults
   The Costs worksheet appears as a table called Costs in the Access database.

 close EE_Project8C.mdb

Figure EP 8-1: Itinerary worksheet

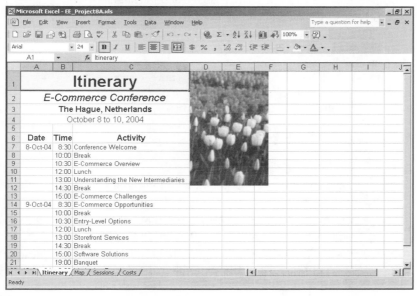

Figure EP 8-2: Map worksheet

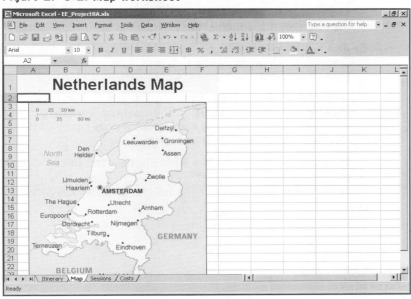

Project for Skill Set 9

Managing Workbooks

Expense Reports for Quito Imports

Quito Imports is a small retail outlet based in San Francisco that sells craft products from Ecuador, Peru, and Colombia. Several times each year, three employees travel to South America to purchase products for the store. As the new office manager, you want to streamline the reporting of travel expenses by creating and modifying a template for the expense reports and then creating a workspace containing each of the expense reports submitted by the three employees. Finally, you want to consolidate inventory data from three worksheets containing data about three of the product lines sold by Quito Imports.

Activity Steps

 open EE_Project9A.xls

1. Save the current workbook as a template called **EE_Project9B.xlt** to the location where you save your project files

2. Open the **EE_Project9B.xlt** template file, remove the **Fuel** column, then save and close the template file

3. Create a new expense report based on the revised template, then enter data in the expense report for **Marianne Bennett**, as shown in Figure EP 9-1

4. Save the workbook as **EE_Project9C.xls**, open **EE_Project9D.xls**, then open **EE_Project9E.xls**
   The Project9D file contains the expense report for Josh Ramirez, and the Project9E file contains the expense report for Yuri Gringko.

5. As shown in Figure EP 9-2, tile the three workbooks vertically, create a workspace called **Expense Statements**, then close all three workbooks

6. Open **EE_Project9F.xls**, then consolidate in the Totals worksheet cells **A3** through **D8** in the **Pottery worksheet**, the **Blankets worksheet**, and the **Jewelry worksheet** using the SUM function and using labels in the top row

7. Click cell **D11**, then use the **AutoSum button** to calculate the grand total
   The grand total for all the consolidated worksheets is $15,403.00.

 close EE_Project9F.xls

Figure EP 9-1: Data for Marianne Bennett

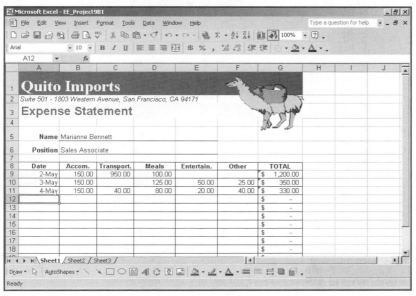

Figure EP 9-2: Workspace with three vertically tiled workbooks

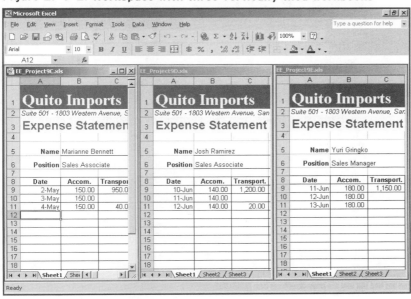

Project for Skill Set 10
Formatting Numbers

Extreme Adventures Tours Sales

You work for Extreme Adventures, a company based in Calgary, Alberta, that specializes in taking clients on physically challenging tours that include activities such as ice climbing, ski touring, and snowshoeing. An Excel workbook contains information about the tours sold on February 15, 2004, along with information about tour distances and durations. In this project, you will format the worksheet by creating, modifying, and applying a variety of custom number formats. You also will apply conditional formatting to highlight tours that generated income over a certain amount.

Activity Steps

 open EE_Project10.xls

1. In the **Tour Durations worksheet**, click cell **D7**, then create a custom number format that matches the number format of the value contained in cell **D6**

2. Apply the new format to cells **D8** through **D11**

3. Click cell **A4**, then create a Custom Date format that appears as **mmmm d, yyyy**
   The Tour Durations worksheet appears as shown in Figure EP 10-1.

4. Display the **Current Tours worksheet**, then apply the custom date format from Step 3 to cell A4

5. Use conditional formatting to automatically apply **Bold** and the **Blue** font color to all values greater than **6** in cells **B6** through **B11**

6. Click cell **E6**, then create a Custom Number format with text that appears as **$0.00" Good";$-0.00" Poor"**

7. Format cells **E7** through **E11** with the new custom number format
   The Current Tours worksheet appears as shown in Figure EP 10-2.

 close EE_Project10.xls

Figure EP 10-1: Revised custom number and custom date formats applied

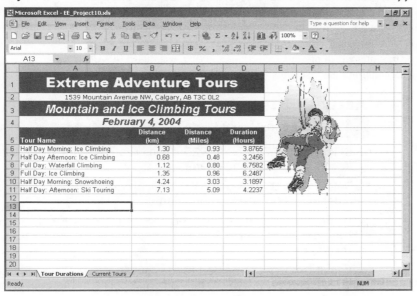

Figure EP 10-2: Conditional formatting and custom format with text applied

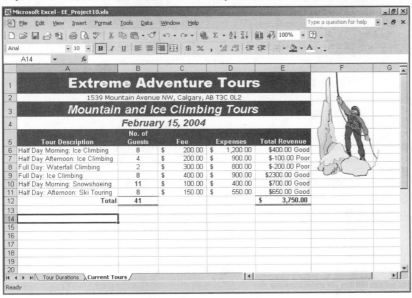

Project for Skill Set 11

Working with Ranges

Inventory Sheets for Vintage Records

You've inherited a great collection of vintage records in both 78 rpm and 33 rpm formats and are interested in trying to sell some of the records in online auctions. You decide to use Excel to create an inventory sheet that organizes your collection into categories. You'll create some ranges, use named ranges in a formula to calculate the total worth of your collection, and then use the HLOOKUP function to calculate appropriate discounts for some of the records.

Activity Steps

 open EE_Project11.xls

1. Select cells **F7** through **F25**, then create a range using the label in cell **F7** as the range name

2. Select cells **G7** through **G25**, then create a range using the label in cell **G7** as the range name

3. Designate **rpm78** as the range name for cells **F8** through **F15**, then designate **rpm33** as the range name for cells **F16** through **F25**

4. In cell **D4**, use the named range **rpm78** in a formula that calculates the total worth of the 78 rpm records in the collection
   The 78s are worth $100.00.

5. In cell **D5**, use the named range **rpm33** in a formula that calculates the total worth of the 33 rpm records in the collection
   The 33s are worth $113.00.

6. Enter an **HLOOKUP function** in cell **G8** to determine the discount by format on each of the records

7. Copy the formula in cell **G8** through to cell **G25**
   The discount percentages appear in columns as shown in Figure EP11-1.

8. In cell **H8**, use the **Price** and **Discount** ranges in a formula that calculates the total price of the first record in the list
   The required formula is Price-(Price*Discount).

9. Copy the formula through to cell **H25**
   The completed worksheet appears as shown in Figure EP 11-2.

 close EE_Project11.xls

Step 6
To complete the HLOOKUP function, you will need to use the table in cells F3 through G4. Remember to make the reference to this table absolute in the formula. The formula required for cell G8 is =HLOOKUP(E8,$F$3:$G$4,2).

Project 11

Figure EP 11-1: Discounts entered

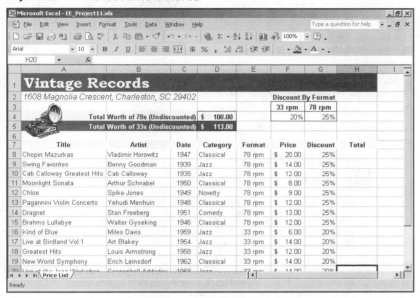

Figure EP 11-2: Completed worksheet

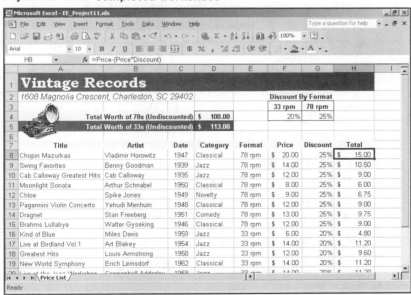

Project for Skill Set 12

Customizing Excel

Payroll Register for Tapestries Bistro

As the manager of Tapestries, a new Bistro in downtown Los Angeles, you have decided to use Excel to keep track of the monthly payroll for the five staff members who work in the restaurant dining room. Before printing all the payroll registers for the year, you decide to customize Excel so that you can format each payroll worksheet in the same way. In this project you will first customize a menu and then add a button to the Formatting toolbar so that you can perform specific formatting tasks quickly. Then, you will create a macro that will fill selected cells with a color and apply the Currency format to selected cells. Finally, you will edit the macro and run the revised version.

Activity Steps

 open EE_Project12.xls

1. Add a new menu called **Payroll** that appears to the right of the Help menu, then add the **Double Underline** command from the Format category and the **Pattern** command from the Format category to the Payroll menu

2. Click cell **A1**, then create a macro called **PayrollFormat** that uses the **Ctrl+F** shortcut key and performs the functions described in Figure EP 12-1

3. Click the **Undo button** several times to undo the macro steps, then click cell **A1** and use **Ctrl + F** to run the PayrollFormat macro

4. Edit the PayrollFormat macro in Visual Basic to change the fill color from **6** to **4**
   The code for the fill color is .ColorIndex = . The new color will be Bright Green.

5. Close Visual Basic, click cell **A1**, then press **Ctrl + F** to run the revised macro

6. Add the **AutoFormat button** to the Formatting toolbar

7. Use the AutoFormat button on the Formatting toolbar to apply the **List 2** AutoFormat to cells A5 through L11

8. Use the Pattern command on the Payroll menu to fill cell A1 with the Thin Horizontal Crosshatch pattern that appears in the bottom row of the pattern pallette, as shown in Figure EP 12-2
   The formatted worksheet appears as shown in Figure EP 12-3.

9. Open the Customize dialog box, then remove the AutoFormat button from the Formatting toolbar and the Payroll menu from the menu bar

 close EE_Project12.xls

Step 1
In the Customize dialog box, you will need to scroll down the Commands list box to find the Double Underlining and Pattern menu items.

Figure EP 12-1: Macro steps

1. Use the Ctrl key to select cells A1, B3, and D3
2. Use the Payroll menu to add Double Underlining
3. Fill the selected cells with the Yellow fill color
4. Select cells D7 to D11, then apply the Currency style
5. Stop the macro recording

Figure EP 12-2: Pattern selection

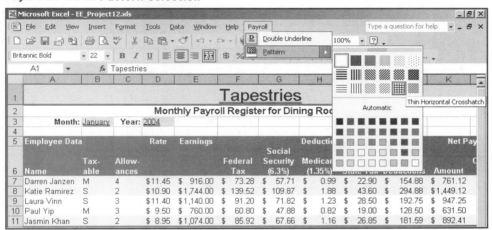

Figure EP 12-3: Formatted payroll worksheet

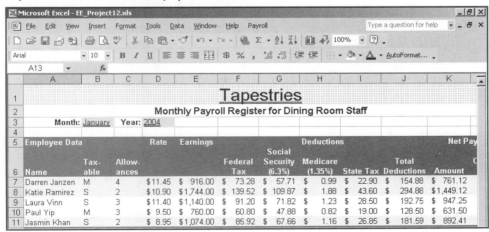

Project for Skill Set 13

Auditing Worksheets

Purchase Orders for Saguaro Art Academy

The Saguaro Art Academy has recently started using Excel to generate its purchase orders. You have been asked to use the formula auditing tools to verify the formulas in two of the purchase order worksheets that are ready to send out.

Activity Steps

 open EE_Project13.xls

1. In the **July 10, 2004 worksheet**, use the Trace Dependents feature to determine which cells are dependent on cell **L24**

2. In the **July 10, 2004 worksheet**, use the Trace Precedents feature to determine which cells are used by the formula in cell **L27**
   The worksheet should appear as shown in Figure EP 13-1.

3. Remove all the arrows

4. In the **August 12, 2004 worksheet**, use the Trace Error feature to identify the cell causing the error in cell **L28**
   The error should appear as shown in Figure EP 13-2.

5. Correct the error by changing the incorrect value in cell J16 to **7.25**

6. Verify that the total is now $412.50, then remove all the arrows

 close EE_Project13.xls

Figure EP 13-1: Traced dependents and precedents

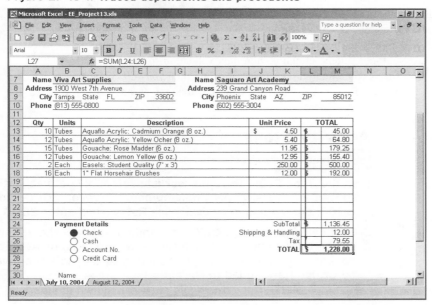

Figure EP 13-2: Error traced

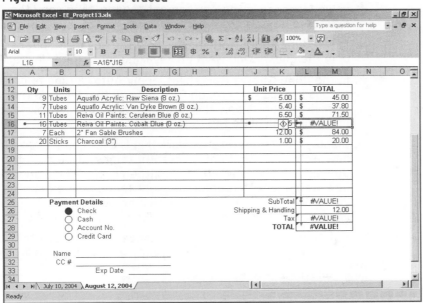

Project for Skill Set 14

Summarizing Data

Guest Information for Glacier Cruises

Each summer, the Glacier Cruises fleet of cruise ships heads north from Vancouver, BC through the scenic Inside Passage to the glaciers of Alaska. At the end of each month, one of your duties in the business office is to use Excel to summarize data related to revenue generated from each cruise. For this project, you will use subtotals, filters, grouping, and data validation to summarize data in three worksheets containing guest information, and then you will create a Web query using data from a weather site, save a worksheet as an XML spreadsheet, and create an XML query.

Step 3
The criteria for the filter appears in cells A21 and A22.
Step 6
From *www.weather.com*, you'll need to search for each city in turn (Juneau and Sitka) and then select the table that shows the current temperature.
Step 7
Enter the exact location of the Tour Revenue.xml file in the Address text box in the New Web Query dialog box. For example, if you have stored the file on a disk in your A:\ drive, the address is A:\Tour Revenue.xml.

Activity Steps

 open EE_Project14.xls

1. In the **June Room Revenue workshseet**, apply data validation to **E4:E27** to allow only whole numbers between **2000** and **8000**, enter 1500 in cell **E5**, click **Retry**, then enter **2000**

2. Sort cells **A3** through **G27** in ascending order by the data in the Cruise Date column and then the data in the Rooms Available column, then use the Subtotal function to calculate the revenue by **Cruise Date** added to **Revenue**
   The top portion of the list should appear as shown in Figure EP 14-1.

3. In the **June Fitness worksheet**, create a custom filter to extract the data from the list range A3 through D19 that contains the value **Massage** in the Assignment column, then copy the extracted data to cell A24

4. In the **June Tours worksheet**, apply the advanced filter to list only the guests who went on kayaking tours (filter in place)

5. In the **June Guests worksheet**, apply Auto Outline to create the groups in cells A4 through C29, hide all the detail so that the worksheet shows only the totals for each location, click cell **C30**, then calculate the total number of guests

6. Display the **Temperatures worksheet**, click cell **A5**, create a new Web query that enters current temperature data for Juneau from *www.weather.com*, then click cell **C5** and create a new Web query that enters current temperature data for Sitka
   Figure 14-2 shows the table selected for Juneau, Alaska and Figure 14-3 shows the completed Temperatures worksheet.

7. Switch to the **Tour Revenue worksheet**, then import the **Tour Revenue.xml** file located from your Project Disk as a Web query

 close EE_Project14.xls

Figure EP 14-1: Subtotals list

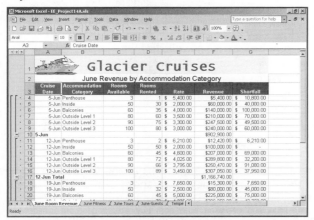

Figure EP 14-2: Web Query table selected

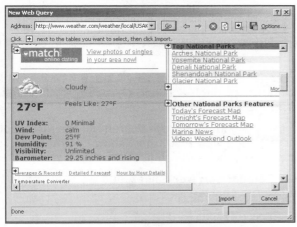

Figure EP 14-3: Completed Temperatures worksheet

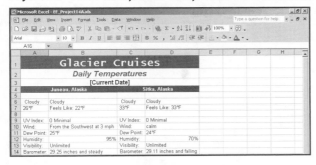

Project for Skill Set 15
Summarizing Data

Analysis of Web Design 101 Class Grades

You are assisting the instructor of Web Design 101 to analyze data related to the marks earned by students in the 2004 class. In this project, you will create a PivotTable to determine the breakdown of grades, and then you will create a PivotChart that displays the results in a pie chart. Next, you will create two scenarios to determine how best to weight the marks earned by students. Finally, you will add a trendline to a chart you created earlier that compares the overall marks earned by students in each of five classes over five years.

Activity Steps

 open EE_Project15.xls

1. From the data in the range **M3:M18** in the Grades worksheet, create a PivotTable in a new worksheet and use the **Grade** data for the Row area and the Data area

2. Click the Chart Wizard button on the PivotTable toolbar to create a PivotChart from the PivotTable
   The chart should appear as shown in Figure EP 15-1.

3. In the **Grades worksheet**, create a scenario called **High Assignments** from the values currently entered in cells I21 through K21

4. Create a second scenario called **Low Assignments** from the values in cells I21 through K21 and change the value in cell I21 to **25** and the value in cell K21 to **50**

5. Show the **Low Assignments scenario**, refresh the PivotTable data (in Sheet1), then view PivotChart shown on the Chart1 sheet
   The revised chart appears as shown in Figure EP 15-2.

6. In the **Class Comparison worksheet**, add a **Logarithmic trendline** to the column chart

 close EE_Project15.xls

Figure EP 15-1: Completed PivotChart

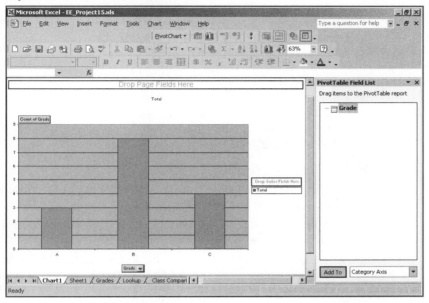

Figure EP 15-2: Revised PivotChart

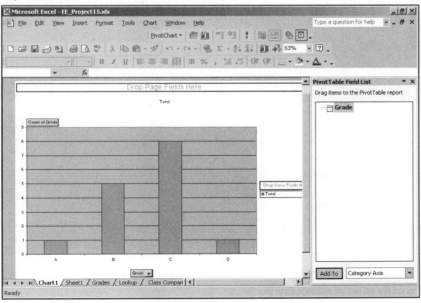

Project for Skill Set 16

Workgroup Collaboration

Sales Projections for Big Sky Campgrounds

Big Sky Campgrounds operates four campgrounds in the state of Montana. To prepare for the Summer 2004 season, you and two colleagues are creating a sales projection worksheet that will show projected sales in July, August, and September. In this project, you will first use the track changes and merge features to develop a final version of a workbook from the worksheets prepared by your colleagues. Then you will open a new workbook containing sales projections for October, November, and December, and set it up for sharing.

Activity Steps

 open EE_Project16A.xls

1. Set the Track Changes option to track all changes and to highlight changes on the screen

2. Change the value in cell **B6** to **35**, then save and close the workbook

3. Open **EE_Project16B.xls**, open the Accept or Reject Changes dialog box, accept the tracked change to **B6**, accept the tracked change to cell **C6**, then reject the tracked change to cell **D6**
   The net revenue in cell F17 is $7,220.00.

4. Merge the current workbook with the files EE_Project16C.xls and EE_Project16D.xls
   Verify that the net revenue in cell F17 is $5,870.00, as shown in Figure EP 16-1.

5. Close the workbook, open **EE_Project16E.xls**, then unlock the cells in the **Sites range**

6. Protect the worksheet, change the value in cell **B11** to **400**, then try entering a new value in cell B12

7. Protect the workbook with the password **camping** to open and the password **bigsky** to modify, then save and close the workbook

8. Open the **EE_Project16E.xls** workbook using the **camping** and **bigsky** passwords, share the workbook by allowing changes to be made by more than one user at a time, then save the workbook when prompted

 close EE_Project16E.xls

Figure EP 16-1: Workbook with merged changes

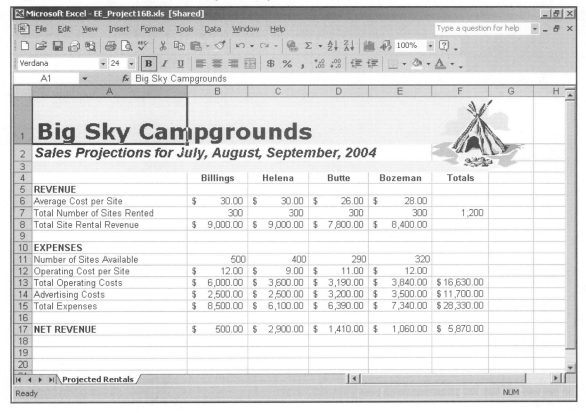

Projects List

Project 1 – Contact Database for Step One Consulting

Project 2 – Event Database for Great Prairie Jazz Festival

Project 3 – Winners Database for Classic Car Races

Project 4 – Photography Database for French Archeology Project

Project 5 – Conference Database for E-Commerce Forum

Project 6 – Properties Database for Powder Trails Realty

Project 7 – Sales Database for Precious Pets

Project 8 – Great Hiking Trails Database

The Access Core skill sets cover the skills you need to create and work with simple Access databases. You learn how to create, format, and modify the principal database objects: tables, forms, reports, and data access pages. You also learn how to import data into Access and how to export data from Access tables into other Office applications. In the following projects, you'll practice your skills by opening and working with databases designed for a variety of purposes.

Project for Skill Set 1

Creating and Using Databases

Contact Database for Step One Consulting

You've just been hired by Step One Consulting, a small firm based in Minneapolis that offers corporate clients seminars in written and oral communications. You've been asked to expand the database the company uses to manage its contacts. To get an idea of the kinds of tables included in a contact database, you'll use the Database wizard to create a Contact Management database. Then you'll open another version of the database, navigate through some of the tables and forms, view and navigate a subdatasheet, and format one of the datasheets.

Step 5
Click the list arrow next to Gerrie Wilcox, then select Susan Ing.

Activity Steps

1. Start Access, click **General Templates**, and then select the **Contact Management** template from the Databases tab

2. Save the database as **Contacts.mdb**

3. Step through the Database wizard, accepting the default for Step 2, selecting the **Sumi Painting** style for screen displays and the **Soft Gray** style for printed reports, and then entering **Step One Consulting Contacts** as the database title

4. From the database window, view the **Calls table**, view the **Contacts form**, explore some of the other tables and forms, then close the database

5. Open **AC_Project1.mdb**, open the **Calls table**, navigate to **Record 26**, then change the name to **Susan Ing**

6. Open the **Contacts form**, navigate to **Record 4**, change **Tom** to **Thomas** in the FirstName field, then close the form

7. Open the **Contacts table**, expand the subdatasheet for Munesh Nanji, compare your screen to Figure AP 1-1, then collapse the subdatasheet

8. Open the Datasheet Formatting dialog box, apply the **Aqua** background color and the **Blue** gridline color, close the dialog box, then compare the formatted datasheet to Figure AP 1-2

 close AC_Project1.mdb

Figure AP 1-1: Subdatasheet for Contacts table

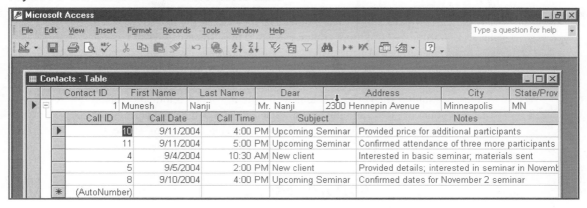

Figure AP 1-2: Formatted datasheet for Contacts table

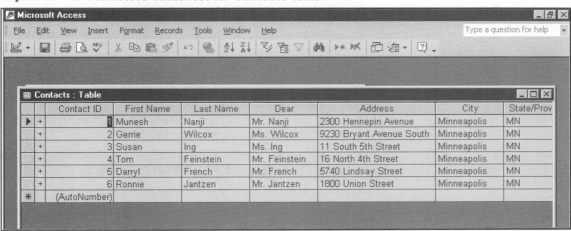

Project for Skill Set 2

Creating and Modifying Tables

Event Database for Great Prairies Jazz Festival

For the past two years, the Great Prairie Jazz Festival in the Red River Valley has welcomed jazz artists from around the world for a three-day festival of the best in avant-garde and mainstream jazz. This year, the festival administration has decided to use Access to organize data about the performers invited to play at 15 venues during the festival. You will help by creating a new database containing two tables. The Performers table will contain contact information about each performer or group, and the Venues table will list the time and place where the performances take place. You will use the Table Wizard to create the Performers table, and then you will work in Table Design view to create the Venues table.

Step 2
Remember to click the Rename Field button to change the name of a field.

Step 8
In the Lookup Wizard, select the I will type in the values I want option, and type the three entries into the cells of one column.

Activity Steps

1. Create a database called **Festival.mdb**

2. Use the Table Wizard to create a table from the **Mailing List** sample that includes the following fields: **FirstName**, **LastName**, OrganizationName changed to **GroupName**, **Address**, **City**, State changed to **State/Province**, **PostalCode**, and **Country/Region**

3. Complete the Wizard by naming the table **Performers** and setting a primary key

4. Enter the data for the first two records shown in the table in Figure AP 2-1, then close the table

5. Create a new table in Design view using the following fields: **Date**, **Time**, **Venue**, **Performer**, and **Phone**

6. Select the **Date/Time** data type for the Date field

7. Save the table as **Venues** and click **Yes** to create a primary key

8. Use the Lookup Wizard to create a lookup field for the Venue field that contains the following three choices: **Main Stage**, **Amphitheater**, and **Lakeside**

9. Add the **Phone Number** input mask to the Phone field, select the option to show symbols, then enter data for the three venues as shown in Figure AP 2-2

 close Festival.mdb

Figure AP 2-1: Records for the Performers table

Record 1		Record 2	
FirstName	Cara	FirstName	Paul
LastName	Hammond	LastName	Robbins
GroupName	Cara Hammond Quartet	GroupName	Paul Robbins Trio
Address	1500 West 9th Street	Address	340 Bathurst Street
City	Vancouver	City	Toronto
State/Province	BC	State/Province	ON
PostalCode	V7H 1E7	PostalCode	M5W 1R7
Country/Region	Canada	Country/Region	Canada

Figure AP 2-2: Records for the Venues table

ID	Date	Time	Venue	Performer	Phone
1	8/3/2004	2 to 4 p.m.	Amphitheater	Paul Robbins Trio	(415) 444-7888
2	8/3/2004	2 to 4 p.m.	Lakeside	The Three Saxes	(604) 555-2344
3	8/3/2004	8 to 10 p.m.	Main Stage	Cara Hammond Quartet	(604) 555-3322
(AutoNumber)					

Project for Skill Set 3

Creating and Modifying Queries

Winners Database for Classic Car Races

Classic sports-racing car drivers compete in races throughout North America from April to October each year. As an avid fan of these races, you've created a database containing a table that lists the winners of the top 25 races in the United States and Canada. In this project, you'll create three queries. The first query will list only winners who drove Ferraris, and the second query will list only winners who drove Aston Martins and competed in the United States. The third query will list all the drivers who won races in Canada and will include a calculated field that calculates the U.S. dollar value of the prize money awarded to the drivers.

Activity Steps

 open AC_Project3.mdb

1. View the contents of the **2004 Winners table** and the **2004 Prize Money table**
   The 2004 Winners table includes the name of the winning driver, the make, model, and year of the winning car, the location of the race, and the Race ID. The 2004 Prize Money table includes the Race ID, the location of the race, and the prize money awarded.

Step 5
The required expression that appears in the blank field to the right of PrizeMoney is USFunds: [PrizeMoney]/1.5 because one U.S. dollar is equivalent to 1.5 Canadian dollars (approximately).

2. Use the Simple Query Wizard to create a detailed query that includes the **FirstName, LastName, Car, Model, Year,** and **Country fields** from the 2004 Winners table and the **Race ID, Raceway,** and **PrizeMoney fields** from the 2004 Prize Money table; accept the default name for the query

3. Modify the query grid so the query lists each winner who drove a **Ferrari**, then save a copy of the query as **Ferraris**
   The completed query appears as shown in Figure AP 3-1.

4. Revise the 2004 Winners Query to list only those winners who drove an **Aston Martin** and who competed at raceways in the USA, then save a copy of the query as **Aston Martins**

5. Open the 2004 Winners Query, remove the current criteria, then create a calculated field named **USFunds** that divides the **PrizeMoney** field by **1.5**

6. Enter **Canada** in the Criteria cell for Country, view the query results, then return to Design view and format the calculated field to display the Currency symbol
   The completed query appears as shown in Figure AP 3-2.

 close AC_Project3.mdb

Figure AP 3-1: Ferrari query results

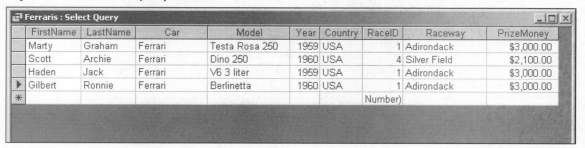

Ferraris : Select Query

	FirstName	LastName	Car	Model	Year	Country	RaceID	Raceway	PrizeMoney
	Marty	Graham	Ferrari	Testa Rosa 250	1959	USA	1	Adirondack	$3,000.00
	Scott	Archie	Ferrari	Dino 250	1960	USA	4	Silver Field	$2,100.00
	Haden	Jack	Ferrari	V6 3 liter	1959	USA	1	Adirondack	$3,000.00
▶	Gilbert	Ronnie	Ferrari	Berlinetta	1960	USA	1	Adirondack	$3,000.00
*							Number)		

Figure AP 3-2: Canadian Winners query results

2004 Winners Query : Select Query

	FirstName	LastName	Car	Model	Year	Country	RaceID	Raceway	PrizeMoney	USFunds
▶	Lundy	Jack	Cooper	Climax 1,100 c.c.	1959	Canada	3	Brantford	$2,400.00	$1,600.00
	Jones	Frank	Jaguar	D-Type	1960	Canada	3	Brantford	$2,400.00	$1,600.00
	Wilkes	Paul	Lotus	Eleven	1959	Canada	6	Westwood	$2,500.00	$1,666.67
	Petersen	Buzz	Corvette	Stingray	1961	Canada	3	Brantford	$2,400.00	$1,600.00
	Phillips	Wally	Porsche	1500 RS	1958	Canada	6	Westwood	$2,500.00	$1,666.67
	Jeffries	Roger	Elva	Mark 2	1960	Canada	6	Westwood	$2,500.00	$1,666.67
	Collins	Alan	Alfa Romeo	Sprint Veloce	1958	Canada	6	Westwood	$2,500.00	$1,666.67
*							Number)			

Project for Skill Set 4

Creating and Modifying Forms

Photography Database for French Archeology Project

As a student of archeology at the University of Victoria, you have created a database that contains data for a history project on archeological sites in France. The database contains three tables: the Sites table lists information about each site you are cataloging, the Photos table lists information about photographs taken at the sites, and the Site Categories table lists the four site categories (Neolithic, Magdalenian, Bronze Age, and Roman). After entering several records in Datasheet view for the Sites and Photos tables, you decide to create forms for entering the data.

Activity Steps

 open AC_Project4.mdb

1. Use the Form Wizard to create a form for the **Sites table** that includes all the fields except the CategoryID field and uses the **Columnar** format and the **SandStone** style, then name the form **Sites**

2. In Design view, select and then fill all the text boxes with **light green**, then apply the **Raised** special effect (middle selection in the top row of Special Effect selections)

3. Select all the labels and text boxes, then increase the font size to **11-point**

4. Enter a new record in the form, as shown in Figure AP 4-1

5. Use the AutoForm tool to create a form for the **Photos table**

6. Save the form as **Site Photos**

7. Reduce width of the ID and CategoryID textboxes to approximately ¾"

8. Enter a new record in the form, as shown in Figure AP 4-2

 close AC_Project4.mdb

Figure AP 4-1: Data for Record 16 of the Sites form

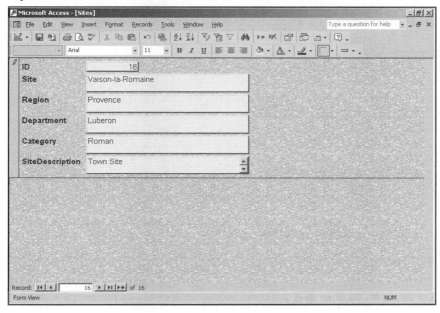

Figure AP 4-2: Data for Record 9 of the Site Photos form

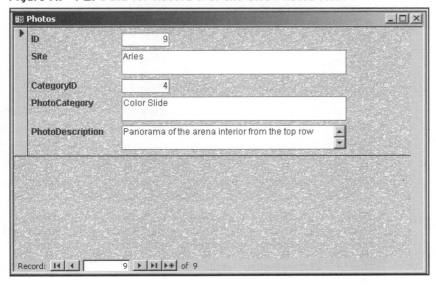

Project for Skill Set 5

Viewing and Organizing Information

Conference Database for E-Commerce Forum

You work for an organization in Mexico City that is sponsoring a two-day forum on e-commerce issues for entrepreneurs from all over North and South America. At present the conference database contains two tables: the Delegates table lists the names and addresses of the people who have signed up for the conference, and the Workshops table lists the various workshops offered at the conference. In this project, you will add two new records to the database as well as edit and delete some other records. You will also create a crosstab query to count the number of delegates from Brazil and Mexico City, and then use the two different filter features to show only records conforming to certain criteria.

Activity Steps

 open AC_Project5.mdb

1. Enter the record for Kevin Sylvano in the **Delegates table**, as shown in Figure AP 5-1

2. Delete the record for **Jorge Ramirez**, edit the record for **Juanita Sanchez** by changing her street address to **av. Angelico 622**, then close and save the Delegates table

3. Open the **Workshops form**, change the text in the **Day 1 Afternoon field** for **Record 2** to **E-Commerce Storefront Services**, enter the data shown in Figure AP 5-2 for **Record 3**, then close the form

4. Use the Crosstab Query Wizard to create a query from the **Brazil and Mexico Delegates query** that designates **Country** as the row heading, **City** as the column heading, and uses the **Count** function
   Figure AP 5-3 shows the results of the crosstab query.

5. Close the query, open the **Delegates table** in Datasheet view, then sort the records in alphabetical order by **Track**

6. Open the **Workshops query** in Design view, sort the records in **Ascending** order by **Country**, then view the query results

7. In the **Delegates table**, use the Filter by Selection button to show only participants who live in **Colombia**

8. Remove the filter, then use the Filter by Form feature to filter the records to show only participants who live in **Mexico City** and are signed up for **Track A**

9. Close the **Delegates table** without saving it

 close AC_Project5.mdb

Figure AP 5-1: New record for the Delegates table

ID	FirstName	LastName	Address	City	Code	Country	Track
1	Pedra	Juarez	Al Maracatins, 1325	Sao Paulo	03088-013	Brazil	A
2	Philippe	Siqueros	Paseo de la Reforma No. 1978	Mexico City	11400	Mexico	B
3	William	Slade	1750 Trade Center Way	Naples, FL	33196	USA	B
4	Astrud	Fernandes	Tr Batuira 18	Guarulhos	7041140	Brazil	C
5	Ramona	Estêves	Sierra Tarahumara No. 345	Mexico City	10500	Mexico	A
6	Alessandro	Almacenes	Av. 10 de Agosto 1545	Quito		Ecuador	C
7	Conchita	Alvarez	Calle 92 no. 14-88	Bogota	90343	Colombia	B
8	Oscar	Tornearia	136 Vila Prudente	Sao Paulo	03638-111	Brazil	B
9	Jorge	Ramirez	Av 6 De Diciembre 125	Quito		Ecuador	A
10	Dawn	Grenville	648 Fifth Ave.	New York, NY	10149	USA	A
11	Maria	Gironella	Calle Shiller 407, Polanco	Mexico City	11580	Mexico	B
12	Carlos	Rivera	Carlos Pellegrini, 1139	Buenos Aires	1028	Argentina	C
13	Pablo	Mendez	Edificio Concasa Carrera 43	Barranquila	4	Colombia	C
14	Manuel	Figuentes	Rio Lerma 41	Mexico City	6580	Mexico	A
15	Juanita	Sanchez	av. Angelica 645	Sao Paulo	2115990	Brazil	B
16	Kevin	Sylvano	1601 42nd Street	New York, NY	10144	USA	C

Record: 17 of 17

Figure AP 5-2: Text added to Record 3 in the Workshops form

Workshops

Session ID	3
Track	C
Day 1 Morning	E-Marketing Made Easy
Day 1 Afternoon	Domain Name Issues
Day 2 Morning	Don't Eat the Cookies
Day 2 Afternoon	E-Mail Marketing Tips

Record: 3 of 3

Figure AP 5-3: Crosstab query results

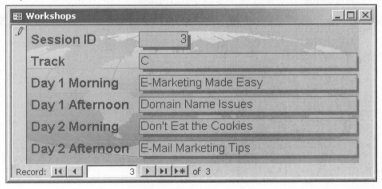

Brazil and Mexico Delegates_Crosstab : Crosstab Query

Country	Total Of FirstNa	Guarulhos	Mexico City	Sao Paulo
Brazil	4	1		3
Mexico	4		4	

Project for Skill Set 6

Defining Relationships

Properties Database for Powder Trails Realty

You work for Powder Trails Realty, a small real estate agency in Whistler, British Columbia that employs five agents. To keep track of which agents are responsible for which properties, you've created a database containing two tables. The Properties table lists the various homes for sale, and the Agents table lists the five agents. You want to create a relationship between these two tables that allows you to quickly determine which agent is responsible for which properties.

Activity Steps

 open AC_Project6.mdb

1. Open the Relationships window, then add the **Properties** and **Agents tables**

2. Create a **one-to-many relationship** from the Agents table to the Properties table using the **AgentID** field
   Compare the Relationships window to Figure AP 6-1.

3. Edit the relationship to select the **Enforce referential integrity** option button in the Edit Relationships dialog box

4. Close the Relationships window, save changes when prompted, then use the Query Wizard to find out which properties are handled by **Mary Gregson** and **Tony Esperanzo**; include all the fields from the Agents table and all the fields *except* the AgentID field from the Properties table and name the query **Mary and Tony Properties**
   The completed query appears as shown in Figure AP 6-2. Mary and Tony are responsible for two properties each.

 close AC_Project6.mdb

Figure AP 6-1: Relationship established

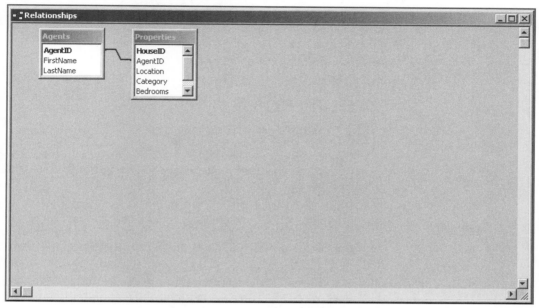

Figure AP 6-2: Completed query

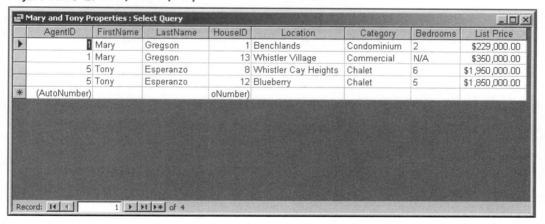

Project for Skill Set 7

Producing Reports

Sales Database for Precious Pets

Precious Pets is a small pet store that caters to pet lovers in Carmel, California. The store sells pets in five categories: cats, dogs, rodents, reptiles, and birds. The owner of Precious Pets has asked you to create reports from two tables in the Precious Pets database. The first report lists all the reptiles and rodents sold from April 1 to 5, 2004, and the second report lists all the pet sales from April 1 to 5, 2004 sorted and totaled according to category.

Activity Steps

 open AC_Project7.mdb

1. Use the Report Wizard to create a report from the **Reptiles and Rodents query** that includes the following fields: **Sale Date, Animal,** and **Price**

2. Make **Sale Date** the grouping level and change the interval for the grouping option for Sale Date to **Day,** sort the records in Ascending order by **Animal,** select the **Outline 1** layout, select the **Soft Grey** format, and name the report **Reptile and Rodent Sales**

3. In Design view, delete the two **Sale Date** labels, then move the two **Animal** labels to the right until the left edge of the labels is even with **3** on the ruler bar and the completed report appears in Print Preview as shown in Figure AP 7-1

4. Preview and print a copy of the report, then save and close it

5. Open the **April 1 to 5 Sales report** in Design view, add subtotals to the Price field, change the label to **Subtotal:,** then format the calculated control with the Currency style

6. Add a date calculated control to the right side of the report header and enter **Current Date:** as the label text

7. Format the Animal categories (e.g., Bird and Cat) with 16 pt and Bold

8. Print preview the report
   The completed report appears in Print Preview as shown in Figure AP 7-2.

 close AC_Project7.mdb

Figure AP 7-1: Reptile and Rodent Sales report

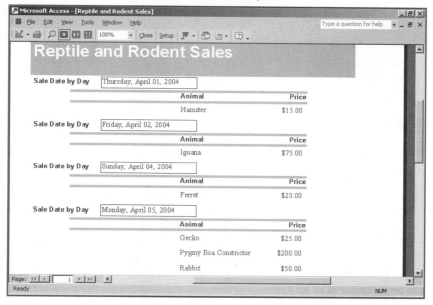

Figure AP 7-2: April 1 to 5 Sales report

Project for Skill Set 8

Integrating with Other Applications

Great Hiking Trails Database

As an avid hiker in the many natural parks throughout North America, you have decided to create a database containing information about your hikes. At present, the data you want to include in your hiking database is saved in two places—an Excel workbook and another Access database. In this project, you will create a new database and then import a file from Excel and a report and table from Access. Then you will import one of the tables into a new Excel workbook and save the report as a Web page. Finally, you will create two versions of a data access page—one that you can enter information into and one that reports up-to-date database activity.

Activity Steps

1. Start a new database and name it **Trails.mdb**

2. Import the Excel file **AC_Project8A.xls** into Access; specify that the first row of the Excel worksheet contains column headings, then accept the remaining defaults and name the table **Day Hikes**

3. Import both the table and the report called **Overnight Hikes** from the Access database **AC_Project8B.mdb** into the **Trails.mdb** database

4. Export the **Overnight Hikes table** to an Excel workbook

5. Export the **Overnight Hikes report** to a Web page called **Overnight.html**, then view the table in your Web browser

6. Use the Data Access Page wizard to create a data access page from the **Day Hikes table** that includes all the fields, has no grouping level, is *not* sorted on any of the fields, and has the title **Day Hikes**

7. Apply the **Watermark** theme to the data access page, enter **Great Day Hiking Trails** as the page title, save the data access page as **Day.htm** and accept the warning, view the page in Page view, then compare it to figure AP8-1

8. Use the Data Access Page wizard to create a data access page for data reporting from the Overnight Hikes table that includes all the fields, designates **State/Province** as the grouping level, is *not* sorted on any of the fields, and has the title **Overnight Hikes**

9. Apply the Nature theme, enter **Great Overnight Hiking Trails** as the page title, then view the first record for British Columbia
The data access page appears as shown in Figure AP 8-2.

10. Save the data access page as Night.htm

Step 4
Click the Save formatted checkbox in the Export dialog box.

Step 9
If the Nature theme is not available, select another theme from the list.

 close Trails.mdb Overnight Hikes.xls, Overnight.html Night.htm

Figure AP 8-1: Great Day Hiking Trails data access page

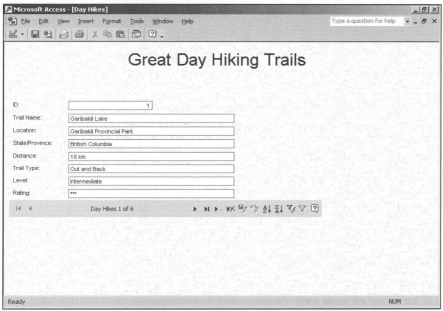

Figure AP 8-2: Great Overnight Hiking Trails data access page

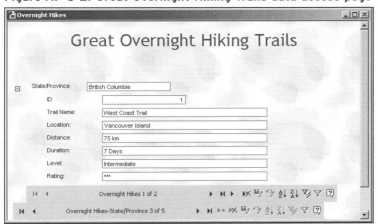

Access 2002 Expert Projects Appendix

Projects List

Project 9 – Database for Italia Vacations, Inc.

Project 10 – Sales Database for Pioneer Antiques

Project 11 – Product Database for Viva Arts

Project 12 – Customer Database for Custom Mouse Pads

Project 13 – Client Database for Fit 'n Fun Health Club

Project 14 – Rentals Database for Classics Plus Video Club

Project 15 – Database of Golden Golf Tours

Project 16 – Product Database for Snaps Photo Supplies

The Access Expert skill sets cover many of the techniques and advanced tools used to create custom versions of database objects. In addition, the skill sets include methods for defining relationships, operating Access on the World Wide Web, using Access tools to perform such activities as encrypting and replicating databases, and using Access to create database applications. In the following projects, you will practice these skills by developing and using databases to maintain information for various business applications.

Project for Skill Set 9

Creating and Modifying Tables

Database for Italia Vacations, Inc.

Italia Vacations Inc., manages a Web site that lists holiday villas for rent in various regions of Italy. The company maintains two databases: one database contains the Villas table, which lists the holiday villas available for rental, and the other database contains the Customers table, which lists the customers who have rented villas. In this project you will first use data validation to ensure that all users enter information consistently in the Villas table, and then you will create a link between the two databases so that information entered in the Customers table is accessible to both databases.

Activity Steps

 open AE_Project9A.mdb

1. In the **Villas table**, create a Validation Rule for the Source field to specify that only **C or W** be entered, then create Validation text that states **Enter C for Catalog or W for Web**

2. Switch to Datasheet view and save when prompted, click **No** when prompted to test existing records, enter **D** in the Source column of the last record, then correct the error by entering **W** when prompted

3. In the **Villas table**, use the Lookup Wizard to create a Lookup field for the Region field that includes the regions shown in Figure AP 9-1

4. In Datasheet view, enter **Tuscany** as the region for the last record in the Villas table

5. Create a custom input mask called **International Phone Number** for the Phone Number field that specifies the settings for a phone number shown in Figure AP 9-2

6. Save when prompted, enter the phone number **(011) (0)343-5569** in the last record, then close the table

7. Use the Link Tables command to link to the **Customers table** in the **AE_Project9B.mdb** database

8. Open the **Customers table** in **AE_Project9A.mdb**, then add a new record for a customer called **Gerry Hansen** who lives at **140 Aspen Way, Boulder, CO, USA 81423**, and will stay for **2 weeks at Villa 14** starting **August 21, 2004**

9. Close the Customers table, close the AE_Project9A.mdb database, then open **AE_Project9B.mdb** and verify that the new record has been added to the Customers table in this database

 close AE_Project9B.mdb

Step 3
Click the I will type the values that I want option button in the first Lookup Wizard dialog box.

Step 5
This input mask will require that phone numbers be entered as (011) followed by a space, followed by a 0 in brackets, followed by three digits, followed by a hyphen, followed by four digits.

Figure AP 9-1: Values for Lookup field

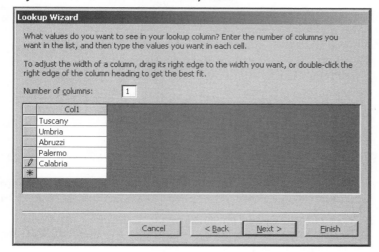

Figure AP 9-2: Custom input mask

Project for Skill Set 10

Creating and Modifying Forms

Sales Database for Pioneer Antiques

Pioneer Antiques sells items from America's past, particularly those items related to the Old West. The company sells its wares from a retail store located in Tuscon, AZ and from its company Web site, www.pioneerantiques.com. The Sales database contains the Sales table, which lists each item sold, and the Customer table, which lists each customer. In this project, you will create a form for entering data in the Sales table and then modify the form by creating a subform that lists the customers. You will then create a switchboard and modify startup options so that a salesperson can quickly access the Sales form to enter new data.

Activity Steps

 open AE_Project10.mdb

1. Using the **Sales table** as the Record Source property, create a form in Design view that appears as shown in Figure AP 10-1

2. Use the form to add a record with the data: **Georgian Candlesticks, Silver, 1792, Gilliam McKim**, buyer ID **20**, then save the form as **Sales**

3. Open the **Customer form**, then add a subform called **Sales subform** under the Zip Code label that contains all the fields from the **Sales table**; accept the default settings in the Subform wizard

4. Navigate to the record for **Gretchen Kingsley**, compare your screen to Figure AP 10-2, adjust column widths in Design view, if necessary, then close and save the form

Step 3
If necessary, increase the width of the Sales subform to approximately 6".

5. Use the Switchboard Manager to create a new switchboard called **Antiques Switchboard** that includes two items: **Open Sales Form** that opens the **Sales form** in edit mode and **Open Customer Form** that opens the **Customers form** in edit mode

6. Close the Edit Switchboard Page dialog box and the Switchboard Manager dialog box, then use the new switchboard to open the **Sales form**

7. Close the **Sales form** and the switchboard, modify the switchboard by moving the Open Customer Form command above the Open Sales Form command, then view the modified switchboard

8. Close the Switchboard, set startup options to display the switchboard on startup, then close the database

9. Open the database, use the command button on the switchboard to go directly to the **Sales form**, then add the following new record: **Punched Tin Lantern, Metalware, 1810, Gail Jenkins**, buyer ID **15**

 close AE_Project10.mdb

Figure AP 10-1: Sales form created in Form Design view

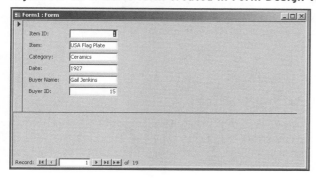

Figure AP 10-2: Customer form with Sales subform

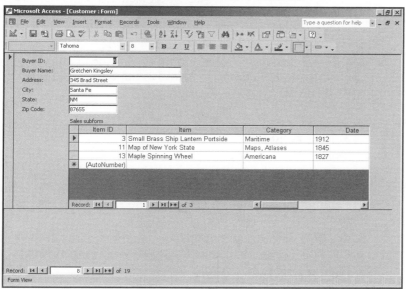

Project for Skill Set 11

Refining Queries

Product Database for Viva Arts

Viva Arts is a wholesale supplier of art materials to artists throughout the United States and Canada. In this project you will modify the Inventory table in the store's database so that the store manager can quickly create queries to obtain specific information about the inventory.

Activity Steps

 open AE_Project11.mdb

1. In Design view, create a query that includes all the fields from the **Inventory table** and finds only the supplies that are in the Paint category AND that cost more than $8.00, then save the query as **Premium Paints**
   The query results list 10 items.

2. In Design view, create a query that includes all the fields from the **Inventory table** and lists all products in the **Canvas** OR **Paper** OR **Canvas Board** categories, then save the query as **Surfaces**
   The query results list 15 items.

3. From the **Inventory table**, create an Advanced filter to select only the **Aquaflo** brand of **paints** in the **6 oz. size** that cost less than **$7.00**
   The criteria for the filter should appear as shown in Figure AP 11-1.

Step 1
Enter >8 in the Price criteria cell.

4. Apply the filter, then save it as a query object called **Aquaflo Acrylic Paints**
   Five items are listed after the filter is applied.

5. In the **Paints query**, create a parameter query that uses the text **[Enter Brand]**, view the query, type **Reiva** in the Enter Parameter Value dialog box, view the six records that appear, then close and save the query

6. Create a new query that includes all the records in the Inventory table, then save the query as **Inventory Query**

7. From the **Inventory Query**, create a Make Table action query that creates a table called **High Cost** containing only items from the Inventory table that cost more than **$100.00**, delete those items from the Inventory table, then view the new table, which contains six records

8. Using the **Categories query**, create a query that uses the **SUM aggregate function** to calculate the total worth of all the items in the query grouped by Category, save the query as **Total Items by Category**, then run the query, and compare it to Figure AP 11-2

 close AE_Project11.mdb

Figure AP 11-1: Advanced Filter query criteria

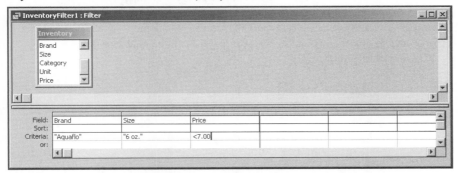

Figure AP 11-2: Total Items by Catetory query

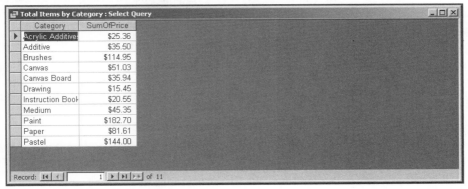

Project for Skill Set 12

Producing Reports

Customer Database for Custom Mouse Pads

Custom Mouse Pads supplies souvenir stores and corporate customers with mouse pads that feature photographic images, reproductions of art work, and logos. You've been asked to create a new report that shows all the mouse pads sold in the Art category and then to modify a report that lists all the mouse pads sold in the Photograph category.

Activity Steps

 open AE_Project12.mdb

1. Create a report in Design view that uses the **Art Mouse Pads query** as the record source

2. Move and size the labels, add **Purchases of Art Mouse Pads** as the Page Header, modify the header by increasing its font size to 18-point and adjusting its size and position, add a text box to the footer that contains **=[Page]**, then remove the label
   Your screen should match Figure AP 12-1.

3. Save the report as **Art Mouse Pads**, then close it

4. Open the **Photograph Mouse Pads report**, add a Report Footer, then add a control in the Report Footer that uses the Sum function to total the quantity of images purchased and includes the label **Total Images**
   The required control is =Sum([Quantity]).

5. View the report in Print Preview, move to the last page of the report, then verify that 25,400 mouse pads have been purchased

6. In Design view, sort the **Photograph Mouse Pads report** in Ascending order by **Country** and show the **Group Header**

7. Move the **Country text box** in the Detail section up into the Country Header section, then move the **CompanyID text box** to close the gap in the Details section

8. Increase the height of the Details section by approximately 3", add a subreport control that shows the **Companies report** for each record (accept all defaults in the SubReport Wizard), then view the report in Print Preview
   The first record appears in Print Preview as shown in Figure AP 12-2.

 close AE_Project12.mdb

Step 2
You separate a label and text box combination by clicking and dragging the large square handle. To increase the size of a label or text box, drag the right middle sizing handle.

Figure AP 12-1: Art Mouse Pads report

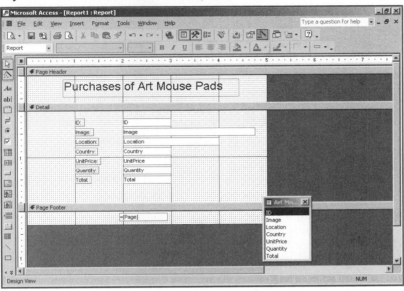

Figure AP 12-2: Photograph Mouse Pads and Companies Report in Print Preview

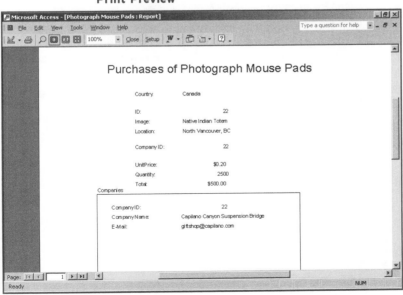

Project for Skill Set 13

Defining Relationships

Client Database for Fit 'n Fun Health Club

The Fit 'n Fun Health Club maintains a database of the various fitness classes offered at the club. This database includes three tables: a list of Members, a list of Classes and Instructors, and a Registration table that identifies the members registered in each class. You first need to create a one-to-many relationship between the Members table and the Registration table. Then you will create a many-to-many relationship between the Members table and the Classes table that uses the Registration table as the junction table.

Activity Steps

 open AE_Project13.mdb

1. Using the **MemberID field**, create a one-to-many relationship with referential integrity enforced from the **Members table** to the **Registration table** to show that one client can take many classes

2. View the **Members table**, then determine how many classes **Ron Dawson** is taking
   Ron takes two classes, as shown in Figure AP 13-1.

3. Using the **Registration table** as the junction table and the **ClassID field**, create a many-to-many relationship with referential integrity enforced between the **Members table** and the **Classes table**
   The relationships should appear in the Relationships window as shown in Figure AP 13-2.

4. In the **Classes table**, determine how many members are taking the Aerobics class taught be Michelle Leung on Wednesdays
   As shown in Figure AP 13-3, two members have registered for Michelle's class.

 close AE_Project13.mdb

Figure AP 13-1: Classes taken by Ron Dawson

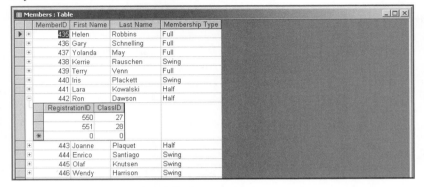

Figure AP 13-2: Relationships established

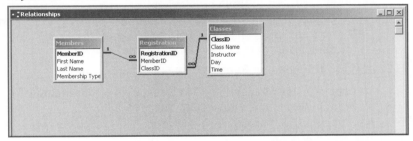

Figure AP 13-3: Members registered in the Wednesday Aerobics class

Project for Skill Set 14

Operating Access on the Web

Rentals Database for Classics Plus Video Club

The Classic Plus Video Club rents classic videos to students at various universities and colleges in the Chicago area. The club's database contains two tables: the Inventory table, which contains the list of videos available, and the Rentals table, which contains the list of students who have rented videos. First, you'll create a data access page from the Rentals table so that club personnel can enter video rental data online. Then, you'll create a data acesss page with a PivotTable and a data access table with a PivotChart.

Step 2
To move both the text box and label, click and drag the text box. To move just the label, click and drag the label.

Step 4
If Drop Areas are not visible, right-click the PivotTable area, then click Drop Areas.

Activity Steps

 open AE_Project14.mdb

1. Create a Data Access Page in Design view that includes all the fields from the Rentals table

2. As shown in Figure AP 14-1, size and position the fields, enter **Video Rentals** as the page title, then apply the **Poetic** theme (or select another theme if Poetic is not available)

3. Save the page as **Rentals.htm**

4. Create a Data Access Page in Design view that includes a PivotTable from the Inventory table as follows:

   a. Remove the **Video ID, Artist or Director**, and **Rentals in 2004** fields

   b. Move the **Category** and **Decade** fields to the Row area

   c. Enter **Videos by Category and Decade** as the title for the data access page

5. Modify the size and position of the PivotTable so that it appears as shown in Figure AP 14-2 in Page view, then save the page as **Categories.htm**

6. Create a Data Access Page in Design view that includes a PivotChart from the Inventory table by doing the following: move the **Category field** into Category, the **Decade field** into Series, and the **Rentals in 2004** field into Data

7. Show only data for the **Comedy** and **Drama** categories

8. Resize the chart and add a title as show in Figure AP 14-3, then save the page as **RentalData.htm**

 close AE_Project14.mdb

Figure AP 14-1: Data Access Page from the Rentals table

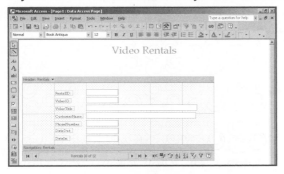

Figure AP 14-2: Data Access Page with PivotTable

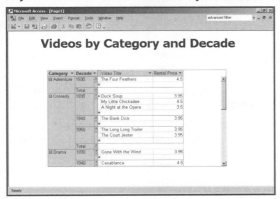

Figure AP 14-3: Data Access Page with PivotChart

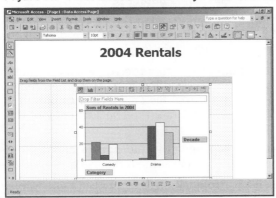

Project for Skill Set 15

Using Access Tools

Database of Golden Golf Tours

Golden Golf Tours offers a wide range of tours to golfers interested in combining travel with golf. In this project, you will work with the company's database to import data currently saved in XML format, export one the of the tables to XML format for transfer over the World Wide Web, and then use Access tools to encrypt the database, compact and reopen it, assign security, and replicate it.

Activity Steps

 open AE_Project15.mdb

1. Import the **Flights.xml** document into the database
   The XML document contains information about flight arrivals and departures for each of the golf tours.

2. Export the **Courses table** to an XML file, click **OK** in the Export XML dialog box to export both the data as an XML document and the schema as an XSD document, then view the XML file in the browser
   The XML file appears in the browser as shown in Figure AP 15-1.

3. Close the browser and return to Access, close the database, open it in Exclusive mode, assign the password **gogolf** to the database, close the database, then open it using the password

4. Create a workgroup called **Golf** with **tours** as the Personal ID that contains two people: **Mark Green** (Personal ID is **soccer**), and **Cheryl Wong** (Personal ID is **snow**)
   Figure AP 15-2 shows Mark Green being added to the Golf workgroup in the User and Group Accounts dialog box

5. Assign the users of the Golf workbook the permission to open and run the AE_Project15.mdb database

6. Close the database, encrypt it using the filename **AE_Project15_Encrypt.mdb**, open the encrypted database, compact and repair it, then close it

7. Remove the **gogolf** password from the **AE_Project15.mdb file**, remove the Golf workgroup and the two users, then replicate the AE_Project15.mdb file to a file called **Replica of AE_Project15.mdb**, without creating a backup copy of the Design Master

8. Open **AE_Project15.mdb**, open the **Tours table**, change **Riviera** to **Lavender** in Record 6, then close the database and exit Access

9. Open **Replica of AE_Project15.mdb**, apply the Synchronize function, then verify that the change was made to Record 6 in the replicated database

 close AE_Project15.mdb

Figure AP 15-1: Courses.xml file shown in browser

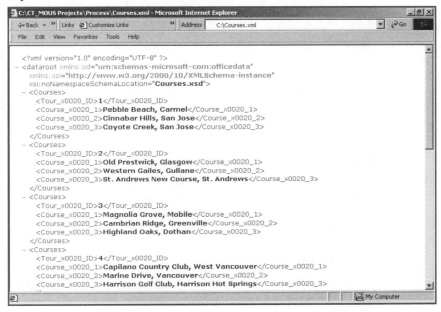

Figure AP 15-2: User and Group Accounts dialog box

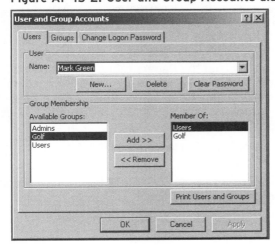

Project for Skill Set 16

Creating Database Applications

Product Database for Snaps Photo Supplies

Snaps Photo Supplies sells cameras, film, and other photographic supplies to photography enthusiasts in Atlanta. You've been asked to create database applications to help automate the form completion process, so that users can quickly enter required information. You'll create two command buttons using the Command Button Wizard, and then you'll create a new Global module that will convert entries in Celsius temperatures to Fahrenheit. This module will be used to calculate the ferotyping temperatures of photographic paper listed in the Papers table.

Activity Steps

 open AE_Project16.mdb

1. Open the **Supplies form** in Design view, then use the **Command Button Wizard** to create a command button called **Add New Record** that uses the pencil image, and a command button called **Delete Record** that uses the trash can 1 image

2. Position the command buttons in the lower right corner of the form as shown in Figure AP 16-1

3. Use the Add New Record button to add a new record with the data shown in Figure AP 16-2, then use the Delete Record button to delete record 15

4. Create a new Global module that consists of the VBA function named **CelsiusToFahr** by entering the VBA code shown in Figure AP 16-3

5. Save the module with the name **Temperature Function**

6. In Query Design view, add the Papers table, add the TempC field to the query grid, click in the **Field cell** in the second column, type **TempF: CelsiusToFahr([TempC])**, run the query, verify that the first temperature is converted to 212, then save the query as **Conversions**

7. Use the Database Splitter to create a back-end database called **AP_Project16_be.mdb**

8. Convert the database to the Access 2002 file format, save the database as **Snaps.mdb**, then close it

9. Make an MDE file for the Snaps.mdb file, then save the file as **SnapsMDE**

 close SnapsMDE.mdb

Figure AP 16-1: Form with command buttons

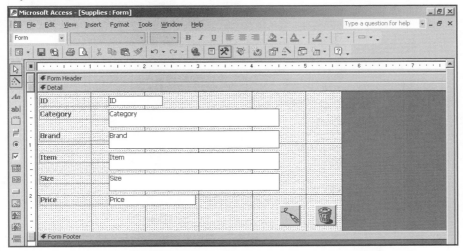

Figure AP 16-2: New record added

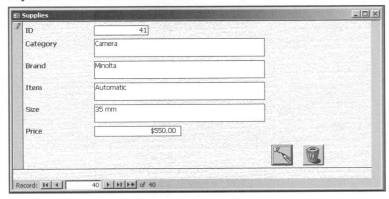

Figure AP 16-3: VBA code for Global module

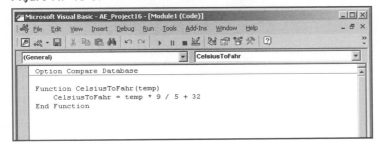

Outlook 2002 Core Projects Appendix

Projects List

Project 1 – E-mail Messages for Vision Productions

Project 2 – Meeting Schedules for Pacific Imports

Project 3 – Message Management for Career Corner

Project 4 – Contact Management for Paradise Realty

Project 5 – Tasks and Notes for Step One Consulting

The Outlook Core skill sets cover a broad range of e-mail and scheduling tasks—from organizing meetings, appointments, and contacts to managing e-mail efficiently. In the following projects, you will use Outlook to create and view e-mail messages, schedule meetings and appointments, manage e-mail messages, create and manage contacts, and work with tasks and notes.

Project for Skill Set 1

Creating and Viewing Messages

E-mail Messages for Vision Productions

As the Office Manager of Vision Productions, located in San Diego, California, your job is to coordinate the activities of the filmmakers involved in shooting a new documentary on the life and work of the artist Michelangelo. The documentary will be set in various locations throughout Italy, and will also involve an Italian film production company based in Florence. In this project, you will receive, read, and send messages to set up meetings between the filmmakers from the home office in San Diego and those from the Italian production company in Florence.

1. Open and read the **Florence shooting schedule message** from Enrico Mazzini, open and print the Word document called **Florence Shooting Schedule.doc** that accompanies the message as an attachment, close the document, then forward the message to yourself

2. Open and read the **Travel Itinerary message** from Mina Harrison, print the e-mail in Memo style over two pages with 1" margins on all four sides of the page, then close the message

3. Open and read the **Hotel in Florence message** from Enrico Mazzini, then add Enrico Mazzini as a new contact to your address book

4. Reply to the message with the text shown in Figure OP 1-1

5. Compose and send an e-mail to Mina Harrison at **minaharrison@hotmail.com** with the subject **Reservations** and the text **I've made the reservations. The hotel will e-mail a confirmation directly.**

6. Create a signature for Mina Harrison that appears as shown in Figure OP 1-2

7. Compose and send an e-mail to Enrico Mazzini at enricomazzini@hotmail.com that includes Revised Itinerary as the subject and the text **Here is a revised version of the travel itinerary.**, attaches the file **Revised Travel Itinerary.doc**, and uses the signature you just created for Mina Harrison

8. Change the Inbox view to view only Sent messages, then customize the view to change the grid line style to **Solid** and the grid line color to **bright blue**

9. Reset the view to the default setting, then remove the signature for Mina Harrison

Figure OP 1-1: Reply message

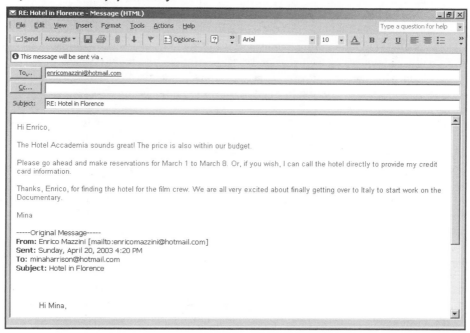

Figure OP 1-2: Signature for Mina Harrison

Project for Skill Set 2

Scheduling

Meeting Schedules for Pacific Imports

Pacific Imports is a small retail outlet based in Seattle, Washington, that sells craft products from various Pacific Rim nations such as Japan, Malaysia, Australia, Chile, and Mexico. Meetings are held frequently to discuss new products and to plan marketing strategies. In this project, you will use Outlook to add appointments to the Calendar, schedule meetings and resources, and manage meeting requests for two managers at Pacific Imports: Derek Thirlwell and Shaun Richter, and for Rie Nishimura, who is in charge of Resources.

1. In the Calendar, enter the appointment **Planning Meeting** at **3:00 pm** for tomorrow; the meeting will last **2 hours** and take place in the **Coral Reef Conference Room**

2. Create a new category called **Planning**, add the Planning meeting to the Planning category, make the meeting one that recurs every month on the same day (e.g., the first Tuesday), save and close the meeting, then apply a conditional format to the Planning Meeting that makes it a **Business** meeting based on the condition that **planning** appears in the subject

3. Schedule an all-day event for next Wednesday called **Employee Appreciation Day** that will take place at **Mayfair Roller Rink**; remove the reminder, show the time as **Out of Office**, label the meeting as **Must Attend**, include the text shown in Figure OP 2-1, then save and close the event

4. Schedule a meeting from **10:00** to **12:00** in the **Pacific Oasis Conference Room** on another free day in your calendar that uses **Rei Nishimura** as the Resource and discusses **Taiwan Imports**, with **Derek Thirlwell** and **Shaun Richter** as required attendees

5. In your Inbox, open the **Product Launch Meeting message**, accept the meeting request, edit the response by adding the message as shown in Figure OP 2-2, send a copy of the message to **Derek Thirlwell** and a copy to yourself, then view the meeting date in the calendar

6. Open the **New Zealand Conference message** in your inbox, decline the meeting request with the message **I'm sorry, Derek. I need to be in Taiwan that week.**, open the **Australia Manager Meeting message**, propose a new meeting time of **1:00 pm** to **2:30 pm**, then send a copy of the message to yourself

7. Print all the appointments in the **Daily Style** for **April 3, 2003**

Figure OP 2-1: All-day event scheduled

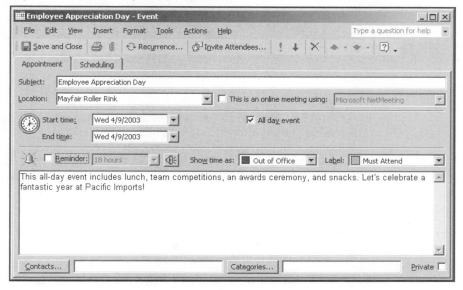

Figure OP 2-2: Reply to Product Launch meeting request

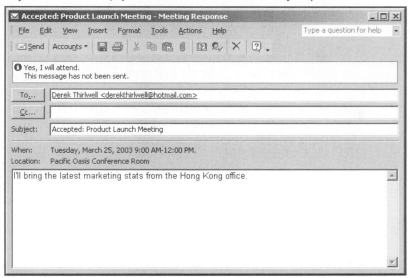

Project for Skill Set 3

Managing Messages

Message Management for Career Corner

Career Corner is an employment agency that finds jobs for people with business administrative skills and provides a variety of career counseling services. The company also maintains an active Web site. As the Administrative Assistant, you use Outlook to manage the many e-mails received from job hunters who browse the Web site. You need to develop an effective system for managing these messages. In this project, you will create a system for managing messages related to positions for Account Managers.

1. Use the Find feature to find all messages in the Inbox that contain **Account Manager** in the Subject line
   You should find three messages containing Account Manager in the Subject line.

2. Select the following messages: **Account Manager Position Available, Account Manager: Regional**, and **Account Managers Needed**

3. Create a new folder in the Inbox called **Account Manager Positions** but do not add a shortcut to the Outlook Bar, then move the selected messages into the new folder

4. Open the **Account Manager Position Available message** from the Account Manager Positions folder, save the message as a Text Only (*.txt) file in the location in which your store your project files, then open the file in Notepad
   The file appears in Notepad as shown in Figure OP 3-1.

5. Open the **Account Managers Needed message**, save it as an HTML file in the location in which you store your project files, then view the file in Internet Explorer

6. Assign all messages in the Account Manager Positions folder to a new category called **Seattle Postings**, then use the Advanced Find feature to display the messages you have assigned to the Seattle Postings category
   The messages appear in the Seattle Postings category as shown in Figure OP 3-2.

7. Send an **Important** and **Confidential** message to Nathan Chang at *nathanchang@hotmail.com* with the subject **New Positions** and the text **Can we meet at 2 pm to discuss the new Account Manager positions?** that uses the voting buttons for a Yes/No response and requests a read receipt for the message

8. Open the Account Manager Positions folder, then modify the AutoArchive properties so that the folder is archived in one week

Figure OP 3-1: Text only file shown in Notepad

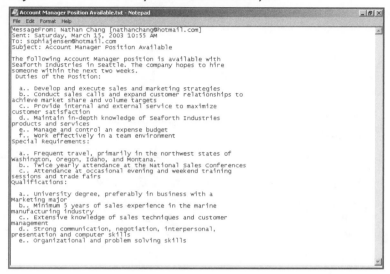

Figure OP 3-2: Messages in Seattle Postings category

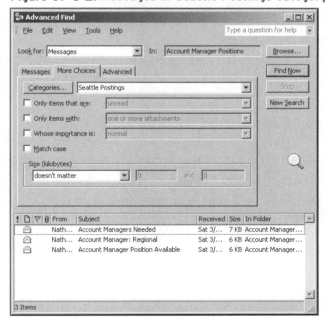

Project for Skill Set 4

Creating and Managing Contacts

Contact Management for Paradise Realty

You work as a realtor for Paradise Realty, a small real estate agency located on Saltspring Island, the largest island in British Columbia's Gulf Islands region. You handle properties located throughout the islands, including Mayne Island, Galiano Island, Gabriola Island and, of course, Saltspring Island. Many of your clients e-mail you for information after viewing your listings on the company's Web site. In this project, you will use Outlook to create contacts for new clients and to organize your existing contacts.

1. Create a contact for **Janice Alton** that appears as shown in Figure OP 4-1

2. In the Contacts folder, find the contact information for **Yves Torandot**, change his job title to **Senior Account Manager**, then flag the contact to call by **March 22, 2004** at **10:00 AM**

3. Create a new category called **Galiano Island**, then assign the following contacts to the Galiano Island category: **Harrison Chan, Dorothea Grunwald, Jamal Leblanc,** and **Wendy Paradou**
Now the Galiano Island category contains all of your clients who are interested in buying property on Galiano Island.

4. View the contacts in your contact list by **Company**, find the contacts from **North Vancouver Regional District**, then return to the default Address Cards view
Both Francis Oleander and Wendy Paradou work for the North Vancouver Regional District.

5. View the category associated with **Jamal Leblanc**, then add him to the Hot Contacts category
Jamal now belongs to both the Galiano Island and the Hot Contacts categories.

6. View **My Shortcuts** on the Outlook bar, then click the **Journal icon**

7. Create a new journal entry that appears as shown in Figure OP 4-2

8. Assign the journal entry to **Harrison Chan** and **Jamal LeBlanc**

9. Open the contact for **Harrison Chan**, then view the activity associated with him

Step 6
If the Journal icon does not appear on the Outlook bar, click Journal in the Folder List pane.

Figure OP 4-1: Contact for Janice Alton

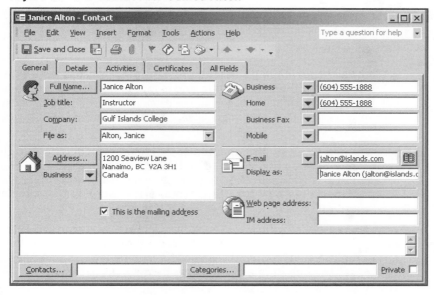

Figure OP 4-2: New journal entry

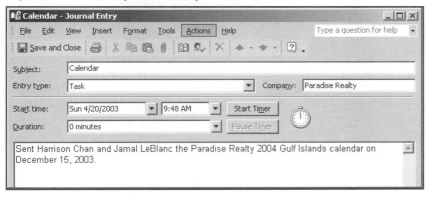

Project for Skill Set 5

Creating and Managing Tasks and Notes

Tasks and Notes for Step One Consulting

Step One Consulting holds full-day and weekend workshops in team building and leadership skills for companies in Dallas, Texas. As one of the company's seminar leaders, you will use Outlook in this project to keep track of your daily tasks and to receive tasks from and assign tasks to various co-workers.

1. As shown in Figure OP 5-1, create an **In Progress task** that starts on the current date and is due on tomorrow's date
This task reminds you to call the caterers who will provide lunch and snacks for the upcoming leadership seminar for employees of Deer Lake Resort.

2. Open the **Web site updates task**, change the due date to tomorrow, change the status to **Waiting on someone else**, set the priority as **High**, set the recurrence to **Monthly**, and select the **Regenerate new task 1 month(s) after each task is completed** option button

3. Create a new task that includes **Seminar Materials** as the Subject and the message **Photocopy materials for the Deer Lake Resort seminar**, assign the new task to Sophia Jensen, set the due date as **tomorrow**, then send the request

4. Open the **Projector for May 3 Seminar** task, delegate the task to **Marcus Branson**, include the text **Can you take care of ordering the projector for your seminar?**, then send the request

5. Create the note shown in Figure OP 5-2, then assign the note to **Sophia Jensen**

6. Select the **May 10 Seminar** and the **June 3 Seminar** notes, then assign them to a new category called **Leadership Seminars**

Step 3
If a message appears telling you that the reminder has been turned off because the task no longer belongs to you, click OK.

Project 5

Figure OP 5-1: Call caterers task

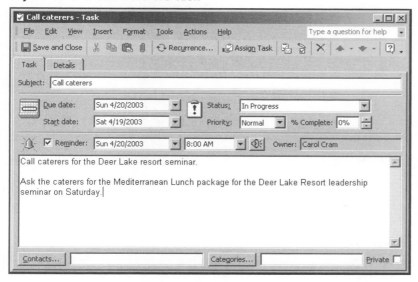

Figure OP 5-2: June seminars note

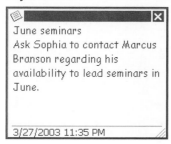

Projects List

Project 1 - Geranium Bistro Business Plan Presentation

Project 2 - Tips for Home Security Presentation

Project 3 - Orientation Presentation for Camp Dream Quest

Project 4 - Great Cathedrals of Europe Tour Presentation

Project 5 - "How to Draw People" Instructional Presentation

Project 6 - Sales Presentation for Road Smart Driving School

Project 7 - Lecture Presentation for E-Commerce Marketing

Project 8 - Rainforest Coalition Web Pages

The PowerPoint MOUS skill sets include the features and functions you need to create, modify, and deliver presentations. In the following projects, you will develop and modify various presentations by inserting and modifying visual elements such as tables, charts, and clip art. You will also explore different presentation delivery options such as transition and animation effects, and enhance a presentation with data from other sources, including Excel charts, Word tables, and sound and video files. Finally, you will work with options designed to facilitate collaboration between two or more people working on the same presentation.

Project for Skill Set 1

Creating Presentations

Geranium Bistro Business Plan Presentation

You've just started working for the Geranium Bistro, a family-style café overlooking a lake in rural Minnesota. The owner would like to obtain financing to expand the café to better serve a large clientele of summer visitors. He asks you to create the outline of a presentation that he can use to describe his business plan to investors. You will start by checking out the Business Plan AutoContent wizard, and then you will create a new presentation containing titles for six slides.

Activity Steps

1. Start PowerPoint, then use the AutoContent wizard to create an onscreen presentation using the Business Plan template; enter **Geranium Bistro** as the Presentation title and **2004 Business Plan** in the footer, along with the default footer options

2. Scroll through the completed presentation to get a feel for its contents, then close the new presentation without saving it
   Now that you have an idea of the contents of a typical business plan presentation, you're ready to create your own version.

3. Create a new blank presentation, apply the **Profile slide design**, then close the Slide Design task pane

4. In the Outline tab, add **five** slides to the presentation for a total of six slides, then enter the text shown in Figure PP 1-1

5. In the presentation footer, add **your name**, the **current date** in the format that corresponds to **July 17, 2004** that updates automatically, and the **slide number**; do not include the footer on the title slide

6. Delete **Slide 3** from the presentation

7. Save the presentation as **PC_Project1.ppt**

8. Compare **Slide 1** to Figure PP 1-2

 close PC_Project1.ppt

Figure PP 1-1: Slide titles for Geranium Bistro Business Plan presentation

Figure PP 1-2: Slide 1 of Business Plan presentation

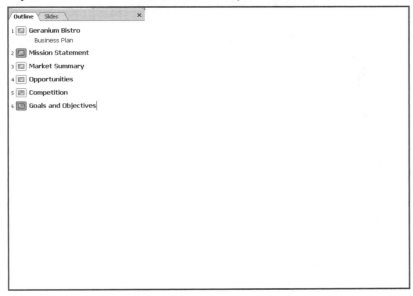

Project for Skill Set 2

Inserting and Modifying Text

Tips for Home Security Presentation

Great Western Security needs to develop a presentation to be delivered to residents of a local condominium complex who are interested in installing a home security system. Most of the content for the presentation is already contained in a Word outline. In this project, you will open the Word outline in PowerPoint, edit selected slides, and add text to some new slides.

Activity Steps

1. Start PowerPoint, then insert the Word outline from the file **PC_Project2.doc** into a blank presentation

2. Delete the first slide in the presentation, apply the **Title slide layout** to the new **Slide 1**, then close the Slide Layout task pane

3. Change the font of the title text to **Arial Black**, then apply Italics to the subtitle text

4. On **Slide 4**, delete the word **personal**, then insert the word **security** before "system"

5. On **Slide 5**, add a bullet with the text **Sign the contract and provide a check for the first and last month's payment**, as shown in Figure PP 2-1

6. Apply the **Blends** slide design to the entire presentation then close the Slide Design task pane

7. View the presentation in Slide Sorter view
   The presentation appears in Slide Sorter view as shown in Figure PP 2-2.

 close PC_Project2.ppt

Figure PP 2-1: Modified Slide 5

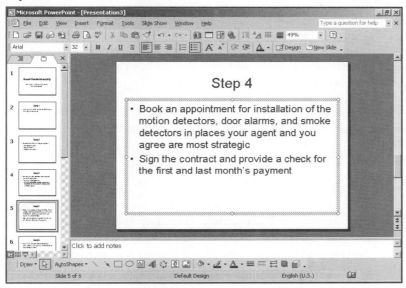

Figure PP 2-2: Home Security presentation in Slide Sorter view

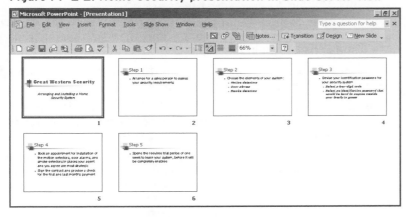

Project for Skill Set 3

Inserting and Modifying Visual Elements

Orientation Presentation for Camp Dream Quest

Camp Dream Quest in Costa Rica provides teens from all over the world with a three-week program of outdoor adventure activities, including hiking and camping in the rainforest and snorkeling, swimming, and sailing in the warm Pacific waters off the Costa Rican coast. The camp administration has prepared a PowerPoint presentation to deliver to school groups throughout the US and Canada. In this project, you will enhance the presentation with graphical elements that include a table, charts, clip art, bitmap images, and drawn objects. The six slides of the completed presentation appear as shown in Figure PP 3-1.

Activity Steps

 open PC_Project3.ppt

1. In Slide Master view, insert the picture file **Hibiscus.jpg** so that it appears in the top right corner of every slide in the presentation, except the first slide

2. Size and position the hibiscus picture as shown in Figure PP 3-1

3. Open the Clip Gallery, search for **Costa Rica**, then insert, size, and position the clip art image of a flag on **Slide 1**, as shown in Figure PP 3-1

4. On **Slide 3**, draw a **sun shape**, fill the shape with the **Papyrus texture** and remove the border line, then size and position the shape as shown in Figure PP 3-1

Step 5
Note that you must be connected to the Internet to insert this piece of clip art from the complete Microsoft Clip Gallery.

5. On **Slide 4**, insert the picture file **Turtle.jpg**, then size and position the picture as shown in Figure PP 3-1

6. On **Slide 4**, insert a text box to the left of the turtle picture, as shown in Figure PP 3-1, enter the text **Meet Tio, our school turtle!** in the text box then enhance it with 40-pt

7. On **Slide 5**, insert a chart using the information shown below, change the chart type to **pie**, change the font color of the chart legend text to black, then remove the border around the pie chart

   16 17 18 19
   25 40 75 60

8. On **Slide 6**, create the table and enter the text shown in Figure PP 3-1

9. Modify the table by reducing its height and width, filling it with light yellow, changing the font color to black, removing the Shadow effect, then changing the border lines to black

 close PC_Project3.ppt

Figure PP 3-1: Completed presentation for Camp Dream Quest

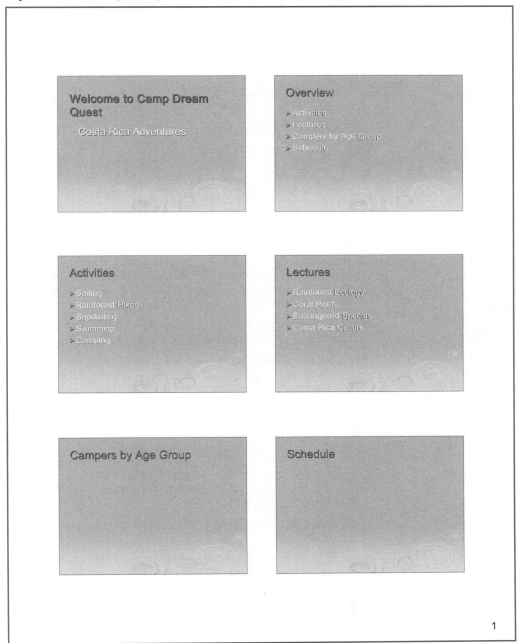

Project for Skill Set 4
Modifying Presentation Format

Great Cathedrals of Europe Tour Presentation

Creative Tours, Inc. puts together customized tours of Europe and Asia for small special interest groups. You have been asked to enhance a presentation that describes a tour of six cathedrals. In this project, you will apply formats to the presentation, apply animation schemes and transition effects, customize slide formats, templates, and the slide master, and then add links to the presentation. Figure PP 4-1 shows the 9 slides in the completed presentation.

Activity Steps

 open PC_Project4.ppt

1. Change **Slide 1** of the presentation so that its background color is a **very light blue**

2. Modify the design template by removing the graphic that appears along the right side of every slide and then apply **bold** to the **title text** on both the slide master and the title slide master

3. In Slide Sorter view, apply the **Watermark** design template to **Slides 5** and **6**, apply the **Pixel** design template to **Slides 7** and **8**, then select the color scheme for the Pixel design template that shows chart elements in **red tones**

4. Apply the **Float** animation scheme to **Slide 1**, then apply the **Zoom** animation scheme to the remaining slides

5. Apply the **Wheel Clockwise, 8 Spokes** transition effect to the last slide in the presentation, then apply the **Shape Diamond** transition effect to **Slides 1** through **8** of the presentation

6. Delete the Slide Master called **Light Text Master**, create a new Slide Master called **Yellow Slide Master** that includes a light yellow background, then apply the Yellow Slide Master to **Slides 2** and **9** in the presentation

7. Move the two slides for **Germany** before the two slides for **France**, then apply the **Title and Text slide layout** to Slide 3 (Cologne Cathedral)

8. On **Slide 2**, make each country name a hyperlink to the first of its related slides

9. Set the time between each slide at **2 seconds**, then rehearse the timing by running the show in Slide Show view, starting from Slide 1

 close PC_Project4.ppt

Step 2
Remember that you need to work in the Slide Master to delete a graphic from every slide in the presentation.

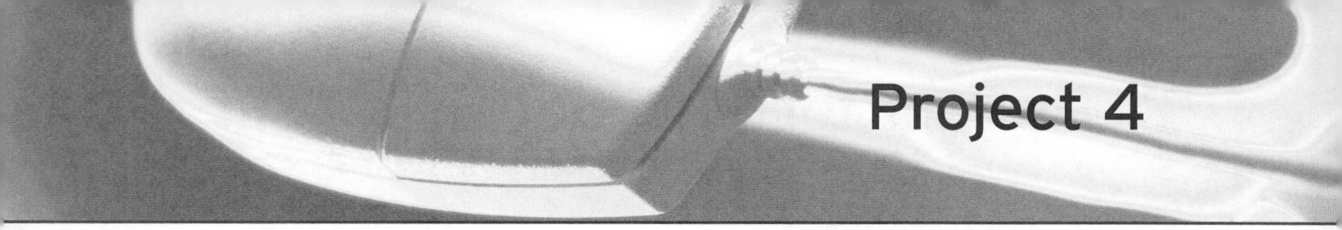

Project 4

Figure PP 4-1: Completed presentation for Cathedrals Tour

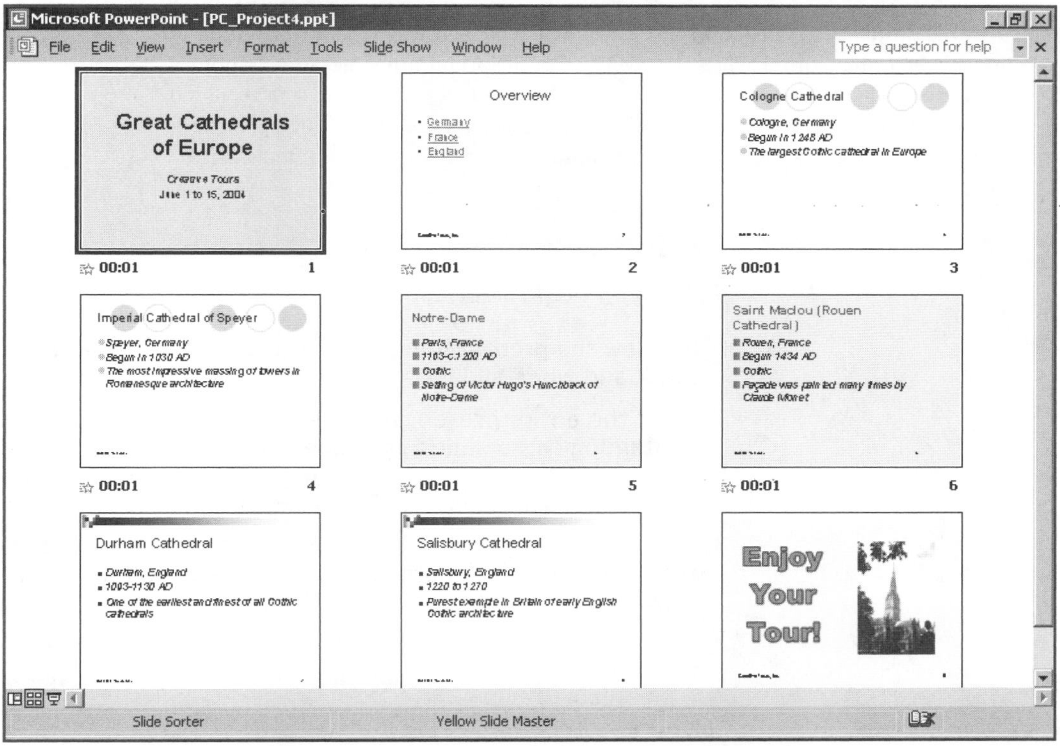

Project for Skill Set 5

Printing Presentations

"How to Draw People" Instructional Presentation

An instructor at a local art school has prepared an instructional presentation to deliver to his portrait class. He asks you to help him print the presentation in various ways. First, you'll print selected slides in black and white, and then you will print the presentation as handouts of three slides per page with space allocated for note-taking. Finally, you'll print the instructor's speaker notes that he plans to refer to while delivering the presentation.

Activity Steps

 open PC_Project5.ppt

1. Preview the presentation, then print **Slides 3** and **4** as pure black and white slides

2. Print the entire presentation as black and white handouts containing three slides per page
   Figure PP 5-1 shows how the first page of the handouts appears. The entire presentation consists of six slides and will print over two pages.

3. In the Notes master, format the speaker notes by changing the font size of the notes to **18 point** and the font to **Times New Roman**

4. Print the speaker notes for **Slides 2** and **3** in Grayscale
   Figure PP 5-2 shows how the speaker notes for Slide 2 appear when printed.

 close PC_Project5.ppt

Figure PP 5-1: Page 1 of the printed presentation

Figure PP 5-2: Notes page for Slide 2

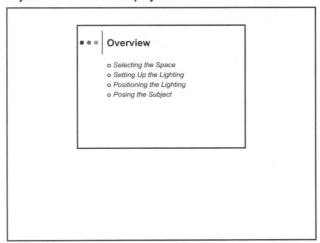

Project for Skill Set 6

Working with Data from Other Sources

Sales Presentation for Road Smart Driving School

Road Smart Driving School in Tulsa, Oklahoma offers four levels of driving courses—from an introductory teen driving course to a commercial driving course. Some of the content for a Road Smart Driving School presentation is contained in Word and Excel files. In this project, you will modify the current presentation by inserting this content, some of which will be linked to source files so that any changes made to the content in the source files also appear in the presentation. You will also insert a sound file and a video file into the presentation. Figure PP 6-1 shows the six slides in the completed presentation.

Activity Steps

 open PC_Project6A.ppt

1. Import the Word file **PC_Project6B.doc** as an embedded object on **Slide 3**, then size and position the table as shown in Figure PP 6-1

2. Start Excel, then open the file **PC_Project6C.xls**, copy the **column chart** and paste it on **Slide 4**, then size and position it as shown in Figure PP 6-1

3. Insert the Excel file **PC_Project6D.xls** as a linked file on **Slide 5**

4. Insert the Word file **PC_Project6E.doc** as a linked file on **Slide 6**

Step 5
To change the media file type in the Insert Clip Art task pane, click the Results should be like list arrow, deselect Clip Art, Photographs, and Movies, then click Search.

5. Insert the sound file **Bulb Horn** in the bottom right corner of Slide 1 by opening the Insert Clip Art task pane, entering the keyword **cars** in the Search text text box, specifying that the results be only **Sounds**, and answering Yes to have the sound played automatically when the slide show is launched

6. In the yellow area on Slide 1, insert the media clip shown in Figure PP 6-1 by searching for **freeway** in the insert Clip Art task pane and specifying that search results should be only **Movies**

7. View the completed presentation in Slide Show view, export the presentation to a Word outline, then save the Word outline as **PC_Project6F.doc**

 close PC_Project6A.ppt   PC_Project6D.doc
PC_Project6B.xls   PC_Project6E.xls
PC_Project6C.doc   PC_Project6F.doc

Figure PP 6-1: Completed presentation for Road Smart Driving School

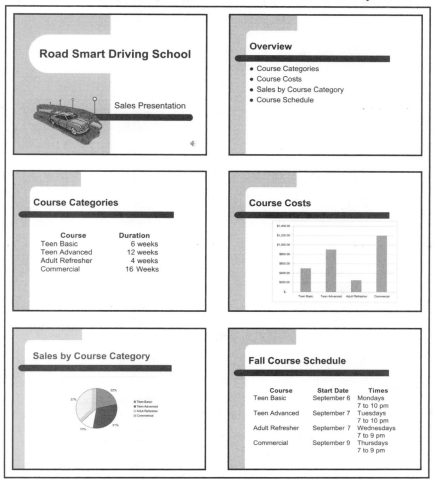

Project for Skill Set 7

Managing and Delivering Presentations

Lecture Presentation for E-Commerce Marketing

You are helping an instructor of a business course in E-Commerce to prepare slides for delivery as part of a lecture. The instructor would like students to view some of the slides in the presentation as a continuous loop on the lab computers. The instructor also wants you to create a folder in which to store the presentation. In addition, the instructor plans to publish the presentation on the World Wide Web for students to review following the in-class lecture. Finally, the instructor plans to deliver the lecture as a self-running presentation from a computer that is not equipped with PowerPoint. Figure PP 7-1 shows the completed presentation.

Activity Steps

 open PC_Project7.ppt

1. Create a new folder called **E-Commerce** on your hard drive or floppy disk, then save the current presentation in this folder

2. Change the pen color to **yellow**, run the slide show, then annotate **Slide 6** of the presentation by drawing an **x** through the **Spam** WordArt object

3. Set up the presentation so that **Slides 3** through **7** can be browsed by an individual in a window, be run continuously until Esc is pressed, and advanced manually

4. View slides **3** through **7** of the presentation in Slide Show view

5. Save the presentation as an HTML file called **Marketing.htm**

6. Set up the presentation so that all slides are run continuously at a kiosk at **3 second** intervals, then view the slide show

7. Use **Pack and Go** to prepare the presentation for delivery on a computer that does not have PowerPoint loaded; choose to copy the file to the A: drive and insert a floppy disk when prompted, select both the **Include Linked Files** and **Embed TrueType fonts check boxes**, and do not include a viewer

 close Marketing.htm

Step 4
To move from slide to slide while viewing the presentation, right-click the slide displayed in the window, then click Advance on the shortcut menu.

Figure PP 7-1: E-Commerce presentation in Slide Sorter view

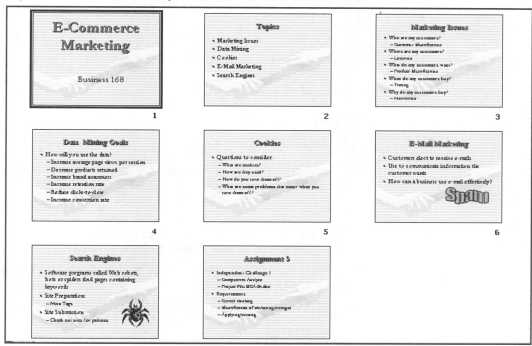

Project for Skill Set 8

PowerPoint Core Projects

Rainforest Coalition Web Pages

Sally Reisman, an administrator at the British Columbia Rainforest Coalition, has put together two slides in PowerPoint that she would like to publish to the coalition's new Web site. She has collaborated with her colleague, Joe Watson, about the content of the two slides. She creates one version of the slides and sends them to Joe. He inserts some comments and makes some changes and then sends the presentation back to Sally. In this project, you will use collaboration options to review the two versions of the presentation.

Activity Steps

 open PC_Project8A.ppt

1. Read Sally's comment on **Slide 1**, enter the e-mail address **info@rainforestcoalition.com** below the text BC Rainforest Coalition on Slide1, then reduce the font size of the e-mail address to 18-point

2. On **Slide 2**, insert a comment in the **Cougars** text box with the text **How about we use a wolf picture instead?**

3. Save the file, click **Tools** on the menu bar, then click **Compare and Merge Presentations**

4. In the Compare and Merge Presentations dialog box, select **PC_Project8B.ppt**, click **Merge**, then click **Continue**

5. On **Slide 1**, show Joe Watson's changes, then accept the **Inserted "British Columbia"** change and the **Deleted "BC"** change

6. On **Slide 2**, accept Joe's changes, then read and delete his comment

7. Replace **Cougars** with **Wolves**, delete the clip art of the cougar, open the Insert Clip Art task pane, search for **sea wolf**, then insert, size and position the clip art, as shown in Figure PP 8-1

8. Delete all the comments in the presentation, then save the presentation as a Web page

9. In the Save as dialog box, click **Publish** to open the Publish as a Web Page dialog box, click the **Open published Web page in browser check box**, click **Publish**, then maximize the Web browser window
   The presentation appears in the Web browser as shown in Figure PP 8-2.

10. Close the browser

 close PC_Project8A.ppt

Figure PP 8-1: New clip art inserted on Slide 2

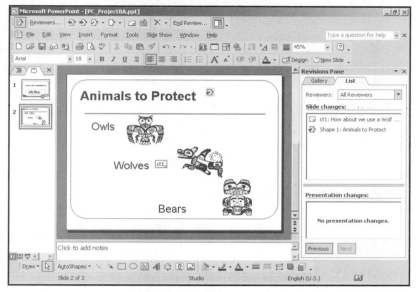

Figure PP 8-2: Presentation displayed in Web browser

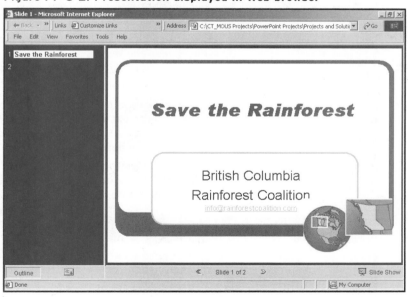

Word 2002 Glossary

.doc filename extension that identifies a file as one created in Microsoft Word

.dot filename extension that identifies a Microsoft Word template file

.htm filename extension that identifies a file as a file created using HyperText Markup Language

.rtf filename extension that identifies a file saved in Rich Text Format

active document the current document; the document in which you are currently entering or editing text

bookmark a named location in a document that you can jump to

cell the intersection of a row and column in a table or a datasheet

centered text or an object that is centered between the left and right margins

chart a visual representation of data in a datasheet

clip (clip art) a drawing, photograph, sound, or movie that you can insert into a document

clipboard an area in the computer in which cut and copied text is stored

comment notes that you add to a document that are not printed unless you specify that you want to print them

comments lines of code in Visual Basic that provide an explanation but do not execute

copy to place a duplicate of text or an object on the system or Office clipboard so that it may be pasted into another location

cross-reference a reference to a figure, table, or other element that appears somewhere else in the document

cut to remove text or an object and store it on the system or Office clipboard so that it may be pasted into another location

data label text that identifies any part of the chart

data marker the bar, column, or point that represents a single piece of data in a chart

data series the collection of all data markers in a row or column in a datasheet

data source the file that contains the list of data to be merged into the main document during the mail merge process

datasheet rows and columns in which you enter data to be graphed in Microsoft Graph

destination file the file into which data, an object, or a link is pasted

digital certificate electronic verification provided by a third-party company that verifies that the person or company whose name appears in the digital signature actually is the creator of the file

digital signature an encrypted key in a file or a macro that identifies the author of the document or macro and verifies that the file has not been changed since it was signed

docked toolbar a toolbar positioned along the edge of the screen

document a file that you create using a word-processing program

Document Map a pane that lists the headings in your document as links in outline form; you can click a heading link to jump to that location in the document

drawing canvas the area in a document in which a drawing or diagram is located or in which you draw a shape

embed to paste an object into a destination file document so that a copy of the object and the source file as well as a link to the source program actually become a part of the destination file

endnotes footnotes that are listed at the end of a document instead of at the bottom of the page on which the note is referenced

field a placeholder for something that might change in a document, such as the page number or the current date

filename extension three letters that follow a period after the filename; the extension identifies the file type, for example, the extension *.doc* identifies a file created using Word

floating object an object that is not anchored to text on a page; you can reposition it by dragging it anywhere on the page

floating toolbar a toolbar positioned in the middle of the screen

followed hyperlink a link formatted with a different color to indicate that it has been clicked

font the design of letters and numbers

font size the size of characters in a document

font style the way characters look, for example, bold, italic, or underlined

footer text that appears at the bottom of every page in a document

footnotes notes at the bottom of the page on which they are referenced

form a method of collecting data in a structured format

form control a field that displays or requests information in a form

format the way something looks; the size, color, and style of a word or paragraph in a document

frame a section of a Web page that acts as if it were a different window or pane on the screen

gutter margin the margin on the binding side of a document

hanging indent a paragraph in which all of the lines following the first line are indented a specified amount

header text that appears at the top of every page in a document

hyperlink (link) specially formatted text or object that, when clicked, moves you to another location in the document, in another document, or on the Web

inactive document an open document in which you are not currently entering or editing text

index entries words in a document that you mark by inserting an index field

index field a field inserted in a document when you mark a word to be part of the index; when you create the index, the words marked with index fields are compiled and sorted

inline object an object that is positioned at the insertion point and is moved with the text around it

insertion point the place on screen where the next character you type will appear

justified text text or an object aligned along both the left and right margins

keywords words that have a specific meaning in a program in Visual Basic

landscape orientation a page set up to print sideways so that the page is wider than it is tall

left-aligned text text or an object aligned along the left margin

link *See* hyperlink

macro a single command that you execute to perform a series of commands

Mail Merge Wizard a series of six steps that leads you through the process of merging a main document with a list of names and addresses from a data source

main document the file (for example, a form letter) that contains the information that will be in every final merged document after merging with a data source

master document a document that contains a set of subdocuments related to it; you can display the subdocuments as part of the master document or as links

merge fields placeholders for the data that you will use from the data source

mirror margins inside and outside margins set up for odd and even pages

object an item that can be manipulated as a whole, for example, an image or a chart in a document

Office Clipboard the clipboard that comes with Office and can store up to 24 of the most recently cut or copied items from any Office program

organizational chart a graphical representation of a hierarchical structure

orphan the first line of a paragraph that is printed by itself at the bottom of a page or column

paste to copy into a document the text or object stored on the system or Office clipboard

pica a measurement for text equal to approximately 12 points

placeholder a section in a template that you can click once to select then type to replace the existing text

point (pt) measurement for text equal to approximately $\frac{1}{72}$ of an inch

portrait orientation a page set up to print lengthwise so that the page is taller than it is wide

pt *See* point

read-only a document that is protected so that users can open it to read the contents but not make any changes or add any comments to it

right-aligned text text or an object aligned along the right margin

section a part of a document with separate page formatting

select to highlight a word or words in a document; also, to click a command

sizing handles small white circles that appear around an object when it is selected; you can drag a handle to resize the object

smart tag a button that appears on screen when Word recognizes a word or phrase as belonging to a certain category, for example, a name or address

source file the file from which data or an object is copied so that it can be pasted into or linked to a destination file

statements lines of programming code in Visual Basic that execute a task

style a defined set of formats that you can apply to words or paragraphs

subdocuments shorter, related documents that are usually referenced in a master document by links

subroutine a series of statements in a program in Visual Basic that, when executed, perform a specific task

symbol a character not included in the standard English alphabet or Arabic numerals

system clipboard the clipboard that contains only the most recently cut or copied item

tab leader a dotted, dashed, or solid line before a tab stop

tab stop the location on the ruler where text moves when you press [Tab]

table of authorities a list of citations in a legal document

table of figures a list of all the illustrations in a document

task pane a panel that appears along the left or right of the screen and contains a set of related hyperlinks to program commands

template a set of styles and formats that determines how a particular type of document will look

theme a background design and set of colors for headings and other text in a Web page or site

toggle turn something on or off; make something, such as a command or toolbar button, active or inactive

toolbar a row of buttons that provide one-click access to frequently used commands

undo to automatically reverse the previous action by clicking the Undo command or button

version a document saved at some point during its creation or while editing it; versions are saved as part of the document in which they are created; they are not saved as separate files

view a way of looking at a document; Word offers four views: Normal, Print Layout, Outline, and Web Layout

widow the last line of a paragraph printed by itself at the top of a page or column

wizard a series of dialog boxes in which you answer questions and choose options to customize a template

word-processing program a program that makes it easy to enter text and manipulate that text in documents

word-wrap the process where the insertion point automatically moves to the next line in a document when it reaches the end of a line

wrap points the vertexes of an object where two lines meet or the highest point in a curve

zoom magnification of the document on screen

Excel 2002 Glossary

#DIV/0! A worksheet error indicating that you have attempted to divide a value by zero; to correct the error, change divisor so it refers to a number.

#N/A A worksheet error indicating that a value is not available to a formula, such as a missing function argument.

#NAME A worksheet error indicating that Excel does not recognize text used in a formula, such as a name that has not been defined.

#NUM A worksheet error indicating that formula numbers are incorrect, such as a function that has a text argument instead of a number.

#REF A worksheet error indicating that a cell reference is incorrect; can occur when you delete cells to which a formula refers.

#VALUE A worksheet error indicating that an operand, value, or argument in a formula is incorrect, such as one value in a function that requires a range.

.bmp The file extension on a Microsoft Windows Bitmap filename.

.emf The file extension on an Enhanced Metafile graphic filename.

.gif The file extension on a Graphics Interchange Format filename.

.jpg The file extension on a Joint Photographic Experts Group filename.

.png The file extension on a Portable Network Graphics filename.

.wmf The file extension on a Windows Metafile filename.

3-D Reference A cell or range reference in a worksheet formula that refers to a cell in another worksheet or set of worksheets, such as January:December!A6.

Absolute reference In an Excel formula, a cell reference that does not adjust when the formula is pasted to a new location; to make a reference absolute, select it, then press [F4] until there are dollar signs before both the row and column references. See also *Relative reference.*

Action menu A menu that appears when you click a smart tag. See also *Smart tag.*

Active cell The worksheet cell with a dark border; text or numbers you type appear in this cell and in the Formula bar; also called the *selected* or *highlighted cell.*

Alignment The placement of cell data in a cell; horizontally, cell contents can be left-, right-, or center-aligned; vertically, cell contents can be aligned with the top, middle, or bottom of a cell.

Area chart A line chart where the areas below the lines are shaded to emphasize their volume.

Argument ScreenTip As you type an Excel function, the yellow ScreenTip that appears to prompt you for each argument; click the function name in the ScreenTip to open a Help window describing the function.

Arguments Values, or cell or range references, usually in parentheses after the function name, on which an Excel function acts.

Arithmetic operators Operators, such as +, -, *, or /, representing addition, subtraction, multiplication, or division, that are used in formulas.

ASCII file Another name for a text file, which contains only data without any formatting.

Audit To analyze and check worksheet formulas and structure.

AutoCorrect Feature that automatically corrects common spelling errors; can be customized by each Excel user.

AutoFilter Data menu command that displays arrow next to field name in a list, allowing you to display a subset of list data.

AutoFit The Excel feature that lets you double-click a column heading to automatically resize the column to the width of its longest entry.

AutoFormat Predesigned combinations of shading, borders, fonts, fills, and alignment that you can apply to a worksheet or a range.

AutoShape Predrawn shapes such as brackets, stars, banners, or arrows that you can insert as objects on any worksheet or chart; insert using the AutoShapes menu on the Drawing toolbar.

AutoSum A button on the Standard toolbar that automatically inserts the SUM function in a cell; also lets you drag to select cells containing the data you want the function to calculate.

Bar chart A chart type that portrays data points as horizontal bars.

Border A line you can place on any or all sides of a worksheet cell using the Border button on the Formatting toolbar or the Border tab in the Format Cells dialog box.

Callout Text boxes with attached lines that you can add to call attention to chart or worksheet features.

Cancel button The X button in the Formula bar that you click to cancel an unentered cell entry and redisplay its original value.

Category axis The x-axis in an Excel chart; usually represents the categories into which data is divided, such as years or stores.

Cell In a worksheet, the intersection of a column and a row, where you enter text or numbers.

Cell address The column letter and row number that describe the exact location of any worksheet cell, such as C5.

Cell range See *Range.*

Cell reference The address of a cell, composed of its column letter and row number, such as C15 or D6; used in formulas to indicate the formula should use the value in the referenced cell.

Change history A worksheet you can have Excel create that lists all changes made in a shared workbook and notes the users who made them.

Chart Sometimes called a graph, a pictoral representation of numeric information; in Excel, you can chart data using presupplied pie, column, bar, line, and scatter charts, in addition to many custom chart types.

Chart sheet A worksheet that includes only a chart.

Chart Wizard A series of dialog boxes that lets you create a chart and customize it as you create it; to start the Chart Wizard, click the Chart Wizard button on the Standard toolbar.

Clear To delete; in Excel, you can clear a cell's content, format, comments or all of these using the Clear command on the Edit menu.

Clip Art Presupplied art organized by topic, that you can insert in your workbooks.

Clipboard See *Office clipboard.*

Close A File menu command that removes a file from your computer's temporary memory but leaves it on your disk; leaves the Excel program running.

Code Text and programming commands written in a programming language, such as **Visual Basic for Applications.**

Column chart A chart that portrays data points as vertical columns.

Column headings The boxed letters at the top of columns that uniquely identifies each one.

Column labels Text or numbers you enter above column data to identify the data in each column, such as "Salary" or "2003".

Comment indicator The small red triangle that appears in the upper right corner of a cell containing a comment.

Comments Electronic notes you can attach to any worksheet cell; useful when sharing documents with others in workgroups.

Comparison values In the VLOOKUP function, the values in a column that Excel compares to a specified value to determine whether it's the value for which you are searching.

Conditional format A format you can create and apply to numbers if a particular condition is true; for example, you can specify that any values over $100 in a selected range be displayed in red.

Consolidate To gather data from other worksheets in a summary worksheet.

Consolidate by category To combine data from multiple worksheets with different layouts and categories; in the summary sheet, Excel creates categories from all the worksheets referenced.

Consolidate by position To combine data from multiple worksheets with the same layout.

Constant A value that does not change; a range name can represent a constant such as a tax rate that you use frequently.

Criteria In an Excel list, conditions for displaying subset records, such as "zip>9000" or "income<20,000". See also *Subset* and *Record*.

Crop To cut off, usually part of a picture or graphic, using the cropping tool on the Picture toolbar.

Custom number formats Special formats you can create and apply to numeric data.

Data consolidation See *Consolidate*.

Data labels In an Excel chart, an option that displays the values, percentages, or other information for each data point.

Data marker In an Excel chart, a graphical representation of a single data point in a worksheet cell, such as a sales figure for a particular store.

Data point In an Excel chart, the representation of a single cell in a worksheet, such as the salary expense for one store for one month.

Data series A group of related data, such as store sales for several locations.

Data table A grid that appears under a chart and that contains the values on which the chart is based.

Data validation An Excel feature that lets you limit cell entries to acceptable values, such as whole numbers or a list of values you specify, such as "Yes" and "No."

Database file A file created in a database program; usually contains related data, such as customer and product information for one company. See also *Database file* and *Database program*.

Database program A program that lets you organize and analyze large amounts of information; see also *Field*, *Record*, and *Table*.

Delimiter In a text file, a character that separates columns of data, such as a tab, comma, space, semicolon, or a character of your choice.

Dependent In worksheet auditing, a cell that uses values in another cell, either directly or via another cell; in the formula =A5+A6, the cell containing the formula is a dependent of both cells A5 and A6. See also *Direct dependent*, *Indirect dependent*, and *Precedents*.

Destination document In object linking and embedding or in a database query, the location to which you link, embed, or export another file.

Direct dependent In worksheet auditing, a cell that uses a value in a selected cell.

Discussion comments Notes relating to a document that you share with others using a discussion server.

Document In the Visual Basic for Applications (VBA) programming language, to add and edit comment lines to describe who created and edited a macro.

Document Recovery task pane The window that opens on the left side of your screen in case your Excel session is interrupted by an unplanned computer shutdown, such as a power interruption; presents workbook version(s) the program "rescued" and prompts you to choose a version to save.

Drop areas In a PivotTable report, special areas representing rows, columns, data, and pages to which you can drag fields from the field list to produce summary information.

Embed To place a copy of a source object (text, graphic, or worksheet, for example) into another file (worksheet, word processing file, for example); changes to the source are not reflected in the destination document because there is no connection between the two.

Enter To accept a cell value; accomplished by clicking the Enter button on the Formula Bar, pressing [Enter], [Tab], or one of the keyboard arrow keys.

Exit To close a program such as Excel; you can use either the Exit command on the File menu, or the Close button on the Excel title bar, which closes both the program as well as any open documents, prompting you to save any changes you have made to them since you last saved them.

Explode To move a pie slice away from a pie chart.

Exponential trendline In an Excel chart, a line chart that projects future values assuming that the series will increase or decrease at an increasingly rapid rate over time.

Export To send data created in Excel to another program in a format it can read.

Extensible Markup Language (XML) A universal data-sharing format that Web designers and organizations use for structured data, such as the data in Excel spreadsheets; instead of being formatted, XML files are "marked up" with tags that describe the type of data they contain. Excel lets you save worksheets in XML format.

Extension See *File extension.*

External data range A range of worksheet data that originated outside of Excel that you can analyze, format, and update. See also *Refresh.*

External reference indicator The exclamation point that separates the sheet name from a cell reference in a 3-D reference. See also *3-D reference.*

Field In an Excel list, a column representing one type of data, such as Last Name. See also *Database file, Database program, Record,* and *Table.*

Field name The label above each column of field information in a list.

File extension The three letters after a filename that identify the program that created it, such as .xls for Excel files; to display or hide extensions on your screen, open any window at the Windows desktop, select Folder Options on the Tools menu, click the View tab, then select Show file extensions for known file types.

File format A file type that is readable by selected software; Excel can open files in the formats listed in the Files of type list in the Open dialog box, and can save files in the formats listed in the Files of type list in the Save dialog box.

Fill color The cell background color; to change, use the Fill Color list arrow on the Formatting toolbar.

Fill handle The small black square on the bottom right corner of a selected cell; drag it to copy cell contents to the dragged area.

Filter In an Excel list, to display only a selected amount of data, such as clients with 96820 showing in a zip code field, or suppliers showing prices less than $10 in a price field. See also *Field*.

Find An Edit menu command that helps you locate worksheet data.

Find and Replace An Excel feature that lets you find data you specify and replace it with other data you specify.

Folder A named storage location on a disk that lets you group and organize files.

Font A letter style, such as Arial, with formatting, such as boldface or italic.

Font size The height of a font, measured in points; one point equals 1/72 of an inch.

Footer Information that prints at the bottom of every worksheet page; can include text you type, the date, time, page number, sheet name, workbook name, or a picture.

Format To change the appearance of cell entries or cells to enhance their appearance and to make data more readily understandable to readers.

Format Painter The Excel feature that lets you click a button to copy a format from one cell and paste it to another.

Formatting toolbar The Excel toolbar that lets you change the font, font size, type style, alignment, number formats, fills, and colors of any selected cell(s); can appear on the same line as the Standard toolbar or below it.

Formula An equation or combination of values, cell references, and operators that calculate a result in the cell containing the formula; changing values or cell references in source cells causes formula to automatically recalculate.

Formula bar The bar that appears above the worksheet column headings; contains the name box, the box displaying formulas and contents of the active cell, and the Enter, Cancel, and Insert Function buttons.

Freeze To keep rows and columns in place while you scroll rows and columns in other parts of a worksheet.

Function An automatic formula supplied with Excel; consists of the function name and selected arguments, which are the cell references or values that the function uses to calculate a result.

Function Wizard A series of dialog boxes that lets you search for a function and then prompts you for each function argument; start the Function Wizard by clicking the Insert Function button on the Formula Bar.

Graphic A picture, photograph, or drawn object; picture formats include .jpeg, .tif, and .bmp. See *Table 8-1* for common formats.

Gridlines In a chart, horizontal or vertical lines that help a reader's eye align a data marker with an axis.

Header Information that prints at the top of every worksheet page; can include text you type, the date, time, page number, sheet name, workbook name, or a picture.

Help system The library of information you access using the Office Assistant, the Type a question for help box, or the Help menu; explains Excel features and commands.

Hide To keep from view, such as a cell formula.

Highlighted cell See *Active cell*.

HLOOKUP function An Excel function that searches horizontally across rows to locate a specific piece of information; for example, you could have Excel search a row of client names for the name "Jones," and then display the number for that client.

Hyperlink Words or graphics that you click to display (or "jump to") another location in a document, another document, or a location on the World Wide Web.

Hypertext Markup Language (HTML) A special file format that lets users view files using a Web browser.

I-beam pointer The I pointer that appears when you hold the pointer over a cell you are editing.

Import To bring data created in another program into Excel.

In-cell editing Double-clicking a cell to enable editing within the cell containing the formula, instead of editing in the Formula Bar.

Indented report formats In PivotTable reports, formats that apply shading and fonts, move column fields to the row area, indent each row field, and show data in a single column.

Indirect dependent In worksheet auditing, a cell that depends on cells, but only via other cells.

Input value In Excel data tables, a value that a formula uses to calculate a result; a data table calculates multiple results for multiple input values.

Insert Function button On the Excel Formula bar, the button that starts the Function Wizard, enabling you to search for, select, and enter any function.

Insertion point The blinking vertical line that appears in the Formula bar or in a cell when you edit cell contents; typed text or clicked cell addresses appear at this location.

Integrate To combine information from one program or document with information from another program or document. See also *Link* and *Embed*.

Interactive workbook An Excel workbook saved in HTML format that users can manipulate using their Web browsers.

Internet The world-wide network of computers and smaller networks.

Internet Explorer The Web browser developed by Microsoft Corporation that lets users explore the World Wide Web.

Intranet Computer networks within organizations used by a group of people, often employees of one company.

Keyword In the Excel online help system, a word you type on the Help tab to find a help topic.

Label See *Column labels* or *Row labels*.

Label prefix A character such as an apostrophe that you type before a number so Excel treats it as a label that will not be used in calculations.

Landscape orientation A worksheet print orientation in which the page is wider than it is tall.

Legend The color key that denotes the colors assigned to each point or data series in a chart.

Line chart A chart type where data points are portrayed as lines.

Linear trendline In an Excel chart, a line chart that projects future values assuming that the trend will continue at a steady rate.

Link To connect a source object (such as text, a graphic, or a worksheet) to a destination file (such as a worksheet, database, or word processing file) so that any changes to the source will automatically update in the destination file.

List A collection of data organized in columns and rows that you can filter or sort; the Excel equivalent of a database.

Lock To prevent cell changes; all Excel cells are locked by default, but locking only takes effect if you protect the worksheet.

Logical test The first segment in the IF function syntax, which states "IF a particular condition is true".

Look in list arrow In the Open and Save dialog boxes, the arrow that you click to navigate to different disks and folders on your computer to locate or save files.

Macro recorder An Excel feature that lets you name and save for reuse a set of worksheet actions you perform; Excel translates your actions into macro code using the Visual Basic programming language.

Macros Named command sequences that quickly and automatically perform common tasks.

Marquee The moving border that surrounds a cell when you click it to include it in a formula.

Menu bar The gray bar below the title bar; contains names of menus, which you click to view and select program commands to manipulate and analyze data.

Merge To combine the changes made by separate users to identical copies of a workbook.

Microsoft Access 2002 The database program that is part of Microsoft Office.

Microsoft PowerPoint 2002 A presentation graphics program that lets you create electronic slides to use as part of a presentation on a standalone computer or over the World Wide Web.

Microsoft Query A program that comes with Excel that lets you connect to a data source, specify the data location, then select the data you need.

Microsoft Word 2002 A word-processing program that lets you enter, edit, and format text, such as letters, reports, and books.

Mixed reference Used in an Excel formula when you need to keep one reference relative and one reference absolute, such as $A4 or A$4; in a mixed reference only the row or only the column reference remains the same when the formula is pasted to a new

location. See also *Absolute reference* and *Relative reference.*

Mode indicator Text on the left side of the status bar in the Excel window that tells which mode, or state, the Excel program is in, such as "Ready" or "Edit."

Module A storage area in a workbook where Excel stores macros.

Name box On the left side of the Formula bar, displays the address of the active cell or the cell name, if any.

New Workbook task pane The window on the right side of the Excel screen that lets you open new or existing documents, or start a new workbook using a template.

Normal Style The default number format, alignment, and font for text and numbers in Excel.

Object An item on a worksheet that you can move and resize, such as a chart or a graphic; a graphic object "floats" over the worksheet, and is not tied to a particular cell.

Object linking and embedding (OLE) A process that lets you import text, objects, or documents to other documents, either with (linking) or without (embedding) a connection between the source and the destination.

Office Clipboard An area in your computer's memory that contains up to 24 copied or cut items; view or select them in the Clipboard task pane.

Online help system The on-screen help capability in Excel that finds answers to your questions about using the program; each Microsoft Office program has an online help system.

Open A File menu command that reads the contents of a selected workbook into your computer's temporary memory, displaying it on the screen.

Operators See *Arithmetic operators.*

Order of precedence The order in which Excel processes operations in a formula with more than one operation, namely: 1) calculations inside parentheses; 2) exponents; 3) multiplication and division; then 4) addition and subtraction.

Page field The area at the top of the PivotTable report where you can place any field to filter the PivotTable data by that field; for example, placing the month field there would allow you to display data for one or more months.

Pane A section into which you can divide your worksheet using the split boxes at the top of the vertical and to the left of the horizontal scroll bars.

Password A word or word/number combination you can assign to a workbook, worksheet, or cell range that must be entered before use.

Pattern A design you can place in a worksheet cell or cell range, using the Patterns tab in the Format Cells dialog box.

Picture toolbar The toolbar that appears when you select a graphic object such as a picture; contains buttons for formatting the selected object.

Pie chart A chart that displays data series as pieces of a pie.

PivotChart report A specially formatted worksheet area to which you can drag fields to chart summary information for an Excel list.

PivotTable Field list In PivotTable reports and PivotChart reports, you can drag the window containing the data fields over the report to produce summary information.

PivotTable report A specially formatted interactive grid in a worksheet to which you can drag fields to produce summary information for an Excel list.

Plot area The area inside the chart axes, where a graphic representation of data appears.

Point A measurement unit equal to 1/72 of an inch; used to measure font height.

Pointer The shape that appears on the screen and moves around as you move the mouse; the pointer takes on different shapes as it moves over different objects—it can be an arrow or a cross, for example.

Pointing A method of including a cell address in formulas; instead of typing the address, you can point to the cell itself to insert its address.

Portrait orientation A worksheet print orientation in which the page is taller than it is wide.

Precedence See *Order of precedence.*

Precedents In worksheet auditing, any cells referred to and used in a formula. See also *Dependent, Direct dependent,* and *Indirect dependent.*

Preview To open the Print Preview window to see how your workbook will look as a printed document.

Primary key In a database such as Microsoft Access, the field that contains unique information for each record or row.

Print area An area you designate that prints when you click the Print button on the Standard toolbar.

Procedure In the Visual Basic for Applications (VBA) programming language, a sequence of statements that performs an action.

Project In the Visual Basic for Applications (VBA) programming language, a workbook.

Properties File features, such as the workbook author and when it was created or last modified, which identify the file and are updated automatically every time a workbook is saved; you can set some properties, such as the workbook author name or summary workbook information.

Protect To prevent locked cells from being changed, using the Protection tab in the Format Cells dialog box.

Publish In Microsoft Excel, to convert a file in Excel format to a file in HTML format that can be viewed on the World Wide Web.

Query In an Excel worksheet or in a database, a request you make to obtain specific data, such as data in particular fields or records; can include filtered and sorted data.

Query Wizard A series of Excel dialog boxes to help you select the fields you want to import from a data source.

Range A group of two or more contiguous worksheet cells, designated by the first and last cell, separated by a colon, such as A1:B6.

Range name A name you can assign to a cell range, such as Expenses or Revenue; you can then use the range names instead of cell references in formulas.

Range reference In a formula, a reference to a range of cells, consisting of the first and last cells in the range, separated by a colon; for example, A6:B6 is the reference for the range of all cells in row 6 under columns A and B.

Record In an Excel list, an individual item represented by a row, such as one customer in a customer list. See also *Database file, Database program, Table,* and *Field.*

Refresh To update Excel data that has been imported from an external source, such as a database, when the source data changes.

Regression analysis In statistics, a method of analyzing data trends that attempts to project future data based on past trends.

Relative reference In an Excel formula, a cell reference that adjusts when the formula is pasted to a new location; the Excel default. See also *Absolute reference.*

Report formats See *Indented report formats.*

Return To find and display; Excel functions return values you can view and manipulate in the worksheet.

Row headings The boxed numbers to the left of each row that uniquely identify each one.

Row labels Text or numbers you enter to the left of row data to identify the data in each row, such as "Expenses" or "3rd Quarter".

Run To have Excel perform the steps of a macro.

Save The File menu command that you use to save an already-named worksheet under the same name.

Save As The file menu command that you use to save a new or existing document under a different name, in a different format, and/or in a different location.

Scenario A named set of formula input values you can name and save so you can apply them to your worksheet and view their effect on formula results.

Scenario Summary A worksheet Excel adds that shows the results of a set of scenarios simultaneously.

ScreenTip A feature of the Excel help system, a yellow box that appears when you point to a toolbar button or a chart element and that contains the name of the element.

Selected cell See *Active cell.*

Sheet tab scroll buttons The buttons to the left of the sheet tabs that let you display sheet tabs that are hidden from view.

Sheet tabs The small tab at the bottom of each worksheet that you click to display that worksheet; double-click then type to rename.

Sizing handles Small black squares that surround a selected object; drag them to resize the object.

Smart tag An icon that automatically appears adjacent to cells after certain Excel actions, such as pasting; click a smart tag to display an action menu that presents options you can take relating to the action, such as retaining source formatting.

Sort To reorder list or database data according to one or more columns of data, such as by Last Name; a multi-level sort reorders first on one column (such as State) then within each state, reorders data on another field (such as Last Name).

Source document In object linking and embedding or in a database query, the original data that you link to, embed in, or import to another file.

Source program The program that originally created data that you import to Excel.

Spell check An Excel feature that lets you automatically check the spelling in your worksheet.

Split To unmerge cells into their original component cells.

Spreadsheet A program that lets you organize and analyze information using a grid of columns and rows, in conjunction with analysis tools, including simple and advanced mathematical and statistical calculations and charting.

Spreadsheet functionality In the Publish as Web Page dialog box, an option that lets users enter, format, calculate, analyze, sort, and filter all kinds of data.

Standard toolbar The Excel toolbar, usually beneath the menu bar, that lets you perform standard Excel program tasks, such as opening, saving, printing, totaling, and charting data.

Start To open a program such as Excel, usually using the Programs subcommand on the Start menu, which is on the left side of the Windows taskbar; procedure may differ for networked computers.

Start menu The button on the far left side of the Windows taskbar; click it to see the Programs submenu, which you click to start any Microsoft Office program.

Statement In a macro, a line of Visual Basic for Applications (VBA) code.

Status bar The bar at the bottom of the Excel screen that displays information such as the program status and the total of selected cells.

Style A named collection of cell or number formats that you can apply to other cells for conveniently formatting worksheets; if you change a style definition, all cells with that style applied are also changed.

Stylesheets Documents that Web developers apply to XML files to specify formatting.

Sub procedure In the Visual Basic for Applications (VBA) programming language, a series of statements that performs an action.

Subset In an Excel list, a group of records that has been filtered to display only selected records. See also *Record* and *Filter*.

SUM The most commonly used function in Excel; sums a range of numbers.

Syntax The arrangement of elements within a function.

Tab split bar The small bar on the left side of the horizontal scroll bar below the worksheet; drag to enlarge tab area or double-click to return to original position.

Tab-delimited text file A text file containing only data but no formatting, in which data columns are separated by a character called a delimiter (such as a tab), and in which lines of data are separated by return characters.

Table In a database, a grid of rows and columns containing all the information for a particular part of a database, such as a company's customers or suppliers; See also *Database file, Database program, Record and Field.*

Table formats In PivotTable reports, sets of formatting features you can apply; table formats leave the PivotTable report data with its original organization.

Target The destination of a hyperlink; the location a hyperlink displays, or "jumps to," when you click the hyperlink.

Task pane A window that opens on the right side of the Excel screen at selected times as you use the Excel program; Excel task panes include the New Workbook, Clipboard, Search, and ClipArt task panes.

Template A workbook file with an .xlt file extension that you use as a basis for creating a new workbook using the same design; can contain text, formatting, formulas, macros, charts, or data.

Text annotations Text in shapes, boxes, or callouts that you can add to a worksheet or chart in Excel.

Text file A file that contains unformatted data.

Threaded Placed one after another, such as discussion comments, so a reader can follow the discussion "thread" or path.

Tick marks Small lines on chart axes that denote measurement intervals.

Title bar The blue bar at the top of the program window; contains the workbook and program titles on the left and the Minimize, Maximize, and Close buttons on the right.

Toggle A button or menu command that works like an on/off switch; click once to activate, then click again to deactivate the feature it represents.

Trace To find, as in tracing dependents when auditing a worksheet.

Tracer arrows In worksheet auditing, blue arrows that connect a selected cell to its dependents or precedents. See also *Dependents* and *Precedents*.

Track To keep a record of workbook changes; to track changes, use the Track Changes command on the Tools menu.

Trendline A special Excel line chart that projects future values based on past trends.

Typeface A style of letters such as Arial or Times New Roman, available from the Fonts list on the Formatting toolbar.

Up One Level button In the Open and Save dialog boxes, the icon that lets you move up one level in the disk structure as you locate disks, folders, and files.

Updating In object linking, the process that replaces the information in the destination object with more current information from the source object.

Value axis The Y axis on an Excel chart; usually contains the values, such as dollars.

Values The numbers in a cell; can be used in calculations.

Variable A value that changes; data tables calculate results based on different possible values for a variable, such as an interest rate.

Visual Basic Editor The Visual Basic program window in which you can enter and edit code to create macros. See also *Macro*.

Visual Basic for Applications (VBA) A programming language Excel uses to create macros.

VLOOKUP function An Excel function that searches vertically through columns to locate a specific piece of information; for example, you could have Excel search a column of client names for the name "Jones," and then display the number for that client. See also *HLOOKUP function*.

Watch window A window you can have appear at the bottom of your screen displaying a cell's address, value, and formula.

Web browser A program that lets you view documents on the World Wide Web, such as Internet Explorer.

What-if analysis An analysis method that lets you explore how changing worksheet values will affect formula results; trendlines are another form of what-if analysis that project values based on trends.

Wildcard In searching worksheets or workbooks, a character that represents one or more characters; the * wildcard represents one or more characters, while the ? wildcard represents any single character.

WordArt Shaped, formatted words that you can add to any worksheet or chart using the Insert WordArt button on the Drawing toolbar.

Workbook An Excel file with an .xls file extension; contains one or more worksheets, which contain columns and rows that enable you to organize and analyze numeric information.

Workgroup A group of people in an organization who work together and who share documents, often electronically.

Worksheet An electronic ledger within an Excel workbook, containing a grid of rows and columns you use to store and analyze data.

Worksheet area In the Excel window, the grid of columns and rows that holds text, values, and formulas you enter.

Workspace An Excel file with an .xlw file extension that contains the location, window sizes, and display settings of workbooks you specify; instead of opening each individual file, you open the workspace file, which automatically opens the workbooks in the arrangement and settings you specified.

World Wide Web (WWW) A series of documents called Web pages, in HTML format, connected by hyperlinks over the Internet.

XML parser A program with the ability to open and display XML code; Internet Explorer 5.5 has an XML parser.

Zoom In Print Preview, the ability to get a closer view of your worksheet.

Access 2002 Glossary

action query one of four queries (make-table, append, delete, or update), all of which change data when you run them

administrator the user who has all permissions to all database activities, including modifying the workgroup information file

aggregate functions functions such as SUM, COUNT, or MAX, that allow you to create statistics on groups of records

Analyze It with Microsoft Excel a tool used to export a set of records to Microsoft Excel

AND conditions two or more criteria entered in the same row of Query Design View, each of which must be true for a given record to display in Query Datasheet View

append query an action query that adds the fields and records selected in the query to the designated table

application an Access database that has been customized to meet the needs of a particular audience

AutoForm a tool used to quickly create a new form based on the selected table or query

AutoFormat a collection of formatting characteristics and design elements that you apply to a given form or report

AutoNumber a data type that Access controls and sequentially increments by one integer for each new record

Avg an aggregate function that averages the values in the given field

back-end database in a split database situation, the database that stores all the table objects

blank database template a template that creates a database with no objects

Briefcase a special type of folder designed to help keep files that are used on two computers synchronized

brown-out a dip in power that sometimes causes computer damage

browser software used to find, download, and display Web pages

calculated control a text box control that contains an expression that calculates a value

calculated field a field created in Query Design View (using an expression) whose contents depend on the values in other fields

Cascade Delete Related Records an option that you can impose on a one-to-many relationship; if a record in the "one" side of the relationship is deleted, all matching records from the "many" table will also be deleted

Cascade Update Related Fields an option that you can impose on a one-to-many relationship; if the value of the linking field in the "one" side of the relationship is updated, all matching fields in the "many" table will also be updated

Category field a field used in the x-axis area on a chart

class modules modules containing VBA code that can be used within a given form or report

client in most client/server computing environments, the user's PC

client/server computing two or more information systems cooperatively processing to solve a problem

combo box a data entry control that provides the features of both the list box control and the text box control

Command Button Wizard a wizard used to create a command button for a form

Compact on Close a feature that automatically compacts and repairs your database every time you close it

Compacting rearranging the database on your hard disk to reuse space formerly occupied by deleted objects

comparison operators characters such as > (greater than) or < (less than) that you can use to further define criteria in a filter or query

constant a value that never changes

control any item on a form or report such as a label, text box, or command button

Count an aggregate function that counts the number of values in the given field

criteria limiting conditions that determine which records are displayed in a particular view

crosstab query a query that creates a summarized presentation of records by grouping data by one or more fields

Crosstab Query Wizard a wizard that helps you create a crosstab query

Currency a data type that allows a field to store only monetary values

custom functions new user-created functions created within a module using VBA code

DAP *see data access page*

data access page a special type of Web page that maintains a connection with the database

data type determines what type of data (text, numbers, dates, pictures) can be stored by a field

data validation a process that compares a field entry with criteria that define a set or range of acceptable entries for a field

database developer one who creates new database objects such as queries, forms, and reports

database normalization the process of determining how tables should be organized and related

database password a password that must be entered to open the database file

Database Splitter a feature that splits a database into two files: the back-end database that stores all the data, and the front-end database that stores all the other database objects

database user anyone who enters, edits, views, or uses database information, but doesn't design or create new database objects

Database window displays the name of the current database in its title bar and has icons that represent the existing database objects

Database window toolbar a toolbar at the top of the Database window that helps you create, modify, or view objects

Database Wizard a wizard that provides sample databases and database options from which you can choose to quickly create a new database

datasheet a spreadsheet-like grid that stores data

Datasheet View a view of a table or query used to enter and edit data in a spreadsheet-like format

date calculated control a text box control that uses an Access function to calculate and display today's date on a report

Date function an Access function that displays today's date in the m/d/yyyy format

Date/Time a data type that allows a field to store only valid dates and times

decrypt to reverse the encryption process

default switchboard the switchboard that opens first when using more than one switchboard in a database

delete query an action query that deletes the fields and records selected in the query

delimited text file a file of unformatted data where each field value is separated by a common character, such as a comma or a tab; used to convert data from proprietary software into a format that other programs can import

Design Master the original database from which replicas are made

Design View a view used to modify the structure of an object

Detail a section that prints once for every record

development database a test database used by a database developer to create and test new objects

dynamic the ability of a Web page linked to a database to reconnect to the database to display up-to-date data every time the Web page is opened or refreshed

encrypt to make database objects indecipherable to other programs

export to convert data from an Access database to an external file, such as a Word document

expression any combination of field names, constants, and operators used to create a value

Extensible Markup Language a standard file format that is used to deliver data from one application to another over an intranet or the World Wide Web; an XML file

Extensible Schema Document a file that accompanies an XML file to further define the structure of the data stored in the XML file; an XSD file

Extensible Style Language a file that accompanies an XML file to further define formatting information about the data; an XSL file

field one category of information such as a person's title, city, or country

field list in Form Design View or Report Design View, a list of fields from the selected record source

file extension one to three characters attached to the end of a filename, which tells the computer what type of information is stored in a file; Access uses the mdb file extension

filter a tool used to temporarily isolate a subset of records in a Datasheet View or in Form View

Filter by Form a filter tool that allows you to specify more than one limiting condition for filter criteria

Filter by Selection a filter tool that allows you to quickly isolate a subset of records that match the value that is currently selected

First an aggregate function that returns the value from the first record in the record source

foreign key field the field on the "many" side of a one-to-many relationship used to tie the "many" table to the "one" table

form an Access object that provides an easy-to-use data entry screen

Form Design View a view used to define the layout and formatting characteristics of a form

Form View a view of a form that is used to enter and edit data

Form Wizard a wizard that helps you quickly create a new form

formatting changes the way something appears, but not its actual value

front-end database in a split database, it stores all the database objects except for the table objects (the front-end database contains linked table objects that link it to data stored in the back-end database)

function a built-in formula that helps you quickly build an expression

global modules appear in the Database window when you click the Modules button on the Objects bar; they contain VBA code that can be used throughout the database

Group Footer a section that prints after every group of records

Group Header a section that prints before every group of records

Grouping sorting records in ascending or descending order based on the value of a field and providing a header and/or footer section before or after the records that contain the same value for that field

Help system a collection of definitions, examples, and linked documents that provide extensive information about Access

HTML *see Hypertext Markup Language*

HTML template a file that contains formatting characteristics, such as font sizes and colors, that you can apply to Web pages in order to give them a consistent appearance

Hyperlink a data type that stores Web page addresses

Hypertext Markup Language the language used to create Web pages

import to convert data from an external data source, such as an Excel workbook into an Access database

Import Spreadsheet Wizard a wizard used to import data from an Excel workbook into an Access database

Input Mask a field property that specifies the number and types of characters that can be entered into a field, and also defines a visual guide as data is entered into a field

Input Mask Wizard a wizard that helps you determine an input mask

junction table a table that establishes separate one-to-many relationships with two tables that have a many-to-many relationship

Last an aggregate function that returns the value from the last record in the record source

Limit to List a field lookup property that limits the values for the selected field to those in the list

linked table a link to data stored in a "real" table in another database

Linked Table Manager a tool used to change the path between the original table and linked table

linking field the field that is common to two tables and used to tie them together in a one-to-many relationship

lookup field a field that contains a drop-down list of values that are provided by Lookup properties

Lookup properties properties which provide a drop-down list of values for a field

Lookup Wizard a wizard that helps you identify the list of values for a lookup field

macro a database object that stores a set of actions that can be automatically replayed by running the macro

Macro Design View a view used to define macro actions

main form a form that contains a subform control

main report a report that contains a subreport control

make-table query an action query that creates a new table of data based on the fields and records selected in the query

many-to-many relationship the relationship between two tables when one record in one table is related to many records in the other table, and vice versa

Max an aggregate function that finds the maximum value in the given field

MDE file a special copy of a database that prevents others from opening or editing a form, report, or module in Design View

Memo a data type that allows a field to store lengthy text beyond 255 characters

Merge It with Microsoft Word a tool used to export Access data to a Microsoft Word document to create a mail merge

Microsoft Visual Basic window a window used to write Visual Basic for Applications (VBA) programming code

Min an aggregate function that finds the minimum value in the given field

module a database object that stores Visual Basic for Applications (VBA) programming code

multi-user a database's ability to support many people entering and updating data at the same time

navigation buttons buttons on the navigation toolbar that help you move through the displayed records

navigation toolbar a toolbar in the lower-left corner of Datasheet View and Form View that contains navigation buttons

Now function an Access function that displays both today's date as well as the current time

Number a data type that allows the field to store only valid numeric entries

objects the major parts of a database; the object types include tables, queries, forms, reports, pages, macros, and modules

Objects bar a bar that is positioned on the left side of the Database window, which gives you access to the seven types of objects used to store and manage data in a database

Office Assistant an animated character that provides tips and interactive prompts that offer assistance while you are working

OfficeLinks a set of tools used to export Access data to Microsoft Excel and Microsoft Word

OLE Object a data type that stands for Object Linking and Embedding; it allows a field to link or embed an external file such as an Excel workbook, a photo, or a sound clip

one-to-many relationship the relationship between two tables when one record in the "one" table is linked to many records in the "many" table

one-to-one relationship the relationship between two tables when one record in one table is related to one record in another table, and vice versa

operators a symbol representative of a particular action, such as + (add), - (subtract), * (multiply), / (divide), and ^ (exponentiation)

OR conditions two or more criteria entered in two or more rows of Query Design View, only one of which must be true for a given record to display in Query Datasheet View

orphan records a record in the "many" table of a one-to-many relationship that doesn't have a matching record in the "one" table

page a database object that creates dynamic Web pages

Page Design View a view used to create and modify data access pages

Page Footer a section that prints at the bottom of every page

Page Header a section that prints at the top of every page (but below the report header on page one)

Page View a view that displays the final data access page just as it will appear in Internet Explorer

Page Wizard a wizard that quickly creates new data access pages

parameter criteria a query criterion that prompts you for the actual criteria entry each time you run the query

parameter query a query that contains parameter criteria

permissions   activities that users are allowed to complete with various objects, as defined by the workgroup information file

PivotChart a graphical presentation of data in a PivotTable that you can use to sort, filter, and analyze data interactively

PivotChart control a control used to add a PivotChart to a DAP (dynamic access page)

PivotTable a presentation of data that calculates statistics about groups of records, and with which you can interactively sort, filter, and analyze the data in new ways

PivotTable List control a control used to create a PiviotTable

Preview a view of an object that shows how it will look when it is printed

primary key field contains unique data for each record

production database a database that's used on a regular basis by database users

properties individual characteristics of an item such as a field, control, or object

Properties button a button on many different toolbars that opens the property sheet for the selected object, control, or section

property sheet a window that displays all the properties for a selected item

Publish It with Microsoft Word a tool used to export data to Microsoft Word

query a database object that selects fields and records from one or more tables and displays them in a datasheet

Query Datasheet View a view used to view, enter, edit, and delete data in a spreadsheet-like arrangement of data compiled by a query

query design grid the lower pane of Query Design View that determines which fields and records (and their order) will be displayed by Query Datasheet View

Query Design View a view used to define the fields and records to be displayed in Query Datasheet View

record all the fields for one item in a table, such as all the fields that describe an employee

record source a table or query that a form, report, or page object is based on

Record Source property a form or report property that determines which record source will be displayed in a form or report

recordset the fields and records that are displayed when you open an object as determined by the object's Record Source property

referential integrity a set of rules that, when applied to a one-to-many relationship, helps you keep inappropriate data from being entered into the database, and helps you from creating orphan records in a database

relational database a database that contains multiple tables linked together in one-to-many relationships

replica a special copy of a database that keeps track of changes so that you can resynchronize the copy with another copy of the database

replica set the Design Master and all replicas created from the Design Master

replication the process of creating copies, called replicas, of a database

report a database object whose main purpose is to create a professional printout

Report Design View a view used to define the layout and formatting characteristics of a report

Report Footer a section that prints at the end of the entire report

Report Header a section that prints at the top of the first page of the report

Report Wizard a wizard that helps you quickly create a new report

ScreenTip descriptive information that automatically appears in a small box when you point to a toolbar button

sections areas of a report that determine where and how often the controls placed within those areas print on the report

security account passwords passwords defined by the workgroup information file that give different users different permissions to various objects

select query a type of query that selects fields and records from one or more tables and displays them in a datasheet

Series field a field used in the legend area on a chart

server in most client/server computing environments, a shared file server, mini-, or mainframe computer

Simple Query Wizard a wizard that helps you build a select query

sorting to arrange records in either ascending or descending order based on the contents of a field

spike a surge in power that sometimes causes computer damage

startup options commands that are automatically applied to your database when you open it

StDev an aggregate function that calculates the standard deviation of the values in the given field

subdatasheet a datasheet within a datasheet

subform a control within a form that displays another form

SubForm Wizard a wizard that assists you in creating a subform control

subreport a control within a report that displays another report

SubReport Wizard a wizard that assists you in creating a subreport control

Sum an aggregate function that totals the values in the given field

surge protector equipment that protects a computer from a power spike

switchboard a special form that helps users navigate through the database

Switchboard Manager a tool used to create and modify switchboard forms

synchronization the process of reconciling the changes between the replicas and the Design Master so that all databases contain the latest updates

table a database object that stores all the data in the database

Table Datasheet View a view used to view, enter, edit, and delete data in a spreadsheet-like arrangement

Table Design View a view used to enter, modify, and delete fields in a table

Table Wizard a wizard that provides sample tables and fields from which you can choose to create a new table

template a sample database for a subject area such as inventory, event, contact, or expense management, which you can use to quickly create your own database

Text a data type that allows a field to store any combination of text or numbers up to 255 characters

Text Box button a button on the Toolbox toolbar that allows you to add a new text box control to a form, page, or report

txt a file extension for a text file

Uninterruptible Power Supply equipment that maintains constant power to computer equipment during power brown-outs, spikes, and total loss of power; UPS

update query an action query that updates field values as defined in the query for the records selected in the query

UPS *see Uninterruptible Power Supply*

Validation Rule a field property used to set criteria for data validation

Validation Text a field property used to display a message if a user attempts to enter an unacceptable value into the field (as determined by the criteria in the Validation Rule property)

value the data that you enter into a field, such as Mark in the FirstName field

Var an aggregate function that calculates the variance of the values in the given field

VBA *see Visual Basic for Applications*

VBA password a password that prevents unauthorized users from modifying VBA code

view a presentation of an object that supports different database activities

Visual Basic for Applications a programming language packaged within each program of the Microsoft Office suite that can be used to extend the features of the software; VBA

W3C *see World Wide Web Consortium*

workgroup a list of database users who have the same needs

workgroup information file a file that contains user IDs, passwords, and permissions; used to create a secure database

World Wide Web Consortium an international league of companies and associations that support initiatives and standards that sustain the growth and health of the World Wide Web; also known as the W3C

XML *see Extensible Markup Language*

XML document a text file that contains data and XML tags to identify field names and field values

XSD *see Extensible Schema Document*

XSL *see Extensible Style Language*

Yes/No a data type that stores only one of two values: Yes or No

Outlook 2002 Glossary

Address Book A collection of names, addresses, phone numbers, and other information that can be used to quickly and easily address e-mail messages and keep track of people.

Answer Wizard tab A tab in the Help dialog box that lets you type a question or keyword in a box and search for related Help topics.

Appointment An Outlook item that is an activity, such as a meeting or phone call, that takes place on a specific day at a specific time.

Appointment area The section of the Calendar that resembles a yellow pad of paper and is divided into time slots where you can enter and view your appointments.

Appointment form A form where you enter detailed information about or make changes to a particular appointment.

Appointment tab The tab on the Meeting Request form used to enter details about a meeting, such as the subject, location, and invitees.

Archive A file for storing old Outlook items that you no longer want in your primary Outlook folders, but want to keep for future reference.

Ask a Question box A box at the right end of the Outlook menu bar into which you can type a question or keywords to access the Help system.

Attachment A file that is sent with an e-mail message to be downloaded or viewed by the recipient.

AutoArchive An Outlook feature that automatically removes files from your Inbox and other folders that you specify and places them in an archive file, where they are still accessible but out of the way.

AutoPreview A way of viewing messages in the Inbox. It displays the first three lines of every message.

Calendar The folder in Outlook used to store information about your schedule.

Category A keyword (or keywords) you can assign to an Outlook item. Categories make it possible to sort items into related groups.

Contact An entry in the Contacts folder that stores information about a particular person such as name, addresses, and phone numbers.

Contacts The folder in Outlook used to store information about people, such as names, addresses, phone numbers, and e-mail addresses.

Contents tab A tab in the Help dialog box that displays a comprehensive listing of all the Help topics available.

Date Navigator A small calendar located in the upper-right corner of the Calendar window. You can go to or display a date in any of the Calendar views by clicking it in the Date Navigator.

Deleted Items A folder in Outlook that stores items that have been removed using the Delete command

Dialog box A window from which you need to make selections or in which you need to type information in order for a task to be completed.

Drafts A folder in Outlook that stores in-progress e-mail messages that have not yet been sent.

e-mail Electronic mail messages transmitted over a computer network.

Event In Outlook, a full-day appointment.

Find bar A bar you open by clicking the Find button on the Standard toolbar. It lets you search for items by typing relevant keywords.

Folder A storage area on a computer disk used to organize files.

Folder banner A horizontal bar located just above the Outlook Bar in the Outlook program window that displays the name of the open folder.

Folder List A list that displays the folders and sub-folders available in Outlook.

Footer Text you can specify to print at the bottom of every page.

Full menu A menu that displays its entire available list of commands. To open a full menu, click the double arrows at the bottom of a short menu.

Header Text you can specify to print at the top of every page.

Index tab A tab in the Help dialog box that lets you search for Help topics by typing particular keywords.

Item A basic piece of information that is stored in an Outlook folder, such as an e-mail message or a Calendar appointment.

Journal A folder in Outlook that stores log entries that describe completed tasks or events that have occurred.

Journal entry An Outlook item that describes how you have spent time, such as the time spent completing a task or the results of a conference call.

Landscape A print orientation that prints a document in a wide format.

Meeting Request A type of e-mail message that requests the presence of the e-mail recipient at a meeting. A Meeting Request informs you of the location and subject of the meeting as well as the date and time. You can accept, decline, or propose a new meeting time for any Meeting Request you receive.

Meeting Request form A form used to invite attendees to a meeting.

Menu bar The bar located below the title bar of the Outlook program window that contains menu names. To open a menu, click a menu name.

Message form A window that displays the full text of an e-mail message and which you can use to write and send an e-mail message.

Note A computerized "sticky note" you can place anywhere on your screen as a reminder or note to yourself.

Note form The form you use to create Notes (computerized "sticky notes") in Outlook.

Notes A folder in Outlook that stores electronic "sticky notes" for recording thoughts, notes, ideas, and reminders.

Outbox A folder in Outlook that stores completed e-mail messages that have not yet been sent to the server for delivery.

Outlook Bar The bar along the left edge of the Outlook program window that contains icons for Outlook folders as well as shortcuts to My Computer, My Documents, Favorites, and other shortcuts you can specify.

Outlook Today folder The folder in Outlook that displays an at-a-glance view of the items in your Calendar, Tasks, and Inbox folders.

Outlook Update A folder in Outlook that opens the Microsoft Office Web site where you access resources, tools, and assistance for Outlook users.

Portrait A print orientation that prints a document in a tall format.

Preview pane A window that opens in the lower half of the View pane when the Inbox is open. It displays the text of the selected message.

Print style A format you choose for printing Outlook items. For example, Print styles for the Calendar include Daily, Weekly, and Monthly, among others.

Profile A group of e-mail accounts and address books set up for a particular user of Outlook.

Resource In Outlook, the name for a special piece of equipment such as a flip chart, monitor, or computer that you need to reserve for a meeting.

Scheduling tab The tab on the Meeting Request form used to view the schedules of all the meeting attendees and then set a meeting time that works for all.

Sent Items A folder in Outlook that stores e-mail messages that have been delivered.

Signature A block of information that is automatically appended to the end of an outgoing e-mail message.

Task An errand or activity you need to perform and that you can track through completion. Tasks are stored in the Tasks folder.

Task form A form you use to enter details about a particular task, including the subject, due date, and start date of the task.

TaskPad A window located in the lower-right corner of the Calendar window that displays a list of the tasks stored in your Tasks folder.

Tasks folder The folder in Outlook that stores information about to-do list items.

Text Only format A format you can save mail messages in that saves the text of a message but does not preserve the formatting of the original message.

Title bar The bar located at the top of the Outlook program window. It contains the name of the open folder or item, and the Minimize, (or Maximize), Restore, and Close buttons.

Toolbar A bar located just above the Folder banner that contains buttons you can click to perform tasks appropriate for the current folder.

View A particular way to display the items in an Outlook folder.

View pane The large area to the right of the Outlook Bar in the Outlook program window, where you view the contents of the current folder.

Voting buttons Buttons that appear in the Message form that let you quickly provide a response to an e-mail message. For instance, Yes/No voting buttons could be included in an e-mail message to make it easy for a recipient to respond quickly to a question.

Ways to Organize pane A window that lets you assign new or existing categories to your Outlook items.

PowerPoint 2002 Glossary

Action button A premade button that you can use to create hyperlinks for commonly used activities such as navigating among slides and playing sounds or video.

Animated gif files Files that contain multiple static images that stream to create an animated effect and that have the file extension .gif.

Animation The motion of text and objects on a slide along with special visual and sound effects.

Animation schemes Preset visual effects that you can apply to text on a slide that make the text move in specific ways. Animation schemes are divided into three categories: Subtle, Moderate, and Exciting, to help you choose just the right animation for your presentation and audience.

Ask a Question box A box on the menu bar in which you can type a question to access the Help system to get help on a topic.

Assistant shape Item at a lower hierarchical level in an organization chart that connects to any other shape with an elbow connector.

AutoContent wizard Series of dialog boxes that asks you to choose your presentation purpose and how you plan to present it, and then creates a presentation with sample content and a professional-looking design.

AutoShapes Group of ready-made graphics that come with PowerPoint and include basic shapes such as squares and circles as well as elaborate shapes such as banners and stars.

Background The color or design that appears as a canvas behind the text on a slide which you can change or modify or to which you can apply one of PowerPoint's special effects.

Bitmap image An image stored as a series of small dots. The most common bitmap image file format is .bmp, but others are .jpg, .tif, .png, and .gif.

Browser Special software used to view Web pages, such as Opera, Internet Explorer, and Netscape Navigator.

Categories Data represented along the horizontal or X-axis of a chart.

Cell The basic unit of a table; the intersection of a column and a row.

Chart A graphic presentation of data useful for showing trends or comparisons.

Clip art A collection of ready made images available through the Clip Organizer that you can use to enhance your presentation.

Clip Organizer The repository for storing, organizing, and retrieving clips in Office XP programs.

Clips Media files such as drawings, images, photographs, sounds and video stored in the Clip Organizer for Office XP programs.

Color scheme A set of eight colors that is consistently applied to fonts, accents, hyperlinks, backgrounds, and fills.

Column head The first row of a table, used to identify the content of each column.

Compressing images Reducing the file size of an image. Does not affect the physical measurements of the image.

Coworker shapes Items in an organization chart that show peers within the hierarchy at an equal level to each other.

Custom show PowerPoint feature that lets you customize a single presentation for several different audiences, letting you show only slides that will be relevant to the needs of a particular audience.

Data series The information in a datasheet row that is represented in a chart with a unique color.

Datasheet A table made up of lettered columns and numbered rows, which intersect to form cells, and which provides placeholder text and numbers that you can replace with new data.

Design template A file that contains all the specifications for how a presentation looks, including background designs, color schemes, fonts, and layout.

Destination file The file that contains a linked or embedded object.

Embedded object An object created in one program (such as a worksheet created in Excel) and placed into another (such as PowerPoint. Clicking the embedded object activates the source program so you can make changes to the object using the source program's tools. Changes to the object in the destination file are not reflected in the source file.

Embedding Inserting an object created in another program, called a **source program,** into your presentation. Once you embed an object into a presentation, the object becomes part of the presentation file and no longer has a connection to the **source file,** where the object was originally created, though it does stay connected to the program where it was created.

Embedding fonts Feature that lets you package the font file that defines a particular set of fonts directly in the presentation file so that all the fonts in your presentation can be displayed on any computer.

Excel 2002 The spreadsheet program included with the Microsoft Office XP software.

Fill effects Special effects such as patterns or shading used to enhance a slide background.

Folder A subdivision on a computer's hard disk used to organize files.

Footer Text information, such as the date, the presentation name, your company name, or the slide number, that appears at the bottom of every slide, notes page, or handout.

Handout Master Specifies how the slides will be positioned on the handouts and also lets you change the header and footer.

Handouts Printed copies of your slides containing 1, 2. 3. . or 9 slides per page that you can provide your audience to help them follow the presentation.

Hidden slides Slides that you designated not to show or print for a particular audience.

Hyperlink Text or an object on a slide that you click to connect to another location. In PowerPoint you can add hyperlinks on a slide to connect to another slide in the same presentation, a slide in another presentation, or a Web page on the Internet.

Hypertext Markup Language (HTML) The computer language format for all pages that are viewed through browsers on the World Wide Web.

Intranet A network of interlinked computers that is restricted to a specific company or group of people.

Kiosk A computer used to display information in a remote setting such as a mall or building lobby.

Layout The organization of text and graphics on a slide.

Legend Identifies each data series and its assigned color in the chart, each of which is identified by the labels in the first row and first column of the datasheet.

Linked object An object created in one program (such as a Word table) that is inserted into another program (such as PowerPoint), where the inserted object remains connected to the source file so that any changes made to the object in the source file are reflected in the object in the destination file.

Lobby page Page created by PowerPoint when you set up an online broadcast that serves as an introduction for your audience and contains information about the title, subject, host name, and time of the broadcast. Appears in the viewer's browser before the broadcast begins.

Meeting Minder Feature that lets you keep track of meeting minutes, or record action items while the slide show is running.

Menu bar Bar located below the title bar in the PowerPoint window that contains the menus for accessing PowerPoint commands. You click a menu to open it.

Normal view The view where you create and modify slides, and which has four work areas: the **Outline tab**, the **slides tab**, the **Slide pane** and the **Notes pane.**

Notes pages Printed pages that contain a copy of the slides along with presenter notes on what to say about each slide.

Notes pane In Normal view, the area below the Slide pane where you type notes for the presentation. Notes appear on the Notes pages.

Online broadcast A live performance of your presentation that is captured and delivered over the Web or a network to viewers through a browser.

Organization charts Graphic diagram used to show the hierarchy of employees in a business or relationships of things or people to each other. Often called **org charts.**

Outline tab In Normal view, the tab that displays all the text that is in text and title placeholders in a presentation.

Pack and Go Wizard Creates a neat package that includes all the required files to run your presentation on any remote computer. You can pack your presentation to a floppy disk, to your hard disk, or across a network to another computer.

Page numbers Slide numbers on printed notes pages and handouts that are contained in the header or footer.

PowerPoint Viewer A special program that makes it possible to run a PowerPoint slide show even if PowerPoint is not installed

PowerPoint 2002 The presentation graphics program that is part of the Microsoft Office XP suite.

Presentation A PowerPoint file, that has a .ppt file extension.

Presentation window Work area in the PowerPoint window where you create the presentation, and which contains three areas, the Slide pane, the Outline tab, Slides tab, and the Notes pane.

Preserve a master Feature that keeps a slide master from being deleted if no slides use it in the presentation. A pushpin icon next to a master indicates it is preserved.

Preview Shows how your slides will print using the current print settings before you actually print them.

Profile A group of email accounts and address books assigned to a single user in Microsoft Outlook.

Publish a presentation Saving a PowerPoint file as a Web page in html format and placing it on a Web server in order to make your presentation available to users on the Internet.

Rehearse timings Feature that lets you view and then set the timings for the amount of time each slide will appear on screen during a slide show that runs automatically.

Review Accept or reject the collective edits and comments of your colleagues after they have reviewed a presentation.

Review cycle The process of routing a file to a specified group of people, and where all reviewer comments and changes are added to the file along with information about each review pass.

Rich Text Format (RTF) files A file format that can easily be imported or transferred between other application formats. PowerPoint files saved as RTF retain text formatting such as font type and font style but lose any graphics or media files that were part of the original file.

Row label The first column of a table, used to identify the content of each row.

ScreenTip A yellow box containing helpful identifying information that appears when you position the pointer over a toolbar button, a design template on the task pane, and in various other places in the program.

Send To Mail Recipient (as Attachment) Command that emails a PowerPoint file to a designated recipient so that the recipient can open, view, and edit it.

Send To Mail Recipient for Review Command that sends a file to an email recipient and automatically includes a message that requests the recipient to review the attachment.

Send To Routing Recipient Command that sends a PowerPoint the file to more than one reviewer, and lets you specify routing recipients in Add Routing Slip dialog box.

Show popup menu Menu that provides navigation commands and other tools to help you as the slide show is running.

Slide master The part of the presentation that specifies how text and graphics appear on each slide. The slide master stores information about the design template, including placeholder sizes, position, background design, and color schemes.

Slide master pair Consists of a slide master and title master in a presentation.

Slide pane In Normal view, the area where you can see and work on the design and text of a slide.

Slide timings The amount of time each slide appears on the screen in a slide show that is set to run automatically. You can specify the same or different timings for each or all the slides in the show.

Slides tab In Normal view, the tab that shows thumbnails of the slides.

Sound file Any file that contains sound such as music, a speech, or a sound effect such as a train whistle, rocket noise, or bells. Most sound files have a .wav or an .mp3 file extension.

Source file The originating file where a linked or an embedded object was created.

Status bar Area at the bottom of the program window that tells you the slide you are viewing, the total number of slides in the presentation, and the design template used in the presentation. The right side of the status bar has several indicators that appear as you create the presentation to help your work.

Subordinate shape Items at a lower hierarchical level in an organization chart, which are connected by lines to superior shapes in the hierarchy.

Summary slide A slide that includes all the titles from selected slides as a bulleted list to provide your audience with an overview of key points in your presentation.

Superior shapes Items at a higher hierarchical level in an organization chart, which are connected by lines to subordinate shapes in the hierarchy.

Table A structure that organizes data in columns and rows.

Title bar Bar that appears at the top of the program window that has displays the Program name as well as the current filename on the left. On the right are three control buttons for controlling the PowerPoint program window: the Minimize button, the Restore button, and the Close button

Title master The part of the slide master that contains the layout and formatting specifications for the title slide in a presentation.

Toolbar Bar that contains buttons that you can click to access common PowerPoint commands.

Transitions Specified display effects for how one slide leaves the screen and a new slide appears.

Values Data represented along the vertical or Y-axis of a chart.

Video files Files that show motion and could be used to make your points stronger in a variety of ways. Video formats include avi, QuickTime, and mpeg.

View buttons Buttons located below the Slides tab that let you quickly switch between the three main views; **Normal, Slide Sorter,** and **Slide Show.**

Web Archive One file that contains all the files required to display Web pages. Web archives can be sent via email and are more easily transported between computers than htm files.

Word 2002 Word processing software program that is part of the Microsoft Office XP suite of programs.

WordArt A text object with highly stylized effects.

X-axis The horizontal axis of a chart, categories of data from the datasheet.

Y-axis The vertical axis of a chart that contains values of data from the datasheet.

Index

target, EX-162
task panes and, WD-6
to documents, WD-266
    followed hyperlink, WD-266
to Web pages, inserting, WD-268
Hypertext Markup Language (HTML),
    AC-104, EX-162, WD-2
Hypertext Markup Language (HTML),
    EX-160. *See also* Extensible Markup
    Language
    saving presentation as, PP-158
hyphens
    line breaks and, WD-174
    manual hyphenation, WD-174

I

icon, understanding file icons, PP-6
IF function, formula creation, EX-134
images. *See also* animation
    clip art insertion with Clip Organizer,
        WD-144–145
    inserting images not stored in Clip
        Organizer, WD-146–147
Import Data dialog box, EX-272
Import Spreadsheet Wizard, AC-98
importing. *See also* exporting
    Access database tables, EX-172
    data, EX-169
        from another Access database,
            AC-100–101
        from Excel workbook, AC-98–99
        from World Wide Web, EX-178
        with query, EX-174
    graphics, EX-176
    text file, EX-170
    XML document, AC-174–175
    Web data, EX-272
        Web query, EX-274
Inbox folder, OL-4
Inbox item, copying to folder, OL-8
indent, hanging indent setting, paragraphs,
    WD-76–77
indentation. *See also* margins
    list, WD-86
    paragraphs

first-line indents, WD-72
    hanging indent, WD-76
    indent entire paragraphs, WD-74
index
    creating, WD-190
    cross-references, WD-190
        creating, WD-198
    format, WD-191
    updating, WD-192
index entries, WD-190
index field, WD-190
Index tabs, WD-20. *See also* Help, tab stops
Input Mask
    adding pre-defined input mask to field,
        AC-36–37
    creating and modifying, AC-120–121
Input Mask Wizard, AC-36
Insert Clip Art task pane, WD-6
insertion point. *See also* pointer
    positioning, WD-12
        shortcut keys for, WD-13
    text, WD-24
integration, data, EX-182
interactivity
    spreadsheet, EX-189
    workbook, EX-190
Internet, EX-159
Internet Explorer, EX-160
Internet Service Provider (ISP), using
    Outlook with, OL-19
intranet, EX-159, PP-163
intranets, EX-159
Invoice for Art Rentals to Movies, EX-172
ISP. *See* Internet Service Provider
items, OL-4
    working with, OL-8
.iqy file format, EX-272

J

Journal, OL-92
    assigning Journal entries, OL-94
    recording items automatically, OL-95
Journal item, copying to folder, OL-10
.jpg file format, WD-146
junction table, AC-162

Microsoft PowerPoint, OL-29
Microsoft Query, EX-174. *See also* query
Microsoft Word, OL-29, PP-39
   importing text from, PP-40
   Word Outline, as presentation, PP-40
Microsoft Word 2002, OL-24
MIN function, formula creation, EX-128
minus sign (-), formula operator, EX-37,
 EX-116
mirror margins, WD-108
mixed reference, EX-124. *See also* cell
 reference
module, EX-240
modules
   creating
       class module, AC-190
       with Command Button Wizard,
         AC-190–191
       global module, AC-190, AC-192–193
mouse pointer
   shape changes, EX-8
   Zoom pointer, EX-16
Move to Folder menu, using, OL-65
My Documents folder, PP-154

N

name, worksheet, EX-106

name list. *See also* list; range names
   creating, EX-225
naming
   folders, EX-13
   worksheet, EX-106
narration. *See also* sound
   for slide show, PP-151
navigating, document window, WD-12–13
navigation toolbar, AC-24
New Document task pane, WD-6
New Object:AutoForm button, AC-54
New Workbook task pane, EX-2, EX-6,
 EX-52. *See also* workbook
Normal view, PP-10
   Notes pane, PP-10
   Outline tab, PP-10
   Slide pane, PP-10

Slide Sorter view, PP-10
   working in, PP-12
Noteform, OL-110
Notes
   assigning categories to, OL-114
   assigning contacts to, OL-112
   copying to folder, OL-10
   creating and editing, OL-110
notes page. *See also* speaker notes
   modifying header and footer, PP-36
Now function, AC-92
NOW function, EX-131
   using, EX-131
number format. *See also* format
   applying, EX-32
numbered list. *See also* lists
   creating, WD-84–85
      in outline style, WD-86–87
   multiple, WD-84
   working with multiple lists, WD-84
numbers
   Custom number formats, EX-209
      conditions, EX-211
      creating and applying, EX-210
      with text, EX-214
   editing, EX-30
   entering in cell, EX-28
   formatting, EX-32
      Custom number formats, EX-209,
      EX-210
   in formula, EX-116
   as text, EX-28

O

object. *See also* database object
   chart as, EX-140, EX-180
   graphic as, EX-176
   page object, AC-106
   source object, EX-180
   types, EX-240
   VBA object, properties, EX-241
   view of, AC-12–13
object linking and embedding (OLE),
 EX-180. *See also* embedding